·········· Industrial Hydraulics Manual

Library of Congress Catalog Card Number 91-121667

Industrial Hydraulics Manual

ISBN-13: 978-0-692-53210-2
ISBN-10: 0692532102
Copyright © 2015 by Eaton Corporation
Training Services — Eaton's Hydraulics Group
1785 Indian Wood Circle
Maumee, OH 43537
1-800-413-8809

6th Edition, 9th Printing

.... Preface

Eaton's (formerly Vickers) Industrial Hydraulics Manual has always been the standard text for the hydraulic industry. Originally developed by instructors employed by the Henry Ford Trade School in 1941, the copyright for this textbook was assigned to Vickers in 1952. Eaton acquired Vickers in 1999. It has since been adopted by colleges, universities, trade/vocational schools and industry throughout the world as the premier text for the Power and Motion Control Industry.

- This text has gone through many revisions and updates since its original development. It was recently decided that another update would not be sufficient and thus a newly revised version to address errors previously found as well as adding metrics would be created.

- It would have not been possible to create this textbook without the watchful eye of its readers. They have notified us of the little discrepancies and hard to find misprints. Because of this, we have been able to improve upon this book even more.

- The basic concepts of controlling hydraulic power transmission do not change and for that reason the reader will see much familiarity in this new text. The advances in control technology, energy savings, and the sophistication of hydraulic applications is what distinguishes this manual from the previous version, as well as any other manual available today.

The standards for graphic symbols and color coding of flows and pressures that were established by ISO are used within this textbook and that is a major update by itself. Significance of the symbols can be found in Chapter 2 and Appendix B. The color key is marked below.

Color Key

	RED	Operating or System Pressure
	BLUE	Exhaust
	GREEN	Intake
	YELLOW	Measured (Metered) Flow
	ORANGE	Reduced Pressure, Pilot Pressure or Charging Pressure
	VIOLET	Intensified Pressure
	BLANK OR BLACK	Inactive Fluid

.... Acknowledgements

This printing of Eaton's Industrial Hydraulics Manual is a result of an exceptional team effort, which included individuals specializing in hydraulics knowledge, graphics, grammar, and publishing.

Thanks to Rod Erickson, Rachel Tranberry, Paul McGavin, Dave Riggenbach, Denis Poirier and Jyotsna Phadke, for their support of this project and their auxiliary efforts on simultaneous projects.

To the readers and educators, we extend an appreciative thank you for their suggestions and constructive comments to improve this manual. We value your commitment in utilizing this text for professional development and educational programs.

Brad Poeth
North America Training Manager
Training Services
Eaton's Hydraulics Operations

Table of Contents

Table of Contents

Chapter 1 .... An Introduction to Hydraulics

The study of hydraulics deals with the use and characteristics of liquids. Since the beginning of time, man has used fluids to ease his burden. It is not hard to imagine a caveman floating down a river, astride a log with his wife and towing his children and other belongings aboard a second log with a rope made of twisted vines.

Earliest recorded history shows that devices such as pumps and water wheels were known in very ancient times. It was not, however, until the 17th century that the branch of hydraulics with which we are to be concerned first came into use. Based upon a principle discovered by the French scientist Blaise Pascal, hydraulics relates to the use of confined fluids in transmitting power, multiplying force and modifying motions.

Pascal's Law

Pascal's Law, simply stated, says this:

> *Pressure applied on a confined fluid is transmitted*
> *undiminished in all directions, acts with equal force*
> *on equal areas, and at right angles to them.*

This precept explains why a full glass bottle will break if a stopper is forced into the already full chamber. The liquid is practically noncompressible and transmits the force applied at the stopper throughout the container (Figure 1-1). The result is an exceedingly higher force on a larger area than the stopper. Thus it is possible to break out the bottom by pushing on the stopper with a moderate force.

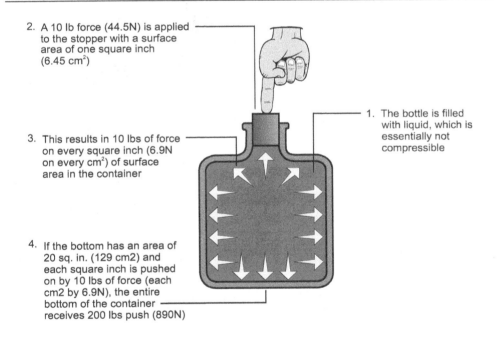

2. A 10 lb force (44.5N) is applied to the stopper with a surface area of one square inch (6.45 cm²)

1. The bottle is filled with liquid, which is essentially not compressible

3. This results in 10 lbs of force on every square inch (6.9N on every cm²) of surface area in the container

4. If the bottom has an area of 20 sq. in. (129 cm2) and each square inch is pushed on by 10 lbs of force (each cm2 by 6.9N), the entire bottom of the container receives 200 lbs push (890N)

Figure 1-1   Pressure (force per unit area) is transmitted throughout a confined fluid

Perhaps it was the very simplicity of Pascal's Law that prevented people from realizing its tremendous potential for some two centuries. Then, in the early stages of the industrial revolution, a British mechanic named Joseph Bramah utilized Pascal's discovery in developing a hydraulic press.

Bramah decided that, if a small force on a small area would create a proportionally larger force on a larger area, the only limit to the force a machine can exert is the area to which the pressure is applied.

Figure 1-2 shows how Bramah applied Pascal's principle to the hydraulic press. The applied force is the same as on the stopper in Figure 1-1 and the small piston has the same one square inch (6.45 square centimeters) area. The larger piston though, has an area of 10 in^2 (64.5 cm^2). The larger piston is pushed on with 10 lbs of force per square inch (0.70 bar, 70 kPa), so that it can support a total weight or force of 100 lbs (445N).

Simple Hydraulic Press

A. SIMPLE HYDRAULIC PRESS

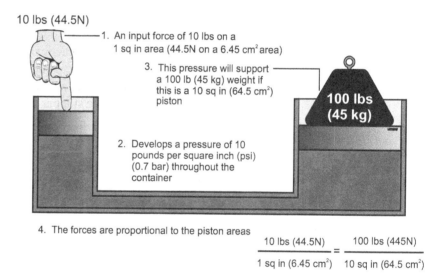

10 lbs (44.5N)

1. An input force of 10 lbs on a 1 sq in area (44.5N on a 6.45 cm^2 area)

3. This pressure will support a 100 lb (45 kg) weight if this is a 10 sq in (64.5 cm^2) piston

100 lbs (45 kg)

2. Develops a pressure of 10 pounds per square inch (psi) (0.7 bar) throughout the container

4. The forces are proportional to the piston areas

$$\frac{10 \text{ lbs (44.5N)}}{1 \text{ sq in (6.45 cm}^2)} = \frac{100 \text{ lbs (445N)}}{10 \text{ sq in (64.5 cm}^2)}$$

Figure 1-2   Pascal's principle applied to the hydraulic press

The forces or weights which will balance using this apparatus are proportional to the piston areas. Thus, if the output piston area is 200 in^2 (1,300 cm^2) the output force will be 2,000 lb (8,900N) [assuming the same 10 lb of push on each square inch (0.70 bar, 70 kPa)]. This is the operating principle of the hydraulic jack, as well as the hydraulic press.

Simple Mechanical Lever

It is interesting to note the similarity between this simple press and a mechanical lever (Figure 1-3).

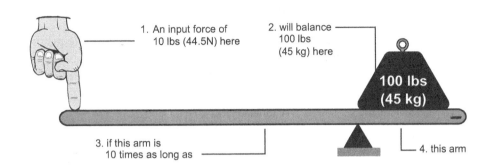

1. An input force of 10 lbs (44.5N) here

2. will balance 100 lbs (45 kg) here

100 lbs (45 kg)

3. if this arm is 10 times as long as

4. this arm

B. SIMPLE MECHANICAL LEVER

Figure 1-3   Similarity between simple press and mechanical lever

Pressure Defined

In order to determine the total force exerted on a surface, it is necessary to know the pressure or force on a unit of area. We usually express this pressure in pounds per square inch, abbreviated psi. It is becoming increasingly common to express pressure in terms used internationally, bar and kilopascals (kPa). Knowing the pressure and the area on which it is being exerted, one can readily determine the total force.

Formula 1-1

Force = Pressure × Area

Conservation of Energy

A fundamental law of physics states that energy can neither be created nor destroyed. The multiplication of force in Figure 1-2 is not a matter of getting something for nothing. The large piston is moved only by the liquid displaced by the small piston, making the distance each piston moves inversely proportional to its area (Figure 1-4). What is gained in *force* must be sacrificed in *distance*.

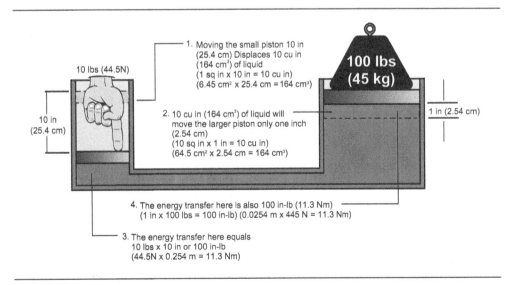

10 lbs (44.5N)

1. Moving the small piston 10 in (25.4 cm) Displaces 10 cu in (164 cm³) of liquid (1 sq in x 10 in = 10 cu in) (6.45 cm² x 25.4 cm = 164 cm³)

100 lbs (45 kg)

10 in (25.4 cm)

2. 10 cu in (164 cm³) of liquid will move the larger piston only one inch (2.54 cm) (10 sq in x 1 in = 10 cu in) (64.5 cm² x 2.54 cm = 164 cm³)

1 in (2.54 cm)

4. The energy transfer here is also 100 in-lb (11.3 Nm) (1 in x 100 lbs = 100 in-lb) (0.0254 m x 445 N = 11.3 Nm)

3. The energy transfer here equals 10 lbs x 10 in or 100 in-lb (44.5N x 0.254 m = 11.3 Nm)

Figure 1-4   Energy can neither be created nor destroyed

Hydraulic Power Transmission

Hydraulics now could be defined as: a means of transmitting power by pushing on a confined liquid. The input component of the system is called a pump; the output is called an actuator.

Most power driven pumps incorporate multiple pistons, vanes or gears as their pumping elements. Actuators are linear, such as the cylinder shown in Figure 1-5A; or rotary, such as the hydraulic motor shown in Figure 1-5B.

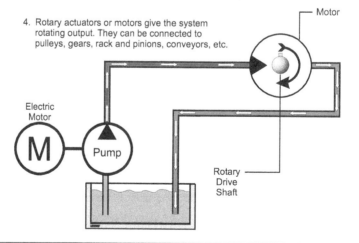

A. Linear Actuator

2. Lines carry the fluid to actuators which are pushed internally to produce a mechanical output which moves the load

Load

1. The pump pushes the hydraulic fluid into the lines

Piston & Rod

To Reservoir

Electric Motor

M

Pump

3. Some actuators operate in a straight line (linear actuators). They are called rams or cylinders. They are used to lift weight, exert force, clamp, etc.

B. Rotary Actuator

Motor

4. Rotary actuators or motors give the system rotating output. They can be connected to pulleys, gears, rack and pinions, conveyors, etc.

Electric Motor

M

Pump

Rotary Drive Shaft

Figure 1-5   Linear and rotary actuator

The hydraulic system is not a source of power. The power source is a prime mover such as an electric motor or an engine which drives the pump. The reader might ask, therefore, why not forget about hydraulics and couple the mechanical equipment directly to the prime mover? The answer is in the versatility and flexibility of the hydraulic system, which gives it advantages over other methods of transmitting power.

Advantages of Hydraulics

As described below, there are several important advantages of hydraulic systems.

Variable Speed

Most electric motors run at a constant speed. It is also desirable to operate an engine at a constant speed. The actuator (linear or rotary) of a hydraulic system, however, can be driven from maximum speeds (Figure 1-6A) to reduced speeds (Figure 1-6B) by varying the pump delivery using a flow control valve. A more complete description of various valves mentioned in this introduction section will appear later in this manual.

A. Maximum Speed

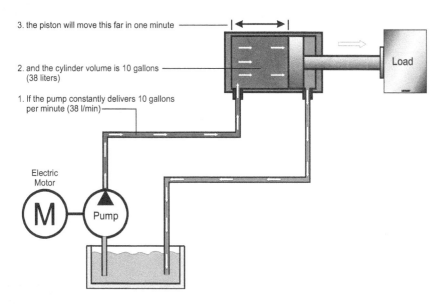

3. the piston will move this far in one minute

2. and the cylinder volume is 10 gallons (38 liters)

1. If the pump constantly delivers 10 gallons per minute (38 l/min)

Load

Electric Motor

M

Pump

B. Reduced Speed

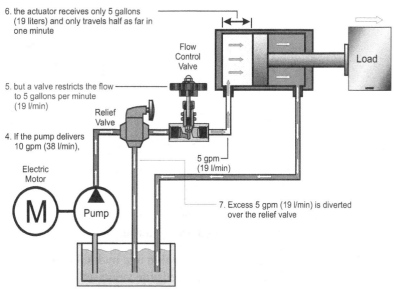

6. the actuator receives only 5 gallons (19 liters) and only travels half as far in one minute

Flow Control Valve

Load

5. but a valve restricts the flow to 5 gallons per minute (19 l/min)

Relief Valve

4. If the pump delivers 10 gpm (38 l/min),

Electric Motor

M

Pump

5 gpm (19 l/min)

7. Excess 5 gpm (19 l/min) is diverted over the relief valve

Figure 1-6   Hydraulic speed control is variable

Reversible

Few prime movers are reversible. Those that are reversible usually must be slowed to a complete stop before reversing them. A hydraulic actuator can be reversed instantly while in full motion without damage to the hydraulic system. A four-way directional valve (Figure 1-7) provides the reversing control, while a pressure relief valve protects the system components from excess pressure.

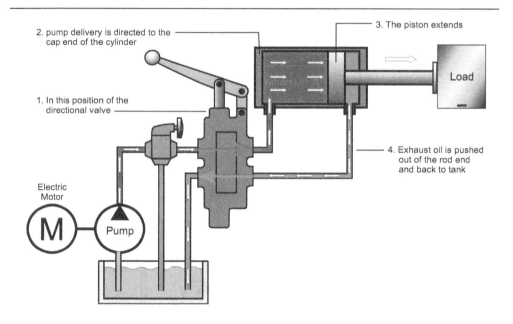

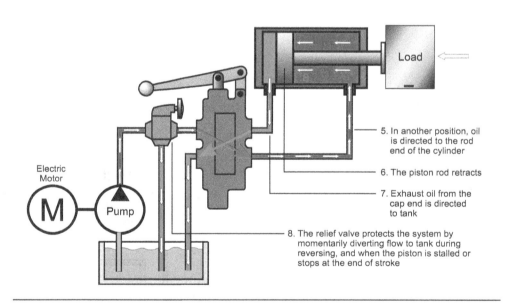

Figure 1-7   Hydraulic drives are reversible

Overload Protection

The pressure relief valve in a hydraulic system protects it from overload damage. When the load exceeds the valve setting, pump delivery is directed to a tank. The result is a definite limit to torque or force output. The pressure relief valve also provides a means of setting a machine for a specified amount of torque or force, as in a chucking or a clamping operation.

Small Packages

Hydraulic components, because of their high speed and pressure capabilities, can provide high power output with very small weight and size.

Can Be Stalled

Stalling an electric motor will cause damage or blow a fuse. Likewise, engines cannot be stalled without the necessity for restarting. A hydraulic actuator, though, can be stalled without damage when overloaded, and will start up immediately when the load is reduced. During stall, the relief valve simply diverts delivery from the pump to the tank. The only loss encountered is in wasted horsepower.

Hydraulic Oil

Any liquid is essentially noncompressible and therefore will transmit power instantaneously in a hydraulic system. The name hydraulics, comes from the Greek, hydro, meaning "water," and aulos, meaning "pipe." Bramah's first hydraulic press and some presses in service today use water as the transmitting medium.

However, the most common liquid used in hydraulic systems is petroleum oil. Oil transmits power readily because it is minimally compressible. It will compress about one-half of one percent at 1,000 psi (70 bar, 7,000 kPa) pressure, a negligible amount in most systems. The most desirable property of oil is its lubricating ability. The hydraulic fluid must lubricate most of the moving parts of the components.

Pressure in a Column of Fluid

The weight of a volume of oil varies slightly as the viscosity (thickness) changes. However, most hydraulic oils weigh from 55 to 58 lbs per cubic foot (880 to 930 kg per cubic meter) in normal operating ranges.

One important consideration of the oil's weight is its effect on the pump inlet. The weight of the oil will cause a pressure of about 0.4 psi (0.03 bar, 3 kPa) at the bottom of a one foot (0.3m) column of oil. For each additional foot (0.3m) of height, it will be 0.4 psi (0.03 bar, 3 kPa) higher. Thus, to estimate the pressure at the bottom of any column of oil, simply multiply the height in feet by 0.4 psi. Similarly, multiply this height in meters by 0.1 bar (Figure 1-8).

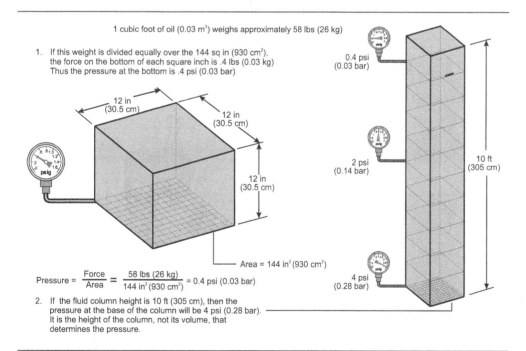

Figure 1-8   Weight of oil creates pressure

To apply this principle, consider the conditions where the oil reservoir is located above or below the pump inlet. When the reservoir oil level is above the pump inlet (Figure 1-9A), a positive pressure is available to force the oil into the pump. However, if the reservoir is located below the pump (Figure 1-9B), a vacuum equivalent to 0.4 psi (0.03 bar, 3 kPa) per foot (0.3m) is needed to "lift" the oil to the pump inlet. Actually the oil is not "lifted" by the vacuum, it is forced by atmospheric pressure into the void created at the pump inlet when the pump is in operation. Water and various fire-resistant hydraulic fluids are heavier than oil, and therefore require more vacuum per foot (0.3m) of lift.

A. Fluid Above Pump Charges the Inlet

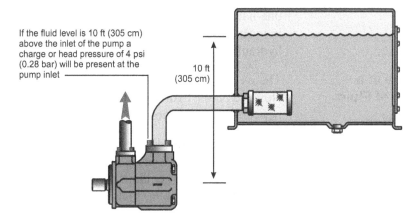

If the fluid level is 10 ft (305 cm) above the inlet of the pump a charge or head pressure of 4 psi (0.28 bar) will be present at the pump inlet

10 ft (305 cm)

B. Oil Level Below

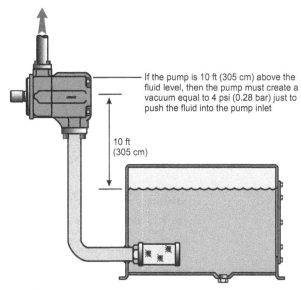

If the pump is 10 ft (305 cm) above the fluid level, then the pump must create a vacuum equal to 4 psi (0.28 bar) just to push the fluid into the pump inlet

10 ft (305 cm)

Figure 1-9   Pump inlet locations

Atmospheric Pressure Charges the Pump

The inlet of a pump normally is charged with oil by a difference in pressure between the reservoir and the pump inlet. Usually the pressure in the reservoir is atmospheric pressure, which, at sea level, is 14.7 psi (1 bar, 100 kPa). It is necessary to have a partial vacuum or reduced pressure at the pump inlet to create flow. Figure 1-10 shows a typical situation for a hydraulic jack pump, which is simply a reciprocating piston. On the intake stroke, the piston creates a partial vacuum in the pumping chamber. Atmospheric pressure in the reservoir pushes oil into the chamber to fill the void. (In a rotary pump, successive pumping chambers increase in size as they pass the inlet, effectively creating an identical void condition.)

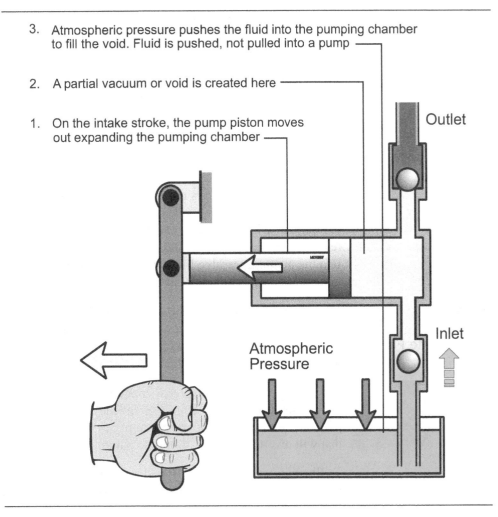

3. Atmospheric pressure pushes the fluid into the pumping chamber to fill the void. Fluid is pushed, not pulled into a pump

2. A partial vacuum or void is created here

1. On the intake stroke, the pump piston moves out expanding the pumping chamber

Outlet

Inlet

Atmospheric Pressure

Figure 1-10   Pressure differences push oil into pump

If it were possible to "pull" a complete vacuum at the pump inlet, there would be available some 14.7 psi (1 bar, 100 kPa) to push the oil in. However, the available pressure difference should be much less. For one thing, liquids vaporize in a vacuum. This puts gas bubbles in the oil. The bubbles are carried through the pump; collapsing with considerable force when exposed to load pressure at the outlet, and causing damage that will impair the pump operation and reduce its life.

Even if the oil has good vapor pressure characteristics (as most hydraulic oils do), too low of an inlet line pressure (high vacuum) permits air dissolved in the oil to be released. This oil-air mixture also collapses when exposed to load pressure and causes the same cavitation damage. Driving the pump at too high a speed increases fluid velocity in the inlet line and consequently, a lower pressure condition, further increasing the possibility of cavitation.

If the inlet line fittings are not tight, air at atmospheric pressure can be forced through to the lower pressure area in the line and can be carried into the pump. This air-oil mixture also causes trouble and noise but it is different from cavitation. When exposed to pressure at the pump outlet, the resulting damage is similar to that of cavitation, but the air does not collapse as violently. It is not dissolved in the oil but passes on into the system as compressible bubbles which cause erratic valve and actuator operation.

Most pump manufacturers recommend a vacuum of less than or equal to 5 inches of mercury (in. Hg), the equivalent of about 12.2 psi (0.84 bar, 84 kPa) absolute at the pump inlet. With 14.7 psi (1 bar, 100 kPa) atmospheric pressure available at the reservoir, this leaves only a 2.5 psi (0.17 bar, 17 kPa) pressure difference to push oil into the pump. Excessive lift must be avoided and pump inlet lines should permit the oil to flow with minimum resistance.

Positive Displacement Pumps Create Flow

Most pumps used in hydraulic systems are classed as positive displacement. This means that, except for changes in efficiency, the pump output is constant regardless of pressure. The outlet is positively sealed from the inlet, so that whatever gets into the pump is forced out the outlet port.

The sole purpose of a pump is to create flow; pressure is caused by a resistance to flow. Although there is a common tendency to blame the pump for the loss of pressure, with few exceptions pressure can be lost only when there is a leakage path that will divert all the flow from the pump.

To illustrate, suppose that a 10 gallon per minute (GPM) (38 liters per minute, l/min) pump is used to push oil under a 10 in^2 (64.5 cm^2) piston and raise an 8,000 lb (35,600N) load (Figure 1-11). While the load is being moved or supported by the hydraulic oil, the pressure must be 800 psi (55 bar, 5,500 kPa).

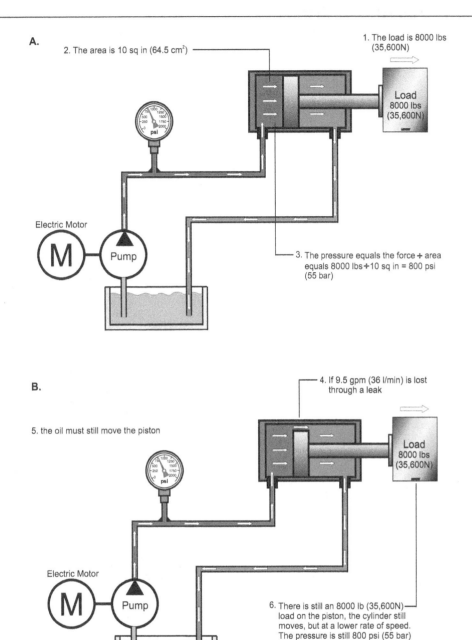

A.

2. The area is 10 sq in (64.5 cm²)

1. The load is 8000 lbs (35,600N)

Load 8000 lbs (35,600N)

Electric Motor

M

Pump

3. The pressure equals the force ÷ area equals 8000 lbs ÷ 10 sq in = 800 psi (55 bar)

B.

4. If 9.5 gpm (36 l/min) is lost through a leak

5. the oil must still move the piston

Load 8000 lbs (35,600N)

Electric Motor

M

Pump

6. There is still an 8000 lb (35,600N) load on the piston, the cylinder still moves, but at a lower rate of speed. The pressure is still 800 psi (55 bar)

Figure 1-11   Pressure loss requires full loss of pump outlet

Even if a hole in the piston allows 9.5 GPM (36 l/min) to leak at 800 psi (55 bar, 5,500 kPa), pressure still will be maintained (Figure 1-11). With only 0.5 GPM (1.9 l/min) available to move the load, it will move very slowly. But the pressure required to do so remains 800 psi (55 bar, 5,500 kPa).

Now imagine that the 9.5 GPM (36 l/min) leak is in the pump instead of the cylinder. There still would be 0.5 GPM (1.9 l/min) moving the load and there still would be pressure. Thus, a pump can be badly worn, losing nearly all of its efficiency, and pressure still can be maintained. Maintenance of pressure alone is no indicator of a pump's condition. It is necessary to measure the flow at a given pressure to determine whether a pump is in good or bad condition.

How Pressure Is Created

Pressure is created whenever the flow of a fluid is resisted. The resistance may come from (1) a load on an actuator or (2) a restriction (or orifice) in the piping.

Figure 1-11 is an example of a load on an actuator. The 8,000 lb (35,600N) weight resists the flow of oil under the piston and creates pressure in the oil. If the weight increases so does the pressure.

In Figure 1-12, a 10 GPM (38 l/min) pump has its outlet connected to a pressure relief valve set at 1,000 psi (70 bar, 7,000 kPa) and to an ordinary water faucet. If the faucet is wide open, the pump delivery flows out unrestricted and there is no reading on the pressure gauge.

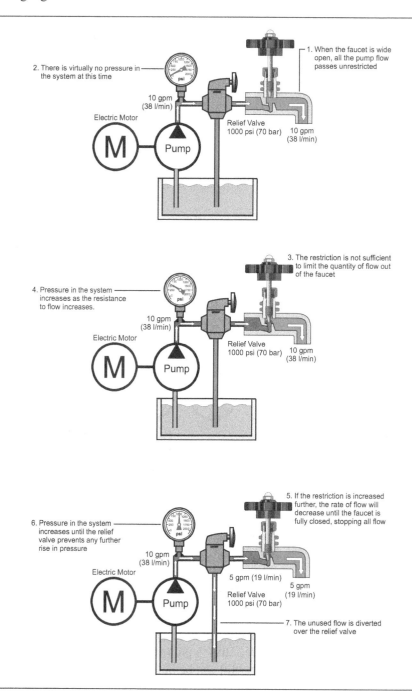

Figure 1-12   Pressure caused by restriction and limited by pressure control valve

Now suppose that the faucet is gradually closed. It will resist flow and cause pressure to build up on the upstream side. As the opening is restricted, it will take increasingly more pressure to push the 10 GPM (38 l/min) through the restriction. Without the relief valve, there would theoretically be no limit to the pressure build-up. In reality, either something would break or the pump would stall the prime mover (electric motor).

In Figure 1-12, at the point where it takes 1,000 psi (70 bar, 7,000 kPa) to push the oil through the opening, the relief valve will begin to open. Pressure then will remain at 1,000 psi (70 bar, 7,000 kPa). Further closing of the faucet will simply result in less oil going through it and more going over the relief valve. With the faucet completely closed, all 10 GPM (38 l/min) will go over the relief valve at 1,000 psi (70 bar, 7,000 kPa).

It can be seen from the above example, a relief valve or some other pressure limiting device should be used in all systems using a positive displacement pump.

Parallel Flow Paths

An inherent characteristic of liquids is that they will always take the path of least resistance. Thus, when two parallel flow paths offer different resistances, the pressure will increase only to the amount required to take the easier path.

In Figure 1-13, the oil has three possible flow paths. Since valve A opens at 100 psi (7 bar, 700 kPa), the oil will go that way and pressure will build up to only 100 psi (7 bar, 700 kPa). Should flow be blocked beyond valve A (Figure 1-13), pressure would build up to 200 psi (14 bar, 1,400 kPa); then oil would flow through valve B. There would be no flow through valve C unless the path through valve B should also become blocked.

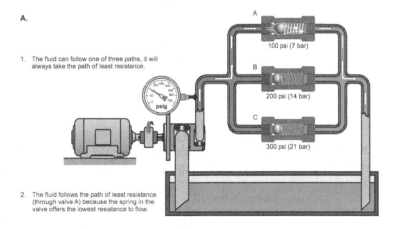

A.

1. The fluid can follow one of three paths, it will always take the path of least resistance.

2. The fluid follows the path of least resistance (through valve A) because the spring in the valve offers the lowest resistance to flow.

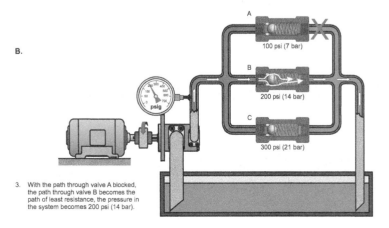

B.

3. With the path through valve A blocked, the path through valve B becomes the path of least resistance, the pressure in the system becomes 200 psi (14 bar).

Figure 1-13   Parallel flow paths

Similarly, when the pump outlet is directed to two actuators, the actuator which needs the lower pressure will be first to move. Since it is difficult to balance loads exactly, cylinders which must move together are often connected to each other mechanically.

Series Flow Path

Pressures are additive when resistance to flow is connected in series. Figure 1-14 illustrates the same valves as in Figure 1-13 but connected in series. Pressure gauges placed in the lines indicate the pressure normally required to open each valve plus back pressure from the valve downstream. The pressure at the pump is the sum of the pressures required to open individual valves.

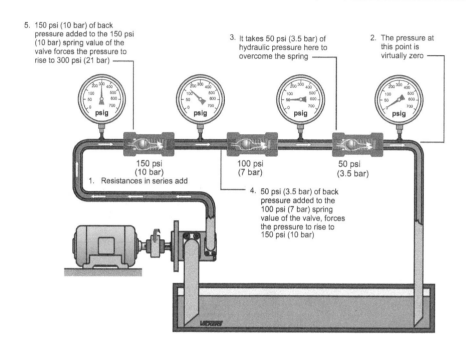

Figure 1-14   Series resistances add pressure

Pressure Drop Through an Orifice

An orifice is a restricted passage in a hydraulic line or component, used to control flow or create a pressure difference (pressure drop).

In order for oil to flow through an orifice, there must be a pressure difference or pressure drop through the orifice. (The term "drop" comes from the fact that the lower pressure is always downstream.) Conversely, if there is no flow, there is no difference in pressure across the orifice.

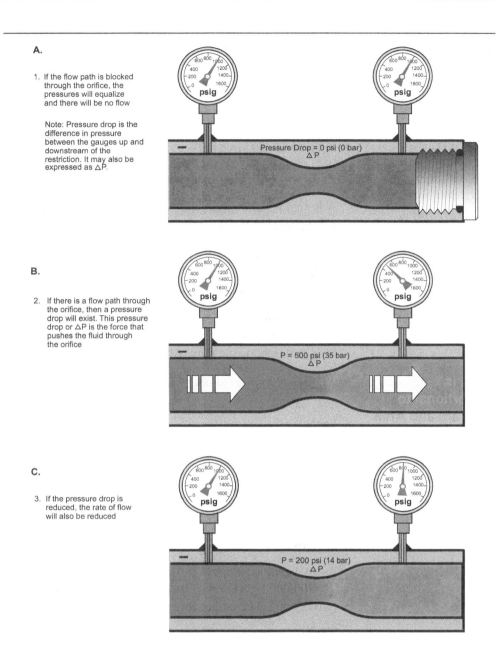

A.

1. If the flow path is blocked through the orifice, the pressures will equalize and there will be no flow

   Note: Pressure drop is the difference in pressure between the gauges up and downstream of the restriction. It may also be expressed as ∆P.

Pressure Drop = 0 psi (0 bar)
∆P

B.

2. If there is a flow path through the orifice, then a pressure drop will exist. This pressure drop or ∆P is the force that pushes the fluid through the orifice

P = 500 psi (35 bar)
∆P

C.

3. If the pressure drop is reduced, the rate of flow will also be reduced

P = 200 psi (14 bar)
∆P

Figure 1-15   Pressure drop and flow through an orifice

Consider the condition surrounding the orifice in Figure 1-15A. The pressure is equal on both sides; therefore, the oil is being pushed equally both ways and there is no flow.

In Figure 1-15B, the higher pressure pushes harder to the right and oil does flow through the orifice. In Figure 1-15C, there is also a pressure drop. However, the flow is less than in Figure 1-15B because the pressure difference is lower.

An increase in pressure drop across an orifice will always be accompanied by an increase in flow.

If flow is blocked beyond an orifice (Figure 1-15A), the pressure will immediately equalize on both sides of the orifice in accordance with Pascal's Law. This principle is essential to the operation of many compound pressure and flow control valves.

Pressure Indicates Work Load

Figure 1-11 illustrated how pressure is generated by resistance of a load. It was noted that the pressure equals the force of the load divided by the piston area. We can express this relationship by the general formula:

Formula 1-2

$$P = \frac{F}{A}$$

In this relationship:

P is pressure [pounds per square inch (Pa)]
F is force [pounds (newtons)]
A is area [square inches (square meters)]
1 Kg per cm^2 = 1 bar

From this can be seen that an increase or decrease in the load will result in a like increase or decrease in the operating pressure. In other words, pressure is proportional to the load, and a pressure gauge reading indicates the work load at any given moment.

Pressure gauge readings normally ignore atmospheric pressure. That is, a standard gauge reads zero at atmospheric pressure. An absolute gauge reads 14.7 psi (1 bar, 100 kPa) sea level atmospheric pressure. Absolute pressure is usually designated "psia."

Force is Proportional to Pressure and Area

When a hydraulic cylinder is used to clamp or press, its output force can be computed as follows:

Formula 1-3

$$F = P \times A$$

Again:

P is pressure [psi (Pa)]
F is force [pounds (newtons)]
A is area [square inches (square meters)]
1 Kg per cm^2 =1 bar

As an example, suppose that a hydraulic press has its pressure regulated at 2,000 psi (13,800,000 Pa) (Figure 1-16) and this pressure is applied to a ram area of 20 in^2 (0.0129 m^2). The output force will then be 40,000 lbs or 20 tons (178,000N).

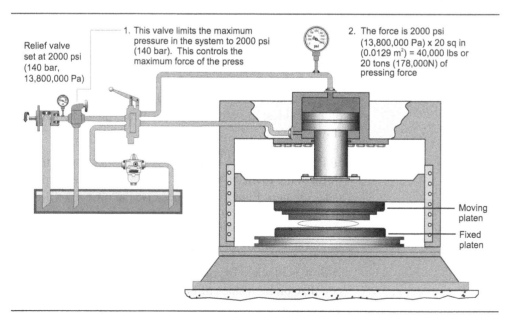

Figure 1-16   Force equals pressure multiplied by area

Computing Piston Area

The area of a piston or ram can be computed by this formula:

Formula 1-4

$$A = \frac{\pi}{4} \times d^2$$

Where:

A = area (square inches or square centimeters)

d = diameter of the piston (inches or centimeters)

$\pi/4$ is 0.7854

These pressure, force and area relationships are sometimes illustrated as shown below to aid in remembering the equations.

Formula 1-5

$$F = P \times A$$

$$P = \frac{F}{A}$$

$$A = \frac{F}{P}$$

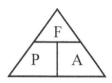

Speed of an Actuator

How fast a piston travels or a motor rotates depends on its size and the rate of oil flow into it. To relate flow rate to speed, consider the volume that must be filled in the actuator to cause a given amount of travel.

In Figure 1-17, note that both cylinders have the same volume. Yet, the piston shown in Figure 1-17B will travel twice as fast as the one shown in Figure 1-17A because the rate of oil flow from the pump has been doubled. If either cylinder had a smaller diameter its rate would be greater, or if its diameter were larger its rate would be less, assuming of course the pump delivery remained constant.

A.

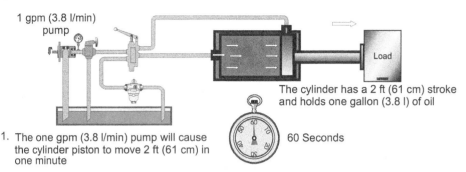

1 gpm (3.8 l/min) pump

The cylinder has a 2 ft (61 cm) stroke and holds one gallon (3.8 l) of oil

60 Seconds

1. The one gpm (3.8 l/min) pump will cause the cylinder piston to move 2 ft (61 cm) in one minute

B.

2. The 2 gpm (7.6 l/min) pump will cause the cylinder piston to move 2 ft (61 cm) in 30 seconds

3. The rate of fluid delivery and its area determine the speed of the cylinder

2 gpm (7.6 l/min) pump

The cylinder has a 2 ft (61 cm) stroke and holds one gallon (3.8 l) of oil

30 Seconds

Figure 1-17   Speed depends on cylinder size and rate of oil flow to it

The relationship may be expressed as follows:

Formula 1-6

$$\text{speed} = \frac{\text{Volume/time}}{\text{area}}$$

$$\text{Volume/time} = \text{speed} \times \text{area}$$

$$\text{area} = \frac{\text{Volume/time}}{\text{speed}}$$

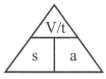

Where:

$V/t = \text{in}^3/\text{minute} \ (\text{cm}^3/\text{minute})$

$a = \text{in}^2 \ (\text{cm}^2)$

$s = \text{in/minute} \ (\text{cm/minute})$

From this we can conclude: (1) that the force or torque of an actuator is directly proportional to the pressure and independent of the flow, (2) that its speed or rate of travel will depend upon the amount of fluid flow without regard to pressure.

Velocity in Pipes

The velocity at which the hydraulic fluid flows through the lines is an important design consideration because of the effect of velocity on friction.

Generally, the recommended velocity ranges are:

Pump Inlet Line = 2 – 4 feet per second *(0.6 – 1.2 meters per second)*

Working Lines = 7 – 20 feet per second *(2.1 – 6.1 meters per second)*

In this regard, it should be noted that:

1. The velocity of the fluid varies inversely as the square of the inside diameter.

2. Usually, friction of a liquid flowing through a line is proportional to the velocity. However, should the flow become turbulent, friction varies as the square of the velocity.

Figure 1-18 illustrates that doubling the inside diameter of a line quadruples the cross-sectional area; thus the velocity is only one-fourth as fast in the large line. Conversely, halving the diameter decreases the area to one-fourth and quadruples the oil velocity.

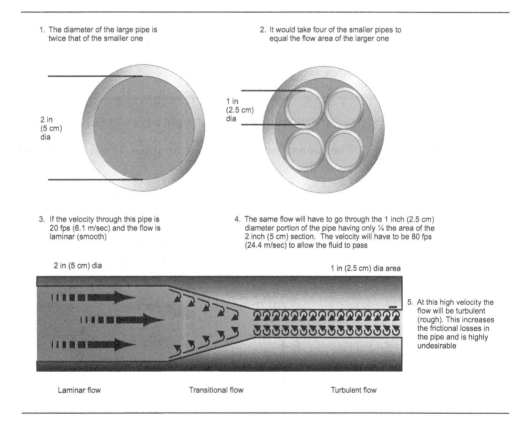

Figure 1-18   Fluid velocity is inversely proportional to pipe cross-sectional area

Friction creates turbulence in the oil stream and resists flow, resulting in an increased pressure drop through the line. Very low velocity is recommended for the pump inlet line because very little pressure drop can be tolerated there.

Determining Pipe Size Requirements

Two formulas are available for sizing hydraulic lines.

If the GPM (l/min) and desired velocity are known, use this relationship to find the inside cross-sectional area:

Formula 1-7
$$\text{Area} = \frac{\text{GPM} \times 0.3208}{\text{Velocity (feet per second)}}$$

When the GPM and pipe sizes are given, use this formula to find the velocity:

Formula 1-8
$$\text{Velocity (feet per second)} = \frac{\text{GPM}}{3.117 \times \text{Area}}$$

Where:
Area = square inches

Formula 1-9
$$\text{Velocity (meters/second)} = \frac{\text{liters per min}}{6 \times \text{Area}}$$

Where:
Area = square cm

In Appendix C you will find a nomographic chart which permits making these computations by laying a straight edge across printed scales.

Size Ratings of Lines

The nominal ratings in inches for pipes, tubes, etc., are not accurate indicators of the inside diameter.

In standard pipes, the actual inside diameter is larger than the nominal size quoted. To select pipe, you'll need a standard chart which shows actual inside diameters.

For steel and copper tubing, the quoted size is the outside diameter. To find the inside diameter, subtract twice the wall thickness (Figure 1-19).

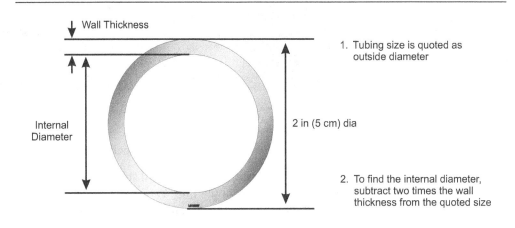

Figure 1-19   Tubing inside diameter

Work and Power

Work is done whenever a force or push is exerted through a distance.

Formula 1-10

$$WORK = force \times distance$$

Work is usually expressed in foot-pounds (joules). For example, if a 10 lb (44.5N) weight is lifted 10 ft (3m), the work is 10 lb (44.5N) x 10 ft (3m) or 100 ft-lb (135J).

The formula above for work does not take into consideration how fast the work is done. The rate of doing work is called power.

To visualize power, think of climbing a flight of stairs. The work done is the body's weight multiplied by the height of the stairs. But it is more difficult to run up the stairs than to walk. When you run, you do the same work at a faster rate.

Formula 1-11

$$POWER = \frac{force \times distance}{time} \ or \ \frac{work}{time}$$

The usual unit of power is the horsepower (watt), abbreviated hp (W). One horsepower is equivalent to 33,000 lb lifted one foot in one minute. (One watt is equal to 1 newton applied over a distance of one meter in one second.) Horsepower has equivalents in electrical power and heat.

$$1 hp = \frac{33,000 \ ft\text{-}lbs}{min} \ or \ \frac{550 \ ft\text{-}lbs}{sec.}$$

$$1 \ hp = 746 \ watts \ (electrical \ power)$$

$$1 \ hp = 42.4 \ BTU/minute \ (heat \ power)$$

It is desirable to be able to convert hydraulic power to horsepower (watt) so that the mechanical, electrical and heat power equivalents will be known.

Horsepower in a Hydraulic System

In the hydraulic system, speed and distance are represented by flow, and force is indicated by pressure. Thus, we might express hydraulic power this way:

Formula 1-12

$$POWER = \frac{gallons}{minutes} \times \frac{pounds}{square \ inches}$$

To change the relationship to mechanical units, we can use these equivalents:

1 gallon = 231 cubic inches (in^3)

12 inches = 1 foot

Thus:

$$POWER = \frac{gallons}{minutes} \times \left(\frac{231 \ in^3}{gallon}\right) \times \frac{pounds}{in^2} \times \left(\frac{1 \ foot}{12 \ in.}\right)$$

$$= \frac{231 \ foot\text{-}pounds}{12 \ minutes}$$

This gives us the equivalent mechanical power of one gallon per minute flow at one psi of pressure. To express it as horsepower, divide by 33,000 pounds/minute:

$$\frac{\frac{231 \ ft\text{-}lbs}{12 \ min}}{\frac{33,000 \ ft\text{-}lbs}{1 \ minute}} = 0.000583$$

Thus, one gallon per minute flow at one psi equals 0.000583 hp (4.347×10^{-4} kW). The total horsepower for any flow condition is:

$$hp = GPM \times psi \times 0.000583$$

or

$$hp = \frac{GPM \times psi \times 0.583}{1000}$$

or

$$hp = \frac{GPM \times psi}{1714}$$

The third formula is derived by dividing 1,000 by 0.583.

These horsepower formulas tell the exact power being used in the system. The horsepower required to drive the pump will be somewhat higher than this since the system is not 100 percent efficient.

If we assume an average efficiency of 83 percent, this relationship can be used to estimate power input requirements:

Formula 1-13

$$hp = GPM \times psi \times 0.0007$$

$$kW = l/min \times bar \times 0.002$$

Horsepower and Torque

It also is often desirable to convert back and forth from horsepower to torque without computing pressure and flow.

These are general torque-power formulas for any rotating equipment:

Formula 1-14

$$torque = \frac{63{,}025 \times hp}{RPM}$$

$$hp = \frac{torque \times RPM}{63{,}025}$$

$$kW = \frac{torque \times RPM}{9{,}550}$$

Torque in these formulae must be in pound-inches or newton-meters.

Designing a Simple Hydraulic System

From the information given in this chapter, it is possible to design a simple hydraulic circuit. Following is a description of how the job might proceed. See Figures 1-20 through 1-22.

A Job to Be Done

All circuit design must start with the job to be done. There is a weight to be lifted, a tool head to be rotated, or a piece of work that must be clamped.

The job determines the type of actuator that will be used.

The first step should be the selection of an actuator.

If the requirement were simply to raise a load, a hydraulic cylinder placed under it would do the job. The stroke length of the cylinder would be at least equal to the distance the load must be moved (Figure 1-20).

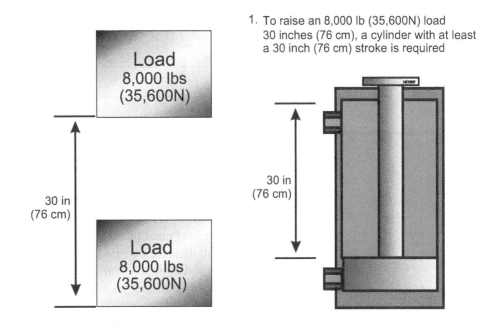

1. To raise an 8,000 lb (35,600N) load 30 inches (76 cm), a cylinder with at least a 30 inch (76 cm) stroke is required

Figure 1-20   Use a cylinder to raise a load

Its area would be determined by the force required to raise the load and the desired operating pressure. Let's assume an 8,000 lb (35,600N) weight is to be raised a distance of 30 in. (0.76m) and the maximum operating pressure must be limited to 1,000 psi (70 bar, 7,000 kPa). The cylinder selected would have to have a stroke length of at least 30 in. (0.76m) and with an 8 in^2 (51.6 cm^2) area piston it would provide a maximum force of 8,000 lb (35,600N). This, however, would not provide any margin for error.

A better selection would be a 10 in^2 (0.00645 m^2) cylinder permitting the load to be raised at 800 psi (55 bar, 5,500,000 Pa) and providing the capability of lifting up to 10,000 lb (44,500N) (Figure 1-21).

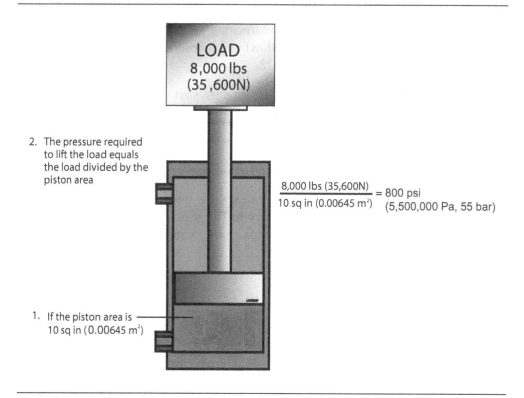

Figure 1-21 Choosing cylinder size

The upward and downward travel of the piston rod would be controlled by a directional valve as shown in Figure 1-22. If the load is to be stopped at intermediate points in its travel, the directional valve should have a neutral position in which oil flow from the underside of the piston is blocked to support the weight on the cylinder. The rate at which the load must travel will determine the pump size. The 10 in^2 (64.5 cm^2) piston will displace 10 in^3 (164 cm^3) for every inch (2.5 cm) it lifts. Extending the piston rod 30 in. (0.76m) will require 300 in^3 (4,900 cm^3) of fluid. If it is to move at the rate of 10 inches per second (0.25m per second), it will require 100 in^3 (1,640 cm^3) of fluid per second or 6,000 in^3 (98,300 cm^3) per minute. Since pumps are usually rated in gallons per minute (liters per minute), it will be necessary to divide 6,000 (98,300) by 231 cubic inches per gallon (1,000 cm^3 per liter) to convert the requirements into gallons per minute (liters per minute).

$$\frac{6,000}{231} = 26 \text{ GPM}$$

The hp (wattage) needed to drive the pump is a function of its delivery and the maximum pressure at which it may operate. The following formula will determine the size of the electric motor required:

Formula 1-15

hp = GPM × psi × 0.0007

hp = 26 × 1,000 × 0.0007 = 18.2

kW = l/min × bar × 0.002

kW = 98 × 69 × = 0.002 = 13.5

To prevent overloading of the electric motor and to protect the pump and other components from excessive pressure due to overloads or stalling, a relief valve set to limit the maximum system pressure should be installed in the line between the pump outlet and the inlet port to the directional valve (Figure 1-22).

A reservoir sized to hold approximately two to three times the pump capacity in gallons per minute (liters per minute), filters and adequate interconnecting piping would complete the system.

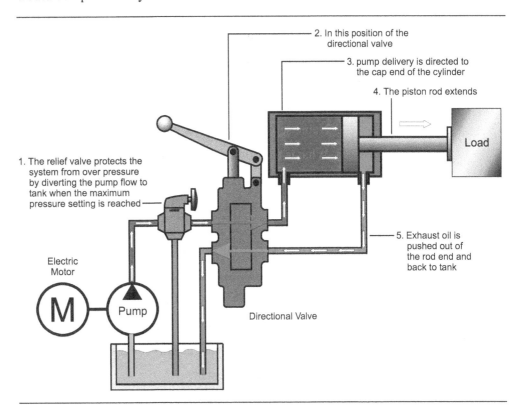

Figure 1-22   Valving to protect and control the system

Conclusion

This chapter has presented a brief introductory overview of hydraulics to demonstrate the basic principles involved in hydraulic system operation. There are, of course, countless variations of the system presented. Many of these will be developed with a more detailed study of operating principles and components in the following chapters.

Industrial Test Questions:
An Introduction to Hydraulics
Chapter 1

1. State Pascal's Law.

2. Define pressure.

3. If a force of 1,000 lb (4,500N) is applied over an area of 20 in^2 (129 cm^2), what is the pressure?

4. What is meant by "conservation of energy"?

5. What is the output component of a hydraulic system named? The input component?

6. What is the prime mover?

7. Name several advantages of a hydraulic system.

8. What is the origin of the term "hydraulics"?

9. What makes petroleum oil suitable as a hydraulic fluid?

10. What is the pressure at the bottom of a 20 ft (6m) column of oil?

11. What can you say definitely about the pressures on opposite sides of an orifice when oil is flowing through it?

12. What pressure is usually available to push liquid into the pump inlet?

13. Why should the pump inlet vacuum be minimized?

14. What is the function of the pump?

15. Why is loss of pressure usually not a symptom of pump malfunction?

16. How is pressure created?

17. If three 200 psi (14 bar, 1,400 kPa) check valves are connected in series, how much pressure is required at the pump to push oil through all three?

18. What is the formula for pressure developed when moving a load with a cylinder?

19. What is the formula for the maximum force output of a cylinder?

20. What determines the speed of an actuator?

21. What is the relationship between fluid velocity and friction in a pipe?

22. What is work? Power?

23. How do you find horsepower (wattage) in a hydraulic system?

24. With which component does the design of a hydraulic circuit begin?

25. What determines the size of the pump needed in a hydraulic circuit?

26. What is the piston area of a 5 in. (127 mm) cylinder?

27. What does the relief valve do?

28. What does a directional valve do?

Chapter 2 . . . . Principles of Hydraulics

This chapter is divided into three sections:

- Principles of Pressure
- Principles of Flow
- Hydraulic Graphic Symbols

The first two sections will further develop the fundamentals of the physical phenomena that combine to transfer power in the hydraulic circuit. The third section, Hydraulic Symbols, will deal with the classes and functions of lines and components. All this material will serve as a background for following chapters on the equipment that makes up a hydraulic system.

Principles of Pressure

A Precise Definition   It has been noted that the term hydraulics is derived from a Greek word for water. Therefore, it might be assumed correctly that the science of hydraulics encompasses any device operated by water. A water wheel or turbine (Figure 2-1) for instance, is a hydraulic device.

The moving water hitting the water wheel turns kinetic energy into useful work

Figure 2-1   Hydrodynamic device uses kinetic energy rather than pressure

However, a distinction must be made between devices which utilize the impact or momentum of a moving liquid and those which are operated by pushing on a confined fluid; that is, by pressure.

Properly Speaking

- A hydraulic device which uses the impact or kinetic energy in the liquid to transmit power is called a hydrodynamic device.

- When the device is operated by a force applied to a confined liquid, it is called a hydrostatic device: pressure being the force applied distributed over the area exposed and being expressed as force per unit area (lbs/in^2 = psi, N/m^2 = Pa, 1 bar = 100 kPa = 0.1 mPa).

Of course, all the illustrations shown so far, and in fact, all the systems and equipment covered in this manual are hydrostatic. All operate by pushing on a confined liquid; that is, by transferring energy through pressure.

How Pressure Is Created

Pressure results whenever there is a resistance to fluid flow or to a force which attempts to make the fluid flow. The tendency to cause flow (or the push) may be supplied by a mechanical pump or may be caused simply by the weight of the fluid.

It is well known that in a body of water, pressure increases with depth. The pressure is always equal at any particular depth due to the weight of the water above it. Around Pascal's time, an Italian scientist named Torricelli proved that if a hole is made in the bottom of a tank of water, the water runs out fastest when the tank is full and the flow rate decreases as the water level lowers. In other words, as the "head" of water above the opening lessens, so does the pressure.

Torricelli could express the pressure at the bottom of the tank only as "feet of head," or the height in feet (meters) of the column of water. Today, with the pound per square inch (psi) (newton per square meter, Pa) as a unit pressure, we can express pressure anywhere in any liquid or gas in more convenient terms. All that is required is knowing how much a cubic foot (cubic meter) of the fluid weighs.

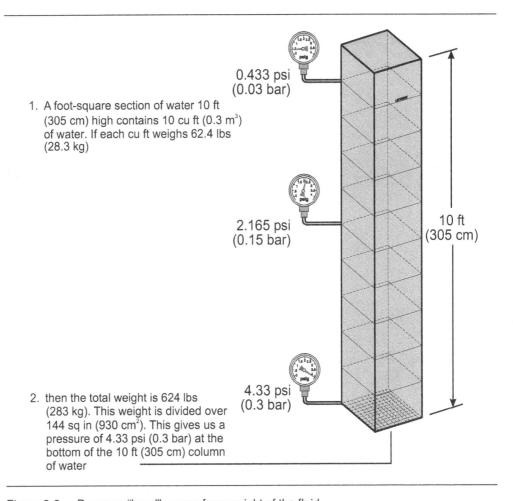

1. A foot-square section of water 10 ft (305 cm) high contains 10 cu ft (0.3 m^3) of water. If each cu ft weighs 62.4 lbs (28.3 kg)

2. then the total weight is 624 lbs (283 kg). This weight is divided over 144 sq in (930 cm^2). This gives us a pressure of 4.33 psi (0.3 bar) at the bottom of the 10 ft (305 cm) column of water

0.433 psi (0.03 bar)

2.165 psi (0.15 bar)

4.33 psi (0.3 bar)

10 ft (305 cm)

Figure 2-2   Pressure "head" comes from weight of the fluid

As shown in Figure 2-2, a "head" of one foot (0.30m) of water is equivalent to 0.433 psi (0.03 bar, 3 kPa); a five-foot head (1.5m) of water equals 2.17 psi (0.15 bar, 15 kPa), and so on. And as shown earlier, a head of oil is equivalent to about 0.4 psi per foot (0.1 bar, 10 kPa per meter).

In many places, the term "head" is used to describe pressure, no matter how it is created. For instance, a boiler is said to "work up a head of steam" when pressure is created by vaporizing water in confinement. The terms pressure and "head" are sometimes used interchangeably.

Atmospheric Pressure

Atmospheric pressure is nothing more than pressure of the air in our atmosphere due to its weight. At sea level, a column of air one square inch (6.45 square centimeters) in cross section and the full height of the atmosphere weighs 14.7 lbs (65N) (Figure 2-3). Thus the pressure is 14.7 psia (1.01 bar, 101 kPa). At higher altitudes, of course, there is less weight in the column, so the pressure becomes less. Below sea level, atmospheric pressure is more than 14.7 psia (1.01 bar, 101 kPa).

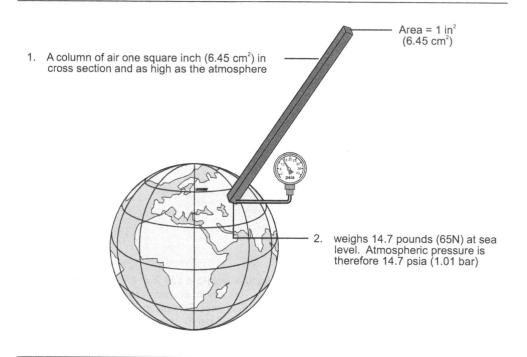

1. A column of air one square inch (6.45 cm²) in cross section and as high as the atmosphere

Area = 1 in² (6.45 cm²)

2. weighs 14.7 pounds (65N) at sea level. Atmospheric pressure is therefore 14.7 psia (1.01 bar)

Figure 2-3   Atmospheric pressure is a "head" of air

Any condition where pressure is less than atmospheric pressure is called a vacuum or partial vacuum. A perfect vacuum is the complete absence of pressure or zero psia (zero bar absolute, zero kPa absolute).

The Mercury Barometer

Atmospheric pressure also is measured in inches of mercury (in. Hg) (millimeters of mercury, mm Hg) on a device known as a barometer.

The mercury barometer (Figure 2-4), a device invented by Torricelli, is usually credited as the inspiration for Pascal's studies of pressure. Torricelli discovered that when a tube full of mercury is inverted in a pan of the liquid, the column in the tube will fall only a certain distance. He reasoned that atmospheric pressure on the surface of the liquid was supporting the weight of the column of mercury with a perfect vacuum at the top of the tube.

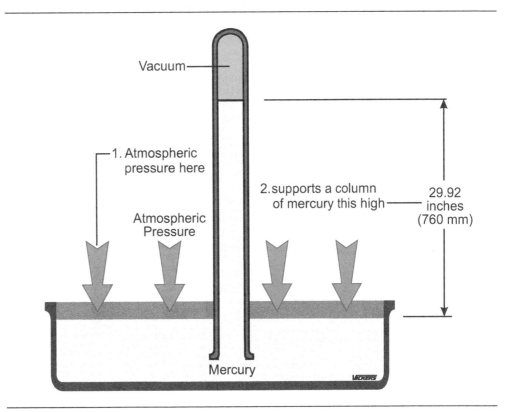

Figure 2-4   The mercury barometer measures atmospheric pressure

At sea level, the column will be 29.92 in. (760 mm) high. Thus, 29.92 (usually rounded off to 30) in. Hg (760 mm Hg) becomes another equivalent of the pressure of one atmosphere.

Measuring Vacuum

Since vacuum is pressure below atmospheric, vacuum can be measured in the same units. Thus, vacuum can be expressed as psia or psi (bar, kPa) (in negative units) as well as in inches of mercury (millimeters of mercury).

Most vacuum gauges, however, are calibrated in inches of mercury (millimeters of mercury). A perfect vacuum, which will support a column of mercury 29.92 in. (760 mm) high is stated as 29.92 in. Hg (760 mm Hg). Zero vacuum (atmospheric pressure) reads zero on a vacuum gauge.

Summary of Pressure and Vacuum Scales

Since a number of ways of measuring pressure and vacuum have been discussed, it would be well to place them all together for comparison. Figure 2-5 presents a summary of pressure and vacuum measurement scales:

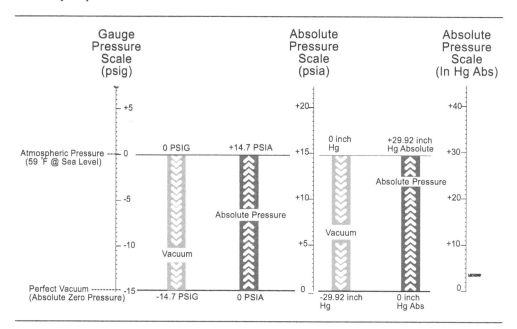

Figure 2-5   Gauge and absolute pressure comparison

1. An atmosphere is a pressure unit equal to 14.7 psi (1.01 bar, 101 kPa).

2. Psia (pounds per square inch absolute) is a scale which starts at a perfect vacuum [0 psia (0.00 bar, 0.00 kPa)]. Atmospheric pressure at sea level is 14.7 (1.01 bar, 101 kPa) on this scale.

3. Psi (pounds per square inch gauge) (bar, kilopascals) is calibrated in the same units as psia but ignores atmospheric pressure. Gauge pressure may be abbreviated psig.

4. To convert from psia to psig:

    Gauge Pressure + 14.7 = Absolute Pressure

    Absolute Pressure - 14.7 = Gauge Pressure

5. Atmospheric pressure on the barometer scale is 29.92 in. Hg (760 mm Hg). Comparing this to the psia scale, it is evident that:

    1 psi (0.07 bar, 7 kPa) = 2 in. Hg (50.80 mm Hg) (approximately).

    1 in. Hg (25.40 mm Hg) = 0.5 psi (0.03 bar, 3.45 kPa) (approximately).

6. An atmosphere is equivalent to approximately 34 ft (10.4m) of water or 37 ft (11.3m) of oil.

Principles of Flow

Flow is the action in the hydraulic system that gives the actuator its motion. Pressure gives the actuator its force, but flow is essential to cause movement. Flow in the hydraulic system is created by the pump.

How Flow Is Measured

There are two ways to measure the flow of a fluid: Velocity is the average speed of the fluid's particles past a given point or the average distance the particles travel per unit of time. It is usually measured in feet per second (fps) (meters per second, m/s), feet per minute (fpm) (meters per minute, m/min) or inches per second (ips) (centimeters per second, cm/s).

Flow rate is a measure of the volume of fluid passing a point in a given time. Large volumes are measured in gallons per minute (GPM) (liters per minute, l/min). Small volumes may be expressed in cubic inches per minute (cubic centimeters per minute).

Figure 2-6 illustrates the distinction between velocity and flow rate. A constant flow of one gallon per minute (3.78 l/min) either increases or decreases in velocity when the cross section of the pipe changes size.

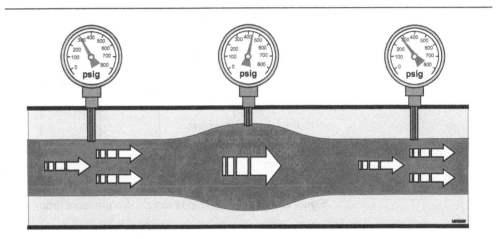

Figure 2-6   Flow is volume per unit of time; velocity is distance per unit of time

Flow Rate and Speed

The speed of a hydraulic actuator, as was illustrated in Chapter 1 (Figure 1-17), always depends on the actuator's size and the rate of flow into it.

Formula 2-1

$$1 \text{ Gallon } = 231 \text{ in}^3 \text{ volume}$$

$$1 \text{ GPM } = 231 \text{ in}^3/\text{minute}$$

$$\text{GPM } = \frac{\text{in}^3/\text{minute}}{231}$$

$$\text{in}^3/\text{minute } = \text{ GPM} \times 231$$

Flow and Pressure Drop

Whenever a liquid is flowing, there must be a condition of unbalanced force to cause motion. Therefore, when a fluid flows through a constant-diameter pipe, the pressure will always be slightly lower downstream with reference to any point upstream. This difference in pressure or pressure drop is required to overcome friction in the line.

Figure 2-7 illustrates pressure drop due to friction. The succeeding pressure drops (from maximum pressure to zero pressure) are shown as differences in head in succeeding vertical pipes.

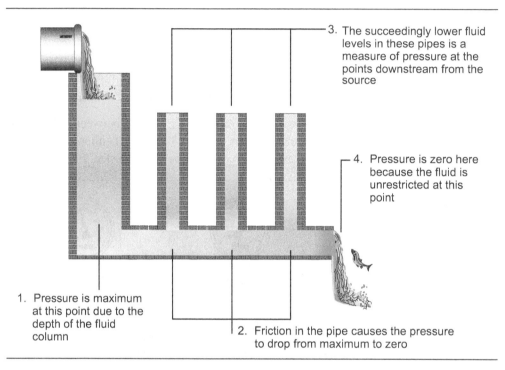

3. The succeedingly lower fluid levels in these pipes is a measure of pressure at the points downstream from the source

4. Pressure is zero here because the fluid is unrestricted at this point

1. Pressure is maximum at this point due to the depth of the fluid column

2. Friction in the pipe causes the pressure to drop from maximum to zero

Figure 2-7   Friction in pipes results in a pressure drop

Fluid Seeks a Level

Conversely, when there is no pressure difference on a liquid, it simply seeks a level as shown in Figure 2-8A. If the pressure changes at one point (Figure 2-8B) the liquid levels at the other points rise only until their weight is sufficient to makeup the difference in pressure. The difference in height (head) in the case of oil is one foot (0.30m) per 0.4 psi (2.76 kPa). Thus it can be seen that an additional pressure difference will be required to cause a liquid to flow up a pipe or to lift the fluid, since the force due to the weight of the liquid must be overcome. In circuit design, naturally, the pressure required to move the oil mass and to overcome friction must be added to the pressure needed to move the load. In most applications, good design minimizes these pressure "drops" to the point where they become almost negligible.

A.

1. The liquid is subject to atmospheric pressure at all points so the fluid is the same level at all points

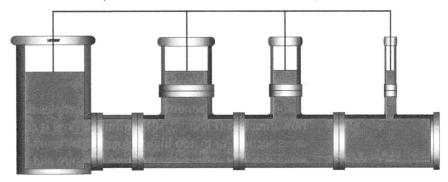

B.

2. The liquid is still subject to atmospheric pressure at all points, so the fluid is higher, but still the same level at all points

1. If the pressure is increased here

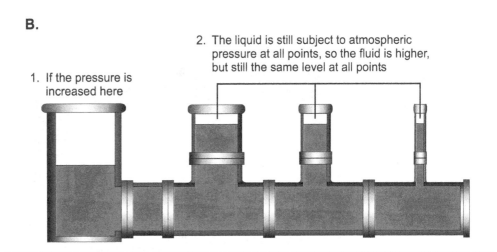

Figure 2-8   Liquid seeks a level or levels depending on the pressure

Laminar and Turbulent Flow

Ideally, when the particles of a fluid move through a pipe, they will move in straight, parallel flow paths (Figure 2-9). This condition is called laminar flow and occurs at low velocity in straight piping. With laminar flow, friction is minimized.

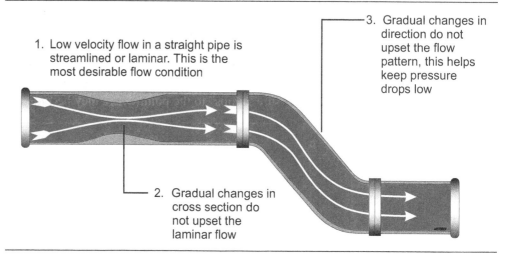

1. Low velocity flow in a straight pipe is streamlined or laminar. This is the most desirable flow condition

2. Gradual changes in cross section do not upset the laminar flow

3. Gradual changes in direction do not upset the flow pattern, this helps keep pressure drops low

Figure 2-9   Laminar flow is in parallel paths

Turbulence is the condition where the particles do not move smoothly parallel to the flow direction (Figure 2-10). Turbulent flow is caused by abrupt changes in direction, cross section, or by too high velocity. The result is greatly increased friction, which generates heat, increases operating pressure and wastes power.

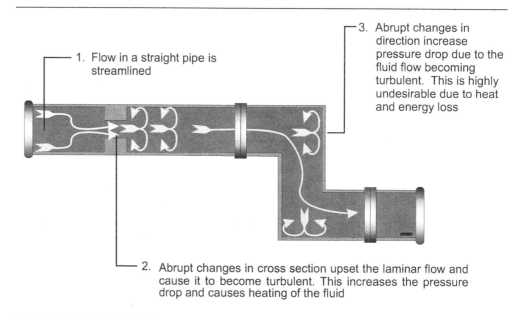

1. Flow in a straight pipe is streamlined

2. Abrupt changes in cross section upset the laminar flow and cause it to become turbulent. This increases the pressure drop and causes heating of the fluid

3. Abrupt changes in direction increase pressure drop due to the fluid flow becoming turbulent. This is highly undesirable due to heat and energy loss

Figure 2-10   Turbulence results in flow resistance

Bernoulli's Principle

Hydraulic fluid in a working system contains energy in two forms: kinetic energy by virtue of the fluid's weight and velocity, and potential energy in the form of pressure.

Daniel Bernoulli, a Swiss scientist, demonstrated that in a system with a constant flow rate, energy is transformed from one form to the other each time the pipe cross section size changes.

As shown in Figure 2-11, when the cross-sectional area of a flow path increases, the velocity (kinetic energy) of the fluid decreases. Bernoulli's principle says that if the flow rate is constant, the sums of the kinetic energy and the pressure energy at various points in a system must be constant. Therefore, if the kinetic energy decreases, it results in an increase in the pressure energy. This transformation of energy from one kind to the other keeps the sum of the two energies constant. Likewise, when the cross-sectional area of a flow path decreases, the increase of kinetic energy (velocity) produces a corresponding decrease in the pressure energy.

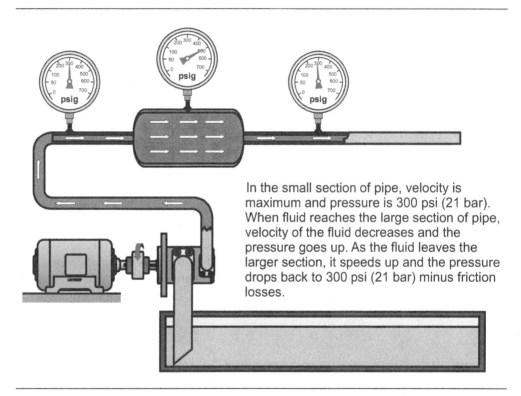

In the small section of pipe, velocity is maximum and pressure is 300 psi (21 bar). When fluid reaches the large section of pipe, velocity of the fluid decreases and the pressure goes up. As the fluid leaves the larger section, it speeds up and the pressure drops back to 300 psi (21 bar) minus friction losses.

Figure 2-11   The sum of pressure and kinetic energy is constant with a constant flow rate

The use of a venturi in an engine carburetor (Figure 2-12) is a familiar example of Bernoulli's principle. Air flowing through the carburetor barrel is reduced in pressure as it passes through a reduced cross section of the throat. The decrease in pressure permits gasoline to flow, vaporize and mix with the air stream.

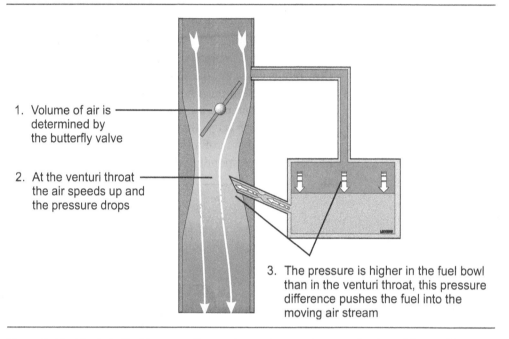

1. Volume of air is determined by the butterfly valve

2. At the venturi throat the air speeds up and the pressure drops

3. The pressure is higher in the fuel bowl than in the venturi throat, this pressure difference pushes the fuel into the moving air stream

Figure 2-12   Venturi effect in a gasoline engine carburetor is an application of Bernoulli's principle

Bernoulli's principle is an important factor in the design of spool-type hydraulic valves. In such valves, changes in fluid velocity are common. If the maximum flow rate of the valve is exceeded, the pressure changes as a result of Bernoulli's principle can produce unbalanced axial forces within the valve. These forces may become great enough to overpower the valve's actuator and cause the valve to malfunction.

Figure 2-13 shows the combined effects of friction and velocity changes on the pressure in a line.

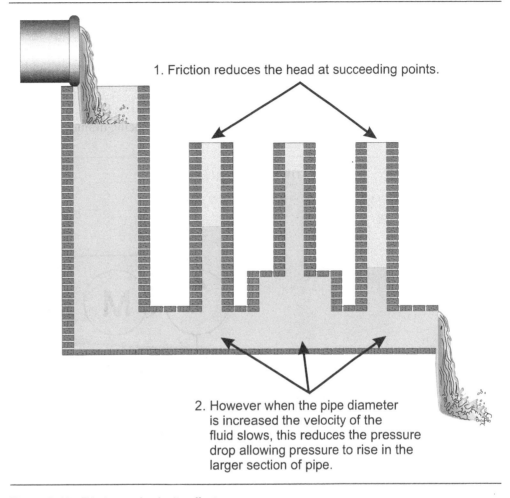

1. Friction reduces the head at succeeding points.

2. However when the pipe diameter is increased the velocity of the fluid slows, this reduces the pressure drop allowing pressure to rise in the larger section of pipe.

Figure 2-13   Friction and velocity affect pressure

Hydraulic Symbols

Hydraulic circuits and their components are depicted in various ways in drawings. Depending on what the picture must convey, it may be a pictorial representation of the components' exteriors; a cutaway showing internal construction; a graphic diagram which shows function; or a combination of any of the three.

All three types are used in this manual. In industry, however, the graphic symbol and diagram are most common. Symbols are the "shorthand" of circuit diagrams, using simple geometric forms which show functions and interconnections of lines and components.

The complete "standard" for hydraulic symbols is reproduced in Appendix B of this manual. Following is a brief exposition of the most common symbols and how they are used, along with an abbreviated classification of some hydraulic lines and components.

Lines

Hydraulic pipes, tubes and fluid passages are drawn as single lines (Figure 2-14). There are three basic classifications:

- A working line (solid) carries the main stream of flow in the system. For diagram purposes, this includes the pump inlet (suction) line, pressure lines and return lines to the tank.

- A pilot, or sensing line (long dashes) carries fluid that is used to control the operation of a valve or other component.

- A drain line (short dashes) carries leakage oil back to the reservoir to prevent a pressure build-up in the area being drained.

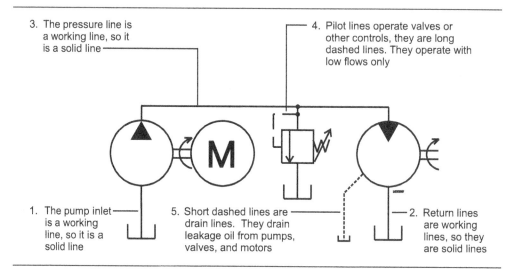

Figure 2-14   Three classifications of lines

Rotating Components

A circle is the basic symbol for rotating components. Energy triangles (Figure 2-15) are placed in the symbols to show them as energy sources (pumps) or energy receivers (motors). If the component is unidirectional, the symbol has only one triangle. A reversible pump or motor is drawn with two triangles.

1. The fluid energy triangle points out showing the pump as a source of flow

Pump

3. The triangle pointing in shows the motor receiving energy

Motor

2. Two fluid energy triangles show the pump to be bi-directional, meaning direction of flow may switch between ports

Bi-directional Pump

4. Two triangles show the motor to be bi-directional, the motor is reversible

Bi-directional Motor

Figure 2-15   A circle with energy triangles symbolizes a pump or motor

Cylinders

A cylinder is drawn as a rectangle (Figure 2-16) with indications of a piston, piston rod and port connection(s). A single acting cylinder is shown open at the rod end and with only a cap end port connection. A double acting cylinder appears closed with two ports. These types of cylinders are explained elsewhere in the text.

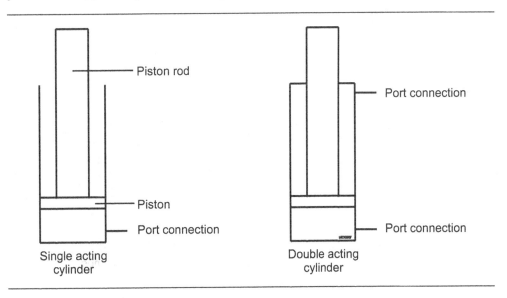

Figure 2-16   Cylinder symbols are single acting or double acting

Valves

The basic symbol for a valve is a square referred to as an envelope (Figure 2-17). Arrows are added to the envelopes to show flow paths and the direction of flow.

Infinite positioning pressure and flow control valves have single envelopes (Figure 2-17A). They are assumed to be able to take any number of positions between fully open and fully closed, depending on the volume of liquid passing through them.

Directional valves are finite positioning valves. Their symbols contain an individual envelope for each position to which the valve can be shifted (Figure 2-17B).

Infinite positioning directional control valves, such as proportional and servo valves, are depicted by two or more envelopes to show the directions of flow and by two parallel lines drawn outside the envelopes to show infinite positioning capability (Figure 2-17C).

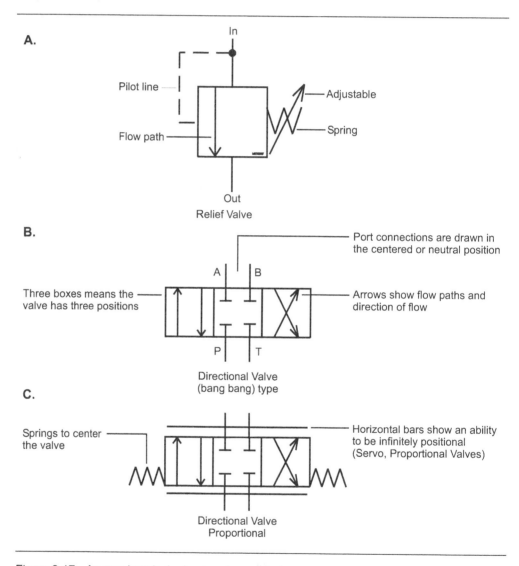

Figure 2-17   An envelope is the basic valve symbol

Reservoir Tank Symbol

The reservoir is drawn as a rectangle with an open top if it is vented and with a closed top if it is pressurized. For convenience, several symbols may be drawn in a diagram even though there is only one reservoir.

Connecting lines are drawn to the bottom of the reservoir symbol when the lines terminate below the fluid level in the tank. If a line terminates above the fluid level, it is drawn to the top of the symbol. The reservoir symbols shown in Figure 2-18 indicate that the reservoir is vented with the lines terminating below the fluid level in the tank.

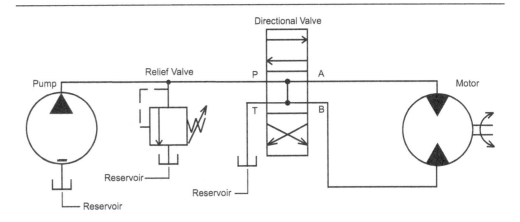

There is typically only one reservoir in a system though the symbol is redrawn for simplicity sake.

Figure 2-18   Graphic diagram of motor-reversing circuit

Conclusion

Figure 2-18 shows a graphic diagram of an entire hydraulic circuit. Note that there is no attempt to show the actual size, shape, location or construction of any component. The diagram does show function and connections, which suffice for most purposes.

Variations and refinements of these basic symbols will be dealt with in the chapters on components and systems.

Industrial Test Questions:
Principles of Hydraulics

Chapter 2

1. What is a hydrodynamic device?

2. How does a hydrostatic device differ from a hydrodynamic device?

3. Name two ways that create a tendency for a liquid to flow.

4. What is a pressure "head"?

5. How much is atmospheric pressure (at sea level) in psia? In bar? In kPa? In psig? In inches of mercury? In millimeters of mercury? In feet of water? In meters of water?

6. How is the mercury column supported in a barometer?

7. Express 30 psig in psia.

8. What are two ways to measure flow?

9. Express 5 GPM in cubic inches per minute.

10. What happens when a confined liquid is subject to different pressures?

11. Pump working pressure is the sum of which individual pressures?

12. What is laminar flow?

13. What are some causes of turbulence?

14. In what two forms do we find energy in the hydraulic fluid?

15. What is Bernoulli's principle?

16. Name three kinds of working lines and tell what each does.

17. What is the basic graphic symbol for a pump or motor?

18. How many envelopes are in the symbol for a relief valve?

19. Which connecting lines are drawn to the bottom of the reservoir symbol?

20. How many positions does the directional valve in Figure 2-18 have? The relief valve?

Chapter 3 . . . . Hydraulic Fluids

There are numerous requirements for a fluid in hydraulic systems, as illustrated in Figure 3-1. Foremost, is the efficient transmission of power to linear and rotary actuators (hydraulic cylinders and motors). In addition to the transmission of power, the fluids are also required to: provide cooling of the system and its components via dissipation of heat through the reservoir and/or cooling devices; lubricate sliding or rotating surfaces in components; seal the running clearances in components to minimize internal leakage; and carry away contaminants in the system to the filter(s) or to the reservoir where they are allowed to settle out of the fluid.

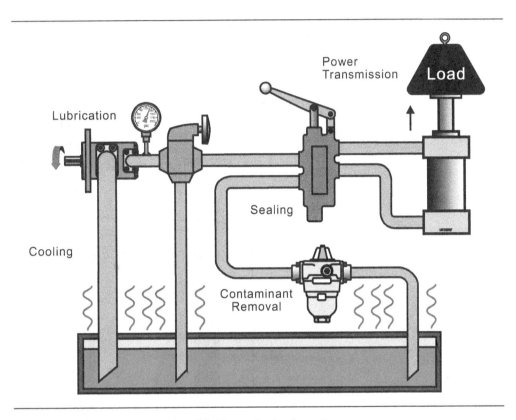

Figure 3-1   Essential properties of fluids in a hydraulic system

In addition to the above listed attributes, fluids used in hydraulic applications are also required to be compatible with component materials such as seals and hose interior linings; resistant to foaming; able to expel air and water and be used over wide operating temperature differentials at acceptable viscosities.

To perform all of these tasks, hydraulic fluids must have the proper characteristics which must be maintained for the life of the fluid in the system. Fluid failure in any of the areas can lead to varying degrees of component or even total system failure. This chapter concerns itself with the variety of fluids used in hydraulic systems, the characteristics and limitations of these fluids and their application advantages and disadvantages, and some of their basic maintenance requirements.

Purposes of the Fluid

The fluids used in mobile and stationary machinery must be effective in the transmission of power from the source of power (e.g., an internal combustion engine in the case of mobile equipment) to provide consistent and reliable response, safe operation and optimum efficiency.

Compressibility

To ensure responsiveness of actuation or "stiffness" in a hydraulic circuit, the fluid must experience very little compression, even under high pressures. Typical petroleum-based fluids are said to be virtually incompressible. In fact, even petroleum-based fluids will compress very slightly -0.4 percent at 1,000 psi (70 bar) and up to 1.1 percent at 3,000 psi (210 bar) operating pressure (Figure 3-2). At a constant operating pressure, the oil remains compressed at a given value. However, with the dynamics of loads in industrial machinery, slight decompression or compression can occur and affect actuation slightly. Typically, this is no cause for concern.

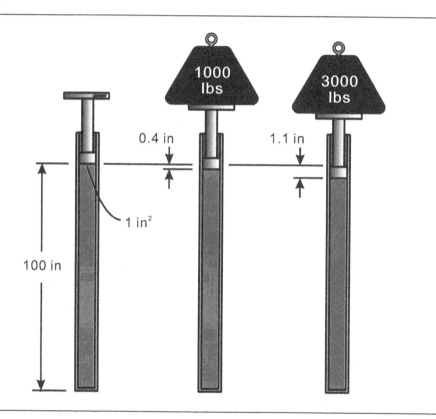

Figure 3-2   Compressibility of fluids

Because of this property of virtual incompressibility, properly maintained hydraulic systems are extremely responsive and reliable.

Lubrication

Lubricity is defined as the property of a fluid to impart low friction under boundary lubrication conditions. Simply put, we want the fluids we use in our hydraulic systems to prevent excess wear of components and excess production of heat via their properties of lubrication.

All hydraulic systems contain components with moving parts that have the potential to come in contact with each other, particularly under pressure. To minimize wear and reduce heat and excessive damage to fluids and components, all fluids used in hydraulics must have the ability to provide lubrication under a variety of operating conditions.

Ideally, we would like always to have what is called "full-film" lubrication between all moving parts as shown in Figure 3-3. This is a condition in which the metal parts of components are held completely apart by a full-film of lubricating fluid. The microscopic peaks on the mating surfaces of the parts, called asperities, cannot come in contact with one another causing wear.

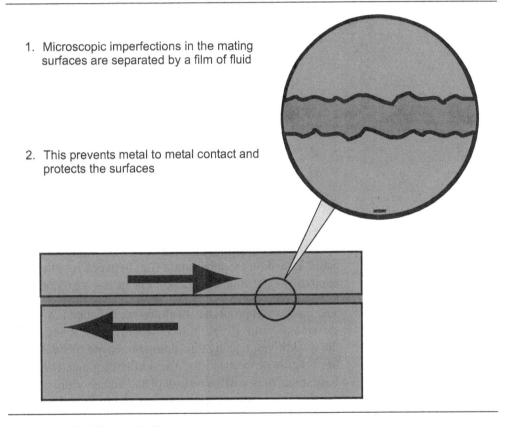

1. Microscopic imperfections in the mating surfaces are separated by a film of fluid

2. This prevents metal to metal contact and protects the surfaces

Figure 3-3   Full-film lubrication

However, with higher pressure demands, the clearances between moving surfaces have been reduced by manufacturers to reduce leakage at higher pressure drops across clearances. This creates a condition called "boundary lubrication." As shown in Figure 3-4, with boundary lubrication the asperities on the surfaces of mated parts can now contact one another. This can cause galling of the component surfaces, which creates work-hardened metal wear contamination, and severe heat, which will increase the oxidation rate of fluids, reducing their useful life.

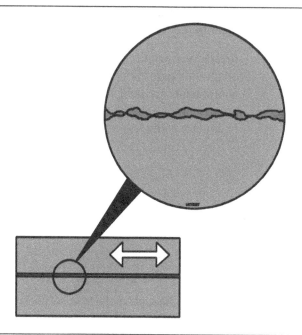

Figure 3-4   Boundary lubrication

Severe working conditions may create pressure "spikes" or transient pressure conditions within components that force a reduction of running clearances. This may cause a break in the lubrication film between running clearances resulting in component and fluid destruction via excess wear and heat.

The lubrication properties of fluids are enhanced by the addition of anti-wear and extreme pressure (EP) additives (Figure 3-5). When using petroleum-based fluids, these additives, usually zinc compounds, are blended into the base stock, which also has specific properties. Because additives typically have a life shorter than that of the base stock, they will become depleted and the fluid must be replaced when determined necessary by competent spectrographic fluid analysis.

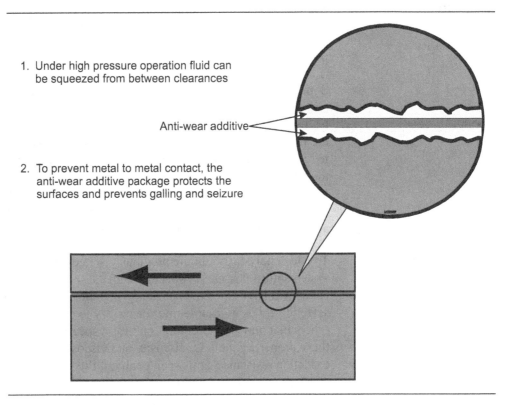

1. Under high pressure operation fluid can be squeezed from between clearances

Anti-wear additive

2. To prevent metal to metal contact, the anti-wear additive package protects the surfaces and prevents galling and seizure

Figure 3-5   Anti-wear action

These types of additives are also present in synthetic and biodegradable fluids.

Sealing

Clearances inside hydraulic components cause internal leakage that affects the efficiency of systems as well as the potential to create excess heat. As shown in Figure 3-6, we rely on the fluid in the system to minimize leakage across these clearances to improve efficiencies and reduce the production of heat. The physical size of clearances, pressure drop across the clearances and the operating viscosity of the fluid determine the leakage rate.

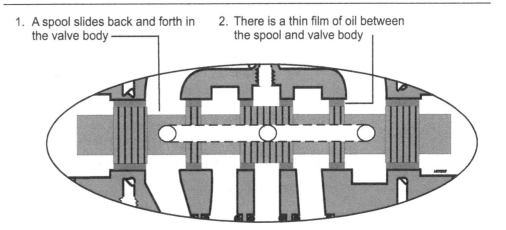

1. A spool slides back and forth in the valve body

2. There is a thin film of oil between the spool and valve body

3. This film of oil lubricates and seals the spool within the valve body

Figure 3-6   Fluid helps to seal between components

Cooling

Any fluid used in hydraulic machinery absorbs and carries heat away from heat generating components such as cylinders and pumps. The fluid then must be allowed to circulate as much as possible against the heat dissipating sides of a reservoir before it is allowed to reenter the pump.

Some system designs may not allow sufficient transfer of fluid to the reservoir, particularly with long lines from the rod end of cylinders. This can cause a buildup of heat and oxidized fluid in an isolated segment of a circuit and result in destruction of the fluid and components. Provision should be made in machine design for the ability to "flush" these segments regularly to prevent cumulative damage to components and the fluid. The transport, filtration and settling out of contamination are important functions of the hydraulic fluid. All types of contamination, solid, fluid or gas, must be dealt with. Baffled reservoir, coolers, strainers and other fluid conditioning devices are designed to maintain fluid quality and ensure long trouble-free operation.

Fluid Properties

To adequately carry out the previously stated purposes, the fluids used in hydraulic systems must possess, to varying degrees, specific desirable characteristics. Not all fluids will have all of the necessary attributes in equal strength. Consequently, when selecting fluids it is sometimes necessary to compromise some properties in favor of others that may be more important for a specific application requirement. In general, these properties include: viscosity and viscosity index, pour point, lubricating ability, oxidation resistance, anti-wear, compatibility with system elements, rust and corrosion protection and demulsibility.

Viscosity and Viscosity Index (VI)

The viscosity of a fluid may be defined as its resistance to flow at a given temperature. If a fluid flows easily, its viscosity is low. A fluid that flows with difficulty would be said to have high viscosity. It has more resistance to flow than the lower viscosity or thinner fluid.

Viscosity

Viscosity affects the fluid's ability to be pumped, transmitted through the system, carry a load and maintain separation (lubrication) between moving surfaces. The selection of proper viscosity is often a compromise in order to optimize system performance. Too high or too low a viscosity for a given system could present problems of performance, leakage, energy usage, etc.

Viscosity too high (fluid is too thick):

- High resistance to flow
- Increased energy consumption due to increased friction, increased input torque requirement at the pump
- High temperatures created by power loss to friction
- Increased pressure drops (Delta P) due to increased resistance to flow
- Slow or sluggish operation/actuation
- Inefficient separation of air from the oil in the reservoir
- Pump cavitation

Viscosity too low (fluid is too thin):

- Increased internal leakage

- Excess wear. Seizure, particularly of pumps, could occur under heavy load because of a breakdown in lubrication film between clearances of moving parts.

- Decreased pump efficiency (volumetric) due to increased leakage and possible cylinder blow-by. This could cause increased cycle times or slower machine operation.

- Internal leakage causing an increase in operating temperatures.

Defining Viscosity

Some methods of defining viscosity are: absolute (dynamic) viscosity in centipoise (cP); kinematic viscosity in centistokes (cSt); relative viscosity in Saybolt Universal Seconds (SUS); SAE numbers (for automotive oils); and ISO viscosity grades. In the United States, hydraulic fluid viscosity requirements are specified in either centistokes, SUS, ISO viscosity grades, or combinations of these. Most hydraulic systems run with oil in the range of 150 to 300 SUS with typical ISO viscosity grade (ISOVG) range of ISOVG-22 to -68.

Absolute Viscosity

Absolute viscosity is defined as resistance encountered when moving one layer of liquid over another. Absolute (dynamic) viscosity is defined as force per unit of area required to move one parallel surface at a given speed past another parallel surface separated by a given fluid film thickness. In the SI system, force is expressed in newtons (N); area in square meters (m^2).

The common SI unit of measurement for absolute viscosity is the centipoise (cP), which is one-hundredth of a poise (P). A corresponding, numerically equal SI unit is the millipascal second (mPa s), which is one-thousandth of a pascal second (Pa s).

Following are conversions between the two units of measure for absolute viscosity in the SI system of measurement:

Formula 3-1

1 Poise (P) = 0.1 Pascal Second (Pa s)

$$1 \text{ Pascal (Pa)} = \frac{N}{m^2}$$

$$1 \text{ Pa s} = \frac{Ns}{m^2}$$

$$1 \text{ Poise} = \frac{0.1Ns}{m^2} = 0.1 \text{ Pa s}$$

1 Centipoise (cP) = 0.001 Pa s = 1 mPa s

Kinematic Viscosity

Kinematic viscosity is the most common way of measuring viscosity. It is measured by the amount of time needed for a fixed volume of oil to flow through a capillary tube. The coefficient of absolute viscosity, when divided by the density of the liquid is called the kinematic viscosity.

The official SI unit for kinematic viscosity is m^2/s (meters squared per second), but the centistoke (cSt), which is mm^2/s (millimeters squared per second), is commonly adopted in the petroleum industry.

The absolute viscosity (cP) of a fluid at any temperature is equivalent to its kinematic viscosity (cSt) at that temperature times its density [(kg/m^3) x 10^{-3}] at the same temperature.

Following are conversions between absolute and kinematic viscosity:

Formula 3-2

Centipoise $=$ Centistoke $\times$ Density

OR

$$cP = cSt \times Kg/m^3 \times 10^{-3}$$

Centistoke $= \dfrac{\text{Centipoise}}{\text{Density}}$

OR

$$cSt = \dfrac{cP}{\dfrac{kg}{m^3} \times 10^{-3}}$$

SUS Viscosity

For practical purposes, it may serve to know the relative viscosity of the fluid. Relative viscosity is determined by timing the flow of a given quantity of the fluid through a standard orifice at a given temperature.

There are several measurement methods in use. A very common method in the United States is the Saybolt Viscosimeter (Figure 3-7).

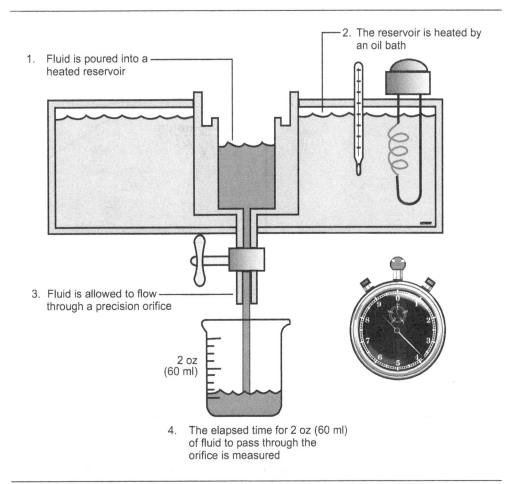

Figure 3-7   Saybolt viscosimeter

The time it takes for the quantity of liquid to flow through the orifice is measured with a stopwatch. The viscosity in Saybolt Universal Seconds (SUS) equals the elapsed time.

A thick liquid will flow slowly, and the SUS viscosity will be higher than that of a thin liquid which flows faster. Since oil becomes thicker at a low temperature and thins when warmed, the viscosity must be expressed as so many SUS at a given temperature. The tests are usually made at 40°C and 100°C (104° and 212°F).

For industrial applications, hydraulic oil viscosities usually are in the vicinity of 150 SUS (32 cSt) at 40°C. It is a general rule that the viscosity should never go below 45 SUS (5.8 cSt) or above 4,000 SUS (860 cSt), regardless of temperature. Where temperature extremes are encountered, multiviscosity grade fluids may be specified (e.g., 5W-30, 15W-30, etc., engine oils or multigrade hydraulic oils with relatively stable viscosity characteristics).

Viscosity Index

The viscosity of virtually all fluids used in hydraulic systems is affected by variations in temperature. Viscosity Index or VI is a dimensionless number that characterizes the variation of viscosity of a fluid with variations of temperature. Simply put, the higher a fluid's VI number, the less change there is in the fluid's viscosity over a given range of temperature as shown in Figure 3-8.

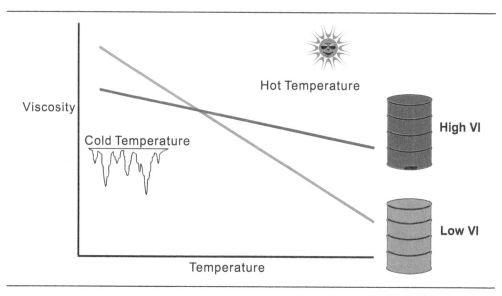

Figure 3-8   The effect of improved viscosity index

Multiple viscosity oils typically include additives (polymers) to improve viscosity index. These oils can exhibit temporary and permanent decrease of viscosity due to oil shear during hydraulic machine operation. Consequently, multiple viscosity fluids with high shear stability are desirable.

Viscosity and Temperature

The viscosity of hydraulic fluids, particularly petroleum-based fluids and vegetable oils, is directly and sometimes adversely affected by changes in temperature. For this reason it is essential that the start-up and operating temperatures of hydraulic machinery be monitored. Machinery should not be put into high speed or heavily loaded operation until the system fluid is warmed up to operating temperatures to provide adequate lubrication.

Excessive heat in a system can cause a loss of viscosity. This will result in severe wear due to a loss of lubricity as well as the destruction of the fluid through oxidation. Severe oxidation, in turn, may cause the fluid to thicken by causing varnish, sludge, corrosive acids, and the destruction of additives.

SAE Viscosity Numbers

The Society of Automotive Engineers (SAE) has established numbers to specify ranges of viscosity for engine oils at specified test temperatures, illustrated in Figure 3-9. Winter numbers (0W, 5W, 10W, 15W, etc.) are specified viscosity ranges at cold temperatures. Summer oil viscosity numbers (20, 30, 40, etc.) are measured at 212°F (100°C).

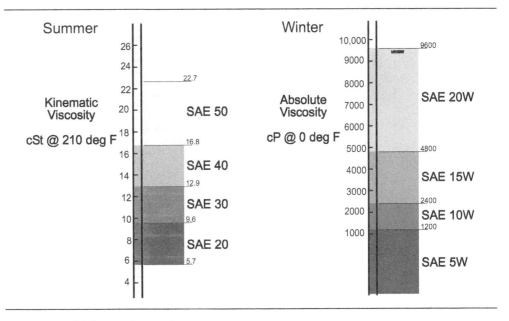

Figure 3-9   SAE viscosity numbers

ISO Viscosity Grades

International Standards Organization (ISO) viscosity grades are shown in Figure 3-10. The ISO viscosity grade number represents a range of kinematic viscosity values at 40°C (104°F), and is the midpoint number of the range. The ISO designation is becoming more popular, and many fluid suppliers are incorporating the designation in their brand description.

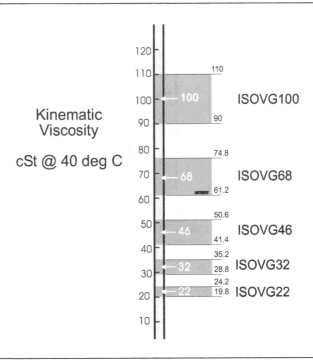

Figure 3-10   ISO viscosity grades

A comparison chart Figure 3-11 shows the common viscosity measurement scales.

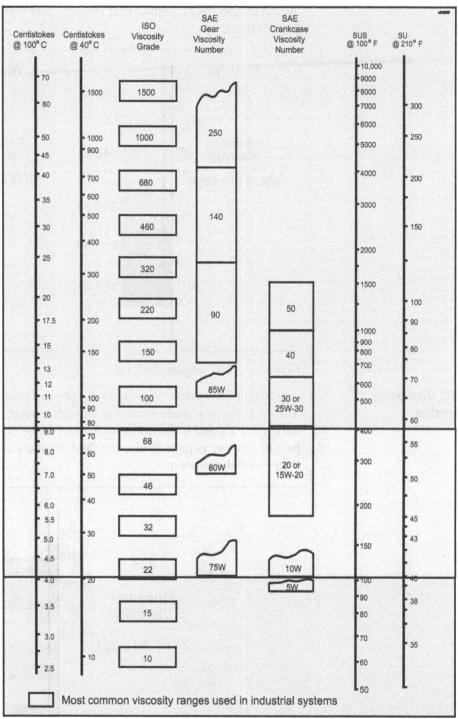

Viscosities at various temperatures assume 95 VI Oils.

NOTE: Viscosities at various temperatures are related horizontally. SAE gear and crankcase specifications are 100° C (212° F) only. Multigrade oil viscosities are not representative at other temperatures.

Figure 3-11   Comparative viscosity classifications

This specified viscosity should be defined within the operating parameters of the application. When viscosity analysis is used as a fluid monitoring tool, you must realize that the actual viscosities of new fluids can vary somewhat from their specifications. Consequently, *changes* in viscosity over a period of time are usually considered more important than an actual reading. Changes of more than 10 percent from the original reading are considered an indication of problems.

Lubricity

As stated under Fluid Properties and illustrated by Figure 3-3, it is desirable for hydraulic component moving parts to have sufficient clearance to run on a substantial film of fluid. This condition is called *full-film lubrication* and does not allow contact between the moving parts. However, in certain types of applications and in higher performance equipment, increased speeds and pressure along with smaller clearances, cause the fluid to be squeezed very thin as in Figure 3-4. This creates the previously described condition called *boundary lubrication.* To prevent excess wear of potential contact between moving parts, extreme pressure (EP) and antiwear additives are required.

Fluid Qualities

The following paragraphs define some of the Fluid Qualities required by hydraulic systems.

Pour Point

Pour point is the lowest temperature at which a fluid will flow. It is an important specification if the hydraulic system will be exposed to extremely low temperatures. Typically, the pour point of a selected fluid should be 20°F (11°C) below the lowest temperature to be encountered. Pump manufacturers provide information about the maximum viscosity acceptable for a specific pump or other components.

Oxidation Resistance

Oxidation, or chemical combination of the oil with oxygen, can seriously reduce the service life of fluids. Both petroleum and vegetable oils are susceptible to oxidation, particularly in hydraulic applications. In petroleum, oxygen readily combines with the carbon and hydrogen present. Low temperature oxidation of vegetable oils is called auto-oxidation and should be prevented by low temperature storage of these oils, generally with nitrogen introduced in the storage vessel to deter oxidation.

Most oxidation byproducts are soluble in oil causing additional reactions to take place that can form gum, sludge and varnish. The first stage products which stay in the oil are acidic and can cause corrosion throughout the system and may increase the viscosity of the oil. Insoluble gums, sludge and varnish can plug orifices, increase wear and cause valves to stick.

Operating temperature of petroleum and vegetable-based oils is important for the prevention of high oxidation rates and the production of destructive oxidation byproducts.

Catalysts in Oxidation

There may be numerous oxidation catalysts present in poorly maintained hydraulic systems, i.e., conditions or elements that increase the potential for oxidation. Heat, pressure, contaminants, water, metal surfaces, some metals, and agitation all accelerate oxidation. Temperature is particularly important. Below 140°F (60°C), petroleum oil oxidizes very slowly. However, the rate of oxidation approximately doubles for every 18°F (10°C) increase in operating temperature above 140°F (60°C).

Rust and Corrosion Prevention

Rust is the chemical union of ferrous metal (iron or steel) with oxygen. Corrosion is a chemical reaction between a metal and a chemical — typically an acid. Acids result from the union of water with some elements (Figure 3-12).

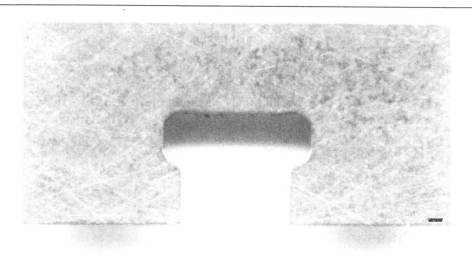

Figure 3-12   Corrosion on vane

Because it is extremely difficult to keep air and airborne moisture out of hydraulic systems, there is always the possibility that rust and corrosion may occur. With corrosion (Figure 3-13), particles of metal are dissolved and washed away.

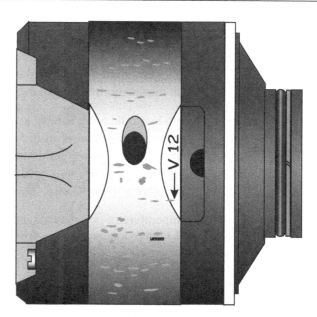

Figure 3-13   Vane pump corrosion

Both rust and corrosion contaminate the system and increase component wear. They may also increase internal leakage past the affected parts causing high temperatures, and may also cause components to seize through heat and closure of running clearances with debris.

Particular care must be taken when operating and cleaning equipment to prevent the contamination of the hydraulic system with water or cleaning solvents — either from the environment or when washing down equipment.

Demulsibility

Demulsibility is the ability of a fluid to separate out or reject water. However, it is desirable when using petroleum or vegetable-based oils that water content be kept to an absolute minimum and that free water not be allowed into the hydraulic system.

Fire Resistance

In some applications, environmental conditions may dictate that the fluid used in hydraulic systems must have fire resistant properties.

The *flash point* or temporary ignition point of typical hydrocarbons (petroleum oils) may be as low as 200°F (93°C) or be higher than 500°F (260°C). It is important to analyze the working environment of your specific application to determine fire hazards. Governmental regulations, local or Federal, could also impact your choices. *Fire point* is the temperature the fluid must attain for continuous burning. Typical petroleum products may continue to burn even after the point of ignition is removed.

Fire resistance in fluids generally means that, while most fluids can be ignited under the right conditions, a fire resistant fluid will not sustain combustion when an ignition source is removed. Resistant fluids will not allow flame to flash back to the ignition source.

Virtually all fluids used in hydraulic systems contain a variety of additives to improve or augment the performance of the fluid under various conditions. It is important that your fluid supplier understand the nature of your application: the environment, the types of components and their manufacturer's specifications relative to fluids. Duty cycles, loads (pressure), storage ability, temperature extremes, and any unusual or special considerations in the operation of your machinery that could affect the life of the fluid or its performance.

Additives

Although additives often enhance the natural abilities of the particular fluid being used, they must be monitored and kept at specified levels to prevent failure of the fluid and eventually the entire system.

Rust and Corrosion Inhibitors

Because virtually every environment contains some moisture, the addition of rust inhibitors to the hydraulic fluid will prevent the formation of iron oxides (rust) in components. Rust inhibitors typically coat metal parts so natural air and moisture do not interact with the metal to form oxide compounds.

Corrosive elements are often created through oxidation, but may be introduced to the system via poor maintenance practices. Care must be exercised whenever the hydraulic system is exposed to atmosphere to minimize the introduction of incompatible elements that may react with the fluid chemistry. Acids formed by the interaction of water in hydraulic fluid can corrode metal components. Corrosion inhibitors either form a protective coating on surfaces or neutralize acids as they form.

Some component materials such as alloys containing magnesium, lead and zinc are very susceptible to corrosion and oxidation and should be avoided in hydraulic systems even if anticorrosion compounds are added.

Antioxidants

Because oxidation is accelerated by the presence of air and excess heat, preventive measures should be taken to complement the antioxidant additives put in the fluid by refiners. Periodic testing of the fluid can indicate problems with fluids that, if detected early, can be corrected and remedied thus extending the life of the fluid.

The presence of some metals, such as copper, will act as oxidation catalysts and should be prevented from induction into hydraulic systems.

Demulsifiers

These are additives that aid the fluid in the rejection of water. Proper maintenance dictates that rejected water contained in reservoirs be removed periodically to prevent re-emulsification and/or reaction with the fluid chemistry. Water in the bottom of a reservoir could freeze in cold weather conditions and cause a serious potential for cavitation of the pump on start-up.

Anti-Wear

Three types of anti-wear additives are used to provide increased wear resistance and enhanced lubrication qualities in hydraulic systems. These additives are classified as: *anti-wear (AW), wear resistant (WR) and extreme pressure (EP)*.

Most anti-wear additives form a protective film on metal surfaces when exposed to low frictional heat. EP types of additive come out of solution when exposed to high frictional heat and either prevent the surfaces from coming in contact or prevent the surfaces from welding to each other. In general, EP additives should be present when operating above 3,000 psig.

Currently, the most common anti-wear additive is zinc dithiophosphate (ZDDP). However, others, such as sulfurized olefins are also used. Fluid suppliers should be contacted to determine the nature of anti-wear additives in your fluid.

Anti-Foaming Agents

Aeration, the introduction of outside air into the hydraulic system is extremely destructive to pumps. Aeration can also create severe safety hazards when air is present in cylinders creating dangerous load dynamics, or being conducted through lines where fluid velocity changes can allow the decompression of the air causing erratic response of actuators and loads. Air in thermoplastic lines, e.g., on utility trucks for high-voltage line work, can compromise the dielectric properties of the hydraulic lines creating a potential for conductivity.

The presence of excess air in fluids also promotes more rapid oxidation and the destruction of the fluid. Anti-foaming agents help prevent foaming and the retention of air in the reservoir. However, close attention must be paid to the integrity of the hydraulic system to prevent the introduction of air in the first place.

Foam and entrained air can be caused by:

• Air leaks, typically at pump inlet (low oil level, leaky fittings) and cylinder rod seals

• High velocities through orifices and servo valve spools

• Rapid discharge of accumulators

Additives typically promote the combination of small bubbles into larger ones that are then more easily forced out of the fluid in the reservoir.

VI Improvers

VI improvers are usually long-chain polymers which help prevent waxes from forming crystalline structures at very low temperatures. Specific attention to viscosity index must be paid when operating machinery at very low temperatures or over a wide range of temperature change.

Fluid Types

The general categories of available hydraulic fluids are: petroleum oils (hydrocarbon-based), fire resistant fluids (high water-based — HWBF; water glycol, phosphate esters and polyol esters) and specialty or biodegradable fluids which include vegetable oils and polyol esters.

Because no single fluid is exceptional in all requirements, some compromise may be necessary when selecting a fluid for a specific application. Since hydraulic applications frequently subject fluids to extremes of temperature and shock, properties of lubricity and a high viscosity index (the ability of a fluid to maintain acceptable viscosity over a wide range of temperature variation) are often important considerations.

Increasing concern about environmental issues has caused heightened interest in biodegradable fluids for use in hydraulic systems, particularly mobile machinery that operates in environmentally sensitive areas such as woodlands, watersheds and farmland. The use of organic vegetable-based fluids such as rapeseed or soy oil has expanded dramatically. Another concern in fluid selection relative to the working environment of machinery is flammability of the fluid. This may be of concern with machinery such as that present in a steel foundry where molten metals are present, other applications may present fire or flammability issues that must be addressed in the selection of hydraulic fluids. The use of synthetic or water-based fluids for their fire-resistant properties may present serious design problems for hydraulic machinery.

Synthetic and water-based fluids are typically heavier than petroleum fluids (specific gravity of these fluids may exceed 1.15) and may require flooded inlet conditions to prevent cavitation of pumps. In the case of water-based fluids, the constant monitoring of water levels to maintain the effectiveness and additive/water ratio of the fluids is a serious drawback. These requirements can be very difficult to accommodate in hydraulic applications.

Hydraulic fluids can be grouped in three general categories: petroleum oils, biodegradable fluids and fire resistant fluids. Figure 3-14 shows the various types of fluids that fall into these categories.

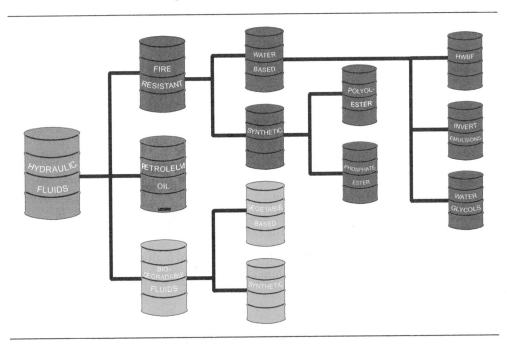

Figure 3-14   Fluid types typically used in hydraulic systems

Petroleum or hydrocarbon-based fluids are most commonly used in hydraulic systems.

Hydrocarbon-Based Petroleum Oil

The advantages of petroleum-based fluids are: low cost, good lubricity, ready availability and relatively low toxicity.

Petroleum oils specifically blended as hydraulic oils, or antiwear hydraulic oils, are the fluids of choice for hydraulic systems. All major oil suppliers produce one or more varieties of this fluid, which have very good VI characteristics as well as additives for antiwear, antioxidation and antirust. The VI improvers used are exceptionally stable and resist shear at the higher temperatures. Oil suppliers conduct the Vickers Pump Test Procedure for Evaluation of Antiwear Hydraulic Fluids for Hydraulic Systems.

ATF (automatic transmission fluid) is sometimes used in hydraulic systems. ATF provides excellent low temperature viscosity and typically has a very high viscosity index, accomplished by the addition of VI improvers. With the exception of demulsifiers, ATFs contain many other hydraulic fluid additives. The presence of high quantities of additives, particularly VI improvers, places the fluid at risk of breakdown (temporary and permanent shear of the VI additive molecular structure) during high temperature operation. Fluid temperatures above 165°F (74°C) should be avoided for any more than very short periods of time. Because hydraulic fluid temperatures can frequently exceed 180°F (82°C) continuously during warm weather operation, the use of ATF should be carefully evaluated.

While ATF is readily available, it is more costly than hydraulic oils. ATF is colored red as are military hydraulic fluids such as MIL-H-5606 and MIL-H-83282. In fact, military fluids are often referred to as *red oil*. Before using MIL-H-5606, you should consult your pump manufacturer as this oil has a very low viscosity and lubricity for compatibility with very low temperature operation.

Crankcase oils can be used in hydraulic applications. Oils used should meet all viscosity requirements, also water content needs to be monitored as engine oils tend to hold water in suspension.

Hydraulic System Operating Temperature Range (Min. Ambient Start-Up to Maximum)*	SAE Viscosity Designation
** -10°F to 130°F (-23°C to 54°C) 0°F to 180°F (-18°C to 82°C) 0°F to 210°F (-18°C to 99°C) 50°F to 210°F (10°C to 99°C)	5W, 5W-20, 5W-30 10W 10W-30 (ensure VI stability) 20 - 20W

NOTE: *The temperatures shown in the above table are cold start-up to maximum operating temperatures. Proper start-up procedures must be followed to ensure adequate lubrication during warm-up.

NOTE: **Arctic conditions represent a specialized field with widely practiced heating of equipment before starting. Oils especially developed for use in arctic conditions such as synthetic hydrocarbons, esters or mixtures of the two may be used.

During cold start-up, avoid high pressure operation of hydraulic systems until the system fluid is at operating temperatures to ensure proper lubrication.

Water-Based Fluids

These fluids are used because of their fire-resistant characteristics. They include *water-in-oil emulsions, oil-in-water emulsions* and *water-glycols*. Because of the increased specific gravity of these fluids, flooded inlet conditions are recommended with a lower allowable pump inlet vacuum than with petroleum.

Although water glycol mixtures have comparable viscosities and additives with hydrocarbon oils, they are more expensive and present considerable maintenance requirements.

These fluids are somewhat fire resistant. They generally have lubrication attributes similar to hydrocarbon-based fluids.

Phosphate Esters

Phosphate esters attack elastomers, some paints and plastics and require special seals such as ethylene propylene rubber (EPR), butyl rubber and occasionally fluorocarbon (Viton).

Synthetics

Most synthetic fluids and blends, typically phosphate esters and chlorinated hydrocarbons or blends come with the same cautions associated with phosphate esters previously mentioned. Some synthetics however are petroleum compatible and offer clear advantages over conventional oils. These advantages include oxidation resistance, reduced friction, better low and high temperature operating characteristics and increased life with longer drain intervals.

Vegetable Oil-Based Fluids

Ongoing research into the viability of vegetable oils as lubricants and power transmitting fluids for industry has created an important option for users of mobile equipment. Problems of heat and oxidation as well as stability are being addressed to enhance the performance of these oils in hydraulic applications.

Vegetable oils achieve superior biodegradability and essentially zero toxicity relative to the environment. These oils are typically more expensive than petroleum-based fluids, but cost much less than synthetics with similar environmental advantages.

Soy, rapeseed and other vegetable-based oils typically have high viscosity indexes (VI) and possess good thermal stability, low volatility and high flash point as well as additive compatibility.

On the negative side relative to petroleum-based fluids, vegetable oils possess poor hydrolytic stability (water degrades the fluid) and poor low-temperature characteristics. Their oxidation stability and response to pour point depressants (cold weather performance additives) are also poor compared to petroleum oils.

Regardless of some of the shortcomings of these vegetable-based fluids, they can provide very good performance in many applications where environmental considerations are important.

Property	Characteristics
Suitable viscosity	The viscosity characteristics of selected fluids must be suitable for all aspects of the application, including pour point, flash point, etc.
Viscosity index	The ability of the fluid to maintain an acceptable viscosity over the operating temperature range of the application is vital for lubrication, efficiency and system longevity.
Chemical/environmental stability	Minimal chemical changes whether in storage or in application. Also, low volatility to minimize evaporation and bubble formation to reduce loss of fluid and potential for cavitation/ aeration damage. Fluids, in some cases, may have to meet safety and environmental regulatory standards for toxicity and biodegradability.
Lubricity	Proper maintenance of adequate lubrication film over the pressure and temperature operating ranges of the application.
System compatibility	Zero or minimum reaction with other system materials such as seals, hose inner tubes and covers, platings and metal components.
Heat transfer	Good thermal conductivity and high specific heat for dissipation and cooling.
Minimum compressibility	High bulk modulus for efficient transmission of energy. Fluid should resist foaming as entrained air increases compressibility.

Table 3-1   Characteristics of Hydraulic Fluids*

* Many of these attributes are augmented by the additives put in the fluid by manufacturers. It is essential that a fluid supplier be aware of all operating parameters of hydraulic applications before a fluid is selected.

The selection of fluids used in hydraulic systems is of considerable importance. When discussing fluid selection with a supplier, it may be useful to keep in mind the following general observations in relation to your application and final fluid selection:

- Temperatures affect viscosity

- Oxidation rates for petroleum-based oils double for each 18°F (10°C) rise in temperature higher than 140°F (60°C). This effectively reduces the life of the fluid by half for each 18°F (10°C) rise.

- Petroleum oil at atmospheric pressure (14.7 psia, 1 bar) contains 8 – 10 percent air in solution. This air cannot be observed and is normal.

- Cold starts at less than 20°F (11°C) above a fluid's pour point can damage components and the system.

- Do not put additives in your fluid.

- Fluids and additives break down and wear out. Laboratory testing and analysis are mandatory, test results should be analyzed by knowledgeable individuals who can then recommend proper action.

Fluid Type (Rel. Cost)	Specific Gravity	Viscosity Index	Lubricity	Oxidation Stability	Fire Resist.	Corrosion Protection	Heat Transfer	Temp. Range °F	Effect on Conv. Elastomers	Effect on Conv. Paints
Anti-wear petroleum (1)	0.85 – 0.89	Good	Excellent	Excellent	Poor	Excellent	Good	20 – 150	Minimal	None
Soybean-Based Oil (2-3)	0.92	Fair	Excellent	Fair	Excellent	Excellent	Good	-13 – 175	Minimal	Minimal
Synthetic Blends (4)	0.8 – 1.0	Good	Good	Good	Fair	Good	Good	20 – 150	Severe	Severe
Phosphate Esters (5)	1.15	Poor	Excellent	Good	Good	Good	Good	20 – 150	Severe	Severe
Water Glycol (2)	1.1	Excellent	Good	Good	Excellent	Fair	Excellent	0 – 120	Minimal	Minimal to Moderate

Table 3-2 Hydraulic fluid comparisons

Water-in-oil (invert) emulsions, oil-in-water emulsions (soluble oil) and water additive fluids are not included because of the problems associated with hydraulic applications. Your fluid supplier should be consulted regardless of the fluid selected.

Proper assembly practices and usage can prevent the existence of any external leakage in modern hydraulic systems. It is estimated by industry analysts that up to 7 million barrels of hydraulic fluid are lost annually via external leaks and line breaks.

Leakage Practices

From 70 to 85 percent of hydraulic problems are associated with contamination of or the improper choice and handling of hydraulic fluids. Proper maintenance practices and the sensible use of hydraulic equipment within manufacturers operating specifications are essential for safety and to prolong the useful operating life of systems and components.

Trained, informed operators and repair crews, as well as purchasing and design personnel are necessary to the effective operation of hydraulic equipment.

Industrial Test Questions:
Hydraulic Fluids

Chapter 3

1. Name the four primary purposes of the hydraulic fluid.

2. Define viscosity. What is the common unit of measuring viscosity?

3. How is viscosity affected by cold? By heat?

4. If viscosity is too high, what can happen to the system?

5. What is the viscosity index? When is the viscosity index important?

6. Which type of hydraulic fluid has the best natural lubricity?

7. Name several catalysts to oxidation of hydraulic oil.

8. How are rust and corrosion prevented?

9. What is demulsibility?

10. What are the four basic types of fire-resistant hydraulic fluid?

11. Which type of hydraulic fluid is not compatible with Buna or neoprene seals?

12. Which type of fire-resistant hydraulic fluid is best for high temperature operation?

13. How does the specific gravity of the synthetic phosphate esters affect the pump inlet conditions?

Chapter 4 . . . . Hydraulic Fluid Conductors and Seals

This chapter is comprised of two parts. First is a description of the hydraulic system "plumbing" — the types of connecting lines and fittings used to carry fluid between the pumps, valves, actuators, etc. The second part deals with the prevention of leakage and the types of seals and seal materials required for hydraulic applications.

Fluid Conductors

Fluid conductors is a general term which embraces the various kinds of conducting lines that carry hydraulic fluid between components plus the fittings or connectors used between the conductors. Hydraulic systems today use principally three types of conducting lines: steel pipe, steel tubing and flexible hose. Pipe may be the cheapest but its use often presents serious leakage problems, especially at higher operation pressures. Pipe is still in use in many installations (which accounts for its inclusion in this chapter) but it is gradually being replaced with tubing and hose. The future may see plastic plumbing which is slowly coming into use for certain applications.

Steel Pipe

Iron and steel pipes were the first conductors used in industrial hydraulic systems and are still used because of their low cost. Seamless steel pipe is recommended for hydraulic systems with the pipe interior free of rust, scale and dirt.

Sizing

Pipe and pipe fittings are classified by nominal size and wall thickness. Originally, a given size pipe had only one wall thickness and the stated size was the actual inside diameter. Later, pipes were manufactured with varying wall thicknesses: standard, extra heavy, and double extra heavy. However, the outside diameter did not change. To increase wall thickness, the inside diameter was changed. Thus, the nominal pipe size alone indicates only the thread size for connections.

Schedule

Currently, wall thickness is being expressed as a schedule number. Schedule numbers are specified by the American National Standards Institute (ANSI).

For comparison, schedule 40 corresponds closely to standard. Schedule 80 essentially is extra heavy. Schedule 160 covers pipes with the greatest wall thickness under this system. The old double extra heavy classification is slightly thicker than schedule 160.

Figure 4-1 shows pipe sizes up to 12 inches (305 mm) (nominal).

		Inside Diameter			
Nominal Size	**Pipe O.D.**	**Schedule 40 Standard**	**Schedule 80 Extra Heavy**	**Schedule 160**	**Double Extra Heavy**
1/8	0.405	0.269	0.215		
1/4	0.540	0.364	0.302		
3/8	0.675	0.493	0.423		
1/2	0.840	0.622	0.546	0.466	0.252
3/4	1.050	0.824	0.742	0.614	0.434
1	1.315	1.049	0.957	0.815	0.599
1-1/4	1.660	1.380	1.278	1.160	0.896
1-1/2	1.900	1.610	1.500	1.338	1.100
2	2.375	2.067	1.939	1.689	1.503
2-1/2	2.875	2.469	2.323	2.125	1.771
3	3.500	3.068	2.900		
3-1/2	4.000	3.548	3.364	2.624	
4	4.500	4.026	3.826	3.438	
5	5.563	5.047	4.813	4.313	4.063
6	6.625	6.065	6.761	5.189	
8	8.625	7.981	7.625	6.813	
10	10.750	10.020	9.564	8.500	
12	12.750	11.934	11.376	10.126	

Figure 4-1   Pipes currently are sized by schedule number

Fluid Conductors and Seals

Fluid conductors: are the means to transport fluid from one point to another in a hydraulic circuit. Connectors fall into one of three broad categories; hose, steel tubing or pipe. There are many sub-categories under each of these, primarily defining the construction, materials and performance criteria.

Connectors: fall into one of two broad categories; port connection — the connection in the hydraulic components or end connectors — how the hose, steel tubing or pipe is connected to what is in the hydraulic component. Port and end connectors are broken into two broad sealing categories, metal-to-metal seals or O-ring seals. Connector types will be discussed later in the chapter.

Pipe: is occasionally used in hydraulic systems, primarily for its relatively low cost and wide availability. Pipe gained its popularity as a conductor for air, water and steam, and so was a natural choice in the early years of hydraulic development. As the sophistication of hydraulics increased, however, pipe became less attractive to designers of hydraulic systems. Pipe is a rather inflexible material, difficult to form and install in close environments. This is particularly important in today's compact machinery.

Selection Criteria

Hose makes a flexible conductor; tubing makes a rigid conductor. Therefore, the **first selection criteria** is:

- Do the components being connected move relative to each other? If so, then hose must be used.

- Is there excessive vibration present? Hose can usually accommodate vibration better than tubing, although proper isolation and clamping can make tube installation successful in many applications.

- Are there frequent pressure pulsations present? Again, hose can usually accommodate pressure pulsations better than tubing, due to the relative movement that takes place. Hose will also tend to absorb and dampen pulsations to some degree. As with vibration, proper isolation and clamping can make for a successful tubing installation in many applications.

The second criteria is the ease of installation. Hose allows the installer to bend and flex the line to install it to fit the application. Tubing may have to be pre-formed or bent prior to installation. Although tubing might make for a neater appearance if installed correctly, it requires a lot of planning and skill to bend tubing correctly. Correctly installed both will normally fill the job requirements.

The third criteria is the space available to accommodate the conductor, which may influence the selection.

Hose

Hose is a flexible conductor that is used when hydraulic lines are subject to movement, flexing or vibration. Figure 4-2 shows the basic elements that makeup a hose. A guideline for hydraulic hose in North America is the SAE J517 Standard. This standard has 100R numbers that define construction, dimension, pressure and temperature specifications. A similar standard was developed in Europe referred to as the CEN (Committee for European Normalization) or EN Standard for flexible hose. Though the SAE and EN construction look similar, only 3 (of the 18 SAE) standards are different and they won't be in a couple of years. Regardless of the country of origin many original equipment manufacturers specify EN rated hose on new equipment. The ISO (International Standards Organization) is also preparing a global standard for hydraulic hose however at the time of printing, those standards were still in committee and in only a draft form. A brief description of both the SAE J517 and EN numbers are provided in Appendix C. As for a safety factor, the burst pressure for hydraulic hose is four times the rated working pressure in all cases with a few exceptions.

Flexible Hose

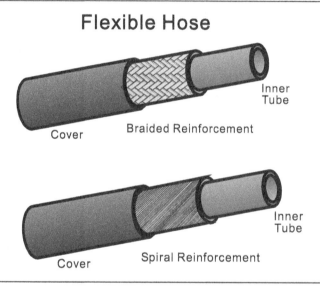

Figure 4-2   Flexible hose is constructed in layers

The tube may be constructed of an oil resistant synthetic rubber material or an oil resistant thermoplastic material. The reinforcement may consist of one or two layers of wire or textile braid, or a combination of both textile and wire braids, or four or six plies of wire wrapped in alternate directions referred to as spiral. The cover consists of an oil and weather resistant material, either synthetic rubber, thermoplastic or textile.

Hose size is designated by a "dash" number, which refers to the inside diameter in sixteenths of an inch. For example, a -6 hose would be 6/16 inch inside diameter, or 3/8 inch I.D. With few exceptions the "dash" number is the actual hose inside diameter.

Hose ends, frequently called fittings, may be reusable (screw together, bolt together) or non-reusable (crimped or swaged) (Figure 4-3). The different end connections will be discussed later.

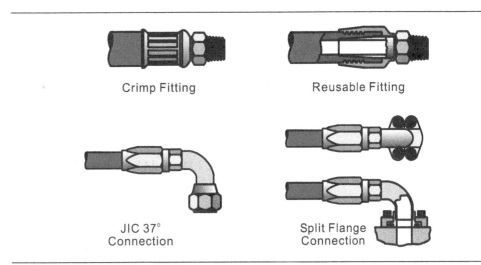

Figure 4-3   Typical hose ends (fittings)

"Don't Mix and Match Hose and Fittings from Two Different Manufacturers"

Reprinted from 1999 SAE Handbook
Hydraulic Hose — SAE J517 FEB 1998

Hose Assemblies

"Hose assemblies may be fabricated by the manufacturer, an agent for or customer of the manufacturer or by the user. Fabrication of permanently attached fittings to hydraulic hose requires specialized assembly equipment. Field attachable fittings (screw style and segment clamp style) can usually be assembled without specialized equipment although many manufacturers provide equipment to assist in this operation.

"SAE J517 hose from one manufacturer is usually not compatible with SAE J516 fittings supplied by another manufacturer. It is the responsibility of the fabricator to consult the manufacturer's written assembly instructions or the manufacturers directly before intermixing hose and fittings from two manufacturers. Similarly, assembly equipment from one manufacturer is usually not interchangeable with that of another manufacturer. It is the responsibility of the fabricator to consult the manufacturer's written instructions or the manufacturer directly for proper assembly equipment. Always follow the manufacturer's instructions for proper preparation and fabrication of hose assemblies."

Steel Tubing

Steel tubing is made from a high ductile, annealed material, which is easily bent and flared. It may be seamless or electrically welded; it usually results in a cleaner looking installation, and properly installed will require less maintenance. It also can be made from stainless steel for highly corrosive fluids and high-pressure applications.

Tubing size is available in 1/16-inch increments from 1/8 inch up to one inch outside diameter, and in 1/4-inch increments above one inch. Various wall thicknesses are available for each size. Tubing is designated by the outside diameter, and depending on wall thickness, the I.D. could be 0.376 of an inch smaller than the O.D., affecting the fluid velocity.

Pressure capability of tubing is based on the diameter and wall thickness. Tubing size charts, as illustrated in Figure 4-4, provide burst and working pressure ratings for each size and wall thickness combination. Burst pressure is some multiple higher than working pressure, usually three and six times. This provides a working pressure "safety factor."

Tubing Table

Nom. Size	Wall (in.)	Burst psi	Working psi	Tubing Oil Flow Capacities (gpm)					
				2 ft/sec	4 ft/sec	10 ft/sec	15 ft/sec	20 ft/sec	30 ft/sec
1/2	.035	7700	1283	.905	1.81	4.52	6.79	9.05	13.6
	.042	9240	1540	.847	1.63	4.23	6.35	8.47	12.7
	.049	10,780	1797	.791	1.58	3.95	5.93	7.91	11.9
	.058	12,760	2127	.722	1.44	3.61	5.41	7.22	10.8
	.065	14,300	2383	.670	1.34	3.35	5.03	6.70	10.1
	.072	15,840	2640	.620	1.24	3.10	4.65	6.20	9.30
	.083	18,260	3043	.546	1.09	2.73	4.09	5.46	8.18
5/8	.035	6160	1027	1.51	3.01	7.54	11.3	15.1	22.6
	.042	7392	1232	1.43	2.85	7.16	10.7	14.3	21.4
	.049	8624	1437	1.36	2.72	6.80	10.2	13.6	20.4
	.058	10,208	1701	1.27	2.54	6.34	9.51	12.7	19.0
	.065	11,440	1907	1.20	2.40	6.00	9.00	12.0	18.0
	.072	12,672	2112	1.13	2.26	5.66	8.49	11.3	17.0
	.083	14,608	2435	1.03	2.06	5.16	7.73	10.3	15.5
	.095	16,720	2787	.926	1.85	4.63	6.95	9.26	13.9
3/4	.049	7187	1198	2.08	4.17	10.4	15.6	20.8	31.2
	.058	8507	1418	1.97	3.93	9.84	14.8	19.7	29.6
	.065	9533	1589	1.88	3.76	9.41	14.1	18.8	28.2
	.072	10,560	1760	1.75	3.51	8.77	13.2	17.5	26.4
	.083	12,173	2029	1.67	3.34	8.35	12.5	16.7	25.0
					3.07	7.67	11.5	15.3	23.0
							10.4	13.9	

Figure 4-4   Size and capability chart for tubing

Tubing Connectors

Tubing end connectors can be a flared type, compression fitting type, and brazed or welded type. These basic types along with both port and end connectors used in today's hydraulic systems will be covered later in this chapter.

Fluid Velocity

Turbulent flow is an undesirable characteristic, as it causes unnecessary friction within the fluid and against the conductor's walls. Excessive fluid velocity is a major contributor to turbulence, which causes unwanted pressure drop between circuit segments. Keeping fluid velocities at reasonable levels is important for maintaining good pump inlet conditions, reducing heat generation and facilitating good component operation (Table 4-1).

Fluid velocity is the speed at which fluid moves past a given point, in a conductor, in connectors or in components. The velocity is most commonly stated in feet-per-second (ft/sec) in customary U.S. units, or in centimeter-per-second (cm/sec) or meters-per-minute (m/min) in metric units. However, velocity may be stated in any dimension per unit of time (Figure 4-5).

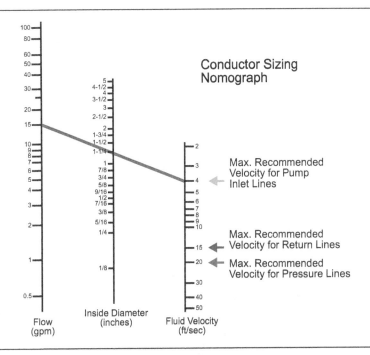

Figure 4-5   Nomograph for determining the inside diameter of a fluid conductor

Conductor Sizing		
Application	**Operating Pressure**	**Maximum Fluid Velocities**
Pump Inlet Line		4 ft/sec
Pressure Line	...0 – 500 psi ...500 – 3000 psi ...over 3000 psi	15 ft/sec 20 ft/sec 25 ft/sec
Return Line		15 ft/sec

Table 4-1 Recommended fluid velocities in conductors

The relationship between fluid velocity and conductor size is:

Flow = Velocity × Area

Care must be taken to assure that units for each of the elements of the above equation are converted correctly to give the desired results. The following formula takes all of the conversion factors into account:

Formula 4-1

$$(V)_{ft/sec} = \frac{0.3208 \times Q_{GPM}}{(A)Area}$$

Where:

V = Fluid velocity in feet-per-second

Q = Fluid flow in gallons-per-minute

A = Inside area of a conductor in square inches

A nomograph in Appendix C shows the recommended velocities of fluid in hydraulic conductors. Velocities in these ranges result in reasonably low pressure drops through conductors and minimal fluid friction.

Fluid velocity varies inversely by the inside area of the conductor, or inversely by the square of the diameter. As Figure 4-6 shows, the velocity of the fluid will increase by 4 if the inside diameter of the conductor is reduced to half its original size.

If the conductor is reduced to half its original diameter, ...

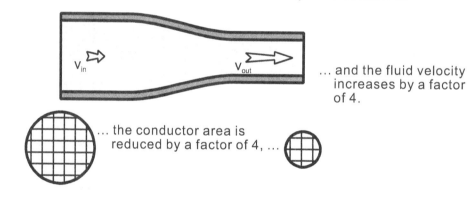

... and the fluid velocity increases by a factor of 4.

... the conductor area is reduced by a factor of 4, ...

Figure 4-6   Fluid velocity is inversely proportional to the conductor diameter squared

Port Connections

Common domestic port connections: National Pipe Tapered Fuel (NPTF), SAE O-Ring Boss (ORB), Split Flange. Common foreign port connections: British Standard Pipe Tapered (BSPT) and Metric. Later in the section will be a brief description on metric port connections.

Pipe Threads

Domestic pipe threads fall into to two types: NPT (National Pipe Tapered) and NPTF (National Pipe Tapered Fuel). The difference between NPT and NPTF is in the quality of the threads and sealing capability (Figure 4-8). A pipe thread's seal is a metal-to-metal type seal, sealing on the threads. Actually NPT pipe threads were designed for water pipe plumbing (60 psi [4.1 bar]) not for hydraulic systems. However they have been used in hydraulic systems for years and they are notorious for leaking. National Pipe Tapered (NPT) requires some kind of thread sealant placed on the threads to create a seal before assembly. A sealing compound can be used for a more effective seal, although this introduces another material that frequently finds its way into the hydraulic system. In an attempt to create a better pipe thread, one that does not require any kind of sealants, the industry introduced what has been commonly supplied for years as National Pipe Tapered Fuel (NPTF), or as it is referred to in the SAE handbook, Dry Seal. Although the NPTF is a better pipe thread, both are common causes for leakage in hydraulic systems and neither is recommended by the National Fluid Power Association (NFPA) for use in hydraulic applications.

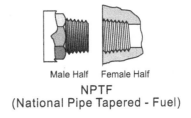

Male Half   Female Half

NPTF
(National Pipe Tapered - Fuel)

Figure 4-7   Male pipe thread

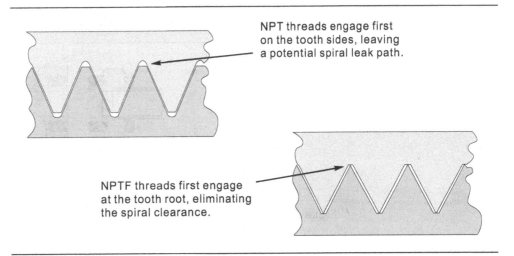

NPT threads engage first on the tooth sides, leaving a potential spiral leak path.

NPTF threads first engage at the tooth root, eliminating the spiral clearance.

Figure 4-8   Pipe threads are not recommended for hydraulic systems — if used, however, they must be NPTF

British Standard Pipe Tapered (BSPT) connection is similar to the NPTF, except that thread pitches are different in most sizes, and the thread form and O.D.s are close but not the same. Sealing is accomplished by distorting the threads. A thread sealant is recommended.

SAE O-Ring Boss

Port connection is recommended by the NFPA for optimum leakage control in medium and high-pressure hydraulic systems. The male connector has a straight thread and an O-ring. The female port has a straight thread, a machined surface (minimum spot face) and a chamfer to accept the O-ring. The seal takes place by compressing the O-ring into the chamfer. The threads hold the connection mechanically together (Figure 4-9).

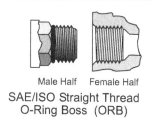

Male Half   Female Half
SAE/ISO Straight Thread
O-Ring Boss (ORB)

Figure 4-9   SAE O-ring boss

Split Flange

This connection is commonly used in fluid power systems at the pump inlet and on hydrostatic systems. There are two pressure ratings, Code 61 is referred to as the "standard" series and Code 62 is the "6,000 psi" series. The design concept for both series is the same, but the bolt hole spacing and flange head diameters are larger for the higher pressure, Code 62 connection. The female port is an unthreaded hole with 4-threaded bolt holes in a rectangular pattern around the port. The male consists of a flange head, grooved for an O-ring, and either a captive flange or split flange halves with bolt holes to match the port. The seal takes place on the O-ring, which is compressed between the flanged head and the flat surface surrounding the port. The threaded bolts hold the connection together.

SAE J518, JIS B 8363, ISO/DIS 6162 and DIN 20066 are interchangeable, except for the bolt sizes. All, but the SAE, use metric-sized bolts.

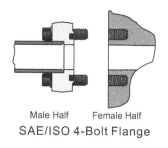

Male Half   Female Half
SAE/ISO 4-Bolt Flange

Figure 4-10   SAE J518 four-bolt flange

Metric Port Connections

The chart below illustrates the various forms and how they seal.

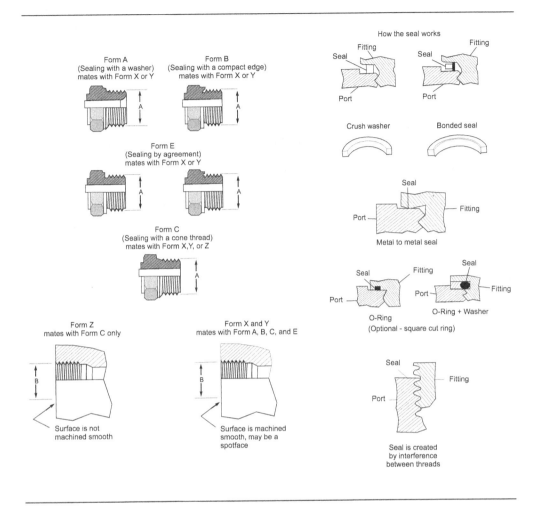

Figure 4-11   Male connectors and female ports

End Connectors

Common domestic hydraulic end connections are either 37 or 45 degree metal-to-metal seals or O-ring seals like an SAE Flat Face O-Ring Seal. Later in this section will be a brief discussion on metric end connections.

45 Degree

This connection is commonly used in refrigeration and automotive and truck systems including air, fuel and lube lines. The connector is frequently made of brass and considered low pressure. The seal takes place between the male flare and the female cone seat. The threads hold the connection mechanically together. The most common sizes are -4 (1/4") up to -12 (3/4") (Figure 4-12).

37 Degree

This connection is very common in fluid power systems. Both the male and female halves of the connection have 37-degree seats. The seal takes place by establishing a line contact between the male flare and the female cone seat. The threads hold the connection mechanically together. The most common sizes are -4 (1/4") up to -32 (2") (Figure 4-13).

Caution: in the -2, -3, -4, -5, -8 and -10 sizes, the threads of the SAE 45 degree flare and SAE 37 degree are the same. However the sealing surface angles are not the same. Intermixing 45 and 37-degree connections could cause hydraulic leakage.

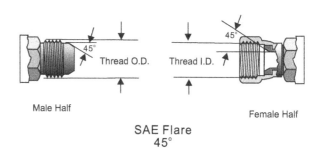

Figure 4-12   SAE 45 degree male and female halves

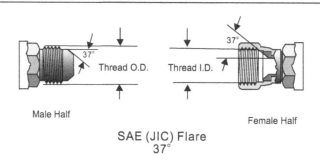

Figure 4-13   SAE 37 degree male and female halves

SAE Flat Face O-Ring Seal

This connection offers the very best in leakage control available today (Figure 4-14). The male connector has a straight thread and an O-ring in the face. The female has a straight thread and a machined flat face. The seal takes place by compressing the O-ring onto the flat face of the female, similar to the split flange type connection. The threads hold the connection mechanically together. The flat face O-ring seal connection is rated to 6,000 psi in sizes up to -16 (1") and the larger sizes -20 (1-1/4") and -24 (1-1/2") are rated to 4,000 psi.

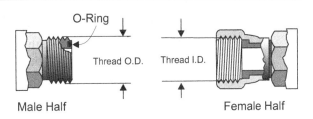

Figure 4-14   SAE J1453 O-ring face seal male and female halves

Metric End Connections

The most common metric connections are 60 and 24 degree inverted seals. The 60-degree is used less in today's newer designed systems and is considered a low-pressure connection. The 24-degree comes in two pressure series: l-Rh, low pressure, and s-Rh, high pressure. Both are very popular on foreign manufactured equipment today. The connection style consists of a common male and three different female halves. The male has a straight thread, a 24 degree included angle and a recessed counter bore that matches the tube O.D. used with it. The female may be a tube, nut and ferrule, a tapered nose/Globeseal flareless swivel or a tapered nose Globeseal flareless swivel with an O-ring in the nose (DKO).

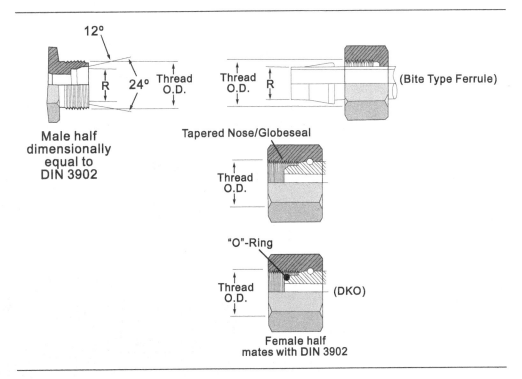

Figure 4-15   Metric 24 degree male and three female halves

O-Rings Basics

For virtually all types of fluid connectors involving O-rings, there are common guidelines that should always be followed:

1. For maximum service, use only O-rings that are made of the material and proper durometer for the application. The most common O-ring for use in petroleum applications is 90 durometer and made of Buna-N material. O-ring materials are also available in Viton, EPR and other materials. Be sure to consult the proper reference material when selecting O-rings for an application.

2. Care should be taken to ensure that the O-ring is properly seated when installing it. Do not twist and do not roll the O-ring when installing it.

3. The O-ring, if used as a dynamic seal, should be lubricated using compatible high shear oil. Lubrication is necessary to prevent rolling or cutting the O-ring upon connection. For EPDM or EPR O-rings, use a vegetable-based lubricant or the system fluid.

4. Keep all connecting surfaces clean and grit free.

5. Never reuse an O-ring. Used O-rings should be replaced before re-installation to help prevent future leakage problems.

Quick-Disconnect Couplings

Frequently, equipment requires hydraulically operated attachments to be repeatedly connected and disconnected from the primary power source. Examples are hydraulically operated power tools, or trail-behind farm equipment that is periodically attached and removed. Quick-disconnect couplings are a convenient method of repeatedly making and breaking the hydraulic connection.

Figure 4-16 illustrates the elements of a quick-disconnect coupling. The male and female portions are pushed together to make the connection and are then held together by a series of balls (bearings) in the female half locking into a recess on the male half. Some couplings screw together, and the advantage of this is the ability to connect against pressures (Figure 4-17). The action of pushing or screwing the two halves together forces the internal valves open, opening a fluid path within the connection.

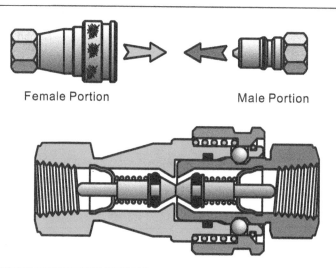

Female Portion   Male Portion

Figure 4-16   Ball latch connection

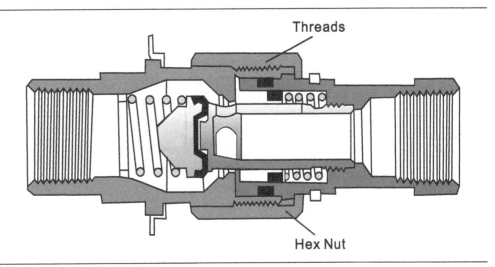

Threads

Hex Nut

Figure 4-17   Threaded connection

The notable advantage quick-disconnects offer is offset by some disadvantages:

- When disconnected, the two halves of the couplings are subject to contamination that will enter a hydraulic system when the two halves are reconnected.

- Poppet and ball valve style quick-disconnect couplings have a small cavity that will allow hydraulic fluid to spill out of, known as "Fluid Loss" upon disconnection. This can be unsightly, cause slippery surfaces and lead to environmental contamination. Also these styles of valves allow for air to be ingested into the system upon connection, called "Air Inclusion."

- If either one or both of the coupling halves are under pressure, it is extremely difficult (if not impossible) to connect the coupling halves.

- Quick-disconnects create a relatively high pressure drop that could cause a significant power loss if not sized correctly.

Manufacturers of quick-disconnect couplings have addressed most of these disadvantages with newer and improved designs.

- Most quick-disconnect coupling manufacturers offer caps and plugs for their products and, if used, they will eliminate or reduce the chance of contamination when disconnected.

- A "flat-faced" design coupling is available, as shown in Figure 4-18, that eliminates the cavity that contains hydraulic fluid or air during disconnection or connection. This design can reduce the amount of fluid leakage during disconnection to near zero and also provides a flat surface that can be wiped free of large contamination particles before being reconnected.

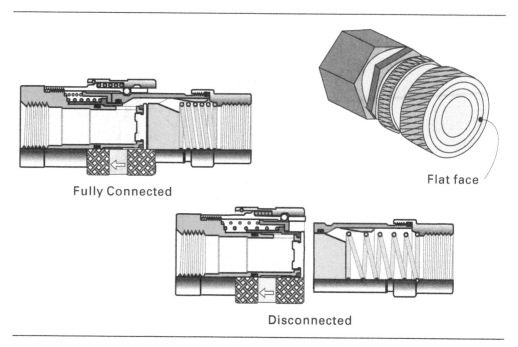

Fully Connected

Flat face

Disconnected

Figure 4-18   Flat-faced coupling

- A screw-together or thread-together type coupling can be used if one of the connectors is going to be under pressure.

Whether using quick-disconnect couplings or not, it is extremely important with today's highly sophisticated hydraulic systems to have a properly designed filtration and reservoirs to address the inherent contamination and air problems.

Dynamic Seals

Dynamic seals are installed between parts which move relative to one another. Thus, at least one of the parts must rub against the seal, and therefore dynamic seals are subject to wear. This makes their design and application more difficult.

O-Ring Seals

Probably the most common seal in use in modern hydraulic equipment is the O-ring (Figure 4-19). An O-ring is a molded, synthetic rubber seal which has a round cross section in the free state.

Note: Clearances greatly exaggerated

O-ring is installed in a groove and compressed

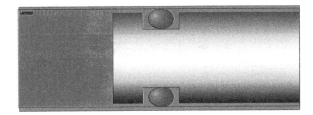

When pressure is applied, the O-ring is forced to the right, providing a positive seal

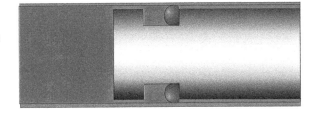

Figure 4-19   An O-ring is a positive seal

The O-ring is installed in an annular groove machined into one of the mating parts. At installation, it is compressed at both the inside and outside diameters. However, it is a pressure actuated seal as well as a compression seal. Pressure forces the O-ring against one side of its groove and outward at both diameters. It thus seals positively against two annular surfaces and one flat surface. Increased pressure results in a higher force against the sealing surfaces. The O-ring, therefore, is capable of containing extremely high pressure.

O-rings are used principally in static applications. However, they are also found in dynamic applications where there is a reciprocating motion between the parts. They are not generally suitable for sealing rotating parts or for applications where vibration is a problem.

Backup Rings (Nonextrusion)

At high pressure, the O-ring has a tendency to extrude into the clearance space between the mating parts (Figure 4-20). This may not be objectionable in a static application. But this extrusion can cause accelerated wear in a dynamic application. It is prevented by installing a stiff backup ring in the O-ring groove opposite the pressure source. If the pressure alternates, backup rings can be used on both sides of the O-ring.

Note: Clearances greatly exaggerated

Increased pressure can cause the O-ring to extrude through the clearance

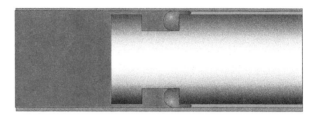

An anti-extrusion backup ring prevents extrusion

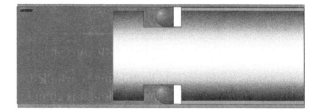

Figure 4-20   A backup ring is a nonextrusion ring

T-Ring Seals

The T-ring seal (Figure 4-21) is used extensively to seal cylinder pistons, piston rods, and other reciprocating parts. It is constructed of synthetic rubber molded in the shape of a "T," and reinforced by backup rings on either side. The sealing edge is rounded and seals very much like an O-ring. Obviously, this seal will not have the O-ring's tendency to roll. The T-ring is not limited to short-stroke applications.

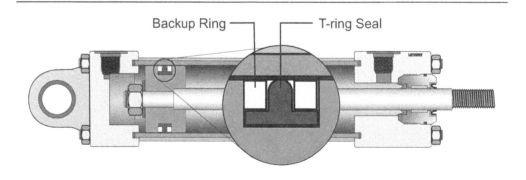

Figure 4-21   T-ring is a dynamic seal for reciprocating parts

Lip Seals

Lip seals are low-pressure dynamic seals, used principally to seal rotating shafts.

A typical lip seal (Figure 4-22) is constructed of a stamped housing for support and installation alignment, and synthetic rubber or leather formed into a lip which fits around the shaft. Often there is a spring to hold the lip in contact with the shaft.

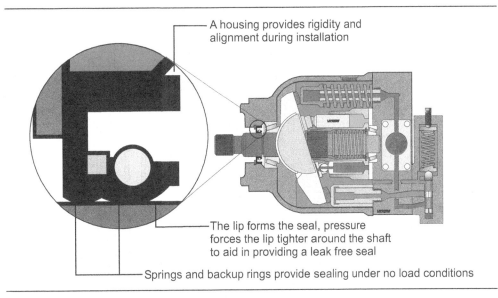

A housing provides rigidity and alignment during installation

The lip forms the seal, pressure forces the lip tighter around the shaft to aid in providing a leak free seal

Springs and backup rings provide sealing under no load conditions

Figure 4-22   Lip seals are used on rotating shafts

Lip seals are positive seals. However, they depend upon the lip riding on a microscopic film of fluid for long life. Sealing is aided by pressure up to a point. Pressure on the lip (or vacuum behind the lip) "balloons" it out against the shaft for a tighter seal. High pressure cannot be contained because the lip has no backup. In some applications, the chamber being sealed alternates from pressure to vacuum condition. Double lip seals are available for these applications to prevent air or dirt from getting in and oil from getting out. Correct installation of lip type seals, avoiding nicks and contamination, is key to successful long life.

Cup Seals

A cup seal (Figure 4-23) is a positive seal used on many cylinder pistons. It is pressure actuated in both directions. Sealing is accomplished by forcing the cup lip outward against the cylinder barrel. This type of seal is backed up and will handle very high pressures.

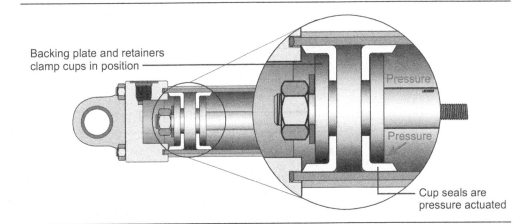

Backing plate and retainers clamp cups in position

Pressure

Pressure

Cup seals are pressure actuated

Figure 4-23   Cup seals are used on cylinder pistons

Cup seals must be clamped tightly in place. The cylinder piston actually is nothing more than the backing plate and retainers that hold the cup seals.

Piston Rings

Piston rings (Figure 4-24) are fabricated from cast iron or steel, highly polished, and sometimes plated. They offer considerably less resistance to motion than leather or synthetic seals. They are most often found on cylinder pistons.

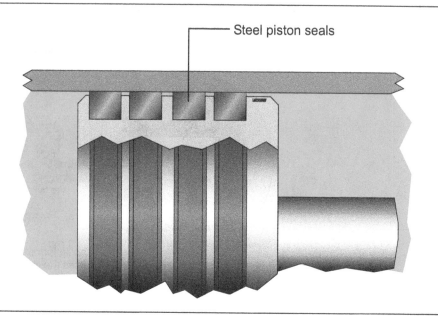

Steel piston seals

Figure 4-24   Piston rings are used for cylinder pistons

One piston ring does not necessarily form a positive seal. Sealing becomes more positive when several rings are placed side by side. Very high pressures can be handled.

Compression Packings

Compression packings (Figure 4-25) were among the earliest sealing devices used in hydraulic systems and are found in both static and dynamic applications. Packings are being replaced in most static applications by O-rings.

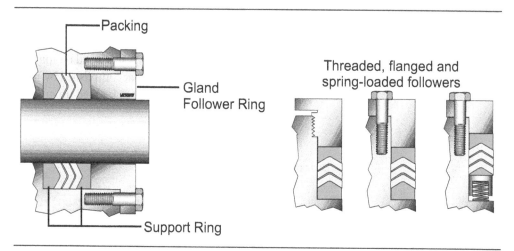

Packing

Gland
Follower Ring

Threaded, flanged and
spring-loaded followers

Support Ring

Figure 4-25   Compression packings

Most packings in use today are molded or formed into "U" or "V" shapes, and multiple packings are used for more effective sealing. The packings are compressed by tightening a flanged follower ring against them. Proper adjustment is critical because excessive tightening accelerates wear. In some applications, the packing ring is spring-loaded to maintain the correct force and take up wear.

Face Seals

Face seals (Figure 4-26) are used in applications where a high-pressure seal is required around a rotating shaft. Sealing is accomplished by constant contact between two flat surfaces, often hard carbon and steel. The stationary sealing member is attached to the housing of the component. The other is attached to the shaft and turns, sliding against the stationary member. One of the two parts is usually spring-loaded to improve contact initially and to take up wear. Pressure increases the contact force and tightens the seal.

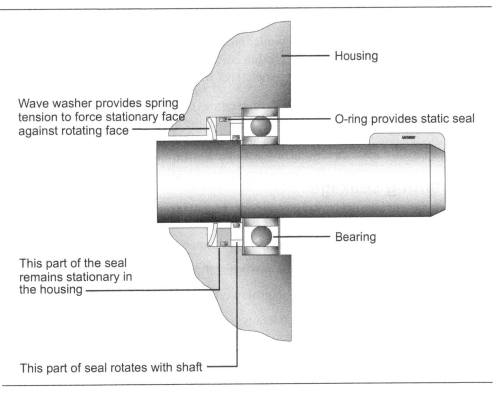

Wave washer provides spring tension to force stationary face against rotating face

Housing

O-ring provides static seal

Bearing

This part of the seal remains stationary in the housing

This part of seal rotates with shaft

Figure 4-26   Face seal for high-pressure sealing of rotating shaft

Gaskets

Gaskets are flat sealing devices, usually fabricated in the shape of the flat mating surfaces to be sealed. Early designs of connection flanges and surface-mounted valves were sealed with gaskets. Today they have been largely replaced in hydraulic equipment by O-rings or formed packings.

Seal Material

Leather, cork, and impregnated fibers were the earliest sealing materials for hydraulic equipment. They were used extensively until after the development of synthetic rubber during World War II. Natural rubber is seldom used as a sealing material because it swells and deteriorates in the presence of oil.

Synthetic rubbers (elastomers), however, are for the most part quite compatible with oil. Elastomers can be made in many compositions to meet various operating conditions. Most of the hydraulic equipment seals today are made of one of these materials: Nitrile (Buna-N), chloroprene (Neoprene), PTFE (Teflon®), EPR/EPDM (also known as EPM), Fluorocarbon (Viton) or silicone.

Nitrile

The elastomer Nitrile (Buna-N) is a widely used sealing material in modern hydraulic systems. It is moderately tough, wears well, and is inexpensive. There are a number of compositions compatible with petroleum oil — most of them easily molded into any required seal shape.

Nitrile has a reasonably wide temperature range, retaining its sealing properties from -40°F to 250°F (-40°C to 121°C). At moderately high temperatures, it retains its shape in most petroleum oils where other materials tend to swell. It does swell, however, in some synthetic fluids.

Chloroprene

One of the earliest elastomers used in hydraulic system sealing was chloroprene. A tough material, it still is used in systems using petroleum fluids.

Plastic, Fluori-Plastics and Fluoro-Elastomers

Several sealing materials are synthesized by combining fluorine with an elastomer or plastic. They include Kel-F, Viton A, and Teflon. Nylon is another synthetic material with similar properties. It is often used in combination with the elastomers to give them reinforcement. Both nylon and Teflon are used for backup rings as well as sealing materials. All have exceptionally high heat resistance (to 500°F) (to 260°C).

At high temperatures, silicone tends to absorb oil and swell. This, however, is no particular disadvantage in static applications. Silicone is not used for reciprocating seals, because it tears and abrades too easily. Silicone seals are compatible with most fluids; even more so with fire-resistant fluids than petroleum.

Preventing Leakage

The three general considerations in preventing leakage are:

1. Design to minimize the possibility (back, gasket or subplate mounting)
2. Proper installation
3. Control of operating condition

Anti-Leakage Design

It has already been noted that designs using straight thread connectors and welded flanges are less susceptible to leakage than pipe connections. Back-mounting of valves with all connections made permanently to a mounting plate has made a great difference in preventing leakage and in making it easier to service a valve (Figure 4-27). Many valves being built today are the back-mounted design. (The term gasket-mounted was originally applied to this design because gaskets were used on the first back-mounted valves. Gasket-mounted or subplate-mounted is often used to refer to back-mounted valves sealed by O-rings.)

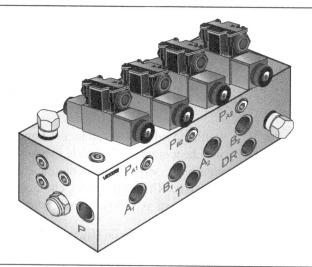

Figure 4-27   Back-mounting leaves connections undisturbed

A further advance from back-mounting is the use of manifolds (Figure 4-28). Some are drilled and some combine mounting plates with passage plates (sandwiched and brazed together), providing interconnections between valves and eliminating a good deal of external plumbing.

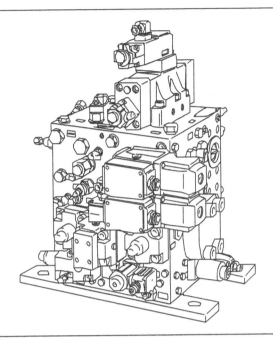

Figure 4-28   Drilled manifold contains interconnecting passages to eliminate piping between valves

Proper Installation

Careful installation, with attention to avoiding pinching or cocking a seal, usually assures a leakproof connection. Manufacturers often recommend a special driver and protective shaft cover for inserting lip-type shaft seals to be certain they are installed correctly. Vibration and undue stress at joints, which are common causes of external leakage, also are avoided by good installation practice.

Operating Conditions

Control over operating conditions can be very important to seal life. A number of factors that can help prevent leakage are discussed below.

Contamination Prevention. An atmosphere contaminated with moisture, dirt or any abrasive material shortens the life of shaft seals and piston rod seals exposed to the air. Protective devices should be used in contaminated atmospheres. Equally important are clean fluid and proper filtration to avoid damage to internal seals and surfaces. O-ring storage should also avoid ultraviolet light exposure.

Fluid Compatibility. Some fire-resistant fluids attack and disintegrate certain elastomer seals. Few seals, in fact, are compatible with all fluids. The fluid supplier should always be consulted when in doubt whether to change seals when a change is made in the type of fluid. (See Chapter 3.) Fluid additives (added by the machine user) also may attack seals and should be used only at the recommendation of the fluid supplier.

Temperature. At extremely low temperatures, a seal may become too brittle to be effective. At too high a temperature, a seal may harden, soften, or swell. The operating temperature should always be kept well within the temperature range of the seals being used.

Pressure. Excess fluid pressure puts an additional strain on oil seals and may "blow" a seal causing a leak.

Lubrication. Latest studies have shown the O-rings used in static applications perform best when installed completely dry — no oil or grease applied to hold in place during assembly. If the O-ring must slide or twist to arrive at its sealing location, a light lube can be used to avoid tearing. Dynamic seals, such as lip-type pump shaft seals should be lubricated during assembly on the dynamic surfaces.

Industrial Test Questions:
Hydraulic Fluid Conductors and Seals

Chapter 4

1. How is a pipe size classified?

2. How does a pipe thread seal?

3. What advantages does tubing have over pipe? Why are pipe thread fittings and plugs not recommended when designing circuits for leak-free operation?

4. To what does the specified size of tubing refer?

5. How are tubing connections sealed?

6. Give two reasons for fluid conductor supports.

7. What is the most common seal used in hydraulics?

8. What is a positive seal?

9. What is a static sealing application?

10. Where are "Lip Seals" typically applied?

11. Why would a backup ring be used with an O-ring seal?

12. Why does using manifold blocks promote leak-free hydraulic circuits?

13. True or False: Static O-ring sealing interfaces should be assembled dry.

14. If the expected flow in one section of a circuit is 60 GPM, what should be the inside diameter of tubing or hose installed to stay below the maximum recommended fluid velocity for pressure lines?

15. How much flow (GPM or l/min) can an intake hose, with a 5 sq. cm inside area, pass without exceeding the maximum recommended fluid velocity (4 fps or 1.2 m/sec.)?

16. Two important considerations in preventing external leakage are: Designing to minimize the possibility; and controlling the operating conditions. What is a third important area to focus on for leak-free hydraulics?

Chapter 5 . . . . Reservoirs

The main function of the reservoir in a hydraulic system is to store and supply hydraulic fluid for use by the system. The chapter discusses this and other reservoir functions such as heat exchange and deaeration. Reservoir components, including air breathers, baffle plates and filler caps are also described. A general discussion on reservoir sizing and reservoir designs is included along with explanations of various fluid temperature conditioning devices.

Functions of Reservoirs

In addition to holding the system fluid supply, a reservoir can also serve several secondary functions. Some system designers feel that the reservoir is the key to effective hydraulic system operation. Some examples of these functions are discussed below.

By transferring waste heat through its walls, the reservoir acts as a heat exchanger that cools the fluid within. As a de-aerator, the reservoir allows entrained air to rise and escape while solid contaminants settle to the bottom of the tank, making it a fluid conditioner.

These are functions that can also be provided to the system by methods that do not involve the reservoir.

In some instances, the reservoir may be used as a platform to support the pump, motor, and other system components. This saves floor space and is a simple way to keep the pumps and valves at a good height for servicing.

Reservoir Components

A typical industrial reservoir (Figure 5-1) is constructed of welded steel plate with end-plate extensions that support the unit. To reduce the chance of condensed moisture within the tank causing rust, the inside of the reservoir is painted with a sealer that is compatible to the fluid being used. Because the reservoir is designed for easy fluid maintenance, a plug is placed at a low point on the tank to allow complete drainage.

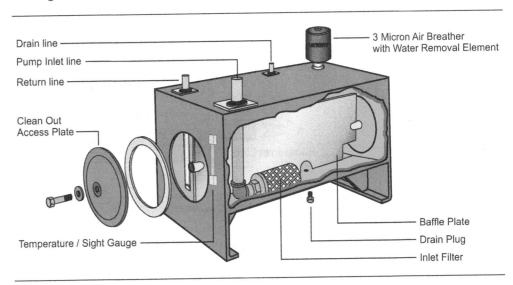

Figure 5-1   Typical industrial reservoir

The various components that makeup a reservoir are discussed in the following sections.

Oil Level Gauge

To check the fluid level in the reservoir, either a sight glass or two small portholes are installed in the clean-out plates. This allows the upper and lower fluid limits to be checked without exposing the reservoir to the contamination that can occur when using a dipstick.

Breather Assembly

A vented breather cap is installed to accommodate the air exchange that results from the constant change of pressure and temperature within the tank. As the hydraulic cylinders extend and retract, air is taken in and expelled through this filter. Generally, the breather must be large enough to handle the airflow required to maintain atmospheric pressure, whether the tank is empty or full (the higher the flow rate, the larger the breather).

On a pressurized reservoir, the breather is replaced by an air valve that regulates the tank pressure between preset limits. An oil bath air filter is sometimes used in atmospheres that are exceptionally dirty.

Filler Opening

The filler opening is often a part of the breather assembly. The opening has a removable screen that keeps contaminants out of the tank when fluid is being added to the reservoir. A cap that will provide a tight seal should be chained to the reservoir.

Another type of filler opening is a quick-disconnect fitting, screwed into a pipe that extends to within a few inches of the bottom of the tank. A portable oil cart, equipped with a small pump and filter, supplies fluid to the tank. This keeps the new fluid clean and prevents contamination of the reservoir.

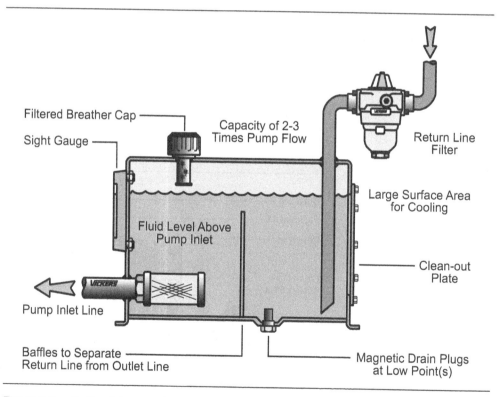

Figure 5-2   Baffle plate controls direction of flow in tank

Clean-Out Plates

Clean-out plates are usually installed on both ends of the tank. This is especially true on reservoirs sized above ten gallons (37.85 liters). The plates are easily removed and large enough to provide complete access when the interior of the reservoir is being cleaned or painted.

Baffle Plate

Because fluid returning to the reservoir is usually warmer than the supply fluid and probably contains air bubbles, baffles are used to prevent the returning fluid from directly entering the pump inlet. A baffle plate (Figure 5-2) is installed lengthwise through the center of the tank, forcing the fluid to move along the reservoir walls, where much of the heat is dissipated to the outer surfaces of the reservoir. This long, low-velocity travel also allows the contaminants to settle at the bottom of the tank and provides an opportunity for the fluid to be cleared of any entrained air. The end result is less turbulence in the tank.

Line Connections and Fittings

Most lines leading to the reservoir terminate below the oil level. The line connections at the tank cover are often packed (sealed), slip-joint type flanges. This design prevents contaminants from entering through these openings and makes it easy to remove inlet line strainers for cleaning.

Connections made on the top of the reservoir are often set on risers to keep them above dirt and other contaminants that may collect on the reservoir.

To prevent the hydraulic fluid from foaming and becoming aerated, pump inlet lines must terminate below the fluid level, usually two inches (5 cm) from the bottom of the tank.

Valve drain lines may terminate above the fluid level, but it is generally better to extend them approximately two inches (5 cm) below the fluid level. In all cases, pump and motor drain lines must terminate below the lowest possible fluid level.

Lines that terminate near the tank bottom and are not equipped with strainers should be cut at a 45 degree angle. This prevents the line opening from bottoming in the tank and cutting off flow. On a return line, the angled opening is often positioned so that flow is directed at the tank walls and away from the pump inlet line.

Standard Reservoir Designs

In addition to the proprietary styles offered by manufacturers, three types of standard reservoir designs are commonly used today.

JIC Reservoirs

The Joint Industry Conference (JIC) reservoir design (Figure 5-3), sometimes referred to as Flat Top, is a horizontal tank with extensions that hold it several inches off the floor or the surface of a drip pan. This design permits increased air circulation and heat transfer from the bottom as well as from the walls of the tank.

JIC reservoirs are usually as deep as they are wide, with the length approximately twice the width. They are generally made from 9 or 11 gauge pickled and oiled steel. Single bolt clean out plates at each end provide access for cleaning. The bottom of the tank is concave and has a drain plug at its lowest point.

Filtered hydraulic fluid is pumped into the reservoir through a filler/breather cap assembly equipped with a fluid strainer. A sight level glass that usually incorporates a thermometer is installed on one or two of the reservoir walls.

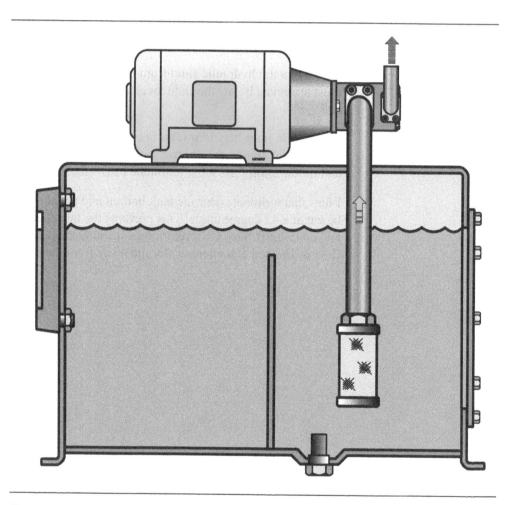

Figure 5-3   JIC reservoir design

L-Shaped Reservoirs

Another standard reservoir design is the L-shaped configuration (Figure 5-4), which consists of a vertical tank mounted to one side of a wide base. The other side of the base is used to mount the pump, motor, relief valve, and if needed, the heat exchanger. Because the fluid level in the tank is higher than the pump inlet, positive inlet pressure is maintained, minimizing the possibility of cavitation and loss of pumping action.

Pressure control and directional valves can be mounted to the side of the tank at the vertical section above the fluid level. If subplate valves are used, nearly all the piping will be inside the reservoir. This arrangement minimizes loss of fluid due to leaks.

The reservoir interior is accessed through a hinged top, which also permits a visual check of the returning fluid while the circuits are in operation. This can aid in system troubleshooting, when it is required.

The L-shaped design provides large surface areas for cooling. To promote air circulation, the base of the reservoir should be raised several inches off the floor.

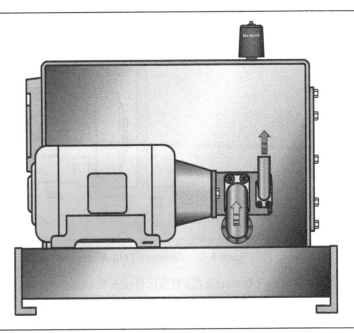

Figure 5-4   L-shaped reservoir design

Overhead Stack Reservoirs

Another reservoir design is the overhead stack (Figure 5-5), which makes use of one or more modular rack type frames stacked vertically with a standard horizontal tank at the top. Each frame is usually set up with one pump motor assembly, with all pumps drawing fluid from the common reservoir at the top.

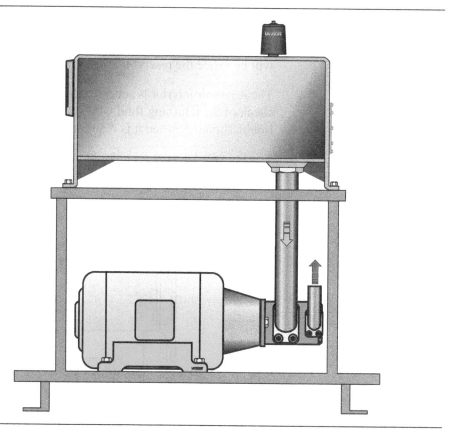

Figure 5-5   Overhead stack reservoir design

Because the HWC (High Water Content) fluids have relatively high density and low viscosity, they should be supplied under positive pressure to prevent pump cavitation. Most manufacturers supply the overhead reservoir as a matter of good hydraulic practice whenever HWCF is specified.

Although there is no limit to the number of stacking levels that can be used, safety and servicing problems may occur when the stack exceeds three levels (two frames plus the tank at the top).

Because the positive head condition is also beneficial to the operation of conventional oil units, the use of the stack configuration in non HWCF applications is growing. The elevated design makes it possible to drain the reservoir easily, without having to pump the fluid out.

The vertical arrangement of the reservoir conserves floor space while providing an economy of scale. Two or more pump motor assemblies with controls can be incorporated in the rack mounting with a common reservoir. The overhead reservoir also provides the capability for an HWCF changeover if necessary.

Vertically Mounted Reservoir Assemblies

Reservoir assemblies are frequently mounted vertically. Several advantages to this design are:

- Reduced floor space

- Increased cooling due to component immersion into reservoir, resulting in heat dispersion into hydraulic fluids directly from pumping system

- Hydraulic fluid acts as a vibration dampener and a noise suppressor

- Reservoir fluid creates a pressure head surrounding the pump and its fitting eliminating the possibility of cavitation and aeration

- Drive force stresses are reduced as a result of gravitational forces (side loading)

- Hydraulic pump system is maintained cleaner in a sealed reservoir.

One potential drawback to this design is a possible maintenance issue. The entire motor/pump assembly has to be removed for any repair or replacement.

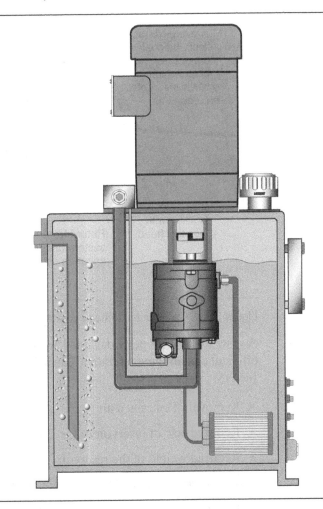

Figure 5-6   Vertical reservoir

Cyclone Tank

A newer type of reservoir design can offer several advantages in a hydraulic system. As noted earlier, a typical hydraulic reservoir for petroleum oil is sized around three times the pump flow. The cyclone reservoir shown in Figure 5-7 is cylindrical in shape and divided into two chambers. The lower chamber contains the pump suction and system return ports. A high-speed rotational fluid spin is created in this chamber as fluid returns to the reservoir. This spin creates centrifugal forces where heavier, non-aerated fluid is pushed to the outside wall of the reservoir interior where it becomes available to the suction port.

The lighter air bubbles migrate to the center of the reservoir by means of the "cyclone" effect. The air bubbles rapidly migrate through the center hole in the baffle, dissipate into the air space above the fluid within the upper chamber and out to atmosphere through the filler/breather cap.

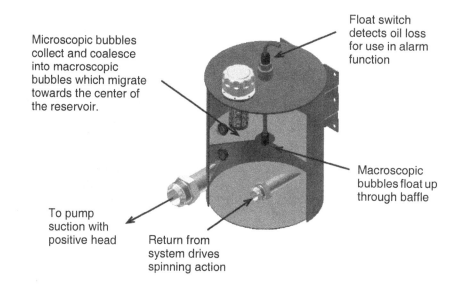

Microscopic bubbles collect and coalesce into macroscopic bubbles which migrate towards the center of the reservoir.

Float switch detects oil loss for use in alarm function

Macroscopic bubbles float up through baffle

To pump suction with positive head

Return from system drives spinning action

Figure 5-7   Cyclone tank (image courtesy of Price Engineering, Hartland, WI)

A system that is properly designed and maintained for minimizing heat generation and efficient contamination removal can achieve the benefits from this type of component, such as:

- Removal of entrained air
- Reduced size of reservoir (up to 20 times smaller)
- Reduced weight of the reservoir
- Faster recovery from large air ingestion
- Reduced sensitivity to machine jostling
- Faster warm up
- Lower installed cost

Reservoir Modifications

Here are some points to keep in mind for cases where these standard reservoir designs cannot be used or modified and a custom design must be developed.

- Make certain the reservoir has ample clean-out openings that will be accessible when the reservoir is in position.

- Be sure the walls and top of the reservoir are strong enough to support any equipment that may be mounted on it.

- Size the reservoir for at least 20 percent overcapacity to provide a reserve against unexpected demands on system capacity.

- Be sure the reservoir is provided with a means of filling, a level gauge, and a drain connection.

Reservoir Sizing

A large tank is always desirable to promote cooling and separation of contaminants. At a minimum, the tank must store all the fluid the system will require and maintain a high enough level to prevent a whirlpool effect at the pump inlet opening. When whirlpooling occurs, air will be taken in with the fluid.

When determining reservoir size, it is important to consider the following factors:

- Fluid expansion caused by high temperatures.

- Changes in fluid level due to system operation.

- Exposure of the tank interior to excess condensation.

- The amount of heat generated in the system.

For industrial use, a general sizing rule is used:

Tank size (gallons) = pump GPM x 2 or x 3

Tank size (liters) = pump l/min x 2 or x 3

In mobile or aerospace systems, the benefits of a large reservoir may have to be sacrificed because of space limitations.

Heat Exchangers

Since no system can ever be 100 percent efficient, heat is a common problem. It is customary to think of cooling when the fluid must be temperature conditioned, but there are some applications where the fluid must be heated. For example, fluids with a low viscosity index will not flow readily when cold and must be kept warm by heaters.

Although the design of the circuit has considerable effect upon the fluid temperature, heat exchangers are sometimes required when operating temperatures are critical or when the system cannot dissipate all the heat that is generated. The three types of heat exchangers, heaters, air coolers and water coolers, are discussed in the following sections.

Heaters

A heater (Figure 5-8) is installed in the reservoir, below the fluid level and close to the pump inlet. The low-heat density design (10 watts per square inch) (1.55 watts per square centimeter) prevents the fluid from burning and a thermostatic control is usually attached.

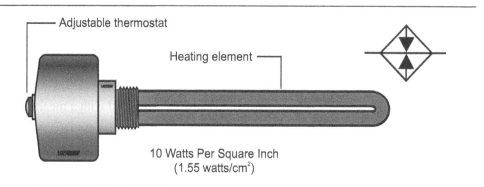

Figure 5-8   Typical heater design

Water Coolers

In a typical water cooler (Figure 5-9), hydraulic fluid is circulated through the unit and around the tubes containing the water. The heat is removed from the hydraulic fluid by the water, which can be regulated thermostatically to maintain a desired temperature. The water is filtered to prevent the cooler from clogging. By circulating hot rather than cold water, this type of temperature control can also be used as a heater.

Water flow requirements are usually equal to between 1/4 and 1/3 of the system oil flow. The availability of cooling towers and water recycling reduces the cost, but water taken from these sources usually has a higher temperature than that of municipal systems.

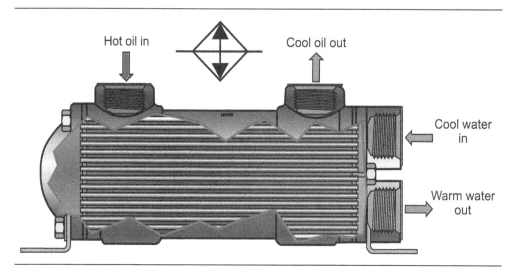

Figure 5-9   Typical water cooler design

Air Coolers

An air cooler (Figure 5-10) is used when water is not readily available for cooling. The fluid is pumped through tubes that are bonded to fins made of aluminum or some other metal that transfers heat to the outside air. The cooler usually has a blower to increase the heat transfer.

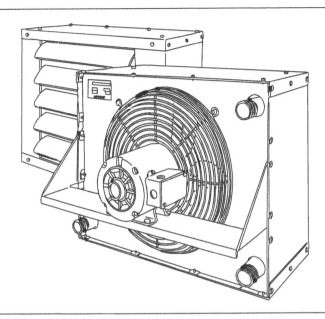

Figure 5-10   Typical air cooler design

Air coolers are less efficient than water coolers and tend to be ineffective in areas of high ambient air temperatures. The initial installation cost is higher than that of water coolers, but the operational costs are usually less.

Industrial Test Questions:
Reservoirs

Chapter 5

1. Name three possible functions of the reservoir.

2. Where should the reservoir drain plug be located?

3. What are the three most common standard reservoir designs?

4. What is the most desirable method of checking fluid level in the reservoir?

5. What is the purpose of the reservoir breather?

6. What is the purpose of using a riser with reservoir connections?

7. What is a reservoir baffle plate used for?

8. Why is a return line often cut at a 45 degree angle?

9. What would probably be an adequate size reservoir for a system with a 5 GPM pump?

10. What is the recommended heat density of a heater?

Chapter 6 . . . . Contamination Control

Contamination control is both a relatively new engineering science and a well established, much practiced art among hydraulics personnel. Although a great deal is known about the prevention and control of contaminant buildup, it is estimated that over 80 percent of hydraulic system failures are due to poor fluid condition.

A contaminant is any material in a hydraulic fluid that has a harmful effect on the fluid's performance in a system. There are several ways to describe the contaminants associated with fluid systems, including their physical state, their originating activity, their properties and characteristics, and their effect on the system. A very complete and detailed treatment of the subject can be found in the Eaton/Vickers manual "Bird bones and Sludge, A Complete Guide To Hydraulic System Contamination Control."

Contaminants can be gaseous, liquid, or solid. Simply stated, contamination is any foreign substance that contributes to or causes harm to the hydraulic or lubrication fluid of the system, or parts of the system, in which the fluid flows.

Obviously, the proper care of hydraulic fluid, both within a system and while stored and handled, has an important effect on machine performance and system endurance. The purpose of this chapter is to provide information that leads to improved control of contamination in the maintenance and operation of systems. This chapter covers the various kinds of contamination, the sources, the effects and the reduction in industrial hydraulic systems.

Sources of Contamination

Sources of contamination in hydraulic systems can be divided into three general categories:

Built-in contamination (Figure 6-1)

Ingressed contamination

Internally generated contamination

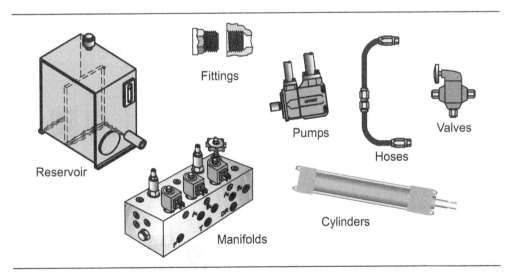

Figure 6-1   Sources of built-in contamination

Built-In Contamination

Hydraulic system manufacturers generally are careful to provide internally clean products to their customers. In spite of these efforts, however, new equipment usually contains some built-in contamination. These contaminants might include burrs, chips, flash, dirt, dust, fibers, sand, moisture, pipe sealants, weld splatter, paints and flushing solutions. New components within a system may also become sources of contamination due to improper storage, handling and installation practices. New directional valves, cylinders, relief valves and pumps may contain contaminants that appear in the system fluid after a very short period of operation.

As the machine is assembled, the reservoir may accumulate rust, paint chips or dust. Although the reservoir is cleaned prior to use, many contaminants are invisible to the human eye and are not removed by wiping with a rag or blowing off with an air hose. Hoses, tubes and fittings that are laying in storage will collect dust and other atmospheric components of contamination, which are then introduced to the hydraulic system at installation.

A frequently overlooked source of contamination is the assembly of fittings. For example: the connecting of one 3/4 inch pipe fitting creates over 60,000 particles greater than 5 microns that become available to the system. Installing several fittings introduces huge numbers of contaminates into the system during assembly.

Contaminants such as weld scale may lay dormant until loosened by the forces of high pressure fluid, or by vibration of the machine while it is running.

Ingressed Contamination

Ingressed, or environmental, contamination is foreign material that is added to the hydraulic system during service or maintenance, or is introduced to the system from the environment surrounding the equipment.

One common source of ingressed contamination is that which occurs when the system is filled with new fluid (Figure 6-2). New oil is refined and blended under fairly clean conditions, but it then passes through many hands as it is delivered to the user. The fluid is pumped from one storage tank to another several times, before being transferred to tankers, trucks, barrels and/or bottles, and finally arriving at the reservoir. Various kinds of contaminants are picked up during this journey, not the least of which is metal, silica and fibers.

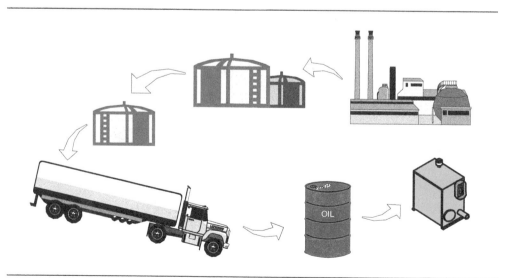

Figure 6-2   New fluid gathers contamination during handling

Dirt and other particles can enter the system during servicing and maintenance. Components are frequently replaced or repaired on site in a soiled environment. Contamination from the area around the equipment can enter the system from any disconnected line or port.

Air enters the reservoir every time a cylinder cycles due to fluid level changes. Or, as the fluid level changes due to, for example, thermal contraction. All reservoirs should have a filter breather installed, but too often, these are inadequate or missing. Airborne particles enter the system in this manner.

Contamination from the environment can also enter the system through power unit access plates that have been removed, and, occasionally, not replaced. If access to strainers or other components depends on the removal of power unit covers, good resealing may not be possible.

Fine particles continuously settle on cylinder rods, and then are pulled into the system when the rods are retracted (Figure 6-3). As seals and wipers on these rods wear, the contamination ingression rate can increase considerably.

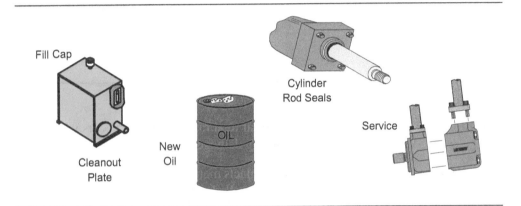

Figure 6-3   Sources of ingressed contamination

Internally-Generated Contamination

This type of contamination is created within the system by the moving parts of hydraulic components. Every internal moving part within the system can be considered a source of self-generated contamination for the entire system. Internal mechanisms of wear include: abrasion, erosion, adhesion, fatigue, cavitation, corrosion and aeration (Table 6-1).

CONTAMINANT — GENERATING MECHANISMS	
Type	**Cause**
Abrasion	Particles grinding between moving surfaces
Erosion	High velocity particles striking surfaces
Adhesion	Metal-to-metal contact
Fatigue	Repeated stressing of a surface
Cavitation	High pump inlet vacuum
Corrosion	Foreign substance in fluid (water or chemical)
Aeration	Gas bubbles in fluid, introduced air to pump inlet

Table 6-1 Contaminant generating mechanisms

Abrasion

Solid particles in the hydraulic fluid grinding between moving surfaces is referred to as abrasion. Abrasion damages the surfaces and can create additional abrasive particles.

Abrasion is categorized into three classes (see Figure 6-4). "One body" abrasion occurs when particulate contamination damages a surface through contact between the fluid and the surface. A "two body" type abrasion occurs when an abrasive particle is embedded in a surface making contact with a second surface. If the hard asperity of one surface contacts a softer surface, a two body abrasion is also said to have occurred. Three body type abrasion refers to loose abrasive particles making contact with two surfaces.

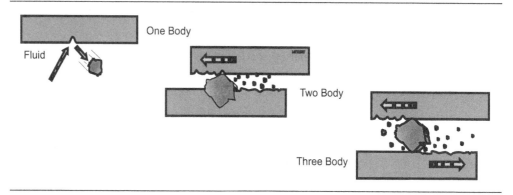

Figure 6-4   Classes of abrasion

Erosion

Erosion is similar to abrasion. Erosion occurs when high velocity particles strike surfaces, causing damage.

Adhesion

When metal contacts metal, due to the loss of a lubricating film, a molecular attraction between them is called adhesion. This will cause small particles of one or both items to dislodge.

Fatigue

Fatigue refers to repeated stressing of a surface (Figure 6-5). This stressing can eventually create cracks in the surface, which will result in particles dislodging and particulate contamination.

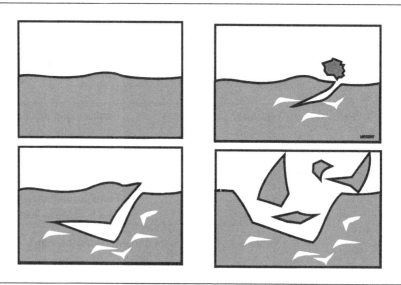

Figure 6-5   Surface fatigue and contaminant generation

Cavitation

Cavitation is caused by a dynamic pressure reduction on hydraulic fluid, typically in a pump inlet, but also in actuators and other circuit elements under certain conditions. This pressure reduction causes vapor-filled cavities to form in the fluid. When the fluid is then pressurized, as in the high pressure side of a pump, these cavities will collapse, causing severe localized shock and heat damage to the metal surfaces (Figure 6-6).

High Velocity Microjet Formation

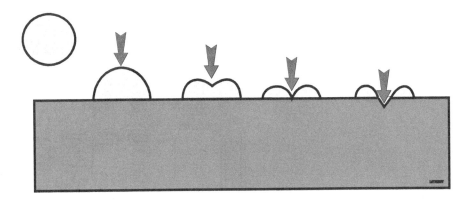

Figure 6-6   Process of cavitation and aeration damage

Pump cavitation is caused by exceeding recommended pump inlet vacuum, which can be caused by overspeeding the pump, restricting inlet lines or air breathers, plugged inlet strainers or high oil viscosity. Typical indications are pump noise and temperature rise in the system. There is little, if any, evidence of cavitation in the downstream fluid as there is with aeration, as illustrated in Figure 6-7.

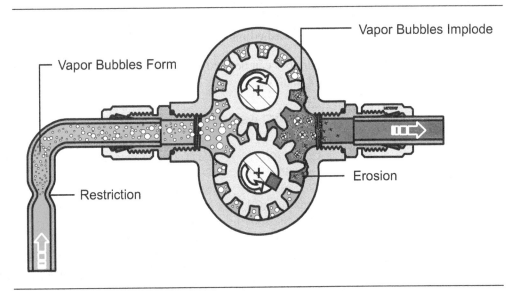

Figure 6-7   Pump cavitation

Corrosion

The deterioration of a surface due to corrosion (such as rust) is often caused by foreign substances in the fluid (e.g. water or chemicals).

Aeration

Aeration is the presence of air or gas bubbles in the fluid. The expansion and compression of these bubbles in the fluid causes the same type of noise and damage as cavitation (Figure 6-8). However, downstream symptoms will often be very noticeable as the air does not dissipate. Spongy cylinder operation and erratic machine performance due to the presence of air will be observed because of the compressibility of gas under pressure and the inability of gas to seal clearances. Poor reservoir design, leaky gas charged accumulators, low fluid level and leaky fittings may all contribute to aeration.

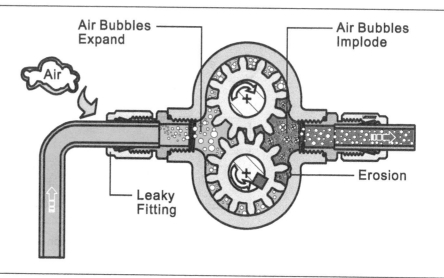

Figure 6-8   Pump aeration

Other

Component housings that are often subjected to flexing and other stresses also can contribute to contamination in the form of metal particles and casting sand. Water vapor that enters the system through the reservoir can condense on the walls of components and conductors during equipment shutdowns. Eventually, rust can form and be washed into the system.

Figure 6-9 can be used to estimate the source of various fluid contaminants found by a fluid analysis.

WEAR METALS, ADDITIVES, AND CONTAMINANTS		
Iron (Fe)	Pumps, valves, cylinders, or oxidation	
Copper (Cu)	Bushings, cylinders, or oxidation	
Lead (Pb)	Bushings	
Tin (Sn)	Bushings or plating	
Chromium (Cr)	Valve spools, cylinders, or plating	
Aluminum (Al)	Gear pumps, valves, or fillers	
Nickel (Ni)	Wear from valves or tubing	
Silicon (Si)	Airborne dirt from process or operation coolant	
Zinc (Zn)	Oil additive, antiwear, or bushings	300-400 PPM typical
Phosphorus (P)	Oil additive, antiwear (Part of ZDP package)	300-400 PPM typical
Calcium (Ca)	Oil additive, detergent	50 PPM typical
Barium (Ba)	Oil additive, detergent	
Magnesium (Mg)	Oil additive, detergent	
Boron (B)	Oil additive, detergent	

Figure 6-9   Sources of wear metals, additives and contaminants

Effects of Contamination

Several factors must be considered when examining the effect of contamination on the life and operation of hydraulic machinery. These factors include how contamination affects the function of hydraulic fluid, how mechanical tolerances in components react to contaminant particles, the effect of various types of contamination, and how components fail when a system contains contamination.

Effect on Functions of Hydraulic Fluid

Recall from an earlier chapter that four primary functions of hydraulic fluid are to:

- Transmit power
- Cool or dissipate heat
- Lubricate moving parts
- Seal clearances between parts.

Solid contamination interferes with the first three of these functions.

Solid contamination interferes with power transmission by blocking or plugging small orifices in devices such as pressure valves and flow control valves. The action of a valve affected by solid contamination in this way is unpredictable and unsafe. A study conducted by Massachusetts Institute of Technology (MIT) found mechanical wear was responsible for 50 percent of surface degradation. The study also found surface degradation responsible for 70 percent of overall loss of machine usefulness (see Figure 6-10).

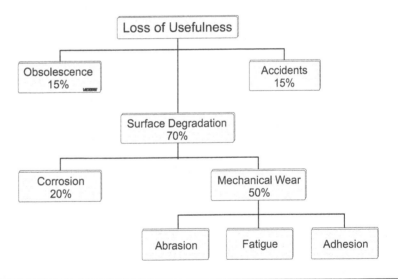

Contamination control in hydraulic systems

Figure 6-10   MIT study of hydraulic system failure

Contamination can form a sludge on the reservoir walls and interfere with the cooling processes. This sludge impedes heat transfer from the fluid to the wall which will eventually result in higher system operating temperatures. Many times the combined effect of several types of contamination damage will cause the heat generating capacity of a normally operating unit to rise significantly.

The most serious effect that contamination has on a system is the loss of lubricating ability of hydraulic fluid. This can occur in several different ways. Very fine particles, smaller than a component's mechanical clearances, can collect in the clearance and eventually block the flow of lubricating fluid into the small space between moving parts and otherwise interfere with the component operation. This accumulation of very fine particulate contamination is called silting.

Silting can cause valves to shift improperly. It can also degrade pump performance, causing a loss of efficiency and the addition of heat. Silting also affects actuators, causing premature wear and degradation in performance efficiency. In rotary actuators, the seals and mating dynamic surfaces can be damaged by the presence of silt. The sealing mechanisms between the opposing sides of pistons in cylinders can be destroyed by contamination.

Mechanical Clearances in Components

Manufacturing clearances within hydraulic components can be divided into two principle zones:

- up to 5 micrometers for high-pressure units
- 10 to 20 micrometers for low-pressure units

The actual clearance may vary widely, depending on the kind of component and the component's operating conditions. Refer to Figure 6-11 for typical clearance values in various components.

COMPONENT	CLEARANCE LOCATION	MICRONS	INCHES	MM
Gear Pump	Gear to side plate	1/2 - 5	0.00002-0.0002	0.0005-0.005
	Gear tip to case	1/2 - 5	0.00002-0.0002	0.0005-0.005
Vane Pump	Tip of vane	1/2 - 1	0.00002-0.00004	0.0005-0.001
	Sides of vane	5 - 13	0.0002-0.0005	0.005-0.013
Piston Pump	Piston to bore	5 - 40	0.0002-0.0015	0.005-0.04
	Valve plate to cylinder	1/2 - 5	0.00002-0.0002	0.0005-0.005
Servo Valve	Orifice	130 - 450	0.005-0.018	0.13-0.45
	Flapper wall	18 - 63	0.0007-0.0025	0.018-0.063
	Spool sleeve	1 - 4	0.00005-0.00015	0.001-0.004
Control Valve	Orifice	130 - 10,000	0.005-0.4	0.13-10.0
	Spool sleeve	1 - 23	0.00005-0.0009	0.001-0.023
	Disk type	1/2 - 1	0.00002-0.00004	0.0005-0.001
	Poppet type	13 - 40	0.0005-0.0015	0.013-0.04
Actuators		50 - 250	0.002-0.01	0.05-0.25
Hydrostatic Bearings		0 - 25	0.00005-0.001	0.001-0.025
Antifriction Bearings		1/2	0.00002-	0.0005-
Slide Bearings		1/2	0.00002-	0.0005-

Figure 6-11 Typical manufactured clearances in hydraulic components

Large particles of solid contamination cannot pass into the clearances between moving parts and normally do not cause abrasion damage to moving surfaces. However, this kind of contaminant can collect at the entrance to a clearance and obstruct the flow of fluid between the moving parts. Large contaminants also jam pumps, valves and motors.

When the particles are about the same size as the clearance they must pass through, they rub against the moving parts, break down the film of lubricant and cause the most wear and damage to the component surfaces (Figure 6-12). Wear generates more contaminants, increases leakage, lowers efficiency and generates heat. The higher the pressure, the greater the problem.

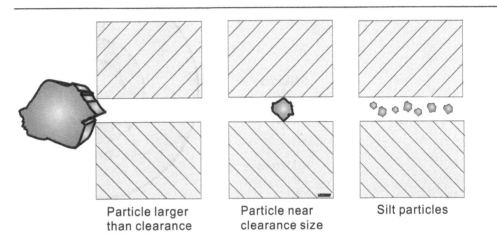

| Particle larger than clearance | Particle near clearance size | Silt particles |

Particles that are the same size or slightly smaller than the clearances between moving surfaces will interact with both surfaces to cause wear. Very large particles do not normally get into critical clearance, but may impede lubrication or cause component malfunction. Very small particles (less than one micrometer) usually flow through without abrading either surface.

Figure 6-12   Behavior of contamination particles in clearances

Clearances between parts in a hydraulic component are usually measured in thousandths of an inch, ten thousandths of an inch or fractions of a millimeter. One micrometer is equal to one millionth of a meter or thirty nine millionths of an inch. To put the size of a micrometer into perspective, consider that the average diameter of a grain of table salt is about 100 micrometers and the average diameter of a human hair is about 74 micrometers. Three micrometers exceeds one ten thousandth of an inch clearance. 25 micrometers is approximately one thousandth of an inch.

A micrometer is also called a micron.

Relative Size of Micronic Particles

The naked eye can normally only resolve size down to about 40 micrometers (Figure 6-13). A single micrometer is too small to be visually detected without the aid of a strong magnifying device. Most of the harmful contamination in hydraulic fluid are less than 40 micrometers in size. This means that contamination cannot be evaluated by a visual inspection.

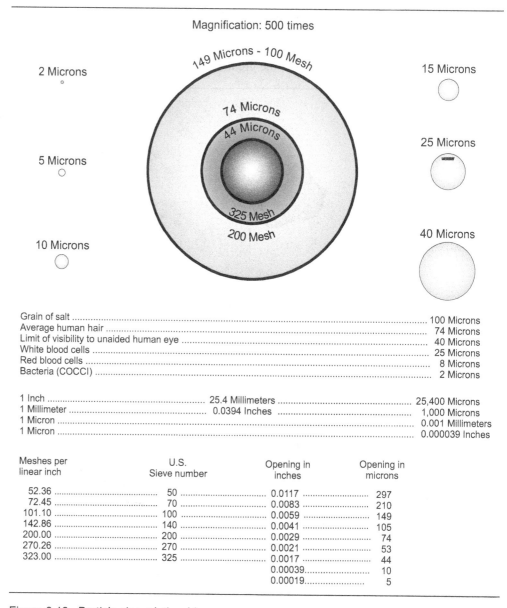

Grain of salt	100 Microns
Average human hair	74 Microns
Limit of visibility to unaided human eye	40 Microns
White blood cells	25 Microns
Red blood cells	8 Microns
Bacteria (COCCI)	2 Microns

1 Inch	25.4 Millimeters	25,400 Microns
1 Millimeter	0.0394 Inches	1,000 Microns
1 Micron		0.001 Millimeters
1 Micron		0.000039 Inches

Meshes per linear inch	U.S. Sieve number	Opening in inches	Opening in microns
52.36	50	0.0117	297
72.45	70	0.0083	210
101.10	100	0.0059	149
142.86	140	0.0041	105
200.00	200	0.0029	74
270.26	270	0.0021	53
323.00	325	0.0017	44
		0.00039	10
		0.00019	5

Figure 6-13   Particle size relationships

Component Failure Modes

Particulate contaminants come in a variety of shapes and sizes. The majority are abrasive and cause wear-related failures in hydraulic components. There are three types of particulate contamination induced failures: catastrophic, intermittent and degradation.

Catastrophic failure is the rapid or sudden, total disabling of a component or system. Catastrophic failures occur, for example, when a large particle gets stuck in a main component. If a particle caused a vane to jam in a rotor slot, the pump or motor could seize. Large size particles could keep a spool valve from shifting. If the pilot orifice of a valve is blocked by particulate matter, a catastrophic failure could occur. Fine particles also can cause a catastrophic failure in a valve due to silt accumulating in the clearances.

Intermittent failures are transitory in occurrence and are most often self correcting or correctable without intrusive maintenance efforts. An intermittent, or transient, failure can be caused when contaminants settle on the seat of a poppet valve and prevent it from reseating properly. If the poppet seat is harder than the contaminant, the particle will probably be washed away when the valve reopens. This kind of problem can cause irregular operation of the valve and is difficult to diagnose.

Another frequent transient failure is a contamination blockage which prevents the solenoid spool from shifting. The cause of this type of blockage is difficult to diagnose as the contaminant is often dislodged during the disassembly of the unit. Subsequent inspection finds the spool to be shifting freely and the valve is returned to service without determining the cause of the failure.

Degradation failure of a component or system simply translates to surface wear. When referring to fluids, degradation relates to additive package depletion or physical/chemical changes to the fluid base stock. Degradation failures are caused by wear, corrosion, cavitation, aeration and erosion. These problems produce internal leakage in system components and surface disruption and deterioration, which progresses until a complete failure occurs. This kind of problem in a rotating group usually results in a catastrophic failure at some point. The contaminants most likely to cause wear are clearance sized particles that barely pass between the moving parts, but bridge the clearance during their passage.

Contamination Failures in Components

Components are affected in different ways by contamination, depending on their design and the function they perform in the hydraulic circuit. Pressure, flow, component load and critical clearance areas are a few of the factors that should be considered when analyzing why and how components fail as a result of contamination.

Hydraulic pumps and motors have component parts that move relative to each other but are separated by a fluid-filled clearance. The components are usually loaded toward each other by pressure forces that also tend to force fluid through the clearances. If the fluid within these clearances is heavily contaminated, rapid degradation and possibly seizure will occur. In low pressure systems, pump design can tolerate relatively large clearances and contamination effects are somewhat lessened. At lower operating pressures, less force is available to drive particles into critical clearance areas. Higher pressures are of greater significance in determining the effect of contamination on a pump or motor because more highly loaded clearances tend to be critical.

Viscosity of the fluid also affects clearances. The film thickness should support loads hydrodynamically, but the viscosity should be low enough to avoid cavitation within the pump or motor. A fluid with viscosity compatible with the pump inlet conditions should be used. Proper temperature control is also important for long life of the component and the fluid.

- Vane pumps and motors (Figure 6-14) vane tip to cam ring; rotor to side plate; vane to vane slot.

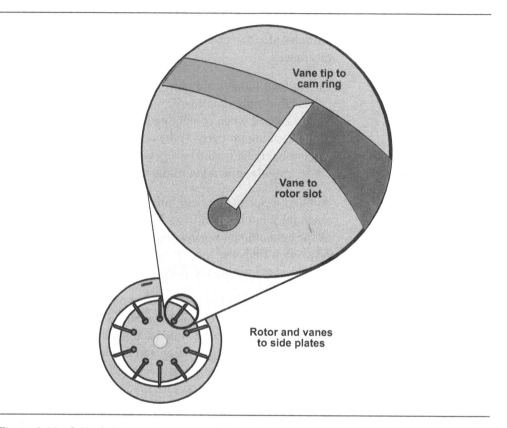

Figure 6-14   Critical clearance areas in a balanced vane pump

- Gear pumps and motors (Figure 6-15) tooth to housing; tooth to tooth; gear to side plate.

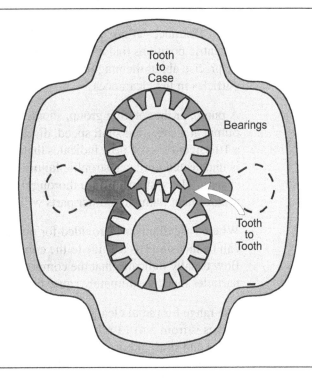

Figure 6-15   Critical clearance areas in gear pumps

- Axial piston pumps and motors (Figure 6-16) shoe to swash plate; cylinder block to valve plate; piston to cylinder block.

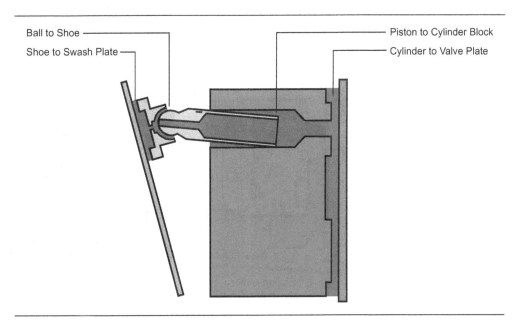

Figure 6-16   Critical clearance areas in piston pumps

Under normal operating conditions, clearances within a pump or motor are self adjusting. With increasing pressure, however, the clearances become smaller. Under adverse operating conditions, particularly when shock loads are present, smaller clearances increase a pump's vulnerability to smaller contaminant particles. Even when clearances are nominally fixed, components under high loads may assume eccentric positions that make them more vulnerable to small particles. It is difficult to be precise about the magnitude of these clearances and the effect of different size particles in the clearances.

A pump, or the rotating group, should be replaced when it cannot deliver the required output at a specified shaft speed, discharge pressure and fluid temperature. Generally, a 10 percent loss of flow indicates that servicing is necessary. Quite often, degradation is undetected until catastrophic failure releases vast quantities of contaminant into the system. The system must be thoroughly cleaned and flushed after such a failure or the replacement pump and other parts will have a shorter than normal life expectancy.

Where case drains are provided for pumps and motors, leakage flow from the drain can be measured as a guide to the component's condition. An increase in case drain flow usually indicates that the component is in a failure mode and has begun shedding particles that can ultimately cause catastrophic failures.

The range for radial clearances between the bore and spool in most directional control valves is from 5 to 13 micrometers. In a practical sense, the production of perfectly round and straight bores is difficult, if not impossible. For this reason, it is not likely that any spool can be positioned in the exact center of the clearance band. For example, in a nominal one eighth inch valve, a good spool fit is likely to have clearances of less than 2.5 micrometers.

The forces acting on the solenoid in an electrically operated valve are shown in Figure 6-17. These forces include flow, spring, friction and inertia. Flow, spring and inertia forces are built-in factors, but friction depends to a large extent on filtration. If the system is heavily contaminated, higher forces are required to move the spool.

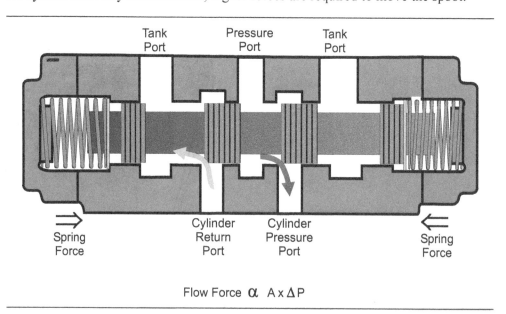

Flow Force α A x ΔP

Figure 6-17   Spool forces in directional valves

Silting produces even more problems as contaminants are driven into clearances under pressure, eventually leading to fluid film breakdown and spool restriction. For example, consider a nominal one eighth inch valve operating at 3,000 psi (210 bar, 21,000 kPa). If this valve is infrequently operated, the area between the spool and bore can silt up. Test data has shown that 30 pounds of force (130N) would be necessary to dislodge the spool. Because the spring and solenoid forces can exert only 10 pounds of force (45N), the silting usually causes problems in the form of a solenoid failure (Figure 6-18).

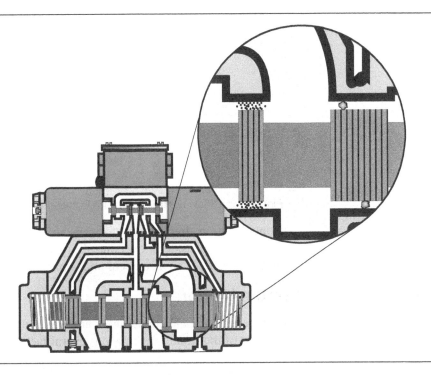

Figure 6-18   Silting leads to spool binding

Erosion of internal valve surfaces by highly abrasive particles suspended in high velocity streams of fluid is a common occurrence in pressure controls (Figure 6-19). This is especially true of relief valves, which are subjected to maximum pressure drops and fluid velocities up to 90 ft/sec (27 m/s). Pilot control stages generally see low volumes at high velocities. Heavy fluid contamination affects both the stability and repeatability of these valves.

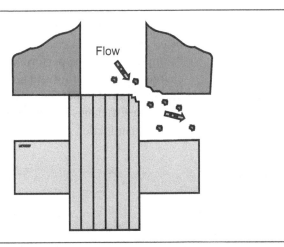

Figure 6-19   High velocity contamination erodes metering surfaces

Orifice configuration is the most important factor in determining the contamination tolerance of flow control valves. Figure 6-20 shows two orifices having different shapes but equal areas. The groove type orifice can tolerate a high contamination level, except when used at a low flow setting. The flat cut orifice is much more susceptible to silting at all settings.

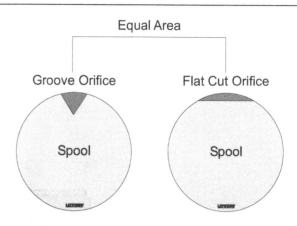

Figure 6-20   Flow control valve throttle sections

Contamination affects the performance of the pressure reducing element in all types of pressure-compensated flow controls, regardless of the valve setting. Damage to the metering orifice can also occur and is particularly apparent at lower flow settings.

Measurement of Contamination

Whenever a particle contaminant analysis is performed on a hydraulic system, the validity of the results depends on several factors, including:

- Cleanliness control over the equipment used to obtain and analyze the fluid sample.
- Cleanliness control over the environment to which the sample may be exposed.
- Method used to obtain the sample.
- Method used to count particles in the sample.
- Accuracy of the equipment selected for the analysis and skill in its use.
- Accuracy in interpreting analysis results and in assessing the contamination in a fluid sample.

Contaminant analysis is a complex process involving many more factors than those listed above. However, knowledge of this process, coupled with an understanding of its importance to the performance of hydraulic systems, can be quite valuable to those charged with operating and maintaining these systems. Contamination control may be the single most important area in which the technician can directly contribute to operating efficiency and improved performance. For this reason, basic information on how contamination data is collected and analyzed is presented in this section.

Cleanliness Control

Prior to obtaining a fluid sample for analysis, certain precautions must be taken to ensure that external contaminants from sampling equipment or from the environment are not introduced into the sample. Cleanliness control must be established for sampling equipment, sample containers and exposed surfaces within the analyzer. In addition, the background contamination level of all fluids used to flush, rinse or dilute the sample must be maintained so that it does not affect the true contaminant makeup of the sample.

Methods of Taking Fluid Samples

The selection of the sampling method and its proper application are critical aspects of the overall analysis effort. The sampling method should be selected on the basis of either the type of sample needed or the purpose of the sample.

If all that is required is a chemical or physical analysis of fluid precipitates and foreign particulates, a static sample is used. These samples are obtained from a fluid body at rest and are normally extracted at the center point of a fluid container. These samples do not reflect the contaminant conditions present in the system under operating conditions, nor are they useful in determining how much particulate contamination is distributed within the fluid. Consequently, dynamic sampling is the preferred method of sampling.

When the important factor in taking a fluid sample is the contamination level that exists within the system under actual operating conditions, then a dynamic sample must be taken from a fluid in motion. Both the location within the system from which the sample is taken, and the period of time during the operation cycle in which the sample is taken, are important in obtaining a representative sample. The preferred location for sampling is directly upstream of the return line filter element.

The basic types of dynamic sampling are laminar and turbulent flow sampling. In laminar flow sampling, the sample is extracted by a probe inserted into a region of the system where the flow of liquid is streamlined. This method can be extremely accurate but is quite difficult to implement. In laminar flow, the large contaminant particles are carried along in the boundary layer, while the small particles tend to flow in the center of the velocity profile. Also, in laminar flow, any dispersed material generally settles. Under these conditions, obtaining a representative sample is no simple matter.

In most situations, turbulent flow sampling is easier to establish and to ensure accurate results than laminar flow sampling. By its very nature, turbulent flow produces a violent mixing action and provides uniform distribution of particles in the sampling field. Sample quality does not depend on the sampling flow or the probe configuration, as long as the sample is taken from the main stream in a turbulent region. In turbulent flow samplings, with dispersed particulate matter generally less than 100 micrometers in size, the quality of the sample is less affected by the sampling system geometry or the withdrawal rate. Therefore, a very simple system can be used to obtain a representative sample from a fluid conductor operating in turbulent flow.

The accepted procedure for extracting a dynamic sample is called in-line sampling. In this procedure, fluid is removed from the mixing zone through fully opened and appropriately flushed ball valves and hypodermic tubing (Figure 6-21). This procedure minimizes the accidental introduction of debris and generated particles from the sampling device. The following guidelines should be followed when using the in-line sampling procedure:

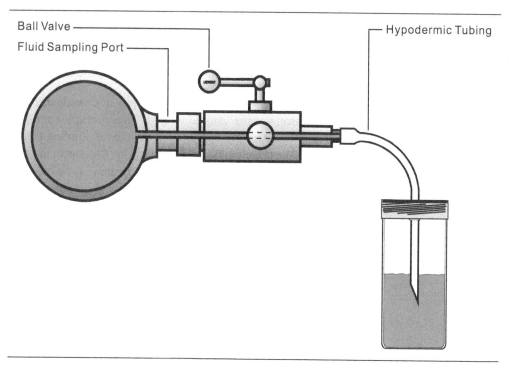

Ball Valve

Fluid Sampling Port

Hypodermic Tubing

Figure 6-21   In-line sampling method

Before the actual sample is obtained, a quantity of fluid (equal to at least five times the volume between the probe or port and the exiting point) should be allowed to flush from the assembly.

The sample bottle should be filled to about 70 percent of its total volume to leave enough room to effectively agitate the sample before it is analyzed.

Extract the sample fluid through fully opened ball valves connected to lines under normal operating conditions. Use a size and length of hypodermic tubing that will give you the fluid velocity you desire.

Particle Size Analysis Methods

The distribution of contaminant particle sizes in a fluid can be analyzed by several different methods. Each of these uses some particular property or combination of properties to distinguish one size particle from another. In some methods, the size dimension is measured directly, while in others, the dimension is derived from the measured physical behavior of the particles. Also, some methods detect and measure each particle, and others measure particles in bulk powder form.

Some industries use an optical method. Fluid cleanliness is measured by pulling a sample of fluid through a submicron filter patch and looking through the patch with the naked eye or under a microscope. A trained technician, using a microscope, counts the number of particles in a given area and estimates the contamination level of the fluid. This process is very tedious and may be unreliable, depending on the skill and experience of the technician.

Modern automatic particle counters can quickly and accurately analyze a sample. Several different optical methods are in use today or are being contemplated for use in the future. Imaging methods with reflected and transmitted light using microscopes have been employed to size particles for quite some time. The image analyzing computer uses television equipment and a minicomputer along with a microscope to count and size particles. Both the conventional electron microscope and the scanning electron microscope are useful instruments in this field. Other optical methods include light extinction, light scattering, diffraction, laser and holographic techniques.

Automatic Particle Counters

The use of Automatic Particle Counters (APCs), particularly portable particle counters, is becoming increasingly popular. There are three basic sensor technologies on the market: flow decay, white light and laser.

In a flow decay instrument, very fine screens collect particulates as a sample of fluid passes through. The pressure drop across the screen is measured, and the quantity of particles is calculated from the pressure drop and a preprogrammed distribution of contamination. These units will indicate whether the fluid in a machine is getting cleaner or dirtier over a period of time, but the accuracy of the actual count may be suspect, as the instrument assumes a standard distribution of contaminants. An advantage of flow decay instruments is that they are unaffected by air bubbles in the fluid.

White light particle counters pass a sample of fluid between a light source and a photo sensor. The "shadows" cast by the particles generate electric pulses in the photo sensor (Figure 6-22). The size of the pulses and number of pulses correspond to the size and number of particles within the fluid sample. The development of white light sensors allowed for the accurate measurement of particles down to 5 microns in size.

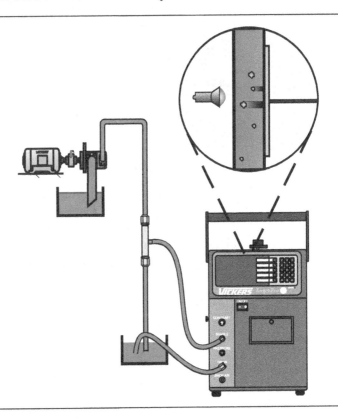

Figure 6-22   White light type of automatic particle counter

Laser counters operate in a manner similar to the white light sensors, but use lasers as the optical source, and can accurately measure particles down to 2 microns in size. They are very stable and require recalibration only once a year.

Portable particle counters are now available with a number of features, including: user friendliness, memory storage capabilities, on-line and off-line sampling, and the ability to download contamination information onto a desktop or laptop computer.

ISO Solid Contaminant Code

To specify the cleanliness level of a fluid, the ISO Solid Contaminant Code (Figure 6-23) was established to express the degree of contamination. The code, which applies to all types of fluid systems, provides a simple, unmistakable, meaningful and consistent means of worldwide communication between suppliers and users.

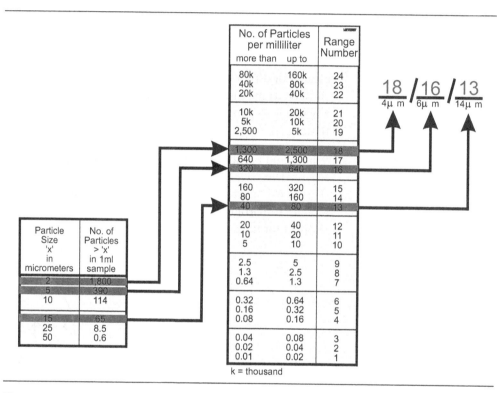

Figure 6-23   ISO solid contaminant code

Description of the Procedure

The ISO contaminant code is constructed by using the results of a particle count analysis to assign a pair of range numbers that represent the cleanliness level of the fluid. First, the contaminant particle size distribution results are used to determine the total number of particles above 4 microns in size, 6 microns and above, and 14 microns and above per milliliter of fluid.

The three values then are plotted on the graph and connected with a straight line (Figure 6-24). The range number for each value is read from the graph and the resultant range of numbers describes the cleanliness level of the fluid. The line connecting the range numbers represents the cleanliness profile of the fluid.

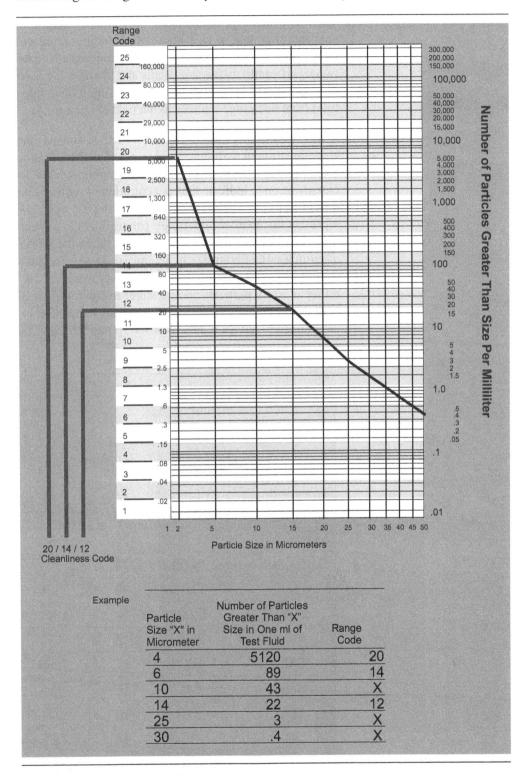

Example			
	Particle Size "X" in Micrometer	Number of Particles Greater Than "X" Size in One ml of Test Fluid	Range Code
	4	5120	20
	6	89	14
	10	43	X
	14	22	12
	25	3	X
	30	.4	X

Figure 6-24   Cleanliness profile

These three particle sizes were selected because they give an accurate assessment of the number of small particulates in the fluid that lead to critical clearance types of failures, and the number of large particles that lead to more general clearance and wear types of failures.

The ISO code range numbers are based on a step ratio of two for particle concentration; that is, each succeeding number represents twice the number of particles present in the fluid. This is considered adequate both to differentiate between two significantly different systems and to allow for reasonable differences in measurement. Note that the numbers defining the range numbers double (step ratio of two) from one range number to the next (Figure 6-25).

It was not until the mid-1970s that a method and accepted standard of assessing solid contamination in hydraulic fluid was established. ISO code 4406 established a range code of particle contamination concentration, independent of particle size, and a classification to indicate the concentration of particles larger than 5 microns and larger than 15 microns. Figure 6-25 illustrates the use of a standard range number to represent the number of particles (of any size) in a specific volume of sampled fluid. The range number for the upper limit of the range is used. For example, if the number of particles of a given size being measured, say 5μ and larger, is 7,800, the range is from 5,000 to 10,000, so the range number would be 20. Indicating an ISO range code rating of 20 for particles 5μ and larger in one milliliter of fluid. Thus a fluid subject to particle count that was determined to have a cleanliness level of 18/16 would be determined to have a range of 18 for 5μ and larger particles/ml, and a range of 16 for 15μ and larger particles per ml.

Number of particles per 1 ml of fluid		Range Code	Number of particles per 1 ml of fluid		Range Code
More Than	Up To		More Than	Up To	
80,000	160,000	24	20	40	12
40,000	80,000	23	10	20	11
20,000	40,000	22	5	10	10
10,000	20,000	21	2.5	5	9
5,000	10,000	20	1.3	2.5	8
2500	5,000	19	.64	1.3	7
1300	2500	18	.32	.64	6
640	1300	17	.16	.32	5
320	640	16	.08	.16	4
160	320	15	.04	.08	3
80	160	14	.02	.04	2
40	80	13	.01	.02	1

Figure 6-25   ISO range code numbers

Example of the Procedure

For this example, the following particle count analysis results are used:

Particle Size Range	No. of Particles per ml
2m and above	5120
5m and above	890
10m and above	192
15m and above	83
25m and above	9
50m and above	0.4

ISO 4406 was unofficially modified in 1987 to include 2μ particles. More recently, ISO has recognized a new certified test dust and better ways of calibrating. This new standard is called ISO 4406 1999. With the development of new technology, particle sizes are now defined differently and more accurately. Instead of reading $\geq 2\mu/\geq 5\mu/\geq 15\mu$, the code will now read $\geq 4\mu_{(c)}/\geq 6\mu_{(c)}/\geq 14\mu_{(c)}$. The subscript $_{(c)}$ denotes that the new code is being used. This new code doesn't change the fluid, the filter, or the target cleanliness requirements (as discussed in the next section). It only changes the language that describes the contamination. In most cases, only the first number will change. Therefore, what was a 19/17/15 under ISO 4406 1987 may become 20/17/15 under ISO 4406 1999.

Figure 6-23 illustrates a cleanliness sample chart used to determine the cleanliness level range code for $\geq 4\mu_{(c)}$, $\geq 6\mu_{(c)}$ and $\geq 14\mu_{(c)}$ particles in a specific sample of oil. While laser light extinguishing technology allows a track of particles from less than 2μ to greater than 50μ, the numbers extracted for the cleanliness level reflect the 4, 6 and 14μ particles.

The three range cleanliness code for this sample may be determined as follows:

1. Determine the particle count per milliliter for particles 4 microns and above. (The particle count is 5,120.) From the chart in Figure 6-25 determine which range code applies. (5,120 falls between 5,000 and 10,000 so this range code number is 20.)

2. Determine the particle count per milliliter for particles 6 microns and above. The particle count is 890. From the chart in Figure 6-25 the number falls between 640 and 1,300. The range code number for this sample of particles 6 microns in size and above is 17.

3. Determine the particle count per milliliter for particles 14 microns and above. The particle count is 83, which falls between 80 and 160. The range code for particles greater than or equal to 14 microns in size is 14.

The three digit cleanliness code for this fluid sample is **20/17/14**. This indicates the range code for contamination.

Particles greater than **4** microns	Particles greater than **6** microns	Particles greater than **14** microns

System Cleanliness

Hydraulic system cleanliness is obtained by utilizing a three-step process (Figure 6-26):

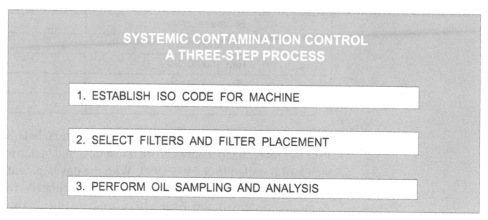

Figure 6-26   Three-step process for system contamination control

Step 1. Establish a Target Cleanliness Level — Based on system characteristics such as operating pressure levels, severity of service, types of products used, operating temperatures, etc., set the ISO cleanliness code value that will achieve acceptable system life.

Step 2. Achieve the Target Cleanliness Level — Install and/or adopt contamination control devices to remove sufficient contamination particles from the system so that the fluid will be within the target cleanliness code.

Step 3. Confirm and Monitor Achievement — Establish a consistent and continuous fluid sampling and analysis procedure to assure target cleanliness levels are maintained.

Establishing a Target Cleanliness Level

All hydraulic systems should have a specific, designated cleanliness level. This desired "target" cleanliness level can be established and maintained for any hydraulic system by first considering such system conditions as environment, pressure, system components and duty cycle, and then specifying and properly locating the system filter(s).

The target cleanliness level is set as follows, using a worksheet similar to that shown in Figure 6-27.

Company Name _____   Date _____

Type of Machine (System) _____

Setting a Target Cleanliness Level

Step One

    Maximum Operating Pressure _____   Pump Flow _____

    Total System Volume (including lines & actuators) _____

    Most Sensitive Component

    Pump Type _____   Target Cleanliness ____/____/____

    Control Type _____   Target Cleanliness ____/____/____

    Actuator Type _____   Target Cleanliness ____/____/____

Step Two

    Fluid Type and Brand _____

    Fluid Adjustment?   _____ Yes   _____ No

Step Three

    Operating Temperature

    High Vibration or Shock?   _____ Yes   _____ No

    Is Machine Critical to Process?   _____ Yes   _____ No

    Could a Hydraulic Failure Cause a Safety Hazard?   _____ Yes   _____ No

    System Stress Adjustment?

Final Systemic Contamination Control Target Cleanliness _____/_____/_____

Recommended Filter Placement and Rating   _____ 3 micron

                                    _____ 5 micron

                                    _____ 10 micron

                                    _____ Pressure Line

                                    _____ Return Line

                                    _____ Off Line

Figure 6-27   Worksheet for setting target cleanliness level

Using the Recommended Cleanliness Code Chart in Figure 6-28, determine the cleanliness level recommended for the most contamination sensitive component in the hydraulic system. All components that draw fluid from a common reservoir should be considered to be part of the same system even if their operations are independent or sequential. The pressure rating is the maximum pressure achieved by the machine during a complete cycle of operation.

	1000 PSI (68.95 bar)	2000 PSI (137.9 bar)	3000 PSI+ (206.8 bar)	4000 PSI (275.8 bar)
Pumps				
Fixed Gear	20/18/15	19/17/15		
Fixed Vane	20/18/15	19/17/14	18/16/13	
Fixed Piston	19/17/15	18/16/14	17/15/13	
Variable Vane	18/16/14	17/15/13		
Variable Piston	18/16/14	17/15/13	16/14/12	
Valves				
Directional (solenoid)		20/18/15	19/17/14	
Pressure Control (modulating)		19/17/14	19/17/14	
Flow Controls (standard)		19/17/14	19/17/14	
Proportional Directional (throttle valves)		17/15/12	15/13/11*	
Check Valves		20/18/15	20/18/15	
Servo Valves		16/14/11*	15/13/10*	
Cartridge Valves		18/16/13	17/15/12	
H.R.C.		18/16/13	17/15/12	
Proportional Pressure Controls	16/14/12*	15/13/11*		
Flow controls (pressure compensating)	17/15/13	17/15/13		
Proportional Cartridge Valves	17/15/12	16/14/11*		
Actuators				
Cylinders	20/18/15	20/18/15	20/18/15	
Vane Motors	20/18/15	19/17/14	18/16/13	
Axial Piston Motors	19/17/14	18/16/13	17/15/12	
Gear Motors	21/19/17	20/18/15	19/17/14	
Radial Piston Motors	20/18/14	19/17/13	18/16/13	
Cam Wave Motors	18/16/14	17/15/13	16/14/12*	
Hydrostatic Transmissions				
Hydrostatic Transmissions (in loop fluid)		17/15/13	16/14/12*	16/14/11*
Bearings				
Ball Bearing Systems		15/13/11*		
Roller Bearing Systems		16/14/12*		
Journal Bearings (high speed)		17/15/13		
Journal Bearings (low speed)		18/16/14		
General Industrial Gearboxes		17/15/13		

* Requires precise sampling practices to verify cleanliness levels.

Figure 6-28   Recommended cleanliness codes for various components

For any system where the fluid is not 100 percent petroleum oil, set the target one range code cleaner for each particle size. For example, if for Step 1 it is determined that the most contamination sensitive component required a cleanliness code of 19/17/15 and phosphate ester is the system fluid, the target cleanliness code becomes 18/16/14.

If any two of the following conditions are experienced by the hydraulic system, set the target one range code cleaner for each particle size.

- Frequent cold starts at less than 0°F (-18°C).
- Intermittent operation with fluid temperatures over 160°F (70°C)
- High vibration levels or high system shock operation

Although the most critical component in many systems is the pump, infrequently operated spool valves which are subjected to continuous pressure must be protected from high silt concentrations. Low setting flow controls, regardless of pressure, must also be protected from silt. Flow control and pressure control valves provide greater operating reliability and repeatability when silt content is under control.

Figure 6-28 shows a chart of recommended cleanliness levels for typical hydraulic components at various operating pressures. The cleanliness level recommendations are based on engineering evaluations that include materials, critical clearances and machining tolerances.

Achieving Target Cleanliness

Filter Location

There are three areas in hydraulic systems for locating a contamination control device: the pressure line (pump outlet line), the return line and an off-loop or kidney loop type filtration/filling circuit.

Strainers are frequently used in the inlet line between the reservoir and the pump. However, these devices are usually a 100 mesh screen that will trap particles larger than about 150 micrometers. It is Eaton's contention that these devices play no part in cleaning a system, or maintaining a clean system, as long as care is taken to keep objects larger than 150 microns out of the reservoir.

Figure 6-29 shows a typical location for a pressure and return filter in an example circuit. A pressure line filter can be considered the "gateway" contamination control device for the system (provided there are no other pumps in the system). However, used by itself, it does not protect the pump from any contamination particles that are returned to the reservoir from the system, and this may increase pump wear. Pressure line filters should always be used in servo or proportional valve systems to protect these products from any wear particles that are generated by the pump.

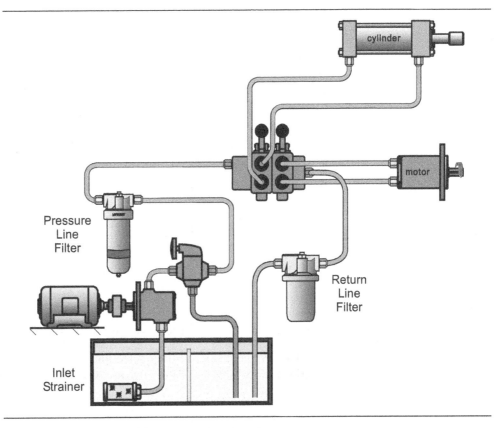

Figure 6-29   Inlet, pressure and return filter locations

Return line filters are an excellent "total system" contamination control device, provided that at least 20 percent of the total system volume passes through the filter every minute. In circuits where a pressure-compensated pump is limiting flow to less than this, an off-line circulating filter should be used.

Care must be taken to size the return line filter for the maximum flow it will experience. Because most cylinders have differential areas, flows greater than pump flow will occur when the cylinder is retracting, and this flow will pass through the return line filter. If the filter is not sized properly, it could rupture, putting large amounts of contamination into the reservoir.

An off-line circulating pump and filter should always be used when a pressure-compensated system is on "standby" for long periods of time. Under these conditions, fluid is not passing the pressure or return line filters, and pump generated contamination is being sent directly to the reservoir. The off-line system will continue to clean the fluid while the system "sleeps."

The chart in Figure 6-30 provides recommendations for filter placement and micron rating in order to achieve the target cleanliness levels. The chart assumes quality filters are used, ingression of contaminants is not excessive, a sealed reservoir with 3 micron air filtration, and good maintenance practices are followed.

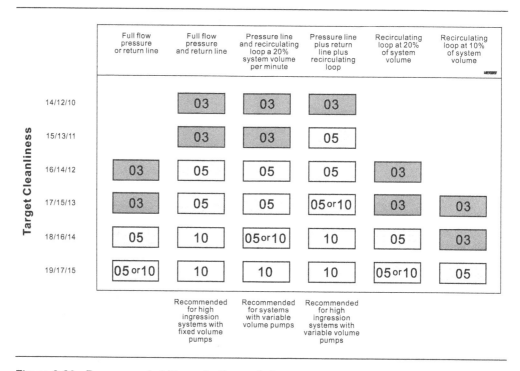

Figure 6-30   Recommended filter selection and placement

Other factors to consider in filter selection, such as steady or pulsating flow conditions, flow rates and filter pressure drop are covered later in this chapter.

Air passing into and out of the reservoir must also be cleaned. Changing fluid levels, caused by cycling cylinders or fluid temperature changes, cause air to enter and leave the reservoir to makeup for the change in volume. The reservoir should be tightly sealed, and all air should pass through a 3-micron filter (Figure 6-31) as it enters.

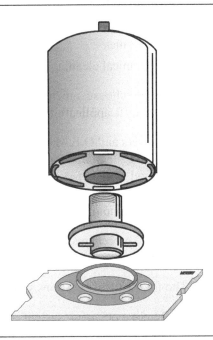

Figure 6-31   Three-micron air filter for reservoirs

Cleanliness of Tubing and Other Conductors

The following information on preparing pipes, tubing, hoses and fittings prior to installation in a hydraulic system should be considered a basic guideline only. Complete procedures are included in Appendix C of this manual.

Iron and steel pipes, tubing and metal fittings must be absolutely clean and free from scale and other foreign matter before they are installed. Metal conductors may be wire brushed, cleaned with a commercial pipe cleaning apparatus or pickled, depending on the amount of scale or rust initially present in the conductor. If pickling is used, the conductor must be degreased prior to the pickling procedure and thoroughly rinsed after it.

The inside edge of tubing and pipe should be deburred after cutting. Tubing must not be welded, brazed or soldered after system assembly as this makes proper cleaning impossible. Hose should be flexed several times to release any trapped dirt and then properly flushed.

Flange fittings must fit squarely on the mounting faces and be properly secured with bolts of the correct length. Threaded fittings should be inspected for metal slivers on the threads before installation. Cover all openings into the system to keep out contaminants during assembly or maintenance.

If conductors are stored for any length of time, they should be plugged to prevent the entrance of foreign matter. Don't use rags or other materials to plug the ends of the conductors as they will only contribute to the contamination problem. Use caps of the correct size for this purpose.

Component Cleanliness

Prior to installation, all components should be cleaned in one or more of the following ways:

- Soap and water
- Acid cleaner
- Alkaline cleaner
- Solvent
- Ultrasonics
- Mechanical cleaning

Be sure to choose a method compatible with existing contemporary standards and your specific application.

Many users and O.E.M.s of large hydraulic components and machinery now specify cleanliness standards for their component and fluid suppliers. This procedure, coupled with good storage practices, assures all incoming parts meet a minimum cleanliness level when introduced to the system. Additionally, today's lower cost of finer filters makes it economically practical to achieve low ISO code levels.

Complete procedures for component cleaning are included in the Appendix C of this manual.

Guidelines for Flushing a System

The following suggestions should be considered whenever a system is to be flushed:

- Remove precision system components before flushing and install spool pieces, flushing plates, jumpers or dummy pieces in their place.
- Remove filter elements from the main lines being flushed.
- Flushing velocity should be two to two and one-half times the anticipated system flow rate.
- Use a low viscosity fluid.
- If possible, use warm flushing fluid; 185°F (85°C).
- Be sure the flushing fluid is compatible with preceding and succeeding fluids.
- Always flush in only one direction of flow.
- Flush each circuit branch off the main branch one at a time, starting with the one closest to the flushing pump and proceeding downstream. It may be necessary to install blocking valves in the system to achieve this pattern.
- In blind runs, provide vertical dirt traps by including short standpipes below the level of the branch piping.
- Do not use the system pump as the flushing pump. Generally, a hydrodynamic pump such as a centrifugal pump provides adequate head and greater flow rates, operates more economically, and has a better tolerance for contaminants that circulate during flushing.
- Use a cleanup filter in the flushing system with a capacity that matches the flow rates used. Micrometer rating should be as fine as practical, but not coarser than the proposed system filter rating.
- If practical, use an auxiliary flushing fluid reservoir to avoid trapping contaminants in the system's reservoir.
- To determine when to stop the flushing procedure, establish a fluid sampling schedule to check contamination levels.
- After flushing, take every precaution to avoid introducing contaminants while reinstalling working components.

Fill with Clean Oil

Contaminants are found even in new hydraulic fluid, so makeup oil should be put through a portable filter when it is added to an operating hydraulic system. Running the new fluid through the filter and then into the machine reservoir ensures contaminant free fluid. Keeping the fluid clean and free of moisture will help it last much longer and avoid contamination damage to close fitting parts in the hydraulic components.

Hydraulic fluid of any kind is not an inexpensive item. Further, changing the fluid and flushing or cleaning improperly maintained systems is time consuming and costly. Therefore, it's important to care for the fluid properly during storage and handling as well as under operating conditions.

Here are some simple rules to prevent contamination of the fluid during storage, handling and servicing:

- Store drums on their sides. If possible, keep them inside or under a roof.
- Before opening a drum, clean the top and the bung thoroughly so dirt and other external contaminants are not introduced into the fluid.
- Use only clean containers, hoses, etc. to transfer fluid from the drum to the hydraulic reservoir. An oil transfer pump (Figure 6-32) equipped with 5 micron filters is recommended. A portable filtration system can provide even finer filtration for critical applications.
- Provide a contaminant-free filling path.
- Be sure the filter is intended for use with the type of fluid required by the system.
- When portable filter hoses are connected to the reservoir, the connections should be wiped clean with a clean, lint free cloth to prevent dirt and other foreign particles from entering the system.

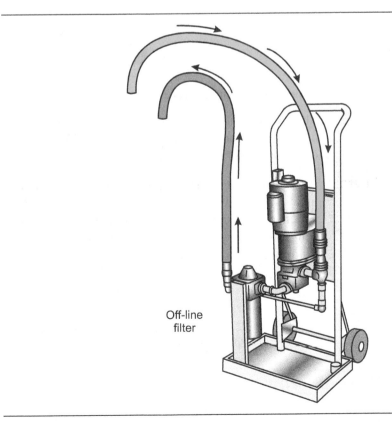

Off-line filter

Figure 6-32   Oil transfer pump and filter

Filtration Products

Inlet Strainers

Figure 6-33 shows a typical strainer of the type installed on pump inlet lines inside the reservoir. Compared to a filter, this type of strainer is relatively coarse, being constructed of fine mesh wire. A 100 mesh strainer protects the pump from particles above about 150 microns in size.

Two important requirements for any inlet strainer (and its associated conductors) are:

- The strainer must pass the full pump volume within the permitted inlet pressure drop for that pump.
- The strainer must provide bypass flow which is still within that limit when the strainer element is blocked.

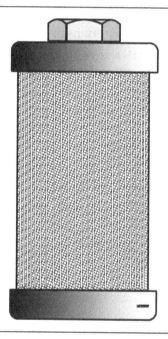

Figure 6-33   100 mesh inlet filter screen

The level of contamination entering the pump is a critical factor. Inlet strainers should only be expected to prevent large particles from entering the pump and causing catastrophic failure.

Pressure Line Filters

A number of filters are designed for installation right in the pressure line and can trap much smaller particles than inlet line strainers. Such a filter might be used where system components are less dirt tolerant than the pump or to protect downstream components from pump deterioration. The filter traps fine contamination from the fluid as it leaves the pump.

Pressure line filters must be able to withstand the operating pressure of the system as well as any pump pulsations. Changing a pressure line filter element requires shutting down the hydraulic system, unless external bypass valves are provided or a duplex filter is used (Figure 6-34).

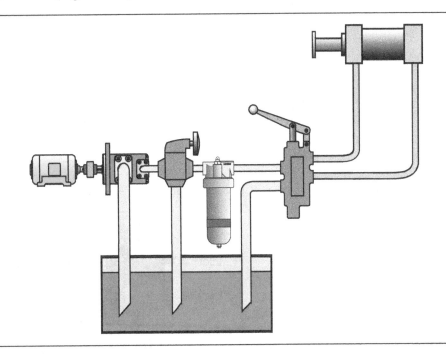

Figure 6-34   Pressure line filter location

Return Line Filters

Return line filters (Figure 6-35) also can trap very small particles before the fluid returns to the reservoir. A return line filter is nearly a must in a system with high performance components which have very close clearances.

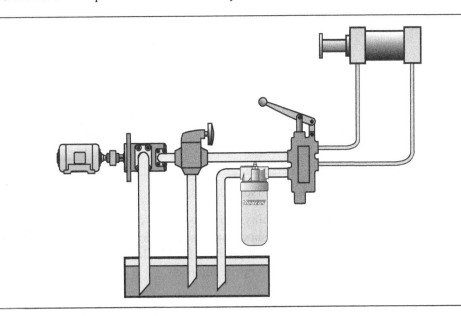

Figure 6-35   Return line filter location

Full flow return filters should have enough capacity to handle maximum return flow with minimal pressure drop. The performance of any return line filter depends on the magnitude of flow, pressure changes and media selected.

The term "full flow" applied to a filter means that all the flow generated by the system passes through the filtering element. In most full flow filters, however, there is a bypass valve preset to open at a given pressure drop to divert flow past the filter element. This prevents the element from being subjected to excessive pressures which could cause it to collapse.

Flow, as shown in Figure 6-36, is outside to inside; that is, from around the element through to its center. The bypass opens when total flow can no longer pass through the contaminate element without raising the pressure above the cracking pressure of the bypass valve.

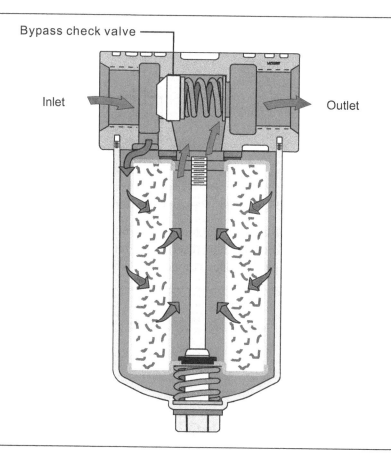

Figure 6-36   Typical filter operation

Off-Line Filter Systems

The desirability and cost-effectiveness of pressure and return line filters can be affected by shock, surges, pulsation and vibration, depending on media types and how well they are supported. Steady flow, relatively free of pressure fluctuations, provides optimum filter performance.

The simplest way to achieve this is to supplement the filter in the main system with an independently powered recirculating system where filter performance is subject to fewer variables (Figure 6-37). Off-line filter systems in which reservoir fluid is circulated through a filter at a constant rate are sometimes used when operating system conditions are severe and the needed quality of filtration is difficult to obtain within the operating system.

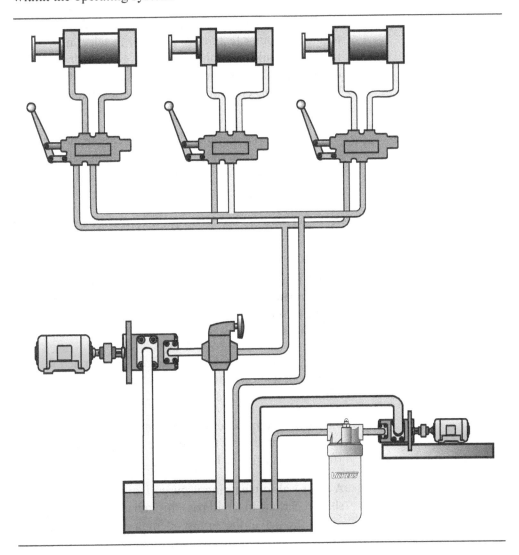

Figure 6-37   Off-line filtration system

With off-line filtration, flow rate or filter type can be altered readily without affecting the design of the main system. Furthermore, the off-line filter system can be run before starting the main system to clean the fluid in the reservoir and reduce the contamination level the pump is subjected to at start-up. A simple valve can be added to filter the initial charge of fluid and any subsequent makeup fluid. Off-line filtration should run continuously to provide clean fluid for every start-up.

Being independent of the main hydraulic system, off-line filters can be placed where they are most convenient to service. Element changes do not affect the main system as the change can be performed at any time without interrupting the operation of the main system.

A typical portable filter package includes the filter, the hydraulic pump and an electric drive motor. The pump is usually protected with its own inlet strainer and a pressure relief valve. All of the components are close coupled and mounted on a hand truck.

Currently available portable filters have pump capacities ranging from 4 to 160 GPM (15 to 620 l/min). Filters used on these packages can have a filtration capability to achieve cleanliness levels of ISO 14/12/9 or finer. Many filters are designed to use disposable and interchangeable elements so that it is simple to change from one rating to another. Other features to consider in selecting a portable filter include integral hoses with quick-disconnect fittings, built-in drip pans, and the availability of spare elements. Consult the manufacturer's specifications and filter guides or contact a knowledgeable contamination control or proactive maintenance specialist to select the appropriate filter media.

Filter or Strainer

There will probably always be controversy in the industry over the exact definitions of filters and strainers. In the past, many strainer devices were named filter, but technically classed as strainers. To minimize the controversy, we offer these definitions:

- *Filter* — a device whose primary function is the retention, by some porous media, of insoluble contaminants from a fluid.
- *Strainer* — a coarse filter, usually metal, with pores larger than 50 microns.

To put it simply, whether the device is a filter or strainer, its function is to trap contaminants from fluid flowing through it. "Porous medium" simply refers to a screen or filtering material that allows fluid to flow through it, but stops other materials above a specific size.

Filter Ratings

A simple screen or a wire strainer is usually rated for filtering pore size by a mesh number or its near equivalent standard sieve number. The higher the mesh or sieve number, the finer the screen.

Filters used to be described by nominal and absolute ratings in microns. A filter nominally rated at 10 microns, for example, would trap at least one particle 10 microns in size or larger.

A filter's absolute rating is purportedly the diameter of the largest hard spherically shaped particle that will pass through a filter under specified test conditions. This is, in effect, the size of the largest opening or pore size in the filter media. This type of rating did not provide any indication of the filter's efficiency in removing these particles, however.

Filter ratings needed to go beyond this basic micron rating, to define the true capability of filter media in cleaning fluids. The Beta Ratio system was developed, and has now replaced essentially all of the micron ratings.

The international standard for rating the efficiency of a hydraulic or lubrication filter is the Multipass Filter Performance Beta Test, ISO 4572 (Figure 6-38). The Beta ratio or rating is determined under laboratory conditions, and the results of the test are reported as a ratio; the number of particles greater than a designated size upstream of the test filter compared with the number of same size particles downstream of the filter. Although not a true measure of how well a filter will do in an operating system, the Beta rating is an indicator of the filtration performance:

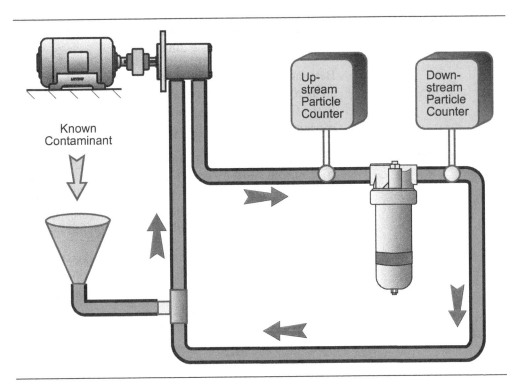

Figure 6-38   Multipass filter performance test

Formula 6-1

$$\text{Beta}_x = \frac{\text{Number of upstream particles} > x}{\text{Number of downstream particles} > x}$$

Where:

x= Particle Size

A Beta ratio of 1.0 means that no particles are stopped by the filter. A Beta ratio of 100 (meaning a ratio of 100 to 1) means that for every 100 particles upstream, 99 particles are trapped for every one that gets through, for an efficiency of 99 percent (Figure 6-39).

Beta Ratio	Efficiency
1	0%
2	50.00%
5	80.00%
10	90.00%
20	95.00%
75	98.70%
100	99.00%
200	99.50%
1000	99.90%
5000	99.98%

Figure 6-39   Beta ratios and corresponding efficiency

To select a filter for silt control, specify a filter with a Beta ratio of $B_3 = 200$. For partial silt control, a filter with a $B_5 = 200$ might be chosen. For chip removal only, the Beta ratio might be $B_{25} = 200$.

Beta ratios are plotted and manipulated in many ways to show separation efficiency, so there may be little correlation between multipass efficiencies and fluid cleanliness. In the final analysis, the goal of a filter is not just high Beta ratios and dirt holding capacity, but properly cleaned fluid.

Holding Capacity

The amount of contaminant particles held by a particular filter is known as the contaminant capacity or dirt holding capacity. The value is obtained under laboratory conditions and is defined as the weight (usually in grams) of a specified artificial contaminant that must be added upstream of the filter to produce a given differential pressure across the filter under specific conditions.

The artificial contaminant is added at a constant rate to a continuously recirculating oil system and the resultant increase in differential pressure is plotted against the weight of contaminant added. The result is a characteristic curve which is constant for a given filter media (Figure 6-40).

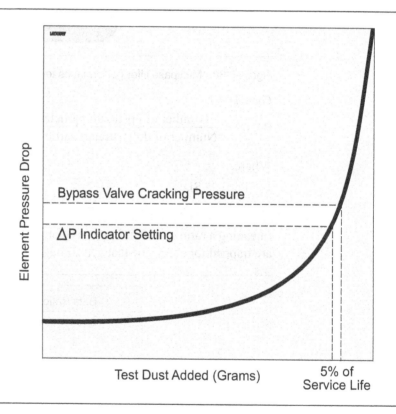

Figure 6-40   Filter media dirt holding characteristic curve

Contaminant capacity is sometimes used as an indication of relative service life. This should only be done when all other variables are constant and equal among the units being compared. Filters must have enough dirt holding capacity to provide acceptable time intervals between element changes. While large capacity filters cost more initially, the differential costs are generally recovered quickly in reduced operating costs. Fewer element changes are required, reducing labor costs and downtime, resulting in higher productivity.

Flow Rate Capacity (GPM or l/min)

Filter manufacturers commonly provide users with flow ratings in GPM or l/min at specific clean pressure drops.

While this information provides a guideline regarding flow capacity, filters which are sized based only on flow rate usually have a short element life. Correct filter sizing requires relating the dirt entering the filter to the effective element area and the maximum allowable pressure drop.

Dirt input is a product of built-in and ingressed contamination, which in turn produces system generated contamination. Figure 6-27 is a tool that can be used to assess the type of contamination controls present in a hydraulic system. After a system evaluation is made using the guidelines in this chart, consult the contamination control guide or a contamination control specialist.

Pressure Rating

Filter specifications include the maximum allowable system pressure that the filter is able to withstand. Pressure line filters must be able to handle full system pressure and are rated under both fatigue and static conditions.

Pressure Drop

The initial and terminal pressure drops (or pressure differentials) across a filter element are important. To minimize energy consumption, the average pressure drop across filters should be as low as possible. A pressure differential of 85 psid at 20 GPM wastes 1 hp at the pump. The maximum pressure drop under bypass conditions should be less than the collapse rating of the element. This maximum value, called the terminal pressure drop [usually 45 psi (3 bar, 300 kPa)], is controlled by the filter manufacturer and depends on media strength and construction details.

Filter manufacturers provide charts, tables and graphs to select filters on the basis of flow and pressure drop. These pressure/flow characteristics refer to a clean element and assembly. The pressure drop across a filter is a measure of the resistance to flow across the filter due to kinetic and viscous effects. In actual service, factors that affect the filter pressure drop include fluid viscosity, fluid specific gravity, flow, operating temperature, filter size, permeability of the filter medium, restrictions in the housing and the degree to which the medium is loaded with contaminant.

Fluid Compatibility

Filter specifications describe the kinds of fluids that are suitable for use with a particular filter. Fluid or material compatibility is one aspect of the structural integrity of a filter. Other structural integrity factors are end load, flow fatigue and collapse burst values. To test for material compatibility, the element is immersed for 72 hours in system fluid that is 59°F (15°C) higher than rated maximum temperature. Other structural integrity tests are then conducted to determine how well the filter media stands up to system forces.

Filter Construction

Filtering Materials

There are two basic classifications of filtering materials; absorbent or adsorbent.

Absorbent filter medium traps particles by mechanical means. Absorbent media are divided into two basic types: surface and depth. Surface media are most commonly used for coarse filtration. Depth media are generally used for finer filtration. The most common hydraulic filter media are cellulose, synthetic, glass fibers or a combination of the preceding. These materials are blended for specific performance characteristics and durability and are usually resin-impregnated to provide added strength.

Adsorbent, or active, filters such as charcoal and Fuller's Earth should be avoided in hydraulic systems since they may remove essential additives from the hydraulic fluid.

Types of Filter Elements

The most frequently used filter element structure is cylindrical in shape. Perforated tubes are used to support the media against pressure differential. The media used is pleated to provide a larger surface area for trapping contaminant, providing greater dirt holding capacity.

As previously mentioned, elements employing surface media are used as strainers for coarse filtration. Due to their relatively large openings, they offer low pressure drops, and because contaminants are trapped on the surface, they may be cleaned for reuse rather than discarded. Pore size is accurately controlled and any contaminant larger than the pores is removed from the fluid. However, this type of filtration will not provide any meaningful control of particles that are smaller than the pore openings.

Stainless steel wire, which offers excellent chemical and temperature resistance characteristics as well as greater strength, is frequently used in weaving surface media. Strainer elements are sometimes constructed to withstand extreme differential pressures. When loaded with dirt they do not permit flow of fluid. This causes loss of equipment function and ensures that the filter is replaced or cleaned. Wire cloth media with the capability for very fine filtration is available but is quite expensive.

Hydraulic filter elements for fine filtration requirements are generally made of depth type media and tend to have a pleated structure. Although the name may be somewhat deceiving, pleated paper type filtration media are considered depth media. Despite the fact that this type medium is quite thin, many particles are captured within the sheet. These filter papers are constructed of randomly laid fibers and do not have an even pore size distribution. Instead, they contain many tortuous flow paths for the fluid and have many areas in which particles can become trapped. These media exhibit greater restriction to flow, but can provide fine filtration and high dirt holding capacity. They are also inexpensive.

Due to the way they are made, some particles smaller than the largest pore are removed from the fluid (Figure 6-41). These elements are not cleanable and must be discarded when saturated with dirt. They do not have the chemical or heat resistivity of mesh and are not as strong. Elements are sometimes constructed of both paper and mesh to provide added strength to the media for more severe service environments.

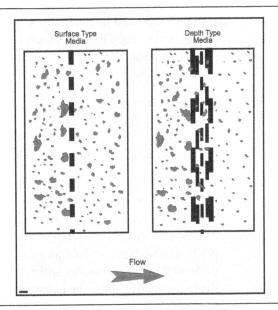

Figure 6-41   Depth versus surface media performance

Hydraulic filter elements for fine filtration requirements are most frequently made of a glass fiber material and also tend to have a pleated structure. This media is also very thin but is most frequently supported upstream and downstream by a strength providing mechanism, usually wire mesh (Figure 6-42). This filter media is constructed of a relatively uniformly laid fiber and tends to have a more even pore size distribution than the above mentioned paper media. Since glass is inert it tends to have a much greater resistance than the paper media to many different fluids and also to the presence of water in the fluid. Unlike the paper media because the fibers are much finer than the paper fiber, sometimes as much as 1/25th to 1/40th the diameter, they tend to have a much lower resistance to flow per unit area than the paper media.

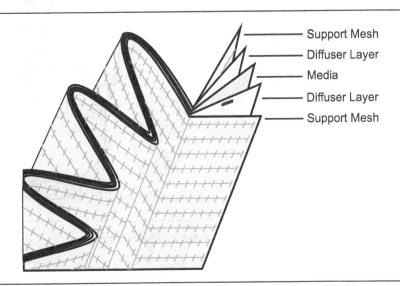

Figure 6-42   Typical filter construction

The glass (microfiber) media elements also tend to have relatively high dirt holding capacity in comparison to strainers and to paper media per unit volume. Advances in the manufacturing processes of glass media have made them extremely competitive with paper media. Because they control much finer particles than paper media, the result is greatly reduced operating expenses and greatly extended component life, filter element life and fluid life. Like the paper element, these elements are not reusable and must be discarded when saturated with dirt. However since they are made of glass they do tend to have a high resistance to chemicals and to heat, and when the mesh is properly supported both upstream and downstream by stainless steel wire mesh, they are quite strong.

Filter Bypass Valves

Generally, a bypass valve is incorporated into the housing to eliminate the possibility of element collapse or rupture when the element becomes clogged or when the fluid is very viscous. The bypass valve is almost a necessity for most filter assemblies operating under cold start-up conditions.

Filter Condition Indicators

It is strongly recommended that all filters include a filter condition indicator so the user will know when the filter element should be replaced (Figure 6-43). The indicators usually operate on element pressure drop (differential pressure) and provide electrical or visual indication when the element is near the end of its service life. There are two basic types of indicators: those that are linked to the filter's bypass valve and those that react only to the differential pressure. Indicators that are linked directly to the bypass valve show the actual position of the bypass valve and indicate movement of the bypass valve. Differential pressure indicators show only that the preset pressure drop has been attained. This type is usually set at a pressure drop somewhat below that at which the bypass valve opens. Both types of indicators are configured in visual and electrical models or a combination of both. The electrical model can be used to light a warning lamp, activate a central buzzer, or even to shut a machine down until the element is replaced, tending to ensure that the system fluid is being filtered.

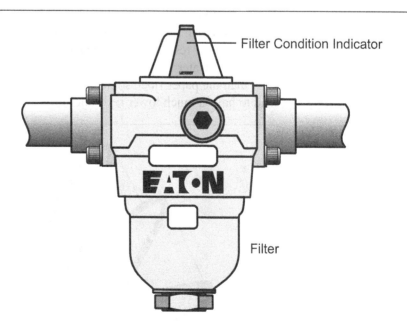

Figure 6-43   Filter with bypass indicator

Summary

Controlling contamination in any hydraulic system is an ongoing process that can greatly improve system performance and extend system longevity. The effort to keep contamination to a minimum begins with the system design process and continues throughout the useful life of the equipment.

The three basic steps are:

- Establish a target cleanliness level.
- Place contamination control devices in the system to achieve the target cleanliness level.
- Monitor fluid condition regularly to ensure that the target cleanliness level is being maintained.

By carefully considering the following key points, system operators and maintenance personnel can contribute significantly to this effort.

In-Operation Care of Hydraulic Fluid

Excerpts from the Standards of the American National Standards Institute, The National Fluid Power Association, The Joint Industry Conference, and the Department of Defense Regarding Filtration, are included in Appendix C.

Key areas for proper in operation care of hydraulic fluid include:

- Preventing contamination by keeping the system tight and using proper air and fluid filtration devices and procedures.
- Establishing fluid change intervals so the fluid will be replaced before it breaks down. If necessary, the fluid supplier can test samples in the laboratory at specific intervals to help establish the frequency of change.
- Keeping the reservoir filled properly to take advantage of its heat dissipating characteristics and to prevent moisture from condensing on inside walls.
- Repairing all leaks immediately.

Filtration System Requirements

In general, the practical and performance requirements of a filtration system can be summarized as follows:

- The system must be capable of reducing the initial contamination to the desired level within an acceptable period of time, without causing premature wear or damage to the hydraulic components.
- The system must be capable of achieving and maintaining the target cleanliness level and must allow a suitable safety factor to provide for a concentrated ingress which could occur, for example, when a system is "topped up."
- The quality of maintenance available at the end user location should be considered.
- Filters must be easily accessible for maintenance.
- Indication of filter condition to tell the user when to replace the unit must be provided.
- In continuous process plants, facilities must be provided to allow changing of elements without interfering with plant operation.
- The filters must provide sufficient dirt holding capacity for an acceptable interval between element changes.
- The inclusion of a filter in the system must not produce undesirable effects on the operation of components, for example, high back pressures on seal drains.
- Sampling points must be provided to monitor initial and subsequent levels of contamination.

Industrial Test Questions: Contamination Control

Chapter 6

1. Describe how contamination can interfere with power transmission.

2. Describe how contamination interferes with the cooling function of hydraulic fluid.

3. Describe how contamination interferes with the lubrication of moving parts.

4. How large is a micron?

5. Define contamination.

6. What areas within a vane pump or motor are the most susceptible to contamination-induced clearance problems?

7. What areas within a gear pump or motor are the most susceptible to contamination-induced clearance problems?

8. What areas within an axial piston pump or motor are the most susceptible to contamination-induced clearance problems?

9. How does pressure influence the effect of contamination on hydraulic components?

10. What type of contamination problem is most common with directional valves?

11. What is the most common type of contamination problem in pressure controls?

12. What is the most important factor determining contamination tolerance of flow control valves?

13. If a fluid sample must be representative of the contamination level that exists within the system under actual operating conditions, what kind of sample would be taken?

14. What are the two types of dynamic sampling methods and which one is the easiest to use?

15. Name the particle size analysis methods.

16. A contaminant particle analysis is conducted with the following results (1 ml sample):

    - Number of particles above 4 microns equals 11,400
    - Number of particles above 6 micrometers equals 4,200
    - Number of particles above 14 micrometers equals 110.
    - What is the ISO code for this sample?

17. A certain in-line piston motor has a contamination tolerance rating of 19/16/13 or cleaner. To safely operate this motor, what are the maximum number of particulates greater than 6 micrometers and greater than 14 micrometers in size for a 100 milliliter sample?

18. What are three sources of particulate contamination in hydraulic systems?

19. Describe proper fluid storage and handling procedures.

20. Name two ways in which a portable filtration unit might be used.

21. Name three possible locations for a filter within a hydraulic system?

22. When might an off-line filtration system be used?

23. What does "full flow" mean?

24. Name five of the seven factors discussed in this chapter that should be considered when specifying a filter.

25. What is used today in place of nominal and absolute ratings for contamination control devices?

26. What is meant by a Beta ratio of $B_3 = 50$ and what is the efficiency?

27. What is the purpose of filter condition indicators?

28. Describe how an electric type filter condition indicator might be used.

29. Describe the difference between surface and depth type filtering material.

Chapter 7 . . . . Hydraulic Actuators

Actuator is the general term used for the output device of hydraulic systems. Two broad categories are linear actuators that deliver power in a straight line, and rotary actuators that deliver their power in a rotating or circular motion. The linear device is called a hydraulic cylinder, and the rotary device is called a hydraulic motor.

Hydraulic Cylinders

Hydraulic cylinders are linear actuators. This means that the output of a cylinder is a straight line motion and/or force. The major function of a hydraulic cylinder is to convert hydraulic power into a linear mechanical force to perform work or transmit power.

There are many types of cylinders, each having its own advantages and typical uses. The general categories are ram, single acting, telescopic and double acting.

Ram

Perhaps the simplest single acting cylinder is the ram type. It has only one fluid chamber and exerts force in only one direction. Most are mounted vertically, as shown in Figure 7-1, and retract by the force of gravity on the load. Practical for long strokes, ram type cylinders are used in elevators, jacks and automobile hoists.

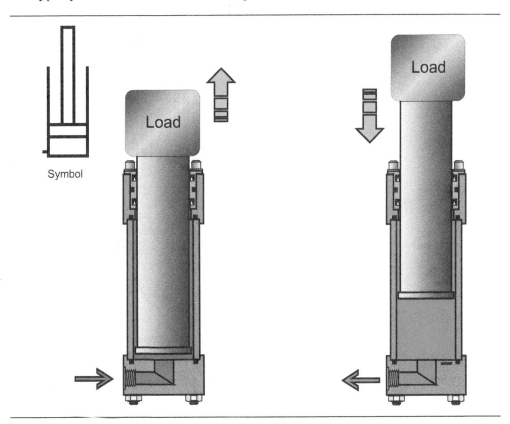

Figure 7-1   Ram cylinder

Single Acting Cylinder

Single acting cylinders operate much the same as rams. They apply a force in one direction, relying on gravity or a counter force to retract. The primary difference between a single acting cylinder and a ram is the single acting cylinder uses a piston, and leakage flow past the piston is ported to the reservoir to minimize external leakage.

Telescopic Cylinders

Telescopic cylinders are most commonly single acting. The telescoping cylinder is equipped with a series of nested tubular rod segments called sleeves. These sleeves work together to provide a longer working stroke than is possible with a standard cylinder. Up to four or five sleeves can be used. The maximum force can be exerted when the cylinder is collapsed. Because the successive cylinder sleeves have smaller diameters, each section has a smaller area and diminished volume. Therefore, the cylinder will increase speed as it is extended and be capable of less force at each stage.

Double acting telescoping cylinders, while not as common, are found in some applications when external forces will not retract the sleeves.

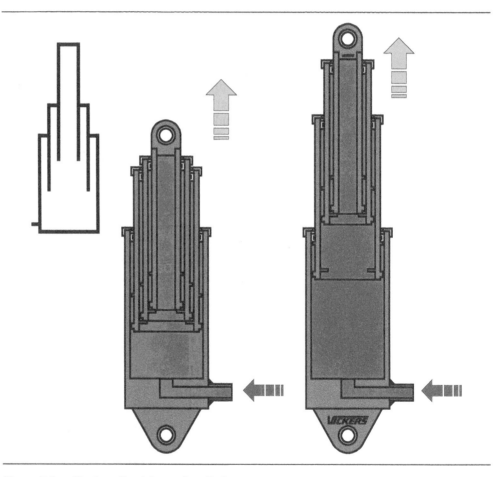

Figure 7-2 Single acting telescopic cylinder

Spring Return Cylinders

A spring return cylinder is also considered a single acting cylinder. Pressure applied to the cap end port compresses the spring as the rod extends. With pressure removed, the spring force retracts the rod. A drain is typically provided in the spring chamber to relieve leakage flow past the piston seal.

Double Acting Cylinders

The double acting cylinder is the most common type used in industrial hydraulics. Hydraulic pressure is applied to either port, providing powered motion when extending or retracting.

The majority of cylinders in use are basic double acting cylinders as shown in Figure 7-3. These cylinders are classed as differential cylinders because there are unequal areas exposed to pressure during the extend and retract movements.

The area of the rod, which reduces the working area of the piston during retraction, causes the difference.

A differential area cylinder will generate more output force during extension than during retraction. When the cylinder is extending, the system pressure will be applied to the full area of the piston, or the effective area; when the cylinder is retracting, the system pressure is only applied to the area of the piston that has not been reduced by the area of the rod, or the annulus area. The output force of a cylinder is equal to pressure multiplied by the working area of the piston. If the effective area is larger than the annulus area, the cylinder will generate more output force on the extension.

The velocity of the cylinder is also related to the working area of the piston. A differential cylinder will retract faster than it will extend if an equal amount of fluid is applied to the rod end, effective area, and the cap end, effective area.

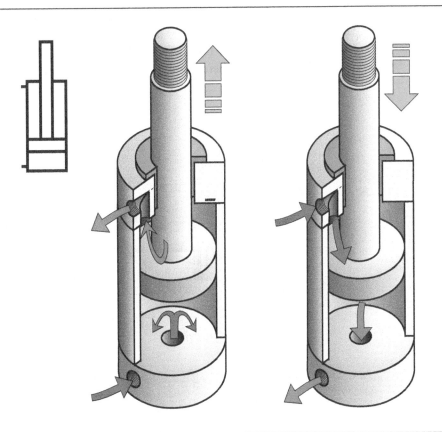

Figure 7-3   Basic double acting cylinder

A double rod cylinder (Figure 7-4) is an example of a nondifferential-type cylinder. There are identical areas on each side of the piston providing the rods are of equal diameter, and they can provide equal forces and speed in either direction. The double rod cylinder is primarily used where it is advantageous to couple a load to each end, or where equal velocities or force capability is required in both directions.

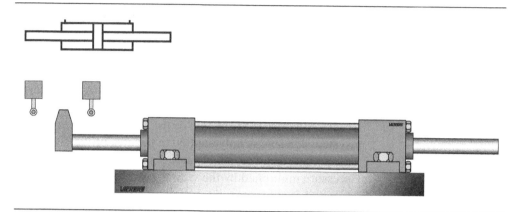

Figure 7-4   Double rod cylinder

By mounting two cylinder pistons in-line to form a tandem cylinder (Figure 7-5) with a common rod, higher forces can be developed with a given pressure and bore size. This cylinder arrangement is mentioned as an example of design flexibility. It is one of many possible techniques that can be considered when applying basic cylinder principles. These types of cylinders are useful for short stroke, high force requirements where there would be insufficient space for a larger diameter cylinder.

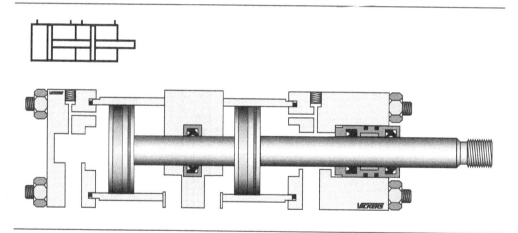

Figure 7-5   Tandem cylinder

Cylinder Construction and Operation

Figure 7-6 shows the cross section of a typical industrial hydraulic cylinder. The chrome plated steel piston rod and piston assembly is the moving part. A cushion collar and/or plunger may be added to the assembly when cushions are desired. The pressure containing assembly is constructed of a steel cap or blind end head, a steel body or barrel with honed finish, a rod end head and the rod bearing.

Tie rods and nuts are used to hold the two heads and body together. Static seals prevent leakage between the cylinder barrel and the heads. The bearing is commonly retained with a plate and screws for easy removal. A rod wiper is provided to keep foreign material from entering into the bearing and seal area. Air bleed valves are frequently added to help purge air from the cylinder.

Sealing of moving surfaces is provided by the rod seal, which prevents external fluid leakage along the rod, and piston seals, which prevent fluid from internally bypassing the piston.

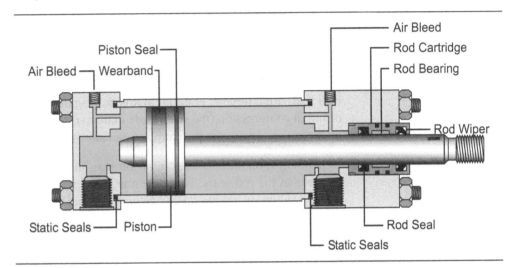

Figure 7-6   Typical cylinder construction

Sealing

Sealing around the piston rod must be done in two directions; the hydraulic fluid must be sealed within the cylinder, and foreign material must be sealed from entering the cylinder from the outside. These are usually two different seals (Figure 7-6), referred to as the "rod seal" and the "wiper seal," and may be replaced individually for service. Integrity of the rod seal is very important as leakage from this area of a cylinder is to the outside, causing loss of fluid to the system (Figure 7-7). The rod wiper sometimes serves the dual purpose of sealing in both directions.

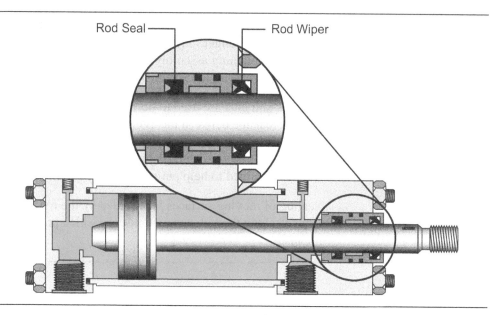

Figure 7-7   Rod seal and wiper design

Rod seals are a flexible material that is held against the rod surface by a combination of initial compression (the seal inside diameter is slightly smaller than the rod outside diameter) and hydraulic pressure acting against it.

Depending upon the application, piston seals may or may not require the same leakage integrity as the rod seals. There are many different designs and materials for piston seals, resulting in a wide range of durability and sealing integrity.

The most durable piston seal is made of cast iron, steel or chrome plated steel (Figure 7-8). An unfortunate characteristic of metal seal rings, however, is a tendency for greater leakage flow than other types. They remain popular due to their durability and their compatibility with high temperatures, and are very satisfactory in applications where a small piston seal leakage is of no concern.

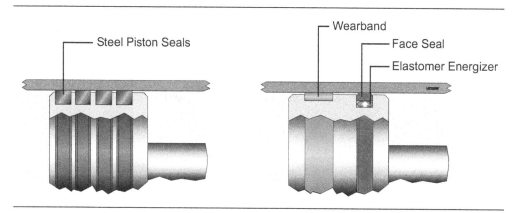

Figure 7-8   Metal sealing rings

U cup and V cup packings are frequently used as piston seals, and are very effective in preventing leakage flow. The seals are installed in sets, consisting of several U shaped or V shaped seals held in place by a gland so that the open face of the seals face the pressure side of the piston. This way, pressure forces the lip of the seal against the body wall, creating a tight seal as shown in Figure 7-9. In a double acting cylinder, two sets of packing are used, each set facing a pressure side of the piston.

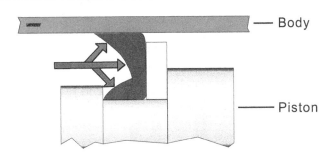

— Body

— Piston

Figure 7-9   Pressure tightens the seal to improve sealing

A "perfect" seal would be one that prevents all leakage. In practice, however, a minute amount of lubrication film must be present for the seal to slide easily over the mating surfaces. In most applications, a seal is considered effective if there is no obviously detected quantity of fluid passing it.

Cylinder Actuation

Fluid is routed to and from the cylinder through ports in each of the heads. The cylinder rod will retract with pressure to the rod end port and the other port connected to the reservoir. To extend the rod, fluid is directed to the cap end port and the rod end port is connected to the reservoir.

Cylinder Mounting

The main function of a cylinder mount is to provide a means of anchoring the cylinder. There are a variety of ways to mount the cylinder including the tie rod, bolt mount, flange, trunnion, side lug and side tapped, and clevis. The tie rod is the most common type of industrial mount. A variety of cylinder mounts are shown in Figure 7-10.

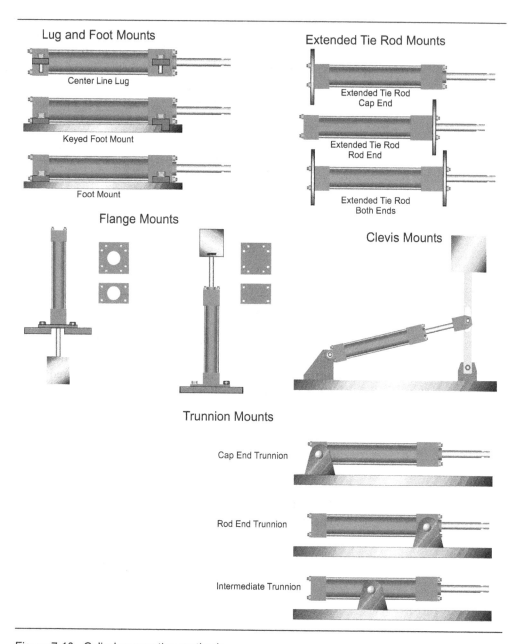

Figure 7-10   Cylinder mounting methods

Cylinder Ratings

The ratings of a cylinder include its size specifications and pressure capability. Principal size features are:

- Piston diameter (bore)
- Piston rod diameter
- Stroke length

The pressure rating is established by the manufacturer. Refer to the cylinder nameplate or the manufacturer's catalog for this information. In application, the maximum continuous pressure rating of a cylinder limits the maximum force capability of the cylinder and is a consideration in sizing for specific load or force requirements.

Cylinder speed, the output force available, and the pressure required for a given load are all dependent on the piston area when extending the rod. When retracting the rod, the effective area of the rod end of the cylinder must be used. This "effective area," or "annulus area," of the rod end is determined by subtracting the area of the rod from the piston area.

Formulas for Cylinder Applications

The following data on cylinder application were developed in Chapter 1:

To find the velocity (speed) of a cylinder when size and GPM (l/min) delivery are known, use the following formula:

Formula 7-1

$$\text{Speed (in/min)} = \text{GPM} \times \frac{231 \frac{\text{in}^3}{\text{Gal}}}{\text{Effective Piston Area (in}^2)}$$

To find the flow required for a given speed, use the following formula:

Formula 7-2

$$\text{Flow (Gal/min)} = \frac{\text{Effective Piston Area (in}^2) \times \text{Speed (in/min)}}{231 \frac{\text{in}^3}{\text{Gal}}}$$

To find the force output for a given pressure, use the following formula:

Formula 7-3

$$\text{Force (lbs)} = \text{Pressure (psi)} \times \text{Effective Piston Area (in}^2)$$

To find the pressure required to exert a given force, use the following formula:

Formula 7-4

$$\text{Pressure (psi)} = \frac{\text{Force (lbs)}}{\text{Effective Piston Area (in}^2)}$$

Table 7-1 is a summary of the effect on cylinder performance for changes in input flow, size and pressure on cylinder applications.

Change	Speed	Load Pressure	Max Force
Increase relief valve setting	No effect	No effect	Increase
Decrease relief valve setting	No effect	No effect	Decrease
Increase GPM	Increase	No effect	No effect
Decrease GPM	Decrease	No effect	No effect
Increase cylinder diameter	Decrease	Decrease	Increase
Decrease cylinder diameter	Increase	Increase	Decrease

Table 7-1   Summary of effects of application changes on cylinder performance

Table 7-2 lists piston areas, output forces and speeds for cylinders of various sizes. To use this table, select the columns and rows that contain the known information about the application and cylinder, and then pick out the remaining information. For example, if cylinder bore, rod diameter and system pressure are known, then other information such as potential extension and retraction forces, piston velocity and inlet flow rate can be determined. A complete chart appears in the Appendix C.

Cyl. Bore Dia. (Inch)	Piston Rod Dia. (Inch)	Work Area (Sq. In.)	Hydraulic Working Pressure (psi)						Fluid Required per In. of Stroke		Port Size Dia. (Inch)	Fluid Velocity @ 15 ft/sec	
			500	750	1000	1500	2000	3000	Gal.	Cu. In.		Flow (GPM)	Piston Vel. (in/sec)
1 1/2	–	1.767	883	1325	1767	2651	3534	5301	0.00765	1.767	1/2	11.0	24.0
	5/8	1.460	730	1095	1460	2190	2920	4380	0.00632	1.460			29.0
	1	0.982	491	736	982	1473	1964	2946	0.00425	0.982			43.1
2	–	3.141	1571	2356	3141	4711	6283	9423	0.01360	3.141	1/2	11.0	13.5
	1	2.356	1178	1767	2356	3534	4712	7068	0.01020	2.356			18.0
	1-3/8	1.656	828	1242	1656	2484	3312	4968	0.00717	1.656			25.6
2 1/2	–	4.909	2454	3682	4909	7363	9818	14727	0.02125	4.909	1/2	11.0	8.6
	1	4.124	2062	3093	4124	6186	8248	12372	0.01785	4.124			10.3
	1-3/8	3.424	1712	2568	3424	5136	6848	10272	0.01482	3.424			12.4
	1-3/4	2.504	1252	1878	2504	3756	5008	7512	0.01084	2.504			16.9
3 1/4	–	8.296	4148	6222	8296	12444	16592	24888	0.0359	8.296	3/4	20.3	9.4
	1-3/8	6.811	3405	5108	6811	10216	13622	20433	0.0295	6.811			11.5
	1-3/4	5.891	2945	4418	5891	8836	11782	17673	0.0255	5.891			13.3
	2	5.154	2577	3865	5154	7731	10308	15462	0.0223	5.154			15.2
4	–	12.566	6283	9425	12566	18849	25132	37698	0.0544	12.566	3/4	20.3	6.2
	1-3/4	10.161	5080	7621	10161	15241	20322	30483	0.0440	10.161			7.7
	2	9.424	4712	7068	9424	14136	18848	28272	0.0408	9.424			8.3
	2-1/2	7.657	3828	5743	7657	11485	15314	22971	0.0331	7.657			10.2

Table 7-2   Data for various size cylinders

Cylinder Features

In addition to the basic size and pressure rating, there are important options and features available for cylinders. The more important items are discussed below.

Seals

Cast iron piston rings are commonly used as the piston seal. Long service life is the important characteristic. However, when an external load acts on the cylinder, these rings also display a characteristic clearance flow that permits slow drifting with the control valve closed. Where such drifting cannot be tolerated, various other seal forms and materials are available. Rubber seals are common, but care must be taken to assure that the seal material is compatible with the fluid and the system temperatures.

Rod seals are most commonly made from rubber-like materials, though polymer (plastic) base materials such as Teflon, are gaining popularity. (Teflon is a DuPont trade name. There are other manufacturers of the same material with comparable performance.)

With few exceptions, a rod wiper or scraper is provided. The importance of this device should not be overlooked. It keeps foreign material from entering the cylinder and the hydraulic system. The materials must be compatible with not only the fluid, but also with the environment that the rod is exposed to such as ice, dirt, dust, steam, water, etc. Maintenance of the scraper/wiper device is important but frequently forgotten.

Cylinder Cushions

Cylinder cushions (Figure 7-11) are often installed at either or both ends of a cylinder to slow down the movement of the piston near the end of its stroke to prevent the piston from hammering against the end cap. The figure shows the basic elements: plunger, adjustable cushion orifice and a check valve. This cushion configuration is used when the cylinder is retracting.

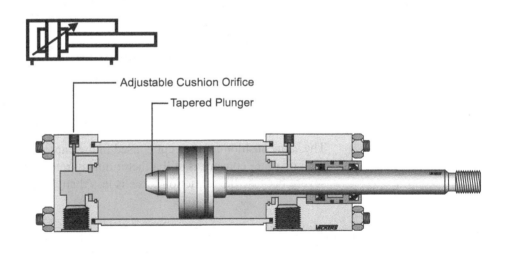

Figure 7-11   Cylinder with extension and retraction cushions

Figure 7-12 shows the rod end cushion operating when the cylinder rod is extending. In this situation, if the adjusting screw is closed it is possible to generate a pressure greater than the system relief setting. Assume 3,000 psi (210 bar, 21,000 kPa) is acting across the diameter of the 4 inch (10.2 cm) bore cylinder used as an example earlier in this section. To slow the motion, the resistive force must be greater than 37,698 lbs (167,688.99N). Because the area is smaller, due to the cushion plunger, the pressure will exceed 3,000 psi (210 bar, 21,000 kPa). Assume the plunger diameter is 2-1/2 inches (6.4 cm). The pressure developed would be 4,920 psi (340 bar, 34,000 kPa). This value would be even larger with a heavy weight attached to the piston rod. Closing of the cushion adjustment screw should be done with care.

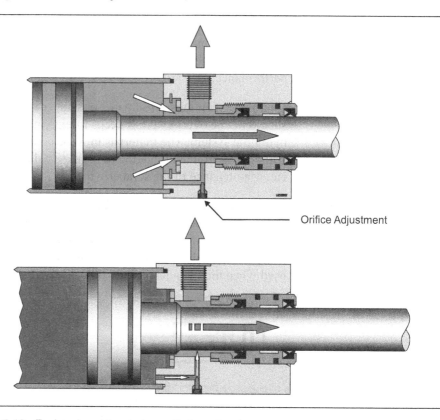

Orifice Adjustment

Figure 7-12   Rod end cushion during cylinder extension

The same cushioning concept is used in the cap end during cylinder retraction. The high pressure concern is still a factor during retraction, although it would not be as severe because the retraction force is less than the extension force.

Stop Tubes

A stop tube (Figure 7-13) is usually a metal collar which fits over the piston rod next to the piston. It is used primarily on cylinders with a long stroke. The main function of the tube is to separate the piston and rod bushing when a long stroke cylinder is fully extended, providing better side load support for the cylinder rod. The majority of hydraulic applications do not require a stop tube. If a stop tube is necessary, it should be mentioned in the manufacturer's catalog.

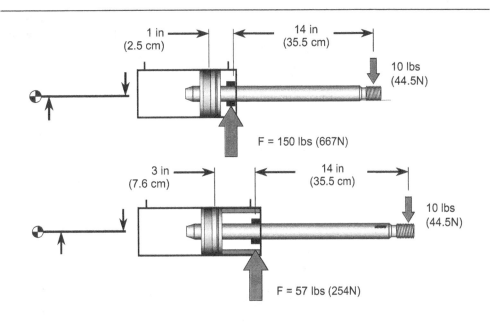

Figure 7-13   A stop tube provides better cylinder rod support

Tie Rod Spacers

Tie rod spacers and center supports are used to improve the structural rigidity of long stroke tie rod cylinders. The spacer (Figure 7-14) keeps the tie rod in the proper position around the center line of the cylinder and acts much like a truss in preventing excessive deflection.

Figure 7-14 also shows a tie rod center support. This support has side mounting lugs similar to side lug mount heads and serves as an additional mounting location. The tie rods are studded into the center support and the support becomes a load carrying component of the cylinder assembly. The exact location of the tie rod center support is generally optional, which greatly increases the flexibility in mounting a long stroke cylinder.

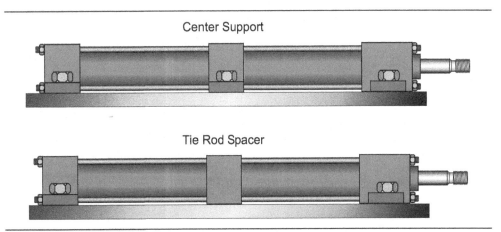

Figure 7-14   Tie rod spacer and center support

Ports

A port is an internal or external opening in a cylinder or valve designed to allow the passing of fluid into or out of the component. Cylinder manufacturers offer a variety of port types and configurations for connection to customer hydraulic systems. Straight thread O-ring fittings are strongly recommended to provide the best probability for a leak-free connection. When the connection of tubing or hose to a port is poorly installed or not fitted properly, it can be a major cause of system leakage.

Bleed Ports

Usually cylinders will bleed themselves of air when ports are vertical, on top. Bleed ports are often desirable to remove entrained air, for example, when the cylinder is installed with the ports on the bottom. High performance and high speed heavy load applications are a few examples where air bleed ports are desirable.

Limit Switches

End of travel limit switches (Figure 7-15) are available that signal rod position to a control circuit or a safety circuit. There are two common types: mechanical and proximity limit switches. Mechanical actuation of an electrical switch is accomplished when the switch is activated by the lead angle on a hardened cylinder cushion. Proximity switches are activated when a metal cushion passes close to the magnetic pickup of the switch. This proximity type is becoming increasingly popular due to its simplicity.

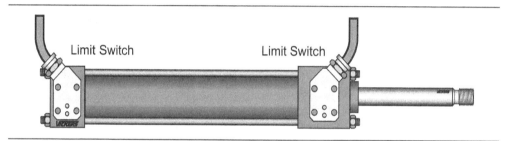

Figure 7-15   Cylinder with limit switches

Cylinder Installation and Troubleshooting

Cylinder application design is a procedure that should be handled by hydraulic engineers, and installation should be handled by seasoned hydraulic technicians. If any problems develop during the installation phase, a hydraulic expert should be consulted.

Proper installation and maintenance is crucial to all hydraulic components in order to achieve maximum efficiency. Recognizing and controlling potential problem areas is the purpose of troubleshooting.

Summary

Hydraulic cylinders are among the simplest of devices in fluid power, having one moving part; the piston and rod assembly. However, forces generated by cylinders are also among the largest found in fluid power systems. Pressures in the cylinders can, and often do, exceed system relief settings. The life of the cylinder and the system can be highly dependent on proper specification and maintenance of a simple element, the rod wiper/scraper.

Like all system components, the cylinder can be damaged by contamination. Contaminants are not as readily flushed out as with rotary devices. General cleanliness practices, such as plugging ports until lines are connected, are important.

Care in alignment at installation is essential to assure minimal loading of bearings and seals.

How the cylinder is used in a system has much to do with its life expectancy and performance. Sudden operation of closed center valves can generate extremely high pressures. Excessive back pressures, due to speed control valves, can cause rapid seal wear. Although cylinders may be simple in design, their proper use requires a consideration of many factors.

Hydraulic Motors

Just as linear actuators convert fluid power to linear motion, rotary actuators convert fluid power to rotary motion. Fluid is pushed into the inlet of the rotary actuator and causes the output shaft to rotate. Resistance to rotation by an external load creates pressure in the hydraulic circuit and in the inlet of the rotary actuator.

Hydraulic motor is the name usually given to a rotary actuator. Motors very closely resemble pumps in construction. Instead of pushing on the fluid as the pump does, they are pushed by the fluid and develop torque and continuous rotating motion as output members in the hydraulic system.

All hydraulic motors have several factors in common. Each type must have a surface area acted upon by a pressure differential. This surface is rectangular in gear and vane motors, and circular in radial and axial piston motors. The surface area in each kind of motor is mechanically connected to an output shaft from which the mechanical energy is delivered. Finally, the porting of the pressure fluid to the pressure surface must be timed in each type of hydraulic motor in order to sustain continuous rotation.

The maximum performance of a motor in terms of pressure, flow, torque output, speed, efficiency, expected life and physical configuration is determined by the:

- Pressure capability of internal and external components
- Internal leakage characteristics
- Efficiency of force and power transmittal

Motor Ratings

Hydraulic motors are rated according to displacement (size), torque capability, speed, and maximum pressure limitations.

Displacement

Displacement is the amount of fluid required to turn the motor output shaft one revolution. Figure 7-16 shows that displacement is equal to the fluid capacity of one motor chamber multiplied by the number of chambers the motor contains. Motor displacement is expressed in cubic inches per revolution (in³/rev) or cubic centimeters per revolution (cm³/rev), and is usually referred to as CIR (cubic inches per revolution), CID (cubic inches displacement) or CCR (cubic centimeters per revolution.

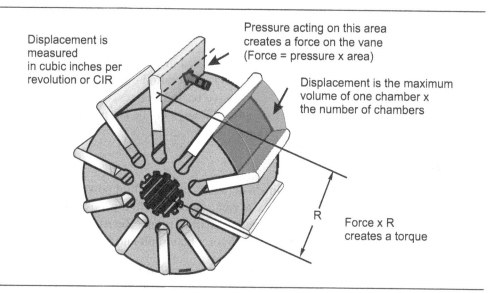

Displacement is measured in cubic inches per revolution or CIR

Pressure acting on this area creates a force on the vane (Force = pressure x area)

Displacement is the maximum volume of one chamber x the number of chambers

R

Force x R creates a torque

Figure 7-16   Displacement is the quantity of fluid that effects one shaft revolution

Displacement of hydraulic motors may be fixed or variable. With input flow and operating pressure constant, the fixed displacement motor provides constant torque and constant speed. Under the same conditions, the variable displacement motor provides variable torque and variable speed.

Torque

Torque is the rotational force component of the motor's output. It is a turning or twisting effort by the output shaft. Motion is not required to have torque, but if the torque is sufficient to overcome any resistance to it, rotary motion will result.

Figure 7-17 illustrates typical torque requirements for raising a load with a pulley. Note that the torque is always present at the drive shaft, but is equal to the load multiplied by the radius. A given load will impose less torque on the shaft if the radius is decreased. However, the larger radius will move the load faster for a given shaft speed.

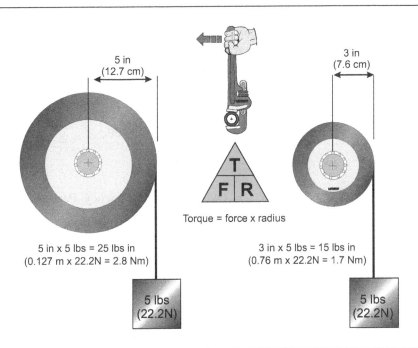

Figure 7-17   Torque equals load multiplied by radius

Torque output of a motor is expressed in pound inches or pound feet (newton-meters), and is a function of system pressure and motor displacement. Motor torque figures are usually given for a specific pressure differential, or pressure drop across the motor. Theoretical figures indicate the torque available at the motor shaft if the motor operated at 100 percent efficiency.

Starting Torque

Friction is the resistance to relative motion between two materials in contact with each other. Static friction is the friction between two materials that have no relative motion, and dynamic friction is the friction between two materials that are moving relative to each other. Because static friction is always higher than dynamic friction, the pressure required to start a hydraulic motor from rest is greater than that required to keep the motor in motion. Starting torque is an important characteristic of hydraulic motors, because it indicates the maximum torque available to begin motion when a mechanism is at rest.

Running torque involves dynamic friction, and is therefore a lower value than starting torque. When sizing a motor for an application, both starting and running torque capability must be taken into consideration. One of the distinct advantages of hydraulic motors is that their running torque is constant at any given pressure throughout most of the speed range. The torque/pressure relationship changes only when the running speed becomes very low, and internal friction begins to approach that of starting torque.

Efficiency

Hydraulic motors have two characteristics that prevent them from delivering all of their torque and speed: internal friction and internal leakage. The effect of internal friction causes a torque loss, and is expressed as a mechanical efficiency of the motor. Internal leakage causes a speed loss, and is expressed as a volumetric efficiency. The product of mechanical efficiency and volumetric efficiency is the overall efficiency.

Formula 7-5

$$\text{Eff}_{oa} = \frac{\text{Eff}_v}{100} \times \frac{\text{Eff}_{mech}}{100} \times 100$$

Where:

Eff_{oa} = Overall Motor Efficiency, Percent

Eff_v = Volumetric Efficiency, Percent

Eff_{mech} = Mechanical Efficiency, Percent

Speed

Motor speed is a function of motor displacement and the volume of fluid delivered to the motor. Maximum motor speed is the speed at a specific inlet pressure which the motor can sustain for an adequate period of time without damage. Minimum motor speed is the slowest, continuous, smooth rotational speed of the motor output shaft. Slippage is the leakage across the motor, or the fluid that moves through the motor without doing any work.

Pressure

Pressure required in a hydraulic motor depends on the torque load and the displacement. A large displacement motor will develop a given torque with less pressure than a smaller unit. Motors will have a maximum pressure rating, which is the highest inlet pressure (and, therefore, the highest torque load) the motor can continuously withstand for an adequate period of time without damage. The size and torque rating of a motor usually is expressed in pound inches of torque per 100 psi of pressure (newton meters per bar).

Formulas for Motor Applications

Listed below are formulas used for applying hydraulic motors and determining flow, pressure and horsepower requirements.

To determine theoretical torque available from a motor with known displacement:

Formula 7-6

$$T = \frac{P_{in} \times \text{Displacement}}{2\pi}$$

Where:

T = Theoretical motor output torque, lb-in

P_{in} = Inlet pressure, psi

Displacement = CIR

As Figure 7-18 shows, this same formula can be used to determine the pressure required to attain a desired torque:

$$P_{in} = \frac{T \times 2\pi}{\text{Displacement}}$$

To find torque rate, use the following:

$$\text{Torque Rate (lb-in/100 psi)} = \frac{\text{Torque Load (lb-in)}}{\text{Desired Operating psi} \times 0.01}$$

The output speed of a rotary actuator is dependent upon flow rate of the fluid into the actuator. The following formula is used to determine the theoretical speed, in RPM, of a hydraulic motor with a known inlet flow:

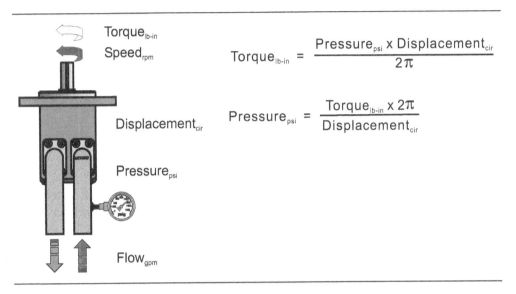

$$\text{Torque}_{\text{lb-in}} = \frac{\text{Pressure}_{\text{psi}} \times \text{Displacement}_{\text{cir}}}{2\pi}$$

$$\text{Pressure}_{\text{psi}} = \frac{\text{Torque}_{\text{lb-in}} \times 2\pi}{\text{Displacement}_{\text{cir}}}$$

Figure 7-18   Hydraulic motor torque formula

Formula 7-7

$$\text{RPM} = \frac{Q \times 231}{\text{Displacement}}$$

Where:

RPM = Motor Output Speed, RPM

RPM = Input Flow, GPM

Displacement = CIR

As Figure 7-19 illustrates, this formula can also be used to determine the theoretical flow required to achieve a desired output speed:

$$Q = \frac{\text{RPM} \times \text{Displacement}}{231}$$

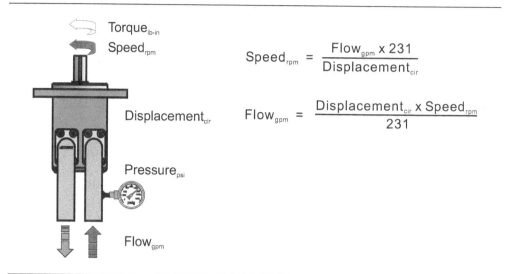

Figure 7-19   Hydraulic motor speed formula

Output horsepower of a hydraulic motor is based on both the torque and the speed. A high speed motor operating at a low torque level may have the same horsepower output as a motor operating at high torque and low speed.

The determination of output horsepower of a hydraulic motor comes from the following formula:

Formula 7-8

$$hp_{out} = \frac{T_{lb\text{-}in} \times RPM}{63,025}$$

Where:

hp_{out} = Motor output horsepower, hp

$T_{lb\text{-}in}$ = Output torque, lb-in

RPM = Output speed, RPM

Figure 7-20 illustrates that if motor output torque is measured in pound-feet instead of pound-inches, the formula becomes;

$$hp_{out} = \frac{T_{lb\text{-}ft} \times RPM}{5,252}$$

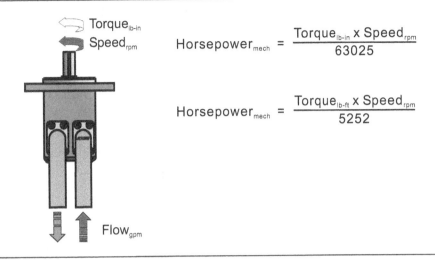

$$\text{Horsepower}_{mech} = \frac{\text{Torque}_{lb\text{-}in} \times \text{Speed}_{rpm}}{63025}$$

$$\text{Horsepower}_{mech} = \frac{\text{Torque}_{lb\text{-}ft} \times \text{Speed}_{rpm}}{5252}$$

Figure 7-20 Hydraulic motor horsepower formula

Efficiency Calculations

To determine the volumetric efficiency of a motor is to compare the actual output speed to the theoretical output speed.

Formula 7-9

$$\text{Eff}_v = \frac{\text{RPM}_{act}}{\text{RPM}_{theo}} \times 100$$

Where:

Eff_v = Volumetric Efficiency, Percent

RPM_{act} = Actual motor output speed, RPM

RPM_{theo} = Theoretical motor output speed, RPM

Theoretical motor speed is the RPM calculated from the displacement and input flow as described above.

To determine the mechanical efficiency of a motor, the following formula can be used.

Formula 7-10

$$\text{Eff}_{mech} = \frac{\text{T}_{act}}{\text{T}_{theo}} \times 100$$

Where:

Eff_{mech} = Mechanical Efficiency, Percent

T_{act} = Actual Output Torque, lb-in or lb-ft

T_{theo} = Theoretical Output Torque, lb-in or lb-ft

Theoretical output torque is the lb-in or lb-ft calculated by knowing the displacement and operating pressure, as described earlier.

The overall efficiency can be determined by multiplying the volumetric efficiency by the mechanical efficiency as described earlier, or by the following formula:

Formula 7-11

$$Eff_{oa} = \frac{hp_{out} \times 100}{hp_{in}}$$

Where:

Eff_{oa} = Overall Motor Efficiency, Percent

hp_{out} = Output Motor Horsepower, hp

hp_{in} = Input Motor Horsepower, hp

Change	Speed	Load Pressure	Max Torque
Increase relief valve setting	No effect	No effect	Increase
Decrease relief valve setting	No effect	No effect	Decrease
Increase GPM	Increase	No effect	No effect
Decrease GPM	Decrease	No effect	No effect
Increase displacement CIR	Decrease	Decrease	Increase
Decrease displacement CIR	Increase	Increase	Decrease
Note: Table assumes constant workload			

Table 7-3 Summary of effects of application changes on motor operations

Table 7-3 summarizes the effects on speed, pressure and torque capacity for changes in motor applications. Note that the basic principles are identical to Table 7-1 on cylinders.

Classes of Hydraulic Motors

Hydraulic motors can be classified by application into three categories:

- High Speed, Low Torque Motors (HSLT)
- Low Speed, High Torque Motors (LSHT)
- Limited Rotation Motors (Torque Actuators)

HSLT Motors

In many applications, the motor operates continuously at relatively high RPM. Examples are fan drives, generator drives and compressor drives. While the speed is high and reasonably constant, the load may be either steady, as in fan drives, or quite variable, as in compressors or generators. HSLT motors are excellent for these kinds of applications. The four primary types of HSLT motors are in-line piston, bent-axis piston, vane and gear.

LSHT Motors

In some applications, the motor must move a relatively heavy load at lower speeds and fairly constant torque. A motor for a crane is one such application. LSHT motors are often used for performing this type of work. Some LSHT motors operate smoothly down to one or two RPM. LSHT motors are simple in design with a minimum of working parts and are quite reliable and generally less expensive than higher speed motors employing speed reducing devices.

Ideally, an LSHT motor should have high starting and stall torque efficiencies, and good volumetric and mechanical efficiencies. They should start smoothly under full load and provide full torque over their entire speed range. These motors should exhibit little or no torque ripple throughout their speed range, and velocity variation at an average speed at constant pressure should be minimal.

Basic LSHT motor designs include: internal gear, vane, rolling vane and radial piston.

Limited Rotation Motors

Modifications of the rotary motor are sometimes found in industrial machinery where special motions are required. One is the limited rotation motor which will not permit continuous rotation in either direction. The vane type version has a movable vane which forms two chambers in an annulus. Pressure exerted against either side of the vane causes it to rotate and turn the rotor and output shaft. Rotation is limited to less than 360 degrees by the width of the body segment containing inlet and outlet porting. Another version of the limited rotation motor is the piston type which converts the linear motion of a cylinder into rotary motion through a crank arm.

Types of Hydraulic Motors

There are a variety of hydraulic motors used in industrial applications. The type of motor used depends on the demands and operating criteria of each individual application. The following motors are reviewed in this chapter:

Gear Motors — external and internal (gerotor and rolator or orbital) motors

Vane Motors — unbalanced, balanced, fixed, variable and cartridge (high performance) types

Piston Motors — in-line, bent-axis, and radial motors (fixed, variable and cam type)

Torque Generators — vane and piston types

Gear Motors

There are two types of gear motors: external gear and internal gear motors.

External Gear Motors

External gear motors consist of a pair of matched gears enclosed in one housing (Figure 7-21). Both gears have the same tooth form and are driven by fluid under pressure. One gear is connected to an output shaft, the other is an idler.

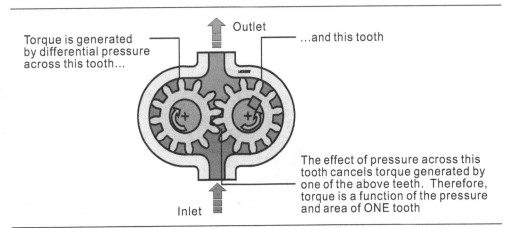

Figure 7-21   Torque generation in an external gear motor

Fluid pressure enters the housing on one side at a point where the gears mesh and forces the gears to rotate, as fluid at high pressure follows the path of least resistance around the periphery of the housing (gray). The fluid exits, at low pressure, at the opposite side of the motor.

Note that torque developed is a function of hydraulic imbalance of only one tooth of one gear at a time: the other gear and teeth are hydraulically balanced.

Close tolerances between gears and housing help control fluid leakage and increase volumetric efficiency. Wear plates on the sides of the gears keep the gears from moving axially and also help control leakage.

Internal Gear Motors

Internal gear motors fall into two categories; direct drive gerotor and orbiting gerotor motors. A direct drive gerotor motor consists of an inner outer gear set, and an output shaft as shown in Figure 7-22. The inner gear has one less tooth than the outer. The shape of the teeth is such that all teeth of both gears are in contact at all times. When pressure fluid is introduced into the motor, both gears rotate. Stationary kidney shaped inlet and outlet ports are built into the motor housing.

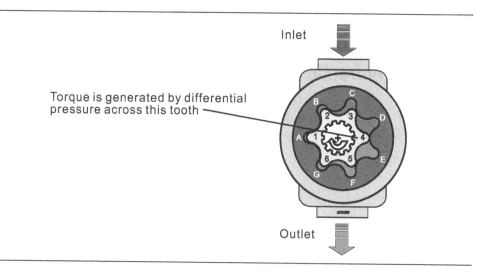

Figure 7-22   Cross section of direct drive gerotor motor

The centers of rotation of the two gears are separated by a given amount called the eccentricity. The center point of the inner gear coincides with the center point of the output shaft. As shown in view A of Figure 7-23, pressure fluid enters the motor through the inlet port. Because the inner gear has one less tooth than the outer, a pocket is formed between inner teeth 4 and 5, and outer socket E. The inlet port is designed so that just as this pocket volume reaches its maximum, fluid inlet is shut off, with the tips of inner gear teeth 4 and 5 providing a seal (view B of Figure 7-23).

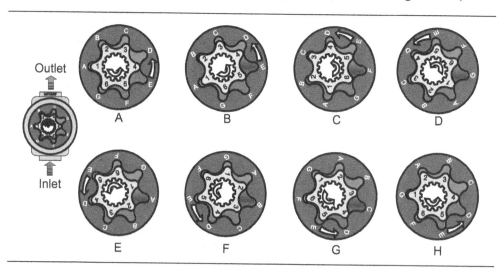

Figure 7-23   Sequence of direct drive gerotor motor

As the pair of inner and outer gears continue to rotate, as shown in view C of Figure 7-23, a new pocket is formed between inner teeth 5 and 6, and outer socket F. Meanwhile, the pocket formed between inner teeth 4 and 5 and outer socket E has moved around opposite the outlet port, steadily draining as the volume of the pocket decreases. The gradual, metered volume change of the pockets during fill and exhaust provides smooth, uniform fluid flow with a minimum of pressure variation (ripple).

Because of the one extra tooth in the outer gear, the inner gear teeth move ahead of the outer by one tooth per revolution. In view A of Figure 7-23, inner tooth 1 is seated in outer socket A. In View H, which is the completion of one cycle, inner tooth 1 is seated in outer socket G, one tooth away from the starting point. This action produces a low relative differential speed between the two gears.

Reversing the fluid flow rotates the motor output shaft in the opposite direction. In this example a 6 tooth inner gear and a 7 tooth outer gear configuration is used. Other combinations of number of teeth can be used, but the outer gear must always have one more tooth than the inner.

An orbiting gerotor motor consists of a set of matched gears, a drive coupling, an output shaft, and a commutator valve plate or valve body (Figure 7-24). The stationary outer gear has one more tooth than the rotating inner gear or rotor. The drive coupling has splines on both ends which match mating splines in the rotor and the shaft, and transmits motion between them. The commutator, which turns at the same rate as the inner gear, always provides pressure fluid and a passage to tank to the proper areas of the spaces between the two gears.

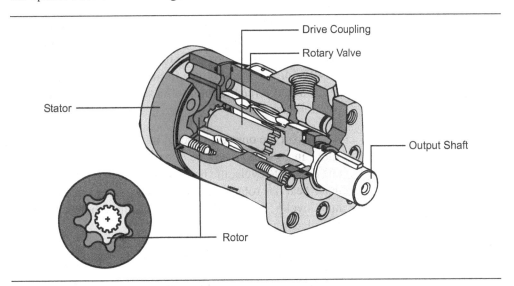

Figure 7-24   An orbiting gerotor motor

As shown in view 1 of Figure 7-25, the tooth of the inner gear with a red "dot" is aligned exactly in socket F of the outer gear. The "+" marks the center of the stationary (outer) gear, and offset to the center of the rotating (inner) gear.

When pressure fluid flows into the lower, left quadrant between the inner and outer gears, the inner gear is forced to the right, as fluid in the lower right quadrant is ported to exhaust. As this gear moves to the right, it rotates about socket F and settles into a new position, with a tooth now aligned exactly with socket G, illustrated in view 2 of Figure 7-25.

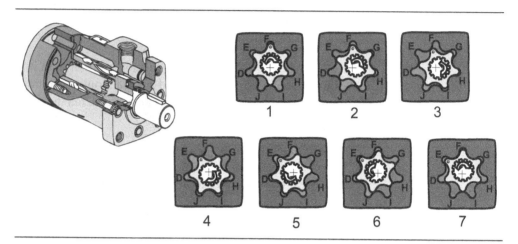

Figure 7-25 Sequence of an orbiting gerotor motor

However, as rotation continues, the inner gear is orbiting clockwise, while it is rotating counterclockwise. As each succeeding tooth of the rotor seats in its socket, the tooth directly opposite on the rotor from the seated tooth always becomes the seal between pressure and return fluid (view 2 of Figure 7-25). The pressurized fluid continues to force the rotor to mesh in a clockwise direction while it turns counterclockwise.

Because of the one extra socket in the fixed gear, the next time the red "dot" tooth aligns in a socket, it will be in socket E (view 6 of Figure 7-5). View 7 shows that after one complete cycle, the next tooth of the internal gear is aligned with socket F, and the inner gear has rotated an angle of 60 degrees from its starting point in view 1. Five more cycles, for a total of six, are required before the inner gear, and shaft, make a complete revolution.

Reversing flow reverses the direction of rotation of the motor shaft.

A Geroler® motor (Figure 7-26) is a variation of the orbiting gerotor motor. Instead of direct contact between the stator and rotor, rollers are incorporated into the displacement chambers. The rollers reduce wear and friction, enabling the motors to be used in higher pressure applications with greater mechanical efficiency.

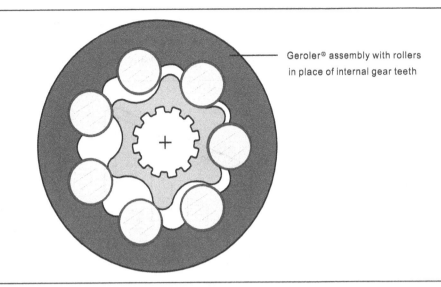

Figure 7-26   Geroler® gerotor motor

Vane Motors

A cross-sectional view of a balanced vane rotating group is shown in Figure 7-27. The elements shown in the view are the cam (or cam ring), rotor and vanes. The output shaft of the motor is connected to the center of the rotor. The vanes slide in and out of the slots in the rotor so as to make contact with the cam surface.

Fluid entering the motor will pressurize two opposite sides of the rotor assembly, and return fluid will exit two opposite sides. This way, equal pressures are always opposite each other, balancing forces across the rotor. This relieves any loading on the drive shaft and bearings caused by internal pressures and forces. Although originally pioneered by Harry Vickers in the mid 1930s, all fixed displacement vane pumps and motors today are of the balanced design.

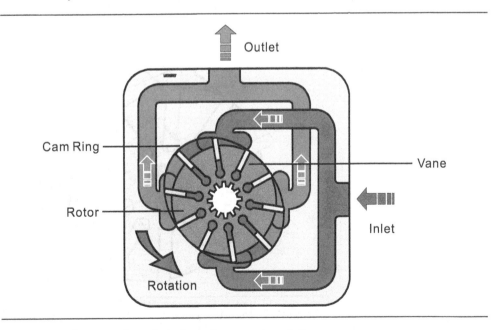

Figure 7-27   Cross section of a balanced vane motor rotating group

A form of spring, either a spring clip or a small coil spring, is placed under the vane to cause it to stay against the cam surface (Figure 7-28). Inlet fluid is also ported under the vanes so as to balance the pressure between the top, and bottom and prevent pressure from pushing the vane back into the slot.

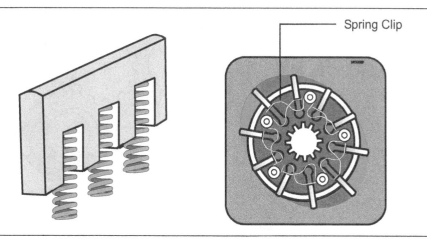

Spring Clip

Figure 7-28   Springs or spring clips keep the vanes against the cam

Figure 7-29 shows how the differential pressure across a vane will create a force on the vane. The amount of vane that is exposed to pressure will determine the magnitude of the force (force equals pressure times area), and the distance from the center of the exposed vane area to the center of the drive shaft will determine the torque that is generated. Therefore, the torque output of a vane motor is dependent upon pressure, size of the vane (height extending above the rotor and width) and radius of the rotor (distance from the centerline of the drive shaft).

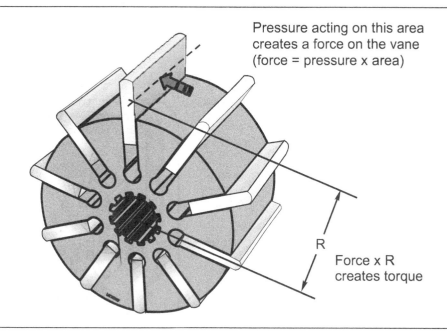

Pressure acting on this area creates a force on the vane (force = pressure x area)

R

Force x R creates torque

Figure 7-29   Pressure acting on a vane creates torque on the drive shaft

The high performance vane motor has significant changes in construction from earlier designs. The entire assembly of ring, rotor, vanes and side plates is removable and replaceable as a unit (Figure 7-30). In fact, preassembled and tested "cartridges" are available for field replacement. These motors also are reversible by reversing flow to and from the ports.

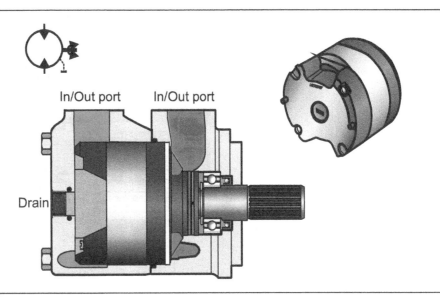

Figure 7-30   High performance vane motor cartridge design

Piston Motors

There are a variety of piston motor designs currently available. The demands of each industrial application determine the correct selection of a piston motor type. Information on the in-line piston motor, radial piston motor, and the bent-axis piston motor is covered in this section.

Piston motors are generally the most efficient of the three types of hydraulic motors to be discussed, and are usually capable of the highest speeds and pressures. For aerospace applications in particular, they are used because of their high power to weight ratio. In-line motor designs, because of their comparatively simple construction and resultant lower cost, are generally preferred for the lower torque, higher speed applications such as machine tools. Radial piston motors are preferred for the higher torque, lower speed applications such as extrusion and rolling.

All three types of motors are available as fixed displacement or variable displacement designs. Both designs will be covered in this section.

In-Line Piston Motors

Piston motors generate torque through pressure on the ends of reciprocating pistons operating in a cylinder block. The motor drive shaft and cylinder block are centered on the same axis in the in-line design (Figure 7-31). Pressure at the piston ends causes a reaction against a swash plate, driving the cylinder block and motor shaft in rotation. Torque is proportional to the area of the pistons and is a function of the angle at which the swash plate is positioned.

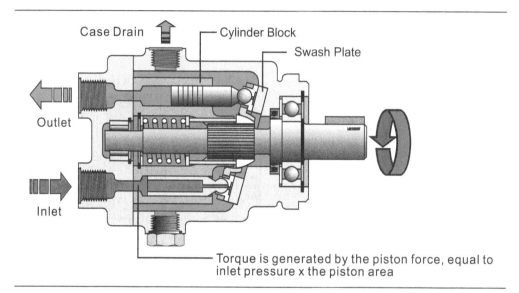

Case Drain — Cylinder Block

Swash Plate

Outlet

Inlet

Torque is generated by the piston force, equal to inlet pressure x the piston area

Figure 7-31   Fixed displacement in-line piston motor

The drive shaft speed is also dependent on the swash plate angle, as well as the flow into the motor. Torque and speed are an inverse relationship to each other; a larger swash plate angle will provide greater torque at a given pressure, but a lower shaft RPM. At the same inlet flow and pressure, a lower swash plate angle will provide a lower output torque, and a higher shaft speed. Figure 7-32 illustrates this concept.

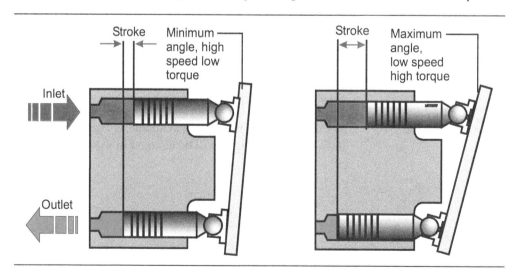

Stroke   Minimum angle, high speed low torque

Inlet

Outlet

Stroke   Maximum angle, low speed high torque

Figure 7-32   Swash plate angle determines the torque and speed relationship

The variable displacement in-line piston motor is shown in Figure 7-33. The swash plate is mounted on a pivoting swash plate, and the angle can be changed by various means ranging from a simple lever or handwheel to sophisticated hydraulic or servo controls. A basic hydraulic compensator control is illustrated in Figure 7-33. As pressure rises to a predetermined setting of the compensator, the compensator spool will shift and allow fluid into the control piston. This will cause the yoke to rotate toward maximum displacement, increasing torque and reducing output speed. When the pressure reduces, the yoke will return to its low torque/high speed configuration. Minimum angle stops are usually provided so that torque and speed stay within operating limits.

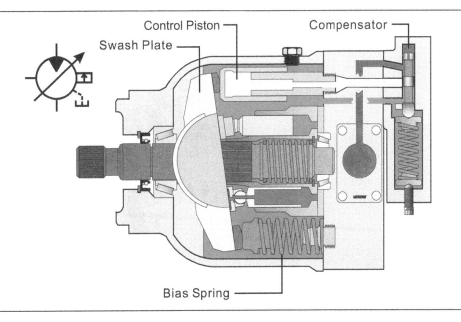

Figure 7-33   Variable displacement in-line piston motor

Radial Piston Motors

A cross-sectioned illustration of a radial piston motor is shown in Figure 7-34. Major components are the cylinders, the pistons, the connecting rods, the crankshaft drum and output shaft. Not shown in the drawing is a rotating valve connected to the output shaft on the reverse side of the motor.

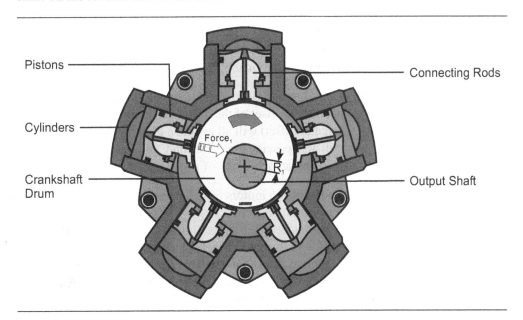

Figure 7-34   Radial piston motor

Fluid enters the motor through the rotary valve, which ports it to the pistons. The force created by the area of the piston under fluid pressure, acting against the offset of the eccentric crankshaft drum, creates a rotation of the output shaft as the piston extends in its bore. As the shaft revolves, it rotates the rotary valve, porting fluid into successive pistons and maintaining a continuous rotary motion. Returning fluid exhausted from retracting pistons is ported through the valve and to the reservoir (Figure 7-35).

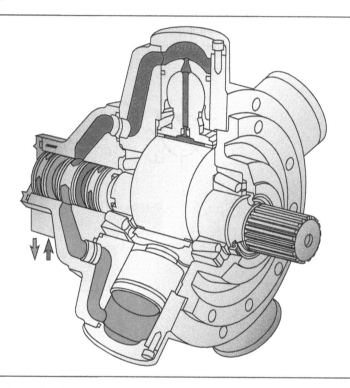

Figure 7-35 Inlet and outlet porting in a radial piston motor

The pressurized fluid also travels through a small orifice in the center of the piston and connecting rod to the surface area between the connecting rod and drum. This surface area is fairly large so that the fluid not only acts as a lubricant, but also reduces contact forces between the mating parts.

As shown in the figure, two or three pistons are pressurized at the same time. This prevents any "dead spots" caused by a single piston being at top dead center, assuring a smooth rotational output.

Output torque is determined by the force of the piston against the drum and by the amount of offset of the drum. Higher pressures, larger pistons and a larger drum (greater offset) will all lead to a higher output torque level. A larger number of pistons will also provide greater torque, and this is accomplished on some very large motors by using a double row of pistons.

Radial piston motors can change their displacement by changing the eccentricity of the drum on the crankshaft. This is done by inserting two pistons, one small and one large, inside the drum as shown in Figure 7-36. The small piston keeps the drum shifted to its maximum displacement, and the large piston shifts the drum to obtain minimum displacement. This shifting can be done while the motor is in motion, and creates a very smooth change in displacement. An outside pilot pressure is applied to provide the shifting force.

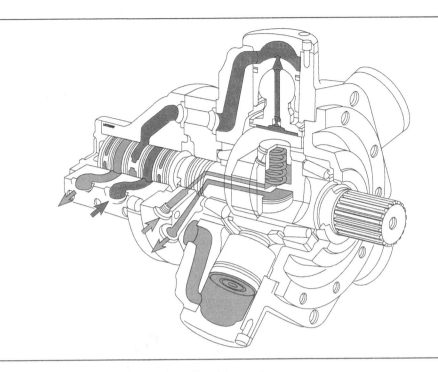

Figure 7-36   Variable displacement radial piston motor

Bent-Axis Piston Motors

A cross-sectioned view of a bent-axis piston motor is shown in Figure 7-37. The main elements are a cylinder block, pistons and shoes, drive shaft and flange, a universal link and a valve plate. The piston shoes are lodged in the drive shaft flange, and the universal link maintains alignment between the cylinder block and the drive shaft so that they turn together.

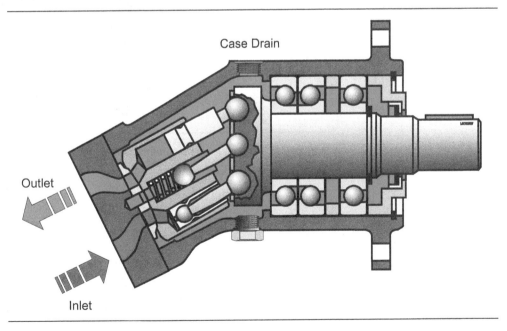

Figure 7-37   Bent-axis piston motor

As fluid is forced through the valve plate into the cylinder block, pistons are forced out of the cylinder block, forcing the drive shaft flange to rotate. This causes the drive shaft to rotate along with the cylinder block and pistons. Pistons are forced back into the cylinder block by the drive shaft flange, and fluid is forced out through the valve plate and back to the reservoir. The entire operation is much the same as the in-line piston motor, except that the cylinder block and piston assembly is angled instead of a swash plate.

The amount of torque that a motor will deliver is based on the force of the piston (pressure times the piston cross-sectional area), the radius of the drive shaft flange (force times distance) and the angle of the cylinder block. The higher the cylinder block angle, the greater the torque output for any given pressure and piston size.

Varying the displacement of a bent-axis piston motor is similar to that of an in-line model, except that instead of moving a yoke to alter the swash plate angle, the cylinder block/piston assembly is moved to alter the angle between the cylinder block and the drive shaft flange (Figure 7-38).

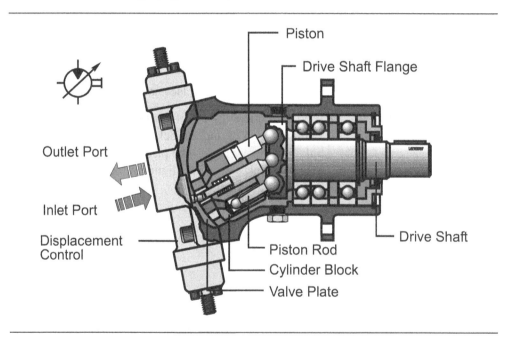

Figure 7-38   Variable displacement bent-axis piston motor

Limited Rotation Actuator

A limited rotation actuator, sometimes called an oscillator, is a form of hydraulic motor designed to rotate less than a full revolution. They are very convenient for use in welding and machining fixtures, for example, where they can clamp, rotate, feed, oscillate, lift, transfer or hold tension. A vane type oscillator is illustrated in Figure 7-39.

In the model shown, the vanes are sealed in a cylindrical chamber and oscillate between stops integral with the housing. To rotate the actuator, a differential pressure is applied across the vanes. The chamber itself has inlet and outlet ports, one on each side of a partition or barrier that seals the chamber into two sections. With this arrangement, it is possible to have output shaft rotary movements of up to about 280 degrees.

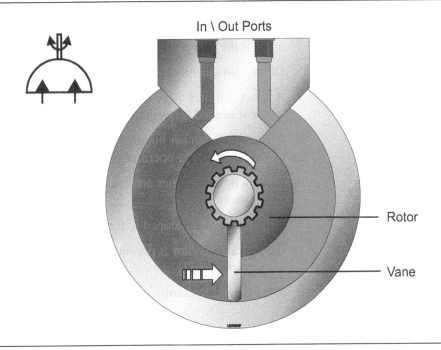

Figure 7-39   Limited rotation actuator

Industrial Test Questions:
Hydraulic Actuators

Chapter 7

1. Describe the operating characteristics of single and double acting cylinders.

2. With an actual delivery of 3 GPM to the head end of a two-inch diameter cylinder, what is the speed of rod travel?

3. A three-inch (7.6 cm) diameter ram can operate up to 2,000 psi (140 bar, 14,000 kPa). What is the maximum output force? In pounds? In newtons?

4. How much pressure is required for a force output of 14,000 pounds (62,275N) if the effective piston area of the cylinder is 7 square inches (45 square centimeters)?

5. What is the primary function of a hydraulic cylinder?

6. Define displacement and torque ratings of a hydraulic motor.

7. A winch requires 50 pound-feet maximum torque to operate. What size hydraulic motor is needed if maximum pressure must be limited to 1,500 psi?

8. A 20 pound inch per hundred psi motor operates with a torque load of 500 pound-inches. What is the operating pressure?

9. Explain how the vanes are held in contact with the cam ring in high performance vane motors.

10. How is torque developed in the in-line type piston motor?

11. If a hydraulic motor is pressure-compensated, what is the effect of an increase in the working load?

12. What type of hydraulic motor is generally most efficient?

Chapter 8 .... Directional Valves

As the name implies, directional valves control the direction of fluid flow in a hydraulic circuit. They also bypass, start, stop, sequence and interlock actuator movement. Although they share this common function, directional valves vary considerably in construction and operation. They are classified according to principal characteristics such as those listed below.

Type of internal valving element — Fluid direction can be controlled by a poppet (piston or ball), rotary spool or sliding spool.

Methods of actuation — Directional valves can be actuated by manual, mechanical, pneumatic, hydraulic or electrical means, or a combination of these.

Number of flow paths — Directional valves can be two-way, three-way or four-way. Eaton references the total number of available flow paths. A four-way, i.e: four flow path, three-position directional control valve is illustrated in Figure 8-1. Some manufacturers may refer to the number of active ports rather than the number of active flow paths. In any case, the graphic symbology reflects the function of the component rather than the construction, and will enhance understanding of the components' effect in a hydraulic circuit.

Three-Position Valve

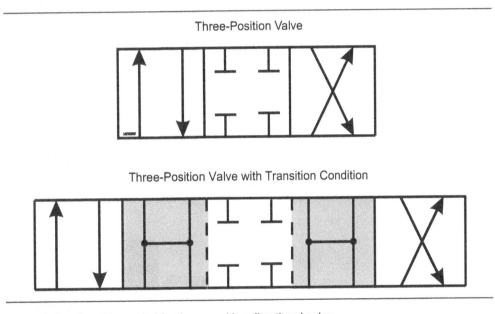

Three-Position Valve with Transition Condition

Figure 8-1   Graphic symbol for three-position directional valve

Size — Valve size may refer to the nominal size of port or flange connections to the valve or its mounting plate, rated GPM (l/min), or with reference to a standard mounting pattern.

Connections — Directional valves may have straight thread, flanged, subplate or manifold, or pipe thread connections. Pipe threads are strongly discouraged due to leakage potential.

This chapter discusses finite positioning directional control valves. These valves direct the fluid by opening and closing flow paths in discrete valve spool positions. For each finite position, the graphic symbol for a directional valve contains a separate envelope or square that shows the flow paths or other port conditions in that position. When needed, this symbol may also indicate transition (crossover) conditions (Figure 8-1) that indicate what happens to the flow path(s) while the valving element is shifting from one finite position to another. Although not typically shown on machine circuit prints, this transition condition can be extremely important relative to acceptable component function, life expectancy, and safety issues.

One example of the importance of the transition condition is the presence of a "hanging" or dynamic load that creates pressure in the system. If a directional valve spool is configured for open crossover, that is all ports are open to tank during shifting, load-created pressure would be released along with a small amount of fluid and the load could fall during the valve shift. This action could cause shock resulting in damage to components and also poses a safety issue. Unless other load-holding designs are incorporated into the circuit, transition for this type of dynamic load should be controlled by a closed crossover spool.

An example of diametrically opposed configuration, that is the open crossover as opposed to closed crossover, would be in the typical use of pressure-compensated pumps. While it is generally accepted that most circuits using compensated pumps have finite closed center conditions, the crossover is typically better suited to an open crossover to prevent the pump trying to compensate every time the valve is shifted. This is particularly true in high cycle operations where a closed crossover would subject the compensated pump to continual high shock and pressure spikes with each valve shift.

Check Valves

In its simplest form, a check valve is a one-way directional valve. It allows free flow in one direction, while blocking flow in the other direction. The graphic symbol for a check valve is a ball and seat (Figure 8-2). A light spring, usually equivalent to 5 psi (0.34 bar, 34 kPa), holds the poppet in the normally closed position. Other spring pressures are available to suit specific application requirements such as providing pilot pressure. In the free flow direction, the poppet cracks open at a pressure equivalent to the spring rating, allowing fluid to pass through the valve.

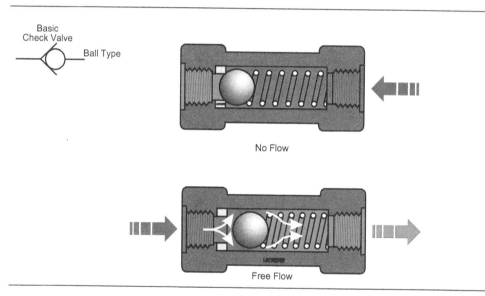

Figure 8-2   A check valve is a one-way valve: ball type is shown

In-Line Check Valves

To allow fluid to flow straight through the valve, an in-line check valve (Figure 8-3) is installed directly in the hydraulic line, preferably with a straight thread connection. The valves are available in a range of flows, up to approximately 100 GPM (380 l/min). One of their design drawbacks is as the flow through the valve increases, the pressure drop through the valve also increases because of the fixed size of the restriction created by the poppet in the fluid flow path.

In-line check valves are not only used for blocking flow, but also as a safety bypass for flow surges through filters and heat exchangers. With a higher spring rating, an in-line check valve can be used as a means of generating pilot pressure.

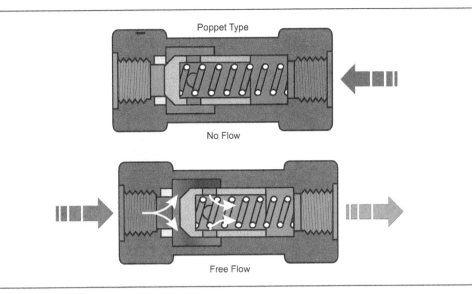

Figure 8-3   In-line poppet-type check valve operation

Right Angle Check Valves

Right angle check valves (Figure 8-4) are designed with the inlet and outlet ports at right angles to each other. This design allows for higher flows with lower pressure drop since the poppet is pushed out of the fluid flow path.

To improve cycle life, these valves generally have hardened steel seats and poppets. This type of valve is available with threaded ports and flanged connections. They are available in flows up to approximately 300 GPM (1,100 l/min).

All types of check valves should be properly maintained to prevent leaks past the ball or piston and seat when loaded. Leaks will create heat as well as cause undesirable movement of actuators, bypass of filter elements, and safety issues where load holding or circuit isolation is a primary function of the check valve.

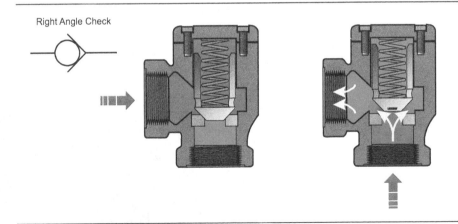

Figure 8-4   Typical right angle check valve

Restriction Check Valves

A restriction or orifice check valve (Figure 8-5), is a variation of a right angle check valve. An orifice plug is placed in the poppet to permit a restricted flow through the valve in the normally closed position. These valves are typically used in controlling the rate of decompression in a large press or other high compression volume application before shifting the main valve. This reduces pressure induced shock in a system caused by high flow rates from high volumes of fluid under pressure. This is important to achieve stability and longer component life.

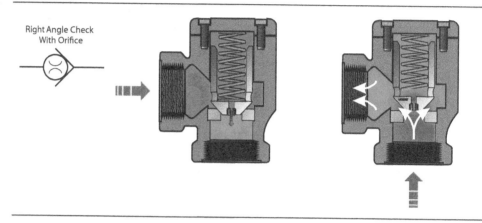

Figure 8-5   Restriction check valve operation

Pilot-Operated Check Valves

The check valves discussed to this point have been direct-operated check valves; that is, they are opened by fluid acting directly against the main poppet or element against the resistive force of a spring. Pilot-operated check valves are acted upon both directly and by a pilot signal, though not necessarily for the same purpose. The two basic types of pilot-operated check valves are pilot-to-open and pilot-to-close.

Pilot-to-Open. Similar to the direct-acting check valve, a pilot-to-open check valve is designed to permit free flow in one direction and prevent flow in the reverse direction. The difference is that reverse free flow is permitted when a pilot pressure signal is applied to the pilot port against the pilot piston (Figure 8-6). These valves have very low internal leakage and are typically used to lock a cylinder in place until the main directional valve shifts.

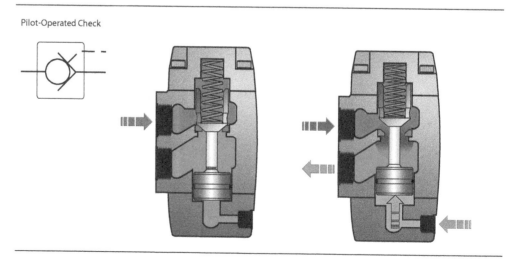

Figure 8-6   Pilot-to-open check valve

Ratios. One of the criteria to consider when applying a pilot-to-open check valve is pilot area and cylinder ratios. The ratio between the pilot pressure area and the main (check) poppet area must be greater than the ratio between the cylinder piston area and the cylinder annulus area. If it is not, the valve will not open. For example, if the cylinder being used has a piston-to-annulus area ratio of 2:1, then the check valve must have a ratio greater than the cylinder (i.e.: 3:1).

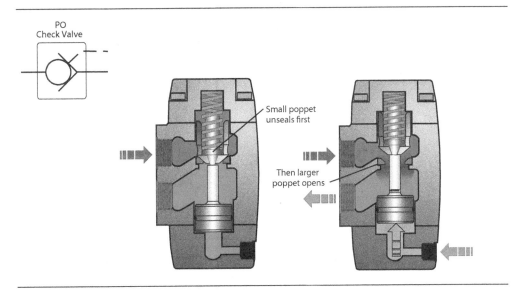

Figure 8-7   Operation of pilot-operated check valve with decompression poppet

With large pilot-operated check valves or with large differential area cylinders, this ratio is sometimes difficult to achieve. For those cases, a pressure breaker or decompression type of pilot-operated check valve (Figure 8-7) can be used. It is designed with a two-stage main decompression poppet that is much smaller than the pilot piston and can have an opening ratio of 12:1 or greater. This poppet opens first, reducing the pressure behind the main poppet that is holding it closed. When the pressure behind the main poppet is low enough, the pilot piston pushes the main poppet into the open position. It is also necessary to consider the dynamic action of loads acting on vertical cylinders and load-induced pressures that may affect the ratio and pilot pressure required to open the check in the reverse free flow condition. Proper circuit design and application of these valves is critical. It must also be remembered that once the valve opens to allow reverse free flow, the load may fall, causing the valve to close again stopping the load from moving. In this case, it may be necessary to incorporate other types of load control components to prevent the load from falling ahead of pump output. Some of these options for load control are discussed in Pressure Controls (counterbalance valves) and Flow Controls (meter-out circuits).

Pilot-to-Close. Less common is the pilot-to-close check valve. It is designed to permit flow in the free-flow direction until a pilot pressure signal is applied to an auxiliary port (Figure 8-8).

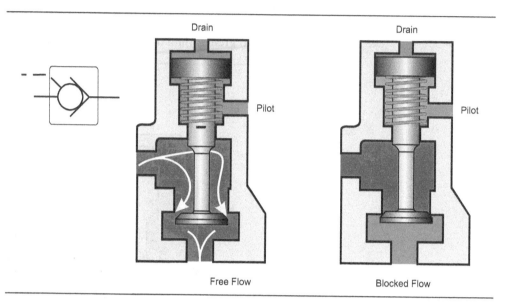

Figure 8-8   Pilot-to-close check valve operation

Figure 8-9 illustrates a common use for a pilot-to-close check valve in an accumulator discharge circuit. While the system is running, system pressure sensed near the pump outlet keeps the check valve closed for normal operation and use of the accumulator. Note that a simple check valve is virtually always used to isolate the accumulator from the pump.

When the machine is stopped and pressure is no longer available at the pump outlet, the check valve opens to allow safe, automatic discharge of the accumulator. This, or some other type of automatic accumulator discharge is essential for maintenance and repair personnel safety when working on machines with accumulators present. Accumulators that must be manually discharged are a serious safety issue.

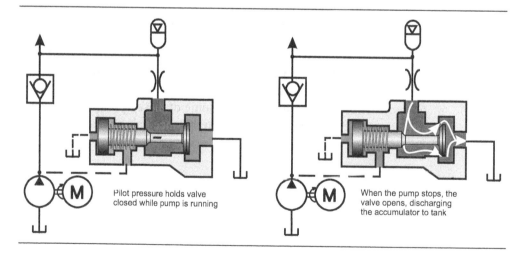

Figure 8-9   Automatic accumulator discharge circuit

Mounting Styles

A variety of mounting styles are available for check valves. They can be line mounted with straight thread ports, pipe thread ports or flanged connections. Subplate or manifold mounted versions are available, along with a cartridge design that screws directly into a block or manifold. Finally, sandwich or modular designs can be stacked between a four-way type valve and the subplate.

Two-Way, Three-Way and Four-Way

The basic function of directional valves is to connect or disconnect two or more ports by shifting or rotating a spool. The number of active ports through which fluid can flow determines if it is a two-way, three-way or four-way valve. The ports of a two-way valve are normally considered "inlet" and "outlet." The ports of a three-way valve are usually labeled "P" (for pressure), "A" and "B." A and B designate the two alternative paths through which the fluid can be directed. The ports of a four-way valve are usually labeled "P," "A," "B" and "T," where T designates the return (or tank) port.

A two-way valve creates or blocks a path between two active ports by shifting or rotating a spool. In one position, the inlet and outlet ports are connected, and in the other position the path between the two ports is blocked.

Three-way valves have spool configurations that permit flow from the pressure port to either port A or port B (Figure 8-10). In one position, the pressure port is connected to port A while port B is blocked. In the other position, the pressure port is connected to port B, while port A is blocked.

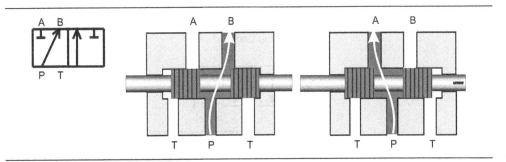

Figure 8-10   Two-position, three-way spool valve

A four-way valve selects alternate ports just like the three-way valve, but the tank port is used for return flow from the opposite port (Figure 8-11). In one position, the pressure port is connected to port A while port B is connected to T. In the other position, the pressure port is connected to port B while port A is connected to T. A four-way valve can be used to move an actuator in either direction.

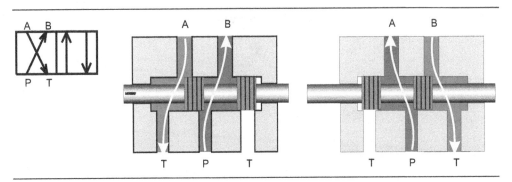

Figure 8-11   Two-position, four-way spool type valve

Spool Positions

Directional valves are designated as having two or more "positions," which refers to the number of specific operating locations the spool can be moved into. Most valves are two- or three-position valves, each position providing a distinct set of operating conditions. Two-way valves are also two-position valves. Three-way and four-way valves can be either two- or three-position valves.

Most four-way valves are available with various spool conditions in each position. Graphical reference to these conditions typically shows the valve in its neutral, or de-energized, condition. To relate valve function relative to actuation, the operator sequence, spool movement, and porting changes must be considered. The following are helpful aids in correctly interpreting the graphic symbols of flow direction (spool position) in directional control valves:

1. The flow direction(s) will be as indicated in the graphic symbol adjacent to the actuating method (solenoid, manual, cam, etc.) symbol.

2. The directional valve symbol usually indicates the de-energized, spool not shifted condition. It is the state that the valve would be in if it were in the shipping box, not installed in the circuit.

For example, for the four-way, two-position valve represented by the graphic symbol in Figure 8-12, P is normally ported to A and B is ported to T. When the solenoid is energized (or the manual override button is pressed) P is ported to B and A is ported to T.

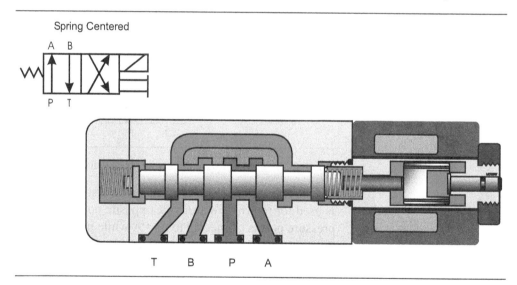

Figure 8-12   Four-way, two-position valve

Spring Centered

Spring centered valves are two- or three-position valves returned to the center position by spring force whenever the actuating force is released. A three-position, spring centered valve has two actuators (except in the case of manually or mechanically actuated valves).

It is wise to keep in mind that the porting condition of the valve relative to a "center" condition relates to the description used for the valve symbol and its function (Figure 8-12 and Figure 8-13). The center condition relates to specific porting conditions discussed further on in this chapter.

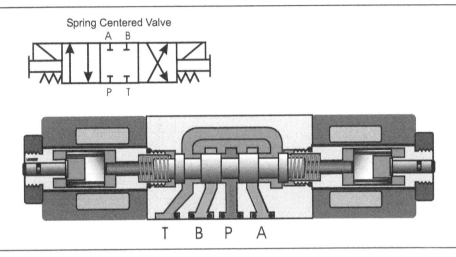

Figure 8-13   Spring centered valve is a three-position valve

Two-Position, Spring Offset

This type of valve (Figure 8-14) is normally offset to one extreme position by a spring. It has one actuator that shifts the spool to the other extreme position. The crossover condition of the spool may also be shown in the valve symbol.

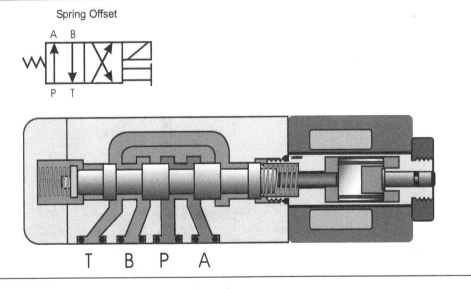

Figure 8-14   Two-position, four-way valve is spring offset

Three-Position, Detented

Similar to the three-position, spring centered valves, this valve also has two actuators. The spool is held by a detent mechanism in one extreme position until shifted by the actuator. This valve will stay in the detented position even after the actuating force is released, in this case a lever. The detent itself is a mechanical device and must be properly maintained.

Wear on the detent pin, spring, or teeth could allow forces within the valve or machine vibration to shift the valve causing a safety hazard and machine or part damage (Figure 8-15).

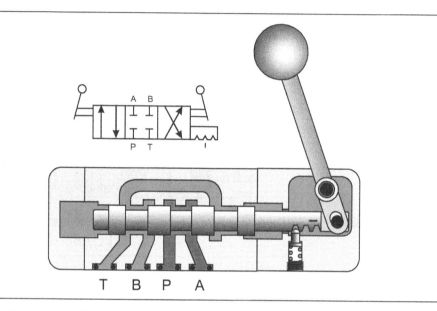

Figure 8-15   Three-position, four-way detented valve

Spool Center Conditions

Most of the standard four-way spools provide the same flow paths when the valve is shifted. However, various center conditions are available to provide specific porting when the valve is shifted to "center" (Figure 8-16).

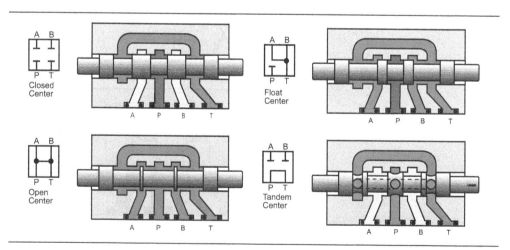

Figure 8-16   Four-way valve center conditions

An open center interconnects all of the ports to tank so that pressure is removed from the circuit, and pump flow goes to the reservoir at low pressure. The closed center spool has all ports blocked from tank. Flow is blocked at all four ports, allowing the pump flow to be used for other operations within the circuit or to be directed over the relief valve. The tandem center spool blocks flow from the cylinder ports while allowing the pump flow to be directed to the tank at low pressure, reducing energy consumption. The tandem center spool can also be used in series circuits. Another common spool has a float center condition. Pressure is maintained on the pressure port while the cylinder ports are open to tank. It is commonly used in circuits that have a pilot-operated check valve. It is also used in the pilot valve of two-stage valves.

Various other spool configurations are available for special circuit requirements. These configurations differ not only because the center condition changes, but also because the shifted conditions change. In addition, it must be remembered that not all spools are symmetrical. When servicing a valve, reversal of a non-symmetrical spool into a valve body will cause machine malfunction. Because of wear-in of valves that have been in service for some time, even the reversal of symmetrical spools could cause excess leakage or binding.

In most cases, the center condition selection of spools is dependent on the application requirements of the machine and the requirements of specific components affected by the center condition. Fixed or variable (pressure-compensated) pumps, cylinder or motor drift, load holding, and many other factors of system dynamics rely on the proper center condition of directional control valve spools. Proper circuit analysis and knowledge of component operation must be considered when selecting spool center conditions as well as transition or crossover.

Direct Acting Valves

What is typically called an operator or actuator shifts the spool or rotating element of a direct acting directional valve. The five categories of actuators (operators) are: manual, mechanical, pneumatic, hydraulic and electrical. Very often specific sub categories are included within these overall categories, e.g.: levers, foot pedals are "manual" operators while a cam roller device would be considered a "mechanical" actuator.

Manual Actuator

A manual actuator is usually a simple lever connected to the spool through some kind of linkage (Figure 8-17). There are also some foot operated valves, but they are generally considered unsafe in today's workplace. While lever operated valves are still quite common in mobile applications, the requirements of repeatability, accuracy and electronic control have eliminated this type of actuation in all but the simplest industrial machinery.

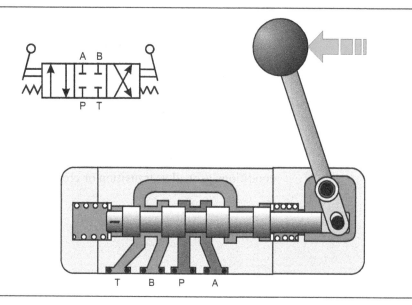

Figure 8-17   Manually (lever) actuated, three-position, four-way valve with spring centering

Mechanical Actuator

Mechanical actuators are either wheel or plunger type devices, as shown in Figure 8-18. When moved by some mechanical device such as a cylinder or cam, mechanical actuators cause the spool to move.

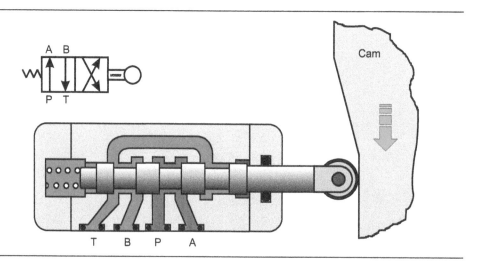

Figure 8-18   Mechanically actuated (cam roller) four-way valve

Pneumatic Actuator

A pneumatic actuator uses air pressure applied to a piston to shift the valve spool (Figure 8-19). The parts in this type of actuator are usually made of aluminum or other non-corrosive material so that moisture in the air lines will not cause the parts to rust and stick. Typically, a small hole in the actuator housing allows accumulated moisture to drain out.

Because air pressure can be quite low, the actuator piston must be relatively large to overcome spring and flow forces. Sealing areas and materials must be properly maintained to prevent aeration of the hydraulic system past the pilot piston(s).

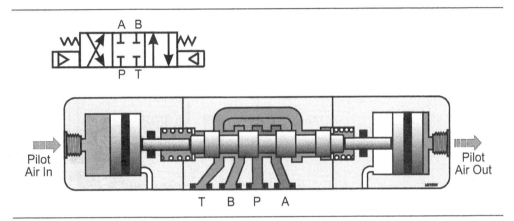

Figure 8-19   Pneumatically actuated four-way valve

Hydraulic Actuator

Hydraulic actuators, like the one shown in Figure 8-20, use pilot oil flow and pressure for shifting the valve spool. The pilot flow and pressure that controls these actuators is often controlled by an additional, typically direct-mounted, directional valve (pilot valve). Hence, these hydraulically operated valves are often called two-stage valves, consisting of the pilot stage and the hydraulically actuated main stage.

While the pilot valve could utilize any type of actuation, it is most often a solenoid-operated valve. This allows the advantages of electrical control of hydraulic circuits where flow requirements are greater than typical single-stage, solenoid-operated valves can handle.

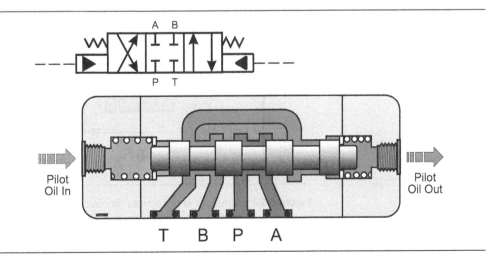

Figure 8-20   Hydraulically actuated, pilot-operated valve

Electrical Actuator

Electrical actuators are commonly called solenoids. The solenoids discussed in this chapter are known as "on-off" solenoids because, upon receiving an electrical signal, the solenoid is either fully shifted or turned off. Proportional valves have unique solenoid characteristics and differ greatly from these "on-off" solenoids.

A solenoid is made up of two basic parts: a coil and an armature. Applying electricity to the coil creates a magnetic field that attracts the armature into it. The armature pushes on the spool, or a small rod called a pushpin, as it is pulled into the magnetic field (Figures 8-21 and 8-22). This causes the spool to shift against a spring at the opposite end of the valve body.

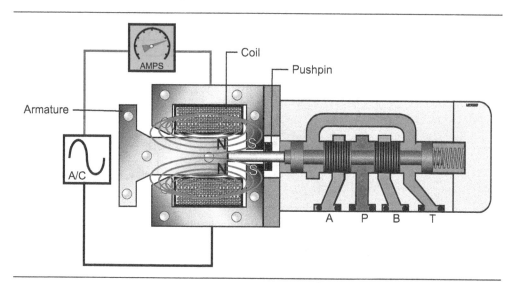

Figure 8-21   Push-type solenoids commonly used to shift spools of small valves

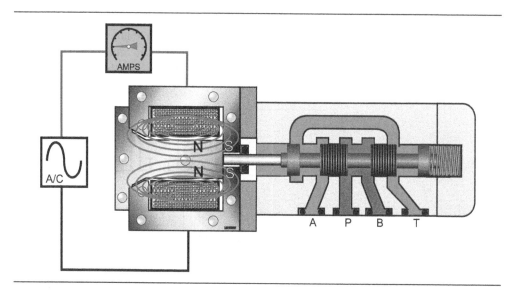

Figure 8-22   Armature is pulled into electromagnetic force of the solenoid, shifting the valve spool

The two-solenoid designs used today are the air gap and wet armature types. In the air gap design (Figure 8-23), air space separates the solenoid from the hydraulic system. To prevent hydraulic fluid leakage, the pushpin is sealed from the valve by a dynamic seal.

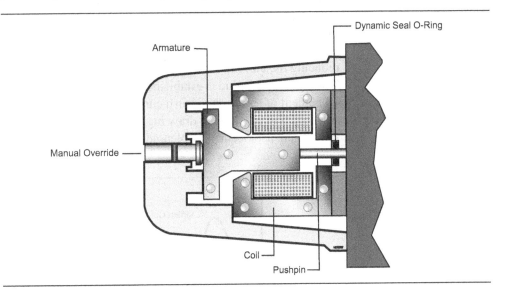

Figure 8-23   Air gap solenoid design

One of the problems of the air gap solenoid is that the dynamic seal eventually wears and starts to leak. In the wet armature design, all of the solenoid's moving parts operate in the system's hydraulic fluid, eliminating the need for a dynamic seal. An encapsulated coil surrounds a core tube that retains the armature and system fluid. Only two seals are used: a static seal where the core tube is screwed into the valve body and a static seal at the manual override pin that only acts dynamically when the manual override is pushed (Figure 8-24). Care should be taken to prevent damage to this seal when using the manual override for machine setup or troubleshooting. Sharp or oversized instruments can damage the seal and create an external leak past the pin seal.

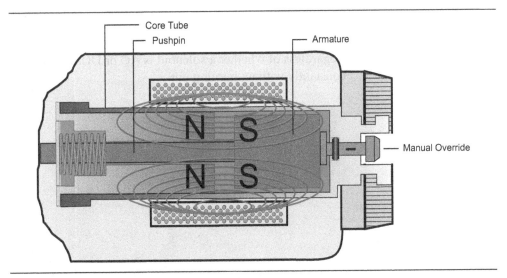

Figure 8-24   Wet armature solenoid design

Another advantage of the wet armature design is that the fluid acts as a cushion for the spool, pushpin, and armature. Although these advantages mean that a wet armature solenoid operates more quietly and usually has a longer life, it requires about 1.6 times more electrical power than the air gap type.

AC/DC Solenoids

Solenoids can be designed to operate on either alternating current (AC) or direct current (DC). The designs are slightly different, but the operating principle is the same.

When energized, an AC solenoid has a high current draw at the beginning of the stroke (inrush current) and a lower draw at the end of the stroke (holding current). Figures 8-21 and 8-22 illustrate this characteristic with ammeters. This is because the armature itself becomes part of the resistance of the solenoid as it is pulled into the coil, reducing the current. Once the armature has moved completely into the coil, the lower holding current value is established (see Figure 8-25). Holding current is typically 10 percent or less of the inrush current. If the armature cannot complete a shift, the solenoid will continue to draw high current, and will eventually burn out. Solenoid failure can also occur if a solenoid is energized and de-energized at very high cycle rates.

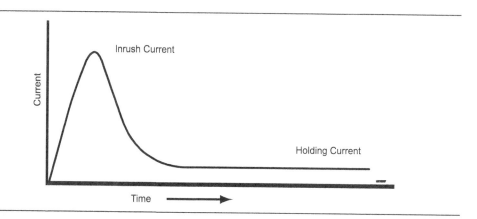

Figure 8-25   Inrush and holding current of energized coil

DC solenoids draw a constant current when energized and are designed to handle high, continuous current. This design avoids burnout as a result of incomplete shifting or high cycle rates since they have no inrush characteristics, but the shift times are slower than that of AC solenoids. DC solenoids are generally safer than AC solenoids because they operate at much lower voltages. DC solenoids are found more often in mobile applications than in industrial ones.

Regardless of whether a solenoid is AC or DC, it is designed to be held energized constantly without burning out.

Two-Stage Valves

Using the flexibility and power of hydraulics, two-stage valves can control large volumes of fluid at high pressures. A direct-acting solenoid valve, used in the same capacity, would be very large and require a great amount of electricity with unacceptable heat generation.

Two-stage valves consist of a pilot-operated main stage and a pilot stage that is usually either electrically or pneumatically operated. They are often referred to as either solenoid-controlled, pilot-operated or pneumatically controlled, pilot-operated valves. When the pilot valve is shifted, it directs fluid at pressure to one end or the other of the main spool while connecting the opposite end of the main spool to the reservoir.

The amount of pressure required to shift the main spool is usually 75 to 100 psi (5 to 7 bar, 500 to 700 kPa), but this varies depending upon the spool configuration, hydraulic spool forces, and the strength of the centering spring which must be overcome to shift the spool. The pilot pressure may be supplied through an internal passage connected to the pressure port inside the valve or from an external source via the "X" port tapped in the bottom of the main stage valve (Figure 8-26).

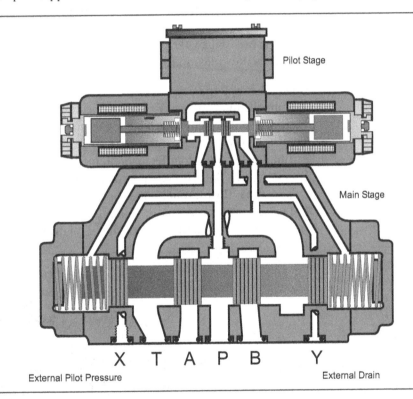

Figure 8-26   Typical solenoid-controlled, pilot-operated valve (two-stage valve)

If the pressure port of the main stage valve is ported to tank, as in the case of tandem or open center spools, a check valve with a heavy spring must be installed in the tank line of an internally piloted valve to create pilot pressure that can be transmitted to the pilot valve (Figure 8-27).

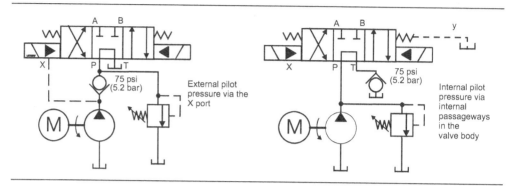

Figure 8-27   Left: External pilot check valve. Right: Return line pilot pressure check valve

When two-stage valves elect the option of being internally drained to the main tank port, a check valve on the tank port will not work, as the constant back pressure created by the pilot check would be transmitted through the pilot valve to both ends of the main stage spool. An alternative is to obtain pilot pressure from a source external to the two-stage valve. This pressure is brought into the two-stage valve via the "X" port as illustrated in Figure 8-30.

Another option on two-stage valves (which is commonly preferred) is to externally drain the pilot valve ("Y" port connection) so that any back pressure in the main return line cannot be sensed and passed on to the main stage spool (Figure 8-28). The tank port interface on top of the main stage allows access to a tapped hole that must be fitted with a plug to affect isolation of the internal main stage tank port from the tank port of the pilot. The "Y" port on the bottom of the main stage must then be allowed to pass drain flow through the subplate and manifold mounting unrestricted to tank. In most instances, externally draining these pilot-operated valves will prevent return line surges and spikes from interfering with the dynamics of the main stage spool.

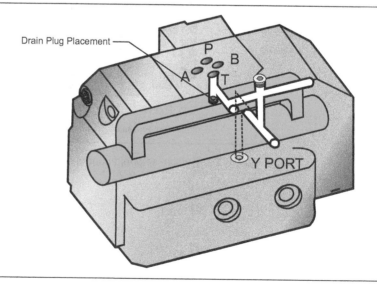

Figure 8-28   Plug options for internal/external drain for pilot valve

Some two-stage valve models create pilot pressure with a check valve built into the main pressure port of the valve (Figure 8-29). The graphic symbol representations of various two-stage valves is shown in Figure 8-30.

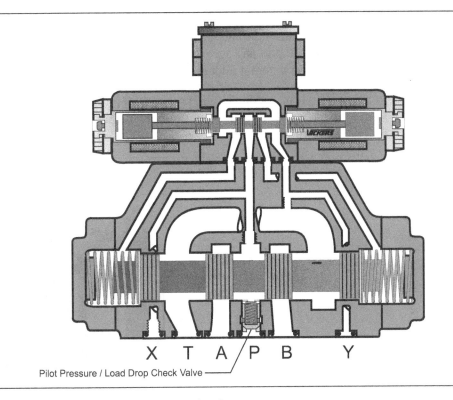

Pilot Pressure / Load Drop Check Valve

Figure 8-29   Integral pilot pressure check valve

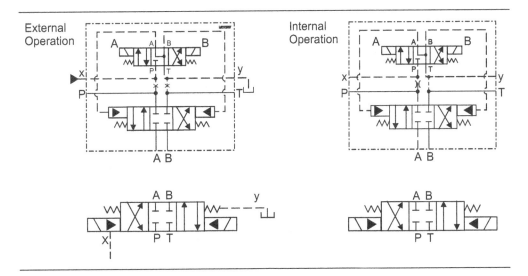

Figure 8-30   Variations of two-stage valve symbols

Pilot Choke Options

To control the shift speed of the main spool, a pilot choke may be incorporated on a two-stage valve. This provides smoother reversals and less hydraulic shock as these valves are used for higher flows and shift very quickly without modification.

Of the various available pilot choke options, one is a fixed orifice fitted between the main stage and the pilot valve. The orifice may be directly screwed into a tap in the "P" port passage of the main stage for internal pilot or placed in the threaded "X" port for external pilot operation.

If placed in the "X" port, a solid plug must be placed in the main stage "P" port tap to isolate pilot pressure from the main stage valve. Figure 8-31 shows the locations of these plugs.

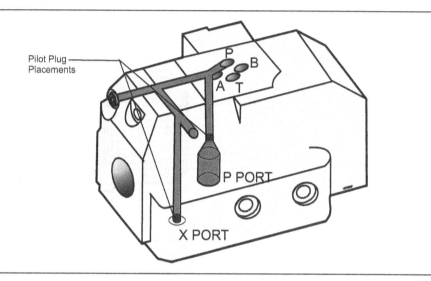

Figure 8-31   Plug options for pilot pressure supply

For discrete control of spool shift in either direction, a pilot choke module may be inserted between the pilot valve and main stage valve. The controls consist of needle valves and reverse free flow checks that are essentially either meter-in or meter-out flow controls for pilot flow affecting spool movement in the main stage.

The meter-out design pilot choke controls the fluid as it is exhausted from one end of the spool. When the valve is energized or de-energized, this type of choke slows down the shifting speed of the main spool. If controlled shifting with fast centering is required, the meter-in design should be used. Figure 8-32 illustrates this option.

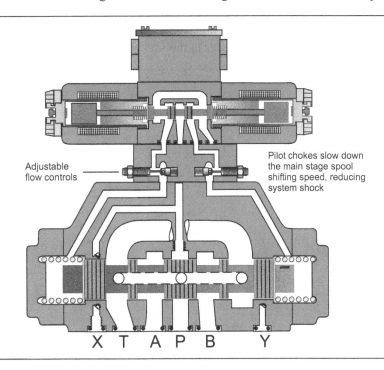

Figure 8-32   Pilot choke mounted on valve

Pilot Piston Options

When it is necessary to increase the main spool shifting speed, pilot pistons (Figure 8-33) can be used. The speed increases because the volume of fluid required to shift the small piston is less than the volume required to shift the main spool. This smaller area requires considerably higher pilot pressures.

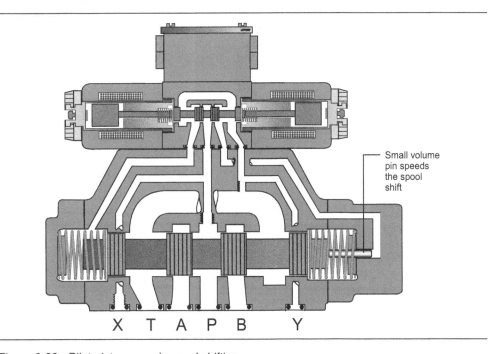

Figure 8-33   Pilot piston speeds spool shifting

Spool Stroke Limiter Options

Spool stroke limiters (Figure 8-34) are a simple method of flow control that restricts the distance the main spool can shift in a given direction offering a "meter-in" effect by reducing the opening(s) in the valve porting. Care must be taken when using this option as mis-adjustments can create excessive heat or failure of the valve to remain shifted due to flow dynamics. It must be remembered that this option does not provide pressure compensation, and variable loads will move at variable speeds with the stroke limiter in the same position.

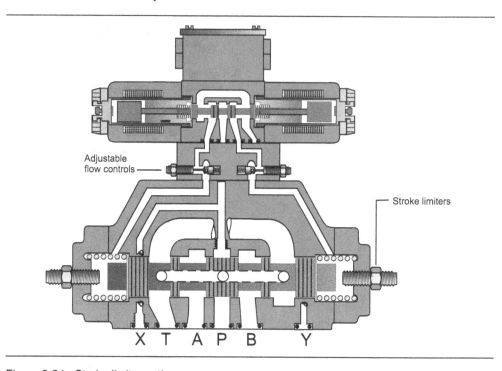

Figure 8-34   Stroke limiter option

Mounting Styles

Sliding spool-type directional valves are available in both line mounted and subplate or manifold mounted designs. Line mounted versions are more frequently found in mobile applications, while the subplate mounted designs are typically used for industrial ones.

Mounting Standards

Standard mounting patterns have been developed to make interchangeability between valve manufacturers more convenient. Figure 8-35 shows various mounting pattern interface names for both United States and international standards. There are also nonstandard patterns that are offered by some manufacturers that will not be covered in this book.

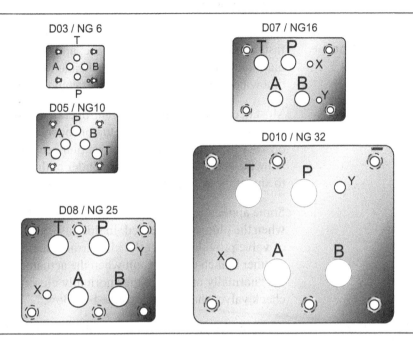

Figure 8-35   Pattern interface terminology for mounting standards

Standards Organizations

National Fluid Power Association. The NFPA sets the standards for the United States. Its pattern conforms to ANSI-B93.7, which is controlled by the American National Standards Institute. Valves conforming to this pattern will also fit on the ISO and CETOP patterns discussed below.

International Standards Organization. The ISO sets the interface pattern for international standardization.

European Oil Hydraulic and Pneumatic Committee. CETOP is the accepted acronym for this European trade organization that represents the organizations of various European countries, similar to the NFPA. These interface standards conform to NFPA and ISO.

Deceleration Valves

Hydraulic cylinders often have built-in cushions that slow down the cylinder pistons at the extreme ends of their travel. An external valve is required when it is necessary to decelerate a cylinder at some intermediate position or to slow down or stop a rotary actuator (motor).

Typical Deceleration Valve Applications

A typical application of a deceleration valve is a machining operation that requires fast speed to move a part into place, and then a slower, controlled speed for the actual machining operation. A simple deceleration valve can be used with a meter-out flow device, or a window type deceleration valve could be used alone to control the slower feed rate.

Most deceleration valves are cam-operated with tapered spools. They gradually decrease flow to or from an actuator for smooth stopping or deceleration. A "normally open" valve cuts off flow when its plunger is depressed by a cam. It may be used to slow the speed of a drill head cylinder at the transition from rapid traverse to feed, or to smoothly stop heavy index tables and large presses.

Some applications require a valve to permit flow during actuation and to cut off flow when the plunger is released. In this case, a "normally closed" valve is used. This type of valve provides an interlocking arrangement that allows flow to be directed to another branch of the circuit when the actuator or load reaches a certain position. Both the "normally open" and the "normally closed" valves are available with integral check valves that permit reverse free flow.

Tapered Plunger Design Deceleration Valve

An early design of deceleration valves used a tapered plunger to reduce flow as it is actuated by the cam. Before the plunger is depressed, free flow is permitted from the inlet to the outlet. Depressing the plunger gradually cuts the flow off. Reverse free flow is permitted by the integral check valve.

The control range of this valve depends on both the flow volume and cam rise. At nearly maximum volume (with an initial pressure drop through the valve), the plunger stroke is completely controlled. One drawback is that at low flow rates, this control is available only from the point where a pressure drop is created. The adjustable orifice design valve compensates for this by allowing the valve to be tailored to any given flow.

Adjustable Orifice Design Deceleration Valve

An adjustable orifice design valve features a closely fitted plunger and sleeve, both of which have rectangular ports or "windows" that control the flow. As the plunger moves inside the sleeve, the ports in each coincide when the open position is reached. Oil entering the inlet flows through the small upper ports in the sleeve and plunger, down through the center of the plunger, and out the large ports to the outlet. When the plunger is depressed, the "window" area is gradually cut off to stop flow. Reverse free flow is allowed by an integral check valve.

Initial Pressure Drop Adjustment

For precise control throughout the plunger stroke, the width of the port openings is controlled by adjusting screws that turn the sleeve. A low flow rate has a narrow opening, while a higher flow requires a wider one. The adjustment is made by attaching a pressure gauge at the side of the valve and turning the screws to obtain the desired initial pressure drop.

This valve also includes an adjustable orifice that allows some flow with the plunger fully depressed. It consists of a small plunger with a chamfered end and a "V" notch that can be set to bypass the spool sleeve closure. During indexing or some similar application, the orifice permits the load to creep to its final position.

The window orifice valve is built in both the threaded and flange mounted versions. Both valves require a drain so that leakage oil can escape from beneath the plunger.

Prefill Valve

Prefill valves are specifically designed to handle large volumes of fluid at low pressure drop. Their flow capacities range from several hundred to several thousand gallons per minute and are typically used on large pressing or die casting machine cylinders. Gravity or atmospheric pressure pushes the fluid through the valve, eliminating the need for large volume pumps. The five operational phases of prefill valves are discussed below. The two essential phases are illustrated in Figure 8-36 and Figure 8-37. Mounting styles that are available for the prefill valves are varied, but typically they are mounted to allow free flow of a large volume of fluid by gravity for filling. Powered retraction of the large volume actuator then pushes the fluid back through the prefill into the reservoir.

Neutral Position

In the neutral position, the valve is held open by pilot pressure. Fluid can flow either into the valve through the prefill and pressure ports before flowing into the main ram cylinder, or vice versa. No pressure can be built up in this phase. The main cylinder is prevented from advancing to the workpiece by other means.

Rapid Advance

During rapid advance, the main ram cylinder exhaust fluid is ported to allow the ram to advance toward the workpiece. This motion causes the fluid to flow from the reservoir and pressure port through the prefill valve and into the ram. Because the fluid is typically gravity fed, little system power is required for this phase. Figure 8-36 illustrates this high flow condition.

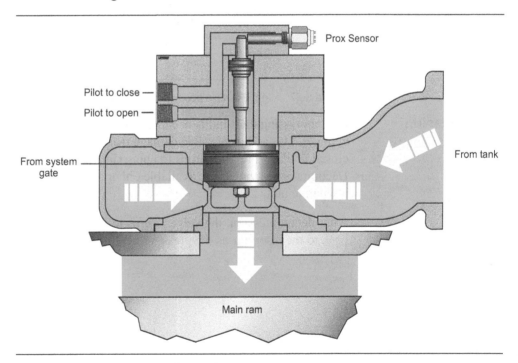

Figure 8-36   High flow position of a prefill valve

Pressing

Pilot pressure is applied to the closing port, shifting the gate assembly into the closed position. This isolates the fluid in the top of the cylinder from the reservoir. Pressure is then applied to the pressure port to perform the pressing function with the proper force requirement. This function is illustrated in Figure 8-37.

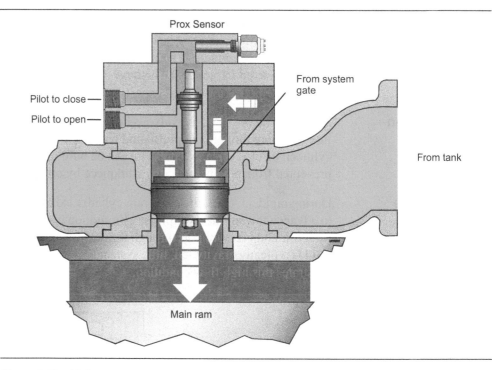

Figure 8-37   High pressure position of a prefill valve

Decompression

Decompressing the fluid is necessary before the valve is shifted to return to the cylinder. This avoids possible damage from hydraulic shock. The prefill valve remains closed until the pressure drops to approximately 250 psi (17 bar, 1,700 kPa). Decompression valves are available either as an integral part of the prefill valve or as a separate unit.

Return

After decompression, the valve returns to its neutral position, allowing fluid to flow back to the reservoir as the press ram cylinder is powered to the up position.

Shuttle Valves

Shuttle valves, using either balls or poppets, are constructed with two opposing inlets that utilize the same ball or poppet. There are two inlet ports and one outlet port. Flow at the outlet port will originate at the inlet port having the highest pressure.

Figure 8-38 illustrates a shuttle valve and its symbol. This device is generally used in a circuit where the higher of two pressures is to be sensed. For this reason they are used in load-sensing systems.

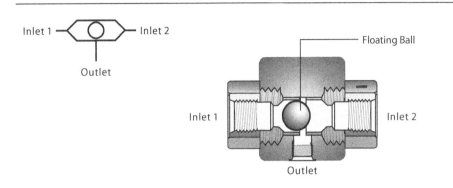

Figure 8-38   Shuttle valve and symbol

Industrial Test Questions:
Directional Valves

Chapter 8

1. What is the function of a directional valve?

2. What is meant by finite positioning?

3. Explain the function of a check valve. Draw the graphic symbol.

4. What is the major consideration when applying a pilot-to-open check valve?

5. List five ways to shift a four-way valve.

6. Describe the "centered" condition of the tandem center spool. A float center spool?

7. How many positions does a spring offset valve have? A spring centered valve?

8. Draw the graphic symbol for a two-position spring centered valve, a spring offset valve, an energize-to-center valve.

9. Describe two ways of obtaining pilot pressure for an open center, two-stage valve.

10. What is the function of pilot chokes? What type would be used to ensure rapid centering in case of an emergency shutdown?

11. What is the purpose of a deceleration valve?

12. How is the adjustable orifice deceleration valve an improvement over the tapered plunger design?

13. List the five basic phases of a prefill valve.

Chapter 9 . . . . Electrical Principles and Operational Amplifiers

This chapter is an introduction to basic electrical concepts and terms, followed by an introduction to operational amplifiers and the electronic control of proportional and servo valves. In particular, those circuits most often associated with hydraulic systems are examined.

Safety First   Though guidelines for using electrical test equipment and working on electrical applications are suggested in this chapter, you should always read and understand any and all instructions that may accompany the equipment you are working on or with.

Electrical Principles

Hydraulics and electricity are often compared because the two types of systems have many similarities. Previous chapters explain that a hydraulic circuit requires a power source (usually a pump), a load device (actuator) and conductors to connect them. Hydraulic circuits differ mainly in the types of devices used to control, direct and regulate the flow of hydraulic fluid and in the type and capacity of the actuators employed to accomplish the work, which varies depending on the application. An electrical circuit has the same basic requirements. There must be a power source (a battery, generator, etc.), a load device (lights, bells, motors, etc.), and proper connections in between. A wide assortment of devices also are incorporated to control, direct and regulate the flow of electrical current.

Hydraulic components are usually represented on diagrams by symbols, which have been standardized to ensure that they will have the same meaning to anyone using the diagrams. Electrical components are represented in the same manner with their own standardized symbols. Electrical diagrams are often called schematics. Many of the illustrations in this and other electrical sections of the manual use these electrical schematic symbols. Figure 9-1 illustrates some of the more common symbols.

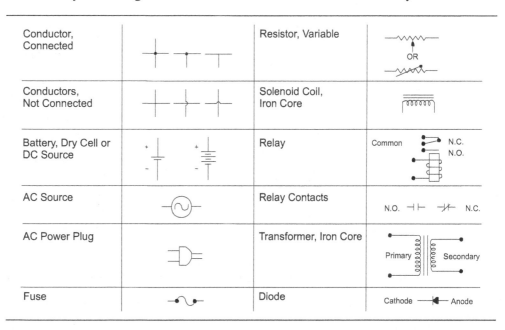

Figure 9-1   Common electrical schematic symbols

Lamp	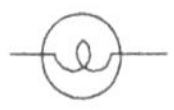	Ammeter	 − —(A)— +
Switch Single Pole, Single Throw	 SPST	Voltmeter	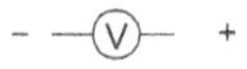 − —(V)— +
Switch Single Pole, Double Throw	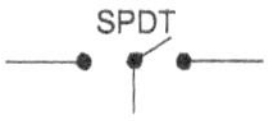 SPDT	Ohmmeter	 − —(Ω)— +
Capacitor		Earth Ground	
Resistor, Fixed		Chassis Ground	
Resistor, Tapped			

Figure 9-1   Common electrical schematic symbols (continued)

There are many important differences between hydraulic and electrical systems and circuits. For example, electrical current is invisible while hydraulic fluid is not, and electrical current flows through solid wires while hydraulic fluid flows through hollow lines. Despite these and other differences, hydraulic and electrical circuits are very similar in a theoretical sense. Figure 9-2 shows symbols for electrical components on the left of the illustration with their hydraulic equivalents shown on the right.

ELECTRICAL		**HYDRAULIC**	
Resistor		Restriction	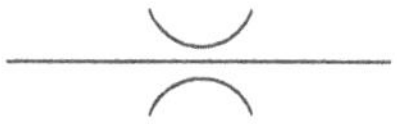
Power Supply	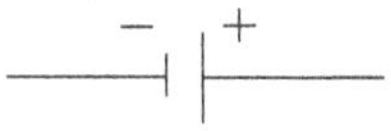 − +	Pump	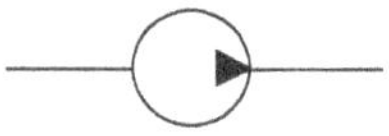
Capacitor		Double Spring Loaded Piston or Accumulator	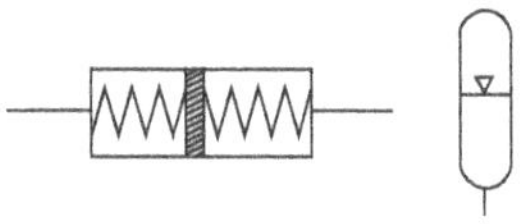
Switch	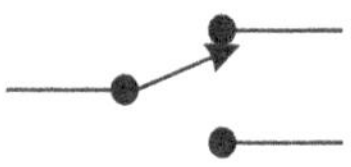	Directional Valve	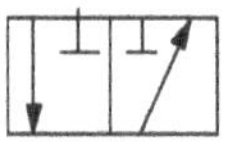
Diode	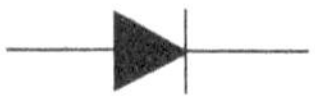	Check Valve	
Transformer	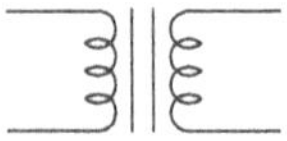	Intensifier	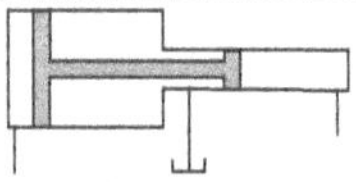
Ground	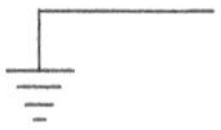	Tank	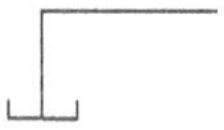

Figure 9-2   Functional equivalence of electrical and hydraulic components

Figure 9-3 illustrates a hydraulic circuit and its electrical counterpart. Either type of circuit could be used to perform the same work; only the cost of operation, the physical construction of components, and the medium being controlled are different. Much of the material on hydraulics presented up to this point can be used to understand electrical circuits as well.

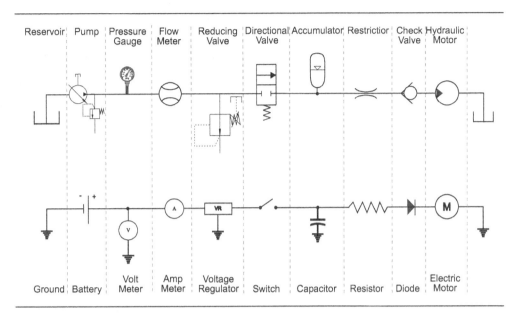

Figure 9-3   Comparison of simple hydraulic and electrical circuits

Basic Electrical Circuit Elements

Every electrical circuit contains measurable quantities of the following four circuit elements:

- Current

- Voltage

- Resistance

- Power

These circuit elements are interrelated, and a change in any one will produce a change in one or more of the others. The interrelationship among current, voltage, resistance and power is explained later in this chapter.

Current

Electrical current is defined as the directed flow of electrical charges from one point to another around a closed electrical circuit. It is the flow of current that accomplishes the work or purpose of a circuit. Electrical charges can be either negative or positive. Conventional current flow consists of the movement of positive charges from positive to negative around a circuit. The direction of conventional current flow is explained by the Law of Electrical Charges.

The Law of Electrical Charges

The Law of Electrical Charges (Figure 9-4) states that:

1. Like charges repel.

    a. Two positive charges will repel each other.
    b. Two negative charges will repel each other.

2. Unlike charges attract.

   a. A positive charge will be attracted to a negative charge.
   b. A negative charge will be attracted to a positive charge.

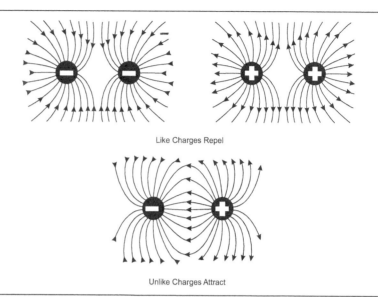

Figure 9-4   The law of electrical charges

The motion of positive charges can be directed and controlled to form conventional current flow. Positive charges will be repelled by the positive power terminal and attracted to the negative power terminal. Therefore, due to the Law of Electrical Charges, conventional current always flows from positive to negative within a circuit. See Figure 9-5.

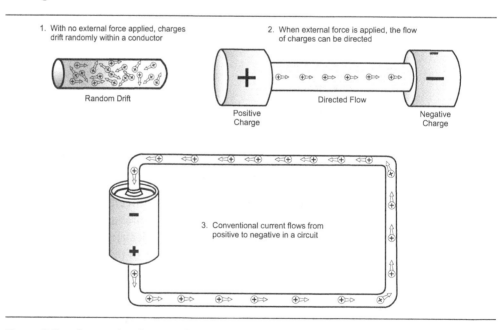

Figure 9-5   Conventional current flow

Unit of Measurement

Current is measured in units called amperes (A). An expression meaning "the current is 2 amperes" would be written I = 2A. Since an ampere is a large quantity of current, current is often measured in smaller units called milliamps (mA), which represent one-thousandth of an amp (0.001A). Therefore, 200 mA = 200/1,000A = 200 x 0.01A = 0.2A.

Conductors

Conductors form the path by which the current can flow from the power source to the load and back. Conductors are materials (usually metals) that support current flow through them without offering much resistance. Conductors are usually wires, but they are also found in other forms such as the metal chassis or skin of an electrical device, or the foil patterns on a printed circuit board.

Insulators

Insulators are made of high resistance materials that prevent current from flowing through them. The rubber or plastic insulating compound covering a wire, for instance, forms a barrier to current flow that provides protection from electrical shocks and short circuits that could cause serious damage to equipment, and physical hazards to the personnel using it.

Open and Closed Circuits

Current can flow through a circuit only when a complete path exists from the positive terminal to the negative terminal of the power source. Such a circuit is called a closed circuit (Figure 9-6A).

If the complete path is accidentally broken or purposely interrupted by switch or relay contacts, current cannot flow in the circuit and work cannot be performed by the load. A circuit in this state is called an open circuit (Figure 9-6B).

A. Current Flows in a Closed Circuit

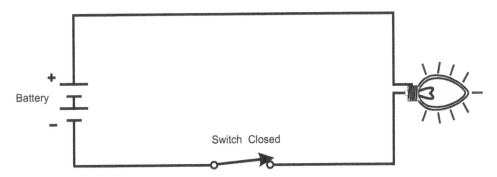

B. Current Cannot Flow in an Open Circuit

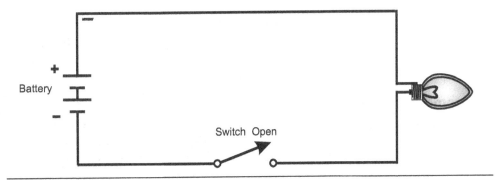

Figure 9-6   Closed and open circuits

Circuit Controls

Circuit controls are devices such as switches, relay contacts and timers, which can be opened or closed either automatically or manually. These devices determine whether or not current can flow and which path or paths the current will follow when it does so. There are other devices, such as rheostats, that are included in a circuit to limit the amount of current that can flow. Some of these devices are examined in more detail later in this chapter.

Voltage

Power sources are devices which convert various other forms of energy into electrical energy. For example, a battery changes chemical energy into electricity and a photocell converts light energy into electricity. During these conversions, negative charges are forced to collect at the negative terminal, while the positive charges are moved toward the positive terminal. This movement of charges creates a difference of potential between the two terminals, with one having an excess of negative charges (- terminal) and the other having an excess of positive charges (+ terminal). See Figure 9-7.

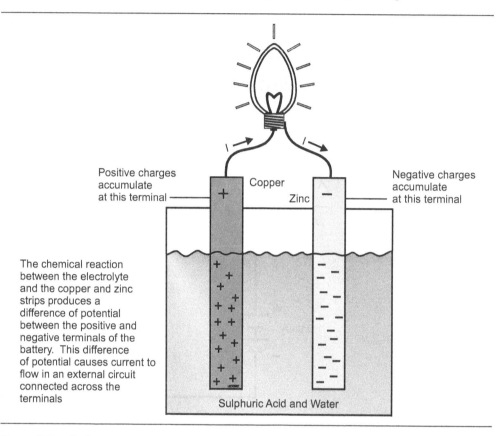

Positive charges accumulate at this terminal

Copper

Zinc

Negative charges accumulate at this terminal

The chemical reaction between the electrolyte and the copper and zinc strips produces a difference of potential between the positive and negative terminals of the battery. This difference of potential causes current to flow in an external circuit connected across the terminals

Sulphuric Acid and Water

Figure 9-7   Battery as a power source

If a path is connected between the positive and negative terminals of the power source, the electrons will try to reach an equilibrium or balancing of charges. This will cause the movement of positive charges (current flow) from the positive terminal, through the external path, to the negative terminal.

Electromotive Force

The force which causes current to flow is called Electromotive Force (EMF), and the amount of EMF produced by the power source is called voltage. The amount of voltage directly depends on the size of the difference of potential which exists between the two terminals of the power source.

Unit of Measurement

Electromotive force is measured in units called volts (V) and is referred to in formulas by the capital letter E. Therefore, the expression, $E = 12V$, means "the voltage equals twelve volts." Large quantities of voltage are often described in units called kilovolts (kV). A kilo represents the number 1,000. Therefore, one kilovolt equals 1,000 volts, or $1kV = 1,000V$.

DC and AC Power Sources

Two types of current can be produced by EMF sources: direct current (DC) or alternating current (AC). Most sources produce DC which is a steady level of current, flowing in only one direction through the circuit. An EMF producing magneto electric device called a generator produces AC, which continuously changes from a positive to a negative peak value, and alternately flows into and out of a circuit. See Figure 9-8.

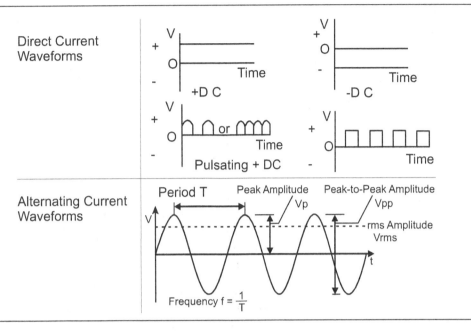

Figure 9-8   DC and AC waveforms

Most of the stationary equipment found in hydraulic applications uses the relatively stable and economical AC voltage supplied by the local power company as its power source. AC voltage is a continous sinusoidal wave that has the properties shown in Figure 9-8. The waveform starts at zero and increases to a positive PEAK amplitude, then decreases through zero to a negative PEAK amplitude. This occurs at a specific time period (T) which can be used to calculate the frequency of the waveform by dividing period (T) into 1. The total difference between the positive and negative peak amplitudes is called the Peak to Peak amplitude, which can only be measured by an oscilloscope or a special peak reading digital meter. The rms amplitude shown above represents the effective current value of the waveform; so a resistor with 70 Vrms across it will have the same current flow as a 70V DC voltage. Rms can be measured only with a meter that has true rms reading cicuits in it and is equal to the Peak voltage times 0.707.

Standard meters that are analog or digital tend to read the Average voltage which equals the Peak voltage times 0.636. There is not a large difference between them but it can result in errors when you are measuring real values.

The AC voltage is converted to DC with a rectifier circuit built into the equipment power supply. The easy to use DC voltage is then distributed by internal wiring to power the various electrical circuits within the equipment. These circuits may process signals that are either AC or DC.

Resistance

Resistance is the opposition to current flow offered by components of the circuit. All electrical load components have some resistance value. A light bulb works only because of the resistance of its filament. The resistance produces the heat which causes the filament to glow.

A fuse provides another example of how resistance can be useful in a circuit. A fuse has a fragile length of resistance wire designed to melt when its current rating is exceeded. The melted fuse opens the circuit and prevents current from flowing until the source of the overcurrent condition is found and corrected. The fuse is then replaced with a new one that has the same current and voltage rating.

Unit of Measurement

Resistance is measured in units called ohms, which can be expressed in terms of current and voltage. One ohm is equal to the amount of resistance which allows one amp of current to flow when an EMF of one volt is applied. The Greek letter omega (Ω) is used to represent the ohm, and the capital letter R represents resistance in circuit formulas. Therefore, "the resistance equals 100 ohms" can be written $R = 100\Omega$.

Resistance values are often quite large. For this reason, the kilohm (kΩ) and the megohm (MΩ) are practical units of measurement for resistance. As mentioned previously, k represents 1,000. Therefore, 100,000 ohms can also be expressed as 100k. Mega (M) represents 1,000,000. So, 7,000,000 ohms can also be written as 7MΩ.

Resistors

The resistor is a device designed to present a specific amount of opposition to the current in a circuit. Fixed resistors are manufactured in many sizes and types, but the opposition to current flow which they present to the circuit remains constant. There are three popular types of fixed resistors: carbon composition, wire wound and deposited film.

Not all resistors have a fixed value; some are variable. A resistor whose value can be changed by rotating a shaft or moving a sliding tap is called a potentiometer if it uses all three available terminals, and a rheostat if it only uses two of the three terminals. Potentiometers are usually connected in parallel to divide circuit voltages, while rheostats are generally connected in series to limit circuit current. See Figure 9-9. Resistors of all types and their uses in electrical circuits are examined in greater detail in a later chapter.

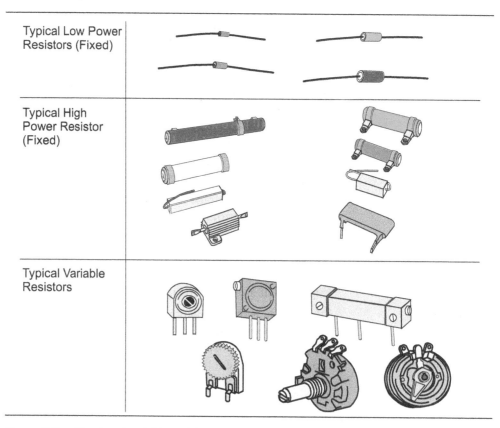

Figure 9-9   Fixed and variable resistors

Power

Power is the amount of work that can be done in some standard unit of time (usually one second). Electrical power is consumed by forcing the current through the resistance of the circuit. The opposition to current flow offered by resistive devices in the circuit produces heat that is dissipated or lost into the surrounding air. This lost energy is called a power loss. The fees charged by the local electrical power company are based on the amount of power consumed over a given amount of time and power losses represent a significant portion of these fees.

Unit of Measurement

Electrical power is expressed in units called watts (W). One watt represents the power used when one ampere of current flows due to an EMF of one volt. It is quite common to see the term kilowatts (kW) used when referring to electrical power. Remember, kilo represents 1,000, so 1 kW is equal to 1,000 watts, or 2.5 kW = 2,500 watts. In formulas, power is represented by the capital letter P. So, P = 2W is the same as saying "the power equals 2 watts." As mentioned earlier in this manual, 746 watts = 1 horsepower (hp). So, to operate a 0.5 hp motor, 373 watts of power are required.

Wattage Rating

The fact that components heat up due to the current passing through them makes it necessary for the circuit designer to consider heat tolerances along with component values for the devices selected for the circuit. This heat tolerance must also be considered when devices are replaced in a circuit. The replacement part must have the same or higher wattage rating as the original part. The heat tolerance is known as the wattage rating of the device and determines how much heat a component can withstand. Generally, the larger the physical size of a component, the higher its wattage rating will be.

Measuring Electrical Quantities

When working with electrical circuits, it is often necessary to know exactly how much current is flowing in the circuit, how much voltage is present, or how much resistance a device is offering to the current flow. When adjusting, calibrating or troubleshooting a circuit, measurements of electrical quantities are made with a device called a meter.

Types of Meters

Some meters are designed to measure only one of the circuit elements. A voltmeter, for example, can only measure the voltage present between two points in the circuit. More commonly, however, a device called a multimeter, or VOM (volt-ohm-milliammeter), is used to make the measurements required. This device is a combination voltmeter, ohmmeter and ammeter; different sections of the meter are used depending on the measurement needed. A function selector switch is rotated or buttons are pushed to select the type of measurement. A range selector switch is used to adjust the meter for reading different amounts of volts, ohms or amps.

There are also two kinds of multimeters: analog and digital. The analog meter has a pointer that moves across calibrated scales (Figure 9-10). The measurement is obtained by reading the appropriate scale. It is important to look directly at the meter face to avoid incorrect readings.

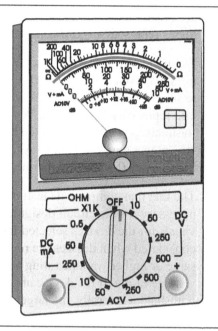

Figure 9-10   Analog meter

A digital meter indicates the measurement on a numerical display (Figure 9-11).

Figure 9-11   Digital meter

Meters are connected to the circuit in different ways depending on the type of measurement being made. There are also several safety precautions that must be observed when using the meter. These safety factors are necessary to protect both the meter and the person using it.

Measuring Current with an Ammeter

Current, or the amount of electrical charge flowing in a circuit, is measured with a device called an ammeter (or milliammeter).

Safety Precautions

Certain precautions must be taken to ensure accurate ammeter readings, to prevent shocks to the technician and to protect the delicate meter circuits. Never exceed the capabilities of the meter being used. All meters have a current rating that indicates the maximum amount of current that can safely be measured. Some meters have a range selector switch which allows the user to adjust the meter for reading different amounts of current. Set this switch to a range that includes the anticipated current to be measured. The highest range shown on the range switch determines the maximum current that can be safely measured.

Prevent electrical shock by always disconnecting the circuit being tested from the electrical power source before measuring current. Before disconnecting, be sure, however, that it is hydraulically safe to do so.

Connecting the Ammeter

Break the circuit at the point where the current flow is to be measured by unsoldering a connection or snipping a wire. Then connect the two meter leads from one side of the break to the other, completing the path for current flow. This is called a series connection (Figure 9-12). When a device is connected in series it means that there is only one path for the current flow. Because the ammeter is inserted directly into the circuit, it is designed to offer very little resistance to the current flowing through it. This is done so that normal circuit operation is not disturbed by the connection of the meter to the circuit.

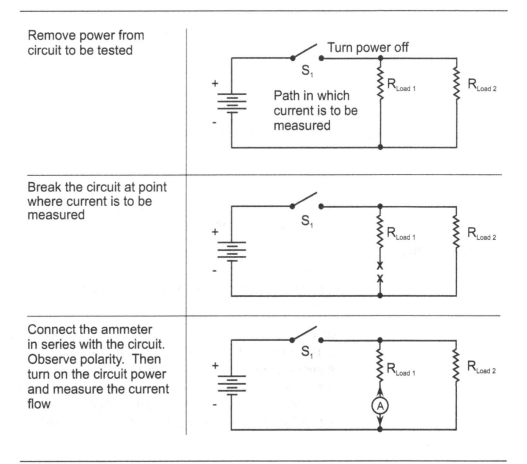

Figure 9-12   Series connection of ammeter

Observing Polarity

The proper placement of the positive and negative meter leads is referred to as observing polarity. When measuring direct current (DC), the meter must be inserted in such a way that the current being measured flows into the positive meter lead, through the meter and out the negative meter lead. If proper polarity is not observed when using an analog meter, the pointer attempts to move backwards on the scale, causing damage to the meter.

When measuring alternating current (AC), it is not necessary to observe polarity as it is normal for the current to flow in both directions. The meter has internal circuits that provide polarity protection when the function switch is set to an AC function.

After correctly connecting the meter in series, turn on the power and note the meter reading. Remember to turn the power off again when disconnecting the meter and reconnecting the break in the circuit that was made earlier.

Measuring Voltage with a Voltmeter

The device used to measure circuit voltage is called a voltmeter. It can be either analog or digital. Voltage is always measured across two points, with electrical ground (zero volts) frequently being one of these points.

Safety Precautions

As with the ammeter, certain precautions should always be taken when measuring voltage. Do not exceed the maximum voltage rating of the voltmeter. If a range switch is incorporated, be sure to set it to a range high enough to include the anticipated voltage being measured. When unsure of the amount of voltage being measured, set the range switch to its highest position and then turn it to a lower range later if possible.

Hold the meter leads only by the insulated portions to avoid electrical shocks. To be completely safe, turn off the circuit voltage and connect both test probes to the circuit with alligator clips. Then reapply the voltage and read the meter.

Be careful when touching the probe to the circuit that two points of different potential are not accidentally connected with a single probe tip. This will cause a short circuit that could damage the equipment.

To avoid shocks and short circuits, remove all rings, watches, necklaces, etc., before testing voltage.

Be sure to set the function switch on the meter to either ACV or DCV as appropriate for the circuit being measured.

Connecting the Voltmeter

When using the voltmeter, the circuit under test need not be broken or disturbed in any way. To measure the voltage between two points, merely touch the two leads of the voltmeter to the two points. Polarity, however, must be observed when measuring DC voltage.

Notice the voltmeter symbol in Figure 9-13A. The negative voltmeter lead (black lead) is connected to the more negative of the two points. The meter is connected in parallel with the points being measured. This means that there are two paths for the current flow, one path through the circuit and another path through the voltmeter. The voltmeter is designed to have a high internal resistance so that very little of the circuit current flows into the extra path created by connecting the meter.

A. Voltmeter Measuring A Voltage Drop
Voltmeter connected in parallel with circuit by touching test leads to each side of component. Meter reads voltage drop if current flows in circuit

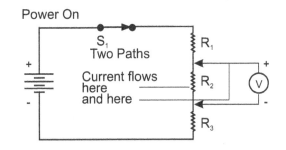

B. Voltmeter Measuring A Voltage Rise
Voltmeter measures voltage rise even though no current is flowing in circuit. Voltmeter provides a path across positive and negative terminals of power source

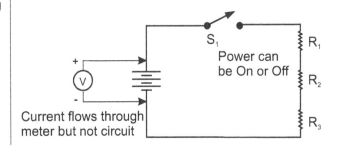

Figure 9-13   Voltmeter measuring voltage drop and voltage rise

Voltage Rises and Voltage Drops

Both voltage rises and voltage drops can be measured with the voltmeter. A voltage rise indicates a point where electromotive force (EMF) is added to the circuit, such as would be measured across the two power source terminals (Figure 9-13B). A reading will be obtained here even if current is not flowing in the circuit attached to the power source. This happens because a complete (closed) circuit is provided by the voltmeter itself.

A voltage drop is a point in the circuit where electrical energy is to be in use by the circuit, such as across the load. A voltage reading here is dependent upon current flowing through the load. When no circuit current is flowing, no voltage can be measured and the meter indicates a zero reading (Figure 9-14).

Voltmeter cannot measure voltage drop if current is not flowing in the circuit

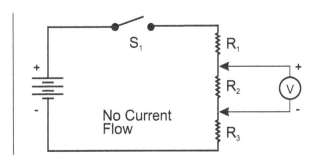

Figure 9-14   Voltmeter across component with no current flowing

In any circuit in which current is flowing, the sum of the voltage drops must equal the sum of the voltage rises.

Measuring Resistance with an Ohmmeter

The device used to measure resistance is the ohmmeter. The ohmmeter has its own internal power source (usually a battery) which is used to force current through the resistance being measured and, as a result, circuit power is not required to operate the meter circuits.

Analog ohmmeters (Figure 9-15) have a nonlinear scale with zero at one end and infinity at the other. A range switch is provided so that a wide range of values can be accurately measured. The switch is marked with settings such as R x 1 and R x 100. To obtain a resistance measurement, the component is connected between the two test probes. A value is read off the resistance scale and then multiplied by the range switch setting. For example, if the reading on the scale was 5 and the range switch setting was R x 1k, the resistance value would be 5 x 1k or 5 kilohms (5,000 ohms).

After zero adjusting the meter and connecting the component between the test probes, the meter pointer indicates 12 on the Ohms scale. Since the range switch is set to R x 1, the resistance equals 12 x 1 = 12 Ohms

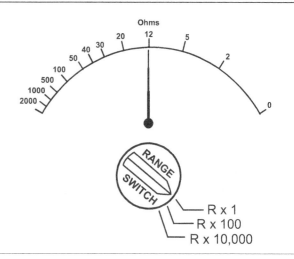

In this measurement, the meter pointer indicates 12, but the range switch is set to R x 100. The resistance being measured equals 12 x 100 = 1200 Ohms

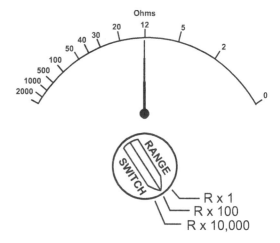

Figure 9-15   Ohmmeter measurements

A zero ohms adjust control is included to compensate for the gradually diminishing internal battery voltage. This control must be readjusted each time the range switch is changed to a new position.

Safety Precautions

Since the ohmmeter has its own source of power, all circuit power must be turned OFF before resistance measurements are taken. Attempting to read resistance with circuit power on may damage the circuit, meter or both! With the circuit voltage removed, there is very little danger involved in measuring resistance. There are, however, several factors that should be considered to ensure accuracy of measurement.

Ohmmeter Accuracy

Always adjust the zero ohms control on the ohmmeter before taking the reading. Touch the two meter probe tips together and then adjust the zero ohms control until the pointer indicates zero ohms. The procedure is the same for a digital meter except that the control is adjusted until the numerical display shows all zeros. If the meter cannot be adjusted to zero, the internal battery is too weak to operate the ohmmeter and should be replaced with a fresh battery.

If the component to be measured is installed in the circuit, one end of it must be disconnected before making the resistance measurement. The reason for this can be seen in Figure 9-16. Notice that when one end is not disconnected there are two paths for the meter battery current to flow: one path through the component and another path back through the rest of the circuit. The ohmmeter will measure the combination resistance of both paths and the result will be a value different than the one intended. If, however, the component is disconnected at one end, there is only one path for the current to follow through the component. This method produces the accurate measurement desired.

When connecting an ohmmeter across a component (R_2) a false reading will be obtained if the component is not disconnected from the circuit. When the ohmmeter is connected as shown, meter current can flow through both R_2 and R_1. The measurement will be a combination of R_1 and R_2 values resulting in a false reading - lower than expected

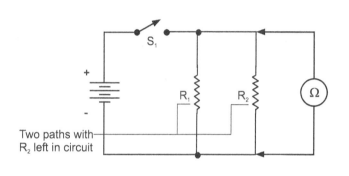

Two paths with R_2 left in circuit

When the component to be measured with the ohmmeter is disconnected from the circuit, meter current has only one path it can follow. This allows a true measurement of the component with the ohmmeter

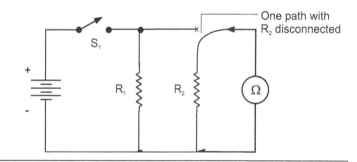

One path with R_2 disconnected

Figure 9-16   False ohmmeter readings

Touching the probe tips with the fingers while taking a resistance measurement also creates an additional path for current flow through the body. While this is not dangerous, it does cause false measurements. Hold the probes by the insulated part only.

While probe polarity does not matter when measuring a resistor, other devices, like diodes, must be measured in both directions to determine if the resistance is within tolerance. (Testing a diode with an ohmmeter is covered later in this chapter.)

Finally, always adjust the range switch until the pointer rests within the middle one third of the ohms scale with the component connected between the two probe tips. This is the most accurate area of the nonlinear ohms scale and should be used if at all possible. Remember to check the zero ohms adjustment after changing range switch settings.

Relationships Among Circuit Elements

As mentioned at the beginning of this chapter, relationships exist among current, voltage, resistance and power in any electrical circuit. These relationships are expressed as a series of simple formulas known as Ohm's Law and Watt's Law.

Ohm's Law

Ohm's Law states that the current in a circuit is directly proportional to the voltage and inversely proportional to the resistance. This means that:

- As the voltage applied to a circuit increases, the current is also increased by a proportional amount. Likewise, if the voltage applied to a circuit decreases, the current also decreases. (If the resistance is held constant.)

- As the resistance in a circuit increases, the current decreases by a proportional amount. Similarly, if the resistance in a circuit decreases, the current will increase. (If the voltage is held constant.)

The relationships should be obvious from the definitions of these electrical circuit elements. Voltage is the force that causes current to flow. If this force is increased, the amount of current flow must also increase. Resistance is the opposition to current flow and must also increase. Resistance is the opposition to current flow. If the opposition is increased, the current must decrease.

Ohm's Law is most often expressed as a formula:

Formula 9-1

$$I = \frac{E}{R}$$

Solving for I

The current in a circuit is equal to the voltage divided by the resistance. For example, consider the simple flashlight circuit of Figure 9-17A. If the battery voltage equals 6 volts and the resistance of the lamp (the resistance of the wires is negligible in this case) equals 120 ohms, how much current will flow when the switch is closed?

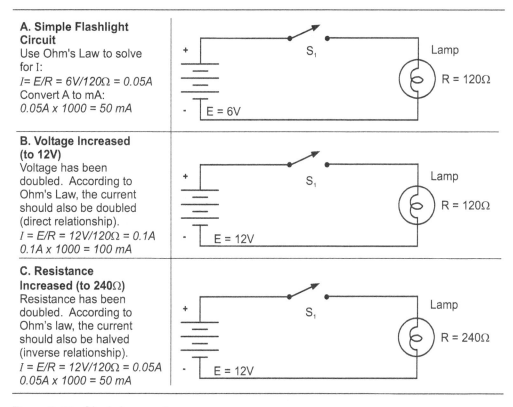

A. Simple Flashlight Circuit
Use Ohm's Law to solve for I:
I= E/R = 6V/120Ω = 0.05A
Convert A to mA:
0.05A x 1000 = 50 mA

B. Voltage Increased (to 12V)
Voltage has been doubled. According to Ohm's Law, the current should also be doubled (direct relationship).
I = E/R = 12V/120Ω = 0.1A
0.1A x 1000 = 100 mA

C. Resistance Increased (to 240Ω)
Resistance has been doubled. According to Ohm's law, the current should also be halved (inverse relationship).
I = E/R = 12V/120Ω = 0.05A
0.05A x 1000 = 50 mA

Figure 9-17   Ohm's law proof

Enter the given values into the formula and divide:

$$I = \frac{6}{120} = 0.05A = 50 \text{ mA}$$

The current flowing through the circuit is 0.050A or 50 thousandths of an amp. Since 1 milliamp (mA) equals 1 thousandth of an amp, the current value could be expressed as 50 milliamps or 50 mA.

It was stated earlier that if the voltage in a circuit increases, the current must also increase by a proportional amount. If the voltage in the flashlight circuit is doubled, then the current should also be doubled. See Figure 9-17B.

$$I = \frac{12}{120} = 0.100A = 100 \text{ mA}$$

The circuit current doubled from 50 mA to 100 mA when the voltage was doubled from 6 to 12 volts. If the resistance of the lamp in the circuit is doubled, what happens to the current? See Figure 9-17C.

$$I = \frac{12}{240} = 0.050A = 50 \text{ mA}$$

When the resistance was doubled from 120 to 240 ohms, the current decreased by half from 100 mA to 50 mA.

The basic Ohm's Law formula can be transposed to also solve for the voltage or the resistance in a circuit. When any two circuit values are known, the third can be calculated using the appropriate formula.

Formula 9-2

$$E = I \times R$$

$$R = \frac{E}{I}$$

Solving for E

Suppose that the current through a device must be limited to one half of an amp, and that its resistance is fixed at 60 ohms. How much voltage should be applied to the circuit to meet these requirements?

$$E = 0.5 \times 60 = 30 \text{ volts}$$

Solving for R

Consider a circuit with a 50 volt power source. How much resistance must be in the circuit to limit the current to one tenth of an amp?

$$R = \frac{50}{0.1} = 500 \text{ ohms}$$

Watt's Law

Watt's Law describes the relationship among power, voltage and current in a circuit. Watt's Law says that 1 watt of power results when 1 volt produces a current of 1 ampere.

Watt's Law is usually expressed in formula form:

Formula 9-3

$$P = I \times E$$

To solve for the power in a circuit, multiply the current times the voltage. For example, if 2 amps of current are produced by a 12 volt power source, the power in this circuit would be:

$$P = 2 \times 12 = 24 \text{ watts}$$

Like the Ohm's Law formula, the formula for Watt's Law can also be transposed into formulas to compute either the voltage or the current in a circuit.

Formula 9-4

$$E = \frac{P}{I}$$

$$I = \frac{P}{E}$$

If any two of the values are known, the third can be calculated using the appropriate formula.

By combining Ohm's Law and Watt's Law, several other formulas can be derived for performing various circuit calculations. For example, two additional formulas for determining power are:

Formula 9-5

$$P = I^2 R$$

$$P = \frac{E^2}{R}$$

The chart in Figure 9-18 is a summary of the information on the four circuit factors or elements and includes definitions, units of measurement, unit symbols, type of meter used to make measurements, and Ohm's and Watt's Law formulas. This information is also shown in Appendix D.

CIRCUIT ELEMENT	DEFINITION	UNIT OF MEASUREMENT	UNIT SYMBOL	MEASURED WITH	FUNCTION SWITCH POSITION	OHM'S OR WATT'S LAW
Current	The flow of electrons from + to - around a circuit	Amperes (amps)	A	Ammeter	ACmA or DCmA	$I = E / R$ $I = P / E$ $I = \sqrt{P/R}$
Voltage (EMF)	The force which causes current to flow	Volts	V	Voltmeter	ACV or DCV	$E = I \times P$ $E = P / I$ $E = \sqrt{P/R}$
Resistance	The opposition to current flow	Ohms	Ω	Ohmmeter	Ohms	$R = E / I$ $R = E^2 / P$ $R = P / I^2$
Power	The rate of doing electrical work	Watts	W	Wattmeter or Calculated	N/A	$P = I \times E$ $P = I^2 R$ $P = E^2 / R$

Figure 9-18   Electrical circuit element summary chart

Electrical Devices

This section contains basic information on several electrical devices commonly found in hydraulic systems and is intended as an introduction only. A comprehensive examination of these devices is beyond the scope of this manual. The basic operation and use of the following devices is described:

- Potentiometer
- Solenoid
- Relay
- Transformer
- Diode rectifier

These devices are available in many different physical sizes, wattage ratings, load capacities, etc., and may serve purposes other than those covered in this manual. The basic principles of operation for a device, however, do not change, regardless of the style.

Potentiometer

The potentiometer is a variable resistive device used to reduce the value of an electrical signal or voltage. It may also be called a gain control, fader, attenuator, or pot (potentiometer) depending on its design and application. The volume control on a radio or TV is a potentiometer. Changing the setting of this control increases or decreases the resistance in the circuit, and raises or lowers the strength of the signal reaching the speaker to the desired sound level.

Potentiometers provide a means of varying the voltage output of one circuit before it is applied as an input to another circuit. In this way, command signals to electrohydraulic valves, feedback signals from transducers or circuit board supply voltages can be adjusted and fine-tuned to allow optimal performance of the equipment.

Potentiometer Operation

Figure 9-19A illustrates a typical potentiometer circuit and also shows the most common schematic symbol for a potentiometer. Notice the three connections or terminals on this device. The voltage or signal to be attenuated (VI) is shown at terminal A. Terminal B is the connection where the output from the circuit is reduced to a percentage of VI (between 0 and 100). The arrow symbol indicates that point B can be moved anywhere between point A and point C. Terminal C is connected to a ground (zero volts) point.

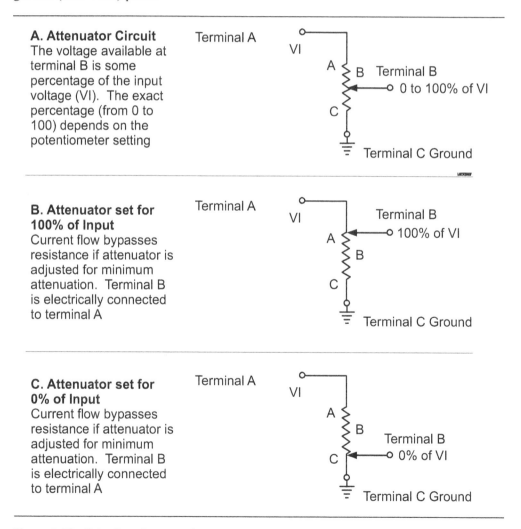

A. Attenuator Circuit
The voltage available at terminal B is some percentage of the input voltage (VI). The exact percentage (from 0 to 100) depends on the potentiometer setting

B. Attenuator set for 100% of Input
Current flow bypasses resistance if attenuator is adjusted for minimum attenuation. Terminal B is electrically connected to terminal A

C. Attenuator set for 0% of Input
Current flow bypasses resistance if attenuator is adjusted for minimum attenuation. Terminal B is electrically connected to terminal A

Figure 9-19 Potentiometer operation

If the potentiometer is set so that point B is at point A (Figure 9-19B), the current flow does not pass through the resistance of the potentiometer and VI is not attenuated. One hundred percent of VI is present at terminal B.

If the potentiometer is set so that point B is at point C (Figure 9-19C), the current must pass through all of the resistance of the potentiometer and VI is attenuated to zero percent. Point B is electrically connected to ground (at Point C) and no voltage is present at terminal B.

Any portion of VI from 0 to 100 percent may be present at terminal B depending on how the potentiometer is adjusted.

For example, if point B is positioned at the midpoint between A and C, 50 percent of the voltage is available at terminal B.

Series Dropping Resistor

The circuit shown in Figure 9-20 illustrates how a fixed resistor can be connected in series with the potentiometer to drop the voltage down to a predetermined level before allowing the potentiometer to provide adjustment over the remaining voltage. In this case, the desired voltage range at terminal B is from 0 to 10 volts and this output voltage must never exceed 10 volts. This means that R^1 must reduce the input voltage by 14 volts (24 - 10 = 14). The total resistance of R^1 and R^2 in series is 1.4 kilohms + 1.0 kilohms = 2.4 kilohms.

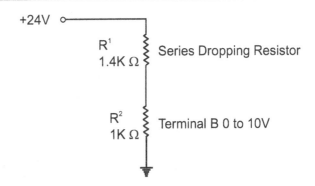

Figure 9-20   Potentiometer with series dropping resistor

The current flowing through both of these resistors can be found using Ohm's Law:

Formula 9-6

$$I = \frac{E}{R} = \frac{24}{2,400} = 0.01A = 10mA$$

The voltage dropped by R^1 can then be calculated using another Ohm's Law formula:

Formula 9-7

$$E = I \times R = 0.1 \times 1,400 = 14.0V$$

In this circuit, the fixed resistance value of R^1 was selected to drop the supply voltage by 14 volts from 24 to 10 volts. R^2 allows adjustment of the remaining voltage between zero and 10 volts.

Solenoid

A solenoid is an electromechanical device that converts electrical energy into linear mechanical motion. In hydraulics, solenoids are most often used to actuate directional valves and are typically on/off devices. Solenoids are available for both AC and DC operation and in all standard voltages. They can be divided into air gap and wet armature types. In order to understand the operation of solenoids it is necessary to briefly examine the principle of electromagnetism.

Electromagnetism

Electric current flowing through a conductor produces a circular magnetic field around the conductor. The direction of the magnetic field depends on the direction of current flow through the wire. Normally, this magnetic field is weak and does not affect the surrounding components.

However, if the conductor is formed into a coil consisting of many loops of the conducting wire (Figure 9-21), the strength of the magnetic field will increase. The field, made up of many magnetic flux lines, forms around the outside and through the center of the coil.

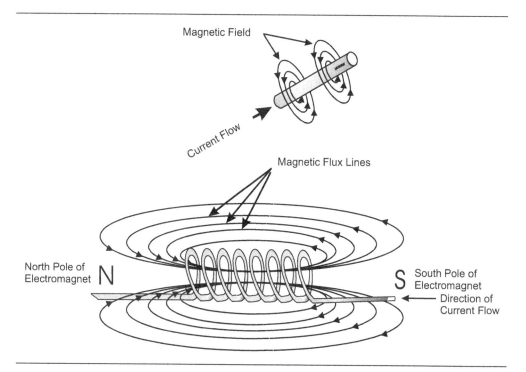

Figure 9-21   Magnetic field around solenoid coil

As long as current is flowing through the wire, the coil acts as an electromagnet and will have north and south poles just like any other magnet. The strength of the magnetic action can be increased by adding more turns of wire to the coil, by increasing the current flow through the coil, or by placing a soft iron core inside the center of the coil. An iron frame surrounding the coil can be added to further intensify the magnetic field.

Magnetic flux lines flow through the iron core and frame material much more easily than they do through air. The iron path both attracts and concentrates the flux lines. If the iron core is allowed to move, it will center itself within the coil when the current flow produces a magnetic action. The stronger the magnetic field, the greater the centering force. This centering action provides the linear mechanical motion required for solenoid operation.

Air Gap Solenoids

Air gap solenoids consist primarily of a T-shaped core or plunger, a wire coil and a C-shaped frame as shown in Figure 9-22. An air gap exists between the plunger and the frame when no current is flowing in the coil. This is because the plunger is held partially out of the coil by a spring and there is no magnetic field to pull it into the center. A solenoid in this position is said to be de-energized.

A solenoid depends on its magnetic field to shift a directional valve spool. A pushpin, also shown in Figure 9-22, is mechanically connected to the end of the valve spool. When current flows in the coil, the resulting magnetic field begins to pull the plunger into the center, overcoming the force of the weak spring (Figure 9-22A). The solenoid is energized but not fully actuated. The directional valve shifts as the plunger hits the pushpin while seating itself within the coil. As the air gap reduces in size, more of the flux lines concentrate in the iron path provided by the plunger and frame. The magnetic force becomes increasingly stronger and holds the solenoid in the energized position (Figure 9-22B).

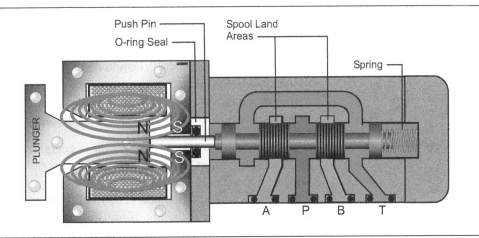

Figure 9-22   Air gap solenoid construction

Wet Armature Solenoids

The wet armature solenoid was developed to overcome some of the problems associated with the air gap solenoid. The wet armature solenoid design has increased reliability as a result of better heat transfer characteristics and the elimination of pushpin seals, which have a tendency to leak.

A wet armature solenoid consists of a coil, a rectangular frame, a pushpin, an armature (plunger), and a tube with one closed end and one threaded end. The rectangular frame surrounds the coil and both parts are encased in plastic. A hole runs through the center of the coil and both ends of the frame. The tube is inserted within this hole when the frame is attached to a directional valve body. The armature is contained within the tube. System fluid from the tank passage within the valve body fills the tube and surrounds the armature (Figure 9-23). Although the wet armature solenoid differs in construction, it operates according to the same electromagnetic principles as the air gap solenoid.

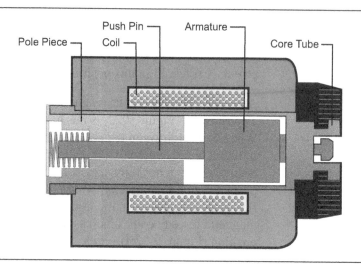

Figure 9-23   Wet armature solenoid construction

DC Operation

DC operation of a solenoid is simpler than AC operation because the current rises to a constant level after coil energization and flows in only one direction. The magnetic field expands and then reaches a steady state condition as the plunger is pulled into the coil. This condition exists until the coil is de-energized. The only resistance to the flow of current is the fixed resistance of the conducting material used to make the coil.

AC Operation

When AC is used as the control power to energize a solenoid, the current is opposed by a factor known as impedance. Impedance is produced by the fixed resistance of the wire used to make the coil winding and, also, by the inductive reactance of the coil, which exists wherever the magnetic field is expanding outward or collapsing inward. Inductive reactance is the opposition developed in a coil to any change of current passing through the coil. The amount of inductive reactance depends on the coil size and the frequency of the AC applied to the coil. It is measured in ohms. Earlier in this chapter it is explained that AC flows first in one direction and then the other, completing this cycle at a rate of 60 times per second. To understand how the AC cycle and impedance affect solenoid operation, it is necessary to examine one complete cycle of the AC applied to the coil.

When the cycle is at zero, the magnetic field does not yet exist and there is only the fixed resistance of the wire in the coil to oppose current flow. The plunger is partially out of the coil. Impedance is at a minimum and, therefore, a high inrush current occurs in the coil windings.

The magnetic field expands outward as the AC cycle rises from zero to a positive peak. Solenoid force is greatest at the peak or maximum value and pulls the plunger into the coil, actuating the directional valve to which it is mechanically connected by the pushpin. Impedance is at a maximum when the plunger is fully centered within the coil. At this time the current is undergoing the most change and that causes the inductive reactance and the impedance to increase to their maximum value. When the impedance is at its maximum value, the AC current is at its minimum value. This minimum amount of current is known as the holding current for the solenoid and is several times smaller than the peak inrush current experienced when the coil is first energized.

As the AC cycle progresses through the positive peak value and returns to zero, the magnetic field collapses, the solenoid force decreases and the plunger is pushed out of the center of the coil by the load (usually a spring biased spool).

The magnetic field expands and the solenoid force builds as the AC cycle increases in the negative direction until the plunger is again pulled into the center of the coil at the negative peak value.

As the AC cycle returns to zero, the magnetic field and the solenoid force decrease and the plunger is once again forced out of the center of the coil by the load.

The continuous alternation of the current produces a constant motion of the plunger in and out of the coil and a chattering noise known as AC hum. This motion is highly undesirable and must be minimized by the use of shading coils.

Shading coils are built into all solenoids that are designed to be powered by AC. In the air gap solenoid, the shading coils consist of copper wire loops attached to the frame. In wet armature solenoids, the shading coil is a copper wire ring installed into the pushpin end of the tube. As the magnetic field from the main coil begins to collapse inward, the moving magnetic flux lines produce a current flow in the shading coil. This current lags behind the main coil current (it is increasing as the main coil current is decreasing) but supports a magnetic field in the shading coil that is strong enough to hold the solenoid in the energized position during the periods when the AC cycle is passing through zero. As a result, the AC hum is effectively reduced to a minimum.

AC Solenoid Failure

Heat is the main problem associated with solenoid failures. Excessive heat in the coil windings melts the thin coat of insulation on the conducting wire and causes the loops of the winding to short circuit. A short circuit creates an unintended path for current flow and causes the coil to malfunction. Solenoids used on industrial directional valves are of the continuous duty type, which can be held energized indefinitely without overheating. The heat dissipating ability of these solenoids is good enough to dissipate most of the heat produced by the coil's low holding current.

Heat problems with solenoids usually occur under one of the following three conditions:

- Blocked plunger or armature
- Low line voltage
- Excessive ambient temperature

Most solenoid electrical failures are a result of a mechanical problem. Either the valve spool is blocked and cannot move when the solenoid is energized, or the plunger (or armature) of the solenoid binds up during energization and does not fully center itself within the coil. When either of these conditions occurs, a continuous high inrush current is present in the coil windings. The coil cannot dissipate the tremendous amount of heat generated by the high current and burns itself out within a short period of time.

Valve spools may stick as a result of contamination of the hydraulic fluid or because of burrs which may form between the spool and the valve body. Valves may also become blocked due to a valve base that is not flat. When the mounting bolts are tightened, the base may warp enough to bind up the spool and cause coil failure when the solenoid is energized.

In an air gap solenoid, plunger movement may become restricted if the iron laminations spread apart due to the wear of repeated contact with the pushpin. Also, if a solenoid is disassembled for cleaning, and then reassembled with the plunger not in its original position, different wear patterns may cause the plunger to bind during actuation.

Failures also occur if the voltage supplied to the coil is too low to produce sufficient solenoid force. In this situation, the plunger is unable to fully center itself within the coil in the designed time frame. Inrush current is present for a longer period of time and, as a result, the coil overheats every time it is energized and eventually fails. Low voltage conditions may occur during brownouts or periods of heavy demand on the local power source.

If the air temperature surrounding a solenoid is excessively high, due to poor ventilation or installation too near another heat source, the solenoid's ability to release heat into the air is greatly reduced. If a solenoid is operated for prolonged periods under these conditions, it will probably fail.

Occasionally, an electrical circuit component failure or an incorrect wiring hookup may cause both solenoids of a double solenoid valve to energize at the same time. These valves have a solenoid installed at each end of the valve spool. The flow paths through the valve depend on which solenoid is energized. If both solenoids are accidentally selected, one solenoid may seat completely and block spool movement in the other direction. Even though the solenoid on the other end of the valve spool has been energized, it cannot move and soon fails due to overheating.

Solenoid Manual Override

Both air gap and wet armature solenoids come equipped with a manual override for checking movement of the directional valve spool without energizing the solenoid. A small metal pin protrudes from the air gap solenoid cover or the wet armature tube. Pressing the override pin causes the plunger or armature to contact the pushpin which moves the spool. If the plunger or spool is blocked, the override cannot be pushed completely into the cover. The override may also be used to check or adjust hydraulic system operation without energizing the complete electrical control system.

Relay

The relay, which operates much like a solenoid, is an electromagnetic device that consists of a coil with a soft iron core and electrical contacts mounted on, but insulated from, the moving armature or plunger. The relay allows one circuit to control another.

As shown in Figure 9-24, the controlling circuit usually contains the relay solenoid, switch contacts and a low voltage power source. The switch contacts in the coil circuit act as a pilot device and may be the contacts of a pushbutton switch, a pressure switch, a timer, a limit switch or the contacts of another relay. The controlled circuit contains the relay contacts, a load device and a separate power source.

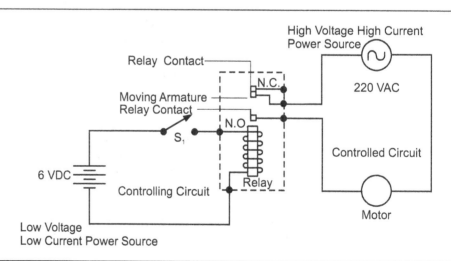

Figure 9-24 Simple relay circuit

Relay Operation

When current is supplied to the coil, the resulting magnetic field pulls the armature and the contacts toward the coil. The relay is in the energized position when the armature is fully seated. Contacts that were open are now closed. These contacts are referred to as the normally open (N.O.) contacts. Contacts that were closed are now open. These contacts are called the normally closed (N.C.) contacts. Therefore, the terms "normally open" and "normally closed" refer to the condition of the contacts when the relay coil is de-energized. A relay may have one or both types of contacts and may also have multiple sets of contacts for controlling several circuits at once.

When the coil circuit is opened, current cannot flow in the coil, the magnetic field collapses and the relay de-energizes. A spring attached to the armature returns the contacts to their normal position.

Relay Applications

The relay can be used to open and close high voltage or high current circuits with relatively little voltage and current in the coil circuit. The controlling circuit is electrically isolated from the controlled circuit. In other words, current from the controlling circuit does not flow in the controlled circuit. The link between the two circuits is strictly magnetic. The relay is also useful for remote control of circuits. The switch contacts in the coil circuit may be located at one point and the other circuit components located some distance away. Because the controlling circuit is usually operated by a low current power source, relatively small gauge wires can be used to connect the remote switch device.

Figure 9-25 shows another application of a relay. In this case, relay contacts are used to switch between two different voltage levels that are applied to a circuit. The two voltage levels may produce two different speeds for a device driven by the circuit board. Attenuators are used to develop the 7.2 volts and the 4.4 volts from the 10 volt source. The upper relay symbol represents a set of normally open relay contacts and the lower relay symbol shows a set of normally closed relay contacts on the same relay. When the relay is de-energized, 4.4 volts are supplied to the board. When the relay is energized, 7.2 volts are applied.

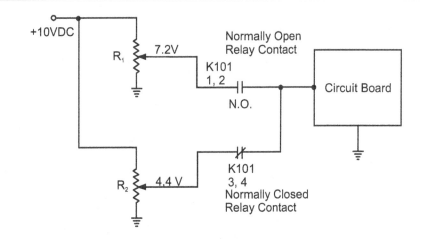

Figure 9-25   Relay controlling two input voltages

A relay which activates or deactivates heavy electrical equipment such as motors and heaters is known as a contactor. The contacts of this device are physically strong enough to switch heavy current flow. The energizing circuit is generally controlled by a pushbutton switch located on an operator's console.

Relays can also be constructed to introduce a time delay when energized (ON DELAY) or de-energized (OFF DELAY). The time delay can be either fixed or variable and may range from a fraction of a second to as much as several minutes. Time delay relays are used primarily for sequence control of a system.

Relay Ratings

Two separate ratings are needed to describe a relay for a given application. The electrical contacts are rated for the voltage and current that they can safely switch. The relay is also rated for the voltage and current required to properly energize the coil. If a time delay is desired, this value must also be specified. The value of these ratings will depend on how the relay is used in the system.

Transformer

The transformer is a device that transfers AC energy from one circuit to another without electrical contact between them. This is accomplished through electromagnetic mutual inductance. Current flowing in a wire produces a magnetic field around the wire. This is the basic operating principle of the relay and the solenoid. The opposite is also true; in other words, magnetic flux lines moving past a conductor will generate a current flow in the conductor. This is the principle used by the transformer to perform its function. An AC signal applied to a coil will produce an alternating magnetic field in that coil. The moving magnetic flux lines will induce an alternating current of the same frequency in a second coil located within reach of the flux lines.

Transformers are constructed so that the two coils are placed quite close to each other. See Figure 9-26. Most often the two coils are wound around the same laminated soft iron core so that all of the expanding or collapsing flux lines from the primary coil will move past all of the windings of the secondary coil. This produces an alternating current in the secondary circuit and also allows maximum transfer of AC energy from the primary circuit to the secondary circuit.

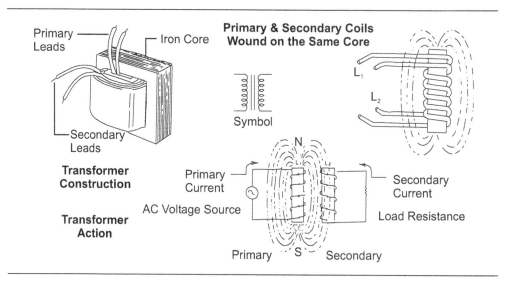

Figure 9-26   Iron core transformer

Transformer Applications

Transformers are very versatile devices. They are used to step up or step down the voltage from the primary to the secondary circuit. They can also be used to step up or down the current from one circuit to another. They are used to match impedances between circuits and also to provide electrical isolation of one circuit from another. They can pass AC signals while blocking DC, and they can provide several different signals at various voltage levels. These functions are determined by the "turns ratio" of the two coils used in the transformer. Turns ratio is defined as the ratio between the number of turns in the secondary winding and the number of turns in the primary winding.

A step up transformer is constructed so that there are more turns of wire in the secondary coil than in the primary coil. A transformer made this way will provide more voltage in the secondary circuit than that supplied to the primary circuit. See Figure 9-29A. This increase in the secondary voltage comes at the expense of a decrease in the secondary current. The total circuit power does not change. *(Remember that P = I x E. If E increases, but I decreases by the same proportion, P remains the same.)*

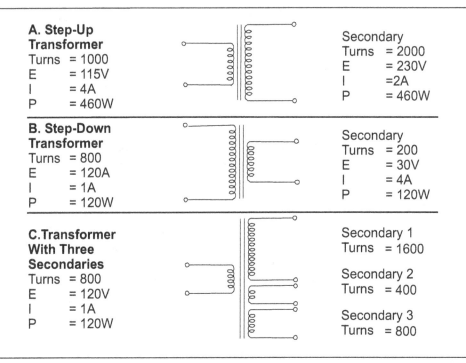

A. Step-Up Transformer
Turns = 1000
E = 115V
I = 4A
P = 460W

Secondary
Turns = 2000
E = 230V
I = 2A
P = 460W

B. Step-Down Transformer
Turns = 800
E = 120A
I = 1A
P = 120W

Secondary
Turns = 200
E = 30V
I = 4A
P = 120W

C. Transformer With Three Secondaries
Turns = 800
E = 120V
I = 1A
P = 120W

Secondary 1
Turns = 1600

Secondary 2
Turns = 400

Secondary 3
Turns = 800

Figure 9-27   Transformer types

In Figure 9-29A, the number of turns in the secondary winding is 2,000, while the number of turns in the primary winding is only 1,000. This is a ratio of 2,000:1,000 or 2:1. This means that the applied AC voltage will be stepped up by a ratio of 2 to 1. In this example, the 115 volts applied to the primary circuit is increased to 230 volts in the secondary circuit. Since the voltage is doubled, the current must be halved from 4 amps in the primary coil to 2 amps in the secondary coil. Note that the power in the primary is equal to 4A x 114V = 460 watts. The power in the secondary must equal the power in the primary, 2A x 230V = 460W. A step up transformer steps up the voltage but steps down the current.

In a step down transformer, the voltage is stepped down by some ratio while the current is stepped up by the same ratio. The transformer is constructed so that the number of turns in the secondary winding is less than the number of turns in the primary winding. In Figure 9-29B the number of secondary turns is 200 while the number of turns in the primary winding is 800. The turns ratio is 200:800 or 1:4. This means that the applied AC voltage will be stepped down by a ratio of 1 to 4. For every 4 volts applied to the primary, 1 volt will be produced in the secondary. If the applied voltage is 120 volts, then the secondary voltage will be 30 volts. Since the secondary voltage is stepped down to one fourth of its primary value, the current in the secondary must be quadrupled, from 1A to 4A. The power in the primary equals 1A x 120V = 120W. The power in the secondary equals 4A x 30V = 120W.

An isolation transformer is constructed so that the number of turns in the primary and secondary windings is equal. The turns ratio is 1:1. The voltage and current is neither stepped up nor stepped down. This type of transformer is used to isolate the voltage and current in one circuit from the voltage and current in another circuit while passing an AC signal from one to the other. The signal is coupled from primary to secondary by the magnetic field through mutual inductance.

Transformers can also be made with more than one secondary winding. See Figure 9-29C. One secondary is a step up, another is a step down, and the third is for isolation. Transformers can produce any desired change in the AC signal applied to the primary circuit simply by winding the primary and secondary coils in the proper ratios.

Diode Rectifier

Although most electrical equipment is connected to an AC source, the circuits within the equipment often require DC voltages for operation. The process of converting the incoming AC voltage into DC pulses is called rectification. The diode is the device used to produce this change from AC to DC.

Diodes are constructed of semiconductor material. This means that the material is normally neither a good conductor nor a good insulator. This material can be given good conducting ability by a process called doping in which certain impurities are added to the base material. There are two types of semiconductor material used in making diodes negative type and positive type. Negative or N type material contains extra negative charges within the structure of the material. Positive or P type material is made so that the structure of the material contains extra positive charges. The negative side of a diode is known as the cathode and the positive side is known as the anode.

For ease of identification, the end of the diode marked with a band of color is the cathode end. The two types of semiconductor material are placed back to back within the diode case and the area where they meet is called the semiconductor junction (Figure 9-31).

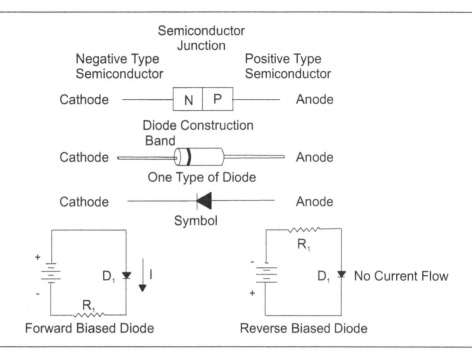

Figure 9-28   Semiconductor diode

Because of the way a diode is constructed, current can flow across the junction and through the diode in only one direction and only under certain circumstances. As shown in Figure 9-28, current flows through the diode from the anode to the cathode only when the anode has a positive electrical potential with respect to the cathode. Current cannot flow from cathode to anode and cannot flow when the cathode is more positive than the anode. Note that when viewing the schematic symbol for a diode, current flows out of the arrowhead if the proper biasing conditions are met. Biasing refers to the application of positive and negative voltage to the ends of the diode. It is the ability to allow current flow in one direction while blocking it in the other that enables a diode to rectify AC into DC pulses.

Half Wave Rectifier

Figure 9-29A shows a transformer, diode and load resistor in a simple rectifier circuit. When the AC voltage is in the positive half cycle, the anode of the diode is more positive than the cathode. Current flows down through the load resistor and from anode to cathode through the diode. The current flowing through the resistor produces a positive pulse across the load.

When the AC input voltage crosses zero and progresses through the negative half cycle, the anode of the diode becomes negative with respect to the cathode and current cannot flow through the diode or in the circuit. A positive pulse is produced for only one half of each AC cycle and no pulses are produced during the other half cycle. This is called half wave rectification and the resulting output of the rectifier is called pulsating DC because it only flows in one direction and does not alternate between positive and negative.

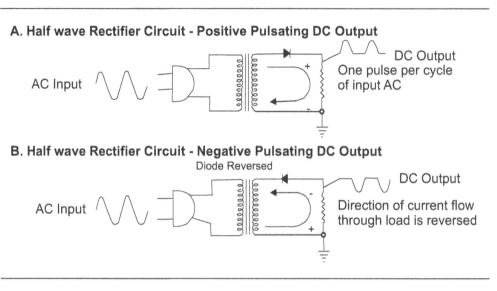

A. Half wave Rectifier Circuit - Positive Pulsating DC Output

AC Input

DC Output
One pulse per cycle
of input AC

B. Half wave Rectifier Circuit - Negative Pulsating DC Output

Diode Reversed

AC Input

DC Output

Direction of current flow
through load is reversed

Figure 9-29   Half wave rectifier circuits

If the diode connections were reversed, as shown in Figure 9-29B, the diode would only conduct current during the negative half cycle of the AC wave and the pulses developed by the load would be negative DC voltage appearing for one half cycle. (If the cathode is more negative than the anode, it's the same as saying the anode is positive with respect to the cathode; the diode will conduct in either case.) The pulses are negative because the current flows through the load resistor in the opposite direction.

Full Wave Rectifier

By using two diodes and a center tapped transformer, full wave rectification of the input AC voltage can be accomplished. As shown in Figure 9-30A, during the first half cycle of the AC input, conditions are correct for diode D1 to conduct and current flows through the load resistor producing a positive output pulse. Diode D2 is improperly biased during this period and cuts off current flow through that part of the circuit.

When the AC input is in the negative half cycle, as shown in Figure 9-30B, diode D1 cuts off, but the conditions are right for diode D2 to conduct. This allows current to flow through the load resistor during this half cycle. Since current flows through the resistor in the same direction as it did in the first half cycle, another positive output pulse is produced. Full wave rectification of the AC input produces two DC pulses for every cycle of AC applied. The amount of pulsating DC voltage available at the output is twice that of the half wave rectifier circuit. As before, reversing the diode connections enables the rectifier to produce negative pulsating DC voltage.

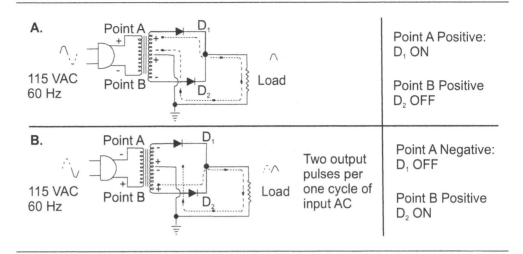

| A. | Point A Positive: D₁ ON |
| | Point B Positive D₂ OFF |

Figure 9-30 Full wave rectifier circuit operation

Filtering Pulsating DC to Pure DC

The pulsating DC produced by a rectifier circuit is not adequate for the proper operation of most DC circuits. Usually DC circuits require pure or unchanging DC voltage levels. The DC pulsations must be smoothed out by filter components connected to the rectifier circuit. The most commonly used component is the capacitor (Figure 9-31). Very simply, the capacitor is a device that has the ability to store an electrical charge and then release it to the circuit when required.

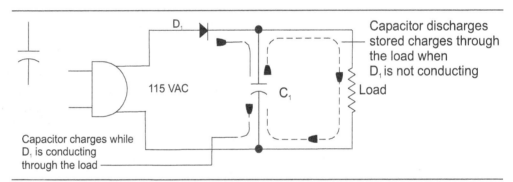

Figure 9-31 Capacitor used as filter for rectifier circuit

When connected across the load of a rectifier, a capacitor will charge up to the peak value of the DC pulse when a diode conducts. Then as the DC pulse begins to return to zero, the capacitor discharges some of its stored charge into the load. The capacitor does not have time to completely discharge before the next peak is felt, so the output is held at a value very close to the peak value. This action is repeated for each pulse and helps to maintain the output at a constant average level. If the capacitor is large enough, the DC output voltage remains essentially free of variations.

Troubleshooting Electrical Devices

Electrical troubleshooting is the process of locating the cause of malfunctions in electrical circuits. This section contains some general troubleshooting information as well as specific tests for determining the status of the previously described electrical devices.

Skill in troubleshooting electrical equipment and circuits requires:

- Enough knowledge of electrical principles to understand how a circuit or device should function.

- Skill in reading and interpreting electrical schematics, diagrams, product data, etc.

- Skill in operating test equipment and interpreting test measurements.

- An ability to analyze problems in a logical manner.

Basic information on the first three of the above items is presented earlier in this chapter. These skills are acquired and developed through experience with electrical circuits. However, if electrical problems are not approached in a logical fashion, a lot of time and effort can be wasted in determining the cause of a malfunction. Following a set of systematic steps that narrow the problem down to an increasingly smaller area of the equipment is much more efficient than trial and error methods. The following logical troubleshooting technique is a time proven procedure that can be very useful in organizing the problem solving effort and reducing equipment downtime.

Logical Troubleshooting Procedure

This procedure consists of five steps that should be performed in order. These steps represent the most reliable method of learning and applying a logical approach to problem solving and can be applied to any equipment, regardless of size.

Step 1: Symptom Identification. Trouble symptoms are external indications that a circuit or device is not functioning correctly. A symptom is identified by investigating the problem with the senses sight, sound, smell and touch. For example, a visual inspection of the equipment may reveal that a circuit component has overheated and changed color, or that an indicator lamp which should be on is not. Perhaps there is a peculiar odor that leads to the discovery of melted insulation or a chattering noise that indicates a solenoid is about to fail. If there are controls or adjusting knobs, moving their position may change the problem or have no effect on the equipment at all, either of which may be a significant factor in finding the problem. Sometimes, even the fact that the equipment is completely inoperable is a good symptom.

If someone else was operating the equipment when it failed, ask if anything unusual was noticed prior to the failure. Funny noises, things that don't look quite right, and improper sequence of operation are all symptoms that may lead to the cause of the problem.

If there are no immediately identifiable symptoms, try operating the equipment after determining that it is safe to do so. Notice what works and what doesn't. Identify the point in a sequence where the problem occurs. Look, listen, smell and touch during this investigation and note anything unusual, no matter how small. It just may be the key to finding the cause of the malfunction.

The time spent on Step 1 is generally more important than that spent on any other step in the process. Frequently, a thorough search for trouble symptoms leads directly to the cause of the malfunction.

Step 2: Symptom Analysis. The purpose of this step is to identify the functions where symptoms indicate a malfunction. Use the symptom information obtained in Step 1 along with schematic and functional block diagrams and knowledge of how the equipment is supposed to operate to make logical technical deduction.

For example, if the equipment with the malfunction is a plastic injection molding machine, the possible functions might include injection forward, injection return, screw run, back pressure control, clamp close, clamp pressurization, prefill shift, mold protect and clamp open. The symptoms observed in Step 1 indicate the clamp will not pressurize. In analyzing the symptoms obtained in Step 1, the problem might be narrowed down to clamp close, clamp pressurization or prefill shift, any one of which may contain the faulty circuit. At this point in the procedure, without using any test equipment, several functions have been eliminated and the problem is isolated to just a few possible circuits.

Step 3: Isolate the Single Faulty Function. In this step, test equipment is used to decide which of the possible faulty functions is actually the cause of the malfunction. In making these tests, follow these guidelines:

- Make only those tests that are safe to make.

- Make the least difficult tests first.

- Test those functions first that will eliminate one or more of the other possible faulty functions.

For example, if an ohmmeter reading can determine the fault, do not take a voltmeter reading as that requires power on the equipment. If half the machine has to be disassembled to reach a test point, perform a simpler test first. Test at a midway point in the circuitry if possible. A good reading at the midway point eliminates the preceding functions and indicates that the problem is in the remaining circuits. A faulty signal at the midway point means the problem is located in the functions that process the signal before the midway point.

In the injection molding example, testing in the clamp pressurization circuits at the point where the clamp fully closed signal is input either eliminates that function or confirms that the cause of the problem is a clamp that is not fully closed and, therefore, cannot be pressurized.

Continue testing inputs and outputs of the suspect functions until the single faulty function is identified and confirmed.

Step 4: Isolate the Faulty Circuit. In this step, the single malfunctioning circuit within a functional group of circuits is located. Use the accumulated symptom and test data to close in on the single faulty circuit. Follow the guidelines from Step 3, but apply them this time to the circuits related to faulty function. Use schematic and block diagrams to locate test points.

Using the injection molding machine example again, assume that the clamp fully closed signal is not present at the input to the clamp pressurization circuits. Test within the clamp close circuits until a single faulty circuit is identified. Perhaps the first test reveals that the output of the clamp fully closed circuit is bad. A check of the inputs to this circuit indicates that the input from a clamp closed limit switch is bad, but all other inputs are good. The problem is now identified as being associated with one of the relatively few parts contained in a single circuit.

Step 5: Locate/Verify Cause of Malfunction. The tests made in this step identify the failing part within the faulty circuit. Test the circuit until the cause of the malfunction is found. Examine and test the faulty part to verify that it has caused the problem and produced the observed symptoms.

In checking out the clamp fully closed circuit, for example, remove the suspect limit switch from the circuit and test with an ohmmeter to determine that the switch contacts are closing correctly to complete the circuit. Connect the ohmmeter across the contacts of the switch and actuate the switch arm several times while the meter reading is checked. If the contacts close properly, the meter should read zero ohms when the arm is in one position and infinity when the arm is in the other position. If the meter pointer does not move when the switch arm is actuated, disassemble and examine the switch. Suppose this last examination reveals that the mechanical linkage connecting the switch arm to the contacts is broken. The cause of the malfunction has been found and a final analysis shows that this cause explains the observed symptoms. However, the procedure is not complete until verification is conducted. In this case, install a new limit switch in the circuit and operate the equipment to confirm that the problem has indeed been fixed.

Electrical circuits are designed, built, and operated in a logical manner. A logical troubleshooting technique takes advantage of this fact and should be used whenever possible to reduce machine downtime.

The next part of this section outlines some basic electrical tests that can be conducted on the devices presented earlier in this chapter. Although they are not described below, mechanical inspections of the devices should also be performed as part of any troubleshooting test. Also, if spare parts are available, substitution of a known good part for a suspect part is often the quickest method of returning equipment to operation. The suspect part can then be tested and either repaired or discarded.

Testing a Potentiometer

Since a potentiometer is a variable resistance device, it should be disconnected from its circuit and tested with an ohmmeter if it is suspect. Only two of the three leads need to be disconnected for this test.

To test a potentiometer, use the following procedure:

1. Determine the expected resistance value from a schematic diagram for the circuit. The value may also be printed on the case of the device.

2. Connect the ohmmeter across the ends of the potentiometer and confirm that the reading matches the expected value.

3. Remove a test lead from one end and move it to the middle terminal. The middle terminal may not be the wiper. (It is often not.)

4. Rotate the shaft or turn the screw that varies the resistance of the device. The ohmmeter reading should indicate zero ohms at one end of the shaft rotation and the full expected resistance value of the potentiometer at the other end. It should also show a smooth change in resistance as the shaft is turned.

5. Move the lead that is still connected to an end terminal over to the other end.

6. Rotate the shaft again while looking for the same smooth transition from zero to maximum resistance.

Be very careful when adjusting small potentiometers installed on printed circuit boards as they are quite fragile and can easily be broken if rotated beyond the end stops.

Testing a Solenoid Coil

When a solenoid is thought to be faulty:

1. Remove it from the machine (plug opened ports on valves if necessary).

2. Disassemble and visually examine the solenoid for signs of overheating or mechanical problems.

3. Test the solenoid coil by attaching an ohmmeter (set to a low resistance range) across the coil terminals. A relatively low reading (a few thousand ohms or less) should be observed on the meter if the coil is good. It should not read zero ohms as this indicates that the coil windings are shorted to each other, probably as a result of melted insulation. If the ohmmeter reads infinity, it means that the coil has opened up and is defective.

Testing a Relay

To test a suspect relay:

1. Remove it from the equipment.

2. Carefully examine it for signs of a mechanical problem.

3. If none is noted, check the relay coil in the same way as a solenoid coil. The electrical contacts can be tested with an ohmmeter in the same way that any switch contacts are tested. The meter should read zero when the contact are closed and infinity when they are open.

Manually actuate the relay armature to conduct these tests. Remember to test both the normally open and normally closed contacts.

Testing a Transformer

When it is determined by voltage readings or symptom information that a transformer may be the cause of a malfunction, check the primary and secondary coil resistance with an ohmmeter. Disconnect one end of the primary winding (coil) and one end of the secondary winding from the rest of the circuit prior to testing. If the failure is the result of an open winding, the ohmmeter will read infinity when connected across the defective winding.

If the failure is caused by shorted turns within a winding, the problem is more difficult to diagnose because the ohmmeter will indicate a very low resistance. Since a winding consists of a length of conductor wound into a coil, the resistance readings are normally quite low anyway. If shorted turns are suspected:

1. Use the expected primary and secondary operating voltages to determine the approximate turns ratio. Divide the secondary voltage into the primary voltage. For example, 120 volts divided by 24 volts equals a ratio of 5:1.

2. Use this ratio to compare the measured primary resistance to the measured secondary resistance. In the example, if the primary resistance is 20 ohms, then the secondary resistance should be approximately 20/5 = 4 ohms. However, this is only if the same gauge wire is measured in both instances.

Be sure to adjust the zero ohms control prior to making the measurement and hold the test probes by the insulated portion only.

It may be quite difficult to determine whether the reading is accurate as the measurement is so near the low end of the ohms scale. Compare the readings to those obtained from a replacement transformer, if one is available. To positively verify that the transformer is faulty, it may be necessary to substitute a known good transformer for the suspect one.

Testing a Diode

A simple resistance check with an ohmmeter can be used to test a diode's ability to pass current in one direction only.

To test a suspect diode:

1. Remove one end of the diode from the circuit.

2. Connect the positive ohmmeter lead to the anode and the negative lead to the cathode. When the ohmmeter is connected this way, the diode is forward biased and the measured reading should be very low. The ohmmeter should be set for the appropriate diode test range.

3. Reverse the ohmmeter connections. When the negative ohmmeter lead is attached to the anode and the positive lead is attached to the cathode, the diode is reverse biased and the meter should read a high resistance.

A good diode should read low resistance when forward biased and high resistance when reverse biased. If the diode reads a high resistance in both directions, it is probably open. If the readings are low in both directions, the diode is shorted.

It is also quite possible for a defective diode to show a difference in forward and backward resistance. In this case, the ratio of forward to backward resistance, known as the diode's front to back ratio, is the important factor. The actual ratio depends on the type of diode. As a rule of thumb, a small signal diode should have a ratio of several hundred to one, and a power rectifier can operate with a ratio as low as ten to one.

Electrical Ground

Every electrical circuit has a point of reference to which all circuit voltages are compared. This reference point is called ground and circuit voltages are either positive or negative with respect to ground. When voltage measurements are taken, the difference of potential between a point in the circuit and a ground point is measured by the voltmeter. This type of ground is referred to as chassis or common ground. Connections to ground are also made for safety reasons and, in this case, ground refers to earth ground.

Earth Ground

In the early days of electricity, ground referred to the earth itself and since then it has represented a point of zero potential or zero volts. Connections to each ground are made primarily for safety and protection purposes. A short circuit within a device that connects live voltage to the frame could cause a serious shock to anyone touching it. However, if the frame is connected to earth ground, it is held at the safe potential of zero volts as the earth itself absorbs the voltage.

A third prong on grounded power plugs connects most stationary equipment in use today to earth ground through the electrical wiring system. Some equipment is connected to earth ground by a conductor that goes from the metal frame of the equipment to a long copper rod driven into the earth. In the home, appliances are often grounded by connecting the conductor to a water pipe running into the ground. In any case, the frames of all equipment connected to earth ground are at the same zero volt potential. This prevents shocks that might occur should a person touch two pieces of ungrounded equipment at the same time.

Chassis or Common Ground

In some cases, electrical circuits used today are not connected directly to earth ground, but still require a point of reference or a common point to which elements of each circuit are connected. For example, a portable battery operated transistor radio does not have a ground conductor connecting it with the earth. A strip of conducting foil on the internal circuit board is used as the common point. In an automobile battery, the negative terminal is generally connected to the engine block or chassis frame by a heavy cable. The connecting point, as well as every other point on the metal frame, is considered to be a ground for the electrical circuits of the vehicle. The rubber tires insulate the vehicle from the earth ground. Ground in these devices is simply a zero reference point within an electrical circuit and is referred to as chassis ground. All voltages in the circuit are measured with respect to this common point.

Importance of a Zero Reference Point

Without a zero reference point, which may be either earth or chassis ground, voltage could not be expressed as a positive or negative value. The schematic diagrams in Figure 9-32 illustrate this point. Figure 9-32A shows a voltmeter connected to the two terminals of a 6V dry cell battery. Without a ground in the circuit, the voltage being measured is simply 6V between the two terminals. It is neither positive nor negative.

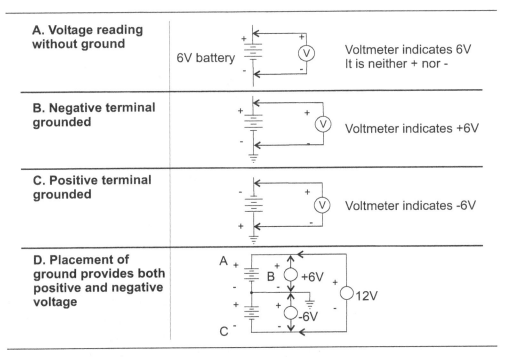

Figure 9-32   Significance of zero reference point

In Figure 9-32B, the negative battery terminal is connected to ground. The voltmeter measures the difference of potential between the positive terminal and the ground point. The voltage measured in this case is +6V because the ungrounded terminal is 6V more positive than the ground or zero reference point.

Figure 9-32C shows that -6V is measured by the voltmeter when the positive terminal of the battery is connected to the zero reference point (ground). The ungrounded battery terminal is now -6V more negative than the reference point.

In Figure 9-32D, the schematic shows two 6V batteries connected in series. The voltage between point A and point C is 12V. When a ground is placed at point B, between the two batteries, +6V is available between point A and point B, and 6V is available between point C and point B. Many modern electronic circuits require both positive and negative voltage for proper operation. This would be impossible without a zero reference point in the circuit.

Isolation Between Earth and Chassis Ground

Industrial equipment often requires both an earth and a separate chassis ground for proper operation. The earth ground represents an actual potential of zero volts, while the chassis ground is used only as a reference point and may be at some potential above or below the earth ground. In these cases, it is important that the earth ground and the chassis ground are not connected together at any point in the equipment. However, during installation or repairs, the chassis ground may be inadvertently connected to the earth ground. A simple way to check for this condition uses a 1.5V "D" cell battery and holder, connecting wires, and a voltmeter. The equipment must be turned OFF to make this test. As shown in Figure 9-33, the battery is installed between the chassis ground and the earth ground.

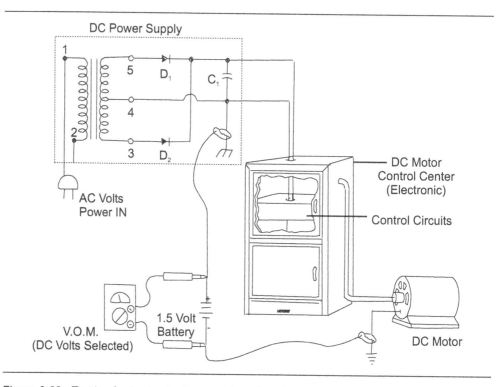

Figure 9-33   Testing for inadvertent connection of earth ground and chassis ground

The voltmeter, set to measure 1.5V DC, is connected across the battery. If a connection exists between the chassis and the earth ground, it will place a short circuit across the battery and the voltmeter will indicate zero volts. If this is the case, temporarily disconnect one end of the battery to keep it from discharging while looking for the improper connection between the grounds. When the connection is found, remove it and reconnect the battery and the meter. The voltmeter should read the battery potential of 1.5V. If the voltmeter reading is still zero volts, an improper connection still exists in the equipment. Repeat the test until the voltmeter reads the battery voltage. Remember to disconnect the battery when the test is complete.

Electrical Wiring

Electrical wires or conductors form the path through which electrical charges are transferred from one point in a circuit to another. Current flows quite easily through a conductor. Insulators, such as the rubber, plastic or nylon coverings on the surface of conductors, confine the flow of electrical charges within the conductor to protect against electrical shocks and short circuits. The current flow in an insulator is so small that for practical purposes it is considered to be zero.

The use of conductors and their insulation is governed primarily by the NATIONAL ELECTRICAL CODE (NEC), sponsored by the National Fire Protection Association. The NEC lists the minimum safety precautions needed to safeguard persons, buildings and their contents from hazards arising from the use of electricity. Various sections of the code cover electrical conductors and equipment installed in industrial plants. While the code is advisory in nature, it should be considered as the authority in all questions regarding the safe and proper use of electricity. Compliance with the NEC, coupled with proper electrical maintenance procedures, results in an installation that is relatively free from electrical hazards.

This section describes the most common conductors and insulating materials, as well as some typical devices used to make wiring connections. It also covers some important wiring considerations like conductor ampacity, voltage drop on long wire runs and electromagnetic interference.

Conductors and Insulating Materials

Wires and cables are the most common conductors used to carry electrical current through all kinds of circuits and systems. Wires and cables are made in a wide variety of types and construction that are suited to many different applications (see Figure 9-34). Differences include the size of the wire used, the kind of insulation covering the wire, the type of outer covering, and the number and makeup of the conductors contained within a wire or cable.

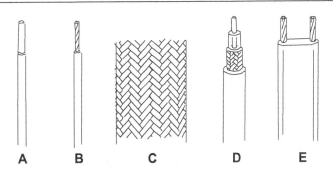

A   B   C   D   E

Figure 9-34   Common types of conductors

Wire Size

Because the diameters of round conductors or wires are usually only a small fraction of an inch, wire diameter is expressed in mils, which are thousandths (0.001) of an inch, to avoid the use of decimals. A diameter of 0.025 inch is equivalent to 25 mils. The cross-sectional area of a wire is usually expressed in units called circular mils. The area in circular mils of a wire is equal to the square of the diameter. A wire having 25 mils of diameter has a cross-sectional area of 25 x 25 = 625 circular mils of area.

Wires are manufactured in specific sizes, called gauge numbers. Figure 9-35A shows characteristics of wire sizes ranging from 0000 to 40. Gauge numbers are listed in the first column. In successive columns are listed the diameter in mils, circular mil area, and the resistance of 1,000 feet (305m) of that size copper wire at 77°F (25°C).

A. Wire Gauge Numbers and Characteristics

Gauge Number	Diameter (mils)	Area Circular mils	Ohms per 1,000 ft. 25° C mils	Gauge Number	Diameter (mils)	Area Circular mils	Ohms per 1,000 ft. 25° C mils
0000	460.0	212,000.0	0.0500	19	36.0	1,290.0	8.21
000	410.0	168,000.0	0.0630	20	32.0	1,020.0	10.4
00	365.0	133,000.0	0.0795	21	28.5	810.0	13.1
0	325.0	106,000.0	0.100	22	25.3	642.0	16.5
1	289.0	83,700.0	0.126	23	22.6	509.0	20.8
2	258.0	66,400.0	0.159	24	20.1	404.0	26.2
3	229.0	52,600.0	0.201	25	17.9	320.0	33.0
4	204.0	41,700.0	0.253	26	15.9	254.0	41.6
5	182.0	33,100.0	0.319	27	14.2	202.0	52.5
6	162.0	26,300.0	0.403	28	12.6	160.0	66.2
7	144.0	20,800.0	0.508	29	11.3	127.0	83.4
8	128.0	16,500.0	0.641	30	10.0	101.0	105.0
9	114.0	13,100.0	0.808	31	8.9	79.7	133.0
10	102.0	10,400.0	1.02	32	8.0	63.2	167.0
11	91.0	8,230.0	1.28	33	7.1	50.1	211.0
12	81.0	6,530.0	1.62	34	6.3	39.8	266.0
13	72.0	5,180.0	2.04	35	5.6	31.5	335.0
14	64.0	4,110.0	2.58	36	5.0	25.0	423.0
15	57.0	3,260.0	3.25	37	4.5	19.8	533.0
16	51.0	2,580.0	4.09	38	4.0	15.7	673.0
17	45.0	2,050.0	5.16	39	3.5	12.5	848.0
18	40.0	1,620.0	6.51	40	3.1	9.9	1,070.0

B. Relationship between Wire Size and Gauge Number

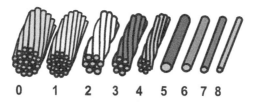

0 1 2 3 4 5 6 7 8

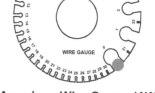

C. American Wire Gauge (AWG)

Figure 9-35   Wire gauge numbers, characteristics and measurement

Note that the gauge number and the diameter of the wire vary in an inverse relationship (see Figure 9-35B). The higher the gauge number, the thinner the wire. Also, note that the thicker wire sizes have the lowest resistances. Thicker conductors have more electrical charges available to support the flow of current. Figure 9-35C shows an American Wire Gauge that can measure wire sizes from No. 36 to No. 0. The wire is measured by the slot into which it will fit, not the hole behind the slot.

Stranded Wire

When considerable flexibility is needed in a conductor, stranded wire is used. Instead of being one solid wire, the conductor consists of many strands of fine wire twisted together (see Figure 9-34B). The gauge number assigned to such a conductor is determined by the total cross-sectional area of all the individual strands added together.

Cable

For many purposes, it is desirable to group two or more insulated wires together in the form of a cable. A cable that contains two No. 14 wires is known as 14-2 cable. If a cable has two insulated No. 14 wires and a bare uninsulated grounding wire, it is called 14-2 with ground. Cables are available in many types including nonmetallic sheathed cable and armored cable. Nonmetallic sheathed cable, shown in Figure 9-36A, contains insulated wires covered with an outer jacket of moisture and fire resistant material which may be fibrous or made of plastic or nylon. As shown in Figure 9-36B, armored cable contains insulated conductors protected by a spiral armor made of galvanized steel.

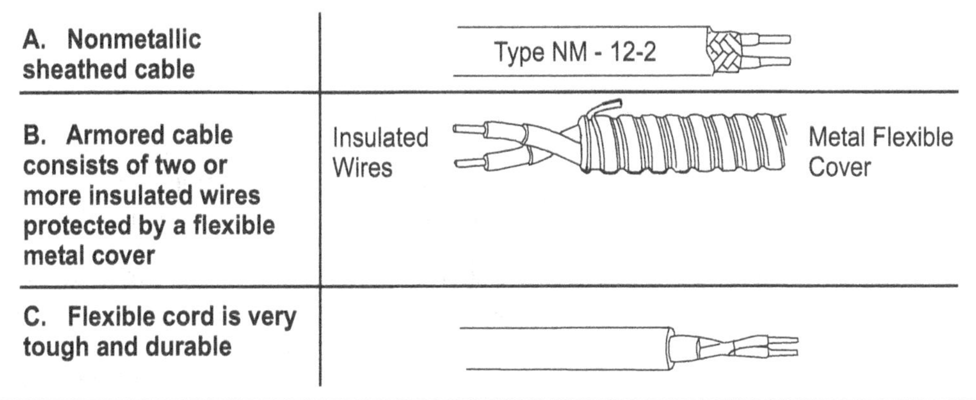

A. Nonmetallic sheathed cable	Type NM - 12-2
B. Armored cable consists of two or more insulated wires protected by a flexible metal cover	Insulated Wires / Metal Flexible Cover
C. Flexible cord is very tough and durable	

Figure 9-36   Types of cable

Flexible Cord

If conductors need to be moved about, as on equipment where the conductors are constantly being flexed by the motion of actuators, etc., flexible cord is used for convenience and to prevent the conductors from breaking (see Figure 9-36C). There are many kinds of flexible cord but the type most often used for industrial applications is Type SO. Constant service Type SO flexible cable uses conductors with many finely stranded wires to provide long cable life. This type of cord is made with a special oil resistant outer jacket to prevent deterioration of the cable from exposure to harsh fluids.

Wire Resistance

The resistance of a wire depends on the material from which it is made, its cross-sectional area, and its length. The most widely used conductor material is copper. It has very good conducting ability and is much more economical to use than slightly better conductors such as gold and silver. Conductors are sometimes made of aluminum when copper is in short supply, but its use is not recommended for most industrial applications.

Wire resistance varies inversely with the circular mil area of a wire. As shown in Figure 9-37A, increasing the diameter of a wire decreases its resistance (as long as other factors, like temperature and length, are held constant). It should be noted that temperature has only a slight effect on conductor resistance and is usually not an important consideration in most applications.

WIRE SIZE	In conduit, cable, or buried directly in the earth		Single conductors in free air		
	Types T, TW	Types RH RHW, THW	Types T, TW	Types RH RHW, THW	Weatherproof
	A	B	C	D	E
14	15	15	20	20	30
12	20	20	25	25	40
10	30	30	40	40	55
8	40	45	55	65	70
6	55	65	80	95	100
4	70	85	105	125	130
2	95	155	140	170	175
1/0	125	150	195	230	235
2/0	165	175	225	265	275
3/0	195	200	260	310	320

Figure 9-37   Ampacity of copper wires

Wire resistance varies directly with the length of a wire. Increasing the length of a wire increases its resistance (as long as temperature and area are held constant). It takes energy to produce current flow along the length of wire. Longer wires require more energy to support the flow of current, and therefore have more resistance.

Conductor Ampacity

Current flowing through a conductor produces heat as it overcomes the resistance of the wire. Heat does not harm the copper conductor, but does harm its insulation. As the temperature of a wire increases, the insulation may become damaged by the heat in various ways dependent on the degree of overheating and the kind of insulation. Some kinds melt, some harden, some burn. In any case, insulation loses its usefulness if overheated, leading to eventual breakdown and fires. With sufficient amperage the conductor itself may get hot enough to start a fire. It is therefore most necessary to carefully limit the amperage to a maximum value, one that is safe for any given size and type of wire.

The maximum number of amperes that a wire can safely carry continuously is called the ampacity of the wire. The ampacity of a given wire is related to its ability to radiate heat into the surrounding atmosphere. The NEC carefully specifies the ampacity of each kind and size of wire for various conditions and methods of installation.

Figure 9-37 shows ampacities for different sizes of copper wire covered with various kinds of insulation and installed in different ways. Note that the larger wires (smaller wire gauge numbers) have a higher ampacity than smaller wires. Larger wires have a greater surface area from which to radiate heat. Also, note that wires with insulation types containing an H in their designations have higher ampacity ratings. These insulations are made to withstand greater amounts of heat than the other types without breaking down. Finally, note that conductors located within enclosed spaces have lower ampacity ratings than conductors suspended in free air. Conductors confined in conduit, cable, or buried in the earth cannot dissipate as much heat as single conductors in free air.

Conductor Voltage Drop

Heat is generated in a conductor as energy is used in overcoming conductor resistance to produce a flow of current. The voltage that is lost in forcing current through a conductor is known as voltage drop. It is wasted power; it merely heats the wires. Wire sizes must be selected for given combinations of voltage and current so that they are big enough to prevent the development of dangerous temperatures, and also big enough to avoid wasted power in the form of excessive voltage drop.

Electrical devices are most efficient when they operate on the voltage for which they were designed. If an electric motor is operated on a voltage 5 percent below its rated voltage, its power output drops by 10 percent. The output decreases at a rate greater than the reduction in operating voltage. For the sake of efficiency, it should be clear that voltage drop must be kept to a minimum. A commonly accepted standard is a voltage drop no greater than 2 percent from power source to load. For a 115 volt circuit, the voltage drop should not exceed 2.3 volts. In some circuits, even a 2 percent voltage drop may drastically affect circuit performance.

The problem of voltage drop increases with long wire runs. For example, assume that a device requiring 460 watts of power is operated at a distance of 50 feet (15.24m) from a 115 volt power source. At this distance, 100 feet (30.48m) of wire is needed. The voltage drop can be calculated using Ohm's Law, $E = I \times R$, if the current and resistance are known. The current can be found by dividing the power by the voltage, $I = P/E$ or $460/115 = 4$ amps.

Taking No. 14 wire as a random size, the table shown in Figure 9-35A shows that 1,000 feet (304.80m) of No. 14 wire has a resistance of 2.58 ohms per 1,000 feet (304.80m). To find the resistance of 100 feet (30.48m), divide 2.58 by 10 (1,000/100 = 10) to get a result of 0.258. The voltage drop equals $4 \times 0.258 = 1.03$ volts. This is well below the recommended voltage drop of 2.3 volts.

Now, assume that the distance between the same device and its power source is increased to 500 feet (152.40m). At this distance, 1,000 feet (305m) of No. 14 wire is required. The calculation for voltage drop in this case becomes $4 \times 2.58 = 10.3$ volts. This is considerably above the recommended voltage drop of 2.3 volts for a 115 volt source.

Voltage Drop Formulas

Suppose that the device in the example above had to be located at the longer distance of 500 feet (152m) and that the voltage drop had to be kept below 2.3 volts. What could be done to solve the problem of the voltage drop being too large? Earlier in this section, it was stated that as the cross-sectional area of a conductor increases, its resistance decreases. If a larger diameter wire is used in the example circuit, the voltage drop can be brought down to the recommended level. The formula shown below is frequently used to solve problems of this type:

Formula 9-8

$$\text{Circular mils} = \frac{\text{Distance*} \times \text{Amperage} \times 22}{\text{Voltage Drop}}$$

* Distance in this formula means the length of the circuit in feet, not the amount of wire required in the circuit.

Substituting the values from the example problem in the formula gives the following result:

$$\text{Circular mils} = \frac{500 \times 4 \times 22}{2.3} = 19{,}130$$

Referring to the table shown in Figure 9-35 note that none of the gauge numbers have exactly the calculated circular mil area of 19,130. The first even wire gauge number having a circular mil area greater than 19,130 is No. 6 with a circular mil area of 26,300. (Odd gauge numbers are not usually used for wiring; they are primarily used for motor and transformer windings.) Since the circular mil area of No. 6 wire is well above the calculated value, the voltage drop for this circuit would be within limits if No. 6 wire is used.

If the actual voltage drop of a given size wire is to be determined, the formula can be transposed to read:

Formula 9-9

$$\text{Voltage Drop} = \frac{\text{Distance} \times \text{Amperage} \times 22}{\text{Circular mils}}$$

To determine the number of feet any given size of wire will carry any given amperage, the formula can be transposed another way to read:

Formula 9-10

$$\text{Distance} = \frac{\text{Voltage Drop} \times \text{Circular mils}}{\text{Amperage} \times 22}$$

All of the above formulas apply to circuits using direct current or single-phase alternating current. Substitute 19 for 22 in these formulas as a correction factor for 3-phase alternating current circuits.

Electromagnetic Interference and Noise

Electromagnetic Interference (EMI) and noise are interference type problems within electrical circuits and associated wiring that can cause erratic or improper operation of equipment. These problems are often hard to locate and correct. EMI and noise can usually be minimized by good circuit design and by proper wiring installation methods. Careful maintenance, repair and replacement procedures must also be followed to prevent EMI and noise problems from occurring after installation of the equipment.

Electromagnetic interference is defined as a modification of signals contained in circuit wiring caused by a strong magnetic field radiated from some other electrical or electronic device or conductor. Previously, it was explained that current flowing through a conductor produced a circular magnetic field around the conductor. It was also explained that devices like transformers, relays and solenoids have coils that intentionally produce a magnetic field as part of normal operation. Devices or conductors carrying a high current produce strong magnetic fields that extend outwards. As the flux lines from these magnetic fields pass through the insulation of nearby wires and components, a current flow is induced that can modify or change the signals already flowing in the conductor. This induced current (EMI) can interfere with command signals going to a device or with feedback signals coming from a device.

Noise is defined as an unwanted disturbance superimposed upon a useful signal which tends to obscure its information content. Random noise is noise that is unpredictable. Noise can be generated in a circuit whenever high currents are switched on or off, such as when relay contacts open and close or when motor armatures make and break contact with brushes. Dirty contacts can cause intermittent current flow and are often the source of many noise problems. The rapid increase or decrease in circuit current produced under such circumstances generates magnetic fields that can cause high amplitude pulses of current (noise spikes) to appear on conductors and cables running to other circuits. These noise spikes, even though very short in duration, add unwanted interference to signals normally present in circuits connected to these lines.

Shielded Conductors

The harmful effects of EMI and noise can be reduced by using shielded conductors and cables and by following proper wiring practices. A shield is a metallic sheath (usually copper or aluminum) applied over the insulation of a conductor during the manufacturing process. It may be a very thin sheet of solid conducting material or a braided wire mesh. It is usually covered by an outer jacket of insulation. The conducting path provided by the shield is generally connected to ground at some point in the circuit. The shield reduces the effect of noise or electromagnetic interference by absorbing random magnetic flux lines before they reach the inner conductor.

When installing a shielded cable or conductor, never ignore the shield connection. Always follow the manufacturer's installation instructions on connecting the end(s) of the shield. Improper connection of the shield can lead to faulty operation of the equipment.

Electrical Safety

Effective safety measures are a blend of common sense, knowledge of basic electrical and hydraulic principles, and knowledge of how a system or circuit operates, including any dangers associated with that operation.

General safety information and safety practices are listed below for personnel who work on electrical circuits and components. The list is by no means all inclusive, is not intended to alter or replace currently established safety practices, and does not include safety practices for hydraulic equipment.

When working with electrical equipment consider the following:

- Injuries associated with electrical work may include electrical shocks, burns, and puncture, laceration, or abrasion wounds.

- Current flow through the body can be fatal. As little as 0.01A produces muscle paralysis and extreme breathing difficulty in the average person. Permanent physical damage and death can result from 0.1A flowing through the heart.

- The amount of current received from an electrical shock depends on the voltage applied and the resistance of that part of the body through which the current flows. For most individuals, 0.1A can be produced by about 30V. Use extreme caution when working in circuits that include voltages higher than 30V.

- Most electrical shocks are unexpected. These shocks, even if they are not particularly dangerous, may cause you to jerk your hand into heavier currents or hit some sharp object. Always check to see that the power is turned off before placing your hand in a circuit.

- Never put both hands in a live circuit as this provides a path for current flow through the heart. Keep one hand behind you or in your pocket when taking measurements with a meter.

- Never work on live circuits when wet as this lowers the body resistance and increases the chance for a fatal shock.

- Never work alone on electrical equipment. Shocks above 0.01A can paralyze your muscles and leave you unable to remove yourself from the source of current flow. Always be sure someone else is around to help in an emergency.

- Use the proper equipment for circuit testing, remembering to check for correct settings of function and range switches, proper insulation on test probes, etc.

- Before starting work on an electrical circuit, remove all watches, rings, chains and any other metal jewelry that may come in contact with an electrical potential or get caught in moving mechanical parts.

- Understand the circuit you are working on, and think out beforehand what you will be doing in the circuit. If your knowledge is not adequate for the task, ask for assistance.

Remember that electrical current can be compared to a rattlesnake without the warning rattle. It is invisible, deadly and ready to strike when least expected. However, the danger associated with electrical work can be reduced if proper safety precautions and practices are observed and applied.

Operational Amplifiers

Many modern electrohydraulic devices, such as proportional and servo valves, servo pumps, pressure and flow control valves, and speed control circuits require relatively high power electrical signals for control and/or positioning. Typically, however, the source of the command or control signal is a device capable of delivering only low power signals. For example, the input signal to control a proportional valve may come from such sources as a:

- Potentiometer

- Temperature sensor

- Pressure transducer

- Tach-generator

- Programmable logic controllers (PLC)

- Microprocessor controlled device, etc.

Since all of these sources produce a low power signal, it is necessary to raise or amplify the electrical level of the signal (in terms of voltage or current, or both) before it is capable of operating the proportional valve.

Because of heat handling and physical size limitations, it is not practical to increase the capacity of the originating device in order to deliver higher power signals. Fortunately, when a low power signal is applied to the input of the electronic circuit known as an amplifier, it can produce the required command signal for electrohydraulic devices at its output. See Figure 9-38.

This chapter provides a brief introduction to amplifier operation and terminology and a more detailed explanation of the Op Amp (Operational Amplifier), which is a special type of amplifier that has several characteristics especially suitable for electrohydraulic applications.

Figure 9-38   Functional block diagram of input device, amplifier and output device

Definition of an Amplifier

An amplifier is a relatively simple circuit used to raise the level (or increase the amplitude) of an electronic signal. The amplified output signal is proportional to the input signal. Various types of amplifiers are used in electrical equipment, but all of them perform this same basic function.

Transistors as Amplifiers

A semiconductor device known as a transistor forms the basic element of most amplifier circuits. Transistors perform many important functions in electronics in addition to amplification and are constructed and configured in many different ways. This chapter does not elaborate on transistor theory or application other than to provide some basic understanding of amplifier operation and terminology.

The schematic symbol for one type of transistor, called an NPN type, is shown in Figure 9-39. The transistor has three terminals labeled emitter (e), base (b), and collector (c) in the figure. The collector is connected to a positive voltage supply, the emitter is connected to a negative voltage, and the base is connected to a voltage slightly higher than the emitter. The main current flow path through the transistor is from the collector to the emitter, with the base acting as a controller in much the same way that a small pilot flow can control a much greater flow of fluid through a hydraulic valve.

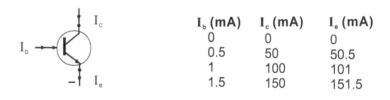

I_b (mA)	I_c (mA)	I_e (mA)
0	0	0
0.5	50	50.5
1	100	101
1.5	150	151.5

Figure 9-39   Schematic symbol and characteristics for a transistor

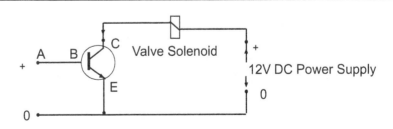

Figure 9-40   Amplifier circuit

In the most common amplifier configuration, a low current input signal applied to the base controls a proportionately larger current output signal flowing between the emitter and collector terminals.

In other words, an increase of current flowing in the base to emitter input circuit will produce a proportional increase in the collector to emitter output current.

For example, consider a transistor with the characteristics shown in Figure 9-39 inserted into the amplifier circuit shown in Figure 9-40. If terminal A of the input is at zero volts, then no current will flow from the base to the emitter, since the emitter is also at zero volts. This means that the transistor is off, so no current passes from the collector to the emitter. In this case, no current flows through the valve solenoid.

If a small positive voltage sufficient to create a base current (I_b) of 0.5 mA is applied to terminal A, the transistor will conduct a current of 50 mA from the collector to the emitter. This means that 50 mA will also flow through the solenoid coil. Increasing the voltage at A so that the base current becomes 1.0 mA creates a 100 mA collector current (I_c) that also flows through the solenoid. Note that, in both of these examples, the collector current is 100 times greater than the base current. Also note that the emitter current (I_e) is equal to the sum of I_b and I_c.

If a low power controlling device such as a potentiometer or temperature sensor were connected to terminal A, its signal would control the amplifier so that a high current output would flow through the transistor and the valve solenoid. In actual practice, the amplifier would consist of many more components than those shown in Figure 9-40 and would usually consist of two or more stages of amplification (see Figure 9-41). The output of the first amplifier is used as the input to the second amplifier. For the purpose of this chapter, it is not necessary to understand the detailed circuitry of the amplifier, and it should be regarded simply as a device that produces an amplified output proportional to its input.

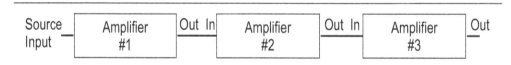

Figure 9-41   Stages of amplification

The schematic symbol for an amplifier circuit is shown in Figure 9-42. The input is connected to the base of the triangle, and the output is taken from the apex. The power supply connections are always there in practice, but are not always drawn on the symbol.

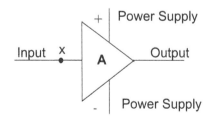

Figure 9-42   Schematic symbol for an amplifier circuit

Gain

The gain of the amplifier is defined as the ratio of output to input:

Formula 9-11

$$\text{Gain} = A = \frac{\text{Output Voltage}}{\text{Input Voltage}}$$

The gain, A, can then be used as a multiplication factor with the input voltage. The gain may be as high as 10^6 (1,000,000). An amplifier may also invert the input signal; that is, a small, positive voltage input produces a large, negative voltage output. Therefore, to find the gain of an inverting amplifier circuit:

Formula 9-12

$$A = \frac{-\text{Output Voltage}}{\text{Input Voltage}}$$

The gain of a non-inverting amplifier can be found by:

Formula 9-13

$$A = \frac{\text{Output Voltage}}{\text{Input Voltage}}$$

The value of A is normally found in the characteristics supplied with a particular amplifier type, but it varies depending on factors like circuit configuration, temperature or power supply voltage.

The input signal is actually the voltage difference across two terminals. The amplifier produces an output in relation to this voltage difference. In most applications, one terminal is permanently grounded so input and output voltages are relative to ground potential (zero volts).

The Op Amp

There are many different types of amplifiers, but the type most often used in control systems is called the Operational Amplifier, or OP AMP.

Figure 9-43 shows the schematic symbol for an Op Amp. The power supply connections are assumed to exist, even though they are not shown. Non-inverting (+) input is shown grounded, and the signal to be amplified is brought in on the inverting (-) input. This common setup is explained later in the chapter.

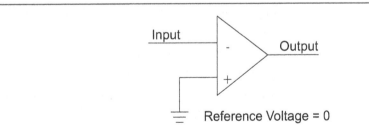

Figure 9-43   Amplifier with grounded input terminal for zero reference

In order to understand the importance of the Op Amp in electronic control, four key features of this amplifier must be explained:

- The input impedance of the amplifier is very high; virtually no current enters the amplifier from its input. NOTE: Impedance is the term used to define the combination of AC and DC resistance in a circuit. It is measured in ohms.

- The output impedance of the amplifier is very low; a relatively large current may be drawn from the amplifier output without affecting the output voltage.

- The Op Amp is a Differential Amplifier. It amplifies any voltage difference applied between its two inputs.

- The gain of the Op Amp is very high. The Op Amp can take a tiny (i.e. microvolt) signal at its input and magnify it to a very large (volts) signal at its output.

Figure 9-44 shows a block diagram of the basic stages within an integrated circuit (IC) operational amplifier. Each stage is a different type of amplifier, and each one provides some unique characteristic.

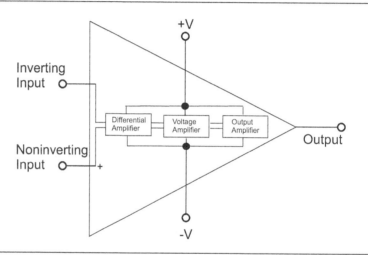

Figure 9-44   Basic operational amplifier

The input stage is a differential amplifier. This type of amplifier has the following advantages:

- High Input Impedance — a differential amp places almost no load on whatever device is connected to it.

- High Common Mode Rejection — the ability to reject unwanted stray electrical noise (appearing as random voltages) at the input.

- Positive and Negative Differential Inputs — the ability to either invert or not invert the polarity of the input signal.

- Frequency Response down to DC — the ability to amplify both AC and DC source signals.

The second stage is a high gain voltage amplifier. This stage is usually composed of several transistors connected in matched pairs. A typical Op Amp may have a gain of 200,000 or more. Most of that gain is provided by this second stage.

The final stage is an output amplifier. The output amplifier usually has a very low gain that may be small as 1. However, the purpose of this amplifier is to give the Op Amp a very low output impedance. A low output impedance means that the Op Amp will itself consume very little of the power it outputs, sending almost all of it to the load.

Due to its small physical size, the IC Op Amp can output about 1 watt of power. However, most valve solenoids require from 5 to 40 watts of power for operation. Therefore, the output of the Op Amp is usually sent on to a Driver circuit, which is composed of large power transistors that can physically handle the current requirements of the solenoid. Op Amps can also be built from discrete components (not in an integrated circuit chip) and can, therefore, use power transistors as components of the output amplifier stage.

Open Loop Gain

When an Op Amp is actually connected as shown in Figure 9-44, the signal applied to the input is amplified at the full gain of the Op Amp. For example, suppose that the Op Amp has a gain of 1,000,000 and is powered by a +10 volt power supply. The maximum voltage output of the Op Amp is limited by its power supply to +10 volts.

Since,

Formula 9-14

$$\text{Output Voltage} = A \times \text{Input Voltage}$$

Then,

Formula 9-15

$$\text{Input Voltage} = \frac{\text{Output Voltage}}{A}$$

Therefore,

$$\text{Input Voltage} = \frac{10 \text{ Volts}}{1,000,000} = .000010 \text{ Volts}$$

This means that if we input as little as 10 microvolts, the Op Amp will give maximum output! Many applications call for amplification of very tiny voltages, but they are usually not encountered in electrohydraulics. When used in this open loop manner, the Op Amp is of little use, since the gain it gives is far too large. Fortunately, the gain of an Op Amp can be very closely controlled through the use of external feedback components.

Closed Loop Gain

A more typical Op Amp circuit is shown in Figure 9-45. Note that one resistor (R_i) is connected to the amplifier input, and a second resistor (R_f) connects the output to the summing junction. R_i is known as the input resistor, and R_f is the feedback resistor. This is known as the Closed Loop configuration, since the feedback resistor forms a loop from output to input. The point where the feedback resistor is connected back to the input resistor is known as the Summing Junction (SJ), and as will be explained later, all inputs connected to this point are added together.

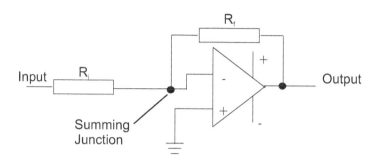

Figure 9-45   Typical Op Amp connections

When connected in this manner, the Op Amp does a very useful thing. It will now attempt to maintain identical voltages at its inputs by changing its output. For example, since the non-inverting (+) input is connected to ground (0 volts), the Op Amp will change its output so that the inverting (-) input and the summing junction connected to it are also at 0 volts.

Op Amps are usually set up to invert the signal being amplified by connecting it to the negative input. This is done to simplify amplifier design. While it is possible to connect an input signal to the positive input and get a non-inverted output, our discussion concentrates on the simpler and more common inverting arrangement.

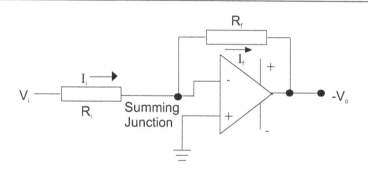

Figure 9-46   Typical Op Amp with voltage applied to input

Suppose that a voltage (V_i) is applied to the input as shown in Figure 9-46. Assuming that the summing junction is at zero volts, the current flow through the input resistor (I_i) can be calculated using Ohm's Law:

Formula 9-16

$$I_i = \frac{V_i}{R_i}$$

Since no current can enter the input to the amplifier, and by using Kirchoff's Law (the algebraic sum of the currents at a junction is zero) at the summing junction, then:

Formula 9-17

$$I_i = I_r = 0$$

so,

$$I_i = -I_r$$

Again using Ohm's Law:

Formula 9-18

$$I_i + I_r = 0$$

so, if

$$I_i = -I_r$$

then

$$\frac{V_i}{R_i} = \frac{-V_o}{R_f}$$

The multiplication factor between input and output is therefore R_f / R_i, which is known as the Closed Loop Gain of the amplifier. Note that this gain value can be varied by changing the value of either R_f or, more commonly, R_i.

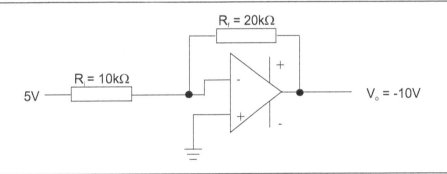

Figure 9-47   Example inverting amplifier circuit

For example, refer to Figure 9-47. Suppose that in this circuit:

$$V_i = +5V$$

$$R_i = 10 \text{ kilo ohms } (10{,}000)$$

$$R_f = 20 \text{ kilo ohms } (20{,}000)$$

then

$$V_o = \frac{R_f}{R_i} \times V_i$$

$$V_o = \frac{20,000}{10,000} \times 5$$

$$V_o = -10 \text{ volts}$$

The gain of the amplifier is therefore -2. If the value of R_i is changed to 5 kilo ohms (5000) then:

$$V_o = R_f \times V_i$$

$$V_o = 20,000 \times 5$$

$$V_o = -20 \text{ volts}$$

so the gain is now -4.

Adjusting the value of R_i therefore adjust the amplifier gain. If R_i is a variable resistor, the amplifier can be adjusted to give the required maximum output voltage when the maximum input signal voltage is applied. In practice, a fixed and a variable resistor would normally be used in series on the input to limit the maximum permissible gain (Figure 9-48).

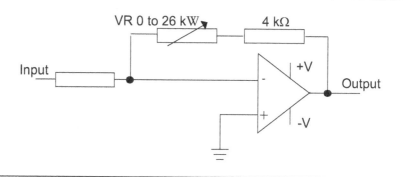

Figure 9-48   Op Amp with variable gain

For example, if R_i equals 5,000 ohms, R_f equals 4,000 ohms, and VR can be adjusted from zero ohms to 26,000 ohms, then the effective feedback resistance ($R_f + $ VR) would be adjustable between 4,000 and 20,000 ohms. This permits a gain adjustment of -0.8 to -6.

While the voltage gain of an amplifier may not be particularly high and may even be less than 1 in some cases, the significant point is that the current drawn from the input source is very small:

If V_i = 5 volts and
R_i = 5,000 ohms

$$I_i = \frac{V_i}{R_i} = 1 \text{ mA}$$

However, the current drawn from the amplifier output can be relatively large, since this current is provided by the power supply.

The important features of this arrangement are:

• The output voltage will normally be the opposite polarity to the input (a positive at the input produces a negative at the output and vice-versa).

• The output voltage will be proportional to the input voltage.

• The input current to the amplifier arrangement will be very small.

• The output current may be relatively large, since it is provided by the power supply.

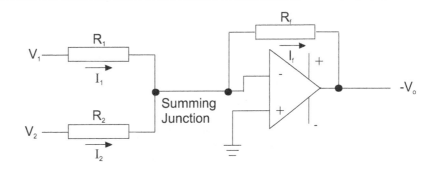

Figure 9-49   Op Amp with two inputs at the summing junction

If the amplifier has two input resistors as shown in Figure 9-49, Kirchoff's Current Law can be applied to the summing junction. For example:

Formula 9-19

$$I_1 + I_2 + I_f = 0$$

So,

Formula 9-20

$$\frac{V_1}{R_1} + \frac{V_2}{R_2} = \frac{V_o}{R_f} \quad \text{(from Ohm's Law)}$$

and

Formula 9-21

$$-V_o = \frac{R_f}{R_1} \times V_1 + \frac{R_f}{R_2} \times V_2$$

The amplifier output is the sum of the two input signals (V_1 and V_2) multiplied by their individual gains (R_f / R_1 and R_f / R_2). If R_1 equals R_2, the gains will be equal. In other cases, the gains may be different to make one signal more dominant than the other. The amplifier may have more than two inputs, but the same principle applies whatever the number. In other words:

Formula 9-22

$$-V_o = (A_1 \times V_1) + (A_2 \times A_2) + (A_3 \times V_3) + \dots$$

where A = individual input gain.

Input Potentiometers

In a great many cases, the input signal to an amplifier comes from a signal potentiometer (variable resistor). A signal potentiometer controls a proportional relief valve to vary the hydraulic pressure in a cylinder.

The machine operator may turn the pot to a position that gives the amplifier (V_i) an input voltage. The amplifier produces a corresponding output voltage (V_o) to drive the relief valve solenoid. See Figure 9-50.

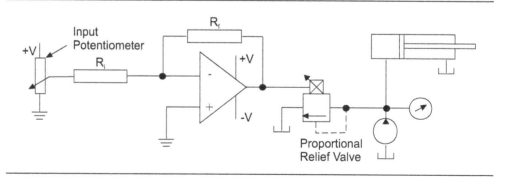

Figure 9-50   Pressure control circuit with Op Amp including input potentiometer

The position of the potentiometer's wiper arm will determine the voltage at the wiper terminal (V_i) (see Figure 9-51), and if no current is drawn from the wiper, a linear relationship exists between the wiper position and the wiper voltage, as shown in Figure 9-52.

Figure 9-51   Potentiometer as a voltage divider

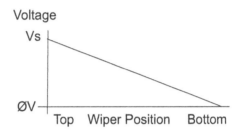

Figure 9-52   Linear relationship between wiper position and wiper voltage

A potentiometer can be regarded as two resistors in series, with the wiper connected between them (see Figure 9-53).

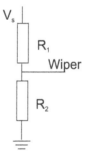

Figure 9-53   Potentiometer shown as two series resistor

The total potentiometer resistance is equal to $R_1 + R_2$. Varying the position of the wiper increases R_1 and decreases R_2, or vice-versa.

Now, let's consider what happens if the potentiometer is used to vary the input voltage to an amplifier as shown in Figure 9-54.

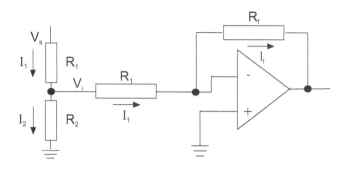

Figure 9-54   Potentiometer used to vary the input voltage

The amplifier input current, I_i, is drawn from the pot wiper, which has the effect of increasing I_i, since:

Formula 9-23

$$I_1 = I_i + I_2$$

An increase current through R_1 creates a large voltage difference across R_1, and so V_i drops. This produces a nonlinear relationship between the wiper position and the wiper voltage as shown in Figure 9-55.

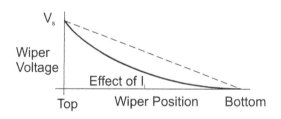

Figure 9-55   Nonlinear relationship between wiper position and wiper voltage

To reduce this nonlinearity, the wiper current (I_i) must be kept small in relation to $I_1 + I_2$. For practical reasons, however, $I_1 + I_2$ must be kept small to reduce power loss and to avoid heat generation; this means that I_i must be smaller still. I_i can be reduced by increasing the value of the amplifier input resistor R_i. A corresponding increase of R_f maintains the amplifier gain.

Although one might be tempted to simply make R_i and R_f very high resistances, there are practical limits to the values of these resistors. It was stated earlier that the inputs of an Op Amp draw virtually no current from the source. In fact, they do draw a tiny amount (nanoamps) of current, called input leakage current. Normally, it is an amount so small that it can be ignored. However, if R_i and R_f are too high in resistance, I_i will be too small.

If I_i is too small, then the assumption that no current enters the amplifier no longer holds true. In other words, the input leakage current starts to become significant relative to I_i causing nonlinearities in the amplifier performance.

In practice, choosing a total potentiometer resistance ($R_1 + R_2$) that is no greater than one tenth of the input resistance (R_i) maintains the nonlinearity with 2 to 3 percent, which is good enough for most applications.

The general rule is:

Formula 9-24

POT RESISTANCE $= 0.1 \times$ INPUT RESISTANCE

In many process control applications, a current input signal is preferred to a voltage signal to avoid voltage drops down long wires. Commonly, a 4 to 20 mA signal is used. The 4 mA represents a zero signal and 20 mA represents a maximum signal. The 4 mA signal is chosen to represent zero for two reasons:

1. It makes the system less sensitive to electrical noise, because any current less than 4 mA is ignored.

2. It provides an indication of malfunction. If the input drops below 4 mA it indicates a fault in the system (such as a broken lead), and the system is usually designed to react accordingly.

The current signal can be converted to a voltage signal very simply by using a resistor arrangement such as that shown in Figure 9-56.

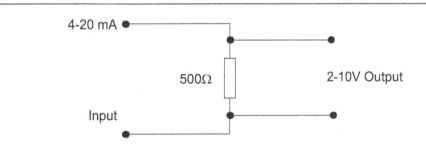

Figure 9-56   Circuit for converting a current signal to a voltage signal

Application Example

Suppose an electrically modulated relief valve such as the one shown in Figure 9-50 requires a current input of 0 to 700 mA. The resistance of the solenoid coil equals 28.6 ohms. A potentiometer supply of 10 volts is available, but it can provide no more than 10 mA of current. Determine the amplifier input, feedback resistor values and the potentiometer resistance.

From the specifications, the maximum potentiometer current equals 10 mA at a voltage of 10 volts. The minimum potentiometer resistance (R_p) can be calculated as follows:

$$R_p = \frac{V}{I} = \frac{10}{0.010}$$

$$R_p = 1,000 \text{ ohms}$$

From the general rule relationship:

$R_i = 10 \times R_p = 10 \times 1000 = 10,000$ ohms

Again, from the specifications, the maximum solenoid current (I_L max) equals 700 mA and the solenoid resistance (R_L) equals 28.6 ohms.

So the maximum output voltage required is:

$-V_o$ max $= I_L$ max $\times R_L$

$-V_o$ max $= 0.700 \times 28.6$

$-V_o$ max $= 20$ volts

Since the maximum input voltage equals 10 volts, the required amplifier gain is:

$$\frac{V_o}{V_i} = \frac{20}{10} = 2$$

Amplifier Gain $= \dfrac{R_f}{R_i}$

so,

$$\frac{R_f}{R_i} = 2$$

or

$R_f = 2 \times R_i = 2 \times 10,000 = 20,000$ ohms

So, the Potentiometer Resistance (R_p) = 1,000 ohms
the Input Resistance (R_i) = 10,000 ohms
the Feedback Resistance (R_f) = 20,000 ohms

General Purpose Amplifiers

Figure 9-57 shows a typical industrial amplifier control module that includes a power output stage, a power stage preamp and a general purpose input amplifier. The input voltage amplifier and the power stage preamp are Op Amps, while the power output stage is composed of an Op Amp driving a transistor power amplifier.

The module contains various potentiometers and switches that allow the module to be used in a number of different applications, while the module contains many functions that have not yet been explained, the input and feedback components on these amplifiers are clearly shown.

The input voltage amplifier, for example, has a 27K and a 270K resistor in series at the input. Switch S5 can be closed to bypass the 270K resistor, allowing the amplifier to be used in high gain applications, or opened to cut down the gain of the amplifier by making R_i greater.

Two input pins (8J and 9K) are provided to the amplifier, connected to a ratio pot that can be used to make one input more dominant than the other. The gain of the amplifier can be adjusted by closing switch S2 and turning the GAIN 2 pot, which adjusts the value of R_f. The power stage preamp also has a feedback pot called GAIN 1, for gain adjustment. Some of the remaining functions, such as dither and limiters, are discussed in Chapter 14 Servo Valves.

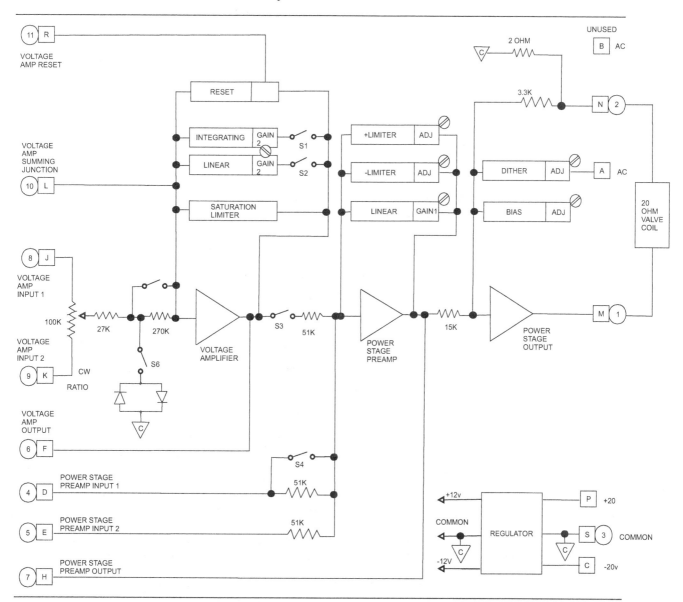

Figure 9-57   Typical industrial amplifier control module

Industrial Test Questions:
Electrical Principles and Operational Amplifiers

Chapter 9

1. Identify the three basic components found in any electrical circuit.

2. Name the four measurable circuit elements contained in an electrical circuit.

3. Define current. What is the unit of measurement for current? In what direction does current flow through a circuit?

4. What is the Law of Electrical Charges?

5. What is the purpose of a conductor? What is the purpose of an insulator?

6. What is a closed circuit? What is an open circuit?

7. Define voltage or EMF. What is the unit of measurement for voltage? What is a voltage drop? What is a voltage rise?

8. Describe the difference between a DC voltage and an AC voltage.

9. Define resistance. What is the unit of measurement for resistance? What is the difference between a fixed resistor and a variable resistor?

10. Convert 2,500,000 ohms to megohms. Convert 6.3 kilohms to ohms.

11. Define power. What is the unit of measurement for power? One horsepower is the equivalent of how many watts? Explain what is meant by the wattage rating of a device.

12. Explain the difference between an analog and a digital meter. What is the name for a combination voltmeter, ohmmeter and ammeter?

13. How is an ammeter connected to a circuit? How is a voltmeter connected to a circuit? What is meant by observing polarity?

14. What is the most important thing to remember about using an ohmmeter? Why?

15. An ohmmeter is set to the R x 10K range. The pointer indicates 5.5 on the ohms scale. How much resistance is being measured by the ohmmeter?

16. Describe how a meter is adjusted for zero ohms.

17. State Ohm's Law and give the formula. If the voltage applied to a circuit is increased, how is the current in the circuit affected? If the resistance in a circuit is increased, how does this affect the current in the circuit?

18. The voltage applied to a circuit is 120V. The resistance in the circuit equals 1,200 ohms. How much current will flow in this circuit? Give answer in milliamps.

19. If a circuit contains 1,000 ohms of resistance and the current in the circuit cannot exceed 0.1A, what is the maximum voltage that can be applied to the circuit?

20. The power source for a circuit supplies 30V. The current in this circuit must not exceed 50 mA. What is the smallest value of resistance that the circuit can contain and still limit the current to 50 mA?

21. State Watt's Law and give the formula. If the current in a circuit is decreased, how is the power affected? If the voltage in a circuit is increased, how is the power affected?

22. What is the purpose of an attenuator? Why would a series dropping resistor be used in a circuit?

23. What is a solenoid? How are solenoids most often used in hydraulic applications?

24. Describe the difference between an air gap solenoid and a wet armature solenoid.

25. Describe the main cause of solenoid failure.

26. What is the purpose of a relay? What is meant by N.O. and N.C. contacts? Explain one way in which a relay might be used.

27. What is the function of a transformer? What is meant by the turns ratio of a transformer? Name two kinds of transformers and explain how they are constructed with respect to turns ratio.

28. Why is a diode called a unidirectional device? How is this characteristic of a diode used to change AC into pulsating DC?

29. What is the difference between a half wave and a full wave rectifier?

30. Name the component most often used to filter pulsating DC to pure DC and explain how it works.

31. Name the four requirements for developing skill in troubleshooting electrical circuits.

32. Name the five steps of the logical troubleshooting procedure.

33. Describe how to test a potentiometer.

34. Describe how to test a solenoid coil.

35. Describe how to test a relay.

36. Describe how to test a transformer.

37. How is a diode tested? What is meant by the front to back ratio of a diode?

38. Name the two types of electrical ground and explain the difference between them.

39. Explain why a zero reference point is so important.

40. Increasing the diameter of a wire (increases/decreases) its resistance?

41. As the length of a wire increases, its resistance (increases/decreases)?

42. What is meant by the ampacity rating of a conductor and why is it important?

43. When using shielded wire or cable, how should the shield be connected to the circuit?

44. Why is it so dangerous to put both hands in an electrical circuit? What is the reason for not working alone?

45. How much current produces muscle paralysis? How much current will cause death? What two things determine the amount of current received in an electrical shock?

46. Name five input signal sources for controlling a proportional valve.

47. Why is an amplifier needed between the input signal source and the electrohydraulic device being controlled?

48. What device forms the basic element of most amplifier circuits?

49. Name the three terminals found on a transistor.

50. Where is the input signal applied in the most common amplifier configuration?

51. Define gain.

52. If the input voltage to an amplifier is 0.05 volts and the output voltage is 5.0 volts, what is the gain?

53. If an amplifier has a gain of 50 and the input voltage is 2 volts, what is the output voltage?

54. What are the four key characteristics of operational amplifiers?

55. Name the three basic stages within an integrated circuit operational amplifier.

56. What elements determine the operational characteristics of an operational amplifier?

57. What is the formula for the multiplication factor when determining closed-loop gain in an Op Amp?

58. If the input voltage (V_i) to an Op Amp is 4 volts, the value of the input resistor (R_i) is 5,000 ohms, and the value of the feedback resistor (R_f) is 20,000 ohms, what is the output voltage (V_o)?

59. What is the closed-loop gain value in Question 58?

60. What device is commonly used to vary the value of R_i or R_f and, therefore, the value of closed-loop gain in an operational amplifier circuit?

61. What is the rule of thumb for choosing a potentiometer resistance at the input to an operational amplifier to reduce nonlinearity of the output signal?

62. Why is a current input signal preferred to a voltage signal in many process control applications?

63. With a current input signal, why is 4 mA chosen to represent a zero signal?

Chapter 10 . . . . Pressure Controls

Pressure control valves perform functions such as limiting maximum system pressure or regulating reduced pressure in certain portions of a circuit, and other functions wherein their actuation is a result of a change in operating pressure. Their operation is based on a balance between pressure and spring force. Most are infinite positioning; that is, the valves can assume various positions between fully closed and fully open, depending on flow rate and pressure differential. Pressure controls are usually named for their primary function, such as relief valve, sequence valve, brake valve, etc. They are classified by size, pressure operating range and type of connections. The valves covered in this chapter are typical of the pressure controls used in most industrial systems.

Relief Valves

The relief valve is found in virtually every hydraulic system. It is a normally closed valve connected between the pressure line (pump outlet) and the reservoir. Its purpose is to limit pressure in the system to a preset maximum by diverting some or all of the pump's output to tank when the pressure setting is reached.

Direct Acting Relief Valves

A direct acting relief valve (Figure 10-1) may consist of nothing but a ball or poppet held seated in the valve body by a heavy spring. In our example circuit, 800 psi is required to extend the cylinder, and the direct acting relief valve is set for 1,000 psi. When the directional control valve is shifted to direct flow into the cap end of the cylinder, system pressure is 800 psi, which is insufficient to overcome the force of the spring (set at 1,000 psi). The valve remains closed and pump flow goes to the cylinder.

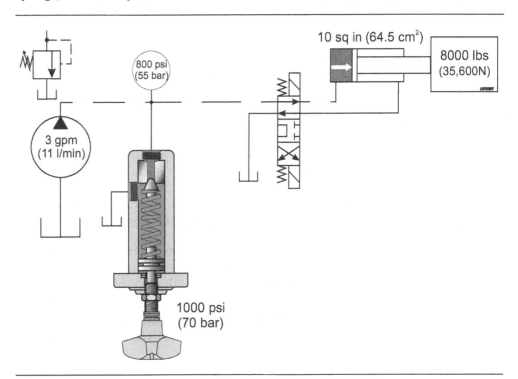

Figure 10-1   Direct acting relief valve

When the cylinder fully extends, system pressure will rise (Figure 10-2). When it reaches 1,000 psi, preset pressure is reached and the ball or poppet is forced off its seat. Flow passes through the outlet to tank for as long as pressure is maintained.

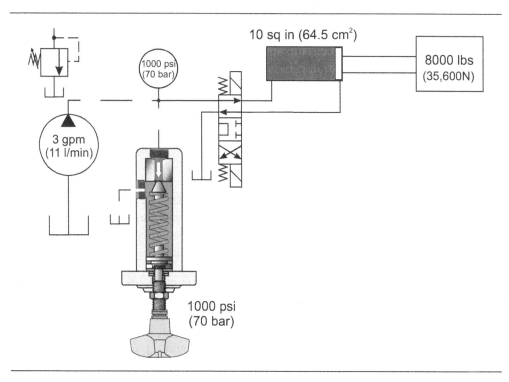

Figure 10-2   Valve opens when preset pressure setting is reached

In most of these valves, an adjusting screw is provided to vary the spring force. Thus, the valve can be set to open at any pressure within its specified range. Some of the terminology used in the adjustment process is:

Cracking Pressure — The pressure at which the valve first begins to divert flow is called the cracking pressure. As flow through the valve increases, the poppet is forced farther off its seat, causing increased compression of the spring. When the valve is bypassing its full rated flow, the pressure can be considerably higher than the cracking pressure.

Full-Flow Pressure — Pressure at the relief valve inlet when the valve is passing its maximum volume is called full-flow pressure.

Pressure Override — The difference between cracking pressure and full-flow pressure is sometimes called pressure override. In some cases, pressure override may not be objectionable. In others, it can result in considerable wasted power due to the fluid lost through the valve before its maximum setting is reached. It can also permit maximum system pressure to exceed the ratings of other components in the system. Where it is desirable to minimize override, a pilot-operated relief valve should be used.

Pilot-Operated Relief Valve

A pilot-operated relief valve operates in two-stages. The pilot stage in the upper valve body contains the pressure limiting valve, essentially a small, direct acting relief valve consisting of a poppet held against a seat by an adjustable spring.

The hydraulic circuit port connections are made in the lower body, and diversion of the full flow volume is accomplished by the balanced piston in the lower body (Figure 10-3).

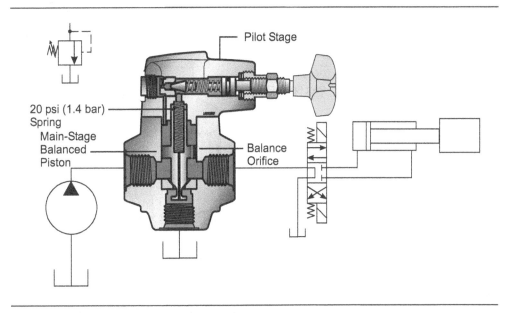

Figure 10-3   A balanced piston, pilot-operated relief valve

The balanced piston is so named because in normal operation (Figure 10-4), it is in hydraulic balance. Pressure at the inlet port acting under the piston is also sensed on its top by means of an orifice drilled through the large land. At any pressure less than the valve setting, the piston is held on its seat by a light spring.

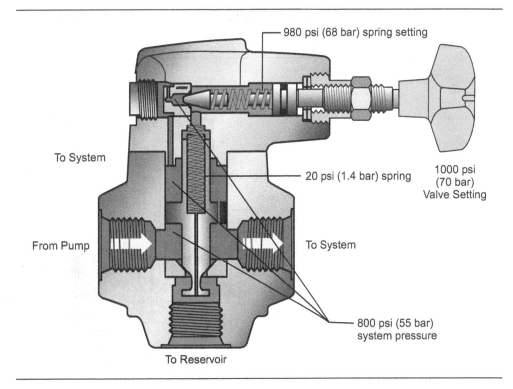

Figure 10-4   Pressure is balanced across the piston

When pressure reaches the setting of the adjustable spring in the pilot stage, the poppet is forced off its seat, limiting pressure in the upper chamber (Figure 10-5).

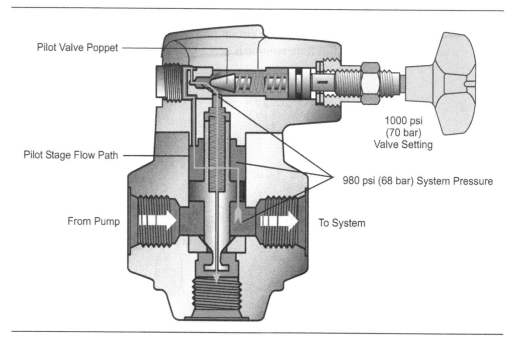

Figure 10-5   Pilot stage pressure setting is reached, and pilot valve opens

The restricted flow through the orifice into the upper chamber results in the pressure in this chamber being controlled at the pilot valve setting. An increase in pressure in the lower chamber causes an unbalance of hydraulic forces, and tends to raise the balanced piston off its seat. When the difference in pressure between the upper and lower chambers is sufficient to overcome the force of the light spring (approximately 20 psi (1.5 bar, 150 kPa), the large piston unseats, permitting flow directly to the reservoir (Figure 10-6). Increased flow through the valve causes the piston to lift further off its seat but since this compresses only the light spring, very little override is encountered.

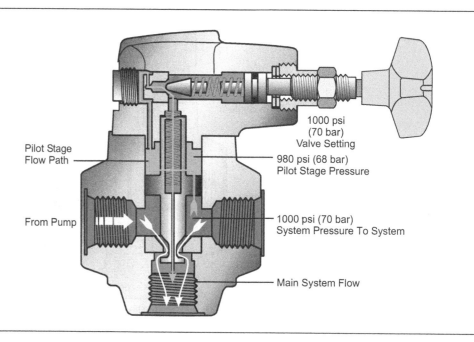

Figure 10-6   Pressure unbalance across piston allows flow to the reservoir

Vent Connection

Pilot-operated relief valves may be remotely controlled by means of an outlet port from the chamber above the piston. When this chamber is vented to tank, the only force holding the piston on its seat is that of the light spring, and the valve will open fully at approximately 20 psi (1.5 bar, 150 kPa). An application circuit is shown in Figure 10-7.

Occasionally, this standard spring is replaced by a heavier one, permitting vent pressures of approximately 80 psi (5.5 bar, 550 kPa) when required for pilot pressure. A second benefit of the heavier vent spring is that it causes faster and more positive seating of the piston.

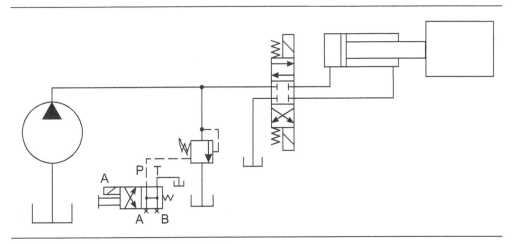

Figure 10-7   Vented relief valve circuit

Remote Control

It is also possible to connect a direct acting relief valve to the vent connection to control pressure from a remote location (Figure 10-8). To exercise control, the remote valve must be set for a lower pressure than the integral pilot stage. An application of remote pressure control is illustrated in Chapter 17.

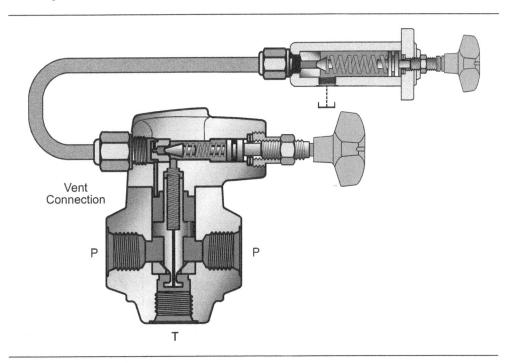

Figure 10-8   Direct acting relief valve connected to venting port

Multiple Preset Pressures

Multi-pressure, solenoid-operated relief valves are also available that provide an ability to electrically select one pressure from a set of given preset pressures. Bi-pressure relief valves can be used to select either of two preset pressures or one pressure and a vent. Tri-pressure relief valves (Figure 10-9) can be used to electrically select any one of three preset pressures, or two pressures and a vent. The main stage in either valve is a balanced piston type relief valve, and the intermediate stages are of the spring loaded poppet-type. Heads in the intermediate stages contain springs with different pressure ratings.

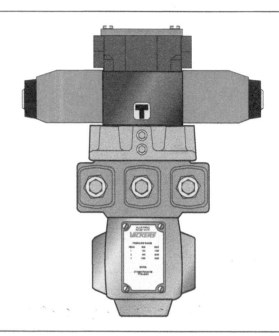

Figure 10-9   Tri-pressure relief valve

As shown in Figure 10-10, pilot head No. 1 will control the pressure when solenoid A is energized. Pilot head No. 3 controls the pressure when solenoid B is energized. With both solenoids de-energized, pilot head No. 2 will control the pressure.

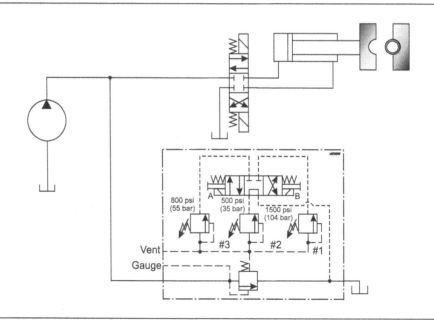

Figure 10-10   Tri-pressure relief circuit

**Electrically
Modulated Relief
Valve**

An electrically modulated relief valve provides the capability to modulate system pressure using a remote electrical controller. The pressure setting of the valve is approximately proportional to the input current; increasing current increases the regulated pressure.

A proportional relief valve (Figure 10-11) consists of three basic parts: a main stage, an intermediate body and the electrically modulated pilot. The main stage is a slip-in cartridge valve with an orifice in the "nose" of the poppet. Between the proportional pilot stage and the main stage, a standard relief valve pilot provides a manual adjustment back-up and has a mounting pad which accepts the electrically modulated pilot. The proportional pilot contains an integrated electronic driver amplifier, a solenoid coil, nozzle and a ferromagnetic plate with an imbedded ball. The manual pilot is set higher than the adjusted pressure range of the proportional pilot, therefore the proportional pilot normally determines the pressure setting of the pilot-operated proportional relief valve.

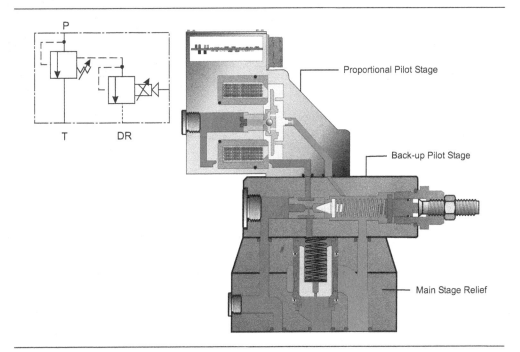

Figure 10-11   Proportional pressure relief valve

This valve provides a self-contained unit that modulates system pressure electrically over a wide range without external feedback devices. The valve has the ability to control system pressure from a distance or remote location. Modulating signals may be derived from potentiometers, analog computer's I/O cards, programmable controllers or any other source that will provide the necessary drive current for the pilot stage.

Refer to Figure 10-11. With zero current to the valve pilot stage, flow and pressure conditions are as follows: fluid flows into the pressure inlet port "P," and this pressure is transmitted to the two pilot stages through the orifice in the slip-in cartridge valve poppet. When the pressure at "P" is less than the setting of either pilot, the pressure at the top of the main stage poppet is the same as the pressure at "P," so the poppet spring holds the main stage poppet closed against the seat.

The following action occurs when current to the coil is increased. When the coil in the proportional pilot is energized, the plate is attracted with greater force, which causes the ball embedded in the plate to block off the nozzle. This creates a higher back pressure at the top of the main stage poppet. This increase in pressure adds again to the slip-in cartridge spring force. A higher pressure is then required at the inlet port to lift the poppet.

Unloading Relief Valve

An unloading relief valve (Figure 10-12) is used in accumulator charging circuits to (1) limit maximum pressure and (2) unload the pump when the desired accumulator pressure is reached.

In construction, it contains a compound, balanced piston relief valve, a check valve to prevent reverse flow from the accumulator and a pressure operated plunger which vents the relief valve at the selected pressure.

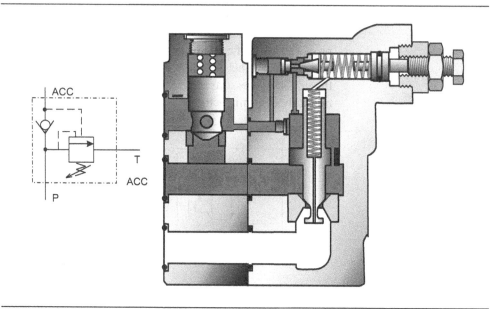

Figure 10-12   Unloading relief valve

Operation

Figure 10-13 illustrates the flow condition when the accumulator is charging. The relief valve piston is in balance and is held seated by its light spring. Flow is through the check valve to the accumulator.

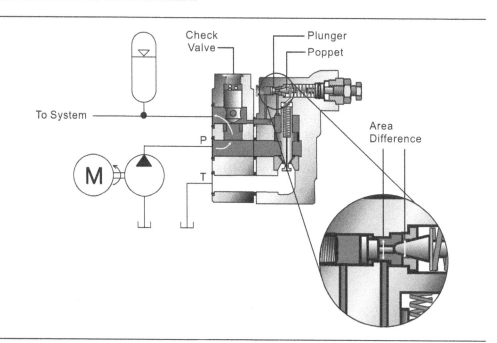

Figure 10-13   Area differential between plunger and poppet

In Figure 10-14, the preset pressure has been reached. The relief valve poppet has unseated, limiting pressure above the piston and on the poppet side of the plunger. Further increase in system pressure acting on the opposite end of the plunger has caused it to force the poppet completely off its seat, in effect, venting the relief valve and unloading the pump. The check valve has closed, permitting the accumulator to maintain pressure in the system.

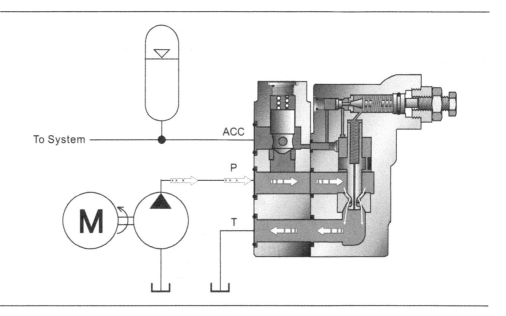

Figure 10-14   Unloading the charging circuit

Because of the difference in area between the plunger and poppet seat (approximately 15 percent), when pressure drops to about 85 percent of the valve setting, the poppet and piston reseat and the cycle is repeated. Figure 10-13 illustrates the 15 percent area differential.

Pressure Reducing Valves

Pressure reducing valves are normally open pressure controls used to maintain reduced pressures in certain portions, or branches, of the system. They are actuated by pressure sensed in the branch circuit and tend to close as it reaches the valve setting, thus preventing further pressure buildup. Both direct acting and pilot-operated versions are in use.

Direct Acting Pressure Reducing Valves

A typical direct acting pressure reducing valve is shown in Figure 10-15. It uses a spring loaded spool to control the downstream pressure.

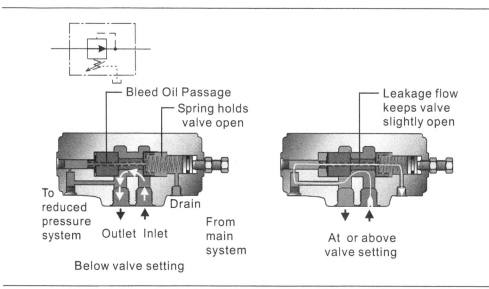

Figure 10-15   Direct acting pressure reducing valve

If the main supply pressure is below the valve setting, fluid will flow freely from the inlet to the outlet. An internal connection from the outlet passage transmits the outlet pressure to the spool end opposite the spring (left view of Figure 10-15).

When the outlet pressure rises to the valve setting (right view of Figure 10-15), the spool moves to partly block the outlet port. Only enough flow is passed to the outlet to maintain the preset pressure. If the valve closes completely, leakage past the spool could cause pressure to build up in the branch circuit. Instead, a continuous bleed to tank is permitted to keep it slightly open and prevent downstream pressure from rising above the valve setting. A separate drain passage is provided to return this leakage flow to tank.

Figure 10-16 illustrates a circuit diagram with a direct acting pressure reducing valve controlling pressure in a clamp cylinder.

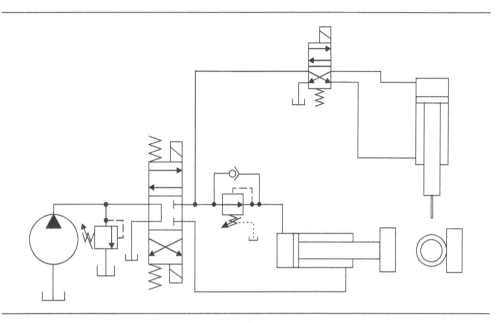

Figure 10-16   Direct acting pressure reducing circuit

Pilot-Operated Reducing Valves

The pilot-operated pressure reducing valve (Figure 10-17) has a wider range of adjustment and generally provides more accurate control than the direct acting pressure reducing valve. The operating pressure is set by an adjustable spring in the pilot stage in the upper body. The valve spool in the lower body functions in essentially the same manner as the direct acting valve discussed previously.

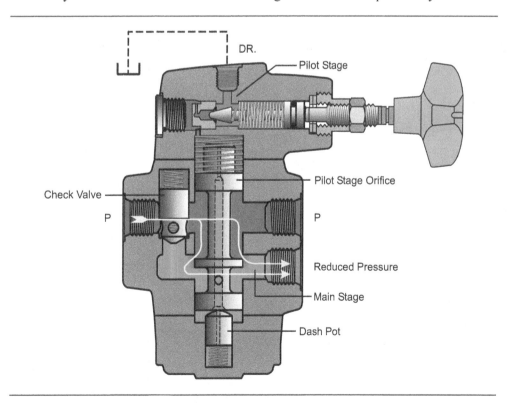

Figure 10-17   Pilot-operated pressure reducing valve

Figure 10-17 shows the condition when supply pressure is less than the valve setting. The spool is hydraulically balanced through an orifice in its center, and the light spring holds it in the wide open position.

In Figure 10-18, pressure has reached the valve setting and the pilot valve is diverting flow to the drain passage limiting pressure above the spool. Flow through the orifice in the spool creates a pressure difference that moves the spool up against the spring force. The spool partially closes the outlet port to create a pressure drop from the supply to the branch system.

Again, the outlet port is never entirely closed. When no flow is called for in the branch system, there is still a continuous flow of some 60 – 90 cubic inches (980 – 1475 cubic centimeters) per minute through the spool orifice and the pilot valve to drain.

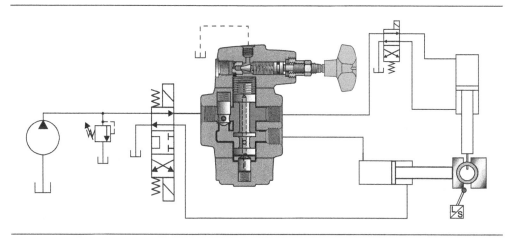

Figure 10-18   Pilot-operated pressure reducing valve regulating in a clamp circuit

Optional Reverse Free Flow Check

The valve illustrated in Figure 10-15 will handle reverse flow only if the system pressure is less than the valve setting. If reverse flow pressure is higher, a bypass check valve is required. This is an integral part of the valve shown in Figure 10-17.

Direct Acting, Spool Type, Pressure Control Valves

A direct acting sliding spool type pressure control valve is shown in Figure 10-19. The spool operates within a valve body and is held in the closed position by an adjustable spring. Operating pressure sensed through a passage in the bottom cover opposes the spring load. The spool area is such that with the heaviest spring normally used, the valve would open at approximately 125 psi (8.5 bar, 850 kPa). To extend their pressure range, most models include a small piston or plunger in the bottom cover to reduce the pressure reaction area to 1/8 [1/16 in the 2,000 psi (140 bar, 14,000 kPa) range] of the area of the spool end. When operating pressure exceeds the valve setting, the spool is raised and fluid can flow from the primary to the secondary port.

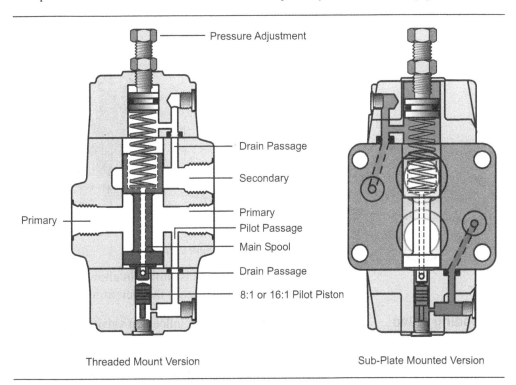

Pressure Adjustment

Drain Passage

Secondary

Primary

Primary

Pilot Passage

Main Spool

Drain Passage

8:1 or 16:1 Pilot Piston

Threaded Mount Version

Sub-Plate Mounted Version

Figure 10-19   A typical direct acting, spool-type, pressure control valve

A drain passage is provided in the top cover to drain the spring chamber. This drain also removes leakage oil from the space between the spool and piston by means of a passage drilled lengthwise through the spool.

Depending on the assembly of the top and bottom covers, this valve can be used as a back pressure valve, unloading valve, sequence valve, counterbalance valve or brake valve. It is built with an optional integral check when reverse flow is required from the secondary to the primary port.

Back Pressure Valve

Figure 10-20 illustrates the valve assembled for back pressure operation. The line that requires back pressure is connected to the primary port and the secondary port is connected to tank. This application permits the valve to be internally drained and the top cover is assembled with the drain passage aligned with the secondary port. The bottom cover is assembled so that operating pressure is sampled internally from the primary port, making it necessary to maintain adequate back pressure to keep the valve open.

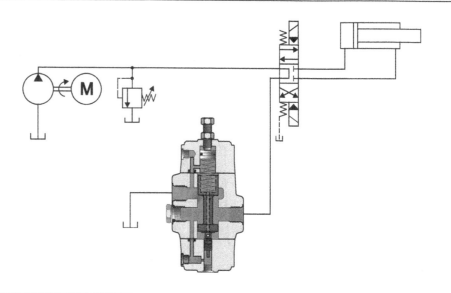

Figure 10-20   Back pressure valve

In Figure 10-20, the spool is shifted to allow flow to the secondary port and to tank when system pressure exceeds that determined by the spring setting.

Unloading Valve

To use the same valve as an unloading valve (Figure 10-21), the lower cover is assembled to block the internal operating pressure passages. An external pressure source is used to move the spool and divert pump delivery to the secondary port. The drain connection remains internal, since the secondary port is still connected to the tank.

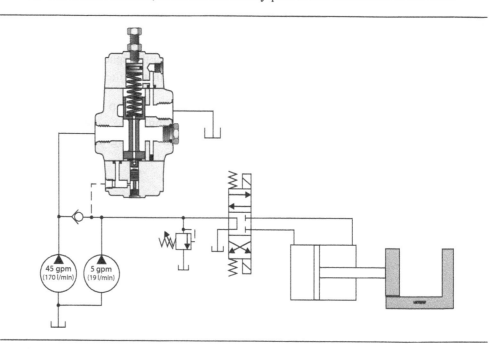

Figure 10-21   Unloading valve configuration

Note the operating difference between the unloading and back pressure valves. The back pressure valve operates in balance, being held open at one of an infinite number of positions by the flow of oil through it. Back pressure maintained at the primary port is determined by the spring adjustment. With the unloading valve (Figure 10-21), however, the primary port pressure is independent of the spring force because the remote pressure source operates the spool. As long as the control pressure is at least 150 psi (10.3 bar, 1,030 kPa) above the spring setting, free flow is permitted from the primary to the secondary port.

In the unloading circuit, Figure 10-21, a simple, load sequenced circuit is shown. A large volume has been specified through the use of two pumps to obtain a desired speed on the large clamp cylinder. Once the clamp has closed, however, the cylinder does not require high volume, but rather higher pressure to provide the high clamping force. The unloading valve directs the large pump flow to the reservoir at low pressure, leaving only the small pump to operate at high pressure. By using a double pump with an unloading circuit, we can save considerable horsepower, reduce heat generation and save on initial installation costs, particularly for the electric motor.

To avoid interaction with other pressure controls in the system, the relief valve should be set some measure (150 psi as a general rule) above the highest working pressure requirement.

Because the unloading valve is ported directly to tank, it may be internally drained to the outlet port and does not require a reverse free flow check valve.

Sequence Valve

A sequence valve is used to cause actions to take place in a system in a definite order, and to maintain a predetermined minimum pressure in the primary line while the secondary operation occurs. Figure 10-22 shows the valve assembled for sequencing. Fluid flows freely through the primary passage to operate the first phase until the pressure setting of the valve is reached. As the spool lifts, flow is diverted to the secondary port to operate a second phase. A typical application is clamping from the primary port and feeding a drill head from the secondary after the workpiece is firmly clamped.

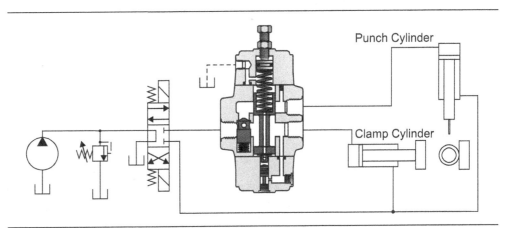

Figure 10-22   Sequence valve in a clamping circuit

To maintain pressure in the primary system, the valve is internally operated. However, the drain connection must be external, since the secondary port is under pressure when the valve sequences. If this pressure were allowed in the drain passage, it would add to the spring force and raise the pressure required to open the valve.

The sequence valve is suitable for systems where it can be installed upstream from the directional valve. If it is installed downstream (in a cylinder line), some provision must be made for return free flow when the cylinder is reversed. Figure 10-22 shows a model with the check valve included.

In some systems, it is desirable to provide an interlock so that sequencing does not occur until the primary actuator reaches a definite position. In these applications, the bottom cover on the sequence valve is assembled for remote operation, as shown in Figure 10-23.

A cam operated directional valve blocks the control pressure from the piston in the bottom cover until the clamp cylinder reaches the prescribed position. Only then is the sequence valve permitted to shift and direct flow to the second operation.

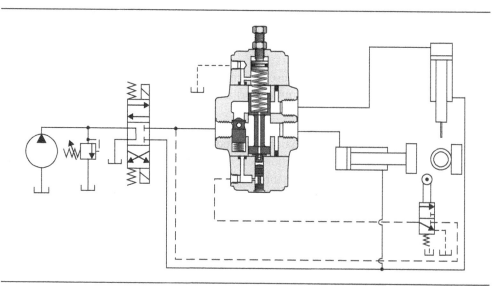

Figure 10-23   Remote controlled sequence valve application

Counterbalance Valve

A counterbalance valve is used to maintain control over a vertical cylinder so that it will not fall freely because of gravity. The primary port of the valve is connected to the lower cylinder port and the secondary port to the directional valve (Figure 10-24). The pressure setting is slightly higher than is required to hold the load from falling.

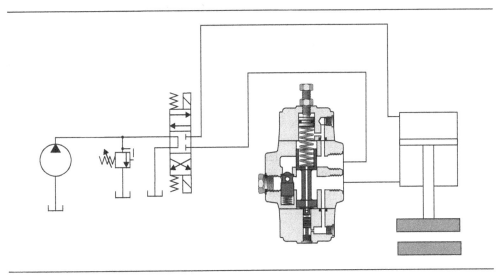

Figure 10-24   Counterbalance valve circuit

When the pump delivery is directed to the top of the cylinder, the cylinder piston is forced down causing pressure at the primary port to increase and raise the spool, opening a flow path for discharge through the secondary port to the directional valve and subsequently to the reservoir. In cases where it is desired to remove back pressure at the cylinder and increase the force potential at the bottom of the stroke, this valve too can be operated remotely, as shown in Figure 10-25.

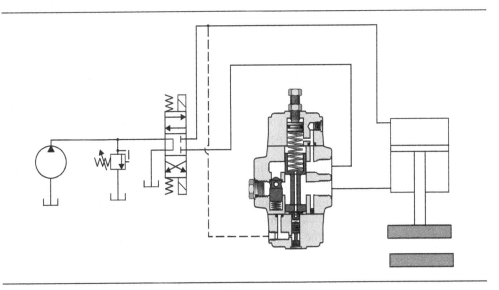

Figure 10-25   Remote piloted counterbalance valve circuit

When the cylinder is being raised, the integral check valve opens to permit free flow for returning the cylinder.

The counterbalance valve can be internally drained. In the lowering position, when the valve must be open, its secondary port is connected to the reservoir. In the reverse condition, it does not matter that load pressure is effective in the drain passage, because the check valve bypasses the spool.

Brake Valve

In any overrunning load application using a hydraulic motor, ensure the motor exhaust line does not become blocked to prevent damage to the hydraulic system, motor, motor shaft or machine. If, however, the load must be brought to a stop quickly, the safe approach is to use a brake valve. A brake valve is used in the exhaust line of a hydraulic motor to (1) prevent overspeeding when an overrunning load is applied to the motor shaft and (2) prevent excessive pressure buildup when decelerating or stopping a load.

When the valve is used as a brake valve, it has a solid spool (no drain hole through the center), and there is a remote operating pressure connection in the bottom cover directly under the spool (Figure 10-26). This port is connected to the supply line of the motor. The internal control connection also is used under the small piston and senses pressure from the exhaust port of the motor.

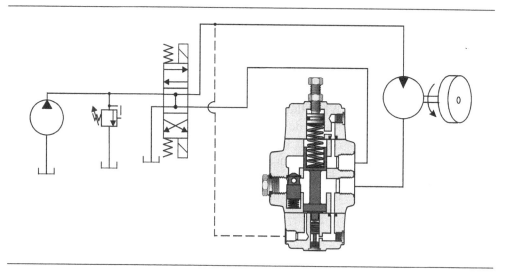

Figure 10-26   Brake valve configuration and circuit

Accelerating. When the load is being accelerated, pressure is maximum at the motor inlet and under the large area of the brake valve spool, holding it in the full open position, permitting free flow from the exhaust port of the motor.

Running. When the motor gets up to speed, load pressure still holds the brake valve open unless the load tries to run away. If this happens, the pressure falls off at the motor inlet and in the remote control pressure passage. The spring force tends to close the valve thus increasing the back pressure. This in turn raises the drive line pressure to the motor and under the small piston, holding the valve at the proper metering position to maintain constant motor speed.

Braking. When the directional valve is shifted to neutral, inertia causes the motor to continue rotating. Until the motor stops turning, it will operate as a pump, drawing fluid from the reservoir through the directional valve and circulating it back through the brake valve.

At this time, pressure at the motor outlet tending to bring it to a stop will be whatever is required under the small piston to overcome the brake valve setting.

Industrial Test Questions:
Pressure Controls

Chapter 10

1. Name three functions of pressure control valves.

2. Where are the ports of a relief valve connected?

3. What is cracking pressure?

4. How could pressure override be disadvantageous?

5. How does the "balanced piston" relief valve reduce pressure override?

6. What is meant by venting the relief valve?

7. When is a high vent spring used?

8. What type of valve provides the ability to electrically select one pressure from a set of given preset pressures?

9. What kind of valve has the capability to modulate system pressure electrically over a wide range without external feedback devices?

10. What is the difference between a pilot-operated relief valve and a pilot-operated sequence valve?

11. What are the functions of the unloading relief valve?

12. What is the purpose of a pressure reducing valve?

13. Which type of pressure control is normally open?

14. Name three applications of the direct acting spool type normally closed pressure control valve.

15. Name three applications of the direct acting spool type normally closed pressure control valve with an integral check.

16. Explain unloading.

17. What does a sequence valve do?

18. Is a sequence valve internally or externally drained?

19. What is the purpose of a counterbalance valve?

20. Explain why a closed center spool in a directional valve cannot be used with a motor driving an overrunning load.

21. What is the purpose of the second pressure control connection in the brake valve?

Chapter 11 . . . . Flow Controls

By controlling the rate of flow in a hydraulic circuit, it's possible to control the speed of hydraulic cylinders or motors. A cylinder's speed is determined by its size and the flow rate of the oil going into or out of it. A large diameter cylinder would hold more oil and take longer to complete its stroke; a smaller one would move faster. Changing the flow rate from the pump would also change the extension time of the cylinder. Changing either the cylinder or pump size to regulate speed would be impractical, especially if a speed change is desired in mid-stroke. A more typical method is to use a flow control valve.

The flow control valve (Figure 11-1), in its simplest form, is nothing more than a variable orifice, and could be as basic as a needle valve. By varying the size of the opening, one can vary the amount of fluid entering the cylinder and thus control its speed. A kitchen faucet is an example of a simple flow control valve.

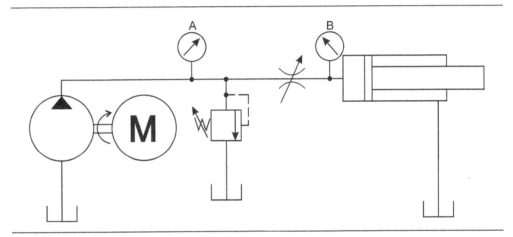

Figure 11-1   Meter-in circuit

Three factors affect flow rate through an orifice or restriction: pressure drop, fluid temperature/viscosity and orifice size. If any one of these factors is increased, the flow rate increases.

Flow Control Methods

Control of flow in hydraulic circuits can be accomplished with a meter-in circuit, with a meter-out circuit or with a bleed-off circuit. Each type of circuit has advantages and disadvantages depending on the type of application.

Meter-In Circuit

In a meter-in operation, the flow control valve is placed between the pump and the actuator (Figure 11-2).

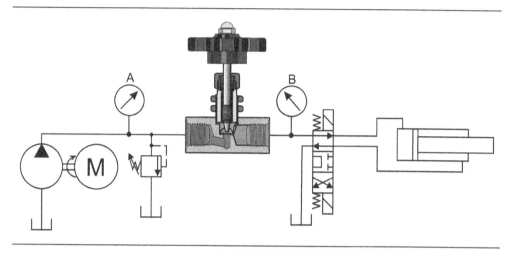

Figure 11-2   Meter-in circuit

In this way, it controls the amount of fluid going into the actuator. Pump delivery in excess of the metered amount is diverted to the tank over the relief valve. If the pump delivered 10 GPM (38 l/min) and the cylinder speed needed to be reduced by half, the flow control could be adjusted to pass only 5 GPM (19 l/min). However, since it's a fixed displacement pump, allowing only 5 GPM (19 l/min) to pass through the flow control into the cylinder means that the other five GPM (19 l/min) has no choice but to go over the relief valve at the relief valve setting. If the relief valve happened to be set at 1,000 psi (70 bar, 7,000 kPa), a pressure gauge at point A would read 1,000 psi (70 bar, 7,000 kPa). The pressure found at point B would be determined by the work load on the cylinder. The difference between the two readings is the pressure drop across the orifice; that is, the pressure required to push the 5 GPM (19 l/min) through the orifice.

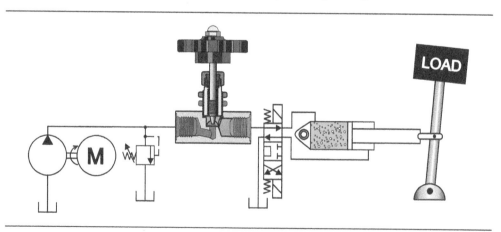

Figure 11-3   Meter-in circuits do not control runaway loads

Meter-in circuits can only be used with opposing loads. If the load in Figure 11-3 should tend to run away, it would pull the cylinder piston ahead of the oil supply. And since the exhaust flow has a free path back to the reservoir, the meter-in circuit could not prevent the load from running away.

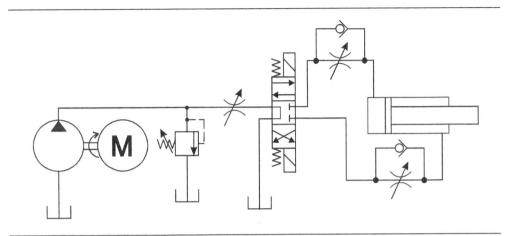

Figure 11-4   Locations for meter-in applications

Figure 11-4 shows three locations where a flow control could be placed in a meter-in circuit. Note that for two of the locations, check valves are included to allow free reverse flow past the flow control. Because the excess flow goes over the relief valve to tank, the meter-in circuit is somewhat inefficient.

Meter-Out Circuit

In Figure 11-5, the flow control is on the outlet side of the cylinder to control the flow coming out. This is known as a meter-out circuit. If the flow control were closed completely, the oil could not exhaust from the cylinder and it could not move. Regulating the size of the opening controls the flow rate, and therefore the speed, of the cylinder.

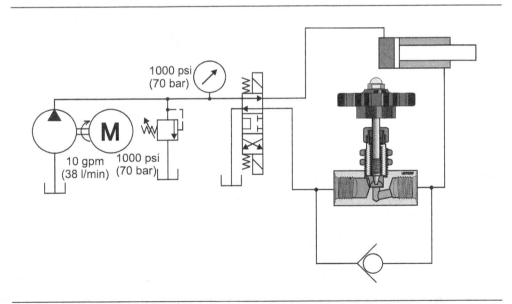

Figure 11-5   Meter-out circuit

If the cylinder in Figure 11-5 has a 2 to 1 ratio, and the outlet flow rate from the rod end is controlled to 4 GPM (15 l/min), the flow rate into the cap end would be 8 GPM (30 l/min). Because the pump is delivering 10 GPM (38 l/min), two GPM (8 l/min) would be forced to return to the reservoir over the relief valve. The pump would be operating at the relief valve setting regardless of how easy or difficult it is to move the load.

Metering into the cylinder works well with an opposing load, but if the load tends to run away, a more positive approach is to utilize a meter-out circuit. Whether the overrunning load is extending or retracting the cylinder, meter-out is a preferable method.

In a meter-out circuit with an overrunning load as shown in Figure 11-5, there is an intensified pressure in the rod end of the cylinder due to the differential area of the cylinder. The overrunning load adds to this intensified pressure. Care must be taken not to exceed safe operating pressures in the rod end of the cylinder when metering-out with an overrunning load. This is an important safety consideration that will be discussed further in following paragraphs.

Figure 11-6 illustrates three possible locations for the flow control valve in a meter-out circuit. In both meter-in and meter-out circuits, the pump is required to operate at relief valve setting because a portion of the flow is being diverted across the relief valve to the reservoir.

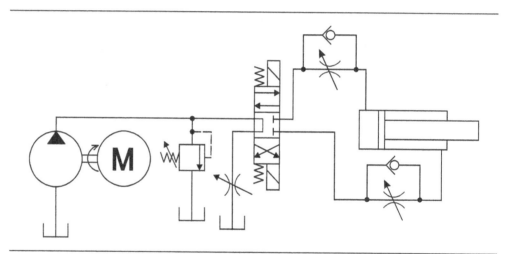

Figure 11-6   Locations for meter-out applications

Pressure Intensification in Meter-Out Circuits

In meter-out circuits using a differential cylinder, it is possible to develop rod end pressures much higher than the system relief valve setting. As shown in Figure 11-7, with no load on the cylinder, the rod end pressure is double the relief valve setting.

To illustrate this principle, Figure 11-7 is showing a force balance across the cylinder, which has no opposing load on it. The speed of the cylinder is being controlled (slowed) by the meter-out flow control. If the flow out of the cylinder is being restricted, then flow into the cylinder is also being restrained. The balance of the flow not going into the cylinder must travel across the relief valve to the reservoir, forcing the system pressure to rise to relief setting, 1,000 psi (70 bar, 7,000 kPa). This pressure, multiplied by the area of the cap end of the cylinder, results in a 2,000 pound (8,900N) load against the cylinder piston.

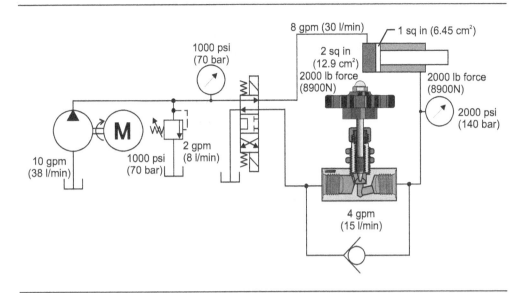

Figure 11-7   Pressure intensification in meter-out circuits

Pressure in the rod end of the cylinder must be sufficient to resist the 2,000 pound (8,900N) load. Whereas the rod end area is half of the cap end area, the pressure must be double [2,000 psi (140 bar, 14,000 kPa)] to provide the same 2,000 pound (8,900N) load. With no load on the cylinder, the rod end pressure is twice system pressure. This phenomenon is called pressure intensification, and will occur any time a meter-out circuit is used on the rod end of a cylinder.

As mentioned previously, any pulling load on the cylinder will also create a pressure in the rod end, which will be additive to the intensified pressure already there. In Figure 11-8, an external load of 1,000 pounds (4,450N) is applied to the cylinder so as to pull to the right (overrunning load). This would add to the 2,000 pounds (8,900N) force applied by system pressure in the cap end. The rod end pressure would then increase to 3,000 psi (210 bar, 21,000 kPa).

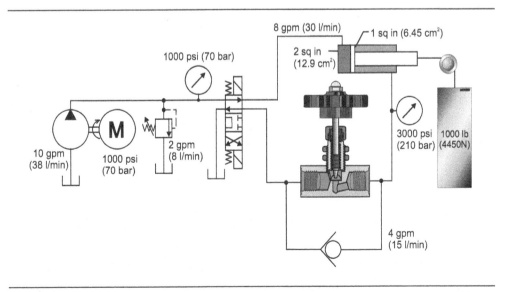

Figure 11-8   Load pressure adds to intensification pressure in meter-out circuits

If an external load is applied to the cylinder to oppose extension (resistive load) with a force of 1,000 pounds (4,450N), this would subtract from the 2,000 pounds (8,900N) force on the cap end. Therefore, the rod end pressure would decrease to 1,000 psi (70 bar, 7,000 kPa).

Bleed-Off Circuit

The third method of applying a flow control is shown in Figure 11-9. The flow control is installed in a branch circuit off the main line to control cylinder speed.

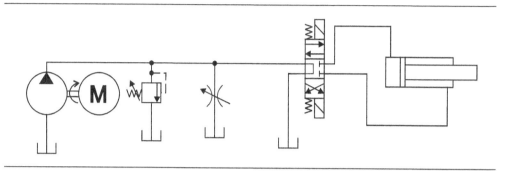

Figure 11-9   Bleed-off circuit

By adjusting the flow control, some of the pump delivery is diverted to the reservoir and the cylinder speed will be affected. Any reduced speed of the cylinder can be attained by this method. Unlike the meter-in or meter-out circuits, there is no flow passing the relief valve, so the pump will operate at the pressure needed to move the load. This can be a considerable saving of energy.

The bleed-off circuit will not prevent an overrunning load from running away. As with a meter-in circuit, it can be used with opposing loads only.

The bleed-off circuit is not as accurate as the meter-in and meter-out circuits because the measured flow is going to the reservoir rather than into the cylinder. This makes the cylinder speed subject to changes in pump delivery and/or system leakage, which vary when the load pressure changes. To minimize these effects, it is recommended to bleed off no more than half the pump delivery and to avoid using a bleed-off circuit when there is a wide fluctuation in the work load pressure. Figure 11-10 shows three possible locations for flow control placement in a bleed-off circuit.

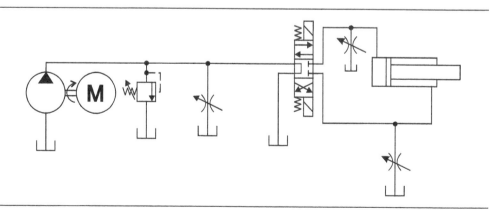

Figure 11-10   Locations for bleed-off applications

Summary

Meter-in and meter-out circuits can be very accurate, but are not very efficient. The bleed-off circuit is efficient, but is not as accurate. The meter-out circuit can control overrunning as well as opposing loads while the other two methods must be used with opposing loads only. The choice of flow control method and the location of the flow control in the circuit are dependent on the type of application being controlled.

Types of Flow Control

Flow controls are of two types: nonpressure-compensated and pressure-compensated. Pressure-compensated flow controls are either the bypass or restrictor type.

The flow control valve used in the preceding examples was a simple variable orifice, such as a needle valve. That makes a good flow control valve as long as the work load does not change very much. However, if the load on the cylinder changes, the amount of fluid flowing through the needle valve will change. It will increase as the load goes down and decrease as the load increases. That's because flow through an orifice, or any other type of opening, increases as the pressure drop across the orifice increases.

In the meter-in example, the relief valve was set at 1,000 psi (70 bar, 7,000 kPa). If the needle valve had been adjusted to pass 5 GPM (19 l/min) to the cylinder when the work pressure was 200 psi (14 bar, 1,400 kPa), and then the work pressure increased to 400 psi (28 bar, 2,800 kPa), the flow would be less than 5 GPM (19 l/min). That's because the pressure drop across the needle valve would have dropped from 800 psi (55 bar, 5,500 kPa) to only 600 psi (40 bar, 4,000 kPa). With a lower pressure drop, there will be less flow (and vice versa).

Pressure-Compensated Flow Control

A pressure-compensated flow control valve automatically compensates for pressure changes and maintains its setting, even as the work load changes.

Bypass Type

A bypass type pressure-compensated flow control is illustrated in Figure 11-11. Inlet flow can pass across the flow regulating piston to the directional valve and cylinder, in this case shown adjusted for 8 GPM (30 l/min), or across the bypass piston to the reservoir. A spring under the bypass piston is equivalent to 20 psi (1.5 bar, 150 kPa), keeping the bypass piston closed. As long as the pressure differential across the throttle (flow control piston) is less than 20 psi (1.5 bar, 150 kPa), the bypass valve will remain closed and all flow will pass to the cylinder. Pressure at the downstream side of the throttle is ported to the spring chamber under the bypass piston, adding to the pressure regulation of the 20 psi (1.5 bar, 150 kPa) spring.

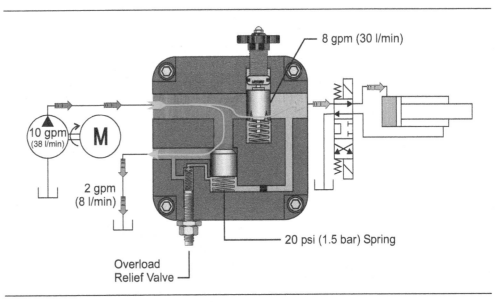

Figure 11-11   Bypass type pressure-compensated flow control

Closing the throttle to limit flow to the cylinder will increase the pressure upstream of the throttle. (It takes more pressure to force fluid through a small opening than through a large opening.)

When the pressure differential across the throttle exceeds 20 psi (1.5 bar, 150 kPa), the bypass valve will begin to open, and will pass enough fluid to the reservoir to maintain the pressure drop across the throttle at 20 psi (1.5 bar, 150 kPa).

Applying load to the cylinder will cause an increase in system pressure. This load pressure is also transmitted to the spring chamber under the bypass piston, attempting to keep it closed. When pressure upstream of the throttle rises to the load pressure plus the spring pressure, the bypass piston will open and divert fluid to the reservoir. The pressure upstream of the throttle, therefore, is always 20 psi (1.5 bar, 150 kPa) higher than the pressure downstream of the throttle, maintaining a constant pressure drop across the throttle. All other things being equal, a constant pressure drop across the throttle will provide a constant flow across the throttle.

Increasing or decreasing the throttle orifice size permits an increase or decrease in the cylinder speed. Maintaining a constant pressure difference across the throttle orifice, regardless of changes in the work load pressure, results in a pressure-compensated flow control.

This control can be modified to include a built-in relief valve for overload protection, as illustrated in Figure 11-11. Pressure in the spring chamber under the bypass piston is limited by means of a small poppet and an adjustable spring. Pressure upstream of the throttle will be regulated at this adjustable spring setting plus 20 psi (1.5 bar, 150 kPa).

Packaging these elements in one unit results in a combination overload relief valve and pressure-compensated flow control. In order for the relief valve to be effective, the flow control valve would have to be placed between the pump and the directional valve.

A bypass type flow control has the advantage of saving energy, in that it does not cause the system to operate at relief valve setting while controlling speed. It can only be used for meter-in applications, however.

Restrictor Type

A restrictor type pressure-compensated flow control is illustrated in Figure 11-12. This type of pressure-compensated flow control can work in a meter-in, meter-out or bleed off function. This flow control operates much like the bypass type, in that a constant pressure drop across an orifice maintains a constant flow. This valve restricts the inlet flow, however, rather than bypassing it.

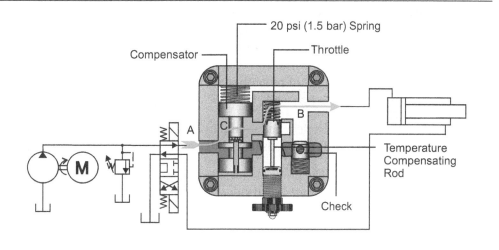

Figure 11-12   Restrictor type pressure-compensated flow control

A 20 psi (1.5 bar, 150 kPa) spring holds the compensator spool in the normally open position. Flow passes the compensator and through the throttle opening to the cylinder. Downstream pressure is ported to the spring chamber acting against the compensator. Upstream pressure is ported through the sensing holes in the compensator spool to the chamber below the compensator spool. As the throttle is adjusted to restrict flow, the upstream pressure rises which increases the pressure under the compensator spool. As the pressure rises above 20 psi (1.5 bar, 150 kPa), the compensator spool will rise and begin to restrict inlet flow until the 20 psi (1.5 bar, 150 kPa) is maintained.

As work pressure (cylinder pressure) begins to rise, this pressure is transmitted to the compensator spring chamber, adding to the spring regulation of 20 psi (1.5 bar, 150 kPa). The pressure differential across the throttle is maintained at 20 psi (1.5 bar, 150 kPa), maintaining a constant flow across the throttle. Pressure upstream will continue to rise until the system relief valve setting is reached. The compensator will continuously adjust, however, to maintain the pressure upstream of the throttle at 20 psi (1.5 bar, 150 kPa) above the pressure downstream of the throttle.

Because flow cannot pass in the reverse direction through the throttle in this valve, a reverse free flow check valve is included so the cylinder can be retracted.

Temperature Compensation

Figure 11-12 illustrates another feature that can be included in this type of valve; temperature compensation. The center rod in the throttle spool expands when heated, such that it will move the throttle slightly toward the closed position as the system temperature rises. Whereas fluid becomes less viscous with higher temperature, the flow across the throttle will increase as fluid temperature rises. By closing off the throttle slightly, this viscosity change is compensated for.

Overspeed Control

When the flow control is sitting idle in a no-flow condition, the compensator is in a full-open position. When flow is suddenly applied, such as when the directional valve is quickly shifted, a momentary high flow will pass through the valve until the compensator moves to its adjusted position. This can cause a momentary actuator overspeed, which may be undesirable in some circumstances.

An overspeed control consists of a threaded rod extending into the compensator chamber to limit how far the compensator will open, thereby reducing the distance and time required for the compensator to regain control.

Proportional Flow Control Valves

Proportional flow control valves provide the ability to control hydraulic flow rates electronically. They can be activated by a remotely located device such as a Programmable Logic Controller and can be programmed for complete automatic cycles. They are called proportional flow control valves because the amount of output hydraulic flow is proportional to the magnitude of the electrical input command signal. The use of any type of proportional valve requires that the equipment contains an electrical power supply and electronic controls. Proportional valves are covered in detail in Chapter 13.

Both cylinders and hydraulic motors can be controlled in applications where precise feed speeds, controlled acceleration or remote electrical programming are required.

The proportional solenoid throttle (Figure 11-13) is a restrictor type nonpressure-compensated valve. A separate hydrostat is required for pressure compensation. It can be used in meter-in, meter-out or bleed-off applications.

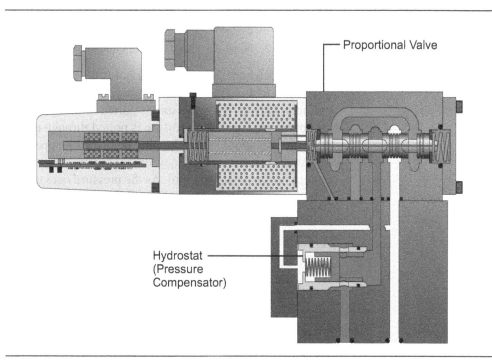

Figure 11-13   Proportional solenoid throttle

Deceleration Valves

Hydraulic cylinders often have built-in cushions that slow down the cylinder pistons at the extreme ends of their travel. An external valve is required when it is necessary to decelerate a cylinder at some intermediate position or to slow down or stop a rotary actuator (motor).

Deceleration valves are restrictor type flow controls and they are usually used in a meter-out configuration. Most deceleration valves are cam-operated with tapered spools. They gradually decrease flow to or from an actuator for smooth stopping or deceleration. A "normally open" valve cuts off flow when its plunger is depressed by a cam. It may be used to slow the speed of a drill head cylinder at the transition from rapid traverse to feed, or to smoothly stop heavy index tables and large presses.

Some applications require a valve to permit flow during actuation and to cut off flow when the plunger is released. In this case, a "normally closed" valve is used. This type of valve provides an interlocking arrangement that allows flow to be directed to another branch of the circuit when the actuator or load reaches a certain position. Both the "normally open" and the "normally closed" valves are available with integral check valves that permit reverse free flow.

Typical Applications

The following figures illustrate a deceleration valve in a typical application. At a preset point, the valve slows a drill head cylinder from rapid advance speed to feed speed. Figure 11-14 shows rapid advance, with exhaust flow from the cylinder passing unrestricted through the deceleration valve.

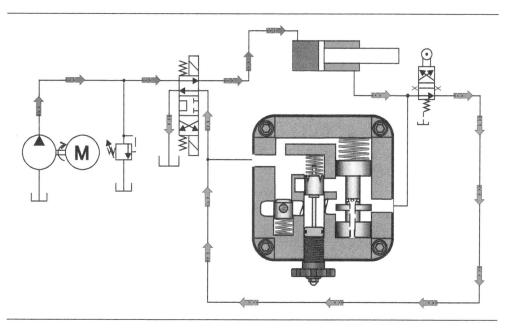

Figure 11-14   Rapid advance

In Figure 11-15, the valve plunger is depressed by a cam mounted on the cylinder rod. Exhaust flow is blocked at the deceleration valve and passes through the flow control valve, which sets the feed speed.

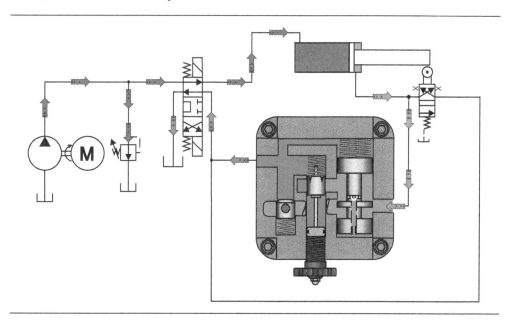

Figure 11-15   Deceleration to feed speed

In Figure 11-16, the directional valve is reversed to return the cylinder. Whether the plunger is depressed or not, oil from the directional valve passes freely through the flow control valve's check valve.

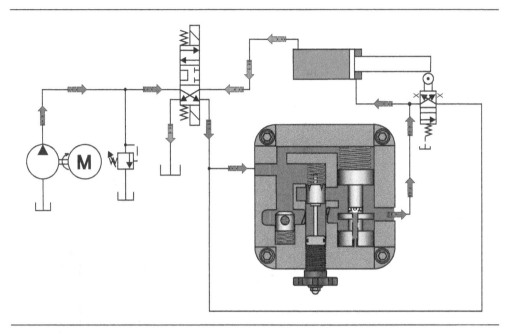

Figure 11-16   Rapid return

In Figure 11-17 the common symbols for flow controls are shown.

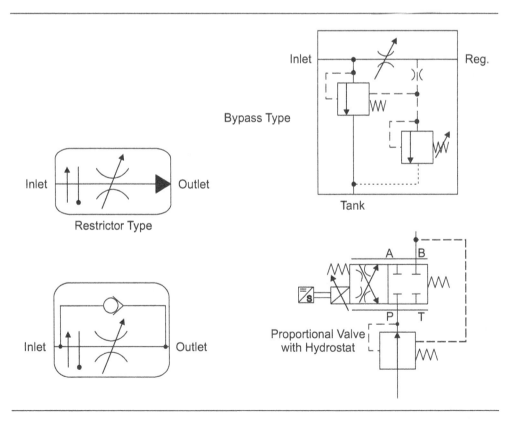

Figure 11-17   Common flow control symbols

Industrial Test Questions:
Flow Controls

Chapter 11

1. Name two ways of regulating flow to an actuator.

2. What are the three methods of applying flow control valves?

3. Under what conditions would you use each of the three methods named in Question #2 above?

4. What is the difference between a bypass and restrictor type flow control?

5. What is pressure compensation?

6. When might temperature compensation be needed?

7. What is the advantage of the flow control with relief valve over a conventional flow control?

8. Why are remote flow control valves called proportional flow control valves?

9. What is the purpose for a deceleration valve?

Chapter 12 . . . . Cartridge and Stack Valves

Refinements in hydraulic system development have led to greater use of manifold blocks. A manifold block greatly reduces the number of fittings required for the interconnecting lines between components in a system. This eliminates many potential leakage points. A cartridge valve is inserted into a standard sized cavity in a manifold block and held in place with either threads or a cover secured with bolts.

Cartridge valves are divided into two basic configurations. One is screw-in cartridge valves, which are commonly used in, but not limited to, low flow systems up to 30 – 35 GPM (120 – 140 l/min). Figure 12-1 illustrates a typical screw-in cartridge valve system installed in a manifold block. The second basic configuration is slip-in cartridge valves, which are used in high flow systems, 40 GPM (150 l/min) and up, where pressure levels are generally 3,000 psi (210 bar) and higher.

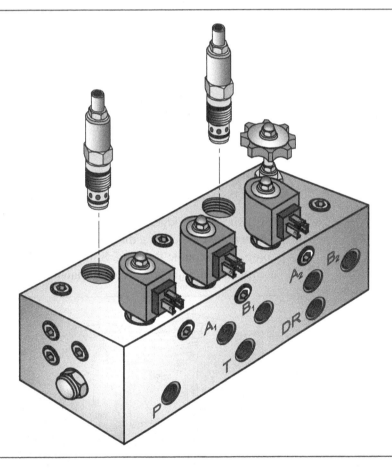

Figure 12-1   Manifold with screw-in cartridge valves

Figure 12-2 illustrates a typical manifold block system using slip-in cartridge valves.

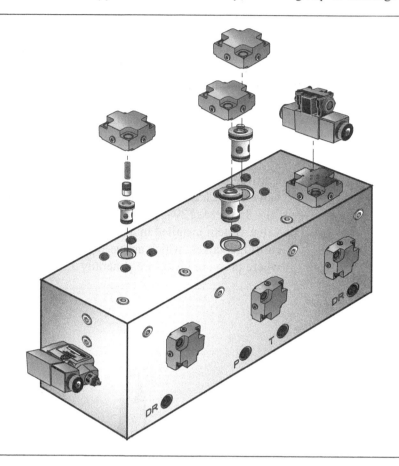

Figure 12-2   Manifold with slip-in cartridge valves

Most slip-in cartridges are poppet-type elements that are normally controlled by another valve (such as a directional, pressure, or flow control valve) to provide a complete hydraulic function. Slip-in cartridge valve systems initially gained acceptance on injection molding machines and steel mill equipment (Figure 12-3).

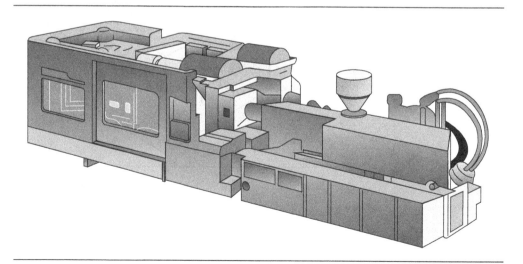

Figure 12-3   Plastic injection molding machines utilize manifolds and cartridge valves

Screw-in cartridge valves initially gained popularity in mobile vehicle and implement applications, but soon found popularity in industrial systems for lower flow circuits and as operators for slip-in cartridge valve systems. Screw-in cartridges can be either spool or poppet-type elements. With a few exceptions, a single screw-in cartridge element provides a stand-alone hydraulic valve function.

This chapter contains information on the construction, operation, and application of these two types of cartridge valves. It also covers a different series of valves, called Stack Valves, that are also used in manifolds and may be used with slip-in cartridge valves.

Cartridge Valve Concept

Manifold Block Systems

Manifold block systems are unique solutions to specific hydraulic circuit or system requirements, using one or more cartridge valves installed into either an aluminum or steel block to perform control or work functions. In addition to free-standing manifold blocks, blocks may be installed on cylinders or hydraulic motors to form integrated, compact, leak-free actuator packages. Figure 12-4 illustrates a cylinder using a screw-in cartridge valve installed in the cylinder head.

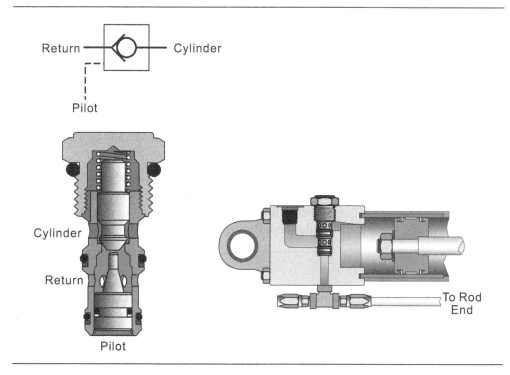

Figure 12-4   A screw-in cartridge valve installed in a cylinder head

Manifold block systems typically use screw-in cartridge valves to form an integral circuit for control of one or more system work functions. Quite frequently, as illustrated in Figure 12-5, one or more directional valves, such as the Eaton DG4V-3, are manifold mounted to the basic screw-in cartridge valve block to provide high performance work valve and control valve packages.

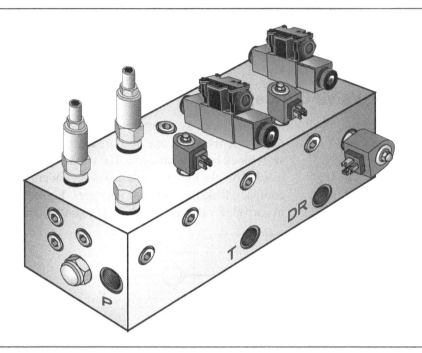

Figure 12-5   Screw-in cartridge valves and high performance directional valves on one manifold

By combining high flow slip-in cartridge valves with a control circuit of screw-in cartridge valves into one package, it is possible to create low cost, high performance solutions for plastic injection molding machines, die cast machines, presses or other similar high flow application requirements (Figure 12-6).

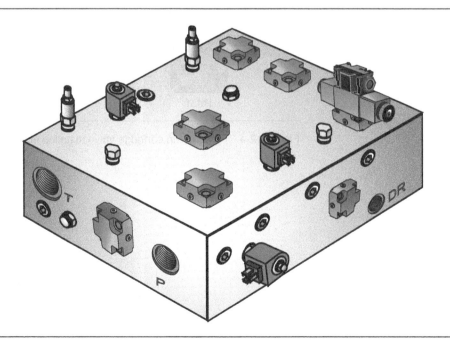

Figure 12-6   Combining screw-in, slip-in and directional valves on one manifold

Consolidating System Segments

As illustrated above, manifold block systems with cartridge valves consolidate system segments by combining valves, plumbing, and diagnostics capability into one complete package (Figure 12-7). Valves can be either all screw-in cartridge valves installed into manifold packages, all slip-in cartridge valves, or any combination of screw-in, slip-in, and manifold type valves mounted internally or externally to the manifold block.

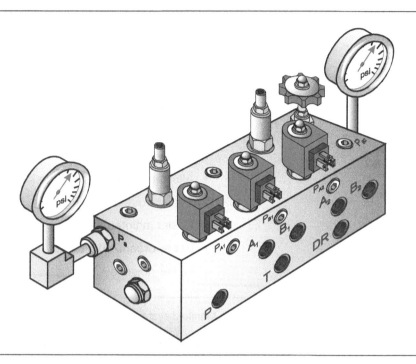

Figure 12-7   Manifold block with diagnostics features and access

A subtle, but significant, difference between the basic types of manifold cartridge valve systems is that in screw-in cartridge valve systems, 100 percent of the circuit is contained inside the block, as illustrated in Figure 12-8. Slip-in cartridge valve/ manifold valve systems typically have only 40 percent of the system contained inside the manifold block; the balance of the valves are mounted externally.

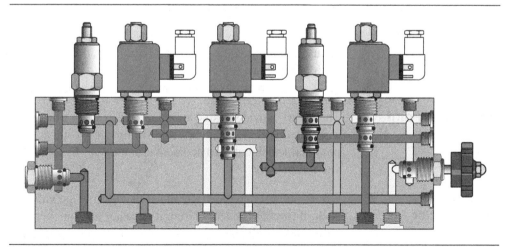

Figure 12-8   Internal plumbing of a screw-in cartridge valve manifold

Simplified installation and Maintenance

Installation and maintenance of cartridge valve manifold blocks is greatly simplified when compared to traditional line mounted valve systems. The necessity of connecting valves by means of hydraulic lines and fittings is greatly reduced by the use of internal passages machined into the manifold block. By combining one or more of the system circuit functions into one or more manifold blocks, the time and cost of installing the hydraulic system on a vehicle or implement is considerably less than traditional line mounted valve systems.

Advantages of Manifold Block Systems

Advantages for an OEM or end user using a cartridge valve manifold block system are (Figure 12-9):

- Greater design flexibility
- Lower installed cost
- Smaller package size
- Alleviated external leakage
- Easier troubleshooting
- Easier maintenance
- Better organized plumbing
- Lower noise levels

Figure 12-9   Manifold system advantages

Design Flexibility

Use of common cavities permits the easy substitution of valves with the same interface, but with either variations on the same functional characteristic or different functional characteristics that provide circuit enhancements or modifications. Also, the hydraulic system designer can incorporate circuit modifications to enhance machine performance by changing only one part (manifold block package).

Lower Cost

Manifold systems permit significant cost savings in terms of: procurement complexity and time, part numbers to be controlled and maintained, inventory complexity, material and labor savings through the elimination of valve-to-valve hydraulic lines and fittings, and simplified field service support.

Smaller Package Size

The use of internally drilled passages to connect two or more valve functions permits the use of common passages and eliminates the space required for hydraulic fittings. Both of these advantages enable the control valves to be packaged into one compact block, which requires a much smaller volume than if line-mounted valves were used.

Fewer Leak Points

The use of cartridge valve and manifold systems eliminates many potential leak points associated with hoses, tubes, and fittings between each valve. It also eliminates potential leakage due to accidental damage to hoses and tubes connecting individual valve functions.

Easier to Troubleshoot

OEMs and users typically treat screw-in cartridge valves as "throw away" items. As such, if trouble is encountered, it is easier and quicker to remove the old cartridge valve and install a new one. For slip-in cartridge valves, economic reasons typically dictate that the valve would be removed and serviced before a replacement is installed. It is significant to note that for either slip-in or screw-in valves, this is normally done without disconnecting hydraulic lines or removing the manifold block from the machine. Figure 12-7 illustrates a screw-in cartridge valve manifold block that has been provisioned for troubleshooting.

Easier to Maintain

Once installed, the manifold package is typically a "care free" item that requires no tightening of fittings or cleaning of oil leaks. If required, it can be serviced by replacing either an individual cartridge valve or the complete manifold package.

Simplified Plumbing

With many of the valve and circuit connections ported inside the manifold block, the number of external lines is markedly reduced. This provides for fewer lines to route and secure, resulting in a more simplified plumbing arrangement.

Reduced Noise Levels

Due to the solid nature of a manifold block system, hydraulic line and valve vibrations are reduced or eliminated.

Screw-In Cartridge Valves

General Characteristics
Variety

Among the first things one notices when looking at a screw-in product catalog is that there is a large variety of basic types of valves. The second thing to be noted is that each basic type has not only the expected spring and/or flow setting options, but also many small modifications that modify the basic function.

Valve design is either spool, poppet, or ball check technology, as shown in Figure 12-10. Spool valves are typically either 2-way, 3-way, or 4-way in function. Through the use of metering notches or grooves, they provide a very smooth operation and control.

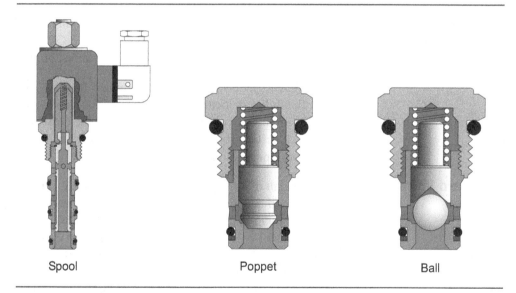

| Spool | Poppet | Ball |

Figure 12-10   Spool, poppet and ball type screw-in cartridge valves

Poppet-type valves provide leak-free operation as an on/off device. Ball-type check valves are low cost, simple versions of poppet-type valves. Because of the rapid, short stroke, non-metering nature, these types of valves potentially can introduce shocks into a hydraulic system.

The attributes of each type of valve make it advantageous for specific applications. While each type is not limited to specific functions, spool valves are typically used for directional, proportional, and flow control; poppet valves for directional, pressure, load holding, and logic control; and, ball check valves for low cost, simple load holding, shuttle, or pressure control.

Actuation of the valves can be by means of a direct acting signal or a pilot signal. These signals can be manual, hydraulic, or electrical. Direct acting valves have fast response, although they are generally limited to flow levels of 10 GPM (40 l/min) due to flow forces acting on the valve. Pilot-operated valves are typically two-stage valves where a very small amount of flow, from fractional up to 3 GPM (12 l/min) is used to control a much larger flow.

Manually operated valves are controlled by either a lever, a knob, or a screw. Hydraulically operated valves are controlled by hydraulic pressure, and electrically operated valves are controlled by electric solenoids having either on/off or proportional control characteristics.

By use of one these methods of actuation, valves are designed to provide flow, pressure, or directional control. Unique to screw-in cartridge valves is an expansion of the general category of "directional control," to include the categories of "load holding valves" and "logic valves." These will be discussed later in this section.

Compact Designs

Screw-in cartridge valves are compact and require a very small space. While this typically limits the upper flow range to 30 – 35 GPM (120 – 140 l/min), it permits the design of very compact, high valve density manifold block packages.

Screw-in cartridge valves are not attitude sensitive. This permits the block designer great flexibility in locating the valves for the smallest package size to accommodate a specific mounting configuration. Typically the only limitation is the necessity to leave one block surface free for mounting purposes; and to accommodate the pressure, tank, and control ports for external connections.

Standard Valve Cavities

The strength of any cartridge valve program is its ability to be easily used by the designer. This requirement covers not only the product range, but also, its ability to be readily used in both simple and complex manifold block systems. While there are proponents of unique cavities for each screw-in cartridge valve function, one of the significant features in the screw-in cartridge valve industry is the use of a standard range of valve cavities. These were first introduced in 1974 by Vickers, and have become the accepted industry standard through their use by most manufacturers today.

Vickers established four standard cavities to service the market. These are the 2-way, 3-way, 3-way short, and 4-way cavities. Figure 12-11 illustrates the similarities in the 2-way, 3-way, and 4-way cavities. 3-way short cavities are similar in design to the standard 3-way cavity, the difference being that Port 3 is manufactured as a pilot port and not as a full flow port. This change permits a shorter cavity depth for use with pilot-operated 2-way valves.

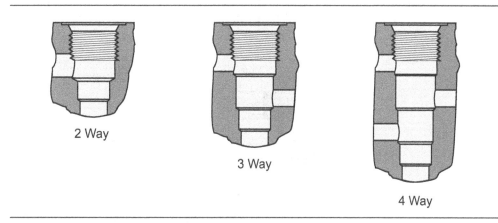

Figure 12-11   Standard cavities for 2-way, 3-way and 4-way screw-in cartridge valves

These 4 basic cavities have provided all the flexibility and freedom necessary to yield both an extensive range of standard valves and a multitude of special valves to satisfy almost any application requirement.

Typical valves used in these cavities are shown in Figures 12-12, 12-13, and 12-14. Figure 12-12 illustrates several 2-way, 2-position valves.

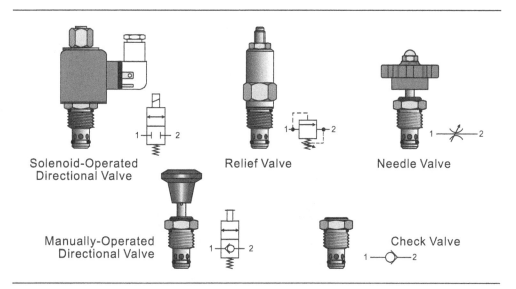

Figure 12-12   Typical 2-way, 2-position screw-in cartridge valves

Figure 12-13 illustrates several 3-way, 2-position valves, including two 3-way short valves (pilot-operated directional valve and pilot-operated check valve).

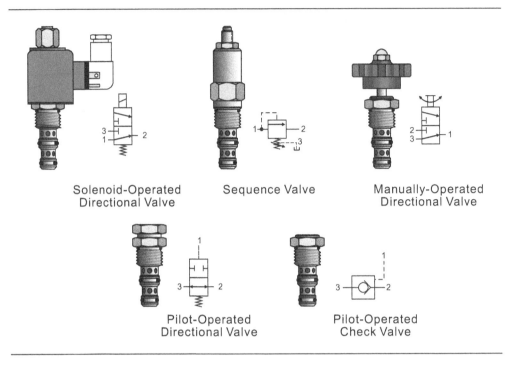

Figure 12-13   Typical 3-way, 2-position screw-in cartridge valves

Figure 12-14 illustrates several 4-way, 2-position valves.

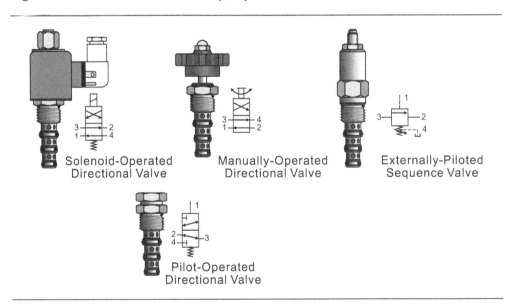

Figure 12-14   Typical 4-way, 2-position screw-in cartridge valves

The standard valve cavity concept is based on two simple principles: dependable repeatability of production, and the ability to interchange any 2-way valve in a 2-way cavity, any 3-way valve in a 3-way cavity, any 3-way short valve in a 3-way short cavity, and any 4-way valve in a 4-way cavity.

Functional Characteristics

Directional Control
Directional control valves determine the path, and therefore both the presence and direction of flow in a hydraulic circuit. They are classified as being either direct operated or pilot-operated valves.

Direct Operated Directional Control Valves
There are three different types of direct-operated directional valves: check valves, shuttle valves, and spool valves.

Check Valves
The simplest form of directional control is a check valve where flow is blocked in one direction and permitted in the other when the hydraulic pressure in the line exceeds a predetermined spring force. While check valves can be either ball type or poppet-type, the ruggedness, and therefore longer life, of the poppet-type makes them the preferred configuration. Figure 12-15 illustrates a typical poppet-type check valve.

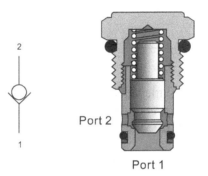

Figure 12-15   Poppet-type direct acting check valve

Poppet-type directional control valves are "On/Off" directional controls. Poppet-type directional valves can also be used very specifically for controlling loads. Their use as load holding devices is covered later in this section.

Figure 12-16 illustrates a typical 2-way, 2-position solenoid-operated directional valve. 2-way, 2-position solenoid-operated directional valves generally are called either normally open or normally closed valves. The valve illustrated in Figure 12-16 is a normally closed valve. Normally open valves permit flow in the non-actuated position while normally closed valves do not permit flow in the non-actuated position.

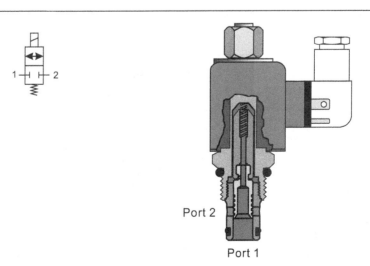

Figure 12-16   Normally closed, solenoid-operated, 2-way, 2-position directional valve

By packaging two 2-way, 2-position poppet valves into a common manifold block, it is possible to create a 3-way, 4-position valve. Figure 12-17 illustrates this valve configuration.

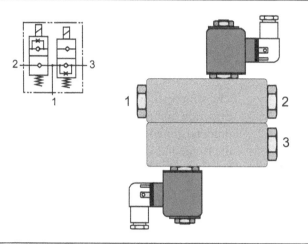

Figure 12-17   A 3-way, 4-position valve assembly

Shuttle Valves

Shuttle valves are also a simple form of directional control and use either a ball or a poppet to direct flow from the higher of two flow/pressure sources to a third opening in the valve housing. Figure 12-18 illustrates a typical poppet-type shuttle directional control.

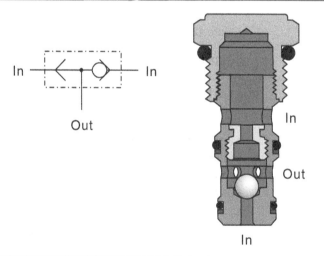

Figure 12-18   Shuttle valve

The shuttle valve shown in Figure 12-19 is a hot oil shuttle valve. This is a pilot-operated, spool type, spring centered valve with three ports. Hot oil shuttle valves are most frequently used in hydrostatic transmission circuits. The term hot oil refers to the valve's cooling function. As is indicated in the closed-loop hydrostatic transmission circuit in Figure 12-20, the hot oil shuttle valve causes a new supply of cool hydraulic oil to enter the system from the charge pump by allowing an equal amount of used, hot oil to exit "P" to "T" and then through the replenishing relief valve.

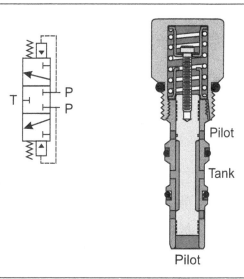

Figure 12-19   Hot oil shuttle valve

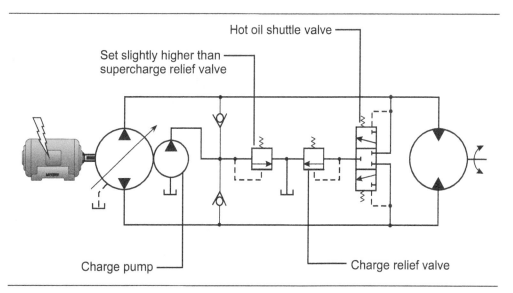

Figure 12-20   Hydrostatic transmission circuit with hot oil shuttle

Shuttle valves are also a simple form of logic valve. Logic valves are covered later in this section.

Spool Valves

The third type of direct operated directional control are spool valves.

One type of direct acting directional control spool valves is a manually operated directional valves. These are either pull-to-open, push-to-open, rotary knob or rotary lever-operated valves. The push-to-open and pull-to-open valves are 2-way, 2-position valves.

Push-to-open and pull-to-open directional control valves are "On/Off" and "Off/On" valves that control the entry of flow to a specific branch of a hydraulic circuit. Figure 12-21 illustrates a manually operated pull-to-open directional valve.

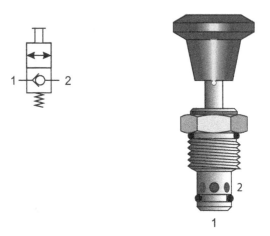

Figure 12-21   Pull-to-open manually operated spool valve

Manually operated rotary valves are used to direct flow from one branch of a hydraulic circuit to a second branch. 3-way, 2-position and 4-way, 2-position valves are typically knob operated; while 3-way, 3-position and 4-way, 3-position valves are lever-operated with a detent. Figure 12-22 illustrates a manually operated 3-way, 2-position rotary directional valve.

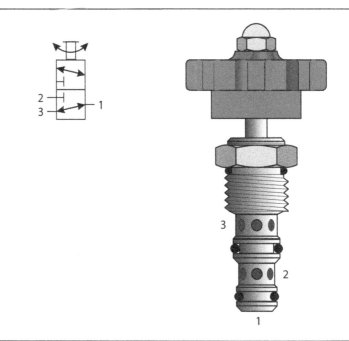

Figure 12-22   Manually operated, rotary, 3-way, 2-position directional valve

A second, and more widely used, form of directional control spool valve is the solenoid-operated directional valve. These valves enable remote control or electrically programmed control of the direction of flow. On/off directional control is provided by 2-way, 2-position spool valves. 3-way, 2-position spool valves direct flow to and from one branch to a second branch of the hydraulic circuit. 4-way, 2-position and 4-way, 3-position valves have a number of spool configurations that create flexibility in controlling the direction of flow in a branch circuit. Figure 12-23 illustrates a 4-way, 2-position solenoid-operated directional control spool valve, and Figure 12-24 illustrates a 4-way, 3-position solenoid-operated directional control spool valve.

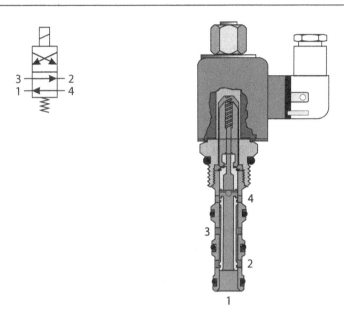

Figure 12-23   Solenoid-operated 4-way, 2-position directional control spool valve

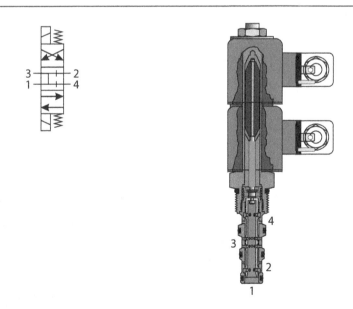

Figure 12-24   Solenoid-operated 4-way, 3-position directional control spool valve

Pilot-Operated Directional Control Valves

There are three basic types of pilot-operated directional control valves. These are check valves, counterbalance valves, and spool valves.

Check valves can be either ball type or poppet-type. Poppet-type valves are more rugged and are usually preferred. Pilot-operated check valves can be either single acting, or packaged as double acting check valves. A significant number of pilot-operated check valve directional control applications are for load holding applications and will be covered later in this section.

Counterbalance valves also control the direction of flow in a hydraulic line. They are better described as a load holding valve, and this subject is addressed later in this section.

The third, and perhaps the most widely used type of pilot-operated directional control valve is the spool valve. Due to flow force considerations, all spool type directional control valves for application with more than 6 GPM (23 l/min) are pilot-operated.

Pilot-operated directional spool valves are similar in operation to direct-acting directional spool valves as described above. The major difference is that the pilot operation feature gives them the ability to perform in systems with flow rate requirements greater than 6 GPM (23 l/min).

Pressure Control

There are four basic types of pressure control valves. These are relief valves, pressure reducing valves (sometimes called pressure reducing and relieving), pressure sequence valves, and unloading valves. Special purpose valves such as accumulator discharge valves and cross line pressure relief valves are also part of the Pressure Control valve family.

Relief Valves

Relief valves are 2-ported, pressure limiting devices and can be either direct-acting or pilot-operated. They can be ball type, poppet-type, or spool type valves. For durability, ball type relief valves should only be used in low flow, 4 GPM (15 l/min) circuit requirements. Vented versions of the basic relief valve should be used when remote control is desired. Vented relief valves require a 3-port cavity.

Figure 12-25 illustrates a typical direct-acting relief valve. When system pressure acting at the "P" port overcomes the valve spring's pressure setting, the valve opens to direct oil from "P" to "T."

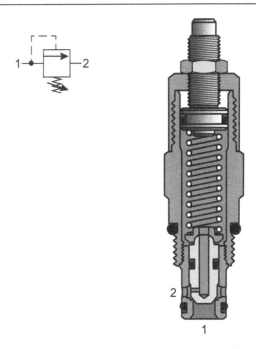

Figure 12-25   Direct acting, poppet-type relief valve

Figure 12-26 illustrates a typical pilot-operated relief valve. System pressure is located at the "P" port, and the "T" port is connected to the reservoir. The main stage spool remains hydraulically balanced until the system pressure reaches the pilot valve pressure setting. Once the system pressure overcomes the pilot valve pressure and the light spring pressure, the main stage spool moves up to direct oil to tank.

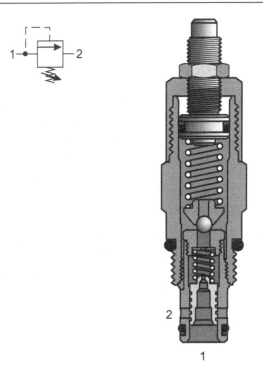

Figure 12-26   Pilot-operated, poppet-type relief valve

Pressure Reducing and Relieving Valves

Pressure reducing and pressure reducing-relieving valves are used to maintain a constant reduced pressure in branch circuits regardless of pressure variations or high settings in the primary system. This is done by means of either a factory preset pressure, or a screw-type or knob-type adjustable pressure setting.

In addition to the pressure reducing function, there are versions of these valves called pressure reducing-relieving valves, constructed with an internal flow path from the reduced pressure port to the tank port. If pressure in the secondary circuit exceeds the selected pressure, the valve opens this flow path to relieve excess fluid to tank. These valves are 3-ported and can be either direct-acting, up to 4 GPM (15 l/min) or pilot-operated. Figure 12-27 illustrates a typical pressure reducing-relieving valve.

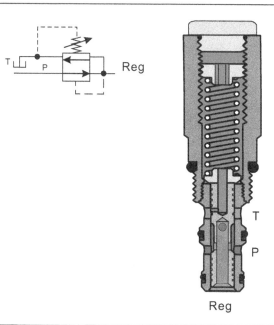

Figure 12-27   Pressure reducing-relieving valve

On this valve, when pressure at the regulated port is lower than the valve's pressure setting, the valve spool moves down to allow unrestricted flow from the primary pressure port "P" to the regulated pressure port "Reg." This blocks the flow to tank. When pressure at the regulated pressure port reaches the pressure setting, the valve spool moves away from the regulated port to partially restrict the flow, thereby limiting the pressure at the regulated pressure port. When pressure at the regulated pressure port exceeds the pressure setting, the valve spool moves further up to open the flow from the regulated flow to the tank. The spool's movement also blocks the primary pressure port.

Sequence Valves

Sequence valves are used to control the sequence of operation for two or more actuators. They typically are 3-port valves, and can be direct-acting, externally piloted; or direct-acting, internally piloted. For applications where trapped pressure in the adjustable spring chamber might be a factor, 4-ported versions are available to drain this chamber. Figure 12-28 illustrates a typical internally piloted pressure sequence valve.

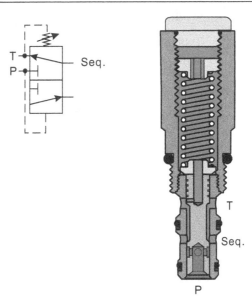

Figure 12-28   Internally piloted pressure sequence valve

When pressure is below the valve's adjustable setting, the primary pressure port is blocked and the sequence port is connected to tank. When the pressure at the primary port reaches the valve's pressure setting, the spool lifts to allow flow from the primary port to the sequence port. The tank port is blocked as this occurs.

Unloading Valve

Unloading valves are used to provide the basic relief function and the means of automatically loading/unloading a fixed delivery pump according to system demands. They are 3-port, spool valves. Figure 12-29 illustrates a typical unloading valve.

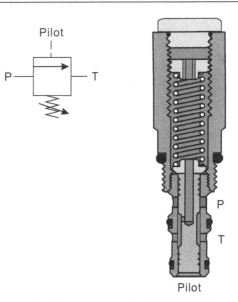

Figure 12-29   Pilot-operated unloading valve

As Figure 12-29 indicates, the pilot port on this valve is the bottom port, the primary pressure port is the upper side port, and the tank port is the lower side port. When pilot pressure is below the valve's adjustable pressure setting, the pressure port is blocked. When pilot pressure exceeds the valve's pressure setting, the valve spool moves up and opens a flow path from the primary port to the tank port.

Flow Control

Flow control valves are available in nonpressure-compensated or pressure-compensated versions.

Needle Valve

Typically, the nonpressure-compensated flow control is a 2-port valve and is also called a flow restrictor valve. The most basic type is the needle valve, although a slotted spool type valve is also available, with or without an integral check valve to provide unrestricted reverse flow. Adjustment of flow restrictor valves is by means of a knob, lever, or adjustment screw. Figure 12-30 illustrates a typical knob-type needle valve without unrestricted reverse flow.

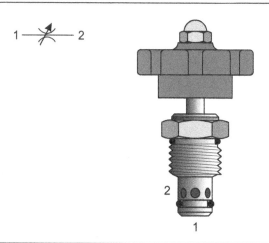

Figure 12-30   Manually operated knob-type needle valve

Pressure-Compensated Flow Regulator Valves

Pressure-compensated flow control valves are used when it is critical to maintain a constant flow regardless of the hydraulic pressure at the valve inlet or outlet. They are 2-way valves with either preset flow or adjustable flow control, and fit into the 2-port cavity. When combined with a priority flow control function, they require a 3-port cavity.

By means of packaging two pressure-compensated flow control valves in one housing, a flow divider/combiner valve is created. Figure 12-31 illustrates a typical flow divider/combiner valve. This valve divides or combines the flow in a specific proportion regardless of changes in system load or pressure.

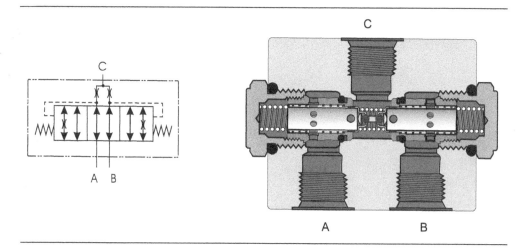

Figure 12-31   Pressure-compensated flow divider/combiner valve

Load Control

Load control valves are used for holding or controlling hydraulic loads by controlling flow. They are important not only for safety, but also to prevent the loss of control of actuators.

There are two basic types of load control: pilot-operated check valves and counterbalance valves.

Pilot-Operated Check Valves

Pilot-operated check valves are used as a low cost alternative to counterbalance valves when control of overrunning loads and/or load release speed is not required. They should only be used for locking a load into position. Figure 12-32 illustrates a typical pilot-operated check valve.

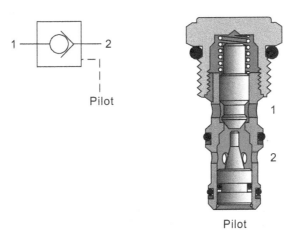

Figure 12-32   Pilot-operated check valve

Counterbalance Valves

Counterbalance valves are available with or without a spring chamber vent and are called either counterbalance valves or vented counterbalance valves. While specific features differ from manufacturer to manufacturer, both configurations are available with different pilot ratios, adjustable operating pressure settings, built-in reverse free flow check valves, different flow ranges, and free flow check valve springs to avoid cavitation. Most manufacturers offer a number of standard housings for multiple mounting configurations that offer maximum design flexibility and minimize installation requirements.

Counterbalance valves should be used with an open center, on/off directional valve for precise control of overrunning loads, protection against system cavitation, prevention of actuators running ahead of the pump supply, and to provide load holding and safety in case of hydraulic line failure.

Figure 12-33 illustrates a typical counterbalance valve.

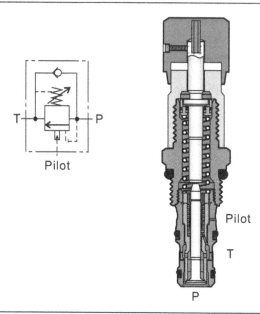

Figure 12-33   Counterbalance valve

Vented counterbalance valves vent the spring chamber in order to ensure stability as a load control, regardless of system back pressure. This insensitivity to system back pressure ensures valve performance in proportional, regenerative, and meter-out control circuits.

Vented screw-in counterbalance valves are available as a 3-port design or a 4-port design. With the fourth port, any oil remaining in the spring chamber is carried back to the reservoir and not vented to atmosphere. Corrosion of the spring and spring chamber is also prevented by keeping atmosphere out of this area.

Logic Elements

Logic elements are switching devices that use an "On/Off" pressure signal to perform a switching function. There are four basic types of logic elements used throughout the screw-in cartridge valve industry. These are: differential pressure sensing valves, modulating orifice cartridges, 2-way hydrostats, and 3-way hydrostats.

Differential Pressure Sensing Valves

Differential pressure sensing valves are used for controlling pressure, flow or direction (including 3-way and 4-way bridge circuits) with the aid of external pilot operators. They are function building blocks which respond to pressure differential signals, providing the capacity to switch or modulate flows and pressure. With logic valves similar to Eaton's DPS2-** Series valves, it is possible to obtain five forms of pressure control functions, eight forms of flow control functions, six forms of directional control functions, two forms of 3-way bridge circuits with four basic flow paths, and two forms of 4-way bridge circuits with 13 basic flow paths.

Figure 12-34 illustrates a typical DPS2 valve.

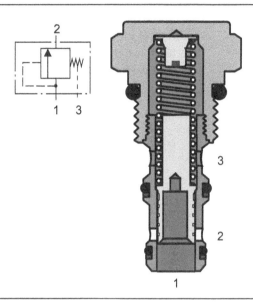

Figure 12-34   Differential pressure sensing valve

Modulating Orifice Valve

Modulating orifice cartridges are 4-ported valves. They modulate flow from Port 3 to Port 2 proportional to a back pressure applied to Port 4. When used with a hydrostat and a suitable back pressure pilot valve connected to Port 4, the modulated flow is pressure-compensated. Figure 12-35 illustrates a typical modulating orifice cartridge.

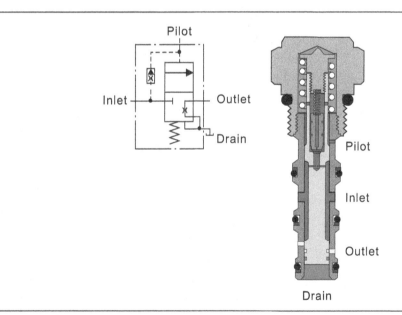

Figure 12-35   Modulating orifice valve

2-Way Hydrostat Valve

2-way hydrostats are an essential component of a pressure-compensated flow control. They are 3-ported cartridges that provide pressure compensation of flow when close coupled in series with a fixed or variable external orifice. A customized housing is required for close coupling the hydrostat and orifice. Excess flow upstream must be diverted through a relief valve to tank. Figure 12-36 illustrates a typical 2-way hydrostat cartridge valve.

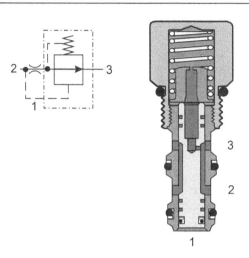

Figure 12-36   2-way hydrostat valve

3-Way Hydrostat Valve

3-way hydrostats with priority are 4-ported cartridges that provide pressure compensation of priority flow from Port 3 while excess input flow is diverted via Port 1 to Port 2. The priority flow rate is controlled by a fixed or variable external orifice close coupled in series with Port 4. A customized housing is required for close coupling the hydrostat and orifice. Excess flow can pass to a secondary circuit or to tank. Figure 12-37 illustrates a typical 3-way hydrostat cartridge valve.

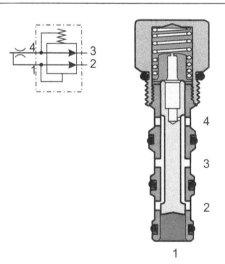

Figure 12-37   3-way hydrostat valve

Valvistor® Screw-In Cartridge Valves

Design Concept

Through its patented Valvistor® technology, Eaton is unique in the hydraulic industry with a series of screw-in cartridge valves that provide a new approach to traditional load control problems. Through means of a unique poppet design which incorporates hydraulic feedback, the new series of valves provide low cost, repeatable, high dynamic performance while simplifying inner loop feedback control requirements. The technology is provided by the "hydraulic transistor" or Valvistor® poppet where small flows control much larger flows in the same manner as the electronic transistor uses a very small signal to control a large current. The name "Valvistor®" is derived from the combination of the words "valve" and "transistor."

These valves are 2-way, 2-position and are electrically controlled by a proportional solenoid. The valve, for flows up to 42 GPM (160 l/min), is available in two different flow path configurations: flow from Port A (Port 1) to Port B (Port 2); and, flow from Port B to Port A. Both valves permit reverse free flow. Figure 12-38 illustrates an EPV16-A series valve.

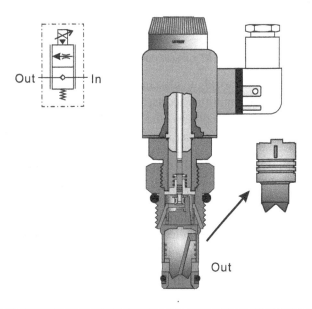

Figure 12-38   Valvistor® flow control screw-in cartridge valve

For flows up to 26 GPM (100 l/min), these valves perform as a pressure-compensated proportional flow control valve. Above this flow rate, they perform as a proportional throttle valve and a separate hydrostat is required for pressure-compensated flow control.

A significant design feature that differs from traditional two-stage proportional flow control valves is that a separate hydraulic pilot supply circuit is not required. Pilot supply is provided by the passageway from the pressure side of the poppet to the milled slot, which meters flow to the pilot chamber. When the solenoid valve is "off," fluid passing to the pilot chamber keeps the poppet closed.

When the solenoid valve opens a path from the pilot chamber to tank, the pilot pressure reduces until it is low enough to allow system pressure to raise the poppet. As the poppet rises, flow from the system to the pilot chamber increases through the slot opening, until there is enough flow to offset the loss to tank. Pressure will again rise in the pilot chamber, and the poppet will be held in this new position.

Slip-In Cartridge Valves

Slip-in cartridge valves are similar to poppet check valves and consist of an insert assembly that slips into a cavity machined into a manifold block. A control cover bolted to the manifold secures the insert within the cavity. As Figure 12-39 illustrates, the insert includes a sleeve, a poppet, a spring, and seals.

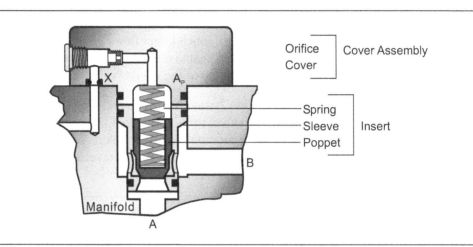

Figure 12-39   Basic components of a slip-in cartridge valve

The cartridge valve insert can be viewed as the main stage of a two-stage valve. It has two main flow ports, "A" and "B." Drilled passages in the manifold connect the "A" and "B" ports to other cartridges or to the operating hydraulic system. Similarly, a drilled pilot passage in the manifold connects the control port "X" as desired.

Notice the orifice in the drilled passage between the "X" port and the spring chamber "A_P." The purpose of this orifice is to reduce the speed at which the valve poppet opens and closes. Various orifice sizes are available to optimize or tune cartridge response in relation to that of the entire hydraulic system. The hydraulic system designer can select the orifice size that provides maximum operating speeds with minimum hydraulic shock.

Area Ratios

As Figure 12-40 indicates, the cartridge valve insert has three areas ("A_A," "A_B," and "A_{AP}") that affect the opening or closing of the valve poppet in the sleeve. "A_A" is the effective area of the poppet exposed to the "A" port. "A_B" is the effective area of the poppet exposed to the "B" port. "A_{AP}" is the effective area of the poppet exposed to the spring chamber "A_P." The "A_{AP}" area is always equal to the sum of the "A_A" and "A_B" areas.

The area ratio of an insert is the ratio of the "A_A" to the "A_{AP}" area. Figure 12-40 illustrates an area ratio of 1:1, meaning the area of "A_A" is equal to the area "A_{AP}." Figure 12-41 shows a cartridge with an area ratio of 1:2; area "A_A" is equal to half the area of "A_P." By changing the ratio between A_{AP} and A_A we can control the action of the poppet for different types of valve functions.

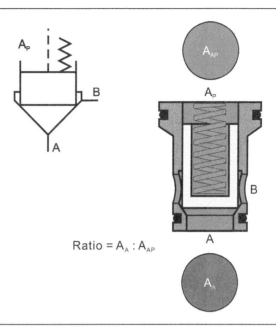

Figure 12-40   Slip-in cartridge valve area designations

A valve with a ratio of 1:1 is used for pressure control. Figure 12-40 illustrates a typical slip-in cartridge valve insert with a 1:1 ratio. A valve with a ratio of 1:2 is used for directional control and/or flow control. Figure 12-41 illustrates a typical slip-in cartridge valve insert with a 1:2 ratio. A valve with a ratio of 1:1.1 can be used for either directional control or pressure control.

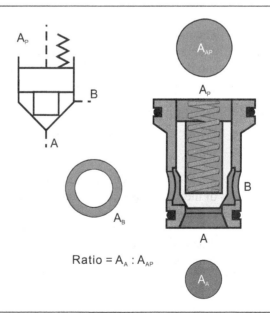

Figure 12-41   Slip-in cartridge valve with 1:2 area ratio

Slip-in cartridge valves are available in three common area ratios, as illustrated in Figure 12-42:

1:1 area ratio, where "A_{AP}" equals the "A_A" area

1:1.1 area ratio, where "A_{AP}" is 1.1 times the "A_A" area

1:2 area ratio, where "A_{AP}" is twice the "A_A" area.

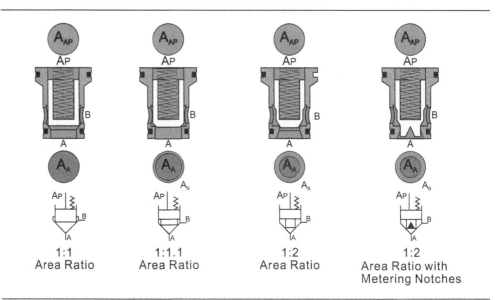

Figure 12-42   Slip-in cartridge valve configurations

Poppet Differences

Figure 12-42 shows the construction of various inserts, the three area ratio relationships and the associated graphic symbols. As the figure illustrates, both the poppet nose design and the sleeve seat change configuration with each area ratio. The first image (area ratio = 1:1) shows a square cornered poppet on the bottom and a sleeve that is chamfered at the point where it touches the poppet.

The insert shown in the second image (area ratio = 1:1.1) has a chamfered poppet and a large diameter, sharp cornered seat in the sleeve. This means there is a relatively small area "A_B" of the poppet on which the pressure in the "B" port can act. The area amounts to only ten percent of the "A" port area "A_A."

The third poppet shown in Figure 12-42 (area ratio = 1:2) also has a chamfered nose, but the sleeve has a sharp edged seat with a smaller diameter than that of the 1:1.1 ratio.

The fourth poppet seat area is the same as the standard 1:2 poppet. However, the nose of the poppet is extended and has a "V" notch cut in it to provide damping or flow metering.

These differences prevent the exchange of sleeves and poppets among the various area ratio inserts.

**Closing Versus
Opening Forces**

To design or troubleshoot a circuit that uses slip-in cartridge valves, one must know how to determine whether the valve should be open or closed under different circuit conditions. One must also know how to calculate the pressure required to open or close the valve. These calculations must take into account the fact that the pressure acts on three areas: "A_A," "A_B," and "A_{AP}." In addition, three different area ratios (1:1, 1:1.1, and 1:2) and different springs are available.

The forces that hold a valve closed are the pressure acting on the "A_{AP}" area plus the spring force. The forces that work to open a valve are the pressures acting on the "A" and "B" port areas. If the sum of the closing forces is greater than the sum of the opening forces, the poppet is closed. In the same way, if the sum of the opening forces is greater than the sum of the closing forces, the poppet is open.

Figure 12-43 is an example of a circuit that uses a 1:2 area ratio cartridge valve with a 40 pound (178N) spring. In this circuit, flow is supplied to a cylinder through the cartridge valve. Notice that the "A_P" area is drained to the tank valve. The only force trying to close the valve is the spring force of 40 pounds (178N). Assume that it takes pressure at 1,000 psi (70 bar, 7,000 kPa) to move the cylinder. This means that there is 1,000 psi (70 bar, 7,000 kPa) of pressure on the "A" area, 1,000 psi (70 bar, 7,000 kPa) of pressure on the "B" area, and zero pressure on the "A_P" area. The following calculations determine if the valve is open or closed.

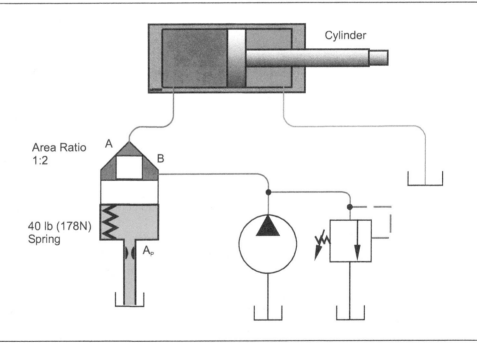

Figure 12-43   Example circuit

Assume that:

A_{AP} = 2 in^2 (12.9 cm^2)
A_A = 1 in^2 (6.45 cm^2)
A_B = 1 in^2 (6.45 cm^2)
Closing forces (F_c) = 40 lbs + (0 psi x 2 in^2) = 40 lbs (178N)
Opening forces (F_o) = (1,000 psi x 2 in^2) + (1,000 psi x 1 in^2) = 3,000 lbs (13,500N)

The opening forces [3,000 pounds (13,500N)] are far greater than the closing forces [40 pounds (178N)]. Therefore, the valve is open.

If the cartridge valve insert in the example had 1:1.1 area ratio, the calculations would be as follows:

Assume that:
$A_{AP} = 1.1$ in^2 (7.1 cm^2)
$A_A = 1$ in^2 (6.45 cm^2)
$A_B = 0.1$ in^2 (0.65 cm^2)
Closing forces (F_c) = 40 lbs + (0 psi x 1.1 in^2) = 40 lbs (178N)
Opening forces (F_o) = (1,000 psi x 1 in^2) + (1,000 psi 0.1 in^2) = 1,000 lbs + 100 lbs = 1,100 lbs (4900N)

The opening forces [1,100 pounds (4,900N)] are much greater than the closing forces [40 pounds (178N)]. Therefore, the valve is open.

Valve Sizes Available

Slip-in cartridge valve configurations are rated by size in accordance with ISO 7368 (DIN 24342) which gives the nominal size of the valve expressed in millimeters. The nominal size relates to the drilled hole (port size) in the manifold that connects one cartridge to another. Each valve has a nominal flow rate that is defined as the rate of flow with a 5 bar (75 psi) pressure drop. Shown in Table 12-1 are typical insert sizes as used throughout the slip-in cartridge valve industry referenced to ISO 7368 (DIN 24342) sizes and the corresponding flow rate. Figure 12-44 illustrates the typical relationships between Size 16 and Size 100 cartridges.

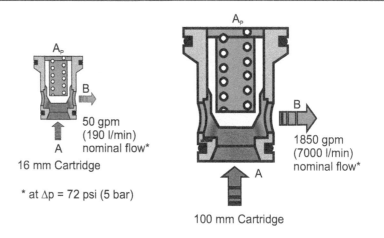

Figure 12-44   Size range of slip-in cartridge valves

Size (mm)	ISO 7368	DIN 24342	l/min	GPM
16	06	NG16	200	53
25	08	NG25	450	119
32	09	NG32	700	185
40	10	NG40	1100	291
50	11	NG50	1700	449
63	12	NG63	2800	740
100	13	NG100	7000	1850

Table 12-1   Typical insert sizes

Cover Configurations

The basic or standard cover configuration is typically a basic check valve function, permitting flow only from Port A to Port B. It contains a pilot pressure passage with an orifice to control the poppet's opening and closing rate.

When the standard cover is used with an internal pilot signal it becomes a pilot-operated check valve that is used to open Port A to Port B or to block Port A to Port B. Figure 12-45 illustrates the standard cover configuration used in this manner as a 2-way, 2-position directional valve.

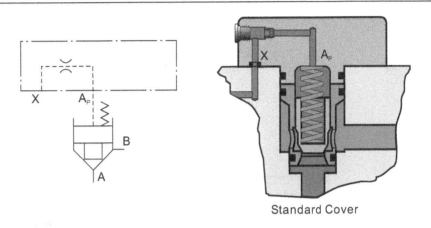

Standard Cover

Figure 12-45   Standard cover configuration

When a pilot-operated check cover is used with a 1:2 area ratio insert, it performs the function of a 2-way, 2-position directional check valve where flow is permitted between either Port A to Port B or Port B to Port A. Flow from Port A to Port B is independent of pilot pressure.

When a shuttle cover is used in combination with a solenoid valve (D03 interface) and a 1:2 ratio insert, the valve acts as a directional valve with flow from either Port A to Port B or from Port B to Port A. When the solenoid is de-energized, the cartridge is shut by the higher of the pressures at Port X or Port Z_1 (Figure 12-46).

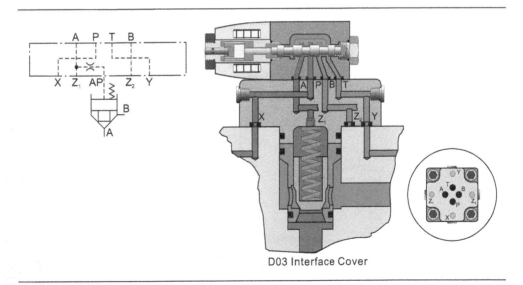

D03 Interface Cover

Figure 12-46   D03 interface cover for mounting a solenoid valve

When a pressure relief cover is used, the insert acts as a pressure relief function with system pressure being determined by manual pilot adjustment as in Figure 12-47.

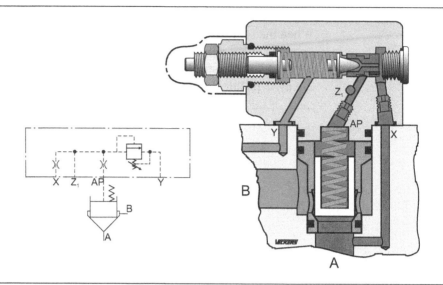

Figure 12-47   Slip-in valve with pressure relief cover

When a pressure reducer cover (typically with a size 03 pilot) is used with a pressure reducer insert, it functions as a manually adjusted pressure relief valve to provide a constant outlet pressure below that of the inlet pressure. Unlike other inserts, pressure reducing inserts contain a spool rather than a poppet.

When a stroke adjuster (flow restrictor) cover is used with a flow restrictor 1:2 area ratio insert, the adjustment that limits the insert poppet opening restricts flow in both directions (Port A to Port B or Port B to Port A). Control is from pilot port X and provides both adjustable flow restrictor and directional functions. Figure 12-48 illustrates a typical adjustable flow restrictor and directional slip-in cartridge valve. With this same combination of cover and insert, it is possible to create an adjustable flow restrictor and check function valve. This is accomplished by connecting the pilot signal Port X to Port B.

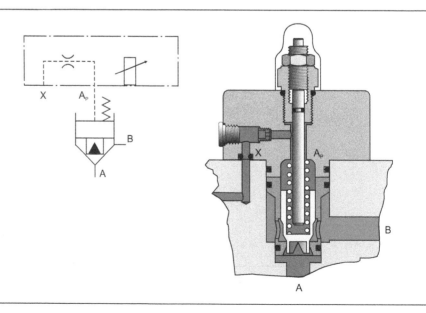

Figure 12-48   Flow control (flow restrictor) cover

Valvistor® Slip-In Cartridge Valves

Hydraulic proportional throttle control is available from Eaton through use of Valvistor® technology, as shown in Figure 12-49. This uses a directional cover with a single proportional solenoid control and a directional insert with 1:2 area ratio. By using a Valvistor® poppet in place of the standard poppet, proportional throttle control with internal hydraulic feedback is achieved. Flow direction is predetermined for either Port A to Port B or from Port B to Port A. Internal hydraulic feedback is provided through means of a metering slot machined into the Valvistor® poppet. This eliminates the necessity of an electrical feedback transducer to obtain servo-like control of the poppet. The operation and features of the slip-in Valvistor® control are similar to those of the screw-in Valvistor® described earlier in this chapter.

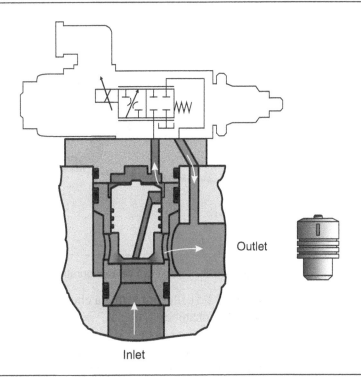

Outlet

Inlet

Figure 12-49   Valvistor® slip-in cartridge valve

Directional Control Configurations

The following section examines the operation of the slip-in cartridge valves that control the direction of the flow of hydraulic fluid.

Check Valve Operation

When a 1:2 area ratio cartridge valve is used as a check valve, as shown in Figure 12-50, it is necessary to connect the "A_p" chamber to the "B" port. If this is not done, any pressure at the "B" port great enough to compress the spring will open the valve. To operate as a check valve, the cartridge should open only when pressure at the "A" port is greater than pressure at the "B" port plus the spring force.

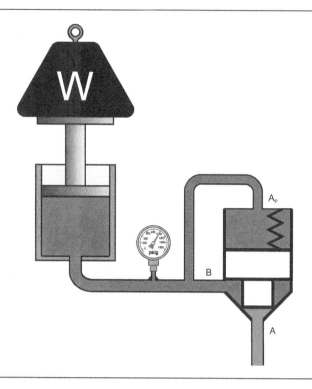

Figure 12-50   Check valve configuration with "B" port pilot

Figure 12-51 illustrates that a check valve function can also be created by connecting the "A_p" chamber to the "A" port. This provides free flow from port "B" to port "A." However, there can be leakage from port "A" through the pilot line to the "A_p" chamber and then through the clearance between the poppet and sleeve to the "B" port. To avoid this, the arrangement in Figure 12-50 should always be used for check valve functions.

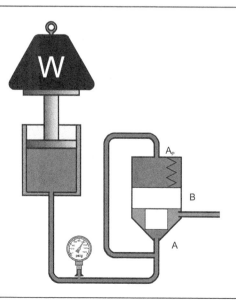

Figure 12-51   Check valve configuration with "A" port pilot

4-Way Directional Control Valve Operation

By definition, four-way directional control valves provide four flow paths, two at a time. One application of a four-way valve is to extend, retract and stop the piston of a double acting cylinder. The following section shows how cartridge valves can be installed to operate together as a single four-way valve.

Figure 12-52 illustrates a circuit in which four cartridge valves are piloted by one double solenoid, spring-centered spool valve. Pilot pressure is obtained by teeing off the main system pressure line and is applied to each cartridge pilot chamber when the pilot valve solenoids are de-energized. The pilot chambers of cartridge valves 1 and 3 are interconnected, as are the pilot chambers of cartridges 2 and 4, so that the paired valves open or close simultaneously. This essentially forms a closed center circuit, because all four cartridges are closed when both solenoids of the pilot valve are de-energized.

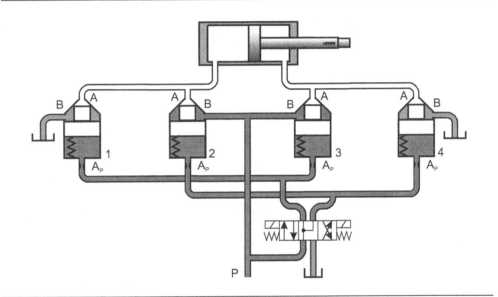

Figure 12-52   Four slip-in cartridges operating as a four-way valve

Energizing the left solenoid drains the "A_P" areas of cartridges 2 and 4 while maintaining pilot pressure on the "A_P" areas of cartridges 1 and 3. System pressure acting over the "B" area of cartridge 2 forces the valve open, directing pump flow to the cap end of the cylinder.

Return flow from the cylinder rod end passes to the tank over cartridge 4 when rod end pressure is high enough to overcome the spring acting against the cartridge valve poppet. The piston of the cylinder moves to the right. Energizing the right solenoid drains the "A_P" areas of cartridges 1 and 3 and applies pressure to the "A_P" areas of cartridges 2 and 4. This causes the piston to move to the left.

Conventional spool valves must be sized for the highest flow at any one port. Cartridge valves, on the other hand, are sized to handle only the flow required through their individual ports. Due to the differential area of the hydraulic cylinder, a flow greater than pump flow will be exhausted from the cap end of the cylinder (through cartridge valve #1) during retraction. Only pump flow will travel through cartridge valves #2 and #3, and less than pump flow will travel through cartridge valve #4. Therefore, three different cartridge valve sizes can be used, whereas the conventional valve would have to be sized for the flow out of the cap end of the cylinder. Economies are realized and system size is optimized.

Four 2-position, single-solenoid valves are used in Figure 12-53 to create an independent pilot control circuit. Operating each cartridge valve with a solenoid valve produces the equivalent of a 16-position spool valve, as shown in Table 12-2. Five of these positions give the same flow conditions, which leaves twelve different possible flow path combinations. This arrangement enables the independent control of each cartridge, which allows a smooth transition from one operating phase to the next.

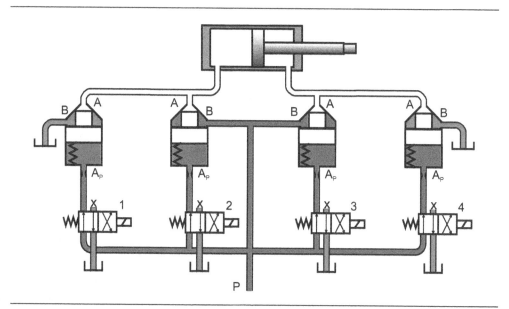

Figure 12-53   Four cartridge valves and four pilot valves will provide 12 different operating combinations

Valve 1 Solenoid	Valve 2 Solenoid	Valve 3 Solenoid	Valve 4 Solenoid	Equivalent Spool Configuration
Off	Off	Off	Off	
On	Off	Off	Off	
Off	On	Off	Off	
Off	Off	On	Off	
Off	Off	Off	On	
On	On	Off	Off	
Off	On	On	Off	
Off	Off	On	On	
On	Off	On	Off	
On	Off	Off	On	
Off	On	Off	On	
On	On	On	Off	
Off	On	On	On	
On	Off	On	On	
On	On	Off	On	
On	On	On	On	

Table 12-2   All spool equivalent combinations of four pilot valves

Stack Valves

Introduction

Stack valves, or stacking valves, are a unique way of assembling a number of operational functions onto a directional control valve. Functions such as relief, sequence, check, and flow control can be mounted, or "sandwiched," underneath a directional control valve to provide a complete control circuit for an actuator. The result is a compact assembly of control functions that negates the need to plumb a series of line valves to accomplish the same purpose.

Stack valves are a very compact design, from about 1-1/4 inches (3.2 cm) to about 3-1/2 inches (9.9 cm) thick, that have two mounting surfaces. They are designed to "stack," one atop the other, in between a directional control valve and the mounting surface. The mounting surface may be a manifold subplate, a multi-station subplate, or a manifold block.

Figure 12-54 illustrates a stack valve arrangement with a solenoid-operated directional control valve on top, and five various circuit functions "sandwiched" below it. This entire assembly would be installed on a mounting surface with four long mounting screws. Stack valves are available with standard interfaces conforming to ISO 4401. Porting usually consists of "P," "T," "A" and "B" ports and may include an "X" (pilot) port and a "Y" drain port. O-rings surround each individual port, ensuring a leak-free interface.

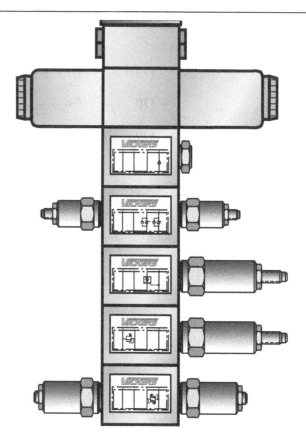

Figure 12-54   Stack valve assembly

| | | Flow and Pressure Capabilities | Stack valves are available in four sizes, in conformance with ISO/DIS 4401 standards: |

Flow and Pressure Capabilities

Stack valves are available in four sizes, in conformance with ISO/DIS 4401 standards:

Size	Designation	Pressure*	Flow
02	ISO 4401-02	3,625 psi (215 bar)**	7.9 GPM (30 l/min)
03	ISO 4401-03	4,500 psi (315 bar)	15.8 GPM (60 l/min)
05	ISO 4401-05	4,500 psi (315 bar)	32 GPM (120 l/min)
07	ISO 4401-07	4,500 psi (315 bar)	53 GPM (200 l/min)

* Eaton pressure ratings   ** Aluminum module housings

Mounting Surfaces

Stack valves assemble onto a single station subplate, a multiple station manifold or on a manifold block that may contain other circuit components such as slip-in or screw-in cartridge valves. Figure 12-55 is a drawing of a multiple station manifold capable of accommodating five function control stacks.

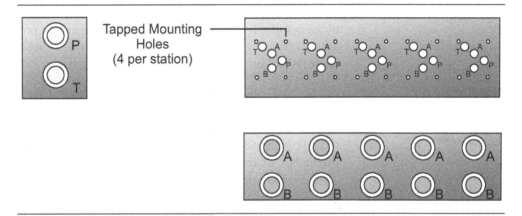

Figure 12-55   Multiple station stack valve manifold

Each position on the subplate has a series of interface ports located in compliance with ISO configurations, such that the control valve or any of the stack valve modules will match the correct porting. Each position also has "A" and "B" outlet ports for serving a specific actuator. Common "P" and "T" ports serve all of the stations on the manifold.

Valve Configurations

Each stack valve is designed to ISO standards so that it will exactly mate with other stack valves and with the directional control valve and manifold. The individual function of each valve will serve one or more of the "P," "T," "A" or "B" ports, depending on the circuit design. Figure 12-56 shows a typical stack valve design. Note that, although this valve is designed to serve only one line of the circuit, all four lines are connected through the valve.

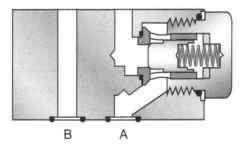

Figure 12-56   Direct acting stacking check valve in port "A"

The following types of stacking valves are available:

Valves Serving "P" or "T" Ports	Valves Serving "A" or "B" Ports
Relief Valve	Relief Valve
Check Valve	Dual Relief Valve
Flow Divider	Flow Divider
Flow Control	Check Valve
Pressure-Compensated Flow Control	Pilot-Operated Check Valve
Sequence Valve	Flow Control
Pressure Reducing Valve	Counterbalance

It is sometimes important, occasionally critical, what order the valves are placed in the stack to prevent pressurized oil from being trapped between components or in-lines tied to actuators. The manufacturer should be consulted in this regard. For example, it is important that a pressure line relief valve be placed at the bottom of a stack, closest to the manifold, to provide the most effective circuit protection. It may be critical that a flow control be placed between a pilot-operated check valve and the actuator in a control ("A" or "B") line so as to avoid chatter.

Symbols and Circuits

Figure 12-57 illustrates the basic hydraulic symbol for a stack valve module, illustrating the port connections and flow paths into and out of each block. All stack valves utilize this basic symbol. It is important to remember that all four flow paths pass through each module in the stack. This figure also illustrates the typical orientation on drawings of the directional control valve mounted on top of each stack. This vertical orientation simplifies print reading.

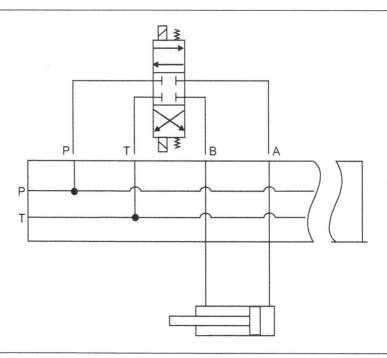

Figure 12-57   Basic stack valve symbol

Figure 12-58 illustrates a typical stack with a relief function, meter-out flow controls, and pilot-to-open check valves. The "A" and "B" ports connect to an actuator. Each module in the stack is outlined individually, and is shown accommodating all four hydraulic lines, "P," "T," "A" and "B." In this drawing, the subplate is not shown.

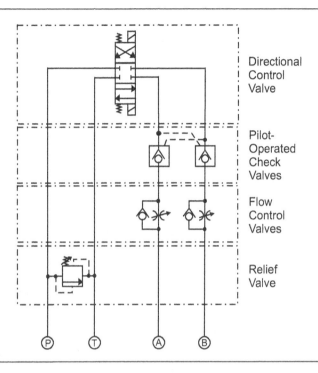

Figure 12-58   Circuit drawing of a single stack valve assembly

Figure 12-59 is a completed control circuit, showing three stack valve assemblies mounted on a four station subplate manifold. A blanking plate is installed on the unused station, which may be retained for the addition of an optional actuator.

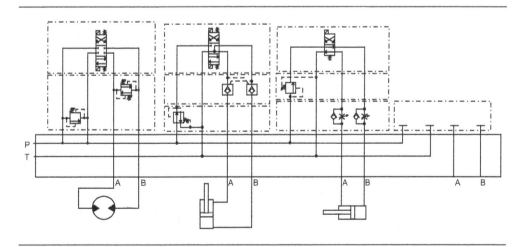

Figure 12-59   Circuit drawing of a three stack valve assembly

Industrial Test Questions:
Cartridge and Stack Valves

Chapter 12

1. Describe three major differences between slip-in and screw-in cartridge valves.

2. List five benefits in using cartridge valves.

3. What hydraulic system functions can screw-in cartridge valves perform?

4. What do the 2-way, 3-way, 3-way short, and 4-way screw-in cartridge valve functions signify?

5. What pressure is required at the pilot port to permit reverse flow through a screw-in pilot-operated check valve?

6. Describe the operation of a screw-in shuttle valve.

7. Briefly describe the operation of a screw-in cartridge that provides a direct acting, normally open, pressure reducing and relieving valve function.

8. How does a screw-in cartridge that is used as a pressure-compensated, nonadjustable flow regulator valve maintain a constant pressure drop across the control orifice?

9. Slip-in cartridge valves are most similar to what other type of conventional valve?

10. What is the significance of the "A_A," "A_B," and the "A_{AP}" areas of a slip-in cartridge valve?

11. How do you designate the area ratio of a valve insert?

12. Are the poppets and sleeves of slip-in type valves with different area ratios interchangeable?

13. What three variables must be taken into account when determining opening and closing forces?

14. Identify the forces that work to open a valve and those that work to close the valve.

15. What determines whether a valve is open or closed?

16. When using a 1:2 area ratio insert as a check valve, why is it better to connect the "A_P" chamber to the "B" port rather than to the "A" port?

17. Explain how sizing a cartridge valve differs from sizing a conventional spool type valve.

18. What is the benefit of an independent pilot control circuit in which each slip-in cartridge valve is operated by a solenoid valve?

19. Briefly describe the two main functions of a basic slip-in valve cover.

20. Explain the additional feature of a pilot valve interface cover.

21. Describe the difference between a conventional relief valve and a slip-in cartridge relief valve.

22. Explain the difference between a nonpressure-compensated flow control slip-in cartridge valve and a typical needle valve that has a similar function.

23. List three advantages of using stack valves in lieu of conventional valves in a circuit.

24. List three advantages of using a multiple station manifold for stack valves.

25. What determines that the porting of stack valve modules will line up at assembly.

Chapter 13 . . . . Proportional Valves

Proportional valves fill a gap between conventional solenoid valves and servo valves. Like conventional solenoid valves, proportional valves are simple in design and relatively easy to service. However, unlike conventional on/off DC solenoid valves, they can assume an infinite number of controlled positions within their working range. Proportional valves have many of the control features without the design complexity, low contamination tolerance, and high cost of the more sophisticated servo valves. They are used in applications where the performance (rapid response time and low hysteresis, etc.) of a servo valve is not required.

Proportional Solenoid Valves

Proportional valves control and vary pressure, flow, direction, acceleration and deceleration electrically from a remote position. They are actuated by proportional solenoids rather than by a force or torque motor.

This chapter concentrates on three types of proportional valves:

- Proportional pressure control valves, including relief and reducing valves with electronically adjusted pressure settings.

- Proportional flow control (throttle) valves, which are proportional valves with electronically varied flow rate through the valve.

- Proportional direction control valves, which can electronically control flow rate as well as for flow direction through the valve.

Remote Control of Hydraulic Flow

Figure 13-1 is a basic proportional solenoid valve that provides remote control of hydraulic flow. As you can see, proportional valves are spool type valves. Typically, the spool is spring centered, or spring offset as shown in Figure 13-1.

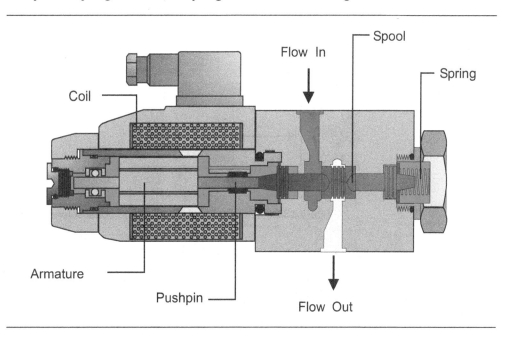

Figure 13-1   Basic proportional valve construction

Output Flow Proportional to Input Signal

Unlike conventional on/off solenoid valves, the proportional solenoid current can be varied to make the spool move variable distances. The term proportional describes the valve's operation. The valve spool moves in proportion to an electrical signal applied to the solenoid; thus, the electrical signal is converted to a mechanical spool motion. In other words, the output flow is proportional to the input signal. By varying the input signal, the solenoid adjusts the spool movement to vary the flow through the valve.

Constant Force Solenoid

On a solenoid, a magnetic force is created when a current is passed through the solenoid coil. This force pulls the solenoid armature toward the pole piece. A pushpin attached to the armature then transmits the force to the valve spool. The major difference between a proportional solenoid and a conventional on/off solenoid is the design of the armature, pole piece and core tube assembly. The proportional solenoid is shaped in a manner that delivers a more constant force over the entire working stroke.

In Figure 13-2, you can see that the proportional solenoid delivers a constant force, regardless of armature position. The coil current alone determines the amount of force transmitted to the valve spool. The solenoid force moves the spool until a balance is achieved between the solenoid force and the valve's spring force.

By varying the current, the solenoid can force the spool to assume a position anywhere within its working range. This operation is called spring feedback, because the valve spring is the only feedback for the solenoid force. Because this operation does not take into account other forces that might affect spool position (such as frictional and flow forces) it is not appropriate for applications that require a high degree of valve performance.

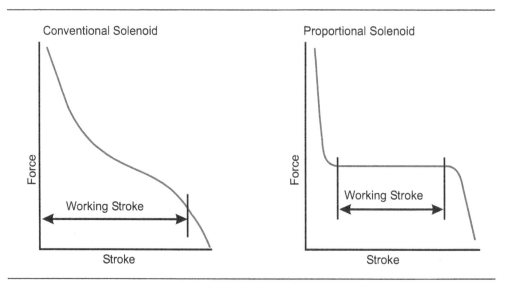

Figure 13-2   Conventional versus proportional solenoid force

Associated Electronic Devices and Controls

Proportional solenoid valves are used with electronic control amplifiers, which provide the power necessary to operate the valve and perform additional functions. Proportional valves can be used in both open and closed loop control systems. These two control methods perform a similar function at two different performance levels. The following sections examine some of the features of electronic control amplifiers and how proportional valves operate within feedback and nonfeedback control systems.

Electronic Control Amplifier

There are many different electronic control amplifiers for proportional valves, but each one provides a portion of one group of functions. The initial input signals that control proportional solenoid valves come from a variety of sources, including:

- Potentiometers
- Temperature sensors
- Pressure transducers
- Tach-generators
- Programmable Controllers

These devices are all low power sources in terms of voltage and/or current. Their power must be amplified before they can operate a proportional valve. To increase power to the required level, a small voltage from one of the sources listed above is sent to an amplifier. The amplifier produces a correspondingly larger current flow that is transmitted to the solenoid. This current flow enables the valve spool to move.

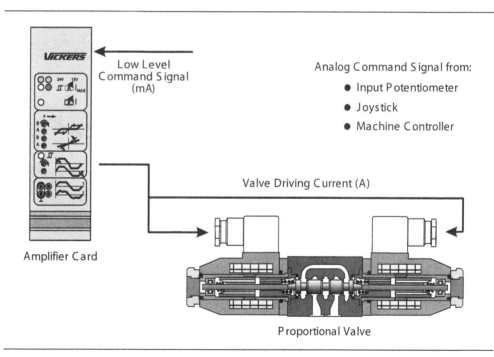

Figure 13-3   Electronic amplifiers control proportional valves

Control Amplifier Functions

Several important control amplifier functions, such as deadband compensation, gain, and dither, are described in this section.

Deadband Compensation

Deadband is primarily caused by the spool overlapping the valve ports. This overlap reduces spool leakage in the null position but now a certain minimum signal level must be provided to the valve before any substantive flow will pass through the valve. Spool overlap is shown in Figure 13-4. As the figure indicates, the spool must be moved a certain amount before oil can pass through the valve. In the example shown, a substantial input signal must be applied to the solenoid to move the spool past the deadband region and to allow flow through the valve. (Close tolerance manufacturing of spools fitted into matched sleeves in some proportional valves and most servo valves reduce spool overlap to almost zero, therefore eliminating deadband.)

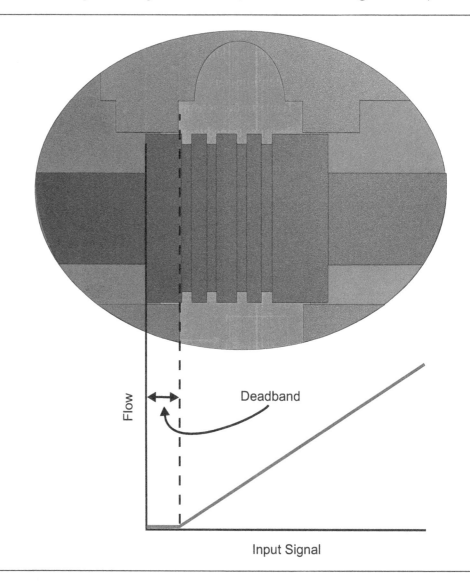

Figure 13-4   Spool overlap causes deadband

Many proportional valve amplifiers have deadband compensation adjustments to electronically cause the spool to jump across the spool overlap region when a threshold voltage is reached. How far the spool jumps when that threshold voltage is input into the amplifier is adjusted with the deadband compensation adjustment. Electrical "noise" or interference must exceed this threshold voltage before the spool motion is affected. Deadband compensation produces the spool motion shown in Figure 13-5. This adjustment dramatically improves valve performance in the deadband region, often producing almost ideal results.

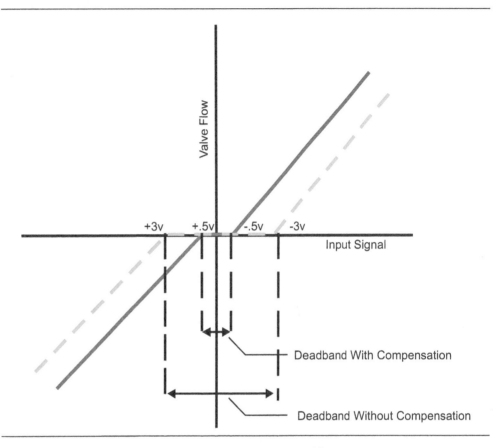

Figure 13-5   Uncompensated and deadband compensated flow curves

Gain

An amplifier's gain, expressed as a multiplication factor, is a measure of the ratio between the amplifier's small input signal and its large output current flow to the valve. The output voltage is proportional to the input voltage. Gain is determined in the following way:

Formula 13-1

$$\text{Gain} = A = \frac{\text{Output Voltage}}{\text{Input Voltage}}$$

Amplifier gain can be in the area of 10^6. In other words:

output voltage $=$ input voltage $\times$ 1,000,000

However, smaller gains are more typical in actual use.

Dither

Dither is a low frequency (50 – 100 Hz), low amplitude AC signal used to offset the effects of a condition known as hysteresis. Hysteresis is caused by friction between a proportional valve spool and bore, flow forces acting against the spool, residual magnetism in the armature, gravity, as well as by the inertia of the spool itself. Friction can be affected by manufacturing tolerance, thermal expansion, wear, fluid viscosity, contamination and other various factors.

When there is friction in a proportional valve, the solenoid force has to overcome the spool spring force and the additional frictional force. Because frictional forces are not evenly distributed within the valve, the same input signal can produce a different amount of spool movement when the signal is increasing compared to when the signal is decreasing (Figure 13-6).

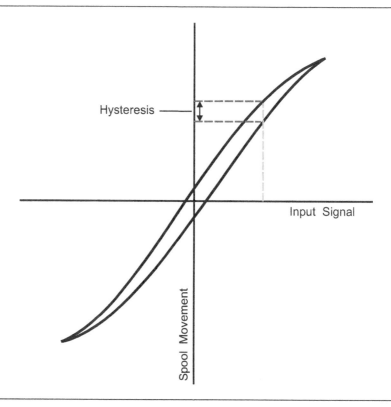

Figure 13-6   Hysteresis causes the same input signal to produce a different amount of spool movement when the signal is increasing compared to when it is decreasing

To reduce hysteresis, a dither low frequency AC signal is superimposed onto the DC signal output to the coil (Figure 13-7). This AC signal reduces the friction within the valve because dynamic friction is lower than static friction.

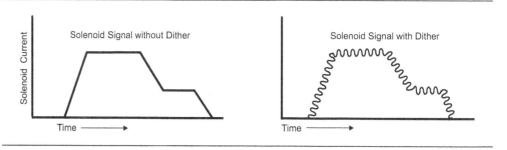

Figure 13-7   Dither is superimposed on the solenoid signal to reduce hysteresis

Ramp Functions

As you have learned, one advantage of proportional valves is that spool speed, in addition to position, can be controlled electronically. This means that the valve can also control the speed, acceleration and deceleration of the final control element, such as a cylinder, hydraulic motor, etc.

To control the speed of the valve spool movement, a gradually increasing or decreasing signal (a ramp function) is fed to the valve coil. The ramp function is illustrated in Figure 13-8. If a switch applies a stepped input to the input of the ramp function (top curve), it will output a voltage that is shaped like that shown in the lower curve. Amplifiers like the one shown in the figure contain ramp functions with separately adjustable acceleration and deceleration ramps; others have only one adjustment that has the same effect on both the acceleration and deceleration side.

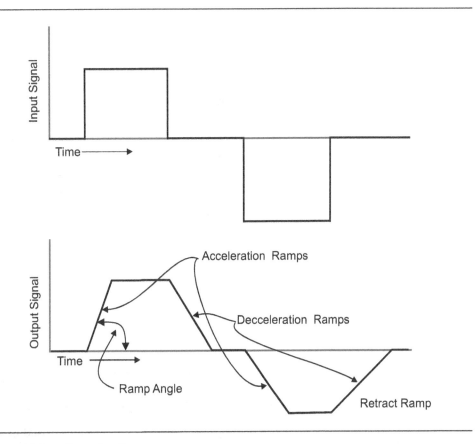

Figure 13-8   Ramp function

Drive Enables

Some amplifier cards have an enable function, which requires a specified voltage to be present at the enable connection before the output stage of the card will output any signal to the valve coils. This can be connected to an emergency stop switch, an output from a programmable controller or master control relay so that if the enable signal is lost, the amplifier immediately produces a zero output and the valve responds accordingly. Normally, it is not recommended that an emergency stop switch be in the power supply line, because the stored charge in capacitors may cause erratic valve operation or maintain the valve signal for some time after the switch is opened.

Current Feedback

In a solenoid, passing a current through the coil generates heat. This heat increases the coil's resistance. For example, a solenoid coil may have a resistance of 26 ohms at 68°F (20°C) and a resistance of 38 ohms at 185°F (85°C). When the solenoid resistance changes, the solenoid current and the valve setting also change. A 50 percent increase in coil resistance as the coil heats up results in a 33 percent reduction in the valve setting.

To compensate for the negative effect of heated coils, some amplifiers have current feedback, in which a low value (1 – 2 ohms) current feedback resistor is added in series with the solenoid coil. The amplifier feedback is taken from a point between the solenoid coil and the current feedback resistor and fed back to the summing junction. This allows the solenoid current to be proportional to the input voltage and independent of solenoid resistance. This provides coil temperature compensation, reducing the effect of spool shifting position as coil temperature changes.

Pulse Width Modulation

When an infinitely variable DC signal is used to operate a proportional valve, the control amplifier has to reduce the voltage from the power supply down to the voltage required by the valve solenoid at any given time. As shown in Figure 13-9, the control amplifier's output transistor acts like a variable resistor. The full solenoid coil current, which may be several amps, also passes through the amplifier's output transistor. High current combined with a relatively large voltage drop produces heat, which wastes energy. Also, a relatively large heatsink is required to dissipate the heat created, which requires considerable space on the electronic card.

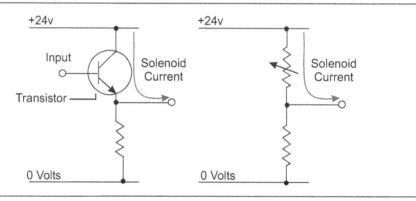

Figure 13-9   The amplifier's output transistor acts like a variable resistor

A technique called pulse width modulation is used in some amplifiers to prevent the creation of heat caused by large voltage drops. With pulse width modulation, the output transistor is used as an on/off switch to feed the valve solenoid with a series of on/off pulses at a constant power supply voltage. The transistor is either fully on or fully off and, therefore, generates much less heat than that created with a DC output signal. (When the transistor is fully on, the voltage drop across it is very low, so it consumes very little power. When the transistor is off, no current flows through it, so it consumes no power at all.)

The pulses are kept at a constant frequency (typically 1 kHz), which is so fast that the solenoid cannot respond to the individual pulses. However, it does respond to the average voltage level of the pulses. The length of the on time in relation to the off time determines the voltage level (Figure 13-10).

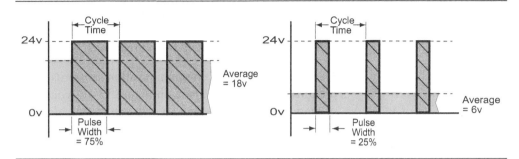

Figure 13-10   The width of the on time in relation to the off time determines voltage level

Open Loop (No Feedback) Control

Proportional solenoid valves and electronic control amplifiers can be used in nonfeedback systems for applications that require smooth control of actuator speed, but only moderately accurate flow control. As you can see in Figure 13-11, an open loop control arrangement has no position sensor to measure the actual movement of the spool. The valve control loop is often called the inner loop. In addition, no feedback signal is sent back from the hydraulic motor to the amplifier for comparison with the command signal. The actuator control loop is often called the outer loop. As you learned in our earlier discussion of spring "feedback," the valve's spring force, which indicates the spool movement, is the only "feedback" provided.

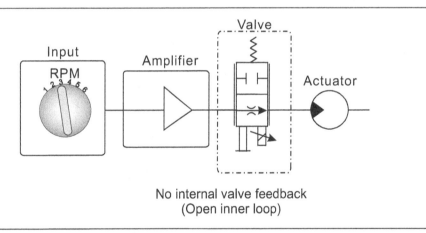

No internal valve feedback
(Open inner loop)

Figure 13-11   Open inner and open outer loop control loops

Linear Variable Differential Transformer Sensing Spool Position

When more accurate control of spool position is needed, a position sensor can be attached to the spool. The sensor sends a signal back to a summing junction, where it is compared to the original input signal. This greatly improves valve performance. To control the spool's stroke, a position sensor called a linear variable differential transformer (LVDT) is attached to the spool to monitor its movement. The LVDT sends a feedback signal to the control amplifier, where it is compared to the input signal. This method ensures more accurate positioning, provides for automatic correction of any disturbances and reduces hysteresis.

The LVDT is the most common position sensor used with spool type valves such as proportional solenoid valves. In Figure 13-12, you can see that an LVDT has one primary coil wrapped around a soft iron core, with two secondary coils also wrapped around the core. The iron core is connected to the solenoid's pushpin. A high frequency AC signal is fed to the primary coil. This power supply creates a varying magnetic field in the iron core, which also induces voltage in the two secondary coils through transformer action.

When the core is centrally positioned and the two secondary coils are connected in opposition, the voltages in the secondary coils are balanced. Therefore, the two voltages cancel out each other to produce a zero output. As the iron core moves away from the center, the voltage induced in one secondary coil increases while the voltage in the second coil decreases. This imbalance produces an output. The magnitude of the output is proportional to the distance the iron core moved from center, and phase shifts indicate the direction of the core's movement. The LVDT's output signal is fed to a demodulator (a phase sensitive rectifier), which produces a DC voltage that accurately reflects the distance and direction of the core's movement.

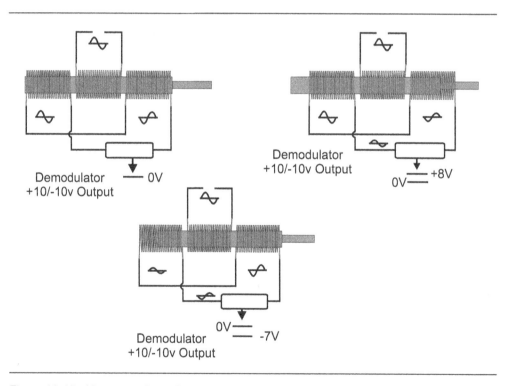

Figure 13-12   Linear variable differential transformer (LVDT)

As the block diagram in Figure 13-13 shows, the input signal is sent first to the amplifier, where the power is amplified. Next, the amplifier outputs a signal to the solenoid, which then transmits a force to the proportional valve spool, causing the spool to move. Then, a position sensor, typically an LVDT, senses the actual valve spool movement. The feedback signal (voltage) is sent back to the summing junction at the amplifier.

At the summing junction, the feedback signal is compared to the input signal. The difference between the two signals produces an error signal. The error signal leaves the summing junction and goes to the voltage amplifier. The amplifier output to the solenoid then changes to reflect the new error signal. This loop continues until the feedback signal balances with the input signal, and the spool reaches the specified position.

Due to the fact that there is a feedback sensor on the valve but not on the actuator (hydraulic motor), this system has an closed inner loop but open outer control loop. If there was a feedback device on the motor, whether or not there was a feedback sensor on the valve spool, it would be considered a closed outer control loop.

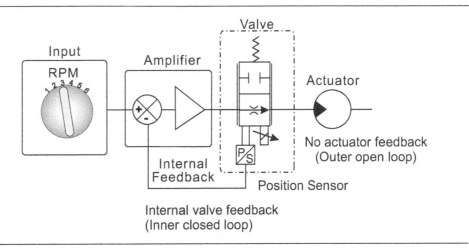

Figure 13-13   Closed inner loop and open outer control loop

Figure 13-14 is a block diagram of a typical amplifier that is used with some proportional valves. In the lower right of the figure (pins z22, b16 and b14) are the feedback connections for the LVDT spool position sensor.

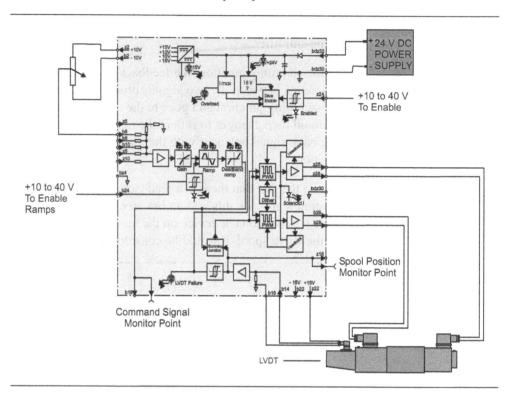

Figure 13-14   Proportional valve amplifier block diagram and connections

Power Supply Requirements

Most proportional solenoid valves require a properly installed DC power supply to provide power to the amplifier. Typically, an amplifier card has two pins for each power connection to increase the reliability of the contact.

The power can be supplied by a battery or by a rectified AC supply. This varies according to the specific application. With either supply, a smoothing capacitor may also be recommended for installation on the power supply connections at the amplifier card. This helps to reduce any rippling effects of a rectified AC supply and filters out any voltage spikes or noise that may be induced in an unshielded power supply line.

Areas of Application

Proportional directional valves can be used to vary, control direction of flow, or both flow and direction in many different applications. Utilizing the ramping function, they can be used to reduce shock caused by rapid pressure changes and the quick starts and stops of a heavy mass. Application examples include controlling hydraulic motors, single and double acting cylinders that move loads, and variable displacement pumps.

Basic Hydraulic Principles of Proportional Valves

A proportional solenoid valve must be properly engineered into a system to perform up to its capabilities. This requires attention to factors that are not present for conventional on/off solenoid valves, such as how flow and pressure act on the valve's variable orifices.

Two Flow Paths Through the Valve

In normal operation, a proportional directional control valve has two flow paths. In Figure 13-15, you can see that there will be flow either from the P port to the A port and the B port to the T port, or from P to B and A to T.

Proportional Valve

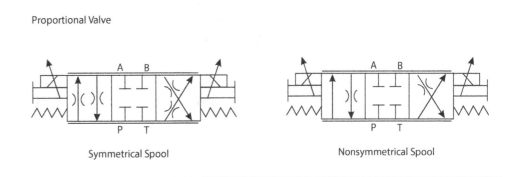

Symmetrical Spool   Nonsymmetrical Spool

Figure 13-15   Symbols for the flow paths through symmetrical and nonsymmetrical spools

Symmetrical and Nonsymmetrical Spools

A proportional valve can have a symmetrical or a nonsymmetrical spool. A symmetrical spool restricts the two flow paths equally, which enables the valve to both meter in and meter out fluid. On a nonsymmetrical spool, the main restriction is in the B to T or the A to T flow path, so the valve will meter out fluid only.

Symmetrical and nonsymmetrical spools are used for different types of applications. In Figure 13-16, a proportional valve is used to control a hydraulic motor, which is an equal area actuator. A symmetrical spool, which provides two restrictions in a series with the actuator, is the practical choice to use, because the actuator area is equal on both sides.

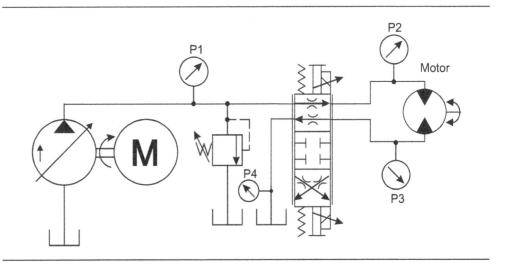

Figure 13-16   A symmetrical spool proportional valve controls an equal area actuator

When the proportional valve spool is in such a position that fluid flows from P to A and B to T and the motor is turning at a constant speed (no acceleration or deceleration), the four pressure gauges shown in Figure 13-16 indicate the following pressures:

- P_1 — indicates main system pressure. Usually determined by the pump relief valve or compensator setting.

- P_2 — indicates pressure needed to turn the load, plus the backpressure on motor outlet port.

- P_3 — indicates backpressure on the motor outlet port created by restricting exhaust flow B to T across the valve, plus the backpressure in tank line.

- P_4 — indicates backpressure in the tank return line caused by pipe work, filters and other restrictions.

Equation for Determining Flow Rate

Flow through each restricted opening in a proportional valve is determined by an equation called the sharp edge orifice equation. This equation is:

Formula 13-2

$$Q = Cd \times A \times \sqrt{\frac{2 \times \Delta P}{q}}$$

Where:

Q = flow rate
Cd = orifice discharge coefficient
A = orifice area
P = pressure drop across orifice
q = fluid density

While you won't need to calculate flow rates on a regular basis, you should understand that flow rate through the valve is proportional to the square root of the pressure drop across the valve:

Formula 13-3

Q is proportional to $\sqrt{\Delta P}$ and

ΔP is proportional to Q^2

In other words, if you *double* the flow rate through the valve, the pressure drop across the valve *quadruples.*

Using the example of Figure 13-16, the following can be stated based on the flow rate equation:

Formula 13-4

$Q_{(P-A)}$ is proportional to $\sqrt{\Delta P_{(P-A)}}$

Where:

$Q_{(P-A)}$ = flow through the valve P to A

And:

$\Delta P_{(P-A)}$ = pressure drop across the valve from P to A

In the same way:

$Q_{(B-T)}$ is proportional to $\sqrt{\Delta P_{(B-T)}}$

Where:

$Q_{(B-T)}$ = flow through the valve B to T

And:

$\Delta P_{(B-T)}$ = pressure drop across the valve from B to T

Since the motor in Figure 13-16 has equal inlet and outlet flows (discounting effects of leakage), then:

Formula 13-5

$$Q_{(P-A)} = Q_{(B-T)}$$

And with equal restrictions on both flow paths,

$$\Delta P_{(P-A)} = \Delta P_{(B-T)}$$

or:

$$P_1 - P_2 = P_3 - P_4$$

Therefore, when a symmetrical spool is used to control an equal area actuator, the pressure drop across each flow path through the valve is the same.

Determining Required System Pressure

Now, let's assume that the hydraulic motor shown in Figure 13-16 has a displacement of 12.2 in^3 (200 cm^3) per revolution and that it needs to turn a load at a torque of 2,655 in-lbs (300 Nm). What system pressure is required in this application?

From available catalog data, we know that the proportional valve has a 116 psi (8 bar, 800 kPa) pressure drop across each flow path when the motor is running at maximum speed. With a backpressure of, for example, 29 psi (2 bar, 200 kPa) in the tank return line, we can determine the system pressure that must be maintained. In these calculations the two restrictions, $P_{(P-A)}$ and $P_{(B-T)}$ must be taken into account.

Known data:

$P_3 - P_4$ = 116 psi (8 bar, 800 kPa)
P_4 = 29 psi (2 bar, 200 kPa)
P_3 = 145 psi (10 bar, 1,000 kPa)
$P_2 = P_L + P_3$
P_L = pressure required to turn the load

The equation needed to calculate load pressure is:

Formula 13-6

$$P_L = \frac{T \times 2\pi}{d}$$

Where:

T = motor torque (in-lb)

π = 3.1416

d = motor displacement (in^3/rev)

$$P_L = \frac{2{,}655 \text{ in-lbs} \times 2 \times 3.1416}{12.2 \text{ in}^3}$$

Therefore:

P_L = 1,367 psi (94 bar, 9,400 kPa)

$P_2 = P_L + P_3$

P_2 = 1,512 psi (104 bar, 10,400 kPa)

From known data:

$P_1 - P_2 = P_3 - P_4$

so:

$P_1 - P_2$ = 116 psi (7.80 bar, 780 kPa)

therefore:

P_1 = 1,628 psi (112 bar, 11,200 kPa)

System pressure must be set at 1,628 psi (112 bar, 11,200 kPa) to turn the load at the specified torque.

Determining Required Braking Pressure

We must determine the maximum braking pressure to decelerate the motor to a stop, assuming that the motor does not require boost pressure when overrunning. To decelerate the motor, the proportional valve spool moves toward the center position to further restrict the flow from B to T. Flow must continue on the P to A flow path to prevent cavitation on the motor's inlet side.

If pressure at the P_1 pressure gauge in Figure 13-16 is 1,628 psi (112 bar, 11,200 kPa) and pressure at the P_2 pressure gauge is zero, the maximum pressure drop from P to A is 1,628 psi (112 bar, 11,200 kPa). This tells us that the maximum pressure drop from B to T is also 1628 psi (112 bar, 11,200 kPa). If the tank line pressure is 29 psi (2 bar, 200 kPa), the maximum deceleration pressure is 1657 psi (114 bar, 11,400 kPa). Braking pressures any higher than this will cause the inlet side of the motor to cavitate, because not enough pressure exists to maintain the flow from P to A.

It might seem appropriate to use a meter-out spool for this application. However, a meter-out spool used in the same system only restricts flow on the outlet side of the motor. This prevents cavitation, but if system pressure at the P port is maintained during deceleration, the flow continues to drive the motor. Having pressure on both sides of the motor at the same time is unacceptable for some motor designs. Therefore, in general, the symmetrical spool, sometimes used with additional braking and anticavitation arrangements, is the best choice for motor drive applications.

Now that we have discussed flow and pressure as they affect an equal area motor, we can address the same issues for a differential area cylinder. In Figure 13-17, a proportional valve is used to control a differential area cylinder. To extend the cylinder, the valve spool moves into a position that allows flow from P to A and from B to T.

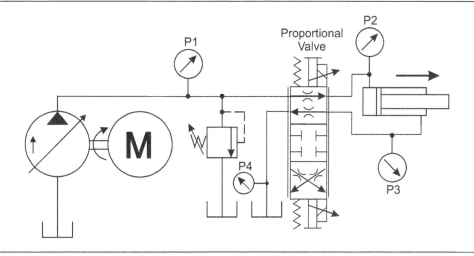

Figure 13-17   A symmetrical spool control cylinder extension

If a symmetrical spool is used and the cylinder's area ration is 2:1, the flow on the full bore side is twice the flow on the rod side of the cylinder. Therefore, the inlet pressure drop from P to A is four times the outlet pressure drop from B to T:

Formula 13-7

$$Q_{(P-A)} = 2 \times Q_{(B-T)}$$

and:

ΔP is proportional to Q^2

then:

$$\Delta P_{(P-A)} = 4 \times \Delta P_{(B-T)}$$

In the same way, as the cylinder retracts (Figure 13-18), the outlet pressure drop from A to T is four times the inlet pressure drop from P to B.

Formula 13-8

$$Q_{(A-T)} = 2 \times Q_{(P-B)}$$

and:

ΔP is proportional to Q^2

then:

$$\Delta P_{(A-T)} = 4 \times \Delta P_{(P-B)}$$

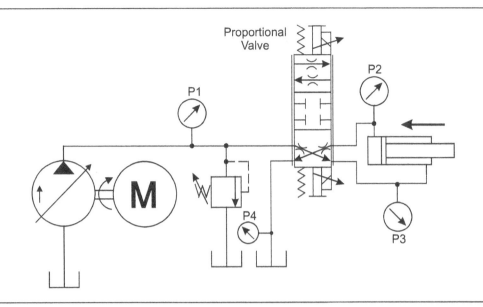

Figure 13-18   A symmetrical spool control cylinder retraction

Now that we have discussed some of the basic principles of proportional valve operation, we can examine the three different types of valves: proportional pressure control valves, proportional flow control valves and proportional directional control valves.

Proportional Pressure Control Valves

Proportional pressure control valves include relief and reducing valves with the same electrically controlled parts. In most pressure control applications, the pilot stage is a small electronically controlled valve, while the main stage is a regular relief or reducing valve sized for the required flow rate. Types of pressure control valves include nozzle-type relief valves, poppet-type relief valves with linear variable differential transformer (LVDT) feedback and plate-type relief valves.

Nozzle-Type Relief Valve

As indicated by the nozzle-type relief valve pictured in Figure 13-19, a proportional solenoid is connected to a spindle, which then presses against the valve's nozzle. The force that pushes the spindle toward the nozzle is proportional to the coil current. To open the valve to allow oil to flow through, the pressure of the fluid (P port) has to be greater than the solenoid force on the spindle. In simple terms:

Formula 13-9

$$\text{Pressure} = \frac{\text{solenoid force}}{\text{nozzle area}}$$

The nozzle opening must be relatively small, because the solenoid is not capable of creating much force. By limiting the nozzle diameter to between approximately 0.04 to 0.08 inch (1 to 2 mm), the valve will be able to reach pressure settings of up to 5,000 psi (345 bar, 34,500 kPa). Because the small valve has a high internal pressure drop, the nozzle-type relief valve is not suitable for applications that require a zero or very low pressure setting.

The small size of the valve also limits its maximum flow rate to approximately 0.8 GPM (3 l/min). The relatively low maximum flow rate of the nozzle-type relief valve means it will be used primarily as a pilot stage for a main stage relief or reducing valve. A nozzle-type valve is also appropriate for controlling compensator settings on pressure-compensated variable displacement vane or piston pumps.

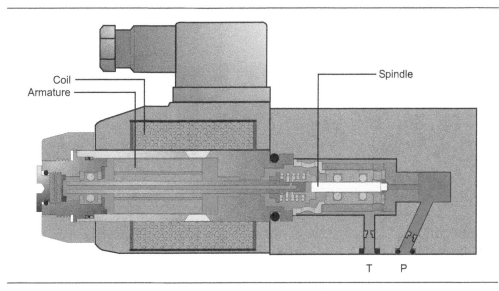

Figure 13-19   Nozzle-type pressure relief valve

Mounting

To ensure greater stability, the nozzle-type relief valve should not be mounted with the solenoid at the top. This prevents air from becoming trapped in the core tube. Also, a damping orifice can be located in the valve tank port to aid stability.

Plate-Type Relief Valve

The plate-type pressure relief valve has a plate-type armature (Figure 13-20). Like the other valves we have discussed, a current is passed through the valve's solenoid coil to create a magnetic field. On this valve, the magnetic field pulls the plate armature toward the coil. A small steel ball is held in the center of the plate, near the valve's nozzle opening.

As the armature is pulled toward the coil, the steel ball at the center of the armature is pushed against the nozzle. This reduces or blocks flow through the nozzle. To create a flow through the nozzle, the fluid pressure must be greater than the force created by the coil current. Therefore, the coil current determines how much pressure is required to allow flow through the nozzle. A variety of ball and nozzle sizes can be fitted for different pressure requirements.

A major benefit of the plate-type relief valve is the absence of springs, which results in less hysteresis, faster response times and better resolution. Also, when the valve plate is energized, there is no mechanical contact between the plate armature and the valve body or nozzle. This valve is very commonly used to control pressures in plastic injection molding machines.

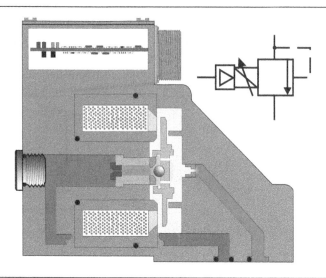

Figure 13-20   Plate-type pressure relief valve

Applications Summary

We have described two types of proportional pressure relief valves. Now, we will discuss the applications in which each pressure control valve works best.

Nozzle-Type Proportional Solenoid Valve

This valve is the simplest and least expensive of the three pressure valves discussed. It is designed for applications that require control of the electronic pressure setting, but do not need low hysteresis or a high degree of accuracy. The nozzle-type valve can be used for pump compensator control and as a soft load and unload feature for a main stage relief valve. In addition, this valve is suitable for use in pressure control systems when used with a pressure transducer that provides a feedback signal.

Plate-Type Relief Valve

This valve can be used in pressure applications that require low hysteresis and smooth linear control. Its onboard electronics make it compatible with microprocessor controls.

Proportional Flow Control Valves

Proportional flow control valves control the flow of hydraulic fluid. A proportional solenoid varies the valve settings for actuator speed, acceleration and deceleration. Proportional flow control valves include nonfeedback throttle valves and throttle valves with feedback.

Nonfeedback Throttle Valve

The nonfeedback throttle valve is very similar to a proportional directional valve. As Figure 13-21 illustrates, the nonfeedback throttle valve has a directional valve spool and body. The spring is extended in the closed position. Therefore, when it is not energized, the valve spool blocks all the ports to prevent any flow through the valve. When a current is passed through the solenoid, the solenoid force causes the spool to move across the valve body. This continues until the solenoid force and the spring compression force are balanced. Varying the coil current varies the spool's position as well as the size of the port openings that allow flow through the valve.

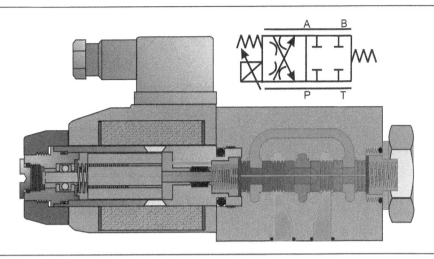

Figure 13-21   Nonfeedback throttle valve

Metering Notches

The edges of the throttle valve's spool lands have machined notches. These notches improve the valve's sensitivity, without reducing the maximum flow rate, when metering flow through very small openings. As you may see from Figure 13-22, the three spools would have different notches on them, allowing different combinations of blocked and restricted flows. In addition, the spools can be sized to meet different flow rate requirements.

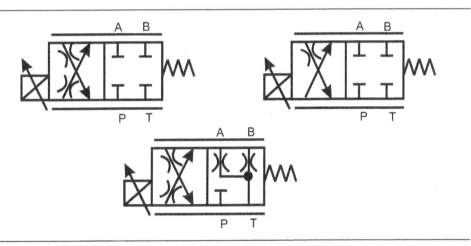

Figure 13-22   Three spool options for a nonfeedback throttle valve

As is true for all throttling valves, the flow rate through the proportional throttle valve is determined by the size of the valve opening and the pressure drop across the valve. Bernoulli's theorem, illustrated in Figure 13-23, states that as the velocity of a flow increases, the static pressure of the fluid decreases. This principle must be accounted for in applying proportional throttle valves in hydraulic systems. The flow forces acting on the spool of a nonfeedback proportional valve give the valve some limited pressure compensation characteristics.

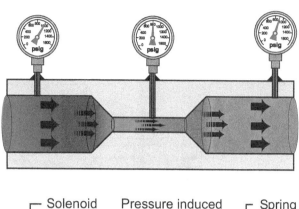

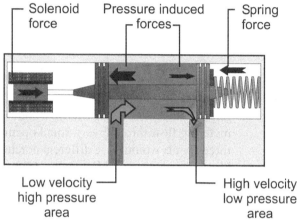

Figure 13-23   Bernoulli forces

When an electrical signal is sent to the solenoid to achieve a particular throttle setting, the solenoid moves the spool until the solenoid force and the spring force become balanced. The flow through the metering notches then produces two additional Bernoulli forces, as shown in the bottom view of the figure. A fluid flows through the restricted area of the notches. A localized pressure drop occurs on one side of the spool face. This drop does not exist on the other side of the spool, so the end effect is that the spool is pushed slightly to the left by the Bernoulli forces. A stable valve setting is achieved when the solenoid force balances exactly with the combined spring and Bernoulli forces.

If something occurs in the hydraulic system that increases the pressure drop across the valve, an increase in flow through the valve might also be expected. However, when the flow attempts to increase, the Bernoulli forces also increase, causing a smaller valve opening and holding the flow rate constant. This effect works best at higher valve pressure drops. In some applications with low valve pressure drops, it may be necessary to install a pressure-compensating hydrostat with the valve.

Throttle Valves with Feedback

When a particular application requires less hysteresis, better repeatability, faster response time and greater power capacity than a nonfeedback valve can provide, a spool position sensor can be used with a throttle valve. The spool position sensor sends a feedback signal to the amplifier's input, which provides for better valve performance. Again, this valve's design is very similar to a directional control valve.

A major difference between nonfeedback and feedback throttle valves (Figure 13-24) is that a balance between the forces of the solenoid and the spring positions the spool on a nonfeedback throttle valve, but only the input signal positions the spool on a feedback throttle valve. The solenoid moves the spool until the input and feedback signals cancel out. This method of positioning the spool is independent of other forces such as flow, system or load pressure, and friction, resulting in very low hysteresis and improved repeatability.

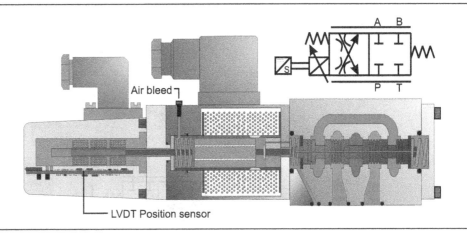

Figure 13-24   Throttle valve with feedback

Because spool position is independent of these forces, there is no pressure compensation like that of the nonfeedback throttle valves. Without any compensation, the flow rate is determined only by the input signal and the pressure drop across the valve.

As the graph in Figure 13-25 illustrates, the flow through the valve will increase as the pressure drop across the valve increases, up to a point, where an further increase in pressure drop actually results in a decrease in flow. At this point, the flow forces (Bernoulli forces) are greater than the solenoid.

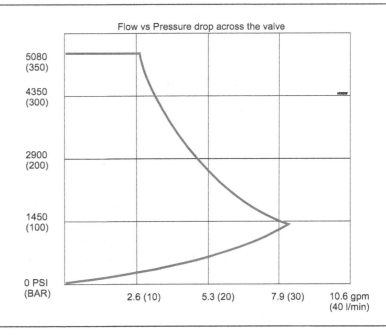

Figure 13-25   A proportional valve with feedback is not pressure-compensated

Hydrostat

When pressure compensation is needed, a hydrostat can be fitted underneath the valve, as shown in Figure 13-26. The hydrostat is a sliding spool type valve which is spring loaded to the open position. When the pressure difference across the throttle valve reaches the hydrostat spring valve, the hydrostat spool begins to move toward the closed position. This reduces pressure to the valve and maintains a constant pressure drop across the throttle valve ports. Using a hydrostat in this manner reduces the maximum flow rate for the throttle valve.

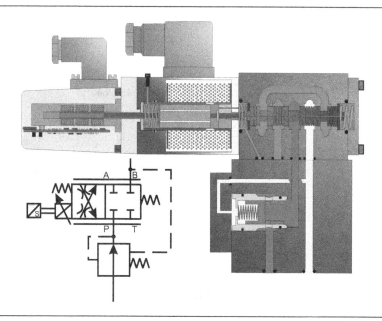

Figure 13-26   Hydrostat module fitted beneath a proportional throttle valve for pressure compensation

Application Summary

The nonfeedback throttle valve can be used in meter-in, meter-out and bleed off flow control applications. When selecting a throttle valve, it is important to remember that the highest degree of control will be achieved by selecting the spool with the lowest flow rating that meets the application's maximum flow requirements. Generally, the throttle valve with feedback is more suitable for applications that require a high degree of valve performance, while the nonfeedback throttle valve is well suited to most common applications.

Proportional Directional Control Valve

Proportional directional control valves control the direction as well as the amount of flow to an actuator in response to an electrical signal. This group of valves includes direct operated valves with or without spool position feedback, and pilot-operated valves, which are used in applications that require higher flow rates.

Proportional Directional Valve without Feedback

The design of a direct operated, or single-stage, proportional directional valve's solenoid, body and spool is very similar to that of the throttle valves we have discussed. One exception is the placement of solenoids at both ends to allow the spool to move in either direction from the center position. The solenoid core tubes have air bleed screws at the end. These screws allow the core tubes to be purged of air when the valve is first installed.

As Figure 13-27 indicates, flow through the valve can be either from the P port to the A port and the B port to the T port, or from the P port to the B port and the a port to the T port. The actual flow paths used depend on which solenoid is energized. The level of the input signal to the energized solenoid specifies the amount of flow through the ports.

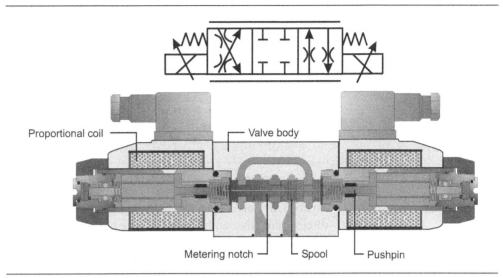

Figure 13-27   Direct operated proportional directional valve without feedback

Once again, different spool constructions and sizes can be used to match the requirements of different applications. Two different spools have different flow conditions in the center position; one blocks flow through all ports, while the other allows the A and B ports to be bled to the tank. Also, spools with different flow ratings, which we will discuss next, can be selected for different maximum flow rates.

Like throttle valves, the nonfeedback, direct operated directional valve provides some degree of pressure compensation. As the pressure drops across the valve and the flow rates both increase, the Bernoulli forces increase to present a greater opposition to the solenoid force. This results in smaller port openings, which prevents an increase in flow rate.

Proportional Directional Valve with Feedback

For applications that require more accurate spool positioning, an LVDT position sensor can be used with a direct operated, proportional directional valve, as shown in Figure 13-28. The spool movement is controlled by the input signal and, therefore, is independent of forces that work on the spool, such as flow, pressure and friction. For this reason, the valve does not make compensations for pressure like the nonfeedback directional control valve. Like throttle valves with feedback, this valve's flow rate is determined by both the input signal and the pressure drop across the valve. Again, the flow rate is approximately proportional to the square root of the pressure difference.

Up to a certain point, the valve's maximum flow rate is determined by the maximum pressure drop across it. However, the combined forces of flow, pressure and friction eventually become so large that they overcome the solenoid force, and the valve stops working properly. Large pressure drops are normally avoided when systems are designed; but when a proportional valve is used, for example, to decelerate an actuator or to control an overrunning load, large pressure drops are unavoidable.

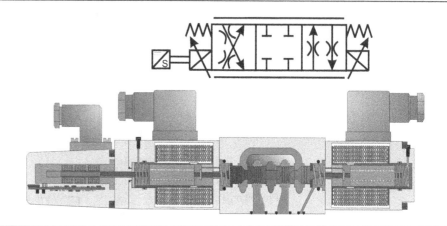

Figure 13-28   Proportional directional valve with LVDT feedback

Hydrostat

To keep the valve's pressure drop constant, a hydrostat can be used with a proportional directional valve with feedback. The hydrostat can be installed in the valve's pressure inlet line. The hydrostat spool senses pressure at port P and, with a shuttle valve, at the A or B port. The shuttle valve automatically picks the higher of the two pressures from lines A and B. This provides for pressure compensation in both flow directions, such as P to A and P to B. For more information on hydrostats, refer to the section on "Load Compensation" that appears later in this chapter.

Pilot-Operated Proportional Directional Valve

When it is necessary to control flow rates that exceed the maximum for direct operated proportional directional valves, a two-stage, or pilot-operated valve can be used. As you can see in Figure 13-29, this valve has a spring centered main stage attached to a position sensor and a solenoid-operated pilot stage with another position sensor. Proportional flow control is achieved by metering notches on the spool lands of the main stage.

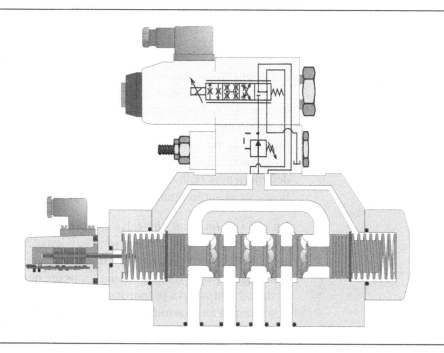

Figure 13-29   Pilot-operated proportional directional valve with feedback

Constant Pilot Pressure

A constant pilot pressure is required for consistent operation of the valve. This is accomplished by placing a pressure reducing valve in the pilot pressure feed line to the pilot stage. The pressure reducer is fitted between the valve's pilot and main stages.

As the symbol in Figure 13-30 represents, the pilot spool has four possible controlling positions. When positioned to the extreme right, the pilot spool is in the fail safe position, which vents both end chambers of the main spool. This allows the springs on the main stage to center the spool, which stops the actuator movement. Under normal operating conditions, the pilot spool operates within the other three positions. The all-ports-blocked position is the null position.

Like other two-stage valves, options are available for internal pilot, external pilot and drain by fitting and removing the appropriate plugs within the valve body.

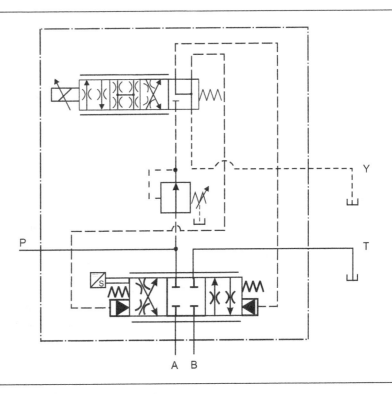

Figure 13-30   Symbol for a pilot-operated proportional directional valve

Hydrostat

The valve's main stage has feedback (an LVDT), so the pilot-operated valve would not be pressure-compensated. To achieve pressure compensation, a hydrostat must be added. Figure 13-31 shows a hydrostat tied to the P port of the main stage, with a shuttle valve between ports A and B. The shuttle valve allows for pressure compensation whether flow is coming from P to A or from P to B. The hydrostat, then senses pressure in the P port and either the A or B port, depending on the main spool movement. Pressure compensation is achieved either P to A or P to B, with a constant pressure drop maintained across the valve spool. As with other valves we have discussed in this chapter, there are two optional spool center conditions. One spool type blocks all ports in the center position, while another spool allows A and B to be bled to the tank when centered.

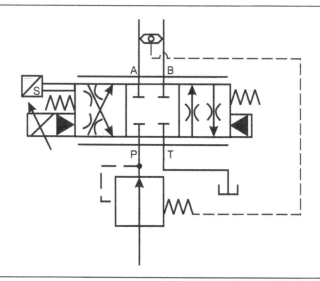

Figure 13-31   Symbol for a pilot-operated proportional directional valve with a hydrostat

Application Summary

A direct operated directional valve without spool position feedback can be used in applications with a moderate accuracy requirement. A direct operated directional valve with spool position feedback should be used in applications that require more accurate spool positioning. Pilot-operated directional valves with feedback can be used in applications that require accurate control of higher flow rates.

Application Guidelines

The following section contains several sample applications of proportional valves. These examples illustrate some of the major considerations involved in the implementation of proportional valves.

Example 1

Figure 13-32 represents an application of a symmetrical spool type valve that controls a positively loaded cylinder with all ports blocked in the center position. When all flow paths are equally restricted, the main control is meter-in on the advancing stroke, and meter-out as the stroke retracts.

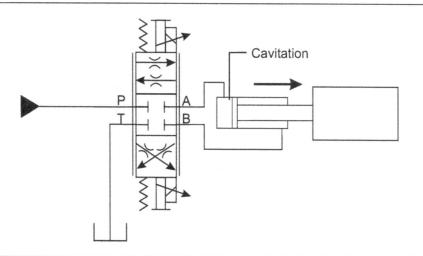

Figure 13-32   Full bore side cavitates with the forward deceleration of a positively loaded cylinder

Like all valves that block all ports in the center position, the piston tends to creep out when the valve is centered. This happens when the spool leaks to one side of the piston, causing it to move slightly.

To decelerate the forward stroke, the spool moves back toward its center position to restrict the flow on the rod side of the cylinder piston. This also restricts the flow on the full bore side of the cylinder piston. The flow rate on the cylinder's full bore side is larger than the flow on the rod side. As you recall, the pressure drop is proportional to the square of the flow. Therefore, this high braking pressure on the rod side of the cylinder causes an extremely high pressure drop in the full bore flow path. This large pressure drop can cause cavitation.

One solution is to install an anticavitation check valve, as shown in Figure 13-33. This reduces the pressure drop on the full bore side and prevents cavitation.

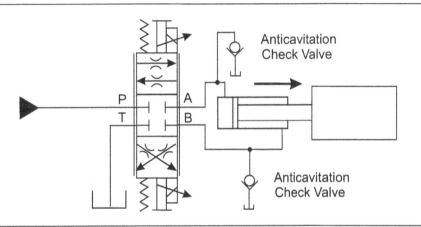

Figure 13-33 An anticavitation check valve reduces high braking pressure drop

A second solution to this problem is to use a meter-out spool instead of a meter-in spool, as shown in Figure 13-34. This allows the inward flow to the cylinder to remain almost totally unrestricted in both the forward and retracting directions. However, this solution does not fully consider the problem of intensified pressure on the rod side of the cylinder piston when decelerating. Also, the meter-out spool cannot be used in a system with some types of hydrostat.

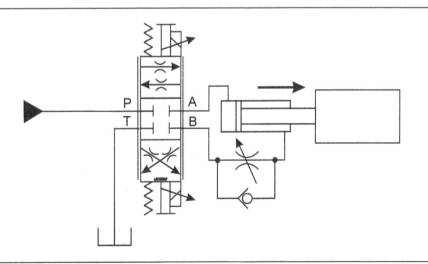

Figure 13-34 A meter-out spool lessens the restriction on entering flow in both directions

Another factor to consider is the sudden loss of power during a power failure or emergency stop conditions. When ramp signals are fed to a proportional valve to decelerate a high inertia load, a sudden loss of power causes the spool to move to the center position very quickly, which will cause peak pressures. The pressure will be greatest on the rod side of the cylinder piston when the cylinder is extended.

To avoid peak pressures, relief and anticavitation valves can be installed, as illustrated in Figure 13-35.

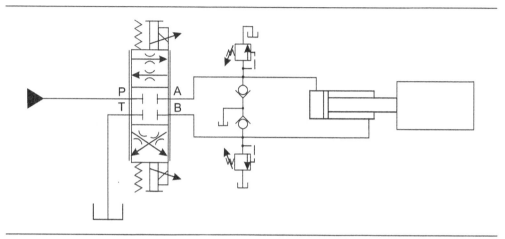

Figure 13-35   Relief and anticavitation check valves prevent peak pressures

Differential creep is unwanted piston movement caused by leakage into lines A and B. To reduce its effect, a spool that bleeds A and B to the tank can be used (Figure 13-36). However, under light load conditions, a high back pressure or peak pressure in the tank can still cause the piston to creep out of position.

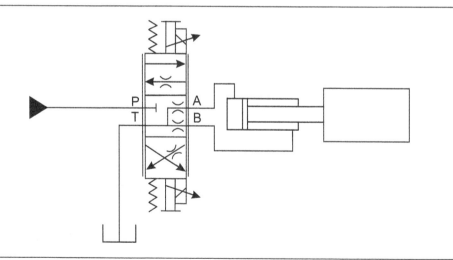

Figure 13-36   A type 33 spool bleeds A and B to the tank in the center position to offset differential creep

Example 2

Figure 13-37 is a schematic of a negatively loaded cylinder, which means that gravity acts on the load. For this type of cylinder, it is important to consider the effects of the load acting on the full bore area or the load acting on the rod side of the cylinder piston. In the arrangement shown in Figure 13-37, the main restriction is meter-in on the forward stroke and meter-out when the cylinder retracts. Because the load naturally decelerates as it moves upward, anticavitation check valves are normally not required.

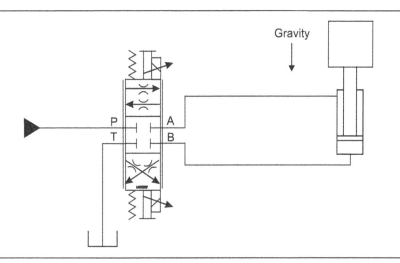

Figure 13-37   The load acts on the rod side of the cylinder in the extending stroke

One problem might occur when the cylinder is held in a partially or fully extended position. The spool would move to its center position, in which all ports are blocked. Line A could leak to the tank, causing the piston to move downward. The amount that leaks depends on variations in the load, fluid temperature and viscosity, valve wear and other influences.

Therefore, an electronic adjustment of the spool's null position to compensate for the leak would not sufficiently solve the problem. A better solution to this leakage problem is to install a pilot-operated check valve (Figure 13-38).

The pilot-operated check valve must be piloted independently. This ensures that the valve will stay open at all times while the cylinder is moving, especially during deceleration. Another important consideration for a negatively loaded cylinder is that, if it requires smooth deceleration when lowered, a spool with all ports blocked in the center position is better than a spool that has A and B bled to tank in the center position.

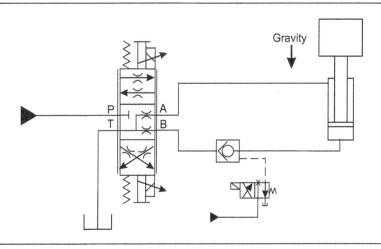

Figure 13-38   A pilot-operated check valve diverts leakage from the proportional valve

If there is leakage across the proportional valve spool, however, the cylinder might move as soon as the pilot-operated check valve is opened. In addition, if the pilot-operated check valve is installed a good distance from the proportional valve, fluid compression in the piping might cause the cylinder to drop momentarily as the pilot-operated check valve is opened.

Therefore, in some applications, it may be necessary to give a small lifting signal to the proportional valve before a lowering signal, the check valve opening speed could be made slower, or a counterbalance valve could be used.

Example 3

When the load acts on the rod side of the cylinder piston, as in Figure 13-39, several different factors must be considered. In particular, the forward extension of the stroke requires special attention.

In the schematic shown in Figure 13-39, the main restriction is the meter-in when the cylinder is extended and the meter-out when the cylinder retracts. However, as we discussed earlier, metering in while the cylinder is lowered can cause cavitation. Therefore, this application requires an anticavitation check valve.

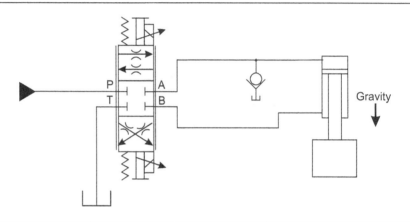

Figure 13-39   The load acts on the rod side of the cylinder in the extending stroke

While simply using a meter-out spool might prevent cavitation in some cases, each application of this kind should be carefully checked out for intensified pressure in the rod side of the cylinder piston.

In some cases, safety considerations require the use of a counterbalance valve (Figure 13-40). This valve ensures that the cylinder is not lowered uncontrollably when the proportional valve is fully opened. Also, the use of a counterbalance valve makes the cylinder positively loaded, so the anticavitation check valve is not required, unless the application demands very rapid deceleration as the cylinder is lowered.

A counterbalance valve would still restrict the A to T flow path when the cylinder is lowered. Therefore, when analyzing circuit operation, the back pressure created across the valve would need to be added to the counterbalance valve setting.

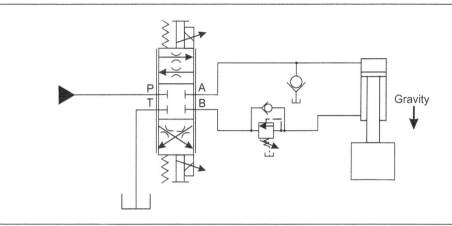

Figure 13-40   A counterbalance valve prevents uncontrolled lowering of the cylinder

Load Compensation

As you have learned, many proportional solenoid valve applications require some degree of pressure compensation. This is especially true for applications that require a constant actuator speed during fluctuations in load or system pressure.

As you recall, nonfeedback type valves compensate for pressure differences to a certain extent. When the built-in pressure compensation does not sufficiently reduce pressure, a hydrostat can be used with the proportional solenoid valve.

In Figure 13-41, a pressure line hydrostat senses the pressure at the P port and either the A or B port of the valve. A built-in shuttle valve picks the higher of the two pressures from A and B and feeds it back to the hydrostat spool. The hydrostat spool then makes any adjustments necessary to maintain a constant pressure drop across the proportional valve. The pressure difference will be equal to the hydrostat spring. This provides for meter-in pressure compensation when the cylinder moves in either direction.

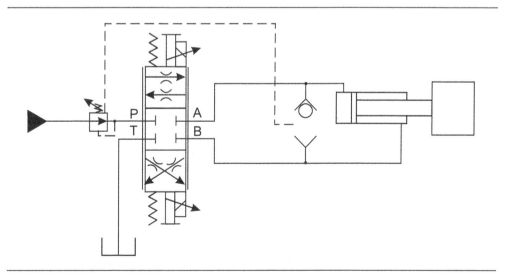

Figure 13-41   Pressure line hydrostat and shuttle valve

When the cylinder moves forward, the A port pressure must be higher than the B port pressure. This is generally true as long as the load does not overrun, except during deceleration. As the cylinder decelerates in the forward direction, pressure in the B port very likely will be higher than in the A port, unless frictional forces acting on the load are high. When this happens, the hydrostat spool moves toward the fully open position to reduce the effect of cavitation on the full bore side of the cylinder.

A hydrostat used for load compensation affects a system's pressure requirements. If the hydrostat in Figure 13-41 has a 60 psi (4 bar, 400 kPa) spring and the cylinder has a 2:1 area ratio, when the cylinder is retracting with a zero load, the pressure drop from P to B will be 60 psi (4 bar, 400 kPa). The pressure drop from A to T will be 232 psi (16 bar, 1,600 kPa) (remember, P is Proportional to Q2), and the pressure in the full-bore side of the cylinder will be at least 232 psi (16 bar, 1,600 kPa). This will require a pressure of 464 psi (32 bar, 3,200 kPa) on the rod-side of the cylinder to overcome the pressure on the other side. Therefore, a system pressure of 522 psi (36 bar, 3,600 kPa) is required [464 psi (32 bar, 3,200 kPa) plus 58 psi (4 bar, 400 kPa) drop from P to B]. If the cylinder is loaded in the retract direction, the load pressure must be added to the total system pressure requirement.

Using a hydrostat also affects a proportional valve's maximum flow rate. A hydrostat has a lowering effect on flow rate, because the maximum flow is the amount that gets through the valve at a pressure difference equal to that of the hydrostat spring. A hydrostat with a variable spring can be used to increase the maximum flow rate. This creates a conventional pressure reducing valve.

Instead of connecting the Drain (DR) port of the reducing valve to the tank, it can be connected to lines A and B using a shuttle valve, as shown in Figure 13-42. Therefore, by varying the setting on the reducing valve, the spring setting of the hydrostat and the pressure drop of the proportional valve can be adjusted. However, the amount of wasted power goes up with the hydrostat setting. In addition, the continual pilot flow from the reducing valve's DR port establishes a specific minimum flow capability.

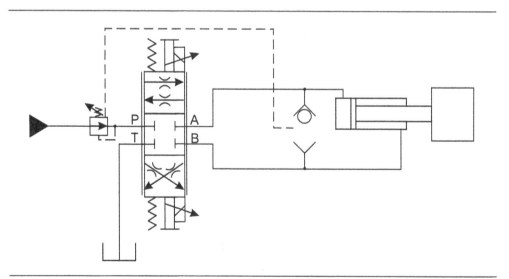

Figure 13-42   A variable spring hydrostat increases the maximum flow rate

If a solenoid valve replaces the shuttle valve, the sensing line can be positively selected at any time (Figure 13-43).

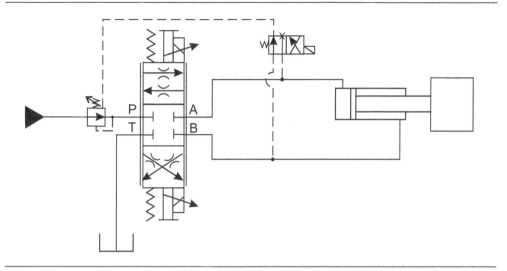

Figure 13-43   A solenoid valve provides load compensation

To achieve proper compensation, negatively loaded cylinders must have a counterbalance valve in the negative load direction when used with a meter-in compensation.

It is possible to build virtually any combination of proportional valve/hydrostat arrangements using independently mounted pressure reducing valves. For example, a full reducing or relief valve assembly can be used if variable hydrostat pressure is required. If the load changes direction while the cylinder is moving, such as during deceleration, the hydrostat sensing line can be independently switched using a solenoid valve.

The same general principles apply when using load sensing with a variable pump. Flow must be metered into the actuator when the load pressure is sensed. Therefore, the meter-out spool should not be used for load sensing.

Summary

Proportional solenoid valves provide solutions to design problems that cannot be resolved using only conventional on/off DC solenoid valves. The replacement of hydraulic valves with electrical control devices simplifies the variable control of pressure, flow and direction. In many applications, proportional solenoid valves are implemented in systems that require various combinations of conventional, cartridge and proportional valves.

Industrial Test Questions:
Proportional Valves

Chapter 13

1. List three major functions of proportional solenoid valves.

2. Explain the expression "output flow is proportional to the input signal" and how a proportional solenoid actuates a proportional valve spool.

3. Explain the significance of a constant force solenoid.

4. Describe deadband compensation.

5. Describe hysteresis and how a control amplifier compensates for it.

6. Explain ramp functions and list the variables they are designed to control.

7. Explain the purpose of current feedback.

8. Describe pulse width modulation.

9. Explain the difference between feedback and nonfeedback proportional valve operation.

10. Explain the difference between symmetrical and nonsymmetrical proportional valve spools.

11. Describe the relationship between flow rate and pressure drop through a proportional valve.

12. Describe two types of proportional pressure valves.

13. Explain the operation of an LVDT.

14. Describe metering notches and their purpose.

15. How can cavitation be prevented when controlling an unequal area actuator, such as a cylinder?

16. Describe some of the special considerations for controlling a negative load with a proportional valve.

17. Describe load compensation and why it is needed.

18. How can a hydrostat affect pressure drop across a proportional valve?

Chapter 14 . . . . Servo Valves

A servo valve is a directional valve that may be infinitely positioned to provide control of both the quantity and the direction of fluid flow. They are unique, however, in that an internal feedback mechanism assures the correct position of the spool relative to the input command. Also, when coupled with the proper outer loop feedback sensing devices, very accurate control of the position, velocity or acceleration of an actuator is provided.

The mechanical servo valve, or follow valve, has been in use for several decades, and is still widely popular for use with power steering actuators. The electrohydraulic servo valve was developed in the 1950s, and originally gained its popularity in aerospace. It is now widely used in electronically controlled industrial systems. The term "servo" has come to mean a component or system that operates as a closed loop control circuit, having feedback of the controlled variable.

Mechanical Servo Valve

The mechanical servo valve is essentially a force amplifier used for positioning control. It is illustrated schematically in Figure 14-1.

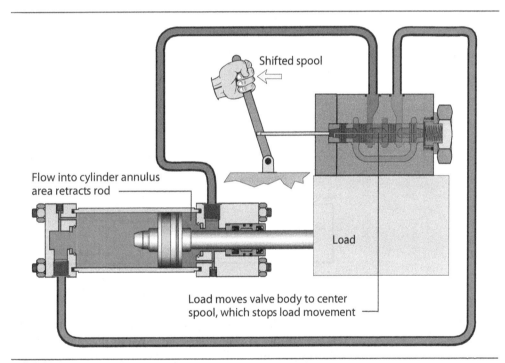

Figure 14-1   Mechanical servo "follow" valve

The control handle or other mechanical linkage is connected to the valve spool. The valve body is connected to and moves with the load. When the spool is actuated, it allows flow to a cylinder or piston to move the load in the same direction as the actuated spool. The valve body follows the spool. Flow continues until the body is centered, or neutral, with the spool. The effect is that the load always moves a distance proportional to the spool movement. Any tendency to move farther would reverse oil flow, moving the load back into position.

The mechanical servo valve is often referred to as a booster. The hydraulic boost provides a considerably greater force than the mechanical input, with precise control of the distance moved.

Some of the first hydraulic steering units were developed by Harry Vickers, founder of Vickers, Incorporated, in the mid 1930s. Power steering today is almost universal on full size passenger cars and widely used on trucks, buses and other large vehicles. At the present time, the many design variations of power steering systems, for the most part, operate on this same principle.

Electrohydraulic Servo Valves

Electrohydraulic servo valves operate on the principle of an electrical input signal establishing a specific spool position within the valve. An internal feedback mechanism assures that the spool position is repeatable and consistent, and exactly proportional to the magnitude of the electrical input signal.

The input signal can come from a variety of sources such as a simple potentiometer or joystick, an electronic controller or a programmable logic controller (PLC). The analog signal is first fed into a servo amplifier, which then powers the servo valve's torque motor coils. The torque motor creates a pressure difference across a spool, which causes spool movement in direct proportion to the input signal. The unique characteristic of servo valves is the internal mechanical feedback mechanism that ensures repeatability of the spool position.

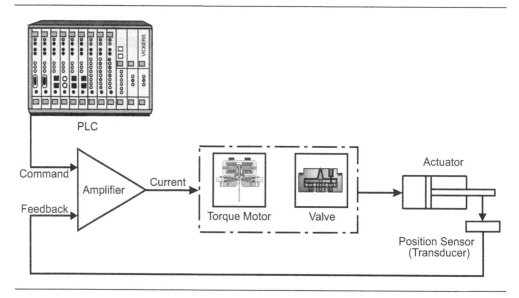

Figure 14-2   Basic servo valve in a closed loop position control circuit

Since servo valves are primarily used in closed loop control systems (Figure 14-2), the servo amplifier also provides the capability to add an external feedback signal that will compare the command signal with the actual controlled variable feedback signal, and make adjustments to the output signal going to the valve to correct any detectable error. This external feedback signal can come from a tachometer generator, encoder, pressure transducer, force transducer, position transducer or any other type of output measuring device that will communicate the controlled variable information back to the servo amplifier.

The various types of electrohydraulic servos can provide very precise positioning or velocity control. Most often, the servo valve controls a cylinder or motor; but it may be also used to operate the displacement control of a variable volume pump (electronic displacement control).

**Flapper Nozzle
Servo Valves**

The flapper nozzle servo valve is actuated by a torque motor. The torque motor includes two separate coils, permanent magnets, an armature which is attached to a flexure tube and a feedback wire which is attached to a hole or slot in the spool (Figure 14-3).

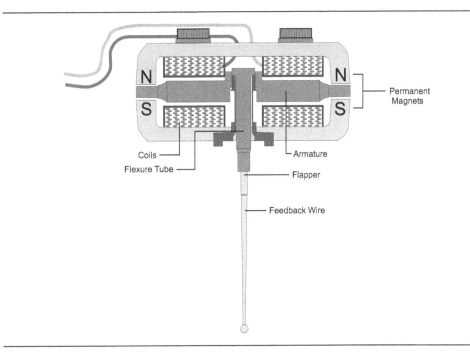

Figure 14-3   Torque motor assembly

When the coils in the torque motor coils are energized, the torque motor armature is magnetized. The magnetic field of the armature reacts to the magnetic fields of the permanent magnets, causing a pivoting of the armature on the flexure tube (torque is produced, hence the name "torque motor"). The amount of torque produced is proportional to the current supplied to the coils, and the direction of pivot is determined by the polarity of the voltage supplied to the coils (Figure 14-4).

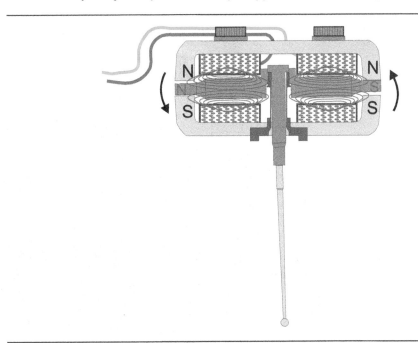

Figure 14-4   Energized coil causes armature to tip

The magnetized armature will be attracted to one side of the permanent magnet and repelled from the other to establish the direction that the armature moves. The armature movement forces the flapper to move toward one of the two nozzles on the pilot stage (Figure 14-5). If current is removed from the coil, the flexure tube flexes back to the center position, centering the flapper between the nozzles once again.

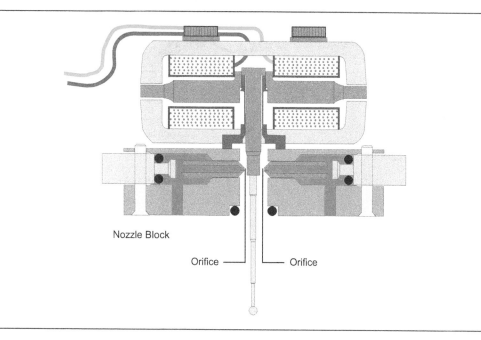

Figure 14-5   Position of the flapper between two nozzles

The torque motor armature is attached to a flapper/feedback wire which is physically connected to the spool via a "ball" attached to the end of the feedback wire. The two ends of the spool have equal pressure when the flapper is centered between the nozzles. Notice that the spool fits within a sleeve. The spool and sleeve are manufactured as a matched set and are not interchangeable with those of other valves.

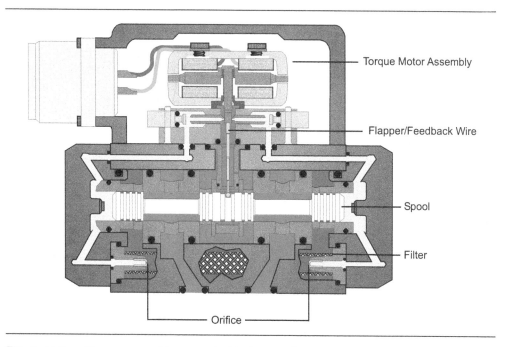

Figure 14-6   Flapper assembly connected to the spool

When the torque motor is energized, as shown in Figure 14-7, the armature will tip (usually less than 3 degrees of rotation). The flapper moves against the nozzle on the left, while moving away from the nozzle on the right. This restricts fluid flow through the left nozzle, which causes pressure to increase behind the nozzle on that side of the valve. While the flapper is moving away from the nozzle on the right, the pressure behind that nozzle will decrease. Notice that the pressure behind each nozzle is connected to an end of the spool.

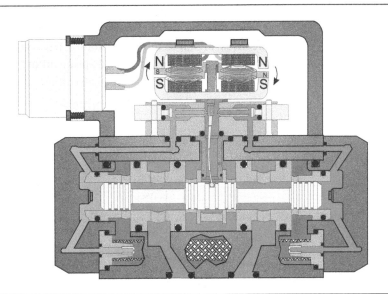

Figure 14-7   Deflected flapper increases pressure behind one nozzle

An increase in pressure on the left end of the spool and a decrease in pressure on the right end of the spool creates an imbalance, which causes the spool to move away from the end with the higher pressure (Figure 14-8). As the spool slides to the right, the feedback wire pulls the flapper to the right until it is again centered between the two nozzles. This highly dependable method of mechanical spool feedback eliminates the need for complex spring arrangements, levers, pilots and other complicated feedback mechanisms.

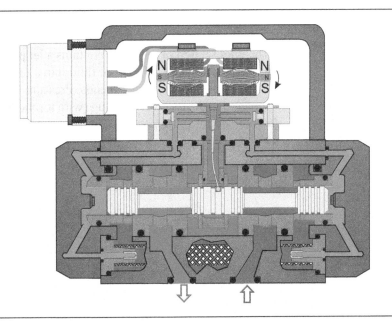

Figure 14-8   Spool movement centers flapper, neutralizing spool forces

Depending on the spool's movement, pressurized fluid flows from one of the valve's two actuator ports (typically labeled port A and port B). Any servo valve can be viewed as a proportional type of valve because the magnitude of the input signal and, consequently the flapper deflection, determine the spool's position as well as the amount of oil flowing through the opened ports. However, the amount of fluid that actually flows to the load depends on the input signal and the additional factors of supply pressure, supplied flow, load pressure drop and the valve's flow rating.

As mentioned earlier, the spool and sleeve are manufactured as a matched pair. To ensure that the spool is centered within the sleeve, and the actuator will stop with no electrical signal to the torque motor, a mechanical null adjustment is often used. While some manufacturers employ a spring adjustment on the torque motor, the null adjuster in Figure 14-9 slides the sleeve to either side to accomplish this adjustment.

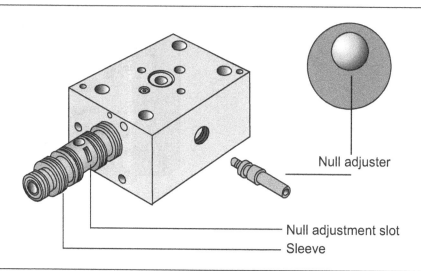

Null adjuster

Null adjustment slot

Sleeve

Figure 14-9   Spool movement centers flapper, neutralizing spool forces

Jet Pipe Servo Valves

Like the flapper nozzle servo valve, the jet pipe servo valve has a torque motor. The jet pipe servo valve also has a valve spool that is shifted by a pressure differential. The distance the spool moves depends on the magnitude of the current flowing through the torque motor coils. This valve also incorporates a feedback spring, providing internal feedback to the feedback arm.

Jet Pipe Operation

The pilot section of the valve contains a jet pipe; a tube with an orifice end that directs a continuing stream of control fluid into a receiver. The receiver has two ports connected to the valve spool ends. Pressure in these ports is equal when the jet pipe is centered in the receiver opening (with torque motor coils de-energized). With pressure at both ends of the spool equal, the spool is centered (Figure 14-10).

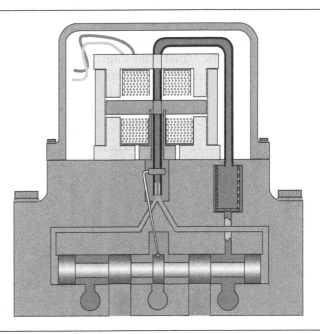

Figure 14-10   Jet pipe servo valve

The torque motor will deflect the pipe in either direction (Figure 14-5), depending on the direction of current in the torque motor coils. When the polarity of the current though the torque motor coils causes the torque motor to pivot clockwise, the deflection of the pipe to the left causes the nozzle jet to increase the pressure at the left end of the spool. As the pipe moves the nozzle jet away from the receiver on the right, the pressure on the right end of the spool decreases (Figure 14-11).

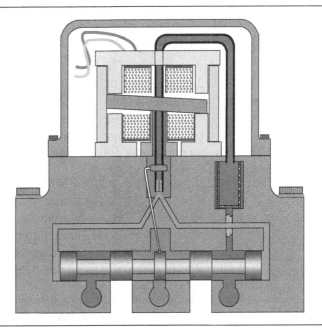

Figure 14-11   Coil current causes the jet pipe to shift

This pressure differential causes the spool to shift to the right, which connects P to A and B to T within the valve. Movement of the spool also moves the feedback wire (Figure 14-12). This force on the feedback arm, in an amount proportional to the electric signal at the torque motor, repositions the nozzle with the receiver and restores a balance of force across the spool. Any attempt by the spool to move from its new position will move the feedback arm, which will correct the spool movement. Thus, the spool will remain in this new position until the current in the torque motor changes.

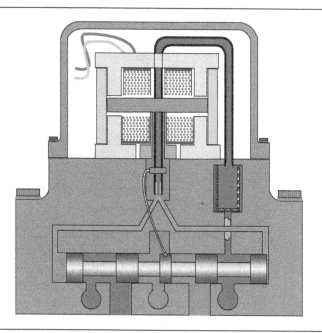

Figure 14-12   Feedback wire centers the jet pipe

High Performance Valve Capacities

The flow capacities of high performance servo valves range from 0.1 to 60 GPM (0.4 to 230 l/min) at 1,000 psi (70 bar, 7,000 kPa) pressure drop across the valve. For more information on servo valve sizing, refer to the Eaton *Closed Loop Electrohydraulics Manual*. A servo valve requires at least 70 psi (5 bar, 500 kPa) supply pressure to assure the spool moves at some reasonable rate, although a minimum pressure of 500 psi (35 bar, 3,500 kPa) is recommended.

Where flows larger than 60 GPM (230 l/min) are required, a three-stage servo valve can be used. This consists of a basic servo valve as a pilot valve on a larger main stage valve. Spool position feedback from the main stage to the torque motor is accomplished via an LVDT (linear variable displacement transformer) which feeds spool position information to the controlling amplifier. Flows can reach as high as 1,000 GPM (3,800 l/min) using three-stage valves.

Servo valves have operating pressure ratings that range from 2,000 psi (140 bar, 14,000 kPa) to 5,000 psi (350 bar, 35,000 kPa).

Fluid Filtration

Contamination is the major contributor to premature failure of most hydraulic components. This is notably true with servo valves. To ensure a long service life, high performance servo valves require adequate fluid filtration to protect them from contamination by very small particles. Filtration is vital because the nozzles, passages and spool clearances are critically dimensioned for performance. In many instances, the critical areas of the valve are protected by a fine filter screen. However, excessive contamination will fill the screens, resulting in sluggish response or in failure of the valve to function properly. An ISO/Vickers cleanliness code of 15/13/10 is recommended to prevent blockages within the servo valve. The filter built into many servo valves is typically 40 – 200 microns. Three micron filtration is generally recommended in a hydraulic system utilizing servo valves, with an additional 3 micron non-bypass filter placed ahead of the servo "P" port.

Electronic Controls

The torque motor of servo valves usually contain an 80 ohm, 40 milliamp coil and provide very satisfactory performance on +/- 0 – 10 volts command signal into the amplifier. Another very popular coil is the 20 ohm, 200 milliamp version. A typical input controlling device is a PLC (Programmable Logic Controller) that provides either voltage or current command input to the servo valve amplifier.

Servo Valve Performance

Servo valves are referred to as high performance valves because of their exceptional performance in the areas of deadband, hysteresis, linearity, frequency response and lower electrical power requirements.

Zero Lap versus Overlap

The edges, or lands, of a conventional valve spool usually have some degree of overlap with the corresponding edges of the valve body ports, as shown in Figure 14-13. This is required for several reasons: 1) overlap helps to prevent flow across the spool when the spool is in neutral, 2) it helps to assure that system flow is zero when the electric signal to the valve is zero, and 3) it helps to assure a degree of safety if the electric power is lost and the spool "springs" back to neutral.

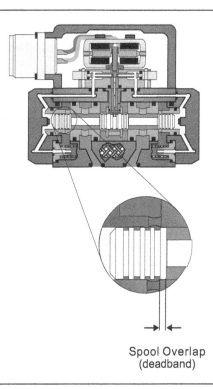

Spool Overlap
(deadband)

Figure 14-13   Overlap of spool and bore lands

The nature of spool overlap, however, means that there will be a defined movement of the spool necessary in the bore before flow begins to take place. This "no-flow" movement is called "deadband," and refers to the amount of movement a valve spool must physically make before any activity (meaning fluid flow) will take place. Figure 14-14 illustrates this characteristic.

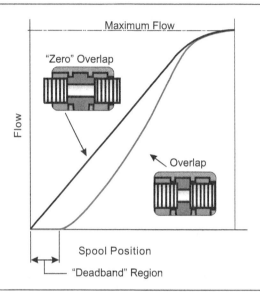

Figure 14-14   Flow vs spool position with overlap and zero lap

The overwhelming majority of servo valves are constructed with, essentially, no overlap ("zero lap"). The deadband is almost zero, as shown in the "zero" overlap curve in Figure 14-14.

Hysteresis

Hysteresis is defined as the difference in the amount of solenoid current necessary for identical spool position when moving in different directions. Figure 14-15 illustrates the spool position difference that can occur when solenoid current is increasing, versus when it is decreasing. At any one point of solenoid current, the flow difference (hysteresis) is usually less than 2 percent, but may be as high as 8 percent of full rated torque motor current.

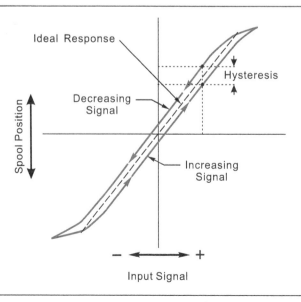

Figure 14-15   The effect of hysteresis on valve spool position

Other factors that contribute to hysteresis are stiction (static friction), flow forces within the valve (forces caused by pressure drops across the spool due to flow), gravity (affected by valve position), contamination (increasing friction), residual magnetism within the torque motor armature (between metal parts), fluid viscosity, etc.

Spool positioning in a servo valve, however, does not depend upon springs, but on the pressure differential between the two ends of the spool. This differential can be quite large, and will generally overcome any tendencies for the spool to lag. Hysteresis in servo valves is minimal.

Linearity

Linearity is a measure of a valve's flow gain, or the relationship between the valve's control flow and its input signal. Every proportional and servo valve should have a control flow that is proportional to its input signal, but the accuracy of the proportional relationship varies between different types of valves. The best possible flow gain is a straight line when plotted on a graph.

Again, because the spool positioning in a servo valve is accomplished by a potentially high differential pressure, the control flow is almost perfectly proportional to its input signal. The valve will perform almost exactly as commanded.

Industrial Test Questions:
Servo Valves

Chapter 14

1. In a mechanical servo valve, what part of the servo valve moves with the load? What part moves with the control?

2. In a single-stage electrohydraulic servo, how is the valve spool actuated?

3. What primary feature makes a servo valve different from an ordinary directional valve? What is the purpose of this feature?

4. Why is there a ball at the end of the feedback wire?

5. How is the spool shifted in jet pipe and flapper nozzle type servo valves?

6. What is the difference between internal feedback and external feedback in servo valves?

7. What ISO/Vickers cleanliness code is required for servo valve systems?

8. Describe zero overlap and how it affects servo valve performance.

9. Explain linearity, comparing that of a servo valve with that of a typical proportional valve.

10. In three-stage servo valves, what is typically used to sense the position of the spool in the main stage?

11. What are the primary differences between proportional valves and servo valves?

12. What is the purpose of the filter typically built into servo valves?

13. What would happen in a flapper nozzle servo valve if one of the nozzles were to be completely blocked with contamination?

14. Are servo valves primarily used in open loop or closed loop control circuits?

15. Are servo valve spools interchangeable from valve to valve?

16. In a jet pipe or flapper nozzle servo valve, what determines which direction the torque motor pivots?

17. What is the purpose of the mechanical null adjustment on servo valves?

18. What is hysteresis?

19. What causes hysteresis within servo valves?

Chapter 15 . . . . Hydraulic Pumps

Hydraulic pumps convert mechanical energy into hydraulic energy (hydraulic horsepower) by pushing fluid into a system.

All pumps work on the same principle. They generate an increasing volume on the intake side of the rotating group and a decreasing volume at the discharge side. However, different types of pumps vary greatly in methods and sophistication.

The hydraulic output horsepower from a pump is determined by the flow provided by the pump and the operating pressure; a common formula is used:

Formula 15-1

Hydraulic Horsepower $=$ GPM $\times$ psi $\times$ 0.000583

Hydraulic Kilowatts $=$ l/min $\times$ bar $\times$ 0.001667

Pump Characteristics

Displacement

The flow capacity of a pump can be expressed as displacement per revolution, or as output in GPM or l/min.

Displacement is the volume of liquid transferred from inlet to outlet in one revolution. It is equal to the volume of one pumping chamber multiplied by the number of chambers that pass the outlet per revolution. Displacement is expressed in cubic inches per revolution (CIR or in^3/rev) or cubic centimeters per revolution (CCR or cm^3/rev).

Delivery

Although a pump can be rated as a 10 GPM (38 l/min) unit, it may actually pump more than that under no load conditions, and less than that at its rated operating pressure. The pump's delivery is also proportional to drive shaft speed.

Most manufacturers provide performance information in the form of a table or graph, showing pump deliveries, horsepower requirements, drive speeds, and pressures under specific test conditions.

There is a direct relationship between pump displacement and theoretical output flow. In traditional units, the theoretical (neglecting internal leakage, etc.) output in gallons per minute is equal to the displacement in cubic inches per revolution multiplied by the speed in revolutions per minute and divided by 231 cubic inches per gallon. That is:

Formula 15-2

$$Q_{Theo} = \frac{D \times RPM}{231 \frac{in^3}{Gal}}$$

Where:

Q_{Theo} = Theoretical output flow (GPM),

D = Displacement (in^3/rev), and

231 = Cubic inches per gallon (in^3/gal)

In metric units, the relationship is:

Formula 15-3

$$Q_{Theo} = \frac{D \times RPM}{1,000\frac{cm^3}{l}}$$

Where:

Q_{Theo} = Theoretical output flow (l/min),

D = Displacement (cm^3/rev), and

1,000 = Cubic centimeters per liter (cm^3/l)

Volumetric Efficiency

Theoretically, a pump delivers an amount of fluid equal to its displacement during each cycle or revolution. In reality, the actual output is reduced because of internal leakage and the requirement for internal lubrication of pump components. As pressure increases, the leakage from the outlet back to the inlet (or to the drain) and the lubrication flow also increases, causing a decrease in pump output. Volumetric efficiency is equal to the actual output divided by the theoretical output. It is expressed as a percentage.

Formula 15-4

$$Efficiency\ \% = \frac{Actual\ out \times 100}{Theoretical\ output}$$

As an example, if a pump presumably delivers 10 GPM (38 l/min) but actually delivers only 9 GPM (34 l/min) at 1,000 psi (70 bar, 7,000 kPa), the volumetric efficiency of that pump at that speed and pressure is 90 percent.

$$Efficiency = \frac{9}{10} \times 100 = 90\%$$

Mechanical and Overall Efficiency

All pumps have sliding surfaces and rotating components that cause friction and generate heat. Heat is also generated by turbulence and friction within the fluid being pumped. These are called mechanical losses.

When heat is generated, there is a loss of power to the system. Combining these mechanical losses with the volumetric losses results in less hydraulic power being delivered by the pump than there is mechanical power being used to drive the pump. The relationship between input and output power may be expressed as:

Formula 15-5

$$hp_{out} = hp_{in} \times Eff_{oa}$$

or:

$$hp_{in} = \frac{hp_{out}}{Eff_{oa}}$$

Where:

hp_{out} = Hydraulic horsepower delivered by the pump, and

hp_{in} = Mechanical horsepower required to drive the pump

Eff_{oa} = Overall efficiency of the pump

The overall efficiency is the product of the mechanical and volumetric efficiencies according to:

Formula 15-6

$$\text{Eff}_{oa} = \text{Eff}_v \times \text{Eff}_m$$

Where:

Eff_v = Volumetric efficiency, and

Eff_m = Mechanical efficiency

Pump Ratings

A pump is generally rated by its maximum operating pressure capability, and its theoretical output flow at a given drive speed or its actual output flow at a given drive speed and pressure.

The pressure rating of a pump is determined by the manufacturer and is based upon reasonable service life expectancy under specified operating conditions. It is important to note that there is no standard industry wide safety factor included in this rating. Operating at higher pressure will result in reduced pump life, and may cause more serious damage.

The flow rating of a pump is expressed in terms of how much fluid is supplied per unit of time. This delivery capability is typically expressed in gallons per minute (GPM) or liters per minute (l/min). It may be a theoretical figure, based on the displacement, or it may be an actual delivery figure determined by test at a nominal pressure, such as 100 psi (7 bar, 700 kPa).

Types of Pumps

There are many different types and designs of pumps used in hydraulics. These can be broken down into categories, however, as shown in Figure 15-1. The broadest categories are positive and non-positive displacement pumps. Positive displacement pumps can further be broken down into gear, vane and piston pump categories. Vane and piston can further be broken into fixed and variable displacement categories.

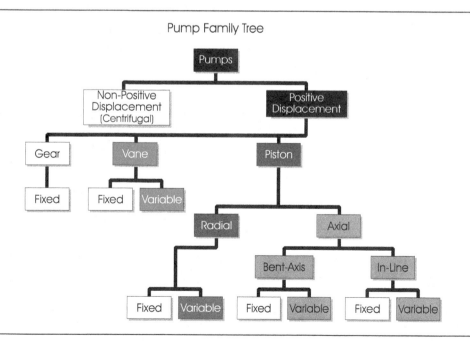

Figure 15-1   Pump categories

Non-positive Displacement

The non-positive displacement pump design is used mainly for fluid transfer in systems where the only resistance to flow is created by the weight of the fluid itself and friction.

Most non-positive displacement pumps (Figure 15-2) operate by centrifugal force. Fluids entering the center of the pump housing are thrown to the outside by means of a rapidly driven impeller. There is no positive seal between the inlet and outlet ports, and pressure capabilities are a function of drive speed.

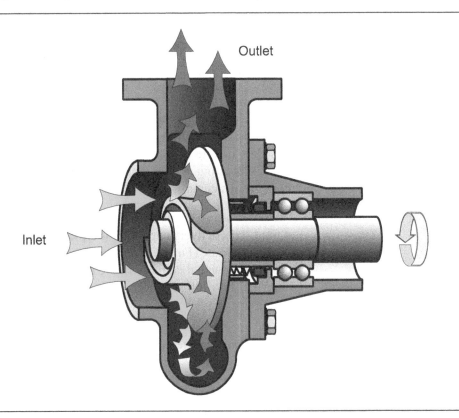

Figure 15-2   Non-positive displacement pump

Although it provides a smooth, continuous flow, the output from this type of pump is reduced as resistance to flow is increased. In fact, it is possible to completely block off the outlet while the pump is running. For this and other reasons, non-positive displacement pumps are seldom used in power hydraulic systems.

These properties make it a more likely choice for a water pump in an internal combustion engine, dishwasher, or washing machine. It could also be used as a supercharge pump for a positive displacement pump.

Positive Displacement

Operation of positive displacement pumps can be seen conceptually in Figure 15-3. This design is typical of hand pumps, such as those used on hydraulic jacks. As the handle is moved to the left, fluid will enter through the lower check valve into the pumping chamber from the reservoir on the lower right. When the handle is then moved to the right, the fluid is forced through the upper check valve to the discharge. The lower check valve prevents fluid from returning to the reservoir.

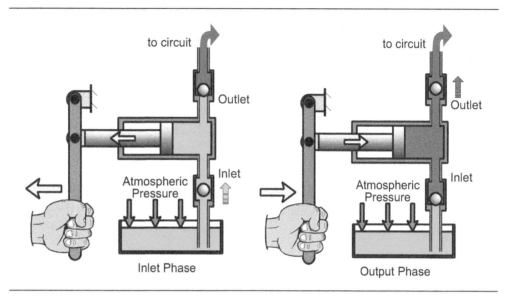

Figure 15-3   Positive displacement pump

This pump has a fixed and predictable displacement. Movement of the handle a certain distance to the right will always generate the corresponding flow out the discharge. Flow per stroke can only be changed by changing the length of the stroke. Delivery in gallons per minute or liters per minute can be changed by changing the length of the stroke or stroke frequency (the number of strokes per minute).

Output of the pump is positive displacement because it is not significantly affected by resistance to flow. Resistance to flow will determine the discharge pressure and the force required to push the handle. However, if the handle is moved, flow will occur or the pump will fail.

This chapter covers the three best known positive displacement pumps: gear pumps, vane pumps, and piston pumps.

Aeration, Cavitation

Aeration and cavitation are two phenomenon that frequently occur in hydraulic systems, and ultimately lead to pump failure. Aeration is caused by air entering the system, and is most pronounced and destructive when passing through the pump. Cavitation is usually caused by inadequate pump inlet conditions, and is equally as destructive. Both are noisy events, not unlike a quantity of steel balls rattling in the system. When this sound is heard, the cause must be identified and corrected as quickly as possible.

Aeration

Aeration occurs when air enters the pump inlet along with the hydraulic fluid. The air can enter due to a leak in the inlet lines (Figure 15-4), or due to a low fluid level in the reservoir. Air bubbles can also be mixed with the hydraulic fluid returning from the hydraulic system, or result from turbulence in the reservoir.

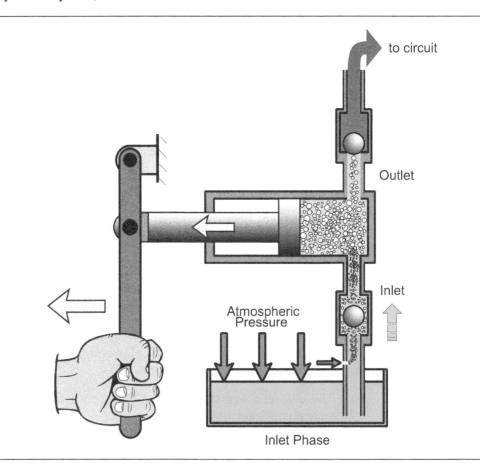

Figure 15-4   Aerated fluid caused by inlet air leak

The low pressure at the pump inlet causes aeration air bubbles to expand. This is illustrated in Figure 15-4; as the handle is moved to the left, pressure is reduced in the cylinder chamber allowing the air bubbles to expand.

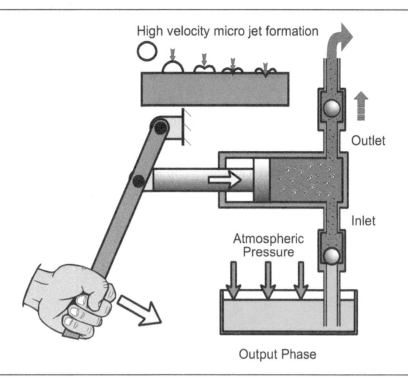

Figure 15-5   Pressurizing the fluid collapses the bubbles

When the handle is moved to the right, closing the inlet check valve and opening the outlet check valve (Figure 15-5), the fluid becomes pressurized which now causes the bubbles to collapse. In the fast moving components of a hydraulic pump, this is a violent collapse, or implosion, and will release large amounts of energy as each bubble forms a micro jet as illustrated in Figure 15-5. This will cause rapid erosion of the internal pump components. Figure 15-6 shows typical short term damage on a piston pump valve plate caused by this erosion.

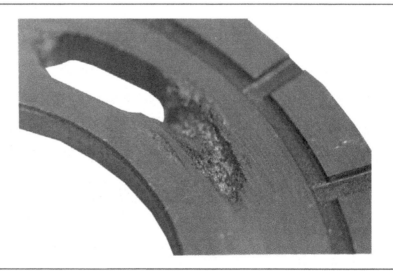

Figure 15-6   Piston pump valve plate erosion caused by aeration or cavitation

Cavitation

Cavitation is similar to aeration, except that rather than already having air bubbles as the fluid approaches the inlet, vapor bubbles form in the fluid at the inlet. These bubbles form due to excessively low inlet pressure (an excessive vacuum) for the fluid being used. The bubbles again collapse violently at the outlet causing component erosion and heat.

A common cause for cavitation is a restriction in the flow of the hydraulic fluid to the inlet side of the pump (Figure 15-7). The inlet hose may be too small, may be bent, or may collapse under vacuum. Excessively clogged inlet screens or filters may not allow fluid to easily reach the pump inlet. Or the fluid may be too viscous to be easily forced into the pump if the fluid temperature is too low or the wrong fluid is used.

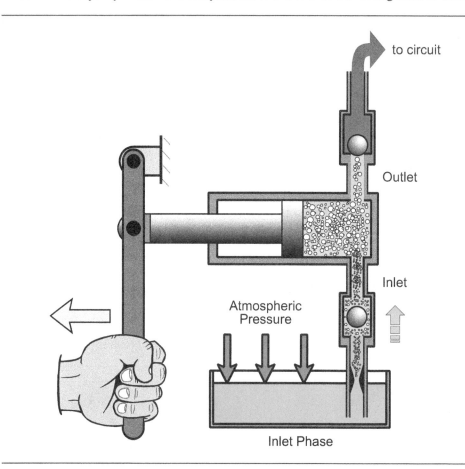

Figure 15-7   Cavitation bubbles formed by a restricted inlet

Cavitation can also occur if the fluid, or part of the fluid, vaporizes too easily. This may happen if the fluid is too hot. Water in the fluid can become water vapor bubbles. Solvent, kerosene, gasoline, diesel fuel and many other volatile liquids that find their way into the hydraulic fluid vaporize easily and lead to cavitation.

Figure 15-8 is a table describing the causes of aeration and cavitation. When either of these events occur, the causes must be investigated and corrected.

Causes of Cavitation and Aeration

Causes of Cavitation	Causes of Aeration
1. Clogged or restricted strainer	1. Low reservoir fluid level
2. High fluid viscosity	2. Defective pump shaft seal
3. Low fluid temperature	3. Return line above fluid level
4. Clogged reservoir breather	4. Improper baffling in the reservoir
5. Pump inlet line too small	5. Loose fitting on pump inlet line
6. Pump too far above reservoir	6. Defective seal on pump inlet line
7. Pump too far from reservoir	7. Incorrect reservoir design
8. Excessive pump RPM	8. Porous hose on pump inlet line
9. Too many bends in pump inlet line	
10. Collapsed hose on pump inlet line	
11. Restriction on pump inlet line	
12. Failure of supercharge pump	

Figure 15-8   Causes of aeration and cavitation

Fixed Displacement Pumps

Fixed displacement pumps have a displacement that cannot be changed without replacing some internal components of the pump. Certain vane and piston pumps, however, can be varied from maximum to zero delivery using an external control mechanism. Some are capable of reversing their flow as the control crosses a center or neutral position. Pumps that can be varied in this manner are called variable displacement pumps.

Gear Pumps

Gear pumps develop flow by carrying fluid between the tooth spaces of two meshed gears. Powered by the drive shaft, the gear known as the drive gear turns the second gear, which is called the driven or idler gear. The pumping chambers formed by the spaces between gear teeth are enclosed by the pump housing, or center section, and side plates (often called wear or pressure plates).

Gear pumps are referred to as an unbalanced design. This is caused by the higher pressures at the pump outlet applying a force on the gears, forcing them toward the lower pressure area of the pump inlet. In addition, there will also be a force generated from the transmission of power from the drive gear to the idler gear. These loads, combined with any external loads, must be borne by the shafts and bearings.

Despite these drawbacks, gear pumps are very popular due to their simplicity and robustness.

External Gear Pumps

The operation of a typical external gear pump (so called because the gear teeth are on the external surface of the hub) is shown in Figure 15-9. The pump carries fluid from the inlet to the outlet in the spaces between gear teeth. The pumping chamber is formed by the gears, pump housing, and side plates. One of the two gears, called the drive gear, is connected to the drive shaft. The other gear, called an idler gear, meshes with the drive gear and is driven by it.

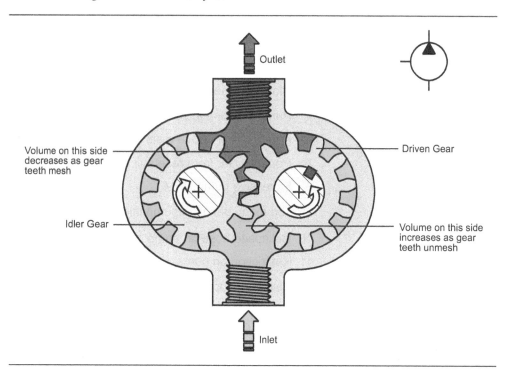

Figure 15-9   External gear pump

As the gear teeth unmesh at the bottom of Figure 15-9, a partial vacuum is created, allowing fluid into the spaces between the teeth. As the gears rotate, the fluid is carried around the housing to the outlet at the top of Figure 15-9. The fluid is expelled from the spaces between the teeth as the gears mesh. The fluid cannot return to the inlet because the spaces between the teeth are filled with a meshing gear as the teeth return to the inlet.

The displacement is equal to the size of each space between teeth multiplied by the number of such spaces which pass in a single input shaft revolution. The number of spaces is equal to the number of teeth on each gear multiplied by two since there are two gears. The flow output of such a pump is equal to the rotational speed (RPM) times the displacement.

Although there can be pressurized wear compensation at the side plates, there is no wear compensation at the cam surface. If the cam ring portion of the housing or the gear teeth wear, the internal leakage of the pump will increase.

As the gears mesh together, any fluid left in the tooth chamber develops a high level of pressure. Decompression notches machined into the side plates relieve this fluid and the corresponding pressure. Any unrelieved fluid is channeled into a groove used to lubricate the bearings.

Multiple and Through Drive External Gear Pumps

External gear pumps are available as single, multiple or through drive versions. The through drive is a single pump with an auxiliary mounting pad and spline coupling in the rear cover. With these accessories, other pumps can be mounted and driven in tandem. This arrangement provides separate inlet and outlet ports for each pump and permits isolation of each circuit. It also allows the use of different fluids for each system.

The double version has two single pumps, each with its own outlet port, but sharing a common inlet port and drive shaft. A double pump can serve two separate hydraulic circuits or supply a single circuit with greater volume.

Multiple units consist of two or more pumping sections driven by a common drive shaft. The double pumps are furnished with a single common inlet, while the triple and quadruple pumps normally have one less inlet than the total number of sections. All inlet ports are internally connected and each pump section has a separate outlet. Multiple pumps save installation costs and space and also offer less chance of leakage.

Certain rating limitations should be observed when multiple pump configurations are used with pumps that have different displacements. The high speed is limited by the lowest high-speed rating of the combination. The low speed is limited to the highest low-speed rating of the combination.

When outlet flows are combined, the pressure limit represents the lowest pressure level of the combination.

Multiple pump configurations with the same displacement use ratings that are common to single pumps. These pressure ratings are also limited by drive shaft torsional loading. The shaft loadings for each pump should be reviewed to ensure that the combined torsional loads do not exceed the drive shaft torsional capability.

Internal Gear Pumps

An internal gear pump replaces the external idler gear with an internal gear (so called because the gear teeth are internal to the gear). A typical type of internal gear pump is the crescent seal pump shown in Figure 15-10. This pump design consists of an external gear that meshes with the teeth that are on the inside of a larger gear. The pumping chambers are formed between the gear teeth. A crescent seal is machined into the pump body between the inlet and outlet where clearance between the teeth is maximum. In this way, the two ports are separated while the gears carry oil past the seal.

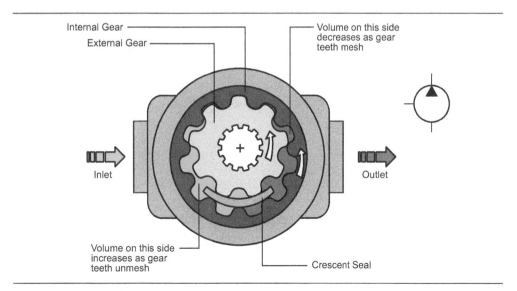

Figure 15-10   Crescent seal type internal gear pump

Like the external type, internal gear drives are fixed displacement and are available in single and multiple configurations.

One of the most common types of internal gear pump is the gerotor pump (Figure 15-11). A gerotor pump combines an external gear inside an internal gear. The inner gear is keyed to the shaft and has one less tooth than the outer gear. As the gears revolve, teeth of the inner gear are in constant contact with the outer gear, but with one more tooth, the outer gear rotates slower. Spaces between the rotating teeth increase during the first half of each turn, allowing fluid in. They decrease in the last half, forcing the fluid into the discharge port.

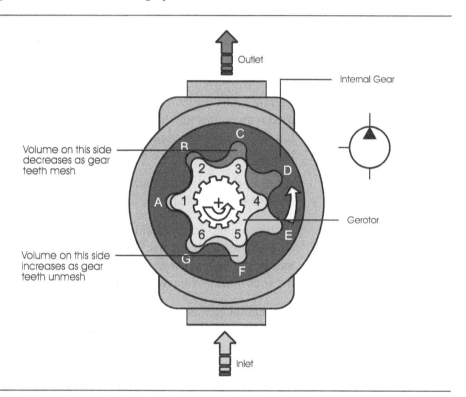

Figure 15-11   Gerotor type internal gear pump

As fixed displacement pumps, gear pumps provide two ways of altering volume levels. The first is to replace the existing gears with gears of different dimensions. The second is to vary the volume by changing the speed at which the drive gear turns.

Vane Pumps

Unbalanced Design Vane Pumps

The basic pumping elements of a vane pump are the slotted rotor, vanes and cam ring, as shown in Figure 15-12. The vanes are fitted to the rotor slots and follow the inner surface of the cam ring as the rotor turns. Generally, a minimum starting speed of 600 RPM throws the vanes out against the ring, where they are held by centrifugal force. Pumping chambers are formed between the vanes and are enclosed by the rotor, ring and two side plates.

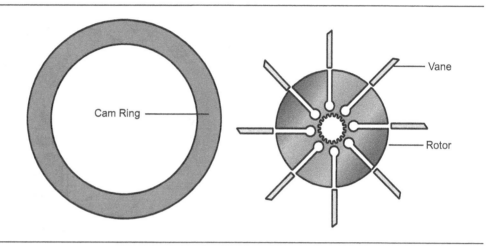

Figure 15-12   Basic pumping elements of a vane pump

The operating principle of a vane pump is illustrated in Figure 15-13. A slotted rotor is splined to the drive shaft and turns inside a cam ring. Because the ring is offset (eccentric) from the rotor centerline, the chambers increase in size on one side of center and decrease in size on the opposite side.

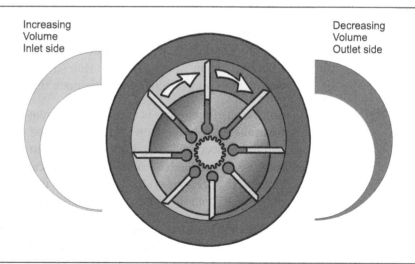

Figure 15-13   Eccentricity between rotor and cam ring

Figure 15-14 shows the relationship between the eccentric rotor and cam ring to the inlet and outlet ports of the pumping chamber. On the left side of Figure 15-14, the chambers are increasing in size, creating a partial vacuum that allows fluid to be forced into the chambers on the inlet side. The chambers become progressively smaller on the right side of the figure, forcing the fluid out the outlet. Displacement of the pump is determined by the difference in volume of the chambers at the inlet and outlet regions, multiplied by the number of chambers.

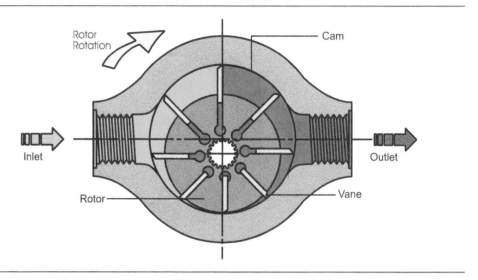

Figure 15-14   Rotating group with inlet and outlet ports

Rotation of the rotor, therefore, causes the fluid to be swept from the inlet to the outlet by the vanes. The vanes contact the cam ring surface, and are lubricated by the fluid. The design compensates for vane tip and cam wear by allowing the vanes to extend farther out of the rotor slots.

The vanes are held against the cam ring surface by centrifugal force. The spinning of the rotor causes a centrifugal force which pushes the vanes out of the rotor slots. Effective sealing at the vane cam ring surface requires that the rotor be turning at a certain minimum speed, depending upon the pump and the operating conditions.

Since centrifugal force is usually insufficient to overcome high pressures at the outer tip of the vane on the outlet side, pressurized oil is also supplied under the vanes. One method of accomplishing this pressure balance is to provide a passageway from the rotor surface to the base of the vane. This causes the pressure under the vane to be equal to the pressure on the top. Another method is to supply pump outlet pressure to the bottom of all the vanes, as illustrated in Figure 15-14.

Pumps of this design are unbalanced, because high (outlet) pressure on one side of the rotor and low (inlet) pressure on the other side, creates a loading on the rotor that must be supported by the shaft and shaft bearings. This leads to larger components, that result in a larger pump.

Balanced Vane Pumps

The difference between the low pressure at the inlet and the high pressure at the outlet will cause a significant force to be transmitted to the rotor and therefore to the pump shaft and bearings. In Figure 15-14 this force will be to the left. To overcome this problem, Harry Vickers introduced the balanced vane design in about 1935. Today, all fixed displacement vane pumps use a balanced design.

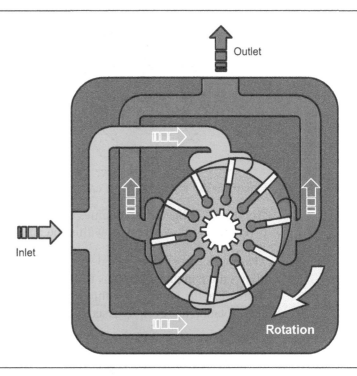

Figure 15-15   Balanced vane pump design

The circular cam ring of the unbalanced design is replaced with an elliptical cam ring in the balanced design. Figure 15-15 shows the balanced design principle. This design has opposing sets of inlet and outlet ports. Since the ports are positioned exactly opposite each other, the high forces generated at the outlet ports cancel each other out. This prevents side loading of the pump shaft and bearings and means that the shaft and bearings only have to carry the torque load and external loads. Reduced loading on the shaft and bearings leads to smaller components, resulting in a more compact pump design.

Since there are two lobes to the cam ring per revolution, the displacement of the pump is equal to twice the amount of fluid which is pumped by the vanes moving from one inlet to its corresponding outlet.

This configuration forms two sets of outlet ports on opposite sides of the rotor that are connected through passages within the housing. Because the ports are positioned 180 degrees apart, forces caused by pressure buildup on one side are canceled out by equal but opposite forces on the other.

The displacement of most balanced design vane pumps cannot be adjusted. Interchangeable rings (Figure 15-16) with different cams are available, making it possible to modify a pump, increasing or decreasing its displacement.

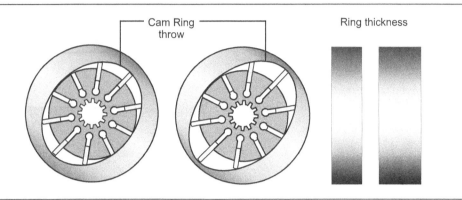

Figure 15-16   Interchangeable cam rings provide a selection of flows

Another modification sometimes used is reversing the drive shaft direction without reversing the flow direction within the pump.

The ring is repositioned 180 degrees from its original position (Figure 15-17). This allows the pumping chambers to increase in size as they pass the inlet porting and decrease at the outlet. Flow through the pump remains the same, even though drive shaft rotation has been reversed.

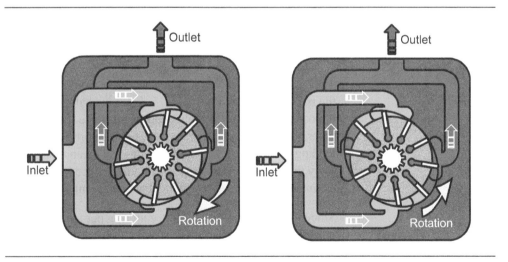

Figure 15-17   Rotating the cam ring 180° reverses the direction of rotation

"Square" vane type pumps (Figure 15-18) are hydraulically balanced and have a fixed displacement.

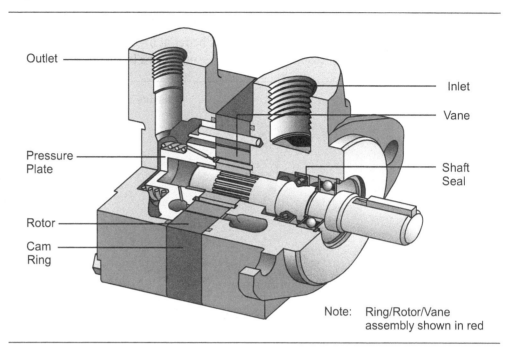

Figure 15-18   Fixed displacement "Square Pump"

The cartridge consists of a ring that is sandwiched between the pump body and cover, a rotor, 12 vanes and a spring loaded pressure plate. The inlet port is in the body and the outlet in the cover, which may be assembled in any of four positions for convenience in piping. The spring holds the pressure plate in position against the ring at all times.

Increasing outlet pressure acts with the spring to offset pressures within the cartridge that can separate the pressure plate from the ring. Proper running clearance is determined by the relative ring and rotor widths.

The pumping action needed for initial starting is generated by spinning the rotor and shaft fast enough for centrifugal force to throw the vanes out against the ring.

An interrupted annular groove in the pressure plate permits free flow of pressurized fluid into chambers under the vanes as they move out of the rotor slots. Return flow is restricted as the vanes move back, holding them firmly against the ring.

High Performance Vane Pumps

Outlet pressure under the vanes causes a greater vane tip force against the cam surface at the inlet side of the pump. Certain high performance pumps seek to optimize the vane extension pressure by using a combination of outlet pressure and surface pressure. The fluid passages in the rotor are designed so that the combination is varied appropriately as the rotor turns.

Figure 15-19 illustrates a high performance pump design in which intra-vanes, or small inserts, are used in the vanes. Full outlet pressure is fed into the intra-vane area continuously to generate enough force to hold the vane tip against the cam ring at all times. Meanwhile, rotor surface pressure is applied to the underside of the vane. This combination can work better at higher speeds and higher pressures than either outlet pressure or surface pressure by itself.

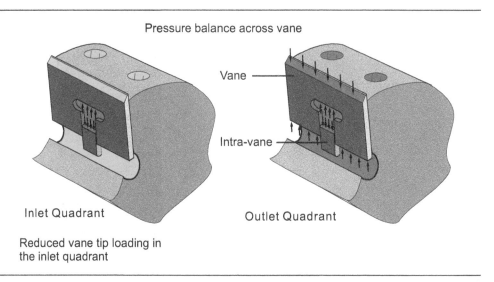

Pressure balance across vane

Vane

Intra-vane

Inlet Quadrant

Outlet Quadrant

Reduced vane tip loading in
the inlet quadrant

Figure 15-19   Vane and intra-vane assembly

Holes drilled through the rotor segments equalize pressure above and below each vane at all times. Outlet pressure is constantly applied to the small area between the vane and intra-vane. This pressure, along with centrifugal force, holds the vanes in contact with the ring in the inlet quadrants to assure proper "tracking" (see Figure 15-20).

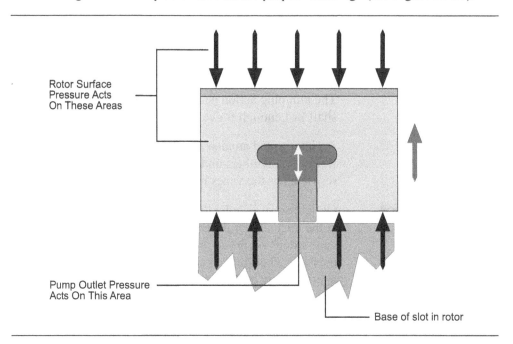

Rotor Surface
Pressure Acts
On These Areas

Pump Outlet Pressure
Acts On This Area

Base of slot in rotor

Figure 15-20   Outlet pressure in the intra-vane area assures vane-cam contact

Passages are formed in the rotor and side plates to port outlet fluid into the intra-vane cavity continuously, while rotor surface fluid is ported into the cavity under the vane. The net effect is a markedly reduced force under the vane while it is traversing the inlet side of the cam ring, because only the intra-vane cavity is pressurized. While the vane is traversing the outlet side of the cam ring, pressurized fluid from the outlet is fed both under the vanes and in the intra-vane cavities, assuring the vane is pressure balanced and will not be forced into the vane slot.

Figure 15-21 illustrates the porting in the rotor that provides this full cycle balance.

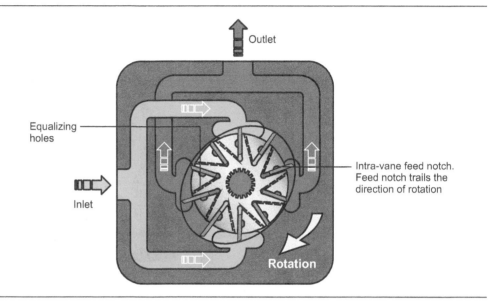

Figure 15-21   Porting in rotor and side plates provides vane pressure balance

For fast replacement, the internal components used in high performance vane pumps are preassembled into a cartridge. The cartridge consists of a ring, rotor, vanes, vane inserts, outlet support plate, inlet support plate, locating pins and attaching screws (Figure 15-22). They are assembled as right or left hand rotating units, but can be reassembled for opposite rotation if required. Arrows and locating pins serve as guides. When properly assembled, flow direction remains the same in both the right and left hand rotating units. The fully assembled cartridge is shown in Figure 15-23, and installed in Figure 15-24.

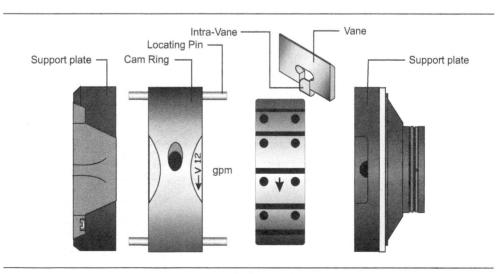

Figure 15-22   High performance pump cartridge components

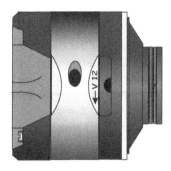

Figure 15-23   Intra-vane pump cartridge assembly

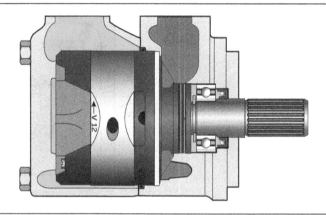

Figure 15-24   Intra-vane pump cartridge installed

Figure 15-25 is a cut away view showing the internal elements of a high performance vane pump. It can be seen in this view, and in Figure 15-24, how the rear cover can be removed and the cartridge extracted without further disassembly of the pump. In many installations, this can be a distinct advantage in that the cartridge can be replaced without removing the pump from the application. This is frequently the solution to a failed pump, as it can very quickly be returned to service.

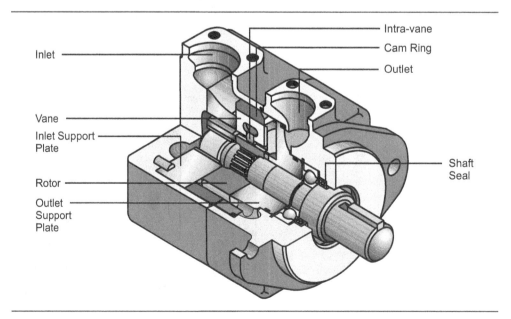

Figure 15-25   Intra-vane pump assembly

Like the square pumps, the high performance pumps are built so that the relative positions of the ports can be easily changed to any one of four combinations. This is done by removing the rear cover assembly bolts and rotating the cover in 90 degree increments, as the four bolt holes are concentric.

Double Vane Pump Assemblies

Double pumps provide a single power source capable of serving two separate hydraulic circuits or providing greater volume through combined delivery. Most double pumps have a common inlet in a center housing, as shown in Figure 15-26. The outlet for one unit, usually the larger of the two is in the shaft end body. The second outlet is in the cover.

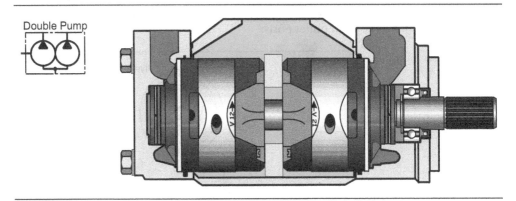

Figure 15-26   A double pump with a single inlet

Some types of double pumps have separate inlets, although they can be mounted in multiples. Both kinds need only one drive motor, however, double pumps that have separate inlets require separate piping. A significant advantage to the tandem style of double pump is that the pumps can be of different types, and more than two pumps can be ganged. A combination of gear, vane and piston can be assembled for operation on one drive shaft in this manner.

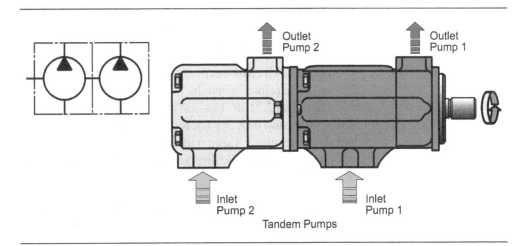

Figure 15-27   A double (tandem) pump with separate inlets

Cartridge construction for double pumps is essentially the same as in single units, making numerous combinations of sizes and displacements possible.

Piston Pumps

All piston pumps operate on the principle that a piston reciprocating in a bore will draw fluid in as it is retracted and expel it as it moves forward.

The two basic designs are radial and axial. Both are available as fixed or variable displacement models. A radial pump has the pistons arranged radially in a cylinder block, while the pistons in the axial units are parallel to each other and to the axis of the cylinder block. Axial piston pumps may be further divided into in-line (swash plate) and bent-axis types.

Figure 15-28 illustrates a conceptual piston pump. As the drive shaft is rotated one revolution, the piston makes one complete cycle in its bore. The check valves at the bottom of the bore assure that the fluid travels in the correct direction through the inlet and outlet ports.

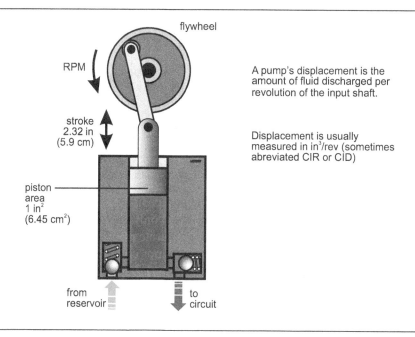

Figure 15-28   The piston pump concept

The piston has a cross-sectional area of 1 in^2 (6.45 cm^2), and a stroke of 2.31 inches (5.9 cm). Therefore, when the piston is withdrawn from its bore, the inlet check valve will open, and 2.31 in^3 (38 cm^3) of fluid will enter the chamber (1 in^2 x 2.31 in). When the piston moves back to its starting position, the inlet check valve will close and the outlet check valve will open, allowing the piston to expel 2.31 in^3 from the chamber. Therefore, the displacement of this pump is 2.31 in^3/rev or CIR (38 cm^3/rev or CCR).

Given a drive shaft speed of 100 RPM, this pump would be delivering 231 in^3 per minute (2.31 in^3/rev x 100 rev/min), the equivalent of one gallon per minute.

Size Range

Piston pumps are an efficient hydraulic power source, available in an exceptionally wide range of flow and pressure capabilities. Model sizes range from less than one cubic inch per revolution (CIR) to several hundred CIR. Pressure ratings range from about 2,000 psi (140 bar, 14,000 kPa) to higher than 7,000 psi (480 bar, 48,000 kPa).

Radial Piston Pumps

In a radial pump, the cylinder block rotates on a stationary pintle inside a circular reaction ring or rotor (Figure 15-29). As the block rotates, centrifugal force, charging pressure, or some form of mechanical action causes the pistons to follow the inner surface of the ring, which is offset from the centerline of the cylinder block. Porting in the pintle (Figure 15-30) permits the pistons to take in fluid as they move outward and discharge it as they move in.

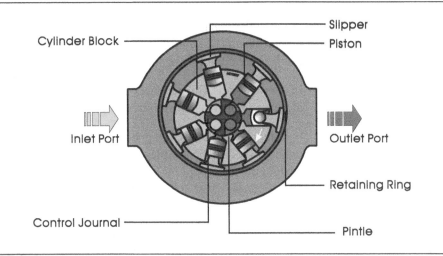

Figure 15-29   Cross section of a radial piston pump

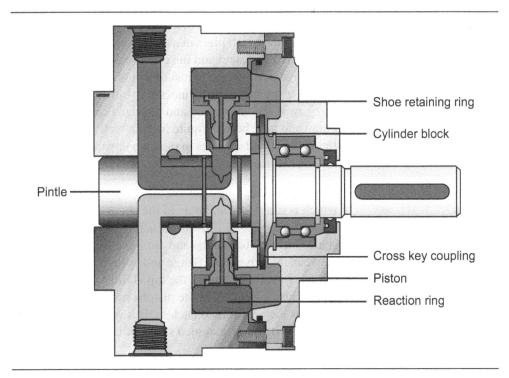

Figure 15-30   Pintle porting in a radial piston pump

Pump displacement is determined by the size and number of pistons and the length of their stroke. Timing of the pump (the point in the circle when the piston is exposed to the pressure port or the inlet port) is such that two or more pistons are discharging their fluid at the same time. Also, two or more pistons may be passing the inlet port at the same time. This provides a very smooth transition of high pressure fluid to the outlet, reducing flow "ripple" and helping to maintain a quiet system.

Displacement of radial piston pumps can be low, but the more popular use of them is in the high displacement range. Large diameter pistons with long strokes can result in displacements of 200 or more CIR (3,275 or more CCR). In addition, sets of pistons can be banked in two or three rows, doubling or tripling the displacement.

In some models, the displacement can be varied by moving the reaction ring to increase or decrease piston travel.

Axial Piston Pumps

In axial piston pumps, the pistons reciprocate parallel to the axis of rotation of the cylinder block. The simplest type of axial piston pump is the swash plate in-line design, the most popular type and produced by a large number of manufacturers. A less common but also viable design is the bent-axis type.

Like radial piston pumps, the displacement of axial piston pumps is determined by the area of the piston, the piston stroke length and the number of pistons. Displacements range from about 0.75 CIR (about 12 CCR) to about 47 CIR (750 CCR). Infrequently, some units are larger.

Piston pumps have several sets of surfaces which move with respect to one another, with the piston motion inside the bore being the most obvious. The sliding of piston shoes on the swash plate in axial in-line pumps is another example. Often one of the surfaces will be steel and the other bronze to lower friction. Care is also taken during the design of the pump to insure that lubrication flow is provided to the surfaces which need it. A pump drain, connected to either the reservoir or pump inlet, is provided to carry away the lubrication and leakage flows. This lubrication fluid also helps cool the pump and may become quite heated itself. Because of the closely fitted parts and finely machined surfaces in piston pumps, cleanliness and good quality fluids are vital to long service life.

Bent Axis Piston Pumps

Bent axis axial pumps rely on the reciprocating motion of pistons in a cylinder block, which is caused by an angle in the connection from the drive shaft to the cylinder block. Figure 15-31 illustrates such a pump. The piston rods are attached to the drive shaft flange by ball joints and are forced in and out of their bores as the distance between the drive shaft flange and cylinder block changes. The piston at the bottom is retracted, while the one at the top is fully forward in the bore. The ports are arranged in the valve plate so that the pistons pass the inlet as they are pulled out and pass the outlet as they are forced back in. It is generally easy to recognize this type of pump due to the distinctive angled shape of the pump housing.

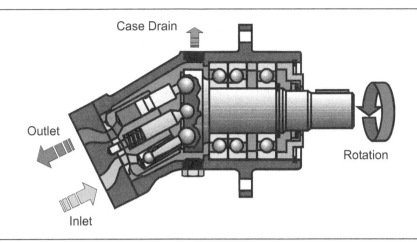

Figure 15-31   A bent-axis piston pump

The angle of the pistons relative to the drive shaft, usually 23 or 24 degrees, but may be as high as 30 degrees, creates high side forces on the shaft, leading to a robust shaft and bearings. This, coupled with the angled housing, results in a larger pump envelope than the equivalent size in-line design. Bent-axis piston pumps are very efficient, however, which provides for a lower start-up torque and less heat generation caused by mechanical losses.

In-Line Piston Pumps

The cylinder block in this pump is turned by the drive shaft. Pistons fitted to bores in the cylinder block are connected through piston shoes and a shoe plate, so that the shoes bear against an angled swash plate. The shoe plate (or retaining ring) makes sure that the piston shoes follow the swash plate.

As the block turns (Figure 15-32), the piston shoes follow the swash plate, causing the pistons to reciprocate. The ports are arranged in the valve plate so that the pistons pass the inlet as they are pulled out and pass the outlet as they are forced back in.

Like all piston pumps, the displacement of axial piston pumps is determined by the size and number of pistons, as well as the stroke length. Stroke length is determined by the angle of the swash plate.

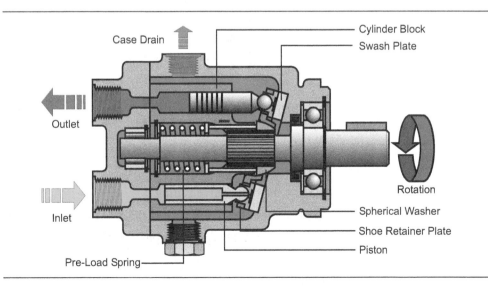

Figure 15-32   An in-line piston pump

The basic components of an in-line piston pump are shown in Figure 15-33. Side forces on the shaft and bearings are lower in the in-line design, which allows for smaller shaft and bearing components, partly because the swash plate angle is less on this type of design. Maximum swash plate angle on an in-line pump is usually 18 or 19 degrees. Although the in-line design is not as efficient as the bent-axis design, it is a more economical design and is therefore more popular.

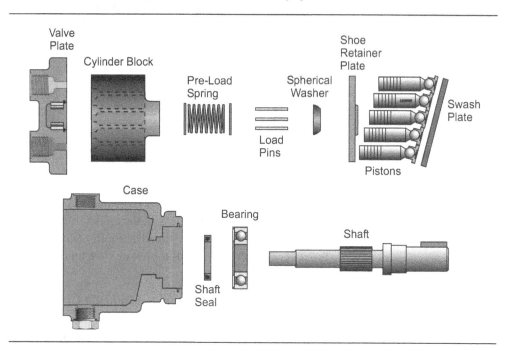

Figure 15-33   Components of an in-line piston pump

Variable Displacement Pumps

Fixed displacement pumps discharge a set volume of fluid regardless of the system requirements. This volume can be changed only by changing the drive speed of the pump, which is impractical when the prime mover is an electric motor. If the system requires less fluid than the pump is discharging, the balance of the flow must find an alternate path which is usually over a relief valve and back to the reservoir.

This amount of excess flow, at the relief valve pressure setting, results in lost energy to the system and heat being added to the fluid and to the reservoir. The amount of heat can be approximated by the formula:

Formula 15-7

BTU/Hr $=$ PSI $\times$ GPM $\times$ 1.5

Where:

BTU $=$ British Thermal Unit

PSI $=$ the relief valve setting

GPM $=$ the flow passing over the relief valve

1.5 $=$ 2,545 BTUs per hour per horsepower divided by 1,714

Frequently, a flow control or directional control valve will be used to reduce the system flow to part of the circuit. When this is done, it is called "metering" the flow. Figure 15-34 illustrates the result of metering flow in a circuit, and the resulting wasted power.

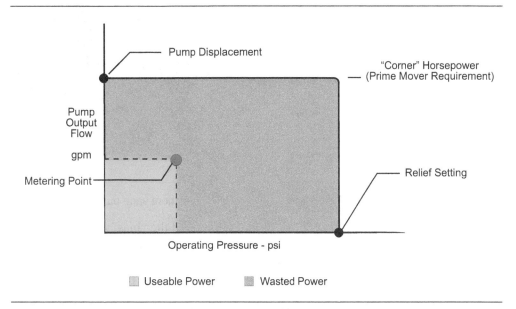

Figure 15-34   Metering losses in a fixed displacement system

To conserve energy and to prevent generating heat, variable displacement pumps are used. These pumps provide a means of changing the pump's displacement so that only sufficient fluid is provided to the system, and no more. The heat formula shows that if the flow passing over a relief valve can be reduced, the heat generated is reduced. Furthermore, the power required to drive the pump is also reduced, based on the formula:

Formula 15-8

$$hp = \frac{P \times GPM}{1,714 \times Eff}$$

Where:

hp = the horsepower to drive the pump

P = the pump output pressure

GPM = the pump output flow

Eff = the pump overall efficiency

1,714 = a constant to resolve the units

Reduced input power, reduced energy loss and less heat generation make the concept of a variable displacement pump quite attractive. Unbalanced vane pumps and all piston pumps lend themselves to a concept of variable displacement.

Variable Displacement Vane Pumps

The variable vane pump is an unbalanced design, and creates the changing displacement by moving the cam ring. Figure 15-35 shows the movable cam ring and the pistons that cause it to move. By moving the cam to the left, the differential volume between inlet and outlet is reduced, because the eccentricity between the cam and rotor is reduced. As the cam is moved back toward the right in Figure 15-35, pump displacement is increased.

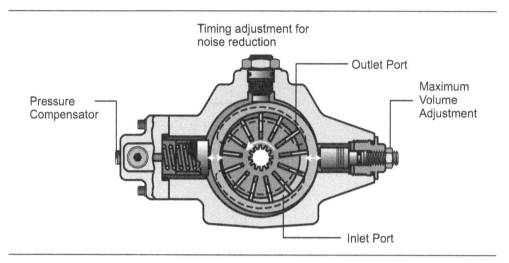

Figure 15-35   Variable displacement vane pump

The piston on the left is called the "bias" piston., and attempts to maintain maximum displacement at all times. The piston on the right is called the "control" piston When system pressure reaches a preset level, the control piston will force the cam to the left. It overcomes the bias piston and the pump displacement will be reduced.

The mechanism that operates the control piston is called a "compensator." There are many versions of compensators, the more common of which will be covered later in this chapter.

Variable Displacement Radial Piston Pumps

Figure 15-36 shows a typical radial piston pump that has been modified for variable displacement. It works on the same principle as the variable vane pump, in that the outer cam is moved left or right to change eccentricity with the cylinder block, and change piston stroke which changes displacement. A bias piston on the left, and a control piston on the right, move the cam left or right to change displacement.

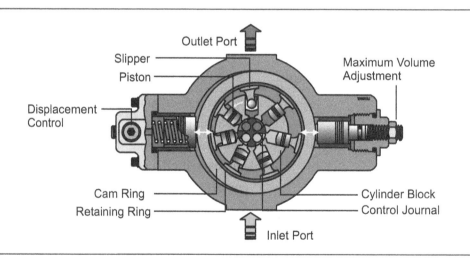

Figure 15-36   Variable displacement radial piston pump

Variable displacement radial piston pumps operate very well, and are usually very reliable and durable. They perform equally as well at high pressures and low pressures, although cost usually prohibits their use in low pressure applications.

Variable Displacement Bent-Axis Piston Pumps

Figure 15-37 shows a cross-sectional view of a bent-axis axial piston pump. Rotation of the drive shaft causes the pistons and cylinder block to rotate, which in turn causes the pistons to move in and out of the cylinder bore. As the angle between the cylinder block and drive shaft (Figure 15-38) changes, the pistons' travel in their respective bores changes, increasing or decreasing the pump displacement.

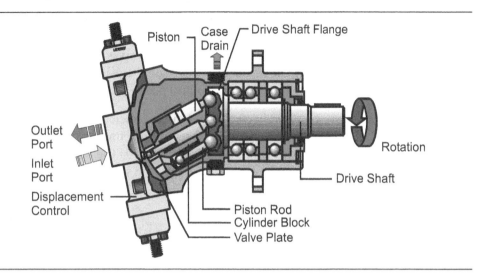

Figure 15-37   Variable displacement bent-axis piston pump

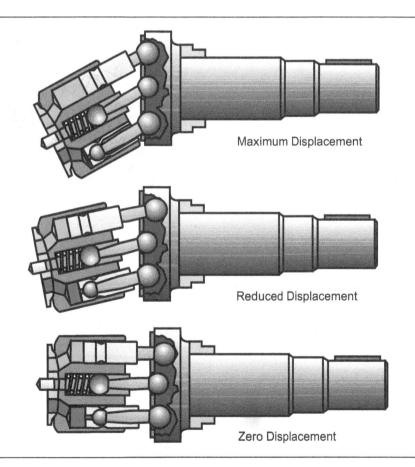

Figure 15-38   Displacement is controlled by the angle of the cylinder block

The displacement angle is controlled by the displacement control valve mounted on the rear of the pump. The displacement control valve consists of a compensator, a bias piston and a control piston. The bias piston attempts to keep the cylinder block at its maximum displacement angle at all times, and the control piston will stroke the cylinder block to a lesser displacement angle as the system requires.

The displacement may also be controlled manually by operating the displacement control valve with a lever. The lever may be a handle, an adjustment knob or a hand wheel, used to control and set speed by controlling pump output. A typical application might be a conveyor drive. The displacement angle of the cylinder block is still governed by the control piston.

A purely mechanical displacement control is viable, and used occasionally. It consists of a handwheel and screw adjustment mechanism connected directly to the cylinder block as shown in Figure 15-39. The handwheel is turned to set the angle of the cylinder block, and thus the system flow.

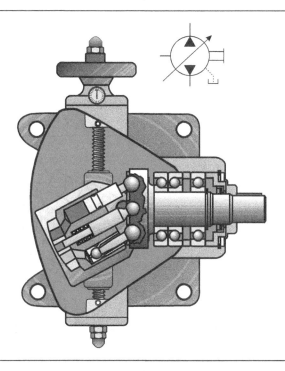

Figure 15-39   Mechanical displacement control

Variable Displacement In-Line Piston Pump

The most popular design of piston pump is the in-line design, so called because the pistons and cylinder block are in-line with the drive shaft. Figure 15-40 is a cross-sectional view of an in-line design.

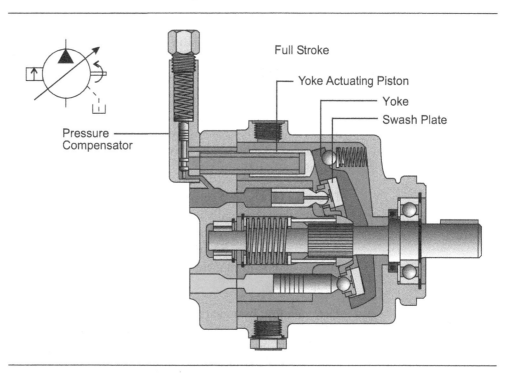

Figure 15-40   Cross section of an in-line piston pump

Rotation of the drive shaft causes the cylinder block and pistons to rotate, which causes the pistons to move in and out of their bores as they slide over the angled swash plate. The swash plate is supported by a yoke, which pivots on bearings. Two types of bearings are prevalent; either a pair of roller or needle bearings on pintles, or a bushing that supports a saddle type yoke. Pivoting the yoke changes the angle of the swash plate, which changes the stroke of the pistons in and out of their bores. Displacement of the pump decreases with a decrease in the swash plate angle (Figure 15-41).

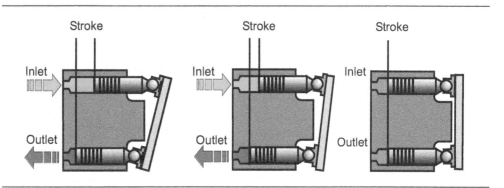

Figure 15-41   Pump displacement is based on swash plate angle

The yoke can be pivoted manually or hydraulically, the most common being hydraulic. Only smaller pumps, about 2.5 in^3/revolution (about 40 cm^3/revolution), can be stroked manually due to the high internal forces on the yoke with larger pumps. Manual operation is popular on smaller hydrostatic transmissions, where the handle becomes the forward reverse and speed control lever for regulating a conveyor drive or mixing drum.

Hydraulic stroke control is accomplished with a control piston working against a bias piston or a bias spring. The bias spring is quite common, as shown in Figure 15-40, although it is limited to pumps with displacements below about 5 in³/revolution (about 82 cm³/revolution) due to the high yoke forces in larger pumps. Both the bias spring and the bias piston perform the same function, to keep the yoke at maximum angle when the control piston is not forcing it back.

Variable Displacement Pump Controls

Controls for in-line piston pumps, called compensators, have one single purpose; to pressurize the control piston and force the yoke to reduce its angle, reducing pump displacement. There are many types of compensators for regulating different parameters of a hydraulic system, but the only control function they perform is reducing pump flow.

Two broad categories of compensators are hydraulic and electrohydraulic. Both types include a valve, usually mounted on the pump, that regulates flow and pressure to the control piston. The hydraulic compensator reacts to hydraulic system parameters such as pressure or flow, and the electrohydraulic compensator reacts to electronic signals that may come from a controller, a transducer, a power amplifier, a control card or computer, etc.

There are four basic variable displacement pump controls. Each type of control has many variations for special or custom purposes, but all are either hydraulic controls (pressure limiting compensators, load sensing compensators or torque limiting compensators) or electrohydraulic controls. Regardless of their circuit function, they all ultimately perform a function as shown in Figure 15-42: they apply a pressurized fluid, either from the pressurized outlet of the pump or from a separate pilot pump, to the control piston to reduce the displacement and the output flow of the pump.

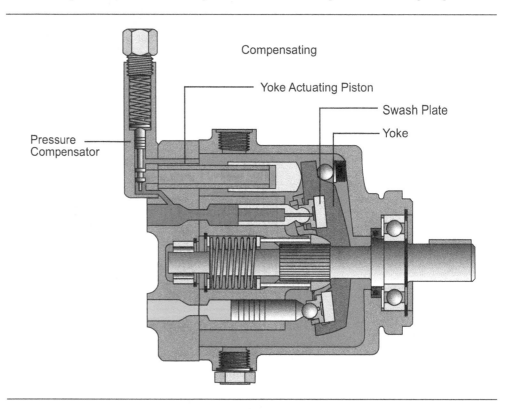

Figure 15-42   Compensators control the stroke adjusting piston

Pressure Limiting Compensator

A pressure limiting compensator is shown schematically in Figure 15-43 with representation of an in-line piston pump rotating group with a stroking piston (large diameter) and "bias" piston (small diameter). The bias piston uses pump outlet pressure to keep the pump "biased" toward full displacement. A directional control valve symbol is also shown, with pump outlet flow connected to the valve inlet, or "P," port.

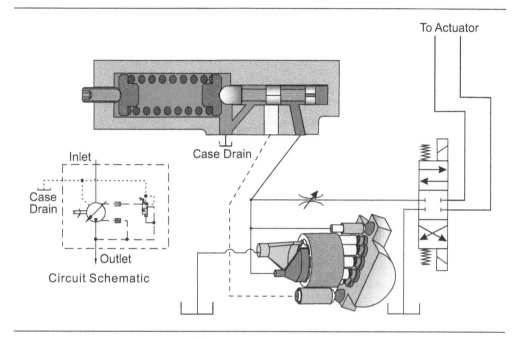

Figure 15-43   Pressure limiting compensator operation

The compensator consists of a housing containing a control spool, a load spring, end caps and a load spring adjustment mechanism. The adjustment sets a pre-load on the load spring, which acts against the control spool, to determine the pressure setting for the pump.

System pressure (pump outlet pressure) is fed to the control spool area and, through small passages, to the right end of the spool. As long as system pressure is below the load spring setting, the control spool will remain to the right, and flow will be prevented from passing through the valve. Any small leakage that may pass the spool will be drained to the pump housing (case drain), which is connected to the reservoir.

As system pressure rises and approaches the setting of the load spring, the control spool begins to shift left, allowing fluid to pass the spool land into the control piston area. Because the control piston diameter (and area) is larger than the bias piston diameter, the pump yoke will begin to reduce its angle. It will continue to reduce its angle as the system pressure rises, until the output flow of the pump is low enough to maintain the system pressure at the load spring setting, or until the pump flow is reduced to zero.

When system pressure decreases, the spool begins to move to the right, closing flow to the control piston and allowing fluid in the control piston to vent to the pump housing. The yoke begins to stroke out, providing more pump output flow. The compensator adjusts the yoke in this manner, regulating the correct amount of pump flow to maintain system pressure at or below load spring setting.

Figure 15-44 shows how the system flow has been reduced to the metering point level, and also shows the energy savings that resulted. Compare this figure to Figure 15-34 to see the difference in wasted energy.

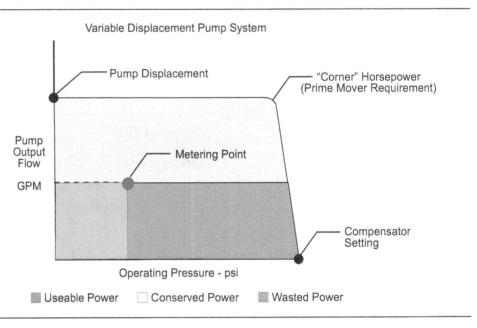

Figure 15-44   Energy saved by pressure compensation

If the system flow requirement is reduced to "zero," such as when the control valve is in neutral or the actuator reaches the end of its stroke, the pressure limiting compensator will cause the pump to reduce the stroke to "zero." This can happen very quickly; typical reaction times may range from 25 to 75 milliseconds (0.025 to 0.075 seconds) to stroke from full displacement to "zero" displacement. In practice, the pump does not stroke to a true "zero," as a small amount of flow is required for lubrication and leakage within the pump.

Load Sensing Compensator

Figure 15-45 shows an in-line piston pump with a compensator containing two spools. The one to the right is a pressure limiting spool, and the one to the left is a load sensing spool. The pressure limiting spool is identical to the pressure limiting spool of Figure 15-42. Because there is no pressure limiting feature to a load sensing compensator, nearly all contain an additional pressure limiting component.

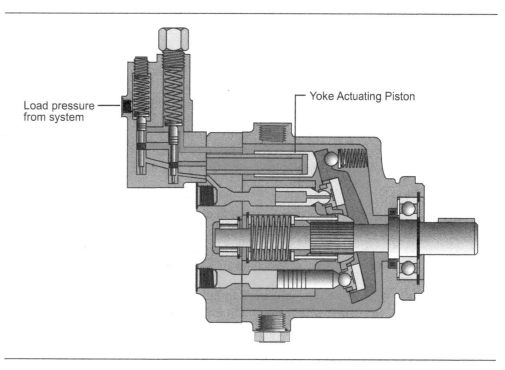

Figure 15-45   Piston pump with load sensing and pressure limiting compensator

Figure 15-46 is a schematic representation of this same dual purpose compensator. The upper spool in the figure is the load sensing spool. It operates basically the same as the pressure limiting spool, with the exception that the spring is light, providing for a load setting of about 200 – 400 psi system pressure. In addition to the spring, however, pressure is sensed downstream of the control valve, and is fed to the spring chamber. The downstream pressure is sensed through a shuttle valve connected to the two sides of an actuator, such that the higher of the two pressures (the loaded side of the actuator) will be sensed by the compensator. The combined load against the load sensing spool is the actuator pressure plus 200 – 400 psi.

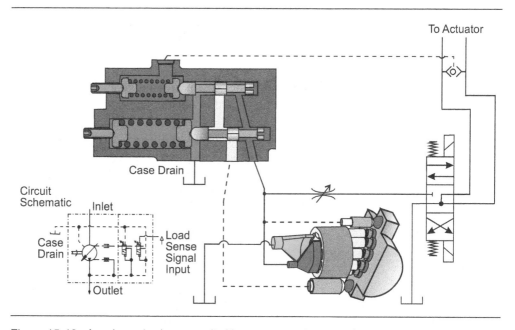

Figure 15-46   Load sensing/pressure limiting compensator operation

The lower spool is the pressure limiting spool, and acts the same as the spool described in Figure 15-43.

Figure 15-44 illustrates the reduction of energy waste by the use of a pressure limiting compensator during a metering operation. There is still a significant amount of lost energy, however, because the pump is operating against maximum system pressure. A load sensing compensator addresses this element of waste.

The pump rotating group (cylinder block and pistons) discharges fluid to the outlet which is fed constantly to the bias piston, the compensator and the system. System flow is through a flow control valve and a directional control valve.

The bias piston is holding the yoke at its maximum angle, such that the pump is discharging maximum flow. Any resistance to the flow, due to the flow control valve, the directional valve or the actuator, will create a pressure at the pump outlet. This pressure will be transmitted into the pressure limiting spool area and the load sensing spool area, and attempt to move both spools to the left against their adjustable springs.

The schematic in Figure 15-46 shows the directional valve centered, such that there is no flow going to the actuator. The actuator pressure is therefore "zero," providing no sensing pressure to the load sensing spool. The spool is regulating the maximum pump pressure at the load sensing spring setting of 200 – 400 psi. This is called "stand-by" pressure, and represents a very significant power savings when the system is doing no work.

The work operation may cause the pressure in either of the actuator lines to rise (depending on which direction the actuator is moving). The shuttle valve detects the highest of the two actuator line pressures, and transmits this pressure to the spring chamber of the load sensing spool. This pressure, plus the equivalent pressure of the load sensing spool spring, now acts upon the load sensing spool to regulate system pressure. Pump outlet pressure will be regulated at the load pressure, plus the value of the load sensing spring. The pressure drop across the flow control and directional control valve will therefore be held constant at the value of the load sensing spring, regardless of changing load pressures.

If working pressure exceeds the pressure limiting spring setting, the pressure limiting spool will move to the right and the pump will now be regulated at the maximum pressure setting.

By regulating the system pressure to a level slightly above the load pressure requirement, an additional element of energy savings has been accomplished during the metering phase, as shown in Figure 15-47. This figure can be compared with Figures 15-34 and 15-44 to illustrate the magnitude of potential energy savings available with the load sensing compensator.

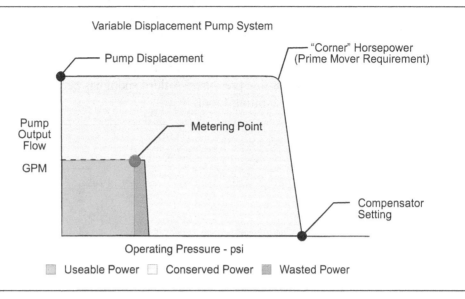

Figure 15-47   Energy savings caused by load sensing

Torque Limiting Compensator

The upper right corner of the curves in Figures 15-34, 15-44 and 15-47 show the maximum power required by the hydraulic circuit, called "corner horsepower." This is a maximum pressure, maximum flow position of the pump for which the prime mover (electric motor) must be sized to prevent stall. The relationship in the hydraulic horsepower formula illustrates how pressure and flow together result in system horsepower. When both pressure and flow are at their highest level, maximum horsepower is absorbed by the system, and the prime mover must be large enough to deliver this horsepower.

There are several industrial applications, however, that never require maximum flow and maximum pressure to occur at the same time. A press brake may need to move into position quickly (high flow, low pressure), and then provide a high shear or bending force (high pressure, low flow). The platen of a die cast machine must move into position quickly (high flow, low pressure), and then clamp (high pressure, low or no flow). A broach may need to cut slowly (high pressure, low flow), but then retract quickly (high flow, low pressure). These are a few simple examples where high pressure and high flow are not required simultaneously, and would benefit from a control that would provide either but not both.

A torque limiting compensator, frequently referred to as a horsepower limiting compensator, is designed to prevent high pressure and high flow from occurring at the same time. Either one can occur independently, that is high flow or high pressure, but not simultaneously. The result is a lower "corner horsepower" requirement, a smaller prime mover requirement and protection against stalling of the prime mover.

Figure 15-48 shows a version of a torque limiting, pressure limiting and load sensing compensator. The upper portion of the assembly is the same pressure limiting and load sensing compensator as described earlier (see Figure 15-46) and operates in the same way to provide the energy conservation characteristics shown in Figure 15-47. The load sensing signal is provided from a shuttle valve which selects the highest of the actuator line pressures. A third spool has been added to the assembly, which is the torque limiting spool.

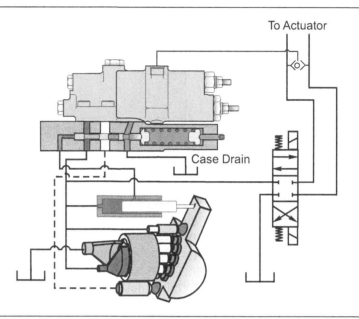

Figure 15-48   Torque limiting compensator operation

The pump rotating group (cylinder block and pistons) discharges fluid to the outlet which is fed constantly to the bias piston, the compensator, the yoke position sensing piston and the system. The bias piston is holding the yoke at its maximum angle, such that the pump is discharging maximum flow. Any resistance to the flow, due to the flow control valve, the directional valve or the actuator, will create a pressure at the pump outlet. This pressure will be transmitted into the torque limiting spool area, as well as the yoke position sensing spool area. The pressure entering the compensator will also enter the load sensing and pressure limiting spools in the same manner as shown in Figure 15-49.

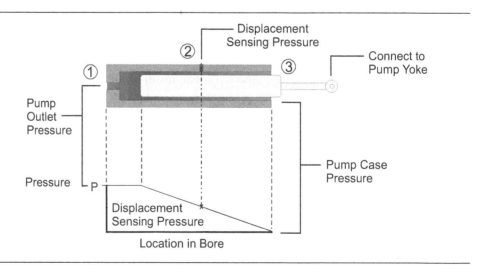

Figure 15-49   Yoke position sensing piston retracted

Figure 15-49 is a cross section of the yoke position sensing piston. It is attached directly to the pump yoke such that it will move right (out of its bore) as the yoke is rotated to maximum angle, and move left (into its bore) as the yoke is rotated to minimum angle. The pressure being applied to the left side of the piston comes from the outlet side of the pump rotating group. The right side of the piston drains into the pump case, which is drained to the reservoir. This pressure is consistently very close to zero, and is considered zero.

There is a small clearance between the yoke position sensing piston and the bore, such that there is a gradual decline in pressure from pump outlet pressure (on the left side) to zero (on the right side). The pressure that will be detected at the displacement sensing port will be in direct proportion to the pump outlet pressure and the location of the piston.

When the yoke is rotated to its maximum stroke angle, the yoke position sensing piston will be furthest to the right (as in Figure 15-50), providing a pressure at the sensing port very close to pump outlet pressure. When the yoke angle is small, the yoke position sensing piston will be furthest to the left, providing a pressure at the sensing port closer to zero.

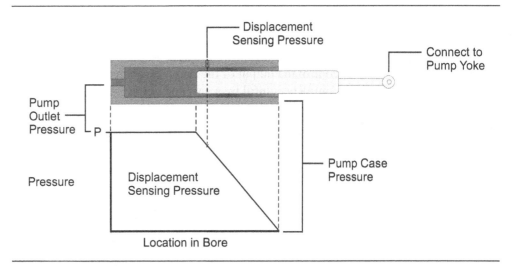

Figure 15-50   Yoke position sensing piston extended

The pressure sensed at the sensing port is fed to the torque limiting spool. The intensity of this pressure depends on the position of the yoke and the pump outlet pressure. When the outlet pressure is high and the yoke is at its maximum displacement angle, the pressure at the torque limiting spool will be great enough to force the spool to the right against the adjustable spring. Flow will then be metered to the displacement control piston, which will reduce the displacement of the pump by rotating the yoke to a lesser angle. As the yoke angle decreases, the pressure from the yoke position sensing piston will reduce until the torque limiting spool returns to the left. The spool will meter flow to the control piston to maintain the reduced displacement position until the pump outlet pressure reduces (due to a drop in load requirement). When pump outlet pressure reduces sufficiently, the torque limiting spool will return to the left, allowing the yoke to rotate to full displacement.

The pressure at which the torque limiting spool begins to regulate a lower displacement is set by the spring adjustment. This is set based on the peak horsepower that the prime mover can be subjected to. When properly set, the machine will be able to produce maximum speed (flow) or maximum force (pressure), but not both at the same time.

Figure 15-51 illustrates the movement of the "corner horsepower" point. The reduced horsepower that results can mean a smaller prime mover, saving machine size and energy consumption.

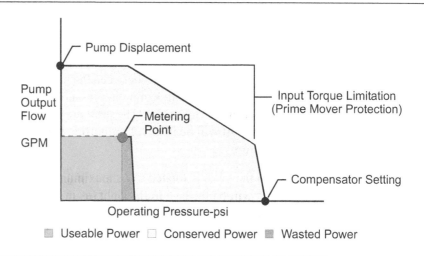

Figure 15-51   Reduced horsepower requirement by reducing corner horsepower

Electronic Displacement Control

The electrohydraulic compensator may also be referred to as an electronic displacement control, or EDC. As with all other compensators, its purpose is to control the output of the pump by controlling its displacement. The EDC provides for complete control by a variable voltage signal.

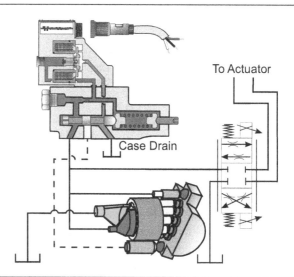

Figure 15-52   Electrohydraulic displacement control

Figure 15-52 is a cross-sectional view of an EDC compensator consisting of a basic compensator valve and an electronically controlled pilot relief valve. The pump rotating group discharges fluid to the outlet which is fed constantly to the bias piston, the compensator and through the proportional directional valve to the system. The bias piston holds the yoke at its maximum angle, such that the pump discharges maximum flow. Any resistance to the flow, due to the valve or the actuator, will create a pressure at the pump outlet. This pressure will be transmitted into the compensator control spool area, and attempt to move the spool to the right against the adjustable spring. The pressure is also transmitted through a fixed orifice into the spring chamber, and to the electronically controlled pilot relief valve. The control spool spring is preset to a "standby" pressure, usually in the 200 – 400 psi range.

Pressure in the control spool spring chamber is controlled by the pilot relief valve. The relief valve will open and meter flow to the case drain (which is directly connected to the system reservoir) in direct proportion to a voltage input. Opening this valve will allow fluid in the control spool spring area to drain out. Flow is also entering the spring chamber through the fixed orifice. By controlling the flow out of the spring chamber relative to the flow in, the pressure in the spring chamber can be controlled. This pressure adds to the equivalent pressure of the spring force, the "standby" pressure, and it is the sum of these two pressures that keep the control spool to the left. As output pressure from the rotating group increases higher than the spring chamber pressure, the control spool will move to the right, metering flow to the control piston to stroke the pump back. Pump displacement will be continuously adjusted to maintain output equal to the pressure in the spring chamber, which is controlled by the level of voltage input to the pilot relief valve.

The voltage input signal to the pilot relief valve can be supplied by any number of sources, such as rheostats, controllers, amplifier cards or computers.

Variable Speed Drives

In a conventional hydraulic system there will be a prime mover, a fixed or variable volume pump, and perhaps a flow control or proportional valve. The pump will be constant speed, and changes in flow or pressure requirements will be controlled by the flow device and/or a displacement control. Using a variable displacement pump in this manner allows for significant energy savings over a fixed displacement pump running at constant speed, and further, by shifting from a "resistive" flow control such as a needle valve or proportional control valve to volumetric flow control, the machine will minimize any unnecessary throttle loss.

A newer alternative to consider is a variable speed drive and a fixed or variable displacement pump. This allows for a minimum Motor Power consumption and eliminates unnecessary loss across a metering device. The benefit to the machine is not only energy savings but also compliance with government regulations on electric motor efficiency.

Some of the benefits that can be realized by using a variable speed drive pump solution include: up to 70% energy savings and 20 decibel lower noise levels; possible use of a smaller pump and/or motor; longer oil and seal life; reduced or even eliminated cooling needs; and lower oil use. The end result is reduced operating costs and a more sustainable operation. Criteria for using a variable speed drive include:

- Presence of low flow in portions of the duty cycle or a significant amount of flow or load variance

- Actuators functioning in sequence rather than parallel

- Common performance problems such as overheating or high noise levels
- Need to fit in a confined space

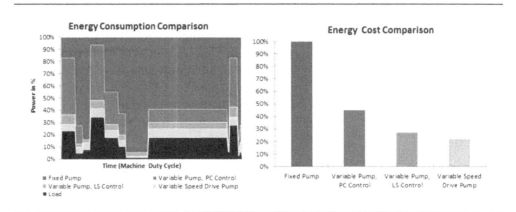

Figure 15-53   Energy consumption comparison of varying methods of pump control

In the chart on the left of Figure 15-53 you see an energy consumption comparison of fixed volume pumps, variable displacement pumps with a pressure compensator control, a variable pump with a pressure compensator and load sense control, and a variable displacement pump using Variable Speed Drive technology. Finally in black is drawn the actual load required by the machine. On the right is an energy cost comparison of the four different control methods utilized. By taking advantage of the variable speed drive's ability to follow the power demand curve more closely, the machine uses less power than would be required by more conventional methods of pump control.

Industrial Test Questions:
Hydraulic Pumps

Chapter 15

1. What are the basic characteristics of positive displacement pumps?

2. What are two ways of expressing pump size?

3. What is the purpose of decompression notches in a gear pump?

4. Which type of pump has automatic compensation for some of its wear?

5. What are two ways of altering volume levels in a gear pump?

6. What type of pumps are available in variable displacement models?

7. Explain the principle of a balanced design vane pump.

8. What holds the vanes extended in a vane pump?

9. What is the purpose of the intra-vane design?

10. What are two ways of positioning a yoke in a variable displacement, in-line pump?

11. How can displacement be varied in an axial piston pump?

12. What causes the pistons to reciprocate in an in-line piston pump? In a bent-axis pump?

13. Why wouldn't a centrifugal pump be used to transmit fluid under pressure?

14. A 5 GPM (18.93 l/min) pump delivers 3.5 GPM (13.25 l/min) at 3,000 psi (210 bar, 21,000 kPa). What is its volumetric efficiency?

15. What tends to limit the pressure capability of a gear pump?

Chapter 16 . . . . Basic Digital Electrohydraulic Devices

Digital electrohydraulic devices are being used in more and more hydraulic systems every day. These devices provide electrical control of hydraulic components such as valves and servos. Digital refers to the type of electrical signal used to actuate these electrohydraulic devices.

The choice of a controlling device used in a given hydraulic circuit is influenced by such factors as safety, flexibility, dependability, initial cost and ease of maintenance. Electrical controls provide a flexibility and convenience that cannot be attained with any other kind of control. In certain applications, digital electrical controls may be the only way to obtain the desired level of performance.

This chapter will provide a basic overview and introduction to many of the concepts encountered in digital electronics as applied to hydraulic components. It covers topics such as the difference between digital and analog devices, basic logic circuits, the binary number system and forms of data representation. This chapter also briefly covers general digital applications in hydraulic systems including microprocessors, industrial controls and relay logic. The chapter concludes with some basic information on specific digital electrohydraulic devices currently used in the industry.

Digital Techniques

Basically, there are two types of electronic signals, analog and digital. Analog signals are the most familiar of the two simply because digital electronics is such a relatively new field and analog devices have been in use for a long time. For this reason, both kinds of signals are briefly examined in this chapter. The emphasis, however, is on digital techniques and applications because the increased use of digital devices in hydraulic circuits is clearly a trend for the future.

Definition of an Analog Signal

An analog signal can be defined as an AC or DC voltage or current that varies smoothly or continuously. Analog signals do not change abruptly or in increments.

The most common type of analog signal is the sine wave shown in Figure 16-1. The voltage or current changes at a regular rate from a positive to a negative value. The positive and negative alternations are symmetrical. Radio signals, audio tones and the AC power supplied by the local power company are all examples of electronic signals or voltages in the form of sine waves.

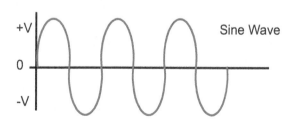

Figure 16-1   A sine wave

Signals do not have to be sinusoidal in nature for them to be considered analog signals. The randomly changing AC signal shown in Figure 16-2 and the varying negative DC voltage illustrated in Figure 16-3 are also analog signals because they change at a fairly smooth rate. Electric circuits that process analog signals are called linear circuits.

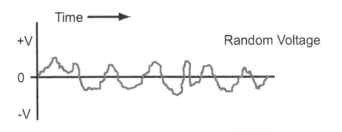

Figure 16-2   Random AC voltage

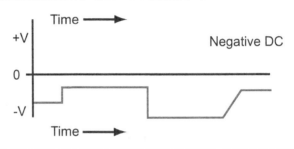

Figure 16-3   Varying negative DC voltage

Definition of a Digital Signal

Digital signals, like those shown in Figure 16-4, almost always vary between two distinct and fixed voltage levels. The digital signal is normally in the form of a series of pulses that rapidly change from one voltage level to the other in discrete steps or increments. Figure 16-4 shows a signal changing between a positive DC level and zero (ground). The voltage levels can also go from zero to a negative voltage, or from a positive to a negative voltage.

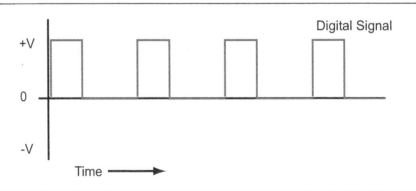

Figure 16-4   Digital signals

Because of the speed at which the signals switch from one level to the other, digital signals are described as two state signals. At any given time, they are either high or low, on or off, up or down. This fast switching characteristic is standard for all digital signals. The circuits that process digital signals are called digital, logic or pulse circuits.

Contrasting Analog and Digital Signals

In the following simple examples, familiar devices and ideas are used to further illustrate the difference between analog and digital methods and techniques.

A light bulb can be either an analog or a digital device depending on how it is used. If the current through the filament of the bulb is varied between maximum and minimum, the brightness level will vary at a proportional rate between full brightness and off. There are virtually an infinite number of brightness levels that can be attained. When used in this way, the light bulb is an analog device.

The light bulb can also be used as a digital device if it's brightness level is only allowed to change in discrete steps. The most common way to use a bulb as a digital device is to permit only two brightness levels, usually full brightness and off. When used this way, the bulb has two states and because of this ON/OFF characteristic the bulb is called binary in nature. The term binary refers to any two-state device or signal.

A watch with hour and minute sweep hands is an analog device. It continuously indicates the time by the positions of the hands on a calibrated dial. To tell the exact time, the hand positions must be estimated. The ability to read the time accurately is limited by the precision of the dial calibration. On a digital watch the time is read directly from decimal number display readouts that change in discrete increments of hours, minutes and seconds. The accuracy is improved because there is no need to estimate the exact time.

A speedometer with a moving needle is an analog device. A speedometer with an LED readout is a digital device. The mechanical channel selector on a television set is a digital device because it changes in discrete positions, i.e. 2, 4, 7, 9, etc. The volume control on the same television set is analog because its position can be changed continuously over a wide range to achieve sound levels from completely off to extremely loud. Any type of switch or relay is a digital device because it has two or more distinct positions. The glass thermometer is an analog device. So is a traditional hiking compass. Money is digital. A pointer type pressure gauge is analog.

General Digital Applications

Digital devices and techniques are being employed in almost every area of electronics from communications to test instruments. Relay logic circuits, microprocessors and industrial controls are devices that are of particular interest to the hydraulics industry.

Relay Logic

A relay can be considered digital in nature because it is basically an ON/OFF device. Figure 16-5 shows a relay and its associated contacts in both the energized and de-energized state. When current is allowed to flow in the coil circuit of the relay, a magnetic field is created that moves the plunger to the energized position. A set of common contacts are connected to the plunger. When the relay is de-energized, the common contacts are connected to the N.C. (normally closed) contacts. In the illustration, contacts 2 and 3 are connected. When the relay is energized, the common contacts are connected to the N.O. (normally open) contacts. As shown in the drawing, contacts 1 and 2 and contacts 4 and 5 are connected. The relay acts like an electrically operated switch.

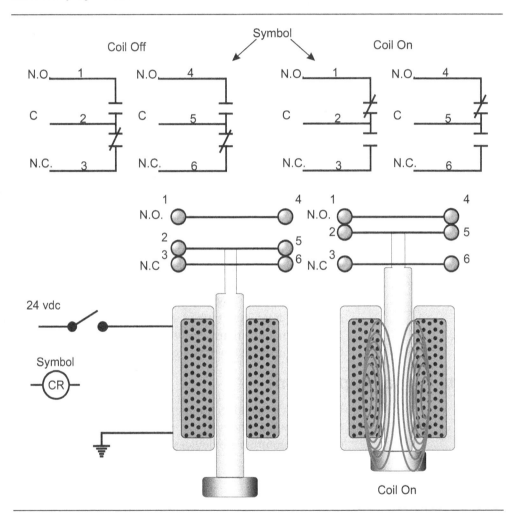

Figure 16-5   Basic relay construction

Relays have been in use in industrial applications for many years and have been quite reliable. The life span of a relay is measured in millions of actuations. Relays are still widely used today for switching or controlling circuits using high voltages and currents, and for controlling high voltage devices with low voltage control circuits.

Figure 16-6 shows a typical basic relay logic circuit. The relays in this circuit operate on 115 volts AC (single phase) and control a 480 volt AC, three-phase motor. The operation of this circuit is described below.

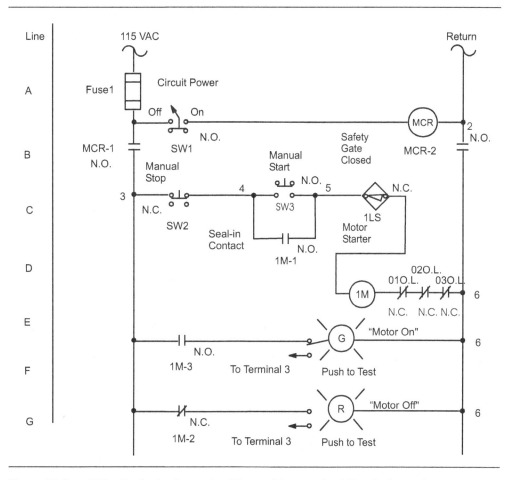

Figure 16-6   115 volt, single-phase circuit is used to control a 480 volt, three-phase motor

Starting with Line A in the figure, Fuse 1 protects the circuit from overcurrent conditions. Circuit power is provided by turning on SW1. This energizes the Master Control Relay (MCR). On Line B, when the MCR is energized, contacts MCR-1 and MCR-2 close, providing power to the rest of the circuit. On Line E, the motor will be started by Motor Starter 1M if conditions on Line C are correct. There are three overload contacts after 1M (one for each phase) that are normally closed. These contacts open if an overcurrent condition exists in the motor itself.

In order to energize 1M, the A Safety Gate Proximity Switch (1LS) on Line C must be closed and the Manual Stop Switch (SW2), must not be depressed. When the Manual Start Switch (SW3) is depressed, 1M is energized. Immediately, seal-in (or holding) contact 1M-1 (on Line D) closes to seal in the 1M relay so that 1M will stay energized when the Start Switch (SW3) is no longer depressed.

The circuit also has red and green lamps to indicate whether the motor is ON or OFF. The red light (Motor Off) is in series with the normally closed (N.C.) contact 1M-2 on Line G. When relay 1M is de-energized, this contact is closed and the red light is ON.

When 1M energizes, the 1M-2 contact opens and turns off the red light. The normally open contact 1M-3 closes when 1M is energized and this allows the green light to illuminate indicating that the motor is ON.

Therefore, the motor is energized by the following logical conditions:

Manual Stop Not Depressed

AND

Manual Start Depressed **OR** Seal-In Contact Closed

AND

Safety Gate Closed

AND

All 3 Overload Contacts Closed

The motor is stopped by the following logical conditions:

Manual Stop Pushed

OR

Safety Gate Open

OR

Seal-In Contact Open **AND** Manual Start Not Pushed

OR

Phase 1 Overload or Phase 2 Overload or Phase 3 Overload.

As machines became more sophisticated and faster, relays proved to be impractical for control purposes. Relay circuits consumed more space and power than the machines they were controlling. Electronic devices, because of their small size, low power consumption and speed, began to appear in industrial controls. The development of the microcomputer accelerated the changeover to electronic control of hydraulic systems.

Microprocessors and Industrial Controls

A semiconductor device developed in the late 1970s called the Solid-State Relay made it possible for low voltage, digital devices to control DC or AC voltages from 5V to 1,000V with no moving parts. The device is an opto-coupled semiconductor that uses a light emitting diode as the transmitter and a light sensitive diode, transistor, FET, SCR or other device as the receiver. Analog outputs are also available now on most computerized controllers, which can be used to directly control a proportional or servo amplifier card. Analog inputs and solid-state relays allow a computer to receive inputs of DC or AC voltage or current from any type of feedback device on the market. This will lead the hydraulics industry down the same path of automation that electronic drives have successfully traveled.

Perhaps the greatest use of digital techniques is in the area of computers. While computers have grown in capability over the last several years, they have also become smaller, cheaper and easier to use.

As a result of advanced semiconductor technology, complete digital computers have been packaged in a single miniature integrated circuit. These devices, called microprocessors, have replaced conventional relay control circuitry in many applications. Figure 16-7 is a comparison of relay control vs. microprocessor control in terms of speed, cost, power consumption, number of components required, size and flexibility.

	RELAYS	MICROPROCESSORS
Speed	Slow response (milliseconds)	Fast response (microseconds)
Cost	$50 and up	$7.50 to $20
Power Use	Watts	Milliwatts
Number of Components Required	Thousands of relays	= 1 microprocessor
Size	0.1 - 6 cubic inches (1.6 - 98 cm^3)	Less than 0.1 cubic inches (1.6 cm^3)
Flexibility	Single function	Hundreds of functions

Figure 16-7   Comparison between relays and microprocessors

Microprocessor control of hydraulic systems offers improved accuracy, efficiency and versatility for two reasons:

- **Programmability**
- **Computational ability**

Programmability gives the microprocessor the ability to change system logic and characteristics with simple software modifications rather than by altering the hardware. The specific details of how the microprocessor and its associated equipment should operate to perform a given device function are contained in the program. If changes occur later in control strategies or equipment output specifications, for example, the new information can be programmed into the microprocessor quickly and efficiently to accommodate the changed conditions. This ability saves a tremendous amount of time and expense and facilitates the use of microprocessors in many diverse applications.

Computational ability allows microprocessors to perform very complex and powerful operations involving logic, probability, computation, decision making and artificial intelligence functions. In these operations, nearly all of the relevant data is represented and processed in a digital form that lends itself to a high degree of precision, speed and accuracy.

Microprocessor based electrohydraulic control systems typically include some or all of the components on the block diagram of the closed loop control system shown in Figure 16-8. The microprocessor is only one component of the system. Other components include analog and digital sensors and transducers, signal conditioning circuits, analog-to-digital and digital-to-analog converter circuits, analog and digital actuators and power supply circuits. The microprocessor handles the logic and decision making requirements. Sensors and transducers report the status of various machine components, including such variables as component positional information, temperature and pressure data, actuator speed and virtually any other type of machine information that can be sensed.

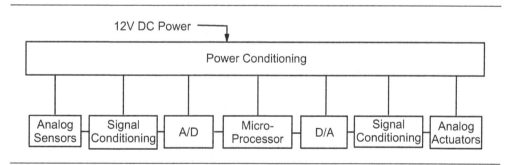

Figure 16-8   Block diagram of a microprocessor based electrohydraulic closed loop control system

Electrohydraulic controls such as solenoids, proportional controls and servos direct the hydraulic actuators in performing the desired operations. Such a system may control several different conditions based on past, present or predicted performance.

PLCs

A programmable logic controller (PLC), like the one shown in Figure 16-9, is a microprocessor-based device that provides the control of a machine or process on the basis of input and output conditions in a manner similar to the electromechanical relay or hard wired printed circuit board. The difference lies in the method used to control the logic and to perform the control sequence which is in the form of a program.

Programmable Logic Controller

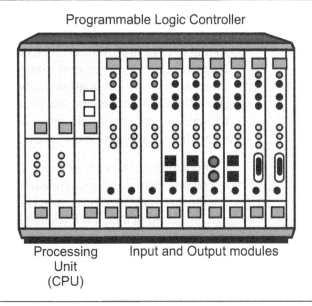

Processing Unit (CPU)   Input and Output modules

Figure 16-9   Programmable logic controller

PLCs generally contain one or more microprocessor chips and are programmed in ladder logic. Figure 16-10 shows the PLC ladder diagram equivalent of the relay logic circuit explained earlier in this chapter.

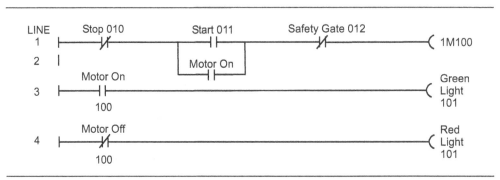

Figure 16-10   PLC ladder diagram for relay logic circuit

Figure 16-11 shows how the PLC would be wired to control the start and stop functions of the motor.

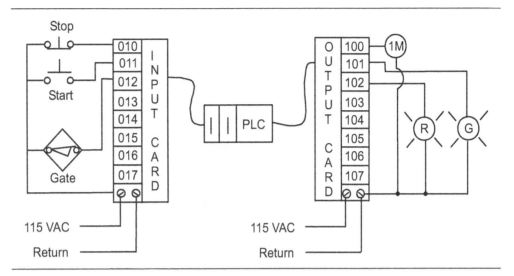

Figure 16-11   PLC wiring diagram for relay logic circuit

With a programmable controller, the sequence of the logic is converted from the symbology of a circuit diagram to data stored on memory chips through an electronic device referred to as a memory loader or programmer. It is comprised of a simplified keyboard with identification characters representing relay ladder diagram symbols and operational instructions. When a chip has been programmed, all of the logic circuitry has essentially been transferred onto solid-state devices. Because these devices can be changed or reprogrammed quite easily, the PLC has the versatility to quickly modify a process or a set of operational parameters that control the machine's function.

A microprocessor is one of many components of a programmable logic controller. It serves as the heart of the microcomputer, allowing it to perform arithmetic calculations, make comparisons and remember what it has done. The use of a microprocessor lends an intelligent capability to an ordinary ON/OFF controller. Other components include input and output conditioning circuits, power supplies, analog to digital and digital to analog converters, and safety and alarm circuits.

PLC inputs can be digital ON/OFF signals from switches, contacts, etc.; analog signals from thermocouples, instruments and transducers, or digital words from other computers or PLCs. Outputs can be digital ON/OFF voltages or currents to relays, lights, starters and other control devices, or analog voltages and currents to such devices as small motors. PLC outputs may also be digital words to LED displays or other PLCs and computers.

PLCs are available in various sizes starting with the smallest versions that can handle three inputs and outputs. The small PLC is basically used to replace or substitute for a few relays and costs around $200. The largest PLCs can handle 3,000 to 6,000 inputs and outputs, have full computer capability, and run entire process facilities. These versions cost anywhere from $10,000 to $100,000.

Digital Data Transmitters

Digital data transmitters are devices that move data between digital devices. They can be built into the digital device or located in separate enclosures. For example, most personal computers have a built-in RS-232 interface which moves data serially (one bit at a time) from the computer to its printer. The term, RS-232, refers to an industry standard which dictates the voltages, number of wires, and definitions of the electrical signals which must be used if the interface is called an RS-232. If data transmission is to be from one computer to another, a modem is used.

A modem, or Modulator Demodulator, is a device used to provide data communications between two separate microprocessing units (Figure 16-12). The modulator portion of the modem converts digital signals into tones that can be transmitted over a telephone line or over any long distance serial line. For example, the modulator might convert the binary output of a circuit into a high tone (1,270 Hz) for logic 1 and a low tone (1,070 Hz) for a logic 0. The demodulator portion of the modem converts the received tones from the telephone line into signals that are once again compatible with the digital circuits of the receiving microprocessor.

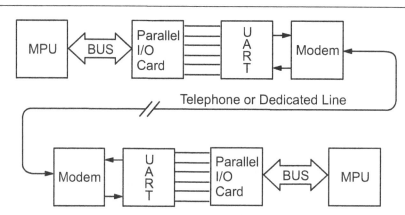

Using modems to communicate over long distances, the modems send and receive digital signals by using different tones for logic "1"s and logic "0"s. NOTE: UART is an acronym for Universal Asynchronous Receiver Transmitter. MPU is an acronym for Microprocessing Unit.

Figure 16-12   Modem used for data transmission

There are many other types of digital data transmission and the method used depends on cost, environment and speed requirements. The RS-232 interface is low cost, good for up to 50 feet (15.24 m) of transmission line, low speed, voltage driven and typically used in an office environment. Parallel interfaces cost more but operate at a very high speed. They are also good for short distances, allow computers to communicate with each other and are found in office environments. The RS-485 interface also costs more, but is current driven, is good for thousands of feet (meters) of distance, has excellent immunity to electrical noise and is typically used in industrial environments. Fiber optics are high in cost, but are very high speed, are totally immune to electrical noise and interference, and are able to handle large amounts of traffic in a very small diameter cable. They are used where absolute data transmission reliability is required.

Other, more sophisticated digital data transmission methods include radio signals, microwave and other industry transmission standards such as RS-422.

Serial and Parallel Transmission of Data

Digital numbers are transmitted, processed or otherwise manipulated in two basic ways. In the serial methods of data handling, each bit of a binary word or number is transmitted serially one at a time. In a parallel system, all bits of a word or a number are transmitted simultaneously.

Figure 16-13 shows a binary number represented in a serial data format that is being sent over a transmission line to a receiving circuit. The binary number exists as a series of voltage levels representing the binary 1s and 0s. Preceding the binary number is a start bit that indicates to the receiver that data is being sent. Following the binary number is a stop bit to indicate to the receiver that the binary number has ended. All of these voltage level changes occur at a single point in a circuit or on a single data line. Each bit of the word exists for a specific interval of time. In this example, the time interval allotted to each bit is one millisecond. The most significant bit (MSB) is the one closest to the start bit. Because this is an 8 bit binary word, it takes 10 milliseconds for the entire word and the start and stop bits to occur to be transmitted. By observing the voltage levels at specific times on the transmission line, the number can be determined. The number in this example is 10101110. This is the binary equivalent of the decimal number 174.

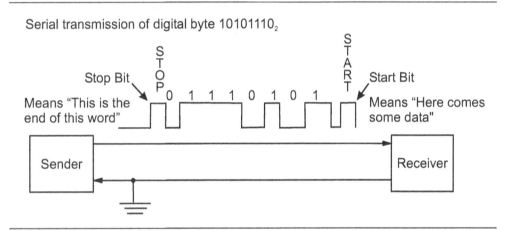

Figure 16-13   Serial data transmission

The main advantage of serial over parallel binary data representation is that it requires only a single line or channel for transmitting it from one place to another. In addition, since each bit on the single line occurs separately from the others, only one set of digital circuitry is generally needed to process this data. For these reasons, serial data representation is the simplest and most economical of the two types. Its primary disadvantage is that the transmission and processing time required for a serial word is longer since the bits occur one after the other.

Binary data may also be transmitted, processed and manipulated in a parallel format. It is called parallel because all of the bits of a binary word are processed or transmitted at the same time. In parallel circuitry, a separate line or channel is required for each bit of the word in transmitting that word from one point to another.

Figure 16-14 shows the digital circuit for parallel processing the binary word 10101110 (174 decimal). The eight bits are available as voltage levels on eight separate output lines for a specific length of time. Since all eight bits are available at the same time, circuitry must be provided to process each of the bits in the word simultaneously. The Request signal is sent to the receiver to announce that data is on the lines. The sender leaves the data on the lines until an Acknowledge signal comes back from the receiver. The Acknowledge signal indicates to the sender that the data has been received.

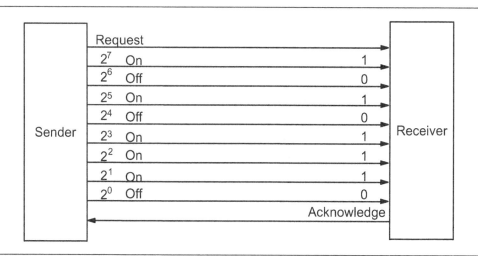

Figure 16-14   Parallel transmission data

The transmission and processing of parallel data is more complex and expensive than that required for serial data. However, the clear advantage of parallel data transmission is its speed. All bits are processed at the same time and the time required for processing is very short. Parallel digital techniques are preferred for high speed applications requiring rapid processing of data.

Advantages of Digital Techniques

Reduction in size, weight, cost and power consumption usually result when analog techniques are replaced by digital methods. This is largely due to advancements in the production of digital integrated circuits or "chips." Other advantages include:

- Greater accuracy — digital techniques allow greater precision and resolution in representing quantities or in making measurements than do analog methods. Accuracy can be verified using parity checking methods.

- Greater dynamic range — dynamic range is the difference between the upper and lower data values that a system or instrument can handle. Analog systems are limited because of component capabilities and noise to a range of something less than 100,000 to 1. With digital techniques practically any desired dynamic range can be obtained.

- Greater stability — analog circuits are subject to the effects of drift and component tolerance problems. Temperature and other environmental factors affect resistor, capacitor and inductance values. Transistor control voltages may vary causing nonlinear operation and distortion. Component imperfections and aging cause drift and resultant problems. Digital methods greatly minimize or eliminate these problems.

- Convenience — digital techniques make instruments and equipment more convenient to use. The direct decimal display of data is not only more convenient, but the error of reading or interpolating analog meters or in setting analog dials is eliminated.

- Automation — many electronic processes can be fully automated if digital techniques are used. Special control circuits or a digital computer can automatically set up, control and monitor many operations. Data is readily recorded, stored and displayed.

- New approaches — digital circuits make it possible to do some things that have no analog equivalent.

Basic Logic Circuits

The two basic types of digital logic circuits are decision making circuits and memory circuits. In all digital circuits, decisions are made based on given information or information is stored for later use. Decision making logic circuits are called gates and usually have two or more inputs and a single output. Both inputs and outputs are in binary form. The gates are combined in a variety of ways to form combinational logic circuits that can perform many complicated decision making functions.

Memory circuits store data in binary form and are commonly called flip-flops. Flip-flops store a single bit of data and are usually combined to form sequential circuits which can store, count and shift larger amounts of binary data. The emphasis in this section is on the two basic decision making circuits or gates, the AND gate and the OR gate.

AND Circuit

A logic gate has two or more inputs and a single output. The gate makes its decision based upon the input states and its particular function, then generates the appropriate binary output. The AND gate operates in such a manner that its output state is a binary 1 if and only if all its inputs are a binary 1 at the same time. If any or all inputs are binary 0, the output of the AND gate is a binary 0. This function can be described by a table of input and output conditions known as a truth table. A truth table for a two-input AND gate is:

INPUTS		OUTPUTS
A	B	C
0	0	0
0	1	0
1	0	0
1	1	1

Figure 16-15 shows a simple electrical equivalent of the AND circuit. Current from the power supply flows through the motor only when both of the electrical switches are closed. If either switch is opened, the motor cannot run.

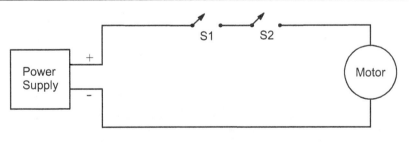

Both S1 and S2 must be closed before motor can run

Figure 16-15   Simple electrical AND circuit

Figure 16-16 shows the hydraulic equivalent of the AND circuit. Manually actuated valves take the place of the switches in the hydraulic circuit, but both valves must allow the flow of fluid through them before the motor can run.

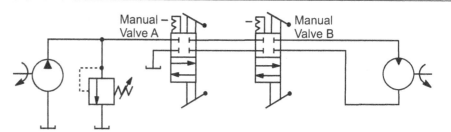

Hydraulic equivalent "AND" circuit. Both valves must be opened to run motor

Figure 16-16   Simple hydraulic equivalent of AND circuit

Figure 16-17 shows a digital circuit for controlling a solenoid valve with an AND gate. Both inputs to the AND gate must be a binary 1 before the solenoid can be actuated. The inputs are logic level pulses of voltage that represent the binary states. They are transmitted to the AND gate by digital circuits in the system controller that determine when the solenoid should be actuated. In this case, two conditions must be met before the solenoid is actuated.

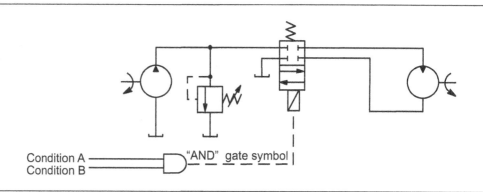

Condition A
Condition B   "AND" gate symbol

Figure 16-17   Digital AND circuit

OR Circuit

The OR gate operates in such a manner that its output state is a binary 1 if either one or both of its inputs are a binary 1. The output of the OR gate is a binary 0 only when both inputs are binary 0 at the same time. A truth table for a two input OR gate is shown below.

INPUTS		OUTPUTS
A	B	C
0	0	0
0	1	1
1	0	1
1	1	1

Figure 16-18 shows a simple electrical equivalent of the OR circuit. Current from the power supply flows through the motor when either one or the other or both electrical switches are closed. The motor stops only when both switches are open.

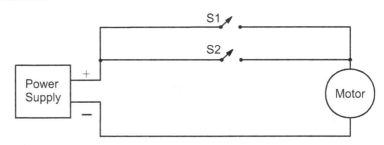

Either S1 OR S2 must be closed before motor can run

Figure 16-18   Simple electrical OR circuit

Figure 16-19 shows the hydraulic equivalent of the OR circuit. Manually actuated valves A and B take the place of the switches S1 and S2 in this hydraulic circuit version. If either valve allows flow, the motor can turn. To stop the motor, the valves must block the flow of fluid.

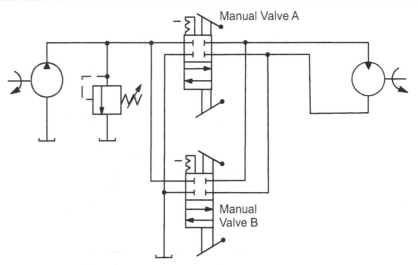

Hydraulic equivalent "OR" circuit. Either valve A or B must be opened to run motor

Figure 16-19   Simple hydraulic equivalent of OR circuit

Figure 16-20 shows a digital circuit for controlling a solenoid valve with an OR gate. If either input to the OR gate is a binary 1, the solenoid is actuated. The inputs are logic level pulses of voltage that represent the binary states. They are transmitted to the OR gate by digital circuits in the system controller that determine when the solenoid should be actuated. In this case, either of two separate signals could actuate the solenoid.

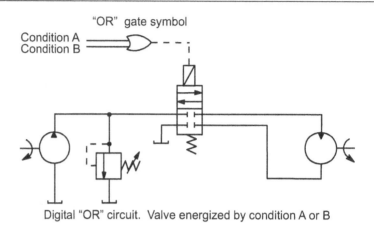

Digital "OR" circuit. Valve energized by condition A or B

Figure 16-20   Digital OR circuit

Machine Interlock Circuit

The following description of a machine interlock circuit is provided as an example of how AND and OR functions can be combined to accomplish a specific task. Following a discussion of how the circuit operates, the logical AND and OR functions are summarized.

The circuit has an electric motor driving a hydraulic pump that provides flow to a hydraulic system. The relief valve protects the system from overpressure conditions. Valves 1 and 2 are solenoid-operated, spring offset valves with a monitor switch. If the monitor switch is in the off position, the valve is off and the oil flow to its associated filter is cut off. There is also a differential pressure switch across each filter that actuates if the pressure difference reaches a level that indicates the filter needs changing.

Valves 1 and 2 select Filter 1 and 2 respectively. When Valve 1 or 2 is energized, it directs flow through its associated filter. When Valve 1 or 2 is de-energized, flow through the associated filter is cut off and the filter is vented to tank. A check valve is provided after each filter to prevent backflushing a dirty filter to tank.

The interlock circuit shown in Figure 16-21, automatically switches to a clean filter when the operational filter becomes dirty. The interlock also shuts down the motor if both filters are dirty.

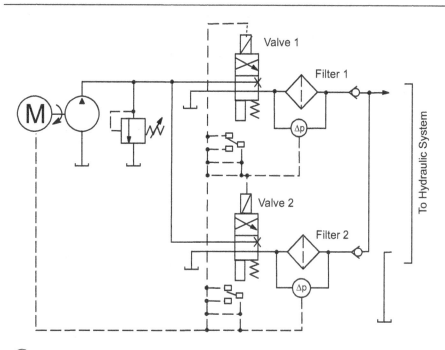

Δp = Differential Pressure Switch. Normal condition = Clean Filter = Low Differential Pressure
Contacts time delayed to avoid triggering due to pressure surges.

Valves 1 and 2 are = Solenoid operated, spring offset with monitor switch.
Switch off = Valve off = Oil flow to filter off.

The above circuit will be interlocked to automatically switch to a clean filter and to shut down the
motor if both filters are dirty.

Figure 16-21   Machine interlock circuit

The sequence of operation is as follows:

- Initially, enable flow to Filter 1, cut off Filter 2, and illuminate green light "Both
  filters clean."

- When Filter 1 is dirty, enable oil flow to Filter 2, cut off Filter 1, and illuminate
  yellow light "Replace Filter 1."

- When Filter 2 is dirty, enable oil flow to Filter 1, cut off Filter 2, and illuminate
  yellow light "Replace Filter 2."

- If both filter become dirty, shut down motor and illuminate red light "Dirty Filter
  Shutdown."

Figure 16-22 is a ladder diagram for the machine interlock circuit that should be used to follow the description of how the circuit works. Beginning with Lines A and B, the motor is started by the Motor Starter Relay, 1M. The following logical requirements must be met before 1M can be energized:

"Pump Stop" button not pushed
AND
"Pump Start" button pushed **OR** 1M-1 "Motor Started" contacts are closed
AND
Valve 1 **OR** Valve 2 ON

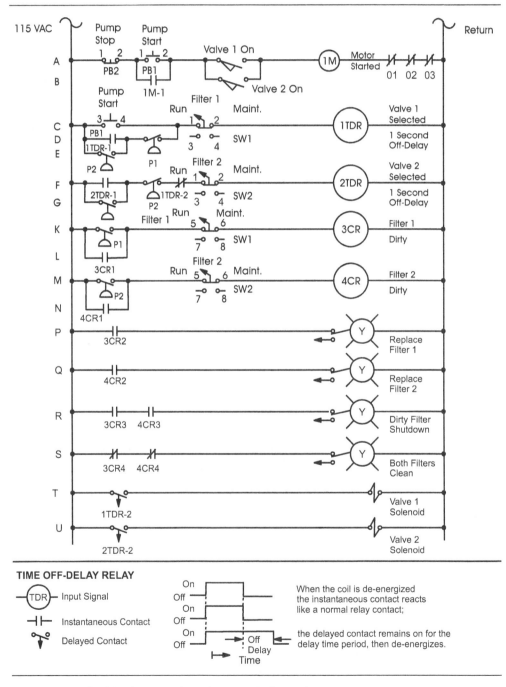

Figure 16-22   Ladder diagram of machine interlock circuit

On Line C, another set of Pump Start contacts selects Valve 1 by energizing relay 1TDR. "Filter 1" switch in the maintenance position, would prevent "valve 1" from being selected if someone is working on it. On Line D, when 1TDR energizes, 1TDR-1 contacts close to hold 1TDR energized, as long as P1 stays closed (differential pressure not high). When Filter 1 gets dirty, the differential pressure goes up and P1 contacts open, deselecting "Valve 1". At the same time, the P1 switch contacts on Line G close. Since Filter 2 hasn't been used yet, the P2 switch contacts are closed. Since "Valve 1" has been deselected, 1TDR-2 contacts are closed and 2TDR is energized, selecting Valve 2.

Lines K through N show the 3CR and 4CR latches, which "remember" when a filter has experienced high differential pressure. For example, if P1 closes, indicating Filter 1 is dirty (differential pressure too high), the 3CR relay is energized. The 3CR-1 contacts close to hold the relay energized until the "Filter 1" selector switch is moved to the "maintenance" (open) position for filter replacement. The 4CR circuit operates in an identical manner for Filter 2. If Filter 1 is replaced while Filter 2 is being used, the 3CR latch (3CR1) is reset by the "Filter 1" selector switch being moved to the "maintenance" position. After Filter 1 is replaced, the Filter 1 switch is turned back to the "RUN" position and P1 on Line D is now closed again. When Filter 2 gets dirty, the P2 switch contacts on Line E closes, selecting Valve 1 again. At the same time, the P2 switch contacts on Line F open, deselecting "Valve 2," and on Line M closes, energizing 4CR "Filter 2 dirty."

On lines C and F valve select relays 1 and 2, shown as 1TDR and 2TDR, are off delay relays. When either valve is selected, its associated TDR is instantly energized. When either valve is deselected, its associated TDR de-energizes **after a short delay** time (approximately one second) to prevent the motor from shutting down during the time period when the filters are switching over by the control circuitry.

If maintenance is careless and dirty filters are not replaced regularly, eventually both filters will be dirty at the same time. In this case, the contacts of P1 on Line D and P2 on line F are both open (differential pressure too high) at the same time. This causes both valves to be deselected and closed. If both valves are closed (off), the Valve 1 and Valve 2 switches on Lines A and B are both open at the same time. This de-energizes Motor Starter 1M, and the motor shuts down. On Line R, if both filters are dirty at the same time, both 3CR and 4CR will be energized. 3CR-3 and 4CR-3 will be closed, turning on the red indicator ("dirty filter shut down"). On Line S, if both filters are clean at the same time, 3CR-4 and 4CR-4 will be closed at the same time, indicating that both filters are clean.

The requirements of the interlock circuit can be written in terms of AND and OR statements in preparation for PLC programming. The following is a sample based on the previous example:

Valve 1 is selected by: Filter 1 Switch in "Run" position
AND
Pump Start **OR** ([Valve 1 Selected **OR** Filter 2 Dirty] **AND** Filter 1 Clean)

Valve 2 is selected by: Filter 2 Switch in "Run" position
AND
Valve 1 not Selected **AND** (Valve 2 Selected **OR** Filter 1 Dirty) **AND** Filter 2 Clean

"Dirty Filter Shutdown" indicator is illuminated by:

Filter 1 Dirty
AND
Filter 2 Dirty

"Both Filters Clean" indicator is illuminated by:

Filter 1 not Dirty
AND
Filter 2 not Dirty

Fundamentals of Digital Design

The following discussion provides insight into the fundamentals used to design digital devices:

Binary Numbers

All digital circuits, instruments and systems work with numbers that represent specific quantities. The most familiar type of numbers are decimal numbers. In the decimal number system, the ten digits 0 through 9 are combined in a certain way so that they indicate a specific quantity. In the binary number system, only two digits, 0 and 1, are used. The binary digits, or bits, when properly arranged can also represent any decimal number. For example, the binary number 110010 represents the decimal quantity 50.

The basic distinguishing feature of a number system is its base. The base indicates the number of digits used to represent quantities in that number system. The decimal number system has a base of 10 because 10 digits, 0 through 9, are used to represent quantities. The binary number system has a base of 2 since only the digits 0 and 1 are used in forming numbers. Figure 16-23 shows binary and decimal equivalents for the decimal numbers 0 through 15.

DECIMAL	BINARY
0	0000
1	0001
2	0010
3	0011
4	0100
5	0101
6	0110
7	0111
8	1000
9	1001
10	1010
11	1011
12	1100
13	1101
14	1110
15	1111

Figure 16-23   Binary and decimal equivalents

All modern digital techniques are based on the binary number system. Since there are only two numbers in this system, data can be represented by hardware devices that only have two states — on and off. Two state devices include switches, relay contacts and transistors. These devices are significantly simpler, less costly, faster and more reliable than devices which would need 10 states to represent the ten different possible digits of a decimal number.

Bit Position Values

The decimal and binary number systems are positional or weighted number systems. This means that each digit or bit position in a number carries a particular weight in determining the magnitude of that number. A decimal number has positional weights of units, tens, hundreds, thousands, etc. Each position has a weight that is some power of the number system base (10 in this case). As shown in Figure 16-24, the positional weights are $10^0 = 1$ (units), 10^1 (tens), 10^2 (hundreds), 10^3 (thousands), etc. (Any number with an exponent of zero is equal to 1.) Note that the weight of each position is ten times that of the weight of the number to the right of it.

DECIMAL NUMBER $3,240,897_{10}$ Denotes base of number system

DIGIT	3	2	4	0	8	9	7
POSITION	7	6	5	4	3	2	1
WEIGHT	10^6	10^5	10^4	10^3	10^2	10^1	10^0
VALUE	3,000,000	200,000	40,000	0	800	90	7

BINARY NUMBER MSB 1101101_2 LSB

DIGIT	1	1	0	1	1	0	1
POSITION	7	6	5	4	3	2	1
WEIGHT	2^6	2^5	2^4	2^3	2^2	2^1	2^0
VALUE	64	32	16	8	4	2	1

Figure 16-24   Bit position values

The total quantity represented by the digits is evaluated by considering the specific digits and the weights of their positions. For example, consider the decimal number 5628 in which there are eight ones, two tens, six hundreds, and five thousands. The number can be written as shown below.

$(5 \times 10^3) + (6 \times 10^2) + (2 \times 10^1) + (8 \times 10^0) =$
$(5 \times 1,000) + (6 \times 100) + (2 \times 10) + (8 \times 1) =$
$5,000 + 600 + 20 + 8 = 5,628$

To determine the value of the number, multiply each digit by the weight of its position and add the results.

Binary numbers work the same way, as each bit position also carries a specific weight. As in the decimal system, the position weights are some power of the base of the number system, in this case 2.

As shown in Figure 16-24, the weights are $2^0 = 1$ (any number to the zero power equals 1), $2^1 = 2$, $2^2 = 4$, $2^3 = 8$, etc. The weight of each position is twice that of the weight of the number to the right of it. Consider the binary number 00110010. This number can be written as shown below.

$(0 \times 2^7) + (0 \times 2^6) + (1 \times 2^5) + (1 \times 2^4) + (0 \times 2^3) + (0 \times 2^2) + (1 \times 2^1) + (0 \times 2^0) =$
$(0 \times 128) + (0 \times 64) + (1 \times 32) + (1 \times 16) + (0 \times 8) + (0 \times 4) + (1 \times 2) + (0 \times 1) =$
$0 + 0 + 32 + 16 + 0 + 0 + 2 + 0 = 50$

The quantity represented by the number is determined by multiplying each bit by its position weight and obtaining the sum. The binary number 1101101 shown in Figure 16-24 has a decimal equivalent of: $64 + 32 + 0 + 8 + 4 + 0 + 1 = 109$.

The eight bits in the binary number for decimal 50 above form what is known as a byte. Bytes can have more or less than eight bits depending upon the hardware used in the specific digital application. Each byte is used to represent a separate piece of information. In the example above, for instance, the bits 00110010 form a byte used to represent the decimal number 50.

MSB / LSB

Often when referring to binary numbers the terms "MSB" and "LSB" are used. MSB stands for most significant bit and refers to the bit position in a binary word or byte that carries the most weight. Normally, binary numbers are shown with the MSB as the left most bit in the byte (Figure 16-24). LSB stands for least significant bit and refers to the bit position that carries the least weight.

Data Representation

Data representation refers to the way in which binary numbers are represented and manipulated by electronic components and circuits. To represent a bit in a binary word, an electronic component must be capable of assuming two distinct states. One of the states will represent a binary 0 and the other a binary 1.

Electromechanical devices like switches and relays are ideal for representing binary data. A closed switch or relay contact can represent a binary 1 while the open switch or contact can represent a binary 0. These logic representations could just as easily be reversed, as long as the way in which the bit value is represented is consistent within the system. Electromechanical devices are still used in places where static binary conditions are required or very low speed operation can be tolerated.

In early computers, vacuum tubes replaced electromechanical devices for representing binary data because they could attain much higher switching speeds. Vacuum tubes are large in size, consume a lot of electrical power and generate a lot of heat, and because of these limitations, they were replaced by transistors in most equipment.

A transistor can readily assume two distinct states, conducting and cut off. When a transistor is cut off it acts as an open circuit, and when it is conducting heavily, it acts as a very low resistance much like a closed contact. Transistors are found in digital equipment both as discrete components or grouped together in integrated circuit chips.

Magnetic cores which can be magnetized in either of two directions are often used to store binary bits in memory. The two directions represent the two binary states, 0 and 1. The direction in which the core has been magnetized can be sensed at a later time when the bit value is needed by the computer.

Logic Levels

Two state devices, whether electromechanical, electronic or magnetic, are the basic element for representing bits of digital information. The exact relationship between the state of the device and the bit condition represented by this state is arbitrary. The digital hardware is not concerned with whether a transistor is conducting or cut off as much as it is with the voltage levels associated with the transistor states. The transistor simply controls these voltage levels which are determined when the circuitry is designed. For example, a binary 0 may be represented by 0 volts or ground. A binary 1 might be represented by a +5 volts. Depending on the equipment power supplies, the design of the circuitry and the application, almost any voltage level assignments may be used.

Positive Logic

When the most positive of two possible voltage levels is assigned to represent a binary 1, positive logic is being used by the circuitry. More often than not, positive logic is employed in digital equipment, however, negative logic level assignments are also sometimes used but are not discussed here in an effort to keep the explanation of logic levels as simple as possible. Several examples of positive logic level assignments are shown below.

Positive Logic Examples

binary 0 = +0.2V binary 0 = -6.0V binary 0 = 0V

binary 1 = +3.4V binary 1 = 0V binary 1 = +15V

Pulse Width and Frequency

When a bit of binary data is represented by a voltage level, the bit is in the form of a logic level pulse and the length of time from the beginning to the end of the pulse is known as the pulse width.

Frequency is defined as the number of pulses per second of time. For example, if each pulse requires 4 ms of time, then 250 pulses could occur each second. The frequency would be 250. If these pulses were transmitted serially, 250 bits per second could be transmitted. If the same information were transmitted in a parallel format, 250 binary bytes could be transmitted per second. This is illustrated in Figure 16-25, along with related definitions.

$$\frac{1,000 \text{ ms/sec}}{4 \text{ ms/pulse}} = 250 \text{ pulses/sec}$$

Figure 16-25 shows the relationship between pulse width, period and frequency.

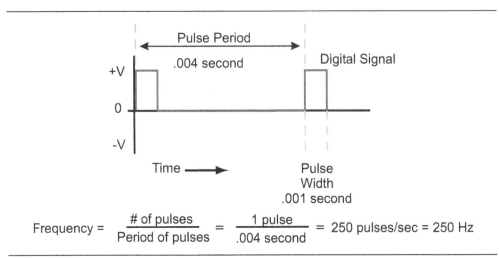

$$\text{Frequency} = \frac{\text{\# of pulses}}{\text{Period of pulses}} = \frac{1 \text{ pulse}}{.004 \text{ second}} = 250 \text{ pulses/sec} = 250 \text{ Hz}$$

Figure 16-25   Relationship between pulse width and frequency

Analog to Digital (A/D) Conversion

Microprocessor-based electrohydraulically controlled systems often contain devices that provide feedback or inputs to the system in the form of analog signals. Because these analog signals cannot be processed by digital microprocessor circuits, the analog to digital converter circuit receives the inputs from the external devices and converts them into digital signals in the form of binary numbers before sending them to the control circuits for processing.

The function of an A/D converter is illustrated in Figure 16-26. Each value of input voltage generates a specific binary output of 1s and 0s. However, the binary number itself does not equal the analog value. The scaling of the analog input is determined by the design of the circuit and/or system. The scaling factors determine the different input voltage ranges to the A/D converter.

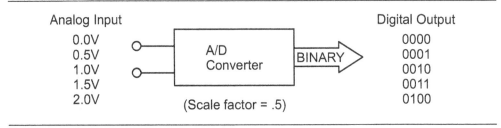

Figure 16-26   Analog-to-digital converter

The circuits for an A/D voltage converter include a sawtooth voltage generator to produce a ramp voltage as a reference and a comparator circuit. The comparator indicates which of its two input voltages is larger and, in turn, whether the output is binary 1 or 0. Then a gate and a counter is used to provide the binary data.

Digital to Analog (D/A) Conversion

Many hydraulic actuators require an analog signal for operation. In a microprocessor based electrohydraulically controlled system, outputs from the system controller are in the form of digital binary data which cannot be sent directly to the actuating devices. A digital to analog converter circuit is used to change the digital pulses into an analog signal.

The function of a digital to analog converter circuit is illustrated in Figure 16-27. Each binary count at the input will generate a specific analog voltage at the output. Higher binary numbers produce higher output voltages. The scaling factor can be set for the system requirements.

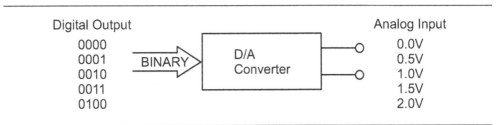

Figure 16-27   Digital-to-analog converter

The circuits of a D/A converter consist mainly of two parts: a resistor network for the binary input and an op amp as a summing amplifier for the analog output. The resistors determine the amount of feedback for the op amp, which controls the amount of gain.

Industrial Test Questions:
Basic Digital Electrohydraulic Devices

Chapter 16

1. Explain the difference between an analog and a digital signal.

2. A point-type pressure gauge is an example of a(n) (**analog/digital**) device, while a two-position electrical switch is an example of a(n) (**analog/digital**) device.

3. Relay logic is still used in hydraulics for what type of applications?

4. Name two reasons why microprocessor control of hydraulic systems offers improved accuracy, efficiency and versatility over relay control.

5. What advantage does programmability allow a microprocessor?

6. What advantage does computational ability allow a microprocessor?

7. What is the difference between a programmable logic controller and electromechanical relay control?

8. What is a modem?

9. Describe the difference between the RS-232 and the RS-485 interface.

10. Describe the difference in how bits are transferred in serial and parallel data transmission.

11. Name three advantages of digital techniques.

12. What are the two basic types of digital logic circuits?

13. What are the two basic decision making logic circuits or gates?

14. Describe the operation of an AND gate.

15. Describe the operation of an OR gate.

16. What binary number is the equivalent of the decimal number 12?

17. Why are modern digital techniques based on the binary number system?

18. MSB ⎍⎍⎍⎍ ± LSB
    What binary number is expressed above? (Start and stop bits are not shown. Assume positive logic.) What decimal number does it represent?

19. What is meant by MSB?

20. If the period of a signal increased, what happens to its frequency?

21. What is positive logic?

22. When is an analog to digital converter used?

23. When is a digital to analog converter used?

Chapter 17 . . . . Accessories

This chapter addresses the various accessories used to perform special functions in hydraulic systems: accumulators, pressure intensifiers, pressure switches, instruments for measuring pressures and flows, and sound dampening devices.

Accumulators

Unlike gases, which are compressible and can be stored under pressure for a period of time, hydraulic fluids are essentially incompressible. Accumulators provide a way to store these fluids under pressure.

Hydraulic fluids enter the accumulator chamber and act on a piston or bladder area to either raise a weight, compress a spring or compress a gas. Any tendency for pressure to drop at the accumulator inlet allows fluid to be forced back into the system.

Hydraulic energy stored in this manner is then available to supplement the system during periods of high demand. When large fluid flows are required in a system infrequently, an accumulator that is filled during periods of low demand can be called upon to discharge its fluid during periods of high demand.

The energy storage capability also makes accumulators capable of acting as shock absorbers. By absorbing a quantity of fluid above a preset pressure, it can help to "cushion" a hydraulic system that is subject to instantaneous pressure surges.

Figure 17-1 lists some of the uses of accumulators.

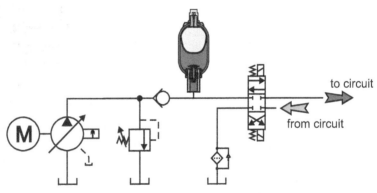

- Energy Source (supplement pump)
- Emergency Power
- Shock Absorption
- Thermal Expansion Protection

- Leakage Compensation
- Pulsation Dampening
- Compensation for Pump Yoke Lag

Figure 17-1   Accumulator applications

Weight Loaded Accumulator

The weight loaded design (Figure 17-2) was the first type of accumulator developed. Adding or removing weights on a vertical ram or piston varies the pressure, which is always equal to the weight imposed divided by the piston or ram area exposed to the hydraulic fluid. This is the only type of accumulator where pressure is constant, whether the chamber is full or nearly empty. Weight loaded accumulators are heavy and cumbersome, making their use limited. They are generally found on heavy presses where constant pressure is required, or in applications where unusually large volumes of fluid are necessary.

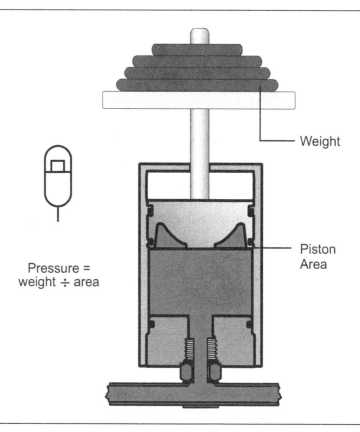

Pressure =
weight ÷ area

Weight

Piston
Area

Figure 17-2   Weight loaded accumulator

Spring Loaded Accumulator

In a spring loaded accumulator (Figure 17-3), compressing a coil spring behind the accumulator piston applies pressure to the fluid. The pressure equals the instantaneous spring force divided by the piston area.

Formula 17-1

$$\text{Pressure} = \frac{\text{Spring Force}}{\text{Area}}$$

Where:

$$\text{Spring Force} = \text{Spring Constant} \times \text{Compression Distance}$$

Since the spring force increases as fluid enters the chamber and decreases as it is discharged, the fluid pressure is not constant.

Spring loaded accumulators can be mounted in any position. However, the spring force (the pressure range) is not easily adjusted. Where large quantities of fluid are required, the forces involved makes spring sizes impractical.

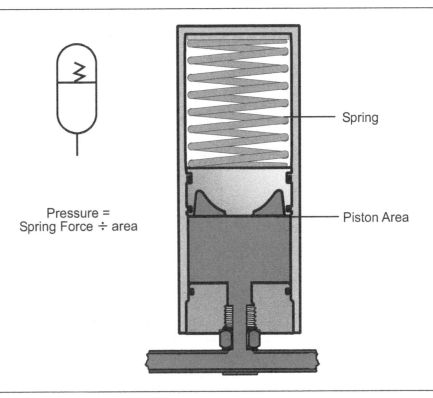

Pressure =
Spring Force ÷ area

Figure 17-3   Spring loaded accumulator

Gas-Charged Accumulator

The most popular type of accumulator has a chamber that is precharged with a compressible gas, usually dry nitrogen. Nitrogen is most commonly used because it is a stable gas that will not react with most fluids used in accumulators. Oxygen should never be used because of its tendency to burn or explode when compressed with oil. For the same reason, air is not recommended, although it is sometimes used with fluids that do not readily react with oxygen.

A gas-charged accumulator should be precharged when it is empty of hydraulic fluid. Precharge pressures vary with each application and depend upon the working pressure range and fluid volume required within that range. It should never be less than 1/4, and preferably 1/3, of the maximum working pressure. Accumulator pressure varies in proportion to the compression of the gas, increasing as fluid is pumped in and decreasing as it is expelled.

Piston-Type Accumulator

Using a free piston (Figure 17-4) is one method of separating the gas charge from the hydraulic fluid. Similar in construction to a hydraulic cylinder, the piston is under gas pressure on one side and constantly tries to force the fluid out of the opposite side of the chamber. Here too, pressure is a function of the gas compression and will vary with the volume of oil in the chamber.

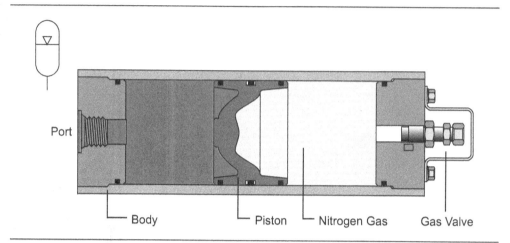

Port — Body — Piston — Nitrogen Gas — Gas Valve

Figure 17-4   Gas-charged piston accumulator

Figure 17-5 illustrates the operating cycle of a gas-charged piston accumulator. In the first step the accumulator is precharged with nitrogen gas, forcing the piston to the bottom of the accumulator. In the second step, fluid from the pump compresses the gas, partially filling the accumulator volume. Although the accumulator is fully charged with fluid, it may only be 40 to 60 percent of the total accumulator volume, the remaining volume being compressed gas. In the final step fluid flows out of the accumulator with the gas acting as a spring, pushing the fluid into the system.

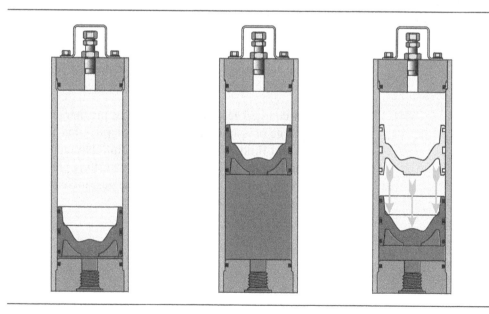

Figure 17-5   Piston accumulator operating cycle

Diaphragm or Bladder-Type

Many accumulators incorporate a synthetic rubber diaphragm or bladder (Figure 17-6) to contain the gas precharge and separate it from the hydraulic fluid. Since certain fire resistant fluids may not be compatible with conventional diaphragm or bladder materials, making the proper material selection is important. Usable fluid can vary between 1/4 and 3/4 of the total accumulator capacity, depending upon operating conditions. Operation beyond these limits can cause the separator to stretch or wrinkle, shortening its life.

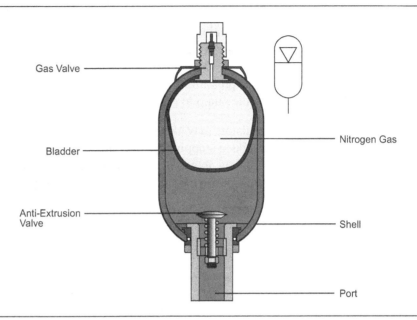

Figure 17-6   Bladder-type accumulator

Figure 17-7 shows the operation of a bladder-type accumulator. In the first step of the operation, there is no fluid present in the accumulator, so the gas precharge pushes the bladder out to fill the entire accumulator volume. In the second step, fluid from the pump pushes against the bladder, compressing the gas. Fluid continues to fill the bladder while pressures within the accumulator increase.

Fluid pressure and gas pressure will always be equal. Again, accumulator volume is not completely filled with fluid, as gas will occupy a portion of the volume. In the final step the fluid flows out of the accumulator with the gas acting as a spring, pushing the fluid into the system.

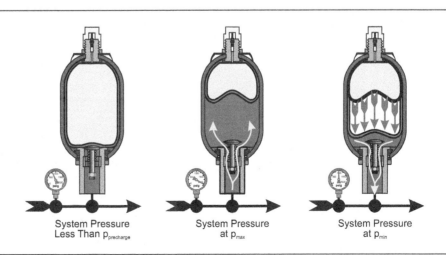

Figure 17-7   Bladder accumulator operation

Applications

In many hydraulic systems, intermittent work done during a machine cycle may require a large volume of fluid. In die casting for example, the "shot" cylinder moves very rapidly while a piece is being formed, but remains idle while the piece is being removed and during the mold closing and opening phases. Rather than use a high volume pump intermittently, such a system can utilize an accumulator to store fluid supplied by a small volume pump, discharging it during the "shot" portion of the cycle.

Some applications require pressure to be sustained for extended periods of time. Instead of allowing a pump to run constantly at the relief valve setting, it charges an accumulator. The pump can then be unloaded to the reservoir while the accumulator maintains pressure (Figure 17-8). Pressure switches, or unloading valves, periodically recycle the pump to replace fluid lost through leakage or valve actuation.

Accumulators may also be installed in a system to absorb shock or pressure surges due to the sudden stopping or reversing of fluid flow. In such cases, the precharge is close to, or slightly above, the maximum operating pressure. This allows it to "pick off" pressure peaks without constant or extended flexing of the diaphragm or bladder.

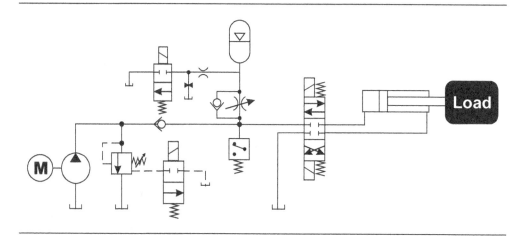

Figure 17-8   Accumulator circuit operation

CAUTION

A word of caution; the accumulator must be blocked out of the circuit or completely discharged before attempting to disconnect any hydraulic lines. Never try to disassemble any weight loaded, spring loaded or gas-charged accumulator without releasing all the pressure.

Intensifiers

An intensifier is a device used to multiply pressure. Certain applications, such as riveters or piercing machines, may require a small amount of high pressure fluid for the final portion of a work cylinder travel. An intensifier can develop pressures several times higher than that developed by the pump. In Figure 17-9, pressure on the large area exerts a force requiring a considerably higher pressure on the small area to resist it. Pressure increases inversely proportionate to the area ratios. However, the volume of fluid discharged at high pressure will be proportionately less than that required at the large end.

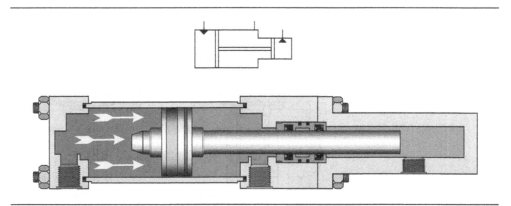

Figure 17-9   Typical pressure intensifier

Pressure Switches

Pressure switches (Figure 17-10) open or close electrical circuits at selected pressures, actuating solenoid-operated valves or other devices used in the system.

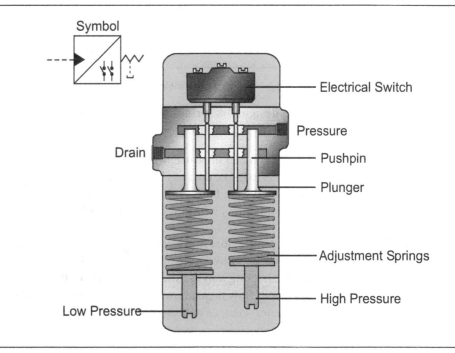

Figure 17-10   Typical pressure switch

Figure 17-11 shows the operating principal of a pressure switch. A push rod operates each of the two electrical switches by bearing against a plunger that is controlled by hydraulic and spring forces. Turning the adjusting screw to increase or decrease the spring force alters the operating pressure of each switch.

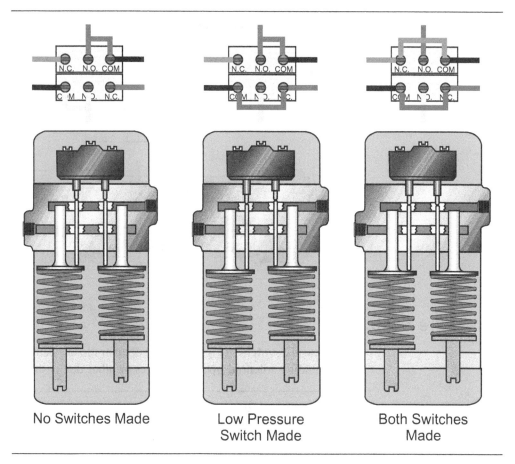

| No Switches Made | Low Pressure Switch Made | Both Switches Made |

Figure 17-11   Pressure switch operation

In this design, the springs actuate the switches when the unit is not under pressure. This leaves the normally open contacts closed and vice versa.

When the preset pressure is reached, the plunger compresses the spring, allowing the push rods to move down. This causes the snap action switches to revert to their normal condition. Using both switches in conjunction with an electrical relay maintains system pressures within widely variable high and low ranges.

Instruments

Flow rate, pressure and temperature measurements are required to evaluate the performance of hydraulic components. These factors are also helpful in setting up or troubleshooting a hydraulic system. Due to the difficulty of installing a flow meter in the circuit, flow measurements are often determined by timing the travel or rotation of an actuator. Gauges and thermometers determine pressure and temperature.

Pressure Gauges

Pressure gauges are used to adjust pressure control valves to required values. They also aid in determining the forces being exerted by a cylinder or the torque delivered by a hydraulic motor.

Two principal types of pressure gauges are the Bourdon Tube and the Schrader type. The Bourdon Tube gauge (Figure 17-12) is a sealed tube formed in an arc. When pressure is applied at the port opening, the tube tends to straighten, actuating linkage to the pointer gear and moving the pointer to indicate the pressure on a dial.

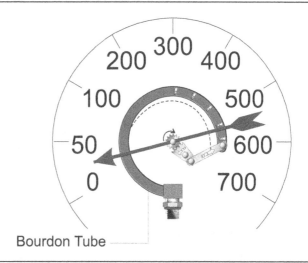

Figure 17-12   The Bourdon Tube gauge

With the Schrader type of gauge (Figure 17-13), pressure is applied to a spring loaded sleeve and piston. When pressure moves the sleeve, it actuates the gauge needle through a linkage.

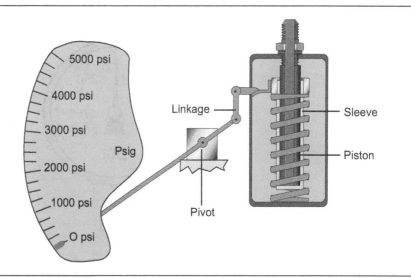

Figure 17-13   Schrader gauge operation

Most pressure gauges read zero at atmospheric pressure. They are calibrated in pounds per square inch (bar, kilopascals), ignoring atmospheric pressure throughout their range.

Pump inlet conditions are often less than atmospheric pressure. They are sometimes measured as absolute pressure (psia [bar, kPa]), but are more often calibrated in inches of mercury (millimeters of mercury) vacuum. 29.92 inches of mercury (760 mm of mercury) vacuum is considered a perfect vacuum. Figure 17-14 shows a vacuum gauge calibrated in inches of mercury and psig.

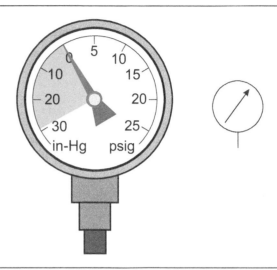

Figure 17-14   Vacuum gauge calibrated in inches of mercury

Gauge Installation

For convenience in setup and testing, it is desirable to incorporate one or more gauge connections in a hydraulic system. This is true even though gauge ports are included in most relief valves and in some other hydraulic components.

When a gauge is permanently installed on a machine, a shutoff valve and snubber (Figure 17-15) are usually installed with it. The shutoff valve prolongs gauge life by isolating it from the system except when readings are being taken.

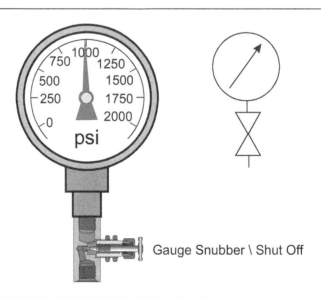

Figure 17-15   Gauge installed with shutoff valve and snubber

The snubber prevents the gauge from oscillating and protects it from pressure surges. A small coil [approximately two inches (51 mm) in diameter] of 1/8 inch (3 mm) tubing makes an effective gauge dampening device when commercially made units are not available.

Flow Meter

Flow meters are usually found on test stands, but portable test units are available. Some include the flow meter, pressure gauge and thermometer in a single unit. They may be connected permanently on a machine. Coupled into the hydraulic piping, flow meters help to check the volumetric efficiency of a pump and determine leakage paths within the circuit.

A typical flow meter (Figure 17-16) consists of a tapered plunger in a calibrated tube. Oil flows into the tube and past the plunger, moving the plunger and the magnetically coupled flow indicator.

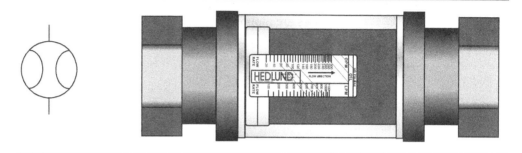

Figure 17-16   Typical flow meter courtesy of Hedland®

More sophisticated measuring devices are available that include a variety of test instruments. They may include a flow meter and transducers to measure horsepower, pressure and temperature (Figure 17-17).

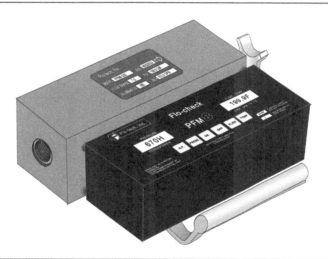

Figure 17-17   Multifunction test instrument courtesy of Hedland®

A more recent development is to use onboard electronic instrumentation. Complete machine operation can be continuously monitored with the inclusion of digital flow, temperature and pressure sensors permanently installed. This instrumentation connected to a programmable logic controller can provide complete machine information during operation and for diagnostic purposes.

Sound Damping Devices

Modern machines operate at higher pressures and more rapid cycle times than those of past years. These higher operating criteria create elevated noise levels, which can be uncomfortable, unhealthy and even dangerous to machine operators. Higher noise levels can be minimized, however, by using sound dampening methods. These include isolating pumps and electric motors from their mounting plates, using proper drive couplings and using hoses for noise isolation.

Pump and Motor Mounting Isolation

This method requires pumps and drive motors to be mounted on a common base. This subassembly is then resiliently mounted on the machine. Isolation theory assumes that isolators are mounted on a stiff structure (Figure 17-18).

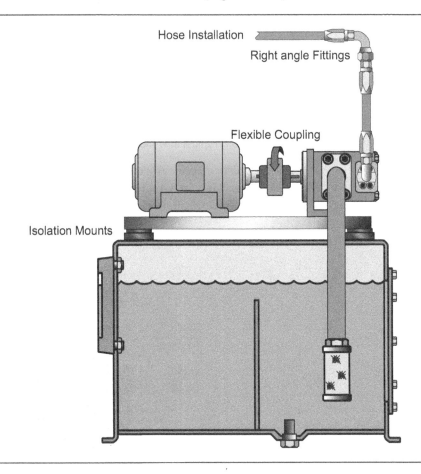

Hose Installation

Right angle Fittings

Flexible Coupling

Isolation Mounts

Figure 17-18   Noise isolation of a typical power unit

Additional control can sometimes be achieved by adding custom tuned pulsation dampening devices to the outlet of the pump. These devices are tuned to the pump and usually use a small accumulator as the noise dampener.

Drive Coupling

Drive couplings provide vibration isolation between the pump and its prime mover and reduce the effect of pump misalignment.

For isolation purposes, couplings with rubber-like material in the drive train are favored. However, many units are all metal and provide adequate isolation. Pump misalignment can cause noise by producing high loads that must be carried by the pump and motor bearings. When good alignment practices are followed, almost any commercial flexible coupling will be satisfactory. When good alignment cannot be provided, or when the torque reaction causes misalignment because only the pump is resiliently mounted, two couplings separated by a short shaft should be used.

Isolation with a Hose

When the noise source is resiliently mounted, a flexible hose must be used to accomplish isolation. Rigid lines attached to the noise source will interfere with the isolating action of the mounts. If used incorrectly, however, flexible lines will actually increase noise rather than decrease it.

Since the hose is so responsive to fluid pulsations, it can be a strong sound radiator if long lengths are used. When bent, the hose acts like a Bourdon Tube, straightening as pressure generates force. These pressure pulsations convert into cyclic forces that can cause vibration in the lines and other machine elements. Similarly, pressure changes the length of the hose. If such changes are unrestrained, forces proportionate to the pressure are generated. This mechanism converts pressure pulsations into vibration forces.

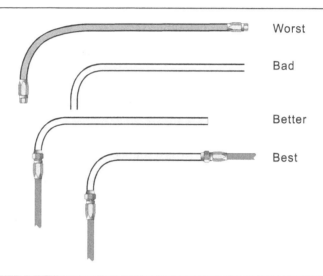

Figure 17-19   Sound and vibration isolation using hose

The best way to maintain noise control while making bends with hose is to use a solid elbow with a hose section on each end. This eliminates problems caused by the Bourdon Tube effect. Any change in length of one hose is accommodated by bending in the other hose.

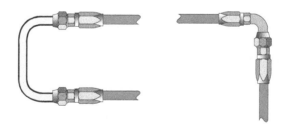

Figure 17-20   Preferred short line configurations

Isolation Line from Machine to Reservoir

Hydraulic lines are frequently responsible for propagating noise energy (line vibrations) from the noise source to the components. These components react to the energy and radiate sound. To prevent the line vibrations from reaching the machine elements, the line can be isolated using commercially available, resilient line supports. These supports suspend tubes or hoses away from the machine, lowering the radiated noise when hydraulic fluid is flowing through them.

Industrial Test Questions: Accessories

Chapter 17

1. Which type of accumulator discharges at a constant pressure? How can the pressure be changed?

2. What type of gas is preferred for gas-charged accumulators?

3. How is fluid forced out of a free piston accumulator?

4. Name two functions of an accumulator.

5. What is the purpose of an intensifier?

6. Knowing the inlet pressure, how can the outlet pressure of an intensifier be determined?

7. How is a pressure switch operated?

8. Give three situations where a pressure gauge might be required.

9. How does a Bourdon Tube gauge reflect pressure?

10. In what units of measure are vacuum gauges calibrated?

11. Why is a snubber used with pressure gauges?

12. How can a flow meter be used to determine the volumetric efficiency of a hydraulic pump or motor?

13. Name three types of sound dampening devices.

14. How does a hose bent at right angles cause hydraulic system noise?

Chapter 18 . . . . Systems

This chapter begins with a section explaining the operation of several generic hydraulic circuits that perform functions such as unloading, venting and clamping. These types of individual circuits are found within hydraulic systems. A description of a complete plastic injection molding system follows these circuit descriptions to illustrate how circuits are combined to form systems.

Industrial Hydraulic Circuits

The circuits described in this chapter are typical of systems used in industrial machinery and illustrate the basic principles of applying hydraulics to various kinds of work.

Because there are so many different applications of the principles and components described in this manual, only a sample will be illustrated here. Many of the circuits include cutaway or pictorial diagrams for ease in following oil flow. Graphical diagrams are shown for all circuits to aid in understanding the use of symbols.

Unloading Circuit

An unloading circuit exists when a pump outlet is diverted to the reservoir at low pressure during part of the cycle. This may occur to prevent load conditions from exceeding the available input power or simply to avoid wasting power and generating heat during idle periods.

Two-Pump Unloading System

While a cylinder is advancing at low pressure, this system combines the delivery of two pumps for maximum speed. When the high speed is no longer required, or the system pressure rises to a point where the combined volume would exceed the input horsepower (wattage), the larger of the two pumps is unloaded.

Low Pressure Operation

Figure 18-1A, shows the arrangement of components in an unloading system with the flow condition at low pressure. Oil from the large volume pump passes through the unloading valve and over the check valve to combine with the low volume pump output. This condition continues as long as system pressure is lower than the setting of the unloading valve.

High Pressure Operation

In Figure 18-1B, system pressure exceeds the setting of the unloading valve which opens, permitting the large volume pump to discharge to the reservoir at very low pressure. The check valve closes, preventing flow from the pressure line through the unloading valve.

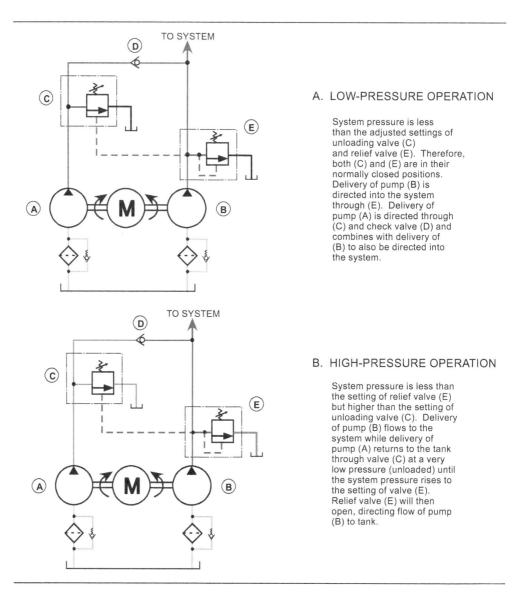

A. LOW-PRESSURE OPERATION

System pressure is less than the adjusted settings of unloading valve (C) and relief valve (E). Therefore, both (C) and (E) are in their normally closed positions. Delivery of pump (B) is directed into the system through (E). Delivery of pump (A) is directed through (C) and check valve (D) and combines with delivery of (B) to also be directed into the system.

B. HIGH-PRESSURE OPERATION

System pressure is less than the setting of relief valve (E) but higher than the setting of unloading valve (C). Delivery of pump (B) flows to the system while delivery of pump (A) returns to the tank through valve (C) at a very low pressure (unloaded) until the system pressure rises to the setting of valve (E). Relief valve (E) will then open, directing flow of pump (B) to tank.

Figure 18-1   Unloading circuit

In this condition, much less power is used than if both pumps were driven at high pressure. However, the final advance is slower because of the smaller volume output to the system. When motion stops, the small volume pump discharges over the relief valve at relief valve setting.

Automatic Venting

In systems where it is not necessary to maintain pressure at the end of a cycle, it is possible to unload the pump by automatically venting the relief valve. Figure 18-2 shows a system of this type, using a cam-operated pilot valve.

Mid Stroke Extending (Figure 18-2A). The machine cycle begins when the solenoid of the spring offset directional valve is energized. The pump outputs to the cap end of the cylinder, while the vent line from the relief valve is blocked at the cam-operated pilot valve. (Note that the pilot valve has only two flow paths instead of the usual four.)

Mid Stroke Retracting (Figure 18-2B). At the end of the extension stroke, the limit switch is contacted by the cam on the cylinder, de-energizing the solenoid. Pump output is then applied to the rod end of the cylinder by the directional valve. The relief valve vent connection is still blocked.

A. MIDSTROKE EXTENDING

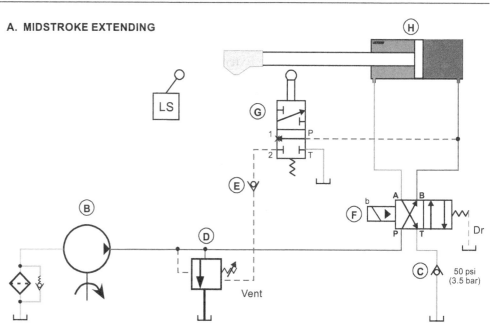

Solenoid "b" of directional control valve (F) is held energized during the extending stroke. Vent line from relief valve (D) is blocked at directional valve (G). Delivery of pump (B) is directed through (F) into cap end of cylinder (H). Discharge from rod end of (H) flows to tank through valves (F) and pilot pressure check valve (C).

B. MIDSTROKE RETRACTING

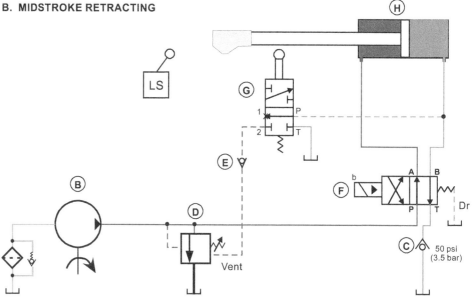

At end of extension stroke, cam on cylinder (H) contacts limit switch LS. This causes solenoid "b" of valve (F) to be de-energized. (F) shifts to the spring offset position and directs delivery of pump (B) into rod end of (H). Discharge from cap end of (H) flows to tank through valves (F) and (C).

Figure 18-2   (A & B) Automatic venting at cycle end

Automatic Stop (Figure 18-2C). At the end of the retraction stroke, the cam on the cylinder opens the relief valve vent through the pilot valve. The relief valve vent port is connected to the line from the cap end of the cylinder and is vented to the reservoir through a check valve, the directional valve, and a tank line check valve. Pilot pressure for the directional valve is maintained at a value determined by the spring load in the balanced piston of the relief valve, vent line check valve and the tank line check valve. (In this circuit, a high vent spring in the relief valve would have eliminated the need for the tank line check valve.)

Pushbutton Start (Figure 18-2D). When the start button is depressed, it energizes the solenoid. The directional valve shifts to direct the pump output into the cap end of the cylinder. This causes the vent line check valve to close, de-venting the relief valve. When pressure builds up again, the cycle is repeated.

C. AUTOMATIC STOP

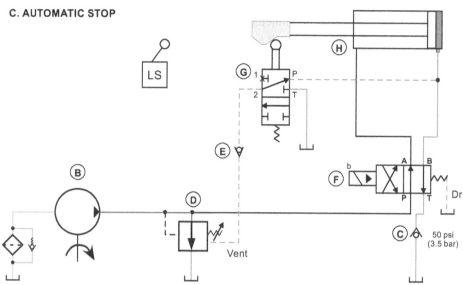

At end of retraction stroke, cam on cylinder (H) depresses valve (G). Valve (D) is now vented through valves (E), (G), (F) and (C). Delivery of pump (B) returns to tank over valve (D) at low pressure. Pressure drop through (C) assures pilot pressure for operation of (F).

D. PUSHBUTTON START

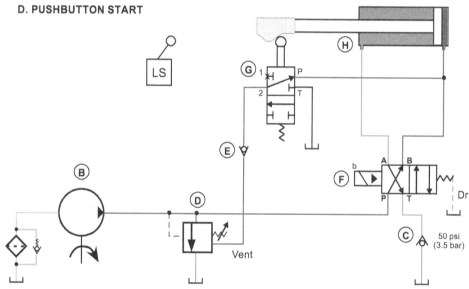

Depressing a pushbutton causes solenoid "b" of valve (F) to be held energized. (F) shifts to connect cap end of cylinder (H) to pump (B), and rod end of (H) to tank. Pilot flow from vent of (D) stops when check valve (E) closes. Pressures equalize through balance hole in hydrostat of (D) causing it to start to close. Acceleration of (H) takes place during the closing of the Hydrostat of (D).

Figure 18-2   (C & D) Automatic venting at cycle end (continued)

Accumulator Pump Unloading — Electric Control

When a preset pressure is reached in an accumulator charging circuit, the pump is unloaded. As pressure drops to a predetermined minimum, the pump cuts back in to recharge the accumulator.

A spring offset, solenoid-operated, directional valve (Figure 18-3), is actuated by a pressure switch. It is used to vent and de-vent the relief valve, as required.

Charging (Figure 18-3A). The two micro switches in the pressure switch are interconnected to an electric relay. This is done so that, at the low pressure setting, the solenoid is energized and the relief valve vent connection is blocked. The pump output flows into the system through the relief and check valve, where it charges the accumulator.

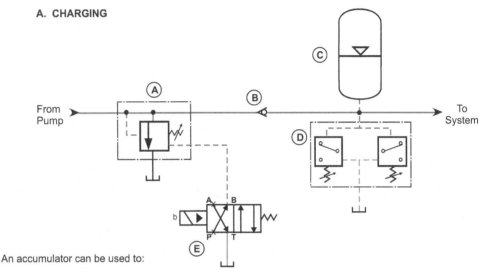

A. CHARGING

An accumulator can be used to:

- Maintain the pressure during a holding operation
- Augment pump delivery during short periods of large volume demand
- Absorb hydraulic shock

This circuit shows one method of unloading the pump when the accumulator is fully charged. It consists of relief valve (A), check valve (B), accumulator (C), dual pressure switch (D) and directional valve (E). Pressure setting of (A) is higher than the setting of (D).

The electric control circuit performs the following operations:
1) energizes solenoid (Eb) when pump motor is started
2) de-energizes (Eb) when system pressure reaches the high setting of switch (D)
3) energizes (Eb) when system pressure reduces to the low setting of the switch (D)
4) de-energizes (Eb) when pump motor is stopped

View A shows circuit conditions when system pressure is below the low setting of the switch (D). Solenoid (Eb) is energized to shift valve (E) and blocks the vent connection of valve (A). Valve (A) is devented and pump delivery is directed through valve (B) into the system. Accumulator (C) is charged with fluid if system volumetric demand is less than delivery rate of the pump.

Figure 18-3 (A) Accumulator pump unloading (electric control)

Unloading (Figure 18-3B). When pressure reaches the maximum setting of the pressure switch, the solenoid is de-energized and the relief valve is vented to unload the pump into the reservoir. The check valve closes, preventing back flow from the accumulator and maintaining pressure in the system.

B. UNLOADING

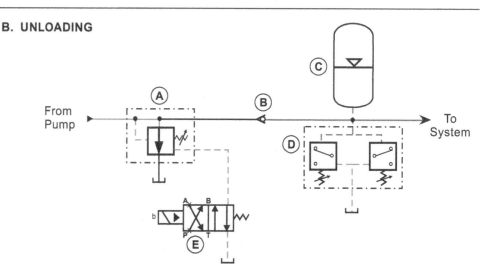

View B shows circuit condition when accumulator (C) is charged and system pressure has reached the high setting of switch (D). Solenoid (Eb) is de-energized to vent valve (A). The pump is unloaded, its delivery being returned freely to tank through valve (A). Check valve (B) closes to permit accumulator (C) to hold pressure and maintain a volume supply to the system.

Charging and unloading continue automatically until pump motor is stopped. The dual pressure switch provides means to adjust the pressure difference between pump "cut-in" and pump "cut-out". The high setting of switch (D) is the maximum pressure control for the system with overload protection provided by valve (A).

Figure 18-3   (B) Accumulator pump unloading (electric control) (continued)

Accumulator Safety Circuits — Bleed Off

When the pump is shut down, the circuit in Figure 18-4 is used to automatically bleed off a charged accumulator. This prevents accidental operation of an actuator and makes it safe to open the system for service. The bleed off is accomplished through a spring offset directional valve and a fixed restriction.

The solenoid for the directional valve is actuated by the prime mover switch so that it energizes whenever the pump is started (Figure 18-4A). During normal operation, this blocks the bleed passage.

The manual valve shown in Figure 18-4 is used to control the accumulator discharge rate into the system. The auxiliary relief valve is set slightly higher than the system relief valve, limiting any pressure rise from heat expansion of the gas charge. The accumulator must have a separator, i.e., diaphragm, bladder or piston to prevent loss of gas preload each time the machine is shut down.

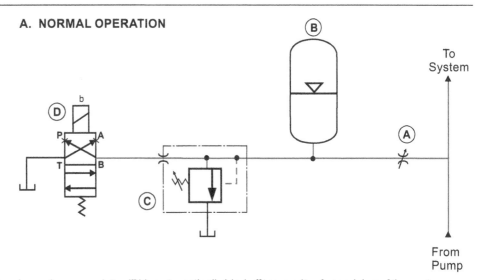

A. NORMAL OPERATION

The charge in accumulator (B) is automatically bled off to permit safe servicing of the system when pump motor is stopped. The circuit consists of needle valve (A), accumulator (B), relief valve (C) and directional valve (D). An electrical control circuit holds solenoid (Db) energized when the pump motor is running and de-energizes it when the motor is stopped.

View A shows circuit condition during normal operation of the system when the pump motor is running. Solenoid (Db) is energized to shift valve (D) and block flow to tank from accumulator (B). Accumulator is charged or discharged through valve (A) as dictated by requirements of the system. Needle valve (A) is often used to control rate of accumulator discharge to the system.

Figure 18-4   (A) Accumulator bleed-off circuit

When the pump is shut down (Figure 18-4B), the spool spring shifts the directional valve and opens the accumulator to the tank through the restriction.

B. BLEED OFF

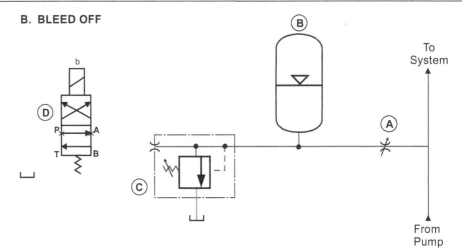

View B shows circuit condition when the pump motor is stopped. Solenoid (Db) is de-energized and the charge in accumulator (B) is bled off to tank through valve (D). Rate of bleed-off is controlled by a fixed restriction at valve (C).

Valve (C) is set slightly higher than the maximum pressure control and provides protection against excessive pressures due to thermal expansion.

Figure 18-4   (B) Accumulator bleed-off circuit (continued)

Reciprocating Circuits

Conventional reciprocating circuits provide reversal through the use of a four-way directional valve, piped directly to a cylinder or motor. When a differential cylinder is used, retracting speed is faster than extending speed because of the rod volume.

A regenerative circuit is a non-conventional, reciprocating hookup that occurs when oil from the rod end of the cylinder is directed into the cap end to increase speed.

Regenerative Advance

The principle of the regenerative circuit is shown in Figure 18-5. Note that the "B" port on the directional valve, which would normally connect to the cylinder, is plugged and the rod end of the cylinder is connected directly to the pressure line (Figure 18-5A). With the valve shifted to connect the "P" port to the cap end (Figure 18-5B), flow out of the rod end joins pump delivery, increasing the cylinder speed. In the reverse condition (Figure 18-5C), flow from the pump is directed to the rod end. Exhaust flow from the cap end returns to the tank through the directional valve.

If the ratio of cap end area to rod end annular area in the cylinder is 2:1, the cylinder will advance and retract at the same speed. However, because the same pressure in the rod end (effective over half the cap end area), opposes the cylinder's advance, the pressure during advance will be double the pressure required for a conventional circuit. With a higher ratio of areas, extending speed will increase proportionally.

A. IDLE

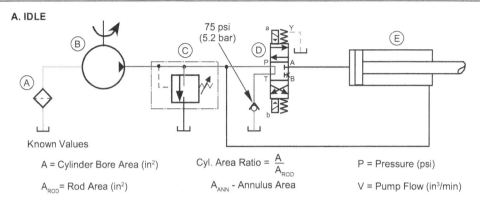

Known Values

A = Cylinder Bore Area (in²)

A_{ROD}= Rod Area (in²)

Cyl. Area Ratio = $\dfrac{A}{A_{ROD}}$

A_{ANN} - Annulus Area

P = Pressure (psi)

V = Pump Flow (in³/min)

View A shows the idle condition of the circuit when solenoids (Da) and (Db) are both de-endrgized. The pump delivery is unloaded through valve (D) and a 75 psi (5.2 bar) check valve.

The formulas shown are used to calculate speeds and forces.

B. ADVANCING

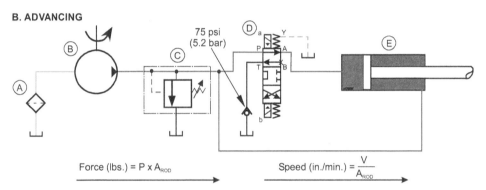

Force (lbs.) = P x A_{ROD}

Speed (in./min.) = $\dfrac{V}{A_{ROD}}$

View B shows the flow and force conditions when solenoid (Da) is energized for regenerative advance. Discharge from the rod end of the cylinder joins the pump delivery at the "P" port of valve (D) to increase the piston speed. However, note that system pressure also acts in the rod end of the cylinder to reduce the output force capability. Formulas shown are used to calculate speeds, forces and flow rates. They also show that, during regenerative advance, Speed increases and force decreases proportionately as the ratio of areas increases.

C. RETRACTING

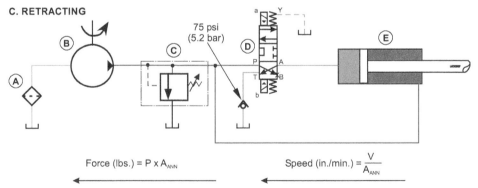

Force (lbs.) = P x A_{ANN}

Speed (in./min.) = $\dfrac{V}{A_{ANN}}$

View C shows the flow and force conditions when solenoid (Db) is energized. The pump delivery is directed into the rod end of the cylinder. The cap end of the cylinder is returned to the tank via "A" to "T" through the valve (D) and a back pressure check valve.

Figure 18-5   (A, B & C) Regenerative circuit

Regenerative Advance with Pressure Changeover to Conventional Advance

The regenerative principle also can be used to increase advance speed with a changeover to conventional advance assuming 2:1 area ratio, to double the final force (Figure 18-6). In this system, a pressure control valve that is normally closed, plugs the "B" port of the directional valve during regenerative advance. When the pressure setting of the valve is reached, it opens, routing oil from the rod end to the tank through the directional valve. The 5 psi (0.3 bar, 30 kPa) check valve permits the oil to join pump delivery during regenerative advance, but prevents pump delivery from taking this route to the tank during conventional advance. When the directional valve shifts to retract the cylinder, the pump outputs to the rod end through the check valve found in the pressure control valve.

A. IDLE CONDITION

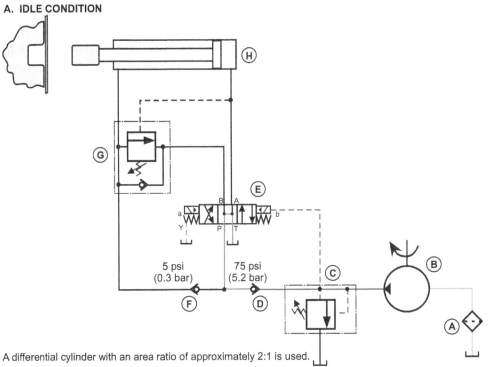

A differential cylinder with an area ratio of approximately 2:1 is used.

In the idle condition, solenoids (Ea) and (Eb) are both de-energized and delivery of the pump (B) is unloaded to the tank through valves (C), (D) and (E). Valve (D) provides pilot pressure for pilot Operation of valve (E).

B. REGENERATIVE ADVANCE

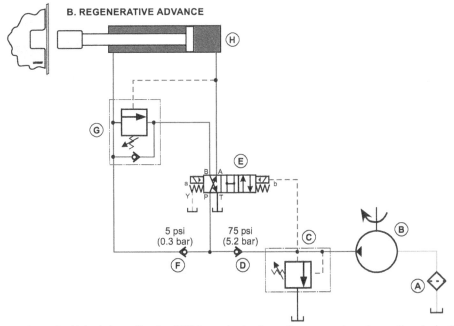

Rapid advance is obtained when, with solenoid (Ea) energized and operating pressure lower than setting of valve (G), pump flow is directed into cap end of (H) with discharge from rod end of (H) directed through valves (G) and (F) to combine with pump flow. Piston speed is determined by pump flow and cross section area of rod (H).

Figure 18-6   (A & B) Regenerative advance with pressure changeover to conventional advance

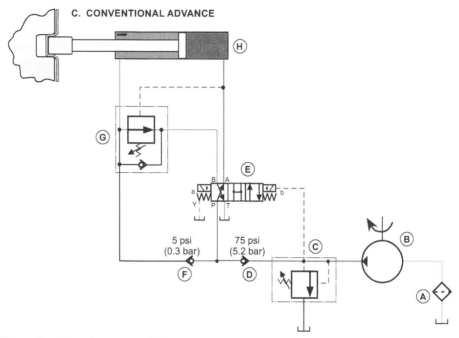

C. CONVENTIONAL ADVANCE

When work resistance is encountered, the pressure increase causes (G) to open, permitting discharge from the rod end of (H) to flow freely to the tank through (G) and (E). Piston of (H) slows to half speed, but potential thrust is now a function of full piston area and maximum operating pressure.

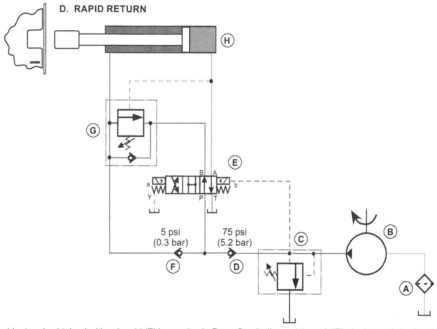

D. RAPID RETURN

Rapid return is obtained with solenoid (Eb) energized. Pump flow is directed through (E), the integral check valve in (G), and into the rod end of (H). Discharge from the cap end of (H) flows freely to the tank through (E). Piston speed is determined by pump flow and the annular area of (H), and is the same as regenerative advance speed.

Figure 18-6   (C & D) Regenerative advance with pressure changeover to conventional advance (continued)

Clamping and Sequence Circuits

In the application of clamping and machining a workpiece, it is necessary to have operations occur in a definite order. The pressure at the first operation must be maintained while the second occurs. One such circuit is shown in Figure 18-7.

Controlled Pressure Clamping Circuit. This circuit provides sequencing plus a controlled clamping pressure, which can be held while the work cylinder is feeding and retracting. Pressing the START button shifts a directional valve and causes the clamp cylinder to extend. Upon contact with the workpiece, a limit switch actuates the solenoid of another directional valve, initiating the work stroke. A sequence valve assures that during the work stroke, the clamp pressure is maintained at a predetermined minimum. When higher pressure is required for the work stroke, a pressure reducing valve limits the clamp pressure to a safe maximum.

Additional electric controls can reverse the work cylinder directional valve while pressure is maintained on the clamp. After the work cylinder is fully retracted, the clamp opens.

A. IDLE CONDITION

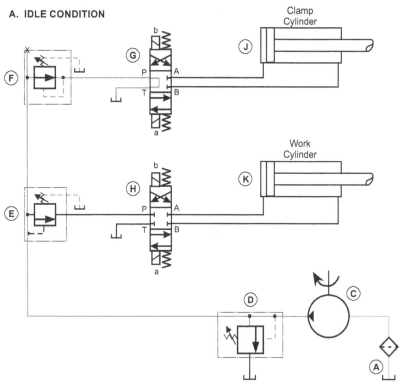

When all solenoids are de-energized, directional valves (G) and (H) are spring-centered and the delivery of pump (C) is unloaded to the tank through valve (G).

B. EXTENDING CLAMP CYLINDER

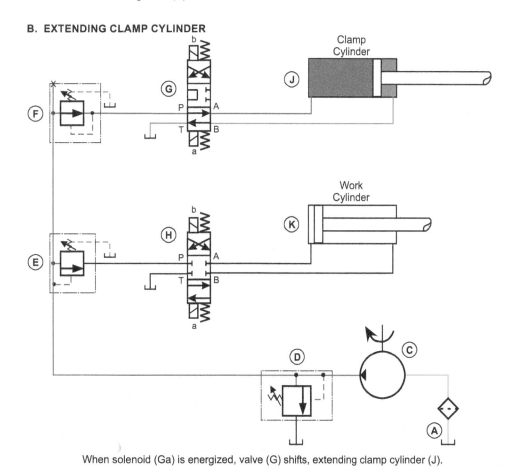

When solenoid (Ga) is energized, valve (G) shifts, extending clamp cylinder (J).

Figure 18-7   (A & B) Controlled pressure clamping circuit

C. EXTENDING WORK CYLINDER

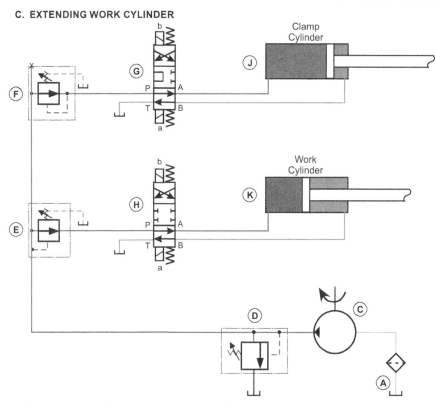

Solenoid (Ha) is energized at the end of the clamp stroke. When pressure in the cap end of clamp cylinder (J) reaches the pressure setting of valve (E), the pump flow will sequence over valve (E), extending work cylinder (K).

Valve (E) ensures a minimum clamping pressure equal to its setting during the cylinder (K) work stroke.

D. LIMITING MAXIMUM CLAMPING PRESSURE

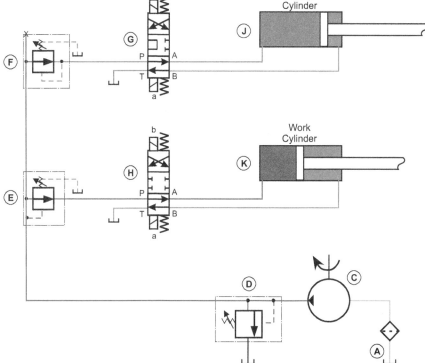

When system pressure exceeds the allowed maximum clamping pressure during the working stroke, pressure-reducing valve (F) moves toward the closed position, keeping the clamping pressure at its pressure setting. System relief valve (D) limits the maximum working pressure.

Figure 18-7   (C & D) Controlled pressure clamping circuit (continued)

E. RETRACTING WORK CYLINDER

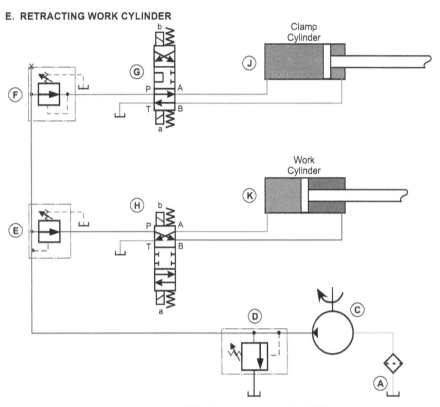

When solenoid (Ha) is de-energized and solenoid (Hb) is energized, work cylinder (K) retracts and sequence valve (E) maintains a minimum clamping pressure. Reducing valve (F) limits maximum clamping pressure.

F. RETRACTING CLAMP CYLINDER

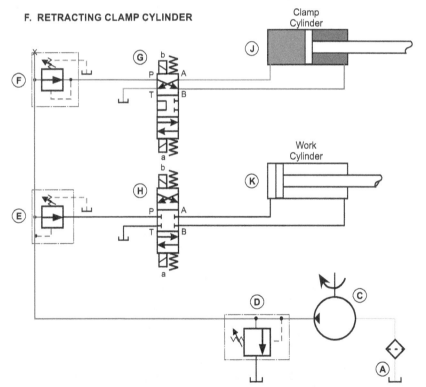

When solenoid (Hb) is de-energized, valve (H) moves to the spring-centered position and stops work cylinder (K).

When solenoid (Ga) is de-energized and solenoid (Gb) is energized, clamp cylinder (K) retracts. Solenoid (Gb) is de-energized at the end of the retraction. Valve (G) moves to the spring-centered position and the system returns to the idle condition.

Figure 18-7   (E & F) Controlled pressure clamping circuit (continued)

Brake Circuits

Figure 18-8 shows an application of a brake valve that holds a back pressure in a rotary motor when needed and brakes the motor when the open center direction valve is shifted to neutral.

Figure 18-8A shows the motor accelerating with the load pressure in the auxiliary remote control connection, holding the brake valve open. Figure 18-8B shows the motor in the RUN mode. Figure 18-8C shows the operation when the motor tries to overrun the pump, creating a lower pressure in the drive line. Neutral braking through back pressure is shown in Figure 18-8D.

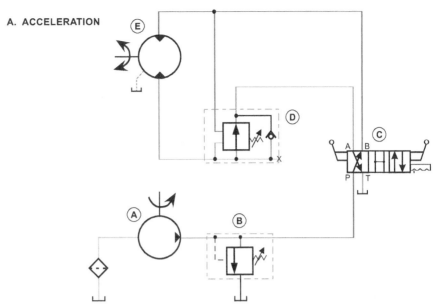

A. ACCELERATION

A brake circuit is used to stop a load with minimum shock when its driving force ceases. It may also be used to maintain control when the force imposed by the load acts in the same direction as motor rotation (overrunning load).

The desired braking force is adjusted by means of a brake valve (D) which is pilot-operated remotely and/or internally.

Remote control pressure is sampled from the input motor line and acts under the full area of the valve spool. Motor outlet pressure acts under the small piston of (D) through an internal passage.

Valve (D) is normally closed. It is opened by either or both of these pilot forces acting against an adjustable spring load.

As motor (E) accelerates, the inlet pressure at (E) and the remote pilot connection of valve (D) are lower than the pressure setting of a relief valve (B). Therefore, valve (D) is held wide open, causing no back pressure at the discharge of motor (E).

Figure 18-8   (A) Brake circuit

B. FULL SPEED RUNNING WITH AN OPPOSING LOAD

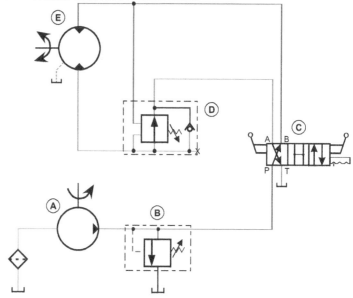

The load opposes the direction of rotation of motor (E) during "run". Working pressure required to drive this load acts under the large spool area of (D) to hold it fully open. Discharge from (E) returns freely to tank through (D) and (C). Delivery rate of pump (A) determines speed of (E).

Figure 18-8   (B) Brake circuit (continued)

C. OVERRUNNING LOAD

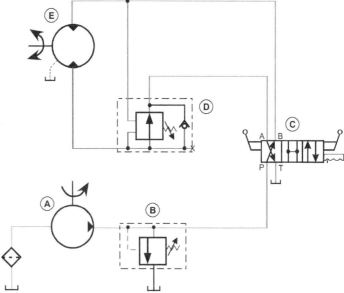

The load may act in the same direction as rotation of motor (E) in certain applications. This "negative load" assumes a portion of the driving force on motor (E) which reduces pressure at the motor inlet.

Reduced pressure at motor inlet, effective under the valve spool of (D), permits the spool to move toward its closed position, thus restricting the discharge from (E).

Restricted flow through (D) creates back pressure in the outlet of (E). This back pressure acts under the small piston of (D).

The sum of the pressures acting under the valve spool and small piston of (D) holds the valve spool at the restricting position required for sufficient back pressure to maintain control of the load on (E).

The extent of negative loading determines the amount of back pressure on (E).

Figure 18-8   (C) Brake circuit (continued)

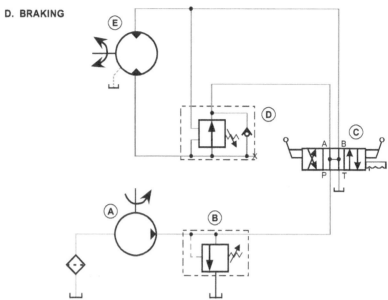

D. BRAKING

Valve (C) is shifted to the "Neutral" position to brake the load on motor (E). Pump (A) delivery is open to tank through valve (C).

Load inertia continues to drive (E) causing it to act as a pump. Inlet fluid to (E) is supplied through (C).

With the inlet of (E) open to tank, pilot pressure under the valve spool of (D) becomes zero, permitting it to move toward the closed position. This restricts discharge from (E) creating back pressure at its outlet.

Back pressure at outlet of (E) acts under the small piston of (D) opposing the spring force. These two opposing forces hold the valve spool at the restricting position. Adjusted setting of (D) therefore determines braking pressure and rate of deceleration.

Figure 18-8   (D) Brake circuit (continued)

Injection Molding System

Injection molding is one of the major processes by which thermoplastics are transformed into usable products. The two basic components of an injection molding machine are the clamp unit and the injection or plasticating unit. (See Figure 18-9.)

The development of cartridge valve and manifold technology has greatly affected the design of hydraulic controls for the injection molding machine industry. Cartridge valve circuits have replaced conventional spool valve circuits because they provide faster response times, less complicated circuitry, less leakage and longer life.

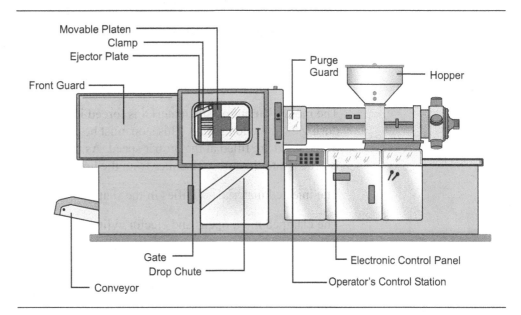

Figure 18-9   Horizontal injection molding machine

Overall Machine Circuit

The injection molding process consists of several sequential stages of operation which are explained below in simplified form:

Powdered or granular thermoplastic material is fed into the injection section of the machine.

The main clamp cylinder moves forward, closing the mold halves.

The full clamp area is pressurized to provide the force necessary to hold the two mold halves tightly together during injection of the molten thermoplastic material and also during the cooling down period.

The material is transported toward the mold and at the same time melted and mixed by the rotating injection screw. The injection screw is turned by the extruder motor. As the screw turns, the plastic pellets are sheared by the flights on the screw and then melted by heaters as they move toward the front end of the screw chamber.

The molten thermoplastic material is forced into the clamped and pressurized mold during the injection stroke. This step must be well controlled to ensure that all sections of the mold are filled at the proper speed. As the screw is retracted, new thermoplastic is drawn into the screw chamber from the hopper.

The injected material solidifies in the shape of the mold cavity.

The clamped mold opens and ejector cylinders push the completed pieces out of the mold.

It is very important to provide good pressure and flow control throughout the entire process. This ensures the repeatable cycle essential for keeping scrap losses to a minimum.

Figure 18-10 shows a block diagram of the overall injection molding machine circuitry. The system has three main manifolds that control the injection molding process. These manifolds and the functions they control are:

Pressure/Flow Control manifold (P/Q manifold) controlling system pressure and flow.

Clamp manifold controlling clamp close, mold protect, clamp pressurization and prefill shift, decompression and clamp open functions.

Injection manifold controlling injection forward, injection return, extruder run and back pressure control functions.

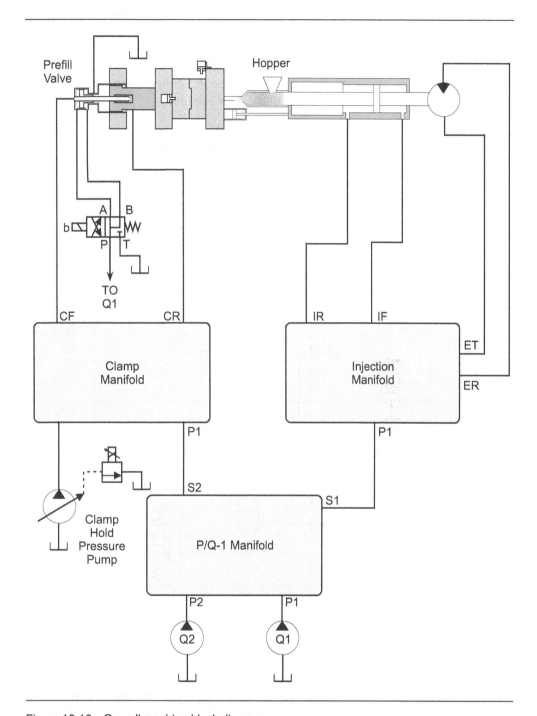

Figure 18-10   Overall machine block diagram

Pressure/Flow (P/Q) Manifold

The P/Q manifold is a flow demand dependent pump control package designed for use with two or more fixed displacement pumps. On/off loading of the larger pump is regulated by hydraulic flow demand; no additional electronic signals are required.

Remotely generated electronic analog command signals provide programmable control of system pressure and flow. The system can easily be adapted for plant computer control of production.

Basic Functions of P/Q Manifold

Figure 18-11 shows components of the P/Q manifold, along with a large pump (Q2) and a small pump (Q1). The ratio of pump flow (Q2:Q1) depends on the machine requirements. Pump flow ratios between 60:40 percent and 85:15 percent may be used. In practice, a ratio of 80:20 percent is a good compromise between energy efficiency and application flexibility. Q2 may represent one or more pumps depending upon the amount of flow required.

The P/Q manifold operates in either a pressure or flow control mode. If the pressure (M1) at the inlet of proportional throttle valve 4.0 is less than the commanded pressure setting of proportional pressure control 2.3, the P/Q manifold operates in a load sensing, pressure-compensated, flow control mode.

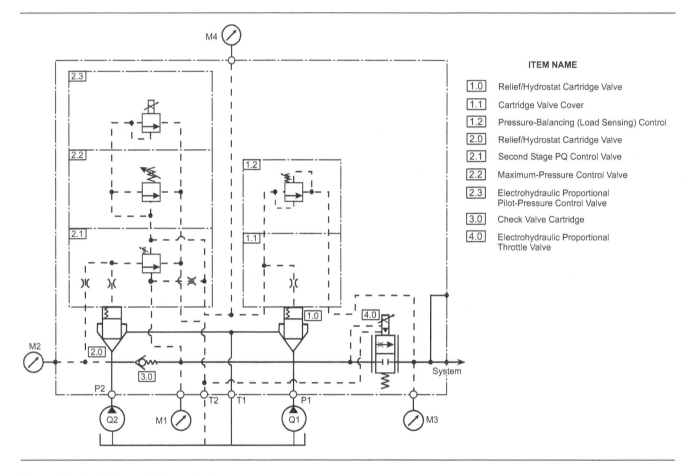

ITEM NAME	
1.0	Relief/Hydrostat Cartridge Valve
1.1	Cartridge Valve Cover
1.2	Pressure-Balancing (Load Sensing) Control
2.0	Relief/Hydrostat Cartridge Valve
2.1	Second Stage PQ Control Valve
2.2	Maximum-Pressure Control Valve
2.3	Electrohydraulic Proportional Pilot-Pressure Control Valve
3.0	Check Valve Cartridge
4.0	Electrohydraulic Proportional Throttle Valve

Figure 18-11   P/Q manifold circuit diagram

If flow to the load is less than commanded flow, for example when a cylinder has reached the end of its stroke, pressure (M1) rises to the commanded pressure setting. In this case, the P/Q manifold operates in a pressure control mode.

Small pump Q1 supplies lower flow functions such as slow movements and pressure holding. If system flow demand is less than the output of Q1, large pump Q2 is unloaded to the tank. If the system requires more flow, Q2 will automatically be loaded. On and off load response times are very short, with minimum pressure overshoot and virtually no shock.

Figure 18-12 shows pressure step response characteristics for a P/Q control manifold with a deadhead load, for example, a cylinder fully extended. Starting from the idle condition with zero command to the pilot pressure valve 2.3, relief valves 1.0 and 2.0 are open, unloading both pumps to tank at about 200 psi (14 bar, 1,400 kPa). A lower idle pressure would adversely affect dynamic performance.

Curves in Figure 18-12 show the results of applying various step pressure commands to pilot valve 2.3 at time zero. During the first 50 milliseconds (ms), relief valves 1.0 and 2.0 are closing to bring the pumps on load and deliver fluid across the open throttle to the system.

The slope of the straight line pressure increase curve reflects the volume of fluid under compression, or stiffness of the system. Systems with smaller compressed fluid volumes will have correspondingly shorter step response times.

As pressure in the system approaches the commanded level, pilot valve 2.3 controls the pressure. The second stage P/Q control valve 2.1 then shifts with a response time of about 10 ms as shown in Figure 18-12. This vents the control fluid of relief valve 2.0 to tank and starts a controlled unloading of pump Q2, which takes 28 ms. At the same time, relief valve 1.0 is also controlled by pilot valve 2.3 to maintain system pressure (M3) at the commanded value. The flow from pump Q1 which is not needed by the system is bypassed to tank at system pressure over relief valve 1.0.

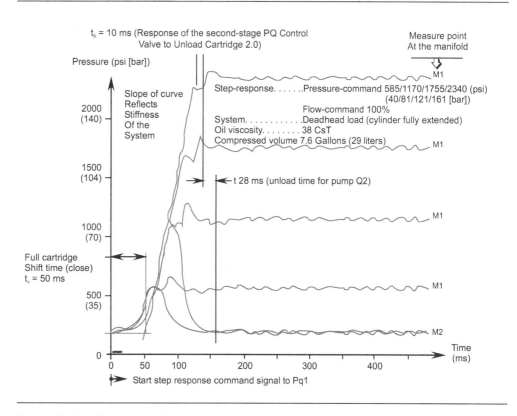

Figure 18-12   Pump unloading/pressure step response

Pressure Control Function

Valve 2.3 is an electrohydraulic proportional pilot pressure valve (Figure 18-13). It controls the pressure at relief valve 1.0 (M1) or relief valve 2.0 (M2). If system flow is less than the output of pump Q1, pressure control is at valve 1.0 and pump Q2 is unloaded to tank over valve 2.0.

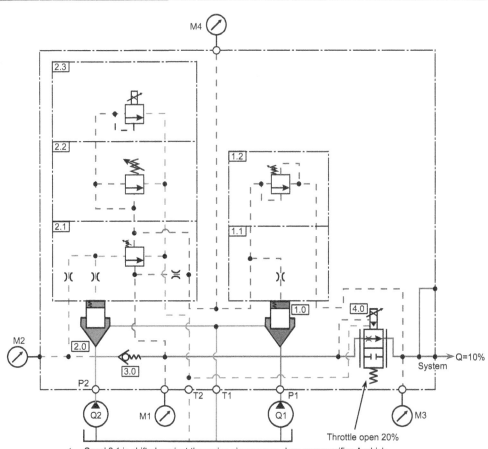

1. Spool 2.1 is shifted against the spring via pressure drop across orifice A which dumps pilot spool flow from top of poppet 2.0.
2. Q2 output is dumped to tank.
3. 2.3 controls pilot pressure on top of 1.0 (System Pressure)
4. 1.0 dumps excess flow to tank at system pressure.
5. 4.0 is open larger than actual flow to system.

Figure 18-13   Pressure control function system flow less than pump Q1 output

When system flow is greater than the output of pump Q1 (Figure 18-14), relief valve 1.0 is closed and system pressure is controlled by relief valve 2.0.

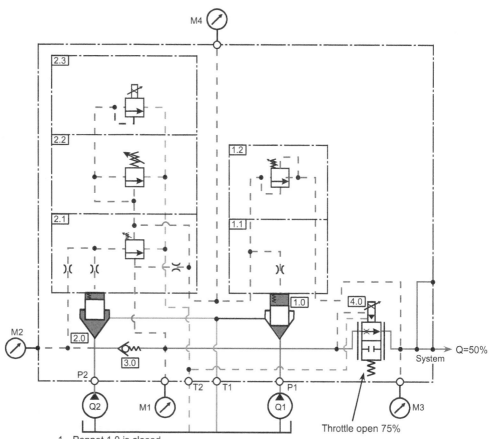

1. Poppet 1.0 is closed.
2. Valve 2.3 modulates 1st-stage pilot pressure on spool 2.1.
3. Spool 2.1 modulates 2nd-stage pilot pressure on poppet 2.0 in combination with spring adjustment and pressure drop across orifice A.
4. Pilot pressure on poppet 2.0 controls 3rd-stage (main stage) pressure.
5. Poppet 2.0 dumps excess flow to tank at system pressure.
6. Throttle 4.0 is open larger than actual flow to system.

Figure 18-14   Pressure control function system flow greater than pump Q1 output

Flow Control Function (Load Sensing)

Load sensing is achieved by a cartridge valve hydrostat combined with a proportional throttle valve that keeps the pressure difference between M1 and M3 almost constant (Figure 18-15). Consequently, there is almost a linear flow/demand signal characteristic within the whole range of load pressure and flow variation. The proportional throttle with feedback position control assures high repeatability.

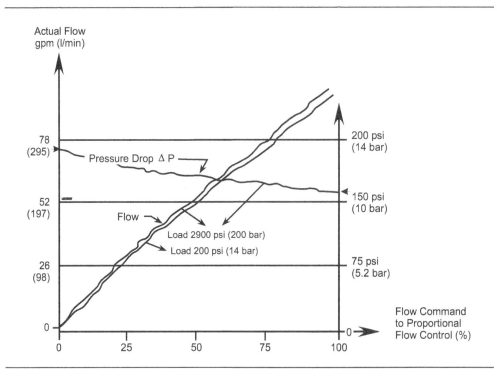

Figure 18-15   Flow and pressure drop vs. flow command

A good match between maximum flow and maximum demand signal can be achieved by selecting the appropriate available flow range for the proportional throttle valve 4.0.

Valve 4.0 (Figure 18-14) is an electrically modulated proportional throttle valve. Combined with cartridge valve 1.0 or 2.0 (acting as a hydrostat), the throttle provides a three-way (bypass type) pressure-compensated flow control or load sensing function.

If the flow command to the throttle 4.0 is less than the output of pump Q1, excess flow from pump Q1 goes over cartridge valve 1.0 to tank. Valve 1.0 acts as the pressure compensating hydrostat to maintain a near constant pressure drop across throttle 4.0 of about 215 psi (14.8 bar, 1,480 kPa) at zero flow. Cartridge valve 2.0 opens to unload pump Q2 to tank.

If the flow command to throttle 4.0 is greater than the output flow of pump Q1, cartridge valve 1.0 is closed and excess flow from pump Q2 goes over cartridge valve 2.0 to tank. Valve 2.0 acts as a pressure compensating hydrostat in this case.

The hydrostatic pressure drop (M3-M1) equals the 100 psi (7 bar, 700 kPa) cracking pressure of valve 1.0 plus the 115 psi (8 bar, 800 kPa) setting of valve 1.2.

The flow vs. command curves of Figure 18-15 show that the P/Q manifold provides excellent pressure compensation. Only a small change in flow results from a large change in load pressure.

Injection Manifold

The injection cycle consists of the following phases:

- Extruder Run/Back Pressure Control
- Melt Decompression (Injection Return)
- Injection Forward

As shown in Figure 18-16, the injection unit consists of a screw and barrel, hopper, extruder motor and injection cylinder which are all mounted on a movable carriage. The screw, extruder motor and injection cylinder form a single unit that is capable of moving while the carriage remains stationary.

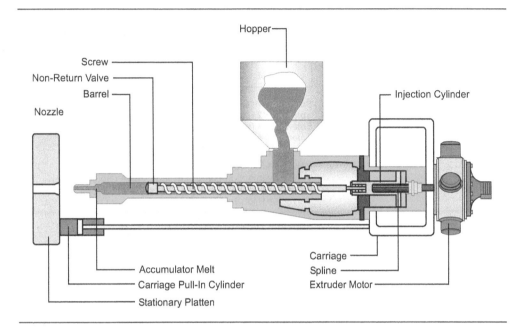

Figure 18-16 Injection unit pictorial diagram

Good control of the injection unit is essential for maintaining a precisely repeatable cycle that ensures the production of quality parts. Because molds are becoming more intricate, surface finish tolerances are more exacting, and the materials being used are more exotic, plastic processing machines in use today require very sophisticated controls.

The injection manifold must be able to control the following injection unit variables:

- Speed of the extruder motor during the melting of the plastic
- The back pressure on the plastic during the melting process
- Barrel heater temperatures
- Speed of injection (injection profiling)
- Pressure control of the mold fill and hold sequences

Figure 18-17 is a solenoid chart that indicates the status of valve solenoids during the various injection phases. Figures 18-18 through 18-20 show the injection unit circuitry during each portion of the cycle. Refer to these diagrams while proceeding through the injection cycle descriptions presented below.

SOLENOID	Y1	Y2	Y3	Y4	Y5
EXTRUDER-RUN/BACK PRESSURE	X				X
INJECTION RETRACT		X			X
INJECTION FORWARD			X		X
CARRIAGE RETURN				X	
CARRIAGE FORWARD & HOLD					X

Solenoid Y1 (Valve 1) = Extruder-Run Cartridge Valve
Solenoid Y2 (Valve 2) = Injection-Back Cartridge Valve
Solenoid Y3 (Valve 3) = Injection-Forward Cartridge Valve
Solenoid Y4 (Valve 7) = Carriage Pull-In Direction Valve
Solenoid Y5 (Valve 7) = Carriage Pull-In Direction Valve

Valve 1 = Extruder-Run Cartridge Valve (Solenoid Y1)
Valve 2 = Injection-Back Cartridge Valve (Solenoid Y2)
Valve 3 = Injection-Forward Cartridge Valve (Solenoid Y3)
Valve 4 = Pilot Shuttle Valve
Valve 5 = 4:1 Back Pressure Cartridge Valve
Valve 6 = Tank Cartridge Valve
Valve 7 = Carriage Pull-In Direction Valve
Valve 8 = Manual Flow Control

Figure 18-17   Injection cycle solenoid chart

In normal operation, the carriage is held in the forward position against the mold by the carriage pull-in cylinder. (See Figure 18-18.) This prevents any backward movement of the carriage that might be caused by the force of injection during the injection forward portion of the cycle. Solenoid Y5 on the carriage pull-in directional valve (7) remains energized throughout the entire injection process.

In the event that material must be cleaned from around the nozzle of the injection barrel, or if maintenance is required on the injection unit, solenoid Y5 is de-energized and solenoid Y4 is energized to produce movement of the carriage away from the mold.

Extruder Run/Back Pressure Control

During this initial phase of the injection cycle, plastic pellets are transformed into a viscous material that can be injected into a mold. The extruder motor is a hydraulic low speed, high torque motor that is coupled to the injection screw. As the motor and screw turn, plastic pellets are gravity fed from the hopper, pushed forward by the motion of the screw across the flights of the screw and directed to the front of the barrel. As the pellets pass between the flights of the screw and the inside of the barrel, shear energy is exerted on the plastic. At the same time, heat energy is added to the polymer from the electrically controlled barrel heaters. The continuously rotating screw provides a mixing action which blends in any colorants and helps maintain a homogeneous melt. Some materials require more heat energy than others for optimum plastification and consistency.

The melting and mixing action of the injection unit can be controlled by regulating screw speed and by exerting a constant back pressure on the screw and melt as the screw turns. In this way, the energy exerted into the material is held constant, resulting in a uniform density of the material before it is injected into the mold.

The screw rotates and pushed the viscous plastic material forward to the front of the barrel where it accumulates. This action produces a pressure on the screw and injection cylinder causing the unit to back away from the nozzle end of the barrel. This movement is slowed and controlled by the opposition of the back pressure on the injection cylinder set up by the injection manifold. Movement continues until the injection unit has moved far enough to reach a preset shot size. The distance that the screw moves backward is usually monitored by some form of stroke transducer or limit switch. Feedback from this device is directed to the electronic controller that sends the run commands to the extruder motor and screw. When the appropriate shot size is reached, the controller turns off the extruder motor.

As shown in Figure 18-18, the extruder motor is activated by controller selection of solenoid Y1. At the same time, the motor speed is controlled by an analog command sent to the flow control circuitry on the P/Q manifold. Extruder motor speed can be controlled either open or closed loop depending on the sophistication needed.

In many cases, a very low back pressure control is needed to provide proper consistency of the melt. Back pressure is regulated by controlling the pilot pressure of cartridge valve 5 on the injection manifold. The controlling pressure is provided by the Auxiliary Pressure Control block through connection S1 on the injection manifold. All pressure valves have a minimum pressure they can control. The back pressure valve shown in Figure 18-18 has an area ratio of 4:1 between the bottom and top of the cartridge. By using this ratio, the minimum controllable pressure can be lowered and a pressure control of 1/4 of the pilot pressure can be achieved. Fluid from the injection cylinder is forced by the backward movement of the screw through valve 5 to tank at a pressure controlled by the valve. The other port (Z2) that closes the valve is vented to tank through a directional valve on cartridge 3 during this cycle.

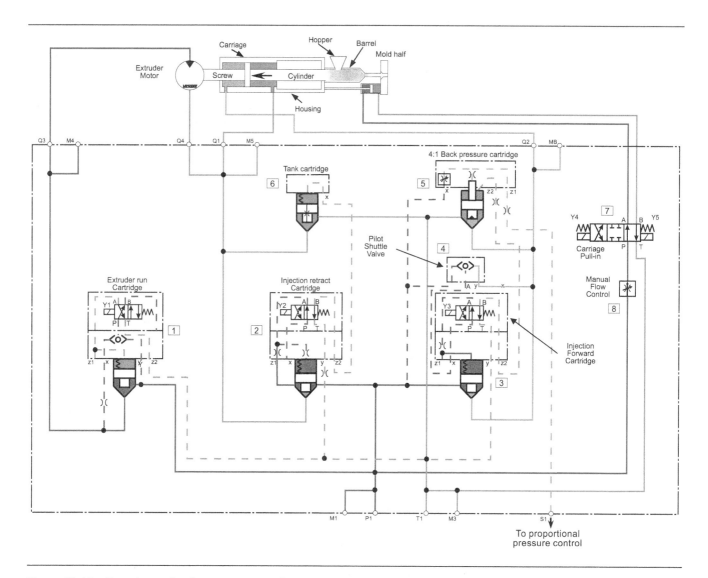

Figure 18-18   Extruder run/back pressure control circuit

Melt Decompression

While the extruder motor and screw are loading the barrel with molten material, the plastic in the mold from the previous shot has hardened. This part must be removed before a new injection forward cycle can be initiated. If the mold opens while back pressure is on the melt in the barrel, plastic material would be forced out of the nozzle end of the injection unit. For this reason, the melt in the barrel must be decompressed before the mold can be opened. This is accomplished by energizing solenoid Y2 on the injection return cartridge valve (2). (See Figure 18-19.) This vents pilot pressure on the A_P area of the valve to tank, allowing the valve to open. Flow through the valve is applied to the screw end of the injection cylinder and moves the injection unit return for a very short stroke while the mold is opened for extraction of the previous part. Back pressure control from the P/Q manifold is removed by the controller and fluid from the other side of the injection cylinder returns to tank through valve 5. The mold is then closed for the injection forward portion of the cycle.

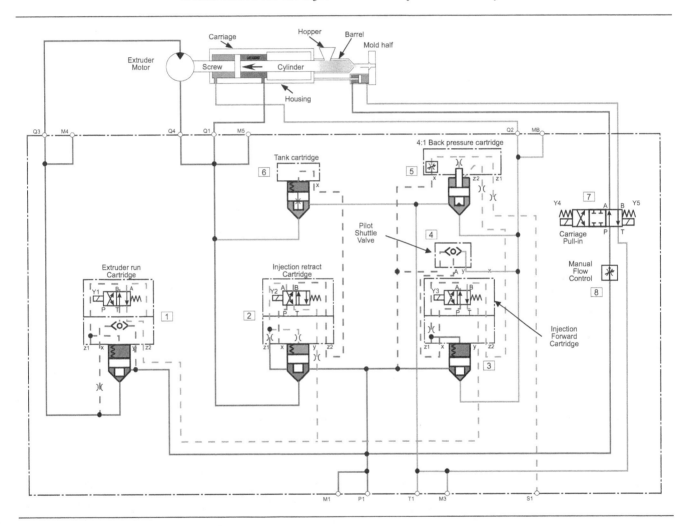

Figure 18-19   Melt decompression control circuit

Injection Forward

The next step is to inject the polymer into the mold at a controlled speed and pressure. (See Figure 18-20.) By energizing solenoid Y3, valve 3 opens and diverts flow from the P/Q block into the injection cylinder. An analog flow command is provided to control the rate at which the plastic fills the various parts of the mold. As the injection cylinder is pushed forward, the oil in the opposite side of the cylinder is diverted to tank across cartridge valve 6. Pilot pressure is applied to both of the closing ports on valve 5, keeping it closed during injection forward. Valves 1 and 2 are also closed while the injection cylinder moves forward.

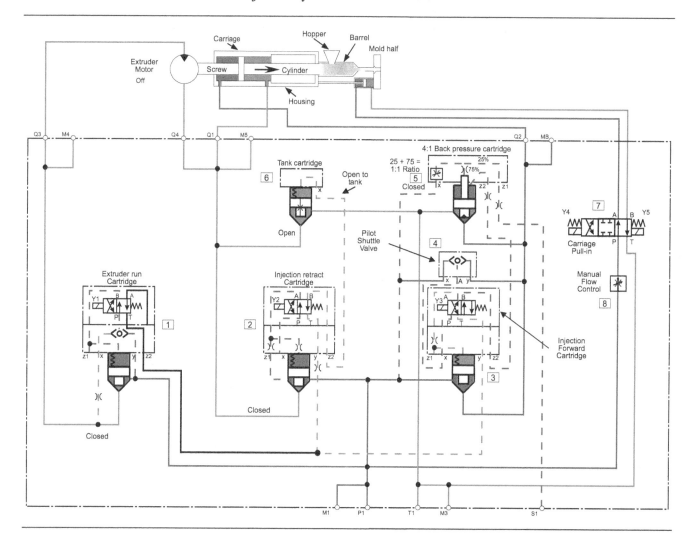

Figure 18-20   Injection forward control circuit

As the viscous plastic is forced into the mold, a resistance is created which tends to push the injection unit away from the mold, so the injection unit must be held forward by applying pressure to the injection unit pull-in cylinder. Solenoid Y5 remains energized to apply this hydraulic pressure through valve 7.

Once the mold is filled with the molten plastic, a pressure must be maintained on the plastic until it is cooled. Solenoid Y3 remains energized and an analog command is maintained on the pressure control on the P/Q manifold to accomplish the pressure profile programmed on the controller.

Clamp Manifold

The clamp manifold controls the direction and speed of clamp motions during the clamping cycle of the injection molding process. This cycle includes clamp close, low pressure mold protection, clamp pressurization and prefill shift, decompression and clamp open with regeneration.

As shown in Figure 18-21, the clamp unit consists of a movable and a stationary platen, the mold halves, an ejector cylinder, a main cylinder, a booster ram, a prefill valve and a reservoir.

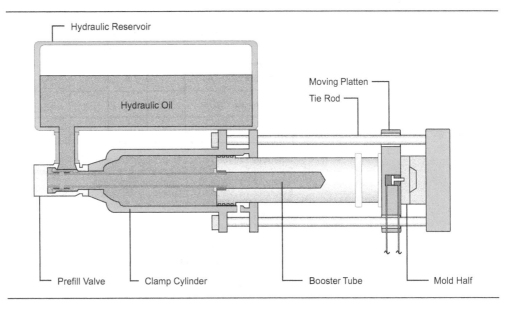

Figure 18-21   Clamp unit pictorial diagram

Figure 18-22 shows a solenoid chart that indicates the status of valve solenoids during the various phases of operation. Figures 18-23 through 18-26 show the clamp directional circuitry for each part of the cycle. Refer to these illustrations while proceeding through the clamp motion descriptions presented below.

SOLENOID	Y1	Y2	Y3	Y4	Y5	Y6	Y7
CLAMP CLOSE		X			X		
LPMP		X			X	X	
PRESSURIZATION		X			X		X
DECOMPRESSION				X			X
CLAMP OPEN/REGEN	X		X				

Solenoid Y1 (Valve 6) = Clamp Open Regenerative Pilot Valve
Solenoid Y2 (Valve 4) = Counterpressure Selection Direction Valve
Solenoid Y3 (Valve 3) = Clamp Open Cartridge
Solenoid Y4 (Valve 9) = Clamp Open to Tank Cartridge
Solenoid Y5 (Valve 1) = Clamp Close Cartridge
Solenoid Y6 (Valve 11) = Low-Pressure Mold-Protection Valve
Solenoid Y7 (Valve 10) = Prefill Shift Valve

Valve 1 = Clamp Close Cartridge (Solenoid Y5)
Valve 2 = Main Stage Interlock Cartridge
Valve 3 = Clamp Open Cartridge (Solenoid Y3)
Valve 4 = Counterpressure Selection Direction Valve (Solenoid Y2)
Valve 5 = Intensification Relief Valve
Valve 6 = Regenerative Pilot Valve (Solenoid Y1)
Valve 7 = Clamp Close to Tank Cartridge
Valve 8 = Regenerative Cartridge
Valve 9 = Clamp Open to Tank Cartridge (Solenoid Y4)
Valve 10 = Prefill Shift Valve (Solenoid Y7)
Valve 11 = Low-Pressure Mold Protection Valve (Solenoid Y6)
Valve 12 = Gate Valve

Figure 18-22   Clamp motion solenoid chart

Clamp Close

Figure 18-23 shows the pressure and return flow paths involved in closing the clamp at the start of the clamping cycle. Fluid at main pressure enters the clamp manifold at P1 and at pilot pressure through the hydraulic interlock valve (12) at R. Valve 12 is shown in the position indicating that the gate in front of the mold area is closed. Pilot pressure works to move the ball in the pilot-operated check valve on top of valve 2 off its seat. This vents the pressure in the A_P area of the cartridge valve to tank and allows valve 2 to open due to the main pressure felt at port B of the cartridge valve. Main flow is blocked at valve 3 because of the pressure on the A_P area of this cartridge combined with the spring force. Main flow is also blocked at valve 11.

Fluid at the main pressure flows through valve 2 and then to valve 1, the clamp close cartridge. At this time, solenoid Y5 is energized opening a path from the A_P area of valve 1 to the low pressure side of the cartridge and allowing the main pressure at port A to lift the poppet off its seat. Fluid at main pressure then flows through valve 1 and on to the booster ram of the clamp cylinder producing a force that causes the clamp to move forward. Solenoid Y4 is energized at this time and keeps pilot pressure on the A_P area of valve 9 which blocks flow through that valve during clamp close. The flow is also blocked at valve 8 and valve 6. Solenoid Y7 is de-energized, allowing pressure to open the prefill valve. This permits fluid from the reservoir to fill the main cylinder area while the clamp is moving forward.

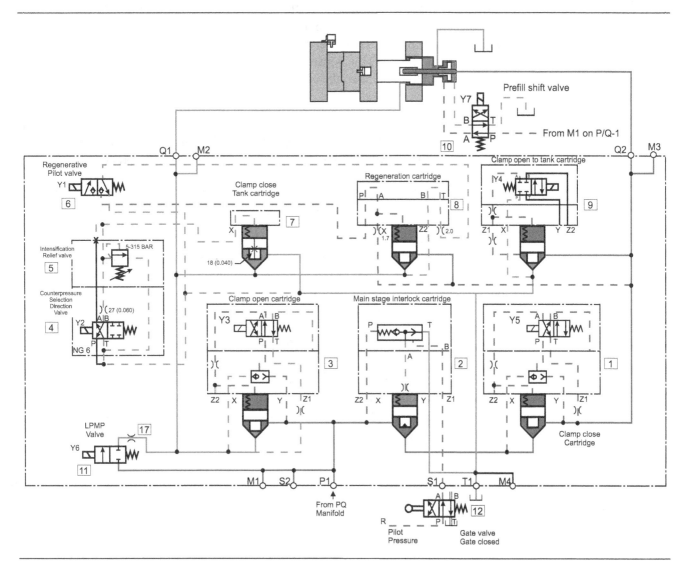

Figure 18-23   Clamp close (without LPMP) control circuit

Fluid from the pullback area of the main clamp cylinder flows through valve 7, the clamp close tank cartridge, and then to tank. The pressure of the return oil permitted through valve 7 is determined by the pilot pressure on the A_P area. The path for pilot flow is through orifice 18 in the insert, through the cover and across orifice 27 to tank through valve 4 (Y2 is energized). Orifice 18 determines the pilot flow, while orifice 27 dictates the pilot pressure on top of cartridge 7. These conditions, in turn, determine the back pressure present during clamp close. This pressure should be just high enough to prevent cavitation from a runaway load as the clamp is closing. Return flow is blocked at both valve 3 and valve 11.

Low Pressure Mold Protection

Low pressure mold protection (LPMP) is a provision in the hydraulic circuit that helps to protect the mold from damage that might be caused by an obstruction between the mold halves or by excessive speed commands. During clamp close fast (before the mold protection stroke) the booster ram moves the clamp mass forward at high speed with a low back pressure on the return line side.

When LPMP is selected (by setting a switch on the control panel) the LPMP circuitry is activated near the end of the clamp close stroke at a point that is determined by the LPMP stroke parameter [e.g., 2 inches (51 mm)]. This parameter is inserted in a microprocessor control program during the machine mold setup procedure.

Figure 18-24 shows the flow paths in the clamp directional circuit during the LPMP stroke, when the overall force on the mold must be limited. When the LPMP circuitry is activated, the flow control valve command on the P/Q block is limited to 10 percent of maximum flow and the pressure command is set at the minimum pressure required to keep the mold moving. These actions limit the flow to the booster ram which reduces the closing speed. At the same time, solenoid Y6 is energized by the LPMP circuitry allowing valve 11 to provide additional flow across cartridge valve 7 to tank. This additional flow maintains a flow across valve 7 to tank at a pressure drop approximately equal to the spring cracking pressure. This occurs whether the clamp is moving or stopped by an obstruction in the mold. The cracking pressure is also seen at the rod end of the clamp cylinder which opposes the force of the booster ram. By increasing the pressure command on the P/Q manifold just high enough to overcome the combination of back pressure and friction, the net force for closing can be controlled to a minimum. Orifice 17 is sized to provide enough flow to produce an additional back pressure that is just low enough to keep the clamp moving.

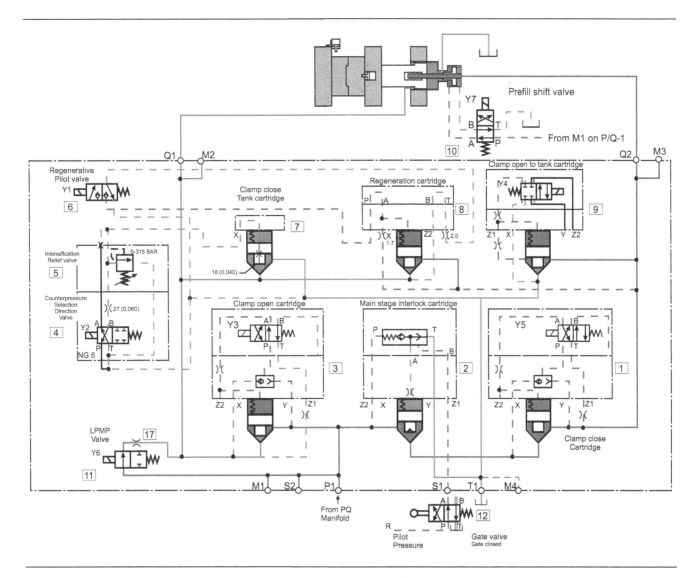

Figure 18-24   Clamp close (with LPMP) control circuit

Normally, obstructions are not encountered and the clamp closes completely under the lower pressure. Under LPMP conditions, any obstruction creates an additional force that, when combined with the existing back pressure force, overcomes the force closing the mold. This prevents the clamp from closing further and protects the mold.

Clamp Pressurization / Prefill Shift

Figure 18-25 shows the clamp directional circuit conditions during the clamp pressurization cycle. The main stage hydraulic interlock cartridge (2) and the clamp close cartridge (1) are still open and allow flow of fluid at system pressure up to the clamp cylinder. Solenoid Y4 is energized keeping cartridge valve 9 closed. Solenoid Y6 is de-energized because LPMP is no longer active once the clamp is fully closed. Other circuit conditions are as before with the exception of solenoid Y7 which is energized during the pressurization cycle. This allows pressure from M1 on the PQ manifold to apply a force to shift the prefill valve to its closed position.

Closing the prefill valve blocks the path between the main clamp area and the reservoir but opens a path between the main clamp area and the booster ram area. The main clamp area can now be pressurized under the control of the PQ manifold and variable pump. The amount of pressure that is allowed to build up is controlled by a microprocessor program. A tonnage build parameter is inserted into the program during mold setup to limit the maximum pressure to a specified value.

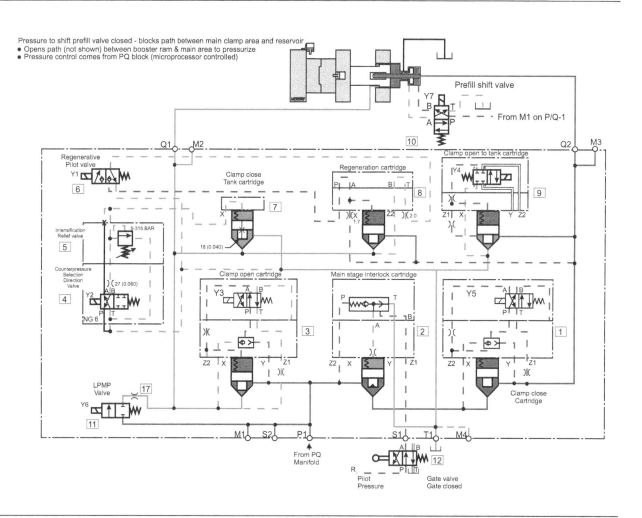

Figure 18-25   Clamp pressurization control circuit

Decompression

The pressurized oil in the main clamp cylinder must be decompressed prior to opening the clamp. Decompression is accomplished by de-energizing solenoid Y4 for a short amount of time to remove the pilot pressure on valve 9, the clamp open to tank cartridge valve, allowing it to open and pass oil to tank. Orifices on this cartridge control the opening speed to regulate the flow velocity of the pressurized oil, keeping it low enough to prevent overheating. When decompression is complete, solenoid Y4 is de-energized for the clamp open with regeneration cycle.

Clamp Open with Regeneration

Figure 18-26 shows the clamp directional circuit during the clamp open cycle. This circuit also includes regeneration circuitry to allow fluid from the booster ram area to assist in opening the clamp. Regeneration ability usually depends on a 2:1 area ratio between the booster ram area and the clamp open (pullback) area and must, therefore, be considered when designing the clamp. Regeneration permits closing and opening the clamp at the same speed even though the opening and closing areas are different.

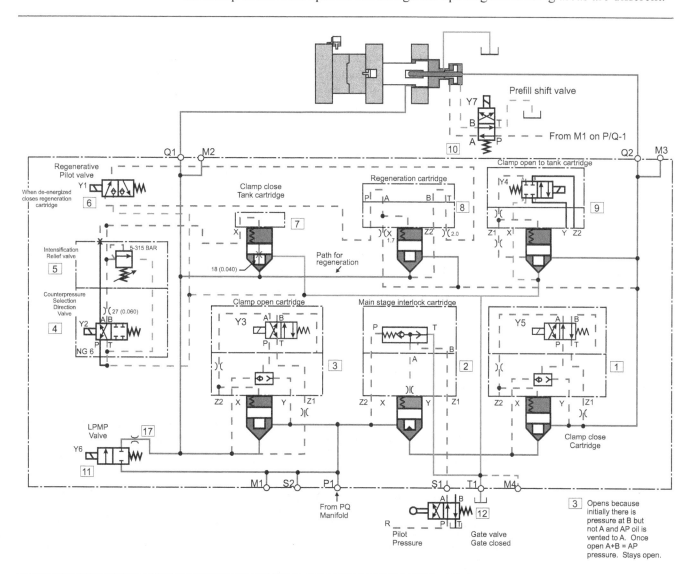

Figure 18-26   Clamp open with regeneration control circuit

At the start of the clamp open cycle, solenoid Y3 is energized allowing the clamp open cartridge 3 to open. Initially, fluid at main pressure is present at port B of valve 3. The A_P area of the cartridge is vented to the line coming from the A port through the directional valve in the cover so the flow at port B opens the valve. The pressure drop from port B to port A causes the pilot fluid from the A_P area to flow to the line connected to port A. The flow through valve 3 goes directly to the pullback area of the clamp cylinder and begins to open the clamp.

Cartridge valve 2 is open if the gate is closed, but cartridge valve 1 will be held closed by the spring force. Valve 1 has a 1:2 area ratio between the A:A_P areas which keeps the valve closed under normal conditions. However, during deceleration of the clamp open movement, the pressure of the booster ram tends to rise above the drive pressure. This places additional pressure at the B port of valve 1, which could open the valve. In this case, however, the shuttle would shift to divert the B port pressure to the A_P area, keeping the valve closed.

Solenoid Y7 is de-energized so the prefill valve is open allowing fluid from the main clamp cylinder to flow back into the reservoir. The path from the main cylinder area to the booster ram area is closed so the fluid in the booster ram area flows out of the cylinder to port B of valve 8, the regeneration cartridge. All other return paths are blocked during clamp open.

Solenoid Y7 is de-energized so the prefill valve is open allowing fluid from the main clamp cylinder to flow back into the reservoir. The path from the main cylinder area to the booster ram area is closed so the fluid in the booster ram area flows out of the cylinder to port B of valve 8, the regeneration cartridge. All other return paths are blocked during clamp open.

Solenoid Y1 is energized during the clamp open cycle so the regeneration pilot valve (6) provides a path for venting the A_P area of valve 8 to the line coming from port A of valve 8. This allows the force at port B, which is produced by the booster ram flow, to open the valve. Because of the pressure drop across the valve, the pressure at port A is lower than the pressure at port B so the pilot flow will join with the main flow through the valve. The flow through the regeneration cartridge is also directed to the pullback area of the main clamp and assists the main flow from valve 3 in opening the clamp.

Clamp Motion Safety Circuitry

Valve 5, the intensification safety valve, prevents damage to the hydraulic components that might be caused by pressure intensification. If valve 4 fails or gets plugged and the prefill is commanded to close before the mold halves touch, the main clamp area would be allowed to pressurize. The only opposition to this force would be the fluid in the clamp pullback area. This area is commonly one-twentieth (1/20) of the main clamp area, so a 2,500 psi (175 bar, 17,500 kPa) clamp pressure setting would cause a 50,000 psi (3,450 bar, 34,500 kPa) pressure on the smaller area. This would definitely cause component failure and, very likely, injury to personnel. Valve 5 is an adjustable pressure relief valve that can be set anywhere between 72 and 4,569 psi (5 bar, 500 kPa and 315 bar, 31,500 kPa). Should pressure intensification occur, the valve opens at the preset pressure level providing a path to tank that prevents any further pressure buildup.

Another safety feature on the clamp manifold is provided by valve 2, the main stage interlock cartridge. Industry safety standards require that both a hydraulic and an electrical interlock must be provided in the circuitry controlling the flow of oil to the clamp close cylinder. When the gate is closed, it creates both a hydraulic and an electrical signal allowing oil to be delivered to the clamp close side of the main clamp cylinder. The electrical signal is provided by a cam on the gate that closes an electrical limit switch.

The hydraulic signal is provided by pilot pressure from gate valve 30 to the pilot-operated check valve on top of the main stage interlock cartridge valve. When the gate is closed, a cam on the gate shifts the directional valve 12 to port the oil to the pilot valve. If the gate is opened or there is a pilot line break, the pilot-operated check valve will close and main pressure will be present on the A_p area of valve 2. This pressure along with the spring force closes valve 2, shutting off the main flow of oil to the clamp close cylinder.

Some circuits also include a proximity switch which senses the spool position to ensure that the poppet on valve 2 does not stick open. If the proximity switch sends a signal to the controller saying that the poppet is open when it should be closed, the software in the controller activates circuitry to shut off the pumps. System operation cannot resume until the error is corrected.

Industrial Test Questions:
Systems

Chapter 18

1. Name two reasons for using an unloading circuit.

2. Why is the high volume pump of a two-pump system often unloaded during high pressure operation?

3. When is it appropriate to use automatic venting?

4. In an accumulator/pump unloading circuit, when is the pump unloaded?

5. If a cylinder in a regenerative circuit has a ratio of cap end area to rod end annular area of 2:1, will the cylinder advance and retract at the same speed? Will a higher area ratio cause the extending speed to proportionately increase or decrease?

6. How can pressure be held on a clamp while the work cylinder is extending?

7. To what degree does the brake valve restrict flow when a motor is accelerating?

8. If the pressure in the injection cylinder rises to the electrically modulated pressure valve setting because the mold is filled, what will P2 pump pressure be?

9. As the extruder motor turns the screw and pellets are being plasticized, how is the density of the melted plastic maintained?

10. What happens to the oil in the booster tube during regenerative clamp open?

Appendix A . . . . . Definition of Technical Terms

A

ABSOLUTE
A measure having as its zero point or base the complete absence of the entity being measured.

ABSOLUTE PRESSURE
The indicated value of the weight of the earth's atmosphere. At sea level this value is approximately 14.65 psi (pounds per square inch).

ACCUMULATOR
A vessel, normally cylindrical, which is used to store fluid and gas for future release of the energy in the compressed fluid and gas. Normally contains a diaphragm or piston between the fluid (liquid) and gas chambers. Fluid is normally introduced at one end and the gas at the opposite end.

ACCURACY
The ability of the servo system to achieve the desired output.

ACTUATOR
A device for converting hydraulic energy into mechanical energy, i.e., a motor or cylinder.

ADAPTER
A mechanical device used to align the shaft of an electric motor (or other rotary device) with the shaft of a hydraulic pump to maintain radial and parallel shaft alignment.

AERATION
Air trapped in the hydraulic fluid. Excessive aeration causes the fluid to appear milky and components to operate erratically.

AIR BLEEDER AUTOMATIC
A valve that is fit into a hydraulic pipe line to facilitate automatic release of air trapped in the pipeline. See also AIR BLEEDER MANUAL.

AIR BLEEDER MANUAL
A valve that is fit into a hydraulic pipe line to facilitate manually initiated release of air trapped in the pipeline. See also AIR BLEEDER AUTOMATIC.

AIR BREATHER
A mechanical device which contains a fine mesh filter element. Normally attached to the top of a reservoir or tank to allow air to pass in and out of the reservoir or tank.

ALTERNATING CURRENT (AC)
A continuously changing magnitude of current, produced by a power source (e.g., generator, alternator).

AMBIENT
The current condition of temperature, humidity and atmospheric pressure.

AMBIENT NOISE LEVEL (BACKGROUND NOISE)
The noise level in the area surrounding the machine or component to be tested with machine being tested not operating.

AMPLIFIER
An electronic device that receives an input voltage or current signal and modifies the signal into a driving voltage or current at a different level.

AMPLITUDE OF SOUND
The loudness of a sound.

ANNULAR AREA
A ring shaped area — often refers to the net effective area of the rod slide of a cylinder piston, i.e. the piston area of the rod.

ANSI FLANGE
A mechanical device that is used to connect two pieces of pipe together to form a pressure tight joint. ANSI flanges are round, use through bolts and/or nuts to attach two matched flanges together or to a valve or other mechanical device. See ANSI standards for pressure and temperature ratings.

ATMOSPHERE (ONE)
A measure of pressure equal to about 14.7 psi.

ATMOSPHERIC PRESSURE
Pressure exerted by the atmosphere at any specific location. [Sea level pressure is approximately 14.7 pounds per square inch (1 bar, 100 kPa) absolute.]

ATTENUATION
Opposite of gain (see gain).

B

BACK CONNECTED
A condition where pipe connections are on normally unexposed surfaces of hydraulic equipment. (Gasket mounted units are back connected.)

BACK PRESSURE
The level of pressure on the return or downstream side of a device or system.

BACKUP BOTTLE
A vessel, normally cylindrical, which is used to store gas for future release of the energy in the compressed gas to an accumulator.

BACKUP RING
A fabric or plastic device that is used with an O-ring or other gasket to prevent extrusion of the O-ring or gasket into an adjacent space or crevice.

BAFFLE
A separator found in a reservoir, tank or other chamber to divert fluid flow in specific direction(s) for de-aeration of moving fluid.

BALL VALVE
A valve that may be used to divert the flow of fluid in a passage. Most normally configured in a two-way pattern which is either open or closed.

BAR
The measure of pressure in the metric system. One (1) bar = 14.5 psig.

BETA RATIO
The amount, expressed as a ratio, of particles in a fluid stream upstream of a filter, divided by the amount of particles downstream, for a particular size particle. See PARTICLE COUNT.

BLADDER
A separator or diaphragm, usually found in a chamber to facilitate separation of two (2) fluids or gases. See ACCUMULATOR.

BLEED-OFF
To divert a specific, controllable portion of pump delivery directly to reservoir.

BOLT KIT
A set of bolts or screws that are selected to suit a particular application, i.e. pre-selected length, threads and strength to match the mounted component.

BRAKE VALVE
A device used in the exhaust line of a hydraulic motor to (1) prevent overspeeding when an overrunning load is applied to the motor shaft and (2) prevent excessive pressure buildup when decelerating or stopping a load.

BREATHER
A device which permits air to move in and out of a container or component to maintain atmospheric pressure.

BURST PRESSURE
The level of pressure at which a component, pipe, tube, hose or other fluid passage will burst during application of internal pressure. Normally 4 – 6 times working pressure. See also PROOF PRESSURE.

BYPASS
A secondary passage for fluid flow.

C

CARTRIDGE
1. The replaceable element of a fluid filter. 2. The pumping unit from a vane pump, composed of rotor, ring, vanes and one or both side plates.

CARTRIDGE VALVE
A valve that is inserted into a standard size cavity in a manifold block and is held in place with either self-contained screw threads or a cover secured with bolts. May be slip-in or screw-in types. Perform directional, pressure or flow control functions.

CASE DRAIN LINE
The line or passage from the internal cavity of a pump or other component that will carry fluid leakage from the device to a low pressure reservoir or tank.

CAVITATION
A localized gaseous condition within a liquid stream which occurs where the pressure is reduced to the vapor pressure.

CHAMBER
A compartment within a hydraulic unit. May contain elements to aid in operation or control of a unit. E.g., spring chamber, drain chamber, etc.

CHARGE (supercharge)
1. To replenish a hydraulic system above atmospheric pressure. 2. To fill an accumulator with fluid under pressure (see PRECHARGE PRESSURE).

CHARGE PRESSURE
The pressure at which replenishing fluid is forced into the hydraulic system (above atmospheric pressure).

CHARGING ASSEMBLY
A system of valves and passages that allow addition or deletion of gas to the gas chamber of an accumulator without discharging any existing gas.

CHECK VALVE
A valve that allows fluid flow in one direction, yet stops flow in the opposite direction.

CHOKE
A restriction, the length of which is large with respect to its cross-sectional dimension.

CIRCUIT
A combination of passages, components and devices that form a working set of logic for a particular application.

CLEAN OUT
A hole in a reservoir or tank that is normally covered with a plate that may be removed to allow cleaning of the interior of the reservoir or tank.

CLOSED CENTER CIRCUIT
One in which flow through the system is blocked in neutral and pressure at the pump outlet is maintained at the maximum pressure control setting.

CLOSED CENTER VALVE
A condition where pump output is not unloaded to pump when the valve is in its center or neutral operating position.

CLOSED CIRCUIT
A piping arrangement in which pump output, after passing through other hydraulic components, returns directly to pump inlet.

CLOSED LOOP
In a control system, a type of control that has an input signal and a feedback of the result of the input signal which is used to modulate the input signal automatically.

COMMAND SIGNAL
An external signal to which the servo must respond.

COMPENSATOR CONTROL
A displacement control for variable pumps and motors which alters displacement in response to pressure changes in the system as related to its adjusted pressure setting.

COMPONENT
A single hydraulic or electrical unit.

COMPOUND GAUGE
A visual indicator of pressure that is set for "zero" psi at atmospheric pressure and includes a dial which will continue to indicate the level of pressure above or below atmospheric pressure.

COMPRESSIBILITY
The change in volume of a unit of fluid when it is subjected to a unit change in pressure (in^3/psi).

COMPRESSION
The name used to describe the change in pressure in a hydraulic system from low pressure to an elevated pressure. Normally the change in pressure is made in a controlled amount of time to cause an even application of energy into the system. See DECOMPRESSION.

CONNECTOR
A mechanical device used to attach two pieces of tubing together or to attach a piece of tubing to a component.

CONTAMINATION
Any material foreign to a hydraulic fluid that has a harmful effect on its performance in a system. Contaminants may be solid particles, liquids or gases.

CONTROL
A device used to regulate the function of a unit.

CONTROLLABILITY
The finest adjustable increment of a system.

COOLER

A mechanical device used to transfer heat from a fluid to air or another fluid. Normally constructed of finned tubes with one fluid on the inside and the other fluid or air on the outside of the tubes.

COUNTERBALANCE VALVE

A valve used to balance the weight of a machine or dead load by causing a back pressure in the system cylinders of sufficient magnitude to support the weight. Normally closed, opened by internal pressure in the counterbalance valve or from a separate source of fluid, that is connected to the opposite end of the balanced cylinder.

COUPLING

A mechanical device used to attach the shaft of an electric motor or other motive power device to a hydraulic pump.

CRACKING PRESSURE

The pressure at which a pressure operated valve begins to pass fluid.

CURRENT

The directed flow of electrical charges from one point to another around a closed electrical circuit. Current is measured in units called amperes or amps.

CUSHION

A mechanical device fitted into a hydraulic cylinder that closes off the flow path of fluid to effect a smooth deceleration and stop of the cylinder at the end of the stroke.

CYCLE

The time of activation of a device or system that is one complete movement from the start position to an extreme position and back to the original position.

CYCLING

A rhythmic change of the factor under control.

CYLINDER, DOUBLE ACTING

A hydro-mechanical device, usually a cylindrical chamber with one closed end and a movable shaft at the other end. When fluid flow is applied to a port in the closed end, the shaft extends until the collar or piston reaches the shaft end. When fluid is applied to the shaft end port, the shaft will retract into the chamber until the piston or collar reaches the closed end. The cylinder will produce an output force at the shaft end in proportion to its internal area multiplied times the pressure potential of the fluid power system.

CYLINDER, DOUBLE ROD

A hydro-mechanical device, usually a cylindrical chamber with movable shafts at the both ends. When fluid flow is applied to a port in either end, the shaft extends until the collar or piston reaches the shaft end. When fluid is applied to the other port, the shaft will retract into the chamber until the piston or collar reaches the opposite end. The cylinder will produce an output force at the shaft end in proportion to its internal area multiplied times the pressure potential of the fluid power system.

CYLINDER, SINGLE ACTING

A hydro-mechanical device, usually a cylindrical chamber with one closed end and a movable shaft at the other end. When fluid flow is applied to a port in the closed end, the shaft extends until the collar or piston reaches the shaft end. When an external weight or load is placed on the shaft, the shaft will retract into the chamber until the piston or collar reaches the closed end. The cylinder will produce an output force at the shaft end in proportion to its internal closed end area multiplied times the pressure potential of the fluid power system.

CYLINDER, TELESCOPING, DOUBLE ACTING

A hydro-mechanical device, usually a cylindrical chamber with one closed end and a telescoping movable shaft at the other end. When fluid flow is applied to a port in the closed end, the telescoping shaft extends until all collars or pistons reach their limit. When fluid is applied to the shaft end port, the shaft will retract into the chamber until all the pistons or collars reach their closed end limits. The cylinder will produce an output force at the shaft end in proportion to its internal area multiplied times the pressure potential of the fluid power system.

CYLINDER, TELESCOPING, SINGLE ACTING

A hydro-mechanical device, usually a cylindrical chamber with one closed end and a telescoping movable shaft at the other end. When fluid flow is applied to a port in the closed end, the telescoping shaft extends until all collars or pistons reach their limit. When an external weight is applied to the shaft end, the shaft will retract into the chamber until all the pistons or collars reach their closed end limits. The cylinder will produce an output force at the shaft end in proportion to its internal closed end area multiplied times the pressure potential of the fluid power system.

D

dB (A) & (C)

A sound level reading in decibels made on the A- & C- weighted network, respectively of a sound level meter.

DEADBAND

The region or band of no response where an error signal will not cause a corresponding actuation of the controlled variable.

DEADTIME

Any definite delay between two related actions. Measured in units of time.

DECIBEL (dB)

A non-dimensional number used to express sound pressure and sound power. It is logarithmic expression of the ratio of a measure quantity to a reference quantity.

DECOMPRESSION

The name used to describe the change in pressure in a hydraulic system from elevated pressure to a lower pressure. Normally the change in pressure is made in a controlled amount of time to cause an even release of energy in the system. See COMPRESSION.

DELIVERY

The volume of fluid discharged by a pump in a given time, usually expressed in gallons per minute (GPM).

DE-VENT

To close the vent connection of a pressure control valve, permitting the valve to function at its adjusted pressure setting.

DEVICE

A combination of individual components that are arranged to form a unit with a specific set of operating parameters.

DIAGRAM

A formal drawing showing the arrangement of components or devices.

DIFFERENTIAL CYLINDER

Any cylinder in which the two opposed piston areas are not equal.

DIFFERENTIAL PRESSURE

The value or magnitude of pressure measured as the absolute difference of the inlet pressure and outlet pressure.

DIRECT CURRENT (DC)

A steady level of electrical current, produced by a power source (e.g. battery, thermocouple, etc.) that flows in only one direction in a circuit.

DIRECTIONAL VALVE

A valve whose primary function is to direct or prevent flow through selected channels.

DIRT CAPACITY

The measure of volume (or weight) of particles that a filter or strainer will hold at the limit of operation.

DISPLACEMENT

The volume for one revolution or stroke or for one radiant when so stated.

DITHER

A cyclic application of voltage across a solenoid or coil. Most often used to assure that the device driven by the coil or solenoid remains in a state of constant motion, thus reducing breakaway friction.

DOWNSTREAM

The passage beyond a device, normally at the outlet of direction of flow.

DRAIN

A passage in, or line from a hydraulic component which returns leakage fluid independently to reservoir or to a vented manifold.

DRIFT

The measure of movement of a device after a preset condition is applied. Normally drift is measured with varying temperature, although drift may be plotted against any variable, such as humidity, etc.

DUROMETER

The measure of hardness of a rubber or other synthetic compound.

DYNAMIC BEHAVIOR

Describes how a control system or an individual unit reacts with time when subjected to an input signal.

DYNAMIC ERROR

The error that results during the transient state, that is, the state when the system is moving from one steady state condition to another.

E

EFFICIENCY

The ratio of output to input. Volumetric efficiency of a pump is the actual output, in GPM, divided by the theoretical or design output. The overall efficiency of a hydraulic system is the output power divided by the input power. Efficiency is usually expressed as a percent.

ELECTRIC MOTOR

An electro-mechanical device that converts electrical power into rotary motion. The resultant power output is measured in horsepower.

ELECTROHYDRAULIC SERVO VALVE

A servo valve which is capable of continuously controlling hydraulic output as a function of an electrical input.

ELECTROMOTIVE FORCE (EMF)

The force produced by a difference of electrical potential that causes current to flow in circuit. EMF is measured in units called volts.

ELEMENT

See FILTER ELEMENT.

ENCLOSURE

A rectangle drawn around a graphical component or components to indicate the limits of an assembly.

ENERGY

See JOULE.

EROSION

Degradation of a surface which is the result of mixtures of fluid and air or fluid and dirt particles passing over the surface at the same time as a change in pressure occurs.

ERROR (SIGNAL)

The signal which is the algebraic summation of an input signal and feedback signal.

EXHAUST LINE

A passage that is open to atmosphere. Normally used in systems using pressurized air or gas which may be dispersed into the atmosphere.

F

FEEDBACK

Part of a closed loop system which monitors back information about the condition under control for comparison.

FEEDBACK LOOP

Any closed circuit consisting of one or more forward elements and one or more feedback elements.

FILLER CAP

A mechanical device which provides an access for filling a reservoir or tank. Normally equipped with a fine screen to strain out dirt particles.

FILTER

A mechanical device used to house a filter element. See FILTER ELEMENT.

FILTER ELEMENT
A series of wire or fabric meshes which are bonded together by caps or perforated cylinders and are fitted into hydraulic system passages to strain fine particles and silt from fluid passed through the passage.

FITTING
A mechanical device used to attach two pieces of tubing/pipe together or to attach a piece of tubing/pipe to a component.

FLOODED
A condition where the pump inlet is charged by placing the reservoir oil level above the pump inlet port.

FLOW CONTROL VALVE, NONPRESSURE-COMPENSATED
A valve used to cause a variable pressure drop in a fluid passage, thus potentially reducing the amount of fluid that may pass through the passage regardless of the pressure level at the inlet of the valve. Varying pressures at the inlet of the valve will change the flow capacity. Often fitted with a check valve that permits free flow of fluid in the opposite direction.

FLOW CONTROL VALVE, PRESSURE-COMPENSATED
A valve used to cause a variable pressure drop in a fluid passage, thus reducing the amount of fluid that may pass through the passage regardless of the pressure level at the inlet of the valve. Often fitted with a check valve that permits free flow of fluid in the opposite direction.

FLOW DIVIDER
A mechanical device used to divide the fluid in a passage into two or more separate fluid streams.

FLOW RATE
The volume mass, or weight of a fluid passing through any conductor per unit of time.

FLOW SWITCH
A digital device that opens or closes a contact when a preset flow passes over the sensing element. Normally mounted in a fluid flow passage with a paddle perpendicular to the fluid stream.

FLOWMETER
An analog device which indicates the volume of fluid passing through its interior passage. The output signal may be a visual one or a low level electrical signal.

FLUID
A media used in a fluid power system for transfer of energy (work). See FLUID POWER SYSTEM.

FLUID FRICTION
The measure of the resistance of flow of fluid in a passage, measured in psi (pounds per square inch) or other measures of pressure. Fluid friction results in increased fluid temperature and loss of work potential in the fluid power system.

FLUID MOTOR
A mechanical device that transforms the flow of pressurized fluid into rotary motion.

FLUID POWER SYSTEM
The term used to describe a system of components that use a pressurized fluid to transfer energy (do work).

FOLLOW VALVE
A control valve which ports oil to an actuator so the resulting output motion is proportional to the input motion to the valve.

FORCE
The measure of the result of pressurized fluid acting upon a chamber in a fluid power system. Normally the measure is in pounds and is most often used to state the force in pounds that will be available at the rod of a cylinder when acted upon by pressurized fluid from a fluid power system. The system of units normally used is square inches, pounds per square inch and pounds.

FOUR-WAY (4-WAY)
A term used to describe a valve that has four ports, normally a pressure (inlet) port, a return (tank) port, an "A" ("1") work port and a "B" ("2") work port. Used to change direction of a cylinder or other output device.

FOUR-WAY VALVE, MANUALLY & DIRECT OPERATED
A valve having a four-way functional capability that may be manually activated to directly control the operating spool. Movement of the spool from extreme end to extreme end reverses the flow paths of the ports. See FOUR-WAY.

FOUR-WAY VALVE, PROPORTIONAL CONTROL & DIRECT OPERATED
A valve having a four-way functional capability that may be proportionately actuated by a solenoid to control the operating spool in infinite resolution. Movement of the spool from extreme end to extreme end completely reverses the flow paths of the ports. See FOUR-WAY.

FOUR-WAY VALVE, SOLENOID & DIRECT OPERATED
A valve having a four-way functional capability that may be solenoid-activated to directly control the operating spool. Movement of the spool from extreme end to extreme end reverses the flow paths of the ports. See FOUR-WAY.

FOUR-WAY VALVE, SOLENOID & PILOT-OPERATED
A valve having a four-way functional capability that may be solenoid-activated to directly control the operating spool which then controls a secondary, larger spool. Movement of the secondary spool from extreme end to extreme end reverses the flow paths of the ports. See FOUR-WAY.

FREQUENCY
The number of times an action occurs in a unit of time.

FREQUENCY BANDS
A division of the audible range of frequencies into sub-groups for detailed analysis of sound.

FREQUENCY RESPONSE ANALYSIS
A control system analysis which by introducing a varying rhythmic change (like alternating current) into a process or control unit observes what effect these changes have on the output. Since the information determines how a system or control unit will react, it is possible to use this method of analysis to predict what the addition of new equipment will mean to an operation.

FRONT CONNECTED
A condition wherein piping connections are on normally exposed surfaces of hydraulic components.

FULL FLOW
A filter in which all the fluid must pass through the filter element or medium.

G

GAIN
Ratio of increase in a signal (or measurement) as it passes through a control system or a specific control element. If a signal gets smaller, it is said to be attenuated.

GAS BOTTLE
See BACKUP BOTTLE.

GASKET
A seal, made from rubber or other synthetic material in the shape of a circle and of polygonal cross section. See O-RING.

GATE VALVE
A 2-way valve that may be opened or closed to block the flow of fluid in a passage. Normally manually operated, but may be automated, especially for larger sizes. Normally designed so that when open, the opening of the passage is not restricted, but there will be some small pressure loss. See GLOBE VALVE and NEEDLE VALVE.

GAUGE (psig) & ABSOLUTE (psia)
The measure of pressure, corrected for atmospheric pressure, that is "zero" psig = 14.65 psia. "Zero" psia = absolute zero vacuum.

GAUGE PRESSURE
A term used to state that any pressure stated is corrected for atmospheric pressure. Normally abbreviated psig (pounds per square inch gauge).

GLAND
A mechanical device that is used to contain a seal, O-ring or gasket in a specified space to result in a leakproof connection between two or more mechanical components.

GLOBE VALVE
A 2-way valve that may be opened or closed to block the flow of fluid in a passage. Normally manually operated, but may be automated, especially for larger sizes. Normally designed so that the flow of fluid must make a non-straight turn inside the valve body which results in a loss of pressure across the valve when open, which is greater than the loss across a gate valve. See GATE VALVE and NEEDLE VALVE.

H

HEAD
The measure of pressure at the base or other reference point of a column of fluid. Normally measured in feet of water.

HEAT
The form of energy that has the capacity to create warmth or to increase the temperature of a substance. Any energy that is wasted or used to overcome friction is converted to heat. Heat is measured in calories or British Thermal Units (BTUs). One BTU is the amount of heat required to raise the temperature of one pound of water one degree Fahrenheit. In the metric system one calorie is the amount of heat required to raise the temperature of one gram of water from 3.5°C to 4.5°C (called a small calorie).

HEATER
An electro-mechanical device that converts electricity into heat, normally for use in raising the temperature of fluid stored in a reservoir or tank.

HEAT EXCHANGER
See COOLER.

HORSEPOWER
The measure of energy used in description of the normal power level in a system. 1 horsepower = 550 lb-ft/min. of work.

HOSE
A passage used to transport fluid between components in a fluid power system. Normally constructed from multiple layers of rubber or other synthetic materials interlaced and bonded with wire mesh to form a flexible passage. Normally fitted with metal end connections to permit connection to pipe threads or other joints.

HUNTING
Tendency for a system to oscillate continuously.

HYDRAULIC BALANCE
A condition of equal opposed hydraulic forces acting on a part in a hydraulic component.

HYDRAULIC CONTROL
A control which is actuated by hydraulically induced forces.

HYDRAULIC MOTOR
See FLUID MOTOR.

HYDRAULIC POWER
See FLUID POWER.

HYDRAULICS
Engineering science pertaining to liquid pressure and flow.

HYDRODYNAMICS
Engineering science pertaining to the energy of liquid flow and pressure.

HYDROKINETICS
Engineering science pertaining to the energy of liquids in motion.

HYDROPNEUMATICS
Pertaining to the combination of hydraulic and pneumatic fluid power.

HYDROSTATICS
Engineering science pertaining to the energy of liquids at rest.

HYSTERESIS
The difference between the response of a unit or system to an increasing signal and the response to a decreasing signal.

HZ (HERTZ)
A measure of the number of cycles that occur in a specific period of time. Usually the time base is the second, but the time base may be any acceptable measure of time. Synonymous term for "cycles per second".

I

INDICATOR
A mechanical device with points to a scale to provide a visual perspective of the state of a component.

INPUT
Incoming signal to a control unit or system.

INTAKE LINE

A passage at the inlet port of a component, normally at the inlet port of a pump.

J

JOULE

A unit of work, energy, or heat. 1J (joule) = 1 Nm (Newton meter).

K

KINETIC ENERGY

Energy that a substance or body has by virtue of its mass (weight) and velocity.

L

LAG

Preferred engineering term for delay in response (usually in degrees).

LAMINAR FLOW

A condition of flow in a passage that is typified by slow movement of fluid in a relatively straight path along the centerline of a passage. See TURBULENT FLOW.

LEVEL SWITCH

An electro-mechanical device which senses the level of fluid in a chamber and opens or closes a digital switch to indicate a change of state. See LEVEL TRANSMITTER.

LEVEL TRANSMITTER

An electro-mechanical device which senses the level of fluid in a chamber and produces an analog signal that corresponds with the change of state in the chamber. See LEVEL SWITCH.

LEVERAGE

A gain in output force over input force by sacrificing the distance moved. Mechanical advantage or force multiplication.

LIFT

The measure of the capability of a pump to raise fluid from a lower to higher level at its inlet port without damage to the pump. Normally expressed in feet of water.

LINE

A connection between components, a passage for fluid or gas transfer. See PIPE, TUBE and HOSE.

LINEAR ACTUATOR

A device for converting hydraulic energy into linear motion, i.e. a cylinder or ram.

LINEAR VARIABLE DIFFERENTIAL TRANSFORMER (LVDT)

An electro-mechanical linear device that produces an analog signal in proportion to the difference in distance between a magnet and a separate fixed coil.

LINEAR VARIABLE TRANSFORMER (LVT)

An electro-mechanical linear device that produces an analog signal in proportion to the difference in velocity between a magnet and a separate fixed coil.

LINEARITY (SERVO VALVE)

The degree of straightness of the hysteresis plot.

LIQUID LEVEL GAUGE

Gauge to visually indicate the fluid level in a reservoir or tank.

LITER

A metric measure of volume. One (1) liter = 0.2642 gallons.

LUBRICATOR

A mechanical device which is used to inject drops or mist of oil into an air line for lubrication purposes.

M

MANIFOLD

A fabricated system of passages to which various components are attached to form a working assembly or sub-assembly.

MANUAL CONTROL

A control actuated by the operator.

MANUAL OVERRIDE

A means of manually actuating an automatically-controlled device.

MECHANICAL CONTROL

A control actuated by linkages, gears, screws, cams or other mechanical elements.

METER

39.37 inches. The measure of distances in the metric system.

METER-IN

To regulate the amount of fluid flow into an actuator or system.

METER-OUT

To regulate the flow of the discharge fluid out of an actuator or system.

MICRON

1/1000th of a millimeter or 0.00003937 inches. The measure used to determine the particle size of contaminants in a fluid system.

MICRON RATING

The size, in microns, of the particles a filter will remove.

MOTOR

A device which converts hydraulic fluid power into mechanical force and motion. It usually provides rotary mechanical motion.

MUFFLER

A mechanical device which provides a complex path for exhaust of air from a pressurized chamber, thus reducing the noise level of the exhausting air.

N

NEEDLE VALVE

A 2-way valve that may be opened or closed to block the flow of fluid in a passage. Normally manually operated, but may be automated, especially for larger sizes. Normally designed so that the flow of fluid must make a non-straight turn inside the valve body which results in a desired loss of pressure across the valve when open which is greater than the loss across a gate valve. See GATE VALVE and GLOBE VALVE.

NEWTON

A unit of force based on the unit of mass, Kg (kilogram), multiplied by the acceleration, m/s^2 (meters per second per second) which produces Kgm/s^2, called the Newton. 1N = 1 Kgm/s^2 = 0.1225 lbs (F) — (pounds force).

NIPPLE

A short length of pipe. May be threaded or plain end.

NITROGEN

An inert gas used to serve as an energy source for accumulators or to be used as a cleaning agent when pure, non-explosive gases are required.

NULL

The position of a device that is its normal or otherwise preset "zero" condition.

O

OPEN CENTER CIRCUIT

One in which pump delivery flows freely through the system and back into the reservoir in neutral.

OPEN CENTER VALVE

One in which all ports are interconnected and open to each other in the center or neutral position.

OPEN CIRCUIT

A circuit in which a complete path for electrical current flow does not exist.

OPERATING PRESSURE

The level of pressure at which a component, pipe, tube, hose or other fluid passage will experience during application of maximum expected fluid pressure. See also BURST PRESSURE and PROOF PRESSURE.

OPERATIONAL AMPLIFIER (OP AMP)

An integrated circuit amplifier with special characteristics (high gain, high input impedance, low output impedance, differential amplification) that make it especially suitable for electrohydraulic control systems.

O-RING

A seal, made from rubber or other synthetic material in the shape of a circle and of circular or other polygonal cross section. See GASKET.

ORIFICE

A narrowing of the passage size. Normally constructed in a connector or fitting of a sharp edged metallic component.

OUTPUT STAGE

A spool or other device that is controlled by a smaller spool or torque motor.

OVERLAP

The condition of a spool and body in a servo valve or other spool valve wherein the spool must move a specified amount (the overlap) before exposing two adjacent cavities.

OVERSHOOT

Occurs when the process exceeds the target value as operating conditions change.

OXIDATION

The absorption of oxygen into fluid and the subsequent plating of the oxygen/fluid mixture onto metal surfaces.

P

PACKING

A seal or gasket. See SEAL, O-RING and GASKET.

PARTICLE

A piece of debris (sand, dirt, metal, fabric, etc.) found in a fluid.

PARTICLE COUNT

The visual or electronic summation of the quantity of particles, grouped by size, in a fluid sample of specified size.

PASSAGE

A hole through which fluid is passed in a fluid power system. See TUBE, PIPE, HOSE and MANIFOLD.

PETROLEUM FLUID

A hydraulic oil (fluid) that is made from a petroleum base. Normally will support combustion if heated to a specific temperature.

PHASE SHIFT

A time difference between the input and output signal of a control unit or system, usually measured in degrees.

PHOSPHATE ESTER FLUID

A hydraulic oil (fluid) that is made from an ester base. A synthetic fluid, manufactured to specific characteristics. Normally will not support combustion if heated to a specific temperature.

PILOT LINE

A passage in a fluid power system that is used to transport a fluid at a pressure lower than the normal operating pressure to facilitate controlled shifting of spool valves.

PILOT-OPERATED CHECK VALVE

A special check valve that may be opened against a check load by applying pilot pressure from a secondary source to open the check to free reverse flow.

PILOT PRESSURE

The pressure in the pilot circuit.

PILOT VALVE

A valve applied to operate another valve or control. The controlling stage of a 2-stage valve.

PIPE

A passage in a fluid power system that is constructed of metal and conforms dimensionally to standards established by ANSI. May be acquired by size and schedule, where increase in wall thickness does not increase the outside diameter. See TUBE.

PISTON

A cylindrically shaped part which fits within a cylinder.

PISTON CYLINDER

A cylinder in which the movable element has a greater cross-sectional area than the piston rod.

PISTON RING

A metal ring that is used to seal high pressure fluid inside a passage to prevent (limit) leakage across the passage. Normally found in cylinders.

PLUNGER CYLINDER

A cylinder in which the movable element has the same cross-sectional area as the piston rod.

POPPET

That part of certain valves which blocks flow when it closes against a seat.

PORT

An internal or external terminus of a passage in a component.

POSITIVE DISPLACEMENT

A characteristic of a pump or motor when a constant volume is delivered for each revolution or stroke.

POWER

Work per unit of time measured in horsepower (hp) or watts (W).

POWER PACK

An integral power supply unit usually containing a pump, reservoir, relief valve and directional control.

POWER SUPPLY

Term used to describe a fluid power source. A hydraulic power unit.

PRE-FILL VALVE

A valve that is arranged so its inlet port is connected to a reservoir or tank and so that fluid will flow from the inlet of the valve into a cylinder or ram when opened. When closed, the valve must close off the ram or cylinder from the reservoir or tank to permit application of high pressure from another source on the cylinder side of the valve. Most commonly used to fill large rams on presses to take up non-operating stroke.

PRECHARGE PRESSURE

The pressure of compressed gas in an accumulator prior to the admission of liquid.

PRESSURE

Force per unit area. Usually expressed in pounds per square inch (psi), bar or kilopascal (kPa).

PRESSURE COMPENSATOR

A hydro-mechanical device fitted to a pump or other flow producing/controlling device that reduces flow when pressure rises and increases flow as pressure decreases, to preset limits.

PRESSURE DIFFERENTIAL (Drop)

The difference in pressure between any two points in a system or a component.

PRESSURE DIFFERENTIAL SWITCH

A digital device that opens or closes a switch when the internal pressure differential changes state. Most commonly used to sense clogging of filter elements.

PRESSURE DROP

See PRESSURE DIFFERENTIAL.

PRESSURE GAUGE

A visual indicator of pressure that is set for "zero" psi at atmospheric pressure and includes a dial which will continue to indicate the level of pressure above atmospheric pressure. See VACUUM GAUGE and COMPOUND GAUGE.

PRESSURE LINE

A passage that carries fluid from the source of flow to various operating elements of a fluid power system. Rated for operating pressure at the maximum expected pressure of the system.

PRESSURE OVERRIDE

The measure of pressure increase over the nominal setting of a device when additional fluid flow is passed over the device after it initially opens.

PRESSURE PLATE

A side plate in a vane pump or motor cartridge on the pressure port side.

PRESSURE REDUCING VALVE

A pressure control valve whose primary function is to limit outlet pressure.

PRESSURE SWITCH

A digital device that opens or closes a switch when the internal pressure changes state.

PRESSURE TRANSDUCER

An analog device that produces a change in voltage or current when the internal pressure changes state. Normally a fast response device for use in servo control systems. See PRESSURE TRANSMITTER.

PRESSURE TRANSMITTER

An analog device that produces a change in voltage or current when the internal pressure changes state. Normally a slow acting device for use in display systems where update time is not crucial. See PRESSURE TRANSDUCER.

PROOF PRESSURE

The level of pressure at which a component, pipe, tube, hose or other fluid passage will not yield during application of internal pressure. Normally 1.5 times working pressure. See BURST PRESSURE.

PROPORTIONAL FLOW

In a filter, the condition where part of the flow passes through the filter element in proportion to pressure drop.

PROPORTIONAL VALVE

A valve which controls and varies pressure, flow, direction, acceleration and deceleration from a remote position. They are adjusted electrically and are actuated by proportional solenoids rather than the input signal. They provide moderately accurate control of hydraulic fluid.

PULSE WIDTH MODULATION

An electronic signal of constant frequency and amplitude that has varying pulse width to control the level of power to the solenoid.

PUMP, AIR-OIL

A mechanical device containing two sets of isolated pistons and control valving that are used to intensify fluid pressure by use of a multiplication effect across the two sets of pistons. The air piston is larger than the fluid piston.

PUMP, FIXED DISPLACEMENT

A mechanical device that creates a flow of fluid when its shaft is rotated in the proper direction and when its inlet is connected to a chamber filled with fluid (a reservoir or tank). The outlet port may be connected to a passage leading to a fluid power system or exhausted into another chamber that is at a higher pressure. The higher pressure chamber must be equipped with a pressure limiting device. The output flow rate is fixed by the pump displacement per revolution.

PUMP, VACUUM

A mechanical device that creates a pressure that is lower than atmospheric at its inlet when the shaft is rotated. The outlet port is normally connected to a higher pressure chamber or atmosphere.

PUMP, VARIABLE DISPLACEMENT

A mechanical device that creates a flow of fluid when its shaft is rotated in the proper direction and when its inlet is connected to a chamber filled with fluid (a reservoir or tank). The outlet port may be connected to a passage leading to a fluid power system or exhausted into another chamber that is at a higher pressure. The higher pressure chamber must be equipped with a pressure limiting device. The output flow rate is fixed by the pump displacement per revolution but variable by the operator in a manual or servo controlled system, depending on the design.

Q

QUICK DISCONNECT

A mechanical device that may be engaged or disengaged to attach two fluid passages. Typically, disengagement is possible by manual means.

R

RAM

A cylinder that has an extend port only. Usually accompanied by auxiliary cylinders that are mechanically linked to the ram to facilitate retraction.

RAMP

The rate of change of a specific output, such as the ramp of a pressure compensator.

RAMP MODULE

An electronic device that controls the rate of rise of a servo or proportional valve by using capacitors to limit the rate of voltage or current change to the servo or proportional valve.

RATED FLOW

The maximum flow that a manufacturer assigns to a specific component as the maximum desirable flow at which the device will function properly. Also the flow that a designer assigns to a system as the nominal maximum flow.

RATED PRESSURE

The maximum pressure that a manufacturer assigns to a specific component as the maximum desirable pressure at which the device will function properly.

RECIPROCATION

Back-and-forth straight line motion or oscillation.

REDUCING VALVE

A valve that decreases the downstream pressure (at the valve outlet) in order to control the flow and therefore the outlet pressure to some preset level. Normally accomplished by balancing the outlet pressure against a precision spring.

REGENERATIVE CIRCUIT

A piping arrangement for a differential type cylinder in which discharge fluid from the rod end combines with pump delivery to be directed into the head end.

REGULATOR

A term used to describe a valve or device that limits the pressure in a passage.

RELIEF VALVE

A valve that limits the pressure at its inlet port by exhausting flow present at its inlet port to another chamber of lower pressure potential through its outlet port.

REPLENISH

To add fluid to maintain a full hydraulic system.

RESERVOIR

A chamber used to store fluid.

RESISTANCE

The opposition to current flow offered by the components of an electrical circuit.

RESPONSE TIME

The elapsed time that occurs after the beginning of a function until its completion. For example, the time elapsed between application of electrical power to a solenoid and its full excursion or stroke.

RESTRICTION

A reduced cross-sectional area in a line of passage producing a pressure drop.

RESTRICTOR

See ORIFICE.

RETURN LINE

A passage that is used to route fluid to a reservoir or tank after use in some function. Normally limited to low pressures of 0 – 150 psig, but may be higher in special applications if so designed.

REVERSING VALVE

A 4-way directional valve used to reverse a double-action cylinder or reversible motor.

ROTARY ACTUATOR

A hydro-mechanical device that converts fluid flow into incremental rotary motion as compared to a fluid motor which produces infinite numbers of turns. See FLUID MOTOR.

ROTARY JOINT

A connector or fitting that is equipped with seals or O-rings that allow it to rotate while passing one or more fluid paths through sealed internal passages.

S

SAE 4 BOLT PORT, CODE 61

A system for flange and surface mounting configurations that are used to attach pipes, tubes or hoses to a component or manifold. Normally rated at 3,000 psig. See SAE 4 BOLT PORT, CODE 62.

SAE 4 BOLT PORT, CODE 62

A system of flange and surface mounting configurations that are used to attach pipes, tubes or hoses to a component or manifold. Nominally rated at 6000 psig, although larger sizes are only rated for 500 psig. See SAE 4 BOLT PORT, CODE 61.

SAE PORT

A threaded hole and stud system that may be used to attach fittings to a component or manifold. Sealed with an O-ring or gasket.

SAFETY FACTOR

The ratio of burst pressure to rated pressure under specific static pressure and temperature conditions. See BURST PRESSURE.

SCRAPER RING

A metal or synthetic ring that is fitted to the shaft of a cylinder to remove particles from the shaft in order to prevent them from entering the cylinder seal chamber.

SEAL

See O-RING and GASKET.

SENSITIVITY

The minimum input signal required to produce a specified output signal.

SEQUENCE

1. The order of a series of operations or movements. 2. To divert flow to accomplish a subsequent operation or movement.

SEQUENCE VALVE

A valve that is normally closed or normally open and changes to the opposite state when pilot pressure is applied to its spring chamber at a preset pressure level. Normally used to initiate a secondary set of operations in a system, based on application of the pilot signal.

SERVO CONTROL
A term used to describe the type of electronic system used for finite, analog control of a function.

SERVO VALVE
A valve that uses a torque motor type coil to control a small stream of fluid. Direction of the fluid stream is used to position a large spool. Therefore a low level power signal may provide precise spool position. Normally, the spool has mechanical feedback of spool position to the torque motor, creating a closed loop spool position system.

SHUTTLE VALVE
A valve that has three ports and a common ball or spool check valve. When flow is applied at either of the two inlet ports, the third or output port receives flow from the higher pressure inlet port.

SILENCER
See MUFFLER.

SILT
Fine particles of debris. Normally found in chambers with little or no circulation, such as at the bottom of a reservoir or tank. See SLUDGE.

SLIP
Internal leakage of hydraulic fluid.

SLUDGE
Partially hardened silt. See SILT.

SOLENOID
A coil of metallic wire, usually copper, wound around a bobbin. Used to magnetize the bobbin and produce linear motion of a companion spool when electricity is applied.

SPOOL
A term loosely applied to almost any moving cylindrically shaped part of a hydraulic component which moves to direct flow through the component.

STABILITY
Ability of a system to maintain control when subject to severe outside disturbances.

STATIC BEHAVIOR
Describes how a control system, or an individual unit, carries on under fixed conditions (as contrasted to dynamic behavior which refers to behavior under changing conditions).

STATIC HEAD
A measurement of pressure that is present when no fluid flow exists in a passage. The static head is normally expressed in feet of water.

STEP CHANGE
The change from one value to another in a single step.

STRAINER
A series of wire or fabric meshes which are bonded together by caps or perforated cylinders and are fitted into hydraulic system passages to strain particles from fluid passed through the passage.

STROKE
1. The length of travel of a piston or plunger. 2. To change the displacement of a variable displacement pump or motor.

SUBPLATE
A metal base to which a specific valve may be attached using a specified bolt kit.

SUCTION LINE
A passage that leads from a reservoir or tank to the inlet port of a pump.

SUPERCHARGE
To replenish a hydraulic system above atmospheric pressure.

SUMP
A reservoir.

SURGE
An increase in pressure that occurs for a specified short period of time over the normal expected working pressure.

SWASH PLATE
A stationary canted plate in an axial type-piston pump which causes the pistons to reciprocate as the cylinder barrel rotates.

SWIVEL JOINT
A connector or fitting that is equipped with seals or O-rings that allow it to partially rotate while passing a fluid path through a sealed internal passage.

SYNTHETIC FLUID
A hydraulic oil (fluid) that is made from a synthetic base. A fluid, manufactured to specified characteristics. Normally will not support combustion if heated to a specific temperature.

SYSTEM PRESSURE
See OPERATING PRESSURE.

T

TACHOMETER
A digital or analog device that produces a pulse train of electrical signals that is proportional to its rotational speed.

TANK
See RESERVOIR.

TEMPERATURE SWITCH
A digital device that opens or closes a switch when the internal temperature changes state to a preset temperature limit.

THREE-WAY (3-WAY)
A term used to describe a valve that has three ports, normally a pressure (inlet) port, a normally closed (N.C.) port and a normally open (N.O.) port. Used to block or open a common flow passage.

THREE-WAY VALVE, MANUALLY AND DIRECT OPERATED
A valve having a 3-way functional capability that may be manually activated to directly control the operating spool. Movement of the spool from extreme end to extreme end reverses the flow paths of the ports. See THREE-WAY.

THREE-WAY VALVE, PROPORTIONAL CONTROL AND DIRECT OPERATED
A valve having a 3-way functional capability that may be proportionately actuated by a solenoid to control the operating spool in infinite resolution. Movement of the spool from extreme end to extreme rod completely reverses the flow paths of the ports. See THREE-WAY.

THREE-WAY VALVE, SOLENOID AND DIRECT OPERATED
A valve having a 3-way functional capability that may be solenoid-activated to directly control the operating spool. Movement of the spool from extreme end to extreme end reverses the flow paths of the ports. See THREE-WAY.

THREE-WAY VALVE, SOLENOID AND PILOT-OPERATED

A valve having a 3-way functional capability that may be solenoid-activated to directly control the operating spool which then controls a secondary, larger spool. Movement of the secondary spool from extreme end to extreme end reverses the flow paths of ports. See THREE-WAY.

THROTTLE

To permit passing of a restricted flow. May control flow rate or create a deliberate pressure drop.

TIE ROD

A metal rod that is used to prevent two or more components from separating. Normally used to restrain the end plates of cylinders against the cylinder tube.

TORQUE

The measure of force applied to a lever arm. Normally expressed in lb-ft (pound-feet) or lb-in (pound-inch).

TORQUE CONVERTER

A rotary fluid coupling that is capable of multiplying torque.

TORQUE MOTOR

A coil of wire and bobbin assembly used in a servo valve that causes the internal mechanism of the servo valve to be offset when current passes through the coil.

TRANSDUCER

An analog device which produces a change in signal level during state changes. Normally used for high speed control systems.

TUBE

A term used to describe a passage for fluid in a hydraulic system. Normally specified by outside diameter, wall thickness, material type and material strength.

TURBINE

A rotary device that is actuated by the impact of a moving fluid against blades or vanes.

TURBULENT FLOW

A condition of flow in a passage that is typified by rapid movement of fluid in a passage, where the fluid is churning and bouncing off the passage walls. See LAMINAR FLOW.

TWO-WAY (2-WAY)

A term used to describe a valve that has two ports, normally a pressure (inlet) port and an outlet port. Used to open or close a flow passage. May be configured as normally closed (N.C.) or normally open (N.O.).

TWO-WAY VALVE, MANUALLY AND DIRECT OPERATED

A valve having 2-way functional capability that may be manually activated to directly control the operating spool. Movement of the spool from extreme end to extreme end opens or closes the flow paths of the ports. See TWO-WAY.

TWO-WAY VALVE, SOLENOID AND DIRECT OPERATED

A valve having a 2-way functional capability that may be solenoid-activated to directly control the operating spool. Movement of the spool from extreme end to extreme end opens or closes the flow paths of the ports. See TWO-WAY.

TWO-WAY VALVE, SOLENOID AND PILOT-OPERATED

A valve having a 2-way functional capability that may be solenoid-activated to directly control the operating spool which then controls a secondary, larger spool. Movement of the secondary spool from extreme end to extreme end opens or closes the flow paths of the ports. See TWO-WAY.

U

UNDERLAP

The condition of a spool and body in a servo valve or other spool valve wherein the spool is displaced a specified amount (the underlap) to expose two adjacent cavities to each other.

UNLOAD

To release flow (usually directly to the reservoir), to prevent pressure being imposed on the system or a portion of the system.

UNLOADING VALVE

A valve that is normally closed and opens from a separate fluid source on rising pressure that is balanced against a precision spring. Re-set point is normally fixed.

UPSTREAM

The passage ahead of a device, normally at the inlet of direction of flow.

V

VACUUM

Pressure less than atmospheric pressure. It is usually expressed in inches of mercury (Hg) as referred to the existing atmospheric pressure.

VACUUM GAUGE

A visual indicator of pressure that is set for "zero" psi at atmospheric pressure and includes a dial which will continue to indicate the level of pressure below atmospheric pressure.

VALVE

A mechanical device that is used in a fluid power system, which is used to provide some change of state of the fluid.

VAPOR PRESSURE

The measure of pressure at which a specific fluid will change to a gas.

VARIABLE

A factor or condition which can be measured, altered or controlled, i.e., temperature, pressure, flow, liquid level, humidity, weight, chemical composition, color, etc.

VELOCITY

The speed of fluid flow through a hydraulic line. Expressed in feet per second (fps), inches per second (ips), or meters per second (mps). Also, the speed of a rotating component measured in resolutions per minute (RPM).

VENT

1. To permit opening of a pressure control valve by opening its pilot port (vent connection) to atmospheric pressure. 2. An air breathing device on a fluid reservoir. 3. To remove trapped air from a component.

VENT VALVE

A valve that may be manually opened to allow air or fluid or a combination of both to be exhausted into a lower pressure chamber or to the atmosphere.

VISCOSITY

The measure of resistance to flow of a fluid against an established standard.

VISCOSITY INDEX
A measure of the viscosity-temperature characteristics of a fluid as referred to that of two arbitrary reference fluids (ASTM Designation D2270-64).

VOLUME
The size of a space or chamber in cubic units. Loosely applied to the output of a pump in gallons per minute (GPM) or liters per minute (l/min).

W

WAFER VALVE
A 2-way valve that may be opened or closed to block the flow of fluid in a passage. Normally manually operated, but may be automated, especially for larger sizes. Normally designed so that when open, the opening of the passage is only restricted by the thickness of the wafer. There will be some pressure loss. See GATE VALVE, GLOBE VALVE and NEEDLE VALVE.

WATER GLYCOL FLUID
A hydraulic fluid that is comprised of a mix of distilled or other pure water and glycol to form a fluid that has enough lubricity to function as a fluid power fluid, but is relatively fire-resistant, i.e., will not support combustion.

WATT'S LAW
States that when one amp of current flows through a device with one volt voltage drop, one watt of power is dissipated in the form of heat (P = I x E).

WIPER RING
A rubber or other synthetic seal that is fitted around a moving shaft to form a low pressure seal. Normally used to prevent fluid from entering the sealed volume.

WORK
The transfer of power from one state to another. The movement of weight over a specified distance.

Appendix B . . . . . ISO/ANSI Basic Symbols for Fluid Power Equipment and Systems

Lines

Line, Working Main	
Line, Pilot, Control Drain	
Flow, Direction of Hydraulic Pneumatic	
Lines Crossing	
Lines Joining	
Line With Fixed Restriction	
Line, Flexible	
Station, Testing, Measurement or Power Take Off	
Variable Component (run arrow through Symbol at 45°)	
Pressure Compensated Units	
Temperature Cause or Effect	
Reservoir Vented Pressurized	
Line, To Reservoir Above Fluid Level Below Fluid Level	
Air Bleed Vented Reservoir	

Pumps

Hydraulic Pump Fixed Displacement	
Variable Displacement	
Electrohydraulic Control	
Load Sensing Pressure Compensator	
Hydrostat	

Motors and Cylinders

Hydraulic Fixed Displacement	
Variable Displacement	
Bi-directional	
Cylinder, Single Acting	
Cylinder, Double Acting Single End Rod Double End Rod Adjustable Cushion Advance Only Differential Piston	

Miscellaneous Units

Electric Motor	
Nonelectric Prime Mover	
Accumulator, Spring Loaded	
Accumulator, Gas Charged	
Heater	
Cooler	
Temperature Controller	
Filter, Strainer	
Pressure Switch	
Pressure Gauge	
Flow Meter	
Temperature Indicator	
Liquid Level Gauge	
Component Enclosure	
Direction of Shaft Rotation (assume arrow on near side of shaft)	

Methods of Operation

Spring	
Manual	
Pushbutton	
Lever	
Pedal or Treadle	
Mechanical – Plunger	
Mechanical – Roller	
Detent	
Pressure Compensated	
Solenoid, Single Winding	
Servo Control	
Pilot Pressure Remote Supply Internal Supply	

Valves

Air Bleed Valve	
Check Valve	
On -- Off Valve (manual shut-off)	
Pressure Relief Valve	
Pressure Reducing Valve	

Valves

Sequence Valve	
Counterbalance Valve	
Unloading Relief Valve	
Flow Control, Adjustable–Non-compensated	
Flow Control, Adjustable (temperature and pressure compensated)	
Two-position Two-way	
Two-position Three-way	
Two-position Four-way	
Three-position Four-way with Closed Center	
Three-position Four-way with Open Center	
Valves Capable of Infinite Positioning (horizontal bars indicate infinite positioning ability)	

Valves

Deceleration Valves	
Proportional Valve	
Servo Valve	
Slip–in Cartridge Valve	
Steering Control Unit	See Chapter 6

Color Code for Fluid Power Schematic Drawings

Function	Color
Intensified Pressure	Violet
Supply	Red
Charging Pressure	Orange
Reduced Pressure	Orange
Pilot Pressure	Orange
Metered Flow	Yellow
Exhaust	Blue
Intake	Green
Drain	Blue
Inactive	Blank

Definition of Functions

Function	Definition
Intensified Pressure	Pressure in excess of supply pressure which is induced by a booster or intensifier.
Supply Pressure	Power-actuating fluid.
Charging Pressure	Pump-inlet pressure that is higher than atmospheric pressure.
Reduced Pressure	Auxiliary pressure which is lower than supply pressure.
Pilot Pressure	Control-actuating pressure.
Metered Flow	Fluid at controlled flow rate, other than pump delivery.
Exhaust	Return of power and control fluid to reservoir.
Intake	Sub-atmospheric pressure, usually on intake side of pump.
Drain	Return of leakage fluid to reservoir.
Inactive	Fluid which is within the circuit, but which does not serve a functional purpose during the phase being represented.

Appendix C . . . . . Fluid Power Data

Formulas and Units

Pascal's Law and the Conservation of Energy

1. Hydraulics is a means of transmitting power. It may be used to multiply force or modify motions.

2. PASCAL'S LAW: Pressure exerted on a confined fluid is transmitted undiminished in all directions, acts with equal force on all equal areas, and acts at right angles to those areas.

3. To find the area of a round piston, square the diameter and multiply by 0.7854.

$$\text{Diameter} = \sqrt{\frac{\text{Area}}{0.7854}} \qquad \text{Area} = \text{Diameter} \times \text{Diameter} \times 0.7854$$

4. The force exerted by a piston can be determined by multiplying the piston area by the pressure applied.

$$\text{Force} = \text{Pressure} \times \text{Area}$$

5. To determine the volume of fluid required to move a piston a given distance, multiply the piston area by the stroke required.

$$\text{Volume} = \text{Area} \times \text{Length} \ (231 \ \text{Cubic inch}_{(in^3)} = \text{One U.S. Gallon})$$

$$\text{Volume} = \text{Area} \times \text{Length} \ (1,000 \ \text{Cubic cm}_{(cm^3)} = \text{One Liter})$$

6. Work is force acting through a distance.

$$\text{Work} = \text{Force} \times \text{Distance}$$

7. Power is the rate of doing work.

$$\text{Power}_{\left(\frac{in\text{-}lb}{sec}\right)} = \frac{\text{Work}_{(in\text{-}lb)}}{\text{Time}_{(sec)}} = \frac{\text{Force}_{(lb)} \times \text{Distance}_{(in)}}{\text{Time}_{(sec)}}$$

$$\text{Power}_{\left(\frac{Nm}{sec}\right)} = \frac{\text{Work}_{(Nm)}}{\text{Time}_{(sec)}} = \frac{\text{F}_{(n)} \times \text{Distance}_{(m)}}{\text{Time}_{(sec)}}$$

Oil and Atmospheric Pressure

8. Hydraulic oil serves as a lubricant and is practically noncompressible. It will compress approximately 0.4 percent at 100 psi and 1.1 percent at 3,000 psi at 120 degrees Fahrenheit (49 degrees Celsius).

9. The weight of hydraulic oil may vary with a change in viscosity. However, 55 – 58 lbs per cubic foot (8,600 – 9,100 N/m³) covers the viscosity range from 150 to 900 SSU at 100 degrees Fahrenheit (30 degrees Celsius).

10. Pressure at the bottom of a one foot column of oil will be approximately 0.4 psi (0.09 bar psia meters of oil). To find the approximate pressure at the bottom of any column of oil, multiply the height in feet by 0.4.

11. Atmospheric pressure equals 14.7 psia at sea level (approximately 1 bar).

12. Gauge readings do not include atmospheric pressure unless marked psia.

Pumping Principles

13. There must be a pressure drop (pressure difference) across an orifice or other restriction to cause flow through it. Conversely, if there is no flow, there will be no pressure drop.

14. A fluid is pushed, not drawn, into a pump.

15. A pump does not pump pressure; its purpose is to create a flow. Pumps used to transmit power are usually a positive displacement type.

16. Pressure is caused by resistance to flow. A pressure gauge indicates the workload at any given moment.

Series and Parallel Circuits

17. Fluids take the path of least resistance. Sum of the pressure drop is equal to total resistance in a series circuit.

Calculating Velocity in a Cylinder

18. Speed of a cylinder piston is dependent upon its size (piston area) and the rate of flow into it.

$$\text{Velocity}_{\left(\frac{\text{in.}}{\text{min}}\right)} = \frac{\text{Flow}_{\left(\frac{\text{in}^3}{\text{min}}\right)}}{\text{Area}_{(\text{in}^2)}} \qquad \text{Velocity}_{\left(\frac{\text{mm}}{\text{min}}\right)} = \frac{\text{Flow}_{\left(\frac{\text{mm}^3}{\text{min}}\right)}}{\text{Area}_{(\text{mm}^2)}}$$

19. To determine the pump capacity needed to extend a cylinder piston of a given area through a given distance in a specific time:

$$\text{Flow}_{(\text{GPM})} = \frac{\text{Area}_{(\text{in}^2)} \times \text{Stroke Length}_{(\text{in.})} \times 60_{(\text{sec/min})}}{\text{Time}_{(\text{sec})} \times 231_{\left(\frac{\text{in}^3}{\text{gal}}\right)}}$$

$$\text{Flow}_{(\text{l/min})} = \frac{\text{Area}_{(\text{mm}^2)} \times \text{Stroke Length}_{(\text{mm})} \times 60_{(\text{sec/min})}}{\text{Time}_{(\text{sec})} \times 106_{\left(\frac{\text{mm}^3}{\text{l}}\right)}}$$

Determining Pipe, Tubing and Hose Sizes

20. Flow velocity through a fluid conductor varies inversely as the square of the inside diameter. Doubling the inside diameter increases the area four times.

21. Friction losses (pressure drop) of a liquid in a fluid conductor vary with velocity.

22. To find the actual area of a pipe needed to handle a given flow, use the formula:

$$\text{Area}_{(\text{in}^2)} = \frac{\text{Flow}_{(\text{GPM})} \times 0.3208}{\text{Velocity}_{\left(\frac{\text{ft.}}{\text{sec}}\right)}} \qquad \text{Area}_{(\text{mm}^2)} = \frac{\text{Flow}_{(\text{l/min})} \times 16.7}{\text{Velocity}_{(\text{m/sec})}}$$

23. The actual inside diameter of standard pipe is usually larger than the nominal size quoted. A conversion chart should be consulted when selecting pipe.

24. Steel and copper tubing size indicates the outside diameter. To find the actual inside diameter, subtract two times the wall thickness from the tube size quoted. I.D. = O.D. − (2 x Wall thickness.)

25. Hydraulic hose sizes are usually designated by their nominal inside diameter. With some exceptions, this is indicated in the inch system by a dash number representing the number of sixteenth inch increments in their inside diameter. (For instance, a No. 16 hose has a 16/16 inch diameter I.D., i.e. 1 inch I.D.)

Power and Torque

26. One hp = 33,000 lbs raised one foot in one minute or 550 lbs raised one foot in one second. One hp = 746 watts. One hp = 42.4 BTUs per minute. One watt = 9.8 Kg weight raised one meter in one second or 1 Newton of force applied over a distance of 1 meter for 1 second.

27. To find the power required for a given flow rate at a known pressure, use the formula:

Pump Output Power (hp) = Flow (GPM) × Pressure (psi) × 0.000583 or

$$\frac{\text{Flow (GPM)} \times \text{Pressure (psi)}}{1714}$$

Pump Output Power (kW) = Flow (l/min) × Pressure (bar) × 0.00167 or

$$\frac{\text{Flow (l/min)} \times \text{Pressure (bar)}}{600}$$

To find the hp required to drive a hydraulic pump of a given volume at a known pressure, use the formula:

$$\text{Pump Input hp} = \frac{\text{Pump Output Power}}{\text{Pump Efficiency}}$$

If actual pump efficiency is not known, use the following rule of thumb formula for input horsepower.

Pump Input (Power) = Flow (GPM) × Pressure (psi) × 0.0007
(assumes 83.3% efficiency)

Pump Input (kW) = Flow (l/min) × Pressure (bar) × 0.002
(assumes 83.3% efficiency)

28. The relationship between Torque and Horsepower is:

$$\text{Torque (lb-in)} = \frac{\text{Power (hp)} \times 63025}{\text{RPM}}$$

$$\frac{\text{Pressure (psi)} \times \text{Pump Displacement (in}^3\text{/Rev)}}{2\pi}$$

$$\text{Power (hp)} = \frac{\text{Torque (lb-in)} \times \text{RPM}}{63025}$$

$$\text{Torque (Nm)} = \frac{\text{Power (kW)} \times 9545}{\text{RPM}}$$

$$\text{Power (kW)} = \frac{\text{Torque (Nm)} \times \text{RPM}}{9549}$$

Metric Units for Fluid Power Applications

Quantity Name		Metric		U.S. Customary Symbols
		Units	Symbols	
Acceleration		meter per second squared	m/s^2	ft/sec^2
Angle, plane		degree	°	°
		minute	'	'
		second	"	"
Area		square millimeter	mm^2	in^2
Bulk Modulus (See Modulus)				
Conductivity, Thermal		watt per meter Kelvin	W/m•K	BTU/hr•ft•°F
Cubic Expansion, Coefficient (Note 8)		per degree Celsius	1/°C	1/°F
Current, Electric		ampere	A	A
Density	hydraulic fluids & other liquids	kilogram per liter	kg/L (Note 1)	lb/gal
	gases	kilogram per cubic meter	kg/m^3	lb/ft^3
	solids	gram per cubic centimeter	g/cm^3	lb/ft^3
Displacement (Unit discharge) (Note 2)	pneumatic	cubic centimeter	cm^3	in^3
		liter (Note 1)	L	gal
	hydraulic	milliliter (Note 1)	ml	in^3
Efficiency		percent	%	%
Energy, Heat		kilojoule	kJ	BTU
Flow Rate, Heat		watt	W	BTU/min
Flow Rate, Mass		gram per second	g/s	lb/min
		kilogram per second	kg/s	lb/s
Flow rate, Volume (Note 3)	pneumatic	cubic decimeter per second	dm^3/s	ft^3/min (cfm)
		cubic centimeter per second	cm^3/s	in^3/min (cim)
	hydraulic	liter per minute	L/min (Note 1)	gal/min
		milliliter per minute	mL/min (Note 1)	in^3/min
Force		Newton	N	lb
Force per Length		Newton per millimeter	N/mm	lb/in
Frequency (Cycle)		hertzreciprocal minute	HZ1/min (Note 4)	HZ (cps) cpm
Frequency (Rotational)		reciprocal minute	1/min (Note 4)	RPM
Heat		kilojoule	kJ	BTU
Heat Capacity, Specific		kilojoule per kilogram Kelvin	kJ/kg•K	BTU/hr•lb•°F
Heat Transfer, Coefficient		watt per square meter Kelvin	W/m^2•k (Note 9)	BTU/hr•ft²•°F
Inertia, Moment of		kilogram meter squared	kg• m^2	lb•ft² lb•in²
Length		millimeter	mm	in
		meter	m	ft
		micrometer	μm	(micron) in

Metric Units for Fluid Power Applications (continued)

Quantity Name		Metric		U.S. Customary Symbols
		Units	Symbols	
Linear Expansion, Coefficient (Note 7)		per degree	1/°C	1/°F
Mass		kilogram	kg	lb
Modulus, Bulk		megapascal	MPa	lb/in² (psi)
Momentum		kilogram meter per second	kg•m/s	lb•ft/sec
Potential, Electric		volt	V	V
Power		kilowatt	kW	hp
		watt	W	BTU/min
Pressure *		kilopascal (Note 5)	kPa	lb/in² (psi)
		bar (Note 5)	bar	lb/in² (psi)
Rotational Speed (Shaft Speed) (See frequency, rotational)				
Stress — Normal, Shear, Strength of Materials		megapascal	MPa	lb/in² (psi)
Surface Roughness		micrometer	µm	in
Temperature, Customary		degree Celsius	°C	°F
Temperature, Thermodynamic (Absolute)		kelvin	K	°R
Time		second, minute, hour	s, min, hr	s, min, hr
Torque (Moment of Force)		Newton meter	N•m	lb•ft lb•in
Volume	pneumatic	cubic decimeter	dm³	ft³
		cubic centimeter	cm³	in³
	hydraulic	liter (Note 1)	L	gal
		milliliter (Note 1)	mL	oz
Volumetric Flow (See flow rate)				
Velocity, Linear		meter per second	m/s	ft/s
		millimeter per second	mm/s	in/s
Velocity, Angular		radian per second	rad/s	rad/s
Viscosity, Dynamic		millipascal second	mPa•s	cP
Viscosity, Kinematic		square millimeter per second (Note 6)	mm²/s	cSt
Work		joule	J	ft • lb

* Measurement of pressure:
     above atmospheric, use — kPa g or bar g — psig
     below atmospheric, use — kPa vacuum or bar vacuum — in Hg or kPa absolute or bar absolute — psi absg

Metric Units for Fluid Power Applications (continued)

NOTES

Note 1

The international symbol for liter is lower case "l" which can easily be confused with the numeral "1." Accordingly, the symbol "L" is to be used for U.S. fluid power.

Note 2

Indicate displacement of a rotary device as "per revolution" and of a nonrotary device as "per cycle."

Note 3

For gases, this quantity is frequently expressed as free gas at Standard Reference Atmosphere, as defined in reference 4.5 and specified in reference 4.6. In such cases, the abbreviation "ANR" is to follow the expression of the quantity of unit (m^3/min [ANR]). See reference 4.1 for more detailed information of the attachment of letters to a symbol.

Note 4

Mechanical oscillations are normally expressed in cycles per unit time and rotational frequency in revolutions per unit time. Since "cycle" and "revolution" are not units, they do not have internationally recognized symbols. Therefore, they are normally expressed by abbreviations which are different in various languages. In English, the symbol for mechanical oscillation is c/min and for rotation frequency, r/min.

Note 5

The bar and kilopascal are given equal status as pressure units. At this time, the domestic fluid power industry does not agree on one preferred unit. The pascal is the SI unit for pressure and a major segment of U.S. industry has accepted the multiple, kilopascal (kPa), as the preferred unit. On the other hand, the majority of the international fluid power industry has accepted the bar as the metric pressure unit. The bar is recognized by the EEC as an acceptable metric unit and is shown in ISO 1000 for use in specialized fields. Conversely, the bar is considered by both the International COmmittee on Weights and Measures and the NBS as a unit to be used for a limited time only. Further, the bar has been depreciated by Canada, ANMC, and some U.S. standards organizations and is illegal in some countries.

Note 6

Viscosity is frequently expressed in SUS (Saybolt Universal Seconds). SUS is the time in seconds for 60 mL of fluid to flow through a standard orifice at a specified temperature. Conversion between kinematic viscosity, mm^2/s (centistokes) and SUS can be made by reference to Tables in references 4.2 and 4.7.

Note 7

The linear expansion coefficient is a ratio, not a unit, and is expressed in customary U.S. units such as in/in and in metric units such as mm/mm per unit temperature change.

Note 8

The cubic expansion coefficient is a ratio, not a unit and is expressed in customary U.S. units such as in in^3/in^3 and in metric units such as cm^3/cm^3 per unit temperature change.

Note 9

In these expressions, "K" indicates temperature interval. Therefore, "K" may be replaced with °C if desired without changing the value or affecting the conversion factor.

English-Metric Conversion Factors

To convert	Into	Multiply by	To convert	Into	Multiply by
Acre	Rods	160.0	BTU	Ergs	1.0550×10^{-10}
Acre	Hectare or		BTU	Foot-lbs	778.3
	Sq. hectometer	0.4047	BTU	Gram-calories	252.0
Acres	Sq. feet	43,560.0	BTU	Horsepower-hrs.	3.931×10^{-4}
Acres	Sq. meters	4,047.0	BTU	Joules	1,054.8
Acres	Sq. miles	1.562×10^{-3}	BTU	Kilogram-calories	0.2520
Acres	Sq. yards	4,840.0	BTU	Kilogram-meters	107.5
Acre-feet	Cu. feet	43,560.0	BTU	Kilowatt-hrs.	2.928×10^{-4}
Acre-feet	Gallons	3.259×10^{-5}	BTU/hr	Foot-pounds/sec.	0.2162
Amperes/sq.cm	Amps/sq.in.	6,452	BTU/hr	Gram-cal./sec.	0.0700
Amperes/sq.cm	Amps/sq.meter.	10^4	BTU/hr	Horsepower-hrs.	3.929×10^{-4}
Amperes/sq.in	Amps/sq.cm.	0.1550	BTU/hr	Watts	0.2931
Amperes/sq.in	Amps/sq.meter.	1,550.0	BTU/min	Foot-lbs/sec.	12.96
Amperes/sq.meter	Amps/sq.cm.	10^{-4}	BTU/min	Horsepower	0.02356
Amperes/sq.meter	Amps/sq.in.	6.452×10^{-4}	BTU/min	Kilowatts	0.01757
Ampere-hours	Coulombs	3,600.0	BTU/min	Watts	17.57
Ampere-hours	Faradays	0.03731	BTU/sq.ft./min	Watts/sq.in	0.1221
Ampere-turns	Gilberts	1.257	Bushels	Cu.ft.	1.2445
Ampere-turns/cm	Amp-turns/in.	2.540	Bushels	Cu. In.	2.150.4
Ampere-turns/cm	Amp-turns/meter	100.0	Bushels	Cu. Meters	0.03524
Ampere-turns/cm	Gilberts/cm	1.257	Bushels	Liters	35.24
Ampere-turns/in	Amp-turns/cm	0.3937	Bushels	Pecks	4.0
Ampere-turns/in	Amp-turns/meter	39.37	Bushels	Pints (dry)	64.0
Ampere-turns/in	Gilberts/cm	0.4950	Bushels	Quarts (dry)	32.0
Ampere-turns/meter	Amp/turns/cm.	0.01	Calories, gram (mean)	BTU (mean)	3.9685×10^3
Ampere-turns/meter	Amp-turns/in.	0.0254	Centares (centiares)	Sq. Meters	1.0
Ampere-turns/meter	Gilberts/cm.	0.01257	Centigrade	Fahrenheit	(C x 9/5) + 32
Angstrom unit	Inch	3937.0×10^{-9}	Centigrade	Kelvin	C + 273
Angstrom-unit	Meter	1.0×10^{-10}	Centegrams	Grams	0.01
Angstrom unit	Micron or (Mu)	1.0×10^{-4}	Centiliters	Liters	0.01
Astronomical unit	Kilometers	1.495×10^{-8}	Centimiters	Feet	3.281×10^{-2}
Atmospheres	Bar	1.013	Centimeters	Inches	0.3937
Atmospheres	Cms. of mercury	76.0	Centimeters	Kilometers	10^{-5}
Atmospheres	Mm of mercury	760.0	Centimeters	Meters	0.01
Atmospheres	Ft. of water (at 4° C)	33.90	Centimeters	Miles	6.214×10^{-6}
Atmospheres	In. of mercury		Centimeters	Millimeters	10.0
	(at 0° C)	29.92	Centimeters	Mils	393.7
Atmospheres	Kgs./sq. cm.	1.0333	Centimeters	Yards	1.024×10^{-2}
Atmospheres	Kgs./sq.meter	10,332.0	Centimeter-dynes	Cm.-grams	1.020×10^{-3}
Atmospheres	Pounds/sq. in.	14.70	Centimeter-dynes	Meter/kgs.	1.020×10^{-8}
Barrels (U.S. dry)	Cu. inches	7056.0	Centimeter-dynes	Pound-feet	7.376×10^{-8}
Barrels (U.S. dry)	Quarts (dry)	105.0	Centimeter-grams	Cm.-dynes	980.7
Barrels (U.S. liquid)	Gallons	31.5	Centimeter-grams	Meter-kgs.	10^{-5}
Barrels (Oil)	Gallons (oil)	42.0	Centimeter-grams	Pound-feet	7.233×10^{-5}
Bars	Atmospheres	0.9869	Centimeters of mercury	Atmospheres	0.01316
Bars	At. (Tech.)	1.0197	Centimeters of mercury	Feet of water	0.4461
Bars	Dynes/sq. cm.	10^{-4}	Centimeters of mercury	Kgs./sq. Meter	136.0
Bars	Kgs./sq. meter	1.020×10^{-4}	Centimeters of mercury	Pounds/sq. ft.	27.85
Bars	Kilopascal	100.0	Centimeters of mercury	Pounds/sq. in.	0.1934
Bars	Newtons/Sq. meter	10^{-5}	Centimeters/sec.	Feet/min.	1.1969
Bars	Pounds/sq. ft	2,089.0	Centimeters/sec.	Feet/sec.	0.03281
Bars	Psi	14.504	Centimeters/sec.	Kilometers/hr.	0.036
Baryl	Dyne/sq. Cm	1.000	Centimeters/sec.	Knots	0.1943
BTU	Liter-Atmosphere	10.409	Centimeters/sec.	Meters/min.	0.6

To convert	into	Multiply by	To convert	into	Multiply by
Centimeters/sec.	Miles/hr.	0.02237	Cubic meters	Gallons (U.S. liq.)	264.2
Centimeters/sec.	Miles/min.	3.728×10^{-4}	Cubic meters	Liters	1,000.0
Centimeters/sec./sec.	Feet/sec./sec.	0.03281	Cubic meters	Pints (U.S. liq.)	2,113.0
Centimeters/sec./sec.	Kms./hr./sec.	0.036	Cubic meters	Quarts (U.S. liq.)	1,057.0
Centimeters/sec./sec.	Meters/sec./sec.	0.01	Cubic yards	Cu. cms	7.646×10^{5}
Centimeters/sec./sec.	Miles/hr./sec.	0.02237	Cubic yards	Cu. feet	27.0
Centipoise	Gram/cm.sec.	0.01	Cubic yards	Cu. inches	46,656.0
Centipoise	Pound mass/ft. sec.	0.000672	Cubic yards	Cu. meters	0.7646
Centistokes	Sq. feet/sec.	1.076×10^{-6}	Cubic yards	Gallons (U.S. liq.)	202.0
Circular mils	Sq. cms.	5.067×10^{-6}	Cubic yards	Liters	764.6
Circular mils	Sq. mils	0.7854	Cubic yards	Pints (U.S. liq.)	1,615.9
Circumference	Radians	6.283	Cubic yards	Quarts (U.S. liq.)	807.9
Circular mils	Sq. inches	7.854×10^{-7}	Cubic yards/min.	Cubic ft./sec.	0.45
Coulomb	Statcoulombs	2.998×10^{-9}	Cubic yards/min.	Gallonssec.	3.367
Coulombs	Faradays	1.036×10^{-5}	Cubic yards/min.	Liters/sec.	12.74
Coulombs/sq. cm.	Coulombs/sq.in	64.52	Days	Seconds	86,400.0
Coulombs/sq. cm.	Coulombs/sq.meter	10^{-4}	Decigrams	Grams	0.1
Coulombs/sq. in.	Coulombs/sq.cm	0.1550	Deciliters	Liters	0.1
Coulombs/sq. in.	Coulombs/sq.meter	1,550.0	Decimeters	Meters	0.1
Coulombs/sq. meter.	Coulombs/sq.cm	10^{-4}	Degrees (angle)	Minutes	60.0
Coulombs/sq. meter.	Coulombs/sq.in	6.452×10^{-5}	Degrees (angle)	Quadrants	0.01111
Cubic centimeters	Cu. feet	3.531×10^{-5}	Degrees (angle)	Radians	0.01745
Cubic centimeters	Cu. inches	0.06102	Degrees (angle)	Seconds	3,600.0
Cubic centimeters	Cu. meters	10^{-6}	Degrees/sec.	Radians/sec.	0.01745
Cubic centimeters	Cu. yards	1.308×10^{-6}	Degrees/sec.	Revolutions/min.	0.1667
Cubic centimeters	Gallons (U.S. liq.)	2.642×10^{-4}	Degrees/sec.	Revolutions/sec	2.778×10^{-3}
Cubic centimeters	Liters	0.001	Dekagrams	Grams	10.0
Cubic centimeters	Pints (U.S. liq.)	2.113×10^{-3}	Dekaliters	Liters	10.0
Cubic centimeters	Quarts (U.S. liq.)	1.057×10^{-3}	Dekameters	Meters	10.0
Cubic feet	Cu. cms.	28,320.0	Drams	Grams	1.7718
Cubic feet	Cu. inches	1,728.0	Drams	Grains	27.3437
Cubic feet	Cu. meters	0.02832	Drams	Ounces	0.0625
Cubic feet	Cu. yards	0.03704	Dyne/sq.cm	Atmospheres	9.869×10^{-7}
Cubic feet	Gallons (U.S. liq.)	7.48052	Dyne/sq.cm	In. of mercury at $0°$ C	2.953×10^{-5}
Cubic feet	Liters	28.32	Dyne/sq.cm	In. of water at $4°$ C	4.015×10^{-4}
Cubic feet	Pints (U.S. liq.)	59.84	Dynes	Grams	1.020×10^{-3}
Cubic feet	Quarts (U.S. liq.)	29.92	Dynes	Joules/cm.	10^{-7}
Cubic feet/min.	Cu. cms./sec.	472.0	Dynes	Joules/meter(newtons)	10^{-5}
Cubic feet/min.	Gallons/sec.	0.1247	Dynes	Kilograms	1.020×10^{-6}
Cubic feet/min.	Liters/sec.	0.4720	Dynes	Poundals	7.233×10^{-5}
Cubic feet/min.	Lbs of water/min.	62.43	Dynes	Pounds	2.248×10^{-6}
Cubic feet/sec	Million gal./day	0.646317	Dynes/sq.cm	Bars	10^{-6}
Cubic feet/sec	Gallons/min.	448.831	Erg/sec.	Dyne-cm./sec.	1.000
Cubic inches	Cu. cms.	16.39	Ergs.	BTU	9.480×10^{-11}
Cubic inches	Cu. feet	5.787×10^{-4}	Ergs.	Dyne-centimeters	1.0
Cubic inches	Cu. meters	1.639×10^{-5}	Ergs.	Foot-pounds	7.367×10^{-8}
Cubic inches	Cu. yards	2.143×10^{-5}	Ergs.	Gram-calories	0.2389×10^{-7}
Cubic inches	Gallons	4.329×10^{-3}	Ergs.	Gram-cms	1.020×10^{-3}
Cubic inches	Liters	0.01639	Ergs.	Horsepower-hrs.	3.7250×10^{-14}
Cubic inches	Mil.-feet	1.061×10^{5}	Ergs.	Joules	10^{-7}
Cubic inches	Pints (U.S. liq.)	0.03463	Ergs.	Kg.-calories	2.389×10^{-11}
Cubic inches	Quarts (U.S. liq.)	0.01732	Ergs.	Kg.-meters	1.020×10^{-8}
Cubic meters	Cu. cms	10^{6}	Ergs.	Kilowatt-hrs.	0.2778×10^{-13}
Cubic meters	Cu. feet	35.31	Ergs.	Watt-hours	0.2778×10^{-10}
Cubic meters	Cu. inches	61,023.0	Ergs/sec.	BTU/min.	$5,688.0 \times 10^{-9}$
Cubic meters	Cu. yards	1.308	Ergs/sec.	Ft-lbs/min.	4.427×10^{-6}

To convert	into	Multiply by	To convert	into	Multiply by
Ergs/sec.	Ft-lbs/sec.	7.3756×10^{-8}	Foot-pounds/sec.	BTU/sec.	4.6263
Ergs/sec.	Horsepower	1.341×10^{-10}	Foot-pounds/sec.	BTU/min.	0.07717
Ergs/sec.	Kg.-calories/min.	1.433×10^{-9}	Foot-pounds/sec.	Horsepower	1.818×10^{-3}
Ergs/sec.	Kilowatts	10^{-10}	Foot-pounds/sec.	Kg.-calories/min.	0.01945
Fahreheit	Centigrade	5/9 (F – 32)	Foot-pounds/sec.	Kilowatts	1.356×10^{-3}
Fahrenheit	Rankine	F + 460	Foot-pounds/sec.	Newton-meters/Sec	1.356
Farads	Microfarads	10^{6}	Furlongs	Miles (U.S.)	0.125
Faraday/sec.	Ampere (absolute)	9.6500×10^{4}	Furlongs	Rods	40.0
Faradays	Ampere-hours	26.80	Furlongs	Feet	660.0
Faradays	Coulombs	9.649×10^{4}	Gallons	Cu. cms.	3,785.0
Fathom	Meter	1.828804	Gallons	Cu. feet	0.1337
Fathoms	Feet	6.0	Gallons	Cu. inches	231.0
Feet	Centimeters	30.48	Gallons	Cu. meters	3.785×10^{-3}
Feet	Inches	12.0	Gallons	Cu. yards	4.951×10^{-3}
Feet	Kilometers	3.048×10^{-4}	Gallons	Liters	3.785
Feet	Meters	0.3048	Gallons	Pints (liq.)	8.0
Feet	Miles (naut.)	1.645×10^{-4}	Gallons	Quarts (liq.)	4.0
Feet	Miles (stat.)	1.894×10^{-4}	Gallons (liq. Br.Imp.)	Gallons (U.S. liq.)	1.20095
Feet	millimeters	304.8	Gallons (U.S.)	Gallons (Imp.)	0.83267
Feet	Yards	1/3	Gallons/min.	Cu. ft./sec.	2.228×10^{-3}
Feet of water	Atmospheres	0.02950	Gallons/min.	Liters/sec.	0.06308
Feet of water	In. of mercury	0.8826	Gallons/min.	Cu. ft./hr.	8.0208
Feet of water	Kgs./sq. cm.	0.03048	Gallons/min.	Pounds of water/hrs.	500.0
Feet of water	Kgs./sq. meter	304.8	Gausses	Lines/sq.in.	6.452
Feet of water	Pounds/sq. ft.	62.43	Gausses	Webers/sq.cm.	10^{-8}
Feet of water	Pounds/sq. in.	0.4335	Gausses	Webers/sq.in.	6.452×10^{-8}
Feet/min.	Cms./sec.	0.5080	Gausses	Webers/sq.meter	10^{-4}
Feet/min.	Feet/sec.	0.01667	Grade	Radian	0.01571
Feet/min.	Kms./Hr.	0.01829	Grains (troy)	Grains (avdp.)	1.0
Feet/min.	Meters/min.	0.3048	Grains (troy)	Grams	0.06480
Feet/min.	Miles/hr.	0.01136	Grains (troy)	Ounces (avdp.)	2.0833×10^{-3}
Feet/sec.	Cms./sec.	30.48	Grains/U.S. gal.	Parts/million	17.118
Feet/sec.	Kms./hr.	1.097	Grains/U.S. gal.	Pounds/million gal.	142.86
Feet/sec.	Knots	0.5921	Grains/Imp. gal.	Parts/million	14.286
Feet/sec.	Meters/min.	18.29	Grams	Dynes	980.7
Feet/sec.	Miles/hrs.	0.6818	Grams	Grains	15.43
Feet/sec.	Miles/min.	0.01136	Grams	Joules/cm.	$9.807/10^{-5}$
Feet/sec./sec.	Cms./sec./sec.	30.48	Grams	Joules/meter (newtons)	$9.807/10^{-3}$
Feet/sec./sec	Kms./hr/sec.	1.097	Grams	Kilograms	0.001
Feet/sec./sec	Meters/sec./sec	0.3048	Grams	Milligrams	1,000.0
Feet/sec./sec	Miles/hrs./sec	0.6818	Grams	Ounces (avdp.)	0.03527
Feet/100 feet	Per cent grade	1.0	Grams	Ounces (troy)	0.03215
Foot-pounds	BTU	1.286×10^{-3}	Grams	Poundals	0.07093
Foot-pounds	Ergs	1.356×10^{-7}	Grams	Pounds	2.205×10^{-3}
Foot-pounds	Gram-calories	0.3238	Grams/cm	Pounds/inch	5.600×10^{-3}
Foot-pounds	Hp-hrs.	5.050×10^{-7}	Grams/cu. cm.	Pounds/cu.ft.	62.43
Foot-pounds	Joules	1.356	Grams/cu.cm.	Pounds/cu.in.	0.03613
Foot-pounds	Kg.-calories	3.24×10^{-4}	Grams/cu. cm.	Pounds/mil.-foot	3.405×10^{-7}
Foot-pounds	Kg.-meters	0.1383	Grams/liter	Grains/gal.	58.417
Foot-pounds	Kilowatt-hrs.	3.766×10^{-7}	Grams/liter	Pounds/1,000 gal.	8.345
Foot-pounds	Newton-meters	1.356	Grams/liter	Pounds/cu.ft.	0.062427
Foot-pounds/min.	BTU/min.	1.286×10^{-3}	Grams/liter	Parts/million	1,000.0
Foot-pounds/min.	Foot-pounds/sec.	0.01667	Grams/sq. cm.	Pounds/sq. ft.	2.0481
Foot-pounds/min.	Horsepower	3.030×10^{-5}	Gram-calories	BTU	3.9683×10^{-3}
Foot-pounds/min.	Kg.-calories/min.	3.24×10^{-4}	Gram-calories	Foot-pounds	3.0880
Foot-pounds/min.	Kilowatts	2.260×10^{-5}			

To convert	into	Multiply by	To convert	into	Multiply by
Gram-calories	Horsepower-hrs.	1.5596×10^{-6}	Joules	Ergs	10^7
Gram-calories	Kilowatt-hrs.	1.1630×10^{-6}	Joules	Foot-pounds	0.7376
Gram-calories	Watt-hrs.	1.1630×10^{-6}	Joules	Kg.-calories	2.389×10^{-4}
Gram-calories/sec.	BTU/hr.	14.286	Joules	Kg.-meters	0.1020
Gram-centimers	BTU	9.297×10^{-8}	Joules	Watt-hrs	2.778×10^{-4}
Gram-centimers	Joules	9.807×10^{-5}	Joules/cm.	Grams	1.020×10^4
Gram-centimers	Kg.-cal.	2.343×10^{-8}	Joules/cm.	Dynes	10^7
Gram-centimers	Kg.-meters	10^{-5}	Joules/cm.	Joules/meter (newtons)	100.0
Hectares	Acres	2.471	Joules/cm.	Poundals	723.3
Hectares	Sq. feet	1.076×10^5	Joules/cm.	Pounds.	22.48
Hectograms	Grams	100.0	Kilograms	Dynes	980,665.0
Hectoliters	Liters	100.0	Kilograms	Grams	1,000.0
Hectometers	Meters	100.0	Kilograms	Joules/cm.	0.09807
Hectowatts	Watts	100.0	Kilograms	Joules/meter(newtons)	9.807
Henries	Millihenries	1,000.0	Kilograms	Poundals	70.93
Horsepower	BTU/min.	42.44	Kilograms	Pounds	2.205
Horsepower	Foot-lbs/min.	33,000.0	Kilograms	Tons (long)	9.842×10^{-4}
Horsepower	Foot-lbs/sec.	550.0	Kilograms	Tons (short)	1.102×10^{-3}
Horsepower (metric) (542.5 ft-lb/sec.)	Horsepower (550 ft-lb/sec.)	0.9863	Kilograms/cu. meter	Grams/cu. cm.	0.001
Horsepower (550 ft-lb/sec.)	Horsepower (metric) (542.5 ft-lb/sec.)	1.014	Kilograms/cu. meter	Pounds/cu.ft.	0.06243
			Kilograms/cu. meter	Pounds/cu.in	3.613×10^{-5}
Horsepower	Kg.-calories/min.	10.68	Kilograms/cu. meter	Poundsmil.-foot	3.405×10^{-10}
Horsepower	Kilowatts	0.7457	Kilograms/meter	Pounds/ft.	0.6720
Horsepower	Watts	745.7	Kilograms/sq. cm.	Bar	0.981
Horsepower-hrs.	BTU	2,547.0	Kilograms/sq. cm.	Dynes	980,665.0
Horsepower-hrs.	Foot-lbs	1.98×10^6	Kilograms/sq. cm.	Atmospheres	0.9678
Horsepower-hrs.	Gram-calories	641,190.0	Kilograms/sq. cm.	Feet of water	32.81
Horsepower-hrs.	Joules	2.684×10^6	Kilograms/sq. cm.	Inches of mercury	28.96
Horsepower-hrs.	Kg.-calories	641.1	Kilograms/sq. cm.	Pounds/sq. ft.	0.2048
Horsepower-hrs.	Kg-meters	2.737×10^5	Kilograms/sq. cm.	Pounds/sq. in.	14.228
Horsepower-hrs.	Kilowatt-hrs.	0.7457	Kilograms/sq. meter	Atmospheres	$9.678.10^{-5}$
Hours	Days	$4.167.10^{-2}$	Kilograms/sq. meter	Bars	98.07×10^{-6}
Hours	Weeks	5.952×10^{-3}	Kilograms/sq. meter	Feet of water	3.281×10^{-3}
Inches	Centimeters	2.540	Kilograms/sq. meter.	Inches of mercury	2896×10^{-3}
Inches	Meters	2.540×10^{-2}	Kilograms/sq. meter	Pounds/sq. ft.	0.2048
Inches	Miles	1.578×10^{-5}	Kilograms/sq. meter	Pounds/sq. in	1.422×10^{-3}
Inches	Millimeters	25.40	Kilograms/sq. mm	Kgs./sq. meter	10^4
Inches	Mils	1,000.0	Kilogram-calories	BTU	3.968
Inches	Yards	2.778×10^{-2}	Kilogram-calories	Foot-pounds	3,088.0
Inches of mercury	Atmospheres	0.03342	Kilogram-calories	Hp.-hrs.	$1.560.10^{-3}$
Inches of mercury	Feet of water	1.133	Kilogram-calories	Joules	4,186.0
Inches of mercury	Kgs./sq. cm.	0.03453	Kilogram-calories	Kg.-meters	426.9
Inches of mercury	Kgs./sq.meter	345.3	Kilogram-calories	Kilojoules	4.186
Inches of mercury	Pounds/sq. ft.	70.73	Kilogram-calories	Kilowatt-hrs.	1.163×10^{-3}
Inches of mercury	Pounds/sq. in.	0.4912	Kilogram-meters	BTU	9.294×10^{-3}
Inches of water (at 4°C)	Atmospheres	2.458×10^{-3}	Kilogram-meters	Ergs.	9.804×10^7
Inches of water (at 4°C)	Inches of mercury	0.07355	Kilogram-meters	Foot-pounds	7.233
Inches of water (at 4°C)	Kgs./sq. cm.	$2,540 \times 10^{-3}$	Kilogram-meters	Joules	9.804
Inches of water (at 4°C)	Ounces/sq. in.	0.5781	Kilogram-meters	Kg.-calories	2.342×10^{-3}
Inches of water (at 4°C)	Pounds/sq. ft.	5.204	Kilogram-meters	Kilowatt-hrs.	2.723×10^{-6}
Inches of water (at 4°C)	Pounds/sq. in.	0.03613	Kiloliters	Liters	1,000.0
International Ampere	Ampere (absolute)	0.9998	Kilometers	Centimeters	10^5
International Volt	Volts (absolute)	1.0003	Kilometers	Feet	3,281.0
International Volt	Joules	9.654×10^4	Kilometers	Inches	3.937×10^4
			Kilometers	Meters	1,000.0
Joules	BTU	9.480×10^{-4}	Kilometers	Miles	0.6214

To convert	into	Multiply by	To convert	into	Multiply by
Kilometers	Millimeters	10^4	Meters/min.	Cms./sec.	1.667
Kilometers	Yards	1,094.0	Meters/min.	Feet/min.	3.281
Kilometers/hr.	Cms./sec.	27.78	Meters/min.	Feet/sec.	0.05468
Kilometers/hr.	Feet/min.	54.68	Meters/min.	Kms./hr.	0.06
Kilometers/hr.	Feet/sec.	0.9113	Meters/min.	Knots	0.03238
Kilometers/hr.	Knots	0.5396	Meters/min.	Miles/hrs.	0.03728
Kilometers/hr.	Meters/min.	16.67	Meters/sec.	Feet/min.	196.8
Kilometers/hr.	Miles/hr.	0.6214	Meters/sec.	Feet/sec.	3.281
Kilometers/hr./sec.	Cms./sec./sec.	27.78	Meters/sec.	Kilometers/hr.	3.6
Kilometers/hr./sec.	Ft./sec./sec.	0.9113	Meters/sec.	Kilometers/min.	0.06
Kilometers/hr./sec.	Meters/sec./sec.	0.2778	Meters/sec.	Miles/hr.	2.237
Kilometers/hr./sec.	Miles/hr./sec.	0.6214	Meters/sec.	Miles/min.	0.03728
Kilowatts	BTU/min.	56.92	Meters/sec./sec.	Cms./sec./sec.	100.0
Kilowatts	Foot-lbs/min.	4.426×10^4	Meters/sec./sec.	Ft./sec./sec.	3.281
Kilowatts	Foot-lbs/sec.	737.6	Meters/sec./sec.	Miles/hr./sec.	2.237
Kilowatts	Horsepower	1.341	Meters-kilograms	Cm-dynes	9.807×10^7
Kilowatts	Kg-calories/min.	14.34	Meters-kilograms	Cm-grams	10^5
Kilowatts	Watts	1,000.0	Meters-kilograms	Pound-feet	7.233
Kilowatts-hrs.	BTU	3,413.0	Micrograms	Grams	10^{-6}
Kilowatt-hrs.	Foot-lbs	2.655×10^6	Microhms	Megohms	10^{-12}
Kilowatt-hrs.	Gram-calories	859,850.0	Microhms	Ohms	10^{-6}
Kilowatt-hrs.	Horsepower-hrs.	1.341	Microliters	Liters	10^{-6}
Kilowatt-hrs.	Joules	3.6×10^4	Microns	Inches	39×10^{-6}
Kilowatt-hrs.	Kg.-calories	860.5	Microns	Meters	1×10^{-6}
Kilowatt-hrs.	Kg.-meters	3.671×10^5	Miles (naut.)	Feet	6,080.27
Knots	Feet/hr.	6,080.0	Miles (naut.)	Kilometers	1.853
Knots	Kilometers/hr.	1.8532	Miles (naut.)	Meters	1,853.0
Knots	nautical miles/hr.	1.0	Miles (naut.)	Miles (statute)	1.1516
Knots	Statue miles/hr.	1.151	Miles (naut.)	Yards	2,027.0
Knots	Yards/hr.	2,027.0	Miles (statute)	Centimeters	1.609×10^5
Knots	Feet/sec.	1.689	Miles (statute)	Feet	5,280.0
League	Miles (approx.)	3.0	Miles (statute)	Inches	6.336×10^4
Light year	Miles	5.9×10^{12}	Miles (statute)	Kilometers	1.609
Light year	Kilometers	9.46091×10^{12}	Miles (statute)	Meters	1,609.0
Liters	Bushels (U.S. dry)	0.02838	Miles (statute)	Miles (naut.)	0.8684
Liters	Cu. cm.	1,000.0	Miles (statute)	Yards	1,760.0
Liters	Cu. decimeters	1.0	Miles/hr.	Cms./sec.	44.70
Liters	Cu. feet	0.03531	Miles/hr.	Feet/min.	88.0
Liters	Cu. inches	61.02	Miles/hr.	Feet/sec.	1.467
Liters	Cu. meters	0.001	Miles/hr.	Kms./hr.	1.609
Liters	Cu. yards	1.308×10^{-3}	Miles/hr.	Kms./min.	0.02682
Liters	Gallons (U.S. liq.)	0.2642	Miles/hr.	Knots	0.8684
Liters	Pints (U.S. liq.)	2.113	Miles/hr.	Meters/min.	26.82
Liters	Quarts (U.S. liq.)	1.057	Miles/hr.	Miles/min.	0.1667
Liters/min.	Cu. Ft./sec.	5.886×10^{-4}	Miles/hr./sec.	Cms/sec./sec.	44.70
Liters/min.	Gals./sec.	4.403×10^{-3}	Miles/hr./sec.	Feet/sec./sec.	1,467
Megohms	Microhms	10^{12}	Miles/hr./sec.	Kms./hr./sec.	1.609
Megohms	Ohms	10^6	Miles/hr./sec.	Meters/sec./sec.	0.4470
Meters	Centimeters	100.0	Miles/min.	Cms./sec.	2,682.0
Meters	Feet	3.281	Miles/min.	Feet/sec.	88.0
Meters	Inches	39.37	Miles/min.	Kms./min.	1.609
Meters	Kilometers	0.001	Miles/min.	Knots/min.	0.8684
Meters	Miles (naut.)	5.396×10^4	Miles/min.	Miles/hr.	60.0
Meters	Miles (stat.)	6.214×10^4	Milliers	Kilograms	1,000.0
Meters	Millimeters	1,000.0	Millimicrons	Meters	1×10^{-9}
Meters	Yards	1.094	Milligrams	Grains	0.01543236

Appendix C Fluid Power Data

To convert	into	Multiply by	To convert	into	Multiply by
Milligrams	Grams	0.001	Pints (liq.)	Liters	0.4732
Milligrams/lliter	Parts/million	1.0	Pints (liq.)	Quarts (liq.)	0.5
Millihenries	Henries	0.001	Pounds (avoirdupois)	Ounces (troy)	14.5833
Milliliters	Liters	0.001	Poundals	Dynes	13,826.0
Millimeters	Centimeters	0.1	Poundals	Grams	14.10
Millimeters	Feet	3.281×10^{-3}	Poundals	Joules/cm.	1.383×10^{-3}
Millimeters	Inches	0.03937	Poundals	Joules/meter (newtons)	0.1383
Millimeters	Kilometers	10^{-6}	Poundals	Kilograms	0.01410
Millimeters	Meters	0.001	Poundals	Pounds	0.03108
Millimeters	Miles	6.214×10^{-7}	Pounds	Drams	256.0
Millimeters	Mils	39.37	Pounds	Dynes	44.4823×10^{4}
Millimeters	Yards	1.094×10^{-3}	Pounds	Grams	453.5924
Millimeters of mercury	Psi	0.0194	Pounds	Joules/cm.	0.04448
Million gals./day	Cu. ft./sec.	1.54723	Pounds	Joules/meter (newtons)	4.448
Mils	Centimeters	2.540×10^{-3}	Pounds	Kilograms	0.4536
Newton	Dynes	1×105.0	Pounds	Newtons (N)	4.44
Newton	Kilograms	0.1020	Pounds	Ounces	16.0
Newton	Pounds	8.85	Pounds	Ounces (troy)	14.5833
Newton/sq. meter	Pascal	1.0	Pounds	Poundals	32.17
Newton-meter	Foot-pounds	0.7375	Pounds	Pounds (troy)	1.21528
Newton-meter	Joule	1.0	Pounds	Tons (shorts)	0.0005
Newton-meter/sec.	Foot-pounds/sec.	0.7375	Pounds (troy)	Ounces (avdp.)	13.1657
Newton-meter/sec.	Watts	1.0	Pounds (troy)	Ounces (troy)	12.0
OHM (International)	OHM (absolute)	1.0005	Pounds (troy)	Pounds (avdp.)	0.822857
Ohms	Megohms	10^{-6}	Pounds (troy)	Tons (long)	3.6735×10^{-4}
Ohms	Microhms	10^{6}	Pounds (troy)	Tons (metric)	3.7324×10^{-4}
Ounces	Drams	16.0	Pounds (troy)	Tons (short)	4.1143×10^{-4}
Ounces	Grams	28.349527	Pounds of water	Cu. feet	0.01602
Ounces	Pounds	0.0625	Pounds of water	Cu. inches	27.68
Ounces	Ounces (troy)	0.9115	Pounds of water	Gallons	0.1198
Ounces	Tons (long)	2.790×10^{-5}	Pounds of water/min.	Cu. ft./sec.	2.670×10^{-4}
Ounces	Tons (metric)	2.835×10^{-5}	Pounds/Inch	newton-meters	0.113
Ounces (fluid)	Cu. inches	1.805	Pound-feet	Cm.-dynes	1.356×10^{7}
Ounces (fluid)	Liters	0.02957	Pound-feet	Cm.-grams	13,825.0
Ounces (troy)	Ounces (avdp.)	1.09714	Pound-feet	Meter-kgs.	0.1383
Ounces (troy)	Pounds (troy)	0.08333	Pounds/foot	Newton-meters	1.356
Ounce/sq. inch	Dynes/sq. cm.	4309.0	Pounds/cu. ft	Grams/cu.cm.	0.01602
Ounces/sq.in.	Pounds/sq. in.	0.0625	Pounds/cu. ft.	Kgs./cu.meter	16.02
Parsec.	Miles	$19. \times 10^{12}$	Pounds/cu. ft.	Pounds/cu. in.	5.787×10^{-4}
Parsec	Kilometers	3.084×10^{13}	Pounds/cu. ft.	Pounds/mil-foot	5.456×10^{-9}
Parts/million	Grains/U.S. gal.	0.0584	Pounds/cu. in.	Gm./cu. cm.	27.68
Parts/million	Grains/Imp. gal.	0.07016	Pounds/cu. in.	Kgs./cu. meter	2.768×10^{4}
Parts/million	Pounds/million gal.	8.345	Pounds/cu. in.	Pounds cu. ft.	1,728.0
Pecks (British)	Cubic inches	554.6	Pounds cu. in.	Pounds/mil-foot	9.425×10^{-6}
Pecks (British)	Liters	9.091901	Pounds/ft.	Kgs./meter	1.488
Pecks (U.S.)	Bushels	0.25	Pounds/in.	Gms./cm.	178.6
Pecks (U.S.)	Cubic Inches	537.605	Pounds/sq. ft.	Atmospheres	4.725×10^{4}
Pecks (U.S.)	Liters	8.809582	Pounds/sq. ft.	Feet of water	0.01602
Pecks (U.S.)	Quarts (dry)	8	Pounds/sq. ft.	Inches of mercury	0.01414
Pints (dry)	Cu. inches	33.60	Pounds/sq. ft.	Kgs./sq. meter	4.882
Pints (liq.)	Cu.cms.	473.2	Pounds/sq. ft.	Pounds/sq. in.	6.944×10^{-3}
Pints (liq.)	Cu. feet	0.01671	Pounds/sq. in.	Atmospheres	0.06804
Pints (liq.)	Cu. inches	28.87	Pounds/sq. in.	Bar	0.0690
Pints (liq.)	Cu. meters	4.732×10^{-4}	Pounds/sq. in.	Feet of water	2.307
Pints (liq.)	Cu. yards	6.189×10^{-4}	Pounds/sq. in.	Inches of mercury	2.036
Pints (liq.)	Gallons	0.125	Pounds/sq. in.	Inches of water	27.7

To convert	into	Multiply by	To convert	into	Multiply by
Pounds/sq.in.	Kgs./sq. meter	703.1	Seconds (angle)	Radians	4.848×10^{-6}
Pounds/sq.in.	Kilopascal	6.895	Slug	Kilograms	14.59
Pounds/sq.in.	Pounds/sq.ft	144.0	Slug	Pounds	32.17
Pounds/hr.	Kilograms/hr.	0.454	Square Centimeters	Circular mils.	1.973×10^{5}
Pounds/sec.	Kilograms/hr.	1,633.0	Square Centimeters	Sq. feet	1.076×10^{-3}
Pounds-sec./sq.ft.	Pound mass/ft. sec.	32.2	Square Centimeters	Sq. inches	0.1550
Quadrants (angle)	Degrees	90.0	Square Centimeters	Sq. meters	0.0001
Quadrants (angle)	Minutes	5,400.0	Square Centimeters	Sq. miles	3.861×10^{-11}
Quadrants (angle)	Radians	1.571	Square Centimeters	Sq. millimeters	100.0
Quadrants (angle)	Seconds	3.24×10^{5}	Square Centimeters	Sq. yards	1.196×10^{-4}
Quarts (liq.)	Cu. cms.	946.4	Square Feet	Acres	2.296×10^{-5}
Quarts (liq.)	Cu. feet	0.03342	Square Feet	Circular mils.	1.833×10^{8}
Quarts (liq.)	Cu. inches	57.75	Square Feet	Sq. cms.	929.0
Quarts (liq.)	Cu. meters	9.464×10^{-4}	Square Feet	Sq. inches	144.0
Quarts (liq.)	Cu. yards	1.238×10^{-3}	Square Feet	Sq. meters	0.09290
Quarts (liq.)	Gallons	0.25	Square Feet	Sq. miles	3.587×10^{-8}
Quarts (liq.)	Liters	0.9463	Square Feet	Sq. millimeters	9.290×10^{4}
Radians	Degrees	57.30	Square Feet	Sq. yards	0.1111
Radians	Minutes	3,438.0	Square Feet/sec.	Centistokes	92,903.0
Radians	Quadrants	0.6366	Square Inches	Circular mils.	1.273×10^{6}
Radians	Seconds	2.063×10^{5}	Square inches	Sq. cms.	6.452
Radians/sec.	Degrees/sec.	57.30	Square inches	Sq. feet	6.944×10^{-3}
Radians/sec.	Revolutions/min.	9.549	Square inches	Sq. millimeters	645.2
Radians/sec.	Revolutions/sec.	0.1592	Square inches	Sq. mils	10^{6}
Radians/sec./sec.	Revs./min./min.	573.0	Square inches	Sq. yard	7.716×10^{-4}
Radians/sec./sec.	Revs./min./sec.	9.549	Square kilometers	Acres	247.1
Radians/sec./sec.	Revs./sec./sec.	0.1592	Square kilometers	Sq. cms	10^{10}
Revolutions	Degrees	360.0	Square kilometers	Sq. ft.	10.76×10^{4}
Revolutions	Quadrants	4.0	Square kilometers	Sq. inches	1.550×10^{9}
Mils	Feet	8.333×10^{-5}	Square kilometers	Sq. meters	10^{6}
Mils	Inches	0.001	Square kilometers	Sq. miles	0.3861
Mils	Kilometers	2.540×10^{-8}	Square kilometers	Sq. yards	1.196×10^{4}
Mils	Yards	2.778×10^{-5}	Square meters	Acres	2.471×10^{-4}
Minutes (angles)	Degrees	0.01667	Square meters	Sq. cms.	10^{4}
Minutes (angles)	Quadrants	1.852×10^{-4}	Square meters	Sq. feet	10.76
Minutes (angles)	Radians	2.909×10^{-4}	Square meters	Sq. inches	1,550.0
Minutes (angles)	Seconds	60.0	Square meters	Sq. miles	3.861×10^{-7}
Myriagrams	Kilograms	10.0	Square meters	Sq. millimeters	10^{6}
Myriameters	Kilmeters	10.0	Square meters	Sq. yards	1.196
Myriawatts	Kilowatts	10.0	Square miles	Acres	640.0
Revolutions	Radians	6.283	Square miles	Sq. feet	27.88×10^{6}
Revolutions/min.	Degrees/sec.	6.0	Square miles	Sq. kms.	2.590
Revolutions/min.	Radians/sec.	0.1047	Square miles	Sq. meters	2.590×10^{6}
Revolutions/min.	Revs./sec.	0.01667	Square miles	Sq. yards	3.098×10^{6}
Revolutions/min./min.	Radians/sec./sec.	1.745×10^{-3}	Square millimeters	Circular mils	1,753.0
Revolutions/min./min.	Revs./min./sec.	0.01667	Square millimeters	Sq. cms	0.01
Revolutions/min./min.	Revs./sec./sec.	2.778×10^{-4}	Square miles	Sq. feet	1.076×10^{-5}
Revolutions/sec.	Degrees/sec.	360.0	Square miles	Sq. inches	1.550×10^{-3}
Revolutions/sec.	Radians/sec.	6.283	Square mils	Circular mils.	1.273
Revolutions/sec.	Revs./min.	60.0	Square mils	Sq. cms	6.452×10^{-6}
Revolutions/sec./sec.	Radians/sec./sec.	6.283	Square mils	Sq. inches	10^{6}
Revolutions/sec./sec.	Revs./min./min.	3,600.0	Square yards	Acres	2.066×10^{-4}
Revolutions/sec./sec.	revs./min./sec.	60.0	Square yards	Sq. cms	8,361.0
Seconds (angle)	Degrees	2.778×10^{-4}	Square yards	Sq. feet	9.0
Seconds (angle)	Minutes	0.01667	Square yards	Sq. inches	1,296.0
Seconds (angle)	Quadrants	3.087×10^{-6}	Square yards	Sq. meters	0.8361

To convert	Into	Multiply by
Square yards	Square millimeters	8.361×10^5
Square yards	Sq. miles	3.228×10^{-7}
Temperature (°C) +273	Absolute Temp. (°C)	1.0
Temperature (°C) +17.78	Temperature (°F)	1.8
Temperature (°F) +460	Absolute Temp. (°F)	1.0
Temperature (F) -32	Temperature (°C)	5/9
Tons (long)	Kilograms	1,016.0
Tons (long)	Pounds	2,240.0
Tons (long	Tons (short)	1.120
Tons (metric)	Kilograms	1,000.0
Tons (metric	Pounds	2,205.0
Tons (short)	Kilograms	907.1848
Tons (short)	Ounces	32,000.0
Tons (short)	Ounces (troy)	29,166.66
Tons (short)	Pounds	2,000.0
Tons (short)	Pounds (troy)	2,430.56
Tons (short)	Tons (long)	0.89287
Tons (short)	Tons (metric)	0.9078
Tons (short)/sq. ft.	Kgs./sq.meter	9,765.0
Tons (short)/sq. ft.	Pounds/sq. in.	2,000.0
Tons of water/24 hrs.	Pounds of water/hr.	83.333
Tons of water/24 hrs.	Gallons/min.	0.16643
Tons of water/24 hrs.	Cu. ft./hr.	1.3349
Volt/inch	Volt/cm.	0.39370
Watts	BTU/hr.	3.4129
Watts	BTU/min.	0.05688
Watts	Foot-lbs/min.	44.27
Watts	Foot-lbs/sec.	0.7378
Watts	Horsepower	1.341×10^{-3}
Watts	Horsepower (metric)	1.360×10^{-3}
Watts	Kg.-calories/min.	0.01433
Watts	Kilowatts	0.001
Watts(Abs.)	BTU (mean)/min.	0.056884
Watts(Abs.)	Joules/sec.	1.0
Watts/hours	BTU	3.413
Watts/hours	Foot-pounds	2,656.0
Watts/hours	Gram-calories	859.85
Watts/hours	Horsepower-hrs.	1.341×10^{-3}
Watts/hours	Kilograms-calories	0.8605
Watts/hours	Kilograms-meters	367.2
Watts/hours	Kilowatt-hrs.	0.001
Watt (International)	Watt (absolute)	1.0002
Yards	Centimeters	91.44
Yards	Kilometers	9.144×10^{-4}
Yards	Meters	0.9144
Yards	Miles (naut.)	4.934×10^{-4}
Yards	Miles (stat.)	5.682×10^{-4}
Yards	Millimeters	914.4

▲ °C = 5° (°F - 32) / 9

Fluid power equivalents

1 bar = 10^5 N/m^2

1 bar = 10 ^{N}/cm^2 = 1dN/mm^2

1 pascal = 1 ^{N}/m^2

1 liter = 10000.028 ^{c}m^3

1 centistoke (cSt) = 1 mm^2/s

1 joule = 1 wattsecond (Ws)

Hertz (Hz) = cycles/second

For multiples

$\times 10^{12}$	tera	T
$\times 10^9$	giga	G
$\times 10^6$	mega	M
$\times 10^3$	kilo	k
$\times 10^2$	hecto	h
$\times 10$	deka	da

For sub-multiples

$\times 10^{-1}$	deci	d
$\times 10^{-2}$	centi	c
$\times 10^{-3}$	milli	m
$\times 10^{-6}$	micro	m
$\times 10^{-9}$	nano	n
$\times 10^{-12}$	pico	p
$\times 10^{-15}$	femto	f
$\times 10^{-18}$	atto	a

Comparative Viscosity Classification

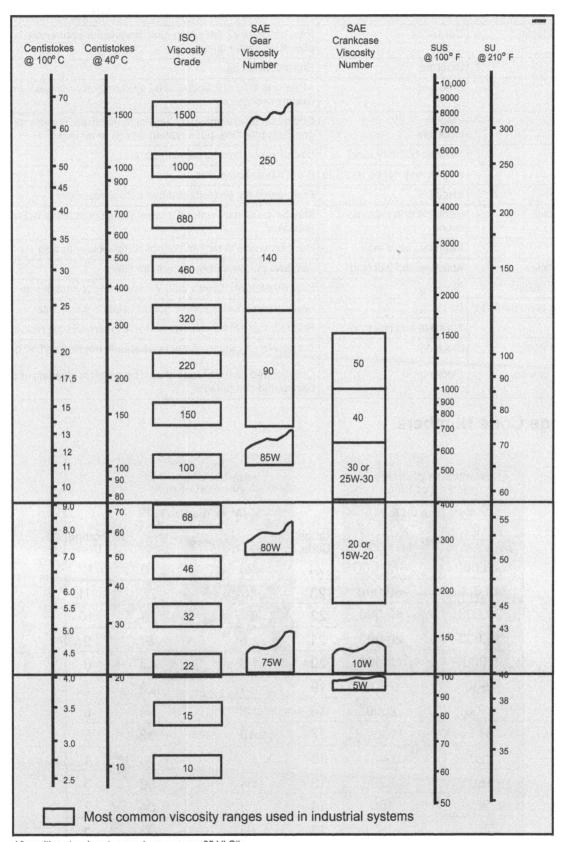

Most common viscosity ranges used in industrial systems

Viscosities at various temperatures assume 95 VI Oils.

NOTE: Viscosities at various temperatures are related horizontally. SAE gear and crankcase specifications
are 100° C (212° F) only. Multigrade oil viscosities are not representative at othe temperatures.

Contaminants in Hydraulic Systems

Contaminant	Character	Source and Remarks
Acidic by-products	Corrosive	Breakdown of oil. May also arise from water-contamination of phosphate-ester fluids
Sludge	Blocking	Breakdown of oil
Water	Emulsion	Already in fluid or introduced by system fault or breakdown of oxidation-inhibitors.
Air	Soluble Insoluble	Effect can be controlled by anti-foam additives. Excess air due to improper bleeding, poor system design or air leaks.
Other oils	Miscible but may react	Use of wrong fluid for topping up, etc.
Grease	May or may not be miscible	From lubrication points
Scale	Insoluble	From pipes not properly cleaned before assembly
Metallic particles	Insoluble with catalytic action	May be caused by water contamination, controllable with anti-rust additives
Paint flakes	Insoluble, blocking	Paint on inside of tank old or not compatible with fluid
Abrasive particles	Abrasive and blocking	Airborne particles (remove with air filter)
Elastomeric particles	Blocking	Seal breakdown. Check fluid, compatibility of seal design
Sealing compound particles	Blocking	Sealing compounds should not be used on pipe joints
Sand	Abrasive and blocking	Sand should not be used as a filler for manipulating pipe bends
Adhesive particles	Blocking	Adhesives or jointing compounds should not be used on gaskets
Lint or fabric threads	Blocking	Only lint free cloths or rags should be used for cleaning or plugging dismantled components

ISO Range Code Numbers

Number of particles per 1 ml of fluid		Range Code	Number of particles per 1 ml of fluid		Range Code
More Than	Up To		More Than	Up To	
80,000	160,000	24	20	40	12
40,000	80,000	23	10	20	11
20,000	40,000	22	5	10	10
10,000	20,000	21	2.5	5	9
5,000	10,000	20	1.3	2.5	8
2500	5,000	19	.64	1.3	7
1300	2500	18	.32	.64	6
640	1300	17	.16	.32	5
320	640	16	.08	.16	4
160	320	15	.04	.08	3
80	160	14	.02	.04	2
40	80	13	.01	.02	1

Guidelines for Controlling Contamination in Hydraulic Systems

Contamination Source	Controller
In built-in components, pipes, manifolds, etc.	Good flushing procedures, system not operated ion load until acceptable contamination level obtained.
plus — Present in initial charge of fluid	Integrity of supplier. Fluid stored under correct conditions (exclusion of dirt, condensation, etc.). Fluid filtered during filling.
plus — Ingressed through air breather	An effective air breather with rating compatible with degree of fluid filtration.
plus — Ingressed during fluid replenishment	Suitable filling points which ensure some filtration of fluid be fore entering reservoir.
plus — Ingressed during maintenance	This task undertaken by responsible personnel. Design should minimize the effects.
plus — Ingressed through cylinder rod seals	Effective wiper seals or, if airborne contamination, rods protected by suitable gaiters.
plus — Further generated contamination produced as a result of the above and the severity of the duty cycle.	Correct fluid selection and properties (viscosity and additives) maintained. Good system design minimizing effects of contamination present on system components.

Preparation of Pipes, Tubes and Fittings Before Installation

Pipe, Tubing and Hose

When installing the various iron and steel pipes, tubes and fittings of a hydraulic system, it is necessary that they be absolutely clean, free from scale and all kinds of foreign matter. To attain this end, the following steps should be taken:

- Tubing, pipes and fittings should be brushed with boiler tube wire brush or cleaned with commercial pipe cleaning apparatus. The inside edge of tubing and pipe should be reamed after cutting to remove burrs. Also remove burrs from outside edge.

- Short pieces of pipe and tubing and steel fittings should be sandblasted to remove rust and scale. Sandblasting is a sure and efficient method for short straight pieces and fittings. Sandblasting should not be used however, if there is the slightest possibility that particles of sand will remain in blind holes or pockets in the work after flushing.

- In the case of longer pieces of pipe or short pieces bent to complex shapes where it is not practical to sandblast, the parts should be pickled in a suitable solution until all rust and scale is removed. Preparation for pickling requires thorough degreasing in a recommended vapor degreasing solvent.

- Neutralize pickling solution.

- Rinse parts and prepare for storage.

- Tubing must not be welded, brazed or silver soldered after assembly as proper cleaning is impossible in such cases. It must be accurately bent and fitted so that it will not be necessary to spring it into place.

- If flange connections are used, flanges must fit squarely on the mounting faces and be secured with screws of the correct length. Screws or stud-nuts must be drawn up evenly to avoid distortion in the valve or pump body.

- Be sure that all openings into the hydraulic system are properly covered to keep out dirt and metal slivers when work such as drilling, tapping, welding or brazing is being done on or near the unit.

- Threaded fittings should be inspected to prevent metal slivers from the threads getting into the hydraulic system.

- Before filling the system with hydraulic oil, be sure that the hydraulic fluid is as specified and that it is clean. DO NOT use cloth strainers or fluid that has been stored in contaminated containers.

- When filling the reservoir with oil, use a filter rated at least the same micron rating as system pressure or return line filters. Use of a Vickers clean cart, porta filtering and transfer unit is recommended. Operate the system for a short time to eliminate air in the lines. Add hydraulic fluid if necessary.

- Safety precautions. Dangerous chemicals are used in the cleaning and pickling operations to be described. They should be kept only in the proper containers and handled with extreme care.

Pickling Process

- Thoroughly degrease parts in degreaser, using a recommended vapor degreasing solvent.

- Tank No. 1 Solution. Use a commercially available derusting compound in solution as recommended by the manufacturer. The solution should not be used at a temperature exceeding that recommended by the manufacturer, otherwise the inhibitor will evaporate and leave a straight acid solution. The length of time the part will be immersed in this solution will depend upon the temperature of the solution and the amount of rust or scale which must be removed. The operator must use good judgement on this point.

- After pickling, rinse parts in cold running water and immerse in tank No. 2. The solution in this tank should be a neutralizer mixed with water in a proportion recommended by the manufacturer. This solution should be used at recommended temperatures and the parts should remain immersed in the solution for the period of time recommended by the manufacturer.

- Rinse parts in hot water.

- Place in tank No. 3. The solution in this tank should contain antirust compounds as recommended by the manufacturer. Usually the parts being treated should be left to dry with antirust solution remaining on them.

- If pieces are stored for any period of time, ends of the pipes should be plugged to prevent the entrance of foreign matter. Do not use rags or waste as they will deposit lint on the inside of the tube or pipe. Immediately before using, pipes, tubes and fittings should be thoroughly flushed with suitable degreasing solution.

Conductor Inside Diameter Selection Chart (Inch)

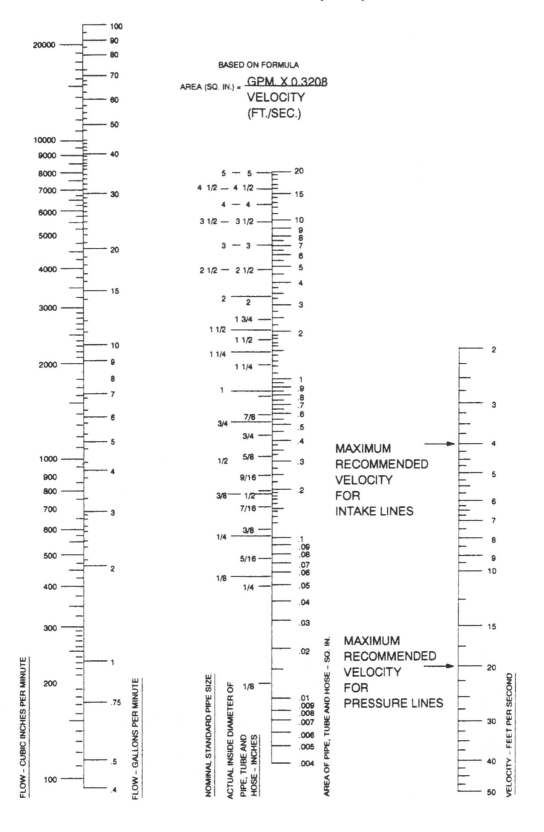

BASED ON FORMULA

$$\text{AREA (SQ. IN.)} = \frac{\text{GPM. X 0.3208}}{\text{VELOCITY (FT./SEC.)}}$$

MAXIMUM RECOMMENDED VELOCITY FOR INTAKE LINES

MAXIMUM RECOMMENDED VELOCITY FOR PRESSURE LINES

Conductor Inside Diameter Selection Chart (Metric)

BASED ON FORMULA

$$\text{AREA (SQ. CM)} = \frac{\text{LPM x 0.1667}}{\text{VELOCITY (METERS/SEC.)}}$$

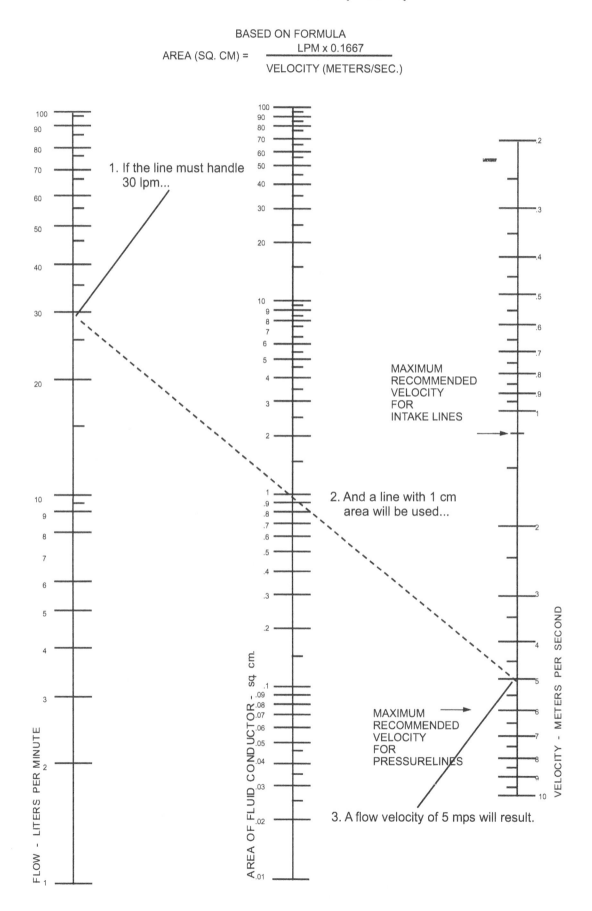

Pipes Currently Are Sized by Schedule Number

Nominal Size	Pipe O.D.	Inside Diameter			
		Schedule 40 Standard	Schedule 80 Extra Heavy	Schedule 160	Double Extra Heavy
1/8	0.405	0.269	0.215		
1/4	0.540	0.364	0.302		
3/8	0.675	0.493	0.423		
1/2	0.840	0.622	0.546	0.466	0.252
3/4	1.050	0.824	0.742	0.614	0.434
1	1.315	1.049	0.957	0.815	0.599
1-1/4	1.660	1.380	1.278	1.160	0.896
1-1/2	1.900	1.610	1.500	1.338	1.100
2	2.375	2.067	1.939	1.689	1.503
2-1/2	2.875	2.469	2.323	2.125	1.771
3	3.500	3.068	2.900		
3-1/2	4.000	3.548	3.364	2.624	
4	4.500	4.026	3.826	3.438	
5	5.563	5.047	4.813	4.313	4.063
6	6.625	6.065	6.761	5.189	
8	8.625	7.981	7.625	6.813	
10	10.750	10.020	9.564	8.500	
12	12.750	11.934	11.376	10.126	

Pressure Ratings of Pipes

Nominal Pipe Size In.	Outside Diameter of Pipe In.	Number of Threads per Inch	Length of Effective Threads Inch	Schedule 40 (Standard)		Schedule 80 (Extra Heavy)		Schedule 160		Double (Extra Heavy)	
				Pipe I.D. in.	Burst Press. psi	Pipe I.D. in.	Burst Press psi	Pipe I.D. in.	Burst Press psi	Pipe I.D. in.	Burst Press psi
1/8	0.405	27	0.26								
1/4	0.540	18	0.40	0.364	16,000	0.302	22,000				
3/8	0.675	18	0.41	0.493	13,500	0.423	19,000				
1/2	0.840	14	0.53	0.622	13,200	0.546	17,500	0.466	21,000	0.252	35,000
3/4	1.050	14	0.55	0.824	11,000	0.742	15,000	0.614	21,000	0.434	30,000
1	1.315	11-1/2	0.68	1.049	10,000	0.957	13,600	0.815	19,000	0.599	27,000
1-1/4	1.660	11-1/2	0.71	1.380	8,400	1.278	11,500	1.160	15,000	0.896	23,000
1-1/2	1.900	11-1/2	0.72	1.610	7,600	1.500	10,500	1.338	14,800	1.100	21,000
2	2.375	11-1/2	0.76	2.067	6,500	1.939	9,100	1.689	14,500	1.503	19,000
2-1/2	2.875	8	1.14	2.469	7,000	2.323	9,600	2.125	13,000	1.771	18,000
3	3.500	8	1.20	3.068	6,100	2.900	8,500	2.634	12,500		

Working pressures for various schedule pipes are obtained by dividing burst pressure by the safety factor.

Oil Flow Velocity in Tubing/Pipe Sizes and Pressure Ratings

Oil Flow Capacity of Tubing

Figures in the chart are US GPM flow capacities of tubing, and were calculated from the formula: GPM = V × A ÷ 0.3208, in which V = velocity of flow in feet per second, and A is inside square inch area of tube.

Figures in Body of Chart are US GPM Flows

Tube O.D.	Wall Thick.	2 Ft/Sec	4 Ft/Sec	10 Ft/Sec	15 Ft/Sec	20 Ft/Sec	30 Ft/Sec
1/2"	0.035	0.905	1.81	4.52	6.79	9.05	13.6
	0.042	0.847	1.63	4.23	6.35	6.47	12.7
	0.049	0.791	1.58	3.95	5.93	7.91	11.9
	0.058	0.722	1.44	3.61	5.41	7.22	10.8
	0.065	0.670	1.34	3.35	5.03	6.70	10.1
	0.072	0.620	1.24	3.10	4.65	6.20	9.30
	0.083	0.546	1.09	2.73	4.09	5.46	8.16
5/8"	0.035	1.51	3.01	7.54	11.3	15.1	22.6
	0.042	1.43	2.85	7.16	10.7	14.3	21.4
	0.049	1.36	2.72	6.80	10.2	13.6	20.4
	0.058	1.27	2.54	6.34	9.51	12.7	19.0
	0.065	1.20	2.40	6.00	9.00	12.0	18.0
	0.072	1.13	2.26	5.66	8.49	11.3	17.0
	0.083	1.03	2.06	5.16	7.73	10.3	15.5
	0.095	0.926	1.85	4.63	6.95	9.26	13.9
3/4"	0.049	2.08	4.17	10.4	15.6	20.8	31.2
	0.058	1.97	3.93	14.8	9.84	19.7	29.6
	0.065	1.88	3.76	14.1	9.41	18.8	28.2
	0.072	1.75	3.51	13.2	8.77	17.5	26.4
	0.083	1.67	3.34	12.5	8.35	16.7	25.0
	0.095	1.53	3.07	11.5	7.67	15.3	23.0
	0.109	1.39	2.77	10.4	6.93	13.9	20.8
7/8"	0.049	2.95	5.91	14.8	22.2	29.5	44.3
	0.058	2.82	5.64	14.1	21.1	28.2	42.3
	0.065	2.72	5.43	13.6	20.4	27.2	40.7
	0.072	2.62	5.23	13.1	19.6	26.2	39.2
	0.083	2.46	4.92	12.3	18.5	24.6	36.9
	0.095	2.30	4.60	11.5	17.2	23.0	34.4
	0.109	2.11	4.22	10.6	15.8	21.1	31.7
1"	0.049	3.98	7.96	19.9	29.9	39.8	59.7
	0.058	3.82	7.65	19.1	28.7	38.2	57.4
	0.065	3.70	7.41	18.5	27.8	37.0	55.6
	0.072	3.59	7.17	17.9	26.9	35.9	53.8
	0.083	3.40	6.81	17.0	25.5	34.0	51.1
	0.095	3.21	6.42	16.1	24.1	32.1	48.2
	0.109	3.00	6.00	15.0	22.4	29.9	44.9
	0.120	2.83	5.65	14.1	21.2	28.3	42.4

Oil Flow Capacity of Tubing (Continued)

Tube O.D.	Wall Thick.	2 Ft/Sec	4 Ft/Sec	10 Ft/Sec	15 Ft/Sec	20 Ft/Sec	30 Ft/Sec
1-1/4"	0.049	6.50	13.0	32.5	48.7	64.9	97.4
	0.058	6.29	12.6	31.5	47.2	62.9	94.4
	0.065	6.14	12.3	30.7	46.0	61.4	92.1
	0.072	6.00	12.0	30.0	44.9	59.9	89.8
	0.083	5.75	11.5	28.8	43.1	57.5	86.3
	0.095	5.50	11.0	27.5	41.2	55.0	82.5
	0.109	5.21	10.4	26.1	39.1	52.1	78.2
	0.120	5.00	10.0	25.0	37.4	50.0	74.9
1-1/2"	0.065	9.19	18.4	45.9	68.9	91.9	138
	0.072	9.00	18.0	45.0	67.5	90.0	135
	0.083	8.71	17.4	43.5	65.3	87.1	131
	0.095	8.40	16.8	42.0	63.0	84.0	126
	0.109	8.04	16.1	40.2	60.3	80.4	121
	0.120	7.77	15.5	38.8	58.3	77.7	117
1-3/4"	0.065	12.8	25.7	64.2	96.3	128	193
	0.072	12.6	25.2	63.1	94.7	126	189
	0.083	12.3	24.6	61.4	92.1	123	184
	0.095	11.9	23.8	59.6	89.3	119	179
	0.109	11.5	23.0	57.4	86.1	115	172
	0.120	11.2	22.3	55.8	83.7	112	167
	0.134	10.7	21.5	53.7	80.6	107	161
2"	0.065	17.1	34.2	85.6	128	171	257
	0.072	16.9	33.7	84.3	126	169	253
	0.083	16.5	32.9	82.3	123	165	247
	0.095	16.0	32.1	80.2	120	160	240
	0.109	15.5	31.1	77.7	117	155	233
	0.120	15.2	30.3	75.8	114	152	227
	0.134	14.7	29.4	73.4	110	147	220

SAE Hydraulic Hose Data

I.D. Inches	Dash No. Ref	SAE No. and Type Spec.	O.D. Max. Inches	Min. Bend (Internal) Rad. In. at Max. Operating Press.	*Max. Operating Press.
3/16	-3	100R1-A	0.531	3-1/2	3,000
3/16	-3	100R1-AT	0.494	3-1/2	3,000
3/16	-3	100R2-A&B	0.656	3-1/2	5,000
3/16	-3	100R2-AT&BT	0.567	3-1/2	5,000
3/16	-3	100R3	0.531	3	1,500
3/16	-4	100R5	0.539	3	3,000
3/16	-3	100R6	0.469	2	500
3/16	-3	100R7	0.423	3-1/2	3,000
3/16	-3	100R8	0.575	3-1/2	5,000
3/16	-3	100R10-A	0.781	4	10,000
3/16	-3	100R10-AT		4	10,000
3/16	-3	100R11	0.906	4	12,500
1/4	-4	100R1-A	0.656	4	2,750
1/4	-4	100R1-AT	0.557	4	2,750
1/4	-4	100R2-A&B	0.719	4	5,000
1/4	-4	100R2-AT&BT	0.619	4	5,000
1/4	-4	100R3	0.594	3	1,250
1/4	-5	100R5	0.601	3-3/8	3,000
1/4	-4	100R6	0.531	2-1/2	400
1/4	-4	100R7	0.513	4	2,750
1/4	-4	100R8	0.660	4	5,000
1/4	-4	100R10-A	0.844	5	8,750
1/4	-4	100R10-AT		5	8,750
1/4	-4	100R11	0.969	5	11,250
5/16	-5	100R1-A	0.719	4-1/2	2,500
5/16	-5	100R1-AT	0.619	4-1/2	2,500
5/16	-5	100R2-A&B	0.781	4-1/2	4,250
5/16	-5	100R2-AT&BT	0.682	4-1/2	4,250
5/16	-5	100R3	0.719	4	1,200
5/16	-6	100R5	0.695	4	2,250
5/16	-5	100R6	0.594	3	400
5/16	-5	100R7	0.590	4-1/2	2,500
3/8	-6	100R1-A	0.812	5	2,250
3/8	-6	100R1-AT	0.713	5	2,250
3/8	-6	100R2-A&B	0.875	5	4,000
3/8	-6	100R2-AT&BT	0.777	5	4,000
3/8	-6	100R3	0.781	4	1,125
3/8	-6	100R6	0.656	3	400
3/8	-6	100R7	0.700	5	2,250
3/8	-6	100R8	0.800	5	4,000
3/8	-6	100R9-A	0.875	5	4,500
3/8	-6	100R9-AT	0.831	5	4,500
3/8	-6	100R10-A	0.969	6	7,500
3/8	-6	100R10-AT		6	7,500
3/8	-6	100R11	1.094	6	10,000
3/8	-6	100R12	0.828	5	4,000
13/32	-6.5	100R1-A	0.844	5-1/2	2,250
13/32	-6.5	100R1-AT	0.744	5-1/2	2,250
13/32	-8	100R5	0.789	4-5/8	2,000
1/2	-8	100R1-A	0.938	7	2,000
1/2	-8	100R1-AT	0.846	7	2,000
1/2	-8	100R2-A&B	1.000	7	3,500
1/2	-8	100R2-AT&BT	0.908	7	3,500
1/2	-8	100R3	0.969	5	1,000
1/2	-10	100R5	0.945	5-1/2	1,750
1/2	-8	100R6	0.812	4	400
1/2	-8	100R7	0.860	7	2,000
1/2	-8	100R8	0.970	7	3,500
1/2	-8	100R9-A	1.000	7	4,000
1/2	-8	100R9-AT	0.958	7	4,000
1/2	-8	100R10-A	1.125	8	6,250
1/2	-8	100R10-AT		8	6,250
1/2	-8	100R11	1.250	8	7,500
1/2	-8	100R12	0.968	7	4,000
5/8	-10	100R1-A	1.062	8	1,500
5/8	-10	100R1-AT	0.971	8	1,500
5/8	-10	100R2-A&B	1.125	8	2,750
5/8	-10	100R2-AT&BT	1.034	8	2,750
5/8	-10	100R3	1.094	5-1/2	875
5/8	-12	100R5	1.101	8-1/2	1,500
5/8	-10	100R6	0.938	5	350
5/8	-10	100R7	0.990	8	1,500
5/8	-10	100R8	1.175	8	2,750

I.D. Inches	Dash No. Ref	SAE No. and Type Spec.	O.D. Max. Inches	Min. Bend (Internal) Rad. In. at Max. Operating Press.	*Max. Operating Press.
3/4	-12	100R1-A	1.219	9-1/2	1,250
3/4	-12	100R1-AT	1.127	9-1/2	1,250
3/4	-12	100R2-A&B	1.281	9-1/2	2,250
3/4	-12	100R2-AT&BT	1.190	9-1/2	2,250
3/4	-12	100R3	1.281	6	750
3/4	-12	100R4	1.375	5	300
3/4	-12	100R7	1.100	9-1/2	1,250
3/4	-12	100R8	1.300	9-1/2	2,250
3/4	-12	100R9-A	1.266	9-1/2	3,000
3/4	-12	100R9-AT	1.255	9-1/2	3,000
3/4	-12	100R10-A	1.469	11	5,000
3/4	-12	100R10-AT	1.450	11	5,000
3/4	-12	100R11	1.594	11	6,250
3/4	-12	100R12	1.241	9-1/2	4,000
7/8	-14	100R1-A	1.344	11	1,125
7/8	-14	100R1-AT	1.252	11	1,125
7/8	-14	100R2-A&B	1.406	11	2,000
7/8	-14	100R2-AT&BT	1.315	11	2,000
7/8	-16	100R5	1.266	7-3/8	800
1	-16	100R1-A	1.547	12	1,000
1	-16	100R1-AT	1.440	12	1,000
1	-16	100R2-A&B	1.609	12	2,000
1	-16	100R2-AT&BT	1.531	12	2,000
1	-16	100R3	1.547	8	565
1	-16	100R4	1.825	6	250
1	-16	100R7	1.420	12	1,000
1	-16	100R8	1.520	12	2,000
1	-16	100R9-A	1.809	12	3,000
1	-16	100R9-AT	1.594	12	3,000
1	-16	100R10-A	1.797	14	4,000
1	-16	100R10-AT	1.790	14	4,000
1	-166	100R11	1.963	14	5,000
1	-16	100R12	1.542	12	4,000
1-1/8	-20	100R5	1.531	9	625
1-1/4	-20	100R1-A	1.875	16-1/2	825
1-1/4	-20	100R1-AT	1.768	16-1/2	625
1-1/4	-20	100R2-A&B	2.062	16-1/2	1,625
1-1/4	-20	100R2-AT&BT	1.053	16-1/2	1,625
1-1/4	-20	100R3	1.812	10	375
1-1/4	-20	100R4	2.000	8	200
1-1/4	-20	100R9-A	2.062	16-1/2	2,500
1-1/4	-20	100R9-AT	1.997	16-1/2	2,500
1-1/4	-20	100R10-A	2.062	18	3,000
1-1/4	-20	100R10-AT	2.060	18	3,000
1-1/4	-20	100R11	2.219	18	3,500
1-1/4	-20	100R12	1.912	16-1/2	3,000
1-3/8	-24	100R5	1.781	10-1/2	500
1-1/2	-24	100R1-A	2.125	20	500
1-1/2	-24	100R1-AT	2.047	20	500
1-1/2	-24	100R2-A&B	2.312	20	1,250
1-1/2	-24	100R2-AT&BT	2.203	20	1,250
1-1/2	-24	100R4	2.250	10	150
1-1/2	-24	100R9-A		20	2,000
1-1/2	-24	100R9-AT	2.312	20	2,000
1-1/2	-24	100R10-A	2.312	22	2,500
1-1/2	-24	100R10-AT	2.310	22	2,500
1-1/2	-24	100R11	2.469	22	3,000
1-1/2	-24	100R12	2.167	20	2,500
1-13/16	-32	100R5	2.266	13-1/4	350
2	-32	100R1-A	2.688	25	375
2	-32	100R2-A	2.594	25	375
2	-32	T100R2-A&B	2.812	25	1,125
2	-32	100R2-AT&BT	2.703	25	1,125
2	-32	100R4	2.750	12	100
2	-32	100R9-A	2.875	26	2,000
2	-32	100R9-AT		26	2,000
2	-32	100R10-A	2.844	28	2,500
2	-32	100R10-AT	2.840	28	2,500
2	-32	100R11	3.031	28	3,000
2	-32	100R12	2.688	25	2,500
2-1/2	-40	100R4	3.250	14	82
3	-48	100R4	3.750	18	56
3-1/2	-56	100R4	4.250	21	45
4	-64	100R4	4.750	24	35

Description of CEN (Committee for European Normalization) Flexible Hoses

EN 853 Wire Braided Hose

Type 1ST — This hose shall consist of an inner tube of oil resistant synthetic rubber, a single wire braid reinforcement and an oil and weather resistant synthetic rubber cover.

Type 1SN — This hose shall be of the same construction as Type 1ST, except having a cover designed to assemble with fittings which do not require removal of the cover or a portion thereof.

Type 2ST — This hose shall consist of an inner tube of oil resistant synthetic rubber, two braids wire reinforcement and an oil and weather resistant synthetic rubber cover. A ply or braid of suitable material may be used over the inner tube and/or over the reinforcement to anchor the synthetic rubber to the wire.

Type 2SN — This hose shall be of the same construction as Type 2ST, except having a cover designed to assemble with fittings which do not require removal of the cover or a portion thereof.

EN 854 — Fabric Braided Hose

Type 1TE — This hose shall consist of an inner tube of oil resistant synthetic rubber, one braided ply of suitable textile yarn and an oil and weather resistant synthetic rubber cover.

Type 2TW — This hose shall consist of an inner tube of oil resistant rubber, two braided ply of suitable textile yarn and an oil and weather resistant synthetic rubber cover.

Type 3TE — This hose shall consist of an inner tube of oil resistant synthetic rubber, three braided ply of suitable textile yarn and an oil and weather resistant synthetic rubber cover.

Type R6 — This hose shall consist of an inner tube of oil resistant synthetic rubber, one braided ply of suitable textile yarn and an oil and weather resistant synthetic rubber cover.

Type R3 — This hose shall consist of an inner tube of oil resistant synthetic rubber, two braided ply of suitable textile yarn and an oil and weather resistant synthetic rubber cover.

EN 855 — Thermoplastic Textile Braid Hose

Type R7 — This hose shall consist of a thermoplastic inner tube resistant to hydraulic fluids with suitable synthetic fiber reinforcement and a hydraulic fluid and weather resistant thermoplastic cover.

Type R8 — This hose shall consist of a thermoplastic inner tube resistant to hydraulic fluids with suitable synthetic fiber reinforcement and a hydraulic fluid and weather resistant thermoplastic cover.

Description of CEN (Committee for European Normalization) Flexible Hoses (Continued)

EN 856 — Spiral Wire Hose

Type 4SP — This hose shall consist of an inner tube of oil resistant synthetic rubber, 4-spiral plies of wire wrapped in alternating directions and an oil and weather resistant synthetic rubber cover. A ply or braid of suitable material may be used over the inner tube and/or over the wire reinforcement to anchor the synthetic rubber to the wire.

Type 4SH — This hose shall consist of an inner tube of oil resistant synthetic rubber, 4-spiral plies of heavy wire wrapped in alternating directions and an oil and weather resistant synthetic rubber cover. A ply or braid of suitable material may be used over the inner tube and/or over the wire reinforcement to anchor the synthetic rubber to the wire.

Type R12 — This hose shall consist of an inner tube of oil resistant synthetic rubber, 4-spiral plies of heavy wire wrapped in alternating directions and an oil and weather resistant synthetic rubber cover. A ply or braid of suitable material may be used over the inner tube and/or over the wire reinforcement to anchor the synthetic rubber to the wire.

Type 13 — This hose shall consist of an inner tube of oil resistant synthetic rubber, multiple spiral plies of heavy wire wrapped in alternating directions and an oil and weather resistant synthetic rubber cover. A ply or braid of suitable material may be used over the inner tube and/or over the wire reinforcement to anchor the synthetic rubber to the wire.

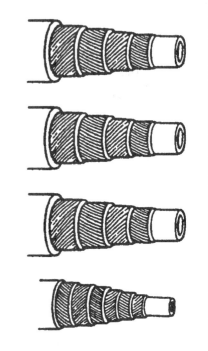

EN 857 — Compact Wire Braided Hose

Type 1SC — This hose shall consist of an inner tube of oil resistant synthetic rubber, 1 wire braid reinforcement and oil and weather synthetic rubber cover.

Type 2SC — This hose shall consist of an inner tube of oil resistant synthetic rubber, 2 wire braid reinforcement and oil and weather synthetic rubber cover.

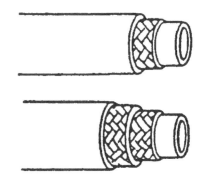

CEN Performance Specifications

**EN 853 — 1 Wire Braid
Type 1ST and 1SN**

Nominal Size (mm)	I.D. (mm)	I.D. (in)	Minimum Bend Radius (mm)	Minimum Bend Radius (in)	Operating Pressure (bar)	Operating Pressure (psi)	Minimum Burst Pressure (bar)	Minimum Burst Pressure (psi)
5	4,8	0.189	90	3.54	250	3625	1000	14500
6	6,4	0.252	100	3.94	225	3263	900	13050
8	7,9	0.311	115	4.53	215	3118	850	12325
10	9,5	0.374	130	5.12	180	2610	720	10440
12	12,7	0.500	180	7.09	160	2320	640	9280
16	15,9	0.625	200	7.87	130	1885	520	7540
19	19,0	0.748	240	9.45	105	1523	420	6090
25	25,4	1.000	300	11.81	88	1276	350	5075
31	31,8	1.252	420	16.54	63	914	250	3625
38	38,1	1.500	500	19.69	50	725	200	2900
51	50,8	2.000	630	24.80	40	580	160	2320

**EN 853 — 2 Wire Braid Hoses
Type 2ST and 2SN**

Nominal Size (mm)	I.D. (mm)	I.D. (in)	Minimum Bend Radius (mm)	Minimum Bend Radius (in)	Operating Pressure (bar)	Operating Pressure (psi)	Minimum Burst Pressure (bar)	Minimum Burst Pressure (psi)
5	4,8	0.189	90	3.54	415	6018	1650	23925
6	6,4	0.252	100	3.94	400	5800	1600	23200
8	7,9	0.311	115	4.53	350	5075	1400	20300
10	9,5	0.374	130	5.12	330	4785	1320	19140
12	12,7	0.500	180	7.09	275	3988	1100	15950
16	15,9	0.625	200	7.87	250	3625	1000	14500
19	19,0	0.748	240	9.45	215	3118	850	12325
25	25,4	1.000	300	11.81	165	2393	650	9425
31	31,8	1.252	420	16.54	125	1813	500	7250
38	38,1	1.500	500	19.69	90	1305	360	5220
51	50,8	2.000	630	24.80	80	1160	320	4640

EN 854 — Fabric Braided Hoses
Type 1TF — 1 Fabric Braid

Nominal Size	I.D.		Minimum Bend Radius		Operating Pressure		Minimum Burst Pressure	
(mm)	(mm)	(in)	(mm)	(in)	(bar)	(psi)	(bar)	(psi)
5	4,8	0.189	35	1.38	25	363	65	943
6	6,4	0.252	45	1.77	25	363	65	943
8	7,9	0.311	65	2.56	20	290	50	725
10	9,5	0.374	75	2.95	20	290	50	725
12	12,7	0.500	90	3.54	16	232	40	580
16	15,9	0.625	115	4.53	16	232	40	580

EN 854 — Fabric Braided Hoses
Type 2TE — 2 Fabric Braid

Nominal Size	I.D.		Minimum Bend Radius		Operating Pressure		Minimum Burst Pressure	
(mm)	(mm)	(in)	(mm)	(in)	(bar)	(psi)	(bar)	(psi)
5	4,8	0.189	35	1.38	80	1160	320	4640
6	6,4	0.252	40	1.57	75	1088	300	4350
8	7,9	0.311	50	1.97	68	986	270	3915
10	9,5	0.374	60	2.36	63	914	250	3625
12	12,7	0.500	70	2.76	58	841	230	3335
16	15,9	0.625	90	3.54	50	725	200	2900
19	19,0	0.748	110	4.33	45	653	180	2610
25	25,4	1.000	150	5.91	40	580	160	2320

EN 854 — Fabric Braided Hoses
Type 3TE — 3 Fabric Braid

Nominal Size	I.D.		Minimum Bend Radius		Operating Pressure		Minimum Burst Pressure	
(mm)	(mm)	(in)	(mm)	(in)	(bar)	(psi)	(bar)	(psi)
5	4,8	0.189	40	1.57	160	2320	640	9280
6	6,4	0.252	45	1.77	145	2103	580	8410
8	7,9	0.311	55	2.17	130	1885	520	7540
10	9,5	0.374	70	2.76	110	1595	440	6380
12	12,7	0.500	80	3.15	93	1349	370	5365
16	15,9	0.625	105	4.13	80	1160	320	4640
19	19,0	0.748	130	5.12	70	1015	280	4060
25	25,4	1.000	150	5.91	55	798	220	3190
31	31,8	1.252	190	7.48	45	653	180	2610
38	38,1	1.500	240	9.45	40	580	160	2320
51	50,8	2.000	300	11.81	33	479	130	1885
60	60,0	2.362	400	15.75	25	363	100	1450
80	80,0	3.150	500	19.69	18	261	70	1015
100	100,0	3.937	600	23.62	10	145	40	580

EN 854 — Fabric Braided Hoses
Type R6 — 1 Fabric Braid

Nominal Size	I.D.		Minimum Bend Radius		Operating Pressure		Minimum Burst Pressure	
(mm)	(mm)	(in)	(mm)	(in)	(bar)	(psi)	(bar)	(psi)
5	4,8	0.189	50	1.97	34	493	136	1972
6	6,4	0.252	65	2.56	28	406	112	1624
8	7,9	0.311	80	3.15	28	406	112	1624
10	9,5	0.374	80	3.15	28	406	112	1624
12	12,7	0.500	100	3.94	28	406	112	1624
16	15,9	0.625	125	4.93	24	348	96	1392
19	19,0	0.748	150	5.90	21	304	83	1203

EN 854 — Fabric Braided Hoses
Type R3 — 2 Fabric Braid

Nominal Size	I.D.		Minimum Bend Radius		Operating Pressure		Minimum Burst Pressure	
(mm)	(mm)	(in)	(mm)	(in)	(bar)	(psi)	(bar)	(psi)
5	4,8	0.189	80	3.15	103	1494	412	5974
6	6,4	0.252	80	3.15	86	1247	344	4988
8	7,9	0.311	100	3.94	83	1204	332	4814
10	9,5	0.374	100	3.94	78	1131	312	4524
12	12,7	0.500	125	4.92	69	1000	276	4002
16	15,9	0.625	140	5.51	60	870	240	3480
19	19,0	0.748	150	5.91	52	754	208	3016
25	25,4	1.000	205	8.07	39	566	156	2262
31	31,8	1.252	255	10.04	26	377	104	1508

EN 855 — Thermoplastic — Textile Braid
Type R7 — Thermoplastic

Nominal Size	I.D.		Minimum Bend Radius		Operating Pressure		Minimum Burst Pressure	
(mm)	(mm)	(in)	(mm)	(in)	(bar)	(psi)	(bar)	(psi)
5	4,8	0.189	90	3.54	205	2972	820	11890
6	6,4	0.252	100	3.94	190	2755	760	11020
8	7,9	0.311	115	4.68	170	2465	680	9860
10	9,5	0.374	125	4.92	155	2247	620	8990
12	12,7	0.500	180	7.08	135	1957	540	7830
16	15,9	0.625	205	8.07	100	1450	400	5800
19	19,0	0.748	240	9.45	86	1247	344	4988
25	25,4	1.000	300	11.81	69	1000	276	4002

EN 855 — Thermoplastic — Textile Braid
Type R8 — Thermoplastic

Nominal Size	I.D.		Minimum Bend Radius		Operating Pressure		Minimum Burst Pressure	
(mm)	(mm)	(in)	(mm)	(in)	(bar)	(psi)	(bar)	(psi)
5	4,8	0.189	90	3.54	345	5002	1380	20010
6	6,4	0.252	100	3.94	345	5002	1380	20010
10	9,5	0.374	125	4.92	275	3987	1100	15956
12	12,7	0.500	180	7.08	240	3480	960	13956
16	15,9	0.625	205	8.07	190	2755	760	11020
19	19,0	0.748	240	9.45	155	2247	620	8990
25	25,4	1.000	300	11.81	138	2001	550	7975

EN 856 — Spiral Wire
Type 4SP — 4 Light Spiral

Nominal Size	I.D.		Minimum Bend Radius		Operating Pressure		Minimum Burst Pressure	
(mm)	(mm)	(in)	(mm)	(in)	(bar)	(psi)	(bar)	(psi)
6	6,4	0.252	150	5.91	450	6525	1800	26100
10	9,5	0.374	180	7.09	445	6453	1780	25810
12	12,7	0.500	230	9.06	415	6018	1660	24070
16	15,9	0.625	250	9.84	350	5075	1400	20300
19	19,0	0.748	300	11.81	350	5075	1400	20300
25	25,4	1.000	340	13.39	280	4060	1120	16240
31	31,8	1.252	460	18.11	210	3045	840	12180
38	38,1	1.500	560	22.05	185	2683	740	10730
51	50,8	2.000	660	25.98	165	2393	660	9570

EN 856 — Spiral Wire
Type 4SH — 4 Heavy Spiral

Nominal Size	I.D.		Minimum Bend Radius		Operating Pressure		Minimum Burst Pressure	
(mm)	(mm)	(in)	(mm)	(in)	(bar)	(psi)	(bar)	(psi)
19	19,0	0.748	280	11.02	420	6090	1680	24360
25	25,4	1.000	340	13.39	380	5510	1520	22040
31	31,8	1.252	460	18.11	325	4713	1300	18850
38	38,1	1.500	560	22.05	290	4205	1160	16820
51	50,8	2.000	700	27.56	250	3625	1000	14500

EN 856 — Spiral Wire
Type R12 — 4 Spiral

Nominal Size	I.D.		Minimum Bend Radius		Operating Pressure		Minimum Burst Pressure	
(mm)	(mm)	(in)	(mm)	(in)	(bar)	(psi)	(bar)	(psi)
10	9,5	0.374	130	5.12	276	4046	1104	16008
12	12,7	0.500	180	7.09	276	4046	1104	16008
16	15,9	0.625	200	8.15	276	4046	1104	16008
19	19,0	0.748	240	9.45	276	4046	1104	16008
25	25,4	1.000	300	11.81	276	4046	1104	16008
31	31,8	1.252	420	16.54	207	3002	828	12006
38	38,1	1.500	500	19.69	172	2494	688	9976
51	50,8	2.000	630	24.80	172	2494	688	9976

EN 856 — Spiral Wire
Type R13 — Multiple Spiral Plies

Nominal Size	I.D.		Minimum Bend Radius		Operating Pressure		Minimum Burst Pressure	
(mm)	(mm)	(in)	(mm)	(in)	(bar)	(psi)	(bar)	(psi)
19	19,0	0.748	240	9.45	345	5003	1380	20010
25	25,4	1.000	300	11.81	345	5003	1380	20010
31	31,8	1.252	420	16.54	345	5003	1380	20010
38	38,1	1.500	500	19.69	345	5003	1380	20010
51	50,8	2.000	630	24.80	345	5003	1380	20010

EN 857 — Compact Rubber Hose Wire Braid
Type 1SC — Wire Braid

Nominal Size	I.D.		Minimum Bend Radius		Operating Pressure		Minimum Burst Pressure	
(mm)	(mm)	(in)	(mm)	(in)	(bar)	(psi)	(bar)	(psi)
6	6,4	0.252	75	2.95	225	3263	900	13050
8	7,9	0.311	85	3.35	215	3118	850	12325
10	9,5	0.374	90	3.54	180	2610	720	10440
12	12,7	0.500	130	5.12	160	2320	640	9280
16	15,9	0.625	150	5.90	130	1885	520	7540
19	19,0	0.748	180	7.08	105	1523	420	6090
25	25,4	1.000	230	9.05	88	1276	352	5104

EN 857 — Compact Rubber Hose Wire Braid Type 2SC — 2 Wire Braid								
Nominal Size	I.D.		Minimum Bend Radius		Operating Pressure		Minimum Burst Pressure	
(mm)	(mm)	(in)	(mm)	(in)	(bar)	(psi)	(bar)	(psi)
6	6,4	0.252	75	2.95	400	5800	1600	23200
8	7,9	0.311	85	3.35	350	5075	1400	20300
10	9,5	0.374	90	3.54	330	4785	1320	19140
12	12,7	0.500	130	5.12	275	3987	1100	15950
16	15,9	0.625	170	6.69	250	3625	1000	14500
19	19,0	0.748	200	7.87	215	3117	860	12470
25	25,4	1.000	250	9.84	165	2392	660	9570

Description of SAE 100R1 through SAE 100R18 Flexible Hoses

SAE 100R1
SAE 100R1s   ISO working pressure (2006, R1 & R2 pressures will be elevated to ISO pressure and the "s" will be dropped)

Type A — (To be discontinued beginning 2005, due to lack of demand.)
This hose shall consist of an inner tube of oil resistant synthetic rubber, single wire braid reinforcement and an oil and weather resistant synthetic rubber cover. A ply or braid of suitable material may be used over the inner tube and/or over the wire reinforcement to anchor the synthetic rubber to the wire.

Type AT — This hose shall be of the same construction as Type A, except having a cover designed to assemble with fittings which do not require removal of the cover or a portion thereof.

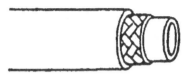

SAE 100R2
SAE 100R2s   ISO working pressure (2006, R1 & R2 pressures will be elevated to ISO pressure and the "s" will be dropped)

The hose shall consist of an inner tube of oil resistant synthetic rubber, steel wire reinforcement according to hose type as detailed below and an oil and weather resistant synthetic rubber cover. A ply or braid of suitable material may be used over the inner tube and/or over the wire reinforcement to anchor the synthetic rubber to the wire.

Type A — (To be discontinued beginning 2005, due to lack of demand.)
This hose shall have two braids of wire reinforcement.

Type AT — This hose shall be of the same construction as Type A, except having a cover designed to assemble with fittings which do not require removal of the cover or a portion thereof.

SAE 100R3

The hose shall consist of an inner tube of oil resistant synthetic rubber, two braids of suitable textile yarn and an oil and weather resistant synthetic rubber cover.

SAE 100R4

The hose shall consist of an inner tube of oil resistant synthetic rubber, a reinforcement consisting of a ply or plies of woven or braided textile fibers with a suitable spiral of body wire and an oil and weather resistant synthetic rubber cover.

SAE 100R5

The hose shall consist of an inner tube of oil resistant synthetic rubber and two textile braids separated by a high tensile steel wire braid. All braids are to be impregnated with an oil and mildew resistant synthetic rubber compound.

SAE 100R6

The hose shall consist of an inner tube of oil resistant synthetic rubber, one braided ply of suitable textile yarn and an oil and weather resistant synthetic rubber cover.

SAE 100R7

The hose shall consist of a thermoplastic inner tube resistant to hydraulic fluids with suitable synthetic fiber reinforcement and a hydraulic fluid and weather resistant thermoplastic cover.

SAE 100R8

The hose shall consist of a thermoplastic inner tube resistant to hydraulic fluids with suitable synthetic fiber reinforcement and a hydraulic fluid and weather resistant thermoplastic cover.

Description of SAE 100R1 through SAE 100R18 Flexible Hoses (Continued)

SAE 100R9 (To be discontinued beginning 2005, due to lack of demand.)

Type A — This hose shall consist of an inner tube of oil resistant synthetic rubber, 4-spiral plies of wire wrapped in alternating directions and an oil and weather resistant synthetic rubber cover. A ply or braid of suitable material may be used over the inner tube and/or over the wire reinforcement to anchor the synthetic rubber to the wire.

Type AT — This hose shall be of the same construction as Type A, except having a cover designed to assemble with fittings, which do not require removal of the cover or a portion thereof.

SAE 100R10 (To be discontinued beginning 2005, due to lack of demand.)

Type A — This hose shall consist of an inner tube of oil resistant synthetic rubber, 4-spiral plies of heavy wire wrapped in alternating directions and an oil and weather resistant synthetic rubber cover. A ply or braid of suitable material may be used over the inner tube and/or over the wire reinforcement to anchor the synthetic rubber to the wire.

SAE 100R11 (To be discontinued beginning 2005, due to lack of demand.)

This hose shall consist of an inner tube of oil resistant synthetic rubber, 6-spiral plies of heavy wire wrapped in alternating directions and an oil and weather resistant synthetic rubber cover. A ply or braid of suitable material may be used over the inner tube and/or over the wire reinforcement to anchor the synthetic rubber to the wire.

SAE 100R12

This hose shall consist of an inner tube of oil resistant synthetic rubber, 4-spiral plies of heavy wire wrapped in alternating directions and an oil and weather resistant synthetic rubber cover. A ply or braid of suitable material may be used over or within the inner tube and/or over the wire reinforcement to anchor the synthetic rubber to the wire.

SAE 100R13

This hose shall consist of an inner tube of oil resistant synthetic rubber, multiple spiral plies of heavy wire wrapped in alternating directions and an oil and weather resistant synthetic rubber cover. A ply or braid of suitable material may be used over or within the inner tube and/or over the wire reinforcement to anchor the synthetic rubber to the wire.

SAE 100R14

Type A — This hose shall consist of an inner tube of polytetrafluorethylene (PTFE), reinforced with a single braid of 303XX series stainless steel.

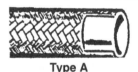

Type A

Type B — This hose shall be of the same construction as Type A, but shall have the additional feature of an electrically conductive inner surface so as to preclude buildup of an electrostatic charge.

Type B

SAE 100R15 — Heavy-Duty, High Impulse Spiral Wire Reinforcement Hose

This hose shall consist of an inner tube of oil resistant synthetic rubber, multiple spiral plies of heavy wire wrapped in alternating directions and an oil-and-weather resistant synthetic rubber cover.

Description of SAE 100R1 through SAE 100R18 Flexible Hoses (Continued)

SAE 100R16 — Compact Wire Braid Hoses of this type are smaller in diameter than two wire braid hoses with similar performance characteristics as 100R2, which gives them the ability to operate at smaller bend radii.

This hose shall consist of an inner tube of oil resistant synthetic rubber, wire braid reinforcement (one or two braids) and an oil and weather resistant synthetic rubber cover.

One Braid

Two Braids

SAE 100R17 — Compact 3,000 psi (21 mPa) maximum operating pressure one and two steel wire reinforced rubber covered hydraulic hose with smaller bend radius.

Hoses of this type are smaller in diameter than one and two braid hoses with similar performance characteristics specified in SAE 100R1 and 100R2 which gives them the ability to operate at smaller bend radii. They are also lighter in weight and their compactness offers advantages when minimal space is available in installations. This hose can be manufactured as either a one braid or two braid design.

One Braid

Two Braids

SAE 100R180 — 3,000 psi (21 mPa) maximum operating pressure

The hose shall consist of a thermoplastic inner tube resistant to hydraulic fluids with suitable synthetic fiber reinforcement and a hydraulic fluid and weather resistant thermoplastic cover.

ISO Performance in psi

Summary of ISO 1436-1 braid wire reinforced, 4079-1 textile reinforced, 3949 Thermoplastic textile reinforced and 3862-1 spiral wire reinforced Series Hose

Maximum Operating Pressures (psi, 14.5 psi = 1 bar)

Nominal - Size (mm)	1436-1				4079-1				
	Type 1	Type R1	Type 2	Type R2	Type 1TE	Type 2TE	Type 3TE	Type R6	Type R3
-2 (5)	3,625	3,045	6,018	5,075	363	1,160	2,320	507.5	1,523
-3 (6.3)	3,263	2,784	5,800	5,075	363	1,088	2,103	435	1,276
-5 (8)	3,118	2,538	5,075	4,307	290	986	1,885	435	1,189
-6 (10)	2,610	2,277	4,785	4,060	290	913.5	1,595	435	1,146
-8 (12.5)	2,320	2,030	3,988	3,553	232	841	1,349	435	1,015
-10 (16)	1,885	1,523	3,625	2,784	232	725	1,160	377	885
-12 (19)	1,523	1,262	3,118	2,277		653	1,015	319	754
-16 (25)	1,276	1,015	2,393	2,030		580	798		566
-20 (31.5)	914	624	1,813	1,639			653		377
-24 (38)	725	508	1,305	1,262			580		
-32 (51)		377	1,160	1,131			479		
-40 (60)							363		
-48 (80)							261		
-64 (100)							145		
Impulse Test Temperature	212°F	212°F	212°F	212°F	212°F	212°F	212°F	212°F	212°F
Impulse Test Pressure*	125%** 100%***	125%** 100%***	133%	133%	N/A	125%	133%** 100%***	N/A	133%** 100%***
Cycles	150,000	150,000	200,000	200,000	N/A	100,000	200,000	N/A	200,000
Length Tolerance****	+2 -4	+2 -4	+2 -4	+2 -4	+2 -4	+2 -4	+2 -4	+2 -4	+2 -4

Summary of ISO 1436-1 braid wire reinforced, 4079-1 textile reinforced, 3949 Thermoplastic textile reinforced and 3862-1 spiral wire reinforced Series Hose

Maximum Operating Pressures (psi, 14.5 psi = 1 bar)

Nominal - Size (mm)	3949		3862-1						
	Type R7	Type R8	Type 4SP	Type 4SH	Type R12	Type R13	Type R15	Type 1SC	Type 2SC
-2 (5)	2,963	5,003	X	X	X	X	X	X	X
-3 (6.3)	2,755	5,003	6,525	X	X	X	X	3,263	5,800
-5 (8)	2,465	X	X	X	X	X	X	3,118	5,075
-6 (10)	2,248	3,988	6,453	X	4,060	X	6,090	2,610	4,785
-8 (12.5)	1,958	3,480	6,018	X	4,060	X	6,090	2,320	3,988
-10 (16)	1,450	2,755	5,075	X	4,060	X	6,090	1,885	3,625
-12 (19)	1247	2,248	5,075	6,090	4,060	5,075	6,090	1,523	3,118
-16 (25)	1001	2,001	4,060	5,510	4,060	5,075	6,090	1,276	2,393
-20 (31.5)			3,045	4,713	3,045	5,075	6,090		
-24 (38)			2,683	4,205	2,538	5,075	6,090		
-32 (51)			2,393	3,625	2,538	5,075	6,090		
Impulse Test Temperature	212°F	212°F	212°F	212°F	250°F	250°F	250°F	212°F	212°F
Impulse Test Pressure*	125%	133%	133%	133%	133%	120%	120%	133%	133%
Cycles	150,000	200,000	400,000	400,000	500,000	500,000	500,000	150,000	200,000
Length Tolerance****	+3 -3	+3 -3	+2 -4	+2 -4	+2 -2	+2 -2	+2 -2	+2 -4	+2 -4

* as a % of Maximum Operating Pressure
** Hose bore 25 mm and smaller
*** Hose bore 31 mm and larger
**** at Maximum Operating Pressure

NOTE: *Minimum burst of ISO hoses is at least 4 times the operating pressure.*

SAE Performance

Summary of SAE J517 100R-Series Hose Maximum Operating Pressures (psi)

Nominal Size	R1[1]	New R1S[2]	R2[1]	New R2S[2]	R3	R4	R5	R6	R7	R8	R9[3]
-3	3,000	3,625	5,000	6,018	1,500		5,000	500	3,000	5,000	
-4	2,750	3,263	5,000	5,800	1,250		3,000	400	2,750	5,000	
-5	2,500	3,118	4,250	5,075	1,200		2,250	400	2,500		
-6	2,250	2,610	4,000	4,785	1,125		2,250	400	2,250	4,000	4,500
-8	2,000	2,320	3,500	3,988	1,000		2,000	400	2,000	3,500	4,000
-10	1,500	1,885	2,750	3,625	875		1,750	350	1,500	2,750	
-12	1,250	1,523	2,250	3,118	750	300	1,500	300	1,250	2,250	3,000
-16	1,000	1,276	2,000	2,393	565	250	800		1,000	2,000	3,000
-20	625	914	1,625	1,813	375	200	625				2,500
-24	500	725	1,250	1,305		150	500				2,000
-32	375	580	1,125	1,015		100	350				2,000
-40			1,000	1,160		62	350				
Impulse Test Temperature	212°F	212°F	212°F	212°F	212°F	N/A	212°F	N/A	200°F	200°F	212°F
Impulse Test Pressure*	125%	125%	133%	133%	133%	N/A	125%	N/A	125%	133%	133%
Cycles	150,000	150,000	200,000	200,000	200,000	N/A	150,000	N/A	150,000	200,000	200,000
Length Tolerance*	+2 / -4	+2 / -4	+2 / -4	+2 / -4	+2 / -4	+2 / -4	+2 / -4	+2 / -4	+3 / -3	+3 / -3	+2 / -4

Summary of SAE J517 100R-Series Hose Maximum Operating Pressures (psi)

Nominal Size	R10[3]	R11[3]	R12	R13	R14	R15	R16	New R16S[4]	R17	R18
-2					1,500					
-3	10,000	12,500			1,500		5,000	6,018		3,000
-4	8,750	11,250			1,500		5,000	5,800	3,000	3,000
-5					1,500		4,250	5,075	3,000	3,000
-6	7,500	10,000	4,000		1,500	6,000	4,000	4,785	3,000	3,000
-7					1,500					
-8	6,250	7,500	4,000		800	6,000	3,500	3,988	3,000	3,000
-10			4,000		800			3,625	3,000	3,000
-12	5,000	6.25	4,000	5,000	800	6,000	2,250	3,118	3,000	3,000
-14					800					
-16	4,000	5,000	4,000	5,000	800	6,000	2,000	2,393	3,000	3,000
-20	3,000	3,500	3,000	5,000	600	6,000		1,813		
-24	2,500	3,000	2,500	5,000		6,000		5,075		
-32	2,500	3,000	2,500	5,000						
-40		2,500								
Impulse Test Temperature	212°F	212°F	250°F	250°F	400°F	250°F	212°F	212°F	212°F	200°F
Impulse Test Pressure*	133%	133%	133%	120%	125%	120%	133%	133%	133%	133%
Cycles	400,000	400,000	500,000	500,000	150,000	500,000	200,000	200,000	200,000	200,000
Length Tolerance*	+2 / -4	+2 / -4	+2 / -2	+2 / -2	+2 / -4	+2 / -2	+2 / -4	+2 / -4	+2 / -4	+3 / -3

* as a % of Maximum Operating Pressure   1 mPa = 145.0377 psi
** at Maximum Operating Pressure   1 bar = 14.50377 psi

[1] R1A, R2A, R2B and R2BT will be discontinued beginning with the year 2005 due to lack of demand. DOD Order after 2004, use R1AT and R2AT to replace R1A and R2A.

[2] R2AT maximum working pressure will be replaced by the type S maximum working pressure beginning 2006, eliminating the need to label R2 as type S. Type S pressures match ISO 1436 for type 1SN and 2SN.

[3] R9, R10 and R11 hose will be discontinued beginning the year 2005, due to lack of demand.

[4] Maximum working pressures will be replaced by type S maximum working pressures with the year 2008, eliminating the need to label R16 as type S.

EN Performance

Summary of EN 853, 854, 855, 856, 857-Series Hose Maximum Operating Pressures in Bar							
Nominal Size in mm	**853**		**854**				
	Type 1	Type 2	Type 1TE	Type 2TE	Type 3TE	Type R6	Type R3
5	250	415	25	80	160	34	103
6	225	400	25	75	145	28	86
8	215	350	20	68	130	28	83
10	180	330	20	63	110	28	78
12	160	275	16	58	93	28	69
16	130	250	16	50	80	24	60
19	105	215		45	70	21	52
25	88	165		40	55		39
31	63	125			45		26
38	50	90			40		
51	40	80			33		
60					25		
80					18		
100					10		
Impulse Test Temperature	100°C	100°C	100°C	100°C	100°C	100°C	100°C
Impulse Test Pressure*	125%** / 100%***	133%	N/A	125%**	133% / 100%***	N/A	133%** / 100%***
Cycles	150,000	200,000	N/A	100,000	200,000	N/A	200,000
Length Tolerance****	+2 / -4	+2 / -4	+2 / -4	+2 / -4	+2 / -4	+2 / -4	+2 / -4

Summary of EN 853, 854, 855, 856, 857-Series Hose Maximum Operating Pressures in Bar							
Nominal Size in mm	**855**		**856**				**857**	
	Type R7	Type R8	Type 4SP	Type 4SH	Type R12	Type R13	Type 1SC	Type 2SC
5	205	345	X	X	X	X	X	X
6	190	345	450	X	X	X	225	400
8	170	X	X	X	X	X	215	350
10	155	275	445	X	276	X	180	330
12	135	240	415	X	276	X	160	275
16	100	190	350	X	276	X	130	250
19	86	155	350	420	276	345	105	215
25	69	138	280	380	276	345	88	165
31			210	325	207	345		
38			185	290	172	345		
51			165	250	172	345		
Impulse Test Temperature	100°C	100°C	100°C	100°C	120°C	120°C	100°C	100°C
Impulse Test Pressure*	125%	133%	133%	133%	133%	120%	125%	133%
Cycles	150,000	200,000	400,000	400,000	500,000	500,000	150,000	200,000
Length Tolerance****	+3 / -3	+3 / -3	+2 / -4	+2 / -4	+2 / -4	+2 / -4	+2 / -4	+2 / -4

* as a % of Maximum Operating Pressure
** Hose bore 25 mm and smaller
*** Hose bore 31 mm and larger
**** at Maximum Operating Pressure

NOTE: *Minimum burst of EN hoses is at least 4 times the operating pressure.*

Cylinder Size Selection

This chart lists the theoretical push and pull forces that cylinders will exert when supplied with various working pressures, plus theoretical piston velocities when supplied with 15 Ft./Sec. fluid velocity through SCH 80 size pipe.

Cyl. Bore Dia.	Piston Rod Dia	Work Area Sq. In.	Hydraulic Working Pressure psi						Fluid Req'd per In. of Stroke		Port Size	Fluid Velocity @15 Ft./Sec.	
			500	750	1000	1500	2000	3000	Gal.	Cu. In.		Flow GPM	Piston Vel. In./Sec.
1-1/2	—	1.767	883	13325	1767	2651	3534	5301	0.00765	1.767	1/2	11.0	24.0
	5/8	1.460	730	1095	1460	2190	2920	4380	0.00632	1.460			29.0
	1	0.982	491	736	982	1473	1964	2946	0.00425	0.982			43.1
2	—	3.141	1571	2356	3141	4711	6283	9423	0.01360	3.141	1/2	11.0	13.5
	1	2.356	1178	1767	2356	3534	4712	7068	0.01020	2.356			18.0
	1-3/8	1.656	828	1242	1656	2484	3312	4968	0.00717	1.656			25.6
2-1/2	—	4.909	2454	3682	4909	7363	9818	14727	0.02125	4.909	1/2	11.0	8.6
	1	4.124	2062	3093	4124	6186	8248	12372	0.01785	4.124			10.3
	1-3/8	3.424	1712	2568	3424	5136	6848	10272	0.01482	3.424			12.5
	1-3/4	2.504	1252	1878	2504	3756	5008	7512	0.01084	2.504			16.9
3-1/4	—	8.296	4148	6222	8296	12444	16592	24888	0.0359	8.296	3/4	20.3	9.4
	1-3/8	6.811	3405	5108	6811	10216	13622	20433	0.0295	6.811			11.5
	1-3/4	5.891	2945	4418	5891	8836	11782	17673	0.0255	5.891			13.3
	2	5.154	2577	3865	5154	7731	10308	15462	0.0223	5.154			15.2
4	—	12.566	6283	9425	12566	18849	25132	37698	0.0544	12.566	3/4	20.3	6.2
	1-3/4	10.161	5080	7621	10161	15241	20300	30483	0.0440	10.161			7.7
	2	9.424	4712	7068	9424	14136	18848	28272	0.0408	9.424			8.3
	2-1/2	7.657	3828	5743	7657	11485	15314	22971	0.0331	7.657			10.2
5	—	19.635	9818	14726	19635	29453	39270	58905	0.0850	19.635	3/4	20.3	4.0
	2	16.492	8246	12369	16492	24738	32984	49476	0.0714	16.492			4.7
	2-1/2	14.726	7363	11044	14726	22089	29542	44178	0.0637	14.726			5.3
	3	12.566	6283	9424	12566	18849	25132	37698	0.0544	12.566			6.2
	3-1/2	10.014	5007	7510	10014	15021	20028	30042	0.0433	10.014			7.8
6	—	28.274	14137	21205	28274	42411	56548	84822	0.1224	28.274	1	33.8	4.6
	2-1/2	23.365	11682	17524	23365	35047	46730	70095	0.1011	23.365			5.6
	3	21.205	10602	15904	21205	31807	42410	63615	0.0918	21.205			6.1
	4	15.708	7854	11781	15708	23562	31416	47124	0.0680	15.708			8.3
7	—	38.485	19242	28864	38485	57728	76970	115455	0.1666	38.485	1-1/4	60.2	6.0
	3	31.416	15708	23562	31416	47124	62832	94248	0.1360	31.416			7.4
	4	25.919	12960	19439	25919	38878	51838	77757	0.1122	25.919			8.9
	5	18.850	9425	14137	18850	28275	37700	56550	0.0816	18.850			12.3
8	—	50.265	25133	37699	50265	75398	100530	150795	0.2176	50.265	1-1/2	83.0	6.4
	3-1/2	40.644	20322	30483	40644	60966	81288	121932	0.1759	40.644			7.9
	4	37.699	18850	28274	37699	56548	75398	113097	0.1632	37.699			8.5
	5-1/2	26.507	13253	19880	26507	39760	53014	79521	0.1147	26.507			12.0
10	—	78.540	39270	58905	78540	117810	157080	235620	0.3400	78.540	2	139	6.8
	4-1/2	62.636	31318	46977	62636	93954	125272	187908	0.2711	62.636			8.5
	5-1/2	54.782	27391	41086	54782	82173	109564	164346	0.2371	54.782			9.8
	7	40.055	20027	30041	40055	60082	80110	120165	0.1734	40.055			13.4
12	—	113.10	56550	84825	113100	169650	226200	339300	0.4896	113.10	2-1/2	199	6.8
	5-1/2	89.34	44670	67005	89340	134010	178680	268020	0.3867	89.34			8.6
	7	74.62	37310	55965	74620	111930	149240	223860	0.3230	74.62			10.3
	8	62.84	31420	47130	62840	94260	125680	188520	0.2720	62.84			12.2
14	—	153.94	76970	115455	153940	230910	307880	461820	0.6664	153.94	2-1/2	199	5.0
	7	115.46	57730	86595	115460	173190	230920	346380	0.4998	115.46			6.6
	8	103.68	51840	77760	103680	155520	207360	311040	0.4488	103.68			7.4
	10	75.40	37700	56550	75400	113100	150800	226200	0.3264	75.40			10.2

Oil consumption in gallons per minute = Gallons per inch x inches per minute of piston travel.
1 gallon = 231 cubic inches. Cylinder bore diameters and piston rod diameters are in inches.

Filtration and Fluid Conditioning

This information is provided courtesy of American National Standards Institute "Hydraulic Fluid Power — Systems standard for stationary industrial machinery." (NFPA/JIC T2.24.1 — 1991)

12.2 Filtration

Filtration shall be provided to limit the in service particulate contamination level to the values listed in table 1 for the given system operating pressure, fluid type and components used.

12.2 Location and Sizing of Filters and Fluid Conditioning

12.2.1 Filters shall be located in pressure, return or auxiliary circulation lines as necessary to achieve the cleanliness levels of filtration during normal equipment operation.

12.2.2 Unless specified in Part B of the Hydraulic equipment data form (or similar document), **filtration on pump suction lines shall not be used.** Inlet screens or strainers are acceptable.

12.2.3 If used, suction filtration devices shall be equipped with an integral bypass valve to limit the maximum pressure drop at rated system flow to a value that insures the requirements of 10.3.5 are satisfied.

12.2.4 Filters shall be sized to provide a minimum of 800 hours operation under normal system conditions.

12.2.5 All filter assemblies shall be equipped with some device which indicates when the filter requires servicing. This device shall be readily visible to the operator or maintenance personnel.

12.2.6 Filter assemblies whose elements cannot withstand full system differential pressure without damage shall be equipped with bypass valves. The bypass valve opening differential pressure shall be at least 20 percent higher that the differential pressure required to actuate the aforementioned indicator.

12.2.7 If specified in Part B of the Hydraulic equipment data form, the fluid system fill ports shall be routed through an auxiliary filter or one of the existing system filters.

12.2.8 Conduit connections to the fluid power filter shall be such as to eliminate external leakage. Taper pipe threads or connection mechanisms which require the use of a nonintegral sealing compound shall not be used, except as noted in 17.3.1.

Reporting Cleanliness Levels of Hydraulic Fluids SAE J1165 OCT80
Cleanliness Level Correlation Table

ISO Code	Particles per Milliliter >10 mm	ACFTD* Gravimetric Level — mg/L	MIL STD 1246A (1967)	NAS 1638 (1964)	Disavowed "SAE" Level (1963)
26/23	140,000	1,000			
25/23	85,000	100			
23/20	14,000		1,000		
21/18	4,500		700	12	
20/18	2,400		500		
20/17	2,300	10	300	11	
20/16	1,400				
19/16	1,200			10	
18/15	580			9	6
17/14	280			8	5
16/13	140	1		7	4
15/12	70			6	3
14/12	40		200		
14/11	35			5	2
13/10	14	0/1		4	1
12/9	9			3	0
11/8	5			2	
10/8	3		100		
10/7	2.3			I1	
10/6	1.4	0.01			
9/6	1.2			0	
8/5	0.6			00	
7/5	0.3		50		
6/3	0.14	0.001			
5/2	0.04		25		
2/0.8	0.01		10		

*ACFTD (Air Cleaner Fine Test Dust) — ISO Approved Test and Calibration Contaminant

Power of Ten Prefixes

Prefix	Symbol	Multiplier
atto	a	10^{-18}
femto	f	10^{-15}
pico	p	10^{-12}
nano	n	10^{-9}
micro	u	10^{-6}
milli	m	10^{-3}
centi	c	10^{-2}
deci	d	10^{-1}
deka	da	10^{1}
hecto	h	10^{2}
kilo	k	10^{3}
mega	M	10^{6}
giga	G	10^{9}
tera	T	10^{12}

Number Conversion Chart

Decimal — Notation	Power of Ten Notation
0.000,000,001	10^{-9}
0.000,000,01	10^{-8}
0.000,000,1	10^{-7}
0.00,001	10^{-6}
0.000,01	10^{-5}
0.0001	10^{-4}
0.001	10^{-3}
0.01	10^{-2}
0.1	10^{-1}
1	10^{0}
10	10^{1}
100	10^{2}
1,000	10^{3}
10,000	10^{4}
100,000	10^{5}
1,000,000	10^{6}
10,000,000	10^{7}
100,000,000	10^{8}
1,000,000,000	10^{9}

Basic Electrical and Electronic Data

This portion of the manual explains the rules, laws, formulas and symbols of basic electrical and electronic data.

OHM'S LAW COMBINED WITH JOULE'S LAW

WHERE:
I = Current in Amperes
P = Power in Watts

R = Resistance in Ohms
E = Potential in Volts

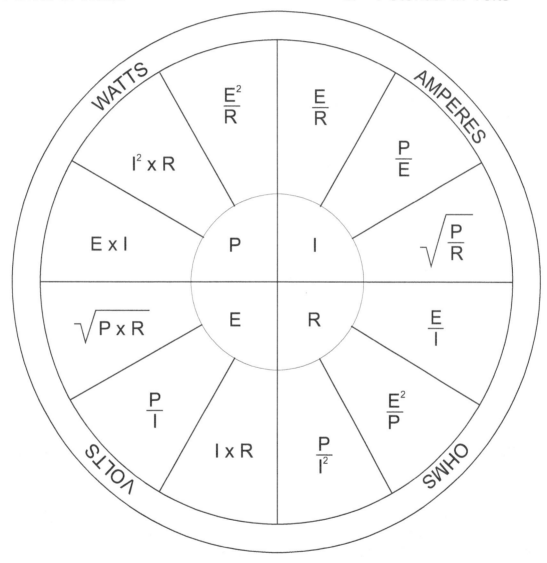

EXAMPLES OF CHART USE:

$$I = \frac{E}{R} = \frac{P}{E} = \sqrt{\frac{P}{R}}$$

$$E = \sqrt{P \times R} = \frac{P}{I} = I \times R$$

$$P = I^2 \times R = \frac{E^2}{R} = E \times I$$

$$R = \frac{P}{I^2} = \frac{E^2}{P} = \frac{E}{I}$$

Rules for Using a Series Circuit

The total resistance in a series circuit is the sum of the individual resistance.

$$R_t = R_1 + R_2 + R_3 + \text{etc.}$$

The current in a series circuit is the same through all components.

$$I_1 = I_2 = I_3 = I$$

The sum of the individual voltage drops will add up to the source voltage.

$$V_t = V_1 + V_2 + V_3 + \text{etc.}$$

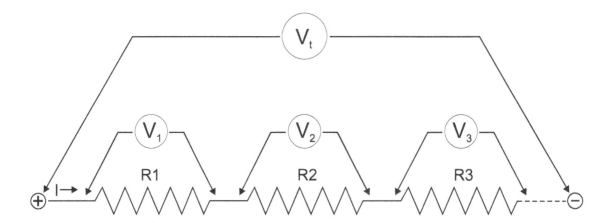

Rules for Using a Parallel Circuit

The formulas listed below are used to find the total resistance of a parallel circuit

With two parallel resistors:

$$R_t = \frac{R_1 R_2}{R_1 + R_2}$$

With more than two parallel resistors:

$$\frac{1}{R_t} = \frac{1}{R_1} + \frac{1}{R_2} + \frac{1}{R_3} + \text{etc.}$$

With identical parallel resistors, divide the value of one resistor by the total number of identical resistors.

Example: For ten, 500 Ohm parallel resistors:

$$500 \div 10 = 50 \quad \text{Ohms}$$

The voltage drop across each branch (resistance) is the same.

The total current in a parallel circuit is the sum of the currents in the individual branches.

$$I_t = I_1 + I_2 + I_3 + \text{etc.}$$

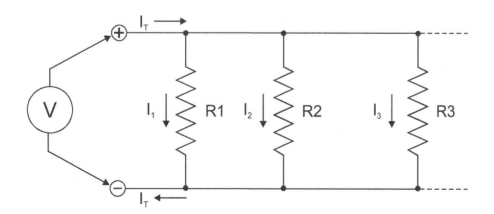

Terms for Electrical Circuits

TERM	SYMBOL	UNIT OF MEASURE	TERM	SYMBOL	UNIT OF MEASURE
Capacitance	C	Farads	Impedance	Z	Ohms
Capacitive Reactance	X_c	Ohms	Power	P	Watts
Charge	q	Coulombs	Resistance	R	Ohms
Current (DC or AC)	I	Amperes	Time Constant	Tc	Seconds
Inductance	L	Henries	Voltage or Potential (DC)	V or E	Volts
Inductive Reactance	X_L	Ohms	Voltage (AC)	V	Volts

Determining Power in AC and DC Circuits

TO FIND	ALTERNATING CURRENT		DIRECT CURRENT
	THREE PHASE	SINGLE PHASE	
Amperes when hp (Watts) is known	$I = \dfrac{746 \times hp}{1.73 \times E \times Eff \times PF}$	$I = \dfrac{746 \times hp}{E \times Eff \times PF}$	$I = \dfrac{746 \times hp}{E \times Eff}$
Amperes when kV is known	$I = \dfrac{1000 \times kW}{1.73 \times E \times PF}$	$I = \dfrac{1000 \times kW}{E \times PF}$	$I = \dfrac{1000 \times kW}{E}$
Amperes when kVA is known	$I = \dfrac{1000 \times kVA}{1.73 \times E}$	$I = \dfrac{1000 \times kVA}{E}$	- - - - - -
Kilowatts input	$kW = \dfrac{1.73 \times E \times I \times PF}{1000}$	$kW = \dfrac{E \times I \times PF}{1000}$	$kW = \dfrac{E \times I}{1000}$
Kilovolt Amperes	$kVA = \dfrac{1.73 \times E \times I}{1000}$	$kVA = \dfrac{E \times I}{1000}$	- - - - - -
Horsepower Output	$hp = \dfrac{1.73 \times E \times I \times Eff \times PF}{746}$	$hp = \dfrac{E \times I \times Eff \times PF}{746}$	$hp = \dfrac{E \times I \times Eff}{746}$

I = Ampers
E = Volts
Eff = Efficiency
    (in Decimals)

kW = Kilowatts
kVA = Kilovolt-amperes
hp = Horsepower Output
PF = Power Factor
    (in Decimals)

NOTE: Efficiency and Power Factor expressed in values between 0 and 1

Horsepower Required to Drive a Hydraulic Pump:

$$hp = \frac{GPM \times PSI}{1714 \times pump\ efficiency}$$

Torque of an Electrical Induction Motor:

$$Torque\,(lb - ft) = \frac{hp \times 5250}{RPM}$$

Speed of an Electrical Induction Motor:

$$RPM = \frac{120 \times Frequency}{no.\ of\ poles}$$

Indicating Light Color Codes

COLOR	CONDITION	SITUATION(S)
Red	Danger, Abnormal, Fault	Fault(s) in air, water, lubricating or filtering system(s). Excess pressure or temperature. Machine has been stopped by a protective device.
Amber or Yellow	Attention, Caution, Marginal	Automatic cycle engaged. Levels are nearing limits. Ground fault indicated.
Green	Machine Ready	All machine functions and auxiliary functions are operating at specified levels. Machine cycle completed and ready for restart.
White or Clear	Normal	Normal air, water and lubrication pressures.
Blue	Any condition not covered by above colors	_____

Pushbutton Color Code

COLOR	CONDITION	SITUATION(S)
Red	Stop, Emergency stop, Off	Motor(s) stopped, Master stop, or Emergency stop.
Yellow	Return, or Emergency Return	Machine elements are returned to a safe position.
Green or Black	Start, On	Cycle or partial sequence is started. Motor(s) started.
White, Gray or Blue	Any condition not covered by above colors	_____

Resistor Color Codes

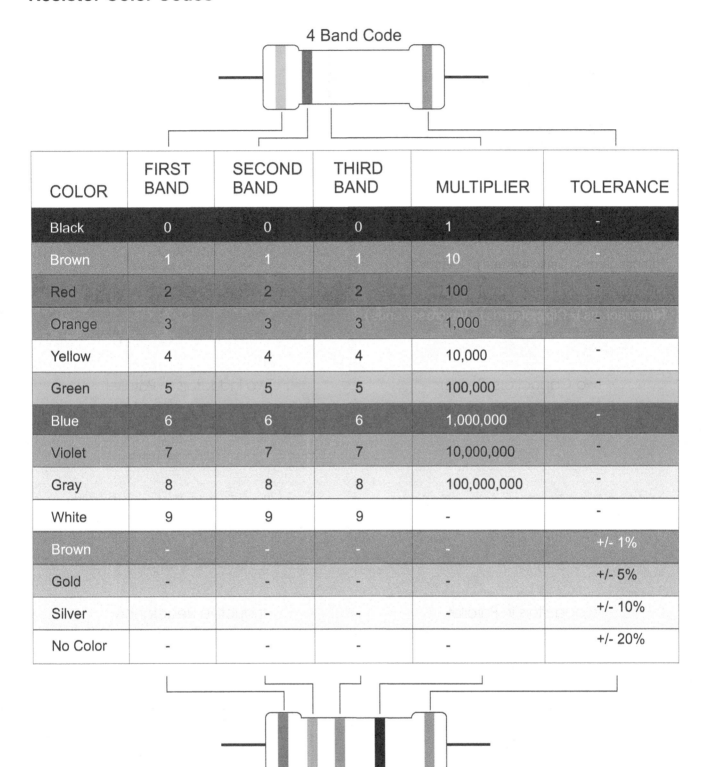

4 Band Code

COLOR	FIRST BAND	SECOND BAND	THIRD BAND	MULTIPLIER	TOLERANCE
Black	0	0	0	1	-
Brown	1	1	1	10	-
Red	2	2	2	100	-
Orange	3	3	3	1,000	-
Yellow	4	4	4	10,000	-
Green	5	5	5	100,000	-
Blue	6	6	6	1,000,000	-
Violet	7	7	7	10,000,000	-
Gray	8	8	8	100,000,000	-
White	9	9	9	-	-
Brown	-	-	-	-	+/- 1%
Gold	-	-	-	-	+/- 5%
Silver	-	-	-	-	+/- 10%
No Color	-	-	-	-	+/- 20%

5 Band Code

Electrical Formulas

RL Circuit Time Constant	RC Circuit (Series) Impedance
$$\frac{L(henrys)}{R(ohms)} = t(seconds)$$ $$\frac{L(microhenrys)}{R(ohms)} = t(microseconds)$$	$$Z = \sqrt{R^2 + (X_C)^2}$$
RC Circuit Time Constant $R(ohms) \times C(farads) = t(seconds)$ $R(megaohms) \times C(microfarads) = t(seconds)$ $R(ohms) \times C(microfarads) = t(microseconds)$ $R(megaohms) \times C(picrofarads) = t(microseconds)$	**RC Circuit (Series) Impedance** $$L_T = L_1 + L_2 + ...$$ (No coupling between coils)
Two Capacitors (Series) $$C_T = \frac{C_1 C_2}{C_1 + C_2}$$	**Two Inductors in Parallel** $$L_T = \frac{L_1 L_2}{L_1 + L}$$ (No coupling between coils)
More Than Two Capacitors (Series) $$\frac{1}{C_T} = \frac{1}{C_1} + \frac{1}{C_2} + \frac{1}{C_3} + ...$$	**More Than Two Inductors in Parallel** $$\frac{1}{L_T} = \frac{1}{L_1} + \frac{1}{L_2} + \frac{1}{L_3} + ...$$ (No coupling between coils)
Capacitors in Parallel $$C_T = C_1 + C_2 + ...$$	**Inductive Reactance** $$X_L = 2\pi f L$$
Capacitive Reactance $$X_C = \frac{1}{2\pi f C}$$	**Q of a Coil** $$Q = \frac{X_L}{R}$$

Electrical Formulas (Continued)

RL Circuit (Series) Impedance	AC CIRCUIT POWER
$$Z = \sqrt{R^2 + (X_L)^2}$$	

R, C and L Circuit (Series) Impedance	Apparent Power
$$Z = \sqrt{R^2 + (X_L - X_C)^2}$$	$$P = EI$$
	True Power
	$$P = EI(\cos\theta) = EI \times P.F.$$
	Power Factor

SINE-WAVE VOLTAGE RELATIONSHIPS	$$P.F. = \frac{P}{EI} = \cos\theta$$
Effective or r.m.s. Value	$$\cos\theta = \frac{\text{true power}}{\text{apparent power}}$$
$$E_{eff} = \frac{E_{MAX}}{\sqrt{2}} = \frac{E_{MAX}}{1.414} = 0.707 E_{MAX}$$	TRANSFORMERS

Maximum Value	Voltage Relationship
$$E_{MAX} = \sqrt{2}(E_{EFF}) = 1.414 E_{EFF}$$	$$\frac{E_p}{E_s} = \frac{N_p}{N_s} \quad \text{or} \quad E_s = E_p \times \frac{N_s}{N_p}$$

AC Circuit Voltage	Current Relationship
$$E = IZ = \frac{P}{I \times P.F.}$$	s = Secondary p = Primary $\quad \dfrac{I_p}{I_s} = \dfrac{N_s}{N_p}$ N = Number of turns

AC Circuit Current	Parallel Circuit Impedance
$$I = \frac{E}{Z} = \frac{P}{E \times P.F.}$$	$$Z = \frac{Z_1 Z_2}{Z_1 + Z_2}$$

Equivalent Logic/Ladder Diagrams

LOGIC DIAGRAMS

LADDER DIAGRAMS

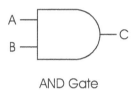

AND Gate

A	B	C
0	0	0
0	1	0
1	0	0
1	1	1

AND Truth Table

Equivalent Circuit

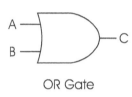

OR Gate

A	B	C
0	0	0
0	1	1
1	0	1
1	1	1

OR Truth Table

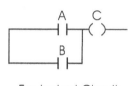

Equivalent Circuit

Exclusive OR Gate

A	B	C
0	0	0
0	1	1
1	0	1
1	1	0

Exclusive - OR Truth Table

Equivalent Circuit

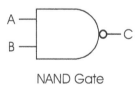

NAND Gate

A	B	C
0	0	1
0	1	1
1	0	1
1	1	0

NAND Truth Table

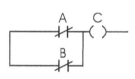

Equivalent Circuit

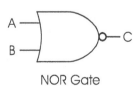

NOR Gate

A	B	C
0	0	1
0	1	0
1	0	0
1	1	0

NOR Truth Table

Equivalent Circuit

Electrical Relay Diagram Symbols

SWITCHES

CIRCUIT INTERRUPTER	DISCONNECT	CIRCUIT BREAKER	PLUGGING	NON-PLUG	PLUGGING W/LOCK-OUT COIL
C1	DISC	CB	PLS F R	PLS F R	PLS F LO

LIMIT

NORMALLY OPEN	NORMALLY CLOSED	NEUTRAL POSITION		MAINTAINED POSITION	PROXIMITY SWITCH		CABLE OPERATED (EMERG.) SWITCH	TEMPERATURE	
			ACTUATED		CLOSED	OPEN		NORMALLY OPEN	NORMALLY CLOSED
LS	LS	NP LS	NP LS	LS	PRS	PRS	COS	TAS	TAS
HELD CLOSED	HELD OPEN								
LS	LS								

LIQUID LEVEL / VACUUM & PRESSURE / FLOW / FOOT / TOGGLE

LIQUID LEVEL		VACUUM & PRESSURE		FLOW (AIR & WATER)		FOOT		TOGGLE
NORMALLY OPEN	NORMALLY CLOSED	NORMALLY OPEN	NORMALLY CLOSED	NORMALLY OPEN	NORMALLY CLOSED	NORMALLY OPEN	NORMALLY CLOSED	
FS	FS	PS	PS	FLS	FLS	FTS	FTS	TGS

ROTARY SELECTOR / SELECTOR / THERMOCOUPLE SWITCH

ROTARY SELECTOR		SELECTOR		THERMOCOUPLE SWITCH
NON-BRIDGING CONTACTS	BRIDGING CONTACTS	2-POSITION	3-POSITION	
RSS	RSS	SS 1 2	SS 1 2 3	TCS OFF 1 2
OR	OR			
RSS	RSS			
TOTAL CONTACTS TO SUIT NEEDS				

Electrical Relay Diagram Symbols (Continued)

COILS						

SOLENOIDS, BRAKES, ETC.				CONTROL CIRCUIT TRANSFORMER	THERMAL OVERLOAD ELEMENT	RELAYS, TIMERS, ETC.
GENERAL	2 POSITION HYDRAULIC	3 POSITION PNEUMATIC	2 POSITION LUBRICATION			

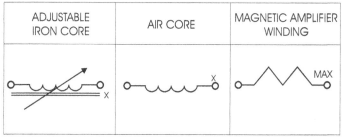

ADJUSTABLE IRON CORE	AIR CORE	MAGNETIC AMPLIFIER WINDING	CONNECTIONS, ETC.				
			GROUND	CHASSIS OR FRAME	PLUG AND RECP.	CONDUCTORS	

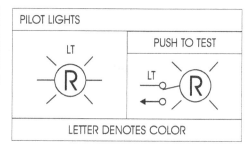

CONTACTS							
TIME DELAY AFTER COIL				RELAY, ETC.		THERMAL OVERLOAD	
NORMALLY OPEN	NORMALLY CLOSED	NORMALLY OPEN	NORMALLY CLOSED	NORMALLY OPEN	NORMALLY CLOSED		
ENERGIZED	ENERGIZED	DE-ENERGIZED	DE-ENERGIZED				

PILOT LIGHTS	
LT	PUSH TO TEST
LETTER DENOTES COLOR	

PUSHBUTTONS		
SINGLE CIRCUIT	DOUBLE CIRCUIT	MAINTAINED CONTACT

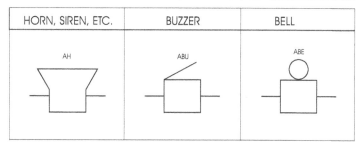

MOTORS	
3 - PHASE MOTOR	D C MOTOR ARMATURE

HORN, SIREN, ETC.	BUZZER	BELL

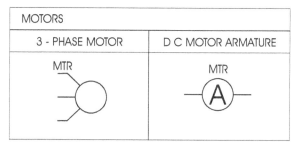

Appendix D . . . . . Logical Troubleshooting

The object of this appendix is to provide a logical approach to hydraulic system troubleshooting which can be extended to cover specific machines in all areas of industry. The fundamentals used to develop this approach (control of flow, pressure and direction) apply equally as well to a rolling mill in a steelworks or a winch drive on a trawler.

Probably the greatest aid to troubleshooting is the confidence that comes with knowing the system. Since every component has a purpose in the system, the construction and operating characteristics of each one should be clearly understood. For example, knowing that a solenoid controlled directional valve can be manually actuated will save considerable time in isolating a defective solenoid.

It is also important to know the capabilities of the system. Each component in the system has a maximum rated speed, torque or pressure. If the system is loaded beyond the specifications, the possibility of failure is greatly increased.

The correct operating pressures of a system must be known and always checked and set with a pressure gauge. The hydraulic schematic should have the correct pressures. If not, assume that the correct operating pressure is the lowest pressure that will allow adequate performance of the system function and still remain below the maximum rating of the components and machine. Once the correct pressures have been established, note them on the hydraulic schematic for future reference.

Understanding the system also includes knowing the proper signal and feedback levels, as well as dither and gain settings in servo control systems.

Occasionally, a seemingly uncomplicated procedure such as relocating a system or changing a component part can cause problems. The points discussed below will aid in avoiding unnecessary complications.

- Each component in the system must be compatible with, and form an integral part of, the system. As an example, placing the wrong size filter on the inlet of a pump can cause cavitation and subsequent damage to the pump.

- All lines should be the correct size and free of restrictive bends. An undersized or restricted line results in a pressure drop in that line.

- Some components are meant to be mounted in a specific position, relative to the other components or lines. The housing of an in-line pump, for example, must remain filled with fluid to provide lubrication.

- Although they are not essential for system operation, having adequate test points for pressure readings will also expedite troubleshooting.

The ability to recognize trouble indicators in a specific system is usually acquired with experience. To help this process, analyze the system and develop a logical sequence for setting valves, mechanical stops, interlocks and electrical controls. Tracing the flow paths can often be accomplished by listening for flow in the lines or feeling them for excessive warmth.

By working regularly with the system, a cause and effect troubleshooting guide, similar to the charts found in this appendix, can be developed. The initial time spent on such a project could save many hours of system downtime later on.

Although troubleshooting and repair are a normal part of operating a system, downtime can be minimized by keeping up on simple system maintenance. Regularly performing the three tasks noted here, the performance, efficiency and life of the system will be greatly improved.

- Maintain a sufficient quantity of hydraulic fluid that is clean and is the correct type and viscosity.

- Change the filters and clean strainers often.

- Keep all connections tight enough so that air is kept out of the system but no distortion is present.

Whenever system troubleshooting is being carried out, the most important consideration is always safety. Although much of practicing good safety habits is common sense, the stress of a breakdown situation may mean that a potential hazard gets overlooked. For this reason, it is a good idea to establish a regular shutdown procedure, like the one shown, which is carried out before beginning work on any system.

These same safety considerations call for a restart procedure which is followed when the repairs have been made and the system is ready to run again.

The following troubleshooting charts are arranged in five main categories. The heading of each is a symptom that indicates some malfunction in the system. For example, if a pump is excessively noisy, refer to appropriate chart. The noisy pump is referenced in Column A below the main heading. Underneath, listed in likelihood of occurrence or ease of checking, there are four probable causes for a noisy pump. Each cause references a remedy that can be found at the bottom of the page. If cavitation is occurring in the system, perform the procedure(s) listed under Remedy A. If not, move to the next cause, continuing until the cause of the problem is determined and eliminated.

Safety Procedure for Shutting Down Machines

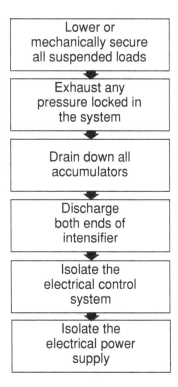

Lower or
mechanically secure
all suspended loads

Exhaust any
pressure locked in
the system

Drain down all
accumulators

Discharge
both ends of
intensifier

Isolate the
electrical control
system

Isolate the
electrical power
supply

Re-start Procedure

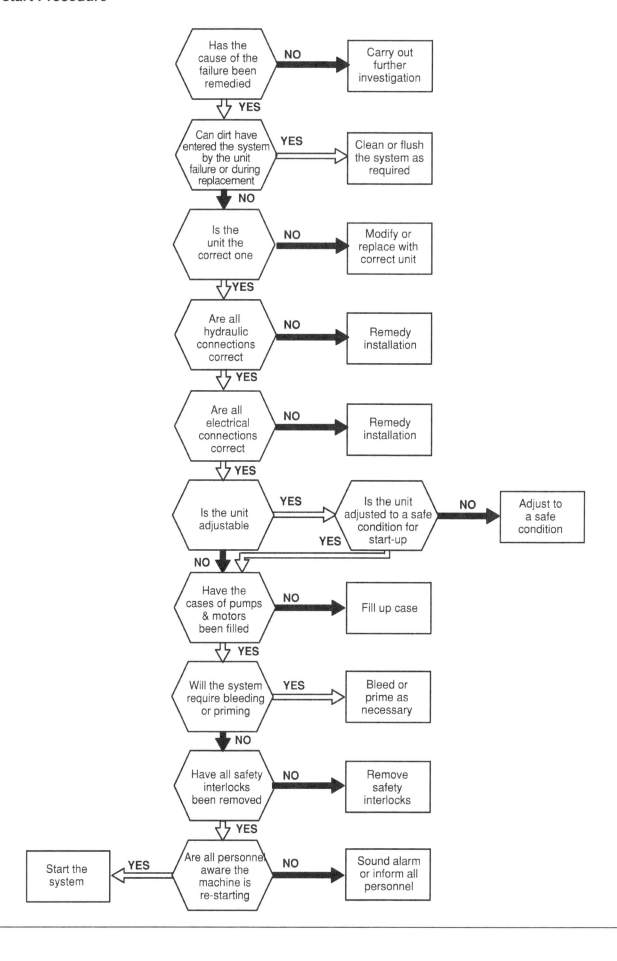

Chart 1

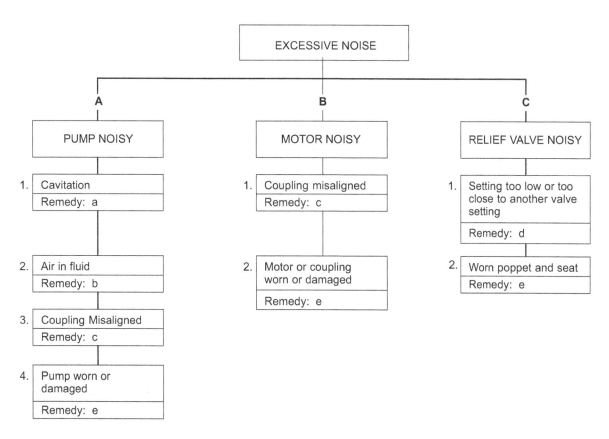

Remedies:

a. Any or all of the following:

Replace dirty filters; wash strainers in solvent compatible with system fluid; clean clogged inlet line; clean or replace reservoir breather vent; change system fluid; change to proper pump drive motor speed; overhaul or replace supercharge pump; fluid may be too cold.

b. Any or all of the following:

Tighten leaking connections; fill reservoir to proper level (with rare exception all return lines should be below fluid level in reservoir); bleed air from system; replace pump shaft seal (and shaft if worn at seal journal).

c. Align unit and check condition of seals, bearings and coupling.

d. Install pressure gauge and adjust to correct pressure.

e. Overhaul or replace.

Chart 2

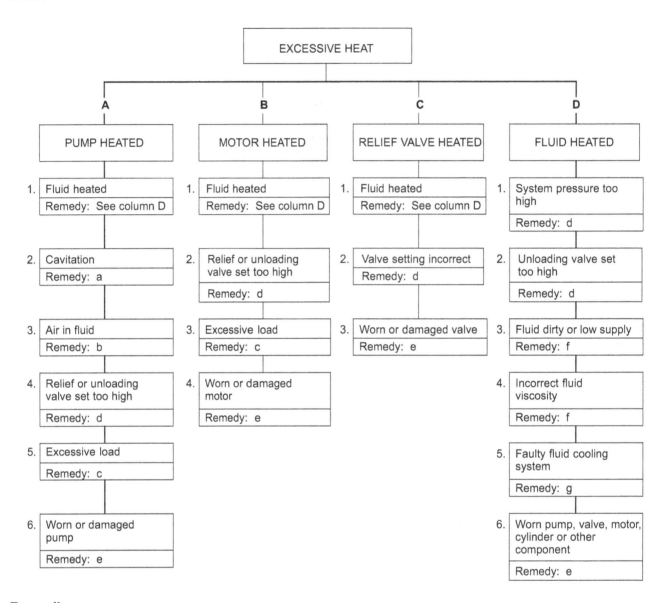

Remedies:

a. Any or all of the following:

Replace dirty filters; clean clogged inlet line; clean or replace reservoir breather vent; change system fluid; change to proper pump drive motor speed; overhaul or replace supercharge pump.

b. Any or all of the following:

Tighten leaking connections; fill reservoir to proper level (with rare exception all return lines should be below fluid level in reservoir); bleed air from system; replace pump shaft seal (and shaft if worn at seal journal).

c. Align unit and check condition of seals and bearings; locate and correct mechanical binding; check for work load in excess of circuit design.

d. Install pressure gauge and adjust to correct pressure (keep at least 125 psi difference between valve settings).

e. Overhaul or replace.

f. Change filters and also system fluid if improper viscosity; fill reservoir to proper level.

g. Clean cooler and/or cooler strainer; replace cooler control valve; repair or replace cooler.

Chart 3

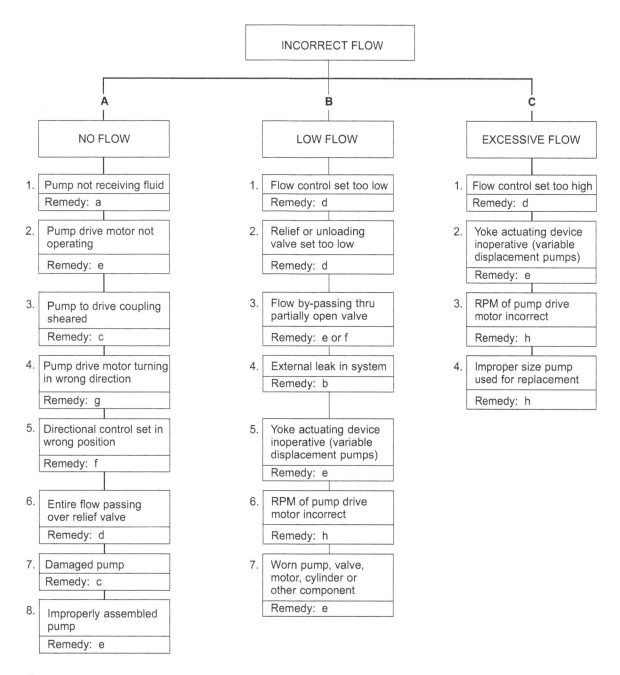

Remedies:

a. Any or all of the following:

Replace dirty filters; clean clogged inlet line; clean or replace reservoir breather vent; fill reservoir to proper level; overhaul or replace supercharge pump.

b. Tighten leaking connections.

c. Check for damaged pump or pump drive; replace and align coupling.

d. Adjust.

e. Overhaul or replace.

f. Check position of manually operated controls; check electrical circuit on solenoid-operated controls; repair or replace pilot pressure pump.

g. Reverse rotation.

h. Replace with correct unit.

Chart 4

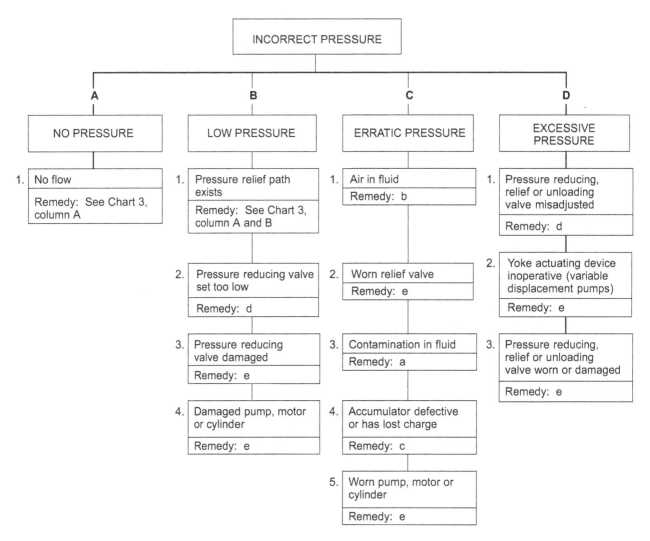

Remedies:

a. Replace dirty filters and system fluid.

b. Tighten leaking connections (fill reservoir to proper level and bleed air from system).

c. Adjust, repair or replace.

d. Clean and adjust or replace; check condition of system fluid and filters.

e. Overhaul or replace.

Chart 5

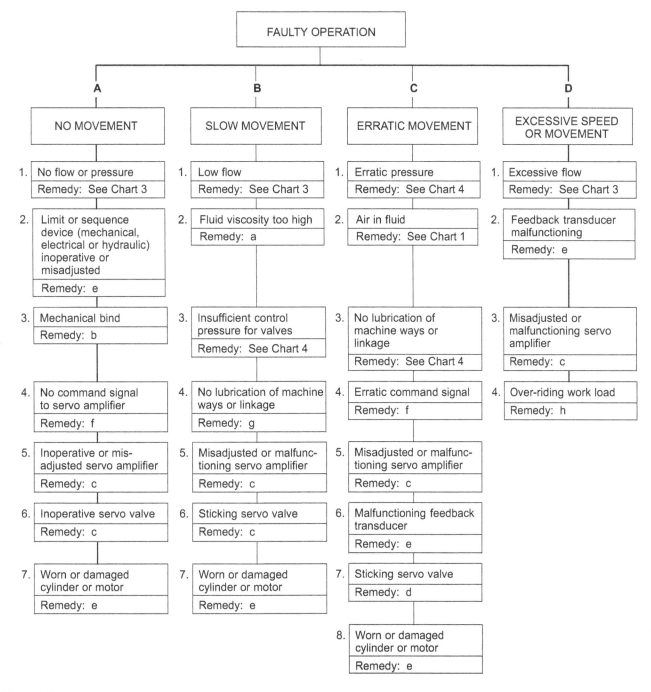

Remedies:

a. Fluid may be too cold or should be changed to clean fluid of correct viscosity.

b. Locate bind and repair.

c. Adjust, repair or replace.

d. Clean and adjust or replace; check condition of system fluid and filters.

e. Overhaul or replace.

f. Repair command console or interconnecting wires.

g. Lubricate.

h. Adjust, repair or replace counterbalance valve.

Appendix E . . . . Noise Control in Hydraulic Systems

Although a certain amount of noise control is required in hydraulic systems just to conform to government regulations, a conscientious noise control program actually provides a competitive edge. The combination of a quiet pump, well-engineered vibration and pulsation controls, and good, economical installation practices will result in a product with a distinct advantage in the marketplace.

The Vickers publication "More Sound Advice," issued in the 1970s, illustrated a variety of machine noise control methods. Because of the nearly infinite variety of hydraulic applications, it's not possible here to discuss the individual features of particular systems. There are, however, a number of installation techniques that can be applied to almost *all* hydraulic systems. When used correctly, these techniques can yield significant reductions in noise.

This publication describes the following:

1. Noise generation and noise control techniques.

2. Noise terms, definition and the use of the decibel.

3. Noise measurement procedures.

Quiet Hydraulics — A Team Effort

A successful noise control program requires a team effort by individuals in several areas of expertise. A quiet hydraulic pump does not guarantee a quiet system. The choice of a quiet pump should be only one part of a multifaceted program that calls upon the talents of the system designer, fabricator, installer and maintenance technicians. And if any member of the team fails to do their job, it can mean failure of the entire noise control program.

The pump and system designers play a key role in achieving successful noise control. They must evaluate every noise control technique available from the standpoints of both cost and practicality. Three of the basic approaches used in quieting hydraulic power systems are:

a. Internal and external pump pulsation control

b. Pump and structure isolation

c. Damping and/or stiffening

Noise Transmission and Generation

Noise is defined as the unwanted by-product of fluctuating forces in a component or system. In a hydraulic system, this noise can be transmitted in three ways: through the air, through the fluid, and through the system's physical structure. We generally think of noise as travelling only through the medium of the air, going directly from its source to some receiver (our ear). This is called *airborne noise*. That airborne noise, however, must have a source within some component of the hydraulic system. That component is normally the pump. Whether it's a piston, vane or gear pump, the internal pumping and porting design can never be perfect. As a result, uneven flow characteristics and pressure waves are created and transmitted through the fluid. This is known as *fluidborne noise*. The pressure wave fluctuations of fluidborne noise in turn create corresponding force fluctuations. These result in vibration, also known as *structureborne noise*. This structureborne noise is transmitted not only through the pump body, but through attached structures as well. These structures then emit an audible sound.

The surrounding structures and surface areas in a hydraulic system tend to be much larger than the pump itself, and therefore radiate noise more efficiently. For this reason, while the pump design should minimize internal pulsations, it's also important to use proper isolation techniques to keep the remaining vibrations from reaching adjoining structures.

Design for Low Noise

An intelligent program of noise control should start at the source: the pump. A quiet pump is the responsibility of the pump manufacturer. The problem for the designer is that although a hydraulic pump is required to perform over a wide range of speeds and pressures, noise control can only be optimized for a relatively narrow portion of that range. The most common strategy is to use porting design to limit the pressure pulsations at the pump's rated speed and pressure. The pulsations are reduced as much as possible without creating a large amount of noise at lower speeds and pressures. Piston, vane, and gear pumps are similar in that their total output flow is the sum of the flows from the individual pumping elements or chambers. Fluid fills the chambers at the pump inlet, is compressed mechanically and/or hydraulically through orifices, and is then combined into a single discharge flow. Each pumping element in a piston pump delivers its fluid to the discharge port in a half-sine profile. The pump discharge is the total of the equally spaced half-sines added in phase. The result is an inherent flow ripple, as shown in Figure E-1 for a nine-piston pump. This ripple is independent of any fluid compression, either through piston motion or any type of internal hydraulic metering. Vane pump flow ripple is more controllable. Cam contours can be designed to reduce mechanical compression effects. This is done by making pressure transitions in the dwell section, where there is controlled change in vane chamber volume. For this reason, vane pumps will normally generate less noise over a wider range of speeds and pressures than piston pumps.

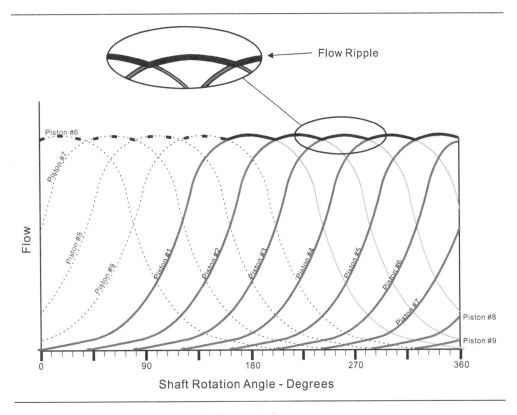

Figure E-1   Inherent piston pump discharge ripple

Noise Frequencies

Pump noise energies are generated in several ways. Vibrational energy is created by an imbalance in the pump, drive motor or couplings. It can also be produced by some undesired interaction in the assembly, but it's rare for any significant audible noise to be generated by these interactions. Nonetheless, care should be taken to minimize its effects on pump or motor life. Figure E-2 shows the frequency spectrum of a ten-vane pump operating at 1,800 RPM with shaft rotation frequency of 30 Hz. Any misalignments in the power train will produce noise components at twice and four times this frequency.

The strongest energy components occur at pumping frequency. This frequency equals the number of pumping chambers times the shaft frequency (300 Hz in Figure E-2). Noise energy is also produced at multiples, or harmonics, of this frequency. 600 Hz and 900 Hz are the second and third harmonics seen in Figure E-2. These harmonics have enough amplitude to produce significant noise. This noise comes not only from the pump itself, but from attached structures which are often more efficient at radiating the noise transmitted from the pump.

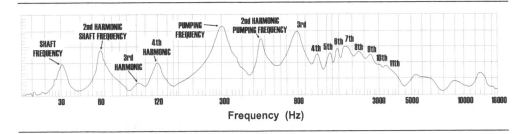

Figure E-2   Structureborne or fluidborne spectrum identifying shaft and pumping frequency and harmonics

Vibration Noise Control

Vibration control is used to prevent pulsation energy from the pump from being transmitted to machine structures. Most pump and drive motor assemblies are attached through a flexible coupling and mounted on a common base to maintain alignment. The common base is resiliently mounted to the support structure, as seen in Figure E-3.

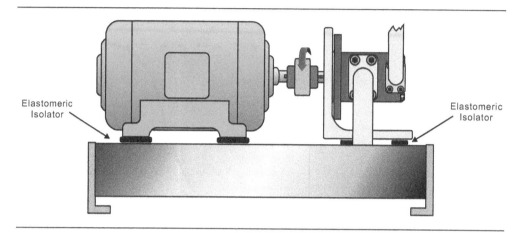

Figure E-3   Pump and motor on subplate, isolated from stiff foundation

An isolator should be selected that has a natural frequency approximately 1/2 or less of the pump's rotational frequency. For example, an isolator with a natural frequency of 10 Hz or less would be appropriate for a pump with a rotational or forcing frequency of 20 Hz at 1,200 RPM, and would work even better for a pump with a frequency of 30 Hz at 1,800 RPM. The higher the ratio between the forcing frequency and the natural frequency of the isolator system, the greater the amount of isolation (see Figure E-4). A typical commercial isolator (which costs about $15 in moderate quantities) can reduce transmitted vibration energy by 10 dB at 1,200 RPM and 15 dB at 1,800 RPM (Figure E-5).

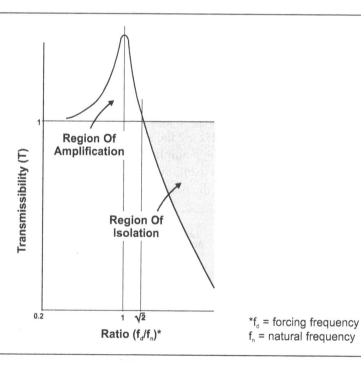

Figure E-4   Typical transmissibility curve for an isolated system

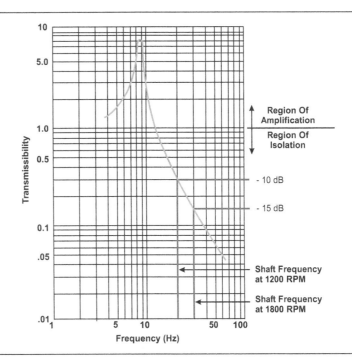

Figure E-5   Transmitted vibration energy reduction using typical commercial isolator

Reservoir Foot on Isolator

Isolators are classified by their load carrying capacity and related natural frequency. When pump, motor and subplate assembly weights are known, the amount of evenly distributed weight on each of the isolators can be calculated. Isolators should be selected that will not be loaded above 60 percent to 70 percent of their capacity. This will allow a sufficient safety margin in the event of shock loading.

The same type of isolators can also be used on power units with overhead reservoirs. Eight isolators can be installed either under the reservoir feet (Figure E-6), or under the upright leg structures supporting the reservoir. The isolators shown would be very effective because the ratio of forcing frequency to natural frequency is very high. For example, a nine-piston pump operating at 1,200 RPM would have a pumping frequency of 9 x 20 rev/sec or 180 Hz. If a 10 Hz isolator system were used, there would be a very low level of vibration transmission, because the ratio between the two frequencies would be 18:1.

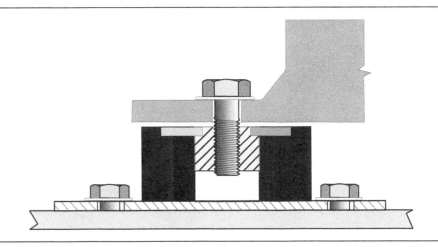

Figure E-6   Reservoir foot on isolator

The chart below lists load ratings of typical isolators with carrying capacities of 60 to 4,400 lbs per isolator.

Load Series	Isolator Number	Max. Static Load per Isolator (lbs)
Light	L1 L2 L3 L4 L5	60 100 130 200 260
Medium	M1 M2 M3 M4	300 450 550 700
Heavy	H1 H2 H3	700 1000 1500
Extra Heavy	EH1 EH2 EH3 EH4	1500 2000 3000 4400

Table E-1   Load ratings of typical isolators

The Table below provides two examples of proper isolator selection:

Pump, motor, and subplate weight Load on each of 6 isolators Maximum static load when loaded to 60 to 70% of capacity **Selection: #L4**	= 800 lbs = 133 lbs = 190 to 222 lbs
Reservoir weight Attached accessories weight 100 gallons oil weight (7 lbs/gal.) TOTAL Load on each of 4 isolators Maximum static load when loaded to 60 to 70% of capacity **Selection: #M3**	= 550 lbs = 150 lbs = 700 lbs = 1,400 lbs = 350 lbs = 500 to 583 lbs

Table E-2   Proper isolator selection

Isolation with Hose

Rubber hose must be used to maintain the vibration isolation afforded when the pump and motor assembly are mounted on isolators. The isolation capabilities of hose will reduce the amount of vibration energy entering the system. Unfortunately, improper use of hose is probably the main cause of noise in many systems.

Although structureborne noise can be reduced by using long lengths of hose, the pressure pulsations from the pump will cause the hose to undergo cyclic radial expansion. One of the drawbacks of hose is that it acts as an efficient radiator in the frequency range where most of the energy is generated: the first few harmonics. Because of these two factors, long lines of hose are less effective for noise reduction than the use of hose at either end of a solid line (Figure E-7).

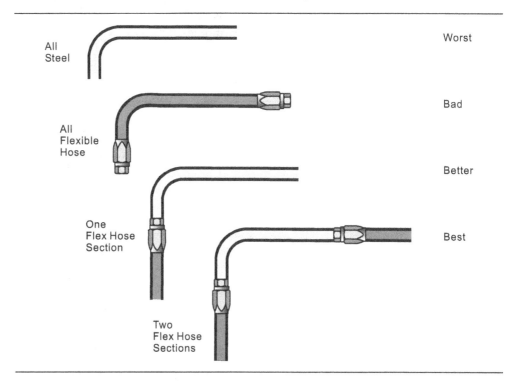

Figure E-7   Long hydraulic line configurations

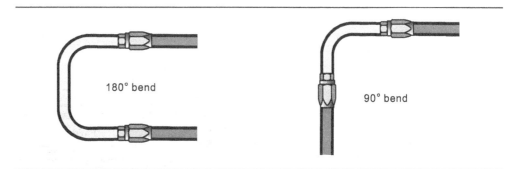

Figure E-8   Preferred short hydraulic line configurations

Two other shortcomings of hose are that its length changes with pressure, and that when it's bent through a radius it acts like a Bourdon tube, trying to straighten out with increasing pressure. Both produce forces that act on connecting structures. The best way to maintain noise control while making bends with hose is to use a solid elbow with a hose section on each end. This eliminates problems caused by the Bourdon tube effect. Any change in the length of one hose is accommodated by bending in the other hose. Figure E-8 illustrates the preferred configurations for 90 degree and 180 degree bends.

Fluidborne Noise Control

Fluidborne noise control begins with a pump's internal design. The ports should be configured so that the lowest practical pressure pulsations are generated. Additional external controls can be added to prevent as much pulsation energy as possible from being communicated to the system. This is usually done by adding expansion volume at the outlet of the pump. These acoustic filters, as they are called, can take many forms. The two most common are gas charged side branch accumulators and flow-through type pulsation filters. Each has its advantages and disadvantages. The side branch type is cheaper, but limited to attenuating pulsations in only a narrow range of frequencies. As a result, it isn't totally effective throughout the first four pump harmonics (where most of the pulsation energy is generated). The flow-through device, although generally larger and more expensive, has a distinct performance advantage: pulsations throughout the spectrum are reduced, including those at the most significant harmonics.

The filters (shown in Figure E-9) have optimum effectiveness when gas charged to 1/3 the maximum operating pressure of the hydraulic system.

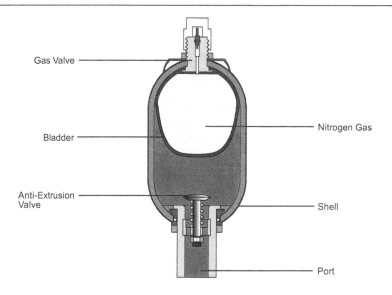

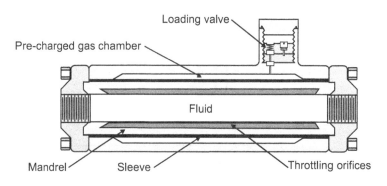

Pass-through gas charged filter

Figure E-9   Acoustic filters

Application of Techniques

Experimental evaluations were made on a typical automotive application: a power unit with a 150 gallon overhead reservoir supplying oil to a piston pump. The pump delivered 40 GPM at 1,200 RPM at a pressure of 750 psi. The noise level, as received, was 88 dB(A). (Standard accepted noise measurement procedures are explained in the subsection entitled System Noise Evaluation.) Four different noise reduction techniques were applied to the system, starting with those that would have the greatest effect on noise levels. The results are shown in Table E-3.

Item	Description	Resulting Noise Level	Change In Noise Level
1	Changed radiused pressure hose to two pieces, separated by right angle fitting.	83 dB(A)	-5 dB(A)
2	Item 1, plus structure isolators under reservoir and upright supports (8 additional isolators).	79 dB(A)	-4 dB(A)
3	Items 1 and 2, plus valve plate designed for 1,000 psi rather than 3600 psi. (Pulsations reduced from 200 psi to 140 psi.)	76 dB(A)	-3 dB(A)
4	Items 1, 2, and 3, plus flow-through pulsation filter. (Pulsations reduced from 140 psi to 35 psi.)	74 dB(A)	-2 dB(A)

Table E-3   Noise reduction techniques

It's important to note that if the changes outlined above had been made in some other sequence, the amount of noise reduction at each step would have been different from that shown — particularly if items 3 and 4 had been evaluated before items 1 and 2. The final noise level of 74 dB(A) would be the same, but the first item tried wouldn't have yielded such a significant reduction. In the example shown, the areas of highest noise radiation were addressed first. This is essential because no appreciable noise reduction can be achieved unless the most significant noise source is identified and its level reduced first.

Noise Terminology

Noise Terms and Equations

Sound at a particular point in air is defined as the rapid variation in air pressure around a steady state value. Sound pressure is measured in the same units as atmospheric pressure. Since it's an alternating quantity, the term "sound pressure" is usually referred to by its root mean square (rms) value. At a frequency of 1,000 Hz, a sound with an rms pressure of 2×10^{-4} microbars (mbar), or about 2×10^{-10} atmospheres, is just below the hearing threshold of someone with good ears. Expressed in more familiar terms, that level of sound pressure would be 2.9×10^{-9} psi. The fact that slightly greater pressures become audible shows the amazing sensitivity of the human ear. It can detect variations in atmospheric pressure as small as a few parts in 20,000,000,000.

In addition to this sensitivity, the human ear has an enormous dynamic range. Not only can it detect sounds as small as 2×10^{-4} mbar, it can accommodate sound pressures as high as 2,000 mbar without being overloaded, i.e. causing pain. That's a dynamic range ratio from threshold to pain of 10,000,000:1 (Figure E-10). Because this range is so large, it's more convenient to express ratios in powers of 10 (hence the use of the log scale). Sound pressure above the reference value of 2×10^{-4} mbar is referred to as sound pressure level (SPL) and expressed in decibels (dB).

Formula E-1

$$SPL = 20 \log \frac{P}{P_0}$$

or

$$SPL = 10 \log \left(\frac{P}{P_0}\right)^2$$

Where:

SPL = Sound pressure level (dB)

P = Sound pressure (bar)

P_0 = Reference pressure (0.0002 ubar)

From this equation, a pressure ratio of 10,000,000 (10^7) would result in the following noise level:

$$
\begin{aligned}
SPL &= 20 \log 10^7 \\
&= 7\,(20) \log 10 \\
&= 7\,(20)\,(1) \\
&= 140 \text{ dB (i.e., painful)}
\end{aligned}
$$

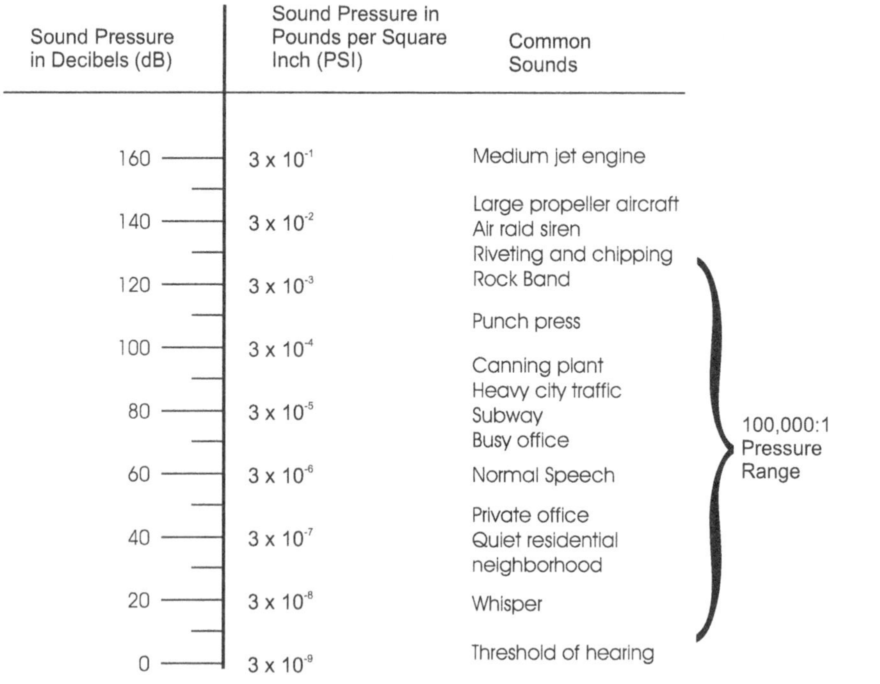

Sound Pressure in Decibels (dB)	Sound Pressure in Pounds per Square Inch (PSI)	Common Sounds
160	3×10^{-1}	Medium jet engine
140	3×10^{-2}	Large propeller aircraft Air raid siren Riveting and chipping
120	3×10^{-3}	Rock Band
		Punch press
100	3×10^{-4}	
		Canning plant Heavy city traffic
80	3×10^{-5}	Subway Busy office
60	3×10^{-6}	Normal Speech
		Private office
40	3×10^{-7}	Quiet residential neighborhood
20	3×10^{-8}	Whisper
0	3×10^{-9}	Threshold of hearing

100,000:1 Pressure Range

Figure E-10   Dynamic range of the human ear

Pressure ratios can also be calculated based on the changes in sound pressure levels (DSPL). For example, what is the pressure ratio (Rp) if the noise level changes by 3 dB?

Formula E-2

$$Rp = 10^{\Delta SPL/20}$$

Where:

Rp = pressure ratio

$$= 10^{3/20}$$

$$= 1.41$$

There are two important conclusions to note here: If the noise level increases from 82 to 85 dB, there's actually a <u>41 percent increase</u> in noise; if the noise level decreases from 85 to 82 dB, there's a <u>29 percent decrease</u> in noise (1/1.41 or 71 percent of the original level).

Table E-4 lists the pressure ratios for changes in SPL from +10 to -10 dB with the previous example in bold:

Change in SPL	Press. Ratio	Change in SPL	Press. Ratio
1	1.12	-1	.89
2	1.26	-2	.79
3	**1.41**	**-3**	**.71**
4	1.59	-4	.63
5	1.78	-5	.56
6	2	-6	.5
7	2.24	-7	.45
8	2.51	-8	.40
9	2.82	-9	.35
10	3.16	-10	.32

Table E-4   Pressure ratios

(A chart of typical noise levels is shown in Figure E-10.)

Human Response to Noise — The "A" Scale

A microphone measures actual sound pressures emitted from a noise source, but the human ear doesn't treat equal levels with equal tolerance over the audible frequency range of up to 12,000 Hz. The ear is more sensitive to noise above 1,000 Hz. This sensitivity is simulated by using the "A" scale filtering system in the signal processing of measured noise.

This internationally standardized system gauges the ear's response to noise through the use of a passive frequency related filter placed between the microphone and output (Figure E-11). The resulting energy, when summed in the respective weighted frequency bands, is then expressed in "A" scale, "A" weighted, or dB(A) levels.

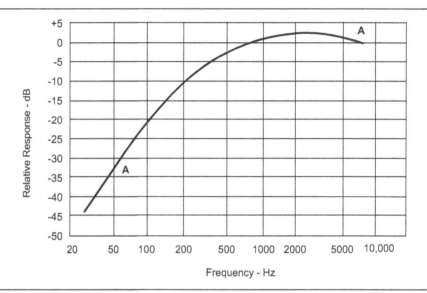

Figure E-11   Response characteristics of standard A filter

Sound Power

Sound pressure levels, in dB(A), are one measure of the noise of a source, but sound can also be expressed in terms of sound power level (PWL), also in dB(A). Sound power is the actual acoustic radiation (though not measurable), expressed in watts. This sound power remains constant, whereas sound *pressure* decays as the distance from the source increases. A good analogy would be light bulbs, which are classified in terms of watts (power) — not illumination level, which falls off with increasing distance.

Sound power levels can be calculated with the following formula:

Formula E-3

$$PWL = 10 \log \frac{W}{W_o}$$

Where:

PWL = sound power level in dB or dB(A)

W = acoustic radiation of source in watts

W_o = reference radiation in watts (10^{-12})

As in the expression of pressure levels, the power level is a logarithmic expression of ratio. Applying the same 3 dB change in power level as was previously calculated for pressure level results in:

Formula E-4

$$R_W = 10^{\Delta PWL/10}$$

Where:

R_W = power ratio

$= 10^{3/10}$

$= 2.0$

In this example, if the power level increases from 82 to 85 dB, the power increases by a factor of 2.0; if the power level decreases from 85 to 82 dB, there's a 50 percent decrease in power (1/2 or 50 percent of the original level).

Table E-5 lists the power ratios for changes in PWL from +10 to -10 dB with the above example in bold:

Change in PWL	Power Ratio	Change in PWL	Power Ratio
1	1.26	-1	.79
2	1.59	-2	.63
3	**2**	**-3**	**.5**
4	2.51	-4	.40
5	3.16	-5	.32
6	4	-6	25
7	5	-7	.2
8	6.31	-8	.16
9	7.94	-9	.13
10	10	-10	.1

Table E-5   Power ratios

Relationship Between Sound Pressure and Sound Power

The correlation between sound pressure and sound power can be seen by comparing the two ratio tables shown above. For an equal change in decibel level the ratios are different. For example:

Change In Db	Pressure Ratio	Power Ratio
3	1.41	2.0

The relationship is such that *power is proportional to the pressure squared*.

Effect of Distance on Noise Levels

In an environment where noise is radiated from a source into a reflection-free space, called a free field, the sound pressure level will vary according to the following formula:

Formula E-5

$$\Delta \text{SPL} = 20 \log \frac{d_1}{d_2}$$

or

$$\Delta \text{SPL} = 10 \log \left(\frac{d_1}{d_2}\right)^2$$

Where:

d_1 = initial distance from sound source
     (noise standards specify either 3 feet or 1 meter)

d_2 = distance of observer (greater than d_1)

This forms the basis for the *inverse square law*. If the distance of observer is doubled, the noise level is decreased by 6 dB.

For example:

d_1 = 3 feet

d_2 = 6 feet

then

$\Delta SPL = 20 \log .5$

$= -6 \text{ dB}$

or

$\Delta SPL = 10 \log (.5)^2$

$= -6 \text{ dB}$

Noise Addition

Noises can only be added or subtracted on the basis of acoustic **power** — *not pressure*. Noise sources of <u>equal</u> sound pressure levels are combined as follows:

Formula E-6

$SPL_2 = SPL_1 + 10 \log X$

Where:

SPL_2 = noise level of all sources

SPL_1 = noise level of 1 source

X = number of sources

For example:

SPL_1 = 80

X = 3 sources

$SPL_2 = 80 + 10 \log 3$

$= 80 + 4.8$

$= 84.8 \text{ dB}$

A chart showing this relationship appears in Figure E-12.

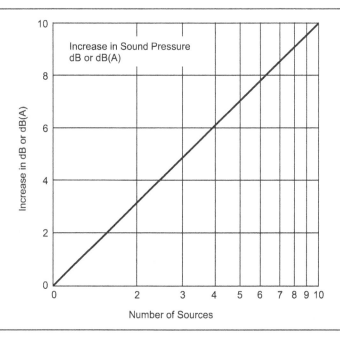

Figure E-12   Addition of equal sounds

Unequal sound pressure levels can also be added. (See Figure E-13.) The difference in the pressure levels of two sounds is used to determine how much their combined level will exceed the higher of the two. To add a third level, use the same process to combine it with the total from the first two levels.

The following example shows the two steps needed to find the total noise from sources of 70, 74 and 77 dB:

A) $74 — 70 = 4$ dB (X Axis) dB to add to larger $= 1.5$ (Y Axis)

    TOTAL $= 75.5$ dB

B) $77 — 75.5 = 1.5$ dB (X Axis) dB to add to larger $= 2.3$ (Y Axis)

    TOTAL $= 77 + 2.3$

    $= 79.3$ dB

The total can also be calculated from the equation:

$$SPL = 10 \log \Sigma \, 10^{SPL/10}$$
$$= 10 \log (10^{7.4} + 10^{7.0} + 10^{7.7})$$
$$= 79.3 \text{ dB}$$

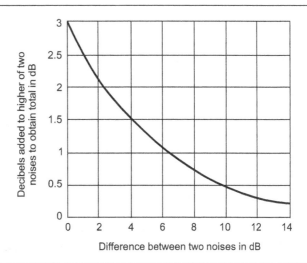

Figure E-13   Addition of unequal sounds

Noise Measurement

Component Evaluation and Rating

To assist machine tool builders in their selection of components on the basis of noise, the National Fluid Power Association (NFPA) developed a standard that assures uniformity in the measurement and reporting of sound levels. This standard, T3.9.12, contains guidelines for obtaining standardized sound ratings. It is concerned only with the radiated noise of components, primarily pumps.

The rating is usually expressed in dB(A) at a distance three feet in a free field above a reflecting plane (semi anechoic). This is a computed figure derived from a mathematical model. This model assumes that all the sound power from a pump is radiated from a single point located in the center of a hypothetical test hemisphere (Figure E-14). The standard allows for masking all parts of the circuit that might contribute to noise. This includes wrapping hydraulic lines and enclosing any load valves.

All radiated noise must be attributable to the pump, with no corrections for background.

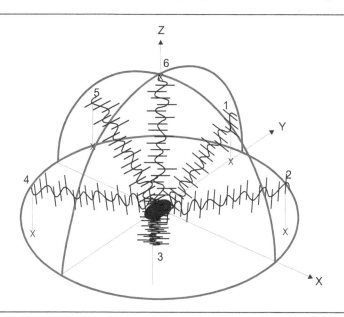

Figure E-14   Microphone positions for measuring pump noise

Microphones are positioned on spatial coordinates, each of which is located at the centroid of equal areas of the hemisphere surface. The rule of thumb is to use one microphone for each square meter of area. With the area of the hemisphere at $2\pi r^2$, and r equal to approximately 1 meter, six microphones are sufficient.

Power is defined as follows:

Formula E-7

$$F = P \times A$$

Where:

F = power
P = sound pressure
A = area acted on by P $(2\pi r^2)$

In terms of decibels:

Formula E-8

$$PWL = \overline{SPL} + 10 \log 2\pi r^2$$

Where:

PWL = sound power level
$\overline{SPL}$ = average sound pressure level of 6 microphones
r = radius in meters (3 feet = 0.914 meters)

Therefore:

$$
\begin{aligned}
PWL &= \overline{SPL} + 10 \log 2\pi + 20 \log 0.914 \\
&= \overline{SPL} + 8 - .8 \\
&= \overline{SPL} + 7.2 \text{ (for 3 feet)}
\end{aligned}
$$

or

$$PWL = \overline{SPL} + 8.0 \text{ (for 1 meter)}$$

System Noise Evaluation

The procedure for measuring system noise is different from the one used for components. Power unit systems are normally located in areas where background acoustics cannot be controlled. Guidelines for measurement in such environments are included in the National Machine Tool Builders Association's (NMTBA) "Noise Measurement Techniques" booklet.

Microphones are positioned *1 meter from the perimeter of the machine and 1.5 meters above floor level*, as shown in Figure E-15. It's extremely important that these distances be measured accurately. This insures uniformity of measurement and comparison, and compliance to customer noise level specifications. A 4-inch position error at a nominal 1 meter distance can result in a 1 dB error in measurement accuracy.

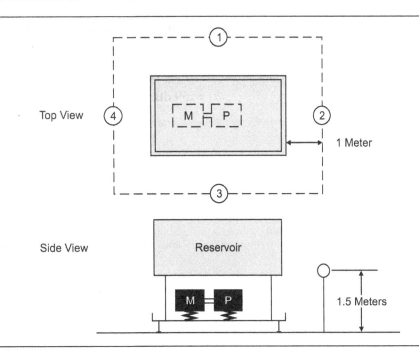

Figure E-15 Microphone positions for measuring system noise

Correction for Background Noise

At the very least, measurements should be taken on all four sides of the machine. It may also be necessary to measure at other locations around the envelope if highly directional noise levels are evident in other spots. Documentation of conditions is also needed to create some reference for comparison to other installations, acoustic environments or pump types. The following conditions should be recorded:

- motor/pump speed
- pump type
- operating pressure
- pump delivery
- fluid type and temperature
- load valve location (if used)

Accurate system noise measurement may involve correcting for the noise of the surrounding area. When ambient sound levels are within 10 dB(A) of the levels when the machine is operating, correction factors may be applied. This is done in accordance with Table E-6, derived from the NMTBA booklet.

Increase in Sound Level Due to Machine Operation [dB(A) Above Ambient]	Correction Factor to be Subtracted from Measured Sound Level [dB(A)]
3 or less	3
3 to 6	2
6 to 9	1
10 or more	0

Table E-6 Background correction factors

One advantage of this chart is that it allows the use of whole numbers for dB(A). It's actually a "rounding off" of the curve shown in Figure E-16 for the subtraction of sound levels. The example shown in the figure can also be expressed as:

$$\text{machine noise} = 10 \log [10^{6.0} - 10^{5.3} \text{ dB}]$$
$$= 59 \text{ dB}$$

Documentation of noise measurements made using four microphone positions might look like that shown in Table E-7.

Noise level should be expressed as the maximum level measured (in this example, 78 dB in position 3) or possibly as the average of the four levels.

Measuring Position	1	2	3	4 dB(A)
Total noise	76	73	79	75
Background noise	70	70	70	65
Background correction	-2	-3	-1	0
Machine noise	74	70	78	7

Table E-7   Noise measurement documentation

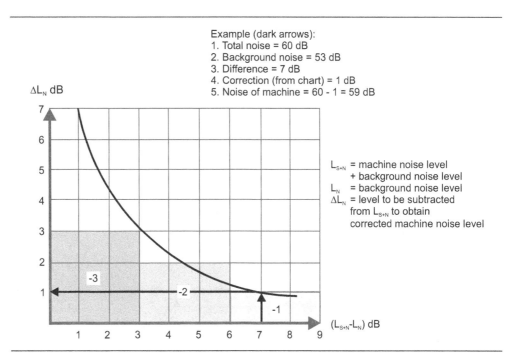

Example (dark arrows):
1. Total noise = 60 dB
2. Background noise = 53 dB
3. Difference = 7 dB
4. Correction (from chart) = 1 dB
5. Noise of machine = 60 - 1 = 59 dB

ΔL_N dB

L_{S+N} = machine noise level + background noise level
L_N = background noise level
ΔL_N = level to be subtracted from L_{S+N} to obtain corrected machine noise level

$(L_{S+N}-L_N)$ dB

Figure E-16   Subtracting sound levels

. . . . Index

W

Y

Z

Numerics

Y0-CRC-174

RECREATIONAL
THERAPY
An Introduction **FOURTH EDITION**

David R. Austin

Michael E. Crawford

Bryan P. McCormick

Marieke Van Puymbroeck

SAGAMORE
PUBLISHING

Publishers: Joseph J. Bannon and Peter L. Bannon
Director of Sales and Marketing: William A. Anderson
Sales Manager: Misti Gilles
Director of Development and Production: Susan M. Davis
Production Coordinator: Amy S. Dagit
Graphic Designer: Julie Schechter

ISBN print edition: 978-1-57167-738-9
ISBN e-book: 978-1-57167-739-6
Library of Congress Control Number: 2014950426

SAGAMORE
PUBLISHING

1807 N. Federal Dr.
Urbana, IL 61801
www.sagamorepublishing.com

CONTENTS

SECTION 3: PROFESSIONAL PRACTICE CONCERNS 279

DEDICATION

To our students, the future of recreational therapy.

The preface to the third edition of this book noted that a revolution has occurred in the depth and breadth of the literature of our ever-evolving and maturing profession, giving testimony to a growing body of knowledge. We believe this fourth edition will play a major role in the continuing advancement in the body of knowledge of recreational therapy.

Our goal in preparing this fourth edition was to provide a book that would clearly define the essence of recreational therapy as a health care profession. Thus, this book is focused on the purposeful use of recreation and leisure as interventions to enhance the health and well-being of clients whom recreational therapists serve. To emphasize this goal, the title used for this edition is *Recreational Therapy: An Introduction*.

To accomplish our goal, we called upon leading authors to join us in writing chapters for this edition. Each author brings his or her expertise to providing the most current information in his or her area of specialization. Readers also may notice that two new editors have agreed to collaborate with the editors of the three prior editions of the book and to author chapters in their areas of expertise. Thus, this new edition benefits from having the best efforts of a team of editors and authors, each of whom brings the most current knowledge available in his or her area of specialization.

Those reading this edition of *Recreational Therapy: An Introduction* will find a continuation of the user-friendly approach employed in prior editions. Chapters begin with a list of learning objectives and end with a series of reading comprehension questions and a complete list of references. This edition also includes the same format being followed in every chapter devoted to a specific client population. This format includes a feature that has been appreciated in prior editions: a case study to illustrate the concepts in each chapter. A unique aspect of this edition is the a chapter on providing recreational therapy for members of the military services as one of the specific client populations.

Instructors using the fourth edition of *Recreational Therapy: An Introduction* as a textbook will have access to an instructor's guide that contains learning activities and examination questions. PowerPoint® slides for every chapter that may be used in classroom instruction are also available to the instructor.

A number of individuals have contributed in many ways to this book. Particular thanks are extended to Joe Bannon and Peter Bannon of Sagamore Publishing, who believed in the unique contribution that this book could make to the practice of recreational therapy. We would also like to express our appreciation to Amy Dagit of Sagamore Publishing for her supreme editorial assistance. Additionally, we wish to acknowledge and thank our coauthors and colleagues who have joined us by providing chapters in their areas of specialization. Their contributions make this fourth edition a truly unique work.

Finally, we would like to express thanks to the scores of individuals who appreciated the format and content of prior editions of the book and who have encouraged us to prepare this fourth edition. Hopefully, this new edition will live up to their expectations and will continue to further the practice of recreational therapy.

David R. Austin, PhD, FDRT, FALS
Michael R. Crawford, ReD, CTRS
Bryan P. McCormick, PhD, CTRS, FDRT, FALS
Marieke Van Puymbroeck, PhD, CTRS, FDRT

David R. Austin, PhD, FDRT, FALS, professor emeritus of recreational therapy, Department of Recreation, Park, and Tourism Studies, Indiana University, Bloomington.

Jessie Bennett, PhD, CTRS/L, clinical assistant professor of therapeutic recreation, Department of Recreation Management and Policy, University of New Hampshire, Durham.

Michael E. Crawford, ReD, CTRS, associate professor in the Department of Pediatric Medicine at the University of Nebraska Medical Center and director of recreational therapy at the Munroe-Meyer Institute at the University of Nebraska Medical Center in Omaha.

Brandi M. Crowe, PhD, CTRS, assistant professor of recreation therapy, School of Health and Applied Human Sciences, University of North Carolina - Wilmington.

Shay Dawson, MA, CTRS, director of Bradford Woods, Department of Recreation, Park, and Tourism Studies in the School of Public Health, Indiana University, Bloomington.

Cara Gray, MS, CTRS, inclusion supervisor, Carmel Clay Parks & Recreation with Carmel Clay Schools, Carmel, Indiana.

Brent Hawkins, PhD, CTRS, assistant professor of recreational therapy, Department of Parks, Recreation, and Tourism Management, Clemson University, South Carolina.

Mark R. James, MS, practitioner with experience in serving clients who have seizure disorders and clients who have psychiatric disorders.

Robin Kunstler, ReD, CTRS, professor in the Department of Health Sciences and director of the recreation education and therapeutic recreation programs at Lehman College in New York City.

Bryan P. McCormick, PhD, CTRS, FDRT, FALS, professor of recreational therapy and chair of the Department of Recreation, Park, and Tourism Studies, Indiana University, Bloomington.

Sandy Negley, PhD, CTRS, instructor and coordinator of therapeutic recreation, Department of Parks, Recreation, and Tourism, University of Utah, Salt Lake City.

Jennifer Piatt, PhD, CTRS, assistant professor of recreational therapy, Department of Recreation, Park, and Tourism Studies, Indiana University, Bloomington.

Nancy Richeson, PhD, CTRS, FDRT, associate professor of therapeutic recreation, University of Wisconsin–La Crosse, and professor emeritus, University of Southern Maine.

Jasmine Townsend, PhD, CTRS, assistant professor of recreational therapy, Department of Parks, Recreation, and Tourism Management, Clemson University, South Carolina.

Marieke Van Puymbroeck, PhD, CTRS, FDRT, associate professor of recreational therapy and recreational therapy coordinator, Department of Parks, Recreation, and Tourism Management, Clemson University, South Carolina.

SECTION 1
THEORETICAL OVERVIEW

1 INTRODUCTION AND OVERVIEW

DAVID R. AUSTIN

OBJECTIVES

- Conceptualize recreational therapy.
- Understand recreation and leisure as they relate to recreational therapy.
- Describe the concept of health.
- Describe the humanistic perspective.
- Describe the perspective of positive psychology.
- Understand the relationship of recreational therapy to a high level of wellness.
- Understand the relationship of recreational therapy to the stabilizing and actualizing tendencies.
- Reduce recreational therapy to a series of tenets.
- Identify kindred professions.
- Assess yourself in terms of competencies needed in recreational therapy.
- Know the plan for this book.

Richter and Kaschalk (1996) wrote that within the field of therapeutic recreation a "confusion over its role and over its very essence" exists (p. 86). The authors' criticism of therapeutic recreation professionals is that they have not clearly identified what they do and the purpose they serve. This failure has plagued the field for some time. For instance, Shank and Kinney (1987) wrote that therapeutic recreation has maintained "one consistent theme: the uneasy fit between recreation as a contributor to the normalization and life quality of persons with disabilities and recreation as a means to improve individuals psychological and physiological functioning" (p. 65). Sylvester (2009) suggested that therapeutic recreation has been "caught between two traditions that have resisted assimilation into a single practice" (p. 19). Furthermore, Sylvester wrote "what appears to be a single practice may actually be two, each practice having its own tradition" (p. 18). He went on to state that *leisure facilitation practice* (i.e., the facilitation of leisure for persons with disabilities) and *recreational therapy practice* (i.e., the use of recreation to bring about therapeutic outcomes) are "fundamentally different practices" (p. 18).

The editors of this text agree with Sylvester's conclusion that the facilitation of leisure for persons with disabilities and recreational therapy (RT) are separate and distinct entities. This book deals with RT.

RECREATIONAL THERAPY: A HEALTH CARE PROFESSION

A number of health care professions exist. RT is one of these. Table 1.1 is a list of several health-related professions, along with their areas of expertise. Each profession has a particular body of knowledge upon which to draw in providing services. This body of knowledge makes the profession unique. In fact, experts (e.g., Schlein & Kommers, 1972; Wilensky, 1964) have long agreed that to claim the title of "profession," an occupational group must have a defined area of expertise. What is the area of expertise of RT? What makes RT unique? The editors of this text believe that RT involves knowledge of recreation and leisure and their applications as these phenomena relate to achieving optimal health and the highest possible quality of life.

Table 1.1
Health-Related Professions

Profession	Expertise
Nurse	Caring for persons
Occupational therapist	Purposeful occupations
Physician	Illness, disease
Psychologist	Human behavior
Social worker	Support systems
Recreational therapy	Purposeful recreation/leisure

RECREATION AND LEISURE AS A BASIS FOR PROFESSIONAL PRACTICE

Inevitably, textbook authors have emphasized recreation and leisure in attempting to define the still relatively new and emerging profession of RT. One of the earliest conceptualizations of RT contained a definition of recreation within it. Davis (1936) wrote,

> Recreational therapy may be defined as any free, voluntary and expressive activity; motor, sensory or mental, vitalized by the expressive play spirit, sustained by deep-rooted pleasurable attitudes and evoked by wholesome emotional release. (p. xi)

More contemporary textbook authors have continued the tradition of including recreation and leisure within their definitions of RT. Two examples follow:

> [Recreational therapy is] the systemic and planned uses of recreation and other activity interventions and a helping relationship in an environment of support with the intent of effecting change in a client's attitudes, beliefs, behaviors, and skills necessary for psychosocial adaptation, health, and well-being. (Shank & Coyle, 2002, p. 54)

Recreational therapy employs purposeful, goal-directed interventions that involve clients in activities that have the potential to produce recreational and leisure experiences that lead them to experiencing what are the optimal levels of health for them as individuals. (Austin, 2013, p. 154)

These definitions of RT both refer to recreation/leisure activities and experiences. Other common themes found in the definitions are the planned and purposeful nature of using recreation/leisure as an intervention and the enhancement of the client's health and well-being as a result of the intervention. In short, these definitions point to the purposeful use of recreation/leisure activities and experiences as means of producing positive health benefits for recipients of RT services. RT practice, then, demands that recreational therapists have a high level of knowledge of recreation and leisure as phenomena, as well as expertise in using recreation/leisure activities to restore health and foster growth.

RECREATION AND LEISURE

Students in college and university departments of recreation, parks, tourism, and leisure studies are asked time and again to define the terms *recreation* and *leisure*. The purpose of the discussion within this textbook is not to cover old ground for those who have undergone the exercise of conceptualizing the meanings of recreation and leisure but rather to discuss these terms, as they form a basis for understanding RT.

Recreation

Voluntary action and activity have been associated with recreation, as have been positive emotions such as enjoyment, fun, and feelings of accomplishment. Recreation has also been perceived to be beneficial or constructive, meeting goals of the participant (Austin, 2011b; Neulinger, 1980; Shank & Coyle, 2002; Smith & Theberge, 1987). Additionally, recreation has been linked with being restorative, offering refreshment or re-creation for the participant (Kelly, 1996). In fact, the view of recreation having a healing function goes back to the writings of Aristotle, who wrote that persons restored their minds and bodies through recreation (Austin, 2011a). This ability to restore or refresh mind and body is perhaps the property that the average person most attaches to recreation.

If recreation is defined as being restorative or re-creative, using the term *therapeutic*, in combination with *recreation* (i.e., therapeutic recreation), seems to be redundant. If all recreation is restorative, is not then all recreation therapeutic? A better term to describe the employment of recreation as a purposeful intervention to promote health outcomes is *recreational therapy*. Today, the terms *recreational therapy* and *recreation therapy* are commonly used and interpret RT as a profession that employs recreation as a planned clinical intervention directed toward health outcomes leading to an improved quality of life.

Leisure

Although many views of leisure exist (Mannell & Kleiber, 1997), authors (e.g., Iso-Ahola, 1980; Neulinger, 1980; Smith & Theberge, 1987) commonly have referred to the factors of "perceived freedom" and "intrinsic motivation" as central defining properties of leisure. Perceived freedom typically is viewed as a person's ability to exercise choice, or self-determination, over his or her own behavior. An absence of external constraints exists. Intrinsic motivation is conceptualized as energizing behaviors that are internally (psychologically) rewarding. Intrinsically motivated behaviors are engaged in for their own sake rather than as a means to an extrinsic reward.

Connected to the phenomena of self-determination and intrinsic motivation found in leisure is the basic human tendency toward developing or fulfilling one's potential. Renowned psychologists Piaget and Rogers both postulated this propensity, which Rogers termed the *actualization tendency* (Deci & Ryan, 1985). The tendency for self-actualization is directed toward stimulation of the organism to promote change, growth, and maturation within the individual.

Intrinsic motivation is seen as the energy basis, or the energizer, of this tendency for growth and development according to Deci and Ryan (1985). Intrinsic motivation itself rests on the organism's innate need for competence and self-determination. These needs in turn motivate persons to seek and to conquer optimal challenges that stretch their abilities but are within their capacities. When persons are able to achieve success, they experience feelings of competence and autonomy, along with accompanying emotions of enjoyment and excitement (Deci & Ryan, 1985).

Leisure seems to be one of the best opportunities for persons to experience self-actualization because it offers opportunities for individuals to be successful in self-selected, pleasurable activities. The Greek philosopher Aristotle held "that leisure is the way to happiness and quality of life because it provides a means to self-fulfillment through intellectual, physical, and spiritual growth" (Austin, 2011a, p. 15).

Self-Determination and Intrinsic Motivation

The concepts of self-determination and intrinsic motivation, which are central to leisure, deserve further consideration. An idea deeply rooted in Western culture is that human beings strive for control over themselves and their environment. The degree of social adjustment is related to the discrepancy that exists between perceived and desired control (Austin, 2002; Grzelak, 1985; Pender, 1987, 1996).

Research (e.g., Langer & Rodin, 1976; Seligman & Maier, 1967; Voelkl, 1986) has found that feeling a lack of control over aversive life situations produces a sense of helplessness. This in turn leads to the development of apathy and withdrawal that, in extreme cases, ultimately may end in death owing to perceived uncontrollability over a stressful environment (Gatchel, 1980). Unfortunately, much of what transpires in modern health leads to feelings of helplessness. Pender (1996) exclaimed that too often interactions with health care professionals foster feelings of helplessness in clients because of condescending behaviors, paternalistic approaches, and the mystification of the health care process.

Fortunately, RT represents the antithesis of the controlling environment often imposed on the individual who has health problems. Rather than being repressive, RT provides opportunities for clients to escape the normal routines of the health care facility to engage in intrinsically rewarding activities that produce feelings of self-determination, competence, and enjoyment.

Recreation/Leisure and Recreational Therapy

Recreational therapists need to have a highly developed understanding of the dynamics of recreation and leisure as potentially powerful forces they apply to practice within their profession. An essential characteristic of recreational therapists is that they hold a strong belief in the positive outcomes that may be derived from recreation and leisure. A basic element in RT is that "recreational therapists prize the positive consequences to be gained through meaningful recreation and leisure experiences" (Austin, 2013, p. 226). Recreational therapists must understand recreation as voluntary activity that has restorative properties and leisure as a phenomenon that provides the individual with perceived control, the opportunity to meet intrinsically motivated needs, and a means to actualize potentials and achieve high-level wellness. In short, both recreation and leisure are means to achieve health enhancement. Recreation participation may be used to restore or maintain health, and leisure experiences may lead individuals toward achieving optimal health and well-being.

HEALTH

Because the ultimate end for RT is achieving as high a level of health as possible for each client, recreational therapists must comprehend fully what is meant by health. The term *health* and related terms are given extensive coverage in the following segment.

For many years, the phrase *absence of disease* was synonymous with health. If you felt "okay" and your doctor did not diagnose you as having medical symptoms, you were perceived to be "healthy." This traditional biomedical model of health dealt strictly with the absence of disease.

Over the years, other definitions of health have evolved. These definitions stipulate a difference between the absence of symptoms of illness or abnormalities and vigorous health. A broad multidimensional view of health is represented in what perhaps is the most cited definition of health; the World Health Organization (WHO, 1947) defined health as "a state of complete physical, mental, and social well-being, not merely the absence of disease or infirmity." The term *biopsychosocial health* has been adopted to encompass the WHO's perspective on health because the WHO definition includes biological, psychological, and social facets of health.

The WHO definition may be criticized as being abstract, vague, simplistic, and unsuitable for scientific interpretation. It does not list specific criteria by which a state of health may be recognized and does not acknowledge the phases of health that persons experience during their life spans (Pender, 1996). Furthermore, the term *complete* in the WHO definition may be questioned as it is unlikely that anyone truly enjoys total or complete "physical, mental, and social well-being"; thus, health under this definition may be considered to be unattainable.

The WHO definition, however, offers concepts essential to formulating a positive conceptualization of health (Austin, 2011a; Edelman & Mandle, 1998; Pender, 1996):

1. It recognizes the interrelated influences of biological aspects, psychological dynamics, and social relationships on health.

2. It displays a concern for the individual as a total system rather than as merely the sum of parts, thus indicating the necessity of taking a holistic view.

3. It places health in the context of internal and external environments.

4. It relates health to self-fulfillment, to creative living.

Health is a complex concept. The following definition of health seems to capture the elements discussed thus far. Jones (2000) wrote,

Health is a positive, balanced state of being characterized by the best available physical, psychological, emotional, social, spiritual, and intellectual levels of functioning at a given time, the absence of disease or the optimal management of chronic disease, and the control of both internal and external risk factors for both disease and negative health conditions. (p. 15)

Good health is a primary requisite to a high *quality of life.* The multifaceted phenomenon of quality of life includes physical, psychological, social, occupational, and leisure functioning, as well as a sense of well-being (Fallowfield, 1990; Jacoby, 1990). To address the total impact of a disease, disorder, or disability, health care personnel with concern for quality of life take a holistic approach that looks beyond primary symptoms. For example, although reduction in the frequency of seizures may be an initial goal in the treatment of a person with epilepsy, quality of life factors such as psychosocial functioning and client satisfaction will also be of concern (Baker, 1990).

At this point, the concept of health within RT will be examined. Often health-related terms such as *functioning, well-being*, and *quality of life* are found in definitions of RT, typically along with the term *health*. For instance, Shank and Coyle (2002) listed "psychosocial adaptation, health, and well-being" (p. 54) as outcomes of RT, and Kunstler and Stavola Daly (2010) listed improvements in "functioning, health and well-being, and quality of life" (p. 380) as outcomes of RT.

The health-related terms such as *functioning, adaptation, well-being*, and *quality of life* in such definitions seem to produce more confusion than clarity. From the information on health presented in this segment of the chapter, these terms may be understood as having application *under the term health* or *as resulting from health*.

These terms may be captured under the concept of health or have health as a basis. First, the term *functioning* will be examined. If RT professionals accept Jones' (2000) definition of health, they see that functioning is a sign of health. Recall that Jones' definition of health stated, "Health is a positive, balanced state of being characterized by the best available physical, psychological, emotional, social, spiritual, and intellectual levels of functioning..." (p. 15). Thus, the term *functioning* reflects health and may be subsumed under health. In short, good functioning indicates good health. Therefore, improved functioning does not need to be listed as a separate outcome of RT. Similarly, does not Jones' term *optimal management*, as an indication of health, incorporate the term *adaptation*? Thus, as with the term *functioning*, the term *adaptation* may be seen as a sign of health to be encompassed under the term *health*.

Now the term *quality of life* will be examined. If RT professionals accept the notions of Fallowfield (1990) and Jacoby (1990) that quality of life includes physical, psychological, social, occupational, and leisure functioning, along with a sense of well-being that results from health, health clearly forms the basis for quality of life, and in fact, good health is necessary for a high quality of life. Using the term *well-being*, in portraying quality of life, expresses a feeling of doing well, satisfaction, or contentment.

Thus, rather than a "laundry list" of terms such as *health, functioning, adaptation, well-being*, and *quality of life* in describing the outcomes of RT, a more succinct expression may be that RT assists clients to bring about health outcomes that permit them to enjoy a higher quality of life or that the ends recreational therapists seek for their clients relate to health and quality of life.

INTERNATIONAL CLASSIFICATION OF FUNCTIONING, DISABILITY, AND HEALTH

Just as the WHO helped persons to take a new view of health in general, it also developed the International Classification of Functioning, Disability, and Health (ICF) to create a new perspective for conceptualizing the health of persons with disabilities. The ICF represents a paradigm change from the traditional medical model to a biopsychosocial model that is focused on functioning, not disability. The ICF emphasizes the importance of functional health. The focus on functioning allows persons with impairments to be viewed as being "healthy" even though they may have a health condition (e.g., a chronic illness, disorder, or injury), as long as they are functioning well. The ICF then is a tool that provides language that is focused on functioning in society, no matter the reason for the individual's impairment (i.e., a problem in body function or structure).

Thus, the ICF emphasizes function rather than the etiology. Instead of having an emphasis the person's disability, the ICF system is focused on the individual's level of functioning as an indicator of health. From the ICF perspective, functioning is the result of the interplay of body functions (physiological or psychological) and body structures (i.e., anatomical parts such as organs or limbs), as well as activities (i.e., executing a task or action) and participation (i.e., involvement in a life situation). The ICF also accounts for environmental barriers and facilitators that impact the person's functioning and for personal factors.

Environmental factors and personal factors are termed *contextual factors* under the ICF. Environmental factors include not only architectural accessibility but also terrain, climate, legal and social structures, and social attitudes. Personal factors are internal and encompass age, gender, coping styles, behavioral patterns, profession, education, and social background, as well as other characteristics that may influence how an individual experiences a disability. Under the ICF, therefore, medical diagnoses are seen as not providing the information needed on which to base the delivery of health care services. Instead, interventions are designed to increase the functional capacity of the individual or bring about environmental modifications that will lead to enhancement in functioning. The question for health care providers then becomes, what interventions may bring about the maximization of functioning?

The WHO (2002) report *Towards a Common Language for Functioning, Disability and Health: ICF* explained interventions that increase functioning:

> Body level or impairment interventions are primarily medical or rehabilitative, and attempt to prevent or ameliorate limitations in person or societal level functioning by correcting or modifying intrinsic functions or structures of the body. Other rehabilitative treatment strategies and interventions are designed to increase capacity levels. Interventions that focus on the actual performance context of an individual may address either capacity-improvement or else seek environmental modification, either by eliminating environmental barriers or creating environmental facilitators for expanded performance of actions and tasks in daily living. (p. 8)

Thus, the ICF provides health professionals with a new way of conceptualizing health and disability. The ICF goes beyond the traditional medical model that viewed interventions only as dealing with the person's impairment. Thus, interventions may be aimed not solely on the individual but also on eliminating barriers to functioning and on developing facilitators to enhance functioning.

Because the ICF does not adhere to the traditional medical model, it fits well with concepts discussed within this chapter as hallmarks of RT, including taking a holistic approach, following a biopsychosocial model, conceptualizing an illness/wellness continuum, acknowledging the effect of the environment, focusing not solely on clients' impairments but also on their functioning, and employing interventions that build strengths and address difficulties (Austin, 2013; WHO, 2002). Furthermore, several RT scholars have described the ICF as being appropriate for incorporation into RT (e.g., Howard, Browning, & Lee, 2007; Porter & burlingame, 2006; Porter & Van Puymbroeck, 2007; Van Puymbroeck, Austin, & McCormick, 2010; Van Puymbroeck, Porter, & McCormick, 2009).

HUMANISTIC AND POSITIVE PSYCHOLOGY PERSPECTIVES

Beliefs and values that flow out of the psychological perspectives of humanistic psychology and positive psychology have and will influence the practice of RT. In the sections that follow, these two perspectives will be introduced.

The Humanistic Perspective

In the 1950s, humanistic psychology came into existence as a "third force" in opposition to Freud's psychodynamic approach and Watson and Skinner's behavioral approach (Austin, 2013). This humanistic perspective recognized the uniqueness of human beings to be self-directed, to make wise choices, and to develop themselves or realize their potentials (i.e., become self-actualized). Humanistic psychologists proclaimed "that striving and growing are essential to human life and health" (Lindberg, Hunter, & Kruszewski, 1983, p. 70).

In general, professionals who embrace the humanistic perspective

- take a holistic view of the person;
- hold that both children and adults are capable of change;
- endorse the concept that individuals are responsible for their own health and possess the capacity to make self-directed decisions regarding their own health;
- follow a developmental model rather than a medical model—the developmental model is focused on client strengths, not pathology;
- see persons as being in dynamic interaction with the environment, not just reacting to the external world;
- view persons who strive for personal satisfaction yet go beyond their own needs to understand and care about others as healthy;
- value a strength-based approach to health enhancement; and
- believe persons express a tendency toward self-actualization. (Austin, 1999, 2011b, 2013)

Halbert Dunn's conceptualization of health grew out of the influence of the humanistic perspective. Dunn (1961) coined the term high-level wellness, which he defined as "an integrated method of functioning which is oriented toward maximizing the potential of which the individual is capable, within the environment where he (or she) is functioning" (p. 4). Dunn's concept of health is centered on the wholeness of the individual and each person's actualizing tendency, which propels each person toward the fulfillment of his or her potential. Furthermore, Dunn's notion implies not only an absence of physical illness but also the presence of positive psychological and environmental wellness. Mental and social well-being join with the physical well-being of the total person in forming Dunn's concept of optimal health, or high-level wellness.

Holistic medicine, as proposed by physicians who have championed high-level wellness, treats the person rather than the disease. Holistic medicine concerns the "whole person" and permits individuals to assume self-responsibility for their own health (Austin, 1999). Ardell (1977) identified the ultimate aim of "well medicine" (in contrast to "traditional medicine" normally practiced by the medical community) to be that of moving individuals toward self-actualization. The sole concern of traditional medicine is illness, whereas well medicine deals with wellness and health promotion.

Extending Humanistic Psychology: The Perspective of Positive Psychology

Positive psychology is focused on the positive side of persons instead of the negative. Similar to humanistic psychology, positive psychology is focused on human strengths and optimal functioning rather than pathology. In fact, positive psychology may be perceived to be an extension or outgrowth of humanistic psychology (Austin, 2013; Austin, McCormick, & Van Puymbroeck, 2010). Joseph and Linley (2004) stipulated that humanistic psychology and positive psychology have more similarities than differences.

Positive psychology came on the scene at the beginning of the 21st century. Championed by Martin E. Seligman, positive psychology developed in response to the orientation of mainstream psychology toward disease and the medical model. As with humanistic psychology, positive psychology is focused on human strengths and optimal functioning rather than pathology (Austin, 2013; Austin, McCormick, & Van Puymbroeck, 2010). Biswas-Diener and Dean (2007) portrayed positive psychology as a "branch of psychology that focuses on what is going right, rather than what is going wrong with people" (p. x).

Briefly, positive psychology is the psychology of human strengths and optimal functioning. Duckworth, Steen, and Seligman (2005) defined positive psychology as "the study of conditions and processes that contribute to the flourishing or optimal functioning of people, groups, and institutions" (p. 629). Linley and Joseph (2004) took an applied approach to positive psychology, stating, "Applied positive psychology is the application of positive psychology research to the facilitation of optimal functioning across the full range of human functioning, from disorder and distress to health and fulfillment" (p. 4). These authors further stated, "Applied positive psychologists may work both to alleviate distress and to promote optimal functioning" (p. 6). Skerrett (2010) explained that "positive psychology is devoted to understanding what goes well in a life and examines how and why, and under what conditions humans flourish." She went on to state that positive psychology is "not a replacement to the more problem focused or deficit-based paradigms.... it is conceptualized as a complementary and important dimension to understand the full range of human experience" (p. 488). The essence of positive psychology is summarized in Table 1.2.

Table 1.2
Positive Psychology in a Nutshell

1. Positive psychology looks at what is right with people, is focused on when people are at their best, and attends to individual and group flourishing.
2. Positive psychology is not the focus of positive at the expense of the negative. Positive psychologists recognize negative emotions, failure, problems, and other unpleasantries as natural and important aspects of life.
3. Positive psychology is, first and foremost, a science. As such, it is principally concerned with evidence, measurement, and testing. That said, positive psychology is also an applied science, and there is a common understanding that research results will lead to the creation of real-world interventions that will improve aspects of individual and social life through evidence-based practice.
4. Interventions produced by positive psychologists are, by and large, positive interventions.

Note. From *Therapeutic Recreation Processes and Techniques* (7th ed.), by D. R. Austin, 2013, Urbana, IL: Sagamore, p. 31, as adapted from *Practicing Positive Psychology Coaching,* by R. Biswas-Diener, 2010, Hoboken, NJ: John Wiley & Sons, p. 5.

Both humanistic psychology and positive psychology likely will influence RT practice as indicated in the following statement:

> It is likely that, as positive psychology becomes better known, recreation therapists will embrace it because positive psychology tends to extend the ideas already accepted by recreation therapists through the influence of humanistic psychology. With the welcoming of positive psychology, recreation therapists will likely more strongly embrace health promotion. Health promotion will then join health protection (i.e., treatment and rehabilitation) to provide two primary thrusts for recreation therapy practice in the years ahead. (Austin, 2005–2006, p. 9)

RECREATIONAL THERAPY: ILLNESS AND WELLNESS

As has traditional medicine, RT has long dealt with problems brought about by illness and disability. Unlike traditional medicine, RT has not dealt exclusively with illness and disability. Instead, RT has historically promoted the facilitation of the fullest possible growth and development of clients. In one respect, RT has been much like traditional medicine in its concern for alleviating the effects of illnesses and disabilities. On the other hand, recreational therapists join physicians practicing well medicine, humanistic psychologists, and positive psychologists in their desire to bring about the growth of clients.

Austin (2011a) summed up this perspective in his book *Lessons Learned: An Open Letter to Recreational Therapy Students and Practitioners*:

We, in recreational therapy, can alleviate distress by helping our clients gain relief from their symptoms, but additionally we can go far beyond this, helping clients to develop and to use their strengths and potentials to deal with barriers to health and to facilitate optimal functioning. We cannot only help our clients to become well again, we can help them to become better than they were before they came to us. (p. 2)

Motivating Forces: The Stabilizing and Actualizing Tendencies

Therefore, recreational therapists help clients to strive for health protection (illness or disability aspects) and health promotion (wellness aspects). Major human motivational forces underlie these two aspects: the stabilizing tendency and the actualizing tendency.

The *stabilizing tendency* is directed toward maintaining the "steady state" of the organism. It is the motivational tendency moving persons to counter excess stress (i.e., distress) to maintain their levels of health. When faced with excessive stress, persons engage in adaptive behaviors to regain their sense of equilibrium. They attempt either to remove themselves from the stress or to minimize the effects of the stressor.

The stabilizing tendency is responsible for persons adapting to keep the level of stress in a manageable range to protect themselves from possible biophysical or psychosocial harm. Potentially harmful stressors may result from internal and external stimuli. Negative forms of tension may come either from within persons or from their surroundings. The stabilizing tendency is the motivational force behind health protection (Pender, 1987).

The *actualizing tendency* is the growth-enhancing force discussed earlier in the chapter, when considering self-determination, intrinsic motivation, the humanistic perspective, and high-level wellness. This actualizing tendency is the motivational force behind achieving optimal health.

IS ILLNESS OR DISABILITY EVER POSITIVE?

Health is a complex concept that encompasses coping adaptively, as well as growing and becoming. When persons are healthy, they can cope with life's stressors. Those who enjoy high-level wellness are free to develop themselves to the fullest. Barriers to actualization do not exist, so such persons are free to pursue personal growth and development. Health makes actualization possible.

 Because of the natural progression from health protection (illness and disability aspects) to health promotion (wellness aspects), Flynn (1980) suggested that an illness or disability may be positive. The occurrence of a health problem may serve as an occasion for clients to take control over their lives and to learn how to strive toward optimal health. An example would be an individual who has a health problem (e.g., cardiac or mental health problem) because of stress. Dealing with this problem forces the person to seek the help of a health care professional, such as a recreational therapist. As a result of treatment involving participation in physical activity, the client may not only overcome the original health concern but also learn to lead a lifestyle that promotes reduced tension and increased enjoyment. By learning how to deal with stress and participate in healthy activities that provide for growth and enjoyment (e.g., walking, yoga, and swimming), individuals not only are able to conquer the initial health problem but also rise to a new level of health that they may not have experienced had the presenting problem not happened.

PRESCRIPTIVE ACTIVITIES, RECREATION, AND LEISURE

Recreational therapists contribute to health by helping persons fulfill their needs for stability and actualization until they are able to assume responsibilities for themselves. This is accomplished through client participation in three interventions: prescriptive activities, recreation, and leisure.

Prescriptive Activity

When individuals first encounter illness or disability, they often become self-absorbed, withdraw from their usual life activities, and experience a loss of control over their lives (Flynn, 1980). To combat such feelings, the recreational therapist selects prescriptive activities to activate clients demoralized by health issues. The rationale for prescriptive activities is that clients must actively engage in life to overcome feelings of helplessness and depression and begin to establish control over the situation. They need to become energized so they are not passive victims of their circumstances but take action to restore their health. Within prescriptive activities, clients begin to experience feelings of fun and accomplishment. They begin to make improvements and to regain a sense of independent functioning and control so they may move past prescriptive activities and engage in recreation. In sum, prescriptive activities become a necessary prerequisite for clients demoralized by illness or disability to move on to voluntary participation in recreation activities that may lead to health restoration.

Austin (2011a) expressed the feelings persons may experience as they gain positive experiences from their prescriptive activities and begin to experience recreation:

> When individuals experience positive emotions, they begin to loosen up, to feel free or less encumbered. They open themselves up so they are more receptive to new thoughts and behaviors. They are far more prone to stretch themselves and to try new experiences that they might avoid if they were not feeling happy or being in a good mood. Think about yourself; are you more open to try new things if you are in a positive, optimistic frame of mind? Of course you are. So are clients. (p. 2)

Recreation

Recreation involves activity as one component, but it is more than activity. As previously discussed, recreation may produce restorative results and help persons to cope with chronic conditions or disabilities. Through recreation activities, clients reach health outcomes and regain their equilibrium. Recreation represents enjoyable activities the client selects in concert with the recreational therapist to meet goals and objectives of the intervention plan. Thus, during recreation, clients are exercising some measure of choice and control.

Leisure

Leisure may be seen as a means to self-actualization. Through leisure experiences, persons meet challenges. These leisure experiences feature self-determination, intrinsic motivation, and mastery and competence—experiences that lead individuals toward feelings of self-efficacy, empowerment, pleasure, and enjoyment (Austin, 2011b, 2013).

A unique virtue of recreation and leisure is that they are components of life free from constraint. In no other parts of their lives are persons allowed more self-determination. During recreation and leisure, individuals may "be themselves." They may "let their hair down." They are allowed to be human with all their imperfections and frailties. The caring, accepting attitude the recreational therapist assumes in creating a free and nonthreatening recreation/leisure environment allows for positive interpersonal relationships and for opportunities for accomplishment. The question has been asked, "in what better atmosphere than that achieved in recreation and leisure could growth be fostered and problems met?" (Austin, 1999, p. 144).

SCOPE OF RECREATIONAL THERAPY

RT may be perceived to be a means to restore oneself or regain stability or equilibrium following threat to health (health protection) and to develop oneself through leisure as a means to high-level wellness (health promotion). Thus, RT has the primary goals of (a) restoring health and assisting clients to cope with chronic conditions and disabilities and (b) helping clients to use their leisure in optimizing their potentials and striving for high-level wellness. RT provides for the stabilizing tendency by helping individuals to restore health or cope adaptively with chronic illnesses and disabilities and the actualizing tendency by enabling clients to use leisure as a means to personal growth.

Figure 1.1 illustrates the Health Protection/Health Promotion Model. This conceptual model for RT was recently reformulated to (a) include clients with chronic conditions and disabilities and (b) reflect theoretical perspectives from positive psychology (Austin, 2011b).

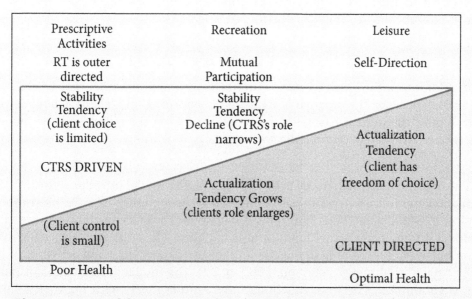

Figure 1.1. Health Protection/Health Promotion Model. TR continuum from *Therapeutic Recreation: An Introduction,* by D. R. Austin and M. E. Crawford, 1996, Needham Heights, MA: Allyn & Bacon. Copyright 1996 by Allyn & Bacon. Reprinted with permission.

In the diagram of the model, as clients move from health restoration toward the achievement of high-level wellness, or optimal health, they exercise greater and greater choice, or self-determination. At the same time, the role of the recreational therapist continually decreases. Clients ideally move to the point that they experience optimal health in a favorable environment and have total self-determination. In this state of optimal health, or high-level wellness, they are free to be self-directed and to pursue self-actualization.

Under the Health Protection/Health Promotion Model, clients may enter the continuum at any point that is appropriate for their needs. Along the continuum are three broad areas. The first area is where the stabilizing tendency is paramount. At the extreme, the client is experiencing poor health in an unfavorable environment, and the recreational therapist helps activate the client. The client's role is relatively passive in terms of selecting activities for participation, as the recreational therapist provides direction and structure for the intervention that involves prescriptive activities.

The next area along the continuum represents mutual participation on the parts of the client and recreational therapist as recreation interventions are selected. The actualizing tendency begins to emerge as the stabilizing tendency starts to decline.

In the third area, the actualization tendency enlarges as the client's health improves and he or she moves toward self-determination. The role of the recreational therapist is to assist the client, who ultimately assumes primary responsibility for his or her own health, to become skilled in and knowledgeable about leisure pursuits and to select leisure opportunities that have the potential to produce high-level wellness.

Thus, the Health Protection/Health Promotion Model reflects the full extent of RT practice. At one extreme of the continuum of service, the recreational therapist is assisting clients in poor environments to restore health. At the other extreme, the recreational therapist is helping clients achieve optimal health, or high-level wellness, in favorable environments (Austin, 2011b, 2013).

ADDITIONAL CONCEPTUAL MODELS

In addition to the Health Protection/Health Promotion Model that I have presented as a basis for the practice of RT, several conceptual models have been developed to offer theoretical bases for the practice of what the authors of the models have termed the field of *therapeutic recreation*.

Leisure Ability Model

The oldest conceptual model is the Leisure Ability Model introduced in 1978 by Gunn and Peterson. This model has been revised through the years. Its most recent revision, by Stumbo and Peterson, appeared in 2009. The mission of the Leisure Ability Model is to help clients with limitations to develop "a satisfying leisure lifestyle, the independent functioning of the client in leisure experiences and activities of his or her choice" (Stumbo & Peterson, 2009, p. 29). The model has three major parts along a continuum. The first, functional intervention, deals with improving functional ability. The second is leisure education, which is focused on the client gaining leisure-related attitudes, knowledge, and skills. The third component, recreation participation, has to do with structured activities that give clients the opportunity to enjoy recreational experiences (Stumbo & Peterson, 2009). Thus, the thrust of the Leisure Ability Model is on facilitating leisure experiences for persons with disabilities.

Other Leisure-Oriented Models

Similarly, the focus of the Self-Determination and Enjoyment Enhancement Model, developed by Dattilo, Kleiber, and Williams (1998), is on leisure for persons with disabilities. This model gives particular attention to promoting participants' self-determination. Likewise, the Leisure and Well-Being Model of Carruthers and Hood (2007) is focused on the leisure experience of persons with disabilities, along with clients' reactions to disability. Practitioners using the model must have understandings of empirical and theoretical knowledge related to the leisure experience. Anderson and Heyne's (2012) Flourishing Through Leisure Model extends the Leisure and Well-Being Model. This model is grounded in the social model of disability that views disability as a social construct in which the social environment (i.e., society's attitudes and practices) is seen as being disabling for persons with impairments. Thus, this model holds that environments need to be changed to allow persons with impairments to enter fully into society and flourish through their leisure participation.

Health-Oriented Models

Two of the conceptual models share the health orientation evident in the Health Protection/Health Promotion Model of Austin (1998, 2001, 2011b, 2013). The Therapeutic Recreation Service Delivery and Therapeutic Recreation Outcome Modelss that Glen Van Andel (Carter & Van Andel, 2011) developed share many of the concepts represented in Austin's conceptual model. Van Andel's models have the purpose of assisting clients to attain their optimal levels of health, well-being, and quality of life. For instance, the Therapeutic Recreation Service Delivery Model uses a continuum that begins with diagnosis/needs assessment and is followed by treatment/rehabilitation, education, and finally, prevention/health promotion. The focus of the Therapeutic Recreation Outcome Models is on improving functional abilities that lead to enhancements in clients' quality of life.

Still another health-related model is the optimizing Lifelong Health Through Recreation Model that Wilhite, Keller, and Caldwell (1999) developed. The purpose of this model is to enhance health and well-being and minimize the effects of illness and disability across the life span, through the use of alternative activities to compensate for impaired abilities.

In summary, Austin's (2011b) Reformulated Health Protection/Health Promotion Model is the only model developed expressly to serve as a conceptual model for RT. Conceptual models developed to serve as theoretical foundations for therapeutic recreation, such as those developed by Van Andel and Wilhite, Keller, and Caldwell, share the health orientation of Austin's Health Protection/Health Promotion Model and therefore may have potential application in RT. Others, such as the Leisure Ability Model, emphasize a leisure orientation. Their focus is on facilitating leisure experiences for persons with disabilities.

RECREATIONAL THERAPY, INCLUSIVE RECREATION, AND SPECIAL RECREATION

RT has been presented in this chapter as a purposeful intervention to assist clients to achieve as high a level of health as possible. You may be asking, "Does RT always involve purposeful intervention for health enhancement? Does RT ever simply involve the provision of recreation services to persons who have an illness or disability?"

Certainly general leisure experiences may bring about benefits for participants. Stumbo, Wang, and Pegg (2011) indicated, "It has been widely acknowledged that leisure experiences and participation provide unique and valuable opportunities that may result in numerous physical, social, and psychological benefits, as well as enhance overall quality of life" (p. 92). Amplifying on the value of leisure in persons' lives, Yalon-Chamovitz and Weiss (2008) stated, "Participation in leisure activities is a fundamental human right and an important factor of quality of life" (p. 273). Based on a review of the literature, Austin and Lee (2013) concluded, "The literature to support the claim that leisure can positively affect people is abundant" (p. 11).

In fact, Austin and Lee (2013) authored an entire book on the need for park, recreation, and tourism professionals to provide leisure services to improve the quality of the lives of all persons by focusing services to encompass underserved diverse populations, including persons with disabilities. The title of that book is *Inclusive and Special Recreation: Opportunities for Diverse Populations to Flourish*.

Within the book, Austin and Lee (2013) employed the terms *inclusive recreation* and *special recreation* to describe the provision of services to persons with disabilities. They wrote, "The term, inclusive recreation, has been used to capture the full acceptance and integration of persons with disabilities into the recreation mainstream" (Austin & Lee, 2013, p. 54). They employed the term *special recreation* to describe programs for individuals with similarities to participate together in recreational experiences. Examples of special recreation programs include wheelchair sports, camps for children with disabilities, the Special Olympics, and the National Veterans' Wheelchair Games.

Persons with disabilities may be recipients of both inclusive and special recreation services and RT services. So what are the differences between the inclusive recreation and special recreation services that the park, recreation, and tourism professions offer and the interventions those in the RT profession provide?

Simply providing recreation services to clients who have an illness or disability does not constitute the delivery of RT. Therapeutic intent has to be involved in RT. Without a planned intervention to produce a health benefit, what is provided is simply a leisure experience even though it is provided to a person who is ill or disabled. Austin (2011a) stated,

> In my mind, to be therapeutic, recreational therapy must display that it is purposeful and goal-directed in terms of supplying health benefits. The outcomes of recreational therapy are not random. They are planned. Recreational therapy employs an evidence-based approach that involves systematically using interventions to bring about specific therapeutic outcomes for clients. (p. 6)

Then what sets RT apart from inclusive recreation and special recreation is both the end sought and the process to achieve that end. The end for both inclusive recreation and special recreation is to facilitate leisure experiences. The end of RT is to help clients achieve specific health-related outcomes through the use of a systematic process employed by credentialed recreational therapists.

The systematic process involves four phases: assessment, planning, implementation, and evaluation. This process is commonly known by the acronym APIE drawn from the beginning letters of each phase and is often referred to as the apie process (pronounced a-pie). More formally, it is known as the recreational therapy process or RT process. An explanation of the RT process follows:

> Through the orderly phases of the recreational therapy process, the client's problems or concerns and strengths and needs are determined (assessment), plans are made to meet the problems or concerns (planning), the plan is initiated (implementation), and an evaluation is conducted to determine how effective the intervention has been (evaluation). (Austin, 2013, p. 156)

The RT process provides a cornerstone for RT. Because of its critical nature, a full discussion of its four phases is provided in Chapter 3.

As a caveat to this discussion, it should be mentioned that occasionally, in settings such as skilled nursing facilities, recreational therapists may be called upon to conduct or supervise general leisure activities (e.g., movie nights, bingo parties) that are not included in the clients' intervention or care plans. Such activities are often conducted by RT assistants, nursing staff, or volunteers and are offered to provide an improved quality of life for participants.

TENETS BASIC TO RECREATIONAL THERAPY PRACTICE

To function as protectors and promoters of health, recreational therapists rest their practice on a belief system. The following statements provide basic tenets for RT practice as perceived by the editors of this book. The tenets are as follows:

1. The basic goal of RT is to achieve the highest possible level of health for each client.
2. Good health provides a basis for a higher quality of life.
3. Illness may be a growth-producing experience for individuals who participate in RT.
4. Every client possesses intrinsic worth and the potential for change.
5. Clients should be treated with dignity and respect.
6. Persons are motivated toward health through the stability and actualization tendencies.
7. Illness (poor health) and high-level wellness (optimal health) are dimensions of health that may be perceived to be on a continuum.
8. RT may assist a wide spectrum of clients along the illness–wellness continuum, including persons with chronic illnesses and disabilities, as well as persons with acute conditions.
9. RT involves planned interventions that are purposeful and goal directed.
10. Persons have social needs that include belonging and feeling valued.

11. Social support often plays a prominent role in maintaining and improving health.

12. Problems and concerns in health produce needs that may be fulfilled through interactions between clients and recreational therapists.

13. Being genuine, nonjudgmental, and empathetic toward clients promotes therapeutic relationships and helps create a safe, caring environment.

14. Warm, positive, accepting, and hopeful atmospheres in programs promote client change.

15. Persons strive to maintain control over their lives and to function independently, so recreational therapists should not be manipulative or controlling.

16. Recreational therapists model healthy behaviors and attitudes while helping clients develop personal competence and intrinsic motivation for participating in healthful activities.

17. Positive emotions, such as pleasure and fun, are means to achieve optimistic views that open persons up to new growth-enhancing experiences.

18. Prescriptive activities have the potential to energize clients and motivate clients to take action to restore their health (in the case of acutely ill clients) or adaptively cope with their chronic condition and disabilities (in the case of clients with chronic illnesses or disabilities).

19. Recreation activities and experiences allow clients choice and control, as well as help clients to restore health or adaptively cope with chronic conditions or disabilities.

20. Leisure experiences, which contain the elements of intrinsic motivation, self-determination, and mastery, produce feelings of self-efficacy, empowerment, and enjoyment that, in turn, move participants toward achieving optimal health, or high-level wellness.

21. Different roles are assumed by recreational therapists who, depending on the needs of clients, may serve as guides providing clients with direction (during prescribed activities), partners in mutual relationships with clients (in recreation), or as facilitators of leisure experiences (during leisure).

22. Recreational therapists assist clients to develop healthy living habits that their clients will take with them once they are no longer in RT.

23. Recreational therapists take a strength-based approach that is focused on abilities and intact strengths of the clients.

24. A strength-based approach helps clients to identify strengths and what works for them.

25. RT is concerned with both treatment/rehabilitation and education/reeducation. Therapeutic outcomes emphasize enhanced functioning and the here and now.

26. Typical outcomes for RT interventions include increasing personal awareness, increasing interpersonal or social skills, developing leisure skills, decreasing stress, decreasing depression, improving physical and mental

functioning, improving physical fitness, and developing feelings of positive self-regard, self-efficacy, perceived control, pleasure, and enjoyment.

27. Recreational therapists have knowledge of the demands inherent in specific activities that are employed as interventions. Activity analysis is used to gain insights into the demands activities make on clients to ensure the careful selection of appropriate activities.

28. Recreation and leisure activities offer diversion or escape from personal problems and concerns and the routine of health care facilities.

29. Recreational therapists employ the RT process (often referred to as the a-pie process).

30. Clients' preferences and perceptions are important in all phases of the RT process.

31. Recreational therapists operate from a theory base provided by the conceptual model of RT that they adopt.

32. Recreational therapists engage in evidence-based practice in their clinical decision making by integrating the most current research findings with their clinical expertise and client values and preferences.

KINDRED PROFESSIONS

Recreational therapists do not work in isolation from other health care professionals. In fact, using interdisciplinary teams composed of personnel from various specializations has become widespread through health care. The establishment of interdisciplinary teams is largely based on the notion that clients are so complex that no profession by itself can offer adequate health care (Austin, 2013; Howe-Murphy & Charboneau, 1987). Team membership will vary as a function of the setting in which services are being delivered (e.g., a center for physical medicine and rehabilitation or a center for psychiatric or mental health care) and as a function of the specific problems or concerns of the client.

Although no attempt is made here to discuss all kindred professions, major professions are covered, including medical doctors, nurses, psychologists, social workers, as well as activity or rehabilitation therapy professions.

Medical Doctors

Medical doctors (MDs) use surgery, drugs, and other methods of medical care to prevent or alleviate disease. In hospital settings, physicians' orders are typically required for off-campus activities. There are over 30 specializations of medical doctors (O'Morrow & Reynolds, 1989). Examples are psychiatrists (who specialize in mental and emotional disorders), pediatricians (who specialize in the care and treatment of children), and neurologists (who deal with diseases of the nervous system).

Nurses

Registered nurses (RNs) are responsible for giving nursing care to patients, carrying out physicians' orders, and supervising other nursing personnel such as licensed practical nurses, nurses' aids, orderlies, and attendants. Nurses may be wonderful colleagues as sources of information for recreational therapists because nurses are typically well informed about clients and progress they have made. Nurses who are enthusiastic about their clients participating in RT may also be invaluable allies for recreational therapists through their encouragement of clients to value and actively participate in RT.

Psychologists

Psychologists usually hold PhD or PsyD degrees in psychology. They engage in psychological testing, diagnosis, counseling, and other therapies. Results from psychological testing may provide important information for recreational therapists to use in assessment. Psychologists may also suggest behavioral interventions for recreational therapists and other members of interdisciplinary teams to follow. Recreational therapists often work closely with psychologists doing group therapy because recreation activities offer real-life means for clients to practice and refine concepts and skills discussed during group therapy sessions.

Social Workers

Social workers use case work and group work methods to assist clients and their families in making adjustments and in dealing with social systems. They prepare social histories of newly admitted clients and are often the primary professionals to assist clients with community reintegration. Social histories may be a particularly valuable resource during the assessment phase of RT. Recreational therapists likely will work closely with social workers when preparing clients for community reintegration.

Physical Therapists

Physical therapists (PTs) are concerned with restoring physical function, reducing pain, and preventing disability following disease, injury, or loss of a body part. They apply therapeutic exercise and functional training procedures in physical rehabilitation. PTs hold either a master's degree or doctoral degree. PTs now entering the profession need a doctorate of physical therapy degree. RT often offers clients opportunities to practice procedures learned during physical therapy sessions.

Occupational Therapists

Occupational therapists (OTs) use purposeful occupations or activities with persons with limitations due to physical injury, illness, psychosocial disorders, developmental or learning disabilities, economic and cultural differences, or aging processes to increase independent functioning in performing all aspects of everyday life, as well as to assist clients in maintaining health and preventing disability. OTs entering the profession need a master's degree in occupational therapy.

Music Therapists

Music therapists (MTs) use music as a medium to reach and involve clients in treatment. Music therapy addresses clients' emotional, cognitive, and social needs through treatments involving creating music, singing, or listening to or moving to music. Music therapy is found primarily in psychiatric treatment programs but may be employed within other settings as well (e.g., long-term care facilities).

Art Therapists

Art therapists use art as a medium to promote self-awareness, nonverbal expression, and human interaction. Art therapy is most widely used within the treatment of persons with problems in mental health. To practice art therapy, art therapists must have knowledge of visual art (e.g., drawing, painting, sculpture) and the creative process, as well as possess understandings of human development, psychological and counseling theories, and related techniques.

Dance Therapists

Dance therapists use movement as a medium to work with clients. Dance therapy is a nonverbal means of expression employed with both individuals and groups. Although not found exclusively in psychiatric treatment programs, it is most commonly used with persons experiencing problems in mental health. Dance therapy, however, may be used to treat any number of illnesses, disorders, and disabilities.

RANGE OF RECREATIONAL THERAPY SERVICES

Settings for Recreational Therapy

At one time, practically all RT occurred within hospitals and institutions. This is no longer true. Today, RT is found in many settings. Although RT is still commonly found in general and psychiatric hospitals and in residential schools for students with disabilities, it also occurs in settings such as skilled nursing facilities, assisted living facilities, home health care, correctional facilities, outdoor recreation/camping centers, rehabilitation centers, community mental health centers, and other community-based health and human service agencies. Even some public park and recreation departments offer RT services (Austin & Lee, 2013).

Clients Served by Recreational Therapists

RT clients may be any persons who desire to recover from an illness or to adaptively cope with a chronic condition or disability (i.e., engage in health protection) or to enhance their own level of health (i.e., pursue health promotion). Persons participating in mental health programs have traditionally been the largest client group of RT. Other major client groups have been persons with intellectual disabilities or physical disabilities, hospitalized children, and aging populations residing in long-term care facilities. Additional individuals who have benefited from RT include persons with autism, persons with substance use disorders or addiction, persons with cognitive impairments (e.g., head injuries), and persons who experience convulsive disorders. Today, a large population of military veterans who require treatment and rehabilitative services also exists.

Structures for Recreational Therapy

RT interventions occur in several formats. These include structures such as classes, clubs, special interest groups, individual and group leisure counseling sessions, adventure therapy groups, informal recreation programs, special events, and contests (Austin, 2013).

Professional Organizations for Recreational Therapy

Two national professional membership societies exist. In the United States, the organization is the American Therapeutic Recreation Association (ATRA). In Canada, the organization is the Canadian Therapeutic Recreation Association. Both national organizations offer continuing education opportunities, publications, advocacy, and other services for their members.

COMPETENCIES RECREATIONAL THERAPISTS NEED

Few professionals would argue with the contention that competencies gained through the professional preparation of recreational therapists differ from those required of park, recreation, and tourism professionals. Certainly both need solid liberal arts preparation. The liberal learning dimension of curricula offers the depth and breadth of education needed for individuals to be contributing citizens of the world and provides a foundation upon which much professional preparation rests. Both also need to gain understandings of the phenomena of recreation and leisure. Beyond these similarities, competencies that students within professional preparation programs need in RT differ greatly from students studying in parks, recreation, or tourism programs because RT is a distinct discipline that requires competencies unique to persons who meet qualifications to enter the RT profession.

Several sources have been drawn upon to develop the areas of competency needed for the practice of RT that follows in this chapter. These include competency areas listed in the third edition of *Therapeutic Recreation: An Introduction* (Austin & Crawford, 2001); *Guidelines for Competency Assessment and Curriculum Planning for Recreational Therapy Practice* published by the American Therapeutic Recreation Association in 2008; *Standards and Guidelines for the Accreditation of Educational Programs in Recreational Therapy* adopted in 2010 by the Commission on Accreditation of Allied Health Education Programs; the results of a job analysis published in 2011 by the National Council for Therapeutic Recreation Certification; and the seventh edition *Therapeutic Recreation Processes and Techniques* (Austin, 2013).

As you review the listing of areas of competency, think about your own preparation for doing RT. Are you personally gaining the competencies necessary to practice RT?

Areas of competency that you, as an emerging recreational therapist, need to evaluate include the following:

- theories/understandings of recreation and leisure;
- human development throughout the life span;
- anatomy and physiology;
- basic assumptions about human nature;
- clients served in RT;
- etiology, course, and prognosis of various diagnostic categories;
- knowledge of the International Classification of Functioning, Disability, and Health;
- disease sequelae;
- effects of stress on individuals;
- theories of helping (e.g., psychoanalytic, behavioral, humanistic, cognitive-behavioral, positive psychology);
- definitions of RT;
- basic concepts/tenets for RT practice;
- facilitation techniques applied as interventions (e.g., horticulture therapy, values clarification, leisure counseling/education, progressive relaxation

training, physical activity, adventure therapy, aquatic therapy, social skills training, animal-assisted therapy, reminiscence therapy);

- perceptions of clients as "whole persons," not just as individuals possessing symptoms;
- conceptual models providing a theory base for RT practice;
- strength-based perspectives in RT;
- evidence-based approaches to RT;
- effects of major drugs;
- health and safety information for working with clients;
- medical and psychological terminology;
- concepts of health and wellness;
- attitudes toward illness and disability;
- self-awareness (e.g., values and beliefs);
- cultural diversity;
- characteristics of effective helping professionals and helping relationships;
- theories and techniques of group leadership;
- concerns and strategies for group leaders;
- leadership skills in using recreation/leisure activities (e.g., arts and crafts, physical activities, sports and games, outdoor activities) as therapeutic interventions;
- activity analysis processes and procedures;
- clinical reasoning skills including identifying activities that hold the potential to meet treatment/rehabilitation aims;
- use of self as a therapeutic agent;
- therapeutic relationship skills;
- therapeutic communication skills;
- therapeutic environments;
- interview skills;
- group processing (debriefing) skills;
- leader transactions with clients (i.e., the social psychology of RT involving concepts such as self-views, helplessness, self-fulfilling prophecy, labeling, loneliness, self-efficacy, and attributional processes);
- advocacy (e.g., client or case advocacy, professional advocacy);
- client assessment;
- formulation of treatment/rehabilitation/wellness goals;
- stating specific behavioral objectives;
- development of treatment/rehabilitation/care/wellness/education/intervention plans;

- implementation of treatment/rehabilitation/care/wellness/education/intervention plans;
- evaluation of intervention processes and outcomes;
- client records and documentation (e.g., charting on clients);
- theories in human behavior and in motivating client change;
- program protocols;
- referral procedures;
- behavioral management techniques;
- learning/teaching principles;
- assistive devices for specific disabilities;
- accessibility and usable recreation environments (e.g., universal design);
- ethical and professional standards of practice;
- legal aspects of RT;
- giving and receiving clinical supervision;
- roles and functions of kindred professionals;
- role and function of interdisciplinary teams;
- interdisciplinary teams and teamwork;
- practice settings;
- structures (formats) for RT programs;
- professional organizations for RT;
- current professional issues and trends (e.g., accreditation, credentialing); and
- historical foundations of RT.

Your self-assessment of the competency areas likely will reveal that, although you have started to gain rudimentary skills and knowledge, you are still in the beginning phase of development as an emerging recreational therapist. This is normal, so do not feel discouraged because you do not yet possess the competencies required for clinical practice in RT.

NATIONAL COUNCIL FOR THERAPEUTIC RECREATION CERTIFICATION

Once you have completed your degree requirements, you will be eligible to sit for a national examination administered by the National Council for Therapeutic Recreation Certification (NCTRC). NCTRC was established in 1981 as a nonprofit organization dedicated to maintaining professional standards to protect consumers through the credentialing of well-qualified recreational therapists. The NCTRC grants professional certification to individuals who apply and meet established standards for certification, which include completing a bachelor's degree in RT or therapeutic recreation and passing the national certification exam. The Certified Therapeutic Recreation Specialist® (CTRS®) credential is offered to qualified individuals who meet all of the requirements to serve as recreational therapists.

PLAN FOR THE BOOK

The editors of this text have attempted to make you, the reader, the focal point of this book. The book is organized with objectives at the beginning of each chapter so you will know explicitly what you should gain from your reading. Another aid to help you in your learning is the reading comprehension questions found at the end of each chapter.

Chapters in Section 1 of the book present the nature, purpose, history, and processes of RT. Section 2 covers areas of practice. Taken as a whole, these chapters illustrate the richness and diversity of RT. To facilitate your learning and ensure completeness in approach, the authors for chapters in Section 2 followed a common outline. For example, in each chapter you will learn about current practices and procedures in that particular area of RT and you will review a brief case study that portrays the actual application of practices and procedures. Section 3 deals with professional practice concerns and contains two chapters. The first chapter covers management, consultation, and research in RT. The second chapter is on issues and trends in RT.

SUMMARY

The purpose of this chapter was to provide an introduction to RT and to offer an overview of its components. The chapter presented definitions of RT and followed with an analysis of common elements found within the definitions. It granted recreation, leisure, self-determination, intrinsic motivation, and health particular attention.

The chapter discussed the relationship of RT to health and wellness, together with the tendencies for stability and actualization. This discussion culminated with the presentation of the continuum of services represented within the Health Protection/Health Promotion Model. Following a description of this conceptual model and others, the chapter further described RT by contrasting it with inclusive and special recreation and by providing basic tenets that guide the practice of RT.

The chapter also offered information on kindred professionals, the range of RT, and areas of competency recreational therapists need. The chapter ended with a brief orientation to the plan for the book.

READING COMPREHENSION QUESTIONS

1. Define RT in your own words.
2. What properties are found in recreation?
3. Do you agree that perceived freedom and intrinsic motivation are the factors that define leisure? Please explain.
4. What is meant by helplessness?
5. Do you agree with the definition of health presented by Jones? Explain.
6. Briefly describe the humanistic perspective.

7. What is high-level wellness?

8. Briefly describe positive psychology.

9. Explain the stabilizing and actualizing tendencies.

10. Is illness ever positive? Explain.

11. Explain the continuum presented in the Health Protection/Health Promotion Model.

12. Do you agree that RT and inclusive and special recreation are separate entities? Please explain.

13. Review the basic tenets of RT. Do you understand each of them? Do you agree with each of them? Why or why not?

14. Name at least five kindred professions of RT.

15. In what settings does RT occur?

16. What types of clients do recreational therapists traditionally serve?

17. Name two national professional membership organizations for RT.

18. How do you assess yourself in terms of moving toward becoming a competent recreational therapist?

19. What is NCTRC?

20. Do you understand the plan of the book? Please explain.

REFERENCES

American Therapeutic Recreation Association. (2008). *Guidelines for competency assessment and curriculum planning for recreational therapy practice.* Hattiesburg, MS: Author.

Anderson, L. S., & Heyne, L. A. (2012). Flourishing through leisure: An ecological extension of the Leisure and Well-Being Model in therapeutic recreation strengths-based practice. *Therapeutic Recreation Journal, 46*(2), 129–152.

Ardell, D. (1977). *High-level wellness: An alternative to doctors, drugs, and disease.* Emmaus, PA: Rodale Press.

Austin, D. R. (1998). The Health Protection/Health Promotion Model. *Therapeutic Recreation Journal, 32*(2), 109–117.

Austin, D. R. (1999). *Therapeutic recreation processes and techniques* (4th ed.). Champaign, IL: Sagamore.

Austin, D. R. (2001). Introduction and overview. In D. R. Austin & M. E. Crawford (Eds.), *Therapeutic recreation: An introduction* (3rd ed., pp. 1–21). Boston, MA: Allyn & Bacon.

Austin, D. R. (2002). Control: A major element in therapeutic recreation. In D. R. Austin, J. Dattilo, & B. P. McCormick (Eds.), *Conceptual foundations for therapeutic recreation* (pp. 93–114). State College, PA: Venture.

Austin, D. R. (2005–2006). The changing contextualization of therapeutic recreation: A 40-year perspective. *Annual in Therapeutic Recreation, 14*, 1–11.

Austin, D. R. (2011a). *Lessons learned: An open letter to recreational therapy students and practitioners.* Urbana, IL: Sagamore.

Austin, D. R. (2011b). Reformulation of the Health Protection/Health Promotion Model. *American Journal of Recreation Therapy, 10*(3), 19–26.

Austin, D. R. (2013). *Therapeutic recreation processes and techniques* (7th ed.). Urbana, IL: Sagamore.

Austin, D. R., & Crawford, M. E. (1996). *Therapeutic recreation: An introduction.* Needham Heights, MA: Allyn & Bacon.

Austin, D. R., & Crawford, M. E. (2001). *Therapeutic recreation: An introduction* (3rd ed.). Needham Heights, MA: Allyn & Bacon.

Austin, D. R., McCormick, B. P., & Van Puymbroeck, M. (2010). Positive psychology: A theoretical foundation for recreation therapy. *American Journal of Recreation Therapy, 9*(3), 17–24.

Austin, D. R., & Lee, Y. (2013). *Inclusive and special recreation: Opportunities for diverse populations to flourish.* Urbana, IL: Sagamore.

Baker, G. (1990). Chairman's introduction. In *Quality of life and quality of care in epilepsy* (pp. 61–62). Great Britain, United Kingdom: Royal Society of Medicine.

Biswas-Diener, R., & Dean, B. (2007). *Positive psychology coaching: Putting the science of happiness to work for your clients.* Hoboken, NJ: John Wiley & Sons.

Biswas-Diener, R. (2010). *Practicing positive psychology coaching.* Hoboken, NJ: John Wiley & Sons.

Carruthers, C., & Hood, C. D. (2007). Building a life of meaning through therapeutic recreation: The Leisure and Well-Being Model, part 1. *Therapeutic Recreation Journal, 41*(4), 276–297.

Carter, M. J., & Van Andel, G. E. (2011). *Therapeutic recreation: A practical approach* (4th ed.). Prospect Heights, IL: Waveland.

Commission on Accreditation of Allied Health Education Programs. (2010). *Standards and guidelines for the accreditation of educational programs in recreational therapy.* Clearwater, FL: Author.

Dattilo, J., Kleiber, D. A., & Williams, R. (1998). Self-determination and enjoyment enhancement: A psychologically based service delivery model for therapeutic recreation. *Therapeutic Recreation Journal, 32*, 258–271.

Davis, J. E. (1936). *Principles and practices of recreational therapy.* New York, NY: Barnes.

Deci, E. L., & Ryan, R. M. (1985). *Intrinsic motivation and self-determination in human behavior.* New York, NY: Plenum Press.

Duckworth, A. L., Steen, T. A., & Seligman, M. E. P. (2005). Positive psychology in clinical practice. *Annual Review of Clinical Psychology, 1*, 629–651.

Dunn, H. I. (1961). *High-level wellness.* Arlington, VA: R.W. Beatty.

Edelman, D., & Mandle, C. L. (1998). *Health promotion throughout the lifespan* (4th ed.). St. Louis, MO: Mosby.

Fallowfield, L. (1990). *The quality of life: The missing measurement in health care.* London, England: Souvenir Press.

Flynn, P. A. R. (1980). *Holistic health: The art and science of care.* Bowie, MA: Brady.

Gatchel, R. J. (1980). Perceived control: A review and evaluation of therapeutic implications. In A. Baum & J. E. Singer (Eds.), *Advances in environmental psychology: Applications of personal control.* (Vol. 2, pp. 1–22). Hillsdale, NJ: Erlbaum.

Grzelak, J. L. (1985). Desire for control: Cognitive emotional and behavioral consequences. In F. L. Denmark (Ed.), *Social/ecological psychology and the psychology of women.* New York, NY: Elsevier Science.

Gunn, S. L., & Peterson, C. A. (1978). *Therapeutic recreation program design.* Englewood Cliffs, NJ: Prentice Hall.

Howard, D., Browning, C., & Lee, Y. (2007). The International Classification of Functioning, Disability, and Health: Therapeutic recreation code sets and salient diagnostic core sets. *Therapeutic Recreation Journal, 41*(1), 61.

Howe-Murphy, R., & Charboneau, B. G. (1987). *Therapeutic recreation intervention: An ecological perspective.* Englewood Cliffs, NJ: Prentice Hall.

Iso-Ahola, S. E. (1980). *The social psychology of leisure and recreation.* Dubuque, IA: Brown.

Jacoby, A. (1990). Chairman's introduction. In *Quality of life and quality of care in epilepsy* (pp. 61–62). Great Britain, United Kingdom: Royal Society of Medicine.

Jones, S. (2000). *Talking about health and wellness with patients.* New York, NY: Springer.

Joseph, S., & Linley, P. A. (2004). Positive therapy: A positive psychology theory of therapeutic practice. In P. A. Linley & S. Joseph (Eds.), *Positive psychology in practice* (pp. 354–368). Hoboken, NJ: John Wiley & Sons.

Kunstler, R., & Stavola Daly, F. (2010). *Therapeutic recreation leadership and programming.* Champaign, IL: Human Kinetics.

Langer, E. J., & Rodin, J. (1976). The effects of choice and enhanced personal responsibility for the aged: A field experiment in an institutional setting. *Journal of Personality and Social Psychology, 34*, 191–198.

Lindberg, J., Hunter, M., & Kruszewski, A. (1983). *Introduction to person-centered nursing.* Philadelphia, PA: Lippincott.

Linley, P. A., & Joseph, S. (2004). Applied positive psychology: A new perspective for professional practice. In P. A. Linley & S. Joseph (Eds.), *Positive psychology in practice* (pp. 3–12). Hoboken, NJ: John Wiley & Sons.

Mannell, R. C., & Kleiber, D. A. (1997). *A social psychology of leisure.* State College, PA: Venture.

National Council for Therapeutic Recreation Certification. (2011). *Information for the Certified Therapeutic Recreation Specialist and new applicants.* New City, NY: Author.

Neulinger, J. (1980). Introduction. In S. E. Iso-Ahola (Ed.), *Social psychological perspectives on leisure and recreation* (pp. 5–18). Springfield, IL: Charles C. Thomas.

O'Morrow, G. S., & Reynolds, R. P. (1989). *Therapeutic recreation: A helping profession.* Englewood Cliffs, NJ: Prentice Hall.

Pender, N. J. (1987). *Health promotion in nursing practice* (2nd ed.). Norwalk, CT: Appleton-Century-Crofts.

Pender, N. J. (1996). *Health promotion in nursing practice* (3rd ed.). Stamford, CT: Appleton & Lange.

Porter, H. R., & burlingame, j. (2006). *Recreational therapy handbook of practice: ICF-based diagnosis and treatment.* Enumclaw, WA: Idyll Arbor.

Porter, H. R., & Van Puymbroeck, M. (2007). Utilization of the International Classification of Functioning, Disability, and Health within therapeutic recreation practice. *Therapeutic Recreation Journal, 41*(1), 47–60.

Richter, K. J., & Kaschalk, S. M. (1996). The future of therapeutic recreation: An existential outcome. In C. Sylvester (Ed.), *Philosophy of therapeutic recreation: Ideas and issues* (Vol. 2, pp. 86–91). Ashburn, VA: National Recreation and Park Association.

Schlein, E. H., & Kommers, D. W. (1972). *Professional education.* New York, NY: McGraw-Hill.

Seligman, M. E. P., & Maier, S. F. (1967). Failure to escape traumatic shock. *Journal of Experimental Psychology, 74*, 1–9.

Shank, J., & Coyle, C. (2002). *Therapeutic recreation in health promotion and rehabilitation.* State College, PA: Venture.

Shank, J., & Kinney, T. (1987). On the neglect of clinical practice. In C. Sylvester, J. L. Hemingway, R. Howe-Murphy, K. Mobily, & P. A. Shank (Eds.), *Philosophy of therapeutic recreation: Ideas and issues* (Vol. 1, pp. 65–75). Alexandria, VA: National Recreation and Park Association.

Skerrett, K. (2010). Extending family nursing: Concepts from positive psychology. *Journal of Family Nursing, 16*(4), 487–502.

Smith, D. H., & Theberge, N. (1987). *Why people recreate.* Champaign, IL: Life Enhancement Publications.

Stumbo, N. J., & Peterson, C. A. (2009). *Therapeutic recreation program design* (5th ed.). San Francisco, CA: Pearson.

Stumbo, N. J., Wang, Y., & Pegg, S. (2011). Issues of access: What matters to people with disabilities as they seek leisure experiences. *World Leisure Journal, 53*(2), 91–103.

Sylvester, C. (2009). A virtue-based approach to therapeutic recreation practice. *Therapeutic Recreation Journal, 43*(3), 9–25.

Van Puymbroeck, M., Austin, D. R., & McCormick, B. P. (2010). Beyond curriculum reform: Therapeutic recreation's hidden curriculum. *Therapeutic Recreation Journal, 44*(3), 213–222.

Van Puymbroeck, M., Porter, H., & McCormick, B. P. (2009). The role of the International Classification of Functioning, Disability, and Health (ICF) in therapeutic recreation practice, research, and education. In N. Stumbo (Ed.), *Client outcomes in therapeutic recreation* (pp. 43–57). Champaign, IL: Sagamore.

Voelkl, J. E. (1986). Effects of institutionalization upon residents of extended care facilities. *Activities, Adaptation and Aging, 8*, 37–46.

Wilensky, H. L. (1964). The professionalization of everyone? *The American Journal of Sociology, 70*, 137–158.

Wilhite, B., Keller, M. J., & Caldwell, L. (1999). Optimizing lifelong health and well-being: A health enhancing model of therapeutic recreation. *Therapeutic Recreation Journal, 33*, 98–108.

World Health Organization. (1947). Constitution of the World Health Organization. *Chronicle of the World Health Organization*, 1(1), 2.

World Health Organization. (2002). *Towards a common language for functioning, disability and health: ICF.* Retrieved from http://www.who.int/classifications/icf/training/icfbeginnersguide.pdf

Yalon-Chamovitz, S., & Weiss, P. L. (2008). Virtual reality as a leisure activity for young adults with physical and intellectual disabilities. *Research in Developmental Disabilities, 29*, 273–287.

2

THE HISTORY OF THERAPEUTIC RECREATION: A HISTORY OF TWO PROFESSIONS

DAVID R. AUSTIN AND MICHAEL E. CRAWFORD

OBJECTIVES

- Name early cultures that employed recreation in health restoration.
- Identify early leaders of the treatment-with-care era.
- Explain the original social welfare motive of the park and recreation movement.
- Identify the perspective the park and recreation movement took once the social welfare motive no longer predominated.
- Discuss the period of rapid growth in therapeutic recreation that has been referred to as "The Great Acceleration."
- Describe the philosophical position of professionals in the Hospital Recreation Section of the American Recreation Society who identified themselves as *hospital recreators*.
- Describe the philosophical position of professionals who identified themselves as recreational therapists and who were members of the National Association of Recreational Therapists.
- Identify the Council for the Advancement of Hospital Recreation.
- Know when the National Therapeutic Recreation Society (NTRS) was formed.
- Name hallmarks in the professionalization of therapeutic recreation.
- Know when the American Therapeutic Recreation Association (ATRA) was formed.
- Agree or disagree that the field of therapeutic recreation should be conceived to be made up of two distinct professions: one representing a leisure facilitation philosophy and the other representing a recreational therapy philosophy.

What if you were to wake up some morning with no memories of who you were, who others were (e.g., family, friends, or strangers), and why you were where you were! It would be frightening as you would have no context for your life, no awareness of yourself or your place in the world. Sylvester (1989) likened such an individual's experience to that of a field missing a history:

> A field without history…is like a person without a memory. Both vaguely recollect coming and having someplace to go; but they have little clue where or why. Without sources of identity drawn from a meaningful past, purposeful direction in unlikely (p. 19).

This chapter will provide you with a meaningful historical account of the broad field of therapeutic recreation[1] so you may grasp the identity of the profession of recreational therapy (RT) and begin to assume your personal identity as a member of it.

Especially if you, as with many students, are not be dedicated to or passionate about the history of RT, this chapter will allow you to develop your personal identity as a fledgling member of a profession that you are perhaps only beginning to understand, as well as to begin to see yourself as a part of a collective of individuals who make up the profession. Hopefully, as a result of understanding the history of RT, you will realize that the profession is one of value and worth, one in which you may take personal pride and joy in becoming a member.

History should involve more than memorizing dates or presenting a chronological list of events. It should help RT professionals to comprehend the antecedents of where they are today through an interpretation of events that have occurred and how these have brought them to where they are now. What has happened in the past causes the present and takes RT professionals forward to their future. Only through history may they grasp how things have changed and how these changes have affected where they are and where they may be headed.

A number of well-prepared histories of therapeutic recreation have been published (e.g., Austin, 2002; Crawford, 2001; Dieser, 2008; Frye & Peters, 1972; James, 1998). Within these accounts, which tend to follow similar patterns, little disagreement was found. These sources provide a synopsis of the history of the broad field of therapeutic recreation.

THE THERAPEUTIC USE OF RECREATION IN EARLY CULTURES

Typically, histories of therapeutic recreation first cover precursors of the organized development of field in the United States and Canada. Frye and Peters (1972) indicated that "the history of therapeutic recreation is as old as antiquity…." (p. 30). In this realm, these authors and others have discussed evidence of recreation being used for restorative purposes thousands of years ago in Egyptian, Greek, Roman, and Chinese cultures. Table 2.1 outlines examples of the use of recreation for health restoration in ancient civilizations.

---

[1]*Therapeutic recreation* has been used as an umbrella term to encompass both the provision of recreation services for persons who are ill or disabled and the use of recreation by recreational therapists as a modality to bring about health enhancement.

Table 2.1
Ancient Cultures Using Recreation for Health Restoration

Egyptian culture
Priests established temples to treat the sick and persons with mental health problems. The therapeutic value of the milieu, or environment (e.g., beautiful lotus gardens), was recognized.
Treatment included dances and ritualistic songs.

Greek culture
Temples for the sick included libraries, stadiums, theaters, and sanatoriums. Treatment for mental disorders included music in conjunction with gymnastics and dancing. A restful, relaxing atmosphere was created.

Roman culture
Physicians prescribed games to relax the body and mind.
The virtues of diet and exercise were heralded as a tonic for the body.

Chinese culture
Activity was used to divert patients' attention from severe primary treatments. Deep breathing and exercise techniques were developed for sedentary older persons (e.g., tai chi).

Note. Adapted from "Organization and Formation of the Profession," by M. E. Crawford, 2001, in D. R. Austin and M. E. Crawford (Eds.), *Therapeutic Recreation: An Introduction* (3rd ed., pp. 22–44), Needham Heights, MA: Allyn and Bacon, and *Therapeutic Recreation: Its Theory, Philosophy, and Practice,* by V. Frye and M. Peters, 1972, Harrisburg, PA: Stackpole Books.

Following discussion of ancient cultures, authors of histories of therapeutic recreation regularly move on to focus on two groups. One of these groups includes individuals who championed using recreation in more modern medical care during the 18th and 19th centuries. The other group is composed of professionals in the park and recreation movement who were inspired by a social welfare motive to use recreation as a social instrument to improve the lives of underserved classes in an increasingly urbanized 19th century America. The employment of recreation in medicine in Europe and the United States and its use as a social instrument in American cities are covered in the following sections.

RECOGNIZING THE THERAPEUTIC VALUE OF RECREATION IN THE 18TH AND 19TH CENTURIES

Reformers of medical practices in the 1700s, and beginning of the 1800s, included noted figures such as Dr. Phillippe Pinel of France, who employed recreation within his humanitarian approach (termed moral treatment) in the treatment of psychiatric patients. Florence Nightingale, widely acknowledged to be the "Mother of Nursing," emerged in the 19th century as a key figure in promoting the use of recreation in rehabilitation. Nightingale strongly advocated using recreation activities for patients in British military hospitals. Not until she employed recreation as a purposeful means to achieve health restoration did the potential for using recreation to bring about healthful outcomes begin to become accepted. Among activities Nightingale used were caring for pets, performing music and drama, listening to music, reading, and playing table games such as dominoes and chess. Dr. Benjamin Rush, the "father of American Psychiatry" ("History of Pennsylvania Hospital," 2013), employed an approach similar to Nightingale's in the United States. Rush, while superintendent of the Pennsylvania Hospital in Philadelphia stressed the need for recreational activities as a part of the treatment of hospitalized psychiatric patients (James, 1998). The contributions of these and other leaders in what Crawford (2001) referred to as the "treatment-with-care era" are noted in Table 2.2.

Table 2.2
Early Leaders of the Treatment-With-Care Era

Phillippe Pinel (French physician)	In the 1700s, advocated recreational activity as a part of his milieu therapy for psychiatric patients.
William Tuck (English philanthropist)	In the 1700s, founded the York Retreat, a country home for the humane treatment of persons with mental illnesses.
Jean Itard (French physician)	In the 1700s, developed training techniques for persons with intellectual disabilities, using games and sport.
Benjamin Rush (American physician)	In the 1800s, advocated the therapeutic value of recreation for psychiatric patients.
Florence Nightingale (British nurse)	In the 1800s, established recreation services for the rehabilitation of soldiers in British military hospitals.

Note. Adapted from "Organization and Formation of the Profession," by M. E. Crawford, 2001, in D. R. Austin and M. E. Crawford (Eds.), *Therapeutic Recreation: An Introduction* (3rd ed., pp. 22–44), Needham Heights, MA: Allyn and Bacon, and "History of Therapeutic Recreation," by R. Dieser, 2008, in T. Robertson and T. Long (Eds.), *Foundations of Therapeutic Recreation* (pp. 13–30), Champaign, IL: Human Kinetics.

INSTRUMENTAL VALUE OF RECREATION: RECREATION AS A VEHICLE FOR SELF-DEVELOPMENT

The park and recreation movement in the United States grew out of the playground movement that is typically traced back to the development of the Boston

Sand Gardens for the underprivileged children of Boston in the late 1800s (Austin & Lee, 2013; Smith & Godbey, 1991). Joseph Lee, who would become a noted figure within the history of parks and recreation, created this sand play area. Neva Boyd also made a noticeable contribution. Austin (2002) noted their efforts:

> Recreation was used as a vehicle for social reform to improve conditions brought about in inhospitable cities during the time many emigrated from Europe to America. Boston's Joseph Lee began the "play and recreation movement" which spread throughout America in the late nineteenth and early twentieth century. To Lee, recreation was a means to self-development. Neva Boyd joined Lee's play and recreation movement, ultimately arriving at Jane Addams' Hull House in Chicago. At this noted settlement house, Boyd used recreation as a medium to help children of recent immigrants adjust within what had to be a hostile environment, and develop themselves as individuals. Hull House eventually became the site of a training program that Boyd initiated for group workers—a program she later moved to Northwestern University. Boyd has been credited as being the originator of theory and techniques that offered a foundation for the practice of Red Cross hospital recreation workers employed in military hospitals during World War I. (p. 275)

The playground movement ultimately expanded beyond its original concern for underprivileged children to a general commitment for serving disadvantaged segments of society. It would mature into the park and recreation movement that would establish services for both youth and adults in cities and other jurisdictions throughout America. As time passed, however, these park and recreation systems began to lose their focus on using recreation as a means to help disadvantaged persons, but instead they adopted the perspectives "recreation for all" and "recreation as its own end." Gray (1969) explained, "Gradually the social welfare mission weakened and a philosophy which sees recreation as an end in itself was adopted; this is the common view of public recreation agencies throughout the country" (p. 23).

The original concept of using recreation as a means to development tied closely to the RT perspective of using recreation as a means to reach its end of helping individuals to achieve health enhancement and well-being. Certainly Neva Boyd's work reflected this. Nevertheless, the park and recreation movement's later philosophical perspectives of recreation for all and recreation as an end would play a much larger role in the history of therapeutic recreation.

"THE GREAT ACCELERATION" AND BEGINNINGS OF PROFESSIONALIZATION

The next era in therapeutic recreation was marked by tremendous growth and the beginnings of professionalization. The field was rapidly expanding, and professionals in it began the process of establishing themselves as a profession. The American Red Cross was at the forefront of this movement as Red Cross recreation workers became a common feature in military hospitals during World War I, which the United States entered in 1917. Neva Boyd's book *Hospital and Bedside Games,* published in 1919, was provided to all Red Cross recreation workers. James (1998) reported that in the foreword of her book Boyd stated she had compiled the recreation activities through the efforts of recreation workers in civilian and military hospitals, who had indicated, "The work that they have done has convinced them that such games have curative value" (p. 14).

Even greater developments in the use of recreation by the Red Cross in military hospitals would arrive during World War II. With World War II came vast acceleration in the use of recreation in military hospitals as more than 1,800 Red Cross recreation workers were employed to serve hospitalized soldiers (James, 1998). Around the same time, the Veterans Administration began recreation programs in its hospitals. Although initially under Special Services (with volunteer services, entertainment, libraries, canteens, etc.), recreation therapy emerged as its own service in 1960 (Frye & Peters, 1972) at which time "its old image of diversionary 'fun and games' changed to one of therapy" (U.S. Department of Veterans Affairs, 2013).

Following World War II, RT services were initiated throughout America in state psychiatric hospitals and state institutions for persons with intellectual disabilities (then termed *mental retardation*). James (1998) commented that such expansion was in part because many medical doctors had seen the benefits of recreational programs in military hospitals and wished to establish similar services as they returned to civilian life. Long-time proponents of RT, such as the noted psychiatrists Karl and William Menninger, who strongly advocated for the clinical application of RT in psychiatric hospitals, aided the cause of RT. The period of rapid upturn in the number of programs during and after World War II has been called "The Great Acceleration" of the broad field of therapeutic recreation (Austin, 2002), a period that culminated with early efforts toward the professionalization of the occupational group whose members were known as either hospital recreators or recreational therapists.

PROFESSIONAL ORGANIZATIONS

As a product of the process of professionalization, occupational groups form professional organizations. This occurred within the field of therapeutic recreation as well. Professionals who perceived themselves hospital recreators were in one organization, and professionals who called themselves recreational therapists were in another.

Persons who called themselves hospital recreators followed the views held by professionals in the park and recreation movement, who believed in recreation as an end in itself and recreation for all. Austin (2002) remarked,

> This perspective believed that the right to recreation was something that all should enjoy, including those who were institutionalized, ill, or disabled. They believed that organized recreation participation was beneficial, and recreation during times of illness or disability would help in the general recovery of the patient or client by providing a healthy daily activity. Provision of a satisfying and enjoyable recreation experience was the central goal under this approach. (p. 277)

Not surprisingly, practitioners who saw recreation as an end in itself and believed in the credo of recreation for all affiliated themselves with the American Recreation Society (ARS), which in the 1940s and 1950s represented professionals in the park and recreation movement who embraced the notions of recreation being an end in itself and the provision of recreation services to all. Within ARS, the Hospital Recreation Section (HRS) was established as a special interest group in 1948.

Those who called themselves recreational therapists thought that recreation was more than wholesome activity. To them, recreation was a tool or modality that they could use to treat illnesses and rehabilitate clients. Professionals with this perspective saw themselves as therapists who used recreation to ameliorate illnesses and aid in the rehabilitation of persons who were ill or had acquired a disability. Thus, to them, recreation was a means, not an end.

The recreational therapists formed into two professional organizations. The largest was the National Association of Recreational Therapists (NART), which came into being in 1952. Members of NART primarily served as recreational therapists in state psychiatric hospitals and state schools for persons with intellectual disabilities (then referred to as state schools for the mentally retarded). A smaller group of recreational therapists formed the Recreation Therapy Section within the Recreation Division of the American Association for Health, Physical Education, and Recreation (Austin, 2002; James, 1998).

In 1953, an effort was made to bring together representatives of the three organizations (i.e., the Hospital Recreation Section of the American Recreation Society, the National Association of Recreational Therapists, and the Recreation Therapy Section of the Recreation Division of the American Association for Health, Physical Education, and Recreation) in the Council for the Advancement of Hospital Recreation. The council successfully established a national registration program, but it failed to unite the organizations (Austin, 2002; Frye & Peters, 1972). According to James (1998), discussion within the council arose about merging the organizations, which included adopting the term *therapeutic recreation*, but representatives did not wish to compromise their distinct positions. The Hospital Recreation Section of the American Recreation Society (HRS/ARS) and the National Association of Recreational Therapists (NART) continued to serve as the major champions for their representative positions until 1966 when they merged to form a branch of the National Recreation and Park Association titled the National Therapeutic Recreation Society (NTRS).

Although professionals holding the polar positions of recreation as an end and recreation as therapy joined together to form NTRS, neither side was willing to break from their philosophical views. These contrasting views would continue to fester for the life of NTRS (Austin, 2007, 2010). Nevertheless, under the NTRS, the field of therapeutic recreation was able to establish hallmarks in its professionalization: (a) establishment of a scholarly journal, *Therapeutic Recreation Journal*, in 1966; (b) publication of guidelines for community-based programs for special populations in 1978 and of clinical standards of practice in 1979; (c) expansion in the number of universities offering therapeutic recreation; and (d) growing publication of textbooks and other professional literature. In 1981, the National Council for Therapeutic Recreation Certification (NCTRC) was established, which would become the credentialing body for therapeutic recreation (Austin, 2002). Even prior to the initiation of NCTRC credentialing, Navar (1979) assessed the professionalization of therapeutic recreation and concluded it had developed into an "emerging profession."

Yet throughout its developmental years, the field of therapeutic recreation was unable to determine whether it stood for recreation as an end (the HRS/ARS position) or recreation as therapy (the NART position). Because the field of therapeutic recreation had not established a single philosophical position to form a basis for its practice, it languished. Hemingway (1986) stated that therapeutic recreation had been absorbed with developing the "trappings of a profession" (p. 4) to the neglect of establishing a philosophical foundation for practice.

The lack of a single solidifying philosophical position for therapeutic recreation has become the focus of a number of authors, particularly since the beginning of the 1980s. Lahey (1987), for instance, lamented over a "lack of philosophical consensus" (p. 24) for the field. In a later publication, she wrote that "as a profession without its own well-defined philosophical consensus, therapeutic recreation is necessarily influenced by the philosophy of care bred into the practical techniques and techno-logical conceptualizations it borrows" (Lahey, 1996, p. 27). Sylvester (2009) likewise wrote about the lack of an integrating philosophy for therapeutic recreation. In his article, Sylvester quoted Peterson as having written that "from the beginning, it appears, there has been debate over the basic issue of whether therapeutic recreation is or should be therapy oriented or leisure oriented" (p. 26).

Of course, practitioners have tried to arrive at one philosophical position for therapeutic recreation. Representatives of what has been termed the "leisure orien-tation" (Dieser, 2008, p. 21) passionately advocated for the positions of recreation as the end in itself and recreation for all that professionals in the Hospital Recre-ation Section of the American Recreation Society had espoused. But these authors used the term *leisure*, rather than *recreation*, in their writings. For instance, Sylvester (1987) wrote that leisure, not health, should be the end professionals in therapeutic recreation seek. Lahey (1996) wrote that therapeutic recreation should be a field that "seeks to open the fullness of leisure to all citizens" (p. 27). In a similar vein, Mobley (1996) wrote that "it seems to me that our job is to stand up for those we serve and advocate for leisure activities for persons with disabilities in all settings, clinical and community" (p. 67).

The leisure orientation position, along with the adoption of the use of the term *leisure*, was codified to some degree in the late 1970s and early 1980s when the first conceptual model for therapeutic recreation appeared. This was the Leisure Abil-ity Model (that focused on the improvement of clients' leisure lifestyles), which was published in Scott Gunn and Carol Peterson's (1978) popular textbook *Therapeutic Recreation Program Design*. Because it was the only conceptual model available and was widely disseminated, many professionals in the field readily accepted it. The philosophical position published early in the 1980s by the National Therapeutic Rec-reation Society (that saw leisure to be at the center of therapeutic recreation prac-tice) also helped bring the leisure orientation to the forefront.

Even with such efforts by professionals holding the leisure orientation, profes-sionals with the "therapy orientation" (i.e., RT perspective) held strongly to their view that recreation was a means to improve clients' health and well-being. Conflicts continued within the National Therapeutic Recreation Society (NTRS) between pro-fessionals holding the leisure orientation and professionals believing in the therapy orientation. Ultimately such philosophical conflicts, coupled with a desire for an au-tonomous professional association, led to the formation of the American Therapeu-tic Recreation Association (ATRA) in 1984 (Austin, 2010).

ATRA quickly established itself. After beginning with 50 founding members, in the space of less than a year, its membership rose to almost 300 (Austin, 2007). In less than 10 years, ATRA's membership had swelled to more than 3,650 (Craw-ford, 2001). ATRA's growth had a profound effect on NTRS. Dieser (2008) indicated, "NTRS clearly suffered when ATRA was formed" (p. 27). NTRS's membership continued to decline over the years. Eventually, in 2010, NRPA decided to do away with its branches (Carter & Van Andel, 2011). With this decision, NTRS was dissolved leaving ATRA as the single professional association representing the field in the United States.

With the arrival of ATRA, the therapy orientation seemed to rise as members of the new professional association increasingly emphasized clinical practice. This shift toward greater emphasis on clinical practice has been reflected in historical accounts by Crawford and Dieser. Crawford (2001) wrote that ATRA provided "for more aggressive growth of clinical practice and specialization within therapeutic recreation" (p. 29). Dieser (2008) wrote about ATRA: "As was the case with NART, the early ATRA leaders felt that therapeutic recreation should emphasize that therapeutic recreation is a treatment for therapeutic change and should separate from its historical roots with parks and recreation and its distinct association with leisure" (p. 27).

Despite its focus on clinical practice, ATRA seemed unable to commit to adopting a clear recreation as therapy philosophical position that would once and for all settle the long-running dispute between the leisure orientation and the therapy orientation. Although coming close to following the clinically focused therapy orientation in defining the field, ATRA did not seem capable of expressing a clearly articulated clinically oriented definition that would guide practice (Austin, 2007, 2010; Dieser, 2008).

Recently, however, ATRA appears to be moving toward expressing a philosophy consistent with the recreation as therapy clinical position, which many members favored when the organization was formed. The following statement has appeared on the American Therapeutic Recreation Association (2009) website:

> The American Therapeutic Recreation Association (ATRA) is the largest national membership organization representing the interests and needs of recreational therapists. Recreational therapists are healthcare providers who use recreational therapy interventions for improved functioning of individuals with illness or disabling conditions.

PHILOSOPHICAL FOUNDATION LACKING FOR THERAPEUTIC RECREATION

Authors such as Lahey (1987, 1996), Mobley (1996), and Sylvester (1989, 2009) have pointed out time and again that throughout its history, therapeutic recreation has lacked a clear philosophical foundation that would serve as a basis to define the field and to guide practice. These authors have made a strong case that every profession needs an agreed upon philosophy that offers a clear position from which it may interpret what it does and on which it may base practice. Yet, as is apparent from reviewing the history of therapeutic recreation, such a philosophical position has been lacking.

Shank and Kinney (1987) commented that the history of therapeutic recreation has "one consistent theme: the uneasy fit between recreation as a contributor to the normalization and life quality of persons with disability and recreation as a means to improve an individual's psychological and physical functioning" (p. 65). Similarly,

Sylvester (2009) suggested therapeutic recreation has been "caught between two traditions that have resisted assimilation into a single practice" (p. 19). These traditions could be aptly termed the practice of leisure facilitation (springing from the leisure orientation) and the practice of RT (coming from the therapy orientation) that have found themselves under the single practice of therapeutic recreation. Most practitioners would agree with Sylvester's (2009) conclusion that these two are "fundamentally different practices" (p. 18).

THERAPEUTIC RECREATION HISTORY: REALLY A HISTORY OF TWO PROFESSIONS

The history of therapeutic recreation clearly shows two practices have existed, each with a distinctive philosophy. One philosophy, which grew out of the traditions of the Hospital Recreation Section of the American Recreation Society, could be termed the *leisure orientation philosophy* or *leisure facilitation philosophy*. This philosophical position perceives leisure as an end, not a means. The second philosophy, which professionals in the National Association of Recreational Therapists embraced, takes the approach of recreation as therapy that sees recreation as a means, not an end. This position could be termed the *recreational therapy philosophy*.

The broad field of therapeutic recreation represents two professions, each of which has its own distinct philosophical foundation. These professions could be termed *leisure facilitation* and *recreational therapy*. Austin (2014) endorsed this position when he wrote:

> Both philosophical positions are strong enough to support two worthy professions, each of which should find their rightful places among kindred professions. Those who hold the "leisure for all" philosophy certainly can have an important place within the leisure service professions. Those who embrace the "therapy" philosophical position can assume their natural position within the healthcare professions.

YOU AND YOUR PERSONAL IDENTITY

This chapter began with a wish that as a result of becoming acquainted with the history of the broad field of therapeutic recreation, you would gain a grasp of the identity of the profession and begin to assume your personal identity as a member of it. If you see yourself becoming a recreational therapist serving in health care, the contents of this book should provide a comprehensive approach that will furnish you with a strong foundation for entering the profession as an emerging professional.

A PERSONAL PERSPECTIVE

Professionals within the field of therapeutic recreation should consider that the field is made up of two distinct professions. Furthermore, the expression *recreational therapy* should be used to interpret the use of recreation as a means to health. Without a movement in which RT separates itself from what has been the fragmented, ill-defined field of therapeutic recreation, RT is in great danger of losing its way and that its potential importance in health care is in danger of being minimized.

Well over 40 years have passed since the founding of the National Therapeutic Recreation Society, at which time RT found itself under the umbrella term of *therapeutic recreation*. The time has come for RT to once again emerge as a separate entity that will advance the cause of using recreation to bring health benefits. In the biblical story, Moses wandered for 40 years. The hope is that RT will not, as did Moses, wander for another 40 years but will step forward now to assume its rightful place as a health care profession.

READING COMPREHENSION QUESTIONS

1. Provide examples of recreation being used for health restoration in early civilizations such as ancient China.
2. For what is Dr. Phillippe Pinel noted? Dr. Benjamin Rush?
3. Who was Florence Nightingale, and what relationship did she have to the use of recreation in hospitals?
4. What has been noted as the beginnings of the playground movement?
5. Who was Joseph Lee? Neva Boyd?
6. What philosophical perspectives did the park and recreation movement adopt once it no longer expressed a social welfare motive?
7. When did "The Great Acceleration" occur within therapeutic recreation?
8. What were the early professional organizations within therapeutic recreation, and when did they form?
9. What philosophical position did professionals who termed themselves *hospital recreators* take?
10. What philosophical position did professionals who termed themselves *recreational therapists* take?
11. When was NTRS founded as a branch of the National Recreation and Park Association?
12. What were indicators of the professionalization of therapeutic recreation?
13. What precipitated the formation of ATRA?
14. Explain why it may be concluded that two distinct professions exist within the field of therapeutic recreation.

REFERENCES

American Therapeutic Recreation Association. (2009). ATRA. Retrieved from http://www.atra-online.com/

Austin, D. R. (2002). A third revolution in therapeutic recreation? In D. R. Austin, J. Dattilo, & B. P. McCormick (Eds.), *Conceptual foundations for therapeutic recreation* (pp. 273–287). State College, PA: Venture.

Austin, D. R. (2007). *ATRA – Famous since 1983 – Founded in 1984 – The early history of the American Therapeutic Recreation Association.* Retrieved from http://www.atra-online.com/associations/10488/files/ATRAHistoryPaper.pdf

Austin, D. R. (2010). ATRA – Famous since 1983 – Founded in 1984 – The early history of the American Therapeutic Recreation Association. *Annual in Therapeutic Recreation, 19*, 1–11.

Austin, D. R. (2014). *Name games: The need for our titles and professional philosophies to coincide.* Manuscript in preparation.

Austin, D. R., & Lee, Y. (2013). *Inclusive and special recreation: Opportunities for diverse populations to flourish* (6th ed.). Urbana, IL: Sagamore.

Carter, M. J., & Van Andel, G. E. (2011). *Therapeutic recreation: A practical approach* (4th ed.). Prospect Heights, IL: Waveland.

Crawford, M. E. (2001). Organization and formation of the profession. In D. R. Austin & M. E. Crawford (Eds.), *Therapeutic recreation: An introduction* (3rd ed., pp. 22–44). Needham Heights, MA: Allyn & Bacon.

Dieser, R. (2008). History of therapeutic recreation. In T. Robertson & T. Long (Eds.), *Foundations of therapeutic recreation* (pp. 13–30). Champaign, IL: Human Kinetics.

Frye, V., & Peters, M. (1972). *Therapeutic recreation: Its theory, philosophy, and practice.* Harrisburg, PA: Stackpole Books.

Gray, D. E. (1969). The case for compensatory recreation. *Parks & Recreation, 41*(4), 23–24.

Gunn, S. L., & Peterson, C. A. (1978). *Therapeutic recreation program design.* Englewood Cliffs, NJ: Prentice Hall.

Hemingway, J. L. (1986). Building a philosophical defense of therapeutic recreation: The case of distributive justice. In C. Sylvester (Ed.), *Philosophy of therapeutic recreation: Ideas and issues* (Vol. 1, pp. 1–16). Alexandria, VA: National Recreation and Park Association.

History of Pennsylvania Hospital. (2013). Retrieved from http://www.uphs.upenn.edu/paharc/features/brush.html

James, A. (1998). The conceptual development of recreational therapy. In F. Brasile, T. K. Skallko, & j. burlingame (Eds.), *Perspectives in recreational therapy: Issues of a dynamic profession.* Ravendale, WA: Idyll Arbor.

Lahey, M. P. (1987). The ethics of intervention in therapeutic recreation. In C. Sylvester (Ed.), *Philosophy of therapeutic recreation: Ideas and issues* (Vol. 1, pp. 17–26). Alexandria, VA: National Recreation and Park Association.

Lahey, M. P. (1996). The commercial model and the future of therapeutic recreation. In C. Sylvester (Ed.), *Philosophy of therapeutic recreation: Ideas and issues* (Vol. 2, pp. 20–27). Ashburn, VA: National Recreation and Park Association.

Mobley, R. E. (1996). Therapeutic recreation philosophy re-visited: A question of what leisure is good for. In C. Sylvester (Ed.), *Philosophy of therapeutic recreation: Ideas and issues* (Vol. 2, pp. 57–70). Ashburn, VA: National Recreation and Park Association.

Navar, N. H. (1979). *The professionalization of therapeutic recreation in the state of Michigan* (Unpublished doctoral dissertation). Indiana University, Bloomington.

Shank, J., & Kinney, T. (1987). On the neglect of clinical practice. In C. Sylvester (Ed.), *Philosophy of therapeutic recreation: Ideas and issues* (Vol. 1, pp. 65–75). Alexandria, VA: National Recreation and Park Association.

Smith, S. L. J., & Godbey, G. C. (1991). Leisure, recreation and tourism. *Annals of Tourism Research, 18*, 85–100.

Sylvester, C. (1989). Therapeutic recreation and the practice of history. *Therapeutic Recreation Journal, 23*(4), 19–28.

Sylvester, C. (2009). A virtue-based approach to therapeutic recreation practice. *Therapeutic Recreation Journal, 43*(3), 9–25.

U.S. Department of Veterans Affairs. (2013). *Recreation therapy: History, patient's needs and VA Roseburg healthcare system.* Retrieved from http://www.roseburg.va.gov/features/Recreation_Therapy_History_Patient_s_Needs_and_VA_Roseburg_Healthcare_System.asp

3

THE RECREATIONAL THERAPY PROCESS

DAVID R. AUSTIN

OBJECTIVES

- Describe the RT process, including its four phases.
- State the rationale for completing client assessment.
- Identify methods for completing client assessment.
- Understand elements of concern during the planning phase, including goals and objectives.
- Know the role of the recreational therapist during the implementation phase.
- Identify characteristics of therapeutic activities.
- Know the purpose of evaluation in the RT process.

Recreational therapy (RT) is a purposeful intervention designed to help clients relieve, or adaptively cope with, health problems and concerns and experience the highest levels of wellness possible for them through participation in recreation and leisure activities. The intervention occurs through a collaborative interaction between a credentialed recreational therapist and a client, who use the recreational therapy process (often referred to as the RT process) as a framework for providing services.

The *RT process* is a systematic problem-solving procedure first introduced into the literature by Gerald O'Morrow in 1976. O'Morrow termed what was then referred to as the therapeutic recreation process to be "a systematic and complex planning process" and listed its "essential characteristics" as being "that it is planned, it is person-centered, and it is goal-directed" (p. 178).

The four phases of the process according to O'Morrow (1976) are

- assessment,
- planning,
- implementation, and
- evaluation.

You may have noticed that the first letters of each word spell out the acronym APIE (pronounced a-pie). Because of this, many practitioners and students use the expression *APIE process* when referring to the RT process. The importance of the RT process to providing RT is emphasized in the following quote from the book *Lessons Learned: An Open Letter to Recreational Therapy Students and Practitioners* (Austin, 2011a):

> It is my view that a recreational therapist who does not follow the recreational therapy process should not claim to be doing recreational therapy. Without the use of the systematic problem-solving process termed the recreational therapy process, no therapeutic intent can exist. (p. 7)

RT practice must transcend the cognition that recreation by its nature is good, so it benefits the well-being of all persons, including those who are ill or have a disability. Justifying the RT profession on the credo of "recreation is good for all" trivializes the profession. RT has instrumental value. Its outcomes are not random and accidental but systematic and purposeful (Mobily, 1987). The RT process is the systematic approach employed in RT to provide purposeful interventions. The RT process is a cornerstone for the delivery of RT. It is the base from which all RT actions proceed.

Although the RT process is commonly associated with entities that are highly clinical in nature, it is not restricted to clinical settings. The RT process is not confined to use in hospitals and rehabilitation centers. It is a systematic process that may guide RT in skilled nursing facilities, assisted living facilities, schools, correctional facilities, community-based programs for persons with disabilities, or wherever recreation is used with therapeutic intent in goal-directed programs.

The systematic phases of the RT process then guide and direct what occurs within RT whatever the setting. First, the recreational therapist collects data and analyzes them to determine the client's problems or concerns and strengths and needs (during assessment). Then, the recreational therapist makes a plan to meet the client's problems or concerns (during planning). Once in place, the recreational therapist puts the plan into action and with the client conducts the designed interventions (during implementation). Finally, the recreational therapist conducts an assessment to determine the validity of the plan and the effectiveness of the interventions (during evaluation). This RT process is cyclical. For example, if the therapist find finds in the evaluation phase that the interventions were not effective, the plan may be revised with new interventions. See Figure 3.1.

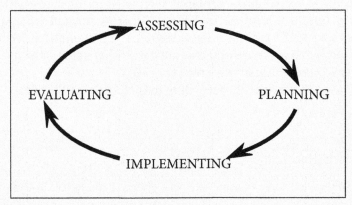

Figure 3.1. Cyclical nature of the recreational therapy process.

Throughout the RT process, recreational therapists work cooperatively with their clients. In doing so, recreational therapists allow as much control as possible to remain with clients. Reasons why the RT process is critically important to both clients and recreational therapists appear in Table 3.1.

Table 3.1
Elements Provided by the Recreational Therapy Process

- Provides a problem-solving structure to accomplish the delivery of effective, customized care
- Involves orderly step-by-step actions directed to achieve stated goals
- Promotes customized care by providing a system to meet specific, unique client needs
- Tailors interventions addressed to the individual's needs (not to the disease or disability)
- Increases client participation in care by collaboration between the client and recreational therapist during each phase of the recreational therapy process
- Offers an efficient, systematic approach where the focus is always on the client
- Allows the delivery of care that is organized, continuous, and systematic
- Leads to a goal-directed approach and measurable outcomes that may be reached through recreational therapy interventions
- Ensures accountability by including the evaluation of sought outcomes
- Through its cyclical nature, establishes interrelationships among and between its phases, which ensures all of its parts work together
- Provides a systematic and logical sequence through which recreational therapy transpires
- Offers a means to interpret to others how recreational therapy contributes to client care

Note. From *Therapeutic Recreation Processes and Techniques: Evidence-Based Recreational Therapy* (7th ed.), by D. R. Austin, 2013, Urbana, IL: Sagamore, p. 155.

ASSESSMENT: THE FIRST PHASE IN THE RECREATIONAL THERAPY PROCESS

The initial phase in the RT process is assessment. It is the foundation for all that follows. A sound assessment identifies the client's health status, environment, needs, and strengths, as well preferences. The assessment directs the planning phase by developing pertinent data about the client.

Recreational therapists should involve the client in assessment as soon and as much as possible. Some clients will be unable to participate temporarily or will be able to participate only partially. Nevertheless, recreational therapists must develop rapport so that clients feel comfortable sharing personal information to the best of their ability. Clients need to have confidence that the information collected is to be used confidentially for the sole purpose of helping them to achieve optimal health.

Even when recreational therapists establish excellent rapport, client assessment is not as straightforward as it may initially seem. That is, sometimes clients tell the recreational therapist what they believe they want to hear or what they perceive a "good" or "rational" client may say. This occurs with regularity with psychiatric clients who have had severe and persistent mental illnesses, according to Kanter (1985), who wrote that professionals may focus too much on expressed wishes for independence to the exclusion of other concerns:

> While we overemphasize the expressed wishes of chronic (psychiatric) patients for independence, we often neglect their unarticulated needs to be cared for, understood, and accepted, as well as their fear of abandonment should they actually achieve a measure of autonomy. (p. 65)

Certainly Kanter's warning may be extended beyond clients undergoing psychiatric care to almost all clients who may tell the recreational therapist what they think he or she would like to hear from them. Thus, the recreational therapist must look past the client's verbalizations to examine behavioral expressions of needs, as well as go beyond the client to seek other sources of assessment data. Although the client is typically a chief source of information, other data sources are observations of clients, interviews with family members and friends, conferences with other health professions, test results, medical records, social histories, educational records, progress notes, and interdisciplinary team meetings.

Clinical Reasoning

RT assessment involves more than data gathering. A critical element of the recreational therapist in doing assessment is to scrutinize the information collected to arrive at clinical judgments. This involves the process of *clinical reasoning*. Clinical reasoning during the assessment phase may be likened to the process of diagnosis in which a medical doctor gathers information by examining and interviewing the patient, forming hypotheses about the symptoms and causes of the patient's complaint, and then often gathering additional data (e.g., running blood tests, talking with other family members, consulting nurses) to substantiate or refute initial impressions.

RT diagnosis (which involves a wide biopsychosocial approach) differs from traditional medical diagnosis (typically limited to a biomedical approach). As with medical doctors, however, recreational therapists must use clinical reasoning to arrive at conclusions (i.e., diagnoses) about what constitutes the client's problem, clarifying factors causing or contributing to the problem, determining the client's needs, and identifying strengths and resources that may be employed as specific means to optimize health. In short, clinical reasoning during the assessment phase allows the recreational therapist to identify client problems/needs and strengths (Austin & Mc-Cormick, 2014).

When applying clinical reasoning to make clinical judgments or conclusions (i.e., derive a client's RT diagnosis), the recreational therapist would benefit from considering the process Alfaro-LeFevre (2014) outlined. This author suggested the process of diagnosis involves (a) creating a list of suspected problems; (b) ruling out similar problems, naming actual and potential problems, and clarifying what is causing or contributing to them; (c) determining risk factors that must be managed; and (d) identifying resources, strengths, and areas to optimize health. Thus, completing such an analysis goes beyond simple data collection.

However, clinical reasoning does not stop with assessment. In addition to arriving at clinical judgments to decide the client's problems/needs and strengths, the recreational therapist must employ clinical reasoning in clinical decisions when determining what to do in planning and interventions, as well as reflect back on the RT process to assess it. For example, during the planning and intervention phases, recreational therapists must consider the client's uniqueness in terms of not only the individual's health status but also the individual's culture, values, desires, and strengths to determine what to do in planning and interventions (Austin & McCormick, 2014).

Theory and Assessment

Although the RT process serves as a cornerstone for practice, theory drawn from the conceptual model of the recreational therapist influences assessment data gathered and decisions made following the examination and analysis of the data collected. Austin and McCormick (2014) listed several ways in which theory affects assessment and clinical reasoning: (a) helps to define which assessment data to collect and analyze; (b) outlines actual and potential problems for consideration; (c) assists in analyzing and understanding health situations; (d) guides formulation of RT diagnoses; (e) clarifies goals and objectives; and (f) specifies interventions that may be provided. For instance, assessment data collected following a health-related conceptual model, such as the Reformulated Health Protection/Health Promotion Model (Austin, 2011b), would emphasize health problems or concerns. In contrast, under a leisure-oriented model, such as the Leisure Ability Model (Stumbo & Peterson, 2009), data would focus on problems or concerns related to leisure functioning rather than health. Another example of theory affecting practice involves sought outcomes derived from assessment data. Outcomes that recreational therapists seek following the Reformulated Health Protection/Health Promotion Model would deal with the client's health status, and those following the Leisure Ability Model would be concerned with leisure functioning.

Methods of Assessment

Observing and *interviewing* are the most common methods of assessment that recreational therapists use. *Secondary sources* of data are also employed in RT assessment.

Observation. Recreational therapists often make observations in unstructured recreational settings (e.g., unstructured recreation by adults in a lounge or children in free play on a playground) where the natural environment is not manipulated or changed. During such naturalistic observations, recreational therapists may note (a) the client's general appearance, (b) how comfortable the client seems, (c) physical functioning, (d) cognitive functioning, (e) interpersonal interactions, (f) verbal communications including speech patterns (e.g., fast, slow), (g) nonverbal communications (e.g., body language), (h) congruence between verbal and nonverbal communications, and (i) the effect of the environment on the client (Austin, 2013; Shank & Coyle, 2002).

Specific goal observations occur in structured situations where the observer sets predetermined goals for the observation. These observations require planning since the observer formulates definite goals for observation to meet a specific purpose or to assess a defined behavior. For example, the therapist may observe the level of cooperation the client displays in a co-recreational game situation or how the client responds to frustration in an athletic contest.

Time-interval observations offer another type of observation. The recreational therapist observes these clients and records the frequency of client behaviors for predetermined times (e.g., 15 minutes, 30 minutes, or any period of the day). For example, the recreational therapist could record the number of aggressive acts occurring during a 1-hour period.

Recreational therapists may use standardized instruments or criterion-referenced tested in *standardized observations*. The standardized instrument, such as a physical fitness test, has *established norms*. Norm-referenced tests provide a way to measure how the client performs in relation to others who are similar (e.g., other children or other adults). *Criterion-referenced tests*, in contrast, measure achievement toward an established standard. For example, the leisure diagnostic battery (Witt & Ellis, 1987), designed to assess leisure functioning, measures whether the client has certain skills and abilities.

When using such standardized instruments, recreational therapists should confirm that they have been established as having reliability and validity. *Reliability* deals with whether the instrument produces consistent results over time. *Validity* answers the question of whether the instrument tests what it sets out to assess or its results are an accurate representation of what is being assessed (Austin, 2013).

Client self-administered *checklists* and *questionnaires* are sometimes used as means to gain specific information and save time in collecting it. At other times, recreational therapists collect the data during the interview process.

Interviews. The *interview* is a time to gather information about the client, clarify items not understood, and observe the client's condition and behavior. A critical competency for recreational therapists is to understand the relationship between recreation and leisure and other aspects of functioning (Long, 2008). With this competency as a basis, the recreational therapist needs to structure the interview to learn about the client's functioning and how recreation and leisure participation may enhance the client's level of functioning. The recreational therapist typically will ask clients about past leisure habits, the activities in which they participate, with whom they usually participate, and recreation interests they may wish to pursue in the future. Regularly used techniques to enhance the interview process are open-ended questions and leisure inventories.

Open-ended questions are used to begin conversations. A general open-ended question is, tell me about yourself? Open-ended questions drawn from Yura and Walsh (1988) follow:

Activity: (a) What do you do in an average day? (b) Do you do anything to keep in shape?

Leisure: (a) What do you do for recreation and leisure? When? How often? (b) What activities are most likely to make you feel refreshed? (c) Are there activities you would like to try?

Wholesome body image: (a) How do you and your body appear to you? (b) How would others describe your body?

Self-control, self-determination: (a) How much ability do you have to be in control of your life or to be responsible for yourself? (b) What within you, or outside you, gives you ability to control and determine things for yourself? What takes control away? (c) How do you account for your state of health?

Acceptance of self and others: (a) What are your personal strengths? How do you feel about them? (b) Have you identified limitations? How do you feel about them? (c) Describe your acceptance by family members, friends, and persons with whom you work. How do you feel about their acceptance?

Appreciation: (a) Which of your positive qualities and accomplishments have been noticed by others? (b) What type of response do you get from others in terms of their appreciation of you?

Autonomy, Choice: (a) Would you describe yourself as being an independent person? (b) When confronted with choices about your leisure, how do you handle these?

Belonging: (a) Describe your relationship with family, friends, and co-workers. (b) With whom do you have your closest relationships? (c) Are you a member of any community or church group?

Challenge: (a) If you had to name a challenging situation in your life, what would you say? (b) Do you get satisfaction from taking on challenges?

Confidence: (a) In what situations do you feel most secure or sure of yourself? (b) What things do you do that make you most confident? Least confident?

Personal recognition and esteem: (a) What do you do that brings you personal recognition and esteem? (b) Who are the persons who provide you with recognition?

Self-actualization, Self-fulfillment: Are you fulfilling your goals in life? (b) What do you see in your future in terms of realizing your potential?

Value system: (a) What beliefs do you hold in terms of taking part in recreation? (b) Identify beliefs you hold in regard to the worth of people and in regard to experiences in your life?

Of course, no recreational therapist would use all these open-ended questions with a client. The questions are only guidelines and should not be strictly adhered to. Therapists pick and choose which questions are appropriate for each client. At times, the therapist will want to follow up with a more probing question to delve more deeply into a particular area.

No matter which questions are used, the therapist should employ good attending or listening skills so clients know they are being heard. The environment in which the interview is conducted is also critical to the success in interviewing. Distractions such as a ringing phone or interruptions from others must be avoided. Psychological privacy should be established by arranging the interview in an area where others cannot hear the conversation. That area may be in an informal setting, such as at a table in a hospital coffee shop, if others are not within listening distance. Sometimes a recreational area is an appropriate place to hold an interview, as long as the client feels comfortable in that setting. Some adolescents, for example, may feel most comfortable talking with the recreational therapist while shooting basketballs in a gym.

Interviews usually begin with a warm-up period with small talk followed by information for the client about confidentiality and the purpose of the interview. The recreational therapist's tone should never be confrontational but should put the client at ease. The working phase of the interview follows when information gathering occurs. The therapist finishes the interview using a closure technique, such as summarizing, to draw the interview to a close.

Most agencies with RT services design or adopt *leisure inventories* appropriate for their clients. Agencies often develop leisure interest checklists or questionnaires that fit the profiles of the clients that they regularly serve. These instruments typically list activities that the recreational therapist reviews with the client and notes whether the client participates in each or has interest in participating. Particularly in cases where clients cannot read or write, are disoriented, or do not have the strength or inclination to fill out the form, recreational therapists may complete inventories with clients during interviews.

Secondary sources. Secondary sources, sources of information not obtained directly from the client, may provide valuable information for the recreational therapist completing client assessments. *Family members and friends* are excellent secondary sources of information. For instance, they may confirm or disconfirm information that the client gave or reveal conditions that exist in the client's home or community. They are often sources to discover a client's strengths. *Client medical records* are another secondary source. Information such as medical precautions, medications, and the client's health status may be found in these records. *Social histories* prepared by social workers provide information on the client's history prior to coming into the treatment, care, rehabilitation, or wellness program. Information in the social history includes where the person was born, raised, and educated; the client's family and home; occupations and income; religious affiliations; and past recreational pursuits. The results of *testing* by psychologists or other clinical staff may provide objective data. *Progress notes* written by other recreational therapists and other staff members often contain information on the client's behavior, particularly regarding deviations from the normal. Members of *interdisciplinary teams* may be rich sources of information about clients either within team meetings or when consulted with individually. Finally, the therapist may learn a great deal by *visiting the client's home and community*. Although making such visits may not be possible for the recreational therapist, social workers are often able to make such visits and share information with the recreational therapist (Austin, 2013).

Areas of Assessment

General information. General information that the recreational therapist normally will gain includes the client's full name, address, telephone number, date admitted, date and place of birth, sex, age, marital or family status, religious preference, language(s) spoken, education completed, occupation, leisure interests briefly noted, medications, why the client is seeking service, and limitations or precautions (e.g., physical restrictions, suicidal).

Settings and models. The setting in which the client is served will affect the assessment data gathered. For example, data collected on psychiatric clients will differ from data collected on clients in physical rehabilitation centers. The setting will also influence assessment as treatment, rehabilitation, care, educational, or wellness programs will have varying concerns. Another factor is the overall model that the agency follows. Data collected at medical centers where a medical model prevails will differ from data gathered under an agency where children's educational needs are being met and an educational model is being followed. So recreational therapists have to adapt their assessment procedures to the setting where the RT service is located and the model that is followed within that setting. Similarly, the conceptual model to which the recreational therapist subscribes will have a bearing on the nature of the assessment data and its analysis (Austin, 2013).

ICF outcome domains. The World Health Organization's (WHO, 2002) International Classification of Functioning, Disability, and Health (ICF) outcome domains offer one means to conceptualize areas for assessment in rehabilitating persons with disabilities. The ICF emphasizes function rather than etiology. Under the ICF, two general categories exist: *medical care* and *socio-cultural care*. Medical care is broken down into *body structure/function* and *activity*. Body structure/function deals with areas such as motor control, vision, strength, flexibility, memory, and problem solving. Under activity are functions such as mobility, climbing stairs, lifting, preparing meals, eating, dressing, and grooming.

The two subareas under the general category of socio-cultural care may garner the most attention from recreational therapists: *participation* and *environment*. Under participation are functions such as fitness activities, leisure/sport activities, social activities, community activities, and religious and spiritual activities. Under the area of environment are aspects such as social support, assistive technology, the natural environment, the built environment, and attitudes (WHO, 2002).

Assessment areas suggested in the recreational therapy literature. Guidelines for specific areas to address in RT assessment have appeared in the literature. Shank and Coyle (2002) listed four areas for assessment: (a) *biological functioning, including physical functioning and health status* (e.g., mobility, muscle strength and muscle endurance, flexibility, cardiovascular endurance, perceptual motor skills, and visual and auditory perception); (b) *psychological functioning, including cognitive and emotional functioning* (e.g., attention, memory, orientation, problem solving, enjoyment, coping); (c) *social functioning* (e.g., behaviors during interactions with others); and (d) *spiritual functioning* (e.g., formal religion, as well as one's personal belief system or philosophical values).

Austin (2013) suggested the following areas for RT assessment:

- Client's general perceptions about their present health status, how they are dealing with their health problems or concerns, and how their health problems/concerns may impact regular recreation and leisure patterns.

- Sensory and motor impairments, cognitive deficits, limitations in activities of daily living, and any precautions (e.g., heart problem) are noted.

- Leisure values, interests, and pursuits are explored, along with client attitudes toward participation in RT programs.

- The developmental level of the client is appraised to determine developmental tasks or issues with which the client may be dealing.

- Problems or concerns are explored in order to reveal needs (e.g., need to belong, for self-esteem) in order to establish a needs list.

- Strengths (e.g., abilities, virtues, support from family and friends) are identified in order to build a strengths list.

- Client expectations and goals are identified. (p. 169)

Strengths assessment. The assessment of client strengths is an area of particular concern to recreational therapists. Austin (2013) described the process of strengths assessment:

> Clients typically require the recreational therapist's help in identifying their strengths because their health concerns or a lack of self-awareness may interfere with the ability of a client to fully appreciate the strengths they possess. Clients often have untapped strengths that the recreational therapist can help them to identify. Strengths include a multitude of characteristics (e.g., persistence, determination, creativity, interpersonal skills, prior life successes), as well as social support (e.g., social networks, environmental resources) and recreational abilities (e.g., skills possessed in recreational activities). Clients' recreational interests need to be explored during assessment as interests are closely tied to client abilities. (p. 210)

Concluding Remarks on Assessment

Assessment forms the foundation of the RT process. To move to the planning phase of the RT process, a complete workup on each client and a thorough analysis of data collected are required. Both *subjective data* gained from the client and *objective data* from other sources are necessary to identify client needs and strengths that will be used in planning—commonly referred to as *needs lists* and *strengths lists*.

Needs are derived from the client's problems or concerns. For example, if the client has a problem or concern with stress, a need would be to achieve stress reduction or relaxation. Strengths the client possesses (enumerated on each client's strengths list) may be examined to determine which may be used to meet the needs identified on the needs list. Categories of strengths that clients may possess include personality traits or characteristics (e.g., resilience, persistence, internal locus of control), recreational skills or abilities (e.g., skills in a sport or creative skills such as writing), and external resources (e.g., support networks of family or friends). The needs list and strengths list, constructed during assessment for each client, form the basis for the customized intervention plan constructed during the planning phase of the RT process (Austin, 2013).

Bullock, Mahon, and Killingsworth (2010) proposed general guidelines for RT assessment that serve as good reminders when approaching RT assessment. These are (a) seek as much input as possible from the individual; (b) assess the physical and human environment as well as the individual's skills and needs; (c) remain focused upon the individual's long-term goals; and (d) assess strengths, abilities, and desires as well as deficits and needs.

PLANNING: THE SECOND PHASE IN THE RECREATIONAL THERAPY PROCESS

After identifying and analyzing the client's needs and strengths during the assessment phase, the recreational therapist and client are ready to move to the second stage of the RT process: the planning phase. During this phase, priorities are set; goals are formulated; objectives are developed; programs, strategies, and approaches are specified; and means of evaluation are determined. When this phase has been completed, the recreational therapist and client have a personalized RT intervention plan to meet the client's needs.

The RT intervention plan usually becomes a component of the client's interdisciplinary intervention plan, sometimes termed a *master treatment plan* or *interdisciplinary treatment plan*. An interdisciplinary team (which may be referred to as the *treatment team* in some settings) develops these plans. The recreational therapist typically works closely with other health care professionals in developing the comprehensive interdisciplinary intervention plan. Team meetings are held to formulate the final plan, which is then reviewed with the client. Depending on the setting, other terms for *intervention plan* may be used such as *treatment plan, rehabilitation plan, care plan, education plan,* or *wellness plan.*

A four-step procedure is followed during the planning phase: (a) setting priorities following examination of the client's needs; (b) formulation of goals and behavioral objectives; (c) determining strategies or actions to meet the goals; and (d) selecting methods to assess progress made toward goals.

Setting Priorities

Setting priorities involves an analysis of the identified needs on the needs list to determine which needs require the professional help of the recreational therapist and which are most urgent. The client should be included in this determination, if possible, because the client should be engaged in the planning process as soon as practical.

Formulating Goals and Objectives

Goals flow directly from the needs list. Goals reflect sought outcomes that are directed toward satisfaction of the client's needs. Therefore, they are stated in terms of the client's behavior and describe proposed changes in the individual in broad terms. Because goals describe client outcomes, they direct the recreational therapist, client, and others in terms of knowing what results are intended from the intervention program.

Objectives are developed to specify client behaviors related to reaching goals. Objectives enable clients to achieve goals and consequently are sometimes referred to as *enabling objectives*. Usually three to six enabling objectives are needed to reach a goal. Therefore, objectives offer a means for the recreational therapist and client to organize their efforts as they break down goals into manageable behaviors that direct program design and offer a basis for evaluation. The acronym SMART is helpful in understanding how to compose well-constructed objectives (see Table 3.2).

While the needs list serves as the basis for the goals, the strengths list is the basis for formulating objectives. That is, objectives take advantage of the strengths of the client.

Table 3.2
SMART Objectives

- **S**pecific (Every objective is in behavioral terms, states only one behavior, and lists associated conditions or criteria.)
- **M**easurable (Objectives provide specific ways to measure behaviors so it is clear the objective is accomplished.)
- **A**ttainable (Objectives are realistic. They are not established just to have something to strive for.)
- **R**elevant (Objectives are relevant to the individual and that individual's needs.)
- **T**imelined (Objectives provide specific deadlines by which they must be achieved.)

Note. From *Positive Psychology Coaching: Putting the Science of Happiness to Work for Your Clients,* by R. Biswas-Diener and B. Dean, 2007, Hoboken, NJ: Wiley.

An illustration may add to a clearer understanding of goals and objectives. A need of a client may be to interact with others through verbal expression. This need could translate into a goal stated as, "Increases verbal interactions with others within 1 week." An enabling objective could be, "Answers questions posed by staff at least 80% of the time." This objective would provide direction so the recreational therapist would know to structure opportunities for this occurrence by scheduling a social activity in which the client has some amount of ability. The objective would also be readily measurable so it could be a basis for evaluating progress toward the goal.

Determining Strategies or Actions to Meet Goals

Programs are interventions that help the client to reach goals and objectives. The recreational therapist provides interventions for client participation that offer opportunities for sought outcomes of the plan (i.e., goals and objectives). The program area selected needs to be one in which the client has skills or the ability to develop skills.

Perhaps another example will be helpful in illustrating the program component. A client who has the goal of learning stress management techniques may be placed in a stress reduction class in which relaxation training techniques are learned and practiced. The strategy used may be to begin with the recreational therapist working with the client in a small group so that the client becomes comfortable in doing relaxation training before moving to the regular stress reduction class that meets daily in the gymnasium, with 15 clients taking part. One element in the plan would be for the recreational therapist to be responsible for determining, with the client, when the client is ready to enter the regular class.

Evidence-based practice. The recreational therapist employs evidence-based practice (EBP) when considering interventions that may be used with a client. EBP involves considering the latest research findings on interventions that represent best practice while considering the clinical expertise of the therapist along with client values and preferences. Melnyk, Fineout-Overholt, and Cruz (2010) provided the following definition of EBP: "Evidence-based practice is a problem-solving approach to the delivery of health care that integrates the best evidence from well-designed studies (i.e., external evidence) with a clinician's expertise and a patient's preferences and values" (p. 302). EBP has become a hallmark within all segments of health care, including RT.

The primary gain found in following the EBP approach is giving full consideration to the best available empirical evidence, thus improving the selection and delivery of RT interventions. Interventions are not recommended to clients "because we have always done it that way" but because of the best research evidence available. Of course, research is not always available to tell the therapist what to do. However, research evidence may exist that informs the therapists what *not* to do (Austin, 2013).

With the emergence of EPB, university professional preparation programs must prepare students with the latest clinical research information. Students also need to learn how to access and evaluate clinical research completed on interventions.

Lee and McCormick (2002) proposed a five-step procedure for implementing EBP in RT. Step 1 is to develop clinical questions concerning the client's problem (e.g., What interventions seem to work best with this type of client?). Step 2 is to locate related research evidence. Textbooks, journals, and databases (e.g., MEDLINE and PsychINFO) are sources for research evidence. Step 3 is appraising the evidence. Step 4 is implementing research findings in practice through selecting an intervention. In doing so, therapists needs to use their clinical judgment and consider the client's preferences. The final step is to evaluate whether the intervention worked.

EBP has come to the forefront of RT and certainly needs to be used when making decisions about the selection of interventions. Law and MacDermit (2008) stated a rationale for using EBP: "The argument for EBP is simple. If there is a better way to practice, therapists should find it" (p. 5).

Selecting Methods to Assess Progress Made Toward Goals

Finally, once the recreational therapist and client have chosen an intervention program, a description of *evaluation* procedures needs to be determined to assess progress toward obtaining stated client goals. The interdisciplinary team typically determines when the client's progress will be followed (e.g., keeping daily or weekly progress notes). Depending on the outcome of the evaluation, the client's goals or schedule of activities may be retained or revised to accommodate the client's needs.

The Planning Phase Provides a Blueprint for Action

The planning phase culminates with the production of the individual intervention plan, which serves as a "blueprint for action." The following elements are commonly found in each client's intervention plan:

- an indication of the client's problems and needs, in order to formulate a needs list (Problems represent obstacles to meeting needs. Therefore, the identification of problems leads to needs.);

- an identification of client strengths (e.g., abilities, virtues, family support) to formulate a strengths list;

- a prioritized goals set appropriate to guide the delivery of RT services;

- a listing of specific objectives for each goal;

- a plan of interventions or programs indicated for participation by the client, approaches to be utilized by staff, and the proper environment in which to facilitate change; and

- a brief description of procedures by which client progress will be periodically evaluated, or a plan for evaluation. (Austin, 2013, pp. 180–181)

IMPLEMENTATION: THE THIRD PHASE IN THE RECREATIONAL THERAPY PROCESS

The implementation phase is the action phase of the RT process. Implementation involves the the recreational therapist and client executing the client's intervention plan. Recreational therapists are responsible for coordinating client-focused and goal-directed activities consistent with the proposed plan of action. They guide the client until he or she can assume self-responsibility. Recreational therapists also ensure that the client's actions and responses are fully documented throughout the implementation phase.

RT programs are interventions tailored to the needs, capacities, and degree of readiness of each client. Programs focus on using existing strengths and interests as foundations for reaching client goals. Progressive, graded programs offer developmental sequencing for clients to acquire skills as they progress. The plan should stipulate the frequency and duration of the client's participation in each activity scheduled.

A number of facilitation techniques, from adventure therapy, animal-assisted therapy, aquatic therapy, and aromatherapy to yoga, values clarification, validation therapy, and video games, are available to be used as interventions to facilitate change. Of course, a primary consideration in selecting a facilitation technique is the research evidence that supports its use with a particular client group to reach a desired therapeutic outcome. Table 3.3 lists facilitation techniques commonly used in RT.

Most would agree that experiencing true recreation or leisure may be unattainable for persons who are severely ill. In fact, it would be naïve to believe that clients who are seriously ill are ready or able to make self-determined choices to enjoy recreation or leisure. For example, clients with neurological dysfunction, Alzheimer's disease, or chronic depression may suffer from impaired functioning to the point that they cannot exercise freedom of choice. Initially, these clients may need to be placed in activities that are not truly recreational or leisure experiences but rather prerequisites to achieving recreation or leisure experiences (Shank & Kinney, 1987).

Helplessness and despair also frequently occur in clients whose coping mechanisms have been severely tested by the stress of dealing with health problems, particularly health problems resulting from chronic conditions. Clients undergoing psychiatric treatment, physical rehabilitation, and nursing home care seem particularly subject to feelings of helplessness. A classic research study by Langer and Rodin (1976) found that helping people regain a sense of control over their lives offers them hope and improves their morale (Bule, 1988). Once individuals begin to experience a restoration of their morale, they develop a renewed sense of resolution or determination to conquer their health problems.

Because of the severity of the client's health condition, or because of feelings of helplessness, the recreational therapist may initially carefully select *prescribed activities,* therapeutic activities that provide the structure and level of demand that may benefit the client. Once clients gain successes in such activities, pleasure and enjoyment gained from these mastery experiences enhance the clients' morale, and they may move to activities that are truly recreational in nature. True recreation represents experiences that are restorative and largely done for pleasure and enjoyment. The most therapeutic activities are those the client chooses in close collaboration with the recreational therapist. Ultimately, the client may be able to exercise a high level of perceived control by selecting leisure activities that represent growth opportunities. The highest form of RT participation is that which the client finds self-rewarding and is not a product of external compulsion.

Table 3.3
Facilitation Techniques

Adventure therapy	Pilates
Animal-assisted therapy	Progressive relaxation training
Aquatic therapy	Qigong
Aromatherapy	Reminiscence therapy
Assertiveness therapy	Remotivation therapy
Autogenic training	Resocialization
Bibliotherapy	Robotic therapy
Biofeedback	Self-massage
Cinematherapy	Sensory training
Cognitive rehabilitation	Snoezelen room
Cognitive stimulation therapy	Social skills training
Creative arts	Stretching
Diaphragmatic breathing	Tai chi
Horticulture therapy	Therapeutic community
Humor	Therapeutic use of touch
Imagery	Yoga
Laughter yoga	Values clarification
Leisure education/counseling	Validation therapy
Meditation	Video games
Physical activity	

Note. From *Therapeutic Recreation Processes and Techniques: Evidence-Based Recreational Therapy* (7th ed.), by D. R. Austin, 2013, Urbana, IL: Sagamore.

Skills Required of Recreational Therapists During Implementation

The recreational therapist needs interpersonal, observational, decision-making, and technical skills during the implementation phase of the RT process. These skills are necessary to put the intervention plan into action.

Interpersonal skills (i.e., relationship skills) are particularly critical to the success of the implementation phase. Interactions need to be goal directed and purposeful within an accepting, nonthreatening atmosphere. Rogers (1961) proclaimed the significance of creating a positive climate:

> On the basis of experience I have found that if I can help bring about a climate marked by genuineness, prizing, and understanding, then exciting things happen. Persons and groups in such a climate move away from rigidity and toward flexibility, away from static living toward process living, away from dependence

toward autonomy, away from defensiveness toward self-acceptance, away from being predictable toward unpredictable creativity. They exhibit living proof of an actualizing tendency. (pp. 43–44)

During interactions with clients, the recreational therapist continually makes observations to document the progress of the client and to verify that the plan of action is correct. Client reactions are charted in the form of progress notes. If a plan is not working as expected, the recreational therapist needs to decide whether to modify the goals and objectives or the approach to achieve the goals and objectives.

Technical skills relate to the recreational therapist's knowledge of the properties of activities and leadership abilities and conducting activities. To demonstrate the therapeutic use of an activity, the recreational therapist must be familiar with the demands it makes on clients and anticipated outcomes from participation. The recreational therapist is action oriented in organizing activities, teaching activity skills, offering feedback, providing psychological support, and completing group processing with clients on their participation as a part of the activities and following activities (referred to as debriefing).

Skills in group processing are particularly important for recreational therapists to develop. A basic tenet in the practice of RT is that the emphasis is always on the client, not the activity. What occurs with the client as a result of participating in an activity is the critical element (Austin, 2011a). The activity is only a vehicle; the end is bringing about therapeutic outcomes for the client. An activity is successful only if clients derive therapeutic benefits by making a connection between their participation in the activity and what they gained from participating. Group processing (i.e., clients discussing the dynamics of their activity participation to gain self-knowledge) led by the recreational therapist permits clients to discuss their participation in an activity, to learn from that discussion, and to extend their learnings to their everyday lives (Austin, 2013). In fact, Austin (2013) said processing is "the most important part of any program and therefore needs to be skillfully and carefully accomplished" (p. 321).

Characteristics of Therapeutic Activities

For activities to hold the potential for therapeutic outcomes, they need to be conducted so that they possess certain characteristics:

1. *Goal directed.* RT activities are directed toward a purpose. They are not "time fillers" but are done for a reason. The goal may be as general as involving the clients in something outside themselves, thus allowing them less time to dwell on problems, or the goal may be specific, such as bringing about stress reduction or learning social skills.

2. *Require participants to actively participate.* Self-determination is important in the sense that clients are active as possible in both choosing activities and having a role in affecting the outcome of the activities. Clients need to be involved to the largest extent possible in determining the activity to exercise control. They need to feel that their participation meaningfully affects the results of the activity to gain feelings of self-efficacy and competence.

3. *Have meaning and value to the client.* The client needs to learn to approach activities not as a requirement but as an opportunity to achieve an end. Recreational therapists process (i.e., discuss) activities with clients so that

clients may gain personal awareness of behaviors, feelings, and outcomes achieved as a result of participating.

4. *Offer potential for pleasure and satisfaction.* Ideally, a primary motivation for the client lies in the pleasurable, satisfying experience gained from participation. Even when gratification is not immediate, activities should make it possible for the client to gain pleasure and satisfaction.

5. *Are selected with the guidance of the recreational therapist.* Gump and Sutton-Smith (1955) wrote, "Activities have a reality and a behavior-influencing power in their own right. An activity, once entered, will exclude some potential behaviors, necessitate other behaviors, and, finally, encourage or discourage still other behaviors" (p. 755). Because activities make inherent demands, recreational therapists need to draw on their professional knowledge of activities to help clients select activities that will possess characteristics suitable to use the client's strengths and meet the client's needs.

Concluding Remarks on Implementation

In sum, the implementation phase of the RT process includes the actions of the recreational therapist in working with clients to execute the intervention plan. The actions of the recreational therapist must be consistent with the plan adopted. Recreational therapists must remain cognizant of the goal-directed nature of their responsibilities in conducting activities so that they are organized and conducted in a purposeful manner and do not become "activity for the sake of activity." Using relationship skills in maintaining a therapeutic relationship with the client is an essential element to the success of the implementation phase as the therapist and client work in a close alliance throughout the RT process, but particularly within the implementation phase. Adequate documentation of client actions and responses as the plan is executed is also necessary. As a result of a high level of performance on the part of the recreational therapist, the client may make positive strides. The direction and amount of these changes are determined during the evaluation phase.

EVALUATION: THE FOURTH PHASE IN THE RECREATIONAL THERAPY PROCESS

Evaluation is the fourth and final phase in the RT process. In this phase, the client's goals and objectives are appraised. The primary question to answer in the evaluation phase is, how did the client respond to the planned interventions?

Evaluation reveals whether the plan has been effective or requires revision. If the planned program has not had the desired effect, it needs to be modified, reimplemented, and reevaluated. This cyclical process continues as long as necessary to achieve the targeted outcomes.

The same methods employed in completing the initial assessment may be used in the evaluation phase. Common means of evaluating are to conduct a review of progress notes, interview clients so they may respond retrospectively after participating in the intervention program, and hold an interdisciplinary team meeting to discuss the progress of each client. Evaluation procedures should retrieve evaluation information from several independent sources to ensure the data are reliable and valid.

As has been indicated, clients must be involved in all phases of the RT process to the fullest extent of their capacities. This principle should be followed in the evaluation phase, where clients can help the recreational therapist determine the effectiveness of the program in achieving sought outcomes (Austin, 2013).

SUMMARY

The purpose of this chapter was to provide an introduction to the RT process as an essential element in RT. The chapter defined the RT process and discussed each of its four components. Furthermore, it emphasized that the RT process may be applied in any setting where therapeutic benefits are being sought to bring about positive outcomes in the health of clients. Finally, the chapter drew attention to the skills required of the recreational therapist to successfully apply the RT process. In this regard, the chapter emphasized the critical aspect of the recreational therapist possessing relationship skills to establish a therapeutic alliance with the client.

READING COMPREHENSION QUESTIONS

1. Do you agree with the definition of RT found at the beginning of the chapter? Explain.

2. Explain why the RT process may be termed the *essence of recreational therapy*.

3. What are the four phases of the RT process?

4. Explain how the RT process may be applied outside of hospitals or treatment and rehabilitation centers.

5. How can recreational therapists emphasize client strengths rather than what is "wrong" with the client?

6. Why is assessment critical to providing interventions?

7. Why should the recreational therapist look beyond client verbalizations in conducting needs assessment?

8. What are data sources for assessment?

9. Describe methods that may be used in RT assessment.

10. What is subjective data? Objective data?

11. What are validity and reliability?

12. What transpires during the planning phase?

13. What is the relationship between goals and objectives?

14. What is the relationship between the list of client needs and goals?

15. What is the relationship between the list of client strengths and objectives?

16. Describe strengths that clients may possess.

17. How would you describe evidence-based practice (EBP)?

18. What is the "big deal" about activities being conducted in a goal-directed, purposeful manner?

19. What makes activities therapeutic?

20. What are common means to completing evaluation?

REFERENCES

Alfaro-LeFevre, R. (2014). *Applying nursing process: The foundation for clinical reasoning* (8th ed.). Philadelphia, PA: Lippincott Williams & Wilkins.

Austin, D. R. (2011a). *Lessons learned: An open letter to recreational therapy students and practitioners.* Urbana, IL: Sagamore.

Austin, D. R. (2011b). Reformulation of the Health Protection/Health Promotion Model. *American Journal of Recreational Therapy, 10*(3), 19–26.

Austin, D. R. (2013). *Therapeutic recreation processes and techniques: Evidence-based recreational therapy* (7th ed.). Urbana, IL: Sagamore.

Austin, D. R., & McCormick, B. P. (2014). Clinical reasoning: A concept for recreation therapy. *American Journal of Recreation Therapy, 12*(4), 31–38.

Bule, J. (1988). Control studies bode better health in aging. *APA Monitor, 19*(7), 20.

Bullock, C. C., Mahon, M. J., & Killingsworth, C. (2010). *Introduction to recreation services for people with disabilities* (3rd ed.). Urbana, IL: Sagamore.

Gump, P., & Sutton-Smith, B. (1955). Activity-setting and social interaction: A field study. *American Journal of Orthopsychiatry, 25*, 755–760.

Kanter, J. S. (1985). Psychosocial assessment in community treatment. In J. S. Kanter (Ed.), *Clinical issues in treating the chronic mentally ill* (pp. 63–75). San Francisco, CA: Jossey-Bass.

Langer, E. L., & Rodin, J. (1976). The effects of choice and enhanced personal responsibility for the aged: A field experiment in an institutional setting. *Journal of Personality and Social Psychology, 34*, 191–198.

Law, M., & MacDermit, J. (2008). *Evidence-based rehabilitation: A guide to practice* (2nd ed.). Thorofare, NJ: SLACK.

Lee, Y., & McCormick, B. P. (2002). Toward evidence-based therapeutic recreation practice. In D. R. Austin, J. Dattilo, & B. P. McCormick (Eds.), *Conceptual foundations for therapeutic recreation* (pp. 165–181). State College, PA: Venture.

Long, T. (2008). The therapeutic recreation process. In T. Robertson & T. Long (Eds.), *Foundations of therapeutic recreation* (pp. 79–99). Champaign, IL: Human Kinetics.

Melnyk, B. M., Fineout-Overholt, E., & Cruz, R. (2010). Correlates among cognitive beliefs, EMP implementation, organizational culture, and job satisfaction in evidence-based practice mentors from a community hospital system. *Nursing Outlook, 58*, 301–308.

Mobily, K. E. (1987). A quiescent reply to Lee. *Therapeutic Recreation Journal, 21*(2), 81–83.

O'Morrow, G. S. (1976). *Therapeutic recreation: A helping profession.* Reston, VA: Reston.

Rogers, C. R. (1961). *On becoming a person: A therapist's view of psychotherapy.* Boston, MA: Houghton Mifflin.

Shank, J., & Coyle, C. (2002). *Therapeutic recreation in health promotion and rehabilitation.* State College, PA: Venture.

Shank, J., & Kinney, T. (1987). On the neglect of clinical practice. In C. Sylvester (Ed.), *Philosophy of therapeutic recreation: Ideas and issues* (pp. 65–73). Alexandria, VA: National Recreation and Park Association.

Stumbo, N. J., & Peterson, C. A. (2009). *Therapeutic recreation program design: Principles and procedures* (5th ed.). San Francisco, CA: Benjamin Cummings.

Witt, P. A., & Ellis, G. D. (1987). *The leisure diagnostic battery users' manual.* State College, PA: Venture.

World Health Organization. (2002). *Toward a common language for functioning, disability and health: ICF.* Retrieved from http://www.who.int/classifications/icf/training/icfbeginnersguide.pdf

Yura, H., & Walsh, M. B. (1988). *The nursing process: Assessment, planning, implementing, evaluating* (5th ed.). Norwalk, CT: Appleton & Lange.

SECTION 2

AREAS OF PRACTICE

BEHAVIORAL HEALTH AND PSYCHIATRIC DISORDERS

BRYAN P. MCCORMICK

OBJECTIVES

- State the two main classification systems for psychiatric disorders.
- State major classifications of psychiatric disorders.
- Identify three changes to mental health services associated with a recovery orientation.
- State common practice settings for recreational therapy in behavioral health.
- Identify evidence-based practices recreational therapists may employ in behavioral health.

The area of behavioral health and psychiatric practice is broad for recreational therapists. This may be one reason that behavioral/mental health is the single largest area of practice for recreational therapists, employing 35% of all nationally certified practitioners (Riley & Connolly, 2007). Although much of the practice sector exists within traditional mental health service providers, recreational therapists also may work within other practice settings providing mental health services. For example, within correctional facilities, approximately 13% of inmates receive mental health counseling and almost 10% receive mental health medications (Substance Abuse and Mental Health Services Administration, 2013a). Another reason that behavioral health and psychiatric practice is such a large area of practice for recreational therapists is that mental illness is relatively common. As much as 26% of the adult population in the United States has reported experiencing at least one mental illness in a year (Kessler, Chiu, Demler, & Walters, 2005).

DEFINITION AND CLASSIFICATION

Mental illness, broadly defined, "refers collectively to all of the diagnosable mental disorders. Mental disorders are characterized by abnormalities in cognition, emotion or mood, or the highest integrative aspects of behavior, such as social interactions or planning of future activities" (U.S. Department of Health and Human Services, 1999, p. 39). Although more than one quarter of the U.S. adult population experiences mental illness, only about 41% of persons with a mental illness receive treatment in a given year (Wang et al., 2005). Such disorders have brain-based origins related to changes in structural, neurochemical, and network aspects of the brain's function. Although some disabilities create clear distinctions between health and illness, this is frequently more difficult to distinguish in mental illness. For example, depression is a common occurrence in humans; however, identifying precisely when it becomes indicative of illness or disability is unclear. Thus, many psychiatric disorders exist on a continuum from disease to health (Cooper & Sartorius, 2013).

Worldwide two main classification manuals of mental disorders have been published: the *Diagnostic and Statistical Manual of Mental Disorders* (5th ed., American Psychiatric Association, 2013), known as the *DSM-5*, and the *International Statistical Classification of Diseases and Related Health Problems* (10th ed., World Health Organization [WHO], 2005), known as the ICD-10. The ICD-10 is more often employed around the world, and the *DSM-5* is the principal classification scheme in the United States. Although the two classification schemes identify specific disorders differently, they may be compared in broad diagnostic categories (see Table 4.1). First, some of these diagnostic categories are addressed elsewhere in this book. Neurocognitive and organic disorders such as dementia are addressed in the geriatric practice chapter (Chapter 9). In addition, substance-related and addictive disorders are addressed in the chapter on substance abuse (Chapter 5). Finally, neurodevelopmental disorders such as autism (Chapter 6), intellectual disability (Chapter 7), and disorders with onset in childhood and adolescence (Chapter 10) are addressed as well.

Schizophrenia Spectrum Disorders

Schizophrenia and related disorders are marked by psychotic features such as delusions, hallucinations, disorganized thought and speech, and disorganized or abnormal motor behavior (American Psychiatric Association, 2013). These symptoms are frequently characterized as positive as they are noted by the presence of thoughts, experience, or behavior that is atypical for other persons (Addington & Addington, 1991). Individuals frequently are confused about the distinction between a delusion and a hallucination. Delusions are beliefs that are relatively fixed and unchanging even in the face of evidence to the contrary that they are incorrect. These beliefs have themes such as persecution (e.g., the belief that you are being surveyed), reference (e.g., belief that a popular song contains a message specifically for you), grandiosity (e.g., belief that you have special abilities), religious (e.g., belief that you are Jesus), and somatic (e.g., belief that you are missing internal organs). In contrast, hallucinations are perceptual experiences that occur in the absence of external stimuli. Although hallucinations may exist in any sensory form, auditory hallucinations are the most common. Furthermore, hallucinations and delusions may occur together such as hearing voices of people outside your apartment talking about kidnapping you. In this example, hearing people talking is the auditory hallucination and the content of the talk—that people are plotting to kidnap you—is a persecutory delusion.

Schizophrenia spectrum disorders may also include symptoms in which certain characteristics of behavior are absent such as blunted affect and diminished emotional expression, the inability to experience pleasure (anhedonia), the lack of motivation and persistence (avolition), poverty of speech (alogia), social withdrawal and avoidance (asociality; Kirkpatrick, Fenton, Carpenter, & Marder, 2006). As these symptoms are noted by their absence, they are frequently referred to as negative. Finally, cognitive symptoms that are characteristic of schizophrenia spectrum disorders may be grouped as universal dimensions of cognition such as attention, working memory and executive function or as higher order dimensions of cognition such as episodic memory, social cognition, and metacognition (see Table 4.2).

Table 4.1

Comparison of Major Classification Systems of Mental Illnesses

Diagnostic & Statistical Manual of Mental Disorders (5th ed., DSM-5)	International Statistical Classification of Diseases and Related Health Problems (10th ed., ICD-10)
Neurocognitive disorders	F00–F09 Organic, including symptomatic, mental disorders
Substance-related and addictive disorders	F10–F19 Mental and behavioral disorders due to psychoactive substance use
Schizophrenia spectrum and other psychotic disorders	F20–F29 Schizophrenia, schizotypal, and delusional disorders
Bipolar and related disorders Depressive disorders	F30–F39 Mood [affective] disorders
Anxiety disorders Trauma- and stressor-related disorders Somatic symptom and related disorders Obsessive-compulsive and related disorders Dissociative disorders	F40–F48 Neurotic, stress-related, and somatoform disorders
Feeding and eating disorders Sleep–wake disorders Sexual dysfunctions	F50–F59 Behavioral syndromes associated with physiological disturbances and physical factors
Personality disorders Gender dysphoria Paraphilic disorders	F60–F69 Disorders of adult personality and behaviour
Neurodevelopmental disorders	F70–F79 Mental retardation F80–F89 Disorders of psychological development
Disruptive, impulse-control, and conduct disorders Elimination disorders	F90–F98 Behavioral and emotional disorders with onset usually occurring in childhood and adolescence
Other mental disorders	F99–F99 Unspecified mental disorder

Table 4.2
Cognitive Functions Implicated in Psychiatric Disorders

Attention/ vigilance	A cognitive function that permits one to be aware of and attend to stimuli. Vigilance is the cognitive function that permits attention for a prolonged period of time.
Fear extinction	The ability to actively suppress response to a stimulus. This is an active function of cognition that involves processes that go beyond forgetting or unlearning a response.
Processing speed	Refers to the relative speed with which cognitive tasks are undertaken and completed.
Verbal memory	Memory of information presented in verbal form. Also involves memory of words and language.
Working memory	The ability to maintain and use recently acquired and stored information to evaluate and integrate ongoing stimuli. Working memory is distinct from short-term memory but interrelated and is implicated in both attention and executive function.
Episodic memory	Relates to the conscious recall of past experiences and places, as well as the ability to project to an imagined future. This ability to project into a hypothesized future is related to social cognition and metacognition.
Executive function	A cognitive process that governs purposeful, goal-directed problem solving and planning. It involves the expression of culturally appropriate responses and the suppression of culturally inappropriate responses.
Social cognition	Mental activities underlying social interaction including understanding the intentions and behaviors of others as well as interpreting and generating responses to those understandings.
Theory of mind	A social cognitive function that reflects one's ability to attribute psychological states to both oneself and other persons.
Metacognition	A social cognitive function that involves thinking about thinking including the recognition of one's thoughts and feelings as well as the synthesis of these thoughts into more complex representations underlying the development of personal meanings.

Note. Adapted from "Metacognitive Capacities for Reflection in Schizophrenia: Implications for Developing Treatments," by P. H. Lysaker and G. Dimaggio, 2014, *Schizophrenia Bulletin, 40,* 497–491, and "Cognitive Dysfunction in Psychiatric Disorders: Characteristics, Causes and the Quest for Improved Therapy," by M. J. Millan, Y. Agid, M. Bruene, E. T. Bullmore, C. S. Carter, N. S. Clayton, . . . L. J. Young, 2012, *Nature Reviews Drug Discovery, 11*(2), 141–168.

Mood and Affective Disorders

Mood and affective disorders are related to problems in regulating one's mood or affective state over time. These mood disruptions are typically accompanied by a change in level of activity (WHO, 2005). In most cases, the disruption has to be constantly present for a minimum of two weeks (American Psychiatric Association, 2013).

Major depressive disorder. Major depressive disorder, also referred to as "major depression," is one of the most characteristic disorders of this group. Major depressive disorder is identified by symptoms such as depressed mood, diminished interest in previously satisfying activities, significant change in weight, sleep disturbance, change in activity level, fatigue, feelings of worthlessness, diminished ability to concentrate, and recurrent thoughts of death (including thoughts of suicide; American Psychiatric Association, 2013). In addition, such symptoms must create significant disruption in functioning in social relations (ICF d7) or other major life areas (ICF d8) and not be attributable to substance use or other medical conditions. Although the majority of symptoms of major depressive disorder are related to mood, cognitive effects (see Table 4.2) may be seen in processing speed, working memory, episodic memory, and executive function (Millan et al., 2012). Depressive disorders may also have a recurrent pattern in which repeated episodes of depression occur, or they may be persistent and last multiple years.

Bipolar disorder. Bipolar disorder is another characteristic mood and affective disorder in which a person experiences episodes of depression and/or mania. Mania is a condition in which a person experiences an elevation of energy and activity as well as enhanced mood and feelings of well-being (WHO, 2005). Although this may sound like a positive state, it is also frequently accompanied by excessive or rapid speech, racing thoughts, motor agitation, and engagement in activities with potentially negative outcomes such as buying sprees, risky sexual activity, and risking financial resources. As with major depressive disorder, these symptoms last for a period of time (a week or more) and create disruptions in functioning in social relationships and major life areas to the degree that hospitalization may be needed to prevent harm to individuals due to their behavior (American Psychiatric Association, 2013). An episode of hypomania may also be observed, in which many of the same manic behaviors are observed, but the duration and degree of functional disruption are lessened. Some individuals may experience periods of mania and hypomania without major depressive episodes, whereas others may experience both mania and major depressive episodes. As with major depressive disorder, in addition to mood disruption, disruptions also occur in cognitive functions in bipolar disorder (Millan et al., 2012). Given the pressured nature of thought and speech in mania, attention and vigilance are diminished. In addition, verbal, episodic, and working memory as well as executive function and social cognition are impaired, but to a lesser degree than in schizophrenia spectrum disorder.

Anxiety, Stress, and Trauma-Related Disorders

Anxiety and stress-related disorders are characterized by fear and anxiety associated with situations that are not currently dangerous (WHO, 2005). The *DSM-5* (American Psychiatric Association, 2013) distinguishes fear from anxiety, noting that fear is characterized by an emotional response to a real or imagined present threat, whereas anxiety is associated with a real or imagined threat in the future.

Included in this group are anxiety and panic disorders as well as disorders that have associated fear and anxiety resulting from exposure to a traumatic or stressful event. Post-traumatic stress disorder (PTSD) is one disorder in this group that recently has received considerable public attention. Disorders associated with obsessive thoughts and compulsive acts are also included in this group. In obsessive and compulsive disorders, anxiety is present either through intrusive thoughts or through the performance of ritualistic behaviors to reduce future anxiety-provoking outcomes (WHO, 2005).

In this group of disorders, fear and anxiety are out of proportion to the actual threat of the situation, and this is frequently the source of interference in functioning. In addition, typically disruptions in sleep and concentration occur, as well as the avoidance of behaviors or situations that may increase the fear or anxiety (American Psychiatric Association, 2013). Cognitive dysfunction associated with this group of disorders is principally associated with heightened attention and vigilance to disturbing stimuli and diminished ability in fear extinction (see Table 4.2).

Behavioral Disorders

Behavioral disorders are principally identified through patterns of behavior that are dysfunctional and may or may not be distressing to the individual such as eating disorders, sleep disorders, and sexual dysfunction. As recreational therapists are more likely to encounter clients with eating disorders as a principal diagnosis compared to other behavioral disorders, eating disorders are presented here.

Among the eating and feeding disorders, bulimia nervosa and anorexia nervosa appear with the greatest prevalence (American Psychiatric Association, 2013). Bulimia nervosa is a condition in which individuals engage in recurrent episodes of binge eating in which persons perceive a lack of control over their eating. This is paired with inappropriate compensatory behaviors to prevent weight gain (e.g., self-induced vomiting, misuse of laxatives, excessive exercise) in a pattern that occurs with some frequency (e.g., at least weekly). Finally, eating disorders have a marked pattern of self-evaluation that relies heavily on body shape and weight. Although less prevalent than bulimia nervosa, anorexia nervosa shares some of the same behaviors (American Psychiatric Association, 2013). Anorexia nervosa has a pattern of self-evaluation highly focused on body shape and weight to the point of disturbance of the way one's weight is experienced. Instead of patterns of binge eating, anorexia nervosa is marked by extreme restriction of energy intake. In addition, inappropriate compensatory behaviors to prevent weight gain or accelerate weight loss are frequently present.

Personality Disorders

Personality disorders are characterized by patterns of experience and behavior that are markedly different from the expectations of one's culture and situation. In addition, the pattern of behavior is enduring, frequently inflexible, and although they affect a range of domains of behavior, they are particularly disruptive to social relationships (WHO, 2005). Personality disorders are diagnosable in approximately 9% of the adult population (Lenzenweger, Lane, Loranger, & Kessler, 2007). Although previous versions of the *DSM* have included more than 10 specific personality disorders, the *DSM-5* offers a dimensional approach to personality disorders in which they are identified by impairments in personality functioning and pathological personality traits (see Table 4.3). Elements of personality functioning include self-oriented aspects of identity and self-direction, as well as interpersonal aspects of empathy and intimacy. Maladaptive personality traits may be grouped into five broad domains: antagonism, detachment, disinhibition, negative affect, and psychoticism (Krueger, Derringer, Markon, Watson, & Skodol, 2012).

Table 4.3
Dimensional Personality Disorders (DSM-5)

Antisocial	Characterized by a failure to follow legal and ethical standards and norms. Demonstrates an egocentric and callous disregard for others. Additional personality traits include deceitfulness and not accepting responsibility for one's actions.
Avoidant	Characterized by feelings of anxiety and inferiority. Although there is a desire for social relationships, there is also a deep concern for negative evaluation and rejection, resulting in avoidance of social situations and relationships.
Borderline	Characterized by instability of personality functions in the areas of self-image, interpersonal relationships, and intimacy. Behavior is frequently impulsive, risky, and/or hostile and may be self-destructive.
Narcissistic	Characterized by grandiose attention and approval-seeking behavior. This is accompanied by a variable and vulnerable self-image.
Obsessive-compulsive	Characterized by rigid perfectionism, preoccupation with details, and inflexibility. Such rigidity disrupts the establishment or maintenance of close interpersonal relationships.
Schizotypal	Characterized by withdrawal from, and diminished capacity for, social contacts and interpersonal relationships. There is also disruption in self-image, cognition, and emotional expression.

Note. From *Diagnostic and Statistical Manual of Mental Disorders: DSM-5* (5th ed.), by the American Psychiatric Association, 2013, Washington, DC: Author.

Serious Mental Illness

Finally, one group of mental illnesses is recognized as serious. Such serious mental illnesses present with symptoms including inappropriate anxiety, thought and perception disturbances, mood disturbances, and cognitive dysfunction. This designation is not meant to imply that other disorders are not serious. For those experiencing a mental disorder, it clearly is perceived as serious. The term *serious* in the case of serious mental illness recognizes that the experience is pervasive, in both duration and impact, and affects multiple areas of functioning. In general serious mental illnesses are characterized by (1) diagnosis, (2) disability, and (3) duration (Schinnar, Rothbard, Kanter, & Jung, 1990). The majority of persons characterized as having a serious mental illness have diagnoses of schizophrenia spectrum disorder or bipolar disorder; however, major depression and severe anxiety disorder are sometimes included (Bond, Drake, Mueser, & Latimer, 2001). The second criterion refers to impairment in major life areas including work and school (ICF d8), interpersonal interactions and relationships (ICF d7) as well as community, social, and civic life (ICF d9). No criterion is set in terms of the number of life areas affected, but generally multiple life areas are disrupted. The third criterion requires that the dysfunction must have been present for a significant period of time. Again, some professionals have disagreed on the length that constitutes a significant period of time, but generally the dysfunction has been present for years as opposed to months (Schinnar et al., 1990).

PURPOSE OF RECREATIONAL THERAPY

General Approaches to Treatment

The purpose of recreational therapy (RT) within psychiatric rehabilitation should be in concert with other health professionals' services and the client's overall plan of care. This may mean that recreational therapists in psychiatric settings focus on reducing symptoms such as mood disturbances or cognitive dysfunction or improving functional abilities such as developing and maintaining interpersonal relationships or developing stress coping skills. In addition, although cure is possible in some disorders, in terms of complete remediation of symptoms and return to pre-disorder function, other disorders such as serious mental illnesses are focused on care to reach the highest possible level of function despite the presence of a persistent mental illness.

Along these lines, an increasing movement in psychiatric rehabilitation has been occurring around the concept of recovery. Peebles et al. (2007) identified that this movement toward a revised approach to rehabilitation began in the mid-1990s and is currently a dominant force in rehabilitation. They noted three fundamental changes implied in this recovery orientation. First, although psychiatric rehabilitation historically has been focused on remediation of symptoms, the recovery approach has added broader goals. For example, although symptom management remains a goal of rehabilitation, it is understood within a larger context of improved life satisfaction, greater client empowerment, the development of natural social supports, and the development of hope. This aspect of the recovery orientation is consistent with the strength-based approach of RT to services (Austin, 2011). Such a strength-based approach "creates as sense of optimism because all people possess strengths that they can develop and use to remove or overcome barriers to health and to promote wellness" (Austin, 2011, p. 3). A second change implied in the recovery orientation is that clients have become collaborators in their own plan of care. Historically, psychiatric rehabilitation has involved patients who were treated by psychiatric professionals; a more current terminology has recognized service recipients as consumers who have considerably more say in the services they receive. The third area of change is the identity of the mental health consumer as a full participant in rehabilitation. Peebles et al. noted that the emergence of the Certified Peer Specialist as a provider of mental health services is indicative of the full participation of persons with mental illnesses as equal partners in the treatment team. Peer specialists are a member of the rehabilitation team and provide support services, but they are also mental health service consumers.

Finally, a focus has been developed on what is termed *integrated care* in psychiatric rehabilitation (Unutzer, Schoenbaum, Druss, & Katon, 2006). This approach seeks to integrate general medicine with mental health services. This has resulted from the recognition that although mental health and physical health are strongly interconnected, their systems of services are segregated. For example, among persons with schizophrenia, life expectancy is reduced by as much as 25 years compared to other adults due principally to cardiovascular disease resulting from an unhealthy lifestyle (Laursen, Munk-Olsen, & Vestergaard, 2012). Thus, negative lifestyle behaviors contributing to secondary health conditions among persons with mental illnesses have been increasingly addressed. These interventions have sought to address issues such as healthy nutrition, smoking cessation, weight control, and increased physical activity.

Empirical Evidence Supporting Practice

Physical activity and exercise. Evidence suggests that physical activity and exercise are beneficial to mental health treatment. First, exercise has been found to reduce symptoms of depression compared to no treatment (Cooney et al., 2013). In addition, exercise appears to have a similar effect in reducing depressive symptoms compared to antidepressants and psychological therapies. Furthermore, although evidence is limited, research suggests that exercise may improve cognitive functions such as attention, inhibitory control, and executive function among adults with major depressive disorder (Kubesch et al., 2003; Vasques, Moraes, Silveira, Deslandes, & Laks, 2011). A number of national practice guidelines have noted exercise as an included component in clinical practice guidelines for the treatment of depression (see National Guideline Clearinghouse, www.guideline.gov).

Behavioral activation. Although the term *behavioral activation* (BA) may not be familiar to recreational therapists as a therapeutic approach, the orientation is highly consistent with RT practice. As a form of treatment for depression, BA was first proposed in 1990 (Dimidjian, Barrera, Martell, Munoz, & Lewinsohn, 2011). Dimidjian et al. (2011) defined BA as

> a structured, brief psychotherapeutic approach to (a) increase engagement in adaptive activities (which often are those associated with the experience of pleasure or mastery), (b) decrease engagement in activities that maintain depression or increase risk for depression, and (c) solve problems that limit access to reward or that maintain or increase aversive control. (pp. 3–4)

Many of the concepts should be familiar to recreational therapists in this approach, particularly the increase in adaptive activities that involve pleasure and mastery, changing behaviors that maintain or enhance depressive experiences (e.g., social isolation) and working to find natural rewards (intrinsically motivating behavior). Research that has compared BA to cognitive-behavioral therapy (CBT) as well as CBT plus BA found that BA alone was as effective as the full CBT with BA (Jacobson et al., 1996). Subsequent research has demonstrated that BA continues to be effective in reducing depressive symptoms (Dimidjian et al., 2011).

Social skills training. As impairments in interpersonal function are seen in many psychiatric disorders, providing social skills training (SST) is appropriate. The general approach in using SST involves cognitive and educational approaches to develop knowledge and skills related to interpersonal interaction (Barth et al., 2013).

Studies of adult depressive disorders have found SST to be as effective as other forms of behavioral and cognitive therapies in reducing depressive symptoms (Barth et al., 2013; Cuijpers, van Straten, Andersson, & van Oppen, 2008). For adults with schizophrenia, SST has been found to be effective in decreasing psychiatric symptoms and improving functioning and life quality (Elis, Caponigro, & Kring, 2013; Granholm, Holden, Link, McQuaid, & Jeste, 2013). SST is a well-documented modality in RT with research from investigators having documented its effectiveness (Austin, 2013).

Commonly Sought Outcomes

Outcomes generally may be considered within three broad domains: clinical status, functional status, and subjective well-being (McCormick & Funderburk, 2000). Clinical status outcomes are directly related to the symptoms of a disorder. For example, Corrigan, Liberman, and Wong (1993) found that RT effectively reduced clinically relevant outcomes such as stereotypic self-talk, rumination, hallucinatory behavior, and inappropriate behavior among adults in inpatient treatment. In addition, although the control of clinical symptoms is typically an important outcome of RT intervention, symptoms alone are insufficient to capture broader outcomes such as functional change.

Functional outcomes include areas such as general tasks and demands, work and educational functioning, self-care, domestic life, interpersonal functioning, and participation in community, social, and civic life. Snethen, McCormick and Van Puymbroeck (2012) found that an RT intervention employing an individualized placement and support design improved community participation, planning skills, and coping skills for community-dwelling adults with schizophrenia.

Finally, although improvements in clinical symptoms and functional performance are clear indicators of the effectiveness of treatment, the intent of most rehabilitation services is to ultimately improve the life quality and well-being of service recipients. Subjective well-being includes outcomes that consider service recipients' perceptions of the impact of services on their lives (McCormick & Funderburk, 2000). For example, Schumacher and Navar (2010) found that an RT intervention that targeted physical activity and social interaction improved psychosocial well-being among adults with mood disorders.

ROLE OF THE RECREATIONAL THERAPIST

In most behavioral health settings, the recreational therapist works as a member of an interdisciplinary team of psychiatrists, psychologists, nurses, social workers, and peer specialists as well as other allied health professions including addictions specialists, occupational therapy, music therapy, art therapy, dance/movement therapy, and counseling. Recreational therapists frequently focus on developing life and coping skills through exercises and activities. Recreational therapists may also use games and activities to identify patterns of interpersonal behavior, as well as dysfunctional cognitive models. In addition, the focus on developing healthy lifestyle patterns is increasing, particularly among persons with serious mental illnesses.

COMMON SERVICE SETTINGS

Overall, mental health services are predominantly provided in privately owned outpatient settings (see Figure 4.1). In 2012 among adults who received mental health services, 52% were treated with only prescription medication, 29% received outpatient services with prescription medication, and 13% received only outpatient services (Substance Abuse and Mental Health Services Administration, 2013b). By comparison, in 2012 among all adults receiving mental health services, only 5% received inpatient services alone or combined with medications and outpatient services. This small number of inpatient services is consistent with trends that have moved services more into clients' home communities. Inpatient beds show that since 1990, the number of beds available has declined in all areas of inpatient services other than in residential treatment centers for children with emotional disturbance, which has had an increase in beds available from 35,170 beds in 1990 to 50,063 beds in 2008 (Substance Abuse and Mental Health Services Administration, 2013a). This is not to say that inpatient services are not in demand. In 2012, just under 1.8 million adults received inpatient services in the United States (Substance Abuse and Mental Health Services Administration, 2013b). In addition, almost half of all inpatient services are provided in general hospitals (Liptzin, Gottlieb, & Summergrad, 2007).

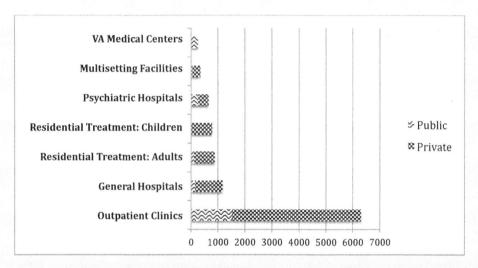

Figure 4.1. Number and type of ownership of mental health facilities in the United States in 2010. From *Behavioral Health United States, 2012*, by the Substance Abuse and Mental Health Services Administration, 2013, Rockville, MD: Author.

Service settings also appear to be interrelated with the type of psychiatric disorder. For adults with serious mental illnesses, almost 48% were treated in outpatient care with prescription medication compared to only 28% of persons with a mild mental disorder. In contrast, 0.8% of adults with serious mental illnesses and 1.8% of adults with mild mental illness were treated in inpatient treatment only (Substance Abuse and Mental Health Services Administration, 2013a).

Bao, Casalino, and Pincus (2013) elaborated a quadrant model that defines populations by severity of their mental health conditions and their insurance status (see Table 4.4). First, they characterized persons with mild to moderate conditions such as anxiety or mild to moderate depression with commercial insurance or Medicare as commonly being served in medical settings (including primary care physicians).

In these medical settings, clients may or may not be seen by a behavioral health specialist. The second quadrant includes clients with mild to moderate conditions who are insured through Medicaid. This distinction is made as these clients are eligible for Medicaid due to their low-income status. As a result, they also tend to have social and support service needs that differentiate them from persons with private insurance or Medicare. This group of clients typically receives care in both medical and behavioral health specialties; however, integration of medical and behavioral health needs is frequently poor. The third quadrant includes clients with severe behavioral disorders such as schizophrenia, bipolar disorder, or major depressive disorders and clients who have commercial or Medicare insurance. Clients in this group typically have health insurance through their own or a family member's workplace. These clients may also be experiencing a first episode of serious mental illness and are typically served in behavioral health specialty settings. As these clients may be served in these settings early in what may be a persistent disorder, chronic physical health conditions may not be present yet. The fourth quadrant represents clients with serious and persistent mental health conditions combined with serious chronic physical health conditions. Given the typically long-term nature of their conditions, these clients are insured through Medicaid (may also be dually insured with Medicare) and are typically served in outpatient specialty behavioral health (e.g., community mental health center). Historically, behavioral health providers have not been able to manage these clients' chronic health conditions (e.g., diabetes, hypertension, cardiovascular disease) effectively.

Table 4.4
Quadrant of Client Needs, Insurance Types, and Service Settings

Commercial insurance or Medicare	Medicaid
Group 1	Group 2
Example disorders: Mild to moderate anxiety, depression **Service setting**: Outpatient primary care	**Example disorders**: Mild to moderate anxiety, depression **Service setting**: Outpatient medical and specialty mental health
Group 3	Group 4
Example disorders: (first episode) Schizophrenia, bipolar disorder, major depressive disorder **Service setting**: Inpatient, specialty mental health	**Example disorders**: (persistent) Schizophrenia, bipolar disorder, major depressive disorder **Service setting**: Outpatient, specialty mental health

CURRENT BEST PRACTICES AND PROCEDURES

Assessment

Within behavioral health care, few standardized assessment instruments exist. Although previous versions of the *DSM* included an assessment of functioning known as the Global Assessment of Functioning (GAF), the *DSM-5* advocates for the use of the WHO's Disability Assessment Schedule 2.0 (WHODAS 2.0). The WHODAS 2.0 covers six functional domains—cognition, mobility, self-care, getting along (with others), life activities (domestic, leisure, work, school), and participation (in community activities)—and examines the degree to which a health condition interferes with functioning in these domains (WHO, 2010). When assessing clients, the recreational therapist should consider functional domains as contained in the International Classification of Functioning, Disability, and Health (ICF). In addition, the National Institutes of Health and Northwestern University jointly sponsor the NIH Toolbox (www.nihtoolbox.org) that lists brief standardized measures for assessing behavioral disorders in cognitive, emotion, motor, and sensation domains. Items within these domains are particularly relevant to RT practice in behavioral health. As most psychiatric disorders have both emotional and cognitive dysfunction, the domain of mental functions (ICF b1) is most relevant within body functions (ICF section b; see Table 4.5). In most cases, recreational therapists will not be the care provider with primary responsibility for assessing mental functions; however, they should be attuned to these areas when conducting their own assessments. In contrast, multiple areas of activity and participation (ICF section d) are relevant to functioning among persons with psychiatric disorders (see Table 4.5). Those areas most implicated in RT services are in the areas of communication, self-care (particularly in diet, fitness, etc.), interpersonal interactions and relationships, and community, social, and civic life. Finally, the ICF considers function to be affected by environmental factors (ICF section e). These factors represent resources and barriers that may enhance or impede functioning. Environmental factors most relevant to RT practice are related to support and relationships, attitudes, and services, systems, and policies. Environmental factors also aid recreational therapists in identifying resources and barriers in their clients' environments. Such factors are particularly relevant for clients already being served in the community and for clients transitioning from an inpatient setting.

Planning

A key concern in planning is the expected length of stay. For clients served in outpatient settings, a longer scope of services and greater focus on functional improvement will lead toward different outcome goals compared to an inpatient setting with a shorter scope of services and outcomes more focused on symptom stabilization. In all cases, planning should be the result of a synthesis of sources of data in decision making related to the plan of care. This approach is characterized as evidence-based practice and involves the intentional use of data from (a) research evidence, (b) clinician judgment, and (c) client values and characteristics as sources of evidence (Frueh, Ford, Elhai, & Grubaugh, 2012). Although recreational therapists historically have been trained to use both client information and clinical judgment in planning, they have been less well prepared to find and employ research evidence as a part of intervention planning. This may be one reason that a recent study found that in a survey of nationally certified RT practitioners in one region, only about 30% of them reported routinely seeking out and using research in their practice (Gerken, Costello, & Mrkic, 2013). Reasons exist to believe that this may change in the future. Given the current level of access to publicly available research studies, clinical practice guidelines, and systematic reviews, barriers to providing evidence-based services have been reduced. Publicly available resources to access research evidence are provided at the end of this chapter.

Table 4.5
ICF Elements of Functioning Relevant to RT Assessment in Psychiatric Disorders

Body Functions (section b)

Mental functions (b1)

Global mental functions

Consciousness (state, continuity, quality) (b110)

Orientation functions (person, place, time) (b114)

Global psychosocial functions (b122)

Temperament and personality functions (b126)

Energy and drive functions (b130)

Sleep (amount, onset, maintenance, quality) (b134)

Specific mental functions

Attention (b140)

Memory (b144)

Psychomotor functions (b147)

Emotion (appropriateness, regulation, range) (b152)

Perception (in relation to hallucination) (b156)

Thought (pace, form, content, control) (b160)

Higher-level cognitive functions (abstraction, planning, cognitive flexibility, insight, problem solving) (b164)

Experience of self and time (including body image) (b180)

Activities and Participation (section d)

Learning and applying knowledge (d1)

General tasks and demands (d2)

Undertaking a single task (d210)

Undertaking multiple tasks (d220)

Carrying out daily routine (d230)

Handling stress and other demands (d240)

Communication (d3)

Receiving nonverbal messages (d315)

Producing nonverbal messages (d335)

Conversation (d350)

Discussion (d355)

Mobility (d4)

Using transportation (car, bus, train, plane) (d470)

Driving (bicycle, motorbike, car) (d475)

Self-care (d5)

Looking after one's health (diet, fitness, health) (d570)

Interpersonal interactions and relationships (d7)

Basic interactions (warmth, appreciation, tolerance, criticism, social cues, contact) (d710)

Complex interactions (forming, terminating, use of social cues) (d720)

Relating with strangers (d730)

Formal relationships (superiors, peers, subordinates) (d740)

Informal relationships (with friends, neighbors, acquaintances, peers) (d750)

Family relationships (d760)

Intimate relationships (romantic, spousal, sexual) (d770)

Major life areas (d8)

Informal education (d810)

School education (d820)

Higher education (d830)

Non-remunerative employment (volunteering) (d855)

Community, social, and civic life (d9)

Community life (formal and informal associations, ceremonies) (d910)

Recreation and leisure (d920)

Religion and spirituality (d930)

Political life and citizenship (d950)

Environmental Factors (section e)

Support and relationships (e3)

Immediate family (e310)

Extended family (e315)

Friends (e320)

Acquaintances, peers, neighbors (e325)

Domesticated animals (e350)

Attitudes (e4)

Attitudes of immediate family (e410)

Attitudes of extended family (e415)

Attitudes of friends (e420)

Attitudes of acquaintances, peers, neighbors (e425)

Societal attitudes (e460)

Social norms, practices, and ideologies (e465)

Services, systems, and policies (e5)

Housing services, systems, and policies (e525)

Transportation services, systems, and policies (e540)

Associations and organizational services, systems, and policies (e555)

Social security services, systems, and policies (e570)

Note. ICF = International Classification of Functioning, Disability, and Health; RT = recreational therapy.

Implementation

In psychiatric and behavioral health settings, nationally certified recreational therapists reported average caseloads of just over 30 clients (Riley & Connolly, 2007). The size of average caseloads in these settings indicates the frequent use of group interventions in psychiatric and behavioral health settings. Austin (2013) identified group types that recreational therapists may use including counseling, stress reduction, self-concept/self-esteem, and problem solving. In addition, Porter and burlingame (2006) noted that additional interventions may include physical activity and exercise, social skills training, family interventions and life/survival skills. A general approach that consistently has found support for effectiveness in almost all psychiatric disorders is a cognitive-behavioral approach. In this approach, therapists assist clients in identifying and challenging cognitive models that may maintain dysfunctional behavior or suppress functional behavior (Austin, 2013). Concrete activities that give evidence of success/failure, acceptance/rejection, pleasure/displeasure are particularly useful aids in helping clients to verbalize their cognitive models about their current and future behaviors.

Evaluation

Austin (2013) identified dimensions of behavior that may be evaluated through group performance such as level and nature of participation, degree of influence and control, observance of group and social norms, degree of integration, expressions of emotion, and many interpersonal behaviors. As evaluation is part of the RT process and feeds back into the previous components, evaluation is inherently tied to clients' functional status identified through assessment. Using appropriate, validated, and reliable measures at assessment enhances the evaluation of outcomes of intervention by ensuring that RT outcomes are in line with the outcomes of services from other professionals.

APPLICATION OF THE RECREATIONAL THERAPY PROCESS: CASE STUDY

Kathy S. is a 45-year-old white female admitted to the community hospital adult psychiatric unit with bipolar disorder I, current manic episode with psychotic features (ICD-10 code F31.2). She was admitted as a result of being reported to and detained by the police as a result of being found outside the public library wearing only a nightgown. When approached, she indicated to the police that Judge Judy (a television personality) had told her that she would win the lottery if "she went to the library right now." She was initially uncooperative with the police and required restraint to transport her to the hospital, expressing extreme agitation that she would not be where Judge Judy told her to be. Upon admission, she demonstrated extremely pressured speech and flight of ideas, with delusions revolving around the messages she receives from Judge Judy on the television.

Ms. S. was first diagnosed with bipolar disorder at age 30 and has had multiple hospitalizations in the previous 15 years. She currently lives in a supervised apartment with an adult roommate and has been volunteering at a community mental health peer help-line 4 hours per week for the past 3 years. Ms. S. presents as obese (height: 5'3", weight: 190 lb, BMI 34) with no history of substance abuse or tobacco use. Ms. S. is divorced with two adult children (a son aged 16 and a daughter aged

18), who have lived with her ex-husband for the past 10 years. Her daughter will be graduating from high school in 1 month and is planning to attend college in another state.

Assessment

The RT assessment found that Ms. S. continued to present with pressured speech and a flight of ideas. Although she expressed no delusional statements during the interview, she was not able to articulate a clear reason for this hospitalization. She exhibited limited ability to sustain attention. When she was focused, she expressed a good relationship with her children and ex-husband. She identified a particularly close relationship with her daughter, who regularly visits her. She identified no close relationships beyond that with her children. She also expressed that she enjoyed her job as a help-line volunteer. Aside from her volunteer work, she had little contact or participation in community or social life. She characterized her time aside from volunteering as "mostly watching television."

Planning

Given Ms. S's projected length of stay of 5 days (typical of this type of unit), the principal focus for RT services is on clinical status, with a secondary focus on functional abilities related to the development of healthy living skills. Treatment goals were related to reducing delusional thought, improving attention and memory, and improving executive function (particularly planning and insight). Additional goals were focused on developing strategies to reduce sedentary time post-discharge and expanding informal relationships.

Implementation

Although Ms. S. is obese, she was referred for the physical activity group. The physical activity group meets daily for 45 minutes in the group room and provides low-impact physical activities and stretching. The group also uses modified elements of yoga and tai chi to engage clients. In addition, clients process activities related to their emotional states pre- to post-activities, as well as discuss strategies for integrating physical activity into their daily lives outside of the hospital. For Ms. S., the goals for this intervention were to reduce sedentary time and improve planning skills to minimize sedentary behavior following discharge. In addition, Ms. S. was referred for the RT cognition group. The cognition group meets every other day for 1 hour and employs table games and/or crafts to engage clients in cognitive processing. These activities are focused on improving attention and vigilance, working memory, and executive function. Through the use of prompts, reflective questioning, and activity processing, the recreational therapists works with clients to remain on task and develop strategies to improve working memory as well as planning and strategizing skills. Ms. S's goals for this group were to improve attention and vigilance on a single task and to improve working memory and executive function.

Evaluation

Over the course of Ms. S's stay, she demonstrated improvements in clinical status, with decreases in delusional thoughts, improved abilities to maintain attention and vigilance to tasks, and improved planning abilities. At the first RT cognition group, Ms. S. had great difficulty in selecting an activity to undertake. Once selected, she began the activity, but she appeared to lose interest and discussed selecting another activity within 5 minutes. At the second RT cognition group meeting, Ms. S. was able to maintain on-task behavior for 15 minutes without prompting while working on a self-selected craft activity. Prompting by the recreational therapist indicated that she was also able to identify immediate next steps in the activity and to project future steps to complete the activity. Ms. S. also participated in the physical activity group daily, although her physical condition limited her ability to participate, particularly in stretching activities. She expressed positive emotional states post-activity sessions and a desire to continue daily physical activity post-discharge. The recreational therapist discussed with Ms. S. strategies to overcome expressed barriers to daily physical activity related to weather, fear of crime in her community, and lack of personal transportation

TRENDS AND ISSUES

One of the most significant trends to affect psychiatric and behavioral health services is the ongoing health care reform. For example, the Affordable Care Act of 2010 (also known as "Obamacare") provided provisions to improve and expand care for persons receiving behavioral health services by expanding Medicaid coverage[1], subsidizing and mandating health insurance coverage, and prohibiting denial of coverage due to preexisting conditions (Mechanic, 2012). The potential expansion of Medicaid coverage is important in behavioral health services because it is the primary source for coverage of health services for persons with serious mental health disorders. In addition to expanding coverage for health services, the Affordable Care Act provides incentives for improving integrated care (combining behavioral and physical health services), a concern that is particularly relevant to adults with serious mental illnesses. Mechanic (2012) asserted that the Affordable Care Act has created conditions that make the reinvention of mental health services likely, among them, incentives and tools to reduce fragmentation of services, provisions that directly address chronic disease comorbidities, better coordination of Medicaid behavioral health services with social services and housing services, and provisions to encourage the integration of and attention to preventative and substance abuse services in behavioral health services. He also noted, "Finally, by extending the concepts of treatment and related supportive care to such entities as health homes, the Affordable Care Act provides new pathways for incorporating evidence-based treatments" (p. 378).

Health homes, one element in the Affordable Care Act, have the potential to change the nature of behavioral health. Such entities seek to fully integrate behavioral and physical health with social and housing supports in a single integrated team of service providers in a single location (Bao et al., 2013). The intent is to integrate primary care (through primary care physicians and nurses) with specialty behavioral health and support services. At present, the role of RT in integrated health is unknown. This integration of physical and behavioral health may create a unique need for RT services, particularly as these services are focused on cost-effective care that minimizes the need for inpatient services. This speaks to the need for develop-

---

[1]The U.S. Supreme Court ruled in 2012 that states could not be required to expand Medicaid coverage. As of June 2014, 26 states and the District of Columbia had adopted the Medicaid expansion, three states were considering adopting the expansion, and 21 states were not expanding coverage at this time (The Advisory Board Company, 2014).

ing evidence-based RT services that address chronic behavioral and physical health conditions.

SUMMARY

This chapter provided an overview of one of the largest areas of RT practice. Psychiatric and behavioral health RT services must be based on a strong knowledge of underlying psychiatric disorder. As such, it provided only the briefest overview of psychiatric disorders, and those seeking to practice in these settings should obtain much greater understanding. Additionally, the chapter noted that the nature of psychiatric and behavioral health services has shifted toward increasing client or consumer input to the nature of care and increasing orientation of services based on concepts of recovery. Another relatively new emphasis in behavioral health is the need to consider integrated care in which behavioral health and physical health are adequately treated. Although recreational therapists continue to practice in inpatient settings, the largest setting for services is the outpatient setting, and this trend is likely to continue into the future. Finally, the Affordable Care Act of 2010 has made significant changes to the incentives for high quality and integrated behavioral health care. Although it is unclear whether the Affordable Care Act will be fully implemented, once the changes have begun, it is unlikely these changes will be reversed. Thus, although the nature of change in behavioral health through the full implementation of the Affordable Care Act may be unclear, what is clear is that change is likely to occur.

READING COMPREHENSION QUESTIONS

1. What are the positive symptoms of schizophrenia?
2. What are the negative symptoms of schizophrenia?
3. What are the characteristics of a major depressive disorder?
4. What are the characteristics of a manic episode?
5. How does fear differ from anxiety?
6. What is the difference between anorexia nervosa and bulimia nervosa?
7. What are the three main changes to psychiatric rehabilitation with the recovery orientation?
8. What are the three characteristic components of behavioral activation?
9. Where are the majority of mental health services provided?
10. How is type of insurance related to diagnosis service settings?
11. What does *integrated care* mean in behavioral health settings?

PUBLIC RESOURCES FOR RESEARCH EVIDENCE

National Library of Medicine: www.nlm.nih.gov

The U.S. National Library of Medicine is a publicly available resource that provides access to health and human services research via the PubMed/MEDLINE index. This resource also provides links to completed and ongoing clinical trials.

National Guideline Clearinghouse: www.guideline.gov

The Agency for Healthcare Research and Quality (AHRQ) provides this public resource to access clinical practice guidelines relevant to a number of illnesses and disorders.

The Cochrane Collaboration: www.thecochranelibrary.com

The Cochrane Collaboration is a nonprofit organization of health practitioners, researchers, and advocates who conduct and publish systematic reviews of research evidence. These may provide a foundation for RT practice.

REFERENCES

Addington, J., & Addington, D. (1991). Positive and negative symptoms of schizophrenia: Their course and relationship over time. *Schizophrenia Research, 5*(1), 51–59.

The Advisory Board Company. (2014, May 28). Where the states stand on Medicaid expansion. Retrieved from http://www.advisory.com/Daily-Briefing/Resources/Primers/MedicaidMap

American Psychiatric Association. (2013). *Diagnostic and statistical manual of mental disorders: DSM-5* (5th ed.). Washington, DC: Author.

Austin, D. R. (2011). *Lessons learned: An open letter to recreational therapy students and practitioners.* Champaign, IL: Sagamore.

Austin, D. R. (2013). *Therapeutic recreation processes & techniques: Evidenced-based recreational therapy* (7th ed.). Urbana, IL: Sagamore.

Bao, Y. H., Casalino, L. P., & Pincus, H. A. (2013). Behavioral health and health care reform models: Patient-centered medical home, health home, and accountable care organization. *Journal of Behavioral Health Services & Research, 40*(1), 121–132. doi:10.1007/s11414-012-9306-y

Barth, J., Munder, T., Gerger, H., Nueesch, E., Trelle, S., Znoj, H., ... Cuijpers, P. (2013). Comparative efficacy of seven psychotherapeutic interventions for patients with depression: A network meta-analysis. *Plos Medicine, 10*(5). doi:10.1371/journal.pmed.1001454

Bond, G., Drake, R., Mueser, K., & Latimer, E. (2001). Assertive community treatment for people with severe mental illness. *Disease Management and Health Outcomes, 9*(3), 141–159. doi:10.2165/00115677-200109030-00003

Cooney, G. M., Dwan, K., Greig, C. A., Lawlor, D. A., Rimer, J., Waugh, F. R., ... Mead, G. E. (2013). Exercise for depression. *Cochrane Database of Systematic Reviews, 2013*(9). doi:10.1002/14651858.CD004366.pub6

Cooper, J. E., & Sartorius, N. (2013). *Companion to the classification of mental disorders.* Oxford, United Kingdom: Oxford University Press.

Corrigan, P. W., Liberman, R. P., & Wong, S. E. (1993). Recreational therapy and behavior management on inpatient units: Is recreational therapy therapeutic? *Journal of Nervous & Mental Disease, 181*(10), 644–646.

Cuijpers, P., van Straten, A., Andersson, G., & van Oppen, P. (2008). Psychotherapy for depression in adults: A meta-analysis of comparative outcome studies. *Journal of Consulting and Clinical Psychology, 76*(6), 909–922. doi:10.1037/a0013075

Dimidjian, S., Barrera, M., Martell, C., Munoz, R. F., & Lewinsohn, P. M. (2011). The origins and current status of behavioral activation treatments for depression. *Annual Review of Clinical Psychology, 7,* 1–38.

Elis, O., Caponigro, J. M., & Kring, A. M. (2013). Psychosocial treatments for negative symptoms in schizophrenia: Current practices and future directions. *Clinical Psychology Review, 33*(8), 914–928. doi:10.1016/j.cpr.2013.07.001

Frueh, B. C., Ford, J. D., Elhai, J. D., & Grubaugh, A. L. (20012). Evidence-based practice in mental health. In P. Sturmey & M. Hersen (Eds.), *Handbook of evidence-based practice in clinical psychology* (Vol. 2, Adult Disorders). Hoboken, NJ: John Wiley & Sons.

Gerken, M., Costello, P., & Mrkic, L. (2013). The prevalence of evidence-based practice by the Certified Therapeutic Recreation Specialist in the intervention planning process for client treatment. *American Journal of Recreation Therapy, 12*(1), 23–30. doi:10.5055/ajrt.2013.0037

Granholm, E., Holden, J., Link, P. C., McQuaid, J. R., & Jeste, D. V. (2013). Randomized controlled trial of cognitive behavioral social skills training for older consumers with schizophrenia: Defeatist performance attitudes and functional outcome. *American Journal of Geriatric Psychiatry, 21*(3), 251–262. doi:10.1016/j.jagp.2012.10.014

Jacobson, N. S., Dobson, K. S., Truax, P. A., Addis, M. E., Koerner, K., Gollan, J. K., . . . Prince, S. E. (1996). A component analysis of cognitive-behavioral treatment for depression. *Journal of Consulting and Clinical Psychology, 64*(2), 295–304. doi:10.1037//0022-006x.64.2.295

Kessler, R. C., Chiu, W. T., Demler, O., & Walters, E. E. (2005). Prevalence, severity, and comorbidity of 12-month DSM-IV disorders in the National Comorbidity Survey Replication. *Archives of General Psychiatry, 62*(6), 617–627. doi:10.1001/archpsyc.62.6.617

Kirkpatrick, B., Fenton, W. S., Carpenter, W. T., Jr., & Marder, S. R. (2006). The NIMH-MATRICS consensus statement on negative symptoms. *Schizophrenia Bulletin, 32*(2), 214–219. doi:10.1093/schbul/sbj053

Krueger, R. F., Derringer, J., Markon, K. E., Watson, D., & Skodol, A. E. (2012). Initial construction of a maladaptive personality trait model and inventory for DSM-5. *Psychological Medicine, 42*(9), 1879–1890. doi:10.1017/s0033291711002674

Kubesch, S., Bretschneider, V., Freudenmann, R., Weidenhammer, N., Lehmann, M., Spitzer, M., & Gron, G. (2003). Aerobic endurance exercise improves executive functions in depressed patients. *Journal of Clinical Psychiatry, 64*, 1005–1012.

Laursen, T. M., Munk-Olsen, T., & Vestergaard, M. (2012). Life expectancy and cardiovascular mortality in persons with schizophrenia. *Current Opinion in Psychiatry, 25*(2), 83–88. doi:10.1097/YCO.0b013e32835035ca

Lenzenweger, M. F., Lane, M. C., Loranger, A. W., & Kessler, R. C. (2007). DSM-IV personality disorders in the National Comorbidity Survey Replication. *Biological Psychiatry, 62*(6), 553–564. doi:10.1016/j.biopsych.2006.09.019

Liptzin, B., Gottlieb, G. L., & Summergrad, P. (2007). The future of psychiatric services in general hospitals. *American Journal of Psychiatry, 164*(10), 1468–1472. doi:10.1176/appi.ajp.2007.07030541

Lysaker, P. H., & Dimaggio, G. (2014). Metacognitive capacities for reflection in schizophrenia: Implications for developing treatments. *Schizophrenia Bulletin, 40*, 497–491.

McCormick, B. P., & Funderburk, J. (2000). Therapeutic recreation outcomes in mental health practice. *Annual in Therapeutic Recreation, 9*, 9–19.

Mechanic, D. (2012). Seizing opportunities under the Affordable Care Act for transforming the mental and behavioral health system. *Health Affairs, 31*(2), 376–382. doi:10.1377/hlthaff.2011.0623

Millan, M. J., Agid, Y., Bruene, M., Bullmore, E. T., Carter, C. S., Clayton, N. S., . . . Young, L. J. (2012). Cognitive dysfunction in psychiatric disorders: Characteristics, causes and the quest for improved therapy. *Nature Reviews Drug Discovery, 11*(2), 141–168. doi:10.1038/nrd3628

Peebles, S. A., Mabe, P. A., Davidson, L., Fricks, L., Buckley, P. F., & Fenley, G. (2007). Recovery and systems transformation for schizophrenia. *Psychiatric Clinics of North America, 30*(3), 567–583. doi:10.1016/j.psc.2007.04.009

Porter, H., & burlingame, j. (2006). *Recreational therapy handbook of practice.* Enumclaw, WA: Idyll Arbor.

Riley, B., & Connolly, P. (2007). A profile of certified therapeutic recreation specialist practitioners. *Therapeutic Recreation Journal, 41*(1), 29–46.

Schinnar, A. P., Rothbard, A. B., Kanter, R., & Jung, Y. S. (1990). An empirical literature review of definitions of severe and persistent mental illness. *American Journal of Psychiatry, 147*(12), 1602–1608.

Schumacher, J. M., & Navar, N. (2010). Promoting physical health and psychosocial well-being through the Sociable Tandem Cycle Recreation Program with adults with mood disorder. *Annual in Therapeutic Recreation, 18*, 114–130.

Snethen, G., McCormick, B. P., & Van Puymbroeck, M. (2012). Community involvement, planning and coping skills: Pilot outcomes of a recreational-therapy intervention for adults with schizophrenia. *Disability and Rehabilitation, 34*(18), 1575–1584. doi:10.3109/09638288.2011.650315

Substance Abuse and Mental Health Services Administration. (2013a). *Behavioral health United States, 2012.* Rockville, MD: Author.

Substance Abuse and Mental Health Services Administration. (2013b). *Results from the 2012 National Survey on Drug Use and Health: Mental health detailed tables.* Rockville, MD: Author.

U.S. Department of Health and Human Services. (1999). *Mental health : A report of the Surgeon General.* Rockville, MD: Author.

Unutzer, J., Schoenbaum, M., Druss, B. G., & Katon, W. J. (2006). Transforming mental health care at the interface with general medicine: Report for the President's Commission. *Psychiatric Services, 57*(1), 37–47. doi:10.1176/appi.ps.57.1.37

Vasques, P. E., Moraes, H., Silveira, H., Deslandes, A. C., & Laks, J. (2011). Acute exercise improves cognition in the depressed elderly: The effect of dual-tasks. *Clinics, 66*, 1553–1557. doi:10.1590/s1807-59322011000900008

Wang, P. S., Lane, M., Olfson, M., Pincus, H. A., Wells, K. B., & Kessler, R. C. (2005). Twelve-month use of mental health services in the United States: Results from the National Comorbidity Survey Replication. *Archives of General Psychiatry, 62*(6), 629–640. doi:10.1001/archpsyc.62.6.629

World Health Organization. (2005). *ICD-10 international statistical classification of diseases and related health problems* (10th revision, 2nd ed.). Geneva, Switzerland: Author.

World Health Organization. (2010). *Measuring health and disability: Manual for WHO disability assessment schedule- WHODAS 2.0.* Geneva, Switzerland: Author.

5

SUBSTANCE USE DISORDERS

ROBIN KUNSTLER

OBJECTIVES

- Understand the scope of substance use disorders.
- Distinguish between casual use, risky use, substance use disorder, and addiction.
- Describe the classifications of drugs and their effects.
- Explain the physical and emotional limitations that accompany substance use disorders.
- Understand the range of treatment approaches and service settings for substance use disorders.
- Evaluate the evidence supporting use of recreational therapy interventions.
- Describe the role and purposes of recreational therapy throughout the treatment and recovery process.
- Apply the recreational therapy process of assessment, planning, implementation, and evaluation.
- Analyze a case study of a client with a substance use disorder.
- Comprehend the trends and issues related to substance use disorders.

Substance use disorders have been an ongoing health concern for decades. Also known as addiction, substance use disorders may present in several settings where recreational therapists work, as it may co-occur with other health conditions. The particular substances that are most used and cause the most harm have changed over time, but regardless of the addiction, recreational therapy (RT) is important in treatment. Although addiction may also be a behavior, such as gambling, this chapter will focus on illegal and legal drugs, including alcohol and prescription medication.

In 2012, an estimated 23.9 million Americans aged 12 or older—or 9.2% of the population—had used an illicit drug or a psychotherapeutic medication (e.g., pain reliever, stimulant, or tranquilizer) for other than its intended use, in the previous month (National Institute on Drug Abuse, 2013). The cost of this substance use in the United States has been estimated at over $600 billion annually due to loss of productivity, crime, and health care (Centers for Disease Control and Prevention, 2014). Nearly one third of all hospital costs are linked to substance use and addiction (CASAColumbia, 2014).

Every day, 105 persons in the United States die of a drug overdose, and this exceeds deaths from motor vehicle accidents (Solomon, 2014). Despite the extent of this public health problem, treatment availability is inadequate to meet the demand. According to the Substance Abuse and Mental Health Services Administration's (SAMHSA, 2012) National Survey on Drug Use and Health, 23.5 million persons 12 years of age and older needed treatment for an illicit drug or alcohol problem in 2009, yet only 2.6 million (11.2%) received treatment at a specialty facility. Only 10% of teens who need treatment receive it (SAMHSA, 2014). More than 1 in 6 (17%) of those with addiction have addiction involving multiple substances (CASAColumbia, 2014). In addition, persons with mental illness have high rates of risky substance use. Results from surveys estimate that 48% of those with schizophrenia, 56% with bipolar disorder, and as many as 65% with severe and persistent mental illness have misused substances (Bellack, Bennett, Gearon, Brown, & Yang, 2006).

Much attention has been given to the use of legal drugs for purposes other than for which, and/or for whom, they were prescribed. This may be considered risky use, which is the use of addictive substances in ways that increase the risk of harm but do not meet the criteria for addiction (CASAColumbia, 2014). The United States has 5% of the world's population and consumes 75% of the world's prescription drugs (United Nations Office on Drugs and Crime, 2011), with the number of prescription medicine risky users in 2010 at 8.76 million (SAMHSA, 2014). For teenagers, although alcohol and cigarette use has decreased, illicit drug use has been increasing, led by marijuana and followed by prescription and over-the-counter (OTC) medications. Based on data from SAMHSA's 2005 National Survey on Drug Use and Health, about 25% of 12- to 18-year-olds reported a moderate level of substance use: they abuse drugs, drink heavily, or drink in binges, but are not physically dependent and still largely can control their intake (Winters, Leitten, Wagner, & Tevyaw, 2007). The legalization of marijuana for medical and recreational use in several states has increased concern over risky use.

The government crackdown on risky use of OTC and prescription medications has led to a rise in the use of heroin. Between 2007 and 2012, heroin use rose 79% nationwide, according to federal data (SAMHSA, 2012). Although a much smaller number of persons use heroin, of particular concern is that 81% of first-time heroin users have used prescription drugs. Emergency room visits due to heroin also have increased. Another drug that is destructive is methamphetamine, but a decrease in its use has been reported. According to the National Institute on Drug Abuse (NIDA, 2012), the number of users decreased from 530,000 in 2007 to 440,000 in 2012. A small decrease also was reported in the use of cocaine.

Alcoholism and alcohol use disorders (AUD) are regarded as the most devastating of all health conditions in terms of economic and social costs, affecting 17 million Americans. Although this reflects a decline from 18.1 million (or 7.7%) in 2002 (NIDA, 2012), approximately 53% of adults in the United States have reported that one or more of their close relatives have a drinking problem. This may be either alcoholism or harmful drinking that does not include dependence. Only 15% with AUD ever seek treatment (National Institute on Alcohol Abuse and Alcoholism, 2014). Alcohol-related problems cost the United States $224 billion per year in lost productivity, health care, and property damage. Alcoholism may affect every bodily system, including the cardiovascular, digestive, and nervous systems resulting in serious diseases such as diabetes, stroke, cancer, hypertension, ulcers, and neuropathy. AUD often co-occurs with anxiety and/or depression and is related to trauma. It may lead to abuse and violence. For college students, alcohol use may result in academic problems, accidents and injuries, sexual assaults, health problems, and suicide (National Institute on Alcohol Abuse and Alcoholism, 2014). Addiction and risky substance use are responsible for more than 20% of all deaths in the United States each year (CASAColumbia, 2014).

One group that has extremely high rates of substance use disorder is prison inmates. Of the estimated 2.3 million incarcerated in the United States, 85% of all inmates in the adult corrections system are substance involved. About 65% of inmates (nearly 1.5 million) have addiction involving alcohol or drugs other than nicotine (CASAColumbia, 2014). Another 458,000 inmates have a history of substance abuse and were under the influence of alcohol or other drugs at the time of their crime, committed their offense to get money to buy drugs, or were incarcerated for alcohol or drug law violations. For young persons apprehended for criminal activity, by the time they enter the juvenile justice system, 78% are substance involved and 44% meet clinical criteria for addiction involving alcohol and drugs other than nicotine (CASAColumbia, 2014). Treatment in prisons would greatly reduce costs and recidivism rates.

Unfortunately, drug misuse in Canada closely parallels the United States. The national government in Canada perceived drug misuse to be a continuing concern, so to combat the harm of substance misuse in Canada, the Canadian Centre on Substance Abuse (CCSA) was established in 1998 (CCSA, 2013).

Similarities exist among the types of addiction in certain effects on the brain, risk factors, behaviors, and common responses to certain treatments. Hopefully this knowledge will lead to expanded and innovative treatment approaches, including RT, and a reduction in the vast human costs of this disorder.

DEFINITIONS

Formerly known as substance abuse, the condition now called *substance use disorders* reflects the assumption that persons who use different substances have different disorders with unique features, which range from mild to moderate to severe. Not everyone who has this disorder suffers from addiction. The word *addiction* is the preferred term for persons who experience compulsive use despite serious health and social consequences. These users engage in a pattern of behavior characterized by overwhelming involvement with a drug and securing its supply regardless of adverse consequences. Addiction is often chronic in nature; it disrupts circuits in the brain that are responsible for reward, motivation, learning, judgment, and memory (CASAColumbia, 2014), making recovery challenging. Some experts believe that addiction is not biologically based or a disease, but that it is a reaction to situational stressors (Peele, 1985). Regardless of the cause of addiction, the diagnostic criteria that have been specified in the fifth edition of the *Diagnostic and Statistical Manual of Mental Disorders* (*DSM-5*) issued in 2013 (American Psychiatric Association, 2014) describe eleven behavioral criteria. Table 5.1 shows the *DSM-5* criteria.

Even persons who are not addicted may experience dependence and withdrawal. Dependence signifies the changes that happen in the body after extended use of alcohol or other drugs, which produces tolerance (need for increased dosage to achieve the desired effect) and withdrawal symptoms when use is reduced or stopped. Withdrawal is the temporary physical and/or psychological symptoms that occur when use of the drug is stopped abruptly (Donatelle, 2004). Each person's response to substance use is unique and depends on many factors: predisposition to a disorder based on heredity, physiology or psychology; the drug itself and its dosage, potency, availability, and means of ingesting; and the individual's attitudes and the attitudes and behaviors of family, friends, and society. Millions of casual users never develop a disorder and risky users may stop harmful use before they develop dependence or addiction.

Table 5.1
DSM-5 Criteria for Substance Use Disorders

1. Taking the substance in larger amounts or for longer than you meant to
2. Wanting to cut down or stop using the substance but not managing to
3. Spending a lot of time getting, using, or recovering from use of the substance
4. Cravings and urges to use the substance
5. Not managing to do what you should at work, home, or school because of substance use
6. Continuing to use, even when it causes problems in relationships
7. Giving up important social, occupational, or recreational activities because of substance use
8. Using substances again and again, even when it puts you in danger
9. Continuing to use, even when you know you have a physical or psychological problem that could have been caused or made worse by the substance
10. Needing more of the substance to get the effect you want (tolerance)
11. Development of withdrawal symptoms, which can be relieved by taking more of the substance

The *DSM-5* allows clinicians to specify how severe the substance use disorder is, depending on how many symptoms are identified. Two or three symptoms indicate a mild substance use disorder, four or five symptoms indicate a moderate substance use disorder, and six or more symptoms indicate a severe substance use disorder.

Note. From "The Symptoms Used for the Diagnosis of Substance Use Disorders," by E. Hartney, 2013, retrieved March 23, 2014, from About.com website: http://addictions.about.com/od/aboutaddiction/a/Dsm-5-Criteria-For-Substance-Use-Disorders.htm.

CLASSIFICATION OF DRUGS

Addiction may occur to one or a combination of drugs. Some are more highly addictive than others, and the extent of withdrawal symptoms also varies. The main categories are depressants, stimulants, opioids, and hallucinogens. Table 5.2 shows the four categories of drugs, with their effects.

Table 5.2
Classification of Drugs

Type of drug	Effects	Addictive potential	Examples
Depressants	Slow normal brain function; drowsiness; calming effect; slurred speech; confusion; poor concentration	High; withdrawal effects can be very severe; barbiturate withdrawal can be life threatening	**CNS depressants** Alcohol; benzodiazepines such as Librium, Ativan, Klonopin; barbiturates such as seconal, luminol, Nembutal; cannabinoid in small doses (marijuana, hashish, THC) **Limbic depressants** Antipsychotics or major tranquilizers such as thorazine, Haldol; antidepressants such as Elavil, Prozac; antimania such as lithium
Stimulants	Speed up motor activity; elevate mood; increase heart rate, respiration, blood pressure, energy, and alertness; may cause feelings of excitability, euphoria, paranoia, agitation, and hostility	High	Amphetamines, cocaine, caffeine, nicotine, ecstasy, Adderall, ritalin
Opioids/ narcotics	Quick, intense feeling of pleasure followed by a sense of well-being and calm; decreases pain, causes lethargy, lack of motivation, drowsiness, slow pulse	High; wide range of physical and psychological withdrawal symptoms	Heroin, morphine, codeine, opium, OxyContin, Demerol
Hallucinogenics/ psychedelics	Alter perceptions, feelings, sense of time; may cause auditory, visual, and tactile hallucinations; may cause panic, paranoia	Moderate risk of addiction; high risk of developing tolerance, few withdrawal symptoms	LSD, PCP, mescaline, psilocybin, peyote, marijuana in larger doses, inhalants

DESCRIPTION OF LIMITATIONS

Recreational therapists should be aware of signs and symptoms of a substance abuse disorder in several populations with whom they work, particularly youth and young adults, adults with psychiatric issues, individuals with intellectual disability, veterans, and senior citizens. Symptoms could include fatigue, unhealthy pallor, change in appetite and grooming, social withdrawal and changes in relationships, and lack of motivation to engage in activities. In addition to appearing under the influence of drugs (e.g., confusion, lack of motor coordination, poor balance resulting in falls, changes in response speed), substance users may be irritable, be jittery, be paranoid, lack impulse control, and demonstrate poor judgment. They may ask for money. They may engage in reckless or dangerous activities such as driving or in risky activities such as unsafe sex or stunts or pranks while under the influence (Drench, Noonan, Sharby, & Ventura, 2012). Recreational therapist should share their observations and concerns with appropriate personnel to address the issue.

If the recreational therapist is working in a substance use disorders treatment facility, clients' limitations will vary based on length of time in treatment. Clients who have just been admitted for detoxification (detox) to rid their body of the drug will begin to go through physical withdrawal. Although symptoms of withdrawal vary based on the substance of use, typical symptoms include anxiety, tremors, muscle pain, nausea, vomiting, sweating, and hallucinations. Emotional withdrawal may be marked by a roller coaster of emotions as the person is flooded with feelings and memories that may have been masked or blocked by the effects of the substances. Once the patient has completed detox, the individual could be anxious, unable to concentrate, confused, guilty, ashamed, withdrawn, depressed, and even suicidal and have other health complications such as infections, injuries, insomnia, unregulated blood sugar, food cravings, weight loss, or fatigue. The individual may be facing legal problems and possibly loss of home, job, and/or family. The condition of the clients and the limitations imposed by the detox and post-detox process will be addressed by the recreational therapist during planning and programming.

Substance users may present in treatment with a variety of health problems, partially due to neglect and lack of self-care. Weight loss, digestive problems, dental disease, diabetes, infections including pneumonia, tuberculosis, hepatitis B and C, HIV/AIDS, damage to internal organs, respiratory problems, and insomnia are some of the physical complications. Long-term use may lead to mood disturbances, anxiety, hostility, paranoia, confusion, and even violent behavior. Also, cognitive impairments in concentration, decision making, and memory often occur. The recreational therapist will need to understand the medical and functional limitations that will affect RT services.

In addition to their health status, these clients also may be facing family, home, job, and/or legal problems. Women in treatment may present a history of abuse and have accompanying psychological issues related to low self-esteem, powerlessness, and guilt. They may be separated from their children. U.S. military personnel may also face unique problems. Although their substance use is lower than among civilians, heavy alcohol and tobacco use, and especially prescription drug abuse, are much more prevalent and are on the rise particularly among combat veterans (NIDA, 2013). These frequently co-occur with post-traumatic stress disorder. With the aging of the baby boomers, the older population also is expected to show an increase in substance use, particularly of antianxiety and pain medications. Persons over 50 account for 10% of all admissions to drug treatment programs (Gross, 2008). This population may be divided into the young-old and the old-old, requiring different treatment approaches. Treatment services are not one size fits all and more options have emerged in the last decade.

PURPOSE OF RECREATIONAL THERAPY

Substance use disorder is a chronic condition that has a high rate of relapse and may require multiple admissions for treatment and ongoing intervention (NIDA, 2012). Treatment for substance use disorders typically begins with medically supervised detoxification to clear the body of the toxic substances. Detox alone does not produce long-term recovery, and patients should be encouraged to continue treatment. Several medications are approved in the United States by the Food and Drug Administration to facilitate recovery (NIDA, 2012), including Antabuse, which makes users sick if they drink alcohol, and naltrexone, which blocks the rewarding effects of alcohol and reduces cravings. For opiate addiction, methadone, Suboxone, and buprenorphine work by reducing symptoms of withdrawal, reducing the cravings for the drug, and blocking the effects of the opiates.

Therapeutic approaches that have been in use for a number of years include therapeutic communities, 12-step support groups, community reinforcement, cognitive-behavioral therapy (CBT), multidimensional family therapy (MDFT), multimodal intervention, and a holistic approach to developing a healthy lifestyle (CASA-Columbia, 2014). Newer methods include screening, brief intervention, and referral to treatment in behavioral health care (SBIRT; SAMHSA, 2014); motivational interviewing (MI) and motivational enhancement therapy (MET; CASAcolumbia, 2014); and multisystemic therapy (MST) and complementary and alternative methods such as massage and yoga ("Treatment programs," 2006) and qigong (Chen, Comerford, Shinnick, & Ziedonis, 2010). Table 5.3 presents current treatments for substance use disorders and their reported efficacy, or effectiveness.

A review of treatment methods found that CBT, 12-step facilitation, MST, psychoeducation, which is educating about substance use, and MI were positively associated with favorable treatment outcomes and that for adolescents, incorporating family-based interventions seemed to consistently provide the best results (Spas, Ramsey, Paiva, & Stein, 2012). In a study of MDFT treatment, Sherman (2010) found that teenage participants treated with MDFT had fewer drug-related problems and improved more on general measures of behavior and mental health than teens treated with CBT. These outcomes were still present a year after treatment. Sherman concluded that MDFT outcomes are among the best for adolescents. However, in another study, 315 drug- and alcohol-involved middle and high school students markedly reduced their substance use following only two 60-minute sessions that combined MI and CBT (Winters et al., 2007).

A meta-analysis literature review of NIDA's recommended principles for treatment found evidence supporting the following practices: matching treatment to the client's needs; attending to the multiple needs of clients; behavioral counseling interventions; treatment plan reassessment; and counseling to reduce risk of HIV. Two of the NIDA principles that are not supported are remaining in treatment for an adequate period of time and frequency of testing for drug use (Pearson et al., 2012). Multiple treatment approaches have positive effects. Different treatment facilities use various approaches and methods that fit well with the RT framework of services.

Table 5.3
Treatments for Substance Use Disorders

Treatment	How it works	Efficacy
Community reinforcement	Provides help from a clinician in the community to assist clients in finding employment, improve family and marital relationships, and enhance social skills; uses a range of recreational, familial, social, and vocational reinforcers, along with material incentives, to make a non-drug-using lifestyle more rewarding than substance use; encourages participation in positive recreation	Facilitates patients' engagement in treatment and successfully aids them in gaining substantial periods of cocaine abstinence. Use of contingencies, or rewards, found to be effective with opiate and cocaine users
Cognitive-behavioral therapy	Learn to identify, recognize, and avoid thought processes, behaviors, and situations associated with substance use; and manage cravings by self-monitoring and developing better problem-solving and coping skills	Skills learned through cognitive-behavioral approaches remain after the completion of treatment
Family behavior therapy	Focus is on improving communication and support among family members and addressing co-occurring problems and disorders; uses behavioral goals and contracting and rewards	More effective for adolescents than supportive counseling
Matrix model	Used with stimulant users; user and therapist develop trusting relationship; therapist teaches about addiction and coaches user to positive behaviors; emphasizes user's dignity and self-worth and can use other techniques	Statistically significant reductions in drug and alcohol use, improvements in psychological indicators, and reduced risky sexual behaviors associated with HIV transmission.
Multisystemic therapy	Takes a total approach to the adolescent with intensive treatment in natural environments; addresses all types of influences including home, school, work, and community	Significantly reduces adolescent drug use during treatment and for at least 6 months after treatment, resulting in fewer incarcerations and out-of-home juvenile placements

Table 5.3 (cont.)

Treatment	How it works	Efficacy
Motivational interviewing and enhancement therapy	Aims to rapidly get user into treatment through discussing motivation, planning for change, developing coping strategies, monitoring progress, and providing ongoing encouragement	Successful with alcohol users, with marijuana users when combined with cognitive-behavioral therapy; most effective at getting people into treatment rather than changing use patterns
Milieu therapy	All aspects of the treatment environment contribute to the client's care including group and individual psychotherapy, support groups, interactions with all staff, social skills development, and vocational rehabilitation, social services, occupational therapy, and recreational therapy as provided	Some promising results when combined with cognitive-behavioral therapy for dual-diagnosed patients
Screening, brief intervention, and referral to treatment in behavioral health care	Comprehensive, integrated, public health approach to the delivery of early intervention and treatment services includes quick assessment, brief intervention to increase insight and awareness and motivate to treatment, and referral to services	Effective in reducing risky alcohol use; growing but inconsistent evidence for users of other drugs; depends on multiple factors
Therapeutic community	Drug-free residential settings focused on psychosocial rehabilitation	Substance use decreased while in therapeutic community, but relapse was frequent after therapeutic community, so long-lasting benefits are uncertain
Twelve-step support groups	Voluntary fellowship open to anyone who walks into a meeting; based on recognition that sobriety and recovery depend on support of others; run by members, no professional staff; includes acceptance, surrender, and active involvement	Efficacy established with alcohol; promising for drug users to sustain recovery

Leisure education is increasingly being included as an essential component of treatment, in the context of either an RT program (Cogswell & Negley, 2011) or some variation offered by other professionals who are recognizing the importance of fun and joy in recovery (Grawe, Hagen, Espeland, & Mueser, 2007; MacLean, Cameron, Harney, & Lee, 2012). For example, a group from the Yale University Department of Psychiatry working with women who were homeless, with mental illness and substance use disorders, recommended pleasure and play as sources of hope, commitment, meaning, and purpose and as a means of discovering individual strengths, talents, sense of control, and mastery (Lawless, Rowe, & Miller, 2009). Another program for adults with mental illness and substance abuse disorders found that teaching skills of "Managing Leisure Time and Friendships," as one of four sets of skills in a life skills program, played a critical role in their first steps toward recovery (Grawe et al., 2007).

EMPIRICAL EVIDENCE SUPPORTING PRACTICE

Many studies have been done that support the use of recreation activities in the treatment of substance use disorders. Evidence of varying quality exists for use of adventure therapy, animal-assisted therapy, horticulture, photography, and physical activity (Austin, 2013), bibliotherapy (Peele, 2014), mindfulness (Wupperman et al., 2012), qigong (Chen et al., 2010; Li, Chen, & Mo, 2002), relaxation and stress management (Drench et al., 2012), and multimodal intervention using recreation such as sports and cultural activities (MacLean et al., 2012). A focus group of treatment providers (SAMHSA, 2013) cited "recreational or social events for the entire family" as a key component to successful client outcomes. Below are examples of research studies supporting recreation as an essential component of substance use disorder treatment:

- Basing their approach on positive psychology and the realization that confrontation strategies often used in treatment were not effective for women, who benefited from a strength-based approach and development of trusting relationships, researchers (Lawless et al., 2009) developed a program that challenged participants to have fun without getting high. The participants were 12 women, eight African American and four Caucasian, who were homeless and diagnosed with substance abuse and mental illness. The components of the program included trying a new activity, giving attention to themselves, having child-like fun, and experiencing the arts. The women ate at ethnic restaurants, went to the theater and art museums, spent a day at the beach and spa, and played board games and flew kites. Lawless et al. (2009) found that play and having fun could be relearned as the women experienced these without getting high, which was their previous source of fun. Positive social pressure and extrinsic rewards were effective motivators. The activities were seen as a source of hope and commitment, a means of discovering strengths and talents, and a means of developing a sense of control and mastery. Outcomes included increased quality of life, hope, trust, and sharing. An unexpected outcome was the value of staff participation in the program. Initially it was designed so staff would take a more supervisory role, but it was discovered not only were they as in need of recreation as the clients, but also their engagement promoted trust and provided social support (Lawless et al., 2009).

- The Better Life Program (Grawe et al., 2007) was implemented with 63 adults with mental illness and substance use disorders. The program covered four skill areas: communication, assertiveness, refusing drugs and resisting cravings, and managing leisure time and friendships. In the leisure time component, the clients identified healthy leisure activities and learned how to invite someone to join them in the activity. Those in the program had a lower dropout rate; and researchers felt that the emphasis on "systematically teaching patients strategies for establishing healthy leisure activities and friendships played a critical role in their first steps toward recovery" (Grawe et al., 2007, p. 632).

- A review of literature (MacLean et al., 2012) analyzed 19 studies reporting interventions for inhalant disorder. MacLean et al. (2012) reported that recreation activities were used frequently as intervention "to engage clients in therapeutic relationships, develop skills and provide alternatives to substance misuse" (p. 284). In one study, cited by MacLean et al. (2012), 175 Mexican American youth, a multimodal intervention including recreation yielded better outcomes at one year post-discharge. The recreation activities included sports, discos, films, cultural activities, beach-going, and rock climbing.

- A study of 248 inpatient (Chen et al, 2010) adults found that practicing qigong meditation, including breathing, guided imagery, empty-mindedness, and a closing strategy with music, helped reduce symptoms of drug withdrawal. Female patients were more successful than males. Chen et al. (2010) concluded that the elements of self-responsibility present in qigong practice were compatible with the aims of recovery.

The results of these studies are exciting for RT practitioners, who may use them as evidence of the value and efficacy of recreation activities and leisure education programs. However, few empirical studies have been completed in the RT field that support use of these and similar recreation activities in the context of an RT program. According to Stumbo and Pegg (2010), the relationship whereby practice is based on research and yields data to demonstrate outcomes "does not currently exist" (p. 15) in the RT profession. Nonetheless, with or without sufficient evidence on which to base practice, recreational therapists should exercise judgment-based practice of care (Polkinghorne, 2004) based on their knowledge, skills, empathy, creativity, and experience to determine what a particular client needs.

Not since the 1990s has a wide-scale effort been made to determine the RT programming offered in substance use disorder treatment facilities. Results from a survey of over 100 facilities found that over three-quarters offered physical fitness, leisure education, and stress management at least once a week (Malkin, Voss, Teaff, & Benshoff, 1993–1994). A subsequent survey of RT programs for adolescents found that the most frequently offered RT programs were leisure education/counseling, individual and team sports, wellness/physical fitness, and arts and crafts/hobbies (Nation, Benshoff, & Malkin, 1996). These programs correlate with the results of the Benefits of Therapeutic Recreation Conference, which found that the four areas of RT practice essential in substance use disorders treatment are leisure education, physical fitness, social skills, and stress management (Coyle, Kinney, & Riley, 1991). These were determined by a review of the evidence up to that time, although the lack of rigor and generalizability of the evidence was noted (Malkin, Coyle, & Carruthers, 1998).

Since that time, RT professionals have had several articles published reporting evidence of efficacy of recreation activities related to substance use disorders, from an RT perspective or in the context of an RT program.

- In a qualitative study of three women, Hood (2003) reported that the women found leisure involvement to be critical to their moving beyond just "not drinking toward true recovery" (p. 51). They saw it as a turning point and a means to learn about themselves, their strengths and talents, and a source of joy that brightened the road to recovery.

- A case report of a creative writing intervention with a 24-year-old woman with alcoholism, codiagnosed with major depression and impulse control disorder (Gillespie, 2003), showed that writing was successfully used as an alternative coping skill and that a shared interest in writing served as the basis for friendship development.

- A seven-session coping skills program, using instruction, homework, and debriefing, was developed and implemented with 56 clients in three alcohol treatment facilities (Carruthers & Hood, 2002). Sessions covered negative thinking, changing a stressful environment through stress management techniques, relaxation, skills for friendship development and assertiveness, coping with high-risk situations, identifying satisfying leisure activities and barriers and developing a plan for leisure after discharge. The clients perceived the importance of developing coping skills and felt they had improved in their coping ability as a result of the program.

- A study was conducted of nine adolescent girls in a psychiatric facility, some of whom also had substance use disorders, who participated in adventure therapy. The study found that adventure therapy had strong, positive impacts on the girls' emotions including coping, control, trust, and teamwork. However, these gains had limited carry over value. Autry (2001) concluded that an ongoing processing of the adventure experience upon return to the facility was needed to maintain the positive benefits.

With the emphasis on evidence-based practice, there are renewed calls for RT research to demonstrate the profession's efficacy in producing sought outcomes. However, Cogswell and Negley (2011) pointed out that the challenges in studies of RT and substance use disorders include participants' compliance, not attending all sessions of RT and dropping out of the study, lack of control groups, difficulty with random selection and assignment to treatment groups, and the mostly descriptive research designs. Nevertheless, based on anecdotal evidence of the value of RT to clients, substance use disorders seem to be an area with strong potential for successful RT intervention that could be documented through well-designed empirically based studies.

COMMONLY SOUGHT OUTCOMES

In substance use disorder treatment, many outcomes are common to all disciplines and specific disorders. These include number of days without a relapse, ability to identify triggers and resist urges, effective use of stress management strategies and coping skills, increased impulse control and frustration tolerance, improved family relationships and communications, developing a support network, acquiring social skills, recognizing strengths and assets, developing trust, and making new friends.

Although RT may contribute to achieving these outcomes, some are more specific to recreation and leisure functioning including increasing awareness of leisure; identifying leisure barriers, interests, skills, and resources; identifying rewarding alternative activities to substance use; acquiring a repertoire of leisure activities to do alone and with others; and implementing a plan for leisure participation. Through RT, clients may come to view leisure as an "opportunity for growth and self-development as opposed to an empty, problematic block of time" (McCormick & Dattilo, 1995, p. 28).

Other outcomes that RT may address are increases in motivation for treatment, self-esteem, intrinsic motivation, internal locus of control, self-awareness, and self-efficacy. Outcomes related to physical health and improved physical fitness may strengthen internal resolve to maintain an overall healthier lifestyle.

ROLE OF THE RECREATIONAL THERAPIST

The purpose of RT in substance use disorders treatment is to focus on promoting a drug-free or sober lifestyle, in alignment with the overall goals or outcomes of the agency or facility. Some programs support the concept of harm reduction, with the goal of reducing the amount of drug use or helping the client to use less damaging or addictive substances. In either case, the recreational therapists role is to assist the clients in overcoming barriers that prevent achieving this goal. These barriers may be internal to the client, external in their environment, or interpersonal in their relationships. RT encourages participation in alternative, non-drug activities that help clients cope and/or obtain enjoyable states, reducing reliance on drugs for the same effect. Stanton Peele (1985), the noted addictions specialist, stated that treatment works best when it requires clients to change attitudes, practice skills, and make life changes that are attributed to the client's efforts. Thus, the goals of RT in Table 5.4 are in alignment with the goals of recovery.

The recreational therapist will assist the client in

- identifying barriers to leisure participation;
- recognizing his or her strengths to reinforce feelings of self-worth as well as using strengths to address unmet needs;
- improving ability to choose healthy alternatives to substance use;
- developing feelings of competence, control, and mastery through participation in RT programs;
- experiencing joy;
- improving functional skills and health status in all behavioral domains;
- developing a supportive social network; and
- reconceiving their identity as a healthy person.

Table 5.4

Goals of Recreational Therapy Compared to Goals of Recovery

Recreational therapy goals	Recovery goals
Self-awareness	Believe addiction is hurting them and wish to overcome it
Self-efficacy	Feel enough efficacy to manage their withdrawal and life without the addiction
Self-rewarding recreation	Find sufficient alternative rewards to make life without the addiction a worthwhile experience

Note. From "TR's Role in Treating Substance Abuse," by R. Kunstler, 1992, *Parks and Recreation, 4,* 58–60.

Mike Tyson (2014), former heavyweight boxing champion, wrote movingly of his own struggles with addiction. To overcome it, he "had to replace the cravings for drugs or alcohol with a craving to be a better person" (p. A19). He recognized that being sober is more than just avoiding drugs or alcohol: "It's a lifestyle focused on making moral choices and elevating the things that make life worth living to the forefront" (p. A19). Tyson cited the needs for a good support system, to talk openly about issues and not keep hidden secrets, and to recognize that focusing on doing and being good are essential strategies for avoiding relapse. Discipline is a day-to-day process of not succumbing to the lure of success and thinking one may relax non-using behavior even once. RT may help clients to understand their values and what matters to them, encourage them to express their feelings, and learn how to develop strong supportive relationships.

Recreational therapists begin their work with substance use disorder clients by providing a natural, supportive environment in which to practice new skills and pursue positive alternative ways of behaving in as typical a setting as possible. This may enhance the client's transfer of learning from the treatment setting to the everyday environment. The RT environment promotes interaction and socialization without the influence of substances. Interacting "straight" may be unsettling and frightening for clients who have used substances to escape uncomfortable emotions and situations. The recreational therapist's role is to be a role model, guide, and support as the clients navigate new feelings and behaviors. Treating clients with dignity and respect will help the recreational therapist to develop a trusting relationship with them.

Recreational therapists are also role models of healthy leisure behavior, participating in recreation with joy and fun. Successful recovery depends on clients finding new ways to have fun, relax, cope with stress, and experience satisfaction. Cogswell and Negley (2011) described RT as a motivator for treatment and a source of opportunities for self-determination and making choices. They found that clients enjoyed the interactive nature of recreational therapy, compared to the more didactic and traditional treatment groups, and valued the well-planned group activities and processes. A structured RT program allows for choice within the necessary limits and regulations of the treatment facility and provides focus toward goals. Clear, matter-of-fact explanations of RT program rules help clients understand boundaries and appropriate behavior.

If the recreational therapist is working in a setting other than a substance abuse treatment facility where individuals could be engaging in harmful use, the purpose of RT would be to deter substance use by promoting a healthy lifestyle, fostering feelings of competence and self-worth, promoting a sense of identity, and helping individuals to develop a repertoire of positive leisure interests.

COMMON SERVICE SETTINGS

In the United States, more than 14,500 specialized drug treatment facilities provide counseling, behavioral therapy, medication, case management, and other services to persons with substance use disorders (NIDA, 2012). Clients are also treated in physicians' offices and mental health clinics by professionals including counselors, physicians, psychiatrists, psychologists, nurses, and social workers. It is recommended that more screening for substance use problems occur in these health care settings as many persons either do not seek treatment or have not revealed their problem to a health care provider. Just as the SBIRT has been designed for use in public health settings, hospital emergency rooms and doctors' offices, the simple CAGE questionnaire (see Table 5.5) is recommended as a cost-effective and quick screening for a substance use problem.

Table 5.5
CAGE Questionnaire for Alcohol Abuse Screening

• Have you ever tried unsuccessfully to Cut down your drinking?
• Does it make you Angry when people suggest that you stop drinking?
• Do you feel Guilty when you drink?
• Do you need an Eye-opener to get started in the morning?

Note. From *Psychosocial Aspects of Health Care* (3rd ed.), by M. Drench, A. Noonan, N. Sharby, and S. Ventura, 2012, Upper Saddle River, NJ: Pearson, p. 308.

One "yes" answer is considered a red flag for problem drinking and two or more "yes" answers are a signal to open a discussion with the goal of encouraging treatment (Drench et al., 2012). Often health care professionals are uncomfortable asking about the use of alcohol and other drugs, but the need is evident.

The main types of specialized treatment facilities include

- long-term residential care in a therapeutic community that is focused on global lifestyle change—treatment includes resocializing the user through groups, structure, a rewards system, self-examination, learning to take responsibility, and learning new skills;

- inpatient hospitalization, typically 28 days—the challenge of treatment in this setting is changing lifestyle after discharge;

- partial hospitalization and day treatment so patients may return home in the evening and apply new skills; and

- outpatient evening treatment that allows clients to continue working or going to school in the day—involves planning for weekend activities and constructive use of leisure time.

Regardless of setting, treatment dropout is a major problem of treatment programs. For residential or outpatient treatment, participation for less than 90 days is considered to be of limited effectiveness, and treatment lasting significantly longer is recommended for maintaining positive outcomes. For methadone maintenance, 12 months is considered the minimum, although some individuals successfully continue on methadone for years. Recreational therapists most often have been employed in inpatient hospital units.

CURRENT BEST PRACTICES AND PROCEDURES

Every RT program should select an appropriate conceptual model as the starting point for designing services. Using a conceptual model helps the recreational therapist define the scope of services to be provided, the nature of the client–therapist relationship, and the desired outcomes. Models ground RT practice in theory and principles and facilitate communication about RT with clients, family, and other professionals (Carruthers & Hood, 2007). Although many RT models may serve as a framework for services in substance use disorders treatment, the following have been selected as particularly relevant to this population: the Leisure and Well-Being Model (LWM; Carruthers & Hood, 2007) and the Optimizing Lifelong Health and Well-Being Through Therapeutic Recreation (OLH-TR) Model (Wilhite, Keller, & Caldwell, 1999).

The LWM (Carruthers & Hood, 2007) is based on the recognition that leisure is a source of well-being along with a strength-based approach. Well-being may be enhanced by recognizing and developing an individual's strengths and potential. According to Carruthers and Hood (2004), clients improve their health and well-being when they are able to

- break patterns of behavior that are not satisfying or productive,

- actively participate in social and physical activities to enhance positive mood,

- maximize positive experiences in daily life that bring pleasure, and

- reflect on the positive and pleasurable aspects of an experience.

These accomplishments fit well with the goals of recovery, as shown in Table 5.4. To achieve the goals, RT services should help clients to

- increase positive emotion and reduce suffering on a daily basis;

- develop and express their full potential, through the development of their psychological, social, cognitive, physical, and environmental resources; and

- create a meaningful and valued life. (Carruthers & Hood, 2013)

LWM also has a strong connection to positive psychology. Table 5.6 shows RT applications of positive psychology strategies.

Table 5.6

Recreational Therapy Applications of Positive Psychology Strategies

Positive psychology strategies	Recreational therapy applications
Break patterns of behavior that are not satisfying or productive	Provide opportunities to try a variety of recreation activities
Actively participate in social and physical activities to enhance mood	Schedule activities that promote social interaction and physical movement
Maximize experiences in daily life that bring pleasure	Support efforts to engage in preferred recreation activities that are fun, enjoyable, and relaxing; provide opportunities to volunteer and be a mentor; assist in creating daily plans that have opportunities for positive engagement
Reflect on the positive and pleasurable aspects of an experience	Provide opportunities to reflect, reminisce, and journal about the effects of participating in different activities; encourage identification of personal benefits derived from recreation participation

Note. From *Therapeutic Recreation Leadership and Programming*, by R. Kunstler and F. Stavola Daly, 2010, Champaign, IL: Human Kinetics.

The OLH-TR Model (Wilhite et al., 1999) is based on three principles: (a) healthy leisure lifestyles may reduce secondary effects of illness or disability and promote health; (b) health promotion may be achieved by individualizing opportunities and resources; and (c) individuals must be flexible to alter their leisure choices as their personal and environmental characteristics change. Kunstler (2004) presented the OLH-TR Model as useful for clients with multiple diagnoses of substance use disorder, HIV/AIDS, and hepatitis C. As these are chronic health conditions that fluctuate over the lifetime, and which are particularly affected by stress, uncertainty, and social stigma, this model's focus on enhancing health and minimizing effects of illness over the life course may be useful. The recreational therapist assists the client with four processes:

1. selecting activities based on interests, abilities, and resources, recognizing that as health status changes the activities may need to be changed;

2. optimizing goal attainment through engaging in activities of choice by maximizing resources needed to facilitate participation;

3. compensating for change in abilities to participate by adapting or modifying activities, selecting alternatives, or learning new approaches; and

4. evaluating the effectiveness of these activities in contributing to a healthy lifestyle.

The recreational therapist should select a model that fits the treatment setting and use it as a helpful framework for services and as a tool for communication about the role of RT.

With the growing recognition of the power of recreation and leisure as components of successful treatment and recovery, a discussion of Csikszentmihalyi's (1990) flow theory is useful. Flow is a state of optimal psychological arousal resulting from intrinsically motivated participation in activities where the challenges posed by the activity and the skills of the individual are ideally matched. If the challenge is too high and the person's skill level too low, he or she may become frustrated or give up; if the challenge is too easy and the person's skill level high, he or she may become bored. The recreational therapist may use flow technology by altering the challenges of the activity and making it more suitable to the skills of the client. The challenge should be slightly above the clients' skill level so they may strive to accomplish the activity, but still perceive it within their reach. When the match occurs, the participant enters the flow state, which is characterized by joy, creativity, a loss of self-consciousness, and depth of involvement in the experience. This is sometimes called being "in the zone" or a "natural high." Csikszentmihalyi acknowledges that both flow and being under the influence of drugs produce euphoria, perceptions of increased self-esteem, and reduced stress; however, he believes drugs produce a shallow or false state of flow in which users are not really in control of their minds and actions. Understanding that the client seeks to experience a flow state, the recreational therapist may guide them to activities that may produce flow. Recreation activities have characteristics that make them ideal for achieving flow: specific skills for participation, rules and goals, immediate and concrete feedback, novelty, and opportunities to experience control. If clients can experience flow through recreation participation, it may assist their recovery. They may be able to give up the rewards they obtain from their substance use when they find new ways to have fun, relax, manage stress, and experience satisfaction (Peele, 1985).

Assessment

Standard assessment procedures are used in RT for all populations and settings. These include conducting the assessment interview, observing the client, speaking with family and friends, receiving reports from other staff, and reviewing the chart with its comprehensive information on demographic background, patient condition, medical and social history, and results of any standardized testing. The recreational therapist will want information on the client's physical and mental status, functional limitations, treatment goals, and other relevant factors that could influence RT programming. Clients' strengths, recreation interests and skills, access to resources, and barriers to participation in recreation and health-promoting behaviors are essential information for the recreational therapist to acquire. However, in substance use disorders treatment, with a focus on recovery, certain adaptations should be made to the traditional assessment process.

Using the recovery model, recreational therapists often start treatment by asking clients what their goals are, rather than formulating goals based on the assessment. Recreational therapists then may focus the assessment on what strengths the client has and what skills and resources he or she needs to develop to reach the self-determined goal. The client then may become more invested in the treatment process. For example, this was effective with a man in recovery from substance use disorders, who also was diagnosed with HIV and hepatitis C (Kunstler, 2004). Despite experiencing frequent bouts of flu-like illness, he was determined to obtain a full-time job. Although the recreational therapist was concerned that his health status would be an obstacle to employment, once the client articulated this goal, he was committed to adjusting his lifestyle to promote his health. With the help of the recreational therapist, he identified needed changes. He planned more rest periods, curtailed evening activities, practiced stress management, and adhered to his medications. Before he set his goal, he would have periods of depression and express low self-esteem; pursuing his dream increased his feelings of perceived competence and his self-worth. He was successful in obtaining a full-time job in his field.

Readiness assessment. Recreational therapist should assess how ready clients are to participate in services that will lead to positive changes in their lives (Kunstler & Stavola Daly, 2010). The stages of change model, developed by Prochaska and DiClemente (1982), offers a useful scale for readiness assessment. The stage of readiness of the client influences the approach the recreational therapist will use. The stages of change and the recreational therapist's role at each stage are as follows:

- Precontemplation: Clients are not ready to think about change due to lack of knowledge, feeling hopeless, feeling they do not need to change or that change is too difficult or was unsuccessful in the past.
  Recreational therapist's role: Do not push; instead offer information of what is available.

- Contemplation: Clients admit they are considering a change in the future; they may be gathering information and weighing the pros and cons of change.
  Recreational therapist's role: Provide information about benefits and consequences of change.

- Preparation or determination: Clients are ready to take action, may have a plan but lack skills and resources to go about making the change.
  Recreational therapist's role: Be encouraging! Assist in planning.

- Action: Clients are fully engaged in the change process.
  Recreational therapist's role: Help client to develop skills and resources.

- Maintenance: Change has been made and new behaviors established. Focus is on preventing relapse by staying vigilant about supporting new behaviors and resisting temptations.
  Recreational therapist's role: Provide opportunities to engage in new behaviors.

- Termination: The new behaviors are fully integrated into the client's lifestyle.
  Recreational therapist's role: Communicate positive feedback about what client has accomplished.

At the initial assessment interview, the recreational therapist should begin to develop a rapport with the client. Building a trusting relationship is the key to successful involvement of the client in the RT program and may influence his attitude toward treatment. The recreational therapist should display warmth, genuine interest, and respect for the client, but not be overwhelming, by stating their name, offeing a handshake, and explaining the purpose of the assessment interview. At this time, the client may be in poor health, be fatigued, have slowed reactions, and demonstrate confusion and disorientation. The recreational therapist may need to reschedule. The recreational therapist will also want to make observations of clients' appearance. How is their grooming and self-care? Are they making eye contact? What is their body posture? How are their communication skills, attention span, and comprehension of the conversation? Can they express their feelings?

Areas to assess that are particularly relevant with this population are their moods, stressors, triggers, social supports, and environment. The recreational therapist should find out when moods occur and what triggers feelings of helplessness, boredom, depression, anger, and/or frustration that may lead to substance use. How does the client deal with these feelings? Has the client tried different strategies, and how effective have they been? What is the client doing when he or she feels good, happy, relaxed? What resources are available to the client for dealing with stress? The recreational therapist should assess the skills the client has in the areas of accessing and using resources. Clients often are referred to 12-step programs, but they may lack the communication and group and social behaviors needed to benefit from participation. They also may lack basic literacy or arithmetic skills that are essential to successful independent functioning. They may lack skills for healthy living such as exercise and preparing and eating nutritious meals. Social supports are vital to successful recovery. Does the client have a network of non-using family and friends?

A basic principle of recovery is to avoid persons, places, and things that are associated with substance use. Therefore, the recreational therapist should assess the client's environment to determine what is needed for the client to either change or resist negative influences. Clients may find themselves in awkward social situations if alcohol is being served. Most important is the RT assessment of leisure functioning, which includes awareness of leisure and its value, past and present leisure interests, leisure skills, knowledge and ability to use leisure resources, ability to identify leisure barriers, participation patterns, and ability to select recreation activities to meet their needs.

The recreational therapist is encouraged to administer appropriate standardized assessment tools such as the Idyll Arbor Leisure Battery, which includes the Leisure Attitude measure, the Leisure Motivation Scale, the Leisure Interest Measure, and the Leisure Satisfaction Scale (burlingame & Blaschko, 2010). The FACTR-R, Functional Assessment of Characteristics for Therapeutic Recreation-Revised, could be used to assess basic functional skills for RT participation and intervention. The Leisure Diagnostic Battery (Witt & Ellis, 1993) has been used with this population and the perceived competence and barriers subscales would be particularly appropriate. These tools may also be used to measure client progress once the planned services are implemented.

Planning

Every substance use treatment program adopts a treatment philosophy and the recreational therapist will want to ensure that RT programming is consistent with the mission and goals of the overall program. Ideally, the recreational therapist is working collaboratively with other members of the treatment team to obtain as complete a picture as possible of the client's status and to ensure consistency in addressing client's needs. Planning involves setting meaningful, achievable goals and developing a schedule of RT programs for the client, with the client's input, all within the time frame of the probable length of stay. Goal-setting should be realistic and offer short-, medium-, and long-term targets. Table 5.7 presents sample goals for substance use disorders treatment.

Table 5.7
Sample Goals

Overall treatment goal: Live a lifestyle that supports ongoing recovery

Long-term goal # 1: Develop and maintain friendships
Intermediate goal: Use appropriate social skills for sustained social interaction
Short-term goals:
- Improve conversation skills as demonstrated by initiating and sustaining a 10-minute conversation with a peer, taking turns, listening, making relevant responses, using nonverbal behaviors appropriately
- Demonstrate cooperation by sharing supplies and information, assisting in setup and cleanup at programs, responding to requests
- Display proper etiquette and behavior appropriate to the situation including cleanliness, appropriate dress, and neatness of clothing

Long-term goal #2: Acquire a repertoire of leisure interests to do alone and with others
Intermediate goal: Develop skills in four leisure activities: two to do alone and two to do with others
Short-term goals:
- Identify leisure interests
- Evaluate your skill level in each activity
- Develop required activity skills to level of performance required for successful implementation

Long-term goal #3: Use range of leisure resources that are economically feasible, accessible via transportation, and fit into your schedule
Short-term goals:
- Acquire skills needed for resource use, including time management, money management, transportation, and assertiveness
- Enroll in two programs in the community
- Obtain supplies for in-home leisure participation

A study identified five priorities for RT intervention in alcohol treatment based on input from 31 experts (Hood & Krinsky, 1997):
- lack of positive coping strategies,
- low self-esteem/feelings of inadequacy,

- lack of knowledge of how leisure may prevent relapse,
- social isolation/loneliness, and
- lack of positive non-using experiences.

These priorities may be addressed through the four areas of programming identified at the Benefits of Therapeutic Recreation Conference. Opportunities to practice new skills and try new behaviors, learn limits, and exercise choice and control should be incorporated into RT programming. Treatment may be frightening, and the client may be resistant to RT (McCormick & Dattilo, 1995). The recreational therapist should determine optimal times for RT services, based on the client's receptiveness and energy levels at different times of day, as well as coordinate with the scheduling of other programs.

RT programs for substance use disorders should be balanced among the behavioral domains. Because of this, many programs lend themselves to collaborating with other disciplines. Exercise specialists, dietitians, occupational therapists, nurses, social workers, counselors, psychologists, and psychiatrists are suitable partners for coleading programs to maximize benefits to clients. Each profession contributes its expertise and specialized knowledge in an integrative approach that may enhance the client's learning and facilitate growth and progress.

The recreational therapist will want to determine the client's most pressing needs that may be addressed through RT programming. Programs such as exercise, fitness, yoga, and relaxation should be implemented as soon as possible on a daily basis. Physical fitness and exercise improve health, increase self-concept, are avenues to reduce stress, and may be a foundation for developing friendships with others who are health oriented. Suggested activities include walking, jogging, swimming, bike riding, weight lifting, sports, outdoor activities, and opportunities to take healthy risks. Most of these require minimal equipment and may be done anywhere. A program at Odyssey House, a treatment center in New York City, called "Skills for Positive Change," includes training to run the NYC Marathon (Johnston, 2005). Running is seen as a metaphor for life, and if the participants can show up, practice, and achieve, it shows them they can manage their lives by persevering. Their self-concept grows as they accomplish a goal, perhaps for the first time in their lives (Butler, 2005).

Mindfulness is being recommended for RT practice in addiction recovery (Carruthers & Hood, 2013). In mindfulness, meditation, breathing, yoga, and other relaxation exercises help to decrease distractions and promote concentration. Mindfulness involves the individual focusing attention, reflecting on values as a basis for a meaningful life, setting goals, and being aware of potential setbacks and barriers. The technique of mindfully navigating urges (i.e., urge surfing) is specifically suggested for RT use. Stress management techniques may be active, soothing, creative, or social. Clients need to try out different strategies for relaxation and managing stress to see what works for them and also to have a few to use in different situations. A breathing technique would be useful in a public place when stress occurs unexpectedly or when the person is entering a stressful situation (Kunstler & Stavola Daly, 2010). The recreational therapist should familiarize himself or herself with activities that may reduce stress and should include them in the RT program.

Cognitive programming may be educational in nature with topics such as substance use and its effects, health practices such as good nutrition, literacy skills of reading and writing, life skills including time management and budgeting, assertiveness training, and leisure education. Leisure education should address structuring free time, substance-free alternatives to boredom, decision making, developing skills in activities of choice, experiencing pleasure and enjoyment, and using affordable community resources. RT must include daily enjoyable recreation participation so clients begin to understand that healthy sources of gratification are available every day. Recapturing a sense of playfulness and feelings of empowerment are essential to recovery.

Many recovery programs are finding success using cognitive-behavioral therapy strategies. These help clients identify faulty thinking patterns that may have led them into substance use, change the ways they think about themselves, and learn and practice new behaviors to avoid relapse. Techniques include cognitive rehearsal, role playing, homework assignments, and social skills training. Positive psychology has also emerged as a relevant approach and has a strong relationship to the strength-based approach in RT. The recreational therapist may incorporate activities that use clients' intact strengths and skills, offer high potential for experiencing positive emotions such as joy and satisfaction, improve mood, provide challenges leading to enhanced self-concept, and afford social support in a caring environment (Austin, 2013). Again, Table 5.6 shows how the recreational therapist may apply positive psychology strategies.

A valuable contribution of RT is the provision of programming that facilitates expression of feelings and emotions in a safe, nonjudgmental atmosphere. Many of these programs are in the arts: drawing, painting, sculpture, pottery, music, poetry, creative writing, and drama. These provide a nonverbal vehicle for communicating what may be difficult for the client to express verbally. As the effects of the substances wear off, the client is flooded with difficult emotions. Finding ways to express these may promote recovery. Through RT, individuals may learn to delay gratification and live with discomfort. Involvement in activities that take time to complete, whether it is doing a craft project, putting on a play, producing a newsletter or magazine, or planning a special event, requires teamwork, patience, and recognition of the process that goes into an accomplishment. For those who never have put impulses into action, beginning to act is a form of taking control of their lives. Learning to socialize without the use of substances is another area RT addresses. RT groups provide opportunities for clients to interact, practice new skills, find common topics of discussion and common interests for friendship development, learn to be a good listener, and develop social intelligence.

Strange as it may sound, substance use involves skill. Users are adept at obtaining substances, preparing and using them, and avoiding detection. Recognizing these as skills may decrease feelings of worthlessness. Of course, this recognition should be accompanied by transferring these skills to developing alternative behaviors. The ritualistic nature of substance use goes beyond the effects of the substance, and many find the ritual reinforcing. That is one reason the "just say no" campaign of the 1980s was not successful. It did not recognize the deep-rooted patterns of behavior that accompanied the substance use. Some clients are successful when they develop recreation interests that have ritualistic elements, such as exercising, doing a hobby, going to school, volunteering, or working.

Planning for those in recovery should account for the chronic or lifelong nature of the illness. RT also considers clients' future after discharge from a program or once they are in their subsequent living situation. Without pre-discharge counseling and guidance, the effectiveness of RT intervention may diminish. The recreational therapist could provide transitional services to assist clients with locating feasible resources and guiding them through the process of establishing healthy lifestyle practices for post-discharge. Linkages with public and private community recreation agencies could be established to facilitate reintegration. The recreational therapist could advise these agencies how to develop programs for individuals in recovery that offer socialization, a place to use new skills, and recreation opportunities in a substance-free environment. The Wellness Recovery Action Plan (Copeland, 2014) is an indispensable tool for developing strategies for staying well.

Implementation

Implementation includes motivating clients to attend the RT programs designated in the individual plan and providing an RT environment that is supportive, offers choices within activities, addresses clients' needs and goals, and uses their strengths, all with a sense of joy and fun. The value of RT is jeopardized if programs are not enjoyable (Mobily & Ostiguy, 2004). The recreational therapist may be the only member of the treatment team who recognizes the value of fun, pleasure, and enjoyment to successful recovery and well-being. Although it may be a controversial concept, clients have the right to enjoy their lives even if they never achieve the goals set in their treatment plan (Sylvester, 2005). It may that "the primary motivation for the client lies in the pleasurable, satisfying experience gained from participation" (Austin, 2001, p. 53). To experience fun without the use of substances is a major contribution of RT to recovery. As the recreational therapist demonstrates genuine enjoyment in recreation, the clients will be observing and learning this behavior.

Implementation requires the recreational therapist to be flexible, adapt quickly to schedule changes, and be creative to adjust programming to participants. Creative contemporary planning considers current recreation program trends. Technology, social networking, the latest fitness crazes, complementary and alternative holistic health practices, and gardening and eating healthy, locally grown foods are trends that the recreational therapist may incorporate into RT to heighten relevance to the client. Programming should also incorporate family members and significant others. When they see their loved one participating in appropriate activities and demonstrating their strengths, relationships and social ties are enhanced. Programming should also occur in the natural environment. If possible, the recreational therapist should implement community-based programs so the clients learn about resources, practice new skills, and evaluate their own comfort levels in a real-world setting.

RT group programs begin with the recreational therapist welcoming the clients, stating the name and purpose of the group, explaining its benefits and rules of behavior, and generally making clients feel comfortable and eager to participate. Instructions should be clear and address multiple learning styles with verbal and written directions, demonstrations, and prompts and cues as needed. Encourage clients to assist and take on as much responsibility as possible, helping with setup and other tasks. During the program, the recreational therapist provides timely, encouraging, and informative feedback to the clients. This helps them identify their strengths and skills and learn new approaches to situations. Throughout the program, the recreational therapist engages the group members, assisting them as needed, and makes connections among members, ideas, and experiences. Quiet members may need encouragement; more active persons may need limits. As the program comes to a close, the recreational therapist lets the clients know it is almost over. At this point, the recreational therapist should use a debriefing technique so clients may evaluate and reflect on their experience in the program and its meaning to them. The recreational therapist may ask questions such as the following: What did you learn from this activity? How did you feel? How can this become part of your future? The group members also may write about their experience. Debriefing reinforces the outcomes the clients gained from the RT experience.

Evaluation

Throughout the client's treatment and participation in RT, the recreational therapist is evaluating the client's progress. Clients should also be encouraged to objectively evaluate their acquisition of new attitudes, knowledge, skills, and behaviors. Ongoing, formative evaluation should lead to needed changes in the client's plan based on response, interest, and progress. The recreational therapist may readminister standardized tests at appropriate intervals to determine progress from the time of assessment. The recreational therapist and other staff make systematic observations. Family, friends, and staff may provide feedback to the recreational therapist based on their interactions with and observations of the client. Clients may provide verbal feedback to the recreational therapist on how they feel, their sense of well-being, and how RT has helped them. With the emphasis on patient satisfaction, clients may be administered a patient satisfaction survey. Private treatment programs are balancing amenities, such as massage therapy and horseback riding, with therapy ("Treatment Programs," 2006) in hopes this increases satisfaction and positive outcomes. At the conclusion of a program, the recreational therapist should conduct summative evaluation to determine program effectiveness in helping clients attain their goals.

Evaluation is not complete without reporting the outcomes. The recreational therapist reports to the team regarding the client's progress toward achieving RT-specific goals as well as overall agency goals. Documentation in patient charts is required by law and regulatory agencies. The recreational therapist should indicate both quantitative outcomes and qualitative benefits the client derived from participation. RT has a unique view of the client, as it is the most typical setting in treatment, the client is often the most relaxed and natural, and opportunities are greatest for displaying strengths and new behaviors. The RT perspective gives a fuller picture of the client to the team.

APPLICATION OF THE RECREATIONAL THERAPY PROCESS: CASE STUDY

The defining characteristic of RT services is the application of the RT process to the design and provision of services. The four steps in the process are assessment, planning, implementation, and evaluation. Each client is unique, but RT professionals must apply the process consistently to all. The following case study illustrates one application of the process, using best practices as described in the chapter.

Bill is a 40-year-old male, admitted for detoxification from alcohol and other drugs after a weeklong binge. His roommate brought him to the emergency room and told staff that Bill has a history of bingeing. Bill remembers smoking marijuana and taking pills and ecstasy. He also made a suicide attempt. He was employed as a coffee shop manager until three weeks ago when his substance use interfered with his work performance; he showed up late several times, missed work one day, and the next time, when he did not call in, he was fired. Highly intelligent, he completed several years of college but has an erratic work history. His roommate suspects that Bill has emotional problems rooted in early family history. The roommate is willing to have him return to the apartment if he can maintain a successful recovery. Bill does not have family nearby.

Assessment

The recreational therapist met Bill following detox, upon admission to the inpatient unit. Bill was neatly dressed and well-groomed but showed signs of fatigue. Although he agreed to speak with the recreational therapist, he did not make eye contact. He appeared anxious; he was fidgety, with his eyes darting around the room. He was talkative at first, but then he would lapse into silence and then abruptly start talking again. He could not focus on the conversation or directly answer the recreational therapist's questions. The recreational therapist determined that Bill was not ready to participate in the assessment process. After 10 minutes, the recreational therapist suggested they meet again in 2 days, and Bill agreed.

The recreational therapist met with Bill as scheduled. Again, he was clean and well dressed and appeared to take care with his personal appearance. He was more subdued, but able to respond coherently, albeit with hesitation. He frequently yawned, although he tried to stifle it. The recreational therapist was able to converse with Bill, after giving a brief introduction about RT. Bill began to mention some of his own interests in reading, writing, cultural activities, and weight lifting. He also said he makes friends easily. He volunteered the information that he smoked marijuana and took pills occasionally, but he had never considered alcohol a problem as it was not his drug of choice. He was just becoming aware that "maybe I shouldn't drink. My father had a drinking problem." His social activities, "partying, staying out late," and casual dating always seemed to involve substance use. What brought him to the hospital was the last binge that he could not control, and it frightened him. When the recreational therapist asked what he would consider to be a goal for himself, he replied to "stop being so crazy, and get back to work."

The recreational therapist rated Bill at the contemplation stage of change because he indicated awareness of his problem and a goal that was oriented toward change. However, she feels he may be close to the action stage and plans to encourage his participation in appropriate RT activities. She used the FACTR-R and assessed his physical skills as intact, his cognitive skills as normal except for decision making, and his social skills as requiring further observation during programs. She also administered the Rosenberg self-esteem scale to develop insight into Bill's underlying feelings about himself that he may be masking with his substance use. She suggested he use a daily stress log to identify when he feels stress over the next few days, what signs of stress he manifests, and what coping strategy he uses. She reviews a list of possible stress symptoms with him.

Bill's strengths include normal physical condition, intelligence, some higher education, good communication skills, sociable, positive leisure interests, supportive roommate, and ability to carry out work responsibilities of a management position. His limitations include a lack of sufficient insight into the causes of his substance use, his socializing includes the use of substances, which seem to be his preferred stress management technique, his roommate is not sure he can trust him if he returns home, and he is currently unemployed.

Planning

The recreational therapist developed an individual, customized plan for Bill, based on concepts from the leisure well-being model, positive psychology, and cognitive-behavioral therapy combined with motivational interviewing and enhancement therapy. She reviewed the plan with Bill to obtain his input and consent to participate. The following goals and RT interventions were set and included in the plan shown in Table 5.8: a schedule of meetings he will attend, a list of his triggers and warning signs, coping strategies to use in different situations, a list of rewarding recreation activities in which to engage, and useful resources with contact information. As part of his WRAP (Wellness Recovery Action Plan), he compiles a crisis plan of what should be done if he needs help, including tasks he may need done and a list of who could do them for him.

Implementation

The recreational therapist reviewed Bill's individual plan with the other treatment staff on the team so they could support his participation as scheduled and discuss his progress in RT with him as it relates to the work they are doing with him. This helps to maintain consistency among the staff on how best to support Bill's recovery process. The team members, including the recreational therapist, suspect that Bill, although admitting his substance use may be a problem, is not fully aware of the extent of it. They agree to help him develop insight into this issue.

During the implementation phase, the recreational therapist reminded Bill of his scheduled activities, encouraged his engagement, provided specific informational and timely feedback, set limits, redirected him, and provided reminders and cues as needed. The recreational therapist assisted Bill in choosing his daily recreation activities. The recreational therapist role modeled playful and joyful participation in recreation and appropriate social behavior; she reinforced his hope for a meaningful and satisfying future. Bill also developed a bond with the trainer in the fitness center, and he was invited to go with Bill on several "walk and talk" sessions. Using flow technology, the recreational therapist and personal trainer increased the challenge of Bill's fitness regimen to meet his skill level. At the end of each program, Bill and the RT, along with the rest of the group, processed the experience discussing what they did, how they felt, what they learned, and how they will use this in the future.

Remember that treatment does not always go smoothly. Clients may lose hope; battle with depression, anxiety, guilt, and self-loathing; lash out in anger; or retreat into themselves. Learning new skills and behaviors takes time and practice. Continual contact by the recreational therapist reflecting and validating feelings and pointing out progress and his strengths may demonstrate to Bill that he is worthy and has the potential and capacity for growth and change.

Evaluation

Evaluation is formative and ongoing during implementation to lead to immediate changes and revisions in the plan and summative at the end of treatment to determine overall effectiveness of the plan and its impact on the client's progress. In Bill's case, formative evaluation led to immediate adjustments in his fitness workout so it was more appropriate to his ability. He rescheduled yoga from the afternoon to the morning, after the second week, as he felt it helped him feel more positive and relaxed during the rest of the day. These changes allowed him to maximize his participation and outcomes.

Table 5.8
Bill's Plan

Goals	Recreational therapy interventions
Increase self-awareness	Journaling about feelings and reactions
Develop positive coping strategies	Daily stress log; attend several relaxation programs such as yoga, mindfulness, qigong; select and use various strategies as appropriate to the setting
Engage in daily recreation activities of choice in a non-using environment	Participate in a variety of RT activities, reflect on their value and incorporate choices into personal repertoire
Develop and maintain friendships with non-using peers	Invite roommate to "family and friends night," attend Sober Dances
Develop support network	Attend 12-step meetings, develop a Wellness Recovery Action Plan
Maintain physical fitness	Use the fitness center 5x per week; attend daily "walk and talk" group

Schedule:
Daily: Keep stress log, do daily journaling, attend relaxation activities, participate in daily "walk and talk," use fitness center, attend 2 recreation activities of choice, attend a 12-step meeting, engage in social recreation in evenings.
Weekly: Attend "Family and Friends Night," Sober Dance, community trip to leisure sites, and Reflections group to review accomplishments and identify areas for continued growth.
Weekend prior to discharge: Camping trip.
In addition to RT programming, Bill will be attending individual and group therapy sessions, and vocational rehabilitation for career development.
Prior to discharge, Bills completes his Wellness Recovery Action Plan (WRAP) (Copeland, 2014) incorporating new persons, places, and things that will support recovery

During the implementation phase, the recreational therapist observes Bill as he participates in programs. She observed that during the first week he seemed less anxious, but was slightly suspicious of others' intentions, asking in discussion groups, "Why are you asking that?" He needed frequent reminders to adhere to his schedule, but he was generally compliant although he complained of fatigue and wanted to nap. He was observed falling asleep in the day room on two occasions. Once he started using the fitness center, he seemed to have more energy and optimism. The personal trainer reported that Bill was open about his problems during the walk and talk sessions. Initially Bill only stayed for 10 minutes in the yoga group, but when it was changed to morning he was able to do 20–30 minutes of postures and was enthusiastic about the mindfulness practice. In leisure education, he expressed that his lifestyle needed changing, but wondered, "What can I do if I don't party?" He attended the weekend Sober Dance; although he did not dance, he said the music was "great." During the third week, his initiative increased and he seemed more comfortable with his schedule, but he would get impatient with himself. He needs to continue working on frustration tolerance and delayed gratification. When this was pointed out to him, he said, "It's true." Always polite, he was helpful to older clients.

During the weekend camping trip at the end of the fourth week of treatment, Bill set up tents, helped with cooking and cleanup, and played new games. "This reminds me of Boy Scout Camp!" he said. He was still wary of some of the trust-challenge activities but was willing to process in the post-session discussions. Upon return to the unit, he seemed more relaxed and laughed more easily.

Bill has made progress toward his goals. Based on his participation in RT, the recreational therapist concludes that Bill has increased his self-awareness as demonstrated by what he has written in and shared in his journal; he reports that he is motivated not to use drugs or drink once he is discharged. He admits it is a bigger problem than he had first thought. He will benefit from ongoing counseling. Bill identified mindfulness, meditation, journaling, and exercise as coping strategies that were beneficial to him, that he may use in a variety of situations, and that were immediately effective for him. He enjoys many recreation activities and was able to make a schedule so he is sure to participate in them and not take the easy way of "getting high" for recreation. To support this, he made a list of friends to contact who are not substance users. He also plans to attend 12-step meetings daily and identified appropriate locations near his home. He needs to look for a job, and in the long-term, he hopes to complete his college degree.

Bill's plans for discharge are essential to successful recovery and serve as a guide for everyday actions that support his goals. The lifestyle of a person with a substance use disorder includes not only substance use, but also language, ethics, behaviors, and relationships that are deeply rooted. Changing this lifestyle includes recognizing the damage caused by substance use and the necessity of changing these habits and patterns of behavior. Even after seemingly successful treatment, a person may relapse many times before sustaining long-term recovery. To maintain change, an individual needs to commit to using daily strategies, believe he is capable of being a better person, and have solid support systems.

Bill represents only one type of client. A person with more limited education, few resources, and a spotty work history may need longer treatment, vocational and life skills training, and social services. They also may have chronic health conditions such as asthma, diabetes, high blood pressure, or tuberculosis and need to learn how to care for these and to comply with medication schedules. Clients with a dual diagnosis of mental illness and substance use disorder may have such a longstanding problem that they have lost valuable personal and community connections. What came first may be unclear: the mental illness that the client attempted to treat with the substance or the substance use that led to depression and/or psychosis. They may have alienated family and friends with behavior such as lying and stealing. Low self-esteem leads them to self-sabotaging, self-defeating behaviors that they then use as proof of their low opinion of themselves. This is a vicious cycle. They are often hopeless. The recreational therapist should provide support for the client's strength of wanting help by being in treatment. Even talking with the recreational therapist is a positive step for which the client should receive positive feedback. Encouragement for any small effort is important. Goals initially should be short term, perhaps in the area of stress management and coping strategies that provide even momentary relief. The recreational therapist should never give up on a client!

TRENDS AND ISSUES

Despite much attention to the problem of substance use and addiction, and the tremendous burden it imposes on society in personal, social, and economic costs, the problem still continues. Although the substances that are used have changed over the years based on price of the drug, means of use, and availability, millions of users suffer physical and emotional effects, as do their families and friends. The need for adequate and sufficient treatment is still unavailable to most users. Treatment programs are under pressure to cut costs and maintain quality services, therefore expanding their treatment slots may be difficult. One solution is computerized interventions that provide quality, low-cost care (Whitten, 2009). Treatment professionals are able to enroll in Web-based training in this area. Technology facilitates one-to-one counseling via computer and Skype as well as provide videos for clients to watch on how to handle triggers and risky situations. Resources then may be reserved for those who respond best to face-to-face treatment or who are unable or unwilling to use computer technology.

Many new treatment approaches have emerged in the last few decades. Emphasis on cognitive-behavioral therapy, positive psychology, motivational interviewing and enhancement therapy, and holistic approaches such as massage, yoga, and mindfulness, are being used more and more and offer greater options for treatment. Twelve-step programs tailored to individual needs, beyond Alcoholics Anonymous and Narcotics Anonymous, are available.

Certain groups are being identified for a rising number of risky users who may require unique approaches to treatment: returning war veterans who may use painkillers to treat painful war injuries or use substances to escape their traumatic memories; aging baby boomers who are more physically active and more comfortable with substance use than previous generations and may become increasingly dependent on painkillers, antianxiety medications, and marijuana; and adolescents whose youth has been marked by prescription drugs use for conditions such as attention deficit hyperactivity disorder. Misuse of painkillers has led to 17,000 deaths from overdose each year, more than deaths from heroin and cocaine combined. A drug overdose treatment device known as Evzio was approved by the U.S. Food and

Drug Administration in 2014 (Tavernise, 2014). This device delivers a single dose of naloxone, which reverses the effects of an overdose and saves lives.

Women have treatment needs and issues that differ from men's. Many women users have responsibility for children or have lost custody of children. The effects on both mother and child point to the need for a concerted, holistic approach that improves the lives of the family both materially and emotionally. Children who are raised in a home where substance use is present are at great risk. A woman may have difficulty leaving a partner who is also using substances and who may sabotage her efforts at recovery. Both men and women may have been abused physically, sexually, or emotionally or have been victims of child abuse, which requires sensitive therapeutic approaches. Persons with disabilities, persons who are homeless, and persons diagnosed with HIV/AIDS have unique concerns that should be addressed in treatment. The growing cultural diversity of society may impact services. Recreational therapists need to be aware of cultural traditions, values, and patterns that influence substance use, attitudes toward treatment, and willingness to access services.

The stigma of being a substance user or being in recovery continues to be of concern to many persons with this disorder. Family, friends, and society may not understand the powerful grip of addiction as a disease and have a negative attitude toward the individual, which may erode a person's confidence and positive attitude toward change. The recreational therapist is encouraged to offer family education and family recreation, through which the successes and strengths of their family member is revealed and recognized.

Focus on a healthy lifestyle has expanded the programming of RT. Fitness, nutrition, alternative practices, stress management techniques, and satisfying leisure experiences are essential components of an RT program. Leisure education may incorporate treatment, recovery, and successful discharge planning, as well as prevention when offered in schools, community recreation centers, and senior centers. Physicians and other health care providers are prescribing time in the park to their patients, as they recognize the benefits associated with nature. One predictor of relapse is leisure activities that are not perceived as satisfying. With the growing recognition of the power and value of play, joy, and fun in recovery, RT has vast opportunities to contribute to the treatment and well-being of this population; if RT does not seize this opportunity now, other professions will certainly take over this essential role. RT research is needed to yield evidence-based practice and ensure that RT remains central to quality treatment and services.

An ethical issue recreational therapists may face in their work in substance use disorders treatment is the use of recreation activities as rewards and punishment. Using reinforcers is a common practice in treatment, especially with youth. Clients may earn points to engage in special events, go on an outing, or participate in certain recreation programs. "Bad" behavior may result in loss of points, which leads to restriction from certain activities. This poses an ethical conflict for RT, as a fundamental belief is in the right of all to recreation. Recreation is the venue for practicing new behaviors and learning to use free time in healthy ways, when much substance use occurs. Using access to recreation as a reward or punishment does not reinforce its essential role in successful recovery. The RT may wish to discuss alternative consequences; at all times, clients should have access to alternative activities; options should be provided even to those who do not earn sufficient points.

Last, recreational therapists must care for their own mental health and well-being. This is good for both the recreational therapist and the patients. One study found that when staff had more influence in their work setting, they tolerated stress better and had less burnout than those who felt they had low influence; when staff members reported lower levels of stress, patients reported more active participation in treatment (Landrum, Knight, & Flynn, 2012). RTs may find their work with substance use disorder clients to be emotionally difficult and frustrating at times. Addressing work stress through clinical supervision and holistic health practices may strengthen the staff's ability to continue being effective and satisfied with their work.

SUMMARY

Substance use disorders, or addictions, continue to be a social issue with vast impacts in the United States and Canada, not only for the user but also for families and society. Not enough treatment programs exist to serve all persons who wish to overcome their disorder. Many new treatment approaches have been developed and may be tailored to inpatient and outpatient settings as well as to the diverse needs of clients based on disorder, individual characteristics, and resource availability. Several RT conceptual models and standardized assessment tools are appropriate for substance use disorders treatment. RT programs across all behavioral domains are available to make a meaningful impact on clients with substance use disorders. Evidence exists to support the use of many recreational activities. In the future, RT should continue to build a body of evidence-based practice to support its contribution to recovery services. Current trends indicate continued need for creative and innovative service approaches to substance use disorders.

As the centrality of leisure skills and play, joy, and fun to successful recovery and quality of life are recognized, RT should be at the forefront of treatment for substance use disorders. The purpose, role, and programming of RT may best be fulfilled by knowledgeable, professional RT practitioners. Justifying RT services continues to be a challenge, but with the growing evidence, RT professionals may advocate so that all who may benefit from their services shall receive them.

READING COMPREHENSION QUESTIONS

1. What are the most common substances misused in the United States? How extensive is this use?
2. Which groups are particularly vulnerable to risky use?
3. Define addiction, substance use disorder, tolerance, dependence, withdrawal, and risky use.
4. Explain the role of RT in early identification and prevention of substance use disorder.
5. Identify the four major classes of drugs, their effects, and the potential for addiction of each.
6. Describe the physical, emotional, social, and cognitive symptoms and effects of substance use disorder.
7. Describe current approaches to treatment and their efficacy.

8. Give examples of research studies that demonstrate evidence of the efficacy of recreation.

9. Explain the role of RT in substance use disorder treatments and recovery.

10. Identify two RT conceptual models that may be applied in treatment settings.

11. What is the relationship between RT and positive psychology? Flow?

12. What areas would RT assess that are unique to this population?

13. How can a recreational therapist use the stages of change (Prochaska and DiClemente, 1982) in the assessment process?

14. State appropriate RT goals for substance use treatment and specify RT programs to meet each goal.

15. Give guidelines for the recreational therapist to follow during the implementation phase of the RT process.

16. Describe the application of the RT process to a sample client.

17. Explain current issues and future trends in substance use disorders treatment.

REFERENCES

American Psychiatric Association. (2014). DSM-5 development. Retrieved from http://www.dsm5.org/

Austin, D. (2001). The therapeutic recreation process. In D. Austin & M. Crawford (Eds.), *Therapeutic recreation: An introduction* (3rd ed., pp. 45–56). Needham Heights, MA: Allyn & Bacon.

Austin, D. (2013). *Therapeutic recreation processes and techniques: Evidence-based recreational therapy* (7th ed.). Champaign, IL: Sagamore.

Autry, C. (2001). Adventure therapy with girls at-risk: Responses to outdoor experiential activities. *Therapeutic Recreation Journal, 35*(4), 289–306.

Bellack, A., Bennett, M., Gearon, J., Brown, C., & Yang, Y. (2006). A randomized clinical trial of a new behavioral treatment for drug abuse in people with severe and persistent mental illness. *Archives of General Psychiatry, 63*(4), 426–432.

burlingame, j., & Blaschko, T. (2010). *Assessment tools for recreational therapy and related fields* (4th ed.). Enumclaw, WA: Idyll Arbor.

Butler, S. (2005, November 3). Rookie marathoners trade addictions. *The New York Times*. Retrieved from http://www.nytimes.com/

Carruthers, C., & Hood, C. (2002). Coping skills for individuals with alcoholism. *Therapeutic Recreation Journal, 36*(2), 154–171.

Carruthers, C., & Hood, C. (2004). The power of the positive: Leisure and well-being. *Therapeutic Recreation Journal, 38*(2), 224–245.

Carruthers, C., & Hood, C. (2007). Building a life of meaning through therapeutic recreation: The Leisure and Well-Being Model, part 1. *Therapeutic Recreation Journal, 41*(4), 276–297.

Carruthers, C., & Hood, C. (2013). Mindfulness-based therapeutic recreation intervention. *Annual in Therapeutic Recreation, 21*, 73–79.

CASAColumbia. (2014). Ending addiction changes everything. Retrieved from http://www.casacolumbia.org/

Canadian Centre on Substance Abuse. (2013). *Canadian Centre on Substance Abuse annual report*. Retrieved from http://www.ccsa.ca/Resource%20Library/2012-2013-ccsa-annual-report-en.pdf

Centers for Disease Control and Prevention. (2014). Persons who use drugs (PWUD). Retrieved March 12, 2014, from http://www.cdc.gov/pwud/

Chen, K., Comerford, A., Shinnick, P., & Ziedonis, D. (2010). Introducing qigong meditation into residential addiction treatment: A pilot study where gender makes a difference. *Journal of Alternative and Complementary Medicine, 16*(8), 875–882.

Cogswell, J., & Negley, S. (2011). The effect of autonomy-supportive therapeutic recreation programming on integrated motivation for treatment among persons who abuse substances. *Therapeutic Recreation Journal, 45*(1), 47–61.

Copeland, M. (2014). WRAP and recovery books. Retrieved from http://mentalhealthrecovery.com/

Coyle, C., Kinney, W., & Riley, B. (Eds.). (1991). *Benefits of therapeutic recreation: A consensus view.* Ravensdale, WA: Idyll Arbor.

Csikszentmihalyi, M. (1990). *Flow: The psychology of optimal experience.* New York, NY: HarperCollins.

Donatelle, R. (2004). *Health: The basics* (6th ed.). San Francisco, CA: Benjamin Cummings.

Drench, M., Noonan, A., Sharby, N., & Ventura, S. (2012). *Psychosocial aspects of health care* (3rd ed.). Boston, MA: Pearson Education.

Gillespie, C. (2003). A case report illustrating the use of creative writing as a therapeutic recreation intervention in a dual-diagnosed residential treatment center. *Therapeutic Recreation Journal, 37*(4), 339–348.

Grawe, R., Hagen, R., Espeland, B., & Mueser, K. (2007). The better life program: Effects of group skills training for persons with severe mental illness and substance use disorders. *Journal of Mental Health, 16*(5), 625–634.

Gross, J. (2008, March 9). New generation gap emerges as older addicts seek help. *The New York Times,* pp. A1, A24.

Hartney, E. (2013). DSM 5 criteria for substance use disorders: The symptoms used for the diagnosis of substance use disorders. Retrieved from the About.com website: http://addictions.about.com/od/aboutaddiction/a/Dsm-5-Criteria-For-Substance-Use-Disorders.htm

Hood, C. (2003). Women in recovery from alcoholism: The place of leisure. *Leisure Sciences, 25*(1), 51–80.

Hood, C., & Krinsky, A. (1997). The use of a Delphi procedure to identify priority client treatment needs for therapeutic recreation intervention in alcoholism treatment. *Annual in Therapeutic Recreation, 7,* 74–82.

Johnston, L. (2005). Lessons for the long run. *amNewYork, 3*(214).

Kelly, J. R. (1996). *Leisure* (3rd ed.). Boston, MA: Allyn & Bacon.

Kunstler, R. (2004). Therapeutic recreation's contribution to living with chronic, stigmatized illness: Health promotion for HIV, HCV and substance abuse. In M. Devine (Ed.), *Trends in therapeutic recreation: Ideas, concepts, applications* (pp. 111–125). Ashburn, VA: National Recreation and Park Association.

Kunstler, R., & Stavola Daly, F. (2010). *Therapeutic recreation programming and leadership.* Champaign, IL: Human Kinetics.

Landrum, B., Knight, D., & Flynn, P. (2012). The impact of organizational stress and burnout on client engagement. *Journal of Substance Abuse Treatment, 42*(2), 222–230.

Lawless, M., Rowe, M., & Miller, R. (2009). New visions of me: Finding joy in recovery with women who are homeless. *Journal of Dual Diagnosis, 5*(3–4), 305–322.

Li, M., Chen, K., & Mo, Z. (2002). Use of qigong therapy in the detoxification of heroin addicts. *Alternative Therapies in Health and Medicine, 8*(1), 50–54, 56–59.

MacLean, S., Cameron, J., Harney, A., & Lee, N. (2012). Psychosocial therapeutic interventions for volatile substance use: A systematic review. *Addiction Review, 107*(2), 278–288.

Malkin, M., Coyle, C., & Carruthers, C. (1998). Efficacy research in recreational therapy. In F. Brasile, T. Skalko, & j. burlingame (Eds.), *Perspectives in recreational therapy: Issues of a dynamic profession.* Ravensdale, WA: Idyll Arbor.

Malkin, M., Voss, M., Teaff, J., & Benshoff, J. (1993–1994). Activity and recreational therapy services in substance abuse treatment programs. *Annual in Therapeutic Recreation,* 4, 40–50.

McCormick, B., & Dattilo, J. (1995). "Sobriety's kind of like freedom": Integrating ideals of leisure into the ideology of Alcoholics Anonymous. *Therapeutic Recreation Journal, 29*(1), 18–29.

Mobily, K., & Ostiguy, L. (2004). *Introduction to therapeutic recreation: US and Canadian perspectives.* State College, PA: Venture.

Nation, J., Benshoff, J., & Malkin, M. (1996). TR programs for adolescents in substance abuse treatment. *Journal of Rehabilitation, 62*(4), 10–17.

National Institute on Alcohol Abuse and Alcoholism. (2014). Alcohol and health. Retrieved from http://www.niaaa.nih.gov/alcohol-health

National Institute on Drug Abuse. (2012). *Principles of drug addiction treatment: A research-based guide* (3rd ed.). Retrieved from http://www.drugabuse.gov/publications/principles-drug-addiction-treatment

National Institute on Drug Abuse. (2013). *DrugFacts: Substance abuse in the military.* Retrieved from from http://www.drugfacts.gov/publications/drugfacts/substance-abuse-in-military

Pearson, F., Prendergast, M., Podus, D., Vazan, P., Greenwell, L., & Hamilton, Z. (2012). Meta-analyses of seven of NIDA's principles of drug addiction treatment. *Journal of Substance Abuse Treatment, 43*(1), 1–11.

Peele, S. (1985). *The meaning of addiction: Compulsive experience and its interpretation.* Lexington, MA: Heath.

Peele, S. (2014). Addiction treatment. Retrieved from http://www.stantonpeele.net/

Polkinghorne, D. (2004). *Practice and the human sciences: The case for a judgment-based practice of care.* Albany: State University of New York Press.

Prochaska, J., & DiClemente, C. (1982). Transtheoretical therapy: Toward a more integrative model of change. *Psychotherapy Theory, Research and Practice, 19,* 276–278.

Sherman, C. (2010). Multidimensional family therapy for adolescent drug abuse offers broad, lasting benefits: An approach that integrates individual, family, and community interventions outperformed other treatments. *NIDA Notes, 23*(3), 13–15.

Solomon, S. (2014, March 8). The heroin epidemic, in Vermont and beyond [Letter to the editor]. *The New York Times,* p. A18.

Spas, J., Ramsey, S., Paiva, A., & Stein, L. (2012). All might have won, but not all have the prize: Optimal treatment for substance abuse among adolescents with conduct problems. *Journal of Substance Abuse Treatment, 43*(1), 1–11.

Stumbo, N., & Pegg, S. (2010). Outcomes and evidence-based practice: Moving forward. *Annual in Therapeutic Recreation, 18,* 12–23.

Substance Abuse and Mental Health Services Administration. (2014). Prevention of substance abuse and mental illness. Retrieved from http://www.samhsa.gov/

Sylvester, C. (2005). Personal autonomy and therapeutic recreation. In C. Sylvester (Ed.), *Philosophy of therapeutic recreation: Ideas and issues* (Vol. 3, pp. 1–31). Ashburn, VA: National Therapeutic Recreation Society.

Tavernise, S. (2014, April 4). Hand-held treatment for overdoses is approved. *The New York Times,* pp. A13, A18.

Treatment programs balance amenities with focus on therapy. (2006). *Alcoholism and Drug Abuse Weekly, 18*(34), 1–3.

Tyson, M. (2014, January 4). Fighting to kick the habit. *The New York Times,* p. A19.

United Nations Office on Drugs and Crime. (2011). *The United States has 5% of the world's population & consumes 75% of the world's prescription drugs.* Retrieved from http://www.unodc.org/documents/data-and analysis/WDR2011/World_Drug_Report_2011_ebook.pdf

Whitten, L. (2009). Computer-based interventions promote drug abstinence: Interactive multimedia therapies may reduce costs and extend access to treatment. *NIDA Notes, 22*(5), 1.

Wilhite, B., Keller, J., & Caldwell, L. (1999). Optimizing life-long health and well-being: A health enhancing model of therapeutic recreation. *Therapeutic Recreation Journal, 33*(2), 98–108.

Winters, K. C., Leitten, W., Wagner, E., Tevyaw, T. O. (2007). Use of brief interventions for drug abusing teenagers within a middle and high school setting. *Journal of School Health, 77,* 196–206.

Witt, P., & Ellis, G. (1989). *The leisure diagnostic battery: Users manual and sample forms.* State College, PA: Venture.

Wupperman, P., Marlatt, G., Cunningham, A., Bowen, S., Berking, M., Mulvihill-Rivera, N., & Easton, C. (2012). Mindfulness and modification therapy for behavioral dysregulation: Results from a pilot study targeting alcohol use and aggression in women. *Journal of Clinical Psychology, 68,* 50–66.

6

AUTISM

OBJECTIVES

- Identify, define, and describe autism spectrum disorder (ASD) as indicated in the *DSM-5*.
- Identify characteristic strengths that may be built upon to achieve outcome goals.
- Identify common standardized assessment tools that recreational therapists may use when working with individuals with ASD.
- Outline the service delivery process for providing recreational therapy services to individuals with ASD.
- Achieve an understanding of how a CTRS® may serve the needs of individuals with ASD and their families.

DEFINITION AND CLASSIFICATION OF AUTISM SPECTRUM DISORDER

Autism (ASD) is a complex neurobiological condition affecting the ways an individual processes and responds to information and sensory stimuli, which may create a "restricted repertoire of activities and interests" as well as impairments in social and communication skills (Janzen, 2003, p. 5). The fifth edition of the *Diagnostic and Statistical Manual of Mental Disorders* (*DSM-5*; American Psychiatric Association, 2013) classifies autism as follows:

Autism Spectrum Disorder, Diagnostic Criteria 299.00 (F84.0)…is characterized by persistent deficits in social communication and social interaction across multiple contexts, including deficits in social reciprocity, nonverbal communicative behaviors used for social interaction, and skills in developing, maintaining and understanding social relationships. In addition to the social communication deficits, the diagnosis of autism spectrum disorder requires the presence of restricted, repetitive patterns of behavior, interests, or activities.

Within the diagnosis of autism spectrum disorder, individual clinical characteristics are noted through the use of specifiers (with or without accompanying intellectual impairment; with or without accompanying structural language impairment; associated with a known medial/genetic or environmental/acquired condition; associated with another neurodevelopmental, mental, or behavioral disorder), as well as specifiers that describe the autistic symptoms (age at first concern; with or without loss of established skills; severity). (pp. 31–32)

ASD appears in early infancy to early adulthood, and prevalence rates do not change based on location, race, or socioeconomic status (SES); although males experience higher prevalence rates than do females (Autism Society, n.d.; Embregts & Van Nieuwenhuijzen, 2009; Indiana Resource Center for Autism [IRCA], 2014; Matson & Ollendick, 1988; Merrell & Gimpel, 1998; Rao, Beidel, & Murray, 2008). ASD is classified as an "Intellectual and Developmental Disability" by the American Association of Intellectual and Developmental Disabilities (AAIDD), the *DSM-5*, and the International Classification of Function, Disability, and Health (ICF). An intellectual disability is "a disability characterized by significant limitations in both intellectual functioning and in adaptive behavior, which covers many everyday social and practical skills. This disability originates before the age of 18" (AAIDD, 2013). These conditions are classified further by "the types of supports individuals need to function on a day-to-day basis": intermittent, limited, extensive, and pervasive (opposed to by the severity of the person's disability; Falvo, 2009, p. 198). The functional ability for individuals with an intellectual and/or developmental disability is identified as mild, moderate, severe, or profound.

ASD is diagnosed in early childhood, if not, in early adulthood. No single etiology is known; however, it is currently understood as a complex compilation of nature (genetics) and nurture (environment), affecting both the central nervous system and digestive system (Batshaw, Pellegrino, & Roizen, 2007; IRCA, 2014; Rapin, 1997). ASD is a lifelong, pervasive condition, with a current prognosis of (1) not having a cure; (2) requiring lifelong management (treatment/services); and (3) not being progressive in nature (does not worsen over time; Batshaw et al., 2007; Hyman & Towbin, 2007). Due to this knowledge, targets for treatment throughout the life span would focus on the remediation of current skills and functioning as well as the enhancement and/or rehabilitation of skills and functioning.

Since psychiatrist Leo Kanner's 1943 publication first identifying and describing this condition (initially identified as "early infantile autism"), autism has had many classifications. Currently, in 2014, autism continues to be defined by the characteristics mentioned above and is simply called autism spectrum disorder (ASD) in the *DSM-5*. Previous versions of the *DSM-5* included multiple diagnoses under the term *ASD*, which at that time described a group of similar conditions. These diagnoses included other health impairment (OHI), pervasive developmental disorder/pervasive developmental disorder-not otherwise specified (PDD/PDD-NOS), childhood disintegrative disorder (CDD), autism spectrum (ASD) with specification of high or low functioning (HFA or LFA), Rhett's syndrome (RS), and Asperger's syndrome (AS). Changes to how ASD was classified were made after years of consultation and input from stakeholders; however, many are still not in agreement about whether all conditions are manifestations of the same condition or whether very separate conditions are only partially related (Matson, 2008; Miller & Ozonoff, 1997; Odom, Collet-Klingenberg, Rogers, & Hatton, 2010; Reichow & Volkmar, 2010; Sansoti, Powell-Smith, & Cowan, 2010; Smith & Matson, 2010). In either case, the defining characteristics of the condition have remained constant, and no single cause of the condition has been identified yet. Nevertheless, the identification of the defining characteristics of ASD, coupled with current research, information within the *DSM-5* and the International

Classification of Function, Disability, and Health (ICF), and interdisciplinary collaboration within multifactored assessment practices, still enables service providers with a consistent and structured starting point for service planning processes and related decisions (American Psychiatric Association, 2013; Merrell & Gimpel, 1998).

STRENGTHS AND CHALLENGES

Because recreational therapy (RT) is a service that builds on an individual's strengths, a glimpse into these strengths is warranted; however, note that these do not reflect every individual who has ASD, and you must respect and learn the uniqueness of every individual to best serve them.

Strengths of individuals with ASD include the following: exceptional visual learners, early development of reading skills, strong memory skills (e.g., words, numbers, dates, sequences, skills), strong literal comprehension skills, fast fact-finding, exceptional spelling skills, good supervisory skills, perfectionism, works well alone and with adults, functions well under stress, sense of humor, perspective, passionate, strong, good endurance and stamina, consistency in skill performance, enjoyment of routine(s), attention to detail, loyal, hardworking, and creative (Attwood, 2007; Bauminger et al., 2008; Cosden, Koegel, Koegel, Greenwell, & Klein, 2006; Gray & Van Puymbroeck, 2012; Students on the Spectrum Club, 2012).

Common challenges individuals with ASD face include staying focused due to level of interest, being over- or underwhelmed from sensory input, waiting patiently due to impulsivity, trying new activities due to a strict adherence to routines or fear, feeling overwhelmed due to hypersensitivity to sensory input (auditory, tactile, taste, olfactory, visual, pain), maintaining good sleep behavior, maintaining good nutrition, excessive fear and/or anxiety, communications (both verbal and nonverbal), social interactions and reading social cues, leisure and recreation participation or pursuits, general comprehension skills, low to moderate processing times, organizational skills, direct application of known skill sets (language, social, stress management, etc.), transitions, large group work, long-term planning, and comorbidities (Bilken, 2005; Bellini & Hopf, 2007; Gray & Van Puymbroeck, 2012; Students on the Spectrum Club, 2012). Crawford, Gray, and Woolhiser (2012) noted the following as well:

> ...many [youth] with ASD develop behavioral excesses, some of which are anxiety-based, rendering them unpredictable social participants or play partners. Facial expressions are often mismatched with their spoken language, vocal quality may be inappropriate to the social space, or they may manifest postures or hand gestures that distract or at times even obscure communication (Autism Society of America, 2008). Most people have experienced anxiety driven motor overflow, in fact it is common to many social situations (e.g., nervous laughter on a first date for instance, or hair twirling during an exam, etc.); however, these experiences are exceptions to their normal social presentation of self. For [youth] with ASD, this motor overflow can be a constant companion, which complicates the social landscape, making acquaintanceship and friendship development difficult. (p. 18)

Overall, these and other challenges may create limitations for individuals with ASD in the areas of "communication, self-care, social situations, school or work activities, and independent living" (Porter & burlingame, 2010, p. 88).

PURPOSE OF RECREATIONAL THERAPY

The definition and classification of ASD and the common characteristic strengths and challenges attributed with having ASD clearly show that services are needed to support these individuals in becoming fully actualized members of the global community throughout their lifetimes. In addition to identifying this basic need for services, within only a 4-year period, the Centers for Disease Control and Prevention–reported statistic has gone from 1 in 110 (2009) to 1 in 50 (2013) individuals diagnosed with ASD annually (Autism Society, n.d.; IRCA, 2014). Due to this increase in prevalence rates, the need for services and access to services also has increased. This has promoted much research and development in the areas of diagnostics, programming, legislation, and beyond (American Psychiatric Association, 2013; Hall, 2013; Hamilton, 2009; Hatton & Henry, 2008; O'Brien, 2011; Ozonoff, Goodlin-Jones, & Solomon, 2005; Paul, 2010). Included in the array of service providers for individuals with ASD are recreational therapists.

Based on the definition of RT provided by the American Therapeutic Recreation Association (ATRA, 2014), the role of RT, in general, is to

> be a treatment service designed to restore, remediate and rehabilitate a person's level of functioning and independence in life activities, to promote health and wellness, as well as reduce or eliminate the activity limitations and restrictions to participation in life situations.

In working with individuals with ASD, the recreational therapist "assists in the development, maintenance and expression of a healthy lifestyle, as well as addresses issues that threaten an individual's health or functioning" (Indiana University, n.d.). In addition to this, recreational therapists want individuals with ASD to be confident in who they are and what they can do and to be able to become self-actualized. Rooted in positive psychology, Abraham Maslow's notion of self-actualization is defined as the "basic human drive toward growth, completeness, and fulfillment" (Austin, 2001, p. 56). This may be achieved through using education, purposeful recreation, and/ or leisure "in the pursuit of developing one's health and happiness" (Austin, 2001; Indiana University, n.d.; Stumbo, 2003).

Since ASD is a lifelong, pervasive condition, and in itself is not progressive, targets or outcomes for treatment, in general, would focus on the remediation of current skills and functioning as well as the enhancement and/or rehabilitation of skills and functioning over an individual's lifetime. Specific outcomes sought for individuals with ASD include reducing impairment in body structures and functions by increasing physical and cognitive functioning; reducing activity limitations and participation restrictions by increasing physical, cognitive, social, psychosocial, and environmental functioning; and identifying, overcoming, and/or removing environmental barriers to participation (American Psychiatric Association, 2013; Crawford et al., 2012; Falvo, 2009). Recreational therapists often achieve these outcomes through facilitation techniques or interventions. Common techniques include leisure education (leisure counseling); purposeful recreation, fitness, and games; support in community recreation; social skills training; biofeedback; progressive relaxation training; aquatic therapy; assertiveness training; animal-assisted therapy; creative arts (dance, music, art); technology; and sensory training (Austin, 2013; Gray, Kavanaugh, & Hunter, in press).

In addition, due to ASD being identified in early childhood and affecting social functioning, services should be addressed in the areas of home, school, and community to help support, reinforce, and sustain behavioral changes over time. These domains also constitute the common service settings in which RT occurs with individuals with ASD: home (i.e., residential), school (K–12 in public/private/charter/alternative, workshop/transition program), and community (camps, parks and recreation organizations, arts programs, etc.); however, Crawford et al. (2012) noted the following concerning services within the school setting:

> The Individuals with Disability Education Act (IDEA) specifically identifies recreation as a related educational service for special needs children and youth. Similar to other related services and/or therapies (e.g. physical therapy, occupational therapy, speech, etc.), if a parent, care-provider, or school staff member believes a student would benefit from said service(s) and it is approved by the multi-interdisciplinary team, services must be provided and formally written into the Individualized Education Plan (IEP). Despite federal legislative support, recreation has yet to be established as an educational service in most public schools. In fact, according to statistics from the National Council for Therapeutic Recreation Certification (NCTRC), less than 2% of all therapeutic recreation specialists work in the public school setting (NCTRC, 2005). Functional barriers to this have included a bias on the part of school personnel regarding the need for such services, parents who have incomplete information regarding the IEP process, and a lack of financial resources to hire certified therapeutic recreation specialists (CTRS's) to deliver leisure education and social skills curriculum (Martin, 2005). (p. 19–20)

CURRENT BEST PRACTICES AND PROCEDURES

The theoretical approaches that recreational therapists use when working with individuals with ASD range from humanistic to multimodal, depending on factors such as where the recreational therapist works, focus of treatment, and needs of the individual. Nevertheless, using a humanistic, biopsychosocial model of care will provide a more holistic assessment and approach when working with individuals with ASD and their families (Austin, 2013; Hall, 2013; Merrell & Gimpel, 1998; O'Brien, 2011; Rao et al., 2008). The approach or approaches used are typically contingent upon the practitioner, the needs of the individual, and the setting in which the services are being performed. Despite the theoretical approach used, recreational therapists use the RT process, or APIE process, as the therapeutic approach and process (see Figure 6.1). The RT process is a cyclical, systematic process of assessment, planning, implementation, and evaluation of service delivery (Austin, 2013; Shank & Coyle, 2002).

Assessment

The first step of this systematic process, assessment, is a phase of gathering information from and about the client. Several modes and methods of collecting information are used to provide the most comprehensive picture of the client and his health status and needs. This may be accomplished by combining interviewing techniques with standardized assessment tools. Standardized assessments are vital due to their reliability and validity for measurement. Recreational therapists want to en-sure the tools used during assessment and evaluation measure what they intended to measure (validity) and will consistently measure what they intended to measure (reliability). Although many practitioners use assessments created specifically for their agency/population, if these assessments have not been tested for reliability and validity, best practices would indicate the use of a standardized assessment along with the agency-based or -created assessment to ensure the proper documen-tation and later evaluation of individual growth, as well as service delivery (Merrell & Gimpel, 1998; Porter & burlingame, 2010; Rao et al., 2008; Ratto, Turner-Brown, Rupp, Mesibov, & Penn, 2010; Volker, 2008).

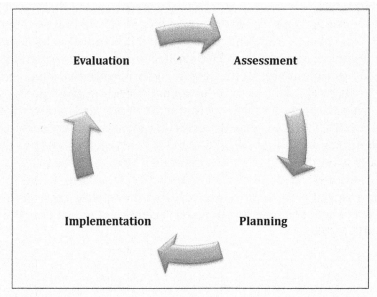

Figure 6.1. The recreational therapy process.

Training and/or expertise in selecting, administrating, scoring, analyzing, and interpreting the assessment and assessment data are also important, as each step in assessment provides a clearer picture of why, if at all, intervention needs to occur and for what purpose. Common standardized assessments used in recreational ther-apy with individuals with ASD include the Childhood Autism Rating Scale (CARS), Adolescent and Adult Psycho Educational Profile (AAPEP), Social Communication Questionnaire (SCQ), Social Reciprocity Scale, Gilliam Autism Rating Scale (GARS), General Recreation Screening Tool (GRST), Functional Assessment of Characteristics for Therapeutic Recreation-Revised (FACTR-R), Leisure Diagnostic Battery (LBD), Comprehensive Evaluation in Recreation Therapy (CERT), Comprehensive Evalu-ation in Recreation Therapy-Psych/Behavioral-Revised (CERT-Psych), Functional Interest Measure (FIM), Test of Gross Motor Development-Second Ed. (TGMD-2), and the School Social Behavioral Scale (SSBS). Selecting assessments specifically de-signed for individuals with ASD is imperative, and many experts consider it a "best practice" (Hall, 2013; Rao et al., 2008).

Assessment and evaluation go hand in hand, in that assessment is a means to identify areas that will be evaluated later for improvement, regress, or no change; therefore, ensuring the validity and reliability of the measure is imperative, especially since the need for services is lifelong, and longitudinal assessment and evaluation should be co-occurring with services in which "change" is the focus. As Rao et al. (2008) stated, "without longitudinal assessment the stability of any positive treatment outcome remains unknown" (p. 359).

Next, after the assessment has been conducted and much information about the individual has been collected, the scoring and/or analysis of all assessment data will ensue. Deeply embedded within the quantitative and qualitative analysis of the information gathered is clinical judgment, or clinical reasoning (Austin & McCormick, 2013; Huckabay, 2009; Levett-Jones et al., 2009; Mattingly, 1991; Shank & Coyle, 2002). This process is similar to both the RT process in that it is reflexive, is dynamic, and uses experience as well as expertise to determine the individual's needs as indicated by the assessment data.

Planning

The next phase in the RT process, or APIE process, is planning. Planning consists of continuing to use clinical judgment in making sense of the information gathered during assessment, as well as creating prioritized lists of needs, writing goals, and objectives and researching therapeutic approaches that will be used to help the individuals meet their needs as indicated by the assessment data. A prioritized list of needs for the individual will help the recreational therapist to identify short- and long-term goals, as well as where referrals may need to be made. After goals or outcomes have been identified, research and planning for intervention occurs. Amid researching therapeutic approaches, recreational therapists want to identify those that are evidence based or have a supporting body of evidence for their use (Bury, 1998; Bury & Mead, 1998; Lee & McCormick, 2002). Once these methods of intervention have been identified, the written plan is created, which is sometimes referred to as the individualized treatment plan (ITP; Austin, 2001), the individualized intervention plan (IIP), or in educational settings, the individualized education plan (IEP; Austin, 2013).

Implementation

After the ITP has been created, discussed, and agreed upon with the client, the implementation phase of the RT process begins. This phase is often called the "action phase," due to clients engaging in the intervention to achieve their goals. Adaptations or modifications are often made within this process, as it is carried out with the individual.

Evaluation

Dynamically interwoven within the implementation phase is evaluation, the next phase in the RT process. Evaluation continuously occurs to identify client and program changes. At the end of every evaluation, reassessment should occur, and the cycle continues until clients have achieved their treatment goals or outcomes.

Examples of Current Best Practices and Evidence-Based Practices

Best and evidence-based practices exist for all practitioners working with individuals with ASD. Best practices include the use of educational/clinical treatment/support teams for multidisciplinary assessment and support, early intervention and lifelong services/programming, selection and use of standardized assessments specifically created for individuals with ASD, family services, use of a multimodal (eclectic) or biopsychosocial approach to care, behavioral therapy—applied behavioral analysis (ABA), social skills training (SST), leisure education (leisure counseling), communications—speech-language pathology (SLPT), education and educational planning (use of IEP, MDT, 504 plans), physical therapy (PT), occupational therapy (OT), music therapy, art therapy, equine therapy, and RT. Evidence-based practices include peer-mediated instruction/intervention (PMII), picture exchange communications systems (PECS), social narratives, structured work systems, visual supports, computer-assisted instruction, pivotal response training, self-management strategies, video modeling, differential reinforcement, joint action routine (JAR), discrete trial training, functional behavior assessment, and functional communications training (IRCA, 2014; Lofland, 2013; Hatton & Henry, 2008).

APPLICATION OF THE RECREATIONAL THERAPY PROCESS: CASE STUDY

Benjamin (Ben) is an 18-year-old male who has autism. He has been working with various therapists and alternative education teachers for the past four years. At present, he only receives speech therapy (SLPT) alongside his alternative education. He is a high school senior and is preparing to enter the school's "transition program" for qualified seniors. This program continues to assist students with increasing their functional skills and exploring more vocational skills/talents. Although Ben is graduating and preparing to enter "transition," he still has underdeveloped social skills, a minimal leisure and recreational repertoire, and minimal involvement with peers outside of school. For these reasons, he requested RT services.

Assessment

Ben stated during his assessment interview that he really enjoys "doing things," but he just would rather do them by himself. He did not answer why he did not like to participate with others in activities; he simply appeared satisfied to remain alone during his free time. When his peers ask him to join in a game, he declines. Ben has no physical limitations and can join in all of the activities that involve his peers with minimal to no modifications; however, he simply chooses not to participate.

Ben still lives at home with both parents, and they are supportive of his education and continued development. He listed activities that he enjoys doing on his own such as drawing, reading, watching video cartoons, researching things on the Internet, math, science, swimming, lifting weights, telling jokes, listening to music, helping his teacher, working with clay and painting, among other things. He also listed that he wishes he could someday ride in a hot air balloon, make a cartoon of his own, and fly a plane.

Ben's parents sat in for the assessment, urged Ben to respond to the questions, and occasionally provided confirmation. The Leisure Interest Measure (LIM) by Regheb and Beard (1992) was used because (a) he could complete it himself with minimal to no assistance and (b) it would provide an overall better understanding of the activities that Ben truly enjoys doing. Once this information is identified, it will help inform the basis for his intervention. The LIM is intended to measure, or rather identify, the degree of interest a person has in each of the eight domains of leisure and is considered valid and reliable per testing and previous research (burlingame

& Blaschko, 2010). The domains of leisure that are included are physical, outdoor, mechanical, artistic, service, social, cultural, and reading.

Ben's results from the LIM:

Physical Domain ((#7 + #14 + #21 + #28) / 4) = 3.75
Outdoor Domain ((#2 + #9 + #16 + #23) / 4) = 3.75
Mechanical Domain ((#3 + #10 + #17 + #24) / 4) = 3.5
Artistic Domain ((#4 + #11 + #18 + #25) / 4) = 4.5
Service Domain ((#6 + #13 + #20 + #27) / 4) = 4.5
Social Domain ((#8 + #15 + #22 + #29) / 4) = 3.25
Cultural Domain ((#5 + #12 + #19 + #26) / 4) = 3.75
Reading Domain (#1) = 3
$X > 4$ = High Interest
$X < 4$ = Low Interest

Ben had similar scores within each domain; however, the areas he scored highest in (Artistic & Service = 4.5) confirmed the preferences he voiced in his assessment interview. Research pertaining to using this assessment instrument has noted that "high scores in all areas may indicate a tendency toward mania, reading comprehension difficulties, or other problems" (burlingame & Blaschko, 2002, p. 248). Ben showed similar scores in each of the eight domains, but higher in two out of the eight. Some of these findings are consistent with what may be considered reading comprehension difficulties; however, after reviewing the questions with what he answered, the recreational therapist found no confusion as far as comprehension, per his explanations and his parents' agreement. He does, however, work on reading comprehension with his SPLT, which indicates difficulty in this area in general. This assessment identified Ben to have high leisure interests in the areas of art and service, which again, was consistent with the findings in his interview.

Socially, Ben keeps to himself and does not initiate interaction with his peers within or outside of class. Emotionally, he appears to have a positive affect, although he does not communicate how he feels verbally (he is more behaviorally reactionary). Ben primarily has behavior problems when he is irritated and cannot adequately express himself. He tested for both the Wechsler Intelligence Scale for Children®, fourth edition, and the Woodcock-Johnson Psycho-Educational Battery and fell within the borderline range of functioning, yet he has displayed excellent academic progress.

Ben requires improvement with his verbal communications. He could better self-manage with coping skills for stress, or stress-management techniques. He has a minimal leisure repertoire and should expand it by incorporating more activities with peer interaction.

Planning

Based on the above assessment data, as well as supplemental documentation from his school and health care providers, the following information was identified to support planning for working with Ben:

Strengths:

1.   Understands tone of voice and body language of others.

2.   Works hard on his course work.

3.   Asks for help.

4. Enjoys participating in recreational and leisure activities.
5. Completes multistep directions well.
6. Does great with overall functional skills (i.e. Activities of Daily Living [ADL]).
7. Has family support.

Needs:

1. Improved verbal communication skills.
2. Improved self-management (feelings).
3. Decrease stress.
4. Increase social interaction.
5. Explore leisure and vocational interests.

Short-term goals (within 2 weeks)
Participation in this IEP will assist Ben with the following:

1. Communication. Increasing unprompted verbal communication skills on a daily basis.
2. Stress management. Displaying better self-management in stressful situations.
3. Leisure repertoire. Increasing participation in new leisure and recreational activities with others.

Long-term goals (within 1 year)
Upon completion of IEP, Ben will do the following:

1. Communication. Increase verbal communication skills with others.
2. Stress management. Display positive self-management skills in stressful situations.
3. Leisure repertoire. Expand leisure and recreation repertoire.
4. Social interaction. Increase social interactions with peers.

Objectives:
Over the course of intervention, Ben will do the following:

1. Communication
    a. Greet CTRS® when he sees her.
    b. Ask questions when he does not understand a directive.
    c. Discuss the "Transition Program" and other post–high school options with CTRS® when asked.
    d. Thank others after they have helped him.

2. Stress management
    a. Take 5 slow, deep breaths when feeling anxious or angry.
    b. Identify and communicate appropriate ways to let others know they are bothering him.
    c. Vocalize what he is feeling or thinking when asked.

3. Leisure repertoire
   a. Investigate other social clubs at school when provided with a list.
   b. Identify whether he likes cartooning activity after two weeks.
   c. Create a plan for pursuing one new activity after intervention.
4. Social interaction
   a. Initiate at least one conversation with CTRS® during each session.
   b. Initiate at least one conversation with one other student during alternative instruction (A.I.) time.
   c. Identify plan for increasing peer involvement.
   d. Participate in at least one social group outside of school.

Plans:

Interventions

- Two 60-min RT sessions twice weekly, during A.I. time.
- Attend bimonthly community-based social club.

Guiding theories:

An eclectic approached was used to compile Ben's ITP. Assessment and intervention techniques based on cognitive, cognitive-behavioral, humanistic, and positive psychology theories were incorporated into creating each objective for him.

Evaluation

Progress will be measured using the following:

- Pre- and post-intervention sociogram "Friendship Circles"
- Daily documentation (SOAP notes)
- Recording times/frequencies Ben engages in each of the objectives in each session.
- Consultation and questionnaire with teacher on record (TOR) prior to intervention and post-intervention.

Sample IEP goals/outcomes

1. Communication. Increase verbal communication skills with others.
   a. Increase use of assertiveness skills in social situations
   b. Demonstrate joint focus of attention in conversations with another peer.
   c. Maintain a conversation with reciprocal communication.
2. Stress management. Display positive self-management skills in stressful situations.
   a. Refrain from being blunt or rude with peers.
   b. Increase use of assertiveness skills in social situations
3. Leisure repertoire. Expand leisure and recreation repertoire.
   a. Identify leisure buddy for activity participation.
4. Social interaction. Increase social interactions with peers.
   a. Increase use of assertiveness skills in social situations.
   b. Identify leisure buddy for activity participation.
   c. Increase ability to build and maintain social networks.

TRENDS AND ISSUES

Community-Based Services

A recent publication by Coyne and Fullerton (2014) recognizes

> an increasing number of human service agencies have placed an emphasis on supporting children and adults with ASD in a wide range of community recreation and leisure activities and settings, on a person-centered, individual basis. At the same time, more community organizations and settings have opened their doors, in inclusive and supportive ways, to participants with ASD. (p. 38)

Despite such increases in opportunities for individuals with ASD, continued public education and advocacy are needed. Challenges also exist in conducting research on autism for many reasons, but specifically due to (a) the diversity of characteristics of each individual, (b) the variance in assessment (tool, processes/procedures, analysis, and use of data), and (c) sampling. In spite of the challenges to this research, more phenomenological and narrative accounts are being published, which provides society with a better perspective of the diversity and experience of ASD, as well as places the voices of persons with ASD at the forefront of the dialogue about themselves. To overcome these challenges, more communications with these individuals into what they want is required (similar to market research) and they must be allowed to be involved in the process of developing and planning new techniques, modalities, and/or programs that would positively assist them with minimizing or eliminating barriers to their ability to self-actualize. Again, they are the best "experts" on themselves and having ASD, so as service providers and a global community, RT professionals should be ready to listen.

Assistive Devices

Assistive devices, once called "adaptive equipment," are identified as "any technology that enables a person with a disability to improve his or her functioning level" and may be used for several needs (Austin, 2001, p. 10). Assistive devices are being used with persons with ASD. Typically, when individuals with ASD use assistive technology, they most commonly use it for social functioning. Common assistive technology individuals with ASD use includes (a) low-tech modalities and techniques (e.g., blinking/physical movement systems, sign language, yes–no system of gestures, storyboards, paper and writing utensils) and (b) high-tech modalities and techniques (e.g., braille, photos, augmented alternative communication [PECS, DynaVox, communication boards], computers), and (c) "fidgets" and other sensory supports (Alant & Lloyd, 2005; Light & Lindsay, 1991; McNaughton, 1993).

Pharmacotherapy

Currently, medication, or pharmacotherapy, is only used to address specific behaviors and secondary conditions in individuals with ASD. Other more medical-oriented approaches to note include laboratory and/or genetics testing and neuroimaging (Batshaw et al., 2007; Hyman & Towbin, 2007).

SUMMARY

Overall, ASD is a complex condition affecting many individuals and families. The diversity that exists among individuals with ASD needs to be recognized as much as the acceptance of those with ASD. For recreational therapists, a client-centered and holistic approach to service delivery supports meeting individuals at their current level of functioning and allowing them a "voice" in their movement toward optimal functioning and fulfillment. Community and collaboration play a large part in the acceptance and assistance of those with ASD and their families; furthermore, to open the dialogue with individuals, organizations and other service providers need to ensure services are of high quality and accessible by both cost and location. Perhaps summing it up best, Hawkins (2001) wrote the following, which still echoes true today:

> For those specialists working with people who have autism and their families, the rewards may be greater than in other areas of human service. Persons with autism are capable of learning and participating in a wide variety of leisure activities that bring both habilitative functions, and moments of joy and pleasure. (p. 126)

These individuals have a lot to share, and if RT professionals take the time to listen and learn, they may see how their skills best support them on the path to self-actualization.

READING COMPREHENSION QUESTIONS

1. How does the *DSM-5* define autism spectrum disorder (ASD)?

2. What are characteristic strengths of individuals with ASD that could be built upon to achieve outcome goals?

3. Name two common standardized assessment tools recreational therapists may use when working with individuals with ASD.

4. What is the service delivery process that recreational therapists use when working with individuals with ASD?

5. What are four ways a CTRS® may serve the needs of individuals with ASD and their families?

REFERENCES

Alant, E., & Lloyd, L. (2005). *Augmentative and alternative communication and severe disabilities beyond poverty*. London, United Kingdom: Whurr.

American Association on Intellectual and Developmental Disabilities. (2013). Definition of intellectual disability. Retrieved August 2, 2014, from http://aaidd.org/intellectual-disability/definition#.U95HPygvFUQ

American Psychiatric Association. (2013). *Diagnostic and statistical manual of mental disorders* (5th ed.). Washington, DC: Author.

American Therapeutic Recreation Association. (2014). Definition statement [Membership packet]. Hattiesburg, MS: Author.

Attwood, T. (2007). *The complete guide to Asperger's syndrome*. Philadelphia, PA: Jessica Kingsley.

Austin, D. R. (2001). *Glossary of recreation therapy and occupational therapy*. State College, PA: Venture.

Austin, D. R. (2013). *Therapeutic recreation: Processes and techniques* (7th ed.). Urbana, IL: Sagamore.

Austin, D. R., & McCormick, B. P. (2013). Clinical reasoning and recreation therapy. *American Journal of Recreation Therapy, 12*(4), 31–38.

Autism Society. (n.d.). *What is autism?* [Pamphlet]. Washington, DC: Author.

Batshaw, M., Pellegrino, L., & Roizen, N. (2007). *Children with disabilities* (6th ed.). Baltimore, MD: Paul H. Brookes.

Bauminger, N., Solomon, M., Aviezer, A., Heung, K., Gazit, L., Brown, J., & Rogers, S. J. (2008). Children with autism and their friends: A multidimensional study of friendship in high-functioning autism spectrum disorder. *Journal of Abnormal Child Psychology, 36*, 135–150. doi:10.1007/s10802-007-9156-x

Bellini, S., & Hopf, A. (2007). The development of the autism social skills profile: A preliminary analysis of psychometric properties. *Focus on Autism and Other Developmental Disabilities, 22*(2), 80–87.

Bilken, D. (2005). *Autism and the myth of the person alone.* New York: New York University Press.

burlingame, j., & Blaschko, T. M. (2002). *Assessment tools for recreational therapy and related fields* (3rd ed.). Ravensdale, WA: Idyll Arbor.

burlingame, j., & Blaschko, T. M. (2010). *Assessment tools for recreational therapy and related fields* (4th ed.). Ravensdale, WA: Idyll Arbor.

Bury, T. J. (1998). Evidence-based healthcare explained. In T. Bury & J. Mead (Eds.), *Evidence-based healthcare: A practical guide for therapists* (pp. 3–25). Oxford, United Kingdom: Butterworth-Heinemann.

Bury, T. J., & Mead, J. M. (1998). *Evidence-based healthcare: A practical guide for therapists.* Oxford, United Kingdom: Butterworth-Heinemann.

Cosden, M., Koegel, L. K., Koegel, R. L., Greenwell, A., & Klein, E. (2006). Strength-based assessment for children with autism spectrum disorders. *Research & Practice for Persons With Severe Disabilities, 31*(2), 134–143.

Coyne, P., & Fullerton, A. (2014). *Supporting individuals with autism spectrum disorder in recreation* (2nd ed.). Urbana, IL: Sagamore.

Crawford, M. E., Gray, C., & Woolhiser, J. (2012). Design and delivery of a public school social skills training program for youth with autism spectrum disorders: A five year retrospective of the school/community/home (SCH) model of social skills development. *Annual in Therapeutic Recreation, 20*(1), 17–35.

Embregts, P., & Van Nieuwenhuijzen, M. (2009). Social information processing in boys with autistic spectrum disorder and mild to borderline intellectual disabilities. *Journal of Intellectual Disability Research, 53*(11), 922–931. doi:10.1111/j.1365-2788.2009.01204.x

Falvo, D. R. (2009). *Medical and psychosocial aspects of chronic illness and disability* (4th ed.). Sudbury, MA: Jones & Bartlett.

Gray, C., Kavanaugh, T., & Hunter, H. (in press). Treatment network update (schools): Survey results. *American Therapeutic Recreation Official Publication.*

Gray, C., & Van Puymbroeck, M. (2012). Social skills identification survey. *Proceedings from the American Therapeutic Recreation Association Research Institute, 2012*, 17–20.

Hall, L. J. (2013). *Autism spectrum disorders: From theory to practice* (2nd ed.). Upper Saddle River, NJ: Pearson.

Hamilton, A. F. C. (2009). Research review: Goals, intentions and mental states—Challenges for theories of autism. *Journal of Child Psychology and Psychiatry, 50*(8), 881–892. doi:10.1111/j.1469-7610.2009.02098.x

Hatton, D. D., & Henry, S. (2008, October 9). *News you can use: Resources and supports for students with autism and their families* (NASDSE Professional Development Series). Teleconference & symposium sponsored by the National Association of State Directors of Special Education, Pittsburgh, PA.

Hawkins, B. A. (2001). Autism. In D. R. Austin & M. E. Crawford (Eds.), *Therapeutic recreation: An introduction* (3rd ed., pp. 113–129). Boston, MA: Allyn & Bacon.

Huckabay, L. M. (2009). Clinical reasoned judgment and the nursing process. *Nursing Forum, 44*(2), 72–78.

Hyman, S. L., & Towbin, K. E. (2007). Autism spectrum disorders. In M. Batshaw, L. Pellegrino, & N. Roizen (Eds.), *Children with disabilities* (6th ed., pp. 325–343). Baltimore, MD: Paul H. Brookes.

Indiana Resource Center for Autism. (2014). Autism awareness month: Facts and tips for working with individuals on the autism spectrum. *IRCA Reporter E-Newsletter, 18*(10), 1.

Indiana University. (n.d.). Notes from a lecture on recreational therapy and autism. Archived Lecture Notes, Indiana University, Bloomington, IN.

Janzen, J. E. (2003). *Understanding the nature of autism: A guide to the autism spectrum disorders* (2nd ed.). San Antonio, TX: PsychCorp.

Kelly, J. R. (1996). *Leisure* (3rd ed.). Boston, MA: Allyn and Bacon.

Lee, Y., & McCormick, B. P. (2002). Toward evidence-based therapeutic recreation practice. In D. Austin, J. Dattilo, & B. McCormick (Eds.), *Conceptual foundations for therapeutic recreation* (pp. 164–183). State College, PA: Venture.

Levett-Jones, T., Hoffman, K., Bourgeois, S. R., Kenny, R., Dempsey, J., Hickey, N., . . . Jeffrey, K. (2009). *Clinical reasoning* [Instructor resources]. University of Newcastle, Australia: School of Nursing and Midwifery Faculty of Health, University of Newcastle.

Light, J., & Lindsay, P. (1991). Cognitive science and augmentative and alternative communication. *Augmentative and Alternative Communication, 7*, 186–203.

Lofland, K. B. (2013). Evidence-based practices for effective communication and social intervention. *IRCA Reporter E-Newsletter, 18*(4). Retrieved from http://www.iidc.indiana.edu/index.php?pageId=3643

Matson, J. (Ed.) (2008). *Clinical assessment and intervention for autism spectrum disorders.* Burlington, MA: Elsevier.

Matson, J. L., & Ollendick, T. H. (1988). *Enhancing children's social skills: Assessment and training.* Elmsford, NY: Pergamon Press.

Mattingly, C. (1991). What is clinical reasoning? *The American Journal of Occupational Therapy, 45*(11), 979–986.

McNaughton, S. (1993). Graphic representational systems and literacy learning. *Topics in Language Disorders, 13*(2), 58–75.

Merrell, K. W., & Gimpel, G. A. (1998). *Social skills of children and adolescents: Conceptualization, assessment, treatment.* Mahwah, NJ: Lawrence Erlbaum.

Miller, J. N., & Ozonoff, S. (1997). Did Asperger's cases have Asperger's disorder? A research note. *Journal of Child Psychology & Psychiatry, 38*, 247–251.

O'Brien, S. (2011). Social assessment in healthcare. In A. Crouch & C. Meurier (Eds.), *Vital notes for nurses health assessment* (pp. 264–287). Retrieved from http://site.ebrary.com/lib/iub/Doc?id=10521362&ppg=280

Odom, S. L., Collet-Klingenberg, L., Rogers, S. J., & Hatton, D. D. (2010). Evidence-based practices in interventions for children and youth with autism spectrum disorders. *Preventing School Failure, 54*(4), 275–282. doi:10.1080/10459881003785506

Ozonoff, S., Goodlin-Jones, B. L., & Solomon, M. (2005). Evidence-based assessment of autism spectrum disorders in children and adolescents. *Journal of Clinical Child and Adolescent Psychology, 34*(3), 523–540.

Paul, R. (2010). *Social skills development, assessment and programming in school-aged speakers with autism spectrum disorders* [Electronic resource]. London, England: Henry Stewart Talks.

Porter, H. R., & burlingame, j. (2010). *Recreational therapy handbook of practice: ICF-based diagnosis and treatment.* Enumclaw, WA: Idyll Arbor.

Rao, P. A., Beidel, D. C., & Murray, M. J. (2008). Social skills interventions for children with Asperger's syndrome or high-functioning autism: A review and recommendations. *Journal of Autism and Developmental Disorders, 38*(1), 353–361. doi:10.1007/s10803-007-0402-4

Rapin, I. (1997). Classification and causal issues in autism. In J. Cohen & F. Volkmar (Eds.), *Handbook of autism and pervasive developmental disorders* (2nd ed.). New York, NY: John Wiley.

Ratto, A. B., Turner-Brown, L., Rupp, B. M., Mesibov, G. B., & Penn, D. L. (2010). Development of the contextual assessment of social skills (CASS): A role-play measure of social skill for individuals with high-functioning autism. *Journal of Autism and Developmental Disorders, 41*(9), 1277–1286. doi:10.1007/s10803-010-1147-z

Regheb, M. G., & Beard, J. G. (1992). Measuring leisure interests. *Journal of Park and Recreation Administration, 10*(2), 1–13.

Reichow, B., & Volkmar, F. R. (2010). Social skills interventions for individuals with autism: Evaluation for evidence-based practices within a best evidence synthesis framework. *Journal of Autism and Developmental Disorders, 40*(2), 149–166. doi: http://dx.doi.org/10.1007/s10803-009-0842-0

Sansoti, F. J., Powell-Smith, K. A., & Cowan, R. J. (2010). *High-functioning autism/Asperger syndrome in schools: Assessment and intervention.* New York, NY: The Guilford Press.

Shank, J., & Coyle, C. (2002). *Therapeutic recreation in health promotion and rehabilitation.* State College, PA: Venture.

Smith, K. R., & Matson, J. L. (2010). Social skills: Differences among adults with intellectual disabilities, co-morbid autism spectrum disorders and epilepsy. *Research in Developmental Disabilities, 31*(6), 366–1372. doi:10.101016/j.ridd.2010.07.002

Students on the Spectrum Club. (2012, April). Notes from a lecture on autism: Autism experts talking points. Archived Lecture Notes, Indiana University, Bloomington, IN.

Stumbo, N. J. (Ed.). (2003). *Client outcomes in therapeutic recreation services.* State College, PA: Venture.

Volker, M. A. (2008). Autism: A review of biological bases, assessment and intervention. *School Psychology Quarterly, 23*(2), 258–270.

7

INTELLECTUAL AND DEVELOPMENTAL DISABILITIES

MICHAEL E. CRAWFORD

OBJECTIVES

- Understand the distinction between intellectual disability (ID) and developmental disability (DD).
- Describe the classification systems for ID and DD.
- Give examples of highly prevalent and rare types of ID and DD.
- Understand the history of social stigma for persons with ID and DD.
- Describe the three levels of recreational therapy intervention.
- Explain the concepts of normalization, least restrictive environment, partial participation, developmental ceiling.
- Explain the differences between task analysis, activity analysis, and environmental analysis.
- Describe common service settings and curriculum differences for recreational therapists working in ID and DD.
- Describe the precision teaching approach used in behavior therapy.
- Identify key issues in service delivery to persons with ID and DD.
- Enumerate individualized adaptation strategies useful in programming.
- Explain the difference between high quality, low quality, and inappropriate leisure behaviors.

DEFINITIONS

Intellectual Disability

Intellectual disability (ID) refers to a group of disorders characterized by a limited mental capacity and difficulty with adaptive behaviors such as managing money, telling time, or handling social interactions appropriately. Intellectual disability originates before age 18 and may result from physical causes as in the case of autism or cerebral palsy or from nonphysical causes such as extreme environmental deprivation, lack of stimulation, and adult responsiveness (American Psychiatric Association, 2013).

Adaptive behavior limitations are linked to underlying intellectual impairment and affect participation in multiple settings, such as home, community, and school. Adaptive deficits include limitations in at least one of the three domains (i.e., conceptual, social, and practical) to the extent that ongoing support is required as compared with others in the same age group. The severity of the ID is defined according to the level of supports needed in each of these domains (Tasse, Schalock, & Balboni, 2012). Intellectual abilities are adversely affected in the areas of learning, reasoning, problem solving, abstract thinking, and judgment. This limitation in intellectual ability typically corresponds to an intelligence quotient (IQ) less than 65–75. Although standardized IQ testing remains pertinent to the diagnostic profile, it is no longer solely used to classify the severity of the impairment.

Developmental Disability

Developmental disability (DD) is a term used to describe a group of conditions that express themselves during periods of time within which key developmental milestones typically are achieved. By interfering with the achievement of developmental milestones, the DD has a significant long-term impact across areas such as physical, social, emotional, cognitive, and communication skill development.

DDs represents a broad umbrella of specific conditions such as cerebral palsy, ADHD, vision and hearing impairments, autism, and intellectual disabilities (Stein & Lukasik, 2009). The term *developmental disability* is used to refer to disabilities affecting daily functioning in three or more of the areas listed in Table 7.1.

Table 7.1
Major Life Activities Functioning Areas

- Capacity for independent living
- Economic self-sufficiency
- Learning
- Mobility
- Receptive and expressive language
- Self-care
- Self-direction

Note. From *Intellectual Disability: Understanding Its Development, Causes, Classification, Evaluation, and Treatment*, by J. C. Harris, 2006, New York, NY: Oxford University Press, pp. 28–42.

CAUSES AND PREVALENCE OF INTELLECTUAL AND DEVELOPMENTAL DISABILITIES

DDs are the result of genetic and/or environmental influences, often a combination of both. Many causes exist, although for some persons a definitive cause never may be determined and may receive the formal diagnosis of idiopathic (i.e., unknown cause). Common factors causing ID and DD are listed in Table 7.2.

The prevalence of DDs is increasing, with the most recent data showing a prevalence rate of 13.87% in the United States (Centers for Disease Control and Prevention, 2011). Researchers from the Centers for Disease Control and Prevention, along with the Health Resources and Services Administration, published the results of a

12-year longitudinal study examining the prevalence of DD in the United States. Significant facts among the findings are included in Table 7.3.

Table 7.2
Causes of Intellectual and Developmental Disabilities

- Brain injury or infection before, during, or after birth
- Growth or nutrition problems
- Abnormalities of chromosomes and genes
- Extreme premature birth
- Drug misuse and/or excessive alcohol intake, smoking, or poor diet during pregnancy
- Child abuse and/or severe environmental deprivation in early years

Note. From "Genetics and Pathophysiology of Mental Retardation, by J. Chelly, M. Khelfaoui, and F. Francis, 2006, *European Journal of Human Genetics, (14)*, 701–709.

Table 7.3
Significant Prevalence Facts Regarding Intellectual and Developmental Disabilities

- Prevalence of autism increased 289.5%.
- Prevalence of attention deficit hyperactivity disorder (ADHD) increased 33%.
- Males had twice the prevalence of any developmental disability than females.
- Males had higher prevalence of ADHD, autism, learning disabilities, and stuttering.
- Children from families living below the federal poverty level had 20% higher prevalence of developmental disabilities.

Note. From *Prevalence of Developmental Disabilities Fact Sheet* (ID4740551), by Centers for Disease Control and Prevention, 2011, Atlanta, GA: Author.

DESCRIPTION OF LIMITATIONS

Associated conditions and comorbidities likely associated with ID and DD (particularly in the severe and profound range of impairment) include neurodevelopmental disorders such as autism and other behavioral disorders, seizure disorders, motor impairments, speech delays, structural abnormalities, and vision, hearing, and other sensory impairments such as tactile defensiveness. Approximately 60% of individuals with DD present with at least one comorbidity (Lott & Dierssen, 2010).

The American Psychiatric Association (APA) and the American Association on Intellectual and Developmental Disabilities (AAIDD) use severity codes; however, the systems are qualitatively different from one another. Although both use adaptive functioning as one criterion to determine severity, the APA system is based on limitations, whereas the AAIDD looks at degree of support needed, sometimes referred to as support intensity. The APA scale recognizes mild, moderate, severe, and profound levels of ID.

Mild Intellectual Disability

This category includes roughly 85% of persons with ID. In many cases, these persons are able to live independently with a minimal level of support, although they may need assistance with major life decisions and help with tasks such as finances, shopping, and transportation.

Moderate Intellectual Disability

This category includes about 10% of persons with ID. Persons at this level may have problems with appropriate social skills. They require regular support for self-care activities in terms of instruction, reminders, and performance cues. A typical residential setting would be a group home with 24/7 staffing.

Severe Intellectual Disability

This category includes 3% to 4% of the ID populations. Communication skills frequently are challenging, often receptive vocabulary is greater than expressive, and survival word training is emphasized (phrases and concepts needed on a daily basis). The incidence of comorbidities in terms of physical and sensory impairments is much higher, leading to the need for high vigilance for safety. Housing is usually a residential center (or group home) with high staffing ratios.

Profound Intellectual Disability

This category includes just 1% to 2% of the ID population. These persons usually require 24-hour care and are highly dependent upon other persons for all aspects of daily routine. High comorbidities with physical and sensory impairments are typically present. Many persons in this category are deemed "medically fragile" and may be tube fed and/or require ventilator assistance with breathing and 24/7 nursing support. The AAIDD (Schalock et at., 2010) severity codes for ID evaluates a person's level of functioning based on the level of support that person needs.

Intermittent Support

These individuals do not require regular support or assistance. They only need help at times of life transition (e.g., changing residences, changing jobs) or during times of high stress (e.g., personal or family illness, crises) or other uncertainties. This level correlates with the APA category of Mild ID.

Limited Support

These are persons who, with extended training, may improve their adaptive behavior. Social and practical skills required for everyday living may be acquired and maintained at a higher level with precision teaching strategies. This level correlates with the APA category of Moderate ID.

Extensive Support

These individuals require intensive support with self-care tasks and basic communication skills. In addition, many may have idiosyncratic behaviors that are self-stimulatory and/or behaviorally challenging for inclusive settings that may require monitoring and behavioral shaping. This category correlates with the APA category of Severe ID.

Pervasive Support

Persons who require pervasive support need daily interventions and monitoring to ensure health, nutrition, and safety. These individuals require lifelong support in virtually every aspect of daily living. Expressive communication is virtually nonexistent for many, and the costs for skilled nursing supervision may be high. This category correlates with the APA category of Profound ID.

Some professionals have argued having two classification systems leads to confusion and problems in providing care for persons with ID and DD. Opponents of the APA classification system have argued that ID continues along a continuum as opposed to four distinct categorical levels and that using level of supports is a more practically based method of determining status. Although a categorical classification may lack individual specificity, its advantage is simplicity in attempting to deal with the marriage of system-based delivery (e.g., staffing ratios, medical supports, transportation needs) and individual care. Individualized support plans (ISPs) are developed with the goal of maximizing the developmental potentials and competencies of each person. The primary objective of the ISP is to optimize functioning and life satisfaction through providing educational supports, improving adaptive functioning (where practical), and providing appropriate levels and types of supports for self-help, social skills, housing, and employment (where practical) and therapies and nursing support depending upon presenting comorbidities.

HISTORY OF SOCIAL STIGMA AND CHALLENGES

Persons with ID (formerly known as mental retardation) also must face challenges based upon stigma, which sometimes leads to social indifference (at best) or occasionally social cruelty (at worst). Stigma may cause marginalization of subgroups from society and stigmatizing language may have a powerful negative effect on the individuals affected. Over the course of history in the United States, many prejudices have been levied against persons with ID and many terms have been coined to describe them, and then later stigmatize them (Wolfensberger, 1972).

Wolfensberger's (1972) extensive research on the history of care and treatment of persons with ID reveals a long period of brutalization (lasting over 100 years) in which many labels were assigned. As early as 1845, Howe's book *On the Causes of Idiocy* (as cited in Wolfensberger, 1972, p. 38) put forward a three-level classification scheme for persons with ID including (1) fools, persons characterized by almost no reasoning skills and possessing major speech delays; (2) simpletons, persons characterized by reasonable motor skills but needing guidance to complete daily living skills; and (3) idiots, persons characterized by some motor control and some cognitive functioning but poor reasoning skills. Originally, these neutral words, used for the purpose of classification by level of severity, were used in the psychology journals of the day. As they were picked up by laypersons in everyday vernacular, they began to take on prejudicial meaning and were used in demeaning terms as insults or judgments of low worth. Other terms that used to have legitimate medical or psychological classification usage include *cretin*, originally reflected the notion that persons with ID were still God's children and should be treated with kindness; *feeble-minded*, referred to persons who were not profoundly disabled but still required some intervention and care; *moron*, developed in part by psychologist Henry Goddard to replace the term *feeble-minded* and to classify persons with mild ID along a three-level continuum including idiot and imbecile; and finally, *retarded*, derived from the Latin *retardare*, meaning to make slow, delay, or hinder. The first record of its use in psychological literature was in 1895 where it was proposed to replace the terms *idiot, moron,* and *imbecile* as classifiers for persons with ID (Wolfensberger, 1972).

Over time, these words were abandoned for the purpose of classification but remain today as socially stigmatizing hate words. The word *retarded* was shortened to *retard* and became such a powerful hate word in contemporary society that advocates lobbied to eliminate it altogether. In fact, in October 2010, President Obama signed a bill known as Rosa's Law, which requires the terms *mental retardation* and *mentally retarded* be stricken from federal records and replaced with the *DSM-5* APA term *intellectual disability.* Unfortunately, if past is prelude, it will be only a matter of time until the RT profession will have to retire the term *intellectually disabled* as someone will eventually figure out a way to wordsmith it into a derogatory term. Common stereotypes that remain today regarding persons with ID are listed in Table 7.4.

Table 7.4
Non-Helpful Social Attitudes Toward Persons With Intellectual Disabilities

1. They are incapable of reasoning.
2. We should pity them and feel sorry for them.
3. They are dumb and cannot learn to read and write.
4. They do not know the difference between right and wrong.
5. They need to be taken care of their entire life.
6. They are eternal children who do not grow up, but live in a child's world.
7. They are less than human.
8. They are a burden to society.
9. They are a social menace and responsible for crimes.
10. They are holy innocents sent by God to teach us to be better Christians.

Note. Adapted from *Normalization: The Principle of Normalization in Human Services,* by W. Wolfensberger, 1972, Toronto, National Institute on Mental Retardation; *Therapeutic Recreation and Adapted Physical Activities for Mentally Retarded Individuals,* by M. E. Crawford and R. Mendell, 1987, Englewood Cliffs, NJ: Prentice Hall; and *Angel Unaware,* by D. Evans-Rogers, 1953, Old Tappan, NJ: Fleming-Revell.

PURPOSE OF RECREATIONAL THERAPY

The Leisure Ability Model (Stumbo & Peterson, 2009) may be used as a conceptual model for recreational therapy (RT) services for persons with ID and DD. Under this conceptual model, Dattilo and Guerin's (2001) narrative regarding the purpose of RT interventions is still pertinent today: "The purpose of recreational therapy is to facilitate the development, maintenance, and expression of an appropriate leisure lifestyle for the person with ID or DD" (p. 136). The phrase *leisure lifestyle* refers to the day-to-day behavioral expression of a person's leisure-related attitudes, awareness, and activities (Peterson, 1981).

Studies have shown that persons with ID and DD can enjoy successful leisure lifestyles, providing them with increases in confidence, skills, and self-esteem (Patterson & Pegg, 2009). Unfortunately, however, research has found that persons with ID or DD participate in fewer leisure activities than persons without ID or DD and predominantly spend their time in passive, solitary pursuits rather than physically active, skill-based activities (Badia, Orgaz, Verdugo, & Ullan, 2012; King, Shields, Imms, Black, & Ardern, 2013; Patterson, 2001; Solish, Perry, & Minnes, 2010). Thus, developing positive leisure lifestyles is a critical element for enhancing the quality of life for persons with ID and DD. Even though the conceptual Leisure Ability Model that underlies the delivery of RT services emphasizes the facilitation of leisure, the development of leisure skills often brings about improvements in other areas. For example, fine motor and gross motor skills, cognitive and affective skills, and social and communication skills may improve as a result of interventions involving leisure facilitation. Three specific areas of professional service are used to facilitate the development of leisure lifestyle: treatment (therapy), leisure education, and recreation participation (National Therapeutic Recreation Society, 1982; Stumbo & Peterson, 2009).

Treatment

At this level of work, the recreational therapist is making activity prescriptions that will, in the long term, increase physical, social, and emotional development related to eventual leisure participation. Recreational therapists must develop interventions and treatments that help persons with ID and DD to develop the functional skills necessary to participate in leisure pursuits. Often referred to as *readiness skills* (Crawford, 1986a), they represent the cognitive and social abilities necessary for instruction to be received. Therefore, attention span, impulse control, eye contact, listening skills, and sequential memory abilities may represent generic abilities that need to be developed prior to or at least simultaneously with leisure skill development. Other maladaptive behaviors may need to be diminished, or even eliminated, such as self-stimulatory behaviors or unnecessary vocalizations.

Another area of treatment with which activity prescriptions are helpful is coping with the disability, comorbidities, or recuperation from medical procedures. The emphasis may be on dealing with stress reduction (perhaps brought on by major lifestyle changes, such as graduation or change in residence), cathartic or emotional venting (perhaps in response to a worsening of a degenerative comorbidity or a grief response), or even preventative care related to aspects of physical health (possibly assisting with range of motion and/or strengthening of certain muscle sets in concert with medical staff, preventing pressure sores, or relieving confining postures via out-of-chair activity work).

Leisure Education

Howe-Murphy and Charboneau (1987) wrote to the importance of cataloging leisure resources available to clients with ID and DD. In addition, they noted knowledge of activities and pursuits available within the local community is also an important part of a comprehensive leisure strategy.

Mundy (1998; as cited in Dattilo & Guerin, 2001, p. 137) identified five essential leisure education goals: (a) enhance their quality of life; (b) identify their leisure values, attitudes, and needs; (c) understand the importance of leisure in their lives; (d) identify and use personal, social, and community resources available for their leisure; and (e) improve mental, physical, social, and emotional development through broad-based leisure experiences. Similarly, according to Dattilo and Williams (2011), leisure education programs may include a number of components to ensure that individuals are prepared to be successful in leisure. The following are helpful for individuals to learn:

1. leisure appreciation,
2. self-awareness,
3. decision making,
4. self-determination,
5. leisure activity skills,
6. community skills,
7. social skills, and
8. leisure resources.

Chronic challenges for persons with ID and DD at the leisure education level of programming are transportation (since most are dependent upon others for travel) and costs (since many are unemployed or underemployed; Hodges & Luken, 2000). Personal, human service agency, and community supports in these areas are a challenge that the recreational therapist must help coordinate and problem solve.

Recreation Participation

According to Dattilo and Guerin (2001), in too many instances families and professionals often make participation choices for persons with ID and DD. Since the goal of leisure education is to help clients achieve the greatest degree of self-initiated leisure choices that is chronologically age appropriate (Wehman & Schleien, 1992), it follows that recreational therapists must help develop these intellectual skill sets to the greatest degree possible. Dattilo and Guerin noted that researchers Palmer and Wehmeyer (1998) and Faw, Davis, and Peck (1996) documented the limited opportunities ID and DD clients have to state preferences, express individual control over daily routine, or even be included in decision-making processes. These are skills important to successful leisure participation that must be added to the leisure education curriculum.

At this level of programming, the recreational therapist is more facilitator than prescriber, more resource problem solver than provider of direct services. Thus, decisions to participate in activities (e.g., Special Olympics, planning a vacation, joining a community gym, or signing up for a pottery class) come with a unique set of participation hurdles requiring different levels of personal support depending upon the person's level of ID or DD and personal resources (e.g., finances, social circle, transportation options).

Least Restrictive Environment Doctrine

Before the normalization movement of the 1960s, the majority of persons with ID and DD in the United States and Canada were served in institutional settings permeated by a custodial philosophy in which recreation services were believed to have no habilitative value. As the normalization movement grew during the 1970s and 1980s, the majority of recreational therapists began providing services according to the least restrictive environment (LRE) doctrine. Under LRE theory, the focus of RT interventions is to prepare persons with ID and DD to function in a variety of environments (Baumgart et al., 1982). According to LRE, only skills or activities that have the potential of being performed in the presence of or in interaction with non-disabled peers should be selected for leisure education.

The second part to the LRE doctrine is frequently forgotten or overlooked, particularly as it applies to persons categorized in the severe and profound levels of ID and DD. The complete LRE doctrine states that services should be provided in the least restrictive environment "that allows for growth and maximization of developmental potential" (Sherrill, 1993 p. 93). Thus, a segregated setting, with special or adapted equipment or exceptional levels of personal support may be preferred over an inclusive setting in some areas of activity prescription. Aquatic activities are an excellent example of this distinction. Teaching swimming as a lifetime leisure skill would be a perfectly reasonable goal for persons with mild or moderate ID and DD and, as such, should occur in inclusive environments within the community. However, for persons with severe spastic cerebral palsy DD, who spend their lives in a wheelchair, participation in aquatics takes on an entirely different priority. The 76°F cold water of YMCAs and city pools is contraindicated for these persons. In fact, immersion in cold water would increase the already present hypertonicity and effectively chill these persons in a matter of minutes due to their inability to move and warm themselves. Thus, a heated therapy pool (93°F as recommended by the National Aquatic Therapy Rehabilitation Institute, ATRI) makes the immersion comfortable, and the warm water reduces hypertonicity, allowing stretching of joints and range of motion activities and also provides extended time out of the wheelchair, which is an important preventative measure against the formation of pressure sores (which may be fatal).

Sometimes the most appropriate application of LRE is a segregated setting because of the level of support needed to accomplish the goal. Over time, many professionals have equated LRE with inclusion-only programming. The important aspect is providing activities that help persons grow and reach their developmental potential. This does not mean exclusive programming in inclusive settings; it means matching levels of support with needs in the most appropriate environment to facilitate growth, learning, and appropriate care.

COMMON SERVICE SETTINGS

Sixty years ago, the majority of persons with ID and DD lived in large custodial institutions. Wolfensberger (1972) and other historians documented in detail the dehumanizing conditions that existed in most facilities. Although the normalization movement has led to the populations of most state-run facilities being drastically reduced (from thousands to hundreds), in favor of community group homes and other residential options, a number of individuals with severe comorbidities are still institutionalized. These individuals fall roughly into two categories: the extreme medically fragile and persons dually diagnosed with mental illness. The extreme medically fragile are individuals requiring 24/7 skilled nursing support, many of whom are bedbound and have comorbidities such as brittle bone disease or hydrocephalus. Others may be deaf/blind and profoundly intellectually disabled. The other dominant population still institutionalized is persons who possess some level of ID or DD and are mentally ill and dangerous to themselves or others by virtue of acts of violence. This population typically is housed in locked units with wall-mounted panic buttons. Recreational therapists working within state institutions today usually must devise ways to deliver services at bedside or on the ward. Frequently the focus of RT with these groups is classic hospital recreation, in that the hospital is home and the purpose of RT is to provide activities that enhance quality of life through sensory rich, often diversional, programming (e.g., aroma and music therapy, tactile stimulation, art activities).

In addition to state-run institutions, a number of private institutions exist, usually church sponsored. These institutions are qualitatively different from state facilities. Many of these campuses date back over 100 years or more to the "happy home era" (Wolfensberger, 1972) and were originally established as a protective community for persons with ID or DD. The prevailing philosophy of the church-based homes was that persons with ID and DD were eternal children sent by God to teach others how to be better Christians. Even today, some families choose to send their children with ID and DD to the safety and security of private institutions. Thus, many of these individuals, in terms of function or level of disability, could do well in the greater community. As a result, recreational therapists working in these settings must offer a greatly expanded curriculum, including leisure education and other skill development activities, since so many of the individuals are in the mild and moderate range of disability.

The normalization movement created the impetus for communities to develop options and supports for families with children who had ID and DD to raise their children at home. This included developing free and appropriate special education services and community group homes, as well as sheltered vocational workshops and day care programs for adults. Recreational therapists have many community and school programs in which they may work including public and private school districts, municipal and county parks and recreation programs, group home and other community residential settings, and adult day care facilities.

Public and Private School Districts

Since the original authorization of the Equal Education Act (PL 94-142) in 1975, therapeutic recreation has been listed as a related service. Because RT is a related service (optional) and not a direct service (as are physical therapy and occupational therapy), budget-minded school districts have been reluctant to include RT in the individualized education plan process (IEP; Turnbull, 1990). Some progressive-minded communities and districts across the United States have set up model programs and employ or contract for RT services, but this is a small number and makes for spotty coverage for families. According to the National Council for Therapeutic Recreation Certification (NCTRC, 2005), less than 2% of all recreational therapists work in the public school setting. The curriculum typically delivered in school settings revolves around social skills training and leisure education skill development.

Municipal and County Parks and Recreation Programs

Mainly as a result of the federal Americans With Disabilities Act of 1990, which requires accessibility and usability of public recreation facilities for persons with disabilities, some cities and counties have developed program options for persons with disabilities, although recreational therapists do not always lead these programs. In fact, a 2012 survey by the National Recreation and Park Association revealed that only 47% of municipal recreation programs nationwide have such programs.

Group Home and Other Community Residential Settings

Group homes vary considerably, from small homes of six to eight residents up to 12 to 20. Some are sex segregated. Typically the residential support staff make decisions in concert with their charges regarding recreation options. However, some state-run group homes and a few more progressive for-profit, private facilities hire recreational therapists to help coordinate programming and services. Typically a single recreational therapist is responsible for covering multiple group homes, and the curriculum will be split between enhancing the quality of recreation inside of the home and planning community inclusion work, usually in small group outings.

Adult day care facilities. As a result of the majority of individuals with ID and DD growing up and living in the community, many individuals have no adult vocational destination (due to the severe and profound level of their ID or DD and co-morbidities). As a result, the industry for private, for-profit as well as state and non-profit adult day care facilities is burgeoning. Nearly 78% of adult day care centers are nonprofit. From a handful of facilities in the late 1960s, adult day care centers grew to approximately 4,600 by 2010 (Met-Life Mature Market Institute, 2010). Typically these facilities serve from 25 to 60 persons, with the national average being 40. Nationwide 51% of all individuals served in adult day care facilities possess an ID. Adult day programs are generally delivered in one of two program models: the social model or the medical model. Although no federal standards of care exist, national standards and guidelines were established in 1997 by the National Adult Day Services Association (NADSA), and 36 states have adopted these standards for regulatory purposes. All day care operations based on the medical model have skilled nursing personnel on-site as well as ongoing therapies (e.g., occupational therapy, physical therapy; NADSA, 1995).

Certainly serving a population with profound disability with an enriched curriculum day after day is challenging. Adding to the challenge is that annual turnover of support staff for this industry exceeds 40% nationwide (Met-Life Mature Market Institute, 2010), which makes for poor continuity in day-to-day operation and puts the facility into a perennial cycle of hiring, training, and being short staffed. Although not required by federal or state laws, many of these providers have added recreational therapists as either programmers or consultants to help enrich the day-to-day environment. Typically RT is a value-added service for which families must pay, meaning that only persons who enroll and pay additional fees benefit from the program. Curriculums in these facilities include center-based sensory activities (e.g., music, art, aroma) and small group community inclusion services.

CURRENT BEST PRACTICES AND PROCEDURES

Many persons with ID and DD present with maladaptive and deficient leisure behaviors. Maladaptive behaviors reduce the likelihood of integration into the community and may include actions such as self-stimulatory hand flapping, body rocking, bizarre vocalizations, and repetitive motions or verbalizations. Deficient behaviors include inappropriate use of leisure materials (e.g., holding a magazine or book upside down, throwing game pieces) or incomplete performances of leisure behaviors (e.g., hitting the ball off the T, but not running to base).

In the 1970s and 1980s, a series of research studies established that maladaptive behaviors may be substantially reduced or eliminated simultaneous to teaching higher quality leisure skills through a combination of precision teaching techniques and behavioral therapy. These studies collectively have established which procedures and techniques represent best practice standards. Some of the more noted studies include teaching table games to adolescents with severe ID (Wehman, Renzaglia, Berry, Schultz, & Karan, 1978), teaching darts to adults with severe ID (Schleien, Wehman, & Kiernan, 1981), teaching video games to teens with severe ID (Sedlak, Doyle, & Schloss, 1982), teaching photography skills to adults with severe ID (Giangreco, 1983), teaching fitness exercises to adults with profound levels of ID (Stainback, Stainback, Wehman, & Spangiers, 1983), teaching sport skills to children with severe ID (Cuvo et al., 1983), normalizing behaviors of teens with moderate ID for inclusion in normal camping programs (Crawford, 1986b), and integrating children with severe ID into community-based recreation programs (Schleien, Tuckner, & Heyne, 1985). As a whole, these studies demonstrate that with the right amount of therapist assistance, environmental or equipment modification, sufficient repetition and/or time at task, and sophisticated behavioral engineering and/or precision teaching techniques, persons with severe and profound levels of ID and DD can achieve relatively high quality leisure behaviors.

Assessment

The first step in developing an individual support plan (ISP) for leisure behavior is for the recreational therapist to conduct a comprehensive assessment. Because of the complexity inherent across individuals with ID and DD, the recreational therapist must be prepared to undertake a long-term and highly individualized planning effort. General guidelines for undertaking assessments include conducting a leisure history, reviewing medical records, interviewing caregivers/staff, observing the client using a structured checklist, and considering environmental factors as they relate to leisure behaviors.

In constructing a leisure history, the recreational therapist catalogs an inventory of existing leisure behaviors and analyzes interactional skills, habit systems, and personal support resources for travel, equipment, money, and so forth. The social circle of friends, acquaintances, play partners, and family members who engage the client is essential to developing the leisure ISP. Some of this information may be gathered by direct client interview; however, when assessing clients in the severe and profound range of disability, the recreational therapist must obtain much of this information secondhand through caregiver (family or staff) interviews.

When interviewing direct care staff, the recreational therapist must talk to more than one person. Responder bias, based on either personality or time of day they supervise the client, may artificially color the assessment if not offset by multiple interviewees. Correspondingly, parents are often eager to please professionals and/or eager to enroll their child in services and may offer only positive pictures or exaggerate the capacities of their child; this "halo" phenomenon of parent interview has existed for a long time, and multiple researchers have documented it (Crawford & Mendell, 1987; McCatchie, 1973; McKinney, 1972).

Review of the medical record is essential in terms of identifying medical limitations or contraindicated activities. Also, understanding medications and possible side effects (e.g., increased photo sensitivity), food allergies, seizure history (if applicable), and other interdisciplinary assessments and goals is also critical. Frequently, RT goals and activity prescriptions provide supportive help to physical, occupational, or speech therapy goals. At the least, the recreational therapist must ensure that the RT plan does not work against the therapeutic goals of other services (e.g., if the physical therapy goal is to stretch calf muscles to achieve a more normal gait, sport activities requiring strong contraction activities are not the best idea for the recreational therapist to pursue).

Client observation and interaction yield the most pertinent information regarding leisure behavior assessment, though it may be time consuming and at times difficult to arrange. As with the interview process, multiple observational periods in different activities and/or environments provide the most accurate picture. Table 7.5 details a personal inventory checklist that illustrates the complexity and many subtleties of observational assessment.

Table 7.5
Personal Inventory Checklist

Interactional capacity
___ Alert to the environment
___ Actively seeks experiences
___ Greets strangers or staff in some fashion
___ Explores new objects or environments
___ Waits for demands to be placed
___ Reacts defensively to new situations
___ Reacts aggressively to new situations
___ Disruptive motor behaviors
___ Talks or verbalizes incessantly
___ Touches everything and everybody
___ Immature responses for age
___ Displays erratic, unpredictable behavior
Comments: _____

Tolerance to task/attention span
___ Physically tires quickly
___ Loses interest rapidly
___ Requires verbal prompting
___ Requires physical prompting
___ Spends a majority of time in self-stimulatory activities
___ Easily distractible
___ Processing delay in responding to prompts or instructions
___ Refuses to try
___ Demonstrates resentful behavior when failing
___ Unable to follow directions
___ Idiosyncratic, insists on a certain order or way of doing things
Comments: _____

Table 7.5 (cont.)

Levels of social and physical tolerance
___ Allows close proximity with strangers ___ with familiar people
___ Shows avoidance response to new environments
___ Demonstrates curiosity with new people
___ Insists on a specific amount of personal space
___ Will initiate interactions with peers ___with staff (positive/negative/neutral)

Reactions to aggression or stress
___ Reacts with counteraggression ___with flight ___with freezing
___ Once upset, emotional makeup is affected for some time
___ Seeks revenge
___ Learning demands (stress) cause the same response patterns as aggression
___ Will actively aggress toward peers ___staff ___strangers
Comments: _____

Expressive and receptive language abilities
___ Understands prepositions of position (on, under, in front of, behind, beside, etc.)
___ Follows simple instructional commands (look at me, sit down, stand up)
___ Can chain up to three verbal instructions into a single action (stand up, go to the chalkboard, draw a circle).
___ Needs peer or trainer modeling to comprehend requests
___ Expresses personal wants and needs (verbally or nonverbally)
___ Unable to express needs
___ Does not respond to requests
Comments: _____

Unusual problem-solving behaviors
___ Displays unusual insights or abilities; explain: _____
___ Displays comforting behavior with upset peers
___ Displays protective behavior with certain individuals or objects
___ Will discipline or correct others inappropriate behavior
___ Will try several solutions when presented with a difficult task
___ Plans manipulative or deviant acts to achieve objects, attention, or other reinforcement
Comments: _____

Relevant reinforcers
___ Responds to social or verbal praise
___ Responds to physical/sensory stimulation (pat on back, pleasant aromas, sounds)
___ Responds to edible/primary reinforcers
___ Requires a combination of reinforcers; explain: _____

Table 7.5 (cont.)

___ Limit setting and/or discipline required for certain times or environments; explain: _____

___ Certain reinforcers are specific to certain individuals, environments, or tasks; explain: _____

___ Responds positively to certain environments ___individuals ___objects; explain: _____

Unusual motor behaviors

___ Hyperextends joints
___ Moves total body for small tasks
___ Very obviously one-sided dominance
___ Switches hands frequently
___ Tremor-like movements
___ Tongue out excessively when working
___ Crossover/overflow or other associated movements
___ Displays motor planning difficulties
___ Difficulty with spatial orientation
Comments: _____

Affective makeup

Which descriptor identifies the dominant or overall affective makeup?

_____

Which descriptors are displayed during periods of stress?

_____

Are any descriptors linked to specific events, objects, or individuals?

_____

___ Confused: Attempted task incorrectly, required assistance to complete.

___ Easily upset: Resisted prompts with any response, refused to enter activity area.

___ Hostile or aggressive: Abused self or others, hit, kicked, bit, pinched, scratched, pulled hair, pushed, took objects or turns from others, threw objects.

___ Anxious: Inappropriately verbalized or laughed, left task area frequently, made repetitive movements unrelated to task (swaying, rocking, hand flapping, etc.).

___ Nervous: Seemed pressured or giggly, covered up mistakes with silliness.

___ Distracted: Often oriented to stimuli other than task materials, must be redirected to task frequently.

___ Elated: Often smiled or laughed appropriately.

___ Shy: Hid face in hands, turned body away, required frequent assurance and coaxing.

Note. From *Therapeutic Recreation and Adapted Physical Activities for Mentally Retarded Individuals,* by M. E. Crawford and R. Mendell, 1987, Englewood Cliffs, NJ: Prentice Hall, pp. 18–21.

Recreational therapists may find few other published assessment instruments helpful. The Fox Activity Therapy Social Skills Baseline represents another approach to the checklist provided in Table 7.5. For younger children, the General Recreation Screening Tool and/or the Ohio Leisure Skills Scales are useful. Also the Comprehensive Evaluation in Recreational Therapy (CERT) and the Leisure Social/Sexual Assessment (LSSA) represent inventories helpful with clients with milder forms of ID and DD (burlingame & Blaschko, 2010). Following the assessment process, the recreational therapist must begin to consider goal setting and activity prescriptions that will facilitate development and expansion of higher quality leisure behaviors.

Environmental factors. Recent studies (e.g., Badia et al., 2012; Rosenberg, Bart, Ratzon, & Jarus, 2013; Rosenberg, Ratzon, Jarus, & Bart, 2011) have emphasized the importance of environmental factors on the leisure participation of children, youth, and adults with ID and DD. Environmental factors often serve as barriers, or facilitators, to leisure participation. In fact, Badia et al. (2012) stated, "Leisure participation among people with developmental disabilities is likely to be more affected by environmental factors than by personal factors" (p. 2061). Thus, recreational therapists need to assess individuals' physical, social, and attitudinal environments to fully understand constraints and facilitators that may influence the leisure participation of their clients with ID and DD.

Planning

Before establishing programming efforts and procedures, the recreational therapist must review assessment materials for significant information that will help in prioritizing goals and objectives. The recreational therapist ultimately must decide this given factors such as the limitations of resources, the client's skills, and programming options. General guidelines relative to human development, social science, and social theory provide clarity.

Recreational therapists often teach specific recreational and leisure skills to improve deficits in other areas such as readiness skills (e.g., tolerance to task, co-active teaching, interactional capacities). Activities such as arts and crafts may help with fine motor deficits. Readiness skills, cognitive skills, and affective skills are the most difficult to teach, maintain, and generalize to other environments or venues. These include expressive language components (spoken or signed); concepts of size, shape, color, or dimension; and appropriate expressions of courtesies, needs, and so on. The recreational therapist may proceed with teaching appropriate leisure skills and work simultaneously on many of these other areas during the activity session.

In establishing a recreational programming hierarchy, the recreational therapist must evaluate information about the client's interactional skills and habit systems with the family unit; the level of social support and available resources may advance or limit long-term goal aspirations. According to O'Connor (1983), "in its simplest sense, social support is made up of the emotional, informational, and material support provided by friends, relatives, neighbors, services providers, and others with whom one has an ongoing relationship, and to whom one can turn in times of need or crisis"(p. 187). In short, the quality of social relationships and interactions is vital to the viability of goal and treatment planning efforts by the recreational therapist. Gresham (1981) conceptualized social skill deficits along three dimensions: skill deficits, performance deficits, and self-control deficits. Given this conceptualization, social skills may be evaluated not only by rate, frequency, and duration of the responses, but also by the situational parameters in which these responses occur such as time, place, and responses of other individuals in the same situation (Foster & Ritchey, 1979). The goal and treatment plan must match the social support resources available.

The normalization principle as articulated by Wolfensberger (1980) attempts to change the perceptions or values of the perceiver and to minimize the stigma of deviancy that activates the perceiver's devaluation. In essence, normalization challenges recreational therapists to enhance the skills and the societal images of their clients. Thus, the normalization principle requires that the recreational therapist ask these central questions about their prescribed activities: Does the activity serve to maximize the developmental potential of the individual through skill development? Does the activity foster a positive societal image of the individual? Thus, attempting to facilitate appropriate spectator social behavior for a teenager who is verbally loud and spontaneous would fulfill both criteria at a hockey game, but would fail the positive image test at an opera or symphony. The social stigma factor must be considered in all goals and objectives related to inclusionary programming.

The four domains of human functioning (cognitive, physical, emotional, and social) combine in different ways and exercise varying degrees of influence across activity pursuits. Everybody has a more or less "dominant" domain to their personal leisure expression (Beard & Ragheb, 1980). Hobbies revolving around collecting, doing crosswords, and playing games of skill such as chess are dominated by the cognitive domain of expression. Similar activity groupings abound for the other domains (e.g., soap operas and trashy novels for affective; sports and exercise for physical; service clubs, social dancing, and reading clubs for social). The subjective process of deciding which domains should have programming priority (sometimes referred to as clinical reasoning) revolves around issues such as the following: Do you build on strengths or deal with weaknesses or both? Where is your best chance to support closing the gap between low quality leisure skills and age-appropriate behavior? What can the family and other social supporters, including school or workshop personnel, do to assist in the ISP? Will the client benefit most from developing skills in domains not currently dominant (improve breadth of expression), or is it better to sophisticate and improve skills already in some evidence (improve depth through quality of expression)?

Writing goals and objectives. Goals and objectives are a necessary element in planning. A goal is an expected result or condition that involves a relatively long period of time to achieve, that is specified in behavioral terms in a statement of relatively broad scope, and that provides guidance in establishing specific, short-term objectives directed toward its attainment. Objectives then specify client behaviors related to reaching goals. Objectives break down goals into manageable and observable behaviors.

Implementation

Implementation is the action part of the RT process in which successfully achieving the specified goals and objectives is the aim. The following segments provide considerations for the implementation phase.

Differentiation between high quality and low quality leisure behavior. High quality leisure behavior includes three basic criteria, all of which must be met: goal-directed recreational activity, chronologically age-appropriate activity, and appropriate use of materials or equipment in a manner consistent with the individual's level of ID. Behaviors representative of high quality leisure behavior include speaking on the telephone, looking through a magazine, taking photographs with a camera, playing cards or a board game, dancing with a partner, and preparing a snack. Low quality leisure behavior includes using materials and equipment in a manner inconsistent with their intention or design, sitting or lying passively without participating in an activity, and engaging alone in an appropriate activity that necessarily requires more than one participant.

Individualized adaptations for recreation participation and the principle of partial participation. High quality leisure behaviors for clients with ID and DD are difficult to achieve for many reasons. One of these is the concept of developmental ceiling. The four-tier classification systems regarding level of disability represent lifelong and permanent barriers to growth. The concept of developmental ceiling is related directly to intelligence capability. Intelligence, as with any other genetically determined trait (e.g., height, eye color, gender), cannot be environmentally amended. In other words, no amount of training, therapy, or environmental nurturance is going to advance an individual with profound ID to the severe level. In other words, the classification levels do not represent a continuum along which movement is possible. That does not mean that growth and learning are not possible within the level; the programming goal is always to maximize developmental potential, but eventually persons will hit the developmental ceiling, or level of functioning, that moving beyond is impossible because of genetic inheritance and/or CNS (central nervous system) injury.

One programming principle that is helpful in dealing with the reality of developmental ceiling is the principle of partial participation (Baumgart et al., 1982). Proponents of this approach believe that participation in chronologically age-appropriate activities, in inclusive settings, even at partial levels, is more advantageous than programming in segregated settings. Through partial participation, the goal of combatting stigma within the lay public is more readily realized as long as the adaptations follow realistic guidelines. Programming for partial participation is done by (a) enhancing the performance of existing skills, (b) compensating for skills that are missing and/or not likely to be acquired (developmental ceiling), and (c) using individualized adaptations such as environmental adaptation or use of alternative skills or modified rules or equipment.

The possible adaptations include (a) using/creating materials and devices (portable objects, equipment, or materials created for instructional purposes, for example, a bus pass rather than coins for fare for persons who cannot count money, nonverbal communication systems, adapted eating utensils, and visual cues to replace auditory ones), (b) using personal assistance (verbal, physical, or supervisory assistance; the selection of appropriate instructional cues, prompts, and guidance techniques and the effective delivery of reinforcers are critical components of personal assistance; examples include the use of two handed scissors in art projects, hand-over-hand guidance, giving concurrent feedback during performance [talking over the actions as they occur]), (c) adapting skill sequences (rearranging the sequence, the type, or the number of skills required by an activity makes possible or enhances partial participation; the instructor must conduct an activity and task analysis of the skill to make informed decisions regarding sequences; an example is having caregivers dress a client for swimming prior to arriving at the pool to not spend half of the time in the dressing room and thus maximize time in the water), (d) adapting rules (rules essentially consist of prescribed guidelines, procedures, or customs for engaging in activities in specified environments; examples are using a t-ball stand instead of swinging at a pitch or using a substitute runner for clients in wheelchairs who are batting), and (e) social/attitudinal adaptations (assumptions, judgments, beliefs, and so on; changes are necessary many times, regarding not only the client's view of the modified activity but also the lay public's attitude toward special considerations or adaptations).

Using individualized adaptations to achieve partial participation may be an effective programming strategy in normalizing leisure behavior. However, the techniques warrant careful consideration before implementing. Adaptations should be used that allow and enhance participation in environment and activities most critical to the quality of life of the client. Clients should not be allowed to become overly dependent on adaptations; over time adaptations should be reviewed for removal or alteration. Patience is important; an adaptation rarely may be judged effective or not in one trial.

Behavioral versus developmental programming. Behavior therapy rests on the premise that psychological disorders represent learned behavior. Thus, the principles of learning may be applied to the modification of these disorders. The recreational therapist applies learning principles in the treatment of psychological disorders that roughly may be classified into two major groupings: deficient behavior and maladaptive behavior. In the former, the client has failed to learn adaptive responses, and the therapeutic task is to teach these responses. In the latter, the client makes responses that are inappropriate to the circumstances and must be taught to modify these responses and to make his or her behavior more adaptive to the demands of the environment. In either case, treatment involves learning, unlearning, and relearning; this corrective action has come to be referred to as behavior therapy (Kennedy & Itkonen, 1993).

Leisure skills training programs often use behavior therapy precision teaching techniques such as prompting, reinforcement contingencies, and shaping (Austin, 2013) to promote the acquisition of recreation skills in specific goal areas. Goal areas are broken down into objectives and steps. Each objective and step should be further broken down via task analysis, forward or backward chained to represent the teaching strategy (Crawford & Mendell, 1987).

Not all maladaptive behaviors, particularly self-stimulatory in nature, are candidates for behavior therapy per se, but rather they are symptoms of further DDs. Many times a perceptual motor or sensory deficit sets up a tension or drive within the individual that seeks release. Many of these comorbidities exert a continuing and considerable influence upon interactional skills as they have become an integral component of the individual's personality and habit system (Smith & Sanderson, 1966).

Task analysis. The learning of a complex skill takes time and practice. Not all of the important elements may be worked on simultaneously; in fact, many build upon one another. The recreational therapist uses the task analysis to break down the whole, or gestalt, of the skill into separate parts. The parts are then introduced, usually in a meaningful sequence, and eventually all the parts are "married together" to produce the total skill.

For example, this type of activity is used to teach YMCA and Red Cross learn-to-swim programs. The skill of swimming the front crawl is a complex movement, requiring attention to body and head position, hand position, breathing rhythm, and coordination of upper and lower extremities in patterns of contralateral flexion and extensions. No one can just watch someone do it and then jump in the pool and perform it. Over time, teachers have perfected a task analysis of the front crawl that involves breaking down the skill of swimming into parts. Thus, children are taught to breathe independent of movement, taught to flutter kick without using their arms with a kickboard, taught proper hand and movement on the deck of the pool, and so forth. Once all of the parts are perfected, the instructor begins to chain them together in different combinations (e.g., kicking on a kickboard and adding in rhythmic breathing) until finally the total skill of swimming is produced and perfected.

Task analysis has been validated over the years in many arenas including special education, vocational education, independent living skills, and leisure education curricula for persons with ID and DD (Dunlap, 1994). The "science" of task analysis is the skill and precision a person is able to employ in developing step-by-step objectives; the "art" of task analysis is deciding how to divide a total skill into sub-wholes, what order in which to present sub-wholes, and when and how to begin to "marry" sub-wholes together to attempt to develop the complete skill. No hard and fast rules exist for this process of teaching as each client will present different abilities, needs, and challenges.

Activity analysis. Activity analysis is the procedure for breaking down and examining an activity to find inherent characteristics (physical, cognitive, affective, and social) that contribute to program objectives (Austin, 2013). The most common application of activity analysis in RT is basic categorizing and ranking of activity participation requirements. This process requires a two-level determination on the part of the recreational therapist. The recreational therapist first decides which domains of functioning make up the majority of participation/performance demands for a particular activity and then determines whether the difficulty level within that domain is appropriate for the client's skills and level of functioning. Thus, if client John Doe has an identified need to improve his recreational skills within the social domain (based on a small social circle identified during assessment), the recreational therapist will first use activity analysis to compile potential social activities in which John can participate. After assembling these activities, the recreational therapist ranks them by level of difficulty so that a sense of clinical progression may be plotted long term. This process may seem elementary; in fact, some detractors of activity analysis have argued that master teachers and experienced clinicians go through this process so automatically and intuitively that to require its documentation on a formal basis is unnecessary. It is certainly true that any skill with proper practice becomes "second nature." But persons, even master clinicians, can and do make mistakes, so documenting intended activity progressions is important an quality control measure.

Environmental analysis. The context of learning and performing the activity may be as critical to success as selection of the activity. Environmental choices include indoor spaces, outdoor areas, custom facilities (e.g., pools, ropes courses, bowling alleys), and private or social spaces (e.g., dining rooms, restaurants, clubs). The recreational therapist also must decide on providing for segregated or integrated opportunities for practice and performance in conjunction with the LRE doctrine and principle of partial participation. In addition, social coding of the activity is important. Will the client work on solitary skills, dual or paired activity, or group settings?

Failure to consider the social and environmental context of performance has resulted in many behavior tantrums and/or unhappy outcomes (e.g., clients running down bowling lanes or being asked to leave a movie for excessive talking). All persons may be intimidated by large groups, new environments, or anything that causes them to react emotionally (excessive noises or auditory overstimulation such as video arcades) because they focus the clients' concentration and render them unavailable for learning. Clients cannot relax and learn when they are emotionally preoccupied.

Environmental analysis inventories provide the recreational therapist with a systematic approach to analyze the leisure context and thus facilitate involvement (Certo, Schleien, & Hunter, 1983). Use of the inventory helps to plan strategies to heighten public awareness and increases the probability of positive inclusive experiences (Schleien, Ray, & Green, 1997). To be most effective, the recreational therapist should conduct a preprogramming site visit not only to assess the configural complexity of the environment (level of visual and auditory distractions), entry/exit and traffic patterns for clients, location of restrooms, refreshments, and so forth, but also to begin the education and sensitizing process with facility managers and staff regarding the RT programming process. A comprehensive community referenced facility inventory may be found in the text by Crawford and Mendell (1987).

Evaluation

An individualized evaluation strategy is essential given the range and complexity of the ID and DD population. Observational strategies (e.g., counting behaviors, number of objectives and goals completed) are among the most reliable methods of evaluation as long as interrater agreement or reliability of tallies is good (Pelegrino, 1979). Some of the same parent/caregiver rating scales discussed in the assessment section of this chapter also may be employed in a pretest–posttest application manner to measure increases in quality of behaviors, growth in diversity of interests, and breadth of engagement opportunities (Crawford & Gray, 2012). A program heavy in behavioral techniques, according to Dattilo (1986), may find that single-subject research designs (e.g., baseline, modification, reversal, remodification) are the most viable method for making summary judgments about the quality of the RT program as it affects the behavioral dynamics of clients.

The validity of social skills instruction ultimately lies in the measurement of the quality and quantity of the client's social network. Measuring changes in the client's social opportunities may be accomplished in several ways. One is for parents/caregivers to keep behavioral diaries of social contacts (e.g., friends coming to the house, invitations to attend parties, go places). Another is to use a pre- and post-friendship circles model (McAfee, 2002) that allows for not only a frequency count of the number of persons involved in the clients life, but also a measure of the importance or the level of intimacy involved (e.g., acquaintance, activity buddy, best friend). Six-month or annual plots with this model provide an important real-world measure of the impact of the social skills training program. Behavioral diaries and the friendship circles model have been proven valid and reliable for clients with ID and DD (Crawford & Gray, 2012).

The process of collecting and analyzing information about clients and program interventions is a critical task for the recreational therapist. If interventions cannot be reliably validated, practice standards, which are the foundation for billable fee-for-service status, will be impossible to develop. If RT is to achieve equal status with occupational therapy and physical therapy and other therapies, or ever achieve direct service status in educational and clinical settings, it must be accomplished through valid scientific evaluation of interventions.

APPLICATION OF THE RECREATIONAL THERAPY PROCESS: CASE STUDY

Greg is a 25-year-old male with severe ID and DD with a number of severely limiting comorbidities. He has semi-lobar holoprosencephaly causing spastic quadriplegic cerebral palsy (CP). He is nonverbal and uses a wheelchair. Medical concerns and precautions include a spinal cord shunt, spinal fusion rods, and an ITP pump for nutrition. Contraindicated postures include no rotation of shoulders and hips in opposite directions (due to placement and length of spinal rods), no prone postures, and when in supine position, he must have his head side turned due to floppy airway syndrome. His allergies include latex and dairy products. Current medications include Zyrtec, Flonase nasal spray, Restasis eye drops, and Optive eye drops. He has a history of seizures, but he has been seizure free for the last 5 years. He can receive nutrition via G-button only as his swallowing muscles are so constricted that he has aspiration difficulties. In short, Greg is one of the most medically fragile clients under care at the university-based habilitation center. On the AAIDD severity code classification scale, he is diagnosed as pervasive support; he is what is commonly referred to as a full assist client, meaning all transfers and lifts are accomplished with a two-person team and all dressing and toileting procedures are accomplished on a gurney.

Assessment

Greg lives at home with his parents, who list his preferred activities as swimming, attending live shows and sporting events, being around other persons, and going to movies. Greg's CP is so severe that he is unable to control his extremities and has no fine motor control in his hands. Greg does not enjoy things that are "loud" as they trigger his already heightened startle reflex. His parents provide him with ear plugs in his chair backpack. He does not enjoy "scary" movies as they give him nightmares.

Greg's expressive communication is limited to eye blinks (one for yes, two for no) a gurgling noise he makes in his throat when he is "happy" or pleased with something, and a frown face (lips tightly pursed, eye brows scrunched) when he is upset or wishes to stop doing something. His receptive vocabulary is limited to about 30 survival words (e.g., toilet, bed, chair, noise); he can answer simple yes–no questions around these concepts (e.g., Greg, do you want out of your chair now?).

Although Greg enjoys being around people and the stimulation they provide, his social circle of friends is limited to his parents, grandparents, and a cousin who lives nearby. Because of the severity of his disabilities, Greg requires constant and close levels of personal support. Expansion of his social circle and more active opportunities in the community (most of his activities are passive spectating) are the primary long-term goals. A secondary quality of life goal is to develop programming that will help him spend more time out of his chair and help combat the formation of pressure sores on his skin.

Planning

Greg and his parents were enrolled in the adapted biking program at the center. This program is designed to help clients who will never be able to be independent riders because of the severity of their conditions to enjoy the freedom and experience of tour biking. Using the principle of partial participation, this program exclusively employs tandem bikes and a riding team consisting of one nondisabled rider and one rider with a disability. Multiple styles of bikes are used. Some are side-by-side tandems and others are front/back; the design of the frames include trike, reverse trike, and quad wheel configurations. Some frames allow for rider participation in steering, pedaling, and braking, and others are designed for a passive rider. Because of the severity of Greg's CP and his inability to use his legs and arms, the Duet wheelchair bike (a reverse trike design with a wheelchair front end) was the best choice. Both of his parents took training as co-riders.

Greg was also enrolled in a year-round medical swim program at the center's therapy pool. Greg does not enjoy YMCA or city park and recreation pools because of how cold the water is and his inability to move to stay warm. The 93°F warmth of the therapy pool allows Greg to extend his swimming time to over 1 hour (instead of minutes) and further the goals of time spent out of his chair.

Greg was also enrolled in a weekly adult "Friendship Club" at the center. The club curriculum of social dancing, music, arts and crafts, and movies provides Greg expanded social time with peers. Because this program is staffed one-to-one with volunteers and activity technicians, Greg is able to get the close and constant level of personal support he needs and still be away from home and his parents.

Implementation

Greg attended all of the seasonal Wheel Club rides (eight sessions in the spring, eight in the fall). The club rotated community trail rides across four parks and trail systems, adding diversity to the scenery and social opportunities of the rides. It was necessary to improvise several pillows and rolled up towel bolsters to provide Greg comfort on the bike once he was out of his custom wheelchair insert. Greg always answered "yes" when asked if he liked the rides and was heard to make his throat gurgling sound during the rides, indicating his enjoyment. His parents' low fitness levels impacted his time on the bike with them. When the RT staff were used as co-riders, Greg was always given a choice on who his new riding partner would be. Greg chose female riding partners 90% of the time.

Greg attended all but two medical swim programs during the calendar year (38 total sessions). He did not enjoy transfers and lifts being done by staff instead of his parents early on (as indicated by his facial expressions). However, after a dozen sessions, the stress in his face all but disappeared. The staff theorized that he may have been afraid of being dropped or hurt by people unfamiliar to him and that once a trust factor was established, he relaxed his guard.

Greg's attendance at the weekly evening social club was perfect. He did not enjoy the social dancing curriculum at first, but once his ear plugs were in place (Session 3) his facial mask relaxed. He enjoyed being given a choice of female dance partners to "wheel his chair" and showed a particular preference for partners with long hair (85% of the time).

Evaluation

Greg's parents enjoyed having a community inclusion option that had a more active element. They were so impressed with the Wheel Club and the Duet bike that they purchased their own so Greg could ride with them in his own neighborhood (a $5,800 purchase). They also befriended several of the activity technicians involved with the Wheel Club and invited them to come to their home as respite care providers so that they could have an occasional evening out. This is a big step for his parents, who have always been extremely overprotective of Greg and have never allowed anyone but nurses to provide respite in the past (an expensive option).

The medical swim program had a positive impact on the quality of Greg's skin as noted by his physician during his annual physical. His parents are now considering the purchase of a hot tub for their home so they can float Greg daily and give him comfortable time out of his chair. Even though the medical swim and social club programs are based at the center, they provide important additional sources of social stimulation and support for Greg, along with curriculum areas that provide a quality of life diversity. His parents and grandparents continue to take him on community outings to inclusive settings, but the peer stimulation and the attention from activity technicians (who are basically his same age and also peers) have provided Greg with activity buddies, which has increased his social circle of friends by 500%. In Greg's example, the least restrictive environments (that supports his growth and development in a meaningful way) are, in several instances, segregated settings with high levels of close personal support, adapted equipment, and modified curriculum.

TRENDS AND ISSUES

Inclusive Programs

Participation in inclusive settings prepares persons with ID and DD to be as independent as possible. It also encourages society to accept individual differences and coparticipate. The recreational therapist, however, is responsible for carefully considering the interactional capacities of clients and how that matches the environmental demands of the setting. When a less than artful match is made, and when clients negatively impact the quality of the leisure experience for the lay public, instead of social support there is social backlash (Crawford, 1986a). Too many instances still occur where concerts, anniversary dinners, movies, and so forth are interrupted or "spoiled" by too large, too loud, or too conspicuous a field trip grouping. The normalization movement is still an active social movement only now entering second generation services; it is important to further that movement by not displaying clients in negative light.

Clients Reside in the Community

For the first time in history of the United States, large numbers of aging and elderly ID and DD clients are living in the community. Many are still with their parents, who are reluctant to place them in group homes or other residential services over quality of care concerns. Because of this, caregiver burnout has become a real phenomenon and potential danger to the older population of persons with ID and DD. Every parent expects to change diapers for the first few years of life, but when parents have been changing diapers for 25, 30, or more years, the stage is more than set for emotional duress. Similarly, most parents look forward to one day being "empty nesters," having time to be a couple again with intimacy, with children being at a distance. This is one of many normal patterns or rhythms of life that are either disrupted or blocked by extended parenting. The research on caregiver burnout is clear (Hodges & Luken, 2000). These families have higher incidences of divorce, mental health problems, drug and alcohol abuse, and domestic violence than families without children with disabilities. Children with a disability are hit more frequently and harder than typically developing children; they push more emotional "buttons" and with higher frequency. The lack of societal supports for families raising children and adults with ID and DD is a primary concern going forward for the normalization movement. RT programs may provide not only meaningful skill development and participation opportunities for clients, but also much needed respite functions for caregivers.

Similarly, adult transition programs must expand their focus from exclusive focus on vocational and/or day care placement and deal with the extreme shrinkage in social circles once a client reaches age 21 and is no longer eligible for public education services. Many adults with ID and DD become socially isolated upon public school graduation. Their opportunities for attending school extracurricular functions disappear and their social calendar shrinks. Their casual acquaintanceships with school personnel (e.g., teachers, lunchroom workers, custodians, bus drivers) and the social stimulation of large groups of typically developing peers virtually disappear. With social isolation comes long periods of idle time and the potential for depression to develop. RT services that focus on social participation are sorely needed in group homes, communities, and adult day care settings. According to NCTRC (2005), less than 10% of the national workforce serve persons with ID and DD. A greater emphasis on this population as a career destination inside university curriculums and a greater lobbying effort for RT services by advocacy groups and professional organizations should be given high priority.

Recreational Therapists in the Schools

No sound reason exists for recreational therapists to abdicate leisure education and social skills instruction in the public schools to psychologists, speech therapists, or special educators, and they should not consider behaviorism to be the only applicable tool for schools to consider for social skills training. Recreational therapists are uniquely qualified to coordinate the long-term delivery of social skills and expansion of social networks for students with ID and DD (Crawford & Gray, 2012). To make a significant difference in the public school settings, educating parents regarding their right to call for RT services in the individualized education plan (IEP) must become a national priority. RT as a profession does not have the national lobby power yet to change the law and make RT a direct (required) service. But RT is already written into the law; a focused, long-term national campaign to educate and arm parents with the knowledge to force the issue inside of IEP meetings is needed. Many parents are reluctant to become confrontational with school administrators over services; they fear that "rocking the boat" may have an adverse effect on their child. These parents need professional "partners" willing to stand with them in the due process hearings when they petition for the services their children need.

Use of Technology

Tanis et al. (2012) wrote, "Advancements of technology in the areas of mobility, hearing and vision, communication, and daily living for people with intellectual and developmental disabilities has the potential to greatly enhance independence and self-determination" (p. 53). Survey research by Tanis et al. has indicated progress made in the uses of technology by persons with ID and DD during the past decade. These researchers noted, "It is particularly promising that computer use has increased substantially during this time and that people with intellectual and developmental disabilities are using new electronic and information technologies, such as cell phones" (p. 65).

Studies conducted thus far on the uses of technology with persons with ID and DD are encouraging. For example, virtual reality technologies have been found to broaden the behavioral repertoires of young adults with ID and physical disabilities (Yalon-Chamovitz & Weiss, 2007). Video modeling procedures were found to be effective in teaching students with DD to use a portable multimedia device (Kagohara et al., 2011). The employment of Photovoice technology was successful in allowing individuals with ID and DD to document their lives and reveal their interests, hopes, and dreams (Schleien, Brake, Miller, & Walton, 2013). Additionally, Snoezelen rooms have been successfully used with persons with DD so they may have novel, stimulating, relaxing, and enjoyable experiences (Patterson, 2004).

SUMMARY

This chapter discussed *developmental disability* as an umbrella term encompassing ID and many other conditions. The complexity of ID and DD with over 200 causes, four major levels, and an unending combination of comorbidities and associated disorders means that individualized approaches to RT are necessary. With over 1 in 6 children falling under the ID and DD category, service is a national priority.

The overall history of care and treatment in the United States, prior to the normalization movement of the 1960s, included mass institutionalization, brutal treatment, and the formation of multiple negative social stereotypes, many of which remain in the lay public today. RT may combat social stigma by providing services at three levels: treatment, leisure education, and recreation participation. The service settings in which RT is involved range from highly specialized services in private and state institutions for dual-diagnosed populations along with programs in public schools, community group homes, medical habilitation centers, and adult day care settings.

Using the normalization principle of providing as normal rhythm of life as possible, the recreational therapist assesses the client's function for high quality, low quality, and inappropriate behaviors through several techniques. Program implementation follows the principle of LRE to devise the best approach to maximizing the developmental potential of the individual. Because of the phenomenon of the developmental ceiling, recreational therapists may have to practice the principle of partial participation and use individualized adaptation strategies to facilitate inclusion. Decisions about behavior therapy versus developmental therapy interventions may be complicated and often require input from other disciplines. The tools of activity analysis, task analysis, and environmental analysis are part of an effective precision teaching approach to ensure program success.

Finally, education of parents and advocacy by the profession is needed in a number of areas. Providing inclusive services with dignity is important to the overall social change movement of normalization. So too is expansion of respite care programs to combat caregiver burnout. An expanded focus for adult transition and school-based services must include RT. With only 2% of all recreational therapists nationally working in the public schools, and with less than 10% working in the ID and DD field (NCTRC, 2005), the profession has a long way to go in providing the number of therapists and the variety of services needed to satisfactorily serve such a highly prevalent group of disabilities.

READING COMPREHENSION QUESTIONS

1. What are the differences between ID and DD?
2. What are the four levels of ID?
3. What are the four levels of social support for DD?
4. What conditions may cause ID and DD?
5. Name comorbidities that may accompany ID and DD.
6. Define the following terms: least restrictive environment, normalization, partial participation.
7. What are the three categories of RT programming?
8. How is task analysis different from activity analysis?
9. What are some of the elements of environmental analysis?
10. How does behavior therapy differ from developmental therapy?
11. Give an example of each of the following: high quality leisure behavior, low quality leisure behavior, inappropriate behavior.
12. How may a behavioral diary be used to evaluate the effectiveness of social skills training?

REFERENCES

American Psychiatric Association. (2013). *Diagnostic and statistical manual of mental disorders* (5th ed.). Arlington, VA: Author.

Austin, D. R. (2013). *Therapeutic recreation processes and techniques: Evidence-based recreational therapy* (7th ed.). Urbana, IL: Sagamore.

Badia, M., Orgaz, M. B., Verdugo, M. A., & Ullan, A. M. (2012). Patterns and determinants of leisure participation of youth and adults with developmental disabilities. *Journal of Intellectual Disability Research, 32*(6), 2055–2063.

Baumgart, D., Brown, L., Pumpian, I., Nishet, J., Ford, A., Sweet, M., . . . Schroeder, J. (1982). Principle of partial participation and individualized adaptations in educational programs for severely handicapped students. *TASH Journal, 7*, 17–27.

Beard, J. G., & Ragheb, M. G. (1980). Leisure satisfaction: Concept, theory, and measurement. In S. Iso-Ahola (Ed.), *Social psychological perspectives of leisure and recreation* (pp. 329–353). Springfield, IL: C. C. Thomas.

burlingame, J., & Blaschko, T. M. (2010). *Assessment tools for recreational therapy and related fields* (4th ed.). Ravensdale, WA: Idyll Arbor.

Centers for Disease Control and Prevention. (2011). *Prevalence for developmental disability fact sheet* (ID4740551). Atlanta, GA: Author.

Certo, N. J., Schleiein, S. J., & Hunter, D. (1983). An ecological assessment inventory to facilitate community recreation participation by severely disabled individuals. *Therapeutic Recreation Journal, 17*(3), 29–38.

Chelly, J., Khelfaoui, M., & Francis, F. (2006). Genetics and pathophysiology of mental retardation. *European Journal of Human Genetics, 14*, 701–709.

Crawford, M. (1986a). Development and generalization of lifetime leisure skills for multi-handicapped participants. *Therapeutic Recreation Journal, 20*(4), 48–60.

Crawford, M. (1986b). Social validation of an integrated camping program for mentally retarded adolescents. *Expanding Horizons in Therapeutic Recreation, 11*, 26–34.

Crawford, M., & Gray, C. (2012). Design and delivery of a public school social skills training program for youth with autism spectrum disorders: A five year retrospective of the school/community/home (SCH) model of social skills development. *Annual in Therapeutic Recreation, 20*, 17–35.

Crawford, M., & Mendell, R. (1987). *Therapeutic recreation and adapted physical activities for mentally retarded individuals.* Englewood Cliffs, NJ: Prentice Hall.

Cuvo, A., Ellis, P., Wisotek, I., Davis, P., Schilling, D., & Bechtal, R. (1983). Teaching athletic skills to students who are mentally retarded. *TASH Journal, 8*, 72–81.

Dattilo, J. (1986). Single-subject research in therapeutic recreation: Implications to individuals with limitations. *Therapeutic Recreation Journal, 20*(2), 76–87.

Dattilo, J., & Guerin, N. (2001). Mental retardation. In D. R. Austin & M. E. Crawford (Eds.), *Therapeutic recreation: An introduction* (3rd ed., pp. 130–156). Boston, MA: Allyn & Bacon.

Dattilo, J., & Williams, R. (2011). Leisure education. In J. Dattilo & A. McKenney (Eds.), *Facilitation techniques in therapeutic recreation* (2nd ed., pp. 187–220). State College, PA: Venture.

Dunlap, G. (1994). The influence of task-variation and maintenance tasks on the learning and affect of mentally retarded children. *Journal of Experimental Child Psychology, 47*, 41–47.

Evans-Rogers, D. (1953). *Angel unaware.* Old Tappan, NJ: Fleming-Revell.

Faw, G. D., Davis, P. K., & Peck, C. (1996). Increasing self-determination: Teaching people with mental retardation to evaluate residential options. *Journal of Applied Behavior Analysis, 29*(2), 173–188.

Foster, S. H., & Ritchey, W. L. (1979). Issues in the assessment of social competence in children. *Journal of Applied Behavior Analysis, 12*, 625–638.

Giangreco, M. F. (1983). Teaching basic photography skills to a severely handicapped young adult using simulated materials. *Journal of the Association for the Severely Handicapped, 8*(1), 43–49.

Gresham, F. M. (1981). Social skills training with handicapped children: A review. *Review of Educational Research, 51*(1), 139–176.

Harris, J. C. (2006). *Intellectual disability: Understanding its development, causes, classification, evaluation, and treatment* (pp. 28–42). New York, NY: Oxford University Press.

Hodges, J. S., & Luken, K. J. (2000). Services and supports as a means to meaningful outcomes for persons with developmental disabilities. *Annual in Therapeutic Recreation, 9*, 47–56.

Howe-Murphy, R., & Charboneau, B. G. (1987). *Therapeutic recreation intervention: An ecological perspective.* Englewood Cliffs, NJ: Prentice Hall.

Kagohara, D. M., Sigafoos, J., Achmadi, D., van der Meer, L., O'Rielly, M. F., & Lancioni, G. E. (2011). Teaching students with developmental disabilities to operate an iPod Touch to listen to music. *Research in Developmental Disabilities, 32*, 2987–2992.

Kennedy, C. H., & Itkonen, T. (1993). Effects of setting events on the problem behavior of students with severe disabilities. *Journal of Applied Behavior Analysis, 24*(2), 321–327.

King, M., Shields, N., Imms, C., Black, M., & Ardern, C. (2013). Participation of children with intellectual disability compared with typically developing children. *Research in Developmental Disabilities, 34*, 1854–1862.

Lott, I. T., & Dierssen, M. (2010). Cognitive deficits and associated neurological complications in individuals with developmental delay. *Lancet Neruology, 9*, 623–626.

McAfee, J. (2002). *Navigating the social world: A curriculum guide for individuals with Asperger's syndrome, high functioning autism and related disorders.* Arlington, TX: Future Horizons.

McCatchie, A. (1973). Parental guide to the auditory training in the deaf-blind child: Not so much a program—more an attitude. In W. Bea (Ed.), *Proceedings of the Southwestern Region Deaf-Blind Workshop.* Houston: University of Texas Press.

McKinney, J. P. (1972). A multidimensional study of the behavior of severely retarded boys. *Child Development, 33*, 923–938.

Met-Life Mature Market Institute. (2010). *Market survey of adult day services and home care costs.* Retrieved from https://www.metlife.com/mmi/index.html

Mundy, J. (1998). *Leisure education: Theory and practice* (2nd ed.). Champaign, IL: Sagamore.

National Adult Day Services Association. (1995). *Your guide to selecting an adult day services center.* Washington, DC: Author.

National Adult Day Services Association. (1997). *Standards and guidelines for adult day services.* Washington, DC: Author.

National Council for Therapeutic Recreation Certification. (2005, July). *Career center link: Newsletter employment update.* Retrieved from http://www.NCTRC.org

National Recreation and Park Association. (2012). *Parks and recreation operating ratio and gis system (proragis): Special populations services report.* Ashburn, VA: Author.

National Therapeutic Recreation Society. (1982). *Philosophical position statement of the National Therapeutic Recreation Society.* Alexandria, VA: National Recreation and Park Association.

O'Connor, G. (1983). Presidential address 1983: Social support of mentally retarded persons. *Mental Retardation, 21*(5), 187–196.

Palmer, S. B., & Wehmeyer, M. L. (1998). Students' expectations of the future: Hopelessness as a barrier to self-determination. *Mental Retardation, 36*(2), 128–136.

Patterson, I. (2001). Serious leisure as a positive contributor to social inclusion for people with intellectual disabilities. *World Leisure, 3*, 16–24.

Patterson, I. (2004). Snoezelen as a casual leisure activity for people with a developmental disability. *Therapeutic Recreation Journal, 38*(3), 289–300.

Patterson, I., & Pegg, S. (2009). Serious leisure and people with intellectual disabilities: Benefits and opportunities. *Leisure Studies, 28*(4), 387–402.

Pelegrino, D. A. (1979). *Research methods for recreation and leisure: A theoretical and practical guide.* Dubuque, IA: Brown.

Peterson, C. A. (1981). *Leisure lifestyle and disabled individuals.* Presentation at the Horizons West Symposium on Therapeutic Recreation, San Francisco, CA.

Rosenberg, L., Bart, O., Ratzon, N. Z., & Jarus, T. (2013). Personal and environmental factors predict participation of children with and without mild developmental disabilities. *Journal of Child and Family Studies, 22*, 656–671.

Rosenberg, L., Ratzon, N. Z., Jarus, T., & Bart, O. (2011). Perceived environmental restrictions for the participation of children with mild developmental disabilities. *Child: Care, Health and Development, 38*(6), 836–843.

Schleien, S. J., Brake, L., Miller, K. D., & Walton, G. (2013). Using Photovoice to listen to adults with intellectual disabilities on being part of the community. *Annals of Leisure Research, 16*(3), 212–229.

Schleien, S. J., Ray, M. T., & Green, F. P. (1997). *Community recreation and persons with disabilities: Strategies for integration* (2nd ed.). Baltimore, MD: Brookes.

Schleien, S. J., Tuckner, B., & Heyne, L. (1985). Leisure education programs for the severely disabled student. *Parks and Recreation, 20*, 74–78.

Schleien, S. J., Wehman, P., & Kiernan, J. (1981). Teaching leisure skills to severely handicapped adults: An age-appropriate darts game. *Education and Training of the Mentally Retarded, 16*, 13–19.

Schalock, R. L., Borthwick-Duffy, S., Bradley, B. J., Wil, H. E., Buntnix, D. L., Coulter, E. M., . . . Yeager, M. H. (2010). *Intellectual disability: Definition, classification, and systems of supports* (11th ed.). Washington, DC: American Association on Intellectual and Developmental Disabilities.

Sedlak, R., Doyle, M., & Schloss, P. (1982). Video games: A training and generalization demonstration with severely retarded adolescents. *Education and Training of the Mentally Retarded, 17*, 332–336.

Sherrill, C. (1993). *Adapted physical activity, recreation, and sport* (4th ed.). Madison, WI: WCB Brown & Benchmark.

Smith, R. E., & Sanderson, R. E. (1966). Relationship of habit training to measured intelligence in severely retarded patients. *California Mental Health Research Digest, 4*, 154–155.

Solish, A., Perry, A., & Minnes, P. (2010). Participation of children with and without disabilities in social, recreational and leisure activities. *Journal of Applied Research in Intellectual Disabilities, 23*, 226–236.

Stainback, S., Stainback, W., Wehman, P., & Spangiers, L. (1983). Acquisition and generalization of physical fitness exercises in three profoundly retarded adults. *TASH Journal, 8*, 46–55.

Stein, M. T., & Lukasik, M. K. (2009). Developmental screening and assessment: Infants, toddlers, and preschoolers. In M. D. Levine, W. B. Carey, & A. C. Crocker (Eds.), *Developmental-behavioral pediatrics* (3rd ed., pp. 785–799). Philadelphia, PA: Saunders Elsevier.

Stumbo, N. J., & Peterson, C. A. (2009). *Therapeutic recreation program design: Principles and procedures* (5th ed.). Boston, MA: Allyn & Bacon.

Tanis, E. S., Palmer, S., Wehmeyer, M., Davies, D. K., Stock, S. E., Lobb, K., & Bishop, B. (2012). Self-report computer-based survey of technology use by people with intellectual and developmental disabilities. *Intellectual and Developmental Disabilities, 50*(1), 53–68.

Tasse, M. J., Schalock, R. L., & Balboni, G. (2012). The construct of adaptive behavior: Its conceptualization, measurement, and use in the field of intellectual disability. *American Journal of Developmental Disabilities, 117,* 291–303.

Turnbull, H. R. (1990). *Free appropriate public education: Law and the education of children with disabilities.* Denver, CO: Love.

Wehman, P., Renzaglia, A., Berry, F., Schultz, R., & Karan, O. (1978). Developing a leisure skill repertoire in severely and profoundly handicapped persons. *AAESPH Review, 1978,* 163–172.

Wehman, P., & Schleien, S. J. (1992). *Leisure programs for handicapped persons: Adaptations, techniques, and curriculum* (2nd ed.). Baltimore, MD: University Park Press.

Wolfensberger, W. (1972). *Normalization: The principle of normalization in human services.* Toronto, Canada: National Institute on Mental Retardation.

Wolfensberger, W. (1980). A brief overview of the principle of normalization. In R. J. Flynn & K. E. Nitsch (Eds.), *Normalization, social integration and community services.* Baltimore, MD: University Park Press.

Yalon-Chamovitz, S., & Weiss, P. L. T. (2007). Virtual reality as a leisure activity for young adults with physical and intellectual disabilities. *Research in Developmental Disabilities, 29,* 273–287.

8

SEIZURE DISORDERS

MICHAEL E. CRAWFORD AND MARK K. JAMES

OBJECTIVES

- State a concise definition of the term seizure.
- Understand the classification of seizures.
- Understand the relationship between seizures and epilepsy.
- Recognize the side effects from anticonvulsant medications.
- Realize that most individuals with epilepsy are able to stabilize their seizures with medications and lifestyle adaptations.
- Recognize the key areas where recreational therapy services are appropriate.
- Understand the possible activity limitations for clients with epilepsy.

DEFINITION OF SEIZURE DISORDERS

The term *seizure* refers to an involuntary spasm or contraction of muscles. Seizures are a symptom of epilepsy, and epilepsy is defined as having at least two seizures. In epilepsy, the brain has an underlying tendency to produce sudden bursts of electrical energy that disrupt other brain functions. Having a single seizure does not necessarily mean a person has epilepsy. High fever, severe head injury, lack of oxygen, and other factors may affect the brain enough to cause a single seizure. Epilepsy, on the other hand, is an underlying condition that affects the delicate systems that govern how electrical energy behaves in the brain, making it susceptible to recurring seizures.

The diagnostic category of epilepsy refers to a heterogeneous group of syndromes unified by their tendency to produce repeated seizures. Epileptic seizures result from temporary chemical imbalances in the brain (as opposed to other chemical imbalances) that cause a rapid discharge of intercellular electrical activity. This electrical overload in turn produces a seizure, which may range from a mild sensory disturbance to loss of consciousness. Epilepsy, or recurrent seizures, is a symptom of disturbed brain functioning.

Prevalence estimates for epilepsy consistently have ranged from 0.5% to 1.5% of the general population (Epilepsy Foundation of America, 2012; Hauser, 1978; Juul-Jensen & Foldspang, 1983; Sander & Hart, 1999). The most recent estimate stands at 2.2 million individuals in the United States (Epilepsy Foundation of America, 2012). More than 45,000 children aged 18 and younger are diagnosed with epilepsy every year. In addition to epilepsy, several other neurological conditions (e.g., stroke) may cause seizures. Thus, the number of individuals impacted by seizure disorders is estimated at 3.9 million (Epilepsy Foundation of America, 2012). Age of onset varies widely; approximately 20% of adult cases have their first seizure before age 10. Another 30% do not experience seizures until the second decade of life. Twenty percent have their first seizure activity in their 30s, and the remainder have relatively late onset at 40 and beyond.

Many negative cultural/social stereotypes about seizure disorders are still in existence among laypersons. Despite that, many famous persons have had seizure disorders such as Alexander the Great, Julius Caesar, Vincent Van Gogh, and Alfred Nobel (Howie, 1994). The history of social acceptance is far from positive. Throughout early European and early North American history, many persons with epilepsy were thought to be "possessed" (their seizures viewed as evidence of demonic possession), and many were summarily "burned at the stake." At the turn of the century to present day, the dominant negative stereotype has been that epilepsy occurs in concert with mental illness and/or developmental intellectual disability. Thus, persons with epilepsy have been individuals to be feared and/or shunned. During the "eugenic scare" of the late 1800s and through the 1920s, many persons were institutionalized and sterilized over fear of transmission.

In addition, many states passed constitutional amendments declaring it illegal to marry a person with epilepsy (Wolfensberger, 1972). (See Wolfensberger for a full historical account of the national eugenic scare of the late 1800s. Mass roundups, brutal institutionalization, and the loss of personal and civil rights depicted care for persons with developmental disabilities, epilepsy, and other socially "deviant" subgroups during this time.) Most of these marriage laws were not removed until the 1960s (Alabama's was not repealed until 1984). Because seizures vary greatly, they may be difficult to recognize. Even in relatively modern times, individuals with epilepsy often are misdiagnosed with learning disabilities by psychologists and educators. Anecdotal accounts also exist of police officers detaining and arresting individuals with epilepsy when seizures have been mistaken as signs of psychosis or public intoxication (Siegler & Osmond, 1974). Many Hollywood science fiction and horror "B" movies of the 1950s and 1960s frequently displayed individuals with epilepsy in horrific caricatures: as villainous despoilers of young girls and similar "innocents," who were best kept locked in the attic or basement (preferably in chains) lest another uncontrollable epileptic "fit" send them into another psychotic "rage" (during which they were visually depicted as frothing and foaming at the mouth). The effect of the dark history of care and negative cultural influences has been to leave many individuals with epilepsy intimidated (or even ashamed). Public opinion regarding epilepsy has taken a long time to change, and pockets of bigotry and resistance still exist. Despite the implementation of the Americans With Disabilities Act in the early 1990s and its many guarantees for personal and civil rights, many individuals with epilepsy continue to be discriminated against vocationally and socially and remain reluctant to disclose their condition.

CLASSIFICATION OF SEIZURE DISORDERS

Of the more than 100 nonepileptic seizure disorders identified in medical literature, some are so rare that only a handful of known cases exist and some are fatal conditions with patients rarely living to adulthood (Marsch & Rao, 2002). Table 8.1

provides an abbreviated list nonepileptic seizure disorders documented in the literature.

Table 8.1
Examples of Nonepileptic Seizure Disorders

Angelman syndrome:
Characterized by unstable jerky gait, hand flapping movements, and frequent laughter/smiling. Intellectual delay and speech problems also usually associated.

Batten disease:
A rare, fatal inherited disease of the nervous system. Onset at age 5 to 10 followed by rapid neurodegeneration and severe total body convulsive seizures.

Alpers' disease:
Also called progressive infantile poliodystrophy, a progressive and degenerative disease of the central nervous system that produces intractable seizures.

Alien hand syndrome:
An unusual neurological disorder in which the patient's hands seem to take on a mind of their own.

Todd's palsy:
Temporary paralysis following seizures (may be partial or complete) that generally occur on just one side of the body.

Alexander disease:
A slowly progressing and fatal neurodegenerative disease, mostly in infants and children causing spastic seizures, intellectual delay, and macrocephaly.

Note. From *Seizures and Epilepsy: Hope Through Research*, by National Institute of Neurological Disorders and Stroke, 2014, Landover, MD: Author.

In 50% of all cases, the cause of epilepsy is idiopathic, or "unknown" (Hanscomb & Hughes, 1999, p. 10). Despite this relatively mysterious nature, parental concerns for "passing" the disorder onto their children may be comforted somewhat by the statistic that only a 6% chance for inheritance exists, even when both parents have the disorder. In the 30% of cases where etiology or cause–effect transmission is clear, 10 factors have been identified as contributory (Bleck, 1987; Sander & Hart, 1999). Seven are clearly implicated in epilepsy, or repeated-seizure syndromes, whereas three are related to episodic, or single-seizure occurrences. Table 8.2 displays these factors.

Table 8.2
Etiological Factors of Seizure Disorders

Epilepsy
1. Genetic influences
2. Birth trauma
3. Central nervous system infections
4. Head trauma
5. Tumors
6. Cerebrovascular diseases or strokes
7. Immunological disorders

Single seizures
1. Drug/alcohol withdrawal
2. Acute drug intoxication
3. Metabolic disorders

Note. Adapted from "Epilepsy," by T. P. Bleck, 1987, *Disease-a-Month, 33*, pp. 601–679; "Epilepsy and Psychiatric Disorders: Epidemiological Data," by P. Vuilleumier and P. Jallon, 1998, *Medline, 154*(4), pp. 305–317.

Recreational therapists should be able to recognize and describe the major seizure types. This knowledge is necessary for proper documentation of seizures that occur during clinical sessions and to give feedback to the appropriate medical personnel who work with the client. Although accurate clinical observations are vital to diagnosis, they do not always clearly indicate the specific disorder; several seizure types may be observed for individual disorders.

The classification of seizure types remains somewhat confusing in the United States because multiple systems remain in use. Many physicians prefer the traditional, or clinical, classification system with its emphasis on terminology such as *grand mal, petit mal, Jacksonian, jackknife,* and *psychomotor seizures.* In fact, many contemporary medical textbooks continue to publish the clinical classification system (Hermann & Jones, 2005; Sherrill, 1993). Advocates for change feel that such terms have become emotionally and negatively charged and now connote negative stereotypes. Their argument is similar to the changeover in classification terminology that has occurred for persons with developmental disabilities (terms such as *imbecile* or *moron* are no longer used even though they were once legitimate psychological IQ classifications). The World Health Organization adopted an international classification system as early as 1970 (Commission on Classification and Terminology of the International League Against Epilepsy, 1981) and has been the preferred system of the Epilepsy Foundation of America since 1995. This system classifies seizure types into partial seizures and generalized seizures. Table 8.3 presents an outline of the international classification system.

Table 8.3
Classification of Seizure Types

A. Partial seizures (begin in one specific body site)
1. Simple partial seizures (consciousness is not impaired)
2. Complex partial seizures (consciousness is impaired)
3. Partial seizure evolving into a generalized seizure

B. Generalized seizures (not confined to one body site)
1. Absence seizures
2. Myoclonic seizures
3. Clonic seizures
4. Tonic seizures
5. Tonic-clonic seizures
6. Atonic seizures
7. Akinetic
8. Infantile spasms

C. Unilateral seizures

D. Unclassified seizures

Note. Adapted from "Proposal for Revised Clinical and Electroencephalographic Classification of Epileptic Seizures," by Commission on Classification and Terminology of the International League Against Epilepsy, 1981, *Epilepsia, 22*, pp. 489–501. Amended according to *Adapted Physical Activity, Recreation, and Sport* (4th ed.), by C. Sherrill, 1993, Dubuque, IA: Brown.

Partial seizures begin in one specific body site and may involve loss of consciousness. If consciousness is not impaired, the term *simple partial* is used. If consciousness is impaired, the seizure is referred to as *complex partial*. A complex partial seizure is the most common type in adults with epilepsy. Under the old clinical classification system, simple partial seizures were referred to as Jacksonian seizures and complex partial seizures as psychomotor, or temporal lobe epilepsy. Simple partial seizures tend to be one sided (involving just one hemisphere of the central nervous system, CNS) and frequently involve simple tremoring of the fingers, hand, and arm. By contrast, the complex partial seizures may produce the specific motor loop behaviors in which automatic activity (which is not remembered because of unconsciousness) is carried out (e.g., sleepwalking, talking, striking, chewing, throwing behaviors). Some partial seizures begin in one body site and progress to a more global type known as a generalized seizure.

Generalized seizures do not start in one isolated body site but rather involve several sites or entire body areas such as the trunk or the extremities. Absence seizures are typified by an abrupt interruption of awareness and behavior, without any loss of muscle tone. Clients with these seizures display slight eye blinking, mouth twitching, and hand movements, which generally last 5 to 30 seconds. Under the old clinical classification system, these seizures were referred to as petit mal. This form of epilepsy frequently has caused individuals to be misdiagnosed with learning disabilities. Since these seizures may occur hundreds of times per day in some individuals, it is easy to see how many of them have difficulty keeping up academically.

The five other subgroups of generalized seizures are differentiated by the display of tonic and clonic movements (tension and relaxation of the muscles). Tonic-only and clonic-only seizures occur but are relatively rare. Somewhat more common are myoclonic seizures (extreme contraction and flexion of muscles). The muscle activity during the seizure is generally violent (often manifested as a sudden head jerk and/or strong dramatic contraction of arm and leg muscles). Atonic seizures affect postural control of the trunk and head and are characterized by a sudden partial collapse or sagging of the affected body part; as with absence seizures, atonic seizures are accompanied by momentary CNS blackout. Akinetic seizures used to be referred to as drop seizures or drop attacks among laypersons. The expression, "He's got a case of the drops!" was born from this rare form of epilepsy (Siegler & Osmond, 1974). The manifestation of akinetic seizures is literally drop to the ground (or down the stairs, depending on where the person happens to be) and is caused by a sudden and complete loss of muscle tone throughout the major antigravity muscle systems. Many individuals with cerebral palsy and other developmental delays have akinetic seizures as an accompanying disorder. These individuals are frequently helmeted when ambulatory to prevent injuries to the face and skull because of the high likelihood for injury that manifestation of this disorder brings. Infantile spasms (which were called jackknife seizures under the old clinical classification system) tend to occur in young children (usually before the first birthday) and in the classic form, look like a jackknife dive off a springboard, a sudden doubling of the trunk (though typically a lesser form involving arm and leg flexion and/or head flexion occurs).

Tonic-clonic seizures are referred to as grand mal under the old clinical classification system. Tonic-clonic seizures drive the majority of laypersons' perceptions and stereotypes of seizures in contemporary society. They are the majority form of the disorder and represent about 30% of all cases (the second most frequent is the absence form, which accounts for 8% to 11%). This version of epilepsy has definite stages to the course of the seizure, and many common safety publications focus on these regarding seizure management (American National Red Cross, 1994; Epilepsy Foundation of America, 2012).

One of the most misunderstood elements of the tonic-clonic seizure is the first stage, or the experience of "aura." Only about half of individuals who have this form of epilepsy are fortunate enough to experience aura, fortunate in the sense that aura is a form of an early warning mechanism regarding seizure activity. Persons experience it most frequently as a sensory perception (e.g., persons may smell an acrid scent such as burning leaves, taste a sickly sweet sensation on the tips of their tongues, or have tingling sensations in their fingers and toes), although anecdotal accounts include other manifestations including feelings/cognitions of euphoria. For persons who experience aura, it represents a brief window of time to find a relatively comfortable position and safe place to experience the rest of the seizure cycle. In the continuous contraction, or tonic phase of the seizure (remember, for some this is the first phase), the CNS blackout occurs and affected muscle systems are flooded with neurological overflow; arms and legs will stiffen, and as a result, if persons are standing, they will lose their balance and frequently fall (this should not be confused with akinetic seizures where individuals also fall, but the fall itself is caused by loss of muscle tone). Some individuals will vocalize; the "shout of rapture" described in the early 1920s was no doubt a clinician's attempt to describe/integrate the phenomenon of emotional aura and the tonic vocalization phenomenon of some patients

(Gastaut, 1970). Occasionally, individuals also will become cyanotic (turn blue due to restriction of respiratory muscles in the chest cavity), particularly if the tonic phase lasts longer than approximately 30 to 45 seconds. In response to occasional cyanosis within the tonic phase, first aid courses in the 1950s urged persons monitoring seizures to place an oral block in the person's mouth. This practice was built on the mistaken notion that persons were turning blue because they had "swallowed their tongue," something that is physiologically impossible (check your mouth; your tongue is attached to the bottom by muscle and thus impossible to swallow). The tongue, however, may fall backward, thus blocking the airway. A simple turn of the head to a side lying position will eliminate tongue block to the airway.

The next phase, the clonic phase, is characterized by arhythmical contraction and flexion of the voluntary muscle sets. This phase may last for several minutes and is the longer, or working, phase of the seizure. During the clonic phase, some individuals injure themselves by biting through their tongues or lower lips as the jaw muscles work up and down. During this phase, many would-be rescuers who were inserting oral blocks (e.g., wallets, combs, or whatever was handy) have lost parts of their fingers or suffered bad bites. Occasionally, the oral block itself causes injury (e.g., wood or plastic items splinter under the force of jaw contractions). The individual may frequently regain consciousness from the seizure with a bloody mouth and embedded particles. Some individuals lose control of their bowel and bladder sphincters during the clonic phase and soil themselves as a result. For most, the active tonic-clonic phase of the seizure cycle lasts only 1 to 5 minutes, stopping spontaneously. Infrequently, seizures will continue beyond 5 minutes. If this occurs, the client is considered to be in a state of status epilepticus. This is a serious condition, and prompt medical attention is needed to prevent residual brain damage or possible death. Evidence has suggested that permanent neuronal damage may occur after about 20 minutes of status epilepticus (Bleck, 1983). Additionally, for some individuals, the active tonic-clonic cycle is so strenuous that the adrenal gland may be triggered and heart rates may accelerate to dangerous levels (over 200 bpm have been recorded), where the likelihood of a heart attack is considerable. Due to the dual risks of permanent neurological damage and/or potentially fatal heart arrest that status epilepticus poses, observers of a tonic-clonic seizure must begin timing the seizure and call for medical assistance if the active part of the cycle exceeds 5 minutes. The final phase of the tonic-clonic seizure is the sleep, or coma, phase. Most persons regain consciousness quickly and only may need assistance in finding a restroom to collect themselves and possibly attend to personal hygiene matters. For others, the seizure is much more draining; they may be only semiconscious and need several hours of sleep to fully recover. In either case, remember that no memory of events during the working phase of the seizure will be available to the person due to unconsciousness that always accompanies tonic-clonic seizures.

In some persons, seizures may be triggered by flashing or flickering light or even by certain geometric shapes and patterns, such as stripes and checks. This is a fairly rare condition and is known as photosensitive epilepsy. Of the 1 in 200 persons with epilepsy, few (less than 5%) are photosensitive; the condition is most common in children and adolescents and becomes less frequent with age, being uncommon from the mid-20s onward. Most persons with photosensitive epilepsy will have seizures with and without this trigger; rarely do persons have seizures triggered by only flashing or flickering lights and at no other time. Photosensitive epilepsy usually responds well to treatment by standard anticonvulsant medication, commonly Eplim (sodium valproate; Hanscomb & Hughes, 1999, p. 61).

DUAL DIAGNOSIS: SEIZURE DISORDERS AND OTHER PERVASIVE CONDITIONS

In addition to the direct consequences of suffering from a seizure disorder, individuals with epilepsy are commonly considered to be at high risk for other psychological and psychiatric problems (Fenton, 1981). These dual-diagnosed clients present difficulties to their interdisciplinary treatment teams in respect to establishing treatment priorities.

Psychopathology related to epilepsy generally refers to psychosis, aggression, sexual dysfunction, affective disorders, significant personality and behavioral changes, and other problems. Research into the correlations between epilepsy and psychopathology has noted specific etiological influences: the seizures themselves, social and environmental stressors, and side effects from anticonvulsant medications (Fincham, 1986). Generally, either singly or in combination, these influences foster the greater incidence of psychopathology in clients with epilepsy.

Psychoses

Of patients with epilepsy, 20% to 30% are estimated to have psychiatric disturbances (Kobau, Gilliam, & Thurman, 2004; Vuilleumier & Jallon, 1998). The most common psychiatric conditions in epilepsy are depression, anxiety, and psychoses (Barry, Lembke, & Gisbert, 2007; Ettinger, Reed, & Cramer, 2004; Tellez-Zenteno, Patten, Jette, Williams, & Wiebe, 2007). Table 8.4 compares the prevalence rates of psychiatric disorders in patients with epilepsy to the general population.

Table 8.4

Prevalence Rates of Psychiatric Disorders for Patients With Epilepsy and the General Population

Psychiatric disorder	General population	Patients with epilepsy
Major depressive disorder	10.7%	37.4%
Anxiety disorder	11.2%	22.8%
Mood/anxiety disorder	19.6%	34.2%
Suicidal ideation	13.3%	25.0%
Others	20.7%	35.5%

Note. From "Psychiatric Comorbidity in Epilepsy: A Population-Based Analysis," by J. F. Tellez-Zenteno, S. B. Patten, N. Jette, J. Williams, and S. Wiebe, 2007, *Epilepsia, 48*(12), pp. 2336–2344.

The risk of psychosis in patients with epilepsy may be 6 to 12 times that of the general population (Torta & Keller, 1999), with half of these patients diagnosed with schizophrenia (Perez & Trimble, 2009). Physicians face a dual treatment problem with this population. Many psychotropic medications used to treat schizophrenia significantly may lower the seizure threshold and provoke epileptic seizures. Similarly, many of the anticonvulsant medicines actually worsen the psychiatric symptoms. Do you choose worsening of behavior over improvement in seizure control, or vice versa? Often, presenting individual patient variables (e.g., frequency and intensity of seizures, duration and frequency of psychotic episodes) are the deciding, albeit subjective, factors in attempting pharmacological treatment (Kanner, 2000).

Depression

Depression is the most frequent psychiatric comorbidity seen in patients with epilepsy. Depression is a mental state or chronic mental disorder characterized by feelings of sadness, loneliness, despair, low self-esteem, and self-reproach. Accompanying symptoms include loss of appetite, insomnia, and withdrawal from social contact. Despite its high prevalence in patients with epilepsy, depression often remains unrecognized and untreated (Kanner & Balabanov, 2002). Multiple reasons exist for failure to treat including patients minimizing their symptoms for fear of further stigmatization, physicians' concern that antidepressant drugs may lower seizure threshold, and certain depressive disorders present differently in patients with epilepsy than within the general population (Boylan et al., 2004).

First and foremost treatment involves seizure control with appropriate anticonvulsant therapies. Some antidepressant medications may be necessary to effectively treat depression; however, the interactional effect on seizure threshold must be monitored closely. Electroconvulsive therapy is not contraindicated and may prove more effective for patients with severe treatment resistant depressions, although some clinicians consider its application controversial (Boylan et al., 2004).

Bipolar Affective Disorders

The incidence of bipolar affective disorder in epilepsy is 1.69 cases per 1,000 persons compared with 0.07 in the general population (Ettinger, Reed, Goldberg, & Hirschfeld, 2005). Bipolar affective disorder is a chronic psychiatric disease with severe changes in mood. Because of the unpredictability of mood swings the quality of life is often suboptimal for patients with epilepsy. Increased financial stress, life stressors, and poor adjustment to lack of seizure control may contribute to extended depressive phases (Harden & Goldstein, 2002). Medical treatment for bipolar disorders occurring with epilepsy parallel those for simple depression.

Suicidal Behaviors

Suicidality (completed suicide, suicide attempt, and suicidal ideation) is significantly more frequent among persons with epilepsy than in the general population (Harden, 2002). The risk of suicide in the general population averages about 1.4%; however, the risk of suicide in patients with epilepsy is about 13% (prevalence rate ranges from 5 to 10 times that of the general population).

The incidence of suicidal phenomena linked to specific antiepileptic drugs (AEDs) has not been systematically well studied. However, in 2008 the U.S. Food and Drug Administration (FDA) issued an alert regarding the association between suicidality and AEDs, concluding that there was a statistically significant twofold increased risk. The FDA decided to insert suicide warnings in the package inserts of all AEDs; thus, physicians need to identify patients with increased risk of suicide (Ettinger, 2006).

Anxiety Disorders

Anxiety is an experience of fear or apprehension in response to anticipated internal or external danger, accompanied by muscle tension, restlessness, sympathetic hyperactivity, and/or cognitive signs and symptoms (hypervigilance, confusion, decreased concentration, or fear of losing control). Anxiety is common in patients with epilepsy. Symptoms of anxiety in epilepsy may result or be exacerbated by psychological reactions, including responses to the unpredictability of seizures and restrictions of normal activities. This results in low self-esteem, stigmatization, and social rejection (Kanner, Barry, & Gilman, 2009). Fear and anxiety often are associated with seizures. Torta and Keller (as cited in Barry et al., 2007) estimated that fear occurs as an aura in as many as 15% of patients, and other studies have concluded that fear is one of the most commonly reported lifestyle emotions (Goldstein & Harden, 2000). Seizure anxiety has a great influence on the quality of life of patients, since most of them have a permanent fear of new discharges; as many as 65% of patients with epilepsy have reported anxiety over fear of seizure recurrence (seizure phobia; Kanner et al., 2009).

Intellectual Disability and Developmental Delay

Recreational therapists who work in a long-term residential treatment center often encounter clients who have epilepsy occurring with significant development delay (approximately one third of persons with severe intellectually disabilities have some form of epilepsy); estimates for adults with cerebral palsy range from 25% to 50% (Sherrill, 1993). In some cases, a single underlying disorder exists (e.g., Lennox-Gastaut syndrome, tuberous sclerosis), and in other cases, two conditions exist. Many metabolic disorders that induce seizures respond poorly to medication and over time will result in residual brain damage. These cases are rare compared with the entire population of individuals with seizure disorders, but they are commonly seen in certain long-term treatment settings (e.g., state schools or developmental centers for the persons with developmental disabilities or chronic psychiatric and/or forensic hospitals and, to a lesser extent, what remains of the old state systems of residential care and education for the persons who are deaf and/or blind).

As many as one third of individuals with autism spectrum disorder also have epilepsy (Tellez-Zenteno et al., 2007). Experts have proposed that some of the brain abnormalities that are associated with autism may contribute to seizures. These abnormalities may cause changes in brain activity by disrupting neurons in the brain. Neurons are cells that process and transmit information and send signals to the rest of the body. So overloads or disturbances in the activity of these neurons may result in imbalances that cause seizures (Tellez-Zenteno et al., 2007).

Description of Limitations

Two key areas present long-term difficulties and challenges to clients with epilepsy: chronic side effects from anticonvulsant medications and lifestyle modifications. Not surprisingly, how clients handle these areas significantly affects the stabilization of their seizures. With careful, ongoing monitoring, most individuals achieve satisfactory freedom from seizures.

Side effects. Clients who have recurrent seizures should be treated with anticonvulsant medications. Many appropriate drugs may be used individually or in combinations (Fincham, 1986; Harden & Goldstein, 2002). Although general guidelines are available for determining which drug works best for specific seizures, working out an effective anticonvulsant treatment regimen is a complex task.

Clients must understand that anticonvulsant medications do not cure or correct epilepsy but rather offer a method of preventing future seizures. The effectiveness of these medications depends on maintaining a stable level of the drug in the blood-stream at all times, hence the need for ongoing monitoring. All anticonvulsant medications may cause side effects. Recreational therapists need to be aware of these to conduct valid assessments and outline appropriate treatment strategies. Table 8.5 identifies common side effects.

Table 8.5
Possible Anticonvulsant Medication Side Effects

Slowed mental processing	Vomiting
Ataxic muscle movements	Unsteady gait
Anemia	Tremors
Slurred speech	Emotional irritability
Drowsiness	Water retention
Fatigue	Cardiac arrhythmias
Vitamin deficiencies	Psychosis
Blurred vision	Hair loss
Depression	Weight gain
Dizziness	Nausea

Note. Adapted from "Epilepsy in Adolescents and Adults," by R. W. Fincham, 1986, in C. Canan (Ed.), *Current Therapy*, Philadelphia, PA: Saunders, and "Psychotropic Effects of Antiepileptic Drugs," by A. B. Ettinger, 2006, *Neurology, 67*(11), pp. 1916–1925.

Lifestyle modifications. Several factors have been identified that are thought to aggravate or spontaneously induce seizures, commonly referred to as triggers (Bleck, 1987; burlingame & Blaschko, 1990; Sherrill, 1993). The majority of these are related to a chemical change in the client's bloodstream. Because the client has partial control of each factor, they may monitor and stabilize them through lifestyle modifications. These factors include the following:

1. Sleep deprivation. Dramatic and rapid changes in sleep habits may hinder stabilization of seizures. Major life stressors and events are a common source of the sleep deprivation trigger.

2. Changes in blood alkalinity. Clients with uncontrolled seizures usually do better with a slightly acidic or ketogenic diet including foods such as high-fat milk, butter, eggs, and meat.

3. Changes in blood sodium levels. Heavy exercise sessions or sitting in high heat conditions, such as spectating at an August baseball game, or specific times of the menstrual cycle for women adversely may affect sodium levels and thus reduce the seizure threshold.

4. Excessive drinking of alcohol. Natural seizure thresholds dramatically may be reduced as alcohol in the bloodstream increases.

5. Avoidance of environments with rapidly oscillating visual effects such as laser light shows, disco dance floors, and rock concerts with strobe light effects. Other documented visual triggers include flickering television sets, certain video games, and looking out of car or train windows sideways at high speeds (Hanscomb & Hughes, 1999). These visual displays may overstimulate and bring CNS seizure potential to threshold. (*Note:* This last caution is particularly important for individuals whose etiology is idiopathic and where seizures remain uncontrolled by medication.)

Lifestyle modifications or limitations also refer to activities that are contraindicated for seizure-prone clients. Contraindicated activities present a health threat to the client and by extension other participants if a seizure were to occur during the activity. Activities in this category include high-risk adventure sports such as scuba diving, sky diving, hang gliding, rock climbing, and unsupervised swimming.

Some physicians take a more conservative stance and restrict involvement in sports that may result in head injuries (e.g., boxing, tackle football, ice hockey, soccer, gymnastics, rugby, lacrosse, and wrestling). Other physicians advocate a more liberal position that allows clients to participate in most activities as long as a non-seizure-prone partner is present. However, activities where delay in assistance may occur (e.g., hang gliding, scuba diving) are still contraindicated.

Many clients with epilepsy are driving restricted. Most states require at least one year of being seizure free prior to obtaining a license. Some require annual certification by an attending physician. The laws vary from state to state, however, which may complicate a client's personal freedom and mobility when moving across state lines.

SEIZURE MANAGEMENT

General first aid precautions to follow during an active seizure are discussed by Austin (1991, 2013) and Crawford (1984) and are also available from sources such as the American National Red Cross (1994) and the Epilepsy Foundation of America (2012). Recreational therapists should not be concerned with trying to stop the seizure but rather with ensuring the clients safety during the seizure and assisting with personal comfort, hygiene, and dignity following the seizure. They should observe the nature of motor movements and the duration of the seizure because this information may be useful to the medical staff regarding changes in treatment.

Important steps to follow, particularly for the tonic-clonic form, are as follows:

1. Assist the client to a comfortable and safe position. Usually a side lying or prone position is preferred. If possible, place a soft object under the head (e.g., a rolled up blanket, towel, or jacket).

2. Check that the mouth and nose are clear and that breathing is unimpaired.

3. Manage the physical environment. Remove furniture or large objects to lessen the likelihood of impact injuries and/or abrasions. If need be, gently drag the client by an appendage or shoulder girdle to an area free from contact from fixed objects such as walls, sharp corners, and handrails.

4. Time the seizure. As soon as you have the client safe and comfortable, note the time on your watch or, if need be, begin a steady count.

5. Manage the social environment. Do not allow a crowd to gather. Ask someone to take responsibility for crowd control, assuring concerned onlookers that everything is under control. The last vision persons coming out of a seizure want to see is a crowd of unfamiliar faces staring down at them.

6. Check for cyanosis. If the seizure is unabated after 2 minutes, check for bluing around the corners of the mouth, nose, or fingers. If there is evidence of bluing and/or signs of labored respiration, adjust the head and trunk position. Elevate by grasping under the armpits and use a shrugging motion several times and then make sure the head is in a side lying position and breathing is unimpaired.

7. React to status epilepticus. If the active phase of a tonic-clonic seizure lasts longer than 5 minute, call immediately for emergency medical assistance. This person is in danger of cardiac failure and/or damage to CNS neurons.

8. Offer reassurance and assistance post-active phase. Check the oral cavity for signs of bleeding on the tongue and sides of mouth or for loose teeth from clenching. Tell them what happened: "You had a brief seizure that lasted ___ minutes." Offer to assist them to a restroom (in case they lost bowel or bladder control) or help them to a quiet place to lie down, rest, and recover (many will need to sleep); remember, some persons may be in the semiconscious coma phase and need your active assistance to be safe during recovery.

Because many recreational therapists use adapted aquatics and forms of aquatic therapy within their programming, and because aquatic facilities are a major feature of private and public recreation (e.g., municipal and YMCA facilities, health clubs, hotel resorts, residential camps, and open water lakes at parks), seizure activity has a distinct likelihood of occurring in these venues. Many individuals are unnecessarily injured during seizures in aquatic settings due to poor seizure management. They are injured as rescuers attempt to pull them onto pool decks or docks or lift them into boats (frequently dropped in the process because they are wet and slippery and therefore hard to hold and also unable to cooperate due to seizure activity).

However, the water is one of the safer places for a seizure to occur if one important condition is maintained: an open airway. Because the water is by nature a non-abrasive environment, many of the associated injuries that accompany strong tonic-clonic seizures are automatically eliminated. Whether recreational therapists are programming in their own facility or in a community facility with their own support staff, a water seizure team needs to be denoted and trained ahead of time (Crawford, 1984). The team should select a distinct audible signal to notify all members of the seizure team that a water seizure is occurring (e.g., three sharp whistle blasts and/or shouting the phrase "water seizure team now."). At this point, team members hand their clients/swimmers off to other staff or volunteers, who should then assist everyone in getting out of the water (to prevent someone else from getting into trouble in the water or being unnoticed because everyone else's attention is naturally focused on the seizure occurring).

The most important first step is ensuring an open airway. The best way to do this is to use a seizure mat or towel. A standard gym exercise or wrestling mat works well for adults or large beach towels may be doubled and used for children. Using a simple four-corner formation, the team should float the mat or towel up underneath the torso and elevate the person to the top of the water. For small children, two persons can accomplish this, each taking two corners. Larger teens or adults may require four persons. An additional team member may need to cradle the head and neck by placing his or her hands/forearms palm up against the shoulder blades (i.e., in instances where the seizure activity is producing extreme head movements).

If the seizure occurs in a swimming pool, the four-corner formation easily may be maintained in the shallows. However, if the seizure occurs in open water, strong and competent swimmers who are capable of treading water for several minutes will be needed to safely manage the seizure in the water. If an insufficient number of strong swimmers are available, the most prudent course of action may be to risk injury by transferring to a boat or dock. Abrasions and broken bones are better than water inhalation and/or drowning.

PURPOSE OF RECREATIONAL THERAPY

Recreational therapists who work with clients with seizure disorders typically are focusing on a secondary diagnosis (e.g., developmental disability, psychiatric or physical disability), the psychopathology associated with epilepsy (e.g., learned helplessness, anger, depression), or specific needs related to lifestyle modifications and restricted leisure activity choices.

In focusing on a second diagnosis, the recreational therapist needs to remain aware of certain activity limitations, medication side effects, and appropriate procedures for handling seizures that may occur during activities. The recreational therapist also should follow appropriate strategies or current best practice standards available for the secondary diagnosis. The latter two areas of concern (psychopathology and lifestyle modifications) are related more directly to clients' seizure activity and may be viewed as specific interventions for recreational therapy.

As noted earlier in this chapter, clients with epilepsy are at risk for other psychological or psychiatric conditions. Recreational therapists should take an active role in addressing some of the psychosocial needs. Three topics will be discussed in detail to highlight this area: stress reduction, leisure lifestyle, and locus of control.

Mittan and Locke (1982) noted that most individuals with epilepsy live with pervasive fears about having seizures, with approximately 70% believing that they may die during their next seizure. In some instances, these fears may be realistic (e.g., persons with a history of strong tonic-clonic seizures or seizures ending in status epilepticus), emphasizing the need for a comprehensive assessment. Recreational therapists should assess these individuals at high risk regarding their knowledge and use of stress reduction and relaxation skills to counteract the effects of chronic stress and reduce potential trigger events. Recreational therapy has a documented research base for promoting healthy, effective stress reduction activities and thus may take a lead on the treatment team in providing intervention in this area (Austin, 2013).

Considerable evidence supports the theory that clients with epilepsy are stigmatized by the disorder, even when the seizures are well controlled (Arangio, 1980; Betts, 1982; Sherrill, 1993). This stigmatization is both real and perceived, indicating that society and the clients need to overcome their stereotypes about seizures. In reaction to perceived stigmatization, clients commonly reflect affective disorders such as anxiety and depression. When social withdrawal and self-enforced social isolation are common parameters, an activity program that is focused on strong experiential work in social settings is the most effective prescription.

Clients with epilepsy also have been shown to reflect higher external locus of control scores (DeVellis et al., 1980). These findings indicate that clients do not believe they have the ability to control their lives. This may be a realistic consequence of having a chronic health problem, but it is nonetheless psychologically debilitating when the feeling of uncontrollability becomes generalized to other aspects of the individual's life and may result in depression and lowered self-esteem. Other authors have discussed locus of control and perceived control in respect to leisure activity (Ellis & Witt, 1984; Iso-Ahola, 1980), and a comprehensive assessment (the Leisure Diagnostic Battery) has been developed for use by recreational therapists (Ellis & Witt, 1990). For external locus and low-esteem parameters, the activity therapy approach should be toward developing mastery experiences. Only through feelings of personal competence and higher levels of skill will individuals be convinced to change their perceptions of locus of control.

The adaptations that relate to clients' leisure lifestyles are appropriate topics for recreational therapy treatment planning. Although certain physical activities may be contraindicated (or need modifications), clients with epilepsy still need a well-rounded leisure lifestyle, including social recreation activities, individual and team sports, and solitary hobbies and interests. Not all clients with epilepsy need leisure counseling, but many benefit from a therapeutic relationship that systematically reviews choices and options for social engagement.

By conducting a comprehensive leisure assessment (e.g., activity checklists, values and benefits questionnaire, locus of control, hobbies and individualized pursuits, social network options), the recreational therapist may develop recommendations based on clients' strengths, focusing on positive choices available rather than dwelling on a few activity limitations.

COMMON SERVICE SETTINGS

Recreational therapists will encounter clients with seizure disorders in all service delivery areas. This is because epilepsy is spread throughout the general population and will be noted randomly in clinical settings. The majority of adult clients with seizure disorders who are in need of recreational therapy services will reside in long-term residential treatment centers, whereas children and youth will occur with greater frequency in community-based group homes and educational centers. Many clients across all age groups will present with comorbidities and have primary developmental or psychological problems in addition to their seizure disorder.

Clients who are not dual diagnosed usually will be able to stabilize their seizures with medications and therefore likely will reside in the community. These individuals intermittently may be referred for recreational therapy services to assist with concomitant psychopathology or lifestyle adaptations as they move through life span developmental stages. Common service settings for these clients include community mental health centers, outpatient clinics in general hospitals, university or medical center clinics, or private practices.

Recreational therapists who work in drug and alcohol detoxification units will witness seizures with chronic alcoholics on a regular basis. These seizures are episodic and are part of the constellation of behaviors probable in alcohol and drug detoxification protocols. Once the client passes through the detoxification stage, the seizures abate, and therefore, the clients are not considered typical of the activity therapy needs of standard seizure disorder clients.

CURRENT BEST PRACTICES AND PROCEDURES

The following sections will discuss appropriate services and will direct special attention toward individuals with concomitant psychopathology or difficulty with lifestyle adaptations. See other chapters in this text for practices and procedures related to secondary diagnoses such as developmental delay and behavioral health and psychiatry.

Assessment

Recreational therapists should consider four global areas when assessing clients with seizure disorders: stress reduction and relaxation training, locus of control, social skills, and leisure lifestyle. Each of these areas provide useful information to document the need for recreational therapy intervention. The topics noted here, as well as suggestions regarding the origins of psychopathology peculiar to individuals with seizure disorders, are derived from common practice. Additional areas (e.g., personal competencies and skill sets) will become evident on an individual basis.

Standardized assessment tools are available for locus of control (Ellis & Witt, 1990; Rohsenow & O'Leary, 1978) and leisure lifestyle concerns (Howe, 1984; Neulinger, 1990). Checklists, questionnaires, surveys, and therapist observations are more commonly used for identifying stress reduction skills and social skills (e.g., communication, cooperation, and leadership skills; Navar, 1990).

Few assessment formats have originated specifically for individuals with seizure disorders, so the recreational therapist will need to be familiar with contraindicated activities when conducting assessments and taking leisure histories. In most cases, no adaptations will be necessary, but the recreational therapist should review the client's medical records and speak to appropriate medical staff prior to beginning an assessment.

Planning

Following the completion of a comprehensive interdisciplinary assessment, the therapy needs must be prioritized and corresponding goals and objectives identified. For most clients, the medical staff will stabilize and monitor the seizures. Other needs then will be prioritized considering their relationship to each client. Lifestyle adaptations that are necessary to help stabilize the occurrence of seizures will be given a high priority. An example of this is establishing a healthy balance between proper exercise and diet. If either of these areas is severely neglected, maintaining the proper anticonvulsant medication level in the client's bloodstream may be difficult. If seizure onset has been late in life, the recreational therapist may have to use continuity–discontinuity theory (Sessoms, 1980) in attempting to reestablish previous activity interests if a more recent activity (e.g., mountain biking, rock climbing) is now contraindicated because of seizure potential.

Relaxation training sessions and physical activities to reduce stress may be presented through therapy sessions (Austin, 2013; Sylvester, 1992) or counseling sessions (assisting the client to fully use the skills already present; Austin, 2013). Experiential group cooperation activities are useful for promoting an internal locus of control and for developing appropriate social skills. The topic of leisure counseling encompasses a broad spectrum of services that basically seek to assist the individual in developing a rewarding leisure lifestyle.

Implementation

The general interaction style of the therapist will vary given the clients' needs. Individuals with severe intellectual deficit and sporadically controlled seizures, needing to develop communication skills, will probably do better with a more structured therapy setting than an adult who is avoiding all physical activities out of fear of having a seizure.

The recreational therapist should continuously monitor clinical strategies to ensure their relevance to the clients' identified needs. The recreational therapist always should remain aware of activity limitations, medication side effects, and appropriate procedures for handling seizures if they occur. Specifically, the recreational therapist should watch for signs of extreme fatigue during and after physical activities, excessive breathing, skipping meals, and other idiosyncrasies identified on an individual basis. Additionally, motor patterns of seizure activity, intensity, duration, and post-seizure state of mind if seizures occur are important priorities in observing and charting.

Evaluation

In instances where standardized assessments are used (e.g., locus of control), a post-therapy assessment is appropriate. The recreational therapist also should monitor check sheets and questionnaires to ensure that the progress stated in the goals and objectives was achieved. One question that is important for this particular clinical population is, did the activities exacerbate the client's condition? The recreational therapist should address this immediately and should highlight this in the clients' evaluation summary and the medical record as well.

APPLICATION OF THE RECREATIONAL THERAPY PROCESS: CASE STUDY

Edward is a 34-year-old single, college-educated client who was referred for outpatient counseling for depression. Edward works as an accounts receivable clerk at an industrial manufacturing company. Edward's epilepsy initially was diagnosed at age 7 and has been stabilized since that time, with the last seizure occurring at age 23 and the one previous to that at age 17. In conjunction with helping a coworker who had a seizure at work, Edward disclosed to his employer that he has epilepsy. This occurred 6 years ago, and Edward attributes this to his being overlooked for job promotions since that time. Feelings of depression, helplessness, and extreme frustration led Edward's physician to recommend outpatient counseling.

Assessment

Edward's physician referred him to a local community mental health center that provided outpatient counseling services. Following an initial screening interview, Edward was advised to attend an outpatient leisure counseling group that met twice weekly. The group used a 12-week program format, which a recreational therapist conducted. As part of the assessment process, Edward completed a nonstandardized leisure interest survey and a questionnaire that identified his current leisure lifestyle: the Perceived Freedom in Leisure Short Form (PFL-SF; Ellis & Witt, 1984) and the Adult Nowicki-Strickland Internal–External Locus of Control scale (ANSIE; Norwicki & Duke, 1974).

The results of the questionnaires indicated that Edward has a well-rounded repertoire of leisure skills and interests but had stopped participating in social activities over the past several years. The PFL-SF noted that Edward felt that he was not able to choose his leisure activities freely and that social and environmental constraints dictated his choices. The ANSIE identified that Edward had a global belief that he did not control his actions and reinforced in general the results from the PFL-SF.

Planning

Based on the results of the assessment battery, physician's comments, the initial screening information, and Edward's own observations, Edward contracted to attend the 12-week, 24 sessions, outpatient leisure counseling group. Edward and the recreational therapist also considered referrals to a clinical psychologist for individual counseling and classes in biofeedback training, guided imagery, and deep muscle relaxation techniques. They decided that these referrals may be appropriate following the 12-week leisure counseling sessions.

Implementation

The 12-week leisure counseling protocol consisted of a structured education/lecture group held biweekly. These groups identified specific interests, skills, and strategies that the individual clients could use immediately. Individual clients presented specific problem areas for discussion and feedback. The clients were responsible to follow up on the suggestions made in groups, relating their experiences in the following sessions. Clients who had difficulty being self-motivated were seen individually by the recreational therapist to provide more structure. Specific topics that were presented during the weekly sessions included the relationship between leisure and work, time management, matching interests with available options, identifying local and regional resources, solitary versus social recreation, and self-responsibility.

The recreational therapist served as the group leader and resource person, offering considerable options and suggestions for the clients to select. The concept of prime importance that was emphasized repeatedly throughout the sessions was that each client take control of his or her leisure activities. As long as the group stayed focused and progressed in a productive manner, the recreational therapist retained the role of resource person.

Evaluation

Edward attended all 24 sessions during the 12-week program without demonstrating the need for individual sessions. Edward actively participated in each group and seemed to begin using the suggestions and feedback roughly around the fifth week. During the course of the program, Edward was confronted with his repeated rationalizations and excuses for making positive changes in his life. Edward appeared to accept this positive criticism, albeit reluctantly.

Post-therapy evaluations included the PFL-SF and ANSIE and a questionnaire covering the main points of the leisure counseling sessions. Edward reflected a more internal locus of control score, was taking more responsibility for his leisure activities, and understood the key concepts of the sessions. Edward noted that he was less depressed and preoccupied about his employment situation and in fact has spoken to his supervisor about a possible promotion. Edward did not receive the promotion but received a minor pay raise and seemed satisfied with his supervisor's comments. Apparently, Edward not only took a more self-responsible, assertive role in his leisure lifestyle but also successfully generalized this concept to other aspects of his life. At a follow-up contact made 3 months later, Edward reported no recurrence of his symptoms of depression. Edward continued to make progress by attending a local biofeedback seminar sponsored by the local community library. He used his guided imagery training when in the workplace, where feelings of being overwhelmed or anxious episodically overtook him. He preferred to begin a moderate exercise regimen 3 days a week to the deep muscle relaxation progression that another therapist taught him.

TRENDS AND ISSUES

Social Stigma

The stigma associated with epilepsy is undoubtedly the greatest issue with which persons with epilepsy must deal. Although the ancient notions regarding possession have disappeared from contemporary society, laypersons continue to associate seizure disorders with other severe psychological and medical problems, including psychopathology and intellectual disability. As discussed earlier in the chapter, even individuals whose seizures are well controlled face stigma. Persons with epilepsy and society in general need to overcome stereotypes held about seizure disorders. A related issue is the lack of understanding on the part of some helping professionals regarding lifestyle modifications for persons who have seizures. Although common sense dictates prudence in selecting recreational activities, excessive limitations are often imposed on individuals with epilepsy. Fortunately, laypersons and helping professionals are becoming more aware that most individuals with epilepsy can achieve freedom from seizures by taking anticonvulsant medication, permitting them to have few lifestyle restrictions.

Seizure Dogs

A breakthrough in the area of companion animal services has potentially liberating ramifications for individuals who continue to suffer from uncontrolled seizures but are not fortunate enough to have the benefit of aura to help them stay safe from uncontrolled collapse or falls. The canine's keen sense of smell (estimated at nearly 200 times that of humans) may be harnessed to help persons with uncontrolled seizures. Scientists have discovered (Lynn, 1998) that a change occurs in a person's biochemistry just prior to seizure activity and is manifested by a slight change in the odor of their skin oil and perspiration. This change, though too subtle for humans to note, may be detected by dogs. The dogs may be behaviorally shaped as companion animals to tug on the person's pant leg or shirt sleeves and, in the case of young children, even taught to gently tug them down to the ground to prevent a potentially harmful unexpected fall when the seizure activity begins.

Although this ability has been reported in a number of breeds, the accuracy of the dog's predictive skills likely will vary considerably for different patients and different dogs. Public and press interest in seizure-alert dogs has led to several commercial groups training and selling dogs; in many cases, the cost exceeds $2,000.

To date, little scientific evidence is available on the quality of the different services and the ability of different breeds (Epilepsy Foundation of America, 2012). Some services are even training dogs to "protect" their owners in the case of a seizure. This could be dangerous to emergency medical services or other persons trying to assist in the case of a prolonged seizure complicated with personal injury.

If this training proves reliable across larger applications, nationwide thousands of children who are "helmeted" (many of whom have intellectual disabilities) could suddenly become much less socially conspicuous and free to move about the community without the many micro-insults visited upon them by laypersons' behaviors of staring and/or commenting.

SUDEP: Sudden Unexpected Death in Epilepsy

In rare cases, epilepsy is fatal. The incidence of sudden unexpected death in epilepsy (SUDEP) ranges from 0.9% (93 cases per 10,000 persons per year) to 1.2% in different studies (Rafnsson, Olafsson, Hauser, & Gudmundsson, 2001). The combination of autism and epilepsy is particularly complicated, often associated with overall poor health and, in extreme circumstances, premature death. SUDEP is more likely in persons with uncontrolled tonic clonic seizures or persons who are having seizures while on AEDs. Causes include pauses in breathing, heart rhythm problems, and damage to the CNS affecting the body's regulatory systems. Various strategies may prevent SUDEP; the most important is gaining control of seizure activity. Several researchers and companies have developed seizure monitors to notify caretakers when a seizure is beginning. Many of these are bed monitors for monitoring nighttime activities; recently a few portable, wearable monitors have been developed to ensure 24/7 coverage (Epilepsy Foundation of America, 2012).

Treatment Options

AEDs eliminate seizures in around two thirds of patients. Patients with more difficult to control cases sometimes respond to combinations of two or more medications. Other treatment options are available. Some physicians have suggested surgery to remove the part of the brain that is causing seizures (Quigg et al., 2011), though this option may result in increased risk of depression and suicidality for a small percentage of cases (Hamid et al., 2011).

Other clinicians have recommended a ketogenic diet. In this diet, each meal has approximately 4 times as much fat as protein or carbohydrates. This diet mimics starvation by burning fat for energy rather than carbohydrates. Physicians are not entirely sure why ketogenic diets have been effective, but about one third of children who try them become seizure free (Epilepsy Foundation of America, 2012).

Yet another relatively recent treatment option is the surgical implant of a vagus nerve stimulator. Once implanted, the device uses electricity to try to stop seizures either before they happen or while they happen (Christmas, Steele, Tolomeo, El-jamel, & Matthews, 2013). The device also helps with depression as a comorbidity in many patients (unlike the brain resection treatment option discussed above, which often increases depression). Patients usually are not considered candidates for this procedure until after all AED treatments and combinations have been exhausted, a process that may take several years.

SUMMARY

Seizures are caused by abnormal amounts of electrical discharge between cells in the brain. As a result of this, the body sites that are controlled by those brain cells will display spasms, or muscle contractions. Epilepsy refers to recurrent seizures. Although between 2.2 and 3.6 million individuals in the United States have epilepsy (or some other form of seizure disorder), most are able to stabilize their seizures through medications and lifestyle modifications alone (Epilepsy Foundation of America, 2012).

Recreational therapy services are typically sought for assistance with a secondary diagnosis, concomitant psychopathology, or specific lifestyle modifications. Certain activity limitations may be recommended because of the individual's seizure history and the nature of the activity. Activity precautions may be instituted to allow individuals with epilepsy to participate in most activities.

READING COMPREHENSION QUESTIONS

1. What is a seizure? Epilepsy?

2. What are the 10 factors that are believed to cause most seizure disorders?

3. What are the differences between the two global seizure classifications?

4. What should the recreational therapist do if a client has a seizure during a session?

5. What are the three areas for which recreational therapists routinely receive referrals?

6. Are medications usually given to individuals with epilepsy? What are possible side effects?

7. Should clients with epilepsy be allowed to scuba dive? Play volleyball? Play tackle football?

8. When would leisure counseling be a recommended approach for clients with epilepsy?

9. List at least three comorbidities common to clients with epilepsy.

REFERENCES

American National Red Cross. (1994). *Instructor's manual for emergency first aid instruction* (Stock No. 421208). Washington, DC: Author.

Arangio, A. (1980). The social worker and epilepsy: A description of assessment and treatment variables. In B. P. Hermann (Ed.), *A multidisciplinary handbook of epilepsy*. Springfield, IL: Thomas.

Austin, D. R. (1991). *Therapeutic recreation processes and techniques* (2nd ed.). Champaign, IL: Sagamore.

Austin, D. R. (2013). *Therapeutic recreation processes and techniques* (7th ed.). Urbana, IL: Sagamore.

Barry, J., Lembke, A., & Gisbert, P. A. (2007). Affective disorders in epilepsy. In A. B. Ettinger & A. M. Kanner (Eds.), *Psychiatric issues in epilepsy: A practical guide to diagnosis and treatment* (pp. 203–247). Philadelphia, PA: Lippincott, Williams & Williams.

Betts, T. A. (1982). Psychiatry and epilepsy. In J. Laidlaw & A. Richens (Eds.), *A textbook of epilepsy* (2nd ed.). Edinburgh, Scotland: Churchill-Livingstone.

Bleck, T. P. (1983). Therapy for status epilepticus. *Clinical Neuropharmacology, 6,* 255–269.

Bleck, T. P. (1987). Epilepsy. *Disease-a-Month, 33*, 601–679.

Boylan, L. S., Flint, L. A., Labovitz, D. L., Jackson, S. C., Starner, K., & Devinshy, O. (2004). Depression but not seizure frequency predicts quality of life in treatment-resistant epilepsy. *Neurology, 62*(2), 258–261.

burlingame, j., & Blaschko, T. M. (1990). *Assessment tools for recreation therapy: Redbook #1.* Ravensdale, WA: Idyll Arbor.

Commission on Classification and Terminology of the International League Against Epilepsy. (1981). Proposal for revised clinical and electroencephalographic classification of epileptic seizures. *Epilepsia, 22*, 489–501.

Crawford, M. E. (1984). Instructional techniques and progressions in water adjustment for the severely disabled. In P. Bishop (Eds.), *Nebraska adapted physical education resource manual* (pp. 225–242). Kearney, NE: Kearney State College Publications.

Christmas, D., Steele, J. D., Tolomeo, S., Eljamel, M. S., & Matthews, K. (2013). Vagus nerve stimulation for chronic major depressive disorder: 12-month outcomes in highly treatment resistant patients with epilepsy. *Journal of Affective Disorders, 28*(1), 32–37.

DeVellis, R. G. (1980). Epilepsy and learned helplessness. *Basic and Applied Social Psychology, 1*, 241–253.

Ellis, G. D., & Witt, P. A. (1984). The measurement of perceived freedom in leisure. *Journal of Leisure Research, 16*, 110–123.

Ellis, G. D., & Witt, P. A. (1990). *The leisure diagnostic battery.* State College, PA: Venture.

Epilepsy Foundation of America. (2012). *Everyday life information about people with epilepsy and seizure disorders.* Landover, MD: Author.

Ettinger, A., Reed, M., & Cramer, J. (2004). Depression and comorbidity in community-based patients with epilepsy or asthma. *Neurology, 63*(6), 1008–1014.

Ettinger, A. B. (2006). Psychotropic effects of antiepileptic drugs. *Neurology, 67*(11), 1916–1925.

Ettinger, A. B., Reed, M. L., Goldberg, J. F., & Hirschfeld, R. M. (2005). Prevalence of bipolar symptoms in epilepsy vs other chronic health disorders. *Neurology, 65*(4), 535–540.

Fenton, G. W. (1981). Personality and behavioral disorders in adults with epilepsy. In E. H. Reynolds & M. R. Bramble (Eds.), *Epilepsy and psychiatry.* Edinburgh, Scotland: Churchill-Livingstone.

Fincham, R. W. (1986). Epilepsy in adolescents and adults. In C. Canan (Ed.), *Current therapy.* Philadelphia, PA: Saunders.

Gastaut, H. (1970). Clinical and electroencephalographic classification of epileptic seizures. *Epilepsia, 11*(3), 102–103.

Goldstein, M. A., & Harden, C. L. (2000). Epilepsy and anxiety. *Epilepsy Behavior, 1*(4), 228–234.

Hamid, H., Devinsky, O., Vickrey, B. G., Berg, A. T., Bazil, C. W., & Langfitt, J. T. (2011). Suicide outcomes after respective epilepsy surgery. *Epilepsy Behavior, 20*(3), 462–464.

Hanscomb, A., & Hughes, L. (1999). *Epilepsy.* London, England: Wellington House.

Harden, C. L. (2002). The co-morbidity of depression and epilepsy: Epidemiology, etiology, and treatment. *Neurology, 59*(6), 48–55.

Harden, C. L., & Goldstein, M. A. (2002). Mood disorders in patients with epilepsy: Epidemiology and management. *CNS Drugs, 16*(5), 391–302.

Hauser, W. A. (1978). Epidemiology of epilepsy. In B. S. Schoenberg (Ed.), *Advances in neurology: Neurological epidemiology.* New York, NY: Raven Press.

Hermann, B. P., & Jones, J. E. (2005). Epilepsy: What is the extent of the current problem? In *Mood disorders in epilepsy: Bridging the gap between psychiatry and neurology* (pp. 3–11). American Epilepsy Society and IntraMed Scientific Solutions.

Howe, C. E. (1984). Leisure assessment instrumentation in therapeutic recreation. *Therapeutic Recreation Journal, 18*(2), 14–24.

Howie, L. (1994, November 14). Society prejudices lull change. *The Missourian*, p. 10a.

Iso-Ahola, S. E. (1980). *The social psychology of leisure and recreation.* Dubuque, IA: Brown.

Juul-Jensen, P., & Foldspang, A. (1983). Natural history of epileptic seizures. *Epilepsia, 24*, 297–312.

Kanner, A. M. (2000). Psychosis of epilepsy: A neurologists perspective. *Epilspsy Behavior, 1*(4), 219–227.

Kanner, A. M., & Balabanov, A. (2002). Depression and epilepsy: How closely related are they? *Neurology, 58*(8), 27–39.

Kanner, A. M., Barry, J. J., & Gilliam, F. (2009). Psychiatric comorbidities in epilepsy: Streamlining recognition and diagnosis to improve quality of life. *Counselling Points, 1*, 1–15.

Kobau, R., Gilliam, F., & Thurman, D. J. (2004). Prevalence of self-reported epilepsy or seizure disorder and its associations with self-reported depression and anxiety: Results from the 2004 Healthstyles survey. *Epilepsia, 47*(11), 1915–1921.

Lynn, G. (1998, October 13). New hope for epileptics: How dogs can help. *USA Today*, p. 3a.

Marsh, L., & Rao, V. (2002). Psychiatric complications in patients with epilepsy: A review. *Epilepsy Research, 49*(1), 11–33.

Mittan, R., & Locke, G. E. (1982). Fear of seizures: Epilepsy's forgotten problem. *Urban Health, 1*, 40–41.

National Institute of Neurological Disorders and Stroke. (2014). *Seizures and epilepsy: Hope through research*. Landover, MD: Author.

Navar, N. (1990). *State and technical institute leisure assessment process*. Ravensdale, WA: Idyll Arbor.

Neulinger, J. (1990). *What am I doing scale*. Dolgerville, NY: Leisure Institute Press.

Norwicki, S., & Duke, M. P. (1974). A locus of control scale for college as well as non-college adults. *Journal of Personality Assessment, 38*(2), 136–137.

Perez, M. M., & Trimble, M. R. (2009). Epileptic psychosis-diagnostic comparison with process schizophrenia. *Psychiatry, 137*, 245–249.

Quigg, M., Broshek, D. K., Barbaro, N. M., Ward, M. M., Laxer, K. D., & Yan, G. (2011). Neuropsychological outcomes after gamma knife radiosurgery for mesial temporal lobe epilepsy: A prospective multicenter study. *Epilepsia, 52*(5), 909–916.

Rafnsson, V., Olafsson, E., Hauser, W. A., & Gudmundsson, G. (2001). Cause-specific mortality in adults with unprovoked seizures: A population-based cohort study. *Neuroepdimiology, 20*(4), 232–236.

Rohsenow, D. J., & O'Leary, M. R. (1978). Locus of control research on alcoholic populations: A review of development, scales, and treatment. *International Journal of the Addictions, 13*(1), 55–78.

Sander, J. W., & Hart, Y. M. (1999). *Epilepsy: Questions and answers*. Coral Springs, FL: Merit.

Sessoms, D. (1980). Lifestyles and life cycles: A recreation programming approach. In T. Goodale & P. Witt (Eds.), *Recreation and leisure: Issues in an era of change*. State College, PA: Venture.

Sherrill, C. (1993). *Adapted physical activity, recreation, and sport* (4th ed.). Dubuque, IA: Brown.

Siegler, M., & Osmond, H. (1974). *Models of madness, models of medicine*. New York, NY: Macmillan.

Sylvester, C. (1992). Therapeutic recreation and the right to leisure. *Therapeutic Recreation Journal, 26*(2), 9–20.

Tellez-Zenteno, J. F., Patten, S. B., Jette, N., Williams, J., & Wiebe, S. (2007). Psychiatric comorbidity in epilepsy: A population-based analysis. *Epilepsia, 48*(12), 2336–2344.

Torta, R., & Keller, R. (1999). Behavioral, psychotic and anxiety disorder in epilepsy: Etiology, clinical features, and therapeutic implications. *Epilepsia, 40*(10), 2–20.

Vuilleumier, P., & Jallon, P. (1998). Epilspsy and psychiatric disorders: Epidemiological data. *Medline, 154*(4), 305–317.

Wolfensberger, W. (1972). *Normalization: The principal of normalization in human services*. Toronto, Canada: National Institute on Mental Retardation.

9

GERIATRIC PRACTICE

NANCY E. RICHESON

OBJECTIVES

- Understand the following vocabulary: acute and chronic conditions, ACE units, activities of daily living, ageism, assisted living, competencies, continuous care retirement community, dementia, demographics, older adults, gerontology, geriatrics, health, health prevention and health promotion, instrumental activities of daily living, medical home, and long-term care.
- Discuss the purpose of the recreational therapist in geriatric practice.
- Identify evidenced-based interventions recreational therapists use.
- Identify useful assessment tools for working with older adults.
- Review current trends and issues in geriatric care.

Due to the unprecedented growth of the population of older adults in the United States, health care professionals, including recreational therapists, will need to develop their knowledge, skills, and abilities to care for older adults. This chapter will provide an overview of the practice of recreational therapy (RT) in geriatrics.

DEMOGRAPHICS

The demographics for the older adult population in the United States suggest that the nation is aging, and the current growth is unparalleled in the country's history. For example, an estimated 89 million Americans are aged 65 and older, more than double the number of older adults in the United States in 2010 (Satariano et al., 2012). The reasons behind the growth are twofold: Americans are living longer, many into their 80s and 90s, and the baby boom, persons born after World War II, has left the nation with more adults than in previous generations (Centers for Disease Control and Prevention [CDC], 2013).

Furthermore, the U.S. population is becoming more racially and ethnically diverse, as demonstrated by the 80% of older adults aged 65 years who are non-Hispanic white (CDC, 2013). According to the CDC (2013), "By 2030 that percentage will have declined and older non-Hispanic whites will make up 71% of the population. Hispanic will make up 12%, non-Hispanic blacks nearly 10.3%, and Asians 5.4%" (p. 1). The demographic shifts will continue, and by 2050, the racial and ethnic diversity of U.S. adults will have changed dramatically. According to the CDC (2013), "non-Hispanic whites will make up 58% of the total population of those 65 years or older and the total proportion of older Hispanics will almost triple" (p. 1).

Canada is also undergoing rapid growth in its aging population. By 2031, a projected 9 million Canadians will be over age 65. This will be 25% of Canada's population, almost double today's aging population of 13% (Austin & Lee, 2013).

DEFINITIONS

Ageism

The term *ageism* was coined by Robert Butler, a geriatrician, to describe the "prejudice and discrimination against older adults" (Ferrini & Ferrini, 2013, p. 6).

Geriatrics

Geriatrics is the study of "health and disease in later life; the comprehensive health care of older persons; and the well-being of their informal caregivers" (Association for Gerontology in Higher Education, 2006, para. 1).

Gerontology

Gerontology is the study of

the aging process and individuals as they grow from midlife through later life including the study of physical, mental and social changes; the investigation of the changes in society resulting from our aging population; the application of this knowledge to policies, programs, and practice. As a result of the multidisciplinary focus of gerontology, professionals from diverse fields call themselves gerontologists. (Association for Gerontology in Higher Education, 2006, para. 1)

Older adults

Older adults or "older persons" may reflect aging as a continuum: young-old (65–74), old-old (75–85), and oldest of the old (85 and above), suggesting that differences exist between groups, although these differences are not definitive. For example, the young-old are more vigorous, have higher incomes, and are more likely to be married (Ferrini & Ferrini, 2013).

ACUTE, CHRONIC, AND COMMON HEALTH CONDITIONS

Older adults have the highest morbidity (illness) rates of all age groups due to the prevalence of chronic health conditions (Ferrini & Ferrini, 2013). Chronic health conditions generally are incurable, worsen over time, and endure over many years, whereas acute conditions have a rapid onset and generally are caused by bacteria or viruses. Older adults typically will recover completely from an acute illness such as the flu, the common cold, bronchitis, gallstones, urinary tract infections, and shingles. However, older adults with acute illnesses need to be monitored because they are more likely to suffer complications.

Many older adults live with chronic health conditions for years. Although some conditions have minimal symptoms, others lead to suffering, disability, and decreased quality of life (Ferrini & Ferrini, 2013). The most common and deadly conditions reported are hypertension (high blood pressure), arthritis, heart disease, cancer, and diabetes. The causes of these conditions vary and are due to a combination of environmental, lifestyle (e.g., diet, cigarette smoking, and inactivity), and genetics (Ferrini & Ferrini, 2013). Other common conditions older adults face include osteoporosis, low back pain, foot problems, thyroid issues, heartburn, constipation, incontinence, varicose veins, itchy skin, cataracts, dizziness, glaucoma, and muscular degeneration (Ferrini & Ferrini, 2013). The focus of treatment is managing the illness by reducing the symptoms.

Chronic health conditions may cause severe limitations resulting in the older adult not being able to perform activities of daily living (bathing, dressing, eating, and getting around the house). Not being able to perform activities of daily living increases older adults' chances of being institutionalized. In addition, older adults visit physicians more often, have longer stays in hospitals, are prescribed more drugs, and use the majority of long-term care services. Long-term care services may be formal or informal and provided at home, in the community, or in an institution.

Mental health conditions also need to be considered in the geriatric population. According to the CDC and the National Association of Chronic Disease Directors (2008), mental health is the ability to engage in productive activities and fulfilling relationships and to cope successfully with change and adversity. Aging leads to a decline in the person's abilities and the person having to face mortality (end of life). Developing ways in which older adults learn to adapt, compensate, and become resilient will aid them in aging successfully and lead them through the transitions or losses associated with this stage of life such as retirement, marital, widowhood, and relationships with children and grandchildren (Ferrini & Ferrini, 2013).

However, when stress becomes unmanageable and the older adult lacks the ability to cope, more serious mental health issues may arise such as mood disorders; mild, moderate, or major depression; and bipolar disorders (National Institute of Mental Health, 2014). Other mental health issues that affect older adults are anxiety disorders, sleep disorders, substance use disorders, and cognitive disorders. According to the National Nursing Home Survey, 66.7% of adults living in long-term care facilities have mental health conditions (CDC, 2014).

Dementia is a cognitive disorder that affects 5.5 million Americans; it is a progressive brain impairment that interferes with memory and typical intellectual functioning (Alzheimer's Association, 2013). The problems are severe enough that they interfere with the ability to perform activities of daily living. According to the Alzheimer's Association (2014), "the symptoms of dementia may vary but two of the following core mental functions must be significantly impaired to be considered dementia: (a) memory; (b) communication and language; (c) ability to focus and pay attention; (d) reasoning and judgment; and (e) visual perception" (para. 2).

Alzheimer's disease, the most common type of dementia, accounts for 60% to 80% of all dementias. Vascular dementia is the second most common type of dementia and occurs after the older adult has had a stroke. Other dementias include dementia with Lewy bodies, Parkinson's disease, mixed dementia, frontal lobe, Creutzfeldt-Jakob disease, Huntington's disease, and Wernicke-Korsakoff syndrome (Alzheimer's Association, 2013). The Alzheimer's Association (2013) stated that

"68% of those living in nursing homes have a diagnosis of dementia" (p. 46). Remember, older adults may be living with multiple physical and mental health conditions, making treatment complicated.

MANAGEMENT OF ACUTE, CHRONIC, AND COMMON HEALTH CONDITIONS

Lifestyle (nutrition, exercise, and managing stress), compared to genetic factors over which a person has no control, plays a major role in risk for disease. According to the CDC (2008),

> more than half of older adults do not get adequate physical activity. Older adults should be getting 2 hours and 30 minutes (150 minutes) of moderate-intensity aerobic activity (i.e., brisk walking) every week and muscle-strengthening activities on 2 or more days a week that work all major muscle groups (legs, hips, back, abdomen, chest, shoulders, and arms). (para. 4)

Another suggestion is to lessen the number of minutes to 75 and engage in vigorous exercise. Yet another proposal is to mix moderate and vigorous activity or break up activity into 10-minute increments.

The ultimate goal, according to Healthy People 2010 (a government-sponsored program to establish priorities and set goals to improve health), is to increase individuals' responsibility for their health and the health of their communities (Ferrini & Ferrini, 2013). The latest initiative, Healthy People 2020, has set goals to improve the health, function, and quality of life of older adults.

To achieve these goals, health promotion programs for older adults may eliminate negative health behaviors and promote positive change. Shank and Coyle (2002) stated, "Generally all health promotion programs include disease prevention activities, activities that focus on preventing illness or disabling condition by getting individuals to take action that will stop the health condition from occurring" (p. 19). These activities are classified as primary, secondary, and tertiary prevention (see Table 9.1).

Table 9.1
Health Prevention

Primary prevention	Interventions are designed to intervene before illness occurs.
Secondary prevention	Interventions are intended for persons who have risk factors for a disease but do not have a diagnosis or symptoms yet.
Tertiary prevention	Interventions are designed to minimize the negative impact of the sickness, restore function, and prevent complications. The goals are to treat and rehabilitate.

Healthy People 2010 and 2020 have set the stage for a more wellness-oriented health care model that includes older adults taking responsibility for their health and making a constant and deliberate effort to stay healthy and achieve the highest potential of well-being (integration and balance of social, mental, emotional, spiritual, and physical health). These national initiatives support a biopsychosocial approach of care embraced by recreational therapists.

ROLE OF THE RECREATIONAL THERAPIST

The recreational therapist is expected to perform many roles in geriatric care. The major roles are the expert clinician, the trainer and educator, the consumer of evidence, and the supervisor and manager (see Figure 9.1). These point toward the role of the recreational therapist as a quality of life advocate and culture change liaison. A quality of life advocate understands the relationship of quality of life to function and health status, realizing that quality of life changes over the life span, and incorporates quality of life issues into clinical practice. A culture change liaison advocates for person-directed values and practices where the voices of older adults and those working with them are considered and respected.

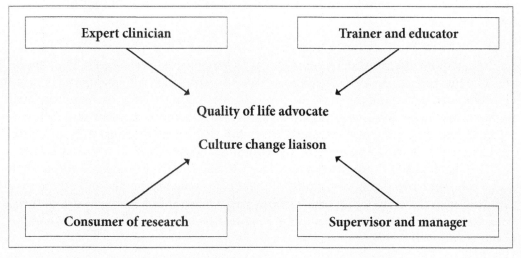

Figure 9.1. Roles of the recreational therapist in geriatrics.

Expert Clinician

The expert clinician uses the RT process of assessment, planning, implementation, and evaluation (APIE) as a basis for practice. In assessment, recreational therapists use standardized (valid and reliable) geriatric assessment tools to develop effective care or treatment plans. They plan and implement RT interventions across interests and needs with increased selectivity to individualized interventions that are ethical, safe, timely, effective, efficient, evidenced based, person centered, strength based, and in compliance with standards of practice, organizational policies, and procedures. They evaluate interventions and report outcomes to stakeholders. They act professionally with all individuals and actively participate in organizational initiatives to improve patient care, practice, and agency performance. They advocate for the profession and are involved with their professional organization, with the aim of advancing the field. The expert clinician uses an ongoing reflection in action approach to treatment that assesses not only the performances of the persons served but also their thought processes and actions.

Trainer and Educator

The recreational therapist working in geriatric care will train and educate service-learning, practicum, and internship students in best practices. Additionally, the recreational therapist will train and educate administrators, staff, and family members at agencies and within communities regarding the role RT may play in health prevention and promotion, treating chronic health conditions, and promoting wellness.

Consumer of Evidence

The recreational therapist will be a consumer of evidence, understanding the use of evidence-based practice in making clinical decisions. Stumbo (2003) described that the application of evidence in practice should follow these steps: "(a) identifying the need of the client; considering the intervention to be used; (b) identifying outcome tools; (c) searching for relevant research; (d) appraising your findings; (e) implementing your findings in clinical practice; and (f) evaluating the process all along" (p. 31).

Supervisor and Manager

Recreational therapists in long-term care settings often are asked to take on the role of department directors. This role includes supervisory and managerial responsibilities such as organizing multiple projects, motivating staff, coaching individual persons and teams, assessing individual skills and weaknesses, hiring and developing staff, fostering accountability and ownership, delegating responsibility, prioritizing tasks, earning trust and respect, and communicating with peers and superiors.

The recreational therapist that works in geriatric care is expected to perform many roles and to do them well. Some of these roles may be obvious and others may not. However, as an emerging professional, you will want to become aware of these roles to be able to define these roles for yourself, the interdisciplinary team, and the administration.

EMPIRICAL RESEARCH IN RECREATIONAL THERAPY

Including research into practice may be challenging for many reasons. Applied research in RT is limited due to the few researchers conducting practice-based studies in geriatrics and research-related skills not being part of the National Council for Therapeutic Recreation Certification job tasks and knowledge areas that are mandatory for practitioners.

However, the RT profession is progressing. Currently, two clinical practice guidelines in geriatric RT are available: *Dementia Practice Guidelines for Recreational Therapy* (Buettner & Fitzsimmons, 2013) and *Recreational Therapy for the Treatment of Depression in Older Adults: A Clinical Practice Guideline* (Buettner, Cummins, et al., 2008). Additionally, research studies completed in several settings (rehabilitation, nursing homes, and community-based settings) have demonstrated that older adults with a variety of conditions benefit from RT services. For example, older adults with chronic health conditions who received physical activity programs experienced significantly increased physical performance and functional mobility (Buettner, Richeson, et al., 2008; Croteau, Richeson, Farmer, & Jones, 2007; Mikula & Smith, 2012; Mikula, Smith, Meuleman, & Levy, 2010; Mobily, 2009; Richeson, Croteau, Jones, & Farmer, 2006; Richeson, Vines, Jones, & Croteau, 2003). Additionally, persons with dementia who received RT programs significantly increased positive behavioral health, that is, experienced decreased depression, agitation, apathy, and passivity and increased self-efficacy (Buettner & Fitzsimmons, 2009; Buettner & Fitzsimmons, 2010; Buettner, Fitzsimmons, & Atav, 2006; Conti, Voelkl, & McGuire, 2008; Kolanowski & Buettner, 2008; Kolanowski, Fick, & Buettner, 2010; Richeson, 2003; Richeson, Boyne, & Brady, 2007; Richeson & Shalek, 2006; Shalek, Richeson, & Buettner, 2004). Although the research above may not be large randomized experimental studies with control groups, the RT profession has an emerging body of evidence that suggests that RT impacts the health status of older adults.

SERVICE SETTINGS

The recreational therapist in geriatric care has the opportunity to work in settings such as home care, medical homes, adult day services, continuous care retirement centers, assisted living, nursing homes, and hospitals. However, recreational therapists also will have the opportunity to work with older adults in settings not listed below, such as rehabilitation and behavioral health agencies.

Home Care

Home-based services typically are provided on a fee-for-service basis. Referrals may come from primary care, home health, and/or community service agencies. RT services promote positive behavior health and encourage physical activity and mobility, daily living skills, and community integration. RT in the home may also provide the caregiver needed respite.

Medical Home

Medical home is a model or philosophy of primary care that is focused on caring for an individual's health conditions. Key philosophical components are patient-centered care, comprehensive care and coordinated care, accessible care, and a commitment to quality and safety (Patience Center Primary Care Collaborative, 2014). The medical home is an accepted model for how primary care should be organized and delivered. It encourages health care providers to meet the patients where they are, from the most simplistic to the most complex conditions. According to Keogh Hoss and Kensinger (2010), "the medical home model provides a rare opportunity for recreational therapists to combine clinical skills with community skills to meet the needs of those individuals in the community with chronic and complex needs" (p. 13).

Adult Day Services

Adult day services are a specialized service for older adults who due to illness or disability require assistance in a supervised and therapeutic environment. They allow individuals to continue to live at home and avoid placement in a nursing home. Two primary models and a mixed model are available for adult day services. The medical model typically provides health, rehabilitative, recreation, and social services to persons who need assistance to live independently, the social model is primarily focused on socializing and interaction and discouraging withdrawal and isolation, and the mixed model is a combination of the medical and social models (AARP Public Policy Institute, 2004).

Continuous Care Retirement Communities

Continuous care retirement communities allow older adults to age in place by offering a tiered approach to addressing the aging process. As persons age and health status changes, their increasing needs may be accommodated. Independent living is for healthy adults who can reside independently in single-family homes, apartments, or condominiums. Assisted living is made available when older adults need help with everyday activities. Many continuous care retirement communities are now offering specialized memory units for persons who need care due to Alzheimer's disease or related dementias.

Assisted Living

The Assisted Living Federation of America (2014) defines assisted living as a "long-term care option that combines housing, support services and health care, as needed" (para. 1). Many older adults who reside in assisted living need support with meals, housekeeping, medication management, mobility, and incontinence. In addition, many have cognitive disorders such as Alzheimer's disease and related dementia. Recreational therapists working in assisted living assess residents and develop plans of care.

Nursing Homes

The highest level of care for older adults, outside a hospital, is provided by a nursing home. Nursing homes provide custodial care and a high level of medical care. Care is supervised by a licensed physician, and a nurse and other medical professionals are on the premises. Skilled nursing care is available on-site, usually 24 hours a day. Medical procedures and rehabilitation therapies are offered on-site (Centers for Medicare and Medicaid Services, 2014).

Hospitals

Acute Care for Elders (ACE) unit is an evidence-based system designed to prevent patients from experiencing functional decline during hospitalization. Hospitals typically identify patients with certain risk factors at admission and who are targeted to receive specific interventions to preserve or restore physical and mental functioning. Interventions include walking, nutritional counseling, medication review, and psychosocial care.

BEST PRACTICES IN ASSESSMENT, PLANNING, IMPLEMENTATION, AND EVALUATION

Evidence-based practice uses the best available evidence in making decisions when caring for older adults. When a recreational therapist chooses to use evidence-based practice, they will be treating an older adult with an approach, technique, or intervention that has been tested by research to be effective (Buettner & Fitzsimmons, 2007). Since the goal for evidence-based practice is to improve the outcome for participants, recreational therapists must know how to use it within the

RT process of assessment, planning, implementation, and evaluation (McCormick, Lee, & Van Puymbroeck, 2009).

Assessment

Understanding standardized (valid and reliable) assessment tools where multiple concerns of older adults may be addressed is key in comprehending the strengths of the person, the need for services, and the development of a coordinated care plan that is focused on interventions that meet the person's needs. Completing an assessment will enable the recreational therapist to determine a baseline for treatment outcomes from interventions (see Table 9.2).

Table 9.2

Resources for Geriatric Assessment Tools

BANDI-RT	http://usm.maine.edu/rls/bandi-rt
Geriatric Assessment Tools	https://www.healthcare.uiowa.edu/igec/tools/
Harford Institute for Geriatric Nursing	http://consultgerirn.org/resources
Rehabilitation Measures Database	http://www.rehabmeasures.org/default.aspx

Planning

After the assessment process is complete, recreational therapists must plan their approaches, techniques, and interventions based on the best available research. McCormick, Lee, and Van Puymbroeck (2009) recommended that the practitioner understand the strengths, needs, and interests of the client; determine goals and objectives; and choose interventions based on the best available information, searching the databases and clinical practice guidelines for relevant research throughout the process. Current RT journals include the *American Journal of Recreation Therapy*, the American Therapeutic Recreation Association's *Annual in Therapeutic Recreation*, and the *Therapeutic Recreation Journal*. Another excellent source for information is the RT Wise Owls (rtwiseowls.com), a website sponsored by Temple University.

Implementation

Evidence-based practice is important during the implementation stage of the APIE process. Recreational therapists need to remember what the research said about implementing the interventions, thus applying research into practice. They must review established protocols from the clinical practice guidelines, as well as techniques and approaches needed. For example, according to the *Dementia Practice Guidelines* (Buettner & Fitzsimmons, 2013), older adults with severe dementia need one-step directions. Therefore, when working with this population, recreational therapists should incorporate these approaches into interventions.

Evaluation

Using standardized outcome tools to demonstrate effectiveness of RT practice is important in determining whether the older adults have met their goals and objectives and improved and/or maintained their health status. Evaluation produces evidence of effectiveness, improves practice, and standardizes outcomes (West, 2009).

APPLICATION: FUNCTIONAL OUTCOMES, ASSESSMENT TOOLS, AND INTERVENTIONS

Recreational therapists have the opportunity to work to maintain and/or increase the functional skills of older adults in several domains including general, cognitive, physical, emotional, and social functioning.

General Functioning

To measure general function, the recreational therapist needs to understand how activities of daily living (ADL) and instrumental activities of daily living (IADL) affect function. ADLs are bathing, dressing, transferring, toileting, grooming, feeding, and mobility and are measured using Katz Activities of Daily Living scale (Katz, 1970; Katz, Down, Cash, & Grotz, 1983). Lawton's IADL Scale determines whether individuals can use the telephone, prepare meals, manage finances, take medications, do laundry, do housework, go shopping, and manage their own transportation (Lawton & Brody, 1969; Lawton, Moss, Fulcomer, & Kleban, 2003). Interventions that are effective for treating general functioning include fall prevention, exercise, relaxation, cooking, brain fitness, gardening, and life skills.

Cognitive Functioning

Due to the incidence of dementia in the United States and Canada, recreational therapists need to understand how to assess cognitive functioning. Common tools are the Mini-Mental State Examination, a 30-point questionnaire test that is used to screen for cognitive impairment. It is commonly used to screen for dementia, to estimate the severity of cognitive impairment, and to follow the course of cognitive changes in an individual over time, thus making it effective for documenting an individual's response to treatment (Folstein, Folstein, & McHugh, 1975). The Dementia Practice Guidelines (Buettner & Fitzsimmons, 2013) uses the Mini-Mental State Examination scores to place participants in appropriate interventions based on level of function. The Global Deterioration Scale (Reisburg, Ferris, deLeon, & Crook, 1982) also identifies stages of dementia. Interventions that assist with maintaining or enhancing cognition are physical exercise, walking, tai chi, brain fitness, games, newsletter, sensory stimulation, relaxation, and simple pleasures.

Physical Functioning

Many chronic health conditions affect physical functioning for older adults. For example, an older adult with osteoarthritis may have limited physical function due to pain and mobility issues. In addition, acute conditions and accidents may contribute to a decline in physical function. An individual recovering from the flu or a fall may need to regain flexibility, endurance, and balance.

Physical functioning assessments measure strength, flexibility, endurance, balance, and risk of falls. An assessment to determine falls risk is the Get-Up and Go test (Podsiadlo & Richardson, 1991) for gait and ambulation, a brief assessment of gait and balance in older adults. The higher the score is, the greater the gait and balance problem and risk of falling (Mathias, Nayak, & Isaacs, 1986). Strength may be measured using a grip strength hand dynamometer or a leg strength push–pull dynamometer. A chair sit-and-reach flexibility test may be used to test hamstring flexibility for older adults (Jones, Rikli, Max, & Noffal, 1998). Distance or timed walks in walking programs and number of repetitions are excellent outcome measures for walking and fitness programs. Interventions that maintain or enhance physical functioning include exercise, tai chi, yoga, dancing, walking, relaxation, animal-assisted therapy, mobility programs, gardening, and aquatics.

Persistent pain is a major clinical problem among older adults, whose functional status and comorbidities present significant challenges to pain diagnosis and treatment. Assessing pain and knowing what pain assessment tool to use is important. According to Herr, Spratt, Mobily, and Richardson (2004), a great tool to assess pain for older adults, including those with mild to moderate dementia, is the Verbal Descriptive Scale (VDS), a series of descriptive phrases that refer to different levels of pain severity or intensity (Herr, Mobily, Kohout, & Wagenaar, 1998). A tool for older adults who have language impairments or who have trouble expressing themselves verbally is the Faces Pain Scale (FPS). Last, the Checklist of Nonverbal Pain Indicators (CNPI) was designed to measure pain in cognitively impaired older adults by observing their behaviors (Feldt, 2000). RT interventions such as gardening, exercise, yoga, tai chi, aquatics, relaxation, breathing exercises, meditation, storytelling, reminiscence, bibliotherapy, animal-assisted therapy, air mat therapy, simple pleasures, and Reiki/therapeutic touch offer an effective non-drug approach to pain management for older adults (Richeson, 2004).

Emotional Functioning

According to Kolanowski and Van Haitsma (2013), many terms are used to describe interventions designed to promote positive behavioral health (PBH). The focus of PBH is to decrease behaviors such as agitation, aggression, apathy, anxiety, and depression and to describe non-drug approaches to treatment. The term *PBH* was used because it is widely accepted, person centered, and understood by most nursing home staff.

According to the National Institute of Mental Health (2014), depression is a common problem among older adults, but it is not a normal part of aging. Unfortunately, it may be overlooked because for some older adults who have depression, sadness is not their main symptom. They may have other less obvious symptoms of depression or they may not be willing to talk about their feelings. Therefore, depression in older adults often remains unrecognized and untreated.

Recreational therapists may assess for depression using the Geriatric Depression Scale, a self-report questionnaire designed specifically to screen for depression in older adults. The scale may be used with cognitively intact patients and patients who have mild to moderate cognitive impairments (Sheikh & Yesavage, 1986). The recreational therapist may provide interventions that focus on strengths and assist with coping and managing depressive symptoms. The clinical practice guide *Recreational Therapy for the Treatment of Depression in Older Adults: A Clinical Practice Guideline* (Buettner, Cummins, et al., 2008) is available through Weston Medical Publishing. Interventions that address depression include relaxation, stress management, expressive arts, reminiscence, storytelling, exercise, outdoor activities, bibliotherapy, wheelchair biking, Reiki/therapeutic touch, and gardening.

The *Dementia Practice Guidelines* (Buettner & Fitzsimmons, 2013) are based on promoting RT interventions to treat agitation and apathy as non-drug approaches to care. The guidelines have useful interventions and assessment tools. Interventions to treat agitation and apathy include coping skills, relaxation, animal-assisted therapy, intergenerational programming, social dance, functional fitness, simple pleasures, cooking, recreation clubs, Reiki/therapeutic touch, brain fitness, and expressive arts.

Social Functioning

Social functioning is the ability of a person to interact in the normal or usual way in society and may be used as a measure of quality of life. According to Healthy People (2013), "quality of life is a multi-dimensional concept that includes domains related to physical, mental, emotional and social functioning" (para. 2). A related concept is well-being, which assesses the positive aspects of a person's life, such as positive emotions and life satisfaction. Recreational therapists may address social functioning (i.e., quality of life, life satisfaction, and well-being) through assessing leisure history using the Buettner Assessment of Needs, Diagnosis, and Interests (BANDI-RT; Buettner, Richeson, & Connolly, 2011). Other excellent quality of life tools include the World Health Organization's Quality of Life Scale (WHOQOL) and the Life Satisfaction Scale by Diener, Emmons, Larsen, and Griffin (1985). Interventions and approaches include friendship groups and activities that allow for resident interaction and preferences, offer choices, provide solitary and group activity, respect interests and wishes of the resident, and focus on the hopes and dreams of the participant.

APPLICATION OF THE RECREATIONAL THERAPY PROCESS: CASE STUDY

Mrs. Melody Jones is an 82-year-old retired school administrator. Her interest inventory stated that she enjoyed walking, biking, gardening, cooking, pets (dogs), singing in the church choir, and social activities with her family. She had a busy work life, but she always made time for the things she enjoyed. She was friendly and her adult children reported that she generally had a positive outlook on life. Melody was placed into assisted living within a continuous care retirement community due to a cognitive impairment. Her children had noticed that she was unable to care for herself and her house after her husband died the previous year. Her cognitive assessment (Mini-Mental State Examination) score was 21; therefore, Melody is considered to be in early stages of dementia.

Due to the loss of her husband and her recent move, Melody had lost all interest in activities. The recreational therapist was consulted, and Melody was screened for depression using the Geriatric Depression Scale. Her score (6) indicated that she had depression, and the recreational therapist referred her to the primary care physician for further evaluation. Due to her low mood, Melody was sitting in her room for hours at a time watching television. Based on the interest inventory, the recreational therapist knew she loved activity, including her pets, and suggested that Melody attend animal-assisted therapy. A service plan was developed, and the primary care physician wrote an RT order that included visiting with the therapy dog Al-e, a yellow Labrador, three times a week, for 30 minutes, for 4 weeks, to decrease depression.

The intervention consisted of walking the dog, playing fetch, grooming the dog, and talking with the dog and handler. Each session she greeted Al-e and the handler, and if the weather permitted, she walked Al-e outside with assistance, recording distance walked each session. She also would take a few minutes to play fetch with Al-e and ended the sessions with grooming her. Melody reminisced about her past pets when prompted and always was eager to participate in this intervention. After 4 weeks, the recreational therapist reassessed her using the Geriatric Depression Scale and noted that her score had dropped 2 points. Her distance walked had increased by 2%, and she was beginning to engage in other activities at the agency. The intervention demonstrates that engaging in meaningful recreation activities may make a difference in the health status and quality of life of persons treated in RT.

TRENDS AND ISSUES

Competencies

According to the Institute of Medicine's (IOM, 2009) report, unless the workforce takes immediate action, the health and human service workforce will not have the knowledge, skills, and abilities to meet the needs of this changing demographic. By 2030, nearly 3.5 million health and human service professionals will be needed (CDC, 2013).

The Bureau of Labor Statistics (n.d.) expects employment for recreational therapists to grow 13% from 2012 to 2022, which is consistent with growth rates of other health professions. This is due to the changing demographic and a need for recreational therapists to help treat age-related injuries and illnesses.

According to the National Council for Therapeutic Recreation Certification (2009), 36% of Certified Therapeutic Recreation Specialists (CTRSs) work in behavioral health, 28% in geriatrics, 22% in physical medicine/physical disabilities, and 14% in developmental disabilities. In reality, a recreational therapist working with any of these populations will work with older adults at some point. For example, persons with intellectual and developmental disabilities are living longer and are expected to live into old age. CTRSs who work in rehabilitation know they will see a large percentage of older adults who are deconditioned or who have had strokes or hip or knee replacements. Last, recreational therapists working in behavioral health will work with older adults with substance abuse issues, older adults dealing with depression, and persons with severe mental illness. Recreational therapists working in pediatrics even will interact with grandparents. As a result, application of geriatric competencies (knowledge, skills, and abilities) will be relevant in several RT practice areas.

Despite the demographic shifts, the growth of RT, and the anticipated shortage of health care workforce, the RT profession has not kept pace. Recreational therapists are not required by the national credentialing body (National Council for Therapeutic Recreation Certification) or the accreditation agencies (Commission on Accreditation of Allied Health Profession, CAAHAP, or Council on Accreditation of Parks, Recreation, Tourism, and Related Professions, COAPRT) to obtain gerontology or geriatric competencies. However, the National Council for Therapeutic Recreation Certification is making strides in this area by offering an optional specialty certification. Therefore, industry competencies as well as specific competencies for recreational therapists need to be outlined. In 2009, the Partnership for Health in Aging identified core competencies in the care of older adults that are relevant to all health professional disciplines, including health promotion and safety, evaluation and assessment, care planning and coordination across the care spectrum, interdisciplinary and team care, caregiver support, and health care systems and benefits. The American Therapeutic Recreation Association's Geriatric Treatment Network currently is working on specific competencies needed for recreational therapists working in geriatrics.

SUMMARY

This chapter provided an overview of current issues and trends in geriatric care, highlighting definitions used, the demographic shifts, and health-related conditions. It focused on the role health prevention and promotion play in geriatric RT. In addition, it discussed practice roles of the recreational therapist and reviewed key assessment and outcome tools used in practice. Moreover, the chapter mentioned two clinical practice guidelines (*Dementia Practice Guidelines* and *Recreational Therapy for the Treatment of Depression in Older Adults*) highlighting evidence-based interventions for the geriatric recreational therapist. Last, it stressed the need for a trained and competent workforce due to the changing demographic and called for recreational therapists to develop the competencies needed to meet the need.

READING COMPREHENSION QUESTIONS

1. What are the common chronic health conditions of older adults?

2. What are the common acute health conditions of older adults?

3. What is the difference between chronic and acute health conditions?

4. Your family member is having memory problems. The individual forgot where he or she put the car keys and could not remember your friend's name. Other family members feel the person has Alzheimer's disease. How would you respond to this reaction?

5. You are being interviewed for a job by the administrator in a long-term care facility. Explain to the administrator how a recreational therapist is a quality of life advocate and a culture change liaison.

6. What are the two clinical practice guidelines in recreational therapy?

7. Why is understanding a variety of assessment tools important when working with older adults?

8. You are hired to provide an evidenced-based RT program in a long-term care facility. What is the first step you would take to complete this task, and why was this your first step?

9. Articulate how you think interventions such as exercise, yoga, tai chi, aquatics, and relaxation programs help older adults to manage and cope with pain.

10. Explain to the director of nursing what type of assessment tool you would use to determine whether the resident is at risk for falling.

11. Your friends ask you, "What is a key issue in geriatric care today?" What is your response?

REFERENCES

AARP Public Policy Institute. (2004). Adult day services [AARP fact sheet]. Retrieved April 21, 2014, from http://assets.aarp.org/rgcenter/il/fs98_service.pdf

Alzheimer's Association. (2013). 2013 Alzheimer's disease facts and figures. Retrieved April 10, 2014, from http://www.alz.org/downloads/facts_figures_2013.pdf

Alzheimer's Association. (2014). What is dementia: Memory loss and other symptoms of dementia. Retrieved July 29, 2014, from http://www.alz.org/what-is-dementia.asp

Assisted Living Federation of America. (2014). Consumer resources. Retrieved April 23, 2014, from http://www.alfa.org/alfa/Assisted_Living_Information.asp

Association for Gerontology in Higher Education. (2006). *Careers in aging: Consider the possibilities.* Retrieved April 22, 2014, from http://www.careersinaging.com/careersinaging/what.html

Austin, D. R., & Lee, Y. (2013). *Inclusive and special recreation: Opportunities for diverse populations to flourish* (6th ed.). Urbana, IL: Sagamore.

Buettner, L. L., Cummins, P., Giordano, J., Lewis, J., Lynch, C., Peruyera, G., & Siegel, J. (2008). *Recreational therapy for the treatment of depression in older adults: A clinical practice guideline.* Weston, MA: Weston Medical Publishing.

Buettner, L., & Fitzsimmons, S. (2007). Introduction to evidence based recreation therapy. *Annual in Therapeutic Recreation, 19,* 25–30.

Buettner, L., & Fitzsimmons, S. (2009). Promoting health in Alzheimer's disease: Evaluation of a 12-week college course for individuals with a new diagnosis. *Journal of Gerontological Nursing, 35*(3), 12–19.

Buettner, L., & Fitzsimmons, S. (2010). Recreational therapy interventions: A fresh approach to treating apathy and mixed behaviors in dementia. *Non-Pharmacological Therapies in Dementia, 1*(1), 27–42.

Buettner, L., & Fitzsimmons, S. (2013). *Dementia practice guidelines for recreational therapy.* Greensboro, NC: Fitzsimmons Publishing.

Buettner, L. L., Fitzsimmons, S., & Atav, A. S. (2006). Predicting outcomes of therapeutic recreation interventions for older adults. *Therapeutic Recreation Journal, 40*(1), 33–47.

Buettner, L., Richeson, N. E., & Connolly, M. (2011). Content validity, reliability, and treatment outcomes of the Buettner assessment of needs, diagnoses, and interests for recreational therapy in long-term care (BANDI-RT). *American Journal of Recreation Therapy, 11*(1), 41–56.

Buettner, L. L., Richeson, N. E., Yu, F., Burgener, S. C., Buckwalter, K. C., Beattie, E., . . . McKenzie, S. (2008). Evidence supporting exercise interventions for persons in early stage Alzheimer's disease (AD). *American Journal of Recreation Therapy, 7*(1), 17–24.

Bureau of Labor Statistics. (n.d.). *Occupational outlook handbook.* Retrieved February 13, 2014, http://www.bls.gov/ooh/healthcare/recreational-therapists.htm

Centers for Disease Control and Prevention. (2008). Physical activity. Retrieved April 10, 2014, from http://www.cdc.gov/physicalactivity/data/facts.html

Centers for Disease Control and Prevention. (2013). *The state of aging and health.* Retrieved February 16, 2014, from http://www.cdc.gov/features/agingandhealth/state_of_aging_and_health_in_america_2013.pdf

Centers for Disease Control and Prevention. (2014). Fast stats. Retrieved April 9, 2014, from http://www.cdc.gov/nchs/fastats/mental.htm

Centers for Disease Control and Prevention & National Association of Chronic Disease Directors. (2008). *The state of mental health and aging in America* (Issue Brief 1: What do the data tell us?) Atlanta, GA: National Association of Chronic Disease Directors.

Centers for Medicare and Medicaid Services. (2014). *Your guide to choosing a nursing home or other long-term care.* Retrieved April 21, 2014, from https://www.medicare.gov/Pubs/pdf/02174.pdf

Conti, A., Voelkl, J., & McGuire, F. (2008). Efficacy of meaningful activities in recreation therapy on passive behaviors of older adults with dementia. *Annual in Therapeutic Recreation, 6,* 91–104.

Croteau, K. A., Richeson, N. E., Farmer, B. C., & Jones, D. B. (2007). Effects of a pedometer-based intervention on the daily step count of community dwelling older adults. *Research Quarterly for Exercise and Sport, 78*(5), 401–406.

Diener, E., Emmons, R. A., Larsen, R. J., & Griffin, S. (1985). The satisfaction with life scale. *Journal of Personality Assessment, 49,* 71–75.

Feldt, K. S. (2000). The checklist of nonverbal pain indicators (CNPI). *Pain Management in Nursing, 1*(1), 13–21.

Ferrini, A., & Ferrini, R. (2013). *Health in the later years.* Columbus, OH: McGraw-Hill Higher Education.

Folstein, M. F., Folstein, S. E., & McHugh, P. R. (1975). "Mini-mental state": A practical method for grading the cognitive state of patients for the clinician. *Journal of Psychiatric Research, 12*(3), 189–198.

Healthy People. (2013). Older adults. Retrieved April 8, 2014, from http://www.healthypeople.gov/2020/topicsobjectives2020/overview.aspx?topicid=31

Herr, K. A., Mobily, P. R., Kohout, F. J., & Wagenaar, D. (1998). Evaluation of the faces pain scale for use with the elderly. *The Clinical Journal of Pain, 14*(1), 29–38.

Herr, K. A., Spratt, K., Mobily, P. R., & Richardson, G. (2004). Pain intensity assessment in older adults: Use of experimental pain to compare psychometric properties and usability of selected pain scales with younger adults. *Clinical Journal of Pain, 20*(4), 207–219.

Institute of Medicine. (2009). *Retooling for an aging America: Building a healthcare workforce* [Report brief]. Retrieved April 22, 2014, from http://www.americangeriatrics.org/files/documents/health_care_pros/PHA_Multidisc_Competencies.pdf

Jones, C. J., Rikli, R. E., Max, J., & Noffal, G. (1998). The reliability and validity of a chair sit-and-reach test as a measure of hamstring flexibility in older adults. *Research Quarterly for Exercise and Sport, 69*(4), 338–343.

Katz, S. (1983). Assessing self-maintenance: Activities of daily living, mobility and instrumental activities of daily living. *Journal of American Geriatrics Society, 31*(12), 721–726.

Katz, S., Down, T. D., Cash, H. R., & Grotz, R. C. (1970). Progress in the development of the index of ADL. *The Gerontologist, 10*(1), 20–30.

Keogh Hoss, M. A., & Kensinger, K. (2010). Medical home: Is there a place for recreational therapy? *American Journal of Recreation Therapy, 9*(2), 13–20.

Kolanowski, A., & Buettner, L. (2008). Prescribing activities that engage passive residents: An innovative method. *Journal of Gerontological Nursing, 34*(1), 13–18.

Kolanowski, A., Fick, D. M., & Buettner, L. (2009). Recreational activities to reduce behavioral symptoms in dementia. *Geriatric Aging, 12*(1), 37–42.

Kolanowski, A., & Van Haitsma, K. (2013). *Promoting positive behavioral health: A nonpharmacologic toolkit for senior living communities.* Retrieved April 10, 2014, from http://www.nursinghometoolkit.com/

Lawton, M. P., & Brody, E. M. (1969). Assessment of older people: Self-maintaining and instrumental activities of daily living. *The Gerontologist, 9*(3), 179–186.

Lawton, M. P., Moss, M., Fulcomer, M., & Kleban, M. H. (2003). *Multi-level assessment instrument manual for full-length MAI.* North Wales, PA: Polisher Research Institute, Madlyn and Leonard Abramson Center for Jewish Life.

Mathias, S., Nayak, U. S. L., & Isaacs, B. (1986). Balance in elderly patients: The "get-up and go" test. *Archives of Physical Medical Rehabilitation, 67*, 387–389.

McCormick, B., Lee, Y., & Van Puymbroeck, M. (2009). Research into practice: Building knowledge through empirical practice. In N. Stumbo (Ed.), *Professional issues in therapeutic recreation* (pp. 447–464, 2nd ed.). Champaign, IL: Sagamore.

Mikula, J., & Smith, P. (2012). Leisure fitness: A recreation therapy concept design. *American Journal of Recreation Therapy, 11*(4), 19–26.

Mikula, J., Smith, P., Meuleman, J., & Levy, C. E. (2010). Effects of a recreation therapy aquatics intervention: A case study on an older adult with uncontrolled orthostatic hypotension. *American Journal of Recreation Therapy, 9*(3), 13–16.

Mobily, K. E. (2009). The role of exercise and physical activity in therapeutic recreation services. *Therapeutic Recreation Journal, 43*(2), 9–26.

National Council for Therapeutic Recreation Certification. (2009). *CTRS™ profile* [Brochure]. Retrieved December 28, 2013, http://www.nctrc.org/standardsandpublications.htm

Partnership for Health in Aging. (2009). *Multidisciplinary competencies in the care of older adults at the completion of the entry-level health professional degree.* Retrieved July 29, 2014, from http://www.americangeriatrics.org/files/documents/health_care_pros/PHA_Multidisc_Competencies.pdf

Patience Center Primary Care Collaborative (2014). *Defining the medical home: A patient-centered philosophy that drives primary care excellence.* Retrieved July 29, 2014, from http://www.pcpcc.org/about/medical-home

Podsiadlo, D., & Richardson, S. (1991). The timed "Up and Go": A test of basic functional mobility for frail elderly persons. *Journal American Geriatric Society, 39*(2), 142–148.

Reisburg, B., Ferris, S. H., deLeon, M. J., & Crook, T. (1982). Global deterioration scale. *American Journal of Psychiatry, 139*(9), 1136–1139.

Richeson, N. E. (2003). The effects of animal-assisted therapy on the agitated behaviors and social interactions of older adults with dementia: A therapeutic recreation intervention. *American Journal of Recreation Therapy, 2*(4), 9–16.

Richeson, N. E. (2004). Recreation therapy as a non-drug approach to pain management for older adults with dementia. *American Journal of Recreation Therapy, 3*(4), 31–36.

Richeson, N. E., Boyne, S., & Brady, E. M. (2007). Education for older adults with early-stage dementia: Health promotion for the mind, body, and spirit. *Educational Gerontology, 33*, 1–14.

Richeson, N. E., Croteau, K. A., Jones, D. B., & Farmer, B. C. (2006). Effects of pedometer-based intervention on the physical performance and mobility-related self-efficacy of community-dwelling older adults: An interdisciplinary preventive health care intervention. *Therapeutic Recreation Journal, 40*(1), 18–32.

Richeson, N. E., & Shalek, M. (2006). The therapeutic use of dolls for older adults with Alzheimer's disease: Dear Aunt Polly and Dear Uncle Pete. *Activities Directors' Quarterly, 7*(3), 42–48.

Richeson, N. E., Vines, S. W., Jones, D. B., & Croteau, K. A. (2003). Pedometer as a minimal intervention to improve physical performance indicators using a multidisciplinary health team approach: Case study. *American Journal of Recreation Therapy, 2*(2), 21–26.

Satariano, W. A., Guralnik, J. M., Jackson, R. J., Marottoli, R. A., Phelan, E. A., & Prohaska, T. R. (2012). Mobility and aging: New directions for public health action. *American Journal of Public Health, 102*(8), 1508–1515.

Shalek, M., Richeson, N. E., & Buettner, L. L. (2004). Air mat therapy for the treatment of agitated wandering: An evidence-based recreational therapy intervention. *American Journal of Recreation Therapy, 3*(2), 18–26.

Shank, J., & Coyle, C. (2002). *Therapeutic recreation in health promotion and rehabilitation.* State College, PA: Venture.

Sheikh, J. I., & Yesavage, J. A. (1986). Geriatric depression scale (GDS): Recent evidence and development of a shorter version. *Clinical Gerontologist, 5*(1–2), 165–173.

Stumbo, N. J. (2003) *Client outcomes in therapeutic recreation services.* State College, PA: Venture.

West, R. (2009). Integrating evidence into recreational therapy practice: An important focus for the profession. In N. Stumbo (Ed.), *Professional issues* (pp. 249–267). College Park, PA: Venture.

10

PEDIATRIC PRACTICE

JENNIFER PIATT AND SHAY DAWSON

OBJECTIVES

- Identify common pediatric diagnoses.
- Describe recreational therapy approaches to pediatric treatment settings.
- Demonstrate best practice approaches in pediatric recreational therapy.
- Review current trends and issues in pediatric settings.
- Understand the role recreational therapy plays in treating pediatric populations.
- Apply the recreational therapy process within a variety of pediatric settings.
- Describe common pediatric service settings where recreational therapy occurs.
- Explain evidence-based practice in the realm of recreational therapy in pediatric settings.

The diagnosis of childhood disability has drastically increased within the past 50 years (Halfon, Houtrow, Larson, & Newacheck, 2012). Some researchers have identified advanced prescreening and better reporting for these increases (Dosreis, Weiner, Johnson, & Newschaffer, 2006; Favis, 2012). More recently, strong causal relationships have been established related to increased percentages of disability due to higher paternal age at childbearing and the subsequent impact on psychological problems including attention deficit hyperactivity disorder (ADHD), autism spectrum disorder (ASD), bipolar disorder, suicide, and academic concerns (D'Onofrio et al., 2014). Moss and Chugani (2014) noted a potential relationship with underweight or obese pregnant mothers and increased rates of ASD diagnosed in their offspring. Opportunities exist for recreational therapy (RT) treatment to address individual and advanced family functioning. This chapter will highlight common diagnoses found in pediatric patients, approaches to RT interventions, and trends and issues in this population.

DEFINITION OF PEDIATRIC DISABILITY

The following definition for pediatric disability will be the context for this chapter: "A disability is an environmentally contextualized health-related limitation in a child's existing or emergent capacity to perform developmentally appropriate activities and participate, as desired, in society" (Halfon et al., 2012, p. 32). The following is a general overview of the most common disabling conditions in pediatric settings. This list is by no means exhaustive, but it is intended to provide a basic overview for the recreational therapist.

Visual Impairments

The Individuals With Disabilities Education Act (IDEA) states that visual impairment, as well as blindness, includes any impairment to vision that directly impacts the educational performance of the child (U.S. Department of Education, 2014). As one of the five senses, vision gives children the opportunity to learn and explore the world. When a visual impairment is present, children have a different perception of the world than their peers do (American Foundation for the Blind, 2014). Although children with vision impairments typically can do everything that their peers can do, they have to establish a different "tool set" to experience life in all areas including the leisure experience. An important step in vision impairment, as with many disabling conditions, is early detection so that early intervention of services occurs immediately. According to the National Dissemination Center for Children With Disabilities (2012), the most well-known vision impairments are near- and farsightedness. Visual impairments that are less common include the following:

- *Strabismus*: The eyes do not focus on a single point, but rather they glance in different directions.

- *Congenital cataracts*: The lens of the eye becomes foggy or cloudy.

- *Retinopathy of prematurity*: This occurs in premature babies when abnormal blood vessels are developed.

- *Retinitis pigmentosa*: The retina is destroyed through this inherited disease.

- *Coloboma*: The structure of the eye is missing a portion.

- *Optic nerve hypoplasia*: This occurs when fibers in the optic nerve are underdeveloped.

- *Cortical visual impairment*: This occurs when the portion of the brain that is associated with vision is damaged.

Visual impairment describes vision loss, whether the person has partial or complete vision loss, whereas blindness indicates limited vision and complete blindness indicates no visual perception, including light. Children under age 15 only account for 5% of blindness worldwide, affecting approximately 1.5 million children (National Dissemination Center for Children With Disabilities, 2014).

Visual acuity is expressed in a numerical ratio identifying lines read on a Snellen chart at a specific distance in relationship to lines readable by persons with typical visual acuity at a distance (Carter & Van Andel, 2011). Individuals with a 20/200 are considered legally blind because their visual acuity at 20 feet is equal to that of persons with typical vision at a distance of 200 feet. Other levels of blindness include travel vision (5/200 to 10/200), motion perception (3/200 to 5/200), light perception (less than 3/200), and tunnel vision, where central vision is limited, resulting in a tunnel-like vision (National Institutes of Health, 2014).

The recreational therapist will want to be aware of the level of vision impairment of the child and the assistive technology available to the child. For example, a child with a mild or moderate vision impairment may need large print items and images enlarged. Children who are blind will not be able to see print or images and may need to have items written or described to them. Several assistive technology devices help individuals with legal blindness. For example, computer programs such as JAWS© will speak the text on the computer screen and screen magnification programs will enlarge the screen from 2x magnification to 20x magnification.

Hearing Impairment

Most recent research has indicated that 40 out of 1,000 newborns fail their initial hearing test. Of these, approximately 38 out of 40 are false positives, leaving a 2 out of 1,000 rate of congenital hearing loss occurrence after retesting (Vohr, 2011). Functionally deaf refers to individuals who have learned primarily from visual input from the environment (Cole & Flexer, 2007). Recreational therapists may consider using amplification devices, written directions, and sign language when appropriate. The definition of hearing impairment, deaf, and hard of hearing continue to be debated without consensus (Cole & Flexer, 2007). In addition to the definitions of this disabling condition, the debate of treatment is unique within this population. A controversial issue is cochlear implants, which typically are considered for clients with severe hearing loss who also do not benefit from traditional amplification. Cochlear implants are implanted as early as age 1. Early intervention is thought to be more efficacious. Hearing aids are used when amplification is beneficial to clients. For children, the majority of rehabilitation is centered on fitting them with hearing aids. Ideally, this occurs up to 6 months of age to improve outcomes (Miller & Schein, 2008). Considering this debate, the following are broadly defined and common categories of hearing impairment:

- *Postnatal hearing impairment* is a temporary loss of hearing after birth but may be pervasive and progressive over time.

- *Permanent childhood hearing impairment* (PCHI) is the ongoing and consistent loss of hearing. Nearly 50% of PCHI is related to genetic factors. (Davis & Davis, 2011)

Recreational therapist should be aware that early detection is important with this population and that nearly 40% of youth with hearing impairment are in need of mental health support or have experienced abuse (Vohr, 2011). Given the high prevalence of mental health issues (up to 40%) in youth with hearing impairment, recreational therapists also should be cognizant of the psychological impact of interventions and the potential need for psychosocial support programming. Activity interventions with youth who have cochlear implants or hearing aids also should be designed to maximize the care for this expensive and highly valuable medical equipment.

Developmental Disabilities

Developmental disabilities (DD) are disorders that present at birth or prior to age 18 (Centers for Disease Control and Prevention, 2013; U.S. National Library of Medicine, 2014) and result in the child not meeting developmental milestones. Children with DD will show limitations within motor performance, cognition, speech, behavior, vision, and hearing (Committee on Nervous System Disorders in Developing Countries, 2001). Intellectual disabilities and DDs often are categorized as one with the acronym IDDs, yet not all children with DD also will have an intellectual disability.

An estimated 10% of children worldwide are diagnosed with a DD, thus making this population a global public health priority (Durkin & Maenner, 2014; Durkin et al., 2006). DDs not only create functional limitations within the areas mentioned above but also impact social interactions with others and create physical barriers to engaging in life activities, including recreation (Durkin & Maenner, 2014). A public health initiative (including RT) is to enhance the quality of life of children diagnosed with a DD through advancing inclusion, equality of engagement in life, and self-determination (Nussbaum, 2002). Following is a list of DDs as identified by the International Classification of Functioning, Disability, and Health. Although autism spectrum disorder (ASD) is under DD, it is discussed in Chapter 6 of this textbook.

- *Learning disabilities:* This condition directly impacts the child's ability to learn. This may include speech, auditory, and verbal and written communication. The most common learning disability is dyslexia (National Institutes of Health, 2014).

- *Cerebral palsy:* This is a neurological disorder that typically occurs at birth or shortly thereafter. It is caused by abnormalities in the brain that control the movement of muscles. The most common cerebral palsy is lack of muscle coordination (ataxia) and spasticity, where the muscles are stiff or tight (National Institutes of Health, 2014).

- *Muscular dystrophies (MD)*: This group of over 30 genetic diseases results in progressive weakness and degeneration of the muscles that control movement. Duchenne MD, the most common, is caused by the absences of protein (dystrophin) in the muscles, is more common in males, and the diagnosis typically occurs between ages 3 and 5. The other two types are facioscapulohumeral (begins in the teenage years) and myotonic (most common in adults; National Institutes of Health, 2014).

- *Spina bifida (SB)*: This condition is the incomplete development of the spinal cord, brain, and/or meninges (covering over the spine and brain). Four types of SB exists. Occulta (mildest and most common) rarely causes disability or symptoms. Closed neural tube defects is the second most common and typically shows few symptoms. The most common symptoms are incomplete paralysis with bowl and bladder dysfunction. Meningocele is when the spinal fluid and meninges protrude through an opening in the spine that is abnormal. Some children may have a few symptoms, whereas others may have complete paralysis and bowl and bladder dysfunction. Finally, the most severe is myelomeningocele, and this occurs when the spinal cord is exposed through an abnormal opening in the spine. This type typically has some form of paralysis as well as learning disabilities or intellectual disabilities (National Institutes of Health, 2014).

- *Spinal muscular atrophies:* This is a genetic disorder affecting the control of the movement of the muscles. It is caused by the loss of motor neurons that leads to weakness and wasting of the muscles used for movement including crawling, walking, sitting, and head movements. Three types of spinal muscular atrophy exist (National Institutes of Health, 2014).

- *Specific speech articulation disorder:* The IDEA defines speech or language impairment as "...a communication disorder, such as stuttering, impaired articulation, a language impairment, or a voice impairment, that adversely affects a child's educational performance" (34 C.F.R. § 300.8(c)(11)).

One of the main concerns in children with DD is social interactions with peers and others who do not have DD. They typically have difficulties making friends and demonstrating age-appropriate social skills. Activity limitations may include mobility impairments and lack of participation in physical activity and sport due to limited financial resources to obtain the correct adaptive sport equipment.

Psychiatric Disorders

Recreational therapists may routinely see pediatric patients in the behavioral health setting with ADHD, ASD, eating disorders, depression, suicidal ideation, and the psychosocial impact of abuse and neglect. Although psychiatric disorders are covered in another chapter, the following highlights psychiatric disorders that are more specific to the pediatric population. See Chapter 4 for a comprehensive review on behavioral health. Recreational therapists working in inpatient acute, outpatient, and partial hospitalization programs positively may impact the pediatric population through techniques such as symptom management, animal-assisted therapy, adventure therapy, stress management, bibliotherapy, leisure education, and family group therapy. Psychiatric disorders include the following:

- *Anxiety disorders:* Internal worrying and disturbing thoughts may end in a common diagnosis of social phobia, generalized anxiety disorder, separation anxiety disorder, or obsessive-compulsive disorder. Self-injurious behavior may result as a negative coping mechanism. Cognitive-behavioral therapy has been the most successful approach (Sarason & Sarason, 2002).

- *Attention deficit hyperactivity disorder (ADHD):* Children have difficulty with paying attention and impulsivity. Stimulants and behavioral therapy are used to assist clients to improve in the academic and social domains of life, areas that tend to suffer the most. Symptoms may continue into adulthood, although the characteristics of those symptoms may change (Sarason & Sarason, 2002). Use of attention restoration theory and nonstructured leisure experiences in green spaces has shown preliminary evidence of improved functioning for youth with ADHD (Taylor, Kuo, & Sullivan, 2001). Therapists also may design programs with outcomes that target improvements in attention and impulse control.

- *Conduct disorder:* This disorder is associated with youth who neglect the rights of others and break societal norms. This diagnosis may correlate to antisocial personality, criminal activity, and substance abuse later in life. Recreational therapists should be concerned with skill building for youth and parents since indicators of this disorder correlate to poor academic skills, social skills, and negative family environments (Sarason & Sarason, 2002).

- *Depressive disorders:* In childhood, these disorders may lead to a bipolar diagnosis later in life or increased reoccurring depressive episodes in adulthood. Recreational therapists should consider that children may be unable to communicate their emotions effectively and are at risk for suicidal ideation (Sarason & Sarason, 2002). Recreational therapists often concentrate on providing coping outlets for emotions, developing interpersonal problem solving, developing social skills, and providing physical activities.

- *Oppositional defiant disorder:* This disorder is characterized by youth who are hostile, defiant, and disobedient. Parent–child relationships and biological influences are thought to cause this disorder. Recreational therapists may benefit from using an ecological perspective to assist with parental skill development, improving relationships within the family, and providing coping skills to youth (Sarason & Sarason, 2002).

- *Tic disorders:* In youth, these disorders consist of involuntary and repeated movements or vocalizations. Tourette's disorder is a common tic disorder. Medications are used to treat tic disorders (Sarason & Sarason, 2002).

- *Reactive attachment disorder:* This disorder occurs due to severe abuse and neglect in young children, resulting in difficulty initiating or responding to appropriate social connections or indiscriminately attaching to others (Sarason & Sarason, 2002). Recreational therapists working with youth in foster care should be aware of this diagnosis and work on developing appropriate social skills.

- *Nonsuicidal self-injurious behavior:* Nonsuicidal self-injury is commonly seen in adolescent behavioral health settings. Sometimes referred to as cutting, it is a common form of self-harming behavior and may be associated with suicidal ideation as many persons use it as a negative coping mechanism (Martin, 2012). Recreational therapists may work with adolescents to supplement this negative coping skill with more positive approaches.

Blood and Immune System Disorders

Common blood and immune system diseases include sickle cell anemia, anemia, hemophilia, and acquired immune deficiency syndrome (AIDS). Recreational therapists typically will work with the pediatric populations impacted in hospital settings and at medically specific camps. The following outlines each of the aforementioned cases in greater detail:

- *Sickle cell disease:* This disease is a hematological disorder where red blood cells "sickle." The disease is found predominantly in individuals with African, Asian, or Mediterranean descent and occurs in 1 in 2,474 births. Vascular injury and dysfunction in organs may occur, as well as stroke when blockage occurs. Acute pain crisis and chronic pain are hallmark symptoms of the disease (Kanter & Kruse-Jarres, 2013).

- *Anemia:* This disease is associated with the reduced presence of hemoglobin, red blood cells, or hematocrit. Iron deficiency is present in 5.5% of inner-city children and is the most prevalent nutritional deficiency in childhood (Lanzkowsky, 2005).

- *Hemophilia:* This is a bleeding disorder consistent with a lack of appropriate clotting mechanism in the blood. Most cases are inherited. Hemophilia A results in 80% of cases, and Hemophilia B makes up the other 20% of cases (Branchford, Monahan, & Di Paola, 2013).

- *AIDS:* AIDS is caused by the human immunodeficiency virus (HIV). A hallmark of the disease relates to the attack of key immune fighting systems within the body (Austin, 2013).

Recreational therapists should be concerned with activities that may induce sickle cell pain crisis. They should avoid client dehydration as well as extreme cold or warm temperatures (e.g., jumping into cold pool water) for these clients. Additionally, recreational therapists should have a risk management plan to avoid injuries that may occur in clients with hemophilia. In the case of injury, the client needs immediate medical attention. Personal protective equipment and procedures for handling fluids are important as AIDS (and other diseases) may be transmitted through body fluids. The recreational therapist should follow universal precautions closely at all times.

Diabetes

A number of major glands make up the endocrine system within the body: hypothalamus, pituitary, thyroid, adrenals, pineal body, and reproductive glands (ovaries and testes). These glands affect growth and development, metabolism, sexual function, reproduction, and mood (U.S. National Library of Medicine, 2014). According to the World Health Organization (2011), the major endocrine diseases in children include thyroidal dysfunctions, diabetes, obesity, precocious puberty, hypospadias and cryptorchidism, and endocrine cancers. The most common is diabetes.

Diabetes occurs when blood glucose (blood sugar) is too high. Two types of diabetes exist: type 1 and type 2. Type 1 diabetes (formally called juvenile diabetes) occurs when the body cannot produce insulin. Type 2 diabetes typically occurs due to poor nutrition and obesity. Within the past few years, the medical field has seen an increase in type 2 diagnosis in youth due to the increase in sedentary lifestyles and obesity. Type 1 diabetes is a complex autoimmune disorder that affects approximately 150,000 youth under age 18, or 1 in every 400 to 500 youth. Approximately 13,000 youth are diagnosed annually with type 1 diabetes (Centers for Disease Control and Prevention, 2013). Unlike type 2 diabetes, which almost always may be managed with lifestyle changes (i.e., exercise and diet), type 1 diabetes is a chronic medical condition when the immune system works against the body, destroying the beta cells of the pancreas. Without pancreatic beta cells the body is unable to produce insulin that regulates blood glucose, thus requiring the child to wear an insulin pump or receive insulin shots. Prior to the discovery of insulin injections in the 1920s, the diagnosis of type 1 diabetes in youth was a terminal illness (Mertig, 2007). Although this is no longer the case, individuals with type 1 diabetes always will require insulin on a daily basis in combination with the monitoring of diet and exercise.

The fear of medical complications makes receiving autonomy support from parents and family members a challenge for youth with diabetes. The medical complications may be extremely serious, and parents often find that taking the primary role in diabetes management is easier, thus leading the child to become more dependent rather than independent within diabetes management. A primary role of the recreational therapist, whether the child is diagnosed with type 1 or type 2 diabetes, is to promote independent diabetes management. Previous RT research has demonstrated that medical specialty camps that focus on diabetes may impact diabetes management and decrease blood glucose levels. Thus, learning the skills to manage diabetes may occur in nontraditional clinical settings, leading to higher levels of autonomy support and independence within leisure pursuits (Hill & Sibthorp, 2006; Taylor, Piatt, Hill, & Malcom, 2011).

Cardiovascular and Respiratory Disorders

The cardiovascular and respiratory systems are unique in that they work collectively to make sure that oxygen is received by the organ tissues. The human body, made up of numerous cells, must work collectively to achieve "health." The respiratory system exchanges carbon dioxide and oxygen through breathing, whereas the cardiovascular system is responsible for transporting blood and other substances throughout the body (U.S. National Library of Medicine, 2014). Although cardiovascular diseases are typically common in adults, they may be problematic in children. Cardiovascular disease in children is either congenital (present at birth with an abnormality of the blood vessels or heart) or acquired (not present at birth). The rise in obesity among youth in the United States also has seen an increase in risk for acquired heart disease earlier in life. Acquired heart diseases in children include the following:

- *Rheumatic heart disease:* This is the most common cardiac disorder in developing countries and is acquired through rheumatic fever. It results in damage to the heart muscle and valves.

- *Kawasaki disease:* The cause of this disease is unknown and typically occurs in boys younger than age 5. Symptoms include fever, rash, swollen hands and feet, bloodshot eyes, swollen lymph nodes, and inflammation of the blood vessels (U.S. National Library of Medicine, 2014).

- *Asthma:* This chronic disease impacts the airway, making breathing difficult. Asthma may be caused by allergens (mold, pollen, and animals), irritants (cigarette smoke, air pollution), exercise, changes in the weather, or infections (flu, common cold). Symptoms include wheezing, coughing, chest tightness, and trouble breathing (U.S. National Library of Medicine, 2014).

- *Cystic fibrosis:* This is a genetic disease of the mucus and sweat glands that affects the lungs, pancreas, liver, intestines, sinuses, and sex organs. When the mucus clogs the lungs, it makes breathing difficult and bacteria easy to grow, leading to infections and lung damage. Some children with cystic fibrosis have severe symptoms, whereas others are mild and do not show up until the teenage years or adulthood. Cystic fibrosis has no cure, but treatments have improved drastically (U.S. National Library of Medicine, 2014).

When working with children who have cardiovascular and respiratory issues, the recreational therapist's main concern should be monitoring physical activity. Recreational therapists may limit the risk of cardiovascular disease by facilitating experiences that promote healthy leisure lifestyles, including physical activity, sport, and nutrition. Children with cystic fibrosis and asthma may have difficulty breathing when participating in moderately active pursuits. Often children with cystic fibrosis will have difficulty keeping weight on and may have digestive issues. This often impacts leisure pursuits.

Musculoskeletal Disorders

With abnormal musculoskeletal conditions accounting for over 427,000 hospitalizations annually, the American Academy of Orthopaedic Surgeons (2014) has made musculoskeletal injuries and conditions in youth a priority. Consisting of the bones, joints, ligaments, tendons, and muscles, the body needs physical activity and nutrition for healthy development. Congenital and acquired illness and injuries that fall under musculoskeletal include clubfoot, hip dysplasia, scoliosis, and sustained injuries (American Academy of Orthopaedic Surgeons, 2014). Each of these conditions directly may impact the normal development of the child. These injuries not only create physical limitations but also impact emotional functioning. The obesity epidemic in the United States has impacted the risk factor of musculoskeletal injuries.

- *Clubfoot:* The most common congenital disorder, this condition may have a genetic predisposition, yet the cause is unknown. At birth, the foot cannot be positioned in a normal position, and the foot and calf muscle may be slightly smaller than normal

- *Scoliosis:* This is characterized by curvature of the spine, often in the formation of the letter S or C. It is more prominent in females with symptoms including leaning to one side and having uneven shoulders and hips.

- *Hip dysplasia:* Affecting one or both hip joints, this occurs when the soft tissues, including ligaments, are loose and allow the femur to shift more than normal. In severe cases, subluxation may occur, which means the femoral head may be dislocated out of the hip socket (U.S. National Library of Medicine, 2014).

- *Sustained injuries:* Sustained injuries are one of the most common causes of death in the pediatric population. The most common injuries include open wounds, contusions, sprains and strains, and fractures or dislocations (Davenport & Nesbit, 2009).

The main concern with musculoskeletal conditions and injuries is monitoring pain and limiting physical activity depending on the limitations of the individual. Children with sustained injuries also commonly experience post-traumatic stress disorder immediately following the injury. In addition, to offset the risk of musculoskeletal injuries, nutrition and exercise are important to counteract obesity and sedentary lifestyles.

Cancer

Malignant neoplasm (cancer) is the leading cause of death for children aged 1 to 14 (Greenlee, Murray, Bolden, & Wingo, 2000). Malignant varieties grow and invade tissues that surround the area where the cancer originated. Metastasis, then, is the growing and seeding of tumors outside of the vicinity of where the cancer originated. Benign tumors do not metastasize and typically are cured through surgical removal (Berman, 2009). Common treatment options in pediatric oncology settings for malignant neoplasm include chemotherapy, radiation, stem cell transplant, bone marrow transplant, and surgery. Common neoplasms include leukemias (blood), bone, muscle, lymphomas, and those located in the nervous system (Howell, 2008). Despite these mortality statistics, pediatric cancer survival rates have improved by as much as 2% to 30% over the last 20 years with an overall cure rate of 80% (Hayat, 2013). As a result, the need for psychosocial intervention by recreational therapists is great (Dawson, Knapp, & Farmer, 2012). Thus, pediatric recreational therapists working with this population may consider the social psychological support of clients in addition to the more obvious medical and physical needs related to the disease. Common cancers in children include the following:

- *Leukemia* is a cancer originating in the blood and is the most commonly diagnosed pediatric cancer. Acute lymphoblastic leukemia (ALL) is the most common form of leukemia, accounting for 75% of leukemia diagnoses. Prognosis is poor in the 20% to 25% of cases resulting in relapse of ALL (Rytting, Choroszy, Petropulos, & Chan, 2005). Acute myelogenous leukemia (AML) accounts for 20% of leukemia, and undifferentiated acute leukemia and chronic myelogenous leukemia (CML) make up the remaining 5% of diagnosed leukemia cases. Overall, leukemias make up 33% of pediatric cancer diagnoses (Imbach, Kuhne, & Arceci, 2006).

- *Lymphomas,* the third most frequently diagnosed cancer in children, account for 10% to 15% of malignancies in pediatric patients. Hodgkin's lymphoma and non-Hodgkin's lymphoma are the most common lymphomas and are also the most curable forms of pediatric cancer (Chan, Petropulos, Change, & Rytting, 2005).

- *Neuroblastoma* is a malignant tumor in the sympathetic nervous system resulting in 7% to 8% of childhood cancer diagnoses. It is most commonly diagnosed in children aged 5 or younger with tumors forming in the nerve tissue of the abdomen, pelvis, or chest after originating in the nerve tissue of the adrenal glands located above each kidney.

- *Brain tumors* are the most prevalent solid tumors found in children and the leading cause of mortality in cancer-related diagnoses (Hayat, 2012).

- *Osteosarcoma* is the most prevalent bone cancer and typically is diagnosed in adolescent patients around the time of puberty and growth spurts. Tumors tend to form around the area of the knee (Howell, 2008).

- *Rhabdomyosarcoma* is the most commonly diagnosed soft tissue cancer in pediatric patients, resulting in nearly 50% of soft tissue cases. Typically impacted muscle groups are around the head area including the skull, neck, or orbital regions and around the ovaries, bladder, testes, and prostate. Overall survival rates approach 70% (Howell, 2008).

Recreational therapists should be concerned with the long-term consequences of childhood cancer. For example, cancer in childhood may result in a decreased likelihood to marry or have a significant other and lower employment rates (Stam, Grootenhuis, & Last, 2005). Thus, recreational therapists may choose to provide treatment with a goal of addressing these potential long-term psychosocial concerns with clients. They should also assess the state of pediatric clients' physical condition including the potential for lowered immunity, risk of infection, and fatigue levels. Great care is needed to balance the physical and medical condition of clients with their psychosocial need for developmentally appropriate play, social opportunities, and other interventions that establish normalcy and improve health-related quality of life.

PURPOSE OF RECREATIONAL THERAPY

The general purpose of RT within pediatric settings is to encourage the most normal developmental process as possible. The recreational therapist within this role has two tasks. First, the recreational therapist should work to minimize risk factors associated with conditions and illnesses, for example, teaching healthy leisure and lifestyle habits so the individual does not participate in substance abuse at an early age or into adulthood. The second key role is teaching adaptations so individuals can participate in the highest level of functioning possible regardless of their health condition.

The editors of this book are of the mind that RT services are not limited to addressing leisure functioning, that they may enhance functioning in many areas. Depending on the setting where the recreational therapist works, cotreatments may occur across disciplines to promote a healthy, positive leisure lifestyle within pediatric rehabilitation. For example, a recreational therapist who is working with children who have orthopedic concerns, burns, or neuromuscular issues may be working directly with the child life specialist to facilitate medical play and family groups and preparing the child to return to the community, school setting, and family environment. If the recreational therapist is teaching life skills to youth currently living in foster care transitional homes, cotreatment within a group therapy session may occur with the social worker, psychologist, and case worker. Whether the recreational therapist is facilitating the treatment independently or with other health professionals, in general, specific clinical outcomes need to be addressed. Common sought clinical outcomes include the following:

1. developing psychosocial coping skills,
2. learning healthy leisure pursuits that decrease alcohol or substance abuse,
3. developing positive social skills that lead to friendship development,
4. identifying adaptive techniques that lead to an increase in physical activity, and
5. understanding the importance of a healthy, balanced lifestyle.

COMMON SERVICE SETTINGS

When providing treatment to the pediatric population, recreational therapists will work within many settings. In recent years, the setting in which RT is provided for the pediatric population has changed significantly. The setting will continue to evolve due to recent and future health care reform. With the Affordable Care Act (U.S. Department of Health and Human Services, 2014) promoting community-based treatment rather than the traditional inpatient rehabilitation stays, recreational therapists will have to be creative in advocacy and awareness of resources to continue to flourish and make sure that the pediatric population is receiving the appropriate RT treatment.

Medically specialized camps have been on the rise, as well as research on the positive outcomes associated with camps. This includes a recent meta-analysis of 31 camp studies (Odar, Canter, & Roberts, 2013) demonstrating that this nontraditional setting may achieve psychosocial outcomes with the pediatric population. Improved compliance with disease care also has been noted. For example, Taylor et al. (2011) found that a medical specialty camp for youth with type 1 diabetes had a direct impact on decreasing blood glucose levels. Other studies have demonstrated that these camps influence autonomy support in diabetes management (Hill & Sibthorp, 2006; Taylor et al., 2011). In addition to diabetes management, medically specialized camps have demonstrated an impact on social acceptance, health-related quality of life, as well as connection with peers who understand the life challenges on experiences while living with a disability (Knapp, Devine, Dawson, & Piatt, 2013).

Recreational therapists also will work in children's hospitals with pediatric populations. Several children's hospitals across the United States have a specific program for mental health and substance abuse. Within these settings, the recreational therapist works with the treatment team to address symptoms associated with the mental illness, behavioral issues, family support, homelessness, as well as coping mechanisms to stay substance free. Recreational therapists who work in children's hospitals that provide care for neuromuscular, orthopedics, and burns may work directly with the child life specialist to prepare the child for surgery or develop a community reintegration program for transition back to the school or home.

Treatment may be provided in more nontraditional clinical settings as well. Recreational therapists have developed life skill classes for youth who are transitioning between their birth families and foster care. Working with adolescents in intensive outpatient programs for mental health and substance abuse, recreational therapists have developed adventure therapy–based programs including ropes course facilitation and wilderness experiences. For example, the University of Utah Neuropsychology Institute Adolescent Intensive Outpatient Services, Salt Lake City, Utah, provides an after-school program for adolescents with a dual diagnosis of substance abuse and mental illness that is grounded in the theory of resiliency and uses low ropes course elements to address problems associated with this diagnosis. A recreational therapist and social worker cofacilitate the program.

Another example is the movement currently occurring at the local level among adapted sport programs. With the goal of achieving Paralympic Sport Clubs in all 50 states (currently sport clubs are active in 48 states and Washington, DC), the United States Olympic Committee, Paralympic Division (2014) is partnering with community-based agencies to promote sport and physical activity for individuals with visual and physical disabilities. This is particularly relevant to pediatric practices as it may provide for expanded RT-facilitated community resources. For adapted sport programs to be called a Paralympic Sport Club, a Certified Therapeutic Recreation Specialist® must be listed on staff providing active RT treatment to the participants.

Finally, with the IDEA listing recreational interventions as one component that may be listed on the individualized education plan (IEP), the field has seen a steady increase in recreational therapists working within the public school setting. These are only a few of the many settings within the pediatric population in which recreational therapists work.

CURRENT BEST PRACTICES AND PROCEDURES

Recreational Therapy Pediatric Treatment Network

The Pediatric Treatment Network, through the American Therapeutic Recreation Association (ATRA), is a group of pediatric RT professionals dedicated to best practices in working with children and adolescents. Monthly conference calls between members address best practices such as using behavior plans, coping with flu season in the hospital, reward systems on units, collaborating with child life specialists, and innovative interventions. Members also review pediatric research and discuss reliable and valid assessment tools (ATRA, 2014).

Youth to Adult Transition Programs

The Freshen Up Program was designed to improve successful youth-to-adult transition related to employment and participation in active lifestyles. The program design connects college students with youth that have disabilities. Each client is assessed, a treatment plan is initiated, 10 weeks of facilitated activities (fitness, recreation, and social skills training) are implemented in a fully inclusive environment, and evaluations are completed. The aim of the program is to transfer learning to outside of the program post-completion including higher levels of self-sufficiency in inclusive settings. Results indicated improved employment, self-esteem, and social skills (Kunstler, Thompson, & Croke, 2013).

School-Based Programming

RT is a related service under the IDEA. In 2013, the U.S. Department of Education used Section 504 of the Rehabilitation Act of 1973 as clarification to include equal access to sports for school-aged children, a major victory for disability sport advocates (Patterson, 2012). This recent court ruling on the requirement of schools to provide equal opportunities in sports and extracurricular activities provides an opportunity for the growth of school-based sport and recreation services.

Project TRiPS (Therapeutic Recreation in Public Schools) is a program partnership between the Recreation and Leisure Studies Department at the University of Tennessee and schools around the Knoxville, Tennessee, area. This innovative approach allows for students to administer standardized RT assessments, write lesson plans, facilitate therapeutic intervention with each student, and document progress while benefiting students with disabilities through RT services. The project coordinator meets annually with the Office of the Superintendent to review service capabilities and to align with students in special education settings that require support. RT is administered to students with the goal of improving independent functioning in the community. In the 2008–2009 school year, this program served 131 students (Waller & Wozencroft, 2010).

Outdoor Recreational Therapy

Bradford Woods is a best practice site for universal accessibility in the outdoor setting (Preiser & Ostroff, 2001), is a national winner of the Eleanor Eells Award for programming innovation (American Camp Association, 2012), and has been highlighted as a best practice site for inclusive recreation services for youth with disabilities and illness (Human Kinetics, 2010). This 2,400-acre outdoor center of Indiana University hosts 800 children with disabilities and chronic illness, children of military personnel, and youth at risk annually. Programming is accomplished through medical specialty summer camps and weekend retreats, adventure therapy, and equine-assisted therapy. The program and facility routinely facilitate adapted scuba diving, equine-assisted therapy and learning activities, aquatics, adapted sport, and an accessible ropes course. Key components of the program include the use of the APIE process (assessment, planning, implementation, evaluation) in therapeutic camps and adventure therapy programming as well as ongoing clinical research on the efficacy of current programming and the development of innovative therapeutic approaches.

Outdoor experiential therapies (wilderness therapy and adventure therapy) have a strong connection to RT practice (Ewert, McCormick, & Voight, 2001). Autry (2001) articulated the value of these services for a large youth at-risk population with tangible evidence of the value for female adolescents. Russell, Gillis, and Lewis (2008) conducted a 5-year follow-up study on 102 North American behavioral health care programs in response to current concerns in the industry regarding safety. Findings indicated that the majority of programs use best practice approaches and licensed mental health professionals. The use of a standardized APIE process in the field is still lacking, and RT professionals can provide a lead in this area. An example of work completed over the last decade at Bradford Woods may be found in the application of the RT process in the next section of this chapter.

Medically Specific Camps

Allsop, Negley, and Sibthorp (2013) identified the benefits of using the RT process in the medical camp setting to improve psychosocial functioning. Studies at Bradford Woods have focused on capturing the therapeutic value of RT-based camps. Benefits include camp as a therapeutic community intervention (Dawson & Liddicoat, 2009) for youth with cerebral palsy transitioning to an adult camp, improved self-esteem and social acceptance for youth with cranial facial disorders (Devine & Dawson, 2010), social comparison opportunities for youth with cancer (Dawson et al., 2012), health-related quality of life and social acceptance improvements for youth with hearing impairments, and improved self-esteem and social connection for youth with physical disabilities, as compared to the community setting (Knapp et al., 2013). Medically specific camps as a pediatric support intervention are becoming more accepted across pediatric helping professions. However, more work is needed in providing a clear therapeutic structure.

Children's Hospitals

Haller, Talbert, and Dombro (1967) referred to the value of RT in children's hospitals over four decades ago. Many programs today are serving the needs of pediatric patients with treatment approaches within rehabilitation, oncology, and pain management programs.

The Pediatric Pain Rehabilitation Program of the Cleveland Clinic Children's Hospital for Rehabilitation serves children and adolescents with functional disabilities associated with chronic headaches, fibromyalgia, back pain, arthritis, regional pain syndrome, and chronic abdominal pain. It is the first and only program of its kind accredited by the Commission on Accreditation of Rehabilitation Facilities (CARF). Many of these youth lack normal participation in school, peer friendships, family activities, and sports. Upon admission, clients are assessed with the Children's Assessment of Participation and Enjoyment and Preferences for Activities of Children (CAPE/PAC), a pie of life (typical day for them), as well as a representative drawing of their pain. Schedules of interventions then are presented to each youth. Subsequently, clients are scheduled for RT interventions such as aquatic therapy, expressive arts, community reintegration, and socialization group. During the second week of treatment, recreational therapists work with clients to set goals for leisure engagement at home. At 6–8 weeks post-discharge, clients return to review progress toward these goals and are remotivated toward home goals for active leisure engagement.

Rainbow Babies & Children's Hospital is a part of the University Hospitals of Cleveland. The rehabilitation therapy program on the Child and Adolescent Psychiatry Unit performs rehabilitation therapy for clients aged 3 to 18, with diagnoses such as depression, anxiety, bipolar disorder, oppositional defiant disorder, conduct disorder, ADHD, ASD, and other pervasive developmental disorders. Rehabilitation therapy groups last for 60 minutes for child and adolescent groups; in addition, adolescents daily participate in 30 minutes of physical activity. Interventions include leisure education and awareness, bibliotherapy, social skills, relaxation techniques, social interaction, coping skills, and sensory stimulation. The APIE process is used throughout inpatient treatment. Each client is assessed through interview, observation, and an assessment tool. An individualized treatment plan is created based on assessed goals and knowledge of the individual patient. After each intervention, the recreational therapist documents within 24 hours verbalization, affect, social behavior, comments, and other observations. At discharge, the recreational therapist initializes a note on goal progression, along with a community referral when needed. Recreational therapists on this unit are part of a treatment team approach along with psychiatrists, nurses, art therapists, mental health workers, a family-centered care team, a licensed school teacher, social workers, and drug and alcohol counselors.

The Recreation Therapy Section within the Rehabilitation Medicine Department at the National Institutes of Health is a leader in pediatric treatment services. Recreational therapists working on the Pediatric Medical/Surgical inpatient and outpatient units serve clients aged 0 to 25 with cancer, infectious diseases, immunological disorders, hematological disorders, endocrine disorders, genetic disorders, and neurological disorders. The Pediatric Behavioral Health unit serves youth aged 7 to 17 with mental illness such as mood dysregulation and childhood onset schizophrenia. Both units use the APIE process by assessing clients through standardized and in-house instruments, individual interviews, observation, input from families, and medical chart review. Individualized treatment plans (short- and long-term stay versions) with specific goals and objectives are written based on assessed need. Interventions include developmentally appropriate and medically based play, community reintegration, relaxation, leisure education, creative and self-expression, animal-assisted therapy, social skill development, and fitness programming. Additionally, the playroom program uses a family-centered care approach that supports pediatric patients, siblings, and children of adult patients. Unique aspects of this program include a strong focus on cultural considerations due to patients and their families arriving from around the world, advanced isolation policies and procedures due to involved cases, and ongoing empirical research to improve medical and therapeutic treatment.

Recreational therapists at Children's Specialized Hospital (Mountainside, New Jersey) serve clients from birth to 12 years of age at their pediatric inpatient rehabilitation hospital, at their two long-term care facilities, and in community recreation programs. Children's Specialized Hospital is the largest pediatric rehabilitation system in the United States, and RT services are provided to children with diagnoses and medical needs such as cardiac conditions, respiratory illness, spinal cord injury, traumatic brain injury, cerebral vascular accident, multiple traumas, autoimmune disorders, autism, and cerebral palsy. A specialization of the inpatient rehabilitation hospital is a program for clients that have chronic illnesses such as uncontrolled diabetes, obesity, and cystic fibrosis. The APIE process is followed through an assessment of physical, behavioral, cognitive, and psychosocial domains, as well as leisure interests and patient and family learning needs. Long- and short-term goals are established, and RT services are documented daily or as necessary. Goals are adjusted as progress is made, and reports are given to the interdisciplinary team weekly. RT treatment consists of 30- to 60-minute group interventions and individual treatment. Common interventions include community reintegration, aquatic therapy, exercise and movement group, developmental play, infant group, animal-assisted therapy, and evening and weekend activities. In collaboration with child life specialists, a playroom and recreation room also are staffed throughout the week, weekends, and evenings.

Family-Based Programming

Zabriskie and McCormick's (2001) core and balance model of family functioning provides support for the assessment and psychoeducation counseling to promote healthy family leisure opportunities. This model is helpful in supporting families with children with a disability or chronic illness and promotes balancing a combination of core (routine) and balance (nonroutine) activities. Therapists using this approach may assess clients using standardized instruments, identify areas for improvement based on these assessments, and educate families on areas of strength and areas for growth. Leisure counseling then may be done with parents to educate on core and balance categories and the value of having both areas present in family life.

Adapted Sport Clubs

Bridge II Sports (B2S) is a community-based adapted sport program that serves 1,400 youth in six counties (Bedini & Thomas, 2012). This program was designed to empower youth with physical disabilities who are 38% more obese, have higher health disparities as a result, and are at risk for psychosocial issues. B2S partners with over 15 community agencies in a hub concept that allows each partner to bring their unique talents with B2S acting as the connecting mediator. Partners are non-profit and for-profit agencies including parks, recreation departments, and university RT programs. Programming includes wheelchair basketball, sit volleyball, goal ball, golf, and rifle. Outcome goals are aimed at improving self-esteem and fostering social capital, self-confidence, hope, and trust.

APPLICATION OF THE RECREATIONAL THERAPY PROCESS: CASE STUDY

Emily is a 13-year-old white female diagnosed with spina bifida at birth. In addition, she has hydrocephalus and a shunt was placed in her skull when she was 5 years old. Little is known about her past medical history at this time, except that she has latex allergies. Sara presents as overweight with poor nutritional skills and minimal physical activity. She currently uses a manual wheelchair independently with strong upper body strength. Emily was raised protestant by her mother, who had full custody, with whom she lived the majority of the time after her parents divorced when she was 7. She is the oldest sibling with a younger brother who is 8 years old and a sister who is 5 years old. Neither sibling has a disabling condition. Her mother works full time and appears somewhat overprotective and hesitant for her daughter to participate independently in recreational activities. She started attending an adapted sport camp located on a university campus when she was 8 years old and continues to attend regularly.

Assessment

The RT assessment found that Emily continued to present herself with little motivation to engage independently in physical activity. Although she attended the adapted sport camp for the past 5 years and engaged socially with peers, she exhibited minimal intrinsic motivation to continue participation in sport and physical activity at the end of the 1-week camp. Of the sports presented to her, she identified most with wheelchair tennis and developed a strong mentor–mentee relationship with the female wheelchair tennis coach, who also had a disability and used a wheelchair. She also verbalized that she enjoyed swimming and water skiing. Although she lives in a small town in a rural area of the Midwest, she made friends easily and kept in contact with several peers she met at camp through Facebook and Skype.

Planning

Given Emily's minimal time at camp to work directly with the RT on her problem areas, the primary focus of treatment was developing skills that may be transferred back to her home living environment. The camp lasted 1 week (Sunday to Saturday), and the principal focus of RT services was to increase sport and physical activity engagement post-camp experience. Treatment goals included improving intrinsic motivation, increasing daily physical activity, and increasing community resourcefulness (particularly advocacy for local sport participation).

Implementation

During the camp experience, Emily participated in individual and team sports. A daily schedule gave her the opportunity to experience each sport. Individual sports included track and field, golf, swimming, cycling, tennis, rock climbing, and water skiing. Team sports that were provided consisted of quad rugby, power soccer, and wheelchair basketball. Adapted sport coaches, who also had a physical disability, facilitated all sport programs. Emily engaged in two to three sport activities per day in 1- to 2-hour increments and in evening social activities including skit night, scavenger hunts, movie night, and a semiformal dance. Daily noon hour educational discussions presented topics on nutrition, athletic training, and community resources related to sport and physical activity for individuals with physical disabilities (this adapted sport camp model was developed by Ability Sport Camp, Chico, California).

Evaluation

During the course of the 1-week adapted sport camp, Emily showed an increase in social interactions with peers and coaches that directly impacted her motivation to engage in sport during the camp. During tennis lessons, Emily was able to engage for the entire session (approximately 45 minutes) with minimal to no prompts. When the coach showed her a new skill to improve, Emily was receptive 4 out of 5 times. She showed hesitation to advocate for herself when discussions occurred about returning to her home community and being able to participate in sport to address her weight and lack of physical activity.

Near the end of camp (Day 5), Emily was able to verbally state that she had a stronger desire than in previous years to continue engagement in sport post-camp. During the fifth day of camp, one of the RTs worked directly with Emily to identify sport programs local to her home in which she could participate. Emily was able to identify two sport programs and directly contact both to obtain information on registration and potential adaptations. She was able to advocate for herself and tell the staff at the sport programs what adaptation she needed. An intake was set up with a date and time 1 week post-camp.

TRENDS AND ISSUES

Learned Helplessness

Learned helplessness occurs when an individual is exposed repeatedly to situations in which they have little control over the outcomes of events and learn to become helpless in responding (Seligman, 1975). Children with disabilities may develop learned helplessness due to the negative impact of having a specific diagnosis that is out of their control, from others doing tasks for them, or from continuous protection from negative outcomes. Learned helplessness may be avoided by promoting self-determination. Recreational therapists ideally are equipped to fight learned helplessness due to the components of leisure that involve free choice and self-determination (Dattilo, 1999). In reference to pediatric populations, recreational therapists may explore ways to involve youth with disabilities in treatment and to assist in overcoming challenges.

Family Context in Treatment

A family context is important in treating pediatric populations impacted by disability and chronic illness. Historically speaking, an emphasis solely on children with disabilities may be problematic and nearsighted. A more comprehensive approach considers the stress of having a child with a disability, the family financial pressures, and the possible disruption on marriages. The impact on siblings due to consistent attention on their brother or sister with a disability or illness also should be considered. Research has shown that sibling groups are at high risk of anxiety and tend to suppress communication of their needs for the fear of adding extra stress to the family (Drotar, Crawford, & Bush, 1984). Recreational therapists may provide programs that specifically target these issues in sibling groups. An ecological model of treatment also should be considered so progress is made not only with the child but also with the child's family members on their need to support these changes. Schleien, Miller, Walton, and Pruett (2014) added that parents of children with disabilities value community programming yet are dismayed at the ongoing battle for access to these programs, negative attitudes from community members, and concerns for the safety of their child. Recreational therapists may assist in the successful implementation of inclusive community-based programming for these families. They may also consider programming targeted at providing respite for these parents.

Consideration of Health and Social Disparities

Health and social disparities are found when examining children with disabilities due to more sedentary leisure lifestyles, decreased vocational engagement, and less postsecondary educational participation (Indjov, 2007; McDonald & Raymaker, 2013). The result is decreased social, emotional, financial, and physical health, as compared to the average population set. This includes 2 to 3 times the rate of obesity, stroke, and heart disease as these youth become adults. High rates of suicidal ideation also exist in youth with illness, disability, and life stressors as evidenced by a 33% increase in suicidal ideation for children in the child welfare system, double the rates for children in the juvenile justice system, and 3 times the rate for suicide attempts for youth with learning disabilities (Chavira, Accurso, Garland, & Hough, 2010). Chavira et al. (2010) also pointed out that one of the highest risk rates are children receiving special education services. Furthermore, youth with chronic illness are less likely to become adults who graduate from college, less likely to gain employment, and at a higher risk for public assistance and lower pay.

Concern for Identity Development

Another trend that has emerged is examining identity development among children and adolescents with disabilities. Identity during adolescence is, in general, a difficult experience, and it is particularly acute for adolescents with physical disabilities (Groff & Kleiber, 2001; Helms, 1990; Steinberg, 1996). Such individuals must negotiate issues related to societal ignorance; internal barriers such as lack of resources, poor social interactions, health concerns, and physical and psychological dependency; and environmental barriers such as negative attitudes, inaccessible building design, transportation, lack of money, and inappropriate rules and regulations (Smith, Austin, Kennedy, Lee, & Hutchison, 2005). These barriers make developing a personalized identity more difficult for persons with disabilities, as compared to their peers without disabilities. Thus, youth with physical disabilities need to have equal or even more experiences (e.g., adaptive sport opportunities) that lead them to develop healthy identities.

Persons with disabilities many times are excluded from rather than included in opportunities in society, including sports, education, and recreation. The lack of acceptance that results from noninclusion of youth with disabilities in all facets of society has directly impacted their participation within all components of life; therefore, one of the challenges becomes providing youth with disabilities life experiences that help develop healthy identities.

SUMMARY

Recreational therapists have several opportunities to provide active treatment to youth with disabilities and chronic illness in pediatric settings. A unique feature of pediatric settings within the past 10 years is the location of treatment and type of RT treatment that is being provided. Recreational therapists, as demonstrated in the best practices section of the chapter, have been creative in advocating for innovative ways to improve the health of youth in the United States. This is an area of the field that will continue to grow with a demand for services to be provided.

READING COMPREHENSION QUESTIONS

1. What is the visual acuity rating that would classify a child as having legal blindness?

2. Name at least two functional domains of disability that would classify a child as having a developmental disability.

3. Name two psychiatric disorders that are specific to the pediatric population.

4. Describe reactive attachment disorder (RAD).

5. What is the difference between type 1 diabetes and type 2 diabetes? Which has an earlier onset?

6. What are the primary concerns for a recreational therapist working with children with musculoskeletal conditions?

7. What is the name for cancer originating in the blood?

8. What are the common clinical outcomes for recreational therapy in the pediatric setting?

9. How has recreational therapy been employed in public education?

10. What is learned helplessness, and how does it affect children with disabilities?

11. How does illness or disability in a child affect the child's family? How does this affect RT interventions?

REFERENCES

Allsop, J., Negley, S., & Sibthorp, J. (2013). Assessing the social effect of therapeutic recreation summer camp for adolescents with chronic illness. *Therapeutic Recreation Journal, 47*(1), 35–46.

American Academy of Orthopaedic Surgeons. (2014). Position statement: Children and musculoskeletal health. Retrieved from from http://www.aaos.org/about/papers/position/1170.asp

American Camp Association. (2012). 2011 Eleanor Eells award winners: Leaders in program excellence. *Camping Magazine, 85*. Retrieved from http://www.acacamps.org/campmag/1207/eleanor-eells-award-winners-leaders

American Foundation for the Blind. (2014). Accommodations and modifications at a glance: Educational accommodations for students who are blind or visually impaired. Retrieved from Family Connect website: http://www.familyconnect.org/parentsite.aspx?SectionID=72&TopicID=347&DocumentID=3820

American Therapeutic Recreation Association. (2014). Getting involved: Treatment networks. Retrieved from http://www.atra-online.com

Austin, D. R. (2013). *Therapeutic recreation processes and techniques: Evidenced-based recreational therapy* (7th ed.). Urbana, IL: Sagamore.

Autry, C. E. (2001). Adventure therapy with girls at-risk: Responses to outdoor experiential activities. *Therapeutic Recreation Journal, 35*(4), 289–306.

Bedini, L. A., & Thomas, A. (2012). Bridge II Sports: A model of meaningful activity through community-based adapted sports. *Therapeutic Recreation Journal, 46*(4), 284–300.

Berman, J. J. (2009). *Neoplasms: Principles of development and diversity*. Sudbury, MA: Jones & Bartlett.

Branchford, B. R., Monahan, P. E., & Di Paola, J. (2013). New developments in the treatment of pediatric hemophilia and bleeding disorders. *Current Opinion in Pediatrics, 25*(1), 23–30.

Carter, M. J., & Van Andel, G. E. (2011). *Therapeutic recreation: A practical approach* (4th ed.). Long Grove, IL: Waveland Press.

Centers for Disease Control and Prevention. (2013). Developmental disabilities. Retrieved from http://www.cdc.gov/ncbddd/developmentaldisabilities/index.html

Chan, K. W., Petropulos, D., Change, E. L., & Rytting, M. E. (2005). *Hodgkin lymphoma and non-Hodgkin lymphoma in pediatric oncology*. New York, NY: Springer Science+Business Media.

Chavira, D. A., Accurso, E. C., Garland, A. F., & Hough, R. (2010). Suicidal behaviour among youth in five public sectors of care. *Child and Adolescent Mental Health, 15*(1), 44–51. doi:10.1111/j.1475-3588.2009.00532.x

Cole, E. B., & Flexer, C. A. (2007). *Children with hearing loss: Developing listening and talking birth to six*. San Diego, CA: Plural.

Committee on Nervous System Disorders in Developing Countries. (2001). *Neurological, psychiatric, and developmental disorders: Meeting the challenge in the developing world*. Washington, DC: National Academy Press.

Dattilo, J. (1999). *Leisure education program planning: A systematic approach* (2nd ed.). State College, PA: Venture.

Davenport, M., & Nesbit, C. (2009). An evidence-based approach to pediatric orthopedic emergencies. *Pediatric Emergency Medicine Practice, 6*(5), 1–16.

Davis, A., & Davis, K. A. S. (2011). Descriptive epidemiology of childhood hearing impairment. In R. C. Seewald & A. M. Tharpe (Eds.), *Comprehensive handbook of pediatric audiology* (pp. 85–112). San Diego, CA: Plural.

Dawson, S., Knapp, D., & Farmer, J. (2012). Camp war buddies: Exploring the therapeutic benefits of social comparison in a pediatric oncology camp. *Therapeutic Recreation Journal, 46*(4), 313–325.

Dawson, S., & Liddicoat, K. (2009). "Camp gives me hope": Exploring the therapeutic use of community for adults with cerebral palsy. *Therapeutic Recreation Journal, 43*(4), 9–24.

Devine, M. A., & Dawson, S. (2010). The effect of a residential camp experience on self esteem and social acceptance of youth with craniofacial differences. *Therapeutic Recreation Journal, 44*(2), 105–120.

D'Onofrio, B. M., Rickert, M. E., Frans, E., Kuja-Halkola, R., Almqvist, C., Sjölander, A., . . . Lichtenstein, P. (2014). Paternal age at childbearing and offspring psychiatric and academic morbidity. *JAMA Psychiatry, 71*(4), 432–438. doi:10.1001/jamapsychiatry.2013.4525

Dosreis, S., Weiner, C. L., Johnson, L., & Newschaffer, C. J. (2006). Autism spectrum disorder screening and management practices among general pediatric providers. *Journal of Developmental & Behavioral Pediatrics, 27*(2), S88–S94.

Drotar, D., Crawford, P., & Bush, M. (1984). *Chronic illness and disability through the life span: Effects on self and family* (Vol. 4, pp. 103–121). New York, NY: Springer.

Durkin, M. S., & Maenner, M. (2014). Screening for developmental disabilities in epidemiologic studies in low-and middle-income countries. In S. O. Okpaku (Ed.), *Essentials of global mental health* (pp. 173–186). Cambridge, United Kingdom: Cambridge University Press.

Durkin, M. S., Schneider, H., Pathania, V. S., Nelson, K. B., Solarsh, G. C., Bellows, N., . . . Hofman, K. J. (2006). Learning and developmental disabilities. In D. T. Jamison et al. (Eds.), *Disease control priorities in developing countries* (pp. 39–56, 2nd ed.). Washington, DC: The World Bank.

Ewert, A. W., McCormick, B. P., & Voight, A. E. (2001). Outdoor experiential therapies: Implications for TR practice. *Therapeutic Recreation Journal, 35*(2), 107–122.

Favis, T. L. (2012). Screening for pediatric bipolar disorder in primary care. *Journal of Psychosocial Nursing and Mental Health Services, 50*(6), 17–20.

Greenlee, R. T., Murray, T., Bolden, S., & Wingo, P. A. (2000). Cancer statistics, 2000. *CA: A Cancer Journal for Clinicians, 50*(1), 7–33.

Groff, D. G., & Kleiber, D. A. (2001). Exploring the identity formation of youth involved in an adapted sports program. *Therapeutic Recreation Journal, 35*, 318–332.

Halfon, N., Houtrow, A., Larson, K., & Newacheck, P. W. (2012). The changing landscape of disability in childhood. *The Future of Children, 22*(1), 13–42.

Haller, J. A., Talbert, J. L., & Dombro, R. I. (1967). The hospitalized child and his family. *The American Journal of the Medical Sciences, 254*(6), 915.

Hayat, M. A. (2012). *Pediatric cancer: Teratoid/rhabdoid, brain tumors and glioma.* New York, NY: Springer.

Hayat, M. A. (Ed.). (2013). *Pediatric cancer: Diagnosis, therapy, and prognosis.* New York, NY: Springer.

Helms, J. E. (1990). Introduction. In J. E. Helms (Ed.), *Black and white racial identity: Theory, research and practice* (pp. 3–8). New York, NY: Greenwood.

Hill, E., & Sibthorp, J. (2006). Autonomy support at diabetes camp: A self determination theory approach to therapeutic recreation. *Therapeutic Recreation Journal, 40*(2), 107.

Howell, D. L. (2008). *My child has cancer: A parent's guide to diagnosis, treatment, and survival.* Westport, CT: Praeger.

Human Kinetics. (2010). *Inclusive recreation: Programs and services for diverse populations.* Champaign, IL: Author.

Imbach, P., Kuhne, T., & Arceci, R. (2006). *Pediatric oncology: A comprehensive guide.* Berlin, Germany: Springer Science+Business Media.

Indjov, D. (2007). *The disability movement* (NATO Security Through Science Series E: Human and Societal Dynamics, Vol. 31). Amersterdam, Netherlands: IOS Press.

Kanter, J., & Kruse-Jarres, R. (2013). Management of sickle cell disease from childhood through adulthood. *Blood Reviews, 27*(6), 279–287.

Knapp, D., Devine, M. A., Dawson, S., & Piatt, J. (2013). Examining perceptions of social acceptance and quality of life of pediatric campers with physical disabilities. *Children's Health Care.* doi:10.1080/02739615.2013.870041

Kunstler, R., Thompson, A., & Croke, E. (2013). Inclusive recreation for transition-age youth: Promoting self-sufficiency, community inclusion, and experiential learning. *Therapeutic Recreation Journal, 47*(2), 122–136.

Lanzkowsky, P. (2005). *Manual of pediatric hematology and oncology* (4th ed.). London, England: Academic Press.

Martin, J. L. (2012). In plain sight: The public secrets of teenage cutting. In P. K. Lundberg-Love, K. L. Nadal, & M. A. Paludi (Eds.), *Women and mental disorders* (Vol. 1, pp. 83–98). Santa Barbara, CA: ABC-CLIO.

McDonald, K. E., & Raymaker, D. M. (2013). Paradigm shifts in disability and health: Toward more ethical public health research. *American Journal of Public Health, 103*(12), 2165–2173.

Mertig, R. G. (2007). *The nurse's guide to teaching diabetes self-management.* New York, NY: Springer.

Miller, M. H., & Schein, J. D. (2008). *Hearing disorders handbook.* San Diego, CA: Plural.

Moss, B. G., & Chugani, D. C. (2014). Increased risk of very low birth weight, rapid postnatal growth, and autism in underweight and obese mothers. *American Journal of Health Promotion, 28*(3), 181–188.

National Dissemination Center for Children with Disabilities. (2012). Categories of disability under IDEA. Retrieved from http://www.parentcenterhub.org/nichcy-resources/

National Institutes of Health. (2014). Blindness and vision loss. Retrieved from http://www.nlm.nih.gov/medlineplus/visionimpairmentandblindness.html

Nussbaum, M. C. (2002). Capabilities and disabilities: Justice for mentally disabled citizens. *Philosophical Topics, 30*(2), 133–165.

Odar, C., Canter, K. S., & Roberts, M. C. (2013). Relationship between camp attendance and self-perceptions in children with chronic health conditions: A meta-analysis. *Journal of Pediatric Psychology, 38*(4), 398–411.

Patterson, L. (2012). Points of access: Rehabilitation centers, summer camps, and student life in the making of disability activism, 1960–1973. *Journal of Social History, 46*(2), 473–499.

Preiser, W. F. E., & Ostroff, E. (2001). *Universal design handbook.* New York, NY: McGraw-Hill.

Russell, K., Gillis, H. L., & Lewis, T. G. (2008). A five-year follow-up of a survey of North American outdoor behavioral healthcare programs. *Journal of Experiential Education, 31*(1), 55–77.

Rytting, M. E., Choroszy, M. S., Petropulos, D., & Chan, K. W. (2005). *Acute leukemia in pediatric oncology.* New York, NY: Springer Science+Business Media.

Sarason, I. G., & Sarason, B. R. (2002). *Abnormal psychology: The problem of maladaptive behavior.* Upper Saddle River, NJ: Prentice Hall.

Schleien, S. J., Miller, K. D., Walton, G., & Pruett, S. (2014). Parent perspectives of barriers to child participation in recreational activities. *Therapeutic Recreation Journal, 48*(1), 61–73.

Seligman, M. E. (1975). *Helplessness: On depression, development, and death.* San Francisco, CA: W.H. Freeman.

Smith, R. W., Austin, D. R., Kennedy, D. W., Lee, Y., & Hutchison, P. (2005). *Inclusive and special recreation: Opportunities for persons with disabilities* (5th ed.). Boston, MA: McGraw-Hill.

Stam, H., Grootenhuis, M., & Last, B. (2005). The course of life of survivors of childhood cancer. *Psycho-Oncology, 14*(3), 227–238.

Steinberg, L. (1996). *Adolescence* (4th ed.). San Francisco, CA: McGraw-Hill.

Taylor, A. F., Kuo, F. E., & Sullivan, W. C. (2001). Coping with ADD: The surprising connection to green play settings. *Environment and Behavior, 33*(1), 54–77.

Taylor, J., Piatt, J., Hill, E., & Malcom, T. (2011). Perception of autonomy support of youth with type 1 diabetes: Medical specialty camps as an intervention. *Annual in Therapeutic Recreation, 20*, 46–58.

U.S. Department of Education. (2014). The Individuals With Disabilities Education Act (IDEA). Retrieved from http://idea.ed.gov/explore/home

U.S. Department of Health and Human Services. (2014). The Affordable Care Act. Retrieved from http://www.HHS.gov/HealthCare

U.S. National Library of Medicine. (2014). MedlinePlus. Retrieved from http://www.nlm.nih.gov/medlineplus/

United States Olympic Committee, Paralympic Division. (2014). *Paralympic Sport Club annual report* (Rev. 1.1). Retrieved from http://www.teamusa.org/US-Paralympics/Community/Paralympic-Sport-Clubs

Vohr, B. R. (2011). Medical considerations for infants and children with hearing loss. In R. C. Seewald & A. M. Tharpe (Eds.), *Comprehensive handbook of pediatric audiology* (pp. 126–136). San Diego, CA: Plural.

Waller, S. N., & Wozencroft, A. J. (2010). Project TRiPS: A school-based learning opportunity for therapeutic recreation students. *Therapeutic Recreation Journal, 44*(3), 223–233.

World Health Organization. (2011). *Endocrine diseases in children.* Retrieved from http://www.who.int/ceh/capacity/endocrine.pdf

Zabriskie, R. B., & McCormick, B. P. (2001). The influences of family leisure patterns on perceptions of family functioning. *Family Relations, 50*(3), 281–289.

11
PHYSICAL MEDICINE AND REHABILITATION PRACTICE

BRANDI M. CROWE AND MARIEKE VAN PUYMBROECK

OBJECTIVES

- Identify at least four populations that are frequently seen in physical medicine and rehabilitation (PM&R) settings.
- Identify at least two characteristics of each population frequently seen in PM&R settings.
- Describe two best practices in assessment, planning, implementation, and evaluation for PM&R settings.
- Apply information to a PM&R case study.

Physical medicine and rehabilitation (PM&R) is a setting in which recreational therapists treat individuals who are recovering from physical injuries, both traumatic (e.g., from an accident) and nontraumatic (e.g., from a surgery). In PM&R settings, recreational therapists work with individuals who have damage to nerves, muscles, bones, and the brain. The focus in PM&R settings is restoring function and helping patients return to being fully involved in their lives.

DEFINITION AND ASSOCIATED LIMITATIONS OF PM&R POPULATIONS

Of the many primary and secondary health conditions in PM&R settings, this chapter will focus on cerebrovascular disease (stroke), traumatic brain injury, spinal cord injury, neuromuscular disorders (including Parkinson's disease, amyotrophic lateral sclerosis, and multiple sclerosis), and joint replacements as they are the most often treated in PM&R settings.

Cerebrovascular Disease

Cerebrovascular accident (CVA), or stroke, is a blockage or rupture of the blood vessels that supply blood to the brain, most often caused by a blood clot. A CVA causes damage to the brain and is considered a nontraumatic brain injury. The level of damage caused by a CVA depends on the part of the brain that is damaged and how long it takes to receive treatment. However, individuals may have a difficult time identifying that they are having a stroke because the symptoms may be thought to be attributed to other conditions. The warning signs of a CVA, as identified by the National Stroke Association (2014), may be remembered by the acronym FAST:

F: Face—Facial drooping.

A: Arms—Can the person hold up both arms evenly?

S: Speech—Is it slurred or strange?

T: Time—Call 911 if any of these signs are seen.

Time is important; if a CVA is treated within 3 hours of the first symptom appearing, an individual may be given a drug to break up the blood clot called tissue plasmino-gen activator (t-PA), or they may be treated with a clot retriever or a system for re-vascularization. According to the American Academy of Emergency Medicine (2014), 8 out of 18 individuals who have a stroke with treatment by t-PA will have little to no significant impairment 3 months following the stroke compared with 6 out of 18 who would recover a similar level of function regardless of t-PA administration.

CVAs are usually classified as Left CVA or Right CVA. A Left CVA means that the clot occurred on the left side of the brain and impacts functioning on the right side of the body, as well as causes difficulty in language, and usually results in slow and cautious movements and behaviors. A Right CVA indicates that the clot damaged the right side of the brain and typically leads to physical problems on the left side of the body, as well as impulsive behavior and visual impairments. Because CVAs damage the brain, the injury and resulting issues are similar to those caused by a traumatic brain injury. See Table 11.1 for information about brain damage.

Table 11.1
Brain Damage and Consequences

	Body function (impairments)	Activity limitations	Participation
Left hemisphere brain damage	Right hemiparesis Communication and language impairment (aphasia, dysarthria, dysphasia) Depression	Speed of activity is slow or may appear confused	Depends on activity limitation and functional impairments
Right hemisphere brain damage	Left hemiparesis Impulsive behavior Impairments in visual function and acuity, including spatial functioning, and visual field deficit (neglect or anosognosia)	Activity may be impulsive or inappropriate for level of function	Depends on activity limitation and functional impairments

Limitations post-CVA depend primarily on where the damage was done to the brain. Individuals who have had a CVA often experience limitations in motor skills and function, cognition, sensory processing and awareness, expression and recep-tion of language, and vision. Many individuals post-CVA experience "emotional labil-ity," which means their emotions may fluctuate, and may experience periods of tearfulness. Other limitations often include bowel and bladder incontinence, problems in sexual functioning, and changes in personality.

Traumatic Brain Injury

A traumatic brain injury (TBI) is caused by an external force to the brain (Brain Injury Association, 2012). A penetrating TBI is caused by something that is able to penetrate the brain, such as shrapnel from a missile, and an injury that does not penetrate the brain is called a closed head injury. The Glasgow Coma Scale (GCS) is used to determine the severity of a TBI. GCS scores range from 3 to 15. A score of 3 indicates deep coma or death, and a higher score indicates more functioning in eyes, verbal responses, and motor responses. Mild TBI is defined as a score of 13–15, moderate TBI is defined as a score of 9–12, and 8 and below is considered a severe TBI (Brain Injury Association, 2012). See Table 11.1 for additional information about the impact that damage to the brain may have on function.

Spinal Cord Injury

A spinal cord injury (SCI) may be classified as incomplete or complete. An incomplete SCI results when the injury to the spinal cord does not result in its complete severing and some motor or sensory function remains below the level of injury. A SCI is considered complete when the spinal cord is completely severed and no function or sensation remains below the level of injury. An additional classification in SCI has to do with the level at which the injury occurred. These classifications are tetraplegia (injury at the cervical spine, C1, to thoracic spine, T1), paraplegia (thoracic spine, T2, to sacrum, S5), and spinal fracture (injury to bone around spinal cord but not to the spinal cord; McKinley, Kulkarni, & Pai, 2013).

Similar to persons who have had a CVA or TBI, individuals with an SCI experience limitations based on the level of damage done to the spinal cord. The higher the injury on the spinal cord, the more functional impairments the individual will have. Individuals with very high level injury may be required to use a ventilator to breathe, and individuals with lower level, incomplete injury may be able to walk. See Table 11.2 for impact of SCI.

Neuromuscular Disorders

As defined by the National Institutes of Health (2014), neuromuscular disorders cause changes to voluntary muscles by impacting the nerves that control them. When these nerve cells are impacted and become unhealthy or die, changes or wasting in the muscles and nervous system result. Many health conditions fall in this category, including amyotrophic lateral sclerosis (ALS), Parkinson's disease (PD), and multiple sclerosis (MS).

Amyotrophic lateral sclerosis. Also known more commonly as Lou Gehrig's disease, named for the baseball player Lou Gehrig, who first brought light to this condition, ALS is a progressive degenerative disease that impacts the brain and spinal cord nerve cells. As the motor neurons (nerve cells that are located in the spinal cord) die, the brain is no longer able to initiate or control the movement of muscles (ALS Association, 2014). ALS has no cure at this time, although one FDA-approved drug (riluzole) has been shown to slow the progression of ALS. Persons with ALS have progressive difficulties with walking, writing, speaking, and eventually breathing.

Table 11.2
Impact of Spinal Cord Injury

Level of injury	Classification	Level of body function (impairments)	Activity limitations and need for adaptation	Participation restrictions
C1–C4	High tetraplegia	C1–C3 damage requires breathing assistance via ventilator	Dependent with mobility and self-care Potential for power wheelchair with sip and puff technology to increase mobility	Many due to dependence on caregiver for most or all care
C5	Tetraplegia	Elbow flexion intact	Able to use assistive devices to groom and feed Can assist in dressing and mobility in bed Power wheelchair Assistance with self-care, transfers required	Able to drive a modified vehicle
C6	Tetraplegia	Wrist extension intact	Highest level of injury to be able to function without constant caregiver (not common) Self-care independence is possible Transfers require device Manual or power wheelchair	Able to drive modified vehicle, use phone, turn pages
C7	Tetraplegia	Elbow extension intact	Typical highest level of injury to be able to function without constant caregiver Self-care independence possible with assistive devices Manual wheelchair possible	Able to drive modified vehicle, use phone, turn pages, use computer
C8	Tetraplegia	Functional finger flexion intact	Self-care independence possible with assistive devices Manual wheelchair possible	Able to drive modified vehicle, use phone, turn pages, use computer
T1–T12	Paraplegia	Feeling and movement of upper extremity	Self-care independence likely Manual wheelchair, potential for minimal mobility depending on level of injury	Able to drive with modifications and navigate wheelchair over various domains
Lumbar	Paraplegia	Self-care independence very likely May be able to ambulate for greater than 150 feet with or without assistive device	Able to drive with minimal modifications

Note. Adapted from "Functional Outcomes per Level of Spinal Cord Injury," by W. McKinley, U. Kulkarni, and A. B. Pai, 2013, retrieved from Medscape website: http://emedicine.medscape.com/article/322604-overview.

Parkinson's disease. This neuromuscular disease usually impacts persons over age 50, although younger persons may get it as well. Early on, the symptoms of PD are difficult to pinpoint. The symptoms most often associated with PD are tremor or trembling of the upper extremities, legs, jaw, or face; stiffness or rigid movements in the limbs or trunk, slow movements; and problems with balance and coordination (National Institute of Neurological Disorders and Stroke, 2014). PD currently has no cure, but medications are available to reduce the symptoms. Individuals with PD often experience tremors, shuffling gait, and balance instability.

Multiple sclerosis. This neuromuscular disease also is progressive and is caused when the covering of the spinal cord and brain are damaged. When the covering is damaged, lesions are formed that cause the individual limitations in functioning, depending on where the lesion is located. Several forms of MS exist, including re-lapsing–remitting (periods of symptoms and periods without new symptoms) and progressive (where symptoms increase over time; National Multiple Sclerosis Society, 2014). MS has no cure, but medications are available to reduce the likelihood of a new attack. Persons with MS may vary in the amount of limitations they experience; their lesions may be numerous and in areas of the brain and spinal cord that greatly limit function, or they may have few lesions and remain ambulatory most of their lives.

Joint Replacement

In joint replacement, a damaged joint is replaced with an artificial joint that is implanted in the body. In PM&R settings, the recreational therapist is most likely to see patients following total knee replacements and total hip replacements, although all joints in the body now may be replaced by an artificial joint, or a prosthesis. Often following a joint replacement, individuals experience limitations in range of motion (ROM) and pain. The limitations in ROM lead to needing to increase mobility and often require short-term modification to enjoyable activities such as adaptive equip-ment. The goal of joint replacement often is for patients to fully function without us-ing an assistive device, although this process is sometimes prolonged. Persons may have lifetime limitations on the amount of weight that should be lifted, and high-im-pact activities such as running and jogging often are prohibited to ensure longevity of the prosthesis.

PURPOSE OF RECREATIONAL THERAPY

The purpose of recreational therapy (RT) in a PM&R setting is to improve func-tional skills so the patient is able to return home and function as independently as possible. In PM&R settings, the recreational therapist collaborates with members of the treatment team, who typically include occupational therapists, physical thera-pists, speech therapists, social workers or case managers, nurses, and physiatrists (medical doctors who specialize in PM&R). Recreational therapists often co-treat with another therapist, meaning that the recreational therapist and occupational therapist may see a patient together, engage the individual in the same activity, and both work on their own treatment goals.

EMPIRICAL EVIDENCE SUPPORTING PRACTICE

Research appropriate for use in PM&R settings may be found in several areas. For example, the RT literature (e.g., *American Journal of Recreation Therapy, Therapeutic Recreation Journal,* and *Annual in Therapeutic Recreation*) publishes intervention studies that could be applied appropriately in the PM&R setting. An additional resource for empirical evidence is current textbooks. In *Therapeutic Recreation Processes and Techniques: Evidence-Based Recreational Therapy,* Austin (2013) analyzed the research support for more than 30 facilitation techniques commonly employed in RT. Similarly, authors in Dattilo and McKenney's (2011) *Facilitation Techniques in Therapeutic Recreation,* 2nd edition, use available research to address the effectiveness of 18 interventions that recreational therapists often use.

Furthermore, professionals in occupational and physical therapies also have published research that provides empirical support for RT practice. For example, a study in a physical therapy journal may demonstrate the use of a Wii™ game to improve balance for patients who have had a stroke. That same study would provide support for the recreational therapist working with an individual who has had a stroke.

A systematic review of leisure therapy[1] and its usefulness in addressing function for persons with CVA was recently published (Dorstyn, Roberts, Kneebone, Kennedy, & Lieu, 2014). This review examined eight manuscripts and found that quality of life was the strongest outcome following leisure therapy and that a reduction in depression was also a short-term impact of leisure therapy. This study also found improvements in leisure satisfaction and leisure participation for persons post-CVA. Furthermore, Williams et al. (2007) found that RT was an important part of improving FIM (functional independence measure) scores for motor, cognition, and overall function for persons post-stroke.

For individuals with TBI, Douglas, Dyson, and Foreman (2006) found that individuals with severe TBI who participate in more recreation had higher mental health and better social integration at 6 months post-injury. Furthermore, individuals with TBI who participated in higher levels of physical activity improved more in areas of mood, including reduced tension, depression, anger, fatigue and confusion, and increased vigor compared with a group who received vocational rehabilitation (Driver & Ede, 2009).

The SCIRehab Project is a large research study involving 1,500 patients with SCI who were admitted to one of six SCI-specific rehabilitation hospitals in the United States to study outcomes related to treatment of SCI and content of therapy provided (Whiteneck, Gassaway, Dijkers, & Jha, 2009). Patients who spent more time in RT were more likely to be working or in school post-discharge; also, the more time that patients spent in RT was found to be related to better social integration and mobility, as well as occupation (Whiteneck, Gassaway, Dijkers, Heinemann, & Kreider, 2012). Furthermore, this study found that more time in RT was associated with better long-term health and quality of life (Cahow et al., 2012).

Recreation and leisure activities have been shown to improve cognitive factors. For example, Radomski and Trombly (2008) suggested that individuals who engage in enjoyable activities may enhance neuroplasticity. Furthermore, they suggested

---

[1]*Leisure therapy* is the term used in Australia and New Zealand to describe the implementation of leisure education, treatment, and recreational services to enhance functioning post-disability.

that leisure therapy may facilitate problem solving related to physical limitations so patients may determine strategies to negotiate the activities. Other researchers have found that a recreation program in conjunction with an exercise program may improve executive function and memory in individuals with chronic stroke (Rand, Eng, Liu-Ambrose, & Tawashy, 2010).

COMMONLY SOUGHT RECREATIONAL THERAPY OUTCOMES

The following are commonly sought outcomes for PM&R patients, described using the International Classification of Functioning, Disability, and Health (ICF) terminology:

Body functions
Orientation functions
Global psychosocial functions
Energy and drive functions
Attention functions
Memory functions
Psychomotor functions
Emotional functions
Perceptual functions
Mental function of sequencing
  complex movements
Experience of self and time
  functions
Proprioceptive function
Exercise tolerance functions
Mobility of joint functions
Stability of joint functions

Activity and participation
Purposeful sensory experiences
Basic learning
Applying knowledge
General tasks and demands
Communication
Mobility
Domestic life
General interpersonal interactions
Community, social, and civic life
  (including recreation)

ROLE OF THE RECREATIONAL THERAPIST

In PM&R settings, recreational therapists must address functional and psychosocial outcomes of their clients. This is because changes in physical functioning may wreak havoc with how individuals feel about themselves, which in turn, may make physical functioning or healing worse or better. Recreational therapists may work on functional outcomes and psychosocial well-being simultaneously by engaging the patient in enjoyable activities that increase functional skills. In PM&R settings, they also need to work on community reintegration, to assist individuals in reentering the community with the new level of ability. Recreational therapists should also address helping family members and patients become aware of resources in the community.

COMMON SERVICE SETTINGS

The most common PM&R setting is an inpatient rehabilitation hospital. In a rehabilitation hospital, the length of stay ranges from a few days to a few weeks, depending on the extent of injury. Some rehabilitation settings specialize in specific rehabilitation health conditions, such as the Shepherd Center in Atlanta, Georgia, which specializes in SCI and brain injury.

CURRENT BEST PRACTICES AND PROCEDURES

Assessment

The purpose of assessment is twofold. First, the recreational therapist needs to learn as much as possible about a client with the intention of providing interventions that best meet the client's comprehensive needs. Second, data collected during assessment may serve as baseline information to which the recreational therapist may refer when determining the client's progress once an intervention has been introduced.

When completing an assessment, the recreational therapist should obtain information from the chart, via conversation with the client, his or her family, and interdisciplinary team members and by observing the individual during interpersonal interactions. Best practice is to use a standardized assessment for identifying the client's strengths, needs, interests, and perceived barriers specific to physical, cognitive, emotional, psychological, spiritual, and leisure functioning.

The Rehabilitation Measures Database (www.rehabmeasures.org/default.aspx) is a great online resource for recreational therapists that provides access to assessments and outcome measures of physical health conditions. The Rehabilitation Measures Database is particularly useful when the recreational therapist would like to assess a specific outcome or area of client functioning throughout the course of treatment. The Rehabilitation Measures Database is user friendly and provides access to assessments that are free to use and tests that require payment for rights to use. The Rehabilitation Measures Database allows the recreational therapist to search for assessments based on a client's diagnosis, client's physical or psychosocial needs (e.g., balance, functional mobility, depression, social support), and the length of time required to administer the test. In addition to the Rehabilitation Measures Database, a number of free measures are available for use in rehabilitation settings; a list of free resources is provided at the end of this chapter.

Planning

When developing a treatment plan, the recreational therapist should consider the results of the client assessment, the client's goals and objectives, the client's length of stay, and the contextual environment to which the client will return post-discharge. In selecting treatment interventions most appropriate for facilitating the client's progress, the recreational therapist should be aware of evidence verifying the effectiveness of selected therapeutic interventions improving functional abilities. The recreational therapist also should consider program logistics (e.g., activity and task analysis) and the interdisciplinary team's focus during planning.

Based on the information obtained as a result of the client assessment, the recreational therapist should develop long- and short-term goals specific to the client and the client's specific needs. Depending on the area and level of need, the recreational therapist should consider what areas of functioning are of greatest priority, and therefore primary goals, and what areas may be secondary or long-term goals.

Once long- and short-term goals have been identified, the recreational therapist should create objectives for each short-term goal. Objectives should be measurable and realistically achievable based on (a) client's strengths and needs and (b) the timeline the recreational therapist will be working with the client. When developing objectives, the recreational therapist should use a strength-based approach in which the client's strengths and interests are incorporated into the treatment plan so the client will feel more confident or motivated to engage in the intervention. For example, while working with Steve during the assessment process, the recreational therapist identified that he needs to improve strength and range of motion in his upper extremities. While completing the assessment, Steve shared with the recreational therapist that he would enjoy playing basketball. It would be appropriate for the recreational therapist to develop an objective that would allow the client to work toward improved physical functioning in his upper extremities (i.e., area of need) while participating in an activity in which he takes pleasure (i.e., playing basketball).

Objectives should support goals, be measurable, and include three components: behavior, condition, and criteria. Behavior identifies the action the recreational therapist expects the client to complete, condition identifies under what circumstances the behavior is to occur, and criteria indicates how the client has to complete the action to achieve the objective (Austin, 2013; Melcher, 1999; Stumbo & Peterson, 2009). The following is an example objective for the goal of improving anger management:

Objective: Following participation in two 60-minute anger management sessions, client will identify two methods for positively expressing her anger and frustration.

Behavior: Client identifies positive methods for expressing anger and frustration.

Condition: Following participation in two 60-minute anger management sessions.

Criteria: Client identifies *two* methods.

Also, the challenge and skill level required of the client in each objective should match the client's skill and perceived ability. The recreational therapist does not want to unintentionally set up the client for failure; this may occur if the recreational therapist creates objectives that are inappropriately sequenced and require too much challenge too soon. For example, if an objective's criteria are too strict, and if the client is unsuccessful in the skill, the individual may experience decreased confidence or self-esteem, causing him or her to be reluctant to attempt the skill again.

The recreational therapist should consult with and collaborate with the client throughout the treatment planning process. A client is more likely to actively engage and work toward improvement during therapeutic interventions if he or she has had an opportunity to provide input into the plan. In contrast, if the client has not had an opportunity to contribute thoughts, concerns, or preferences during the treatment planning process, the individual is likely to be more hesitant or unwilling to participate in individual and group interventions.

Implementation

The recreational therapist executes the treatment plan by implementing the selected therapeutic interventions with the client in individual or group sessions. Sessions first may be provided in a controlled setting to allow the client to build up functional skill and competence. When it is appropriate, the recreational therapist may work with the client in a community setting so the client may practice learned functional skills in an environment with natural supports and barriers. By encouraging the client to transfer and use skills, behaviors, and attitudes learned during rehabilitation into the community setting, the recreational therapist may facilitate the client's reintegration into his or her everyday environment. Working through this transition promotes the client's independent functioning and allows the person to problem solve or adapt to unanticipated situations.

During and upon completion of each therapy session, the recreational therapist formatively should evaluate (and document) the client's progress toward goals and objectives, as well as changes or developments in contextual factors, the client's health condition, attitudes, or behaviors regarding the rehabilitation process. Based on the client's progress in reaching intended outcomes, the recreational therapist should revise existing goals and objectives, or create new ones as needed, to consistently reflect the client's needs.

Evaluation

Once a client has reached the end of a rehabilitation stay or has completed goals and objectives, the recreational therapist should document a discharge summary and transition plan based on the results of a summative evaluation regarding the client's progress and response to treatment.

The discharge summary should outline the areas of client functioning that have been addressed successfully, as well as those that still need improvement. Such progress may be evaluated by comparing the client's original assessment data to the client's current status. The recreational therapist should comment on which goals and objectives the client has achieved or made progress toward and identify what existing or newly developed goals and objectives still remain. The discharge summary should also address how receptive the client was to selected interventions, including which therapies were most effective regarding functional improvement.

The transition plan should be tailored specifically to the individual client, and the recreational therapist should create it with the client's reintegration into his or her home community in mind. A transition plan may include action-oriented goals and objectives for the client to work toward once the individual returns home. The transition plan also may identify natural supports and community-based resources to which the client has access and should pursue to further the recovery process, independent functioning, leisure lifestyle, and overall quality of life.

Prior to the client's discharge, the recreational therapist should discuss the transition plan with the client; this reassures clients that they have the necessary skills and supports to successfully return to their everyday life and home community. Reviewing supports and resources with clients and identifying action-oriented goals encourages clients to work toward their maximum potential post-rehab, potentially decreasing the risk of secondary health conditions and poor quality of life.

APPLICATION OF THE RECREATIONAL THERAPY PROCESS: CASE STUDY

The following case study illustrates the use of the RT process with an individual who has a spinal cord injury. The four steps of the RT process include assessment, planning, implementation, and evaluation. Each step of the RT process will be discussed as it applies to the case study provided.

Eli is an 18-year-old male who has recently sustained a T4 SCI as a result of a diving accident. Prior to his injury, Eli identified as being an athlete; he participated in triathlons, ran on his university cross-country club team, and enjoyed going to the lake to water ski with friends on the weekend. As a result of the accident, Eli is paralyzed from the waist down; he experiences less control and stability in his chest and abdominal regions, but he has strong functioning in his arms and hands. Post-injury, Eli has become fairly sedentary and keeps to himself. He wants to spend less time with friends and is unsure about whether he should return to college. He watches television and visits with family in his room, but he rarely participates in community outings or other programs sponsored by Billings Ridge Rehabilitation Hospital, where he currently is receiving therapy. Eli uses a manual wheelchair and is working toward being able to independently transfer himself.

Assessment

Prior to meeting with Eli, the recreational therapist reviewed the client's chart and the data already entered by interdisciplinary team members. Understanding Eli's background provided the recreational therapist with further insight into Eli (his attitude, behavior) and the personal/environmental contexts that influence his life; this equipped the recreational therapist with knowledge for which to probe for additional client perspectives during the assessment process. The recreational therapist, in collaboration with Eli, completed the Comprehensive Evaluation in Recreational Therapy (CERT-Physical Disabilities) standardized assessment for the purpose of generally evaluating Eli's strengths and needs regarding his functional abilities and adjustment to his SCI. In addition, the recreational therapist completed the standardized Idyll Arbor Leisure Motivation Scale (LMS) with Eli to gain more specific in-depth knowledge about his interests, satisfaction, and motivation levels regarding leisure (burlingame & Blaschko, 2002).

From the assessment, the recreational therapist learned that Eli was having a difficult time adjusting to his health condition. Eli identified that he was hesitant to socialize with friends because they will treat him differently and because he feels he will no longer be able to participate in the activities that they typically do together (e.g., running, waterskiing, triathlons). His lack of confidence in his abilities and his perception of his health condition and how others may respond to him are also the reasons he is unsure as to whether he wants to return to college. In completing the LMS, Eli identified that prior to his injury he was most interested and motivated in group and social settings where physical activity and friendly competition were present. Post-injury, Eli reported that he was "not sure" he had the functional skills necessary to return to similar activities.

Planning

Based on the results of the assessment, the recreational therapist and Eli agreed that his greatest needs relate to his (a) coping with and accepting his health condition, as it has caused him to isolate himself from friends and community opportunities; (b) lack of confidence regarding his abilities, which has decreased his motivation to attempt activities for fear of failure; and (c) lack of awareness and knowledge regarding adaptive sports, including collegiate adaptive sport programs, and elite-level competitions. As a result, the recreational therapist developed the following goals for Eli:

Goal 1: Increase knowledge of adaptive sports.

Goal 2: Increase endurance necessary for independently maneuvering wheelchair.

By educating and exposing Eli to adaptive sports, the recreational therapist used Eli's interests (e.g., social involvement and competitive physically active sports) to work toward improved physical functioning and independence using a wheelchair, which may build his confidence and competence regarding his functional abilities and improve his perception of how friends and family will respond to him post-injury.

The recreational therapist developed the following measurable objectives specific to Eli's goals:

Goal 1: Increase knowledge of adaptive sports.

Objective 1: Within 1 week of completing leisure education session, client will verbally identify three adaptive sports he would be interested in learning more about (via spectatorship or participation).

Objective 2: During participation in the Abilities Expo sports demonstrations, client will try using five pieces of adaptive equipment specific to the three adaptive sports in which he indicated he was interested.

Goal 2: Increase physical endurance necessary for independently maneuvering wheelchair.

Objective 1: During wheelchair basketball scrimmage, client independently will push his wheelchair up and down the court for 10 minutes, stopping only when game play indicates the need to do so (e.g., ball goes out of bounds, coach calls time-out).

Objective 2: During 60-minute accessible air travel exercise, client will park in airport parking deck, bring one carry-on bag and independently push his wheelchair through all checkpoints required for boarding plane (ticket counter, security, and terminal gate), taking no more than five 1-minute rest breaks.

Eli's goals and objectives (based on his greatest area of need) guided the recreational therapist in selecting appropriate treatment interventions intended to facilitate Eli's progress toward achieving his goals.

Implementation

Eli participated in several leisure education courses specific to his learning about adaptive sports, including opportunities for participation in his home community, the variety of adaptive sports available, the types of equipment offered to aid in his being able to independently participate, and the university programs with adaptive sport teams in which he could transfer to and complete his undergraduate degree while competing at the collegiate level. Many of these sessions involved experiential learning opportunities in the community and involved Eli's natural support system. This allowed Eli to socially interact with friends and family while participating in activities that are of shared interest to all involved.

At the conclusion of each treatment session, the recreational therapist completed a progress note, documenting subjective and objective information, provided an overall analysis of how the session went for Eli, what goals and objectives were achieved, and identified how the progress of the session informed the implementation of the next scheduled treatment session. During this process, if the recreational therapist realized that Eli's goals and objectives need to be modified, or if new goals needed to be created, the recreational therapist did so accordingly.

Evaluation

The recreational therapist was made aware of Eli's scheduled discharge and confirmed that Eli will be reintegrating into his hometown community and moving back in with his parents until he is able to locate an accessible apartment in which to live and feels confident in his abilities to independently do so.

The recreational therapist completed a discharge summary, documenting the interventions in which Eli participated during his inpatient stay and the goals and objectives achieved as a result. Additionally, the recreational therapist worked with Eli to develop a transition plan that identified supports and resources available to Eli in his home community, as well as long-term goals for Eli to work toward once he returned home to ensure maintained and improved functional abilities and quality of life. These goals included signing up and participating in an adaptive sport program at least twice a week, traveling to participate in sport-specific camps and clinics, and learning to drive using hand controls for the purpose of furthering his independence and ability to join friends in social and leisure-based activities.

TRENDS AND ISSUES

International Classification of Functioning, Disability, and Health

The International Classification of Functioning, Disability, and Health (ICF) continues to become the accepted global classification system for organizing health conditions across health care providers and settings. To maintain relevant with medical and allied health professionals, recreational therapists need to incorporate the ICF into their terminology and practice.

Rather than being focused solely on an individual's disability, the ICF is a strength-based approach that is focused on functional abilities. In addition, the ICF classification of an individual's health condition is based on personal factors, environmental factors, and participation in activities. This aligns well with RT in that RT professionals also strive to operate from a strength-based lens, consider the whole person (including contextual factors) when developing a treatment plan, and promote active participation in activities of daily living and leisure throughout the continuum of care and during transition from hospital to community-based settings (Howard, Browning, & Lee, 2007; Porter & Van Puymbroeck, 2007; Reed et al., 2005; Rimmer, 2006).

Continuum of Services

As the health care system in the United States continues to evolve, clients receiving RT services in a clinical setting likely will experience shortened length of stays. As a result, the probability of RT services becoming outpatient oriented with programs being delivered in community-based settings increases.

Recreational therapists should be proactive in recognizing this shift in how, where, and why services are delivered. For some clients, RT services will be preventative; for others, services will be focused on recovery and rehabilitation; and for others, the purpose will be improved quality of life and well-being. Regardless of the intended outcome, format, or environment in which services are delivered, recreational therapists must be acknowledged as a vital member of the multidisciplinary team across the continuum of care.

A Need for Standardized Assessment

As RT professionals continue to lobby for consideration and ultimate approval for RT to be a covered service among insurance companies and the Center for Medicare and Medicaid Services, they must justify the functional outcomes (e.g., measurable change in physical, cognitive, social, and emotional performance) that clients experience as a result of programs and services delivered (Passmore, 2007; Stumbo & Hess, 2001; Thompson, 2001).

At present, recreational therapists use standardized assessments from external professions, as well as nonstandardized, agency-specific assessments. This use of nonstandardized assessments potentially prevents recreational therapists from being able to determine conclusively client outcomes and discredits the validity and reliability of RT services as services and treatment approaches may differ.

Thus, recreational therapists need to establish and consistently use standardized assessments across the continuum of care. In doing so, professionals could articulate more clearly via measurable data the benefits of RT with regard to functional outcomes and an individual's health, well-being, and quality of life (Stumbo & Pegg, 2010). In addition, having a standardized assessment process would promote global consistencies with regard to terminology, treatment approaches, and philosophies of care. The first step is recognizing the need for standardizing the professional field; however, identifying where to begin, what content to include or exclude, and who is responsible for leading such a task is a greater challenge (Hood, 2001).

Innovative Assistive Technology

With the advancement of medical expertise and computer-based technology, the progression and availability of innovative adaptive equipment and assistive technology continues to become more accessible in clinical and community-based settings. Due to the fast pace in which technology is introduced into the mainstream, recreational therapists must remain up to date in their knowledge and expertise regarding the diverse technologies available to clients that promote independent functioning (Jans & Scherer, 2006; McNaughton et al., 2009).

Recreational therapists may learn and remain informed about modern technology through demonstration expos, conference workshops, and in-service trainings. In turn, the recreational therapist is better prepared to create awareness of and educate clients about available assistive technologies and available resources for loaning or purchasing equipment for long-term use.

SUMMARY

In PM&R settings, recreational therapists have a great deal of evidence from which to draw to implement in practice. Recreational therapists in a PM&R setting will work with several populations, including those with CVA, TBI, SCI, neuromuscular disorders, and joint replacements. By focusing on functional outcomes, recreational therapists may improve their clients' lives dramatically. Recreational therapists should use current best practices and procedures and be aware of current trends and issues.

RESOURCES

For a comprehensive list of appropriate rehabilitation measures that the user may search by categories such as ICF category, diagnosis, length of test, and cost, visit the Rehabilitation Measures Database website (www.rehabmeasures.org).

For a list of geriatric assessments in functional domains visit the Geriatric Assessment Tools website (www.healthcare.uiowa.edu/igec/tools/) and the Hartford Institute for Geriatric Nursing website (consultgerirn.org/resources).

READING COMPREHENSION QUESTIONS

1. Name four populations frequently seen in PM&R settings.
2. Name two characteristics of persons with CVA.
3. Name two characteristics of persons with TBI.
4. Name two characteristics of persons with SCI.
5. Name two characteristics of persons with MS.
6. Describe one research finding related to RT and spinal cord injury.
7. Develop two additional goals for Eli based on the case study information provided.
8. Describe two trends for RT in PM&R settings.

REFERENCES

ALS Association. (2014). *What is ALS?* Retrieved from http://www.alsa.org/about-als/what-is-als.html

American Academy of Emergency Medicine. (2014). *t-PA for stroke: Potential benefit, risk and alternatives.* Retrieved from http://www.aaem.org/UserFiles/file/tpaedtool-AAEM.pdf

Austin, D. R. (2013). *Therapeutic recreation processes and techniques: Evidence-based recreational therapy* (7th ed.). Urbana, IL: Sagamore.

Brain Injury Association. (2012). About brain injury. Retrieved from http://www.biausa.org/about-brain-injury.htm#definitions

burlingame, j., & Blaschko, T. M. (2002). *Assessment tools for recreational therapy and related fields* (3rd ed.). Ravensdale, WA: Idyll Arbor.

Cahow, C., Gassaway, J., Rider, C., Joyce, J. P., Bogenschutz, A., Edens, K., . . . Whiteneck, G. (2012). Relationship of therapeutic recreation inpatient rehabilitation interventions and patient characteristics to outcomes following spinal cord injury: The SCIRehab project. *The Journal of Spinal Cord Medicine, 35*(6), 547–564.

Dattilo, J., & McKenney, A. (Eds.). (2001). *Facilitation techniques in therapeutic recreation* (2nd ed.). State College, PA: Venture.

Dorstyn, D., Roberts, R., Kneebone, I., Kennedy, P., & Lieu, C. (2014). Systematic review of leisure therapy and its effectiveness in managing functional outcomes in stroke rehabilitation. *Topics in Stroke Rehabilitation, 21*(1), 40–51.

Douglas, J. M., Dyson, M., & Foreman, P. (2006). Increasing leisure activity following severe traumatic brain injury: Does it make a difference? *Brain Impairment, 7*(2), 107–118.

Driver, S., & Ede, A. (2009). Impact of physical activity on mood after TBI. *Brain Injury, 23*(3), 203–212.

Hood, C. D. (2001). Clinical practice guidelines: A decision-making tool for best practice? In N. J. Stumbo (Ed.), *Professional issues in therapeutic recreation: On competence and outcomes* (pp. 189–214). Champaign, IL: Sagamore.

Howard, D., Browning, C., & Lee, Y. (2007). The International Classification of Functioning, Disability, and Health: Therapeutic recreation code sets and salient diagnostic core sets. *Therapeutic Recreation Journal, 41*(1), 61–81.

Jans, L. H., & Scherer, M. J. (2006). Assistive technology training: Diverse audiences and multidisciplinary content. *Disability and Rehabilitation: Assistive Technology, 1*(1–2), 69–77.

McKinley, W., Kulkarni, U., & Pai, A. B. (2013). Functional outcomes per level of spinal cord injury. Retrieved from Medscape website: http://emedicine.medscape.com/article/322604-overview

McNaughton, D., Rackensperger, T., Benedek-Wood, E., Krezman, C., Williams, M. B., & Light, J. (2008). "A child needs to be given a chance to succeed": Parents of individuals who use AAC describe the benefits and challenges of learning AAC technologies. *Augmentative and Alternative Communication, 24*(1), 43–55.

Melcher, S. (1999). *Introduction to writing goals and objectives: A manual for recreation therapy students and entry-level professionals.* State College, PA: Venture.

National Institute of Neurological Disorders and Stroke. (2014). NINDS Parkinson's disease information page. Retrieved from http://www.ninds.nih.gov/disorders/parkinsons_disease/parkinsons_disease.htm

National Institutes of Health. (2014). Neuromuscular disorders. Retrieved from http://www.nlm.nih.gov/medlineplus/neuromusculardisorders.html

National Multiple Sclerosis Society. (2014). Symptoms and diagnosis. Retrieved from http://www.nationalmssociety.org/Symptoms-Diagnosis

National Stroke Association. (2014). Warning signs of stroke. Retrieved from http://www.stroke.org/site/PageServer?pagename=SYMP

Passmore, T. R. J. (2007). *Coverage of recreational therapy: Rules and regulations.* Alexandria, VA: American Therapeutic Recreation Association.

Porter, H. R., & Van Puymbroeck, M. (2007). Utilization of the International Classification of Functioning, Disability, and Health within therapeutic recreation practice. *Therapeutic Recreation Journal, 41*(1), 47–60.

Radomski, M., & Trombly, C. (2008). *Occupational therapy for physical dysfunction* (6th ed.). Philadelphia, PA: Lippincott Williams & Wilkins.

Rand, D., Eng, J. J., Liu-Ambrose, T., & Tawashy, A. E. (2010). Feasibility of a 6-month exercise and recreation program to improve executive functioning and memory in individuals with chronic stroke. *Neurorehabilitation and Neural Repair, 24*(8), 722–729.

Reed, G. M., Lux, J. B., Bufka, L. F., Trask, C., Peterson, D. B., Stark, S., . . . Hawley, J. A. (2005). Operationalizing the International Classification of Functioning, Disability and Healing in clinical settings. *Rehabilitation Psychology, 50*(2), 122–131.

Rimmer, J. H. (2006). Use of the ICF in identifying factors that impact participation in physical activity/rehabilitation among people with disabilities. *Disability and Rehabilitation, 28*(17), 1087–1095.

Stumbo, N. J., & Hess, M. E. (2001). On competencies and outcomes in therapeutic recreation. In N. J. Stumbo (Ed.), *Professional issues in therapeutic recreation: On competence and outcomes* (pp. 3–20). Champaign, IL: Sagamore.

Stumbo, N. J., & Pegg, S. (2010). Outcomes and evidence-based practice: Moving forward. *Annual in Therapeutic Recreation, 18*, 12–23.

Stumbo, N. J., & Peterson, C. A. (2009). *Therapeutic recreation program design: Principles and procedures* (5th ed.). San Francisco, CA: Benjamin Cummings.

Thompson, G. T. (2001). Reimbursement: Surviving prospective payment as a recreational therapy practitioner. In N. J. Stumbo (Ed.), *Professional issues in therapeutic recreation: On competence and outcomes* (pp. 249–264). Champaign, IL: Sagamore.

Whiteneck, G., Gassaway, J., Dijkers, M. P., Heinemann, A. W., & Kreider, S. E. (2012). Relationship of patient characteristics and rehabilitation services to outcomes following spinal cord injury: The SCIRehab Project. *The Journal of Spinal Cord Medicine, 35*(6), 484–502.

Whiteneck, G., Gassaway, J., Dijkers, M. P., & Jha, A. (2009). New approach to study the contents and outcomes of spinal cord injury rehabilitation: The SCIRehab Project. *Journal of Spinal Cord Injury Medicine, 32*(3), 251–259.

Williams, R., Barrett, J., Vercoe, H., Maahs-Fladung, C., Loy, D., & Skalko, T. (2007). Effects of recreational therapy on functional independence of people recovering from stroke. *Therapeutic Recreation Journal, 41*(4), 326–332.

12

MILITARY SERVICE MEMBERS

JASMINE TOWNSEND, BRENT HAWKINS, AND JESSIE BENNETT

OBJECTIVES

- Identify the ways injured service members are impacted by their military experiences and injuries.
- Describe differences and similarities between the three generations of military service members.
- Describe the physical and emotional/psychological injuries associated with military service.
- Identify evidence-based interventions and programs that a recreational therapist may implement to improve the functioning and quality of life of injured service members and their families.
- Identify commonly sought outcomes associated with recreational therapy with injured service members.
- Describe the role of the recreational therapist in each phase of the treatment process.
- Identify settings in which a recreational therapist may work with injured service members and their families.
- Describe trends in services for injured service members and their implications for recreational therapy.

The U.S. Armed Forces consists of five main branches of service (Air Force, Army, Coast Guard, Marines, and Navy), as well as National Guard and Reserves components. The first military branches were established in 1775 to protect the United States during the American Revolution (U.S. Department of Defense, n.d.) and have evolved to meet the country's national security needs in the face of global conflict. Currently, approximately 1.4 million men and women are serving in active duty roles in the U.S. Armed Forces, with a population of approximately 22.6 million living veterans of conflicts since World War II. Of these, approximately 10% are female (U.S. Department of Defense, n.d.; U.S. Department of Veterans Affairs, 2013).

The profile of veterans in the United States is diverse and ever changing. Figure 12.1 shows an estimate of living veterans of America's wars, as well as veterans of peacetime, as of 2013 (National Center for Veterans Analysis and Statistics, 2013). To best understand and meet the needs of this dynamic group of military service members, they should be classified into generations. The oldest generation includes the remaining World War II veterans, the middle generation includes the Vietnam and Korean War veterans, and the newest or youngest generation includes veterans from the Gulf Wars (Desert Storm/Desert Shield and the Global War On Terrorism [GWOT]).

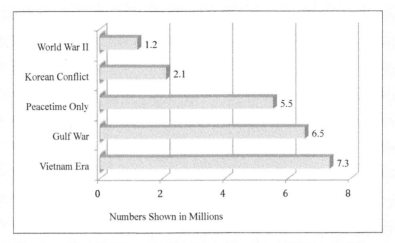

Figure 12.1. Estimate of living veterans of U.S. conflicts.

The term *injured service member* will be used frequently throughout this chapter, as it reflects the greatest proportion of military service members with whom a recreational therapist would work. As of this writing, more than 1 million men and women are currently serving in active duty roles (U.S. Department of Defense, n.d.) and may receive services from a recreational therapist as well. A recreational therapist may work with a service member at any point during the stages of service. More often than not, however, recreational therapists work with service members following their discharge from the military and, in many cases, especially in more recent times, following discharge due to traumatic injury.

Traumatic injury and death among service members is a sobering and unfortunate artifact of a nation at war. Military conflicts and rebuilding efforts that follow have left many service members to sustain the brunt of the violence that accompanies the conflicts. In the most recent conflicts in Iraq and Afghanistan, an increased survival rate has been reported due to improvements in body armor, advancements in emergency medical services, and immediate access to life-saving medical attention to service members injured in the combat location (Fitzpatrick & Pasquina, 2010). Therefore, more service members are returning with traumatic physical, emotional, and psychological injuries than in past conflicts. Injury type and severity vary greatly among injured service members.

DEFINITIONS AND DESCRIPTION OF LIMITATIONS

Service members often sustain more than one injury. Frequently, service members experience complex physical injuries, emotional and psychological injuries, and other health conditions that affect all life domains and, consequently, their ability to participate in life activities. To properly treat this population, recreational therapists need to understand common combat-related injuries. The following sections will provide an overview of common injuries of service members.

Physical Injuries

Blast injuries account for the largest number of injuries among injured service members during the recent combat operations in Iraq and Afghanistan and were common in previous conflicts as well. *Blast injury* is an overarching term that includes injuries from artillery, mortar shells, mines, booby traps, aerial bombs, improvised explosive devices (IEDs), and rocket-propelled grenades; this type of injury accounts for approximately 90% of all casualties (Sayer et al., 2008; U.S. Department of Defense, 2014a). Blast injuries include categories of physical injuries such as limb loss, bone fractures, sensory impairments, burns, spinal cord injury (SCI), crushing injuries, brain injury (BI), and polytrauma. However, not all injured service members sustain their injuries in combat; many are injured in military trainings and during times of nondeployment.

Polytrauma is a combination of injuries that affects at least two body regions, in which one of the injuries was life threatening and resulted in multiple impairments or disability (U.S. Department of Veterans Affairs, 2014). Polytrauma is associated most commonly with BI due to the multidimensional nature of blast injuries. The combination of injuries creates a complexity of impairments that are challenging to address during and after rehabilitation. Since polytrauma is defined by multiple injuries, the recreational therapist needs to understand other individual categories of injury to better indicate how the injuries affect the service member.

BI has been considered the signature injury of the GWOT in particular, but it also has been an issue in previous conflicts (Fitzpatrick & Pasquina, 2010; Sandberg, Bush, & Martin, 2009; Sayer et al., 2008). Any injury to the brain may affect a person's physical, cognitive, and psychological functioning depending on the severity of the injury. Both closed and open BIs are prevalent during war. Closed BIs are likely to result from concussive injuries from blast waves or impact injuries that do not penetrate the skull. Open, or penetrating BIs, are likely to occur from shrapnel from bombs, artillery, or other outside objects that break through the skull and damage the brain. Depending on the severity of damage to the brain, complications may include seizures, loss of consciousness, spasticity, and loss of physical functioning such as balance and functional strength, loss of memory, problems with attention span, anxiety, and depression (Fitzpatrick & Pasquina, 2010).

SCI also is common among injured service members and generally results from vehicular accidents, blasts, and gunshot wounds that damage the spinal cord (Fitzpatrick & Pasquina, 2010). These injuries result in paresis (i.e., incomplete impairment) or paralysis (i.e., complete impairment) below the level of injury and may affect muscular and sensory/sensation and functioning. Injuries in the thoracic or lower region of the spine often result in paraplegia (i.e., impairment in two extremities, typically the trunk and legs), whereas injury to the thoracic or higher region of the spine often results in tetraplegia (i.e., impairment in all four extremities). These impairments lead to difficulty with ambulation, activities of daily living, bowel and bladder functioning, increased risk for autonomic dysreflexia, and adjustment to disability. Other injuries to the spine also occur and may result in paresis or paralysis, such as bulging discs due to overuse or an accident from lifting heavy equipment.

Limb loss is another common injury. The causes of amputation include traumatic injury from a gunshot or bomb that causes immediate amputation or leads to further complications that result in medical amputation (Fitzpatrick & Pasquina, 2010).

Limb loss includes amputation of the leg above or below the knee and amputation of the arm above or below the elbow. In addition, amputation of phalanges or portions of the foot or hand are common. Prosthetics often are used as assistive devices to replace the missing limb depending on the condition of the residual limb (Fitzpatrick & Pasquina, 2010; Reznick, 2008). Impairments tend to include adjustment to limb loss, difficulty with ambulation and other activities of daily living, and skin breakdown.

Emotional/Psychological Injuries

Mental health conditions may be the most prevalent injury associated with injured service members, especially those who have served in the GWOT. These injuries are considered invisible, as their signs and symptoms are not as obvious to other service members, family members, or friends as are physical injuries such as amputations or SCIs (Hoge, Castro, Messer, & McGurk, 2004; Tanielian & Jaycox, 2008). Common psychological issues that accompany traumatic injury or result from witness of traumatic events are post-traumatic stress disorder (PTSD), depression, and generalized anxiety disorder. These disorders may manifest into comorbid issues such as alcohol and drug abuse and dysfunctional social skills if not addressed appropriately. The counts of psychological injuries may be inaccurate due to the high number of service members who are not diagnosed as a result of delayed onset of the injury, symptoms that are not always observable, and the stigma of reporting mental health issues in the military (Hoge et al., 2004; Sandberg et al., 2009; Seal et al., 2008).

PTSD is a serious issue among injured service members, as many experience traumatic events during their military service. The *Diagnostic Statistical Manual* (*DSM-5*; American Psychological Association, 2013) identifies four symptom clusters for PTSD: re-experiencing, avoidance, negative cognitions and mood, and alterations in arousal and reactivity. Many injured service members do not have a clinical diagnosis of PTSD, but they may have post-traumatic stress symptoms such as feeling on edge, startling at sudden noises, spending more time at home rather than participating in community activities, and feeling that they have no control over what is happening in their lives. In addition to PTSD, many injured service members are struggling with depression. Symptoms of depression include sadness, poor mood, loss of interest, lack of motivation, and feeling hopeless. These symptoms vary day by day but are more present than not for 2 weeks or longer and interfere with daily activities such as taking care of the family and going to work or school. Finally, generalized anxiety disorder presents symptoms of excessive worry or anxiety about large and small issues, difficulty concentrating due to worry, irritability, muscle tension, and sleep difficulty. These symptoms usually last for at least six months or longer before diagnosis (American Psychological Association, 2013; Anxiety and Depression Association of America, 2014; U.S. Department of Veterans Affairs, 2012a, 2012b).

Other Threats to Health

Substance use is a common and easily accessible way for all service members to cope with the stressors of military service. Unfortunately, substance use disorders may develop quickly and may persist long after a deployment has ended. Studies over the last decade of the United States' involvement in Iraq and Afghanistan have demonstrated a relationship between deployments and combat exposure with increases in alcohol consumption, binge drinking, and misuse of prescription drugs

(Barlas, Higgins, Pflieger, & Diecker, 2013; Jacobson et al., 2008; National Research Council, 2013; Santiago et al., 2010; Spera, 2011). Among a sample of almost 18,000 veterans aged 21 to 39 who sought substance abuse treatment in a non-Veterans Affairs (VA) facility, 50.7% reported alcohol as being the primary substance of abuse (Substance Abuse and Mental Health Services Administration [SAMHSA], 2012). Alcohol is not the only substance that is abused among military members, however, and the GWOT is not the only conflict in which substance abuse has been an issue. Service members during Vietnam frequently used heroin and opium, and an estimated 43% of service members used those drugs at one point during their deployment, and of those, half were thought to be dependent on them (National Research Council, 2013; Robins, 1974).

During the course of military service, especially overseas deployments, many service members are exposed to environments, contaminants, and diseases that have lasting negative health effects. For example, Agent Orange was an herbicide used frequently during Vietnam to kill vegetation. The negative health impacts from exposure to Agent Orange include increased incidence of ischemic heart disease, diabetes, and birth defects in children (Kim, Lim, Cho, Cheong, & Lim, 2003; Office of Public Health, 2014; Young, 2002). Negative health impacts also have been reported among Gulf War veterans who served in Desert Storm and Desert Shield, including fatigue, joint pain, headaches, rash and dermatitis, and memory loss (Proctor et al., 1998). Exposure to neurotoxicants such as anti-nerve gas pills, nerve agents such as sarin gas, pesticides and insect repellents, and toxins in the smoke from oil well fires and burning human waste have been determined to contribute to these health conditions (Proctor et al., 1998). Therefore, in conjunction with more typical combat-related injuries (e.g., BI, PTSD), many injured service members are living with other medical conditions that are a direct outcome of their military experiences.

Age-Related Health Conditions

Age-related health conditions must not be forgotten in this discussion and are especially prevalent among the older and middle generations of service members. Older service members may experience health conditions associated with advanced age, such as changes in cognitive functioning, physical functioning, and social interaction patterns. These include conditions such as visual and hearing impairments, mobility issues, stroke, dementia, delirium, depression, arthritis, and cardiovascular disease. A contributor to many of these conditions is the process of secondary aging. Secondary aging refers to environmental and behavioral factors, such as stress, smoking, and unhealthy lifestyle behaviors, that further contribute to the primary or biological aging process (McGuire, Boyd, Janke, & Aybar-Damali, 2013).

PTSD also is common among injured service members who served in earlier conflicts such as World War II, the Korean War, and the Vietnam War. As their younger counterparts do, the older generation service members experience the effects of PTSD beyond the symptoms of PTSD alone. For example, research studies have suggested that male and female Vietnam service members who experienced combat exposure and PTSD had significantly poorer health outcomes including more functional impairment, lower well-being and quality of life, physical health problems, physical impairments, increases in interpersonal violence, and other health problems (Wolfe, Schnurr, Brown, & Furey, 1994; Zatzick et al., 1997). The relationship between age-related and combat-related health conditions is tenuous, as each likely exacerbates the other. As time goes on, service members of the younger generation (Gulf Wars) likely will deal with these health conditions as well. See Chapter 9 for a more in-depth discussion of age-related health conditions.

PURPOSE OF RECREATIONAL THERAPY

Recreational therapy (RT) with injured service members consists of providing therapeutic interventions designed to improve functional capacity, promote independence in life activities, increase home and community participation, and increase quality of life for injured service members and their supporters through health-promoting treatment modalities. The recreational therapist may take many approaches to treatment and program provision depending on factors such as injuries sustained, nature of injury or disorder, purpose of the service organization (e.g., medical center, community program), and the generation of injured service member being treated.

General Approaches to Treatment

Injured service members may receive RT treatment during rehabilitation programs, the transitional phase between rehabilitation and home, or after they have returned to their home and community. In any phase, recreational therapists address the injured service member's functional strengths and limitations. The following sections will be focused on general approaches to treatment in the areas of physical, cognitive, emotional/psychological, and social functioning, as well as home and community functioning. Table 12.1 provides specific examples of RT treatment approaches and their physical, cognitive, emotional/psychological, and social outcomes.

Physical functioning. Due to the high prevalence of BI, SCI, amputations, and other orthopedic injuries, a recreational therapist may choose interventions and other therapeutic approaches that are focused on improving specific neuromuscular functioning, such as muscle power, tone, endurance, control of voluntary movement, gait pattern, fine and gross motor skills, flexibility, and range of motion. Commonly used interventions include adaptive recreation, leisure, and sport activities specifically targeting the recovery and promotion of physical functioning. Yoga also is becoming a commonly used intervention to improve physical functioning by improving balance and reducing pain.

Cognitive functioning. Service members with mild to severe BI, in particular, may exhibit limitations in cognitive functioning, such as limited ability to sustain attention, impaired memory, abstract thought, mental organization, time management, problem-solving, judgment, and ability to understand and express language appropriately. Many recreation and leisure activities that recreational therapists provide as interventions require the use of these cognitive processes, and when adapted to match and challenge the client's functional abilities and meet the interests of the injured service member, they may improve their cognitive skills.

Emotional/psychological functioning. Recreational therapists working with injured service members always should consider the potential emotional and psychological injuries that may be present, even when the primary referral for care may be for another health condition. All generations of injured service members may benefit from RT that teaches effective health-promoting coping mechanisms and stress management techniques. These treatment approaches are likely to help older and younger service members with combating PTSD symptoms and likely will lead to improvement in other health outcomes and prevention of secondary health conditions. Therapeutic approaches used with injured service members may lead to improved emotional and psychological functioning, such as increased motivation, regulation of emotions, emotional expression, self-efficacy, perceived competence, post-traumatic growth (i.e., positive psychological change and personal development after trauma), and the ability to cope effectively with stress and mental health condition symptoms. For example, participation in adaptive recreation, leisure, and sport activities may provide injured service members opportunities for challenge and success, which may increase enjoyment and self-efficacy, reduce PTSD symptoms, and lead to the injured service member adopting the activity as a health-promoting coping mechanism.

Social functioning. Many injuries service members experience lead to decreased social functioning, especially BI and PTSD. Depending on the injury sustained, many injured service members socially isolate themselves and demonstrate difficulty with appropriate emotional expression of anger, sadness, and happiness toward others; relating to other persons; establishing and maintaining conversations; and effectively communicating with family, friends, coworkers, and others in authority positions. Various RT interventions and approaches may assist the injured service member with learning specific social skills and increasing comfort with interacting with others. For example, therapeutic camps may offer injured service members and their families opportunities to learn more effective communication techniques, increase processing of emotions, and promote family bonding in a fun camp environment. RT services that involve groups of injured or noninjured service members may help service members adjust to injury and reestablish a sense of camaraderie once experienced during their military service. Service members typically feel a strong sense of identity with their military service. Connecting with other service members (injured or not) may facilitate a level of openness and comfort not experienced with civilians, including friends and family members, and improved overall social functioning.

Home and community functioning. Due to increases in the quality and availability of medical care and rehabilitation programs in military health care, most injured service members are discharged back to their home and community. An important purpose of RT in rehabilitation programs is to assist the injured service member with readjusting to normal life and reintegrating into home and community environments, which is a critical aspect of participation in life activities. The recreational therapist may use community outings and other recreation and leisure interventions to assist injured service members with increasing specific physical, cognitive, and emotional/psychological skills to decrease barriers and increase facilitators to participation in home and community activities. Recreational therapists help injured service members with understanding how to negotiate structural accessibility issues, overcome stigma associated with mental health conditions (or other injuries), control mental health symptoms, learn how to use healthy stress management and coping techniques, and assist the service member with becoming more confident and competent with participating in home and community activities.

Table 12.1
Recreational Therapy Treatment Approaches and Associated Outcomes

Therapeutic approach	Physical	Emotional and psychological	Cognitive	Social	Home and community
Recreation, leisure, and sport (including outdoor recreation)	Increased muscle power, tone, endurance, movement, motor control, mobility, skills specific to the activity	Improved regulation of emotion, motivation, self-efficacy, resilience, perceived competence, stress management	Improved organization and planning, improved judgment, problem-solving, calculation, learning and applying knowledge	Increased interpersonal interactions; social integration; improved communication, teamwork, and sportsmanship; relationships with family, friends, peers, and others	Engagement in associations with others with similar interests (e.g., military and recreational interests), promotion of participation in recreation and leisure activity
Therapeutic camps	Depending on camp activities: increased muscle tone, endurance, movement, motor control, skills specific to the activity	Improved expression of emotions, provide time for self-reflection and self-awareness, post-traumatic growth, decreased PTSD and depression symptoms	Improved communication skills	Improved effective communication skills, family functioning, restored sense of camaraderie with other service members in the home	Increase recreation and leisure skills and participation, connection with other service members in the community, family cohesiveness in the home
Yoga	Improved balance and pain management, muscle power, tone, endurance, movement, motor controls, skills specific to the activity	Improved self-awareness, stress management, mindfulness, emotional regulation	Increased sustained attention	Increased interactions with others in group setting; opportunities for positive social comparison	Improved connection between self, larger existence, and community
Virtual reality	Increased balance, endurance, fine and gross motor skills	Increased appropriate expression of emotion, healthy processing of traumatic events, mood, PTSD symptoms, coping skills	Improved thought functions to relearn appropriate responses to stressors		Reduced psychological barriers associated with PTSD/depression to participate in home and community activities
Leisure education	Various depending on focus of leisure education session	Increased awareness of positive health-promoting leisure activity	Improved organization and planning, judgment, problem-solving	Increased interpersonal interactions	Increased knowledge of associations with others with similar interests, promotion of participation in recreation and leisure activity

Table 12.1 (cont.)

Therapeutic approach	Physical	Emotional and psychological	Cognitive	Social	Home and community
Community outings	Increased ability to apply motor skills in home and community environments	Increased self-efficacy in home and community environments	Improved organization and planning, judgment, problem solving	Improved self-advocacy skills, social skills in applied and community environments	Increased competence in accessing and using home and community resources, decrease barriers to participation in home and community activities
Animal-assisted therapy	Increased fine and gross motor skills	Improved trust, ability to cope with mental health symptoms (e.g., PTSD), mood	Improved expressive and receptive communication skills	Increased ability to express emotions without fear of judgment	Increased comfort at home and in the community
Art and music	Increased fine and gross motor skills, motor control	Increased appropriate expression of emotions, healthy processing of traumatic events, mood, decreased depression symptoms	Improved expressive and receptive communication skills	Increased interpersonal interactions	Creative expression of stressful home experiences

Similar to interventions targeting social functioning, recreation and leisure programs, both therapeutic and recreation based, may create connections with other injured service members who have shared similar military experiences, have similar injuries and symptoms, and may be experiencing similar difficulties with fitting back into their homes and communities. Recreational therapists may find that injured service members are willing to share their personal stories, struggles, and successes with other injured service members in a recreation activity that they have not shared with their therapists or family members, which promotes reintegration into home and community environments by building supportive networks.

Empirical Evidence Supporting Practice

Demonstrating the effects of RT interventions on the functioning of injured service members is important to improving the lives of these individuals and for supporting RT practice with this population. Much of the research literature on the effects of RT interventions and other recreation programming has focused on emotional/psychological, social, and home and community functioning, although some research has documented the effects on physical functioning. A small amount of research has investigated the effects of RT interventions on cognitive functioning of injured service members. More research is needed to clearly demonstrate RT's effects on the many areas of functioning, especially cognitive and physical functioning outcomes. The following sections highlight and summarize the research supporting RT interventions and programs.

Recreation, leisure, and sport. Involvement in recreation and sport has been demonstrated to create and strengthen social and emotional/psychological functioning of injured service members by developing social supports and improving their perception of disability. Hawkins, Cory, and Crowe (2011) interviewed participants in a weekend Paralympic program for injured service members. For these participants, social support and social comparison with other service members motivated them to improve personally and continue to participate in recreation and sport activities. Continued participation in recreation and sport led to development of additional social supports, positive changes in perception of disability, increased knowledge and skills in recreation and sport, and improved health and overall well-being. In addition, Sporner et al. (2009) studied the effects of participation in a veterans wheelchair games event and a winter sports clinic. They found that the outcomes associated with service members' participation in the recreation and sport events included improved quality of life, mobility, social integration, quality of life, and self-esteem.

Outdoor recreation. Of the outdoor recreation activities that may be implemented with service members, fly-fishing and river running (e.g., boating and kayaking) have been the most researched in regard to emotional/psychological and social functioning. Benefits associated with these outdoor recreation services include increased sense of camaraderie, opportunities for reflection and reconciling of memories, a more positive outlook on treatment and life post-treatment, increased confidence, development of new skills, and the chance to reconnect with other persons and nature (Bennett, Van Puymbroeck, Piatt, & Rydell, 2014; Mowatt & Bennett, 2011). Other research has examined the psychosocial outcomes of participating in a fly-fishing program for military service members. Researchers found a decrease in negative mood states, depression, anxiety, PTSD symptoms, and somatic symptoms of stress and perceptual stress, along with improvements in attentiveness, positive mood states, and sleep quality (Vella, Milligan, & Bennett, 2013). Researchers examining a 4-day river running trip found decreased symptoms of re-experiencing, avoidance and numbness, and hyperarousal (Dustin, Bricker, Arave, Wall, & Wendt, 2011). Finally, during a weeklong adaptive kayaking program researchers found improvements in depression, anxiety, PTSD, and social interaction scores for the injured service members (Scherer, Gade, & Yancosek, 2014).

Therapeutic camps. RT in the form of a couple's therapeutic and adapted recreation and sport programs in a therapeutic camp setting also has been linked to benefits for injured service members and their significant others. In a study by Lundberg, Bennett, and Smith (2011), this program resulted in significant decreases in tension, depression, and anger and increases in vigor and perceived competence in sport. In a follow-up study using a comparison group, Bennett, Lundberg, Zabriskie, and Eggett (2014) found decreases in PTSD symptoms and increases in marital satisfaction compared to a wait-list control group of injured service members and their significant others who had not yet completed the program.

Yoga. Recent research has suggested yoga to be a beneficial treatment for injured service members and has been shown to improve emotional/psychological and physical functioning. These changes in functioning include decreases in depression symptoms; reductions in pain; decreases in PTSD symptoms; increases in energy; and improvements in sleep quality, balance, and overall mental health (Carter et al., 2013; Groessl, Weingart, Johnson, & Baxi, 2012; Schmid et al., 2012; Staples, Hamilton, & Uddo, 2013; Van Puymbroeck, Allsop, Miller, & Schmid, in press).

Virtual reality. An emerging area of study is the use of virtual reality exposure therapy to improve emotional/psychological functioning by decreasing PTSD symptoms of injured service members. This consists of exposing the participant to a virtual war scenario in a safe environment for increasing lengths of time and usually includes the education and use of an immediate coping strategy when emotional or psychological symptoms are exposed. This gradual exposure in small successful sessions may help the service member with controlling PTSD symptoms. Although a few studies have presented initial support for the use of virtual reality in treatment for service members with PTSD (Botella et al., 2010; Gerardi, Rothbaum, Ressler, Heekin, & Rizzo, 2008; Ready, Pollack, Rothbaum, & Alarcon, 2006), more research is necessary to demonstrate its comparative efficacy (Motraghi, Seim, Meyer, & Morissette, 2014). As with any intervention, the recreational therapist should become knowledgeable and competent in developing programs and providing treatments prior to implementing treatments.

Support for other interventions and therapeutic approaches. Leisure education, community outings, animal-assisted therapy, art and music, and other interventions and therapeutic approaches benefit many populations, as seen in research and in other chapters in this textbook. These treatments and approaches are likely to produce positive therapeutic outcomes in injured service members; however, no research studies were found reporting their effects with this population. Additional research is needed to determine the effects of these interventions and approaches.

COMMON SERVICE SETTINGS

Recreational therapists may work with service members in many treatment settings including the following:

- VA medical centers;

- VA polytrauma centers;

- long-term care facilities (e.g., assisted living, nursing home);

- mental health and substance abuse programs (e.g., inpatient, outpatient, residential);

- branch-specific transitional programs (e.g., Army Warrior Transition Units, U.S. Marine Corps Wounded Warrior Battalions);

- soldier and family Morale, Welfare, and Recreation (MWR) programs; and

- adapted recreation and sport programs (e.g., Paralympic Sport Clubs and community park and recreation programs).

CURRENT BEST PRACTICES AND PROCEDURES

The rise in the number of injured service members as a result of the United States' current conflicts has increased the demand for programs for military members past and present. Unfortunately, this increase has resulted in an overload of the VA system (Korb, Duggan, Juul, & Bergmann, 2009). In response to the increased demands placed on VA resources, programs have been created to lessen the burden on the VA system and assist in providing care for the growing number of injured service members who may need it. Along with acute and post-acute rehabilitation services for injured service members, community-based RT programs have become viable health care options. In addition, family member involvement has been recognized as an important factor in positive outcomes for service members (Evans, Cowlishaw, Forbes, Parslow, & Lewis, 2010; Evans, Cowlishaw, & Hopwood, 2009; Khyalis, Polusny, Erbes, Gewirtz, & Rath, 2011). Providing RT for this group of individuals should take a multifaceted, holistic approach that uses the RT process (assessment, planning, implementation, and evaluation).

Assessment

Using the assessment process to determine functional impairments due to an injury enables recreational therapists to gather vital information for the planning process. Recreational therapists should use standardized instruments to assess injured service members whenever possible. As discussed in Chapter 1, the International Classification of Functioning, Disability, and Health (ICF) allows recreational therapists to gain a more comprehensive profile of the functioning level of an injured service member (World Health Organization, 2002). The ICF comprises body structure and functioning, activities and participation, and contextual factors (i.e., environmental and personal factors). Starting with body structure and functioning, the recreational therapists will be able to determine the body parts that may be impaired (e.g., limbs, organs, brain) and the extent, nature, and location of the impairment. The recreational therapist determines the level of functioning by assessing the amount of impairment in the physiological and psychological functions of the body systems. For injured service members, this may include assessing the impairment level in consciousness, psychic stability, energy level, motivation, attention, memory, muscle tone, regulation of emotions, and cognitive functioning.

To assess activity and participation, the recreational therapist determines how much difficulty the service member has in performance and capacity in tasks and life situations. This could include assessing the limitations and restrictions injured service members experience with thinking, problem solving, decision making, carrying out their daily routines, handling stress, carrying on a conversation, hand and arm use, walking, using transportation, self-care, interpersonal interactions, employment, and recreation. Assessing the contextual factors that are facilitators or barriers to functioning addresses the third component of the ICF. This includes personal and environmental factors such as age; gender; prescription and nonprescription drug use; technology for daily use or mobility; accessibility in their community and home; attitudes of family, friends, community members, and health professionals; and health services systems and policies.

The focus of the assessment process is to develop a comprehensive view of the injured service member to determine the areas of functioning that may be influenced through RT interventions. The assessment process should include observation, review of medical charts, discussions with family and friends, an interview with the service member, and administration of valid and reliable instruments. The service member and family members may withhold information on the severity of symptoms due to the stigma of having psychological and physical disabilities in the military. In addition to using valid and reliable instruments to collect this data, recreational therapists need to develop rapport with the injured service member and their supporters to gather accurate and appropriate assessment information.

Many of the reliable and validated instruments available to recreational therapists in the book *Assessment Tools for Recreational Therapy and Related Fields* (burlingame & Blaschko, 2009) may be used with the military population. Those that are especially useful in assessing the functional components of the ICF include the Comprehensive Evaluation in Recreational Therapy - Physical Disabilities (CERT-P), which measures functional skills related to leisure activities; the Functional Assessment of Characteristics for Therapeutic Recreation - Revised (FACTR), which measures basic functional skills and behaviors in the physical, cognitive, and social/emotional domains; the Therapeutic Recreation Activity Assessment (TRAA), which measures basic functional skills as demonstrated in a group setting; and the Assessment of Leisure and Recreation Involvement (LRI), which measures a participant's perception of his or her involvement in leisure and recreation. Other valuable tools are available in this book that would help assess the activity and participation components of the ICF as well.

Additional instruments that are highly valuable during the assessment process include the Posttraumatic Stress Disorder Checklist, Military Version (PCL-M), which examines PTSD symptoms (Forbes, Creamer, & Biddle, 2001); the Short Form-12 Health Survey (SF-12), which measures physical and mental health (Ware, Kosinski, & Keller, 1996); and the Patient Health Questionnaire-9 (PHQ-9), which measures depression (Kroenke, Spitzer, & Williams, 2001). Other useful instruments to use with this population include the Community Reintegration for Service Members (CRIS), which measures elements of community reintegration (Resnik, Plow, & Jette, 2009); the Complicated Family Reintegration Scale - Veteran (CFRS-V), which measures elements of reintegration into the family for veterans (Sayers, Farrow, Ross, & Oslin, 2009; Sayers, Farrow, Oslin, & Jacques, 2009); and the Family Leisure Activity Profile (FLAP), which measures the amount, frequency, and duration of participation in family leisure activities (Zabriskie & McCormick, 2001). The PCL-M and PHQ-9 may be accessed on the Internet for free. The other instruments may be found by contacting the authors of the scale.

Planning

After completing the assessment phase, the recreational therapist and injured service member should develop and prioritize treatment goals. Areas that typically require improvement include functional skills in physical, cognitive, emotional/psychological, and social domains. A focus on home and community functioning is also present in RT services with this population; however, they are not generally the primary focus following a referral to a recreational therapist. All injured service members experience their injuries differently; therefore, involving the client in every step of the process to provide the best treatment possible is important. Working with the injured service member, the recreational therapist will develop goals and objectives during the planning phase, which work as a road map and help guide the selection of therapeutic modalities to be used to address the client's needs.

Appropriate goals for this population may include the client will (a) increase the range of motion in the affected limb (physical), (b) demonstrate improved problem-solving skills (cognitive), (c) increase stress management coping skills (psychological), (d) demonstrate the ability to communicate appropriately with others (social), and (e) participate in more recreation and leisure activities with their family and friends (home and community). Therapeutic modalities that would be useful in addressing these goals include an aquatics program for increasing range of motion, challenging brain games for cognitive development, physical activity or workout programs for stress management, group activities using art and music for developing communication skills, and family leisure activities for developing participation in the home and community.

Implementation

When implementing programs for injured service members, the recreational therapist must fully understand the needs of the client. The recreational therapist makes accommodations and modifications to the activities, the instruction, and the environment to best meet those needs. The therapist also must be cognizant of his or her behaviors and modify them as necessary when implementing programs to reduce the possibility of exacerbating symptoms of emotional/psychological injuries and trauma. Injured service members may not mention their anxiety with a situation due to the stigma that often is associated with mental illness, especially in the military. The recreational therapist should be able to read the clients nonverbal communication patterns and be aware of how they may be contributing to the stress and anxiety. Small changes to implementation styles may help tremendously in diffusing stressful situations (e.g., approaching injured service members from the front to not catch them off guard, positioning activities so the clients' backs are not facing entrances, and avoiding touching clients without permission). The recreational therapist should create a relaxing atmosphere for the injured service member to allow the individual to engage fully in the activity and gain the full benefit of participation in the program. Recent research examining beneficial staff characteristics has suggested that injured service members value recreational therapy staff who genuinely care for them, who are patient with them and their situations, who are knowledgeable about how to instruct them in the activity, and who are aware of the intricacies of combat-related injuries and know how to work with them (Bennett, Van Puymbroeck, et al., 2014).

Other implementation strategies that may be unique to this population include having small group activities, as opposed to large groups, which may contribute to stress and anxiety; including other injured service members who have successfully progressed through their recovery to allow for positive social comparison, bonding, and the development of social support networks; and including family members in activities to allow for the redevelopment of personal relationships that may have been strained due to deployment and injury. An important implementation strategy that must be addressed concerns substances commonly used for self-medication (i.e., alcohol). In some program settings (e.g., river rafting, camping, and other social activities), instances may occur where the flow of the activity is such that participants are looking for ways to relax and unwind. Having a drink around the campfire after a day on the river may seem harmless; however, alcohol use has been shown to impede recovery from psychological injury by exacerbating symptoms and serving as an avoidance mechanism to therapeutic work (Schumm & Chard, 2012). Alcohol and other substances should never be a part of any RT program, especially those that serve injured service members.

Evaluation

Similar to the assessment process, the evaluation process must evaluate the outcomes of the intervention holistically; this may be accomplished by using the three components of the ICF. Therefore, the recreational therapist should examine the outcomes related to body structures and functioning, activity and participation, and contextual factors. This may be done through observing clients' functioning throughout their participation in the program, which may be compared to observations performed during the assessment process. Assessment scales should be readministered when injured service members complete a program or intervention to quantitatively measure changes in functional levels.

APPLICATION OF THE RECREATIONAL THERAPY PROCESS: CASE STUDY

Frank is a 32-year-old white male who is in the process of being medically discharged from the Marines. He was deployed three times to Iraq, and midway through his third deployment, an IED detonated under his Humvee, and he sustained an injury to his left leg that resulted in a unilateral amputation below the knee as well as a mild brain injury. Frank has completed inpatient physical rehabilitation and is able to ambulate using his prosthetic leg. Frank is continuing his recovery in outpatient rehabilitation at Walter Reed National Military Medical Center and has been demonstrating symptoms of PTSD and depression. He rarely leaves his home for anything other than his physical therapy, is on edge, and has exaggerated stress responses to everyday situations. Frank believed he would be in the Marines his whole life and is having difficulty finding his purpose in life now that he is being discharged from the military and has a new and stressful situation with which to deal including his amputation. He also is having difficulty finding the motivation to focus on reintegration into his home and community. He is married with two children, aged 7 and 10. Frank's wife Monica is 30 years old and works full time. He is concerned with his inability to control his emotions and the difficulty he is having relating to his wife and children. The only time he feels better is when he is drinking. He used to be an avid outdoorsman, mostly hunting and fishing, but he is hesitant to participate in these activities due to his BI, as he quickly loses focus on the task at hand and has difficulty with being motivated to put effort into the activities. Frank is being treated primarily for his ongoing physical and psychological injuries (e.g., amputation, BI, PTSD, depression).

Assessment

Using ICF components as a guideline, the recreational therapist should review his medical records to gain a better understanding of his body structures and functioning and then interview Frank and administer valid and reliable scales to understand how he performs activities and participates in life situations. Next, the recreational therapist may interview family members to start determining which contextual factors could be acting as barriers and facilitators of his ability to participate in life activities with his physical and psychological injuries

Frank's medical records indicate that due to his BI, he has impairments in memory, attention span, and regulation of emotions. Fortunately, he is experiencing little physical impairment as a result of his amputation and BI because he has been working with a rehabilitation team to further develop his proficiency with his prosthetic device. During the assessment interview with Frank, the recreational therapist found he has limitations with problem solving, handling stress, interpersonal interactions, and participating in recreation. The CERT-P, PCL-M, PHQ-9, FLAP, and LRI are used to assess the level of impairment in these areas. Results of these assessments indicate that Frank can solve one-step problems, but he terminates his activities after a few minutes due to frustration and short attention and memory span. His PCL-M and PHQ-9 scores indicate that his psychological and emotional functioning also are impaired, as demonstrated by a heightened stress response to everyday situations resulting in withdrawal from many of his relationships. The FLAP and LRI indicate that he neither participates in an adequate amount of personal or family recreation nor draws much pleasure from participation in his current activities. The CFRS-V results indicate that he feels his children are afraid of him, do not act warmly toward him, and turn more to his wife to have their needs met; he is unable to discuss with his wife the effects of his deployments on their relationship; and his family members do not understand what he went through while deployed.

During the interview and assessment, Frank seemed hesitant to talk to the recreational therapist about his BI or what he liked to do. He was more willing to talk about his family but would lose focus and have to be redirected back to the topic of the conversation. He clearly loves his children and wife but is having a hard time connecting with them since he returned home. He spoke fondly of the time he took his family fishing five years ago but has not gone fishing with them since then. His wife indicated that she is frustrated that he is unemployed because he could go back to work, but all he does is sit at home and drink alcohol. She also explained that his attitude about life has changed since his injury, and he is not motivated to accomplish tasks that he was once able to accomplish.

Planning

The treatment team in the outpatient rehabilitation program developed the following discharge goal for Frank:

Long-term goal: Frank will be discharged to his home with the ability to independently use his prosthetic device and cope with residual symptoms of his brain injury and other psychological injuries with the help of his family.

Informed by the assessment findings and with the help of Frank, the recreational therapist determined that the immediate treatment goal for recreational therapy was to reduce PTSD and depression symptoms through the use of yoga. The second goal was to increase participation in recreational activities he used to enjoy to further promote overall functioning (e.g., physical, emotional/psychological, social) and adjustment. A third goal was to increase participation in recreational activities with his family to redevelop their relationships and promote his reintegration into his home. Objectives for these goals include the following:

Goal 1: Reduce PTSD and depression symptoms according to Frank's scores on the PCL-M and PHQ-9.

Objective 1.1: Following 1 month of treatment, Frank will experience a reduction in PTSD symptoms, as measured by a 10-point reduction of PCL-M scores.

Objective 1.2: Following 1 month of treatment, Frank will experience a reduction in depression symptoms, as measured by a 10-point reduction on the PHQ-9.

Goal 2: Increase participation in recreational activities to promote overall functioning and adjustment.

Objective 2.1: Following 1 month of treatment, Frank will verbally identify five activities that he has participated in independently.

Objective 2.2: During the first month of treatment, Frank will participate in a nature hike outside for 1 hour once a week, to increase overall recreation participation and promote overall functioning and adjustment.

Goal 3: Increase participation in recreation with Frank's family members to increase family functioning and promote reintegration.

Objective 3.1: Following 1 month of treatment, Frank will demonstrate an increase in family leisure participation, as measured by a 30-point increase on the FLAP.

Objective 3.2: Following 1 month of treatment, Frank will experience improvements in elements of his family relationships, as measured by a 10-point increase on the CFRS-V.

Implementation

The recreational therapist needs to understand that even though the only visible sign of Frank's injuries is his amputation, he still is experiencing debilitating effects that are impairing his cognitive, social, and emotional functioning. The recreational therapist should educate any other staff who may be working with him on these issues if they are not aware of his impairments. Frank also may be having difficulty accepting that his impairments are due to symptoms of PTSD, depression, BI, or his amputation. During sessions, the recreational therapist needs to help him recognize when the symptoms are occurring and what may be triggering them.

After the first visit with Frank, the recreational therapist should invite him to participate in small group activities with his family. He should be encouraged to involve his family whenever possible. In addition, he will be given information about the fishing group that meets once a week. Another military service member with similar injuries could be used to encourage Frank to go to the fishing group and plan to meet with him regularly. Having this peer supporter should help him see that he still can participate in his favorite outdoor activities even with a BI and amputation.

To increase Frank's interest in participation in yoga, the recreational therapist may introduce him to a few simple moves and breathing exercises one-on-one during one of their sessions. A peer supporter also could talk to him about the benefits he has experienced with yoga. In addition, this peer supporter could attend the yoga sessions with Frank to offer encouragement and support.

Evaluation

The overall purpose of the evaluation stage is to determine whether the goals the client and recreational therapist set have been met. The evaluation process begins in the documentation stage. The recreational therapist should keep detailed progress notes. This will allow the recreational therapist and Frank to follow his progress and keep him motivated toward continued treatment. His goals need to be realistic so he does not lose motivation but challenging enough so he does not feel patronized. If Frank still is having difficulty relating to his family, treatment sessions with his family on communication skills and the importance of participation in family recreation may be necessary.

The recreational therapist may readminister the CERT-P, PCL-M, PHQ-9, FLAP, LRI, and CFRS-V given in the assessment phase and reinterview Frank and his family members to determine whether his goals have been accomplished. Depending on how he is progressing toward his goals, the recreational therapist either may write new goals or may expand upon the previous goals. In addition to determining whether he has accomplished his goals, the recreational therapist will make other determinations about Frank's treatment by evaluating whether he needs continued services, needs decreased services, or is ready for discharge from the program. Discharge decisions are not be up to the recreational therapist, but the recreational therapist still should develop and write a discharge note detailing his progression through treatment, as well as goals and future needs.

TRENDS AND ISSUES

Injured service members face many issues as a result of their military experiences, and those have been discussed in this chapter; however, five areas of concern require a focused effort to best support military service members and their families: psychological injuries, suicide rates, female-specific issues, military sexual trauma, and military families.

Psychological Injuries

PTSD and BI have been characterized as the signature injuries of the GWOT, with reported prevalence rates ranging from 6% to 24.5% and 19% to 37%, respectively (Litz & Schlenger, 2009; Tanielian & Jaycox, 2008; Vanderploeg & Cornis-Pop, 2010). Because of the prevalence of these psychological injuries and the pervasive impact they have had on the lives of the younger generation of service members, the focus has been brought back to the experiences of the older generation of service members, mostly those who served in Vietnam, who comprise the largest segment of living service members. Current efforts to address PTSD and BI in service members should extend beyond the younger generation to include the remaining members of all generations of veterans, as the older generations likely are living with the negative outcomes of the traumatic experiences they encountered in combat.

Suicide Rates

Untreated psychological injuries may have serious, long-lasting impacts on service members and their support systems. Although suicide is not a psychological injury, it often results from uncontrolled psychological distress, as does PTSD. The rate of suicide among service members is higher than that of the civilian population, and as of 2010, the rate of suicides was 22 per day, with an average veteran age of 59 years, which highlights that this epidemic, as it is being referred to, cuts across the generations of service members (Kemp & Bossarte, 2013). Suicide also accounted for more military deaths than service members killed in action (Hoge & Castro, 2012; Iraq and Afghanistan Veterans of America, 2011; Kemp & Bossarte, 2013). Unfortunately, the stigma attached to a mental health diagnosis and the seeking of treatment for such conditions often are barriers for many veterans who could benefit from mental health care.

Returning veterans face unique challenges following deployment to a combat zone, but their issues may extend beyond direct combat issues such as a mental health or physical injury and include finding employment, redeveloping family relationships, and reintegrating into communities. The Iraq and Afghanistan Veterans of America (2011) put it succinctly: "Fighting suicide is not just about preventing the act of suicide; it is providing a soft and productive landing for our veterans when they return home" (Overview section, para. 3). Recreational therapists are employed in many settings that lend themselves to interacting with service members in the early stages of returning from deployment. These settings may provide an opportunity to help service members develop the coping skills necessary to reassess their situations and move toward positive outcomes following deployment.

Female-Specific Issues

The number of female service members has increased steadily over the last few decades. Although their exposure to combat has been similar to their male comrades (Kelley et al., 2013), females often differ in their injury compositions and readjustment needs. Female service members often experience sexual assault and harassment (see below for more information on military sexual trauma), interpersonal stressors such as sexism, and limited positive interpersonal interactions prior to and during their military service. After their service, many female service members experience difficulty with returning to previous family roles, such as being a mother or wife. They also have reported difficulties with receiving the appropriate medical and support services and have less supportive homecomings (Street, Vogt, & Dutra, 2009). Due to these differences in their military and post-military experiences, VA programs and other nongovernment-supported programs are offering female-specific services. Gender-specific programming may provide female service members with the opportunity to seek medical services and other programs where they may share openly about their experiences with other female service members who may be experiencing similar difficulties and successes in a safer environment to limit discrimination or judgment by their male counterparts. Programmatic examples range from women-specific VA health care programs to community-based camps for female service members.

Military Sexual Trauma (MST)

Military sexual trauma (MST) has been found to be a significant source of traumatic stress for many service members, both male and female (Hyun, Pavao, & Kimerling, 2009). According to the *Department of Defense Annual Report on Sexual Assault in the Military: Fiscal Year 2013* (U.S. Department of Defense, 2014b), 5,061 sexual assaults were reported involving service members, which is a 50% increase over reports from 2012. Out of the more than 5,000 reports, 2,149 service members received disciplinary action from U.S. Department of Defense commanders, which means that approximately 42% of sexual assaults that service members reported in 2013 were committed by fellow service members (U.S. Department of Defense, 2014b). Research has indicated that 4.2% of men and 71% of women seeking treatment for PTSD reported experiencing a sexual assault during their military service (Murdoch, Polusny, Hodges, & O'Brien, 2004). In addition to psychological impacts, MST has been found to be associated with other mental health conditions such as anxiety disorders, depression, dissociative disorders, eating disorders, bipolar disorder, substance use disorders, and personality disorders, as well as physical health conditions including poor health-related quality of life, liver disease, pulmonary disease, obesity, and hypertension (Hyun et al., 2009).

Self-blame and social stigmas associated with MST are often barriers to reporting the assault and seeking services. According to Pentagon estimates, as few as 13.5% of sexual assaults are reported (Tsongas, 2014). Sexual assault in the civilian population has been shown to negatively impact the lives of the victims; however, research has indicated that the stressor of a sexual assault in combination with the stress of combat-related experiences results in greater negative mental health consequences for military service members who experience sexual trauma, especially for women (Street et al., 2009). The U.S. Department of Defense (2014b) report also indicated that 62% of service members who reported a sexual assault also experienced retaliation. Recent legislation has been introduced that limits the ability of commanders to reverse decisions made by juries in military sexual assault cases and allows victims to request expedited transfers from their units or the commander to transfer the perpetrator elsewhere so the victim does not have to continue to serve alongside his or her perpetrator (Tsongas, 2014). Recreational therapists working with service members who have experienced a sexual trauma while in the military, especially women, must consider the military culture and its impact on the experience, which oftentimes exacerbates the traumatic aspects of the assault.

Focus on Military Families

The U.S. Department of Defense (2014a) reported that approximately 80% of service members injured during the GWOT were under age 30 at onset of injury. Given this timeframe in a person's life, many service members are growing their families and taking on new familial roles, such as spouse or significant other, parent, and role model. Onset of injury, such as PTSD or BI, may cause significant changes in the family unit that affects not only service members but also their family and friends. Many military families are able to navigate successfully the challenges associated with military service during conflict and peacetime; however, existing literature has painted a picture of the negative impacts of military service on families. Increases in marital conflict and partner distress levels have been associated with repeated deployments. Emotional and behavioral disruptions, heightened anxiety, and academic difficulties have been reported in children of deployed military families, and the cumulative length of parental deployments has been correlated with increased risk for depression and behavioral disruptions in children (Lester et al., 2012; Sayers, 2011).

Family services long have been called for in the RT literature, with recent work providing guidelines for developing such programs (Townsend & Van Puymbroeck, 2012). Camps and retreats provide an ideal setting for recreational therapists to work with service members and their families on issues such as problem solving, decision making, anger management, financial management, relationship (re)building, and spending time together, among others. These settings are invaluable in their ability to remove the family from a stressful home environment for a small period of time to allow important family recovery work to occur in a safe, accepting, and often restorative, natural environment.

SUMMARY

Military service members represent a growing segment of the population, and although not all have sustained injuries related to their service, many have had life-changing experiences that may have resulted in physical or psychological injury. This chapter reviewed some of the more common combat-related injuries that have resulted from involvement in military conflicts, such as PTSD and BI. Although some service members may have incurred only one injury (e.g., amputation), they may be dealing with comorbid conditions as well (i.e., substance abuse, depression, and anxiety). This chapter also discussed common treatment options for working with injured service members.

Due to the overwhelming demand for health services on the VA system, RT is a viable and complementary treatment option for working with injured service members. Yoga and outdoor recreation pursuits such as fly-fishing have been found to be especially impactful with this population. Efforts toward community reintegration are vital to the well-being of service members and their supporters, regardless of whether those supporters are family or community members, as the impacts of military service extend beyond the boundaries of a home, and have lasting effects on society as a whole. The ability of a recreational therapist to work with service members in health-related settings (e.g., community recreation centers, VA and rehabilitation hospitals) creates a unique opportunity to ensure a continuum of care that is crucial to the long-term recovery of injured service members. Working with military service members, especially those who have experienced a combat-related injury, is simultaneously challenging and highly rewarding. Recreational therapists will be successful in their endeavors with this group if they are committed to understanding the complexities of combat-related injuries and the toll they take on the individual and their families and communities.

READING COMPREHENSION QUESTIONS

1. In what ways are service members' lives impacted by their military experience?

2. Describe two differences and two similarities between the three generations of military service members.

3. Other than loss of physical functioning due to injuries sustained during military service, what other areas of functioning could be impacted?

4. What are three ways recreational therapist may improve the quality of life for injured service members?

5. Discuss two trends in services for military service members and their implications for RT.

REFERENCES

American Psychological Association. (2013). *Diagnostic and statistical manual of mental disorders* (5th ed.). Arlington, VA: Author.

Anxiety and Depression Association of America. (2014). Understanding the facts: Generalized anxiety disorder. Retrieved May 12, 2014, from http://www.adaa.org/understanding-anxiety/generalized-anxiety-disorder-gad

Barlas, F. M., Higgins, W. B., Pflieger, J. C., & Diecker, K. (2013). *2011 Department of Defense survey of health related behaviors among active duty military personnel.* Retrieved from Tricare website: http://tricare.mil/tma/dhcape/surveys/coresurveys/surveyhealthrelatedbehaviors/downloads/Final%202011%20HRB%20Active%20Duty%20Survey%20Exec%20Summary.pdf

Bennett, J. L., Lundberg, N. R., Zabriskie, R., & Eggett, D. (2014). Addressing posttraumatic stress among Iraq and Afghanistan veterans and significant others: An intervention utilizing sport and recreation. *Therapeutic Recreation Journal, 48*(1), 74–93.

Bennett, J. L., Van Puymbroeck, M., Piatt, J. A., & Rydell, R. J. (2014). Veterans' perceptions of benefits and important program components of a therapeutic fly-fishing program. *Therapeutic Recreation Journal, 48*(2), 169–187.

Botella, C., García-Palacios, A., Guillen, V., Baños, R. M., Quero, S., & Alcaniz, M. (2010). An adaptive display for the treatment of diverse trauma PTSD victims. *Cyberpsychology, Behavior and Social Networking, 13*(1), 67–71.

burlingame, j., & Blaschko, T. (2009). *Assessment tools for recreational therapy and related fields* (4th ed.). Ravensdale, WA: Idyll Arbor.

Carter, J. J., Gerbarg, P. L., Brown, R. P., Ware, S., Ambrosio, C. D., & Anand, L. (2013). Multi-component yoga breath program for Vietnam veteran post traumatic stress disorder: Randomized controlled trial. *Journal of Traumatic Stress Disorders & Treatment, 2*(3), 1–10.

Dustin, D., Bricker, N., Arave, J., Wall, W., & Wendt, G. (2011). The promise of river running as a therapeutic medium for veterans coping with post-traumatic stress disorder. *Therapeutic Recreation Journal, 45*(4), 326–340.

Evans, L., Cowlishaw, S., Forbes, D., Parslow, R., & Lewis, V. (2010). Longitundinal analyses of family functioning in veterans and their partners across treatment. *Journal of Consulting and Clinical Psychology, 78*(5), 611–622.

Evans, L., Cowlishaw, S., & Hopwood, M. (2009). Family functioning predicts outcomes for veterans in treatment for chronic posttraumatic stress disorder. *Journal of Family Psychology, 23*(4), 531–539.

Fitzpatrick, K. F., & Pasquina, P. F. (2010). Overview of the rehabilitation of the combat casualty. *Military Medicine, 175*, 13–17.

Forbes, D., Creamer, M., & Biddle, D. (2001). The validity of the PTSD checklist as a measure of symptomatic change in combat-related PTSD. *Behaviour Research and Therapy, 39*(8), 977–986.

Gerardi, M., Rothbaum, B. O., Ressler, K., Heekin, M., & Rizzo, A. (2008). Virtual reality exposure therapy using a virtual Iraq: Case report. *Journal of Traumatic Stress, 21*(2), 209–213. doi:10.1002/jts.20331

Groessl, E. J., Weingart, K. R., Johnson, N., & Baxi, S. (2012). The benefits of yoga for women veterans with chronic low back pain. *Journal of Alternative and Complementary Medicine, 18*(9), 832–838. doi:10.1089/acm.2010.0657

Hawkins, B. L., Cory, A. L., & Crowe, B. M. (2011). Effects of participation in a Paralympic military sports camp on injured service members: Implications for therapeutic recreation. *Therapeutic Recreation Journal, 45*(4), 309–325.

Hoge, C. W., & Castro, C. A. (2012). Preventing suicides in US service members and veterans: Concerns after a decade of war. *Journal of the American Medical Association, 308*(7), 671–672. doi:10.1001/jama.2012.9955

Hoge, C. W., Castro, C. A., Messer, S. C., & McGurk, D. (2004). Combat duty in Iraq and Afghanistan, mental health problems, and barriers to care. *The New England Journal of Medicine, 351*(1), 13–22.

Hyun, J. K., Pavao, J., & Kimerling, R. (2009). Military sexual trauma. *PTSD Research Quarterly, 20*(2), 1–8.

Iraq and Afghanistan Veterans of America. (2011). Issues and campaigns: Suicide and mental health. Retrieved April 13, 2014, from http://iava.org/issues-and-campaigns/suicide-and-mental-health

Jacobson, I. G., Ryan, M. A. K., Hooper, T. I., Smith, T. C., Amoroso, P. J., Boyko, E. J., . . . Bell, N. S. (2008). Alcohol use and alcohol-related problems before and after military combat deployment. *JAMA, 300*(6), 663–675.

Kelley, M. L., Runnals, J., Pearson, M. R., Miller, M., Fairbank, J. A., & Brancu, M. (2013). Alcohol use and trauma exposure among male and female veterans before, during, and after military service. *Drug and Alcohol Dependence, 133*(2), 615–624. doi:10.1016/j.drugalcdep.2013.08.002

Kemp, J., & Bossarte, R. (2013). *Suicide data report, 2012.* Washington, DC: Department of Veterans Affairs.

Khyalis, A., Polusny, M. A., Erbes, C. R., Gewirtz, A., & Rath, M. (2011). Posttraumatic stress, family adjustment, and treatment preferences among National Guard soldiers deployed to OEF/OIF. *Military Medicine, 176*(2), 126–131.

Kim, J. S., Lim, H. S., Cho, S. I., Cheong, H. K., & Lim, M. K. (2003). Impact of Agent Orange exposure among Korean Vietnam veterans. *Industrial Health, 41*(3), 149–157. doi:10.2486/indhealth.41.149

Korb, L. J., Duggan, S. E., Juul, P. M., & Bergmann, M. A. (2009). *Serving American's veterans: A reference handbook.* Santa Barbara, CA: ABC-CLIO.

Kroenke, K., Spitzer, R. L., & Williams, J. B. (2001). The PHQ-9: Validity of a brief depression severity measure. *Journal of General Internal Medicine, 16*(9), 606–613.

Lester, P., Saltzman, W. R., Woodward, K., Glover, D., Leskin, G. A., Bursch, B., . . . Beardslee, W. (2012). Evaluation of a family-centered prevention intervention for military children and families facing wartime deployments. *American Journal of Public Health, 102*(Suppl. 1), S48–S54.

Litz, B. T., & Schlenger, W. E. (2009). PTSD in service members and new veterans of the Iraq and Afghanistan wars: A bibliography and critique. *PTSD Research Quarterly, 20*(1), 1–8.

McGuire, F. A., Boyd, R. K., Janke, M., & Aybar-Damali, B. (2013). *Leisure and aging: Ulyssean living in later life* (5th ed.). Champaign, IL: Sagamore.

Motraghi, T. E., Seim, R. W., Meyer, E. C., & Morissette, S. B. (2014). Virtual reality exposure therapy for the treatment of posttraumatic stress disorder : A methodological review using CONSORT guidelines. *Journal of Clinical Psychology, 70*(3), 197–208. doi:10.1002/jclp.22051

Mowatt, R., & Bennett, J. (2011). War narratives: Veteran stories, PTSD effects, and therapeutic fly-fishing. *Therapeutic Recreation Journal, 45*(4), 286–308.

Murdoch, M., Polusny, M. A., Hodges, J., & O'Brien, M. (2004). Prevalence of in-service and post-service sexual assault among combat and noncombat veterans applying for Department of Veterans Affairs posttraumatic stress disorder disability benefits. *Military Medicine, 169*, 392–395.

National Center for Veterans Analysis and Statistics. (2013). *Department of Veterans Affairs: Veteran period of service statistics at a glance.* Retrieved from http://www.va.gov/vetdata/docs/Quickfacts/Homepage_slideshow_12_31_13.pdf

National Research Council. (2013). *Substance use disorders in the U.S. Armed Forces.* Washington, DC: The National Academies Press.

Office of Public Health. (2014). Public health: Diseases & conditions. Retrieved March 7, 2014, from http://www.publichealth.va.gov/diseases-conditions.asp

Proctor, S. P., Heeren, T., White, R. F., Wolfe, J., Borgos, M. S., Davis, J. D., . . . Oznoff, D. (1998). Health status of Persian Gulf War veterans: Self-reported symptoms, environmental exposures and the effect of stress. *International Journal of Epidemiology, 27*(6), 1000–1010. doi:10.1093/ije/27.6.1000

Ready, D. J., Pollack, S., Rothbaum, B., & Alarcon, R. (2006). Virtual reality exposure for veterans with posttraumatic stress disorder. *Journal of Aggression, Maltreatment & Trauma, 12*(1–2), 199–220. doi:10.1300/J146v12n01

Reznick, J. S. (2008). Beyond war and military medicine: Social factors in the development of prosthetics. *Archives of Physical Medicine and Rehabilitation, 89*(1), 188–193. doi:10.1016/j.apmr.2007.08.148

Resnik, L., Plow, M., & Jette, A. (2009). Development of CRIS: Measure of community reintegration of injured service members. *Journal of Rehabilitation Research & Development, 46*(4), 469–480.

Robins, L. N. (1974). *The Vietnam drug user returns: Final report.* Washington, DC: U.S. Government Printing Office.

Sandberg, M. A., Bush, S. S., & Martin, T. (2009). Beyond diagnosis: Understanding the healthcare challenges of injured veterans through the application of the International Classification of Functioning, Disability and Health (ICF). *Clinical Neuropsychologist, 23*(8), 1416–1432. doi:10.1080/13854040903369425

Santiago, P. N., Wilk, J. E., Milliken, C. S., Castro, C. A., Engel, C. C., & Hoge, C. W. (2010). Screening for alcohol misuse and alcohol-related behaviors among combat veterans. *Psychiatric Services, 61*(6), 575–581.

Sayer, N. A., Chiros, C. E., Sigford, B., Scott, S., Clothier, B., Pickett, T., & Lew, H. L. (2008). Characteristics and rehabilitation outcomes among patients with blast and other injuries sustained during the Global War on Terror. *Archives of Physical Medicine and Rehabilitation, 89*(1), 163–170. doi:10.1016/j.apmr.2007.05.025

Sayers, S. L. (2011). Family reintegration difficulties and couples therapy for military veterans and their spouses. *Cognitive and Behavioral Practice, 18*, 108–119.

Sayers, S. L., Farrow, V. A., Ross, J., & Oslin, D. W. (2009). Family problems among recently returned military veterans referred for a mental health evaluation. *Journal of Clinical Psychiatry, 70*(2), 163.

Sayers, S. L., Farrow, V., Oslin, D. W., & Jacques, N. (2009). *The complicated family reintegration scale for military veterans returned from Iraq and Afghanistan.* Symposium presentation at the annual meeting of the Association for Behavioral and Cognitive Therapies, New York, NY.

Scherer, M. R., Gade, D. M., & Yancosek, K. E. (2014). Efficacy of an adaptive kayaking intervention for improving health-related quality of life among wounded, ill, and injured service members. *American Journal of Recreation Therapy, 12*(3), 8–16.

Schmid, A. A., Van Puymbroeck, M., Altenburger, P. A., Dierks, T. A., Miller, K. K., Damush, T. M., & Williams, L. S. (2012). Balance and balance self-efficacy are associated with activity and participation after stroke: A cross-sectional study in people with chronic stroke. *Archives of Physical Medicine and Rehabilitation, 93*(6), 1101–1107. doi:10.1016/j.apmr.2012.01.020

Schumm, J. A., & Chard, K. M. (2012). Alcohol and stress in the military. *Alcohol Research: Current Reviews, 34*(3), 401–407.

Seal, K. H., Bertenthal, D., Maguen, S., Gima, K., Chu, A., & Marmar, C. R. (2008). Getting beyond "Don't ask; don't tell": An evaluation of US Veterans Administration postdeployment mental health screening of veterans returning from Iraq and Afghanistan. *American Journal of Public Health, 98*(4), 714–720. doi:10.2105/AJPH.2007.115519

Spera, C. (2011). Relationship of military deployment recency, frequency, duration, and combat exposure to alcohol use in the Air Force. *Journal of Studies on Alcohol and Drugs, 72*(1), 5–14.

Sporner, M. L., Fitzgerald, S. G., Dicianno, B. E., Collins, D., Teodorski, E., Pasquina, P. F., & Cooper, R. A. (2009). Psychosocial impact of participation in the National Veterans Wheelchair Games and Winter Sports Clinic. *Disability and Rehabilitation, 31*(5), 410–418. doi:10.1080/09638280802030923

Staples, J., Hamilton, M., & Uddo, M. (2013). A yoga program for the symptoms of post-traumatic stress disorder in veterans. *Military Medicine, 178*(8), 854–860.

Street, A. E., Vogt, D., & Dutra, L. (2009). A new generation of women veterans: Stressors faced by women deployed to Iraq and Afghanistan. *Clinical Psychology Review, 29*(8), 685–694. doi:10.1016/j.cpr.2009.08.007

Substance Abuse and Mental Health Services Administration. (2012). *Data spotlight: Half of substance abuse treatment admissions among veterans aged 21 to 39 involve alcohol as the primary substance of abuse.* Retrieved February 25, 2014, from http://www.samhsa.gov/data/spotlight/Spot106VeteransAlcoholAbuse2012.pdf

Tanielian, T., & Jaycox, L. (2008). *Invisible wounds of war: Psychological and cognitive injuries, their consequences, and services to assist recovery.* Santa Monica, CA: Rand.

Townsend, J., & Van Puymbroeck, M. (2012). Development and evaluation of a family recreation intervention for families with an adolescent with an autism spectrum disorder. *American Journal of Recreation Therapy, 11*(4), 27–27. doi:10.5055/ajrt.2012.0032

Tsongas, N. (2014). Issues & legislation: Military sexual trauma. Retrieved May 15, 2014, from http://tsongas.house.gov/military-sexual-trauma/

U.S. Department of Defense. (n.d.). About DoD. Retrieved February 25, 2014, from http://www.defense.gov/about/

U.S. Department of Defense. (2014a). Conflict casualties. Retrieved March 07, 2014, from https://www.dmdc.osd.mil/dcas/pages/casualties.xhtml

U.S. Department of Defense. (2014b). *Department of Defense annual report on sexual assault in the military: Fiscal year 2013.* Washington, DC: Author.

U.S. Department of Veterans Affairs. (2012a). Mental health: Generalized anxiety disorder. Retrieved February 25, 2014, from http://www.mentalhealth.va.gov/generalizedanxiety.asp

U.S. Department of Veterans Affairs. (2012b). National Center for PTSD. Retrieved February 25, 2014, from http://www.ptsd.va.gov/index.asp

U.S. Department of Veterans Affairs. (2013). *Profile of veterans 2011.* Retrieved February 25, 2014, from http://www.va.gov/vetdata/docs/SpecialReports/Profile_of_Veterans_2011.pdf

U.S. Department of Veterans Affairs. (2014). Polytrauma/TBI system of care: Terminology and definitions. Retrieved February 25, 2014, from http://www.polytrauma.va.gov/news-and-resources/terminology-and-definitions.asp

Vanderploeg, R. D., & Cornis-Pop, M. (2010). *Traumatic brain injury.* Birmingham, AL. Retrieved from Department of Veterans Affairs website: http://www.publichealth.va.gov/docs/vhi/traumatic-brain-injury-vhi.pdf

Van Puymbroeck, M., Allsop, J., Miller, K. K., & Schmid, A. (in press). ICF-based improvements in body structures and function, and activity and participation in chronic stroke following a yoga-based intervention. *American Journal of Recreation Therapy.*

Vella, E. J., Milligan, B., & Bennett, J. L. (2013). Participation in outdoor recreation program predicts improved psychosocial well-being among veterans with post-traumatic stress disorder: A pilot study. *Military Medicine, 178*(3), 254–260.

Ware, J. E., Kosinski, M., & Keller, S. D. (1996). A 12-item short-form health survey of scales and preliminary construction tests of reliability and validity. *Medical Care, 34*(3), 220–233.

Wolfe, J., Schnurr, P. P., Brown, P. J., & Furey, J. (1994). Posttraumatic stress disorder and war-zone exposure as correlates of perceived health in female Vietnam War veterans. *Journal of Consulting and Clinical Psychology, 62*(6), 1235–1240.

World Health Organization. (2002). *Towards a common language for functioning, disability, and health.* Geneva, Switzerland: Author.

Young, A. L. (2002). Vietnam and agent orange revisited. *Environmental Science and Pollution Research, 9*(3), 158–161.

Zabriskie, R., & McCormick, B. (2001). The influences of family leisure patterns on perceptions of family functioning. *Family Relations, 50*(3), 281–289.

Zatzick, D. F., Marmar, C. R., Weiss, D. S., Browner, W. S., Metzler, T. J., Golding, J. M., . . . Wells, K. B. (1997). Posttraumatic stress disorder and functioning and quality of life outcomes in a nationally representative sample of male vietnam veterans. *American Journal of Psychiatry, 154*(12), 1690–1695.

SECTION 3
PROFESSIONAL PRACTICE
CONCERNS

13

MANAGEMENT, CONSULTATION, AND RESEARCH

MARIEKE VAN PUYMBROECK, SANDRA K. NEGLEY, AND JUDITH E. VOELKL[1]

OBJECTIVES

- Describe how the management of a department or facility may influence the professional growth of a recreational therapist.
- Explain the difference between general supervision and clinical supervision.
- Define consultation.
- Define evidence-based practice.
- Describe how to implement an evidence-based recreational therapy practice.
- Name resources that provide recreational therapists with information on current research studies.

This book has presented information on using the recreational therapy (RT) process with individuals who have illnesses, disorders, and disabilities. As a result of these readings and possibly previous experiences, many readers may have identified a specific group of individuals with whom they would like to work. Future coursework and practical experiences may be planned to allow a student to gain specialized skills in the provision of services for a particular group of individuals. Many students, however, may not have considered the ways entry-level recreational therapists attain and enhance their clinical knowledge and skills. By continually attaining high-level knowledge and skills and refining previously learned skills, the recreational therapist will be able to provide quality services for clients.

As specified in the Code of Ethics of the national organization, the American Therapeutic Recreation Association (ATRA), as well as the standards of the National Council for Therapeutic Recreation Certification (NCTRC), recreational therapists have a responsibility for maintaining and improving their clinical knowledge and skills. Principle 9 (Competence) in ATRA's (2009) Code of Ethics states, "Recreational Therapy personnel are responsible for complying with local, state and federal laws, regulations and ATRA policies governing the profession of Recreational Therapy." Additionally, NCTRC (2014) places consequential importance in maintaining professional competence

---

[1]Judith E. Voelkl was an author on the original chapter in the third edition of this text and remains as an author here posthumously due to her substantial contributions on the original chapter.

by requiring recertification every 5 years. Thus, RT students need to consider what processes inherent in the workplace will support and enhance their professional growth.

The purpose of this chapter is to consider several processes within the workplace and the profession that support the professional growth of recreational therapists. The first section will reflect upon how management and the supervision process may enhance the further development of clinical skills, the second section will focus on the consultation process, and the third section will address the role research plays in furthering professional knowledge.

MANAGEMENT

Mary Parker Follett, a management theorist and early American social worker, defined management as "the act of getting things done through other people" (Wren, 1979, p. 3). Carter and O'Morrow (2006) synthesized that management is "a process of working with others to achieve organizational goals in a changing environment" (p. 4). In RT management, managers are often first-line managers because they provide treatment services and are responsible for human resources issues in the department, including the oversight of RT staff, interns, and volunteers. Managers of RT departments oversee not only human resources, such as recreational therapists, but also nonhuman resources, such as equipment, supplies, and space or work areas available to staff members (Keller, 1985). This section will explore how management influences the job responsibilities, availability of resources, professional participation, and supervision that a staff member receives. Furthermore, it will examine briefly how these areas influence a recreational therapist's opportunities for professional growth in an agency.

Most entry-level recreational therapists report to or are directly responsible to a supervisor who is in a management position. The manager may be the director of RT services, the director of rehabilitation or therapy services, or a director or chief of a unit within a hospital or agency. The manager is an important person when an entry-level recreational therapist is interviewing for a position at an agency. Entry-level recreational therapists should ask the following questions to discover the viewpoint of the manager and how this viewpoint may influence their job responsibilities and opportunities for professional growth:

- What is the mission of the recreational therapy department?

- What are the goals of the manager in relation to the department or unit?

- How does the manager interpret the supervisee's job description and role within the department/unit/agency?

- How does the manager influence the supervisee's access to equipment, supplies, or moneys for new items?

- What types of supervision are provided for the staff?

- Does the department or agency support the staff's participation in professional organizations, conferences, and workshops?

The way in which the manager interprets an employee's job description and the goals the manager has for the department directly may influence a staff member's job responsibilities. For instance, a recreational therapist interested in developing a stress management program within a rehabilitation program for adults with a chemical dependency may not feel professionally challenged or fulfilled while working under a manager who believes that the job responsibility of the staff member is to provide general recreation programs. This work situation most likely would prevent recreational therapists from further developing their skills as stress management facilitators. When considering an RT position, an individual needs to "interview" the manager carefully by asking questions regarding the philosophy, purpose, and support for the RT program and the associated job responsibilities.

Another area that may influence a recreational therapist's provision of treatment services is the availability of resources such as equipment, supplies, space for running activities, and money for the purchase of new equipment and supplies. A recreational therapist without the proper resources or equipment may be unable to facilitate an effective intervention. Recreational therapists considering a potential job must ask the manager about the availability and allocation of nonhuman resources.

The supervision a department or agency provides is another area for a potential employee to consider when applying for a professional position. Most recreational therapists receive general supervision, which entails a supervisor directing and evaluating employees' work and informing employees of policies, procedures, standards, or legislation that affect the provision of services (Austin, 1986). Many health care disciplines, including RT, recognize clinical supervision as a key element in successful clinical practice (Austin, 2013).

Clinical Supervision

Clinical supervision is a dynamic process in which the supervisor, often a person different from the individual providing general supervision, works with recreational therapists to identify their strengths and weaknesses in regard to clinical practice (Munson, 1993). The purpose of clinical supervision is twofold: to help develop the professional skills and strengths of the recreational therapist and to enhance client care via enhanced skills (Austin, 1986, 2013).

The clinical supervisor should possess extensive experience, skills, and knowledge in terms of the practice of RT. Together the clinical supervisor and the recreational therapist identify skills that the recreational therapist would like to improve. Clinical skills, which are addressed in the clinical supervision process, include charting, developing individualized treatment plans, selecting and applying a counseling approach (e.g., behavioral, client centered, cognitive-behavioral), or developing skills in a new facilitation technique for an RT group. As part of the process, the clinical supervisor and the recreational therapist decide how they will work together and how to evaluate progress. Throughout the clinical supervision process, the supervisor and the recreational therapist discuss the difficulties of learning new skills and acknowledging areas of weakness. Clinical supervisors seek to support and acknowledge a recreational therapist's progress and feelings about clinical supervision.

The benefits of participating in clinical supervision are evident and have been found to influence employees' work satisfaction positively (Cherniss & Egnatios, 1977; Munson, 1993). Furthermore, the positive outcomes of clinical supervision include an improved level of services for clients, which enhances the achievement of organizational goals and the provision of professional growth for recreational therapists (Austin, 1986, 2013).

Professional Organizations

Participation in professional organizations is another way recreational therapists may enhance their professional growth. In the United States, numerous state RT chapters are affiliates of the national organization, ATRA. In Canada, provinces have professional societies and the national professional organization is the Canadian Therapeutic Recreation Association (CTRA). Furthermore, numerous specialty organizations (e.g., Council for Exceptional Children, American Congress of Rehabilitation Medicine, American Public Health Association) provide support for recreational therapists specializing in particular populations. Professional organizations are instrumental in disseminating information regarding new developments and issues in the field (Keller, 1989). For example, members of professional RT organizations may receive information regarding how standards, legislation, and research influence professional practice. Many professional organizations sponsor yearly conferences with sessions on topics such as innovative programs or interventions, tips for devising effective treatment plans, or practical approaches for working with specific individuals. Information received from professional organizations directly may influence and enhance the recreational therapist's delivery of service in the workplace. Entry-level recreational therapists considering a position need to discover how the management of a department and agency views professional involvement. More specifically, recreational therapists need to clarify whether management will provide time and possibly financial support for membership in professional organizations and attendance at professional meetings.

The management of a department (departmental philosophy, mission, vision, and goals; design of job descriptions; availability of equipment, resources, and facilities; the type of supervision offered; and support for participation in professional organizations) influences the opportunities staff members have for developing clinical knowledge and skills. Therefore, these areas directly influence opportunities for professional growth in the workplace. Recreational therapists seeking positions need to consider how the management of a specific department or agency will enhance or hinder their professional growth and development.

CONSULTATION

Consultation involves a process in which a consultant, a professional with specialized knowledge, works with an individual or group seeking that knowledge (known henceforth as client). The client may be a recreational therapist, an RT department, or an agency that has RT personnel. The client usually enters into the consultation process on a voluntary basis. The purpose of consultation is for the consultant to help the client enact change in the agency (Block, 2011).

This section will explore the conditions under which an entry-level recreational therapist may work with a consultant. Furthermore, it will present information on the types of consultation, the consultation process, and several roles that the consultant may use during the process.

Undertaking work with a consultant typically involves a five-stage process, including entry and contracting, discovery and dialogue, feedback and the decision to act, engagement and implementation, and extension, recycle, or termination (Block, 2011). The first stage in the consultation process allows a client to find the best consultant for a specific job. This occurs during the entry and contracting stage of the consultation process. This stage allows the consultant and client to size each other up. If both parties agree that they could work well together, a contract is drawn up. Most entry-level recreational therapists would be involved in meeting potential consultants, even though supervisory personnel usually draw up the contract.

After the consultant and the client work out an agreement, they enter the discovery and dialogue stage. They work together to identify the facts surrounding the problem or issue that has brought them together. They want to discover the reasons for the problem. The consultant will ask questions, observe, ask clients to keep records surrounding the problem issues, and interview individuals and groups of employees.

The consultant will present the results of the discovery and dialogue stage to the client. The challenge in the feedback and decision to act stage is for the consultant to provide the feedback in a manner that is well received by the client.

After correctly identifying the problem, the client and the consultant must decide on an intervention in the engagement and implementation stage. An intervention is a plan of action outlining the changes that will occur, the tasks related to each area of change, and the parties responsible for each task. How actively involved the consultant is in this decision will depend on the role the individual has taken. If a consultant is serving as a mediator or collaborator, the individual will support the client in making decisions. However, if the consultant is serving as a provider of specialized information, the individual will take a more active role in identifying the appropriate intervention. When deciding on an intervention, the client and the consultant need to discuss each person's role, a timeline, and how the intervention will be evaluated.

The final phase, extension, recycle, or termination, starts with an evaluation of what occurred in the fourth phase (engagement and implementation). If the evaluation indicates that the outcome of the intervention is not satisfactory, changes need to be made. Occasionally, the real issues take time to emerge. In this case, the contract needs to be recycled, and the process starts over. In instances where the outcomes are positive, the intervention is seen as working as anticipated.

When positive outcomes are found from an intervention, the consultant and client must decide how long the consultant will work in the system. Plans for termination of the consultant's services need to be made. Plans will identify tasks to which the client needs to attend rather than the consultant. The client and the consultant also may decide that the consultant will conduct periodic checkup visits with the client to ensure all is running smoothly.

Much information regarding consultation and the stages of the consultation process have been reviewed. Many entry-level recreational therapists will participate in a consultation process. To clarify how an entry-level recreational therapist will experience the aspects of consultation, the case study in Table 13.1 shows the steps in the consulting process.

Table 13.1
Consultation Process and Roles: Golden Acres Long-Term Care Facility

Sarah: Director of recreational therapy
Connie: Consultant

Current situation
A 160-bed long-term care facility, the Golden Acres Long-Term Care Facility was recently reviewed by the state. The recreational therapy department was cited for failing to comply with several standards. While talking with the administrator, Sarah stated that her department is doing the best it can with limited resources, and she feels unsure of how to meet all the standards. The administrator suggests that a consultant be hired to help Sarah evaluate current services and consider alternatives that would ensure meeting all of the standards that the state set.

Entry and contracting phase
Sarah searches the Internet for long-term care consultants in her area. She is pleased when she finds Connie, a recreational therapist, who specializes in helping recreational therapy programs meet all standards. Sarah and Connie meet to discuss problems. Connie explains her approach as a consultant is collaborative and that she will need Sarah's assistance in collecting enough information to make appropriate suggestions. Following the meeting with Connie, Sarah recommends to the administrator that Connie be hired as the consultant. Sarah and Connie then agree upon the contract and clearly lay out the purposes of the consultation.

Discovery and data collection phase
Sarah and Connie review the report that the state inspector filed and the job description/responsibilities of each employee in the recreational therapy department. Connie interviews the employees and asks them to keep a diary of how they spend their time.

Feedback and the decision to act phase
Connie and Sarah meet to discuss findings and alternatives. Connie and Sarah meet with the department to discuss findings. The department decides on an intervention that alters each person's job responsibilities to ensure that state standards are met. While planning the intervention, the department decides that Connie will conduct monthly reviews on employees' progress and that they will meet after 3 and 6 months.

Engagement and implementation phase
As part of the intervention, Connie provides an in-service training session on treatment plans and progress notes. Sarah institutes and monitors the changes in the job responsibilities.

Evaluation, recycle, or termination phase
Improvement was noted at both the 3- and 6-month reviews. At the 6-month review, the department decided that Sarah would take over monthly reviews. Connie is then no longer an official consultant with the facility. However, she talks with Sarah periodically to check on how the recreational therapy department is getting along. The recreational therapy department receives an excellent report during the next state inspection and no citations.

In the case of the Golden Acres Long-Term Care Facility discussed in Table 13.1, Connie, the consultant, spent approximately 9 months in the facility. This is an example of a short-term consultation process. Some consultation processes may span several years and are considered long-term consultation.

As discussed in this section, consultation is a process that involves a consultant assisting a client in making changes. The consultation process allows the client to learn new skills and approaches to problem solving that will assist staff members in functioning more competently as a recreational therapist.

RESEARCH

Research is defined as a systematic and well-planned process that allows the researcher to gather information about a phenomenon (Babbie, 2004). Research in RT typically enhances a recreational therapist's understanding of a recreation activity or experience as a therapeutic intervention for individuals with illnesses, disorders, or disabilities. For example, a research study may examine the effects of an 8-week yoga intervention on the perceived health benefits for breast cancer survivors (Van Puymbroeck, Burk, Shinew, Kuhlenschmidt, & Schmid, 2013) or the development of an RT intervention for children with autism and their families (Townsend & Van Puymbroeck, 2013).

Entry-level practitioners and students of RT may have questions regarding research in RT such as the following:

- What is the link between research and practice in RT?

- What is evidence-based practice?

- How do practitioners stay informed on current research?

Each question will be explored in the following sections.

Link Between Research and Practice

Leaders in the field have discussed the importance of research in RT (cf. Bedini, 2009; Coyle, Kinney, Riley, & Shank, 1991; McCormick, Lee, & Van Puymbroeck, 2009; West, 2009). The entry-level practitioner who is faced with learning the ropes of a new position, however, may struggle with finding time to read published research. Entry-level practitioners may wonder what motivates practitioners to stay up to date on current research findings in RT. Many recreational therapists find that their knowledge of RT research increases their understanding of the effectiveness of RT interventions and helps them find areas for potential collaboration with other treatment team members.

Knowledge of research that examines the effectiveness of RT interventions will aid recreational therapists in designing interventions. If a research study finds that a sensory stimulation program decreased the number of agitated episodes among older adults with dementia (Buettner, Lundegren, Lago, Farrell, & Smith, 1996), recreational therapists who work with similar clients may consider providing such an intervention. Research also supports developing protocols. Protocols are standardized sets of steps implemented to achieve an outcome. For example, in a sensory stimulation program, a recreational therapist may develop a protocol of sensory stimulation activities for clients who display agitation. As research efforts increase, recreational therapists will be better able to develop protocols to address clients' specific behaviors, characteristics, and diagnoses. In the field of RT, one published set of protocols, or guidelines, exists to guide practice with persons with dementia. The *Dementia Practice Guidelines for Recreational Therapy* (Buettner & Fitzsimmons, 2008) are theoretically grounded, evidence-based protocols based on research that guide treatment intervention selection for persons with dementia. These guidelines are the first in RT and translate existing research into practice recommendations.

Evidence-Based Practice

Evidence-based practice (EBP), in this case RT practice, is based on research evidence. Although practitioners across all health care disciplines are pushing for EBP, practice based on research evidence is a surprisingly recent trend in health care. Today the focus is on EBP because it helps to streamline practice by reducing variations in care and because interventions that are evidence based consistently produce specific outcomes (West, 2009).

McCormick et al. (2009) recommended a specific approach to including evidence in a recreational therapist's whole RT practice, not only in the choice of interventions. First, they recommended using a valid and reliable assessment tool that examines the outcomes the recreational therapist is interested in changing. This assessment would be administered prior to initiation of therapy and at specific set points established in the treatment plan. Second, the recreational therapist would choose an intervention based on the existing literature that demonstrates changes on the outcome he or she is interested in changing. Third, the recreational therapist would evaluate the changes in the outcome, using the same assessment in the first step. The scenario in Table 13.2 illustrates this process. Although the idea of incorporating evidence into practice may be intimidating, the process, as outlined in Table 13.2, is feasible, and management likely would applaud it because it is interdisciplinary and evidence based.

Staying Informed on Current Research

Striving to stay informed of current research allows recreational therapists to be aware of innovative and unique approaches to conducting the RT process. Furthermore, research findings allow recreational therapists to begin to understand under what conditions RT interventions are effective.

A number of journals are available for RT students and professionals who are interested in keeping themselves informed of the research findings in the field. The *American Journal of Recreation Therapy, Therapeutic Recreation Journal*, and *Annual in Therapeutic Recreation* publish RT-specific studies. Readers of broader journals, such as the *Archives of Physical Medicine and Rehabilitation*, may find articles of interest written by and for recreational therapists. Research findings to support evidence-based practice also appear in textbooks, for example, Austin's (2013) *Therapeutic Recreation Processes and Techniques: Evidence-Based Recreational Therapy*. Recreational therapists also may stay informed of current research in the field by attending national and regional conferences where research is presented. The Leisure Research Symposium, which is part of the National Recreation and Park Association Congress, and the American Therapeutic Recreation Association Annual Conference sponsor presentations of RT research. In Canada, research findings are presented at the Canadian Therapeutic Recreation Association Annual Conference. Recreational therapists also may find beneficial research presented at conferences that are focused on a specific population, such as the National Autism Conference.

Table 13.2
Evidence-Based Recreational Therapy Scenario

Background
John is a recreational therapist who works in an outpatient rehabilitation facility. John's patient, Curt Tiger, had a stroke that impacted his left side. He has left hemiplegia, poor balance, difficulty with gait, and reduced inhibitions. John consults the rehabilitation literature and finds that several studies support using yoga as a therapeutic intervention to improve balance and gait for persons with stroke (Schmid et al., 2012; Van Puymbroeck, Allsop, Miller, & Schmid, in press). One research paper in particular talked about the collaboration in a yoga intervention among recreational therapists, occupational therapists, and physical therapists (Van Puymbroeck et al., in press). After reading this, John approaches the physical and occupational therapists on his team, and they jointly design a treatment approach for Curt.

Assessment
First, the team of therapists will measure balance, gait, and inhibitions using standardized outcome measures. They found these assessments by searching www.rehabmeasures.org.

Intervention
Next, the team facilitates a series of yoga interventions, following the published protocol.

Evaluation
The team evaluates Curt's progress after 8 and 16 yoga sessions. They determine that he had clinically meaningful changes in each outcome measure.

As mentioned earlier, entry-level recreational therapists need to understand the link between practice and research, to understand how to implement EBP, and to know how to stay current on the research in the field. Research is another way recreational therapists may enhance their knowledge and seek professional growth.

SUMMARY

Recreational therapists are committed to improving their clinical knowledge and skills continually. Numerous opportunities are available for recreational therapists, offered by employers and professional organizations, to increase their professional growth. The management of the department or agency in which a recreational therapist works will influence staff members' job descriptions, resources, and supervision. Recreational therapists who finds themselves in a position with a job description that matches their professional interests, provides adequate resources, and offers general and clinical supervision may be in an optimal environment for professional growth. The consultation process is another area in which staff members may have the opportunity to develop their professional skills further. Finally, research is an essential tool for use in practice, and recreational therapists need to understand the process to have an EBP.

READING COMPREHENSION QUESTIONS

1. What is meant by human and nonhuman resources?

2. What questions would a job applicant want to ask a manager/supervisor to obtain information on opportunities for professional growth?

3. What is the difference between general and clinical supervision?

4. Name several clinical skills that may be evaluated during the clinical supervision process.

5. In what contexts does clinical supervision occur?

6. Outline a situation that calls for a consultant. What type of consultation would you need in this situation?

7. Why is it important for a consultant to act as a catalyst of change?

8. Define research.

9. Explain EBP.

10. What are the steps to incorporating evidence into everyday RT practice?

11. How do recreational therapists stay informed of research being conducted in the field?

REFERENCES

American Therapeutic Recreation Association. (2009). Code of ethics. Retrieved April 16, 2014, from https://www.atra-online.com/welcome/about-atra/ethics

Austin, D. R. (1986). Clinical supervision in therapeutic recreation. *Journal of Expanding Horizons in Therapeutic Recreation, 1,* 7–13.

Austin, D. R. (2013). *Therapeutic recreation processes and techniques: Evidence-based recreational therapy* (7th ed.). Urbana, IL: Sagamore.

Babbie, E. (2004). *The practice of social research* (10th ed.). Belmont, CA: Thomson Wadsworth.

Bedini, L. (2009). Status of therapeutic recreation research. In N. Stumbo (Ed.), *Professional issues in therapeutic recreation* (2nd ed., pp. 403–414). Champaign, IL: Sagamore.

Block, P. (2011). *Flawless consulting: A guide to getting your expertise used.* Hoboken, NJ: John Wiley and Sons.

Buettner, L., & Fitzsimmons, S. (2008). *Dementia practice guidelines for recreational therapy.* Alexandria, VA: American Therapeutic Recreation Association.

Buettner, L., Lundegren, H., Lago, D., Farrell, P., & Smith, R. (1996). Therapeutic recreation as an intervention for persons with dementia and agitation: An efficacy study. *American Journal of Alzheimer's Disease, 12,* 4–12.

Carter, M. J., & O'Morrow, G. S. (2006). *Effective management in therapeutic recreation service* (2nd ed.). State College, PA: Venture.

Cherniss, C., & Egnatios, E. (1977). Styles of clinical supervision in community mental health programs. *Journal of Consulting and Clinical Psychology, 45*(6), 1195–1196.

Coyle, C. P., Kinney, W. B., Riley, B., & Shank, J. W. (Eds.). (1991). *Benefits of therapeutic recreation: A consensus view.* Philadelphia, PA: Temple University Press.

Keller, M. J. (1985). Creating a positive work environment for therapeutic recreation personnel. *Therapeutic Recreation Journal, 19*(1), 36–43.

Keller, M. J. (1989). Professional leadership: Honor or responsibility? In D. M. Compton (Ed.), *Issues in therapeutic recreation: A profession in transition* (pp. 35–48). Champaign, IL: Sagamore.

McCormick, B., Lee, Y., & Van Puymbroeck, M. (2009). Research into practice: Building knowledge through empirical practice. In N. Stumbo (Ed.), *Professional issues in therapeutic recreation* (2nd ed., pp. 447–464). Champaign, IL: Sagamore.

Munson, C. E. (1993). *Clinical social work supervision.* Binghamton, NY: Haworth Press.

National Council for Therapeutic Recreation Certification. (2014). *Certification standards: Part III—Recertification and reentry.* Retrieved April 13, 2014, from http://nctrc.org/documents/3RecertInfo.pdf

Schmid, A. A., Van Puymbroeck, M., Altenberger, P., Schalk, N., Dierks, T., Miller, K., . . . Williams, L. (2012). Post-stroke balance improves with yoga: A randomized pilot study. *Stroke, 43*(9), 2402–2407.

Townsend, J. A., & Van Puymbroeck, M. (2013). Understanding the intentions of families with a child with autism to participate in a family recreation program: A pilot study. *American Journal of Recreation Therapy, 12*(1), 16–22.

Van Puymbroeck, M., Allsop, J., Miller, K. K., & Schmid, A. (in press). ICF-based improvements in body structures and function, and activity and participation in chronic stroke following a yoga-based intervention. *American Journal of Recreation Therapy.*

Van Puymbroeck, M., Burk, B. N., Shinew, K., Kuhlenschmidt, M. C., & Schmid, A. A. (2013). Perceived health benefits from yoga among breast cancer patients. *American Journal of Health Promotion, 27*(5), 308–315.

West, R. (2009). Integrating evidence into recreational therapy practice. In N. Stumbo (Ed.), *Professional issues in therapeutic recreation* (2nd ed., pp. 249–268). Champaign, IL: Sagamore.

Wren, D. A. (1979). *The evolution of management thought* (2nd ed.). New York, NY: John Wiley and Sons.

14

ISSUES AND TRENDS

BRYAN P. MCCORMICK, MICHAEL E. CRAWFORD, AND DAVID R. AUSTIN

OBJECTIVES

- Describe the three periods in recreational therapy (RT).
- Differentiate between issues and trends.
- Identify three issues for RT.
- Understand the trends in RT presented in the chapter.

THREE PERIODS IN RECREATIONAL THERAPY

Austin (2013b) proposed that the recreational therapy (RT) profession has gone through three distinct periods: the 1950s and 1960s, when RT professionals displayed passion for caring for underserved populations; the 1970s, 1980s, and 1990s, which saw the professionalization of RT; and the temporary state of equilibrium experienced during the 21st century.

In the 1950s and 1960s, RT professionals displayed their passion for caring for underserved populations in hospitals and institutions. During this time, recreational therapists initially based practice on the intrinsic value of recreation for persons who were ill or had disabilities and later began to see themselves as clinicians that used recreation as a tool for treatment in individualized care plans.

The 1970s, 1980s, and 1990s saw the professionalization of RT. Many markers of professionalization were achieved. A body of knowledge was developed. University professional preparation programs were developed. Ethical standards were established. Continuing education was offered at the national, regional, provincial, state, and local levels. A credentialing program administered by the National Council on Therapeutic Recreation Certification began. In addition, in the United States, the American Therapeutic Recreation Association (ATRA) was formed as the professional membership society for recreational therapists in 1984. ATRA's sister organization in Canada, the Canadian Therapeutic Recreation Association (CTRA), has existed since 1995.

Austin (2013b) suggested that any system has three basic directions in which to move. It may grow, decline, or temporarily reside in a state of equilibrium. He posited that RT in the 21st century is in a temporary state of equilibrium, at which point RT must grow, or it will decline. Austin (2013b) rested his belief that RT in the United States is in a state of equilibrium on the following:

Over 30 years ago we met the criteria to be considered an emerging profession (Navar, 1979). Back then, as previously indicated, we had a developing body of knowledge, professional literature, university curricula, professional associations, a code of ethics, and other markers of professionalization. Some gains have been made since but, in the main, RT in the United States has remained stagnant and some areas even have shown decline (e.g., a reduced number of research universities with RT curricula). If we are to break out of the state of equilibrium, our future will have to be much different than what our profession has been in the past. (p. 14)

Now is time for the RT profession to rejuvenate itself—or to take a leap forward in its development. Austin (2013b) wrote, "I believe our profession is in the position to move to new heights but only if we examine ourselves and commit ourselves to advancing our profession" (p. 14). That is what this chapter is about: moving the profession forward by meeting the issues with which it is faced and reacting positively to trends that will influence its practice.

WHAT ARE ISSUES AND TRENDS?

Before delving into specific issues and trends, the terms *issues* and *trends* will be discussed. Issues involve problems or concerns over which two opposing points of view often exist. On the other hand, trends are developing tendencies that are taking RT in new directions. They indicate emerging changes.

ISSUES IN RECREATIONAL THERAPY

Defining the Profession: A Critical Issue

Austin (2013b) suggested that to move out of the temporary state of equilibrium—to reinvigorate the profession—RT professionals need to clearly define the profession and their role in it. Every profession needs to be able to provide a succinct definition to interpret the profession to themselves, other practitioners, administrators, students, legislative bodies, regulating agencies, and the public in general. To be successful as a profession, RT professionals need to settle the issue of who they are and what they do so their value and worth are clear to everyone. Kunstler and Stavola Daly (2010) proclaimed that "our value to the public has not been clearly established in the world of practice or clearly articulated" (p. 354).

Any definition of RT needs to define the boundaries of the profession. Austin (2002) wrote that clearly demarcated boundaries are needed "because carefully defining the profession will ultimately lead to the expansion of a focused and documented body of knowledge, [and] provide students with a clear sense of mission and purpose...." (p. 2). Finally, Austin and Lee (2013) indicated RT needs to be differentiated from the facilitation of leisure services for persons with disabilities, or what has been termed *inclusive and special recreation*.

Thus, RT must be clearly defined as a means to reaching therapeutic outcomes with clients. Austin (2013b) wrote,

Some may argue that recreation therapy can operate as both a means and as an end. That is, recreation can be seen as both an end in itself and a means to client change. Such dual use of the term recreation is however confusing to external publics – and I might add it would be confusing to us as we define who we are. (p. 19)

Likewise, an occupational therapist wrote about the similar means–end debate in occupational therapy: "Metaphorically speaking, one simply cannot have one's cake and eat it too" (Royeen, 2003, p. 610). As do occupational therapists, RT professionals must declare that RT is a health care profession that employs recreation and leisure as means to achieve specific health-related outcomes.

An Issue: Not Professing for the Recreational Therapy Profession

Once RT professionals have clearly articulated what RT is, recreational therapists need to declare a commitment to the profession as they have defined it. As professionals, recreational therapists need to see themselves as therapeutic agents who positively impact persons by helping them achieve therapeutic outcomes, and accordingly, they should profess the value and worth of their profession. Austin (2013b) wrote,

> We should have great respect for ourselves and our profession. We should earnestly believe in ourselves as professionals and we should proclaim allegiance to our profession of recreational therapy, a profession in which we should take our responsibilities very seriously. (p. 16)

Yet the charge has been made that too many recreational therapists do not take themselves and their work seriously. They devalue their profession by not realizing the potential that RT has to change lives (Austin, 2013a). Some even may practice without therapeutic intent and without theory to support their practice as was done when the profession was first emerging during the 1950s and 1960s (Austin, 2013b). Austin (2013b) wrote,

> Practicing at what years ago we termed a "fun and games" level, I can see would not be respected by colleagues in health care—and practitioners practicing at that level might be apt to suffer from low self-regard. In fact, I can see how a lack of respect for what they do could lead those practicing at a shallow level to feel dispirited and demoralized. Being dispirited and demoralized might naturally produce low self-regard with resulting unprofessional behaviors—a downward spiraling effect if you will. (pp. 16, 17)

Respect for their own dignity and worth, or self-respect, is a value that recreational therapists should hold. Recreational therapists who serve as therapeutic agents are persons of value and worth and should hold themselves and their profession in high regard. As such, they should exhibit a sense of dedication and commitment to the profession that they value. Translating this into action, recreational therapists should, at a minimum, belong to and support their professional membership organizations. At the national level, this means being a member of the American Therapeutic Recreation Association (ATRA) or the Canadian Therapeutic Recreation Association (CTRA).

True professionals seem to see involvement in their national professional organization as a personal responsibility and a moral obligation. Furthermore, belonging to their professional society allows them to work toward advancing the profession to meet their vision of what they see as the preferred future of their profession. Yet in the United States, only about 15% of Certified Therapeutic Recreation Specialists® (CTRS®) belong to ATRA (Austin, 2013b).

The editors of this textbook desire that students preparing for careers in RT understand the value and worth of the profession and act accordingly by becoming involved as members of their campus, state, and/or national professional membership organizations. Such engagement seems to be the right thing to do.

Lack of PhD-Prepared Faculty: A Key Issue

Austin and McCormick (2011) identified a severe shortage of RT faculty with terminal degrees (i.e., doctoral degrees). This is an issue for the profession because well-prepared faculty are necessary not only to teach in university professional preparation programs but also to contribute to the literature of the profession through research and scholarship.

Two major reasons exist for the shortage of faculty possessing terminal degrees. The first is that too few practitioners have chosen to go on for advanced degrees. This is perplexing because the potential benefits for those who gain credentials to become academics are great, and the profession direly needs individuals to assume faculty roles. The second reason is that the number of universities that offer the doctoral degree in RT has declined, so the availability of academic opportunities for potential students who wish to pursue terminal degrees is limited. This issue is becoming apparent to RT professionals and must be addressed (Austin & McCormick, 2011). Without an adequate number of well-prepared faculty members, the profession is unlikely to move forward to reinvigorate itself.

Degree Level for Entrance to Practice

Curricular requirements for recreational therapists were developed first in the 1940s and have been evolving since then (Stumbo, Carter, & Kim, 2004). Although the types and number of courses and practical experiences that constitute students' professional preparation have expanded, the bachelor's degree has remained the entry-level degree for the profession. Thus, the basic educational requirement for recreational therapists has not changed in more than 70 years even though the knowledge and skills required for persons entering into RT practice have expanded.

To take advantage of the growth in knowledge and sophistication in skills, the educational requirements of other health care professions have been extended. Cases in point are the professions of occupational therapy and physical therapy. Both require degrees beyond baccalaureate degrees. In fact, both no longer have accredited baccalaureate degree programs. Today, entry-level occupational therapists must possess a master's or a doctor of occupational therapy (OTD) degree. Similarly, those who wish to enter into careers in physical therapy must obtain a master's or a doctor of physical therapy (DPT) degree (Skipper & Lewis, 2005).

Will the depth and breadth of requirements for entry into the RT profession be expanded? Will RT professionals be required to have at least a master's degree as an entry-level degree? Only time will tell. However, sometime in the near future, individuals may have to obtain a master's degree to become a certified recreational therapist.

TRENDS AFFECTING RECREATIONAL THERAPY

A number of trends today are impacting the RT profession. Each of these trends is discussed in the following section of the chapter.

Increasing Use of the Term *Recreational Therapy*

The term *recreational therapy* is enjoying greater use. For example, the symposium that once had been named the Southeast Therapeutic Recreation Symposium recently changed its name to the Southeast Recreational Therapy Symposium. The rationale for the change was that "most individuals, who hold the title of CTRS®, are employed in the provision of recreational therapy treatment services" (Southeast Recreational Therapy Symposium, 2012). Another example is the use of the term *recreational therapists* in the title of the recently established honorific society for the profession, the National Academy of Recreational Therapists (Austin & West, 2011). The states of New Hampshire and North Carolina have used the term *recreational therapy* in their licensure laws, and Washington, D.C., has employed the expression *recreation therapy* in its licensure law (National Council for Therapeutic Recreation Certification, 2007). An analysis of the titles of state and regional professional societies that are chapters of ATRA revealed the terms *recreational therapy* or *recreation therapy* now appear in the titles of 37% of these organizations (ATRA, 2009). A number of universities now use either *recreational therapy* or *recreation therapy* to describe their professional preparation programs, including California State University, Chico; Clemson University; East Carolina University; Indiana University; Radford University; San Jose State University; Shaw University; University of North Carolina, Wilmington; and Western Carolina University (B. P. McCormick, personal communication, April 12, 2013). Although these examples of the employment of the terms *recreational therapy* and *recreation therapy* are small in number, they are indicative of a trend toward increasing use of these terms.

Uniform and Rigorous Professional Preparation Programs

University professional preparation programs appear to be trending toward uniformity and being more rigorous. Recently universities have employed several resources as a basis for improving university RT curricula, including *Guidelines for Competency Assessment and Curriculum Planning for Recreational Therapy Practice* (ATRA, 2008), *Standards and Guidelines for the Accreditation of Educational Programs in Recreational Therapy* (Commission on Accreditation of Allied Health Education Programs, 2010), and the results of a job analysis by the National Council for Therapeutic Recreation Certification® (2014). Among these, the development of an independent committee on accreditation specific to RT education indicates that the preparation of RT professionals should be independent of the preparation of parks and recreation professionals.

Theory-Based Practice

Austin (2013c) emphasized the relationship between theory and practice. He explained the interrelation of philosophy, theory, and practice based on Smith and Liehr's (2008) Ladder of Abstraction. This ladder has three rungs. The top rung is philosophy. The middle rung is theory. The lowest rung is the empirical level, the most concrete level of abstraction.

Philosophy consists of the values and beliefs held in regard to RT. Theory is the structuring of concepts derived from philosophical perspectives to produce a systematic view of a phenomenon such as RT practice. Theory is an explanation of RT practice so RT professionals understand that RT may guide their actions. Theories then reflect the purpose and nature of RT practice. Austin (2013c) wrote, "Theory becomes the lens through which practice is viewed" (p. 198).

Within RT, theories are represented by conceptual models, such as the Reformulated Health Protection/Health Promotion Model (Austin, 2011), the Leisure Ability Model (Gunn & Peterson, 1978; Stumbo & Peterson, 2009), and the Flourishing Through Leisure Model (Anderson & Heyne, 2012). Traditionally, these conceptual models for RT have been represented by graphic representations, or diagrams. McEwen and Wills (2011) stated that the narratives that accompany conceptual models represent theory. Austin (2013c) commented on the writings of McEwen and Wills. He wrote, "Further, these authors have declared that theories define and clarify the nature of the profession and its purpose, distinguishing it from other helping professions by marking professional boundaries" (p. 198).

Because conceptual models are the theoretical basis for RT, they serve to define and guide the practice of RT. Thus, conceptual models are a theoretical basis for the practice of RT.

Due to the Leisure Ability Model (Gunn & Peterson, 1978; Stumbo & Peterson, 2009) being the only conceptual model available in the 1970s, many professionals used it to define and direct their practice. Today, however, practitioners may adopt a number of models as the theoretical basis to define and guide their practice. Thus, several theoretical bases for practice are available, and recreational therapists are tending to choose to embrace a conceptual model that best provides a basis for their practice.

Evidence-Based Practice

In addition to theory as a basis for practice, evidence-based practice (EBP) also has been increasing. Concepts of EBP have existed in the RT literature for more than a decade (Lee & McCormick, 2002; McCormick & Lee, 2001; McCormick, Lee, & Van Puymbroeck, 2009; Stumbo, 2003a) and have been a part of the literature of medicine for more than two decades. Lee and McCormick (2002) defined EBP as "practice that is continuously informed and guided by the systematic collection and inclusion of research and practice evidence in clinical work" (p. 168). Such a definition recognizes that a number of sources of evidence must be considered in effective RT practice. This increasing recognition of the importance of EBP in RT is reflected in the subtitle of Austin's (2013c) seventh edition of *Therapeutic Recreation Processes and Techniques: Evidence-Based Recreational Therapy*.

The concept of EBP began within medicine (then known as evidence-based medicine) during the late 1970s and was focused principally on integrating clinical research evidence into the practice of medicine (Wyer & Silva, 2009). One of the first formal statements of evidence-based medicine was offered in 1992 (Guyatt et al., 1992), and subsequently expanded to evidence-based health care in 1994 (Evidence-Based Medicine Working Group, 1994); however, it remained largely focused on integrating research evidence into practice. Critics of this original conceptualization asserted that research evidence alone is insufficient to make clinical decisions (Haynes, Devereaux, & Guyatt, 2002). Thus, definitions of EBP expanded to include clinical knowledge and client characteristics in clinical decision making. The three principal sources of evidence identified were practitioner expertise or judgment; client characteristics, needs, and preferences; and research findings (Malloch & Porter-O'Grady, 2009).

Akobeng (2005) stated that the reason to provide EBP was "to improve quality of care through the identification and promotion of practices that work, and the elimination of those that are ineffective or harmful" (p. 837). Ultimately, this is the reason to pursue evidence-based RT practice as well. With the increasing focus on cost-effectiveness in health and human services, RT professionals may demonstrate the contribution of RT to overall quality of care through identifying and implementing services with demonstrated effectiveness. The implication for RT practice is that EBP should be an explicit concept included in preprofessional preparation programs. Thus, in addition to students learning to collect information directly from clients and make clinical judgments about that information (largely through the assessment and planning processes), they will need to have the skills to find, evaluate, and translate research findings into practices (thus informing planning and implementation of services).

Outcome Measurement

A key component of EBP is the use of outcomes as a basis for evaluating the quality and effectiveness of care. Most simply, outcomes reflect a recipient's status following services (Stumbo, 2003b). Furthermore, outcomes are multidimensional and may include clinical status, functional status, quality of life, satisfaction, and resource consumption (McCormick & Funderburk, 2000). For example, an RT gross motor activity intervention for an adult post-stroke may produce outcomes related to improved vestibular functions of balance and position as well as gait pattern (clinical status). Yet the intervention may fail to produce outcomes related to mobility, self-care, and participation in community life (functional status) without attention to environmental factors that may be barriers to full participation. Outcomes also may be contradictory. Ware (1992) cited a classic case in which three antihypertensive medications were compared. Although all were found to effectively reduce hypertension (clinical status), one of the three was found to significantly reduce quality of life for persons taking it due to multiple discomforting side effects.

Although outcome measurement may seem like a straightforward phenomenon as it relates to determining a client's status post-service, it is inherently related to the quality of initial assessment (Beidas et al., 2014). The importance of assessment to outcome measurement has led to an approach to assessment that advocates for evidence-based processes and instruments (Hunsley & Mash, 2007). For recreational therapists, this speaks to the need for a systematic EBP for assessment and the use of valid and reliable instruments in collecting baseline status. Although resources are available for identifying standardized assessment instruments related to RT (e.g., burlingame & Blaschko, 2002; Porter & burlingame, 2006), established validity and reliability of these measures is more limited. Furthermore, evidence-based assessment also implies that instruments are validated for use with specific diagnoses or health conditions. Again, many standardized RT measures have limited information available to indicate their appropriateness across a number of diagnostic categories.

Although high quality instruments may be few for RT, a model for compiling outcome measurement instruments has been developed through the Rehabilitation

Institute of Chicago (2010) and is available at www.rehabmeasures.org. Led by Dr. Alan Heinemann, this initiative has brought together allied health professionals to identify, evaluate, and catalog appropriate instruments for outcome measurement in physical medicine and rehabilitation (more about this resource may be found at the end of this chapter). Instruments are categorized under many areas of functioning that are appropriate for recreational therapists to use such as cognition, mobility, life participation, mental health, quality of life, and social relationships, to name a few.

The National Institutes of Health has headed another initiative to create a toolbox for assessing neurological and behavioral functioning. This consensus set of measures assesses function in cognitive, emotional, motor, and sensation domains. Of particular relevance to RT practice may be measures in the cognitive, emotional, and motor domains. For example, within the emotional domain, instruments are available to assess well-being, social relationships, stress, efficacy, and negative affect, and RT services may affect these aspects of functioning.

This trend, with increasing demands for accountability and EBP, will require recreational therapists to become more sophisticated in measuring the outcomes of their services. Again, RT professionals will need to be strongly prepared in understanding and measuring outcomes for RT to remain a relevant allied health and human service profession.

Positive Psychology and Strength-Based Approach

The elements of positive psychology and a strength-based approach are apparent in the most recent conceptual models: the Reformulated Health Protection/ Health Promotion Model (Austin, 2011) and the Flourishing Through Leisure Model (Anderson & Heyne, 2012). Positive psychology came about late in the 20th century as a response to the perception that psychology had been embracing a disease and medical model. Rather than being focused on pathology, positive psychology is concerned with human strengths and optimal functioning. Biswas-Diener and Dean (2007) stated that positive psychology is a "branch of psychology that focuses on what is going right, rather than what is going wrong with people" (p. x). In positive psychology, the emphasis is on the full range of human functioning. Linley and Joseph (2004) stated, "Applied positive psychologists may work both to alleviate distress and to promote optimal functioning" (p. 6). Skerrett (2010) indicated that "positive psychology is "not a replacement to the more problem-focused or deficit-based paradigms, it is conceptualized as a complementary and important dimension to understand the full range of human experience" (p. 488). The inclusion of positive psychology, with its strength-based approach, as an element affecting the theory and practice of RT is a definite trend within RT today.

For additional information on positive psychology, readers may wish to refer to the discussion of positive psychology in Chapter 1 of this book, to a summary of positive psychology found in *Therapeutic Recreation Processes and Techniques* (Austin, 2013c), and to the article "Positive Psychology: A Theoretical Foundation for Recreation Therapy Practice" (Austin, McCormick, & Van Puymbroeck, 2010).

International Classification of Functioning, Disability, and Health

The World Health Organization (2002) developed the International Classification of Functioning, Disability, and Health (ICF) to provide a common language for functioning, disability, and health. The ICF model is focused on functioning, not disability. Its emphasis on functioning allows persons with impairments to be viewed as being "healthy" even though they may have a health condition (e.g., chronic illness, disorder, or injury) as long as they are functioning well. The ICF is a tool that provides language that is focused on functioning in society, no matter the reason for the individual's impairment (i.e., a problem in body function or structure).

The ICF is a departure from the traditional medical model. Because of this, it fits well with trends in the way RT is viewed today such as following a biopsychosocial model, conceptualizing an illness–wellness continuum, acknowledging the effect of the environment, being focused not solely on clients' impairments but on their functioning, and employing interventions that build strengths and address difficulties (Austin, 2013c). The embracing of the ICF by RT professionals is reflected by Porter and burlingame's (2006) *Recreational Therapy Handbook of Practice: ICF-Based Diagnosis and Treatment* and in articles found in RT books and journals (Porter & Van Puymbroeck, 2007; Van Puymbroeck, Porter, & McCormick, 2009).

Technology

The therapeutic use of technology in RT is an emerging trend. Austin (2013c) discussed applying video games, video production, computers, Snoezelen rooms, robotic therapy, and assistive technology in RT interventions. He suggested that using video games holds great promise. He warned, however, that recreational therapists need to consider the clients' preferences when applying technology. For example, although using technology may appeal to younger clients and recreational therapists, it may not have the same appeal to older clients.

Aging Population and Chronic Conditions

The populations of the United States and Canada are aging. In the United States, between the years 2000 and 2010, the population of persons 65 and older grew at the rate of 15.1% to 40.3 million older adults, or 13% of the total population (U.S. Census Bureau, 2011). This population only will continue to grow; by 2030, the number of older Americans is expected to increase from today's 40 million to 72 million, or from 13% to 20% of the population (Friedman, 2011). Similarly, Canada will experience a rapid growth in the number of older Canadians. By 2031, an estimated 9 million Canadians will be older than age 65, more than doubling the number of 4 million older Canadians in 2005 (Public Health Agency of Canada, 2006).

Accompanying the aging process are chronic conditions such as arthritis, multiple sclerosis, obesity, cardiovascular diseases, strokes, cancer, diabetes, asthma, chronic obstructive pulmonary disease (COPD), Parkinson's disease, Alzheimer's disease, and muscular dystrophy (Austin, 2013c). Thus, to meet the health needs of the increasing elderly population experiencing chronic conditions, recreational therapists must expand services to this population. See Chapter 9 on geriatric practice in RT for more information.

Growing Number of Persons with Disabilities

The United States and Canada have large and growing populations of persons with disabilities. According to the U.S. Census Bureau, 56.7 million (18.7%) Americans have some level of disability and 38.3 million (12.6%) have severe disabilities (Brault, 2012). The *2009 Federal Disability Report* (Human Resources and Skills Development Canada, 2009) reflected that the disability rate in Canada in 2006 was 14.3% of the population, up from 12.4% in 2001. This is 4,353,150 Canadians out of 30,581,240.

Thus, a trend for recreational therapists will be serving the growing number of persons with disabilities. Many of these persons will be veterans who served in combat. See Chapter 12 for additional information on RT for veterans.

Community-Based Services

The majority of elderly individuals with chronic health concerns and persons with disabilities will reside in the community rather than in institutions. To serve these and other populations needing health care, recreational therapists will have to follow a health care trend already apparent in Canada and the United States to offer community-based services. However, a number of individuals will continue to require institutional care to ensure their safety and well-being. The need for long-term care services likely will call for growth in the number of long-term care beds in coming years (Austin, 2013b).

Illness Prevention and Health Promotion

Particularly in the area of mental health, prevention programs are being seen as means to prevent mental, emotional, and behavioral disorders before they begin (Beardslee, Chien, & Bell, 2011). The trend toward the provision of illness prevention and health promotion in mental health is largely interdisciplinary in nature and certainly should involve RT. Among other areas of illness prevention and health promotion are the provision of physical activities to combat obesity (Austin, 2013c). Recreational therapists likely will offer physical activity programs to help clients with weight reduction and to promote physical fitness.

Health Care Reform

Many of the preceding trends have contributed to an ever-increasing need for the United States to examine its health care system. Most notably among these reforms was the passage in 2010 of the Patient Protection and Affordable Care Act, also known as Obamacare. Although the future of this particular act is not known, it has been characterized as "the most fundamental change to the structure of health care regulation since the introduction of Medicare and Medicaid" (Savel & Munro, 2014, p. 100). It was proposed to address fundamental problems in the U.S. health care system such as out-of-control costs, inconsistent access to services, and problems in quality (Feldman, 2012).

Among these reforms have been changes to the way private health insurance is offered, for example, eliminating preexisting condition clauses, mandating coverage of dependents to age 26, and prohibiting dropping policyholders who develop costly diseases. In addition, revisions to both Medicare and Medicaid have resulted in new structures to address the health care needs of populations who have higher rates of chronic and multiple health conditions. Examples include the creation of Medical Homes, in which primary care physicians (PCP) work with a team of nurses and other allied health professionals to provide and coordinate services for patients across the entire spectrum of illness and disease from prevention to end-of-life care (Feldman, 2012). Although such care coordination entities may afford new opportunities for recreational therapists in service provision, this may be possible only in larger practices serving a large patient population.

Another change has been the creation of accountable care organizations (ACO), groups of doctors, nurses, hospitals, and other health care professionals who work to integrate care from inpatient to outpatient services (Feldman, 2012). The rationale for ACOs is that through greater coordination of care and reductions in unnecessary costs, care will be improved and costs reduced. Again, recreational therapists may be a part of ACOs principally through hospital settings, but they should be aware that high quality, cost-effective services will be valued in such organizations.

Perhaps a key element of the current health care reform initiative is the belief that reducing the cost of health care may be achieved through providing high quality services in the least costly setting (home and community), with a focus on maintaining health and preventing disability and (re)hospitalization. Regardless of whether the Patient Protection and Affordable Care Act is fully implemented, modified, or repealed in the future, the principles of reform on which it is based are likely to remain. The future of health services in the United States will continue to value care that is supported by evidence, integrated across all service providers, provided in the least costly environment, and focused on maintaining health over treating disease.

SUMMARY

This chapter provided an overview of both issues and trends that are likely to affect the profession of RT as well as the location and nature of practice. It advanced the notion that the profession of RT is in a state of temporary equilibrium that will require a collective commitment to advancing the profession if it is to progress. Critical to this advancement will be a common definition and understanding of what constitutes RT and a commitment of practicing professionals to that common understanding. Finally, RT professionals will have to support the preparation of professionals at all levels of academic credentials, including those at the doctoral (PhD) level. At the same time, the chapter identified trends that may provide opportunities for advancing RT as a profession. The historical commitment of RT professionals to a strength-based orientation in services is highly consistent with new approaches to health and healing. In addition, an increasing movement to provide services in the communities in which clients reside is highly consistent with historical practices in RT. At the same time, other trends will demand that RT professionals prepare and practice RT differently. Theory and EBP will be required to advance RT as a rehabilitation service on par with others. RT professionals will have to become more rigorous in using outcome measurement to demonstrate the effectiveness and value of their services to the stakeholders affected. Both of these trends will require preprofessional and continuing education programs that improve the scientific orientation to RT practice. Finally, although challenges certainly exist, RT is poised to break out of the equilibrium and fully realize its potential contributions to health and human services by improving clinical status, functional abilities, life participation, and quality of life for clients.

READING COMPREHENSION QUESTIONS

1. Describe the three periods in RT that Austin (2013b) identified.
2. Differentiate between the terms *issues* and *trends*.
3. Name qualities that recreational therapists should demonstrate if they are to support the profession.

4. How could practicing at a shallow level lead to an undermining of the RT profession?

5. What are the causes of the shortage of doctorally-prepared (PhD) personnel in RT?

6. What are the implications of a shortage of doctorally-prepared (PhD) personnel in RT?

7. Should RT require a master's degree for entry-level practice? What is your argument to support your position?

8. What are the principal indicators of an increasing consistency of professional preparation programs in RT?

9. What is the value of theory-based practice?

10. How are conceptual models of RT related to theory?

11. Identify and describe the three forms of evidence that comprise theory-based practice.

12. What skills are needed in RT training to implement EBP?

13. How is outcome measurement related to the process of assessment?

14. Describe limitations of currently available RT-specific assessment measures in outcome measurement.

15. What is positive psychology, and how does it integrate with RT services?

16. How does the International Classification of Functioning, Disability, and Health (ICF) change the orientation to disability and health?

17. What are the population, disease, and demographic factors that may affect the future practice of RT?

18. How will the location and nature of RT services likely change in the future?

19. What are the main changes to health services that the Patient Protection and Affordable Care Act of 2010 have created?

EXTERNAL RESOURCES

Rehabilitation Measures Database: www.rehabmeasures.org

The database was developed through a grant to Dr. Alan Heinemann through the Rehabilitation Institute of Chicago, Center for Rehabilitation Outcomes Research, Northwestern University Feinberg School of Medicine Department of Medical Social Sciences Informatics group. This database provides information on outcome measures that expert panels have reviewed for validity, reliability, and appropriateness for use in many domains and client characteristics.

NIH Toolbox: http://www.nihtoolbox.org

This resource, created by the National Institutes of Health and Northwestern University, provides a set of consensus assessment tools for measuring neurological and behavioral function. These instruments are freely available with associated training manuals. In addition, instruments are specified for use with different age groups. Some of the instruments also are available in Spanish.

REFERENCES

Akobeng, A. K. (2005). Principles of evidence based medicine. *Archives of Disease in Childhood, 90*(8), 837–840. doi:10.1133/adc.2005.071761

American Therapeutic Recreation Association. (2008). *Guidelines for competency assessment and curriculum planning in therapeutic recreation: A tool for self evaluation.* Hattiesburg, MS: Author.

American Therapeutic Recreation Association. (2009). ATRA. Retrieved from http://www.atra-online.com

Anderson, L. S., & Heyne, L. A. (2012). Flourishing through leisure: An ecological extension of the Leisure and Well-Being Model in therapeutic recreation strengths-based practice. *Therapeutic Recreation Journal, 46*(2), 129–152.

Austin, D. R. (2002). Conceptual models in therapeutic recreation. In D. R. Austin, J. Dattilo, & B. P. McCormick (Eds.), *Conceputal foundations for therapeutic recreation* (pp. 1–30). State College, PA: Venture.

Austin, D. R. (2011). Reformation of the Health Protection/Health Promotion Model. *American Journal of Recreation Therapy, 10*(3), 19–26.

Austin, D. R. (2013a). On not taking ourselves seriously as individuals working in a vital profession. *American Journal of Recreation Therapy, 12*(1), 7–9.

Austin, D. R. (2013b, May). *Perspectives on our profession: A 50 year journey.* Paper presented at the Canadian Therapeutic Recreation Association Conference, Halifax, Canada.

Austin, D. R. (2013c). *Therapeutic recreation processes and techniques: Evidenced-based recreational therapy* (7th ed.). Urbana, IL: Sagamore.

Austin, D. R., & Lee, Y. (2013). *Inclusive and special recreation: Opportunities for diverse populations to flourish* (6th ed.). Urbana, IL: Sagamore.

Austin, D. R., & McCormick, B. P. (2011). Recreation therapy scholarship: A necessary contribution to the future of recreation therapy. *American Journal of Recreation Therapy, 10*(1), 5–6.

Austin, D. R., McCormick, B. P., & Van Puymbroeck, M. (2010). Positive psychology: A theoretical foundation for recreation therapy practice. *American Journal of Recreation Therapy, 9*(3), 17–24.

Austin, D. R., & West, R. (2011, August). The beginnings of NART. *NART Newsletter, 1,* 1–2.

Beardslee, W. R., Chien, P. L., & Bell, C. C. (2011). Prevention of mental disorders, substance abuse, and problem behaviors: A developmental perspective. *Psychiatric Services, 62*(3), 247–254. doi:10.1176/appi.ps.62.3.247

Beidas, R. S., Stewart, R. E., Walsh, L., Lucas, S., Downey, M. M., Jackson, K., . . . Mandell, D. S. (2014). Free, brief, and validated: Standardized instruments for low-resource mental health settings. *Cognitive and Behavioral Practice.* doi:10.1016/j.cbpra.2014.02.002

Biswas-Diener, R., & Dean, B. (2007). *Positive psychology coaching: Putting the science of happiness to work for your clients.* Hoboken, NJ: Wiley.

Brault, M. W. (2012). *Current population reports.* Washington, DC: U.S. Department of Commerce, Economics and Statistics Administration.

burlingame, j., & Blaschko, T. M. (2002). *Assessment tools for recreational therapy and related fields* (3rd ed.). Ravensdale, WA: Idyll Arbor.

Commission on Accreditation of Allied Health Education Programs. (2010). *Standards and guidelines for the accreditation of educational programs in recreational therapy.* Clearwater, FL: Author.

Evidence-Based Medicine Working Group. (1994). Evidence-based health care: A new approach to teaching the practice of health care. *Journal of Dental Education, 58*(8), 648–653.

Feldman, A. M. (2012). *Understanding health care reform: Bridging the gap between myth and reality.* Boca Raton, FL: Taylor & Francis.

Friedman, M. (2011). Meeting the mental health challenges of the elder boom. *The Huffington Post.* Retrieved from http://www.huffingtonpost.com/michael-friedman-lmsw/meeting-the-mental-health_b_804725.html

Gunn, S. L., & Peterson, C. A. (1978). *Therapeutic recreation program design: Principles and procedures.* Englewood Cliffs, NJ: Prentice Hall.

Guyatt, G., Cairns, J., Churchill, D., Cook, D., Haynes, B., Hirsh, J., . . . Tugwell, P. (1992). Evidence-based medicine: A new approach to teaching the practice of medicine. *JAMA, 268*(17), 2420–2425.

Haynes, R. B., Devereaux, P. J., & Guyatt, G. H. (2002). Physicians' and patients' choices in evidence based practice: Evidence does not make decisions, people do. *British Medical Journal, 324*(7350), 1350–1350. doi:10.1136/bmj.324.7350.1350

Human Resources and Skills Development Canada. (2009). *2009 federal disability report: Advancing the inclusion of people with disabilities.* Retrieved from http://publications.gc.ca/pub?id=358988&sl=0

Hunsley, J., & Mash, E. J. (2007). Evidence-based assessment. *Annual Review of Clinical Psychology, 3,* 29–51.

Kunstler, R. A., & Stavola Daly, F. (2010). *Therapeutic recreation leadership and programming.* Champaign, IL: Human Kinetics.

Lee, Y., & McCormick, B. P. (2002). Toward evidence-based therapeutic recreation practice. In D. R. Austin, J. Dattilo, & B. P. McCormick (Eds.), *Conceptual foundations for therapeutic recreation* (pp. 165–181). State College, PA: Venture.

Linley, P. A., & Joseph, S. (2004). Applied positive psychology: A new perspective for professional practice. In P. A. Linley & S. Joseph (Eds.), *Positive psychology in practice* (pp. 3–14). Hoboken, NJ: Wiley.

Malloch, K., & Porter-O'Grady, T. (2009). *Introduction to evidence-based practice in nursing and healthcare* (2nd ed.). Sudbury, MA: Jones & Bartlett Learning.

McCormick, B. P., & Funderburk, J. (2000). Therapeutic recreation outcomes in mental health practice. *Annual in Therapeutic Recreation, 9,* 9–19.

McCormick, B. P., & Lee, Y. (2001). Research in practice: Building knowledge through empirical practice. In N. J. Stumbo (Ed.), *Professional issues in therapeutic recreation* (pp. 383–400). Champaign, IL: Sagamore.

McCormick, B. P., Lee, Y., & Van Puymbroeck, M. (2009). Research in practice: Building knowledge through empirical practice. In N. J. Stumbo (Ed.), *Professional issues in therapeutic recreation: On competence and outcomes* (2nd ed., pp. 447–464). Champaign, IL: Sagamore.

McEwen, M., & Wills, E. M. (2011). *Theoretical basis for nursing* (3rd ed.). Philadelphia, PA: Lippincott Williams & Wilkins.

National Council for Therapeutic Recreation Certification. (2007). *NCTRC position paper on the legal regulation of the practice of recreation therapy.* New City, NY: Author.

National Council for Therapeutic Recreation Certification. (2014). *Certification standards: Part V— NCTRC National job analysis.* New City, NY: Author.

Porter, H., & burlingame, j. (2006). *Recreational therapy handbook of practice.* Enumclaw, WA: Idyll Arbor.

Porter, H. R., & Van Puymbroeck, M. (2007). Utilization of the International Classification of Functioning, Disability, and Health within therapeutic recreation practice. *Therapeutic Recreation Journal, 41*(1), 47–60.

Public Health Agency of Canada. (2006). *Healthy aging in Canada: A new vision, a vital investment, from evidence to action—A background paper.* Retrieved from http://www.phac-aspc.gc.ca/seniors-aines/alt-formats/pdf/publications/public/healthy-sante/vision/vision-eng.pdf

Rehabilitation Institute of Chicago. (2010). Rehabilitation measures database. Retrieved from http://www.rehabmeasures.org/default.aspx

Royeen, C. B. (2003). Chaotic occupational therapy: Collective wisdom for a complex profession. *American Journal of Occupational Therapy, 57*(6), 609–624.

Savel, R. H., & Munro, C. L. (2014). Current state of health care reform: Dysfunctional government, divided country. *American Journal of Critical Care, 23*(2), 100–102. doi:10.4037/ajcc2014289

Skerrett, K. (2010). Extending family nursing: Concepts from positive psychology. *Journal of Family Nursing, 16*(4), 487–502. doi:10.1177/1074840710386713

Skipper, A., & Lewis, N. M. (2005). A look at the educational preparation of the health-diagnosing and treating professions: Do dietitians measure up? *Journal of the American Dietetic Association, 105*(3), 420–427. doi:10.1016/j.jada.2004.12.004

Smith, M. J., & Liehr, P. R. (Eds.). (2008). *Middle range theory for nursing* (2nd ed.). New York, NY: Springer.

Southeast Recreational Therapy Symposium. (2012). History of SRTS. Retrieved from http://srts.info/10.html

Stumbo, N. J. (2003a). The importance of evidence-based practice in therapeutic recreation. In N. J. Stumbo (Ed.), *Client outcomes in therapeutic recreation services* (pp. 25–48). State College, PA: Venture.

Stumbo, N. J. (2003b). Outcomes, accountability, and therapeutic recreation. In N. J. Stumbo (Ed.), *Client outcomes in therapeutic recreation services* (pp. 1–24). State College, PA: Venture.

Stumbo, N. J., Carter, M. J., & Kim, J. (2004). 2003 national therapeutic recreation curriculum study part A: Accreditation, curriculum and internship characteristics. *Therapeutic Recreation Journal, 38*(1), 32–52.

Stumbo, N. J., & Peterson, C. A. (2009). *Therapeutic recreation program design: Principles and procedures* (5th ed.). San Francisco, CA: Pearson.

U.S. Census Bureau. (2011). 2010 census shows nation's population is aging. Retrieved from http://www.census.gov/newsroom/releases/archives/2010_census/cb11-cn147.html

van Puymbroeck, M., Porter, H. R., & McCormick, B. P. (2009). The role of the International Classification of Functioning, Disability and Health (ICF) in therapeutic recreation practice, research and education. In N. J. Stumbo (Ed.), *Professional issues in therapeutic recreation* (2nd ed., pp. 43–58). Champaign, IL: Sagamore.

Ware, J. E., Jr. (1992). Measures for a new era of health assessment. In A. L. Stewart & J. E. Ware, Jr. (Eds.), *Measuring functioning and well-being: The medical outcomes study approach* (pp. 3-11). Durham, NC: Duke University.

World Health Organization. (2002). *Toward a common language for functioning disability and health: ICF.* Retrieved from http://www.who.int/classifications/icf/training/icfbeginnersguide.pdf

Wyer, P. C., & Silva, S. A. (2009). Where is the wisdom? I – A conceptual history of evidence-based medicine. *Journal of Evaluation in Clinical Practice, 15*(6), 891–898. doi:10.1111/j.1365-2753.2009.01323.x